California Gold Camps

California Gold Camps

A Geographical and Historical Dictionary
of Camps, Towns, and Localities Where
Gold Was Found and Mined; Wayside
Stations and Trading Centers

Erwin G. Gudde

Edited by

Elisabeth K. Gudde

University of California Press
Berkeley   Los Angeles   London

University of California Press

Berkeley and Los Angeles, California

University of California Press, Ltd.

London, England

Copyright © 1975, by

The Regents of the University of California

ISBN 0-520-02572-5

Library of Congress Catalog Card Number: 73-85788

Printed in the United States of America

Designed and Produced by Dave Comstock

Illustrations on pages 28, 161, 260, and 296 are reproduced through the courtesy of the University of California Library at Berkeley; those on pages 77, 224, 343, and 357 are from the California State Department of Parks and Recreation; those on pages 57, 155, and 284 are reproduced courtesy of the Los Angeles office of the Union Title and Trust Company, and the San Diego office of that firm provided photos on pages 89 and 180. The drawings of Bridgeport and Sierra were done by George Mathis of Coloma. The photo of Rough and Ready is from the private collection of Don Schmitz of Nevada City, and the Bodie photo is from the Los Angeles County Museum. All other illustrations are reproduced through the courtesy of the Bancroft Library, University of California, Berkeley.

Contents

Preface

THIS book is an outgrowth of my *California Place Names*. Soon after the publication of that work in 1949, I received numerous inquiries, especially from natural scientists who had hoped that the dictionary would not only contain current geographical names, but also the obsolete, or vanished place names that were needed for identifying geological formations, the habitats of trees and plants, the early occurrence of native animals, and so forth. Historians, librarians, and general readers too, had hoped to find these names. I realized the justification for such a demand, and in the preface to the second edition of *California Place Names* I promised to publish a dictionary and gazetteer of obsolete and vanished names.

When I started the work in 1960 on the basis of notes that I had accumulated in the course of my work on living names, I soon realized that it would not be feasible to create an all inclusive dictionary as I had promised. The various types of vanished names would have to be treated in separate monographs: the names of Indian rancherias, the topographic names bestowed by the original inhabitants, the large number of settlements and subdivisions later absorbed by cities, and the even greater number of mining camps and localities. However, such an undertaking would not be consonant with my line of research; hence, I decided to concentrate on two projects: one, to add to the third edition of *California Place Names* a reference list of all the obsolete and vanished names mentioned within the text and not otherwise alphabetized, and another, to compile a gazetteer and historical dictionary of places where gold was found and mined in California.

The book is written for the geographer, the historian, the scientist interested in geographical distribution, as well as the general reader interested in California history. It is not written for the geologist, the mining engineer, the student of economic development, or the etymologist.

In the Introduction I have given a brief sketch of the California Gold Rush, which will add nothing new to the scholar but which might help the general reader to use and read the book with more pleasure and understanding. I have also outlined the purpose and scope of the book and have added a bibliography of the books, maps, and manuscripts cited in the text, combined with a glossary of mining terms mentioned in the text and some expressions current in the Gold Rush.

The project was carried out by us independent of financial assistance or subsidy. Numerous are the historians, colleagues, and friends, however, who have supported us with information and advice. We express our gratitude to all of them. The errors that are apt to occur in an undertaking of this kind are all ours, to be sure.

ERWIN G. GUDDE

Eichenloh, April 6, 1969

Note to Preface

---◦⌒⌒◦---

Mr. Gudde had completed, before his death in May 1969, the major research and writing of this dictionary and gazetteer of California gold camps and mining localities. Since I had assisted my husband in his research for several years and was familiar with his concept and plan, I undertook to prepare this present manuscript for publication. This entailed examining certain sources marked "to be checked" and others published after 1969, checking for duplication and errors, and editing.

For Mr. Gudde and myself I wish to acknowledge the generous assistance given us by colleagues, librarians, friends, official agencies, and state and private libraries. Particular thanks are due members of the staff of the Bancroft Library, the General Library of the University of California at Berkeley, the California State Library, the California Historical Society Library, the California Pioneer Society Library, the Huntington Library, and county libraries throughout the state, as well as the members of the staff of the California State Bureau of Mines and Geology, the Department of Parks and Recreation, the U.S. Forest Service, and the U.S. Geological Survey.

Among individuals we wish to thank are James D. Hart, Director, and George P. Hammond, Director Emeritus of the Bancroft Library; J. S. Holliday, Director of the California Historical Society; and the following friends and colleagues: James Abajian, Richard C. Bailey, Trinda L. Bedrossian, Robert H. Becker, L. Burr Belden, Oscar Berland, Richard Bernard, Clyde R. Berriman, Frances E. Bishop, Leonard Booth, Marie Byrne, F. D. Calhoon, Charles L. Camp, Edwin Carpenter, Larry Cenotto, Cecil Chase, William B. Clark, Alma Compton, Carlo M. De Ferrari, Sheila Dowd, Ruth Drury, Mary Dunn, Barbara Eastman, Richard B. Eaton, Elizabeth Egenhoff, Peter A. Evans, Marilyn Ferguson, Soledad Fernandez, Vivian Fisher, Doris Foley, Mildred Forester, Claire Freeman, Mary Isabel Frye, Susan Gallup, Vincent P. Gianella, Helen S. Giffen, Hal E. Goodyear, Robert Greenwood, Merrilee Gwerder, Arda Haenszel, Peter Hanff, Leon Harte, O. F. Heckelman, Mary Hill, Philip Hoehn, Patricia Howard, Mary Ellen Jones, J. R. K. Kantor, Andrew Karpenstein, Katherine Karpenstein, Milton Kenin, Gary Kurutz, Julia Macleod, Joseph A. McGowan, Margaret Mason, Irene Moran, Adrienne Morgan, Andrea Nakagawa, Dolores Nariman, John H. Nopel, Allan R. Ottley, Kenneth I. Pettit, Miriam T. Pike, Victor R. Plukas, George P. Poore, Earl Ramey, Eletha Rea, Estelle Rebec, William Roberts, John W. Robinson, Colonel F. B. Rogers, Shirley Sargent, Esther Schenk, Jane Schlappi, Bertha Schroeder, Robert I. Slyter, William M. Smith, George R. Stewart, Lois Stone, Maud Swingle, Bernita L. Tickner, Elizabeth Todd, John B. Tompkins, Robert M. Wash, Frank Wedertz, Lyle L. White, Norman Wilson, R. Coke Wood. We appreciate also the assistance given us by the late Helen Bretnor and Dale L. Morgan. August Frugé, Joel F. Walters, Susan Peters, John Enright, Susan Taha, Harlan Kessel, David Comstock, and other members of the staff of the University of California Press were generous in their assistance, and to them we express our thanks. Also to Adrienne Morgan, who made the maps, we extend our thanks. Finally, to our faithful secretaries Phyllis Dexter and Doris Sandford, we are grateful for their patience and skill.

ELISABETH K. GUDDE

April 6, 1974

Introduction

————·⟨∞⟩·————

Gold is the Cornerstone is the title of John W. Caughey's book on the California Gold Rush, and there could be no better slogan for the edifice we call California History. Our state is today known over the world by many products of her soil and by many activities of her population. As early as 1849 Joseph Warren Revere prophesied: "A hundred years hence it will be apparent that the wealth of California did not lie in her shining sands." That prophecy has long ago been proved to be right. Yet the discovery of gold, the gold rush, and the subsequent events will remain the cornerstone of the modern great commonweath, California.

A large number of books and monographs besides Caughey's excellent work have treated the same subject, but a geographical-historical dictionary of the localities where gold was found, washed, and mined has been lacking. Our account tries to fill the gap. A book of this kind which could claim to be complete and final will have to be written by a younger scholar who is willing to make it his *magnum opus*, and it would also have to wait until more regional monographs will have been published.

Scope and Compass

Quite naturally our book deals chiefly with places that originated in the wake of Marshall's discovery at Sutter's Mill. That gold was present in the soil of what is now our State of California had been surmised long before the first grains were picked up on the South Fork of the American River on January 24, 1848. Some historians and also some government officials even maintain that gold was actually mined in the 1820s or earlier, but except for the discovery of the placers in the San Fernando foothills in 1842, no documentary evidence satisfactory to the historian has been presented so far.

Chronological Aspect

While the beginning of California gold geography may be chronologically assumed to be the year 1848, with the Los Angeles prelude in 1842, no terminal date could be established for our account. In general the historical part covers what we may call the romantic period of the golden age, the age during which the camp was really the signature of gold mining. This period was short-lived and includes at most the first two decades after 1848. The later years are more sketchily covered, except for intermittent gold rushes caused by the discovery of new deposits. For the sake of completeness, an attempt has been made to add references to mining and dredging activities in the twentieth century and also to make mention of the highly productive mines in the latter part of the nineteenth century and in the twentieth century. To give a complete account of gold mining to modern times, however, is not within the compass of this book.

This dictionary cannot present a logical and chronological entity. It is a long road from the time when gold flakes were picked from the soil with finger nails or pocket knives or washed from the river sand with *bateas*, caught in long toms or sluice boxes, obtained by hydraulic methods and by crushing the ore in arrastres and stamp mills, to the modern methods of extracting the metal by chemical-electronic processes. The lone prospector who sat patiently with his basket or pan along the tributaries of the Tuolumne or the Trinity, the men who formed "companies" of two or more for mutual protection and cooperation have long been anachronisms. Although new discoveries and the subsequent establishment of transitory camps reach way into the twentieth century, the big gold mining establishments of later days may have been in the hands of capitalists who may never have seen their mines or even have known the first thing about the process of gold production. There are gradual and overlapping periods of economic development of gold mining, and there is no way of drawing a line indicating when the old individualistic and cooperative phase turned into capitalistic undertakings.

Geographical Aspect

The gazetteer or geographical part of the dictionary gives the location of the place in relation to towns or topographical features as found on modern maps or in relation to places listed in this dictionary. Distances are generally "as the crow flies." We have indicated the earliest record on a map or in a book or a manuscript, whenever possible. Many of the abandoned camps were situated on streams with a different name or on roads that have long disappeared and can be found only on old and not always reliable maps. Where out of the way places are still recorded on detailed maps of today, like the topographical quadrangles of the U. S. Geological Survey, these maps are indicated at the end of the entry. The source of the information is given whenever possible for the benefit of readers who seek more detailed information.

The word "camp" is used more or less for the sake of convenience. Some camps became towns, even cities. The greater number of camps of the years of the gold rush have long disappeared, often without a trace, and the exact location can no longer be established. One of the best narrators of the gold rush, Prentice Mulford, wrote in his charming account: "The California mining camp was ephemeral. Often it was founded, built up, flourished, decayed, and had weeds and herbage growing over its site and hiding all of man's work inside of ten years." Often camps grew up along a stream or on a hill and did not focus around a central point that had a name. Hence, a number of items are listed not with the name of a camp or settlement but with the name of a topographical feature. Again for the sake of completeness, some places are listed that could not be identified but that are included in Hittell's roster, in Bancroft's sixth volume of his *History of California*, in Coy's *In the Diggings in Forty-nine*, or in other lists of mining camps. Finally, we have included a number of fictitious names in literature, some places that did not have a name and had to be described, and some trading centers, wayside inns, ferries, etc., where no gold was found but that played an important role during the gold rush. No attempt was made to list all of the hundreds of individual mines, but mines that were highly productive and some early mines of historical interest are mentioned.

Sources

The sources for a book which deals with many minute details are so extensive, varied, and widespread that we cannot possibly claim to have exhausted them. The rich manuscript material of the Bancroft Library has been gratefully used, as well as selected materials in the Huntington, the California State, the California Historical Society, and the California Pioneer Society libraries. But manuscripts in other important depositories, and many diaries, letters, or reminiscences still in private hands we were not able to consult. Likewise, we have not been able to examine the still existing county archives, except where they are preserved in the Bancroft Library. A number of our informants, however, have examined their local archives in the county recorders' offices and have provided information not found elsewhere. The amount of newspaper and other periodical literature is so enormous that we found it impossible even to attempt to cover it. Only the most important ones such as *Alta California* and the *Mining and Scientific Press* were checked for the years that came into consideration. Fortunately the Bancroft Library possesses a large number of scrapbooks of clippings and notes referring to the California gold mining regions. Of books and other monographs, we believe that we have consulted most if not all of the important ones that give original and dependable information. Like other historians we were often obliged to depend on some manuscripts and books whose authenticity or reliability may be doubtful. Although we have tried to sort the chaff from the wheat, discrepancies may certainly have occurred.

The historical part of the entries may be found too meager by many, but it was necessary to keep it within the range of a gazetteer and dictionary. As well as the dates, development, and productiveness of the places, we have added literary and folkloric elements.

In checking our manuscript we discovered many errors, and more will be discovered when the book appears in print. Some places may not have been placed in the right county because county boundaries have undergone considerable changes during more than a century. Some of the localities not definitely identified may in fact have produced not gold but silver or copper, or may not have been mining localities at all. There were a number of camps too insignificant and transient to have received a name. Some places may be duplicated because they had more than one name or the original name was lost or transferred to an entirely different region. In many cases, the sources were so confusing and contradictory that no definite conclusion about the location could be reached. Neither the early maps nor the early reports are entirely dependable and consistent in giving the alignment of streams and the location of camps.

In view of the above-mentioned limitations, we hope that our account can be considered, not definitive, but basic. We believe that it will be of help to all who are interested in California gold lore, and that it will stimulate more intensive regional studies and encourage and assist the scholar who will some day write a complete and definitive dictionary of our gold geography.

Elisabeth K. Gudde is the co-author of this dictionary, as she was of *California Place Names*.

ERWIN G. GUDDE

Eichenloh, April 6, 1969

INDEX
SHEET

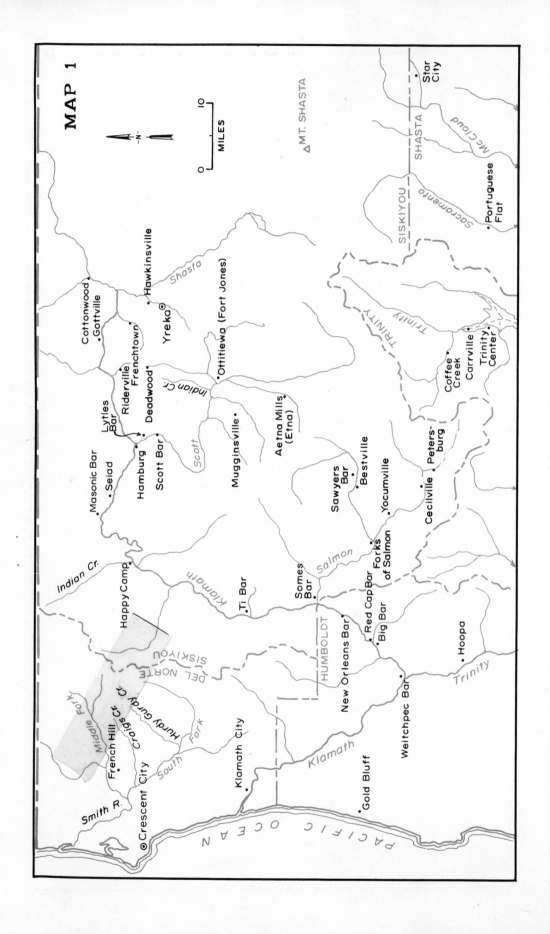

MAP 1

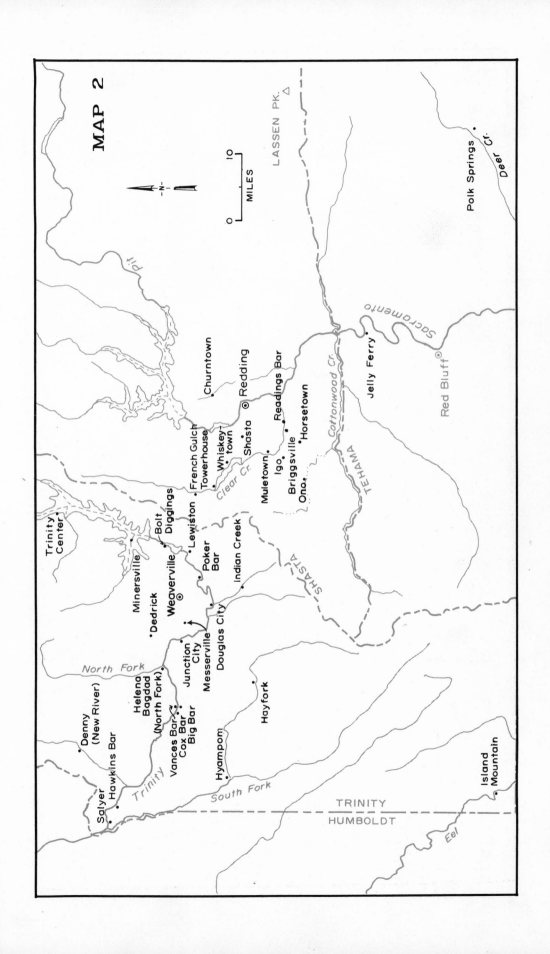

MAP 2

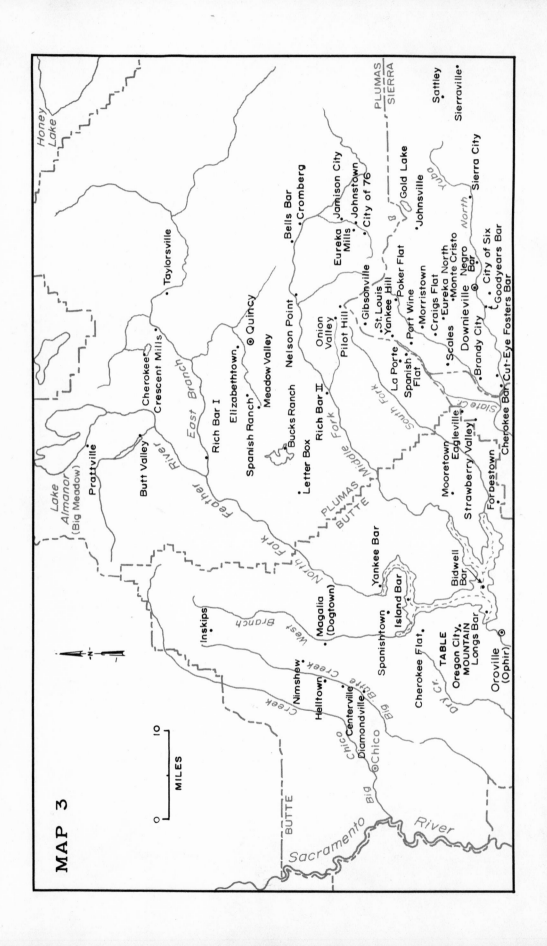

MAP 3

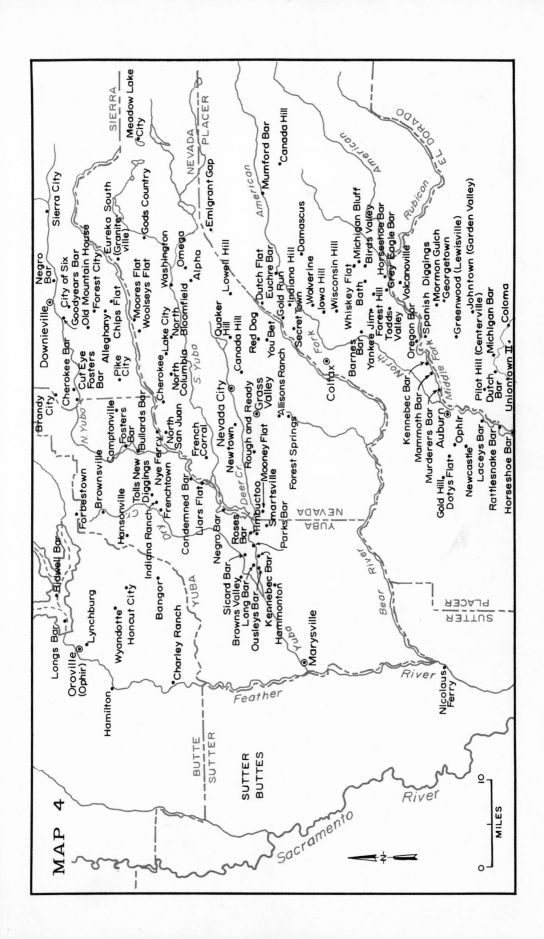

MAP 4

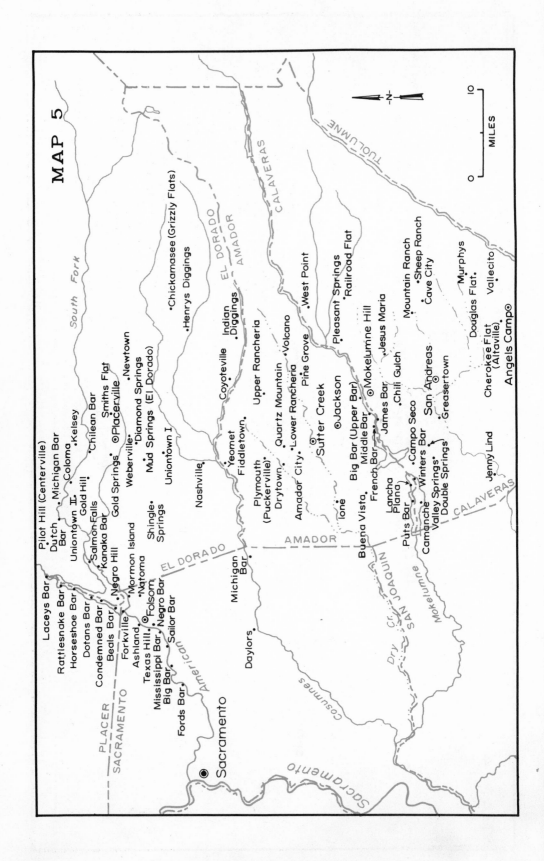

MAP 5

Sacramento

Daylors•

Michigan Bar•

Laceys Bar•
Pilot Hill (Centerville)•
Rattlesnake Bar• Dutch Michigan Bar
Horseshoe Bar• Bar• •Bar •Kelsey
Dotans Bar• Uniontown II• Coloma• Chilean Bar•
Condemned Bar• •Salmon Falls Gold Hill• Smiths Flat•
Beals Bar• Kanaka Bar• Gold Springs• •Placerville •Newtown
Forkville• Negro Hill• Weberville• •Diamond Springs
Ashland• Mormon Island• Shingle• Mud Springs (El Dorado)•
Texas Hill• •Folsom Springs Uniontown I•
Mississippi Bar• •Natoma
Big Bar• Negro Bar•
Fords Bar• Sailor Bar•

Nashville•

•Henrys Diggings

•Chickamasee (Grizzly Flats)

South Fork

EL DORADO
AMADOR

CALAVERAS

TUOLUMNE

Coyoteville• Indian
•Diggings
Yeomet• Upper Rancheria
•Fiddletown •West Point
Plymouth• Quartz Mountain• Pine Grove• •Pleasant Springs
(Puckerville)• •Volcano •Railroad Flat
Drytown• •Lower Rancheria
Amador City• Sutter Creek• Mokelumne Hill Mountain Ranch•
•Ione •Jackson Big Bar (Upper Bar)• •Jesus Maria •Sheep Ranch
Middle Bar• James Bar• •Cave City
Buena Vista• French Bar• •Chili Gulch •Murphys
Lancha •Campo Seco San Andreas• Douglas Flat•
Plana• Winters Bar• Greasertown• •Vallecito
Puts Bar• Camanche• Cherokee Flat
Valley Springs• (Altaville)•
Jenny Lind• •Double Springs Angels Camp⊙

American River

SACRAMENTO
PLACER

EL DORADO

AMADOR

SAN JOAQUIN
Dry Cr.
Mokelumne

CALAVERAS

Cosumnes

Sacramento

⊙Sacramento

MILES
0   10

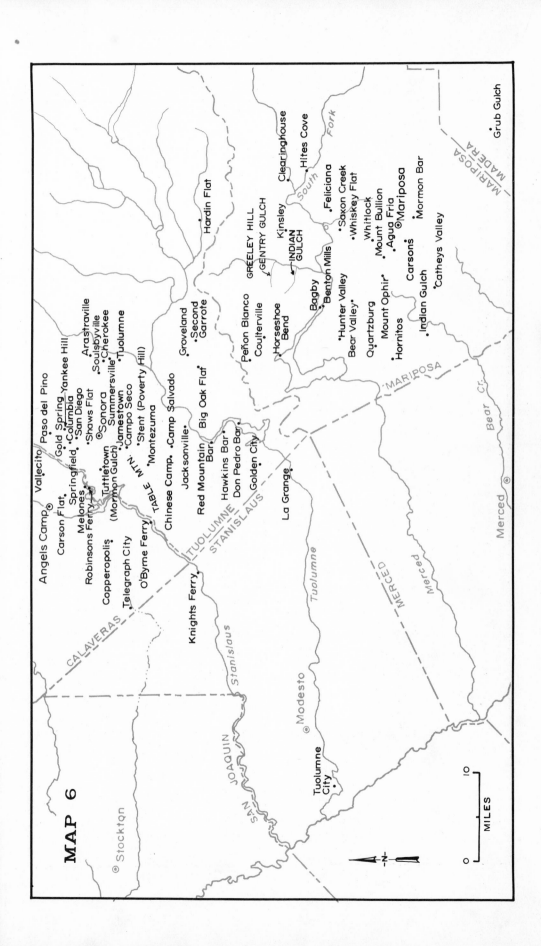

MAP 6

MAP 7

-N-

0   40
MILES

ALPINE
Mogul
Monitor
Kongsberg
Star City
Monoville
Lundy
Bodie
Tioga
Leevining
Benton
Mammoth City
Grub
Gulch
Coarse Gold
(Texas Flat)
Quartz
Mountain
Fine Gold
MADERA
FRESNO
Millerton
(Rootville)
San Joaquin
MONO
INYO
Owens
Big Pine
Kings
Kearsarge
Bend City
Mineral King
ALABAMA HILLS
Lone Pine
Keane Wonder
Globe
Skidoo
Darwin
TULARE
KERN
White River
Panamint
Ballarat
Amargosa
Kernville (Whiskey Flat)
Keyesville
Petersburg
Isabella
Havilah
INYO
SAN BERNARDINO
Bakersfield
Kern
Claraville
Goler
Garlock
Randsburg
Johannesburg
Salt Springs
Neenach
Tropico
Silver Lake
Ivanpah
SAN FELICIANO CAN.
CASTAIC CAN.
Barstow
Calico
SAN FRANCISQUITO CAN.
Mojave
Daggett
Kelso
BOUQUET CAN.
SOLEDAD CAN.
Acton
PLACERITA CAN.
MT. GLEASON
Ludlow
MT. BALDY
Rochester (Stedman)
Holcomb
Cushenbury
Los Angeles
SAN GABRIEL CAN.
Valley
City
Bagdad
Needles
Eldoradoville
Lytle
Belleville
LOS
ANGELES
Cr.
Clapboard Town
San Bernardino
Riverside
RIVERSIDE
New Dale
Pinecate
(Perris)
SAN DIEGO
Dos Palmas
CHUCKWALLA
MTNS.
MULE
MTNS.
Coleman
City
Julian
Banner
City
IMPERIAL
CHOCOLATE
MTNS.
San Diego
Mesquite
Picacho
Hedges (Tumco)
Ogilby

California Gold Camps

Abbeys Ferry [Calaveras, Tuolumne]. On the Stanislaus River, two miles above Parrots Ferry bridge. License to operate was granted in April, 1852. The ferry was probably discontinued when access to Parrots Ferry was improved (R. C. Wood, p. 139).

Abbotts [Yuba]. Near the junction of the North Fork of the Yuba River and Slate Creek, east of Forbestown. Recorded on Goddard's map, 1857. It was probably named for John M. Abbott of the Oak Grove House.

Abrams [Trinity]. On the upper South Fork of Salmon River, near the source of Coffee Creek, in the Salmon-Trinity Alps. James Abrams had a summer trading post here from 1850 to about 1860 for miners on their way to the diggings on the Salmon and Trinity rivers. Abrams carried mail from Carrville to Cecilville between 1877 and 1892. (*Siskiyou Pioneer*, I:5, pp. 39 ff.) There was a post office between 1895 and 1902, and it was a trading center for quartz and hydraulic mines in the vicinity (*Register*, 1898). Abrams Cabin, shown on the USGS Etna 1942 quadrangle, is still standing at the Mountain Meadow Ranch Resort.

Achinsons Bar [Yuba]. *See* Atchison Bar.

Acton [Los Angeles]. Twenty miles north of Los Angeles. The place dates back to 1875, when the Southern Pacific came through Soledad Canyon and named the station Acton. Miners began coming to the area about 1877 to work the Red Rover and New York mines. The Red Rover had been worked previously with arrastres. About 1892 a rich quartz vein was struck, and the mine continued to operate until 1940. The New York Mine was opened in the 1880s. Between 1895 and 1932 it was operated by Henry T. Gage, attorney, businessman, and governor of California, 1899–1903. In 1932 it was reopened by his son, Francis Gage, who renamed it Governor Mine and developed it extensively. At its closure in 1942, it had yielded more than 1.5 million dollars, which represented more than half the total production of the entire county. Mining was carried on in the area on a small scale into the 1950s. An account is given by J. W. Robinson (pp. 27 ff.) and descriptions of the various mines in the district may be found in *Mining Bureau*, L (pp. 497 f., 499 f., and 612 ff.).

Adams [Stanislaus]. On the south bank of Tuolumne River, between Tuolumne City and Empire City. It was not a gold town but a way station on the road to the Southern Mines. It was a short-lived town, and in 1854 it served briefly as the county seat. (Rensch-Hoover.)

Adams Bar, Adamsville [Butte]. *See* Adamstown.

Adams Diggings [Placer]. Near Michigan Bluff. The diggings were discovered by Captain W. G. Adams, a forty-niner. The place was apparently at or near Ground Hog Glory, according to the correspondence of the "Clipper" in the Sacramento *Union*, December 23, 1852.

Adamstown [Butte]. On the Feather River, about two miles above Oroville. The camp was established in 1848 by George Adams shortly after Bidwell's discovery of gold on the Feather River. It was also known as Adams Bar and Adamsville. A story of the camp is given by Mansfield (p. 6).

Adelaide and Anderson Mine [Mariposa]. *See* Coulterville.

Aetna Mills [Siskiyou]. *See* Etna Mills.

African Bar [Placer]. On the Middle Fork of American River, between Spanish Bar and

Drunkards Bar. Hutchings lists it in 1855. It is mentioned in El Dorado County History, 1883 (p. 84) and in Bancroft, VI (p. 354).

Agua Caliente District [Kern]. Along Caliente Creek, about six miles east of Bakersfield. Its best producer was the Amalie Mine, yielding ore valued at more than half a million dollars. The post office from 1894–1908 was Amalie. *Agua caliente* is the Spanish term for 'warm or hot water'.

Agua Fria [Mariposa]. West of Mariposa, on Agua Fria Creek, tributary to Mariposa Creek, shown on Butler's map, 1851. It was possibly here that Alexis Godey, one of Frémont's men, discovered gold in 1849. The camp was one of the earliest settlements that developed on Frémont's grant. Eccleston, in his description in *Mariposa Indian War* (October 20, 1950), states that the name, spelled Agua Frio by him, is derived from two springs of cold (*frio*) water (*agua*), which are situated at the bend in the creek. The lower, or principal camp was about a quarter mile above the springs, and at the time of Eccleston's writing it had about a dozen stores, monte and faro banks, a billiard room, bowling alley, and hotel. It served briefly as the county seat: February 18, 1850 to November 10, 1851. The post office was established October 7, 1851. Like all Mariposa placer camps, it soon declined, and the contemporary accounts of Allsop, Eccleston, Evans, Christman, McIsaac, Knoche, and D. B. Woods all report poor

Agua Fria Valley, Mariposa Co.

results. The first 6-stamp quartz mill, driven by a 12-horsepower engine, began operations at Upper Agua Fria in 1853, and the development of quartz mining brought temporary prosperity. Upper Agua Fria was about one mile northwest of the main camp (Lower Agua Fria). It was the site of the quartz mine operated by the Agua Fria Mining Company, described in its prospectus published in London in 1851, as being on a hill on the east side of the creek. Upper Agua Fria had fewer stores than Lower Agua Fria, according to Eccleston, and it did not develop into as large a camp as Lower Agua Fria. Both places are shown on the *Las Mariposas Map*, 1861. The spelling of the name varies in the literature. When the lower camp was named county seat by act of the legislature (February 18, 1850), the name was misspelled Aqua Fria. As early as 1850 the place also became known as Agua Frio (Derbec, p. 92). Eccleston called it Agua Frio in 1850; Gibbes used this spelling on his *Map of the Southern Mines*, 1850, and it persisted for many years. Butler's map of 1851, however, used the proper spelling, Agua Fria, and the Post Office Department, likewise, spelled it properly in 1851. The place is Historic Landmark 518.

Ah-Moon Bar [Butte]. On the Big Bend of the North Fork of Feather River. It is recorded on the map in the County History, 1882 (p. 209).

Alabama Bar [El Dorado]. On the upper Middle Fork of American River, near the junction of the forks of the Middle Fork, above New York Bar. Sioli's El Dorado County History, 1883 (p. 84) and Angel's Placer County History, 1882 (p. 10) both locate it above Junction Bar. A claim is recorded in the El Dorado County Mining Locations, I (p. 10) on October 8, 1850.

Alabama Bar [Sacramento]. On the American River, near the confluence with the South Fork, a half mile above Beam's Bar. The name was applied by prospectors from Alabama (Sacramento *Bee*, April 2, 1887). The diggings were opened in 1850 but abandoned in 1856, according to the County History, 1880 (p. 229).

Alabama Bar [Yuba]. On the North Fork of Yuba River, near the mouth of Hampshire Creek. Shown on Trask's map, 1853, and on Wescoatt's County Map, 1861. The County History, 1879 (p. 97), reports mining activities in 1852, but early exhaustion of deposits. However, De Long still collected miners' taxes here in March, 1855.

Alabama Flat [El Dorado]. On Johntown Creek, near Irish Creek. It is mentioned by Stephen Wing, when he and other miners built a road in the vicinity (Journal, II, p. 42). W. A. Goodyear mentioned it in 1871 (Whitney, *Auriferous Gravels*, p. 85).

Alabama: Gulch, Hill [Calaveras]. The Gulch is a tributary to the Mokelumne River, below the junction of the North and South forks. There was considerable mining around 1850. A well-known figure in the community was Charles Grunsky. He was a member of the Eutaw Company of Alabama and had a store in nearby Pleasant Springs. *See* Pleasant Springs; Kohlbergs Humbug. A good account of the Gulch is given by Doble (pp. 35 ff. and 297 f.). The Gulch was also known as Spring Gulch, according to Doble. It is shown on Camp's map in his edition of Doble.

Alabama Hills [Inyo]. There was silver, gold, and lead mining here. The trading center and post office for the area was at Lone Pine City. The name was given to the range during the Civil War by Confederate sympathizers after the Confederate raider *Alabama* had sunk the Union man-of-war *Hatteras* off the coast of Texas, January 11, 1863.

Alabama Mine [Placer]. *See* Penryn.

Alaska Mine [Sierra]. *See* Pike City.

Albany Flat [Calaveras]. South of Angels Camp on Highway 49. It was "among the hot spots in early days" (Demarest, p. 9), but the pay dirt soon gave out, and Heckendorn in 1856 lists three miners and one merchant as sole inhabitants. According to Demarest, like many other camps it was "a favorite stopping place" of the bandit Murieta. Shown on map 3 of the *Guidebook*.

Albany Hill [Nevada]. Near Little York. The first mill to crush the "blue cement" was erected here in the summer of 1857 (Bean, p. 58).

Albion: Diggings, Hills [Nevada]. Near Bear River. The place was apparently abandoned in 1857 and left to Chinese miners who struck it rich (*Alta*, steamer edition, March 20, 1857). *See* Long Hollow.

Alder: Creek, Springs [Sacramento]. The Creek flows past Prairie City about two miles south of Folsom and enters the American River opposite Mississippi Bar. Judah's map, 1854, shows Alder Springs as a station, near the junction, on the Sacramento Valley Railroad, but later maps show it as Alder Creek (Doolittle, 1868). The County History, 1880 (p. 224), mentions Alder Creek as a mining camp near Prairie City. Hutchings saw many Chinese working on the creek when he passed there April 21, 1855. According to an item in Bancroft Notes taken from the Folsom *Telegraph*, March 30, 1867, gold was struck in March, 1867, a half-mile south of Alder Creek, and within one week one hundred shafts were sunk in an area of two and a half acres of ground. Historic Landmark 746, at Nimbus Dam a few miles to the north, marks the old Coloma Road, which ran from Sutters Fort through Alder Creek to Coloma and was used by Marshall when he brought the first gold from Sutters Mill to the Fort. California's first stageline was established by James E. Birch in 1849 on the well-traveled route to the diggings.

Alder Grove [Placer]. South of the present town of Colfax. It was also known as Upper Corral and later as Illinoistown. Mahlon Fairchild (p. 15) spent several days here in August, 1849, en route to the mines. *See* Colfax and Illinoistown.

Alex Ranch [Amador]. In the Volcano post office district. Ben Bowen mentions Toby Moor's diggings on Alex Ranch, January 18, 1855.

Algerine Camp [Tuolumne]. Five miles south of Sonora. The diggings were first called Providence Camp, then Algiers, and finally Algerine Camp. The gulch in which the camp was situated was for many years called Algiers Gulch. The deposits were discovered in February, 1853, by a Frenchman, who with one or two companions took out 200 ounces of gold in a few days, including an 8-pound lump (De Ferrari in *Chispa*, V, p. 137). Successful mining and the finding of a 14-ounce piece of solid gold on the surface by two boys were reported in the Sonora *Herald* (Hittell Clippings, p. 26, apparently February 11, 1854). Browne (p. 38) states that in 1867 the placers were nearly exhausted, and the 800 voters had dwindled to a few score. According to *Mines and Minerals* (p. 358), the entire output was 2.5 million dollars. Shown on the USGS Sonora 1939 quadrangle.

Algiers [Tuolumne]. *See* Algerine Camp.

Alhambra Mine [El Dorado]. Two miles northeast of Kelsey. It was developed in 1883 and worked intermittently until the late 1950s. The total production by 1955 was reportedly 1.25 million dollars (*Mining Bureau*, LII, p. 404).

Alleghany: Tunnel, town, **District** [Sierra]. On the north slope of San Juan Ridge, south of Downieville, on a branch of Kanaka Creek. Shown on Doolittle's map, 1868, and on the County Map, 1874. Alleghany is a popular American name, derived from the Delaware Indian name for the river in Pennsylvania. The Alleghany Company tunnel was begun in April, 1853, and tapped the pay streak in 1855. In early spring, 1856, the town was laid out (Co. Hist., 1882, pp. 473 ff.). On November 19, 1857, the post office was transferred from Chips Flat. The place is described, or mentioned in Vischer (p. 240); *Transactions*, 1858 (p. 189); *Annual Mining Review*, 1876 (p. 23). The decline of the tunnel mines began in 1862, but the district remained one of the richest (*Mining Press*, May 16, 1862). According to the San Francisco *Bulletin*, July 6, 1867, there were still thirteen tunnels north of Kanaka Creek, varying in length from 1,200 to 2,000 feet (Bancroft Notes). The mines of 1867 are listed in Browne (pp. 147 f.); modern mines are described in *Guidebook* (pp. 78 f.); *Mining Bureau*, LII (pp. 237 ff.); and *Bulletin*, 193 (pp. 19 ff.). Among the rich lode mines near Alleghany, the largest was the Sixteen-to-One, which yielded with consolidated mines more than 25 million dollars and was in operation until the early 1960s. Other productive lode mines included the Brush Creek Mine, which yielded more than 4 million dollars; the Plumbago, 3.5 million; the Oriental, 2.85 million; the Rainbow, 2.5 million; and the Kenton between 1 and 1.25 million. At the Kenton Mine a high-grade pocket valued at 100 thousand dollars was found in the 1930s. North of Alleghany, on the Great Blue Lead, there were a number of productive drift mines, among which the Bald Mountain yielded 3.1 million dollars; the Ruby more than 1 million; and the Live Yankee almost 1 million. The above mentioned mines (except Plumbago and Kenton) are listed separately in this dictionary. A geologic map of the district may be found in *Bulletin*, 193 (p. 22). The town Alleghany is shown on the USGS Colfax 1938 quadrangle.

Allison: Ranch, Diggings [Nevada]. On Wolf Creek, two miles below Grass Valley. Allison Ranch and Quartz Mine are shown on Doolittle's map, 1868. The Ranch was named for a farmer before the gold deposits were discovered. The rich Phoenix ledges were struck in 1852. In 1858 the yield was estimated at 1.5 million dollars (Hittell Clippings, pp. 41, 77). Vischer (p. 244) reports in April, 1859, a profit of 42 thousand dollars in twelve days. In 1865 about 300 miners were still listed (*Grass Valley Directory*, 1865). The mine was reported idle between 1871 and 1896, and later, in 1918, it was reopened with a 20-stamp mill (MacBoyle, pp. 112 ff.). The total production was 2.7 million dollars (*Bull.*, 193, p. 59).

Alpha [Nevada]. Two miles southeast of Washington, near Scotchman Creek. Shown on Doolittle's map, 1868. The origin of the two neighboring camps bearing as names the first and last letters of the Greek alphabet is shrouded in mystery. According to one source ("The Knave," September 15, 1946), the places were early mining towns called Hell-Out-For-Noon and Delirium Tremens, but this explanation may be just as questionable as several others. The name Alpha was in use in 1854, and the post office was established as Alpha in 1855. The *Alta*, February 27, 1854, reports that during the wet season the average earnings were one ounce to the hand, but sometimes they were as high as fifty to seventy dollars a day. The *Mining Press*, July 31, 1862, states that a miner picked up a lump of gold worth 729 dollars. The fineness of gold was high, 968° (*Mining Bureau*, IV, p. 220). According to Bean, the place had yielded 1.25 million dollars by 1867, and one hydraulic claim was in operation at that time. The total production of the Alpha Mine exceeded 2 million dollars (*Bull.*, 193, p. 128). The name Alpha Diggings is recorded on the USGS Alleghany 1950 quadrangle. Historic Landmark 628. *See* Omega and Hell-Out-For-Noon City.

Alpine Mine [El Dorado]. Two miles southeast of Georgetown. It was first worked in the late 1860s (Logan, p. 15). In 1884 the yield was reported at seventy-two dollars per ton, the highest in the county. In 1888 a 10-stamp mill was in operation. From 1933 to 1938 the production was nearly half a million dollars. (*Mining Bureau*, IV, p. 223; LII, p. 406.)

Alta [Placer]. Near Canyon Creek, east of Dutch Flat. At the end of the nineteenth century it was the headquarters of the extensive drift mining of the Alta Gold Mining Company (*Mining Bureau*, XIII, pp. 272 f.).

Alta [Sierra]. The location was not determined. It is mentioned in *Illustrated Spirits* (Bancroft Scraps, V, p. 1803). The Spanish adjective *alta* for 'high' or 'upper' is a popular element in California geographical names.

Alta Hill [Nevada]. Northwest of Grass Valley, on the road to Rough and Ready. Shown on Hoffmann and Craven's Great Gravel Map, 1873. Several shafts were sunk, but the mines were not very extensive (Whitney, *Auriferous Gravels*, p. 182).

Altaville [Calaveras]. Four miles north of Angels Camp, and now a part of it. Former names were Forks of the Road, Winterton, Cherokee Flat. *See* Cherokee Flat. It was important as a point for supplies and machinery. A foundry was established in 1854 by D. D. Demarest, and it is still operating today as California Electric Steel (G. Poore). In the 1870s the place was the center of silk culture. Historic Landmark 288.

Althouse, Althouse Creek [Del Norte]. The creek is a tributary to Illinois River in Oregon and extends into California. It is recorded on Goddard's map, 1857. The mining camp was ten miles from Sailor Diggings, which was across the Oregon state line, on the Crescent City Plank and Turnpike Road (Historic Landmark 645). A letter from W. T. Patterson to Asa H. Thompson is datelined Althouse, July 8, 1854 (Letters of Asa H. Thompson).

Alto Mining District [Calaveras]. In the southwest corner of the county, about six miles south of Copperopolis. The Alto Mine, from which the district takes its name, was discovered in 1886 and operated until 1907. There had been placer mining during the Gold Rush period, when the gravels under nearby Table Mountain were worked by drifting. (*Bull.*, 193, p.24.)

Altons Bar [Mariposa]. On the Merced River, below the junction with the South Fork. Recorded on Trask's map, 1853. No other record was found.

Alturas [Sierra]. Apparently in the vicinity of La Porte. It is mentioned in an extract from the San Francisco *Bulletin*, July 30, 1862 (Bancroft Notes). Tunnel work and hydraulic mining are reported in the item.

Alvord District [San Bernardino]. In the southern part of the Alvord Mountains, about twenty-five miles northeast of Barstow. Shown on the County Map, 1892. It was named for Charles Alvord of New York, who is said to have discovered "wire gold" somewhere in the Panamint Mountains in 1860 or 1861. The story is told by Weight (pp. 48 ff.). According to *Mining Bureau*, VIII (p. 499) and XLIX (p. 70), the major mine, the Alvord Mine, was not located until 1885. The ore was reduced at a 5-stamp mill at Camp Cady in

1888, and the mine continued to operate intermittently until 1952.

Amador City [Amador]. On Highway 49, three miles north of Sutter Creek. It was one of the richest mining towns of the state. On Trask's map, 1853, the name is recorded as Amidor on Amidor Creek. Cool calls it Amadore City in his diary, June 10, 1850, and Morgan refers to it as Amadore in 1850–1852. South Amadore is the name given in an article in the *Christian Advocate*, November 11, 1851. On Sherman Day's map, 1856, the spelling is Amador. The place developed around the camp of José Maria Amador, major-domo of Mission San Jose and grantee of San Ramon land grant. He must have reached the place shortly after June 15, 1848, for on that day he camped with Chester Lyman on Dry Creek (*CHSQ*, II, p. 185). The first permanent cabin was built in the fall of 1848 by James Wheeler and his party from Oregon. In the fall of 1849 Bayard Taylor, the renowned poet and literary critic, traveled in the area and found the creek lined with tents and winter cabins (Chapter 25). The placers soon gave out, but the striking of lode gold in 1851 started the town on its phenomenal development. In the fall of 1859 three quartz mills were operating; the oldest one, the Spring Mill with a 60-HP engine and 28 stamps, crushed forty tons a day (*Transactions*, 1859, p. 81). The principal mines of the area in the 1860s are shown on the County Map of 1866 and are listed by Browne in 1867. In 1881 there were still six mills with 116 stamps in operation (Co. Hist., 1881, p. 161). The total production of the Keystone Mine is given as approximately 24.5 million dollars, that of Bunker Hill Mine (formerly Ranchoree or Rancheria) as 5 million, and of Original Amador Mine as 3.5 million. Several other mines in the district, including South Spring Hill and Treasure, produced one million dollars or more. (*Guidebook*, p. 65; *Mining Bureau*, L, pp. 173, 185; *Bull.*, 193, p. 76.) *See* Spring Hill Mine; Ministers Claim.

Amador Crossing [Amador]. East of Amador City, on the stage road from Jackson to Dry Creek, at the crossing of Amador Creek. The camp was also known as Upper Crossing (Cenotto).

Amalie [Kern]. North of Mojave, between Jawbone and Lone Tree canyons. In 1904 a Huntington mill and an arrastre were still in operation. From 1894–1900 it was the post office for Agua Caliente Mining District. *See* Agua Caliente District; Caliente.

Amargosa District [San Bernardino]. *See* Salt Springs.

Amazon Gulch [Tuolumne]. Southeast of Sonora. It is mentioned by Heckendorn (p. 89) in 1856.

American Bar [Butte]. On the Middle Fork of Feather River, above Evans Bar, near the Plumas County line. Shown on Goddard's map above Sucker Riffle, on the east side of the river. It may be the American Bar at which Noblet Herbert and his company built a wing dam, which was washed out by a heavy rain in September, 1850 (*CHSQ*, XXIX, p. 299). The editor of Herbert's letter, however, suggests a location near Rich Bar on the East Branch of the North Fork of Feather River.

American Bar [Nevada]. Shown on Trask's map, 1853, as the farthest east bar on the South Fork of Yuba River.

American Bar [Placer]. On the Middle Fork of American River, above Gray Eagle Bar. Recorded (below Horseshoe Bar) on Trask's map, 1853. In 1855 a 12-stamp mill was erected (*State Register*, 1859). Here a wire rope was used for the first time, in 1856, to transport ore to the mill. The originator, Andrew Smith Hallidie, became the builder of suspension bridges and later the developer of the San Francisco cable car system. (*CHSQ*, XIX, p. 146.) In 1856 or 1858, the "Judge Chambers process" was introduced, whereby the tailings were subjected to a chemical process, which was reported to have increased the maximum from 15 to 130 dollars per ton (Co. Hist., 1882, p. 195). According to Bancroft, VI (p. 354), American Bar was credited with an output of 3 million dollars. It is possible that there were two different American Bars in the same region. Doolittle's map, in fact, shows one on either side of Pleasant Bar. Trask's map shows American Slide opposite American Bar.

American Bar [Placer]. On the North Fork of American River; a newspaper article of August 13, 1864, reported the discovery of a nugget weighing six and a half pounds (Co. Hist., 1882, p. 228).

American Camp [Tuolumne]. About five miles northeast of Columbia, north of the South Fork of Stanislaus River. According to an undated clipping from the Stockton *Republican*, a nugget of 161 ounces, worth 3 thousand dollars, was found here in April, 1858. Shown on the USGS Big Trees 1941 quadrangle. American Camp was also a former name of Columbia and of Jamestown.

American Flat [Amador]. Near Fiddletown. It is mentioned as a camp in *Amador Ledger*, June 20, 1857 (Cenotto).

American Flat [El Dorado]. Eight miles north of Placerville. Shown on Doolittle's map, 1868. On a Sunday in June, 1852, a crook sold some of the claims, including tools, to Chilenos. This would have caused another Chileno war if the Americans had not succeeded in driving away the foreigners by strategy. Steele (pp. 264 ff.) gives an interesting account of it. In 1855 water was brought from the Pilot and Rock Creek Canal (Hittell Clippings, p. 73). Shown on the USGS Placerville 1931 quadrangle.

American Girl Mine [Imperial]. *See* Cargo Muchacho; Ogilby.

American Hill [Amador]. Early hill mining was reported in the County History, 1881 (p. 126). The location was not determined.

American Hill [Nevada]. Just northwest of Nevada City and now a part of it. Shown on Doolittle's map, 1868. It was here that Edward E. Matteson in April, 1853, "invented" the method of hydraulic mining by attaching a nozzle to the end of a hose, thereby improving the method introduced by Anthony Chabot a year earlier at Buckeye Hill. The force of the water directed against the bottom of the gravel bank undermined it and caused it to cave in and break down, making it easy to sluice the gravel. Details of the "invention" vary in different accounts. *Hutchings' Illustrated California Magazine*, July, 1857 (p. 12) and *Miners' Own Book* (pp. 28 ff.) give the date as February, 1852. Other accounts, giving the date as 1853, are found in *Bean's History* (pp. 62 f.); Browne (p. 119); *Mining Bureau*, II (Part 2, p. 149). *See also* the recently published monograph of Philip R. May, *Origins of Hydraulic Mining in California*. A similar method with crude apparatus and limited capacity was reportedly used about a year earlier in 1852, at Yankee Jims in Placer County (*Mining Bureau*, II, Part 2, p. 149), but credit for the invention is usually given to Matteson, with Chabot as the forerunner. *See* Buckeye Hill [Nevada] near Quaker Hill; Buckeye: Hill, Ravine [Nevada]; Yankee Jims [Placer]. The last hydraulic mining around Nevada City after its prohibition was at the so-called Hirshmann's Cut in the extreme northwestern corner of American Hill (Lindren, *Gold-Quartz Veins*, p. 19).

American Hill [Nevada]. Near North San Juan, at the upper end of the large body of gravel adjoining Manzanita Hill. Hydraulic mining operations in the early 1870s are described in Raymond, VIII (p. 95), where it is stated that the estimated gold production by 1875 was more than 2.5 million dollars. Pettee in his discussion of the area in 1879 reports that a tunnel 4,000 feet in length had been completed, reaching a depth of 190 feet below bedrock at one shaft (Whitney, *Auriferous Gravels*, p. 389).

American Hill [Sierra]. South of Downieville, near the Middle Fork of Yuba River. Shown on Doolittle's map, 1868, and the County Map, 1874. The camp prospered in 1861 (*Mining Press*, November 30, 1861). For references to the district, *see Mining Bureau*, XVI (Sierra, p. 5).

American Hollow [Placer]. Hutchings lists it along with places on the Middle Fork of American River in 1855. It is also included in Hittell's roster.

American House [El Dorado]. A place on the Sacramento River, mentioned by Crockett (p. 42) in 1856.

American House [Plumas]. Five miles from Sears Diggings, on Charles McLaughlin's stage line (Hale & Emory's *Marysville City Directory*, 1853, pp. 64 f.). It is shown on Wescoatt's map, 1861, and on the USGS Bidwell Bar 1944 quadrangle, about three miles southwest of La Porte.

American Rancho [Plumas]. *See* American: Valley, Ranch.

American Slide [Placer]. On the south side of the Middle Fork of the American River, just above American Bar. It is shown on Trask's map, 1853.

American: Valley, Ranch [Plumas]. The region surrounding Quincy on the north, west, and south is designated as American Valley. It is recorded on Goddard's map, 1857, south of Quincy. Browne (p. 167) mistakenly places it in the Plumas-Eureka area. The American Ranch was visited by Windeler (p. 130) in January, 1852, about the time miners were prospecting in the vicinity. Later, the town of Quincy developed at the site of the Ranch. *See* Quincy. In February, 1852, there was a great rush for the quartz mines near by, apparently the result of a hoax (Dame Shirley, Letter of February 27, 1852; Steele, p. 188). Dame Shirley, who refers to the place as American Rancho, spent three weeks there in the fall of 1852, while attending a political convention, and she gives a detailed account of the visit in her letter of October 16, 1852. At the turn of the century unsuccessful attempts were

made to work the bedrock of Spanish Creek, which runs through the Valley north of Quincy. A shaft sunk below Elizabethtown Flats, on a tributary to Spanish Creek, however, reportedly yielded 200 thousand dollars (*Bull.*, 92, p. 111). American Valley is shown on the USGS Downieville 1907 quadrangle.

Americaville [Placer]. Three miles from Oak Grove, apparently near the North Fork of the Middle Fork of American River. An item in the Sacramento *Union*, December 12, 1852, reports that a slide prevented miners from working, but a 3-mile long ditch was being built from the North Fork at Oak Grove to Americaville, to provide water for mining.

Anada [Trinity]. An unidentified mining camp, listed by Gannett.

Ancho-Erie Mine [Nevada]. *See* Graniteville.

Andrews Creek [Shasta]. A branch of Clear Creek, north of Igo. It was mined in the 1850s by A. R. Andrews, signer of the California Constitution of 1879 (Steger).

Angelo [Calaveras]. Near Angels Camp and possibly named after it. According to Browne (p. 63), there were some heavily yielding mines here in the 1860s.

Angels: Camp, Creek [Calaveras]. On Highway 49, between Carson Hill and Altaville. It was incorporated as Angels in 1912, but the post office and popular usage preferred the original name Angels Camp. It was one of the earliest and best known settlements of the Southern Mines. George (or Henry) Angel settled at the Creek in June, 1848. The name Angels Camp is already recorded on Derby's map of 1849 (*Sketch*). William Shaw (p. 87) gives an interesting description of the same year, mentioning many English sailors and "celestials." Other early accounts are given by Audubon in 1850 (p. 210), by Demarest in 1850, by Borthwick in the spring of 1853 (pp. 318 ff.), and by Vischer in 1859 (p. 324). A modern account is given in Buckbee, *Pioneer Days*. At first there was good placering in the area, then mainly quartz mining. In 1857 there were eight water-driven mills with seventy stamps and four steam mills with forty-eight stamps (*State Register*, 1859). By 1885 the region had become one of the major gold producing districts in the state. The chief mine was the Utica, which had begun operations in the 1850s, and between 1893 and 1895 produced more than 4 million dollars worth of gold. During World War I most of the mines were closed, but some were reactivated in the

Angels Camp, Calaveras Co.

1930s and there has been intermittent prospecting in recent years. The mines are listed in *Bulletin*, 193 (p. 28), and their locations are indicated on the geologic map (*ibid.*, p. 26). The total yield of the Utica Mine was 17 million dollars. Among other productive mines were the Angels Mine, which yielded 3.25 million dollars; the Lightner, more than 3 million; the Gold Cliff, more than 2.8 million; and the Madison, more than 1 million. A high grade pocket valued at 100 thousand dollars was found in the Angels Mine in 1910. The estimated total production of the district was 30 million dollars or more. (*Bull.*, 193, pp. 11, 25 ff.) Angels Camp is Historic Landmark 287. It is the setting for Mark Twain's story "The Jumping Frog of Calaveras County." Since the late 1930s there has been an annual Jumping Frog Jubilee at a place called Frogtown, between Angels Camp and Carson Hill. It is shown on map 3 in the *Guidebook* and on the USGS San Andreas 1962 quadrangle.

Angier House [Calaveras]. In the spring of 1852 Doble and company had their headquarters here and prospected various gulches near by. *See* Pleasant Springs.

Antelope [Sierra]. This place is frequently mentioned as a town or precinct until the late 1870s, but the location is not indicated.

Antelope Ravine [Placer]. It is listed as a mining camp by Hittell in *Mining Bureau*, IV (p. 221).

Antelope Spring [Butte]. Shown on the von Leicht-Craven map, 1874, near the Tehama County line. It was apparently a mining camp.

Anthony House [Nevada]. Eight miles west of Grass Valley, on Deer Creek. Shown on Doolittle's map, 1868. The rich gold-bearing belt apparently has its western

terminus here. It is mentioned in *Bean's Directory*, 1867 (p. 354) and is recorded in *Mining Bureau*, XVI (Nevada, p. 54). Shown on the USGS Smartsville 1943 quadrangle.

Antoine [Calaveras]. *See* San Antonio.

Antoine or Antone Canyon [Placer]. A tributary to the North Fork of the Middle Fork of American River. It is shown as Antoine Canyon on Goddard's map, 1857. According to Rensch-Hoover (under the entry Last Chance), it was named for a half-breed Crow Indian named Antoine, who mined here in 1850. James Marshall also mined here in the summer of 1850 (Parsons, pp. 135 ff.). Steele was here May 18, 1853, but too early in the season to mine. Hittell lists the name as Antone (*Mining Bureau*, IV, p. 221). It is also recorded as Antone Canyon on the County Map, 1887, and the USGS Colfax 1938 quadrangle, but on the Duncan Peak 1952 quadrangle it appears as Antoine Canyon.

Applegate [Placer]. Applegate Station is shown on the County Map, 1887, about four miles south of Colfax. It is not a real gold town, but the *Mining Press*, January 4, 1861, printed a report from the Jacksonville *Sentinel*, stating that samples of quartz showed ninety-six dollars per ton at or near the place. According to the *Register*, 1902, there was still some quartz mining in the twentieth century. The place was named for Lisbon Applegate, who established his Bear River House here in the 1850s.

Applesauce Bar [Siskiyou]. On the North Fork of Salmon River, above Sawyers Bar and opposite Eddys Gulch. Near by is Slapjack Bar. (Tickner.)

App Mine [Tuolumne]. At Quartz Mountain, two miles south of Jamestown. There were three profitable chimneys, and the average yield between 1863 and 1866 was fifteen dollars per ton. A 1,500-foot tunnel never paid anything. An account is given in Browne (pp. 41, 43). In 1871 there were 25 stamps, but the mill was idle. A description as of 1873 is found in Raymond, VI (pp. 70 f.). The mine was reopened several times and was in operation until the 1940s. A detailed account is given in Logan (p. 161). *See* Dutch-App Mine and Heslep Mine.

Aqueduct City [Amador]. At the head of Grass Valley, three miles south of Volcano. It was named because the Ham ditch crossed the Mokelumne Divide here over a 130-foot high aqueduct. Gold was discovered in 1850. The town grew fast and at one time had three hotels, three stores, and numerous saloons. Details are given in the County History, 1881 (p. 215). Albert Leonard mined here without success in 1854. The County Map of 1866 shows the place and surrounding mines. When the placers in the gulches gave out and hill mining proved unprofitable, the town declined rapidly. Browne (p. 72) reports that in 1868 the mines were worked out. Shown as Aqueduct on the USGS Jackson 1938 quadrangle.

Arastraville [Tuolumne]. About three miles north of Tuolumne. The name is a misspelling of Arrastreville, from the Mexican *arrastre*. *See* Glossary. The Easton claim was said to have assayed eighty-five to one hundred dollars per ton. No effort was being made to develop it, though it was a promising mine, and 50 thousand dollars was being demanded for it (Co. Hist., 1882, p. 453). Shown on the USGS Sonora 1939 quadrangle.

Arbuckle Diggings [Shasta]. On a branch of the Middle Fork of Cottonwood Creek, near Harrison Gulch. Gold was discovered in the early 1850s (Steger).

Arctic Group [Nevada]. *See* Gods Country.

Argentine [Plumas]. Twelve miles east of Quincy. The original name, Greenhorn Diggings, was changed to the silvery name when a silver-bearing ledge was discovered. In the 1860s there was extensive quartz and hydraulic gold mining (Raymond, VI, p. 140).

Argonaut Mine [Amador]. Northwest of Jackson. The name of the seekers of the Golden Fleece in the pre-Homeric legend was applied to the searchers for gold in California in 1848 and 1849. Of a number of mines so named, the one west of Highway 49 proved to be the richest, the total production to 1942 reaching 25 million dollars. It operated from 1850, first as Pioneer Mine and after 1893 as Argonaut Mine. It had a 60-stamp mill until 1942, when a ball mill was installed, raising the recovery of gold to 94 percent. The lowest level reached was 6,300 feet. A fire in 1922 at the 3,350-foot level was the most disastrous in modern California gold mining, with forty-seven miners killed. A detailed description of the mine is given in *Mining Bureau*, L (pp. 168 ff.). Recorded on map 5 of the *Guidebook*. Argonaut and Kennedy mines are Historic Landmark 786. *See* Jackson.

Argus Mountains [Inyo]. In the early 1890s there was gold mining in Argus Canyon, on the west slope of the mountains. Later, in the 1930s, gold was mined on the east slope of the range, at the Arando, Mohawk, and Ruth mines. The most productive mine was the Ruth Mine, which yielded an estimated 750 thousand dollars. (*Mining Bureau*, XII, p. 136; XXXIV, pp. 381, 411 f., 416 ff.).

Arica District [Riverside]. In the Arica Mountains, in the northeastern part of the county. Several mines were active in the early 1900s and again in the 1920s and 1930s (*Bull.*, 193, p. 153).

Aristocracy Hill [Nevada]. Now a part of Nevada City. It was named because some southern "aristocratic" residents in the early 1850s refused to mingle with the ordinary miners.

Arkansas [Yuba]. Shown as Arkansan on Milleson and Adams map of 1851, about twenty-two miles northeast of Marysville, where trails to Rich Bar and Downieville fork.

Arkansas Bar [Placer]. The Bar was just above Horseshoe Bend on the Middle Fork of American River (*Mining Bureau*, IX, p. 275).

Arkansas Canyon [Nevada]. Tributary to Greenhorn Creek; near Red Dog. Shown on Pettee and Bowman's map, 1879, and mentioned by Pettee in Whitney, *Auriferous Gravels* (p. 173).

Arkansas: Dam, Bar [Trinity]. Between Canyon and Dutch Creeks. The story of the dam is told by John Carr's *Pioneer Days in California* (pp. 141 ff.). In the summer of 1850 a company, including many men from Arkansas, built the "Arkansaw" dam to divert Trinity River from its bed. The dam broke, apparently in the fall of 1851 (Knapp, p. 509), but was rebuilt. According to Cox (pp. 53 ff.), it was rebuilt several times, and the claims paid richly.

Arkansas Bar is shown on Goddard's map, 1857, just south of Weaverville. It may not be the same site as Arkansas Dam, which is several miles as the crow flies southwest of Weaverville (H. E. Goodyear).

Arkansas Diggings [Amador]. On Arkansas Creek, about three miles northwest of Forest Home. Recorded on the County Map, 1866. According to the County History, 1881 (p. 231), it was "so called because no Arkansaw traveller ever came this way." W. I. Morgan found only one old tent, but no house at the Arkansaw Encampment, near Willow Springs, in the middle of May, 1850. Arkansas Creek is shown on the USGS Sutter Creek 1944 quadrangle. Arkansas Ferry on the Mokelumne River is shown on the County Map, 1866, near French Camp and Camp Union.

Arkansas Flat [Mariposa]. Two miles west of Mariposa, on a ridge between Carson Creek and McBrides Gulch. Shown on the Las Mariposas map, 1861. According to *Mining Bureau*, LIII (p. 235), a pocket mine on Las Mariposas grant was active between 1906 and 1908 and again in 1911.

Arlington District [San Bernardino]. *See* Black Hawk Canyon District.

Armstrong's Mill [Amador]. A half mile from Pine Grove, on the Volcano-Jackson stage road. There was a store at David Armstrong's mill and camp in 1857 (Cenotto).

Arrastre Creek [Mono]. Near Bodie. It was named for the large arrastres which were used there to crush ore from the Bodie mines in the 1860s and 1870s (F. S. Wedertz).

Arrastre Flat [San Bernardino]. In Holcomb Valley, about one and a half miles east of Belleville. The settlement, around which there was both placer and quartz mining, is mentioned by Belden, March 2, 1952 and October 16, 1966. *See* Holcomb Valley.

Arrastre Spring [San Bernardino]. In the Avawatz Mountains. According to the *Death Valley Chuck Walla*, March 1, 1907, prospectors found here an old Mexican gold camp, including the remnants of an arrastre, and they tried to revive mining activities.

Arrastreville [Tuolumne]. *See* Arastraville.

Arrowhead District [San Bernardino]. At the southeast end of the Providence Mountains, adjoining the Trojan District. The Hidden Hill Mine was located in 1882, and for several years considerable work was done by Mexicans using arrastres. In 1913

a rich pocket in the mine yielded 13 thousand dollars. The Big Horn Mine was worked on a large scale in 1918–1919 and was reactivated in the 1920s and 1930s. (*Mining Bureau*, XV, pp. 800 f.; XXVI, p. 222; XXVII, p. 301; *Bull.*, 193, p. 153.) Other mines are listed in *Mining Bureau*, XLIX (table following p. 257).

Arroyo Seco [Amador]. The Spanish name for Dry Creek.

Arum City [El Dorado]. *See* Aurum City.

Ash Hollow [Trinity]. On the north edge of Weaverville townsite; it drains into Sidney Gulch, tributary to Weaver Creek. It is mentioned in 1858 by Cox (p. 131), but no other record was found.

Ashland [Amador]. Three or four miles from Volcano, between the Middle and North forks of Sutter Creek. It is mentioned in the *Amador Ledger*, March 8, 1856, as having been worked for three or four years, whenever water was available. In an earlier issue, February 9, 1856, the camp is described as a "large district," with thirty or forty cabins, housing nearly one hundred miners, and prospects for mining were good. Ashland Creek is shown on the USGS Jackson 1938 quadrangle.

Ashland [Sacramento]. On the north bank of American River, opposite Folsom. Shown on Doolittle's map, 1868. Former names were Big Gulch, Bowlesville, and Russville. The name Russville was given for Colonel Russ, a colorful entrepreneur who came here in 1857 but failed in his gold mining and granite quarrying ventures. After his departure around 1860, the name was changed to Ashland. (Co. Hist., 1880, p. 220; 1890, p. 202.) The place was a station on the California Central Railroad between Folsom and Lincoln.

Askews Bar [Placer]. At the junction of Bear River and Rock Creek, seven miles east of Wheatland. A wire bridge crossed the river here. Shown on the Yuba County Map of 1879.

Atchison Bar [Yuba]. On the North Fork of Yuba River, opposite Fosters Bar. Shown as Achinson Bar on Trask's map, 1853, and on Wescoatt's map, 1861, as Atchisons Bar. Newton Miller mined here and built a wing dam in July, 1851. De Long collected miners' taxes at the place on March 20, 1855. According to the *Marysville Directory*, 1858 (p. xxvii), it was named for J. H. Atchison, and since 1849, it had yielded with fair success, some portions having been very rich.

Atlanta [Nevada]. *See* Fordyce Valley.

Auburn: town, **Ravine, District** [Placer].

Auburn, Placer Co.

Claude Chana (or Charnay), a French prospecter, is credited with having discovered gold in the ravine, May 16, 1848 (*Mining Bureau*, XXIII, p. 261). The County History, 1882 (pp. 66 f.) gives a lengthy story of the discovery and even states that Chana cut a tree on Bear Creek and made *bateas* to wash gold. *See* Rich Flat and Rich Ravine. The place was known successively as Rich Dry Diggings, North Fork Dry Diggings, and Woods Dry Diggings. It was named Auburn in August, 1849, after Auburn, New York. According to Letts (p. 77) and Mahlon D. Fairchild (pp. 15 f.), the "town" consisted of three or four tents at that time. The U. S. Bureau of the Census lists the names of 1,302 inhabitants at Auburn and vicinity for the 1850 census. John Banks was in Auburn in September, 1850, and in *The Buckeye Rovers* (p. 139) he tells an amusing story of a doctor who was condemned by a jury to refund his exorbitant fee. The name Auburn is recorded on Butler's map of 1851; a post office was established July 21, 1853. Browne (pp. 108 and 109) mentions three active mines in the vicinity of Auburn in 1867, and the *Register* of 1902 still lists four stamp mills and one Huntington mill. The mines of the district are described in Raymond, VII (pp. 109 f.). The town is Historic Landmark 404.

Auburn Station [Placer]. *See* Secret Ravine.

Augustaville [Yuba]. *See* Hammonton.

Auram City [El Dorado]. *See* Aurum City.

Aurora [Mono]. The Latin name for the northern lights was repeatedly used for mines. Gold and silver were discovered on a tributary to Bodie Creek, north of Mono Lake, in August, 1860 (Maule, p. 25; *Mining Press*, December 7, 1860; Browne, p. 178). In 1862 the town had 5,000 resi-

dents. It is shown as a place of considerable size on Clayton's map, about 1865. From 1861 to 1864 it was the county seat of Mono County, but in 1864, as the result of a boundary survey, it was determined that Aurora was in the state of Nevada. The Esmeralda District in Nevada had its headquarters here. Mark Twain prospected in Aurora (or Esmeralda) from February to August, 1862, and his experiences there form the basis of the "blind lead" story in his *Roughing It*. Details of the Esmeralda or Aurora experience may be found in Effie Mona Mack, *Mark Twain in Nevada* (pp. 155 ff.).

Aurum City [El Dorado]. About a mile and a half southeast of El Dorado. Shown as Auram City on Doolittle's map, 1868. A 14-stamp steam-driven quartz mill was established as early as 1852 (Hittell Clippings, p. 74; *State Register*, 1857). However, in 1866 the Jamison Mine still used an arrastre (Browne, p. 89). The name is sometimes spelled Auram and Arum.

Austin [El Dorado]. South of Diamond Springs. The name is recorded on Goddard's map of 1857.

Avawatz Mountains [San Bernardino]. At the southeast corner of Death Valley National Monument. There was apparently intermittent gold mining since the 1850s. Both slopes of the range reportedly have gold and silver containing quartz deposits. A detailed description is given in *Mining Bureau*, IX, (pp. 216 f.). A variant form of the name, Ivawatch, is used in *Mining Bureau*, VIII (pp. 501 f.). For the origin of the name, *see California Place Names*. *See* Arrastre Spring and Crackerjack.

Ave Maria [Mariposa]. About one mile

south of the town of Mariposa, at the junction of Stockton Creek (originally called Ave Maria River) and Mariposa Creek. Recorded on Trask's map, 1853, and on Goddard's, 1857. It was doubtless named by Mexican miners. There was a store and a corral here before the influx of the gold seekers. The British Ave Maria Company worked here in 1852 (Crampton, p. 64). *See* Stockton Creek.

Average [Calaveras]. Listed in Hittell's roster (*Mining Bureau*, IV, p. 219).

Ayres Diggings [Placer]. On El Dorado Canyon, tributary to the North Fork of the Middle Fork of American River, north of Michigan Bluffs. Shown on Doolittle's map, 1868.

B aboon Gulch. An unidentified locality mentioned by Knapp (p. 517).

Bachelor Hill [Placer]. On El Dorado Canyon, tributary to the North Fork of the Middle Fork of American River, above Michigan Bluffs. Shown as Batchelors Hill on Doolittle's map, 1868. It is mentioned by Lindgren (*Tertiary Gravels*, p. 156) as a gravel hill that had been hydraulicked.

Backbone: Creek, District [Shasta]. At the northeast corner of Shasta Lake. According to old newspaper reports, a party of German prospectors discovered rich gold placers here and named the Creek after the mountain called Backbone. The district, which produces gold and silver, is along Squaw and Backbone Creeks (*Mining Bureau*, XI, p. 46). The Uncle Sam Mine, the largest producer in the district, has yielded more than a million dollars, according to *Bulletin*, 193 (p. 133).

Backs [El Dorado]. The place is recorded on Gibbes' map, 1851, as a town near or on the Rubicon River.

Bacons Placer [El Dorado]. An unidentified place near Placerville. Edward Wilson (p. 36) claims that he and a partner took out seven hundred dollars in nine days in the summer of 1850.

Badger. Only a few mining places are named for this valuable animal because it was almost extinct at the time of the Gold Rush.

Badger Bar [Placer]. Below the junction of the North and Middle forks of American River. According to *Placer Nuggets*, October, 1971, miners had a flume there in July, 1853, and were doing well.

Badger Hill [El Dorado]. Seven miles east of Placerville. There was profitable placering

by drifting and sluicing. A mine was still listed in 1956 (*Mining Bureau*, LII, p. 541).

Badger Hill [Plumas]. About fifteen miles northwest of Sawpit Flat. In 1867 four piping and five drifting companies were in operation. The output, however, was only five dollars to the man per day. (Browne, p. 167.)

Badger Hill: settlement, District [Nevada]. Near the Middle Fork of Yuba River, four miles east of North San Juan. Shown on Doolittle's map, 1868. Several companies were operating in 1867 (Bean, p. 341). The area was on the Great Gravel Deposit (Raymond, VI, p. 108). Badger Hill District, which includes Cherokee Diggings, was hydraulicked from the 1850s through the 1880s, and later Chinese miners worked the tailings (*Bull.*, 193, p. 28). Badger Hill is shown as a settlement on the USGS Smartsville 1943 quadrangle.

Badger Mine [Mariposa]. *See* Hornitos.

Bagby [Mariposa]. *See* Benton Mills.

Bagdad [Butte]. A mining camp of the 1850s on Feather River, south of Oroville. Windeler (pp. 149 ff.) mined here briefly in the winter months of 1852–1853.

Bagdad [San Bernardino]. The station on the Santa Fe Railroad, east of Barstow, was not a gold town, but it was one of the principal gold shipping points in the state between 1900 and 1910. From the south an important wagon road came in from Twentynine Palms and the Dale District, and from the north a road connected with the Orange Blossom Mine in the Bristol Mountains. It grew to be a thriving town; but when the Bagdad-Chase mines were developed at Stedman, the mining railroad was built to the closer Santa Fe connection at Ludlow. (Belden, April 3, 1960; Haenszel.) *See* Stedman District.

Bagdad [Trinity]. *See* North Fork.

Bagdad-Chase Mines [San Bernardino]. *See* Stedman District.

Bailey Bar [Trinity]. On Cañon Creek. Miners were making regularly 100 to 150 dollars a week to the hand (*Trinity Journal*, February 18, 1860).

Bairdstown [San Bernardino]. Near and west of Gold Mountain Mill, in eastern Holcomb Valley. A town was laid out and named for Samuel H. Baird, who had staked a claim on a ridge between Holcomb Valley and Bear Valley in 1873. The town flourished briefly; boasting a store, hotel, restaurant, ten or more saloons, and fifty houses (La Fuze, I, p. 132). It had a short-lived post office from February to September, 1875. By 1888 the town was deserted (Hale, p. 42). *See* Holcomb Valley; Gold Mountain.

Bakers Claim [Calaveras]. Near Jesus Maria. In 1853 water was brought to the camp, and the average earning was thirty dollars a day to the hand (Letter of W. H. Moore, July 17, 1853).

Bakers Ranch [Placer]. On the divide between Shirttail Canyon and the Middle Fork of American River, near Michigan Bluffs. Shown on Doolittle's map, 1868. It was a stopping place operated by J. Hull Baker, who lived there since 1850 (Hutchings' Diary, May 6, 1855). Shown on the USGS Colfax 1938 quadrangle.

Balaklala Mine [Shasta]. *See* Balaklava Hill [Calaveras].

Balaklava [Nevada]. Shown on Doolittle's map, 1868 as a settlement about four miles northeast of Quaker Hill. *See* Balaklava Hill [Calaveras].

Balaklava Hill [Calaveras]. Two and a half miles south of Vallecito. Like a number of gold and copper mining places, it was named after Balaklava, a seaport on the Black Sea, where a battle took place in 1854 during the Crimean War. The place is listed by Hittell in 1884 (*Mining Bureau*, IV, p. 219) and a drift and hydraulic mine there was reported as idle in 1936 (*Mining Bureau*, XXXII, p. 326). The Balaklala Mine in Shasta County, west of Kennett, on the South Fork of Squaw Creek, which carried iron, copper, gold, and silver but produced mainly copper, was listed as Balaklava in 1892–94 (*Mining Bureau*, XII, p. 245). It appears as Balaklala on the USGS Weaverville 1942 quadrangle.

Bald Eagle Diggings [Nevada]. Northeast of Remington Hill. Shown on Doolittle's map, 1868. Hydraulic mining in the 1870s is recorded in Raymond, VI (p. 117). The name of the well known American bird was used to designate a number of mines and mining localities. *See* Consolidated Index.

Bald Hill [Calaveras]. North of Angels Camp. The south side of the hill is now covered with brush; hence, the name is no longer applicable. The Calaveras Central Mine, situated on the north side of the hill, was reactivated early in 1948 but was soon closed. According to *Guidebook* (p. 56) and other sources, the "Calaveras Skull," now generally considered a hoax, was found at the bottom of a shaft on Bald Hill in 1866. The "Skull" is now at the Peabody Museum of Archaeology and Ethnology, Harvard University.

Bald Hill [El Dorado]. In the Hornblende Mountains, near Otter Creek. There was mainly seam digging here and on Little Bald Hill (Raymond, IV, p. 105; VII, pp. 84, 94). In 1857 a steam-driven, 12-stamp mill and two arrastres were in operation (*State Register*, 1859).

Bald Hill [Placer]. Near Ophir, in the Lone Star District. In 1856 a company of German miners had a quartz mine and a water-driven 8-stamp mill here. The quartz yielded twenty-eight dollars per ton. (Co. Hist., 1882, p. 193.) According to an extract from the Grass Valley *Union* in a clipping marked December, 1864 (Hayes Scrapbooks: Mining, IV, sec. 20), miners prospecting in the vicinity of Bald Mountain (doubtless Bald Hill), near Auburn, struck a rich pocket and took out as much as 5 thousand dollars in a few hours. Notices of numerous mining claims are recorded in December, 1864, and January, 1865, in Placer County Records, V (pp. 145, 155, 341).

Bald Mountain [Sierra]. North of Forest City. The deposits were apparently discovered during the Gold Lake hunt. The name is listed by Hittell (*Mining Bureau*, IV, p. 221). The Bald Mountain drift mine, developed in 1864, yielded 2 million dollars before it closed ten years later, according to *Mines and Minerals* (p. 383). The figure given in *Bulletin*, 193 (p. 24) is 3.1 million dollars for the Bald Mountain and between one half and one million dollars for the Bald Mountain Extension. The activities before 1875 are described in detail by Raymond, VII (pp. 152 ff.).

Bald Mountain [Tuolumne]. About three miles northeast of Sonora. It was also known as Bare Mountain for the lack of vegetation, when the first settlers came, and sometimes as Bear Mountain for the grizzly bears found there. The place was connected with the Columbia and Stanislaus River Water Company (Heckendorn, p. 25). It produced the very finest gold quartz, measuring as high as 960°. In 1867 Browne (p. 49) reported all mines as good yielders, but they were idle at that time. The most famous was the Ford Mine or Lead, discovered by William Ford, an early Sonora desperado. For details on Ford's career, *see* William Perkins (p. 230). The Ford Mine is still worked occasionally. (De Ferrari.) The Bald Mountain or Austrian Mine is listed in Mining Bureau reports until 1927. Shown on the USGS Big Trees 1941 quadrangle.

Bald Point [Trinity]. On the Trinity River, east of Douglas City. There was rich hydraulic gravel mining here. The claims of the district are listed in Mining Bureau, XIII (p. 459). The Bald Point Mine was still listed in 1941.

Baldwin [Mariposa]. The place is recorded on Butler's map of 1851, just west of Quartzburg. No mining record was found.

Baldwin Lake District [San Bernardino]. In the San Bernardino Mountains. The claim that Mexicans mined here as early as 1800 has not been authenticated. American miners first worked the Rose Mine probably in the 1860s, but the main activity was between 1895 and 1903. The mines in the district are listed in *Bulletin*, 193 (p. 170) and are described in *Mining Bureau*, XLIX (pp. 69 ff.). *See* Doble; Gold Mountain. The lake was named for E. J. ("Lucky") Baldwin, spectacular promoter in the latter part of the nineteenth century (*California Place Names*).

Baldy Notch [San Bernardino]. *See* Mount Baldy District.

Ballarat [Inyo]. In Panamint Valley, west of Death Valley. The town, named after the gold-mining center in Australia, developed in the 1890s. On June 21, 1897, a post office was established, and in 1900 seven mills with a total of about sixty stamps were in operation. The gold producing mines are listed and mapped in the *Register* of 1902. The most productive was the Ratcliff, discovered in 1897 and active to about 1915 and again between 1927 and 1942, with intermittent work since that time. The total production was more than 1.3 million dollars. (*Bull.*, 193, p. 146). Modern mines around Ballarat are listed in *Mining Bureau*, XXVIII (pp. 364 ff.) and XLVII (pp. 45 ff.). The place is now a ghost town.

Ballards Humbug [Amador]. South of Volcano. Shown on Camp's map opposite p. 99. Named for A. M. Ballard, who found a rich lead on a tributary to Sutter Creek. His discovery caused great excitement, but the lead did not produce as was expected; hence, the name. Doble and others mined here with moderate success (Doble, August 11, 1852 and later). He mentions it as Humbug Gulch, December 28, 1852. Humbug is listed by Hittell.

Ballena Placers [San Diego]. South and east of Ramona. The placers are in an old river bed and extend about four miles. They were worked as early as 1890 and probably before. The main recorded activity was between 1906 and 1914 and again in the 1920s. The production was small, mainly

because of the lack of water to wash the gravels. (*Mining Bureau*, XIV, p. 652; *County Report*, III, p. 122.)

Bally Choop District [Trinity]. *See* Bully Choop.

Balsam Flat [Sierra]. One mile east of Alleghany. The *Mining Press*, June 22, 1861, reported that the place was on the decline but still going. In the issue of October 19 of the same year, it was further stated that seven tunnels were running, but only two of these were paying — "the others were living on hope." The *Sierra Democrat*, December 8, 1862, reported that one company took out fourteen ounces and another thirty-seven ounces in one week.

Balsam Hill [Butte]. Northeast of Stirling City, on Kimshew Creek. It was named after the balsam spruce, which grew in the gold region. The County Map of 1861 shows a sizeable settlement. No mining record was found.

Baltic Mine [Nevada]. *See* Gods Country.

Baltic Peak [El Dorado]. North of Grizzly Creek, tributary to the Steele Fork of the North Cosumnes River. The Baltic Mine north of the peak had a 10-stamp mill built about 1895 (*Mining Bureau*, XIII, p. 133). It ceased operation in 1907 (*California Place Names*). The name of the Baltic Sea between Scandinavia and Germany was a favorite for gold mines during the Gold Rush. The U. S. Forest Service named the peak after the mine. It is shown on the USGS Placerville 1931 quadrangle.

Baltimore City [Nevada]. At Meadow Lake. It was founded in 1865 and was first known as Wightman Camp. Wightman was a broker and instigator and first president of the Excelsior Company (Foley). There were once five or six buildings here, according to the County History, 1880 (p. 196), but in 1880 the site was marked only by a single, deserted house.

Baltimore: Hill, Ravine [Placer]. Near Ophir. Gold was first discovered in the area at the junction of Baltimore Ravine and Auburn Ravine, and newspapers of the 1850s reported rich finds (Gianella; Co. Hist., 1882, p. 227). Ravine and Hill claims of 1851 and 1852 are recorded in Placer County Records, I (pp. 31, 75). According to a correspondent to *Stars and Stripes* writing August 4, 1870, a group of Austrian prospectors found a hunk of quartz, of which ninety-seven pounds [!] was gold. The piece was found near the surface in a ravine that had been considered exhausted, and the finders kept it a secret for sometime. (Unidentified clipping in Hayes' Scrapbooks: Mining, IV, sec. 119.)

Bandarita Mine [Mariposa]. *See* Gentry Gulch.

Bandereta [Mariposa]. *See* Coulterville.

Bangor [Butte]. Between North and South Honcut creeks. Shown on Doolittle's map, 1868. It was named in 1855 by the Lumbert Brothers after their hometown in Maine. In 1857 a rich channel was struck, which yielded at first one hundred dollars per day to the hand. The place is shown as a sizeable town on the County Map of 1861. A fairly good chronicle of the place is given in the County History, 1882 (pp. 264 ff.). One drift mine was in operation until 1918. The Bangor-Wyandotte District was dredged in the early twentieth century and again in the 1930s (*Bull.*, 193, p. 29).

Banks Mine [Los Angeles]. *See* Mount Baldy District.

Banner. A folk name used frequently for mines that yielded or were expected to yield well.

Banner: City, Creek, Canyon, District [San Diego]. About three miles southeast of Julian. Gold was discovered in August, 1870, by a party of men from Julian, who were looking for wild grapes in San Felipe, now Chariot Canyon. Soon afterwards the Redman Mine was discovered near by and a mining district was formed. After 1881 the district was combined with Julian District. (*Mining Bureau*, VI, Part 1, pp. 86 ff.; XXX, p. 350.) A town called Banner City was laid out and for a period of time it rivaled Julian. It had a post office intermittently between 1873 and 1906. Among the mines that developed were the Ready Relief, Hubbard, Hidden Treasure, and Golden Chariot. Mining soon declined, but after 1888, when the Gold King and Gold Queen mines were discovered southeast of Julian, there was a brief renewal of activity in the Julian-Banner District. Mines and mills are listed in the *Register*, 1903. Descriptions of the mines are given in *County Report*, III (pp. 124 ff. and Tables, pp. 136 ff.). An interesting account is also given in Ellsberg, *Mines of Julian*. The "City" has now disappeared and today only a part of the foundation of a stamp mill is a reminder of the once lively town (Ellsberg, p. 46).

Banner Ledge [Butte]. In Oregon Gulch, six miles from Oroville. The ledge was discovered and prospected in 1850, and it yielded profitably until 1881. Detailed description may be found in County History, 1882 (pp. 214 ff.). The claims are listed and described in *Mining Bureau*, XV (pp. 211 f.). The Banner Mine yielded an estimated one million dollars (*Bull.*, 193, p. 93).

Banner Mine [Nevada]. *See* Nevada City.

Bannerville [Nevada]. About two miles southeast of Nevada City. Banner Butte and Bannerville are shown on Doolittle's map, 1868. The place was the site of the (Star Spangled) Banner mine. The camp is long vanished, but the Consolidated Banner Mines are listed in *Mining Bureau* until 1941; their total production was more than 1 million dollars (*Bull.*, 193, p. 99). Banner Hill is shown on the USGS Colfax 1938 quadrangle.

Bardee Bar [Butte]. On the North Fork of Feather River. Shown on the County Map, 1877. It is probably the same as Bartees Bar, which is mentioned in the County History, 1882 (p. 253) as a once flourishing mining camp in Concow township, north of Oroville.

Bardwells Bar [Placer]. On an affluent of the South Fork of the North Fork of American River. Shown on Doolittle's map, 1868.

Barefoot Diggings. An unidentified location, listed in the Work Projects Administration project.

Bare Mountain [Tuolumne]. *See* Bald Mountain.

Barley Flat [El Dorado]. Mentioned as an early mining locality in Kelsey township (Co. Hist., 1883, p. 191).

Barlows Bar [Yuba]. On the North Fork of Yuba River, below Fosters Bar. It is listed by Theodore Johnson in 1849 and is recorded on Jackson's map of 1850.

Barnards Diggings [Plumas]. Southwest of La Porte. Shown on Crossman's Map of Sierra County, 1867. There was hydraulic mining as early as 1856. The place is described in *Transactions*, 1858 (p. 201). It is mentioned as Bernard Diggings in Raymond V, 1872 (p. 87) and in the *Register* of Plumas County, 1892.

Barnes Bar [Placer]. On the North Fork of American River, above the junction with the Middle Fork, near Mineral Bar. Shown on Goddard's map, 1857. The bar was discovered in the spring of 1849 and was named for George A. Barnes, who opened a store here. Judge Robert Thompson mined here in July, 1849, and averaged one ounce a day (*CHSQ*, XXX, pp. 237 ff.).

Barnwell [San Bernardino]. *See* Manvel.

Barra Rica [Plumas]. *see* Rich Bar.

Barrett City [Mariposa]. About six miles north of Exchequer; now under Lake McClure. The Mariposa *Gazette*, Centennial edition, 1954 (p. 51) mentions it along with another settlement, Pleasant Valley. No contemporary record was found, and the tales told about its size and importance do not ring true.

Barric Mine [Los Angeles]. The place where the first known gold deposit in California was discovered is designated on Duflot de Mofras' map of 1844 as *Mine d'or de M'Baric*. It is in almost complete alignment with San Fernando Mission and Los Angeles. These placers were obviously the same that were discovered by Francisco Lopez who exploited them with Charles Barric, a native of France. *See* Placerita and San Feliciano.

Barrys Halfway House [Tuolumne]. *See* Halfway House.

Barstow [San Bernardino]. Around 1880 it was the center of the gold and silver mines north of the Mojave River, and in 1886 a post office was established here to serve these mines. The mines are listed and mapped in the *Register*, 1902. A mill here in the early 1890s served the Bagdad-Chase mines at Stedman (Belden, November 23, 1952). *See* Grapevine District; Waterman; Daggett.

Bartees Bar [Butte]. *See* Bardee Bar.

Bartons Bar [Yuba]. On the main Yuba River, between Parks Bar and Rose Bar. Shown on Milleson and Adams' map, 1851, and Wescoatt's, 1861. It was named for Robert and John Barton who had a store here in the 1850s. In 1855 miners were doing only moderately well (Hutchings' Diary, September 25, 1855). According to the *Alta*, November, 1867, and the County History, 1879 (p. 88), it was a rich bar but was soon buried by gravel.

Bassetts Gulch [Tuolumne]. A former name

Bartons Bar, Yuba Co.

of Sonora Creek. It was named for Charles Bassett, who discovered gold here while leading a party of sailors in the spring of 1849. Stoddart (pp. 82 ff.) gives an interesting account of the place.

Bassetts Station [Sierra]. Five miles east of Sierra City. It was a well-known inn and rest stop on the road across the Yuba Pass. When the inn was opened in the early 1860s, it was known as Hancock House. About 1865 the name was changed to Howard Ranch, for the owner, Howard Chris Tegerman, and in the 1870s the name Bassett's Station was applied, for Jacob and Mary Bassett. (Sinnott, *Sierra City*, p. 131). It is said that many miners were grubstaked at the inn.

Bates [Trinity]. On the East Fork of Stuarts Fork, sixteen miles from Weaverville. The place is mentioned as a trading post in 1858 by Cox (p. 89). Hutchings spent the night here, January 11, 1855. The Bates and Tourtellote Mine, listed by the Mining Bureau in 1896, may be at the same site.

Bath [Placer]. One mile above Forest Hill. It drains into Volcano Canyon and was originally (1850) called Volcano, according to the County History, 1882 (p. 375). The name was changed to Sarahsville in 1851 and to Bath in 1858, when the post office was established. Doolittle's map, 1868, shows "Bath P. O." with Sarahsville as an alternate or former name. For many years it was an important gold mining town. A 20-stamp mill was built at the Paragon Mine in 1864 (Browne, pp. 97 f.). In 1869 there were two steam-driven mills with thirty stamps and one hurdy-gurdy mill with five stamps, all idle except the Paragon (Raymond II, p. 41). The gravels mined at the Paragon are part of the Tertiary river channel (Gianella). The total yield to 1868 has been estimated at 2.5 million dollars, according to *Mining Bureau*, XXIII (p. 262). By 1870 the town had dwindled to 100 inhabitants (Raymond, VII, p. 106), but the post office remained active until 1899, and the *Register* of 1902 still reports sluicing operations. Bath Mining District is mentioned in Placer County Records, IV (pp. 55 f.), in connection with the sale of a tunnel mining claim, August 3, 1859. Browne (pp. 97 ff.) describes mining activities in the various claims in the district in the 1860s.

Batharac [Sierra]. This strange name is shown on Raymond's map opposite p. 88, volume V (published in 1873), in the midst of placer mines in the Slate Creek Basin, north of Potosi.

Bayecito [Calaveras]. *See* Vallecito.

Bayles [Shasta]. In 1884 a post office was established here for the mines along Dog Creek. The trading center for the area was Delta. *See* Delta.

Beals Bar [Placer]. A short-lived camp on the north bank of the North Fork of American River, near the junction with the South Fork. Recorded on Jackson's map, 1850; Goddard's, 1857; and other early maps. In the summer of 1849 a company of thirty men worked here on shares; each share was worth 2 thousand eight hundred dollars and the profits were twenty dollars per day to the man (Letts, p. 91). Notice of intention to build a ditch here is dated September 28, 1852, in Placer County Records, I (p. 122). According to the *Placer Herald*, September 22, 1856, claims located here and near by were still yielding well. The U. S. Bureau of the Census lists the names of 378 miners at Beals Bar (Forksville) in the population schedule for 1850. According to Hutchings (Diary, April 25, 1855) there were 170 inhabitants, mainly Americans, in 1855.

Beams Bar [Sacramento]. On the south side of American River, below Alabama Bar. The place was named for Jerry Beam, and it was a gold producer from the summer of 1849 until 1863 (Co. Hist., 1880, p. 225).

Bean Hill [El Dorado]. Near Placerville. It is mentioned in 1859 by Crockett (p. 95). Whitney, in *Auriferous Gravels* (p. 101), locates it northeast of Sugar Loaf, at Diamond Springs, and describes the extent of hydraulic mining by 1871.

Bean Poker Flat [Placer; El Dorado]. On the North Fork of American River, on both sides of the river. It is mentioned in *Placer Nuggets*, February, 1964, by May W. Perry.

Bear. More than 500 geographic features in California are named for our most notable wild animal. In the gold regions there are comparatively few Bear names. The miners, given to exaggeration, often called any bear a grizzly.

Bear Creek [Mariposa]. There are two streams in the county named Bear Creek. One heads in Bear Valley on Highway 49, northwest of the town of Mariposa and flows west and southwest; the other heads about three miles northeast of Mariposa and flows northerly, emptying into Merced River at Briceburg. It is probably the latter from which Allsop datelines one of his letters: Bear Creek, September 14, 1852. Near Bear Creek, about one and a half miles south and east of Briceburg, is the old Piedra De Goza lode mine, later known as the Roma Mine, which was discovered in the 1850s or early 1860s by Spanish Californians. Close by were the King Solomon and Sierra Rica mines, both of which were operated at one time with the Roma Mine. Descriptions are given in *Mining Bureau*, LIII (pp. 164 f.; pp. 274, 304).

Bear Creek [Santa Barbara]. Along the ocean beach from Bear Creek to Surf, gold was extracted from the black beach sand with moderate success in the twentieth century (*Mining Bureau*, XXI, p. 541).

Bear Creek [Siskiyou]. On the Klamath River, near Gottville. The Lee Han Mine, owned by Chinese, was still in full operation until the end of the nineteenth century (*Mining Bureau*, XIII, p. 412).

Bear Mountain [Tuolumne]. *See* Bald Mountain.

Bear: Mountains, Creek [Calaveras]. South of Calaveras River, parallel to Highway 49. There was intensive mining in the foothills from San Andreas to Angels Camp as early as 1849. The mountains are said to have been the hideout of Joaquin Murieta in the winter of 1852–53, when quite a few misdeeds were committed and blamed on Murieta. The highest peak is still named for him, Mount Joaquin. According to the San Francisco *Bulletin*, December 1, 1856, a rich deposit was discovered, when a prospector, who fell into a ravine while pursuing a grizzly, scratched out nine dollars worth of gold with his hunting knife. In 1856 there was a water-driven 8-stamp mill (*State Register*, 1859). A Bear Mountain mine is listed in 1936 (*Mining Bureau*, XXXII, p. 297).

Bear River District [Yuba]. *See* Wheatland District.

Beartrap Flat [Kern]. A mining camp in Greenhorn Gulch (Boyd, p. 29).

Bear Valley [Mariposa]. Twelve miles north of Mariposa, on Highway 49. Shown prominently as a settlement on Trask's map, 1853. The camp was first known as Haydensville for David, Charles, and Willard Hayden, who with James C. Higginbotham in October, 1850 purchased or leased part of the Great Johnson Vein, known as the Hayden Division and the Spring Division, from John F. "Quartz" Johnson, the discoverer. The Hayden Division later became the Josephine Mine when the Nouveau Monde Gold Mining Company acquired the property. The first post office of the county was established here as Haydensville, January 21, 1851, with Higginbotham as post master. Hayden and associate soon went bankrupt, however. The post office was discontinued August 20, 1852, and the same year the camp and election precinct were called Biddle's Camp, Bear Valley, for William C. Biddle. It is mentioned as Biddleville in the Report of the Nouveau Monde Gold Mining Company, September, 1854 (p. 28). Another unofficial name was Simpsonville, for Robert Simpson, who with Robert W. Hammath had a store here. In 1856 the town was surveyed and subdivided and was named Johnsonville, for John F. "Quartz" Johnson. On June 21, 1858, when the post office was reestablished, the name was changed to Bear Valley, its present name. Mexican miners discovered gold here in 1850, but they were soon forced out after having found a quarter million dollars worth of gold within a few weeks, according to a report in the *Alta*, November 27, 1851. A short phenomenal boom followed and the town had several thousand inhabitants in 1851, but as early as March 22, 1852, the *Alta* reported that the placers were exhausted. This report could have referred only to the placers because quartz mining continued to keep the place alive. In 1854 a Mexican is said to have found a lump of pure gold "weighing fully three pounds" (*Alta*, March 15, 1854). In 1855 a 10-stamp mill was in operation (*Annual Mining Review*, 1876, p. 21), and in 1859 John C. Frémont also had an 8-stamp mill in operation built by J. F. Johnson (*Hutchings Illustrated California Magazine*, September, 1859, p. 105; *Alta*, August 11, 1860). The place was the headquarters of Frémont's 44,386-acre Las Mariposas Estate, and it was the home of the Frémont family from 1858 to 1861 (Jessie B. Frémont, *Mother Lode Narratives*). The *Register*, 1903, still lists a mill in operation. Additional references to Bear Valley may be found in Crampton.

Bear Valley [San Bernardino]. A mining district in the San Bernardino Mountains. An undated clipping from the Los Angeles *Star* of 1855 reports that the average daily earning was only four dollars to the man. However, State Geologist Trask stated in the 1850s that the region north of San Bernardino "abounds in gold." In 1860 W. F. Holcomb, for whom Holcomb Valley was later named, placer mined at Starvation Flat (Poverty Point), between present-day Big Bear Lake and Big Bear City (Leadabrand, p. 72; Hale, p. 15). The *Mining Press*,

May 1, 1861, reports that the richness of the mines is exaggerated and only a few claims were worked. A 40-stamp mill was built in 1875 by E. J. ("Lucky") Baldwin, which proved to be a failure (*Annual Mining Review*, 1876, p. 21; Co. Hist., 1883, p. 57). In the 1890s commercial mining in the district was reported in *Mining Bureau*, XXVII (pp. 280 ff.). *See* Holcomb Valley. Since 1884 the lower part of Bear Valley has been inundated by the Old Bear Valley Dam, Historic Landmark 725.

Bear Valley, Mariposa Co.

Beaver. This beautiful and interesting animal was at the time of the Gold Rush almost extinct, thanks to the mass destroyers of California wild life, the American, Canadian, and Russian trappers. Beaver River was the old name of Scott River [Siskiyou], when the wealth of the stream lay in beaver dams and not in gold bars. Goddard's map, 1857, still shows both names.

Beaver Bar [El Dorado; Placer]. On the North Fork of American River, below Rattlesnake Bar. It is mentioned in the El Dorado County History, 1883 (p. 83) and Placer County History, 1924 (p. 176). An alternate name was Rich Bar, applied to the bars on both sides of the river, according to *Placer Nuggets*, February, 1964 (p. 6).

Beaver Creek [Siskiyou]. A tributary to Klamath River, which rises in the Siskiyou Mountains. The *Mining Press*, May 1, 1862, reports good success with the washings of tailings left by previous mining operations. There was intermittent placer mining as late as 1914 (*Mining Bureau*, VIII, p. 591; XIV, p. 814).

Beaver Ranch [Yuba]. On Willow Glen Creek, tributary to Dry Creek. Named for David Beever, part owner in 1854. The

County Map of 1879 has the correct spelling of the name, but most other sources misspell it. De Long repeatedly collected the miner's tax here (January 25, 1856 and *passim*). Shown on the USGS Smartsville 1943 quadrangle.

Beckmans Flat [Nevada]. On Deer Creek, about five miles downstream from Nevada City and about one mile southeast of Newton, below Pleasant Flat. It was a small camp, located in the winter of 1851–1852, at which time the lynching of an innocent man was averted. The story is told in the County History, 1880 (p. 106). Shown on the Hoffmann-Craven Gravel Map, 1873.

Beckville [Nevada]. On Deer Creek. It is mentioned by Sargent in Brown's *Directory*, 1856 (p. 19) as the name of the settlement where Dr. Caldwell built his store. Dr. A. B. Caldwell had several stores in the 1850s at different locations on Deer Creek. *See* Rensch-Hoover's entry Nevada City.

Beckworth [Plumas]. In the southeastern part of the county, near present day Hawley. Successful mining was reported here in the summer of 1858, according to a newspaper in Hittell Clippings (p. 54). The place was named for "Old Jim" Beckwourth, who was in this area in the 1850s and had a trading post in Sierra Valley in 1852. In 1851 he had discovered the pass which bears his name. The name is variously spelled — Beckwith, Beckworth, Beckwourth. *See California Place Names* under the entry Beckwith.

Bedbug [Amador]. This name is said to have been one of the early names of Ione.

Beebee Bar [Siskiyou]. On the Scott River below Scott Bar. No early reports were found, but a hydraulic mine owned by Chinese was still in operation in 1896 (*Mining Bureau*, XIII, p. 388).

Beebe Mine [El Dorado]. *See* Georgetown.

Bee Ranch [Sierra]. *See* Kanaka: Flat, Ravine.

Beever [Yuba]. *See* Beaver Ranch.

Beldens Bar [Plumas]. On the North Fork of Feather River, above the mouth of Rock Creek. Shown on the Butte County Map, 1877. No mining record was found.

Belfort [Mono]. Two and a half miles west of Star City, at the eastern base of Mount Patterson. It is listed as a mining camp of the 1880s (Nadeau, p. 210). The name was apparently given quite late as there is no reference to it in early county records (F. S. Wedertz). Shown on the USGS Bridgeport 1911 quadrangle.

Belleville [San Bernardino]. In upper Holcomb Valley, and sometimes called Upper Holcomb. It was named for Belle, daughter of Jed Van Dusen, town blacksmith and builder of a supply road down the north side of the mountains. By July, 1860, Belleville was the principal town in Holcomb Valley, and in 1861 it almost became the county seat. The early workings were mostly placer. (Drake, pp. 16 ff.; La Fuze I, 56; Haenszel.) Raymond, III (p. 13) mentions quartz operations here in 1870.

Bell Hill [Tuolumne]. *see* San Diego.

Bells Bar [Plumas]. On the Middle Fork of Feather River, between Nelson Point and Cromberg. It is listed in the Giffen file and is shown on the USGS Downieville 1907 quadrangle.

Bells Diggings [El Dorado]. Six or seven miles northeast of Georgetown, at the head of Missouri Canyon. The place is described by Raymond, IV (p. 103) and VII (p. 93). It had been prospected by tunnels and many shafts but awaited water for development of its riches. It is shown on Bowman's map, 1873.

Belvedere Flat [Tuolumne]. South of Jamestown. It is mentioned by Hutchings in his diary, July 20, 1855, by Heckendorn in 1856 (pp. 89 and 104), and in retrospect by Gardiner, who was there in the 1850s (pp. 255 ff.).

Bend City [Inyo]. On Owens River, about four miles east of Independence. A soldier from Camp Independence discovered gold near the river in 1862, and the San Carlos Mining and Exploration Company was formed to exploit the lode. A vein of galena was also found, and soon afterwards the towns of San Carlos and Bend City were prospering and Chrysopolis showed promise. *See* Chrysopolis. Bend City had between sixty and seventy buildings, including two hotels, and it became the provisional county seat of the newly organized Coso County. The boom was short-lived, and by 1865 Bend City and San Carlos were deserted. The rich Eclipse Mining Claim, which had been active at the beginning of the boom, and the Brown Monster were worked again between 1880 and 1914 and for an extended time after 1935 (De Decker, pp. 41 ff.). An interesting account is given in *Mining Bureau*, VIII (pp. 265 ff.).

Bendigo District [Riverside]. In the northeast corner of the county. Gold was discovered in 1898 and mining continued until about 1920; in the 1930s there was again some activity (*Bull.*, 193, p. 153).

Ben Lomond Mountain [Santa Cruz]. In the

Santa Cruz Mountains. According to *Mining Bureau*, XVII (p. 235), there were reports that a large amount of gold was taken from a huge boulder in a creek issuing from the mountain. The gold was purportedly the nucleus of a fortune developed by the discoverer, a Mr. Hihn of Santa Cruz. *See* the entry Capitola in *California Place Names*, 3rd ed. The gold was discovered apparently in the 1870s or 1880s. *See also* Grahams Ranch and Gold Gulch [Santa Cruz].

Bennets Ranch [Yuba]. Near Fosters Bar. De Long collected the miners' tax here, March 21, 1855.

Bennettville [Mono]. At the summit of Mono Pass, on the old Mono Trail. In 1882 a mining camp was established and named for Thomas Bennett, president of the Great Sierra Consolidated Mining Company, owners of claims on the Sheepherder and Great Sierra lodes. A tunnel was in the process of construction, but financial disaster caused suspension of work in 1884, and it was never completed. There was a post office between 1882 and 1884. Some of the old buildings are still standing. (F. S. Wedertz; *Mining Bureau*, VIII, pp. 371 f.; De Decker, p. 22.)

Benshy [Placer]. In Benshy Canyon, two miles from Forest Hill. According to the *Annual Mining Review*, 1876 (p. 52), the Josephine Company developed a 1,200 foot tunnel here in the 1870s, with capital stock of 5 million dollars (!).

Bensonville [Tuolumne]. A half mile below Columbia, on the road to Springfield. References to Pierson Hill and Rhode Island Hill, south of St. Anne's church, are to the same place. Rich yields are repeatedly reported in the newspapers, 1853–1855. Many miners were making ten to forty dollars per day (Columbia *Gazette*, April 9, 1853), and one man took out three pounds in one day (*Alta*, May 5, 1853). A company at Pierson Hill struck a lead which prospected one to four dollars per pan (Columbia *Gazette*, November 11, 1854). Webster's claim averaged seven dollars per day to the man one week (*San Joaquin Republican*, May 22, 1855). McKenna had a splendid hydraulic hose and fixings in full operation (*Alta*, April 25, 1856). In 1861 the place was still considered to have the best claims on Columbia Gulch because it was situated lower than the flume (*Mining Press*, November 23, 1861).

Benton [Mono]. On State Highway 120, about seven miles from the California-Nevada border. The town was founded in 1865, and a post office was established in 1866. The place was the supply and milling center for nearby mines, mainly silver. The period of greatest activity was between 1862 and 1888, when the production was more than 4 million dollars, most of which was from the Blind Springs District, east of the town. A contemporary account of the region is given in *Mining Bureau*, VIII (pp. 376 ff.) and a recent account by De Decker (pp. 25 ff.). According to De Decker, the place was first called Hot Springs.

Benton Mills [Mariposa]. On the south bank of Merced River, opposite modern Bagby and now under the backwaters of Lake McClure. From 1850 to 1860 the place was known as Ridleys Ferry, for Thomas E. Ridley, who operated a ferry here from 1850 to 1852. It was on Frémont's claim, and it is generally assumed that the name Benton Mills was given for Frémont's father-in-law, Senator Thomas Hart Benton of Missouri, but it may have been given for the man who built the quartz mill there for Frémont in 1859. At that time the Mariposa *Gazette* referred to it as a type of mill, "The Benton Quartz Mill." *Transactions*, 1859, (p. 91) reports that a 16-stamp mill crushed 130 tons every day and a 48-stamp mill was under construction. For many years the ore of a number of mines was crushed here. There were barnlike mill buildings, boarding houses, cabins, and a store "finely situated on both sides of the river," which Frémont had dammed to produce power for the mills (*Hutchings' California Magazine*, September, 1859, pp. 101, 103; *Alta*, August 11, 1860). The mills went the way of all of Frémont's mines and millions. In 1920 the last remaining one was destroyed by fire (*Mining Bureau*, XXIV, p. 80). In 1890, when the post office was established, the place was renamed Bagby for a hotel owner. The mines in the Bagby District in the vicinity of the towns of Bagby and Bear Valley are listed in *Bulletin*, 193 (p. 29) and in *Mining Bureau*, LIII (pp. 232 ff.). The Red Bank, one and a half miles northwest of Bagby, was worked intermittently for almost one hundred years. There was placering and sluicing in the late 1860s, brief hydraulic mining in 1881, and extensive underground mining in the late 1890s and intermittently into the 1960s (*Mining Bureau*, XVII, p. 135; XXXI, p. 43; LIII, pp. 162 ff., p. 299; *Bull.*, 193, p. 29). The famous Pine Tree and Josephine Mine is treated separately in this dictionary.

One mile east of the Pine Tree is the French Mine, one of the earliest mines in the county, which operated intermittently to 1948 (*Mining Bureau*, LIII, pp. 99 f.). The Mexican Mine, also one of the earliest, was discovered by Mexicans and worked by them until 1859, when undisputed title was given to Frémont. It was reactivated in 1908 and again briefly in the 1930s (*ibid.*, p. 132). The Mountain King Mine, six miles east of Bagby, on the Merced River, was not developed until 1899. It became idle in 1925 after having produced about a million dollars worth of gold and silver (*ibid.*, pp. 140 f.). It is shown on the USGS Sonora 1939 quadrangle.

Berdan [Butte]. Southwest of Inskip, between Chico and Butte creeks, on the old Humboldt Road. From 1878 to 1916 it was the trading center and post office for the surrounding quartz mills (*Register*, 1903).

Bernard Diggings [Plumas]. *See* Barnards Diggings.

Bernard Flat [Butte]. It is mentioned by Asa B. Smith in a letter to his brother Seth, datelined Enterprize, November 13, 1859.

Berrington Hill [Nevada]. *See* Burrington Hill.

Berry Creek Bar [Butte]. At the confluence of Berry Creek and the North Fork of Feather River, on the Big Bend. The creek was named for Henry Berry. Shown on the County Map, 1862. It is mentioned by Asa B. Smith in letters to his brother datelined McCabe Creek, October 29, 1858 and March 14, 1859. A mill and post office, established May 10, 1875, were located at Virginia Mills two miles upstream. In 1903 a 15-stamp mill and one arrastre were still in operation (*Register*). The Berry Creek Mine was still being worked in the late 1920s (*Mining Bureau*, XXVI, p. 370) and is still listed in 1949. Berry Creek Bar is shown on the USGS Bidwell Bar 1944 quadrangle.

Bertrands Bar [Trinity]. On the lower Trinity River. It is mentioned by Cox (p. 83) in 1858.

Bests Bar [Siskiyou]. W. A. Knapp (pp. 510 ff.), who mined here in 1851, gives a good description. It is doubtless the same place as Bestville, though Knapp locates it on the Klamath River. *See* Bestville.

Bestville [Siskiyou]. On the North Fork of Salmon River, about a mile below Sawyers Bar. Recorded on Goddard's map, 1857. E. M. Anthony, in his "Reminiscences of the Early Days of Siskiyou," states that in June, 1850, the town was founded by miners from Trinity who were prospecting

on the Salmon River. They named the town for a member of the party, Captain Best, a trader and miner on Trinity River. The miners were led to the place by an Indian called Squirrel Jim, who lived at the mouth of Little North Fork of Salmon River (Tickner). The place was mentioned and described by George Gibbs, October 11, 1851 (Schoolcraft, III, p. 150). In 1855 it was reported that mining in the bedrock had been resumed, using old holes, and that dirt paid as high as eight dollars to the bucket (Hittell Clippings, p. 28). W. M. Smith states that most of the mining here was by "wing damming and ground sluicing, or just shovelling the dirt into the sluice box."

Betsyburg [Plumas]. *See* Elizabethtown.

Beveridge District [Inyo]. On the eastern slope of Inyo Mountains, north of New York Butte. It is in a remote area, accessible only by trail. Gold was discovered in 1877 by W. L. Hunter, and the district was named for John Beveridge, discoverer of mines east of Cerro Gordo. The chief source of gold was the Keynot Mine, from which the ore was packed by mules a distance of three miles to a 5-stamp mill. The mine was worked from 1878 to 1886 and intermittently to 1907, with an estimated total production of half a million dollars. An account of the district is given in De Decker (pp. 49 ff.). It is recorded on Keeler's map, *ca.* 1884.

Biacete [Calaveras]. *See* Vallecito.

Biddles Camp [Mariposa]. *See* Bear Valley.

Biderman, Mount [Mono]. Near Mono. Named for Jack Biderman, an early miner at Bodie. The name is misspelled on several maps. (F. S. Wedertz.)

Bidwell Bar [Butte]. On the Middle Fork of Feather River, near the junction with the North Fork. Recorded on Butler's map, 1851. John Bidwell was Sutter's closest associate and one of the best known pioneers of northern California. He was at Sutter's Fort on February 28, 1848, but he did not mention Marshall's discovery of gold in his letter to Larkin written a little later (Larkin, VII, p. 154). He decided, however, that the shores of the Feather River might offer the same chances of finding gold as the American River. In March, 1848, he and his companions found "color" at or near Hamilton Bend. *See* Hamilton. Bidwell then moved farther upstream and settled on the Middle Fork, near the junction with the North Fork. Bidwell Bar flourished, and by 1853 it reportedly had a tributary population of

3,000 (Bancroft, VI, p. 490). A post office was established July 10, 1851, and in 1853 it became the second county seat. It was soon to be surpassed by its rival Oroville, to which it lost the county seat in 1856. The decline continued, and in 1857 Pringle Shaw could mock in these words: "the Cayotas will soon play hide and seek through the streets of this deserted village." The site of Bidwell Bar is Historic Landmark 330 and that of the old suspension bridge is Historic Landmark 314. The place is now under Oroville Lake.

Bifogle Flat [Sierra]. *See* Breyfogle Flat.

Big Bar [Amador]. On the Cosumnes River, about eight miles below the forks. Shown on the County Map, 1866. Most of the miners were Chinese (*Amador Ledger*, June 13, 1857).

Big Bar [Amador, Calaveras]. On the Mokelumne River, five miles southeast of Jackson, on the Amador-Calaveras line. Recorded on Butler's map, 1851, and on Trask's, 1853. Bayard Taylor mentions it as Upper Bar in August, 1849 (Chapters 3 and 9), and it was also known as Upper Ferry (Cenotto). Burns & Pope were issued a ferry license September 14, 1850. *See* Whaleboat Ferry. Doble mentions a rope ferry here, April 12, 1852. In 1853 Soher & Parrish's Bridge was built (Amador Co. Hist., 1881, p. 179). A water-driven mill with six stamps and two arrastres was in operation in 1856 (*State Register*, 1859). According to an item in the *Picayune*, August 31, 1850, a piece of quartz containing eight pounds of gold was found here. Historic Landmark 41.

Big Bar [Butte]. On the Middle Fork of the Feather River, near the Plumas County line. Recorded on the County Map, 1861. The original name was apparently Pulga Bar. The USGS Bidwell Bar 1944 quadrangle shows another Big Bar on the North Fork of Feather River, about seven miles above the Big Bend of the river.

Big Bar [El Dorado]. On the Cosumnes River. The place is mentioned in the County History, 1883 (p. 85).

Big Bar [El Dorado]. On the Middle Fork of the American River, below Volcano Bar. Recorded on Jackson's map, 1850, and Trask's map, 1853. It is mentioned as early as 1849 by Wierzbicki (p. 41) and re-

Big Bar, Butte Co.

peatedly in the following years by Buffum (pp. 69, 77), Haskins (p. 138), Barstow (p. 6), and others.

Big Bar [Humboldt]. On the south side of the Klamath River, above Bluff Creek. Recorded on Trask's map, 1853. The hydraulic mine here was still productive in 1888 (*Mining Bureau*, VIII, p. 219).

Big Bar [Sacramento]. On the American River, below Sailor Bar and Mississippi Bar. Shown on Doolittle's map, 1868.

Big Bar [Trinity]. On the south bank of Trinity River, twenty-five miles west of Weaverville, above Cox Bar. Shown on Goddard's map, 1857. According to Cox (p. 73), it was discovered by a Mr. Jones in 1849 and named because of the extensive bars of placer gravel there. De Massey (pp. 87 ff.) gives an almost classical account of the district. It is the locale of Avery's delightful story, "The Trinity Diamond," in which he describes the camp a few miles upstream from Big Bar. In 1858, Cox (pp. 73 ff.) gives a rambling account of the place where the "Diamond" was found. According to Bancroft, VI, (p. 371), there were already 600 miners at the bar in the spring of 1850 with average earnings of twenty-five to fifty dollars a day. A post office was established October 7, 1851. This Big Bar was the most enduring of the many Big Bars and remained the center of placer and hydraulic mining into the twentieth century (*Register*, 1898). According to Robert J. Morris (*Trinity*, 1967, pp. 18, 20), the post office at Big Bar was moved to Cox Bar at one time but retained the name. Cox Bar, Big Flat, Manzanita Flat, and Vances Bar are a part of present day Big Bar community. Big Bar Creek and Big Bar are shown on the USGS Big Bar 1930 quadrangle.

Big Bar [Tuolumne]. On Sullivan Creek; just below the mouth of Sullivans Dry Arroyo and between Sonora and Kincaid Flat. It is mentioned by Stoddart (p. 81) as existing in 1849 and was probably the richest bar on Sullivan Creek (De Ferrari).

Big Bend [Butte]. The Big Bend of the North Fork of Feather River is about thirteen miles long, in the shape of a horseshoe. Extensive mining was begun in the days of the Gold Lake hunt. The camps on the Bend are listed separately. *See* Island, Lattimores, Berry Creek, Wild Yankee, Huffs, and Whiskey bars. In the 1880s a big tunnel was built to divert water from the North Fork through Dark Canyon to the West Branch, but it was a failure. A de-

scription and map of the tunnel are give in *Mining Bureau*, VI, Part 2 (pp. 25 f.). The area of the Big Bend Mining and Tunneling Company is also shown on the County Map, 1886.

Big Bend Bar [Siskiyou]. On the South Fork of Salmon River, below the junction, and six miles from Big Flat. There was mining here as early as 1851 or 1852 (W. M. Smith).

Big Betsy. An unidentified place, listed in the Work Projects Administration project. It is probably only a mine.

Big Blue Lead. This is the biggest of all "dead" rivers containing auriferous gravel, cement, and quartz. It reaches from Grizzley Peak (lat. 39° 45') in Sierra County to Forest Hill (lat. 38° 45') in Placer County.

Big Blue Mine [Kern]. *See* Cove District.

Big Bottom [Siskiyou]. On the Klamath River, near Murderers Bar (later Happy Camp). The place is described by George Gibbs in his journal, 1851 (Schoolcraft, III, pp. 154 ff.).

Big Canyon [El Dorado]. The canyon is formed by a tributary of the Cosumnes River, south of Shingle Springs. Lucius Fairchild mined here without success (*California Letters*, May 20, June 6, 1850), and Samuel F. Pond earned about seven dollars per day in 1851 (Diary, April 4, 1851). In later years the mines were very productive. The Oro Fino or Big Canyon Mine, which operated intermittently from the 1880s to 1940, had two modern ball mills and produced more than 3 million dollars worth of gold (*Mining Bureau*, LII, p. 408). Sometimes this Big Canyon was confused with Big Canyon north of Placerville. Both Canyons are recorded on the USGS Placerville 1931 quadrangle. *See* El Dorado Canyon.

Big Canyon [El Dorado]. The canyon is formed by a tributary to the South Fork of the American River. It is sometimes called Big Ravine. It is mentioned repeatedly by Haskins (pp. 120, 137) as very rich in 1849–1850. It is also mentioned by Crockett between 1854 and 1859 (p. 3, *passim*). In 1857 a mill with two mule-driven arrastres was in operation (*State Register*, 1859). In 1874 the Gross Mine assayed as much as 160 dollars per ton (Raymond, VII, p. 88). Shown on the USGS Placerville 1931 quadrangle.

Big Canyon [Trinity]. On the Trinity River, between Big Flat and North Fork. David Leeper and companions settled here in the late summer of 1850. One afternoon

Leeper took out eighty dollars worth of gold by scooping water from the river (Leeper, p. 112). In September, 1854, the men of the Eagle Flume Company averaged thirty dollars a day to the hand (Hittell Clippings, p. 20).

Big Canyon [Tuolumne]. A tributary to the Tuolumne River, north of Groveland. It is also called Big Creek. Goddard records it as Big C--- on his map of 1857. Successful mining here was mentioned in the *Alta*, December 16, 1851. The Hunter Mine reportedly produced the almost incredible amount of 300 dollars per ton of quartz before 1867 (Browne). Big Creek is shown on the USGS Sonora 1939 quadrangle. The lower end of Big Creek, where it debouches into Tuolumne River, runs through a very steep walled canyon called Big Creek Canyon, below which were the famous Mary Ellen and Mohican mines. Big Creek rises in Savages Flat. The Big Creek Indian Rancheria was situated at the confluence with Second Garrote Creek. (De Ferrari)

Big Creek District [Fresno]. In the eastern part of the county, fifty miles northeast of Fresno. "Superficial placer mining was done during the early days and sporadic lode mining from the 1890s to around 1915." (*Bull.*, 193, p. 30).

Big Crevice [Placer, El Dorado]. The gold bearing "crevice" crosses the Middle Fork of American River diagonally at Murderers Bar and extends over into the El Dorado side back under the hill, according to the description in Placer County History, 1882. The rich deposits, which were on the bottom of an ancient river bed, were covered by a stratum of soapy, sedimentary "slum," hence they were difficult to work. They were first worked in 1850 by J. D. Galbraith and later, in 1878, by the American River Dredging Company. A detailed account is given on pages 229 f. of the Placer County History, 1882.

Big Dipper Mine [Placer]. *See* Iowa Hill.

Big Dry Creek District [Fresno]. In the northeastern part of the county, about ten miles northeast of Clovis. There was placer mining on a small scale during the Gold Rush and lode mining from the 1870s to the end of the century (*Bull.*, 193, p. 30).

Big Flat [Calaveras]. Near West Point, on a rich quartz lode. According to the *Mining Press*, April 25, 1862, one company took out 12,000 dollars worth in one season. It is also mentioned in the *Calaveras Chronicle* in

May, 1878 ("The Knave," September, 1939).

Big Flat [Del Norte]. On Hurdy Gurdy Creek. Mining of coarse gold started apparently in the 1850s. The County History, 1881 (p. 135), gives an account of mining activities in the district in the late 1870s and the subsequent decline. According to *Mining Bureau*, XIII (p. 127), a hydraulic mine was in operation in 1896. In 1945 an attempt was made to reopen a part of it with modern equipment but failed within two years (*Mining Bureau*, XLVIII, pp. 277 f.).

Big Flat [Trinity]. On the Trinity River, above present day Big Bar Creek, formerly Little Weaver Creek, about twenty-two miles west of Weaverville. Recorded on Goddard's map, 1857. According to Cox (p. 71), Weaver (of Weaverville) had discovered the deposits in 1850, and in 1851 he and his company constructed a flume from Little Weaver Creek and took out 100 thousand dollars in a short season. James William Denver (of Denver, Colorado) settled here in 1850 and earned his first political spurs as California state senator in 1852. An item in Hittell Clippings (p. 60) gives a lengthy report on the Trinity mines, datelined Big Flat, December 3, 1854. The population was estimated at 250 in 1855, and 412 in 1856 (Cox, p. 71). *See* Big Bar [Trinity].

Big Gulch [Sacramento]. *See* Ashland.

Big Gun [Sacramento]. On the American River, opposite Negro Bar. Shown on Trask's map, 1853.

Big Gun Mine [Placer]. *See* Michigan Bluff.

Big House [El Dorado]. *See* Mosquito Valley.

Big Kimshew [Butte]. *See* Little Kimshew.

Bigler Canal [Placer]. The canal supplied water from the North Fork of American River to the camps between the forks. Recorded on Goddard's map, 1857. It was named after nearby Lake Bigler (now Lake Tahoe), which had been named for John Bigler, governor of California, 1852–1856.

Biglers Diggings [El Dorado]. This is not a recorded name but the identification of the first prospecting that was carried on away from Sutter's Mill tail race. On February 6, 1848, Henry Bigler and a fellow Mormon "mined" on the north side of the South Fork of the American River opposite the Mill and gained ten dollars worth of gold with the use of pocket knives. On February 12, Bigler discovered gold a half mile west of the Mill and averaged one ounce a day on three different days. (Bigler's *Chronicle of the West*, pp. 99 f.).

Big Meadows [Plumas]. North of Butt Valley, on the North Fork of Feather River, now largely inundated by Lake Almanor. Recorded on Goddard's map, 1857. Rich deposits were discovered in the fall of 1850 after the failure of the Gold Lake hunt. Shown on the map in the County History, 1882, and on the County Map, 1886. *See* Prattville.

Big Negro Hill [El Dorado]. This was actually part of the settlement at Negro Hill. In 1852 two negroes from Massachusetts opened a store here, around which quite a negro village developed. (Co. Hist., 1883, p. 201). *See* Negro Hill [El Dorado].

Big Oak Bar [Placer]. On the south side of the North Fork of the American River, six miles above the mouth of the South Fork. Recorded on Trask's map, 1853. The boundary of a claim was recorded on December 18, 1851 (Placer County Records, I, p. 53).

Big Oak Flat [Siskiyou]. On the Klamath River, above Wingate Bar. It was a river bar, named before 1851 "from a superb live oak tree growing upon it" (School-craft, III, p. 154).

Big Oak Flat [Tuolumne]. About two and a half miles southwest of Groveland. The deposits were first located by James D. Savage, one of Sutter's men, a shrewd trader and later the commander of the Mariposa Battalion, which entered Yosemite Valley in 1851. He opened the mining district in 1849, employing friendly Indians (CHSQ, XXVIII, p. 325). The U. S. Bureau of the Census lists 210 inhabitants in the camp in April, 1851, in the population schedule for the 1850 census and gives the name as Oak Flats. In 1852 a post office was opened, and the same year the name is shown on Gibbes' map of the Southern Mines. Goddard's map, 1857, shows it as Oak Flat. After a rich vein was discovered between Big Oak Flat and Deer Flat, about 1855, and after a ditch later brought water to the place, a period of prosperity set in. In 1856 Heckendorn's *Directory* shows quite a large population, with a strong German element. Browne (p. 50) lists the principal mines in 1867. De Ferrari mentions two important mines, The Longfellow and the Mack, on Cerro Gordo, the mountain between Big Oak Flat and Deer Creek. The Mack Mine was named for August and Albert Mack, early German merchants. The Mississippi, at the western or lower end of the camp, was another important mine. According to the *Pacific Coast Annual Mining Review*, 1878 (p. 174), some of the biggest mines were consolidated, and the assay was as high as eighty-nine dollars free gold per ton. *Mines and Minerals*, 1899, (p. 358) estimated the output of Big Oak Flat, Deer Flat, and Groveland at 25 million dollars. *See* Savage Flat. In 1903 there were still three stamp mills in operation in the area (*Register*, 1903). *See also* C. G. Crampton. Stories differ about the enormous oak that gave the name to the place. According to tradition, miners secretly removed the soil from around its roots to pan for gold, and eventually the tree died. Pancoast (p. 209), who mined here in the winter of 1850–1851, tells a somewhat romantic tale of a Norwegian woman who hollowed out the rotten trunk and established a boarding house in it. The 1863 fire, which almost destroyed the town, charred the trunk, and in 1869 the top fell off, leaving only the lower trunk, a picture of which is in the Schlichtmann collection in Bancroft Library. Brewer, who saw the tree shortly before the fire, describes it in his diary, June 10, 1863, as having been a grand old tree, more than 28 feet in diameter, once protected by town ordinance but dilapidated at that time. In 1900, according to Paden-Schlichtmann, a camper accidentally set fire to the tree and fled. (Paden-Schlichtmann, pp. 129, 135, 141.) Some of the buildings erected in 1852 were still standing in 1949 (*California Historical Landmarks*). Historic Landmark 406.

Big Pine [Inyo]. It is listed in *Bulletin*, 193 (p. 147) as a district on the west slope of the White Mountains, southeast of Bishop, in which there are several quartz mines and prospects.

Big Ravine [El Dorado]. *See* Big Canyon.

Big Rich Bar [Sierra]. On the North Fork of Yuba River, west of Downieville. The first diggings were in 1849, according to the County History, 1882 (p. 419).

Big Rock Creek [Butte]. It is listed in the County History, 1882 (p. 253), as a once flourishing mining camp in Concow Township.

Big Sandy Mine [El Dorado]. *See* Kelsey.

Big Spring [Placer]. Near Forest Hill. Stephen Wing in a letter of October 2, 1856, states that he had one-third interest in the Spring Tunnel, which had already cost 25 thousand dollars at the time of his writing.

Big Stony Bar [Butte]. On the east side of the Middle Fork of Feather River. Recorded on Trask's map, 1853, and on Goddard's, 1857. The place was named by analogy with nearby Stony Bar. *See* Stony Bar [Butte] on the Middle Fork of Feather River.

Big Tujunga Canyon [Los Angeles]. In the San Gabriel Mountains. It is the site of the legendary Los Padres Mine, where the Indians supposedly mined for the San Fernando Mission padres in the 1790s. Authenticated mining began in the 1860s, with major activity from 1889 to about 1896. The most productive mine was the Monte Cristo, which operated possibly as early as 1867 and was closed in 1942. A summary of the mining activity in the area is given in J. W. Robinson (pp. 31 ff.).

Big Valley [Mendocino]. On the Eel River, forty miles from the town of Mendocino. The *Alta*, June 13, 1854, reported that gold was discovered here and that prospectors averaged ten dollars per day.

Bingham Bar [Plumas or Butte]. On the Middle Fork of Feather River. It is mentioned in Bancroft, VI (p. 363) as a "noted bar." It is also mentioned by Hutchings on his way to Fall River House, November 2, 1855.

Birchville [Nevada]. Eight miles northwest of Nevada City. Shown on Doolittle's map, 1868. It is said to have been named for a prominent citizen, L. Birch Adsit. Until 1853 it was also called Johnson's Diggings for David Johnson, first prospector (Co. Hist., 1880, p. 61). The deposits were discovered in 1851. Prosperity started in 1857, when a ditch of the Middle Yuba Canal Company brought water to the place and hydraulic mining replaced placering. In 1865–1866 five companies showed a profit of 327 thousand dollars (Bean, p. 343). A rapid decline followed, but according to the *Register* of 1898, there was still a stamp mill in operation at that time. Shown on the USGS Smartsville 1943 quadrangle. A Birchville mine, south of Graniteville, was in operation until the 1940s (*Mining Bureau*, XXXVII, p. 386).

Bird: Flat, Gulch [Placer]. East of Iowa Hill; two miles from Wisconsin Hill. Recorded on Goddard's map, 1857. It was named apparently for Mr. Bird, who kept a store here. The place is mentioned as Bird's by Henry Spiegel in a letter dated June 7, 1850. Various newspaper clippings reported rich yields, especially by hydraulic mining. The Bird Flat Company started a tunnel in 1854 and spent twelve years and 50 thousand dollars before striking the quartz lead between the North and Mid-

dle forks of the American River (Bancroft Scraps, LI:1, p. 8). Hutchings describes it as a pleasant little village in 1855 (Diary, May 5, 1855). On August 17, 1855, a 33-ounce lump of gold was found, according to a newspaper report cited in the County History, 1882 (p. 227). The drift and hydraulic mines are listed in the same County History (p. 216).

Birdseye Creek [Nevada]. A tributary to Steep Hollow, south of You Bet. In 1866 the Greenwell claims yielded 96 thousand dollars from tailings alone (Raymond, VI, p. 21). The Birdseye Mine is still listed in the *Register* of 1900.

Birds Valley [Placer]. One mile southwest of Michigan Bluffs. It is shown on Trask's map, 1853, as an important trail junction, but east of Michigan Bluffs. Doolittle's map, 1868, and other later maps show it as Byrds Valley, west of Michigan Bluffs. The *Alta*, November 15, 1852, reported rich gold deposits in 1849 and 1850, but no profits were shown until a ditch was built from El Dorado Canyon. The Birds Valley Quartz Mining and Lumber Company was incorporated in April, 1850 (Placer County Records, I, p. 215). Hutchings states that the deposits had been worked out by 1855, and that where there had been 3,000 persons working in 1850, five years later there were only three houses (Diary, May 7, 1855). The place is mentioned again on March 28, 1863, in Placer County Records, IV (pp. 84 ff.).

Bishop Creek District [Inyo]. On the east flank of the Sierra Nevada, about fifteen miles southwest of the town of Bishop. The principal gold mine was the Cardinal or Wilshire-Bishop Creek Mine, which operated in the early 1900s and again between 1933 and 1938. The total production is estimated at about one million dollars. (*Mining Bureau*, XV; p. 85; XXXIV, pp. 389 f.; *Bull.*, 193, pp. 30 f.). *See* Gospel Swamp.

Black Bart Mine [Mariposa]. *See* Solomon Gulch.

Black Bear [Siskiyou]. On Black Bear Gulch, a tributary to the South Fork of Salmon River. The place was the trading center for a number of quartz mines, and in 1869 a post office was established here. Gold was discovered in 1860, and in 1865 the Black Bear Mine was opened. It had the second quartz mill in the Salmon River country — one which was brought by oxen over the old Deacon Trail in 1871. *See* Eddys Gulch. The mine yielded 1.5 million dollars in thirteen years, and the total production is estimated at 3.1 million dollars (*Bull.*, 193,

p. 139). Detailed accounts are given in the *Pacific Coast Mining Review*, 1878 (pp. 175 f.), and in Raymond, V (p. 101) and VII (p. 165). According to the *Register*, 1898, a 32-stamp mill was active in that year. The Black Bear post office was not discontinued until 1941. *See* Liberty District.

Black Creek [Calaveras]. On the Stanislaus River, one mile west of Byrnes Ferry. According to an item in the Sonora *Herald* about 1858 (Hittell Clippings, p. 66), three Chinese companies were doing well.

Black Gulch [Del Norte]. Apparently near Crescent City. A lump of gold weighing twenty-six ounces was taken from this place, according to a report in the Sacramento *Union*, June 15, 1855 (Bancroft Notes).

Black Gulch [Siskiyou]. The camp is mentioned by E. M. Anthony in his "Reminiscences," in connection with the 1851 discovery of gold at the upper flats near Shasta Butte City (later named Yreka).

Black Hawk Canyon District [San Bernardino]. On the north slope of the San Bernardino Mountains, about five miles north of Baldwin Lake and nine miles southeast of the town of Lucerne Valley. The district was opened in 1870 and was developed on a large scale in 1890. The principal mines are listed and described in *Mining Bureau*, XXVII (pp. 282 ff.), and an account of mining activity to 1940 is given in *Bulletin*, 193 (p. 170). Shown on the County Map, 1892. It is also known as the Arlington District (*Mining Bureau*, XXVI, p. 222).

Black Hawk Diggings [Plumas]. Northwest of Quincy, near Keddie. Windeler (p. 178) locates it near Snake Lake in his diary entry of May 24, 1853. Black Hawk Creek is shown on modern maps between Snake and Butterfly valleys.

Black Leg Gulch [Tuolumne]. The *Alta*, June 18, 1854, reprinted an item from the Sonora *Herald*, according to which rich deposits were discovered on a hill between this place and Sullivans Dry Arroyo. The miners went down twenty feet and the deposits paid from the top down. A similar strike had been made the previous year. De Ferrari locates the Gulch about one mile southeast of Sonora and indicates that the location given above is incorrect.

Black Oak Mine [El Dorado]. Between Garden Valley and Meadowbrook. There was mainly drift mining, and according to the *Guidebook* (p. 70), the production was more than one million dollars. It was originally a pocket mine, was reopened in 1934 and operated until 1942 (*Mining Bureau*, LII, p. 409).

Black Oak Mine [Tuolumne]. One mile west of Soulsbyville. The mine was located in 1878, and it is said to have produced 3.5 million dollars. It was in operation with modern equipment until 1918. Details are given in *Mining Bureau*, VIII (pp. 665 f.) and XXIV (pp. 9, 10). *See* Soulsbyville.

Black Rock [Plumas]. Between the North and Middle forks of Feather River, adjacent to Walkers Plains, near the Butte County line. The discovery of gold and silver deposits in the early 1860s caused an excitement reminiscent of the Gold Lake hunt, according to a report of the Quincy *Union* which appeared in the San Francisco *Examiner*, March 17, 1866 (Hayes Scrapbooks: Mining, II, sec. 153). A correspondent of the Sacramento *Union* states that "the hill" was known to be rich in its understrata, and in 1864 it was tunneled for gold and a ditch was in process of being built (undated clipping in Hayes Scrapbooks: Mining, IV, sec. 15). The Black Rock hydraulic mine, near Merrimac, took its water from Marble Creek.

Blacks Bridge [Nevada]. *See* Edwards Crossing.

Blacks Gulch [Amador]. On the Mokelumne River, above Lancha Plana, where the river crosses the Mother Lode. It is listed in Coy's *In the Diggings* (p. 42) and is shown on his map.

Blacksmith Flat [Placer]. On the Ralston Divide, in the southeastern part of the county, on a Tertiary river channel. Shown on Doolittle's map, 1868. There was hydraulic mining here in the early 1870s, according to Warren T. Russell. *See* Ralston Divide.

Bladderville. An unidentified place, listed in the Work Projects Administration project.

Blair [Shasta]. *See* Whiskeytown.

Blairtown [Butte]. It is listed in the County History, 1882 (p. 253), as a once flourishing mining camp in Concow Township, north of Oroville.

Blake [San Bernardino]. Twenty-five miles northwest of Needles, on the Atlantic and Pacific Railroad (later Santa Fe). The name of the station was Goffs, but from 1896 to 1911, the post office was called Blake. *See* Goffs. The name Blake was given for Isaac E. Blake, Standard Oil tycoon, who beginning in 1892 built the Nevada Southern Railroad north from Goffs to Purdy, and then to Manvel, to serve his mines in the

New York Mountains (Haenszel). The *Register* of 1902 lists and maps the mines in the area.

Blanchard Diggings [Placer]. Notice of a quartz claim at the head of the diggings is recorded in Lone Star District Book of Claims, February 8, 1873 (Placer County Records, V, p. 430).

Blanket Creek [Tuolumne]. An intermittent stream, tributary to Rough and Ready Creek. It was so named because Indians stole a miner's camp, including all the blankets (Dexter, p. 132). It is listed by Hutchings in 1855; mentioned by Heckendorn in 1856; and recorded by Goddard, 1857. The diggings are described as rich in *Mines and Minerals* (p. 358). Dexter tells two delightful stories about the place in "The Major's Plum Pudding" and "A Christmas Day." Blanket End, listed without identification, is presumably the same place.

Bleakly Point [Butte]. An unidentified place, mentioned by Asa B. Smith in a letter to his brother dated August 30, 1859.

Blind Mans Flat [El Dorado]. An unidentified place on the South Fork of the American River, east of Placerville.

Blizzardville. An unidentified place mentioned by Guinn (p. 43), with reference to an undated issue of the *Golden Era* (1856?).

Blood Gulch [Amador]. On Dry Creek, probably in the vicinity of Fiddletown. Bancroft mentions it in volume VI (p. 372). It may be the same place mentioned in *California Place Names*, according to which miners gave the name when they noticed blood in the waters of the creek and discovered the body of a murdered man upstream. This creek may have been in Bloody Gulch. *See* Bloody Gulch.

Bloody. A frequently occurring adjective in California geographic names, used in the descriptive sense or as a slang word.

Bloody Bend. An unidentified place mentioned by Helper in 1855.

Bloody Canyon [Mono]. On the old Mono Trail across the Sierra Nevada. The name is derived from the red metamorphic walls of the canyon. The first gold was found here in the fall of 1852 by soldiers of Lieutenant Tredwell Moore's detachment, who were pursuing Indians. *See* Leevining. In 1879 the deposits were rediscovered, and the mines were operated by the Great Sierra Mining Company, the same company that operated the Sheepherder Lode. *See* Bennettville. A number of log cabins built at that time

are still standing. (Sierra Club *Bulletin*, XIII, p. 42; F. S. Wedertz.)

Bloody Gulch [Amador]. A tributary to Indian Creek, west of Fiddletown. Shown on the County Map, 1866. The name is listed in the *Guidebook* (p. 65), with other placer mining localities in the area. *See* Blood Gulch [Amador].

Bloomer: Bar, Hill [Butte]. On the east side of the North Fork of the Feather River, about fifteen miles from Oroville. Bloomer Hill Creek is shown on the County Map, 1877. At the end of January, 1861, three unsuccessful miners built a ditch for their claim and accidentally cut across a vein of decomposed granite, which yielded about 20 thousand dollars in two weeks (*Mining Press*, February 8, 1861). The Bloomer Mine had an 8-stamp mill in 1868, but the yield was very irregular because the deposits were in pockets (Browne, p. 163). According to *Mining Bureau*, XXIV (p. 179), the Bloomer Hill Mine, with 15-stamps, operated with fair success until about 1915. It is still listed in 1949. Bloomer Hill is shown on the USGS Bidwell Bar 1944 quadrangle.

Blue. The adjective is used frequently in California place names. In mining districts the word is especially common because of the many "blue leads," the discolored strata of auriferous gravel or cement.

Blue Bank [Sierra]. On the North Fork of the North Fork of the Yuba River, east of Downieville. The place is shown on Trask's map, 1853.

Blue Bar [Siskiyou]. On the Klamath River. It is mentioned in a clipping in Bancroft Scraps, LI:1 (p. 240).

Blue Bar [Yuba]. Near Fosters Bar. Most of the claims were apparently held by Chinese miners. The place was mentioned by De Long, June 19, 1857.

Blue Belly Ravine. An unidentified mining locality, listed in the State Library roster and in Hittell, *Resources*.

Blue Bluffs [Placer]. Between Bear River and the North Fork of American River; about five miles northeast of Dutch Flat, near Shady Run. Shown on Doolittle's map, 1868. A description of the diggings in 1870 is given in Whitney, *Auriferous Gravels* (p. 163). Mining activity is also described by Lindgren, *Tertiary Gravels* (p. 146).

Blue Canyon [Placer]. On Blue Canyon Creek, about eight miles northeast of Dutch Flat. It was named for "Old Jim" Blue, who mined here in the 1850s. The canyon crossed an immense ledge of slate and quartz. (Loye Miller.) A post office was established at the camp in 1867. According to the *Register*, 1902, it had two stamp mills, and various types of mining were carried on. The extent of hydraulic mining by 1870 is described in Whitney, *Auriferous Gravels* (p. 162). An active mine is listed until 1936 by the Mining Bureau. Shown on the USGS Colfax 1938 quadrangle.

Blue Gouge Mine [El Dorado]. *See* Grizzly Flats.

Blue Gravel Mine [Shasta]. In the city of Redding. This was the only municipally owned gold mine in the United States and was operated by lessees on a royalty basis intermittently between 1927 and 1942, according to a report given in the *Redding Searchlight* (R. B. Eaton). It was on land purchased by the City for the airport (*Mining Bureau*, XXIX, p. 59; XXXV, pp. 133, 177).

Blue Gulch [Placer]. Listed by Hittell in *Mining Bureau*, 1884 (IV, p. 221). It is perhaps the same place as Blue Canyon.

Blue Gulch [Siskiyou]. Gold mining started here soon after the discovery of gold at the upper flats in 1851 near Shasta Butte City (later Yreka). It is mentioned by E. M. Anthony in his "Reminiscences" and by Hutchings as a town in 1855.

Blue Gulch [Tuolumne]. The Gulch heads northeast of Chinese Camp on the opposite side of Woods Creek, with the intervening canyon carrying that stream in the direction of Jacksonville. The brothers Smith had a claim on the Gulch as early as 1856 (letter datelined Texas Hill, January 2, 1856). Two water-driven 10-stamp mills were in operation at the nearby Eagle and Shawmut mines in July, 1869 (Raymond, II, p. 26). The *Annual Mining Review*, 1876, also lists two mills (pp. 21, 23) at these locations. *See* Eagle-Shawmut Mine.

Blue Mountain: City, District [Calaveras]. North of the bend of the South Fork of Mokelumne River. The town called Blue Mountain City was on the Licking Fork, tributary to the South Fork; it had a post office between August 19, 1863 and August 8, 1864, and was the center for gold and silver mines (mainly silver) in the vicinity. In the 1870s fourteen water-driven stamps were in operation (*Annual Mining Review*, 1876, p. 22). The Heckendorn, or Blue Mountain Mine, near Creighton, twelve miles east of West Point, was an old mine reported closed in the 1870s; it was reopened in 1935 (U.S. *Bull.*, 413, p. 130; *Mining Bureau*, XXXII, pp. 263 f.). Apparently operations were suspended at

the opening of World War II. A resumé of mining in the area is given in *Las Calaveras*, October, 1961. Blue Mountain and Creighton are shown on the USGS Big Trees 1941 quadrangle.

Blue Nose [Siskiyou]. Eighteen miles north of Somes Bar. It was named after the Blue Nose gold mine. This and several other features in the mining districts bear the nickname of the Nova Scotians (*Bull.*, No. 85, p. 68; *Mining Bureau*, XXI, p. 465; XXXI, p. 315). *See Consolidated Index*.

Blue Tent [Nevada]. Four miles northeast of Nevada City. Shown on Doolittle's map, 1868, and the County Map, 1880. The place existed in 1850, according to Canfield (p. 60), and it is listed in *Bean's Directory* of 1867. A post office was established March 21, 1878. Raymond (VI, p. 19) reports that in 1873 the Blue Tent Company had taken out 780 thousand dollars by an unimproved hydraulic process. The Blue Tent Consolidated Hydraulic Gold Mines of California, a British company, was in operation here until 1890 (microfilmed copy of the company's records in Bancroft Library). The *Nevada Directory* of 1895 mentions four active mines in the district. The *Register* of 1900 still lists the place as a center of quartz mining. Blue Tent School is shown on the USGS Colfax 1938 quadrangle.

Boalts Hill [Trinity]. *See* Bolt Diggings.

Bob Ridley Flat. Unidentified place, listed in Hittell, *Resources*.

Bodfish: Canyon, Creek, Camp [Kern]. On the Kern River. Mining in the canyon is mentioned in *Mining Bureau*, VIII (p. 316). A post office was established at the camp in 1892. The place was probably named for a pioneer placer miner, Orlando Bodfish, who died in Havilah in 1868. George H. Bodfish, who owned a mine in Keyesville (Boyd, p. 44), was probably his son. A mine is still listed in the *Register*, 1904 (p. 18).

Bodie [Mono]. About eighteen miles east of Bridgeport. The story about the discovery of gold at Bodie varies, but credit is generally given to W. S. (William S. or Waterman S.) Body and his partner, E. S. "Black" Taylor. They were among the prospectors who came across the Sierra Nevada from Sonora after gold was discovered at Dogtown and Monoville. In the fall of 1859 they found gold in a gulch that was later named Taylor Gulch. Bodey lost his life in a snow storm soon afterwards, and his name was given to the camp that developed near by. The Bodie Mining Dis-

Bodie, Mono Co.

trict was formed in the summer of 1860, but the rich strike which led to the great bonanza was not made until 1874. By the summer of 1878 the population was reportedly 3,000 and by 1880 it reached 10,000, according to some estimates. At the peak of the boom, between forty and fifty mines and ten mills, aggregating 162 stamps, were in operation. By 1882–1883 the boom had ended, and in 1888 only three mines were being worked. Today Bodie is a ghost town. It is Historic Landmark 341 and since 1962 a state park. There are many accounts of Bodie and its mines. A brief account is given in *Mining Bureau*, VIII (pp. 382 f.). Joseph Wasson gives the early history in his *Bodie and Esmeralda* and his *Complete Guide to the Mono County Mines*. A detailed and well documented account was written by Frank S. Wedertz in his book entitled, *Bodie, 1859–1900*. Warren Loose, in his *Bodie Bonanza*, has also written a detailed history of the place, based largely on contemporary newspapers and reports. *Bulletin*, 193 (p. 148) gives a brief resumé of Bodie District, with a list of the most productive mines and estimates of their production. By far the most productive were the Standard Consolidated Mines, with an estimated yield of more than 18 million dollars. Listed as having produced more than one million dollars are the

Southern Consolidated Mines and the Syndicate Mine.

Bogardus Ranch [Yuba]. About two miles southwest of Camptonville. It was a well known stopping place on the road to Bullards Bar and was also known as Junction House, as shown on Doolittle's map, 1868. De Long mentions it, January 10, 1854. *See* Junction House.

Bogus. A name occasionally used because of disappointment or sometimes used in fun, instead of the more common humbug. "Bogus gold dust" is described in *Mining Bureau*, II, pt. 1 (p. 138).

Bogus Creek [Siskiyou]. The name goes back to mining days, but no gold mining record was found. The place is said to have been so named because counterfeiters operated here (*Western Folklore*, VI, pp. 376 f.).

Bogus Thunder Bar [Placer]. On the North Fork of the Middle Fork of American River, northeast of Michigan Bluff. It was named by the miners because a nearby waterfall produced a sound like thunder. Bogus Thunder is listed by Hutchings as a town in 1855. The mine is still listed in 1936 (*Mining Bureau*, XXXII, p. 87). Recorded on the USGS Duncan Peak 1952 quadrangle.

Bolly Choop [Trinity]. *See* Bully Choop.

Bolt: Diggings, Hill [Trinity]. Opposite

Eastman Creek or Gulch, a tributary to the Trinity River, north of Deadwood Creek. The diggings were prosperous in the early 1850s, according to Cox (p. 24). In 1861 a 12-mile ditch from Buckeye Gulch brought new life to mining here (*Mining Press*, November 2, 1861). A news item, apparently of 1872, from the *Trinity Journal* in Hayes Scrapbooks: Mining, II (sec. 14) claims that a miner averaged eighty-five dollars per day one season on a claim on Bolt Hill. Boalt's Hill is mentioned as a gold mining district in *Mining Bureau*, II, Part 1 (1880/82, p. 189).

Bonanza King Mine. *See* Providence Mountains [San Bernardino]; Trinity River [Trinity]; Carrville.

Bonanza Mine [Tuolumne]. In the northern portion of the town of Sonora. This was a noted pocket mine discovered in 1851, which yielded more than 1.5 million dollars (*Mining Bureau*, XXIV, p. 10). *See* Priest.

Bondurant [Mariposa]. The *Annual Mining Review*, 1876 (p. 23), gives Bondurant as the name of the place where the Shimer Company built a 10-stamp mill in 1863. Browne (p. 33) states that the Shimer lode was discovered in 1858 when miners were digging a ditch, and it yielded as high as 500 dollars a ton! There is a Bondurant Mine west of the North Fork of Merced River, about twelve miles east of Coulterville, which was named for Judge James A. Bondurant, first county judge of Mariposa County and owner of the mine. It is the second oldest patented mine in the county, the patent having been issued in 1856. The mine was in operation intermittently until 1942. A detailed description is given in *Mining Bureau*, LIII (pp. 79 ff.).

Bondville [Mariposa]. One mile east of Benton Mills, on the south side of Merced River. Placering was carried on after 1850. Stephen Bond established a store here, shown on the Las Mariposas map, 1861. Bond also served as postmaster of the short-lived post office (1855–1860), and in 1856 he was authorized to build a toll road and to collect tolls (Mariposa County Board of Supervisors Minutes, vol. A, p. 123).

Boneyard [Butte]. On Butte Creek, near Helltown. It is mentioned in *Diggin's*, IV: 2 (p. 13). It is usually referred to as Boneyard Flat, so named because of the Indian burials that were unearthed in the mining operations (Nopel).

Booker Flat [Mono]. A claim was located near by in 1877–1878 by S. M. Booker. The

Flat later became part of the town. (F. S. Wedertz.)

Boomville; Boonville [Amador]. *See* Butte City.

Boones Bar [Plumas]. On the South Fork of the Feather River, a half-mile below Stony Point. It is listed in the Giffen file.

Boone Valley [Yuba]. An abundance of water in the winter of 1871–72 brought activity to surface mining with varying success, according to a report of the *Appeal*, printed in an unidentified clipping in Hayes Scrapbooks: Mining, II, sec. 13.

Borrjes Ranch [Nevada]. An unidentified place listed in Hittell's roster.

Boston Bar [El Dorado]. On Horseshoe Bend of the Middle Fork of the American River, below Michigan Bluff (*Mining Bureau*, IX, p. 275). Doolittle's map, 1868, shows it above Horseshoe Bar, below Pleasant Bar; Bowman's map, 1873, shows it just above Pleasant Bar. The El Dorado County History, 1883 (pp. 84, 85), locates it between Eureka Bar and Pleasant Bar. The same source states that the first mining company to receive a charter in the state was the Boston Bar Company of the American River. The charter, granted in 1850, extended over the entire Boston Bar.

Boston Companys Bar [Calaveras]. Boston Company and New Boston Company are shown on Trask's map, 1853, on the South Fork of Mokelumne River, about two miles above the junction.

Boston Flat [Placer]. On the North Fork of American River, above Rattlesnake Bar. It is mentioned as a river bar by May W. Perry in *Placer Nuggets*, February, 1964 (p. 6).

Boston Hill [Nevada]. Northeast of Red Dog and south of Buckeye Hill. The extent of hydraulic mining by 1879 is shown on Pettee and Bowman's map.

Boston Mine [Calaveras]. *See* Mokelumne Hill.

Boston Ranch [Butte]. *See* Hurleton.

Boston: Ravine, Flat [Nevada]. Now a part of Grass Valley. The diggings were started in 1849 by Bostonians. According to Bancroft, VI (p. 357), within six years several placers in the Ravine yielded nearly four million dollars. Edwin Morse, who lived here from 1850 to 1896, gives the best account (pp. 222 ff.). The claims, mines, and mills in 1867 are listed by Bean (pp. 202 ff.).

Boston Store [Amador]. There were two settlements so named in the county. One was in Ione Valley at the junction of the stage road to Muletown and Dry Creek.

The other, also known ~_____, was in Jackson Valley, at the ju._____ f the Jackson Valley and Stony Creek roads. (Cenotto.) Boston House is shown on the USGS Jackson 1938 quadrangle.

Bostwick Bar [Calaveras]. Near Reynolds Ferry, on the Stanislaus River. According to a Hittell clipping from the Sonora *Herald* of 1858 (p. 66½), it was one of the largest bars on the river with well-paying claims. Heckendorn in 1856 lists it with Reynolds Ferry. In 1861 two miners took out twenty-one ounces in two days (*Mining Press*, March 16, 1861). The site is shown on the USGS Copperopolis 1939 quadrangle as Bostick Bar.

Bottileas [Amador]. The diggings around which the town of Jackson developed were called Bottileas. According to the often repeated story, the name originated because the many bottles (Spanish *botillas*), which had been thrown away by campers, accumulated there around the spring. *See* Jackson.

Bottle Hill Diggings [El Dorado]. In the Hornblende Mountains, three miles north of Georgetown. Recorded on Goddard's map, 1857. According to the County History, 1883 (p. 190), the name was given in 1851 because of the numerous bottles found at the place. The mines were doing well in 1855, according to Hutchings (Diary, May 12, 1855). The diggings were hill diggings until 1856, when water was brought to them by Pilot and Rock Creek Canal. The extensive tunneling is described by Raymond (IV, p. 105; VII, p. 95). The gravel deposits are mentioned in 1911 (*Professional Paper*, 73, p. 169), and the mine is still listed in 1956 *Mining Bureau*, LII, p. 543). The hill is shown on the USGS Placerville 1931 quadrangle.

Boulder Bar [Nevada]. At the mouth of Scotchman Creek, tributary to the South Fork of Yuba River. *See* Rocky Bar.

Boulder Creek District [San Diego]. In the central part of the county, five miles west of Cuyamaca. Gold was discovered about 1885 and mined intervals and on a small scale to about the 1920s (*Bull.*, 193, p. 170). The claims and mines along the stream are listed in *Mining Bureau*, XIV (p. 662).

Boulder Flat [Mono]. In the Patterson Mining District, at the eastern base of Mount Patterson. It was a small camp of the 1880s, between Star City and Belfort. The name is derived from the large gold and silver boulders found there. (F. S. Wedertz.) Shown on the USGS Bridgeport 1911 quadrangle.

Boulder Hill [El Dorado]. *See* Bowlder Hill.

Bouquet Canyon [Los Angeles]. North of Saugus. This is one of the places where gold is said to have been mined before 1842. There has been small-scale mining here since the 1880s (J. W. Robinson). When the St. Francis dam broke in 1933 and the rush of water eroded the sides of this canyon and San Francisquito Canyon, the little gold that was found there caused a minor run (*Mining Bureau*, XXX, p. 247). The excitement brought about the renewal of the rumors about early gold deposits that had been worked here before 1842.

Bourbon Hill [Nevada]. Near Nevada City. The place is mentioned as a mining settlement in *Bean's Directory*, 1867. In 1870 a Welsh company made a rich strike on claims they had worked for years (Hayes *Scrapbooks*: Mining, IV, sec. 120).

Bovyers [Nevada]. On the South Fork of Yuba River, near Jones Crossing. David Bovyer established a trading post here in September, 1849, for the purpose of trading with Indians, according to Brown's *Directory*, 1856 (p. 9), and in October of the same year he moved to White Oak Springs. *Bean's Directory*, 1867 (pp. 358 f.), locates White Oak Springs, named by Bovyer probably in the summer or early fall of 1849, midway between Jones Bar and Newtown. Both places may have been known by the name Bovyers, as they were both established as trading posts.

Bowens Bar [Plumas]. On the Middle Fork of Feather River. It is mentioned in the County History, 1882 (p. 288), as one of the chief camps on the Middle Fork.

Bowery Bar [Sacramento]. On the American River, between Sacramento River and Negro Bar. It is mentioned in C. S. Wilson's *Report* to the stockholders of the Sacramento Valley Railroad, October 20, 1854. No mining record was found.

Bowlder Hill [El Dorado]. Between Otter and Canyon creeks. Shown on Bowman's map, 1873, northeast of Georgetown. The name is also spelled Boulder Hill. Extensive deep deposits were mined by the hydraulic process (Raymond, IV, p. 105; VII, p. 91). A Boulder Placer Mine at Pilot Hill is described in *Mining Bureau*, XXXIV (p. 243).

Bowlesville [Sacramento]. *See* Ashland.

Bowling Green [Nevada]. Near Rough and Ready. The U. S. Bureau of the Census in the population schedule for the 1850 census lists 126 inhabitants, mainly miners, five tavern keepers, and one physician.

Bowmans Ranch [Nevada]. About six miles

north and east of Graniteville, south of Poorman Creek. Shown on Doolittle's map, 1868, on a toll road. It is mentioned as a settlement with a hotel in 1867 (*Bean's Directory*, p. 402).

Box [Plumas]. Between the North and Middle forks of Feather River, five miles from Butte County line. This was the trading center for numerous quartz mines in the vicinity, and from 1896 to 1901 it served as the post office for these mines. In 1900 three stamp mills were still in operation, one Huntington Mill, and one arrastre (*Register*, 1900). The name is shown on the map of the *Register* and on the USGS Bidwell Bar 1944 quadrangle as Letter Box, which was obviously the original name.

Boxes Bar. An unidentified place on the ancient channel of Yuba River. It is mentioned in an undated Hittell clipping, (p. 61), probably in 1854.

Boyers Bar [Tuolumne]. On the south bank of the Tuolumne River, west of Jacksonville. Shown on Trask's map, 1853.

Bradshaws Bar [Placer]. On the North Fork of American River, twelve miles north of Auburn. It is mentioned in the notice of a claim recorded January 15, 1855 (Placer County Records, I, p. 276).

Branches: Bar, Ferry [Tuolumne]. On the Tuolumne River, above San Pedros Bar. Shown on Goddard's map of 1857. It is often mentioned by Stephen Davis in 1852 in *California Gold Rush Merchant*. The name sometimes appears as Branch Bar.

Brandons Bar [Siskiyou]. One mile above Happy Camp. In January, 1852, miners made ten dollars a day to the hand (*Alta*, February 18, 1852).

Brandy: City, Gulch [Sierra]. On Cherokee Creek, tributary to the North Fork of Yuba River. Recorded on Wescoatt's map, 1861. The original name of the place was Strychnine City (R. Drury). Gold was discovered here after the Gold Lake hunt of 1850. Good prospects were reported in the 1855 *Report of the California State Surveyor General* (p. 202). De Long describes the place on June 16, 1857. A rare picture of the enormous suspension flume over Brandy Gulch was published in *Hutchings' Magazine*, September, 1857. *See also* the illustration in Ernest Seyd (p. 42). In 1857 Downie (p. 137) had a share in the Hagler Tunnel here. The place was situated above a channel of the Blue Lead, which was not heavily covered by earth and lava; hence, there was extensive hydraulic mining (Browne, p. 138). There was a renewal of mining in the early 1920s. There was still a

school then and the post office existed until 1926. The name is shown on the USGS Bidwell Bar 1944 quadrangle. On some maps it is placed in Yuba county, apparently by mistake. Modern mining operations in the district are described in *Mining Bureau* XVI (Sierra, pp. 6 ff.).

Brandy Flat [Nevada]. Near Alpha, opposite the mouth of Poorman Creek. A letter written by Frederick Shaw and datelined Brandy Flat, February 14, 1857, is in the Bancroft Library collection. The place is mentioned in *Bean's Directory*, 1867 (pp. 286 f.) It was once quite a mining camp, according to the County History, 1880 (p. 205), yielding about 150 thousand dollars, and was being hydraulicked in 1880.

Branson City [San Diego]. About one mile east of present-day Julian. In 1870 a town was laid out as a rival to Julian by a San Diego lawyer, Lewis C. Branson (Ellsberg, p. 18). *See* Julian.

Brass Wire Bar [Nevada]. On the South Fork of Yuba River, opposite Washington. It was a small bar, having yielded about 50 thousand dollars, and was being worked by Chinese miners in 1880 (Co. Hist., 1880, p. 205).

Brays Bar [Plumas]. On the Middle Fork of the Feather River (Bancroft Notes). It is mentioned as one of the chief mining camps on the Middle Fork of Feather River in the Plumas County History, 1882 (p. 288).

Brazoria Bar [Tuolumne]. On the south side of Tuolumne River, a short distance above its confluence with Moccasin Creek. The first residents were apparently Texans, and the name was probably derived from Brazoria, Texas. It is mentioned by De Ferrari in *Chispa*, IV (p. 130) and again in an anonymous article in *Chispa*, VIII (p. 286), where it is stated that it was later also known as Missouri Bar.

Brazos [Tuolumne]. A camp on Moccasin Creek. Shown on Goddard's map, 1857. The name is the Spanish word for 'arm', and may designate here 'arms of a river'. The place may, however, be the same as Brazoria Bar (De Ferrari).

Brewster [El Dorado]. Near Coloma. Stephen Wing mined here occasionally in the winter of 1855–56 (Journal, II, pp. 81, 85, 87).

Breyfogle Canyon [Inyo]. In Death Valley. Charles C. Breyfogle left the mines on the Yuba River in December, 1850, and settled in Oakland, California. From 1854 to 1859 he was assessor and treasurer of Alameda County. Then he went to Austin, Nevada, and in 1863 he prospected for gold in Death Valley. The same year he claimed that he discovered a rich gold deposit but was wounded and held captive by Indians. After his recovery and release from captivity, he could not recall the site of the gold deposit. In the jargon of Death Valley prospectors the term "breyfogling" later became the synonym for hunting lost mines. According to a somewhat questionable report in the *Pioche Record*, reprinted in the Stockton *Daily Herald*, February 3, 1873, Breyfogle rediscovered the deposits but was again attacked and crippled by Indians. In the spring of 1873, this newspaper report resulted in a stampede for the "lost mine." Numerous articles have been written about the Breyfogle Mine, especially in the *Desert Magazine* and in *Westways*. However, the truth of the story remains doubtful. According to the *Death Valley Guide* (p. 20), the first name of Breyfogle was Jacob, and he was a gunsmith from Austin, Nevada. In the magazine *Death Valley Chuck-Walla*, April 1, 1907, the man is called Anton Breyfogle, a German from Austin. The most detailed stories about Breyfogle are told by L. Burr Belden, March 22 and March 29, 1964, and by H. O. Weight (pp. 12 ff.).

Breyfogle Flat [Sierra]. On the South Fork of the North Fork of Yuba River, about eight miles east of Downieville. The name is spelled Bifogle on Trask's map, 1853. In October, 1859, "Major" Downie ((pp. 40, 49) mined at this site and claims to have taken out forty ounces in four days. Joshua D. Breyfogle, at times in partnership with his brother Charles and another relative, mined here with moderate success from March to November, 1850. The Breyfogles, Pennsylvania Germans, arrived in California in 1849 and first mined on the Trinity River, but without success. (Diary of Joshua D. Breyfogle.)

Brickville [Shasta]. *See* Briggsville.

Bridgeport [Amador]. On the South Fork of Cosumnes River, north of Fiddletown. Shown on the County Map, 1866; Doolittle's map, 1868; and the USGS Placerville 1931 quadrangle. A few good cabins and a tavern constituted the mining camp, situated here where the two branches of the South Fork unite and the road to Centreville crosses the river (*Amador Ledger*, June 20, 1857). There was also a good ranch here, part of which was in El Dorado County (Berriman).

Bridgeport [Mariposa]. About five miles southwest of Mariposa, on Agua Fria Creek. Shown on the Las Mariposas map, 1861. In May, 1852, Andrew Church opened a store, erected a frame house, and named the place (p. 188). There were some promising early reports, but in 1867, Browne (p. 34) reports the 8-stamp mill as idle. The mill was on the creek, very near the southern border of Frémont's grant. Shown on the USGS Indian Gulch 1920 quadrangle.

Bridgeport [Nevada]. On the South Fork of the Yuba River just above the junction. Shown prominently on Trask's map, 1853. It was so named because there was a wooden bridge across the river at this point. Urias and Manuel Nye had built a trading post here in 1849, and the place was then known as Nyes Landing. The first bridge was built by David Woods; in 1862 it was replaced by a covered bridge, recognized as a remarkable engineering feat. It is one of the longest covered bridges in existence (Nevada County Historical Society *Bulletin*, November, 1957). When Mrs. D. B. Bates saw the place in 1851, it consisted of three shanties and a toll bridge (Bates, p. 179). In March of the same year a drunken crowd hanged an innocent man here, according to Bean (p. 362). The place was short-lived. The name still appears on the USGS Smartsville 1943 quadrangle.

Briggsville [Shasta]. On Clear Creek, west of Redding. Recorded on Goddard's map,

Bridgeport, Nevada Co.

1857. It is mentioned in a letter of June 13, 1853 from one named Evoy to John Bidwell (Bidwell Collection, California State Library, California Section). In the summer of 1862 a company of fifteen hands was working here with good prospects (*Mining Press*, August 8, 1862). Hutchings in his Diary, December 20, 1855, mentioned a place near Horsetown named Brickville, which consisted of three stores, two cabins, and "the balance Chinese and Indian tents and huts." This was probably Briggsville, where lime was produced for the brick buildings at Horsetown and elsewhere (R. B. Eaton).

Brills Diggings [El Dorado]. Probably on Dutch Creek, between Kelsey and Coloma. The place is mentioned by De Long, March 2, 1854.

Bristol Mountains [San Bernardino]. About fourteen miles northeast of Amboy. Gold was discovered on the northeast slope in 1897 by a Chemehuevi Indian named Hicorum. The Orange Blossom Mine developed here and produced copper as well as gold. By 1907 there was a little settlement here, unusual in that it had no saloon, according to Belden, who gave an account of it February 7, 1954. When the Great Gold Belt Mine was opened in 1907, old arrastres in the wash proved that it was old mining ground. The mine was relocated in 1923 as Camp Castle Mine and equipped with a Herman ball mill. In 1931 it was idle again. (*Mining Bureau*, XV, p. 789; XXVI, p. 217; XXVII, pp. 276, 290.)

Brocklis Bar [El Dorado]. Shown on Goddard's map of 1857 on the South Fork of the American River, east of Silver Creek. A settlement, Brocklis, is shown on the road to Slippery Ford on the same map.

Brookland [Nevada]. The name is mentioned in a letter of Jacob Young, dated November 7, 1852 (in the California State Library, California Section). The reference is apparently to Brooklyn in Nevada County. *See* Red Dog [Nevada].

Brooklyn [Nevada]. *See* Red Dog.

Brown Bear Mine. *See* Deadwood: Creek, District [Trinity]; French Gulch [Shasta].

Browns Bar [El Dorado]. Shown on Trask's map, 1853, on the south side of the South Fork of the American River, above Iowa Bar.

Browns Bar [Placer]. On the Middle Fork of the American River, below Kennebec Bar. It was the terminal of a 4-mile flume from Poverty Bar (San Francisco *Bulletin*, September 10, 1857). Shown on Doolittle's map, 1868; Bowman's, 1873; and the County Map, 1887. A dragline dredge was operated in 1946 (*Mining Bureau*, LII, p. 549).

Browns Bar [Plumas]. On the North Fork of Feather River, near the junction with the East Fork, in the vicinity of Rich Bar. The place is mentioned by Dame Shirley, I (p. 42) and was apparently of little importance in September, 1851. It is probably the same bar that is described in a letter by Rodney P. Odall written May 18, 1851.

Browns Bar [Trinity]. In New River District, near Denny. It was a small but apparently productive camp, originally called Hackerman Bar (*Mining Bureau*, XIV, p. 903).

Browns Cut [Placer]. On the Middle Fork of the American River, between Murderers Bar and Kennebec. It was apparently a section of the Big Crevice. Rich ancient river deposits were worked by a complicated system of dredging (Co. Hist., 1882, p. 230).

Browns Flat [Tuolumne]. Between Columbia and Sonora, with its lower extremity adjacent to present-day northern boundary of Sonora. At its upper end was Squabbletown, and to the east is Bald Mountain. Mining began in the early 1850s. In June 1854 two claims reportedly yielded one and a half pounds daily (Columbia *Gazette*, June 24, 1854). In 1855 water was supplied by the canal of the Columbia and Stanislaus River Water Company. Details concerning the place are given in Heckendorn (pp. 25, 77). Browne (p. 38) states that the pay dirt was hoisted by a wheel into dump boxes and washed there. In 1862 a chunk of gold weighing almost three pounds was found (*Mining Press*, May 1, 1862). *Mines and Minerals* (p. 358) gives the total output until 1899 at 4.5 million dollars. The mines are indicated on Dart's map, 1879. Shown on the USGS Big Tree 1941 quadrangle.

Browns Hill [Nevada]. About one-quarter mile east of You Bet. It was named for Giles S. Brown, one of the brothers who owned the mine which took up most of the hill. It was one of the richest mines in the You Bet — Red Dog area. In 1862 one claim which had opened in 1853 and considered worthless yielded 30 thousand dollars within a year (*Mining Press*, August 30, 1862). In 1867 five mills with forty-two stamps were in operation, all run by hurdy-gurdy wheels (Bean, pp. 372 f.). The hill, part of the You Bet Hydraulic Excavation, one of the largest in California, is now almost washed away (Foley).

Browns Ravine [Butte]. It is listed in the County History, 1882 (p. 253), as a once flourishing mining camp in Concow Township, north of Oroville.

Browns Valley [Yuba]. About fifteen miles northeast of Marysville. Shown on Wescoatt's map, 1861. It was first settled in 1850 and became one of the richest gold towns in the county. Ida Pfeiffer visited the place in 1853 and gives an interesting account in her book (chapter 13). Three mills are listed in 1859 (*State Register*, 1859) and four in 1869 (Raymond, II, p. 71). The Dannebroge Mine reportedly yielded 250 thousand dollars by 1865. Among other mines in the vicinity were the Jefferson, the Pennsylvania, the Sweet Vengeance, and the Rattlesnake (Browne, pp. 152 ff.). The decline began about 1875, and by 1885 only six miners are listed among a population of about 100 (Co. Dir., 1884–85). Accounts of mining in the area may be found in the County History, 1879 (p. 87) and in Browne (pp. 152 ff.). The place is recorded on the USGS Smartsville 1943 quadrangle.

Brownsville [Calaveras]. Near Murphys, at the junction of Pennsylvania and Missouri gulches. According to *California Historical Landmarks*, the camp was named for an early settler, Alfred Brown. It was a thriving placer mining camp in the 1850s and 1860s. There is still one plot of graves enclosed by an iron fence, all that remains of a large cemetery (R. C. Wood). Historic Landmark 465.

Brownsville [El Dorado]. Between Indian and On It creeks, on the Cedar and Indianville Canal, which was built in 1852 to bring water from the Middle Fork of the Cosumnes River. It was named for Henry Brown, one of the locators of the Volcano claims, according to *Resources* (p. 77). It is recorded on Goddard's map, 1857, and is described in 1867 by Browne (pp. 85, 87) as "deep diggings which will not be exhausted for many years." On December 2, 1867, a post office was established and named Mendon, since there was a post office Brownville in Yuba County. *See* Mendon. In 1905 a 10-stamp mill was still in operation (*Register*, 1905).

Brownsville [Sierra]. *See* Forest City.

Brownsville [Siskiyou]. On the East Fork of Salmon River. It was a mining camp which developed in the 1860s and was named for George Green Brown (Tickner; *Siskiyou Pioneer*, II:10, p. 21). William M. Smith suggests that the reference may be to Browns Store on the South Fork of Salmon River, at the mouth of Plummer Creek. The place was raided and burned by Indians from the Hoopa Reservation in the late 1870s, according to his report.

Brownsville [Yuba]. On the old road from Marysville to Rabbit Creek. The place was named for I. E. Brown, who built the first sawmill here in 1851. It is mentioned by De Long, February 2, 1856, and is shown on Goddard's map, 1857. There were mainly ravine diggings, and in 1867 the deposits were nearly exhausted, after which the place was known for its orchards (Browne, p. 148). In later years mining is again reported in the newspapers. Rich ore was found in the Apple Tree Mine in 1909, according to a report in the Marysville *Appeal*, April 25, 1909, and the same newspaper, beginning with the issue of April 26, 1908 and continuing into 1909, tells of the excitement caused by the sheriff attaching ore from the Solano Wonder Mine and holding it under arrest in the Yuba County jail. (Ramey.)

Brules Bar [Placer or Sacramento?]. The location is undetermined. A notice of intention to build a ditch from Miners Ravine to Brules and Mississippi bars was recorded in Placer County Records, I (p. 165).

Brunswick [Nevada]. Two miles east of Grass Valley. Mining began in the "early days," and a 20-stamp steam-driven mill is described in 1887/88 (*Mining Bureau*, VIII, pp. 431, 693). The mine and mill are frequently described in the Mining Bureau reports until 1941.

Brush Creek [Butte]. Brush Creek and Rush Creek are not clearly identified. There was a Brush Creek post office in 1856, apparently between the North and Middle forks of Feather River, near Berry Creek, to which it was later moved. *See* Frickstad. The USGS Bidwell Bar 1944 quadrangle shows Brush Creek as a settlement near Mountain House Creek, but an earlier map, the County Map, 1862, shows the place as Rush Creek P.O.

Brush Creek [Nevada]. A tributary to the South Fork of Yuba River, northwest of Nevada City. There was some mining here as early as 1850, but the rich vein was not discovered until 1854 (*Alta*, June 4, 1854). Canfield mentions the creek, and *Bean's Directory*, 1867, states that the shallow diggings had produced an estimated three million dollars by ground sluicing. The stream is sometimes confused with Rush Creek, which is also a tributary to Yuba River but farther to the west. Both streams are shown on the USGS

Smartsville 1943 quadrangle. *See* Rush Creek [Nevada].

Brush Creek [Sierra]. For the early history, *see* Mountain House. By 1875 the Brush Creek Mine had produced one million dollars, and it continued to be a heavy producer, with interruptions. By 1955 the total output was about 4 million dollars (*Mining Bureau*, LII, p. 248). The mine was closed in 1964 (*Bull.*, 193, p. 21).

Brushville [Calaveras]. South of the Calaveras River, near Quail Hill, in the copper belt. In the 1860s there were several mines here which had two mills with a total of 30 stamps (Browne, pp. 69 f.). According to an item in the San Andreas *Independent*, January 19, 1861, the average pay was only seven dollars per day to the hand.

Brushy Canyon [Placer]. East of Yankee Jims on the lead between the North and Middle forks of the American River. A legal notice to convert Brushy Canyon into a ditch is recorded in Placer County Records, I (p. 247) on September 11, 1854. According to Hittell Clippings (p. 63 and 64), the place was an important mining center in 1855. It is mentioned again December 21, 1861 in the *Mining Press*.

Bryden [Yuba]. *See* Honcut.

Buccleughs [Yuba]. Near New York Ranch. The place is mentioned by De Long, February 3, 1856, but no mining records were found.

Buchanan Hill [Butte]. In Concow Township, north of Oroville. It was once a flourishing mining camp, according to the County History, 1882 (p. 253).

Buck [Plumas]. *See* Bucks Ranch.

Buckeye. The tree or shrub, *Aesculus californica*, which is common in the foothills, has given names to many places and mines in the gold district. Some of the names, however, were given by miners from Ohio, the Buckeye State.

Buckeye [Shasta]. North of Redding. In the 1850s a Mr. Johnson discovered a quartz lead between Buckeye and Churntown, "the richest of any as yet known in California" (Hittell Clippings, p. 43) — a slight overstatement. The place is recorded on Goddard's map, 1857, and it is reported in the *Mining Press*, April 6, 1861, as yielding twenty dollars a day to the hand. Shown on the USGS Redding 1944 quadrangle. Buckeye or Old Diggings District is described in *Bulletin*, 193 (p. 104). *See* Old Diggings [Shasta].

Buckeye [Tuolumne]. In Table Mountain District. It was developed in 1854 and mentioned in Heckendorn, 1856 (p. 104). Browne states that by 1867 the expenditure exceeded the profit by far (p. 41).

Buckeye [Yuba]. On Strawberry Ridge. De Long mentions it February 1, 1856. It is possibly the same as Buckeye Bar on the North Fork of Yuba River, shown on Trask's map, 1853.

Buckeye Bar [Placer]. On the Middle Fork of American River, above Kennebec Bar. Shown on the County Map, 1887. It is listed in the County History, 1882 (pp. 401 f.), beyond Kennebec Bar, above Poverty Bar.

Buckeye Bar [Placer]. On the North Fork of the American River. Notices of claims here were filed May 5, 1852, in Placer County Records, I (pp. 92, 130). Another claim on Buckeye Bar below Auburn is mentioned in a notice filed on February 23, 1854 (p. 219).

Buckeye Bar [Plumas]. On Nelson Creek. It is mentioned in the County History, 1882 (p. 288), as one of the important mining points along the creek.

Buckeye Bar [Sacramento]. On Laguna Creek, near the present town of Carbondale on the Ione Valley Road. Shown on Goddard's map, 1857, and on the map in the County History, 1880.

Buck-Eye Bar [Trinity]. Near Douglas City. Good wages were paid here in 1854, according to Cox (p. 40).

Buckeye District [Mariposa]. A small district about eight miles south of Mariposa. The *Annual Mining Review*, 1876 (pp. 22 f.), states that a 4-stamp mill was in operation in 1869 and one of eight stamps in 1870. According to *Bulletin*, 193 (p. 132), two mines in the district were active from the 1870s to the early 1900s and again from 1938 to 1941.

Buckeye District [San Bernardino]. South of Ludlow. It included the Bagdad-Chase mines and the town of Stedman. Shown on Crowell's map, 1903. *See* Stedman District.

Buckeye Flat [El Dorado]. Southwest of Placerville, on the Eureka Canal. The first miners came from Ohio (Hittell Clippings, p. 73). They may have been a group of the mining company called "Buckeye Rovers," who prospected between Auburn and Placerville.

Buckeye Flat [Placer]. Notice of a surface claim was recorded June 19, 1852, in Placer County Records, I (p. 94).

Buckeye: Flat, Hill, Gulch [Calaveras]. Two miles east of Mokelumne Hill. The Hill was named in 1849 by people from Ohio, who kept a store here. In 1852 Doble (p. 34) purchased lumber from a sawmill at Buckeye Gulch to build his long tom. In 1854 a claim was sold for thirty dollars, and the purchasers dug up six pounds of gold the following day (Hittell Clippings, p. 20). Browne (p. 56) mentions several hydraulic claims after 1861. The *Annual Mining Review*, 1876 (p. 21), lists a mill with forty stamps capacity at Buckeye Gulch in Calaveras County, but the exact location is not indicated.

Buckeye Hill [El Dorado]. About six miles north of Georgetown. It is shown on Doolittle's map, 1868, and is mentioned in Raymond VII (p. 91). The diggings were mainly seam and gravel diggings. A placer mine is still listed in 1938 (*Mining Bureau*, XXXIV, p. 227).

Buckeye Hill [Nevada]. Between Birchville and Sweetland, on the gravel ridge between French Corral and North San Juan. Shown on Hoffmann and Craven's Great Gravel Map, 1873. In 1874 the ground was worked by an English company, reportedly with good success. The mine had a tunnel 5,000 feet in length and an outlet on the Middle Fork of Yuba River. (Raymond, VII, pp. 126 f.). In 1879, when Pettee visited the region near by, the gravel was not yet worked out (Whitney, *Auriferous Gravels*, p. 389).

Buckeye Hill [Nevada]. In the Greenhorn District, southeast of Quaker Hill and opposite Hunts Hill, on the other side of Greenhorn Creek. Shown on Doolittle's map, 1868. According to the reminiscences of Eli Miller, as recounted to George E. Poore (reprinted in Philip R. May, *Origins of Hydraulic Mining in California*, pp. 67 ff.), the Hill was named in the spring of 1852 by Eli Miller and Anthony Chabot. They were joined in the fall by E. E. Matteson, who had travelled overland to California with them and with whom they had worked as day laborers in Nevada City during the dry summer season. The trio devised a method of washing the loose gravel on Buckeye Hill with a water hose and a nozzle, and later when Matteson returned to the Nevada City area, he applied the method on a claim on American Hill and took full credit for the "invention." As in many reminiscent accounts and as pointed out by May, there are discrepancies in Miller's story. Whether or not the first hydraulic process took place at Buckeye Hill, or Ravine near Nevada City, or at Buckeye Hill in the Greenhorn District, Matteson's contribu-

tion, namely, the idea of attaching a nozzle to a hose, seems to be adequately documented in early accounts. *See* American Hill [Nevada] and Buckeye: Hill, Ravine [Nevada]. *See also* the analysis of the various accounts in May's monograph cited above. When Pettee visited the Greenhorn District in 1879, he found the gravels of Buckeye Hill practically exhausted, with only a few Chinese at work at that time (Whitney, *Auriferous Gravels*, pp. 422 f.). Similar reports are given by Lindgren, *Tertiary Gravels* (p. 144) and in *Mining Bureau*, XXIII (p. 100). The Hill is shown on Pettee and Bowman's map, 1879. *See* Yankee Jims.

Buckeye: Hill, Ravine [Nevada]. The site of the Hill was north of Nevada City (now within the limits of the town), east of Oregon Hill and American Hill. These hills were completely washed away by the hydraulic operations by 1870, when Pettee visited the area (Whitney, *Auriferous Gravels*, p. 188). According to various accounts, about April, 1852, Anthony Chabot, a Frenchman, for whom the observatory and lake in Oakland were later named, used a water hose in the Ravine, or the Hill, in sluicing off earth and gravel that had been picked off and in cleaning up the bedrock. This innovation led to the introduction or "invention" of hydraulic mining the following year by E. E. Matteson at nearby American Hill. *See* American Hill [Nevada]. The details as given in the early accounts vary, but the story of Chabot's and Matteson's contributions is essentially the same (*Bean's History*, p. 62; *Mining Bureau*, II, part 2, p. 149; *Mines and Minerals*, p. 266; Browne, p. 110). In a more recent account, *Gold Rush Days in Nevada City* (p. 22) written by H. P. Davis, the author gives credit to Chabot for the "first step" in the new method, namely the use of the hose, but he concedes that the locale may possibly have been at Buckeye Hill near Red Dog in the Greenhorn district and not in Buckeye Ravine near Nevada City. For the "second step," the use of the nozzle with the hose, which took place on a claim on American Hill near Nevada City, Davis gives credit to three partners, Chabot, Matteson, and Eli Miller. *See* Buckeye Hill [Nevada] in the Greenhorn district. The account and analysis as given in Philip R. May, *Origins of Hydraulic Mining in California*, gives further details. *See also* Yankee Jims.

Buckeye Ranch Dry Diggings [Plumas]. About twelve miles east of Oroville. It is mentioned by Steele, February 24, 1851 (p. 199), and is shown on Milleson and Adams' map of 1851. The post office was established in 1861 using the popular name Bucks Ranch. It was changed to the present (and proper) name when a post office was established in 1868 at Bucks Ranch, ten miles to the north. *See* Bucks Ranch.

Buckeye Ridge [Trinity]. South of the junction of Trinity River and Stuarts Fork. Very rich gold bearing gravel, washed by ground sluicing, was reported in the 1850s. On Boalt's Hill, on the eastern end of Buckeye Ridge; successful mining was carried on for many years and continued into the 1870s (Raymond, VI, p. 154).

Buckeye Tent [Sierra]. Ten miles southwest of Downieville, near the South Fork of the Feather River. Recorded on Milleson and Adams' map of 1851.

Buckners Bar [Placer]. On the north side of the Middle Fork of American River, near the junction with the North Fork, opposite Murderers Bar. It was named in 1848 for Thomas M. Buckner, a Kentuckian who had come to Oregon in 1847 (Co. Hist., 1882, pp. 69 ff.). The miners, in cooperation with those at Murderers Bar, constructed an enormous flume here, which was swept away in September, 1850, after the last nail had been driven.

Bucks Bar [El Dorado]. On the south side of the North Fork of Cosumnes River, southeast of Diamond Springs. Bucks Bar Bridge is shown on Doolittle's map, 1868. A letter of James Carson datelined Bucks Bar, August 15, 1856, is in the Bancroft Library collection. A gravel deposit was worked by dragline in 1938 (*Mining Bureau*, XXXVIII, p. 363). The place was still listed in 1956. Shown on the USGS Placerville 1931 quadrangle.

Bucks Ranch [Plumas]. On Bucks Creek, tributary to the North Fork of Feather River. Shown on the County Map, 1886. Horace Bucklin and Francis Walker located the Ranch in 1850 (*California Historical Landmarks*, pp. 42 f.). Windeler (p. 113) prospected here in the spring of 1852 on his way to Rich Bar on the East Branch of the North Fork of Feather River. The place became the trading center and the post office (1868–1894) for a number of quartz and drift mines (*Register*, 1900). The name of the post office was changed to Buck in 1894. The place is sometimes confused with Buckeye, which was ten miles southwest and was first called Bucks Ranch. The name is shown on the USGS

Bidwell Bar 1944 quadrangle. The site is inundated by Buck's Dam and Reservoir. It is Historic Landmark 197.

Budeville [El Dorado]. Shown on Gibbes' map, 1851, between the North and Middle forks of American River.

Buells Flat [Siskiyou]. On the upper South Fork of Salmon River, at the confluence of Big Bend Creek. It was named for William M. Buell, who came to the Salmon-Trinity Alps with James Abrams in 1850 and had a trading post here until the bar was worked out, about 1860 (*Siskiyou Pioneer*, I:5, p. 40; II:10, p. 10).

Buena Vista. This was a very popular name in the United States after General Taylor's victory over Santa Anna at Buena Vista in the state of Coahuila, February 23, 1847. Some places might have been named because they commanded a "beautiful view."

Buena Vista [Amador]. A camp north of Jackson Creek, south of Ione. Goddard records Buena Vista south of Jackson Creek on his map of 1857; the County Map, 1866, shows Buena Vista Peak about one and a half miles south of the Creek and Buena Vista as a camp less than a half mile north of the Creek. Cenotto points out that it was the site of the Hitchcock Ranch, mentioned by Alfred Green in the fall of 1848 (pp. 12 f., 17) when he was mining at the diggings on the lower Mokelumne. There were several traders there at that time. It was an election precinct in November, 1849. The settlement was also known as The Corners, at the junction of the roads to Lancha Plana, Ione, Jackson, and Stockton. In 1868 the placers were worked out (Browne, p. 72; Co. Hist., 1881, p. 189). The post office was discontinued in 1878. The settlement and the Peak are shown on the USGS Jackson 1938 quadrangle.

Buena Vista [Nevada]. On the Colfax-Grass Valley road, between Peardale and Chicago Park, about one-quarter mile southeast of the junction of the You Bet and Colfax roads. Buena Vista Ranch is shown on Doolittle's map, 1868. The camp was in existence in 1850 and later received water from the Greenhorn Ditch (Sacramento *Daily Union*, December 9, 1854).

Buena Vista District [Humboldt]. The *Mining Press*, August 31, 1861, reprinted an item from the Red Bluff *Independent*, according to which the Abba Nueva Ledge was yielding gold and silver. The location was not determined.

Buena Vista Flat [Stanislaus]. Near Knights Ferry. It was a prosperous camp around

1860, averaging twenty dollars per day to the hand (*Mining Press*, March 16, 1861; Heckendorn, p. 104).

Buena Vista Hill [Calaveras]. Four miles northeast of Mokelumne Hill. The deposits are reported to have been rich, but it was almost impossible to get water to the top of the hill. (Browne, p. 56.) Only a dozen miners are listed as residents of the place by Heckendorn (p. 103) in 1856. A report in an undated newspaper clipping claims, however, that after 1857, four hydraulic claims were in operation. A Buena Vista group of mines, three miles west of West Point, is listed in 1916 (*Mining Bureau*, XIV, p. 72).

Buena Vista Mine [Mariposa]. *See* Colorado.

Buffalo Gulch [Mariposa]. On the Feliciana vein. A 5-stamp steam-driven mill was erected here in 1865 (*Annual Mining Review*, 1876, p. 21).

Buffalo: Hill, Creek [El Dorado]. On the Georgetown Divide, northeast of Georgetown. Prominently marked on Bowman's map, 1873. The place is mentioned in Raymond (IV, p. 106; VII, p. 91) as the site of one of the principal gravel mines of the region.

Buffs Bar [Butte]. *See* Huffs Bar.

Buljon Gulch [Shasta]. *See* Bullion Gulch.

Bullards Bar [Yuba]. On the North Fork of Yuba River, about a mile below Fosters Bar. Recorded on Milleson and Adams' map, 1851. In June, 1849, a Dr. Bullard of Brooklyn, New York, and three partners dammed up the river after a fortnight of hard labor and netted 15 thousand dollars worth of gold in less than two months (Buffum, p. 105). In July of the same year William Downey of Downieville opened a store here, and thus started on his remarkable career. By 1858 there were few residents left with the exception of some Chinese, according to the *Marysville Directory*, 1858 (p. xxv). In 1866 the post office was transferred from Fosters Bar and continued until 1914. There was, however, little mining after 1870. The place is now covered by Bullards Reservoir.

Bull Creek [Butte]. An extract from the Chico *Review*, January 27, 1872, printed in the San Francisco *Bulletin*, February 2, 1872, reports that one company had been averaging twenty dollars per day to the hand (Hayes Scrapbooks: Mining, II, sec. 24). The location is not indicated.

Bull Creek District [Mariposa]. *See* Kinsley.

Bull Diggings [El Dorado]. On the ridge between Illinois and Oregon canyons, north

of Mameluke Hill. The place was discovered in May, 1851, by Greenfield and Edward Jones, brothers, who cleared 20 thousand dollars between May and August of that year. It was so named because a yoke of bulls was used to haul the gravel to the canyon for washing. (W. T. Russell, p. 97.)

Bullion Gulch [Shasta]. Near Briggsville. According to Steger, it was also known as Buljon Gulch. In early years it was a rich channel, which in the early 1900s was dredged profitably.

Bullion Knob [Mariposa]. About five miles northwest of Mariposa. Shown on Goddard's map, 1857, and the Las Mariposas map, 1861. This is not the same place as Mount Bullion.

Bullpen Gulch [Tuolumne]. Northeast of Sonora, and now a part of it. The Sonora *Herald*, February 11, 1854 (?) mentioned successful prospecting (Hittell Clippings, p. 26).

Bully Choop District [Trinity]. At the foot of Bully Choop Mountain, near Shasta County Line. One mine with a 30-stamp mill is listed by the Mining Bureau until 1940. The name is often spelled Bally or Bolly, the Wintun Indian name for 'mountain'. *See California Place Names.*

Bully Hill [Shasta]. *See* Delamar.

Bummerville [Calaveras]. East of West Point. Shown on the USGS West Point 1948 quadrangle. No mining record was found. *See* Camp Flores and Camp Spirito.

Bunchs Bar [Placer]. On Bear River. It is mentioned in *Placer Nuggets*, June, 1959 (p. 3).

Bunker Hill. This has been a popular place name in the United States because of the Battle of Bunker Hill in the American Revolution. In California a number of mines, hills, and ravines were so named during the Gold Rush era.

Bunker Hill [Nevada]. Northeast of Red Dog and Independence Hill. Recorded as a settlement on Doolittle's map, 1868. Pettee and Bowman's map, 1879, shows the area on Williams' claim mined by hydraulic operations.

Bunker Hill [Sierra]. Six miles southeast of Downieville, near the Middle Fork of Yuba River. Shown on Doolittle's map, 1868.

Bunker Hill Mine [Amador]. *See* Amador City.

Bunker Hill Mine [Mariposa]. *See* Hites Cove.

Bunker: Hill, Ravine [Sierra]. Between Portwine and Whiskey Diggings. An unidentified clipping in Hayes Scrapbook: Mining (I, sec. 44) contains a report from the *Mountain Messenger* dated January 15, 1859, that tunnel operations in the Hill unexpectedly reached pay dirt yielding as high as eleven dollars to the pan, resulting in a rush to the place, with about fifty claims staked off in less than twenty-four hours. According to the San Francisco *Call*, May 18, 1879, an 800-acre claim paid up to 100 thousand dollars yearly. The Bunker Hill Gold Quartz Company, a British concern (1873–1885) may have operated at this location. There were several Bunker Hill drift mines in the region. A Bunker Hill Mine is listed in the *Register*, 1903.

Bunkerville [Nevada]. One-half mile south of Nevada City, on Little Deer Creek. Shown on a map in the Book of Preemptions, I (p. 34) in Nevada County Records.

Bunkumville. An unidentified place listed as a mining locality on an illustrated letter sheet published by Hutchings in 1855.

Buntys Gulch [Calaveras]. Near Cave City, four and a half miles from San Andreas. It is mentioned in the San Franciso *Bulletin*, January 18, 1858.

Burks Bar [Nevada]. On the south side of the South Fork of Yuba River, three miles above Relief. Recorded on Trask's map, 1853.

Burleys Bar [Plumas]. On the North Fork of Feather River, nine miles below Rush Creek. Recorded on Trask's map, 1853.

Burns & Pope Ferry [Amador, Calaveras]. *See* Big Bar.

Burns: Camp, Creek, Diggings, Ranch [Mariposa]. Southwest of Hornitos. Named for John and Robert Burns, New Englanders, who settled here in 1847, and on whose ranch gold was discovered (Burns, pp. 13 ff.). James H. Carson (p. 9) states that gold was discovered here in 1849, and Enos Christman (p. 122) mentions the digging on March 19, 1850. Eccleston (*Mariposa War*, p. 28) mentions Burns Town, on February 28, 1851. The creek is recorded on Gibbes' *Map of the Southern Mines*, 1852, and by Goddard on his map of 1857. There was placering until 1851, followed by quartz mining. It may have been this camp that was later known as Quartzburg (*Alta*, October 24, 1851). In the same year the Burns Ranche Gold Mining Company was formed (Burns, pp. 13 ff.). Mining in the district continued until recent years. Between 1949 and 1951 almost five million yards of gravel were processed by dredging, yielding about 650

thousand dollars (*Mining Bureau*, LIII, p. 319). Burns Creek is shown on the USGS Haystack 1919 and the Sonora 1939 quadrangles. *See* Quartzburg [Mariposa].

Burnt Ranch [Trinity]. Near the confluence of the Trinity and New rivers, on Highway 299. It was so named because an Indian village here had been burned by Canadian miners in 1849. Cox (p. 84) gives a long story about the place in 1858. According to his informant, the place was so named because in 1854 Indians burned the buildings of a farmer, C. W. Durkee. But the burnt ranch was really an Indian rancheria. (De Massey, p. 100; Schoolcraft, III, p. 135). The post office was established October 18, 1858. In 1898 the place was still an important center and post office for hydraulic mines in the vicinity (*Register*, 1898). The Burnt Ranch District is described in *Bulletin*, No. 92 (p. 92). *See* Canadian Camp.

Burrington Hill [Nevada]. Three miles south of the Missouri Bar on the South Fork of Yuba River. It is shown as Burrington Hill on Doolittle's map, 1868, but is mentioned as Berrington Hill in Raymond, VI (p. 117).

Burtons Gulch [Plumas]. About two miles northeast of Spanish Peak. J. A. Edman mapped and listed it among the prosperous camps in the area, which produced well in the early days of surface mining and at which there was still profitable placer mining in 1875 (Raymond, VIII, pp. 110, 115).

Burwells Bar [Butte]. On the Feather River. According to Ferguson (p. 132), the place was two miles below the junction of the Middle and South forks. This may have been a misunderstanding on the part of Ferguson, and the reference may be to Bidwell Bar (Nopel).

Burying Ground Hill [Sacramento]. Above Mormon Island. The diggings were first worked by Patterson in August, 1849 (p. 37), yielding "rich returns" in later years.

Buster Flat [Trinity]. On the Trinity River, above the junction with the South Fork. It is mentioned in 1858 by Cox (p. 83).

Busters Gulch [Calaveras]. Near San Antone Camp, on San Antonio Creek, ten miles southeast of San Andreas. John W. Winkley ("The Knave," March 5, 1961) tells a story about a negro called Buster, who is said to have mined 40 thousand dollars worth of gold and buried it here.

Butchers Ranch [Placer]. East of Auburn; near the El Dorado County line. The *State Register*, 1859, lists a 2-stamp steam-driven

Butte City, Amador Co.

mill. From 1871 to 1935 the post office served several quartz mines. The Butcher Ranch District is described in *Mining Bureau*, XV (p. 316). It is listed in the *Register*, 1902, and recorded on the USGS Placerville 1931 quadrangle as Butchers. According to May W. Perry in *Placer Nuggets*, February 1, 1963 (pp. 4 f.), several large masses of gold were found in a drift mine that was located in 1856, one of which weighed twenty pounds.

Butte. This typical western American term, usually designating an isolated hill or mountain, was frequently found in geographic names in the gold region. For the meaning of the name, *see California Place Names*.

Butte [Sierra]. It is mentioned as a settlement or precinct in *Illustrated Spirits*, December 25, 1877 (Bancroft Scraps, V, 1803).

Butte Bar [Plumas]. On the south side of the Middle Fork of Feather River, a half mile above Onion Valley. It is listed in the Mining Bureau *Report* of 1890 and later years.

Butte City [Amador]. Three miles southeast of Jackson, at the foot of Jackson Butte, on Highway 49. Shown on Goddard's map, 1857. It was also called The Bute, and it was an early election precinct in Calaveras County (Cenotto). Rev. I. B. Fish preached at Bute City in December, 1851, between two gambling houses. In the spring of 1852 Doble passed through Butte City, which was "on a small flat about a mile from the ferry and consists of some 50 canvas tents and clapboard houses" (April 12, 1852). In the August 15, 1852 issue of the Volcano *Weekly Ledger* the "Traveler" found some non-English speaking foreigners building a store. This may have been the Ginnochio Store, an empty building still standing in 1962 (Camp, p. 299). Pringle Shaw mentions it as a "lively place" in 1854 (p. 116), and in *Transactions*, 1859 (p. 83), it is described as "a small village doing vast business." Vischer mentions it in 1859 (p. 322). The original name is said to have been Boomville, or Boonville, but no contemporary record was found. In the early 1850s it was probably called Greasertown, or Greaserville, at least by the owners of the ferry at Big Bar, who called it Greaserville early in 1852 (Berriman). Camp places the name Greaserville tentatively east of Butte City. There was mainly placer mining, but in 1855 a 12-stamp mill was in operation. The post office of 1857 was of short duration, but the *Mining Press*, January 18, 1861, reports that the mines were still yielding well. The County Map of 1866 shows the principal mines in and around the "city." The place is now a ghost town, and the name does not even appear on the USGS Jackson 1938 quadrangle. The building which housed a store and bakery in 1854 is Historic Landmark 39.

Butte Creek District [Butte]. Butte Creek, extending from near Chico to Whiskey

Flat, above Helltown, was very rich in gold. Asa Smith, however, in a letter to his father, datelined Butte Creek, September 4 and 22, 1853, stated that he and his brother made only a dollar a day. The *Mining Press*, March 23, 1861, reported profitable hydraulic mining; one chunk was valued at four hundred dollars. The creek was dredged in later years, between 1900 and the 1930s and again from 1945 to 1949. The district is described in *Bulletin*, 193 (p. 32). Placer mining during the Gold Rush was followed by hydraulic mining and some drift mining of the Tertiary gravels. At the beginning of the twentieth century it was worked with power shovels, then by dredging to the early 1920s, and later in the 1930s and 1940s.

Butte Flat [Calaveras]. On the Mokelumne River, south of Jackson Butte. Recorded on Goddard's map, 1857.

Butte Flat [Nevada]. West of Grass Valley. There was placer mining in the 1850s (Bean, p. 356).

Butte Mills [Butte]. The site is under Magalia Reservoir. The place had a post office between 1857 and 1861. *See* Dogtown [Butte] and Magalia.

Butte Mine [Kern]. *See* Rand District.

Butte Mountains [Sutter]. *See* Sutter Buttes.

Butterfield Flat [Tuolumne]. West of Jamestown, on Peppermint Creek Ditch. It is mentioned by Heckendorn in 1856 (p. 54) and was named for Benjamin F. Butterfield, pioneer of Jamestown (De Ferrari).

Butterfly: Creek, Valley, Diggings [Plumas]. The diggings here were apparently worked in the early 1850s but were soon abandoned. About 1860 two prospectors struck rich-paying dirt and soon thereafter about sixty miners were at work there and were doing well. (*Mining Press*, September 28, 1861.) Butterfly Creek and Valley are shown on modern maps west and south of Keddie.

Buttes Flat [Sierra]. *See* Kane Flat.

Butte Valley [Plumas]. *See* Butt Valley.

Butt Valley [Plumas]. South of Lake Almanor. It is shown as Butte Valley on the von Leicht-Craven map of 1874. The gravel deposits were worked for many years, according to *Mining Bureau*, XVI (Plumas, p. 1); and lode gold mining began in the 1850s and continued to about 1940, with later intermittent prospecting (*Bull.*, 193, p. 32). Drift, placer, and quartz mines are listed in the *Register*, 1898. The place was named for Horace Butts, early miner, and it had a post office, 1887–1912.

Buzzards [Nevada]. Northeast of Graniteville, between Milton and Weaver Lake, near the Sierra County border. It is mentioned as a settlement by Foley. No mining records were found.

Byrds Valley [Placer]. *See* Birds Valley.

Byrnes Ferry [Calaveras]. Patrick O. Byrne first built a ferry and later (in 1852) a bridge, at the point where the road from Copperopolis to Mountain Pass crossed the Stanislaus River. The ferry was also known as O'Byrne or O'Byrne's Ferry (*California Place Names*). In 1862 a covered bridge was built to replace the one that was washed away in a flood. A picture of it appears in S. G. Morley's *Covered Bridges of California*. In 1849–1850 a mining camp developed at the river and was called Byrnes Ferry. Pringle Shaw (p. 116) states that it was one of the principal bars on the Stanislaus River. According to the Sonora *Herald*, one company nearby was making ten to twenty dollars per day to the hand (Hittell Clippings, p. 66½). O'Byrne Ferry is Historic Landmark 281. The camp is believed by some to be the setting of Bret Harte's "The Outcasts of Poker Flat."

Cabbage Patch [Yuba]. It was on Dry Creek, tributary to Bear River, near the Nevada County line. Recorded on Wescoatt's map, 1861, and the County Map of 1879. Mining activities were apparently only on a small scale; mainly copper, between 1870 and 1890. According to the County History, 1879 (p. 79), the name arose when two negroes planted a cabbage field here in 1852. The name was changed to Waldo when a post office was established on December 29, 1898. (Marysville *Appeal*, December 29, 1898).

Cache Creek [Yolo]. Flows from the northwest corner of the county through the center of the eastern side and toward the Sacramento River. Early placering was carried on in a small way, according to *Mining Bureau*, XIV (p. 367).

Cactus Queen Mine [Kern]. *See* Mojave Mining District.

Calaveritas: Creek, Hill [Calaveras]. Southeast of San Andreas. The name is a diminutive form of Calaveras. A mining camp on the creek developed probably in 1849. Jacob H. Bachman worked here without success in April, 1850. In 1850 there was an Upper Calaveritas about three and a half miles east of Lower Calaveritas. Upper Calaveritas is still a small town; Lower Calaveritas has vanished. Murders and depredations in the spring of 1853 were promptly credited to Murieta (J. R. Ridge, p. 110). In 1857 Calaveritas became the seat of the Georgia Canal Company (Hittell Clippings, p. 48), and in the same year a French company erected a mill for 110 thousand dollars, which never crushed a pound because the vein was exhausted (Browne, p. 71). A detailed account of hydraulic mining in the district is given in Raymond, IV (pp. 71 f.). Hydraulic mining continued without much success until the 1930s (*U.S. Bull.*, no. 413, pp. 93 f.). A "doodle-bug" dredge operated on the creek in the 1930s (Poore). The site is Historic Landmark 255.

Caldwells Garden [Tuolumne]. In Shaws Flat, on the road from Sonora to Sprinfield. In 1855 a shaft was sunk in the garden of a Mr. Caldwell, and rich gravel deposits were discovered, yielding the owner 150 thousand dollars' worth of gold before he sold his claim (Co. Hist., 1882, pp. 478 ff.). The *Alta*, March 3, 1856, reported that from March 5 to March 21, 15,250 dollars in gold dust was taken out of the Caldwell claim; and the Sacramento *Union* February 2, 1856 reported that W. O. Sleeper purchased twenty-nine pounds of gold that were taken out of the same claim in four days. *See* Shaws Flat.

Caldwells Upper Store [Nevada]. *See* Nevada City.

Caledonia Flat [Nevada]. Three miles northwest of Meadow Lake. It was reported prosperous in an undated *Sierra Citizen* clipping, probably about 1854. A description of a quartz gold mine in the 1870s is given in Mining Bureau, XIII (p. 238).

Calf Bar [Placer]. On the North Fork of the American River, near the junction with the Middle Fork. Hutchings lists it in 1855; and it is mentioned in the County History, 1882 (p. 402). Notice of a claim was recorded October 21, 1852, in Placer County Records, I (p. 132). A Calf Pasture Mine, north of Auburn, is listed as late as 1936 (*Mining Bureau*, XXXII, p. 43).

Calico [San Bernardino]. In the Calico Mountains; four miles northwest of Yermo. For the origin of the name, *see California Place Names*. The silver and gold deposits were discovered in 1880 and paid well from the start. In 1881 there were already twenty-five houses and some tents here (Co. Hist., 1883, p. 57; Bancroft Notes); and in 1882 five saloons took care of the thirst of the miners. The County

Map, 1892, shows some sixty mines in the Calico Mining District. The volume of silver production exceeded by far that of gold. An undated clipping indicates that many of the houses of the old camp were moved to Barstow, apparently about 1890. In 1953 Walter Knott bought the ghost town to restore what has been called "the greatest southern California silver camp." It is now a San Bernardino County Regional Park and Historic Landmark 782.

Caliente [Kern]. A Southern Pacific station near Highway 466, east of Bakersfield. The name was taken from nearby Agua Caliente (Spanish for 'hot water' [spring]). The place was not a gold town, but it was the trading center and after 1875 the post office for the mines to the east. It had three custom stamp mills (*Register*, 1904). The Engels Mining Company operated until 1942 (*County Report*, I). *See* Agua Caliente: Amalie.

California Bar [El Dorado]. Near Coloma. Stephen Wing began working on a claim here in July, 1854, and he sold it September 16th of the same year (Journal, II, pp. 2, 14).

California Bar [Siskiyou]. On the Klamath River, nine miles southwest of Hornbrook. No early records were found, but a mine is listed in *Mining Bureau* from 1896 to 1935.

California Consolidated Mine [Nevada]. *See* Nevada City.

California House [Yuba]. On a tributary to Dry Creek, eight miles west of North San Juan. It is mentioned by De Long, January 24, 1856.

Calistoga District [Napa]. *See* Silverado.

Callahans Ranch [Siskiyou]. At the southern end of Scott Valley; at the junction of the East and South forks of Scott River. Gold was discovered in 1851, and the place was named for the first hotel keeper, M. B. Callahan. A post office was established in 1858; in 1892 the name was changed to Callahan. By the 1890s the mines were worked out. (*Mining Bureau*, XI, pp. 433 f.) The river below Callahans Ranch was dredged until about 1950 (W. M. Smith).

Callahans Station [Mono]. It was not a gold camp but a stage station in the 1880s on the Lundy Road (F. S. Wedertz).

Camanche [Calaveras]. About one and a half miles south of the Mokelumne River. The name is sometimes spelled Comanche. Shown on Goddard's map, 1857. It was once called Limerick, and later was named Camanche after a town in Iowa. No early reports of mining were found. In 1868

water was brought to the district and prospects for success were reported to be good at this camp and neighboring Cat Camp and Haightsville, according to a correspondent of the Sacramento *Union* writing January 20, 1868 (Clipping in Hayes Scrapbooks: Mining, IV, sec. 7). Marriage records indicate that the place was inhabited mainly by Chinese in 1871. Considerable dredging was carried on until 1936 (U.S. *Bulletin*, No. 413, pp. 76 ff.; *Mining Bureau*, XXXII, p. 336); and some dredging continued until 1951 in the Camanche-Lancha Plana District (*Bull.*, 193, p. 33). Camanche is now covered by Camanche Reservoir. Historic Landmark 254. Camanche and Camanche Creek are shown on the USGS Jackson 1938 quadrangle.

Camden [Nevada]. In the vicinity of Hunts Hill. It is mentioned as a mining camp by Foley.

Cameron [Mono]. Twelve miles north of Bridgeport, in Frying Pan Canyon. It was a mining camp in the Patterson district and was first called Newburg. When a post office was established August 6, 1887, the name was changed to Cameron, for Robert A. Cameron. Later all the buildings in the town were moved to Clinton and Bridgeport. Cameron Canyon, southwest of Bridgeport, was also named for R. A. Cameron, who mined there, 1897–1900. (*Mining Bureau*, VIII, p. 358; F. S. Wedertz.)

Camp Beautiful [Nevada]. When A. J. McCall left the charming spot, October 1, 1849, he applied this name. The location is not indicated.

Campbell Creek [Trinity]. A tributary to Trinity River, at Cox Bar. The miners averaged ten dollars a day in 1851, according to the Sacramento *Transcript* (steamer ed.), February 14, 1851 (Bancroft Notes).

Campbells Flat [Tuolumne]. On the north bank of Sullivan Creek, east of Campo Seco. One week 3,900 dollars were washed up from the tailings of twelve companies, which were dumped into the flume on an average of every thirty-five days (Sonora *Union Democrat*, May 20, 1860). In 1861 the Northern Light Company conducted large-scale tunnel mining here (*Mining Press*, August 31, 1861).

Campbells Halfway House [Tuolumne]. *See* Halfway House.

Campbell Springs [Shasta]. *See* Olney Creek.

Camp Cady [San Bernardino]. Twenty miles east of Daggett. In 1889 it had a 5-stamp mill, which crushed the ore from the Alvord mine, nine miles to the north (*Mining Bureau*, IX, p. 238). The place was formerly a military post on the Old Government Road.

Camp Catarrh [Calaveras]. Near West Point and Bummerville, on a rich quartz lode. It is mentioned in the *Calaveras Chronicle*, May 1, 1878.

Camp: Creek, Springs [El Dorado]. A tributary to the North Fork of the Cosumnes River. It was named in 1848 by Mormons on their trek from Sutters Fort to Salt Lake, when they camped here (Bigler, p. 114). Rich auriferous deposits were reported. Recorded on Goddard's map of 1857 and on detailed modern maps.

Camp Far West [Yuba]. About four miles east of Wheatland. In 1876 there was dry washing of gold here, but little production. It is the site of the military post established in 1849 by the United States government for the protection of settlers; it was abandoned in 1852. (Ramey; Wheatland *Free Press*, February 12, July 22, December 16 and 30, 1876; March 17, 1877).

Camp Flores [Calaveras]. Near West Point and Bummerville, on a rich quartz lode. It is mentioned in the *Mining Press*, April 25, 1862, and the *Calaveras Chronicle*, May 1, 1878.

Camp Hill Springs [Shasta]. *See* Olney Creek.

Campo. The name is the Spanish word for 'field', but at the time of the Gold Rush it was used in the sense of 'camp' by American as well as Mexican miners.

Campo de los Muertos [Calaveras]. Between Angels Camp and Carsons. It is mentioned in a letter to the editor of the San

Calico, San Bernardino Co.

Andreas *Independent*, dated April 20, 1858. The name is derived from the complete destruction of a camp of some 3,000 Mexicans by 800 Americans in 1851. The place was once called Indian Creek. (*Las Calaveras*, July, 1955). See Los Muertos.

Camp Opera [Amador]. Southeast of Ione, between Mokelumne River and Jackson Creek. Shown on the County Map of 1866. It was a Mexican camp which developed when the Lancaster ditch brought water in 1853. In 1857 the camp had several stores and saloons, but there was soon a rapid decline. The camp had the reputation of harboring outlaws, including Murieta, of course. (Co. Hist., 1881, p. 202.)

Campo Salvador [Tuolumne]. see Camp Salvado.

Campo Seco [Calaveras]. Eight miles southwest of Mokelumne Hill. Recorded on Goddard's map, 1857. *Campo seco* is Spanish for 'dry field', used here in the sense of 'dry camp, or place'. A. Lascy in his "Reminiscences" reports that in the winter of 1850 quite a town had sprung up, but lack of water made it necessary for the miners to turn back to the river bars. As a result Campo Seco had lost more than half its population by the end of the year. The camp prospered nevertheless. About the first of February, 1853, the mines yielded several large lumps of gold, one of which was sold for 940 dollars (*Alta*, February 15, 1853), and in 1854 a 93-ounce nugget was found (*Bull.*, 193, p. 10). The post office was established in 1854 and was never discontinued. In 1856 the Mokelumne Water Company provided the camp with water. The quartz mines of the place are described by George Lundy Hunt in his diary, 1867. The *Register*, 1899, lists it as the center of quartz and drift mines, and *Mines and Minerals* of the same year places the output at 5.5 million dollars. In later years the place was known mainly for its production of copper and zinc, mainly from the Penn Mine. Historic Landmark 257.

Campo Seco [Tuolumne]. One mile south of Jamestown, near Woods Creek. Recorded on Trask's map, 1853. On Dart's map, 1879, it is abbreviated to Seco. Peter Justeson mined here with fair success in 1850, but James Carr (pp. 157 ff.) claimed that some days he and his companions washed out as much as 220 dollars. The brothers Smith mined in nearby Blue Gulch in the 1850s, and their letters are of considerable interest. In 1853 two lucky Mexicans struck a pocket near the camp on the other side of Sullivans Gulch, and by noon one day they took out 5,700 dollars, one piece of which weighed eight pounds. In one hour they washed out 200 ounces with their bateas. (Columbia *Gazette*, February 19, 1853.) *See also* County History, 1882 (pp. 96, 126). At one time the camp had two hotels, a theater, and "enough bars to go around" (De Ferrari). The Chapman family are said to have played the opening engagement. Shown on the USGS Sonora 1939 quadrangle.

Camp Rochester [San Bernardino]. See Stedman.

Camp Salvado [Tuolumne]. Less than a mile east of Chinese Camp. Shown on a map in Whitney, *Auriferous Gravels* (p. 132). According to De Ferrari (Book Club of California, Keepsake Series, 1972), the first Chinese to come to the California mines were thirty-five men, who arrived in the summer of 1849, under contract to mine for English speculators from Hong Kong. They were first directed to a dry tributary of Woods Creek by Mexican miners. Soon they were driven out by white miners, and the camp became known as old Chinese Diggings or Camp Salvado. In a variant version, Paden and Schlichtmann (pp. 68 f., 306) attribute the name given as Camp Salvador, to San Salvador, the home of the founders, and they give East Chinee as the name sometimes used after the Chinese were forced to leave. *See* Camp Washington and Chinese Camp. Camp Salvado, after the departure of the Chinese, was populated mainly by Americans, Germans, and Chileans, according to Paden and Schlichtmann, and for a few years had the reputation of being a rough and tough town. After its demise, some Chinese returned to sluice the tailings, but the camp was never revived.

Camp Senorita [Calaveras]. Near Marble Springs. It was deserted in 1858, according to a letter to the San Andreas *Independent* dated April 20, 1858, cited in *Las Calaveras*, July, 1955.

Camp Spirito [Calaveras]. North of Bummerville. It was an early mining camp, according to *Las Calaveras*, July, 1957.

Camp Stick-in-the-Mud. An unidentified place, listed in the Works Project Administration project.

Camptonville [Yuba]. Between the North and Middle forks of Yuba River, northeast of Fosters Bar. Shown on Goddard's map, 1857. The diggings developed around the Nevada House, a hostelry built in 1850 or 1851, on the Nevada City-Downieville

Road, and the place was named in 1854 for Robert Campton, the blacksmith (Co. Hist., 1879, p. 98). However, it was named earlier, according to William Bull Meek, who states that the miners drew up resolutions to form the Camptonville Mining District on December 6, 1852 ("Reminiscences," pp. 22 f.). The camp is also mentioned in a letter of C. G. Whitcomb dated November 23, 1853. Prospectors had sunk a shaft in 1852 and discovered a rich lode (*Marysville Directory*, 1858, p. 28). It was on the rich Blue Lead, which stretched from Brandy City [Sierra] to North San Juan [Nevada]. A post office was established February 18, 1854. In 1855 the population of the town and vicinity was about 1,300, according to Hutchings (Diary, October 27, 1855), who prophesied that "Years will elapse before the diggings can be worked out." In 1858 the Sierra Mountain Water Company proposed the building of a canal to bring the needed water (*Sierra Citizen* in Hittell Clippings, p. 44). According to Browne (pp. 134, 148) the lead was not covered much and hydraulic mining was extremely profitable. The shipment of gold reached the figure 600 thousand dollars for the year 1860. Brewer (*Up and Down California*, p. 455) calls it "a miserable, dilapidated town" in 1862, with immense hydraulic diggings. "Bluffs sixty to a hundred feet thick have been washed away for *hundreds of acres together*." In 1905 there was an electric-powered mill with three stamps (*Register*). It was here that Lester A. Pelton invented his famous water wheel.

Camp Union [Amador]. Two and a half miles above Lancha Plana, near the Mokelumne River. It is shown on the County Map, 1866.

Campville [Butte]. An indefinite location on Butte Creek. Windeler (pp. 159 ff.) mined in the vicinity from March 3 to May 15, 1853, with poor results.

Camp Washington [Tuolumne]. Between Montezuma and Jacksonville. According to Paden and Schlichtmann (pp. 68 f.), it was a small American camp, which absorbed the Chinese miners who had been forced out of nearby Camp Salvado, and it became the nucleus of Chinese Camp. *See* Camp Salvado. The name does not appear on early maps, but it is retained in the name of Washington Street in Chinese Camp. *See* Chinese Camp. The place was also known as Washingtonville, according to De Ferrari.

Camp Watson [Sierra]. Near Goodyears Bar.

The place is mentioned as "florishing" about 1865 in a clipping from the *Mountaineer* (Bancroft Scraps, LI:1, p. 237).

Canacer: Bar, Creek [Sierra]. The bar is on the Middle Fork of Yuba River, to which Canacer Creek is a tributary. Shown on Milleson and Adams' map, 1851. No later recording was found, but there was a Kanaka Creek in the Eureka Diggings area (Eureka North), according to R. Drury, and the spelling Canacer is probably a misspelling of Kanaka.

Canada Hill [Nevada]. Southeast of Nevada City. The French Mill here was built by French Canadians in 1861 and was limited mainly to custom work (Bean, p. 114). For later development *see* Canada Hill Consolidated Group in *Mining Bureau*, XVI (Nevada, p. 132). The total production is given as 1.13 million dollars in *Bulletin*, 193 (p. 99).

Canada Hill [Placer]. On Forest Hill Divide, about six miles northeast of Last Chance. Recorded on Goddard's map, 1857. The place had a number of promising quartz lodes, but the Secret Mill, built in 1864, was already idle in 1866. In 1867 there were mainly Mexican miners here. (Browne, p. 110.) Some mines at Canada Hill were listed until 1935. Shown on the USGS Colfax 1938 quadrangle.

Canadian Bar [Trinity]. Opposite Taylors Flat, where Canadian Creek joins the Trinity River. Recorded on Goddard's map of 1857. In 1858 it was "crowded with Chinamen" (Cox, p. 82).

Canadian Camp [Trinity]. On the Trinity River, close to the Humboldt County line. Named for French Canadian trappers who had mined with good success in 1849 at Big Bar and Long Bar and in 1850 had their camp here. Their story is interestingly told by Massey (pp. 98 ff; 102 ff.). The Indian village which they burned in retaliation is probably the "burned ranch" which George Gibbs noticed in 1851. *See* Burnt Ranch.

Canal Bar [Nevada]. On the South Fork of the Yuba River, south of Canyon Creek (Bancroft Notes). According to an extract from the Nevada *Transcript*, April 29, 1867 (Hayes Scrapbooks: Mining, IV, sec. 61), miners were sinking shafts for the old river bed and prospects were good.

Canal Gulch [Siskiyou]. In Hawkins Mining District, north of Yreka. Mining began here soon after the discovery of the rich diggings in the upper flats near Shasta Butte City (later Yreka). The place is mentioned by E. M. Anthony in his "Reminiscences." Notice of the sale of a claim in the Gulch, dated March 10, 1855, is recorded in "Siskiyou County Land Papers." The gold yield in the Gulch was as high as sixty dollars for a pan of dirt, according to the *Mining Press*, May 1, 1862.

Cantil [Kern]. On the Southern Pacific Railroad, west of Randsburg. It was a station and post office for numerous mines in the El Paso Mountains. Individual mines are listed in *County Report*, I.

Canton [El Dorado]. Near Coloma. Stephen Wing mined here without much success in February, 1856. He had mentioned going there in 1853 with the "foreign tax collector," who sold part of the foreigners' belongings since they — the "Maccao Chinamen" — generally refused to pay the tax (Wing's Journal, I, p. 57). Canton is mentioned in a communication from Wetmore & Company to Messrs. Davis and Carter, July 23, 1849 (California State Library, California Section).

Canyon. A common generic term often used as a specific name in gold districts. It is sometimes spelled cañon, the original Spanish way, and occasionally canon or cannon.

Canyon [El Dorado]. South of Shingle Springs. It was named after Big Canyon Creek, tributary to the Cosumnes River. Samuel F. Pond mined here in 1850 with little success, according to his diary, August 24, 1850, and later entries. There were two stamp mills in the district in 1902, and the place was the trading center for the mines in the area (*Register*, 1902).

Canyon Creek [El Dorado]. Tributary to the Middle Fork of American River. It was probably near this confluence that Buffum and his partners mined successfully in the latter part of December, 1848. Buffum gives a delightful description of the place. (1959 ed. pp. 52 ff.). The Gold Bug Mine on lower Canyon Creek, near Georgetown, produced more than 1.5 million dollars, largely from the tailings of Georgia Slide (*Mines and Minerals*, p. 315). It was worked intermittently by several owners from 1896 to 1934 (*Mining Bureau*, LII, p. 550). The Goldbug Mine, an exhibit in Bedford Park in Placerville, was a consolidation of the Vulture and Hattie lode mines located in 1888 and relocated in 1926 (Schlappi-Ferguson).

Canyon Creek [Placer]. Tributary to the North Fork of the American River, south of Gold Run. Notice of intention to build a dam below the mouth of Cañon Creek was given November 24, 1850, and re-

corded November 3, 1851 (Placer County Records, I, p. 34). Browne (p. 103) lists six claims, the oldest one dated 1853, and fifteen companies which tailed into two sluices of the Canyon. Shown on the USGS Colfax 1938 quadrangle.

Canyon Creek [Sierra]. Tributary to the North Fork of the Yuba River. Orlando Hodges (pp. 5 f.) mined here in 1851. About 1855, one of Downie's many companies started to build a tunnel but gave up (Downie, p. 135). Pringle Shaw (p. 123), however, called it a most profitable district in 1855. In March, 1862, two men took out ninety ounces from one crevice (*Mining Press*, March 8, 1862).

Canyon: Creek, City [Trinity]. The Creek is an important tributary to the Trinity River, northwest of Weaverville. Recorded on Goddard's map, 1857. Placer mining was apparently carried on as early as 1850. The "city," founded in 1851, was near modern Dedrick, and according to Cox (p. 98), was originally called Jackass Gulch; this name was probably changed when the post office was established in 1856. In 1855 it had 400 inhabitants, and the *Alta* (steamer ed.), March 20, 1857, as well as other newspapers before and after this date, reported good yields. A lengthy, loquacious account is given by Cox in 1858 (pp. 97–101). A report of hydraulic mining in later years may be found in *Mining Bureau*, XXXV (p. 308) and a picture in *Bulletin*, 109 (p. 35).

Cape Claim [Butte]. *See* Cape River Claim.

Cape Cod Bar [Amador]. On the south side of the Cosumnes River, northwest of Plymouth. Shown on the County Map, 1866. The camp, which was opposite Poverty Bar, was reported as having only one cabin in 1857 and practically no mining activity (*Amador Ledger*, June 20, 1857).

Cape Horn. A typical name given where the going was tough, used especially by people who reached the mines via Cape Horn.

Cape Horn Bar [Placer]. On the North Fork of the American River. The place is mentioned in the Placer County Records, I (p. 103, July 31, 1852, and p. 351, February 2, 1856).

Cape Horn Bar [Trinity]. About a half mile by road west of Douglas City, near the confluence of Trinity River and Weaver Creek. Cox (p. 39) gives a flattering picture of the German miners here in the 1850s.

Cape Horn Bar [Yuba]. On the main Yuba River, just above Corduas Bar. It was started by a company from Connecticut who had come around Cape Horn in the summer of 1849. (Co. Hist., 1879, p. 84).

Cape River Claim [Butte]. On the main Feather River, about three miles above Oroville. Also known as Cape Claim. In 1852 they "had turned the stream and were taking out gold by the bucket-full" (Knapp, p. 514). Mansfield (p. 5) claims that the place yielded one million dollars in sixty days of operation. In 1857 a 3,200-foot flume was built to divert the water. The cost was 120 thousand dollars, but before the placers were flooded again, 680 thousand dollars were taken out in forty days. (*Mining Bureau*, IX, p. 273). If these reports are reliable, this place must have yielded more than any other in the county. *See* Union Cape Claim; Golden Gate Flume.

Cap Orsburne's Ravine [Plumas]. *See* Carriboo.

Capulope [Calaveras]. The doubtful name of a small place near Angels Camp. It is mentioned by Ridge (p. 130 f.).

Cardinal Hill [Nevada]. Near Nevada City. Gold was discovered in March, 1851, by Luther M. Schaeffer and his party. Numerous claims were registered because prospectors believed, in vain, that the yield would be as rich as on nearby Gold Hill. (Schaeffer, pp. 122 f.).

Cardinal Mine [Inyo]. *See* Bishop Creek District.

Cargo Muchacho: Mountains, Mining District [Imperial]. Formerly in San Diego County. The mountain range is twelve miles from the Colorado River, near the Ogilby station of the Southern Pacific. It is rich in gold but could not be exploited by placer mining because of the lack of water. According to *Mining Bureau*, IV (p. 217), this was the first site in the present state of California where gold was allegedly found in 1775. In the 1870s lode mining developed in the district, and in 1882 the Yuma Mining Company operated a stamp mill which crushed 167 thousand dollars worth of gold from 14,000 tons of quartz. In 1938 the discovery of a rich pocket caused a short-lived excitement. The American Girl Mine produced an estimated one million dollars and the Golden Cross more than 3 million (*Bull.*, 193, p. 154). The best account of modern gold mining operations in the range until 1942 may be found in *Mining Bureau*, XXXVIII (pp. 112 ff.). The origin and etymology of the name could not be determined.

Cariboo, Caribo, Caribou. The name of the finest representative of Canada's fauna, the caribou, was used for several camps and mines and probably arose when California prospectors returned from the famous Caribou mines of 1858 in British Columbia. The name is also spelled Carribo and Carriboo.

Cariboo [Nevada]. On the Blue Lead, northwest of Dutch Flat. In 1863 a "Spaniard" dug a 12-foot shaft and found a rich pocket of gold (Bean, p. 369). *See* Cariboo: Ravine, Diggings [Nevada].

Cariboo [Plumas]. On the North Fork of Feather River, between Marion Flat and Junction Bar, marked Carriboo on von Leicht-Craven map, 1874. It was a flourishing mining camp of the 1870s, or earlier, according to a letter of Verne Richards published in Plumas County Historical Society *Publications*, no. 11 (p. 1, April, 1963). The local name was Cap Orsburne's Ravine for a former sea captain who was the first to strike it rich here. Mrs. Elsie Ellis, who was born in Carriboo, states that the former name was French Bar (*ibid.*, p. 28). Richards' sketch map, however, shows French Bar above Carriboo. Present day Caribou is two miles above the old place. Contemporary records describe old Cariboo. According to Hayes Scrapbooks: Mining, IV (sec. 17 and 59), the bar and hill diggings were paying good wages in 1867, although they were not rich.

Cariboo: Ravine, Diggings [Nevada]. The Ravine heads at or near the summit of Manzanita Hill near Little York and empties into Steep Hollow Creek, tributary to Bear River. Shown on Pettee and Bowman's map, 1879. Pettee describes the gravels in the area and states that the quality of the gold found here was poorer than elsewhere in the vicinity (Whitney, *Auriferous Gravels*, pp. 158 f.). *See* Cariboo.

Caribou [Plumas]. *See* Cariboo.

Carlyle [Nevada]. Near Meadow Lake. The camp was named for Thomas Carlyle, one of the locators of the U. S. Grant claim in 1866. Mining activities are described in the County History, 1880 (p. 196). In 1870 a 15-stamp mill was in process of being constructed, according to an unidentified clipping in Hayes Scrapbooks: Mining, IV (sec. 127). The name is sometimes spelled Carlile.

Carmel River [Monterey]. In 1854 Trask (p. 58) reported that Mexican miners using "the battaya" were working placers on upper "Carmello," the old name of Carmel River. Mining was mainly around

Rancho Tulecita and along Francisquito Creek.

Caroline Diggings [Placer]. Twelve miles northeast of Michigan Bluff. The original name of the camp was Last Chance and was later changed to Caroline Diggings in honor of "a worthy and beautiful young lady." The diggings were discovered in the early 1850s and proved to be rich. According to an item in the *Placer Democrat*, reprinted in the *Alta*, June 30, 1854, one company took out 2 thousand dollars and another 15 hundred dollars in one week. Carolineville, listed by Hutchings in 1855, may be the same place.

Carpenters Bar [Butte]. Shown on Trask's map, 1853, on the south side of the northern branch of Butte Creek, above the junction.

Carpenters Bar [Placer]. In Green Valley, on the North Fork of the American River. It is mentioned in Placer County Records, I (p. 181, September 13, 1853).

Carpenters Flat [Butte]. Near Oroville. The place is mentioned by John Clark in his journal, September 16, 1856.

Carr Diggings [Butte]. About four miles north of Kimshew Table Mountain, at an elevation of 6,200 feet. The gravel formation is described in Lindgren, *Tertiary Gravels* (p. 97).

Carrier Gulch [Trinity]. A tributary to the Hayfork of Trinity River. In 1858 there were a considerable number of miners during the rainy season who earned ten to twelve dollars per day to the man. The camp had a store, butcher shop, and blacksmith. (Cox, p. 111.)

Carrolton [Placer]. On the North Fork of American River, opposite Condemned Bar. Shown on Doolittle's map, 1868. According to Hutchings' diary, April 25, 1855, the place was formerly also called Condemned Bar, but this appears doubtful. After the introduction of water in 1855, within six weeks it grew from three houses to a bustling town.

Carrs Diggings [Sierra]. Southeast of Scales Diggings and Mount Pleasant Ranch. Shown on Crossman's map, 1867. On the USGS Downieville 1907 quadrangle Cars Creek is shown in this vicinity as a tributary to Canyon Creek.

Carrville [Trinity]. On the Trinity River, a half mile south of the confluence with Coffee Creek. It was the trading center and the post office (1882–1943) for the quartz, placer, and hydraulic mines in the vicinity. The rich Bonanza King lode mine near by yielded 1.25 million dollars. Trinity

River was dredged here until fairly recently. (*Bull.*, 193, p. 143.) The mines and the dredges are listed and described in *County Report*, IV.

Carrysville [Butte, or Yuba]. A mining camp near Forbestown. Huntley (p. 62) states that it consisted of four or five shanties in January, 1852, and that it was named for Mrs. Caroline P——n.

Cars Creek [Sierra]. *See* Carrs Diggings.

Carson Creek [Mariposa]. *See* Carsons.

Carson: Creek, Hill, Flat, town [Calaveras]. About four miles south of Angels Camp. Carson Creek and Hill are shown on Gibbes' map, 1852. The mining camp was on the north slope of the hill. It is said that Mexican miners discovered gold in the hill early in 1848. Gold was discovered in the creek in the summer or fall of the same year by James H. Carson, a sergeant in the third U. S. Artillery, who was on furlough from Monterey with George Angel (*see* Angels Camp) and other soldiers. According to Carson's somewhat questionable *Recollections*, it was in the fall of 1848 that an Indian directed him to the creek, where he and his partners each took out 180 ounces in ten days. Instead of following up his discovery, he returned to Monterey. Carson claimed that he discovered many more deposits in 1849 but left the exploitation to others. The richness of Carson Creek is recorded in the diary of Levi Stowell (*CHSQ*, XXVII, p. 160) in 1849. The fame of the place, however, was not in the placers of the creek but in the rich lodes in the hill. In February, 1850, John Hance and William Morgan founded the Union Company and "hit the richest deposit of quartz gold ever known." A piece of metal weighed 112 pounds and one blast threw out 110 thousand dollars worth of gold. From February, 1850 to December, 1851, a total of 2.8 million dollars was netted by arrastres. (Bancroft Notes: Calaveras County.) In 1854 a mass of gold weighing 195 pounds troy was taken out of the hill. It was the largest mass of gold ever taken out of California, and its value at the time was more than 43 thousand dollars. (*Guidebook*, p. 55.) The newspapers of the early 1850s were filled with reports of astonishing finds, many obviously exaggerated. The *California Courier*, August 9, 1850, reports that one miner took out 19 thousand dollars worth in less than three days. The nuggets were valued from twenty dollars to one thousand and more apiece, according to the report. (Bancroft Notes: Calaveras County.) The

Picayune, September 6, 1850, reports the finding of a 12-pound lump at Carson Flat. The *Alta*, December 1, 1851, states that a San Francisco firm made an offer of 500 thousand dollars for a quartz mine, but it was refused. Other more reliable, contemporary or almost contemporary accounts and reports may be found in Borthwick (pp. 323 ff.); Heckendorn (p. 97); *State Register*, 1859; Browne (p. 62); *Annual Mining Review*, 1876 (pp. 21, 23). Marryat (p. 362) gives an account in 1855, but it is based on the questionable account of James Carson. The *Guidebook* (p. 55) gives a brief account. It mentions that Billy Mulligan and his gang jumped some claims in 1852 and held them for nine months until they were forced out by legal process. — The Carson Hill Mines, which included the Calaveras, Melones, Morgan, Reserve, Stanislaus, and Finnegan, produced an estimated 26 million dollars in gold, and the Carson Creek Mine around one million dollars (*Bull.*, 193, p. 36). Carson Hill is Historic Landmark 274. *See* Melones; Morgan Ground.

Carson Flat [Nevada]. The *Picayune* of September 16, 1850, reported that on the fourth of July a 12-pound solid gold nugget had been dug up.

Carsons or Carson [Mariposa]. About four miles west of Mariposa, on Highway 140. Alex Godey discovered the gold deposits on Frémont's grant in the summer of 1849, and he probably named Carson Creek for his friend, Kit Carson. The Creek is mentioned by Thomas Allsop in December, 1851 (p. 32). In his diary entry of February 19, 1853, Angus McIsaac describes the place Carsons as follows: "It is about as large as Mariposa and consists of all cotton houses, except two, which are of wood and better furnished than any of the houses in Mariposa. They are used as public houses as well as gambling and another ill-famed business which I do not choose to mention." The Mariposa *Chronicle* reported in the spring of 1854 that miners averaged fifteen to twenty dollars per day to the hand. The *Alta*, June 24, 1854, reprints an item from the Mariposa *Chronicle* which states that many miners had left Carsontown because of the lack of water. It is probably the same place as Carsons. The town was well known as the site of Louis de Blainville's tannery, which is indicated on the Las Mariposas map, 1861. Another map of the area, dated March, 1859, is in the Mariposa County Records, Deeds (book G, p. 81).

Carters [Tuolumne]. *See* Summersville.

Cart Wheel Valley [El Dorado]. *See* White Oak Flat.

Cascade Diggings [Nevada]. About three and a half miles northeast of Quaker Hill. Shown on Doolittle's map, 1868. It is apparently the camp mentioned as the Cascades in Raymond, VI (p. 117).

Cascade Valley [Butte]. At the head of Fall River, on the Yuba County line. No mining record was found. There was a post office at Cascade City, December, 1858 to September, 1860, and the name Cascade still appears on modern maps.

Casco Mill [Amador]. Three miles from Jackson. In 1869 there was a 12-stamp mill here. (*Annual Mining Review*, 1876, p. 21). The Hardenberg and Zeila mines were near by.

Cassadys Bar [Fresno]. On the San Joaquin River, above Millerton. Rich placers in 1850 are reported. Many of the prospectors joined the Mariposa Battalion in the spring of 1851.

Castaic Creek [Los Angeles]. Also spelled Castaca. This canyon at the Santa Clara River, northwest of Newhall, is one of the places where gold was discovered in 1834, and the deposits were exploited for a number of years by the priests of San Fernando Mission, according to *Reports* of the Mining Bureau. This claim has not been authenticated. However, there is evidence that there was placering in the region beginning in 1842. *See* San Fernando Placers; Placerita Creek; San Francisquito; San Feliciano Canyon.

Castle Bar [Yuba]. On the main Yuba River, below the confluence of the South Fork, and just below Nigger Bar. The place is now under water (J. C. Merriam, p. 2).

Castle Mountains District [San Bernardino]. *See* Hart district.

Castle Peak District [Mono]. About twelve miles northwest of Leevining. The district was organized in July, 1867, by the discoverer of the lode, Charles Snyder. The lode was rich, according to Browne (p. 179), but the output was small. However, a small mining camp developed, and it even had a post office (1871–1872) named Munckton for the owner of the claims, Dr. George Munckton of Nevada City. The refractory ore led to the closing of the mines, and they lay idle until 1891, when they were developed by an English syndicate. (F. S. Wedertz.) In 1878 the Wheeler Survey changed the name of the peak to Dunderberg Peak, after the mine on the north slope. *See California Place Names*.

Cat Camp [Calaveras]. About a mile east of the western line of the county, near Camanche. Browne (p. 51) states that there was a lack of water, but 350 claims were laid in the 1860s in anticipation of the building of a ditch. A correspondent to the Sacramento *Union* reported on January 20, 1868, that water had reached the place (unidentified clipping in Hayes Scrapbooks: Mining, IV, sec. 7). Professor Camp shows it on his map as Catt Camp, and Walter Haddock in his "Recollections of Wallace" (*Las Calaveras*, July, 1970) states that it had been named for Samuel Catts, who operated a trading post for the miners. The name was changed to Wallace when the Sierra Railroad was built in 1883, and the place is now the site of a saw mill.

Catgut Canyon. A fictitious name created by Mark Twain when he wrote a satire on the extraction of gold from sulphur water, published in the New York *Evening Post*, September 17, 1880, and reprinted in *Rushing for Gold* by J. W. Caughey (pp. 110 ff.).

Catheys Valley [Mariposa]. West of Guadalupe Mountains. It was named for Andrew Cathey of North Carolina, who settled here in 1852. It is a rich farming country, but there was also some quartz mining for free gold and sulphides. The *Register*, 1903, lists one stamp mill. Several mines in the Cathay (Cathey) District were worked until the 1930s (*Bull.*, 193, p. 35). The name is often misspelled Cathay, as on the USGS Indian Gulch 1920 quadrangle. Between 1879 and 1881 the post office name was Catheys Valley; in 1882 it was changed to Cathay. The valley, however, continued to be called Catheys Valley.

Cat Town [Mariposa]. In Solomon Gulch. It is described as an "old mining camp" in *Bulletin*, 193 (p. 36) and elsewhere in Mining Bureau reports, where it designates a mining district. Shown on the USGS Buckhorn Peak 1949 quadrangle.

Catts Camp [Calaveras]. *See* Cat Camp.

Cave City [Calaveras]. Eight miles by road east of San Andreas. Situated at the end of an ancient river bed that started from the Calaveras River. Recorded on Goddard's map of 1857. The deposits were discovered in 1852. According to *Transactions*, 1859 (p. 84), the place had been a mining town until 1859, when it was nearly deserted. Browne (p. 58) states that the rich placers were almost exhausted in 1867. The diggings are listed until 1928, but now the place is chiefly known by the manganese mine. Shown on the USGS Jackson 1938 quadrangle. Cave City Cave was a noted early day tourist attraction; no buildings remain today.

Cave Valley [El Dorado]. The place is shown as a settlement on Trask's map, 1853, southwest of the junction to the North and Middle forks of American River.

Cayote or **Cayute** [Calaveras]. *See* Coyote: Gulch, Creek.

Cecilville [Siskiyou]. On the South Fork of Salmon River, near the junction with the East Fork. Shown on Goddard's map, 1857. The place was named for John Baker Sissel, who came to Shasta Valley before 1849 (*California Place Names*). It was the trading center for a number of quartz and hydraulic mines in the area (*Register*, 1908); a post office was established in 1879. A Cecilville placer is listed by the Mining Bureau until 1935. Cecilville was the second in size and importance to Petersburg on the South Fork and the only remaining town which developed on this river. Of interest to folklorists is the saga of the "Lifting Rock" connected with Cecilville. It is told in the *Siskiyou Pioneer* (II:6, pp. 45 ff.; IV:1, pp. 33 ff.). The place is shown on the USGS Sawyers Bar 1945 quadrangle.

Cedar Bar [Yuba]. This is last bar on the main Yuba River before it enters the valley. It is mentioned by Morse (p. 218).

Cedarbergs Quartz Lode [El Dorado]. Near the Middle Fork of the American River, northwest of Georgetown. Recorded on Bowman's map, 1873. There was only seam mining until Mr. Cedarberg discovered a rich lode (Raymond, VII, p. 89). In 1870 there was a 10-stamp mill called Cedarburg Mill (*Annual Mining Review*, 1876, p. 21). The Cedarberg Mine, which yielded an average of sixty-five dollars per ton (*Mining Bureau*, II, pt 1, p. 175), is listed until 1940.

Cedar Creek [Placer]. In the Dutch Flat district. There was extensive hydraulic mining by a British firm in the 1870s (Raymond, VII, p. 105). Mines at this location are listed in *Mining Bureau*, 1936.

Cedar Grove [Nevada?]. Four and a half miles from Nevada City. It is mentioned in Brown's *Directory* of 1856 (p. 133).

Cedar Grove [Sierra]. On Slate Creek, four miles east of La Porte. Shown on Crossman's map, 1867. There was active mining here in 1859, according to an item in the San Francisco *Call*, May 18, 1859. Browne states that drift mining stopped in 1868; however, on the County Map, 1874, the place seems to be quite a settlement. Shown on the USGS Downieville 1907 quadrangle.

Cedar: Ravine, Springs [El Dorado]. The ravine is formed by a tributary to Hangtown Creek, south of Placerville. The camp developed around the Dickerhoff Mine (Co. Hist., 1883, p. 88). It may be the same place as Cedar Canyon and Flat mentioned in 1856 by Crockett (p. 40). The Cedar Ravine Drift Mine was worked intermittently to about 1911, but it is still listed in 1956.

Cedarville [El Dorado]. Near the Middle Fork of Cosumnes River, on the Cedar and Indianville Canal. Shown on Doolittle's map, 1868. It is mentioned in the *Alta*, December 21, 1853, and it is included in Hittell's roster.

Celestial Valley [Yuba]. Three miles south of Camptonville, on Oregon Creek. De Long mentioned it as a settlement, August 23, 1855. It was doubtless named because of the presence of Chinese miners. A little mining was still reported in 1877. Shown on *Guidebook* map 9.

Celina Ridge [Nevada]. West of Canyon Creek, in Gods Country, Washington Mining District. Two quartz mines are listed in the report of the Mining Bureau, 1941. Shown on the USGS Colfax 1938 quadrangle.

Cement Hill [El Dorado]. Near Bottle Hill, north of Georgetown. Shown on Bowman's map, 1873. There was mainly gravel and drift mining. It was so named because the surface was covered by a cement or mixture of clay with volcanic ejections. In 1850 there were sixteen tunnels, five of which paid. A detailed description may be found in Patterson (pp. 43 ff.). Raymond refers to the immensely rich deposits in 1874, and states that "the auriferous earth was found under a thick deposit of fine clay, 30 feet thick, in which whole trees were embedded" (Raymond, VII, pp. 94 ff.). A Cement Hill drift mine, active between 1894 and 1896, is still listed in 1956.

Cement Hill [Nevada]. About two miles northwest of Nevada City. Shown on Doolittle's map, 1868. It is mentioned repeatedly in Pettee's discussion of the ancient river channels in the area (Whitney, *Auriferous Gravels*, pp. 184 ff.).

Centerville [Butte]. South of Helltown, on Butte Creek. Shown on the County Map, 1877. It was mentioned as a small producer in *Mining Bureau*, II, Part 1 (p. 188). There were several small hydraulic cuts near Centerville, but the gravel was reportedly low grade except in some places along the rim, according to Lindgren in 1911 (p. 91), and no work was being carried on at that time.

Centerville [El Dorado]. About six miles southeast of Auburn. Doolittle's map, 1868, shows Centreville as an alternate name for the settlement Pilot Hill; Bowman's map, 1873, shows both places as separate settlements. Centerville is listed in Hittell's roster. It was still an active mining district in 1874 (Raymond, VII, p. 77). *See* Pilot Hill.

Centerville [Shasta]. In the center of the Clear Creek mining district. In 1892 the town was described as of considerable size in early days when there was extensive placer mining, but by the early 1890s the site had almost disappeared (*Mining Bureau*, XI, p. 40). The Yankee John lode mine nearby operated intermittently from the 1850s, and was reactivated in the 1930s (*Mining Bureau*, XVII, p. 524; XIX, p. 11; XXII, p. 185; XXIX, p. 57; and Steger).

Centerville [Sierra]. Near Alleghany. An item in the *Mining Press*, June 22, 1861, reported that the place was almost deserted in 1859, when an abandoned tunnel caved in and revealed rich gravel. According to another item in the same newspaper, August 31, 1861, two tunnel companies took out sizeable amounts of gold.

Centipede Hollow. An unidentified mining locality, listed in the State Library roster.

Central Eureka Mine [Amador]. *See* Eureka Mines.

Central Ferry [Tuolumne]. It was an important crossing over Stanislaus River above Peoria, and in the mid-1870s there was extensive placer mining here by companies using Chinese labor. At one time it was bridged. (De Ferrari.) It is mentioned in 1899 as rich (*Mines and Minerals*, p. 358).

Central Hill, Central Hill Channel [Calaveras]. Central Hill is northwest of San Andreas, and the ancient channel system bearing its name extends southeast to the vicinity of Altaville and Angels Camp, turning northeast toward Vallecito and Murphys. A description and map are found in *Mining Bureau*, XII (pp. 482 ff.). Central Hill, according to Heckendorn, was "the greatest mining attraction in 1851–52." The San Andreas *Independent*, January 5, 1861, stated that two miners working in a tunnel on the hill averaged thirty-five dollars per day for the past year. A few months earlier 400 dollars worth of gold had been taken from one pan and as much as eleven hundred dollars per week from the claim. The Harkins Mine near Central Hill, "the richest in the county," continued to pay well in 1870, according to an unidentified clipping in Hayes Scrapbooks: Mining, IV (sec. 127). The drift mines on the channel are listed in *Mining Bureau*, XIV (pp. 114 ff.) and in U. S. *Bulletin*, 413 (pp. 60 ff.). The Central Hill Mine, one mile southwest of Murphys, was an important hydraulic mine in the 1870s and 1880s. Water was brought from the Stanislaus River through the North Ditch to operate the monitors and was drained through the hill to Douglas Flat. The mine was reactivated in 1936. Today it is a county rubbish dump. (*Mining Bureau*, XXXII, p. 335; R. C. Wood.)

Central House [Amador]. About two miles southwest of Puckerville. It was a major stopping place on the stage road from Sacramento to Jackson (Cenotto).

Centre Diggings [El Dorado]. Near Coloma. A letter written by Hiram G. Ferris to J. T. Barnett is datelined from here December 29, 1850. This may be the same place as Centerville.

Centreville [El Dorado]. *See* Centerville and Centre Diggings [El Dorado].

Centreville [Nevada]. *See* Grass Valley.

Centreville [Placer]. West of the North Fork of American River, immediately west of Interstate Highway 80, south of Newcastle. Trask's map, 1853, shows it prominently northwest of Auburn, and Goddard's map, 1857, shows it south of it. Trask also mentions the place in 1854 (doc. 9, p. 70). The Alabama Quartz Mining Company opened the diggings in 1851. Its constitution and by-laws are recorded on November 10, 1851, in Placer County Records, I (pp. 42 ff.).

Centreville Ravine [Nevada]. Near Grass Valley. By 1856 200 thousand dollars worth of gold was taken from the Ravine (Foley). *See* Grass Valley.

Cerro Gordo [Inyo]. Northeast of Keeler, in the Inyo Mountain district. Shown on the County Map, 1884. *Cerro gordo* is Spanish for 'big mountain'. There was mainly silver production but also gold, in paying quantities. According to the *Inyo Independent*, August 22, 1874, a Mexican who had been a prisoner of a Paiute Indian tribe, discovered the deposits in 1868 or earlier and led Americans to it. Around 1870 there was a town Cerro Gordo, and from 1869 to 1895 it had a post office. One of the principal tunnels was the Freiberg

Tunnel, named after the famous German mining school where Alexander von Humboldt, as well as Rossiter Raymond and many other engineers of the Gold Rush period, had studied. A detailed description is given in Raymond (II, p. 17; VII, p. 27). *See also* Hayes Scrapbooks: Mining VI for contemporary newspaper clippings.

Chalk: Mountain Range, Bluffs [Nevada]. The Chalk Mountain Range, also called Chalk Bluffs, lies for the most part between Bear River and Greenhorn Creek. At the southwestern extremity, at Red Dog and You Bet, and along the margins of the ridge, the auriferous gravels were hydraulicked, but the large part required drifting. Browne (pp. 126 f.) describes the area and the workings of the Chalk Mountain Blue Gravel Company, which began in 1866. The extent of the company's holdings is shown on Doolittle's map, 1868, and a settlement is shown east of the southern end, between the ridge and Steep Hollow Creek. This settlement is also shown on Hoffmann and Craven's Gravel Map, 1873, north of Sugar Loaf, at the terminus of the Yuba Company Ditch. *See* Red Dog; You Bet.

Challenge [Sierra]. Two miles south of St. Louis, on a tributary to Slate Creek. The mills are recorded on Wescoatt's map of 1861.

Chambers Bar [Tuolumne]. A half mile above Swetts Bar. The place is mentioned by Mulford (p. 120). About 1860 it was apparently a Chinese camp. Gardiner (pp. 243 ff.) mined here with good success between 1855 and 1857 with the help of Chinese whom he employed as laborers.

Chambers: Bar, Creek [Plumas]. The creek is a tributary to the North Fork of Feather River, north of Rock Creek. Shown on the Butte County Map, 1877. No record of mining was found.

Chambers Ravine [El Dorado]. South of Diamond Springs. A 5-stamp steam-driven mill was erected in 1857, according to the *State Register*, 1859. Crockett (p. 95) mentions it as a mining locality. A deed to part interest in a quartz vein about one and a half miles south of Diamond Springs in Chambers Ravine is recorded in El Dorado County Deed Book C (p. 379).

Chamisal [Mariposa]. Also spelled Chemisal and Chimesal. On Temperance Creek, a tributary to the Merced River, and now under Lake McClure. For the name, *see California Place Names*. There was placer mining in the 1850s and quartz mining fol-

Chalk Bluffs, Nevada Co.

lowed. In 1861 a 10-stamp steam-driven mill was built (*Annual Mining Review*, 1876, p. 23). Shown on the USGS Sonora 1939 quadrangle.

Champion Mine. *See* Nevada City and Coulterville.

Chanchelulla [Trinity]. Near Knob Gulch and Harrison Gulch. This place, as well as the mountain in Shasta County, was named after the extensive Chanchellula geological formation (*Mining Bureau*, XXIX, pp. 18, 85). The name is probably Wintu Indian.

Chandlerville [Sierra]. Northeast of La Porte in Slate Creek basin. Shown on Trask's map, 1853. Rich hydraulic claims were reported from 1853 to 1857, but in 1868 they were worked out (Browne, p. 138). However, Raymond's map in Volume V (opposite p. 88) shows seven placer mines in 1872. According to the San Fransico *Call*, May 18, 1879, it had been a prosperous town in the 1850s with stores, hotels, and saloons, but no trace was left in 1879.

Chandlerville Diggings [Yuba]. Between Browns Valley and Long Bar, ten miles from Marysville. The Diggings were mentioned by De Long, July 31, 1858, as Chandlerville Quartz Diggings. They were reported as very rich but short-lived in the Marysville *Daily News*, July 25 and 28, 1858.

Chaparral. The name is from the Spanish *chaparro* and designates a place where evergreen scrub oak grows. At the time of the Gold Rush it had already taken on the meaning of a place densely covered with brush.

Chaparral Hill [Amador]. *See* Lancha Plana.

Chaparral Hill [Calaveras]. In the vicinity of Carson Hill. The mines are described in *Mining Bureau*, XIV (p. 73) and are still recorded by the Mining Bureau until 1936.

Chaparral Hill [Nevada]. Near Nevada City. The placers were first worked in 1853. A detailed description of the method of hydraulic mining used here is given in the San Francisco *Bulletin*, July 21, 1857.

Chaparral Hill [Sierra]. On Goodyear Creek, northwest of Downieville. In 1859 Vischer (p. 240) reports mainly tunnel work. The place is shown on the County Map of 1874. The Blue and the Eureka lodes run together here (Monroe Thomson, p. 20).

Chaparral House [Butte]. A mining settlement between the Feather River and Butte Creek; north of Inskip. Shown on the County Map of 1861.

Chaparral Tunnel [Calaveras]. Probably near Chaparral Hill. According to Hittell (*Mining Bureau*, IV, p. 223), the yield was 240 dollars per ton of quartz.

Charcoal; Flat, Ranch [Sierra]. Six miles east of Downieville, where Charcoal Ravine joins the North Fork of the Yuba River. Shown on Doolittle's map, 1868. The flat was first prospected in 1851 (Co. Hist., 1882, p. 470). Mines at this location are listed in *Mining Bureau* until 1942.

Chariot Canyon [San Diego]. Leading off from Banner Canyon. The gold deposits were discovered by George N. King on February 13, 1871, and the canyon was named after the Golden Chariot Mine (*California Place Names*). A detailed account of the mine is given by Ellsberg (pp. 46 ff.). It is also described in *County Report*, III (pp. 124 ff.).

Charleys Ranch [Butte]. *See* Veazie City.

Chelalian Bar [El Dorado]. *See* Chili Bar.

Cherokee. The name of the tribe of the southern Appalachian region is not only the most frequently used Indian place name in the United States but also the most popular Indian name used for gold towns and mines in California. The spelling often differs, and in view of the frequency of the name it might sometimes refer to eastern United States Indians in general.

Cherokee [Nevada]. On Shady Creek, three miles east of North San Juan. Recorded on Trask's map, 1853. It was prospected by some Cherokee Indians in 1850. In 1852 the Grizzly Ditch brought water from Bloody Run and Grizzly Canyon. A period of prosperity followed, and it was reported that some companies made fifty dollars a day to the hand. (Brown, *Directory*, p. 12.) Hutchings found it a "small, dried-up place with few people and those not far from 'broke' " (Diary, October 12, 1855). The *Mining Press*, June 22, 1861, calls the town almost dead, but Bean in 1867 still lists it as a sizeable town. A post office was established in 1855 named Patterson (*see* Patterson), but most letters continued to be datelined Cherokee. The USGS Smartsville 1943 quadrangle shows the name of the post office but spells it Paterson.

Cherokee [Plumas]. South of Greenville, near Round Valley. A. R. Bidwell (*in* Plumas County Historical Society, *Publication*, no. 4, April 1961) states that the mining camp Cherokee, near the Round Valley Dam, flourished from about 1865 to 1870. The Kittle Mine had a 10-stamp mill and the Caledonia (owned by Bidwell's father) had a 20-stamp mill. The place is mentioned by Theodore Hittell (III, p. 102). In the *Annual Mining Review*, 1876 (pp. 21, 41) it is reported that the Cherokee Gold Mining Company was developed with capital stock of 6 million dollars, but since the exact location is not given, it may not refer to the same place.

Cherokee: Bar, Crossing [Yuba, Sierra]. On Cherokee Creek, a tributary to the North Fork of the Yuba River, near Cuteye Fosters Bar. Recorded on Trask's map, 1853. Wescoatt's map, 1861, shows Cherokee Creek and Bridge. De Long collected taxes here August 19, 1855. The Crossing is shown on the *Guidebook* map and Cherokee Bridge on the USGS Bidwell Bar 1944 quadrangle.

Cherokee Camp [Tuolumne]. Two miles north of Tuolumne. It was apparently an early gold camp, but it did not develop until the Blakely and Vincent lode was discovered in 1858 on the slope of Turnback Creek, one and a half miles southwest. In a letter to the *Courier* dated April 25, 1858, it was claimed that the discovery almost equalled the rich Solsbury (Soulsby) claim (Hittell Clippings, p. 41). A 10-stamp water-driven mill was erected the same year (*Annual Mining Review*, 1876, p. 23). The Cherokee Gravel Mine was still in operation in 1914 (*Mining Bureau*, XIV, p. 166). The name appears on the USGS Sonora 1939 quadrangle and on the map in *Mining Bureau*, XLV, where the mines are also indicated. Historic Landmark 445.

Cherokee; Cherokee: Flat, Ravine [Butte]. Ten miles north of Oroville, at the northern extremity of Table Mountain. Cherokee is not recorded on the maps of Trask and Goddard, 1853 and 1857, but the County maps of 1862 and 1877 show it as a large town. Gold may have been discovered here as early as 1849. Windeler placed a claim in Cherokee Ravine, December 16, 1850, describing it as "a fair prospect." A post office was opened August 17, 1854. Work on the Charity Blue Gravel Claim started in 1856, but in 1867 it had not yet reached the pay streak, in spite of heavy investment. In 1870 the famous Cherokee siphon, a thirty-inch iron pipe, nearly two and a half miles long, brought water from Concow Valley and instilled new life into the town. Detailed descriptions of the activities are given in Browne (pp. 157 f.); Raymond, III (p. 49); *Mining Press*, January 7, 1871; J. W. Johnson (pp. 196 f.); and Jack D. Sturgeon in *Diggin's*, X:4 (pp. 3 ff.). The Cherokee and Spring Valley Mine was worked by the hydraulic process from 1858 to 1890. The production by 1886 is estimated at more than 10 million dollars, and the total production reached about 15 million. Intermittent mining continued until 1944. It is one of the few places in California where real diamonds were found. (*Mining Bureau*, XXIV, p. 195; *Bull.*, 193, pp. 36 f.).

Cherokee: House, Creek, Flat [Calaveras]. On Cherokee Creek, northwest of Angels Camp. The camp Cherokee Flat became Altaville, now a part of Angels Camp. Rich pockets, the "richest of the state," were discovered here by French and Italian prospectors, February 17, 1854 (Hittell Clippings, p. 56; Browne, p. 70). The *Mining Press*, April 13, 1861, reports that the diggings "yield more this season than ever." However, the 16-stamp mill was already idle in 1867, according to Browne (p. 70). The famous and controversial Calaveras skull, now in the Peabody Museum of Archaeology and Ethnography, Harvard University, was discovered nearby (Smithsonian *Report*, 1899, pp. 454 ff.). *See* Bret Harte's story "To the Pliocene Skull." In this region the bandit Murieta played such an important role, that Joaquin Mountain, northwest of the creek, was named for him (Ridge, p. 124; Demarest, p. 4). The creek is shown on the USGS Jackson 1938 quadrangle.

Cherokee Mine [Mariposa]. *See* Gentry Gulch.

Cherry: Creek, Hill [Siskiyou]. In Greenhorn District, southwest of Yreka. Hutchings mentions Cherry Creek as a town in 1855. The mines were doing well in 1862, according to the *Mining Press*, May 16, 1862. The Cherry Hill Mine was apparently in operation in 1935 (*Mining Bureau*, XXXI, p. 276).

Chichi [Calaveras]. Two miles northwest of Mountain Ranch. It is a placer mining area (G. Poore), listed in Hittell's roster.

Chickamasee [El Dorado]. On Grizzly Creek, a tributary to Steely Fork of the North Cosumnes River. It is an Indian place name, probably that of a rancheria, recorded by Doble (p. 80) in April, 1852. *See* Grizzly Flats.

Chicken Flat [El Dorado]. North of the South Fork of American River, one mile west of Spanish Flat. A lump of pure gold weighing four pounds and one ounce was found here about 1854, according to an item in the Placerville *American* (Hittell Clippings, p. 29). A deed to a quartz lead here is recorded in El Dorado County Deed Book E (pp. 358 f.) on December 12, 1859.

Chicken Point [Nevada]. East of You Bet. It is a high gravel east of Wilcox Ravine, tributary to Steep Hollow Creek. Hydraulic mining operations are described by Pettee in Whitney, *Auriferous Gravels* (pp. 164, 168, 422).

Chicken Ranch [Tuolumne]. About three miles west of Jamestown, on the southern slope of Table Mountain, at the site of the Chicken Ranch Indian Reservation (De Ferrari). Heckendorn mentions it as a large claim (p. 104); Bennett and Company struck paying dirt at 300 feet in their tunnel (*San Joaquin Republican*, November 20, 1855); two tunnels were built in the 1860s at the cost of 20 thousand dollars, but yielded no profit (Browne, p. 41).

Child Bar [El Dorado]. On the South Fork of American River, five miles above Coloma (Giffen file).

Chile. Of all the South American countries Chile sent the largest contingent of gold diggers to California. The name was often spelled Chili and even Chilie.

Chilean Bar [El Dorado]. The older form of the name Chili Bar; sometimes also spelled Chelalian, Chillean, Chillian. *See* Chili Bar.

Chilean Bar [Placer]. On the American River, below the junction of the North and Middle forks. Shown on Trask's map, 1853.

Chilean Gulch [Calaveras]. *See* Chili Gulch.

Chile Bar [El Dorado]. Apparently near Massachusetts Flat and Condemned Bar, near the confluence of the North and South forks of American River. It is mentioned in the County History, 1883 (p. 201).

Chilian Camp or **Diggings** [Tuolumne]. *See* Chili Camp.

Chili Bar [El Dorado]. On the South Fork of the American River between Placerville and Kelsey. Recorded on Goddard's map, 1857. Chile Bar bridge is shown on Doolittle's map, 1868. Steele mentions the place (pp. 270, 280). This may be the same place which Ely and his party passed in the middle of October, 1851. Ely (pp. 146 f.) calls it Chillian Bar and gives a charming description of the place. Later it was known mainly by the slate quarry. At the same time he mentions the prices of prostitutes (not necessarily at this place): 100 dollars for a young woman from New Orleans, 50 dollars for girls from Hawaii. County records indicate that the early name (1852) was Chilean Bar and later (1857) Chili Bar (Schlappi-Ferguson). The name is also spelled Chelalian and Chillean. Shown on the USGS Garden City 1950 quadrangle.

Chili Camp [Calaveras]. East of Lancha Plana. Goddard, on his map of the Mokelumne Hill Canal, shows the camp as a sizeable place near the rich Camanche Diggings. This recording of the name has apparently caused the confusion with Chili Gulch, about ten miles to the east, south of Mokelumne Hill. *See* Chili Gulch. Chile Camp is mentioned by Lascy as the site of a trading post in 1850. The ground was rich but hard to wash, and most miners had left for the river. The San Andreas *Independent*, October 27, 1860, reported that new mining ground was struck, and shafts were sunk as deep as 150 feet from which prospects as high as twenty dollars to the pan were obtained.

Chili Camp [Tuolumne]. West of Campo Seco. Recorded prominently as Chilli on Trask's map, 1853. In April, 1851, the U. S. Bureau of the Census lists eighty-four inhabitants in the population schedule for the 1850 census and gives the name as Chilian Camp. Daniel B. Woods, who prospected here early in January, 1851, calls it Chilian Diggings (pp. 99 f.). The place is mentioned by Stephen Davis in April and May, 1852. It is listed by Heckendorn (p. 104). When first discovered, it reportedly was so rich that for a period of time claims were limited to 100 square feet (De Ferrari). According to *Mines and Minerals* (p. 358), the production with Poverty Hill reached 4 million dollars in 1899.

Chilie Camp [Yuba]. Near the North Fork of the Yuba River, north of Camptonville. It is mentioned in a letter of December 10, 1851, as Chilleon Camp by Stephen Jackson. De Long, September 22, 1855, calls it Chilie Camp.

Chili Gulch [Calaveras]. The gulch extends from the town of North Branch, about three miles east of San Andreas, to the southern end of the town of Mokelumne. The name was apparently Chilean Gulch originally and was so mentioned in the *Alta*, January 6, 1852. Trask records it as Chilean Gulch on his map of 1853. Goddard shows it as Chili Gulch in 1857, and this form has prevailed. There were three small camps along the gulch, and at one of

them a post office named Chili was established on October 10, 1857. The gulch was occupied and mined by Chinese peons who had been imported by a Dr. Concha. This led to the "Chilean War" early in 1850, of which Ayers gives the best account, from memory, to be sure. All contemporary accounts attest to the richness of the deposits. In the spring of 1853 Borthwick (p. 311) saw about 200 Chilenos panning gold in large flat wooden dishes. At the end of 1860 new discoveries were made, a dozen shafts were sunk up to 130 feet, and the lead was traced for miles. (*Mining Press*, December 14, 1860; April 6 and October 26, 1861.) One company in 1867 worked its claim night and day in the gulch, employing twenty-five men in the mine and mill, reportedly with good results, according to an extract from the *Chronicle* (Hayes Scrapbooks: Mining, IV, sec. 47). In 1869 Browne (p. 55) mentions a 10-stamp mill operated by a hurdy gurdy wheel. A Chile Gulch Chalk Hill Mine is listed by the Mining Bureau until the 1930s. Chili Gulch is shown on the USGS Jackson 1938 quadrangle. Historic Landmark 265. *See* Chili Camp [Calaveras].

Chillean Bar [El Dorado]. *See* Chile Bar.

Chilleon Camp [Yuba]. *See* Chilie Camp.

Chilli [Tuolumne]. *See* Chili Camp.

Chillian Bar [El Dorado]. *See* Chili Bar.

Chimney Hill [Nevada]. Between Cherokee and North Columbia. It is listed in *Bean's Directory*, 1867, as a mining settlement. Hydraulic mining is mentioned in the *Mining Press*, February 1, 1861. After his visit in 1879, Pettee reports that much work had been done in the mines there but was suspended at that time (Whitney, *Auriferous Gravels*, p. 395).

Chimney Hill [Yuba]. On the main Yuba River, between Long Bar and Parks Bar. According to the *Marysville Directory*, 1858 (p. xxviii), the river had been flumed at this point at great expense, and the rich deposits in the hill awaited hydraulic mining.

China, Chinese. Chinese miners played an important role in the Gold Rush, and their presence is attested by numerous place names.

China Bar [Calaveras]. On the Calaveras River, northwest of San Andreas. It is shown on Trask's map, 1853.

China Bar [El Dorado]. On the South Fork of American River, eight miles from Chile Bar. Mining was reported fair in 1856 (Sacramento *Union*, August 27, 1856).

China Bar [Siskiyou]. On the Klamath River,

Chinese Camp. Location not determined.

apparently in the neighborhood of Meads Bar, below the mouth of Scott River. It is mentioned in Bancroft, VI (p. 367).

China Bar [Trinity]. A camp on New River. It is mentioned by Cox (p. 106) in 1858. A China Bar placer mine that was in operation in 1940 (*Mining Bureau*, XXXVII, p. 76) was apparently in a different location.

China City [Amador]. On the Mokelumne River, about a mile above Whites Bar. Shown on Camp's map.

China Creek [Siskiyou]. A hydraulic mine about six miles northeast of Happy Camp was reported as a good producer in Chinese ownership, but about 1914 it was idle (*Mining Bureau*, XIV, p. 845). China Creek, a tributary to the Klamath River, above Happy Camp, is shown on the USGS Seiad 1945 quadrangle.

China Flat [Sierra]. On the North Fork of the Yuba River, three miles east of Downieville. Shown on Doolittle's map, 1868, as China Flat and on the County Map of 1874 as Chinese Flat. Placering started in the 1850s. Chinese Mine is listed in reports of the Mining Bureau until 1942. The place is shown on *Guidebook* map, no. 10. One of the first "auto camps" in the area was built here, and it is still operating (R. Drury).

China: Gulch, Hill [Amador]. Near Vol-

cano. Doble (June 25, 1853, and later) had several claims here. Browne (pp. 72 f.) mentions that some hydraulic claims on the hill were still active in the 1860s, but that the yield was moderate and exhaustion was near.

China Town [Butte]. On Butte Creek, below Helltown and Centerville. It is shown on the County Map, 1877. On Trask's map, 1853, it appears as Chinees Cp., adjacent to Rich Bar. *See* Rich Bar and Diamondville.

China Town [Placer]. Just below Dotans Bar, on the North Fork of American River. Shown on the County Map, 1887.

China Town [Placer]. In a ravine north of Newcastle. It is described in Rensch-Hoover as a picturesque old mining camp with its "balconied upper stories overshadowed by an avenue of giant cottonwoods," all now destroyed by the construction of a freeway.

Chinese Camp [Butte]. *See* China Town.

Chinese Camp [Sierra]. In the Slate Creek Basin, on the road from La Porte to Portwine. Shown on Raymond's map in volume V.

Chinese: Camp, Diggings [Tuolumne]. Between Montezuma and Jacksonville. It is the oldest and best known California gold town named for the Chinese miners.

When and how the first celestials came here has not been definitely established, but doubtless they belonged to the earliest importation of Chinese laborers in 1849. According to Paden-Schlichtmann (pp. 68 f., 306), the Chinese miners, when forced out of Camp Salvado, came over the hill to the camp of American miners called Camp Washington (or also Washingtonville according to De Ferrari). The camp grew and became known as Chinee or Chinese Camp, one of the streets of which still bears the name Washington. *See* Camp Washington and Camp Salvado. The camp is mentioned as Chinese Diggings by Daniel B. Woods (p. 94) in December, 1849, and as such it appears in early diaries: Audubon, January, 1850; Dart, winter 1850/51; Stephen Davis, April 12, 1852. It also appears as Chinese Diggings on the early maps: Gibbes, 1851; Goddard, 1857. Dart (p. 207) and Heckendorn (1856, p. 83) give the population at 1,000. The post office was established as Chinese Camp April 18, 1854, and its brick building is still standing. According to the County History, 1892, four of the six Chinese companies had agents here, and a tong war is said to have occurred in September, 1856 (Rensch-Hoover). In 1859 Vischer records that it "bore the characteristics of the celestial empire" (p. 336), and Mulford about 1860 describes it as the metropolis for the district, with many urban comforts. According to Browne (p. 38), there was still placer mining around 1870. The geology of the district is described in *Bulletin*, 92 (p. 150). The total production of gold was estimated at 2.5 million dollars in 1899 (*Mines and Minerals*, p. 358). Historic Landmark 423.

Chinese Station [Tuolumne]. *See* Shoemake.

Chioko Bar [Placer]. On the North Fork of American River. Notice of a claim dated July 2, 1855, is recorded in Placer County Records, I (p. 294).

Chipsegs Flat [Sierra]. *See* Chips Flat.

Chips Flat [Sierra]. North of the Middle Fork of Yuba River, near Minnesota. Shown on Doolittle's map, 1868, and on the County Map, 1874. It is doubless the same as Chipsegs Flat mentioned by Trask in his *Report* of 1854 (doc. 9, pp. 63 and 64). The camp is also mentioned in Brown's *Directory*, 1856 (p. 133) and by Vischer in 1859 (p. 240). The Plumbago Mine, southeast of Chips Flat, produced an estimated 3.5 million dollars (*Bull.*, 193, pp. 11, 24).

Chivalry Hill. An unidentified locality, listed by Guinn (p. 42).

Chloride Cliff District [Inyo]. In the eastern part of Death Valley National Monument, in the Funeral Range. The Chloride Cliff and Keane Wonder mines were operated from about 1900 to 1916. *See* Keane Wonder Camp. The camp at the Chloride Cliff Mine was called Chloride City. (*Bull.*, 193, p. 148; Nadeau, p. 267.) Shown on the USGS Chloride Cliff 1952 quadrangle.

Chocolate Mountains [Imperial]. On Riverside County line. Largescale mining in the mountain range has been carried on at various times since 1878. The Mary Lode and other gold-producing geological formations were apparently not discovered until the beginning of the twentieth century (*Mining Bureau*, XXXVIII, pp. 112 f.).

Chowchilla District [Madera]. On the lower Chowchilla River. There was placer mining during the Gold Rush, and in recent years small amounts of gold have been recovered by dredging (*Bull.*, 193, p. 37).

Chris Ranch [El Dorado]. *See* Jackass Flat.

Christian: Flat, Hill. An unidentified place, listed in Hittell, *Resources*. Hutchings includes a Christian Valley as a town in Placer County in 1855.

Christmas Hill [Nevada]. Northeast of Little York. Recorded on Pettee and Bowman's map, 1879, where a large part of the gravel is shown as "more or less completely hydraulicked away." The place is listed in Hittell's roster. The gold mined there had a fineness of 980°. A description of the area is given in Whitney, *Auriferous Gravels* (pp. 156 f.) and in *Mining Bureau*, XXIII (p. 98).

Chrysopolis [Inyo]. North of San Carlos and Bend City. Shown on Keeler's map, *ca.* 1884. It was a gold and silver mining camp, which had a short-lived post office from May 1866 to March 1867. The *Annual Mining Review*, 1876, lists a 20-stamp water-driven mill in operation in 1866. The name is the Greek equivalent for 'golden city'. *See* Bend City.

Chub Gulch [Butte]. A mining camp in Concow Township, north of Oroville. It is mentioned in the County History, 1882 (p. 253).

Chuchilla Diggings [Mariposa]. Probably named after the Chowchilla River. The place is mentioned repeatedly in 1853 by Thomas Allsop.

Chucklehead Diggings. An unidentified place, listed in the State Library roster.

Chuckwalla District [Riverside]. In the southeastern part of the county. There was gold mining here in the 1880s and 90s, and again in the 1930s. For a list of the mines, see *Bulletin*, 193 (p. 156). The name is derived from a species of lizard, native to the southeastern part of the state.

Church Hill [Nevada]. In Grass Valley township. Mining was active at this site in 1851–1852. The present-day Catholic Church and St. Mary's Convent are situated here. (Foley.)

Churchman Bar [Yuba]. On the east bank of the North Fork of Yuba River, near the junction with the Middle Fork. Shown on Trask's map, 1853.

Church Mine [El Dorado]. *See* Springfield District; Uniontown; El Dorado.

Churchs Corners [Sierra]. About four miles northwest of Sierraville, at the junction of present-day Highway 49 and Highway 89 leading to Blairsden. After 1884, when the post office was established, the name was changed to Sattley. The place is not recorded on the County Map, 1874, and no mining records were found.

Churn Creek Diggings [Shasta]. North of Redding, near Buckeye. In a letter to his wife and daughter dated January 19, 1851, Epaphroditus Wells states that the diggings are "not very rich but something can be made at it every day." *See* Churntown.

Churntown [Shasta]. East of the Sacramento River, about six miles north of Redding. The settlement was named after Churn Creek, which received its name from a waterfall resembling the movements of an old-fashioned churn. Churn Creek is mentioned in the Sacramento *Union*, July 9, 1851. The diggings at Churntown were still holding their own in the spring of 1864, according to an item written in April of that year in an unidentified clipping (Hayes Scrapbooks: Mining, IV, sec. 5). The place was never really a town. There was a mining claim or two, the farm of an Irishman named Mahan who came there in 1855, a school, and a store (Louise Murphy in *Covered Wagon*, 1948). Churntown is shown on the USGS Redding 1944 quadrangle.

Cigan Bar [Yuba]. On the main Yuba River, west of Parks Bar. Recorded on Milleson and Adams' map, 1851. The name is probably a misspelling of Sicard Bar.

Cihota Bar [Placer]. On the North Fork of American River. Notice of a claim laid November 27, 1852 is recorded in Placer County Records, I (p. 144).

Cin Bar [Nevada]. *See* Cincinnati Bar.

Cincinnati [El Dorado]. Apparently near Dryer Creek, a tributary to Dutch Creek, northwest of Coloma. The U. S. Bureau of the Census lists the names of 168 inhabit-

ants at Cincinnati and vicinity in the population schedule for the 1850 census.

Cincinnati Bar [Nevada]. On the Yuba River, probably on the South Fork. Peter Decker repeatedly mentions the place, abbreviated Cin Bar, in 1850, and notes that it had a store (Diary, May 12, 1850 and later).

Cincinnati Hill [Nevada]. In Grass Valley District. A steam-driven 16-stamp mill was erected in 1855 (*State Register*, 1857). A quartz mine is listed on the County Map, 1880, with location shown directly west of Grass Valley. A mine is still listed in 1941 (*Mining Bureau*, XXXVII, p. 448).

Cisna Hill [Calaveras]. On Old Gulch Creek, northeast of Calaveritas. The old river channel was struck with signal success in 1857 (San Francisco *Bulletin*, January 18, 1858).

City of 76 [Plumas]. On Jamison Creek, below Eureka Peak. Shown as Seventy-Six on Trask's map, 1853, and on Goddard's map, 1857. The name is derived from a company of seventy-six men who had given the name Washington to their location on Eureka Peak soon after the rich quartz ledge of the Eureka Company was discovered in 1851 (Co. Hist., 1882, pp. 241 f.). Browne (p. 168) describes the workings, which were equipped with three arrastres, to which the rock had to be carried on mule-back. The arrastres were later replaced by a 16-stamp mill on the flat below the creek, and it was at this site that a town was laid out and given the name City of 76. The venture soon failed, and the grounds were taken over by the Sierra Buttes Company of London, which gained possession of all the quartz locations on the peak. *See* Eureka [Plumas].

City of Six Diggings [Sierra]. On Slug Canyon, southwest of Downieville, situated on the main Blue Lead. Recorded on Doolittle's map, 1868, and on the County Map, 1874. An item in the *Alta*, June 27, 1852, reprinted from the Downieville *Echo*, states that the diggings paid well at that time, but there was a scarcity of water. According to Browne (p. 138), there was mainly drift mining, and it declined in the 1860s. Chauncey Canfield was intrigued by the name and wrote a novel entitled *The City of Six*, which was centered around it. A city of Six Mine is listed in the Mining Bureau reports until 1942. *See* Jackassville.

Clapboard Gulch [Amador]. Tributary to Sutter Creek. This was one of the rich gulches in Volcano Valley, mentioned by Doble, who mined here successfully

(January 25, 1853, pp. 102, 140). Clapboard Gulch is mentioned as a town by Hutchings in 1855.

Clapboard Town [San Bernardino]. About a half mile south of Lower Holcomb, just east of Poligue Canyon Road. Six hundred miners were working and living here in 1861 (La Fuze, I, p. 62). *See* Holcomb Valley; Union Town.

Claraville [Kern]. In the Ticknor Basin, east of Piute Mountains, half way between Bakersfield and Johannesburg. The place developed in 1861 as a trading center of the Mount Sinai District which produced mainly silver. It was named for a girl, Clara Munckton (Boyd, p. 34). The *Register* of 1904 lists one stamp mill. A mine was operating in 1933 (*Mining Bureau*, XXIX, p. 296) and is still listed in 1949. Shown on the USGS Mojave 1923 quadrangle.

Claraville [Placer]. Near the mouth of Squaw Creek. Gold and silver were discovered north of Lake Tahoe in 1861, and Claraville was one of several short-lived settlements which developed in the area (*Bull.*, 193, pp. 124 f.).

Claremont Hill [Plumas]. About four miles southwest of Quincy. According to an unidentified clipping marked 1870 in Hayes Scrapbooks: Mining, IV, (sec. 125), one company discovered deposits with "flattering indications" after having prospected here for ten years. Another company struck "excellent prospects." The name is sometimes spelled Clermont.

Clark Mountains District [San Bernardino]. North of U. S. Highway 15, near the Nevada state line. It was mainly a silver producing district, with a little gold (Raymond, III, pp. 13 f.). On the County Map, 1892, eight mines are listed. Some mines operated into the 1930s. The district and the mountains were named in honor of William A. Clark, United States senator from Montana and the "copper king" of Montana. The Colosseum Mine in the northern part of the district produced mainly silver, but also gold, assayed as high as thirty dollars per ton. Details are given in *Mining Bureau*, XXVII (p. 291). The mines in the district are listed in *Bulletin*, 193 (p. 156).

Clarks Canyon [Sierra]. Seven miles north of Downieville. Downie (p. 134) struck it rich here but had to give up because of the lack of water. Shown on the USGS Downieville 1907 quadrangle.

Clarkson [El Dorado]. Shown on Goddard's map of 1857 on the Sacramento County line. It is probably the same as Clarksville.

Clarks Run [Yuba]. Enters the main Yuba River twenty miles above Marysville. According to Pringle Shaw (p. 124), as many as 700 miners were at work around 1855.

Clarksville [El Dorado]. Six miles east of Folsom. Shown on Doolittle's map, 1868. A five-stamp mill is listed in 1887 (*Resources*, p. 21). In 1923 a drag-line dredge operated on Carson Creek near by (*Mining Bureau*, LII, p. 434). *See* Clarkson.

Classic Hill [Siskiyou]. On Indian Creek, above Happy Camp. Hydraulic mines in the district were worked for a number of years by Chinese, probably before 1900 (*Mining Bureau*, XIV, p. 825).

Clawhammer Bar [[Siskiyou]. Below Sawyers Bar, just around the bend of the Salmon River. It was one of the richest bars on the river. The place was named for a miner who was dressed in a "clawhammer" coat (swallow-tailed coat) at the Fourth of July celebration in 1854. (*California Place Names*.) It is now the residential part of Sawyers Bar.

Clay Hill [El Dorado]. Between the South Fork of American River and Weber Creek, south of Indian Hill. It is situated on a spur of the Blue Channel of the county. Recorded on Bowman's map, 1873. It is listed in Hittell's roster, *Mining Bureau*, IV (p. 219), and it is mentioned in the County History, 1883 (p. 88).

Clays Bar [Calaveras]. On the Mokelumne River, above the confluence with Jackson Creek. Shown on Trask's map, 1853. It is mentioned by Browne (p. 51).

Clays Ranch [Yuba]. On Willow Creek, near Garden Valley. It was named for the owner, John Clay. The place is mentioned by De Long, August 30, 1857, and the name is shown on the County Map of 1879.

Clayton [Yuba]. On New York Creek, tributary to Dry Creek. Recorded on Goddard's map, 1857. It is mentioned by De Long, January 28, 1856. J. C. Clayton settled here in 1853 (Co. Hist., 1879, p. 92). The place is also known as Clayton Ranch. Shown on the USGS Smartsville 1943 quadrangle.

Clear Creek [Shasta]. A tributary to the Sacramento River. Recorded on Goddard's map, 1857. Pierson B. Reading discovered gold here near his land grant on his return from a visit to Sutter's Mill in March of 1848. The site of the discovery is Historic Landmark 78. *See* Readings Bar [Shasta] and Horsetown. The creek was still paying well in 1861 (*Mining Press*, March 23, 1861). In 1872 a steam-driven 6-stamp mill crushed ore containing gold and silver (*Annual Mining Review*, 1876, p. 22). Dredging a few miles below Redding was reported in 1913/14 (*Mining Bureau*, XIV, p. 777) and later, 1918, for platinum (*Bull.*, 85, p. 38).

Clear Creek [Yuba]. Tributary to Willow Creek, two and a half miles west of Camptonville. Clear Creek and Green Mountain Ditch are mentioned by De Long, June 30, 1857.

Clear Creek Mining District [Kern]. West of Havilah. There was extensive mining here during the Kern River rush in the 1860s. The Drunkards Dream Mine was still active in 1933, but by 1949 most mines in the district were idle (*Mining Bureau*, XLV, pp. 233 f.). For a collection of contemporary newspaper clippings about the Clear Creek area see Hayes Scrapbooks: Mining, VII, sec. Clear Creek.

Clearinghouse [Mariposa]. On the Merced River, six miles west of El Portal. The deposits were discovered about 1860, probably by the Ferguson brothers, and the mine was first named for them. In 1867 an 8-stamp mill and later a 15-stamp mill were erected. In 1907 the place was named Clearinghouse by Frank X. Egenhoff, after his mine, which was a clearinghouse for gold bullion during the panic of 1907. The total production of the mine reached more than 3 million dollars. The Clearinghouse or Original Mine operated with modern equipment until the late 1950s. (*Mining Bureau*, XXIV, pp. 107 f.; LIII, pp. 60, 85 ff.)

Clements [San Joaquin]. Limited placer mining was carried on before 1900 on the Mokelumne River near this place, mainly by Chinese. From 1935 to 1951 the Gold Hill Dredging Company was in operation here, apparently with moderate success. (*Mining Bureau*, LI, p. 37.)

Clingmans Point [Yuba]. See Klingermans Point.

Clinton [Amador]. On the South Fork of Jackson Creek about eight and half miles east of Jackson. Recorded on Goddard's map, 1857, and on the County Map, 1866. Between 1856 and 1859 it was also known as Sarahville (or Sarahsville, according to the *Amador Ledger*, August 1, 1857), the name of the short-lived post office. It is mentioned by Doble, April 12, 1852, and again by Borthwick (p. 309) in the spring of 1853. The miners were chiefly Mexicans, Chileans, and French. Ben Bowen

describes the place, January 25, 1855. The County History, 1881 (p. 209) states that hydraulic mining was introduced in 1853–1854. According to a letter from Whites Bar, October 30, 1855, to an unidentified newspaper (Hittell Clippings, p. 63) a young man, Thomas H. Loehr, discovered a rich vein north of Clinton. In 1857 two mills with 26 stamps were in operation (*State Register*, 1859). In the winter of 1867–68 a 9-pound nugget was picked up in a claim that had been considered worthless (*Amador Ledger*, March 14, 1868). Browne (p. 72) reports that the deposits were considered worked out in 1869, but according to an account in the *Amador Dispatch*, February 3, 1872, reprinted in the San Francisco *Bulletin*, a surface claim had recently yielded fourteen and a half ounces as the result of one day's work of three men (Hayes Scrapbooks: Mining, II, sec. 12). Historic Landmark 37.

Clinton [Mono]. About three miles north of Cameron, in Ferris Canyon. Clinton was the first settlement in the Patterson Mining District and the only one which held the status of a town (F. S. Wedertz). It had a post office from 1882 to 1884. Mining here was mainly silver, with some gold. A description is given in *Mining Bureau*, VIII (pp. 358, 360).

Clinton [Nevada]. The post office at Moores Flat was named Clinton from 1854 to 1857. See Moores Flat.

Clinton Bar [Placer]. On the North Fork of the American River. Notice of intention to flume and dam the river at this point, dated August 30, 1852, is recorded in Placer County Records, I (p. 109). It is probably the same as Clinton Bar mentioned in the same Records, I (p. 214).

Clio [Plumas]. See Wash.

Clipper The term, made famous by the American clipper ship, was used occasionally for mines and mining localities in the gold regions.

Clipper: Canyon, Hill [El Dorado]. About three miles northwest of Georgetown. Shown on Bowman's map, 1873, with indication of sites of quartz mines and "old mining claims."

Clipper Mills [Butte]. About two miles northeast of Woodville, near the Yuba County line. Shown on Wescoatt's map, 1861, as Clipper Mill, on the old La Porte turnpike. It was the trading center for a number of hydraulic and drift mines in the vicinity (*Register*, 1905), but it was primarily a lumbering community. A post office was established in 1861.

Clover Patch District [Mono]. In the southern part of the county, about twelve miles southwest of Benton. The area also includes the Chidago and Indian districts. Some gold was mined here before 1900 and again in the 1930s. The mines are listed in *Bulletin*, 193 (p. 148).

Cluna Bar [Siskiyou]. On the Klamath River, below the mouth of Scott River (Bancroft Notes).

Clydesdale Diggings [Placer]. Between Long Canyon and the South Fork of the Middle Fork of American River (Rubicon River); south of Blacksmith Flat. Shown on Doolittle's map, 1868. They are mentioned in 1911 by Lindgren (*Tertiary Gravels*, p. 169) as "old" diggings in a gravel region poor in gold.

Coal Canyon [Sierra]. In Poker Flat District. Rich gold yield is reported in an undated clipping of the Downieville *Democrat*, apparently June, 1858. A Coal Canyon claim, listed in *Mining Bureau*, XVI (Sierra, p. 68) might be the same site.

Coarse Gold: Creek, Gulch [Madera]. A tributary to Fresno River. Recorded on Gibbes' map, 1852, and on Goddard's map, 1857. The deposits were apparently discovered by Mexicans. It was the same creek which was called by the Mexicans Oro Grosso, as is evident from two letters written by Derbec, October 23 and 27, 1850. *See* Oro Grosso. The place was mentioned repeatedly by Eccleston in his Mariposa War diary in March, 1851. On July 10, 1852, the *Alta* reports that there were only a few miners here at that time because of Indian attacks. At one time it was called Texas Flat for miners from Texas who found coarse gold there. There has been intermittent mining and prospecting in the district to the present time (*Bull.*, 193, p. 38). Coarse Gold is shown as a stream on the USGS Mariposa 1938 quadrangle.

Cobbs Creek [Tuolumne]. A branch of Moccasin Creek, south of Big Oak Flat. It is mentioned as having been very rich by the "Mountaineer" in the *San Joaquin Republican*, December, 16, 1851. Shown on the USGS Sonora 1939 quadrangle.

Cock-a-doodle Creek. An unidentified place, listed by Marryat (p. 373).

Coeur [Trinity]. At the source of New River, close to Siskiyou County line. The name is the French word for 'heart' and was probably applied by French miners, who were very active in the region. It was a trading center and from 1885–1896 the post office

for quartz mines in the area. In 1898 there were still three stamp mills in operation.

Coffee Creek [Trinity]. A town on Coffee Creek, a tributary to Trinity River, four miles from the confluence. According to Cox (p. 11), the creek was so named because a sack of coffee was spilled at the mouth of the creek. The place is mentioned by Hutchings in 1855. A post office was established in 1882, and it was the trading center for numerous quartz mines in the area (*Register*, 1899). *See* North Fork of Coffee Creek.

Coffin Bar [El Dorado]. On the South Fork of American River, probably at the mouth of Coffin Creek or Ravine, about three miles southeast of Coloma. Coffin Ravine is shown on Bowman's map, 1873. Two mining locations are recorded in El Dorado County Records, Mining Lcoations, Book I (pp. 112, 172), one between Eagle and German Mining companies, the other between the mouth of Coffin Creek and French Company claim (Schlappi-Ferguson).

Colburg [Calaveras]. *See* Kohlbergs Humbug.

Cold Canyon [Sierra]. On the ridge between Slate and Canyon creeks, opposite Howland Flat. In 1856–1857 the Fashion Company built a 700-foot tunnel at considerable cost before pay dirt was reached. In 1861 the *Mountain Messenger* reported all business at a standstill, except the tunnel of Fashion No. 2. (*Mining Press*, May 11, 1861). A description and a list of mining companies before 1869 is found in Browne (pp. 141 f.).

Cold Spring [Placer]. Near the confluence of Canyon Creek and the North Fork of American River. Notice of intention to build a ditch from Canyon (or Cañon) Creek to Indiana Hill and vicinity, datelined Cold Spring, September 7, 1852, is filed in Placer County Records, I (p. 114). Hutchings lists Cold Spring as a town in 1855. Cold Spring Hill is shown south of Gold Run on the USGS Colfax 1938 quadrangle.

Cold Spring [Sierra]. About two and a half miles southwest of Chips Flat. Cold Spring Hotel is shown on Doolittle's map, 1868. Hutchings was here October 25, 1855 (Diary).

Cold Springs [El Dorado]. About three miles northwest of Placerville, near the confluence of Hangtown and Weber creeks. Shown on Doolittle's map, 1868. Haskins (p. 62) states that the camp consisted of a cluster of tents in the fall of

Coloma, El Dorado Co.

1849. In October, 1849, the Buckeye Rovers made their headquarters here. John E. Banks tells of the rapid growth of the place and the rich profits made within one year (*Buckeye Rovers*, pp. 98 ff., 141 ff.). A post office was established January 21, 1852. In 1855 a 10-stamp water-driven mill was erected (*State Register*, 1857). In 1860 the place was a "dilapidated village," near which a German miner had planted several thousand grapevines and worked his claim only in his spare time (*Transactions*, 1860, p. 60). According to Frickstad, the name of the post office was changed to Granite Hill in 1874. However, Granite Hill, as shown on the USGS Placerville 1931 quadrangle, is at or near the site of Gold Hill. The post office may have been moved to Granite Hill rather than have changed its name. The name is preserved in the name of Cold Springs Road, but only the grass-grown cemetery remains at the site of the once flourishing camp. On Trask's map, 1853, and on Bowman's, 1873, the name appears as Gold Springs. *See* Gold Springs.

Coleman City [San Diego]. Late in 1869 A. E. (Fred) Coleman, a negro, discovered gold in a creek near present-day Julian. The mining camp that developed nearby was first called Emily City, then Coleman City. (Ellsberg, pp. 15, 18.) *see* Julian. Coleman Creek is shown on the USGS Santa Ysabel 1960 quadrangle.

Coleridge [Trinity]. On the East Fork of the North Fork of Trinity River. It was a trading center, and from 1889–1907 it had a post office. In 1898 two stamp mills and three arrastres were still in operation. (*Register*, 1898). Shown on the USGS Big Bar 1930 quadrangle.

Colfax [Placer]. About fifteen miles northeast of Auburn. It was named in 1865 for Schuyler Colfax, who became vice president of the United States under Grant in

1868 (*California Place Names*). The place was not a mining town but the trading center for placer and quartz mines in the vicinity. It absorbed nearby Illinoistown and Alder Grove and continued to be a trading center for the miners into the twentieth century. One and a half miles west of it was the famous Rising Sun lode mine, which operated from 1866 to 1884, with a total production of more than 2 million dollars. (*Annual Mining Review*, 1876, p. 23; *Mining Bureau*, XXIII, p. 252; *Register*, 1902). Colfax or Illinois District is described in *Bulletin*, 193 (p. 38). *See* Illinoistown; Alder Grove.

Collierville District [Calaveras; Tuolumne]. In the East Gold Belt of the Sierra Nevada, in the south central part of Calaveras County and the north central part of Tuolumne County; east of Murphys. The chief source of gold was the Collier Mine, which was discovered in 1878 and active until 1899; in 1925–1926 it was again worked on a small scale (*County Report*, II, p. 51; *Bull.*, 193, pp. 38 f.).

Collins Riffle [Yuba]. Near Hampshire Mills. It is mentioned as a mining camp in the County History, 1879 (p. 97).

Coloma [El Dorado]. The site of Sutter's mill on the South Fork of American River, where James Marshall's discovery of gold on January 24, 1848, inaugurated the Gold Rush. The name is that of a Maidu Indian village near the site; the meaning 'beautiful vale' attributed to the name is the figment of American romanticists. The earliest detailed reports are in Bigler (pp. 88 ff.) and in Mason's *Report*, July, 1848. Other early reports are in Buffum (p. 49) and in the statements of Barstow and Bayley. The name is shown on Derby's Sacramento map and on all other early maps, where it is spelled Culloma, Colluma, Cul-lu-mah. The present spelling was first used on Tyson's map of 1849. The post office, established November 8, 1849, was Culloma until January 13, 1851. The name is spelled Coloma by the U. S. Bureau of the Census in its 1850 population schedule. As early as 1852 Martin Allhoff planted a vineyard, and it appeared that horticulture might overshadow the golden glimmer. In *Transactions*, 1859, it is stated that it would be worthwhile traveling 500 miles to see the Coloma gardens. However, it remained a mining town. Quartz mining later replaced placering. In 1864 a water-driven 5-stamp mill was built (*Annual Mining Review*, 1876, p. 22) and a Coloma Quartz Mining District was in existence until 1870. In the 1930s and 1940s there was some gold dredging in the river (*Bull.*, 193, p. 39). — Some of the old buildings in the town, including the school in which Edwin Markham taught, are still standing on Main Street. Studebaker's shop, where the later automobile builder made wheelbarrows for the miners around 1853, is Historic Landmark 142; the Gold Discovery Site is no. 530. The famous nugget found at Sutters Mill known as the Wimmer Nugget is in the Bancroft Library. Another specimen, a flake of gold reputedly the first one to have been picked up by James Marshall, is in the Smithsonian Institution.

Colorado [Mariposa]. About two miles east of Sherlock and five miles north of Mariposa, at the headwaters of Saxton (or Saxon) Creek. Goddard's map, 1857, shows it at the head of Stockton Creek. Allsop visited the placer camp in January, 1852, and again in October of the same year. He called it a "very rich spot," and like Goddard located it at the head of Stockton Creek. Later records indicate that the camp was moved to Saxton Creek. It was a lively place as early as 1855, and it had a post office from June 2, 1858 to March 26, 1860. The camp, or town, no longer exists, but local residents call the district Colorow (*Mining Bureau*, XXIV, p. 84). The Colorado Quartz Mine, on Long Gulch, had a 10-stamp mill and operated apparently to the 1940s (*Mining Bureau*, XIV, p. 579; XVII, p. 111; XXIV, p. 83; LIII, pp. 90 f.). The Buena Vista mine in the area had one of the first quartz mills, built in 1851. Its history from the early 1880s to the depression in the 1930 s is given in *Mining Bureau*, LIII (p. 80). The Mocking Bird Mine was noted for specimens of wiry and arborescent gold (*Mining Bureau*, X, p. 304; LIII, pp. 132 f.).

Other mines in the area are listed and mapped in the 1957 (LIII) report of the Mining Bureau. *See also* Sherlock Creek and Saxton Creek. The site of Colorado is shown on the USGS Yosemite 1938 quadrangle.

Colorow [Mariposa]. *See* Colorado.

Colton Hill [Nevada]. South of the South Fork of Yuba River, one and a half miles west of Washington. Shown on Doolittle's map, 1868. It is listed in Hittell's roster. *See* Cotton Hill.

Columbia [San Bernardino]. On the eastern slope of Providence Mountains, north of the town of Providence. Shown on Crowell's map, 1902. It was a small mining community, with a post office listed, 1901–1902. In the 1920 *Report* of the Mining Bureau the Columbia Mine is listed as idle.

Columbia [Tuolumne]. Three miles northwest of Sonora; on the limestone belt. The town, once known as the "gem of the Southern Mines," is probably the best preserved mining camp in California. Since 1945, when it was made part of the California park system, it has become a sort of show window of the gold region. The name appears on Gibbes' Map of the Southern Mines, 1852; on Trask's map, 1853; and on Wallace's map of the Tuolumne Water Company, 1853. Later, in 1879, it appears on Dart's Map of the Principal Quartz and Gravel Mines in Tuolumne County. In 1871 Dart had made a detailed plat of the town, showing the layout of streets, lots, and names of their owners at that time. The various stories about the discovery of gold at Columbia are somewhat contradictory. See Rensch, "Columbia, a Gold Camp"; Heckendorn (pp. 6 ff.); Stoddart (pp. 119, 127, 139 f.); County History, 1882 (pp. 22 f.); Eastman, in *Chispa* (IV, pp. 131 f.; VI, pp. 177 f.; XI, pp. 357 ff.). It has now been established that Mexicans from the nearby San Diego camp mined at the foot of Kennebec Hill in Columbia Gulch (Main Gulch in the later town of Columbia) in 1849, and that in March, 1850, Dr. Thaddeus Hildreth and party followed the trail from Pine Log Crossing down the hill to Columbia Gulch. They may have seen Mexicans mining there; in any event, one of the party raised the color on March 27 (or 29), 1850, at the place where the Mexicans had mined. The rich find brought a rush to the place. It became known as Hildreths Diggings, and in newspaper accounts it was also sometimes called American Camp and Dry

Diggings. By April the population reportedly reached 6,000 to 8,000 according to Stoddart, doubtless an exaggerated figure. A more realistic figure of 3,000 is given in a letter written from Columbia, May 13, 1850, cited by Eastman, in *Chispa*, XI (p. 358). On April 29, 1850, Majors Farnsworth and Sullivan and D. G. Alexander named the town Columbia (County History, 1882, p. 26). The post office was established on November 16, 1852. Contemporary newspapers were filled with reports of the finding of many large nuggets and lumps of gold in the town and vicinity. The largest was perhaps the 72-pound lump of almost pure gold picked up by a loafer and valued by Wells Fargo at 14 thousand dollars (Hittell Clippings, p. 26). Another lump which yielded 33.5 pounds of gold was bought by William O. Sleeper and Company for $7,438.50 (*Tuolumne Courier*, September 11, 1858). Other large nuggets were found at nearby Knapps Ranch, Gold Hill, and Spring Gulch (*Mining Bureau*, II, part 1, pp. 148 f.). Several factors contributed to the early decline in the population of Columbia. The most important was the lack of water for placering. The foreign miners' tax doubtless was also a factor, but less so than in neighboring Sonora. For a discussion of the tax and its effect on the mining population in California in general, *see* Rensch, "Columbia, a Gold Camp" (pp. 14 f.); Heckendorn (p. 6); E. D. Perkins' diary (pp. 153 ff. and introduction, pp. 43 ff.). The lack of water was remedied when water was brought from Five Mile Creek by the Tuolumne Water Company. The ditch was started in 1851, and the first

water was brought to Columbia in May, 1852. This feat was accomplished with the financial help of D. O. Mills, founder of the Bank of California, who opened a bank and assay office in Columbia in 1852. (Heckendorn, p. 9; Co. Hist., 1882, pp. 170 f.; and Brockman, p. 11.) The survey of the ditch was made by John Wallace, whose map of 1853 shows the installations of the Water Company. Later, in 1854, after the first disastrous fire, the Columbia and Stanislaus Water Company was formed to bring water from the South Fork of Stanislaus River. *See* Rensch's account in his chapter "The Boon of Water." The temporary prosperity which Columbia regained soon declined again. Between 1853 and 1857 it shipped 100 thousand dollars in gold weekly, but by 1868 the shipments decreased to around 50 thousand dollars monthly (Browne, pp. 36 ff.) Browne lists (p. 37) a number of important claims in the Columbia Basin, showing the decrease in earnings between 1853 and 1867. He includes Columbia Boys Claim, Tiger Claim, Cascade Claim, Burns Claim, Main Claim, and Millington Claim. A few other early important claims not listed by Browne include the Cannonade, the Columbia, the Luddy, the "Old Hildreth" (same as "Maine Boys"), and the Pat Smith. *See* Columbia Gulch; Main Gulch. The Columbia district as described in *Bullein*, 193 (p. 39) comprises Columbia, Yankee Hill, Sawmill Flat, Browns Flat, Squabbletown, and Springfield. The estimated production of gold in this district is 87 million dollars or more, some estimates reaching as high as 150 million dollars. The town of Columbia is Historic Landmark 123, and

Columbia, Tuolumne Co.

as previously stated it is a part of the California state park system.

Columbia Bar [Amador]. On the Mokelumne River, four miles south of Jackson. Shown on Trask's map of 1853. A. Lascy locates it below Middle Bar on the Mokelumne, about five miles from Campo Seco, and describes it as a very rich, lively camp in the winter of 1850–1851. The average yield was five dollars to a bucket, the richest pay dirt Lascy saw on the Mokelumne. The diggings were originally worked by Mexicans. Charles Peters mined there in 1849 (Berriman). It is mentioned by Logan Fay in letters to his family dated May 28, 1851 and January 28, 1852 (Fay Collection, California State Library, California Section).

Columbia Flat [Butte]. On the Middle Fork of the Feather River. It is apparently the same as Columbiaville. In 1858 there were three mills with twenty-four stamps and four arrastres in operation (*State Register*, 1859). The same year it was reported that a lump of forty-one ounces, worth 540 dollars, was found here.

Columbia Flat [El Dorado]. Near Kelsey. According to Warren T. Russell (p. 123), it was also known as Lawrenceberg. The place is mentioned as an early mining locality in the County History, 1883 (p. 191).

Columbia Flat [Tuolumne]. Between Columbia and Springfield, near the entrance to Columbia airport. Rich yields were reported in the newspapers of 1854 to 1857. In the spring of 1856 the Able, Duchow claim yielded 800 to 1,000 dollars per week from dirt that had been "thrown up" during the previous fall (*Alta*, April 21, 1856). The following March the same company averaged eight ounces per day to the man washing the gravel they had "housed" the previous fall (*San Joaquin Republican*, March 10, 1857). The Eddy claim, near the Duchow, paid six to ten dollars a day to the hand in 1857 (*San Joaquin Republican*, May 31, 1857). The New York claim had to pulverize the clay before it could be washed. It paid regularly twelve dollars a day to the man in May, 1857 (*San Joaquin Republican*, May 31, 1857). Other paying claims in Columbia Flat in 1854 and 1855 were the Hawkes, Murphy; the Ives, Glass; the Shaw, Austin; the Turner; and the Wells (Columbia *Gazette*, July 8, August 8, 1854; *San Joaquin Republican*, July 15, 1855).

Columbia Gulch [Tuolumne]. *See* Main Gulch.

Columbia Hill [Nevada]. Between North Bloomfield and Cherokee, on the San Juan Ridge. It is mentioned by De Long, January 17, 1856, and by Raymond (VI, 108). *Bean's Directory* of 1867 still shows a large miners' population, but the place declined with the prohibition of hydraulic mining. In the *Register* of 1900 two stamp mills are listed. According to the Nevada County Historical Society (*Bulletin*, May, 1951), the Tisdale brothers began mining here in 1853, and though the name was changed to North Columbia when the post office was established in 1860, the place was still known as Columbia Hill or "The Hill." *See* North Columbia. The Columbia Consolidated Mining Company operated until about 1920 (*Mining Bureau*, XXVI, p. 136).

Columbia House [Sierra]. The location could not be determined. The finding of a large lump of gold in October, 1858, is reported in Hittell Clippings (p. 34).

Columbia Ranch [El Dorado]. John Steele (p. 234) speaks of a small Pah Ute Indian village known as Columbia ranch, near Coloma, and gives an account of the Indians mining in a primitive way in the early 1850s without the white man's interference (p. 276). No other reference to Columbia Ranch was found.

Columbiaville [Butte]. *See* Columbia Flat.

Comanche [Calaveras]. It is mentioned in *Pacific Coast Mining Review*, 1878 (p. 185). The name Comanche is a misspelling of Camanche.

Concord Bar [Nevada]. On the Middle Fork of Yuba River. It is mentioned in Brown's *Directory*, 1856 (p. 133). A bridge was built in 1857 (Co. Hist., 1880, p. 132). Stewart Sheldon recalls in 1890 (pp. 66 ff.) his trip to Concord Bar in 1850 (?). According to Bancroft, VI (p. 486), the original name of Orleans Flat was Concord.

Concow: Valley, Township [Butte]. North of Oroville. Recorded on the County Map of 1861 and on von Leicht-Craven's map of 1874. It is the site of the Concow Reservoir. There was considerable quartz mining as early as 1850 (Co. Hist., 1882, p. 214). For the origin of the name see *California Place Names*.

Condemned Bar [El Dorado, Placer]. On the North Fork of American River, about two and a half miles above the confluence with the South Fork, as shown on the maps of Doolittle, 1868, and Bowman 1873. On Trask's map (1853) and Goddard's (1857) it is shown farther upstream, above Horseshoe Bar. E. S. Holden came here in 1849, when 200 miners were at work. He gives an interesting account of the life of a miner. (*CHSQ*, XII, pp. 312 ff.). Stephen Wing visited the place on March 19, 1852, when there were about fifty miners at work, averaging five dollars per day (Journal, I, p. 12). According to the Placer County History, 1882 (p. 226), however, the Condemned Bar Company distributed to its members in October, 1852, 20 thousand dollars from one week's work. In 1855 Hutchings reported it not as flourishing as formerly, but with a population fairly permanent (Diary, February 25, 1855). *See* Carrolton. Now under Folsom Lake. The site is Historic Landmark, 672.

Condemned Bar [Yuba]. At the confluence of Dobbins Creek and the main Yuba River. Shown on Milleson and Adams' map, 1851, Trask's map, 1853, and Goddard's, 1857. Joseph A. Stuart mined here and had a trading post in 1851. He gives a good account of Condemned Bar and nearby Klingerman Point. In the 1870s only three white men and three Chinese were left, according to the County History, 1879 (p. 94). The name is recorded on the USGS Smartsville 1943 quadrangle. The site is very near the site of the first hydroelectric generator on the Yuba River and of the present-day Colgate Power House of the Pacific Gas and Electric Company.

Confidence: Flat, District [Tuolumne]. On Turnback Creek, eleven miles east of Columbia. Shown on Dart's map, 1879. The Confidence Mine, which gave the name to the settlement and to the post office (1899–1906), started in 1853. A 30-stamp steam driven mill was built in 1869 (*Annual Mining Review*, 1876, p. 21). Raymond, IV (p. 69), records that forty stamps were in operation in 1871 and that the daily yield was as high as 12 hundred dollars. The mine was one of the best in the state and was said to have produced more than 3 million dollars in the early years. Another period of prosperity was from 1896 to 1912, when a production of more than one million dollars was reported. Later attempts at revival failed in spite of heavy investments (*Mining Bureau*, XLV, p. 61). Confidence is shown on the USGS Big Trees 1941 quadrangle.

Conn Valley [Napa]. East and south of Saint Helena. Named for John Conn, a pioneer of 1843. The discovery of some gold and silver at the head of the valley caused a moderate rush in 1860 (*Mining Press*, March 1, 1861).

Contreras [Amador]. On the North Fork of Mokelumne River, about four miles southeast of Volcano. Shown on the County Map, 1866. The quartz vein was discovered by a Baptist preacher in February, 1851, but the camp was named for Pablo Contreras. The attempts to crush the rock were futile until a German miner from Peru introduced the arrastre. (Bancroft, VI, p. 273.) In 1857 four arrastres and two water-driven mills with ten stamps were in operation (*State Register*, 1859). Gold was found in pockets and was worked mainly by Mexicans. The *Amador Ledger*, September 19, 1857, refers to the "new town," at which there were about 100 Mexicans, two stores, and "any number of brush houses." The place is mentioned in the *Mining Press*, May 11, 1861; in 1880 it was almost dead, and now it is vanished. It is described in the County History, 1881 (pp. 215 ff.). The painter and caricaturist Tavernier "operated" here for a while.

Convicts Bar [Sierra]. *See* Pierces Bar.

Cooks Bar [Sacramento]. On the south side of the Cosumnes River, west of Michigan Bar. Shown on Goddard's map, 1857. The place was named for Dennis Cook, who had a trading post here in 1849. At times the Bar had a population of 500, but mining ceased about 1860 (Sacramento Co. Hist., 1880, p. 214). Hutchings mentions it March 24, 1855. It is also mentioned in the Jared Sheldon's papers in a document dated July 6, 1851 (California State Library, California Section).

Cookseys Diggings [Trinity]. The place is mentioned in the *Mining Press*, February 15, 1862, but the location is not indicated.

Cool [El Dorado]. On Highway 49, where the road from Georgetown joins the highway. It was a placer camp of the 1850s and apparently lasted until about 1900 (*Register*, 1902). A post office was established in 1885. The place is shown on the *Guidebook* map No. 7.

Cooley Hill [Nevada]. Listed in Hittell's roster, *Mining Bureau*, IV (p. 220).

Cooleys Bar [El Dorado]. Near Coloma. Stephen Wing worked here as a wheelwright in July and August, 1857. The Bar may have been named for Carlos Cooley of Uniontown, mentioned in Wing's diary, June 24, 1857 (Journal, III, pp. 69, 72.)

Coolgardie Placer [San Bernardino]. Fifteen miles north of Barstow. It was named after a mining town in Australia. There was no water for mining, but dry mining started in 1900. By 1915 the total production reached 100 thousand dollars, a respectable sum under the circumstances. (*Mining Bureau*, XXVII, p. 293; XXX, p. 250).

Coon. The popular name for the raccoon, one of the best known North American carniverous mammals, is frequently used as a place name in the gold region and elsewhere. Coon is also a colloquial connotation for a negro, and this usage may well account for some of the place names.

Coon Creek [Placer]. This was once a rich camp, but already in 1855 it was dying "a natural death" (Pringle Shaw, p. 121). Coon Creek and School District are shown on the County Map, 1887, northwest of Ophir.

Coon Flat [Del Norte]. Five miles from Gasquet. Placering was carried on by ground sluicing (*Mining Bureau*, XXIX, p. 143).

Coon: Hollow, Hill [El Dorado]. Southwest of Placerville. Shown on Bowman's map, 1873. Apparently the two places were in the same rich area on the Placerville Divide. Coon Hill is listed in Hittell's roster, with the fineness of the gold given as 965°. Raymond VII (p. 96) states, in what he believes reliable authority, that the gravel from twenty-five acres around Coon Hill yielded 25 million dollars worth of gold(!). Other claims are more modest, although in *Transactions*, 1860 (p. 60), it is stated that "the amount of gold taken out [of Coon Hollow] is fabulous." According to *Mining Bureau*, LII (p. 433), the Coon Hollow Mine, including the Excelsior Claim, yielded 10 million dollars. Coon Hollow, listed by Hutchings as a "town" in 1855, is shown on the USGS Placerville 1931 quadrangle.

Coopers Bar [Trinity]. On the Trinity River, between Canyon Creek and the North Fork. It is mentioned by Cox in 1857. The place was also known as McGillivrays Bar.

Coopers Bridge [Nevada]. *See* Illinois Bar.

Coopers Flat [Tuolumne]. About a half mile below Jamestown, on the north bank of Woods Creek, east of Whiskey Hill. It is mentioned in the San Francisco *Herald*, November 6, 1855, and by Heckendorn (p. 89). The place was named for a pioneer merchant, Ezra Cooper, who had a hotel there (De Ferrari).

Copley [Shasta]. On the Sacramento River, north of Redding. The production was mainly copper and a little gold. Around 1900 there were two stamp mills and one Huntington mill in operation (*Register*, 1902).

Copper. The prospecting for gold led to the discovery of rich copper deposits. Some gold was always found even where copper production predominated. For modern copper production *see* Consolidated *Index*.

Copper City [Shasta]. In Pitsburg (or Pittsburg) mining district at the foot of Killinger Hill, near the junction of Pit and McCloud rivers. According to an unidentified clipping marked April, 1864, the town had 600 inhabitants (Hayes Scrapbooks: Mining, IV, sec. 3); another clipping, marked March 25, 1865, in section 5 of the same volume indicates that gold and silver were mined at the place. According to Steger, activities ceased in 1920 after several periods of boom and depression. Shown on the USGS Redding 1944 quadrangle.

Copperopolis [Calaveras]. About twelve miles southwest of Angels Camp. The copper deposits were discovered in 1860 by prospectors searching for gold. The production was mainly copper, but there were some lode mines in the vicinity, for which the town was the trading center. A post office was established in 1861, and in 1868 it is said to have had a population of nearly 2,000. A major asbestos mine, about five miles south of the town, is now active. Copperopolis is Historic Landmark 296.

Coral Gulch [Tuolumne]. *See* Corral Gulch.

Corbet Creek [Mariposa]. Between El Dorado and Bear creeks, east of Hornitos. A water-driven quartz mill was reported in operation in 1857 on Corbitts Creek (*State Register*, 1857). In the early 1940s there was dredging along the creek (*Bull.*, 135, p. 262).

Corcoran Diggings [Placer]. Between Wallace Canyon and Rubicon River; south of Blacksmith Flat. The gravel diggings, mentioned by Lindgren (*Tertiary Gravels*, p. 169) are in an area poor in gold.

Cordua Bar [Yuba]. On the north bank of the main Yuba River, northwest of Timbuctoo. It was named in 1848 for Theodor Cordua, a native of Germany, on whose property the city of Marysville now stands. It was named for him because he kept a trading post here (*Memoirs*). Shown on Ord's map (1848) as the only bar on the Yuba River, and on all other early maps. It is mentioned by Stephen Davis, September 19, 1850, as Corduways Bar. The bar paid richly at low water (Raymond, VII, p. 144). Later it was completely covered by the hydraulic tailings from Smartsville and Timbuctoo (Co. Hist., 1879, p. 84). It was still mentioned as a settlement in 1877 (*Illustrated Spirits of the Times*, December 25, 1877, in Bancroft Notes), and it is recorded on the County Map of 1879.

Cornish House [Sierra]. *See* Nebraska Diggings.

Cornish Mine [Nevada]. *See* Ural.

Corons [Calaveras]. A doubtful name shown on Derby's map 1, 1849, eight miles north of Angels Camp, near the town of Fourth Crossing.

Corral Flat [Calaveras]. Near Mokelumne Hill. The place is mentioned by "Judge" Robert Thompson (p. 241) in the fall of 1851. According to an unidentified item in the *Calaveras Chronicle*, probably in 1852, the place was "famed for its monster nuggets." A lump of pure gold weighing eighty ounces was picked up from twenty-five to thirty feet under the lava (Hittell Clippings, p. 27). A news item in the San Francisco *Bulletin*, September 22, 1871, reports that one company took out 500 dollars after a short run but averaged only six dollars per day to the hand (Hayes Scrapbooks: Mining, II, sec. 10). A drift mine, one mile southwest of Mokelumne Hill, was in operation in the beginning of the twentieth century (*Mining Bureau*, XIV, p. 116).

Corral Gulch [Tuolumne]. Also spelled Correll and Coral. In the northeast corner of Columbia. The *Alta*, July 7, 1854, has an item from the *Mountain Messenger* stating that twenty-eight ounces were taken out in one claim one day, one nugget weighing thirteen ounces. The *Mining Press*, November 23, 1861, reported that the claims were worked out because of lack of cheap water. The Schilling claim was reported as one of the richest claims in the Columbia area (*Alta*, April 27, 1867).

Correll Gulch [Tuolumne]. *See* Corral Gulch.

Cosmopolite Mining District [Placer]. Notice of a claim for right of way to construct a ditch from Duncans Canyon through Millers Defeat to the district is recorded July 18, 1854 (Placer County Records, 1, p. 237).

Coso District [Inyo]. This is the general term for the region between Owens Lake and Death Valley. For the etymology of the name, *see California Place Names*. The silver and gold deposits were discovered in 1859 by Dr. Darwin French and his party, who were hunting for the lost gunsight lode (*Panamint News*, March 9, 1875). A map in the *Mining Press*, December 21, 1861, shows the district as a silver district only.

The Lone Star Company was active until 1900 but, again, mining only silver (*Register*, 1902). It is now in the territory of the Naval Ordnance Test Station. Shown on the USGS Ballarat 1939 quadrangle. Before the advent of the Naval Ordnance Test Station, the area was known for its hot springs and thermal baths. *See* De Decker (p. 39).

Cosumne [Sacramento]. *See* Daylors.

Cosumnes [El Dorado]. On the Cosumnes River; two and a half miles north of Grizzly Flat. In 1866 a water-driven 4-stamp mill was in operation (*Annual Mining Review*, 1876, p. 23). The Cosumnes (formerly Melton) Mine had a 15-stamp mill, which operated intermittently from 1880 to 1943. The sulfide concentrates yielded 100 to 200 dollars worth of gold per ton at times (*Mining Bureau*, LII, p. 413).

Cosumnes River ferry.

Cottage Grove [Siskiyou]. On the Klamath River. The mining camp was established in 1852 and mining continued intermittently until the 1930s (Vera Toleman, in *Siskiyou Pioneer*, I:1, pp. 6 ff.). A post office was established November 18, 1857.

Cotton Creek, Cottonville [Mariposa]. The creek is a tributary to the section of Merced River which is now Lake McClure. Cottonville was named for G. T. Cotton, who placer mined here in 1849. It was one of the three voting precincts in the county for the general election of November 13, 1849. The steam-driven quartz mill reported in the *State Register*, 1857, as having been on Colton Creek may have been on Cotton Creek. In the 1930s a

Cotton Creek Mine was in operation on the creek just east of the Hunter Valley Road (*Mining Bureau*, LIII, p. 91). Cotton Creek is shown on the USGS Sonora 1939 quadrangle.

Cotton Hill [Nevada]. Mentioned with Gold Hill and Jefferson Hill in the vicinity of Washington. It was the scene of extensive mining, according to the County History, 1880 (p. 206). The Nevada City *Daily Miner*, December 19, 1905, reports that a 1,200-foot tunnel showed a rich body of cemented gravel (Foley). It may be the same as Colton Hill shown on Doolittle's map, 1868, west of Washington.

Cottons New Ferry [Stanislaus]. On the Stanislaus River, between Hyslips (Islips) and Taylors ferries. It is mentioned in the Stockton *Times*, April 20, 1850, as a newly established ferry to the Southern Mines.

Cottonwood [San Bernardino]. Southwest of Barstow, at or near the site of the Santa Fe Railroad siding Hodge. The mill and the trading center for the mines west of Highway 390 was at Cottonwood. It is listed and mapped in the *Register*, 1902. The place, also called Point of Timbers, is historically interesting. It was known to the mission padres and is mentioned by early immigrants, wagon freighters, and other travelers on both the Santa Fe-Salt Lake Trail and the Government Road from Fort Mohave, which merged near present-day Daggett (Haenszel).

Cottonwood [Siskiyou]. At the junction of Klamath River and Cottonwood Creek. Recorded on Goddard's map, 1857. On February 4, 1850, the Cottonwood Prospecting Expedition set out from Clear Creek to a distant volcano which was supposed to be the fountainhead of gold. John S. Hittell accompanied the expedition as the "historiographer" and told the story in the *Alta* (undated clipping in Bancroft Notes). Their phantom dream did not come true, but they came upon Cottonwood Creek, which yielded richly for some time (Petty, pp. 45 ff.). According to the County History, 1881 (p. 210), a thriving camp developed in 1852 and flourished for five years as the center of mines in the vicinity. When the post office was established January 3, 1856, it was called Henley, but the name Cottonwood prevailed among the people. The later development of the district is described in detail in *Mining Bureau*, VIII (pp. 586 ff.). The mines in the Henley-Hornbrook area are described in *Siskiyou Pioneer*, II:10 (pp. 48 ff.).

Cottonwood: Creek, District [Shasta]. The Creek is a tributary to the Sacramento River and forms the southwest border of the county. There was productive mining in the past, and in the 1930s dragline and bucket-line dredges were in operation (*Bull.*, 193, pp. 134 f.). The dredging is described in *Mining Bureau*, XXXIV (pp. 114 ff.).

Coulterville [Mariposa]. On Highway 49, twenty-eight miles north of Mariposa. Recorded on Trask's map, 1853. This was one of the most important trading centers of the southern Mother Lode. It was named for George W. Coulter of Pennsylvania, who opened a trading place in a tent here in the summer of 1850, or earlier (Church, p. 183). No contemporary evidence could be found for the often repeated story that the place was first called Bandereta. Stephen Davis had a store in Coulterville from May, 1852, to April, 1854. In his interesting account of the place he tells about the opening of a large quartz mill with an 80-horse power engine in the spring of 1854 (Davis, pp. 72–96). The post office was established in 1852 as Maxwells Creek, named for Coulter's partner (*see* Maxwell Creek), but the name was changed to Coulterville in 1872. The mines in the area are described and mapped in *Mining Bureau*, LIII. Probably one of the first claims located in the 1850s was the Louisa, one quarter mile south of Coulterville. Next to Penon Blanco it is the most conspicuous vein system in the area. The main period of activity was 1894–1900, after which little sustained work was done. (*Mining Bureau*, LIII, pp. 119 f.) West of Coulterville is the Malvina Group, in which the Potosi is included. From the time of its opening in 1852 to 1942 it produced more than one million dollars (*ibid.*, pp. 123 ff.). The Tyro (Rittershoffen) Mine, adjoining the Malvina, was discovered probably in the early 1850s and was worked until the early 1900s, with little production since then (*ibid.*, pp. 175 f.). The Mary Harrison Group, one mile south of Coulterville, consisted of a large number of claims, the first of which was discovered about 1852, and operated to the early 1900s, producing a total of 1.5 million dollars (*ibid.*, pp. 130 ff.). One of the first patented claims was the Virginia Mine, four miles south of Coulterville, discovered in 1850 and worked as late as the 1950s (*Guidebook*, p. 40; *Bull.*, 153, pp. 41 f.; *Mining Bureau*, LIII, pp. 176 f.). To the northeast of Coulterville is another early mine, the Champion, which operated to 1938 (*Mining Bureau*, LIII, pp. 83 f.). Discovered later, in the late 1860s or early 1870s is the Adelaide and Anderson Mine in the southern end of the Big Bend Mountains, which was worked intermittently to the 1940s (*ibid.*, pp. 72 f.). For a listing and description of other mines, placer as well as lode, consult the *Register of Mines*, 1903; *Bulletin*, 193 (pp. 41 f.), and *Mining Bureau*, LIII. *See also* Flyaway; Penon Blanco; Maxwell Creek. Catherine Coffin has written a lengthy account in her Coulterville *Chronicle* (San Francisco, 1942). Coulterville is Historic Landmark 332.

Council Hill [Nevada]. Near Little York, or a part of it. The *Alta*, April 8, 1854, reprinted an item from the Grass Valley *Telegraph* stating that new diggings were discovered on the "celebrated" hill, and one small company took out five pounds of gold dust in a single day.

Council Hill [Sierra]. Between Scales Diggings and Brandy City, above Canyon Creek. Shown on the County Map, 1867. It is mentioned as an extensive mining locality in the 1855 *Report of the California State Surveyor General* (p. 202). In the 1870s there was hydraulic mining here, and a description of the gravel deposits is given in Whitney, *Auriferous Gravels* (pp. 453 f.).

Cove District [Kern]. Between Kernville and Isabella, on the west side of Isabella Reservoir. The deposits were discovered in 1861. A 16-stamp mill was operating in 1874 (Raymond VII, p. 49). The Big Blue Mine was the best producer but became idle in 1943. The total production of the District was estimated to have been between 5 and 8 million dollars (*Mining Bureau*, XXIX, p. 278). Big Blue Mine is shown on the USGS Kernville 1908 quadrangle.

Cow Wells [Kern]. *See* Garlock.

Cox Bar [Sierra]. On the north side of the North Fork of Yuba River, two miles west of Downieville. Recorded on Trask's map, 1853, as Cox's Bar. Downie (p. 63) mentions the place, and Pringle Shaw (p. 124) refers to it in 1856 as Coxe's Bar, a "bustling little town." Cox's Bridge is shown on Doolittle's map, 1868.

Cox Bar [Trinity]. On the south bank of Trinity River, below the original site of Big Bar. It is shown as Cox's Bar on Goddard's map, 1857. Major Isaac Cox, sometimes spelled Coxe, of Illinois, kept a store here from 1853 to 1857. In 1858, he published *The Annals of Trinity County. (CHSQ*, XXI,

127 f.) According to Robert J. Morris (*Trinity*, 1967, pp. 19, 20), the post office at the original site of Big Bar was moved to Cox's Bar but retained the name Big Bar. It is included in the present day Big Bar community along with Vances Bar, Big Flat, and Manzanita Flat.

Cox Bar [Yuba]. On the north side of the main Yuba River, below the confluence of the South Fork. Recorded on Trask's map, 1853. The name is misspelled Coy's Bar on Goddard's map, 1857. Sherman P. Sumner reports that fifteen to twenty men were employed here by one company at seven dollars per day (letter to his brother, dated September 7, 1851).

Cox Station [El Dorado]. About two miles west of Kyburz, on the Placerville-Carson Valley Road, west of Whitehall Hotel or Perrins Hotel. The *Alta*, March 29, 1854, reprints an item from the Placer *Herald* that states that new and rich diggings were reported within a mile of Cox Ranch. The *Mining Press*, May 4 and 25, 1861, reports that the discovery of a rich gold and silver lode caused a moderate rush. It may be the same place as the Cox Claim, where the "Cox pan," run by an 8-foot hurdy-gurdy, reportedly did the work of a 15-stamp mill. (Browne, pp. 83 f.) Coxes Station is mentioned in the El Dorado County Records, Mechanics Lien Book III (p. 126) and in a deed filed September 27, 1864, Deeds Book I (pp. 629 f.). Coxville is mentioned in a deed filed September 28, 1860, Book F (p. 83). (Schlappi-Ferguson.)

Coyote. The western American name for the *Canis latrans*, from Aztec *coyote*, was applied to numerous place names in the gold regions, and the term "coyoteing" was used to designate a method of placer mining by which shafts and tunnels were burrowed in the ground.

Coyote Bar [Placer]. On the North Fork of the American River. Notice of a claim here was recorded January 26, 1852, in Placer County Records, I (p. 70). It is mentioned in the County History, 1924 (p. 179), as a bar between New York Bar and Oregon Bar.

Coyote Diggings [Nevada]. *See* Coyoteville.

Coyote Diggings [Plumas]. On the North Fork of the Feather River, near The Meadows, the exact location of which could not be determined. The diggings were discovered in 1850 in connection with the Gold Lake hunt. The San Francisco *Evening Picayune*, August 31, 1850, reports that 23 thousand dollars worth of gold was taken out in two days. This may be an exaggeration, as was common in the days of the Gold Lake hunt.

Coyote Diggings [Tuolumne]. At the northwest corner of Columbia. Perkins mentions the place in 1853. *See* Los Coyotes. In many places the pay was as high as fifty to one hundred dollars per day to the man (Columbia *Gazette*, June 22, 1853).

Coyote: Gulch, Creek [Calaveras]. The Creek enters the Stanislaus River near Robinsons Ferry. There was early rich placering here. Bachman worked at this place in April, 1850, and Audubon gave a brief but interesting account dated March 23, 1850. They spelled the name Cayote and Cayute. In 1853 a Mexican company built a tunnel and sluices, and rich finds were reported. A letter from Vallecito, May 3, 1854 (Hittell Clippings, p. 21), gives a descriptive list of the various lumps and nuggets found here — probably greatly exaggerated. Borthwick, July, 1853, gives a classic description of the tunnel and of the miners. Heckendorn in 1856 (p. 104) spells the name Coyota. In 1857 it was the seat of the Italian Canal Company (Hittell Clippings, p. 48). Shown on the USGS Big Trees 1941 quadrangle.

Coyote Hill [Nevada]. On the Coyote Lead and now a part of Nevada City. In March of 1850, a ditch was built from Mosquito Creek to supply the long toms with water, and in September, 1850 a longer ditch was built from Rock Creek (Brown, *Directory*, 1856, pp. 10, 11). These ditches doubtless

also supplied the water for Coyote Diggings and Coyoteville. According to the *Guidebook* (p. 31), the ditch from Mosquito Creek is claimed to have been the first mining ditch in California to supply water for the miners' long toms. *See* Coyoteville [Nevada].

Coyoteville [El Dorado]. Between Bridgeport and Cedarville. On the North Fork of Cedar Creek, tributary to the South Fork of Cosumnes River. Shown on Doolittle's map, 1868, and on the USGS Placerville 1931 quadrangle.

Coyoteville [Nevada]. Northwest of Nevada City and now a part of it. It is situated at the end of the famous rich Coyote Lead, one mile long and 100 yards wide, which was struck in May, 1850, and was said to have produced 8 million dollars by 1856 (Brown, *Directory*, 1856, pp. 21 f; Bancroft Notes). Peter Decker in his diary of September 25, 1850, mentions that the town called "Kiotaville," was laid out on Buckeye Hill. The "Kiota Diggins" near which Alex Barrington worked with success in the summer of 1850 were probably at or near the same place (*Miscellany*, pp. 5 f.). The U. S. Bureau of the Census lists 168 inhabitants for "Coyota City" in the population schedule for the 1850 census. Brown and Dallison's *Directory* lists it as a separate camp in 1856, but it later became a part of Nevada City. The name was derived from the method of mining termed "coyoteing," likened to the burrowing of the prairie wolf, called coyote in the West. An interesting description of the method

Coyote Diggings. Location not determined.

is given by Lorenzo Sawyer (pp. 118 ff.) in a letter datelined Nevada City, November 25, 1850. He found the "Cayote diggings of great extent" on the hills around the city. At the foot of the hill the shafts were sunk only six or eight feet deep, but as they ascended the hill they had to be sunk deeper, sometimes as much as 100 feet. When bedrock was reached the miner worked on hands and knees in each direction to the extent of his 30-foot claim, brought the dirt to the surface by means of a windlass, and hauled it one-half to one and a half miles to Deer Creek to be washed. Sawyer was told that not more than one in fifteen or twenty shafts paid, but occasionally one turned out a fortune. Another early description of "coyoteing" may be found in the Sacramento *Transcript*, steamer ed. January 14, 1851. *See* Coyote Hill.

Coyoteville [Sierra]. One mile west of Downieville on the North Fork of Yuba River. Shown on the County Map, 1874. The camp was founded in 1850, and in 1852 the diggings were reported as doing well, according to the *Mountain Echo*, September 20, 1852 (Sinnott, *Downieville*, p. 145). The name is retained in a motel-type settlement on Highway 49 (R. Drury).

Coys Bar [Yuba]. *See* Cox Bar.

Crab Hollow Diggings [Los Angeles]. At the headwaters of the East Fork of San Gabriel River. The Los Angeles *Star*, September 21, 1854 (Hayes Scrapbooks: Mining, V, sec. 143) reports the excitement caused by the discovery of new diggings here. This was the site of the original discovery of gold on the East Fork of San Gabriel River (J. W. Robinson). *See* San Gabriel: Canyon, River.

Crackerjack [San Bernardino]. In the Avawatz Mountains, about twenty-five miles northwest of Baker. It was a short-lived gold town mentioned repeatedly in the *Death Valley Chuck Walla*, 1907. This was just before the 1907 financial panic, which ended its life. Supplies were brought from Silver Lake by motor stages (Belden, January 24 and June 21, 1961). There was a post office in 1907–1908.

Craggs Flat [Sierra]. *See* Craigs Flat.

Craigs Creek [Del Norte]. Southwest of Gasquet. Bars, including Hueniche, were worked by ground sluicing with cradle and rocker in the 1890s (*Mining Bureau*, XIII, p. 129) and are still listed in 1952.

Craigs Flat [Sierra]. Near Canyon Creek, northwest of Downieville. Situated on the branch of the main Blue Lead (Browne, p.

138). Recorded as Craigs on Goddard's map, 1857; also shown on the County Map, 1874. The *Alta*, December 30, 1853, reported mining here as "very dull." The place is mentioned by John Clark in his guide, January 3 and May 20, 1853; by M. Thomson as Craigs Diggings in 1855 (p. 16); in *Transactions*, 1858 (p. 197); by Vischer (spelled Craggs Flat) in 1859 (p. 240). According to a clipping from the Sacramento *Daily Union*, July 1, 1856, this mining locality had been monopolized by a single company, which had nearly mined out the whole area, and only a few miners were living there at that time.

Cranes Gulch [El Dorado]. South of Georgetown. Crane's Gulch Ditch and Mine are shown on Bowman's map, 1873. The "district" is mentioned in 1875. The Whiteside Mine took out 100 thousand dollars from a pit seventy feet deep (Raymond, VII, pp. 77, 84). W. A. Goodyear, in 1871, describes the seam diggings on a hill at the head of the Gulch, from which gold was obtained from the quartz by blasting, sluicing, and by using the hydraulic process (Whitney, *Auriferous Gravels*, p. 116). A Cranes Gulch Mine is listed in the Mining Bureau reports until 1938.

Crane Valley [Butte]. Successful mining was reported in May, 1858 (Hittell Clippings, p. 54). According to the County History, 1882 (p. 253), the camp was extinct in 1880.

Cranwells Bar [Placer]. On the American River. The place is unidentified, but a picture of it as a large camp in 1856 was published in Nadeau's *Ghost Towns*.

Crater City [Amador]. *See* Volcano.

Crater Hill [Placer]. A few miles west of Auburn. In 1870 there was a 20-stamp steam-driven mill here (*Annual Mining Review*, 1876, p. 23). The place is mentioned in a notice of a claim recorded October 4, 1851 (Placer County Records, I, p. 7).

Craycroft [Sierra]. Between Downieville and Goodyears Bar. M. Thomson (p. 21) called it a "new place" in 1856. It is listed in Hittell's roster. Pettee described the gravel deposits here and the tunnel work carried on in one of the mines he visited in 1879. Good pay was also found high on the rimrock where the gravel was only two to three feet deep. (Whitney, *Auriferous Gravels*, pp. 465 f.) A mine is listed in the Mining Bureau reports until 1942.

Crazy Gulch [Tuolumne]. Apparently near Jacksonville. According to Mulford, a San

Francisco company had bought the Crazy Gulch quartz lead and intended to build a 10-stamp mill (*Prentice Mulford's Story*, 1913 ed., p. 24).

Creek Bar [Siskiyou]. On the Klamath River, below Scotts Bar (Bancroft Notes).

Crees Flat [Placer]. On the road between Auburn and Ophir. According to the County History, 1882 (p. 227), a nugget of pure gold worth 110 dollars was found in December, 1855.

Crescent City [Del Norte]. Gold has been mined mostly on a small scale on the beaches south of Crescent City since the 1850s. In the 1890s and again in 1913/14 several large operations were attempted without success. Most of the gold was probably washed down from the Smith River to the north and the Klamath River to the south. (*Bull.*, 193, p. 178.)

Crescent City [Stanislaus]. On the south bank of Tuolumne River, two miles below Empire City. Shown on Butler's map, 1851. It was a short-lived town on the way to the Southern Mines, at the site of Ripperdan's ranch (Stoddart, p. 107).

Crescent Mills [Plumas]. On Indian Creek, southeast of Lake Almanor. The deposits yielded moderately but steadily. In 1868 there was one 32- and one 24-stamp mill. A detailed description is given by Browne (pp. 168 f.). A post office was established July 14, 1870, and the place remained the trading center for a number of quartz mines of Indian Valley. The *Register* of 1900 still lists two mills with 35 stamps. The production of the district is estimated at almost 7 million dollars (*Mining Bureau*, XVI [Plumas], pp. 4 ff). The most productive mines were the Crescent, 500 thousand dollars; the Green Mountain, between one and two million; and the Indian Valley, 1.8 million (*Bull.*, 193, p. 42). *See* Green Mountain.

Croesus [Placer]. On October 24, 1851 a company of thirty-nine men organized for the purpose of quartz mining here (Placer County Records, I, p. 37). The location is undetermined.

Cromberg [Plumas]. On the Middle Fork of Feather River, about ten miles north of Johnsville. The Americanized form of the German name Krumberg, 'curved mountain', was applied to the old Twenty-Mile House when the post office was established on March 10, 1880. It became the trading center for drift and hydraulic mines in the area (*Register*, 1900).

Crooked Bar [Plumas]. On the Middle Fork

of the Feather River. Listed in the Giffen file.

Crow City [Sierra]. *See* Jim Crow Ravine.

Crows Bar [Trinity]. Opposite the junction of Trinity River and Rush Creek. Listed by Cox (p. 27).

Crows Flat [Placer]. Notice of the sale of a water ditch from Miners Ravine to Crows Flat and Taylors Ravine was given by the owner, William George of Secret Ravine, and recorded April 8, 1854, in Placer County Records, I (p. 227).

Cruce del Pino [Tuolumne]. The place is mentioned by W. P. Perkins (p. 85). Apparently it is the same as Pine Log Crossing.

Crumbecker Ravine [Nevada]. A branch of Scotchman Creek, just below Alpha. It was named for the first man to mine there in 1850, who reportedly took out 100 thousand dollars in one season and then returned to his home in Kentucky (Nevada City *Transcript*, 1891). The place is listed as Crumbeck Ravine in Hittell's roster (*Mining Bureau*, IV, p. 220).

Crusen Mine [El Dorado]. *See* Oak Ranch.

Crystal Mine [El Dorado]. *See* Shingle Springs.

Crystal Peak [Sierra]. It is mentioned as a town or precinct in *Illustrated Spirits*, December 25, 1877 (Bancroft Scraps V, pp. 1803 f.).

Crystal Springs [Tuolumne]. Three miles southwest of Columbia. Productive placering was reported in the 1850s and 1860s. There were several later attempts to open the mines (*Mining Bureau*, XLV, p. 62). Shown on the USGS Columbia 1948 quadrangle.

Culbertsons Station [Nevada]. On the South Yuba River, above Washington and Doolittle's suspension bridge. James Culbertson built a bridge here, according to the County History, 1880 (p. 132).

Culloma, Cullumah [El Dorado]. *See* Coloma.

Cumberland Ravine [Sierra]. The location was not determined. In 1858 there were three "very fine" claims in the Ravine (unidentified clipping). The *Mining Press*, August 10, 1861, reports the finding of a 37-pound lump of gold and quartz. On May 16, 1862, the same periodical mentions that the claims were still paying well.

Cunningham Rancho [Mariposa]. Near Princeton. According to Bancroft, VI, (p. 378), it was a gold producing place in 1854.

Curley Flat [Butte]. Apparently in the vicinity of Stringtown and named for a miner

Cuyamaca, San Diego Co.

from there. Asa B. Smith mentions the place in a letter datelined McCabe Creek, October 29, 1858; and in a letter of May 1, 1859, he reports that the miners were making five to six dollars a day per hand washing the tailings from the Flat.

Curtis Creek, Curtisville [Tuolumne]. The creek is a tributary to Woods Creek, south of Sonora. Recorded on Gibbes', 1851, and Trask's, 1853 maps. Derby's map of 1849 (*Sketch* 2) shows a place "Curtis" ten miles *north* of Sonoran Camp. In November, 1849, Benjamin Harris found "the richest mine I ever owned" on a bar on Curtis Creek (*The Gila Trail*, p. 124). Daniel Woods and partners mined at the creek with moderate success in January and February, 1850, and Woods gives an interesting account (pp. 97–113). In April, 1851, the U. S. Bureau of the Census listed 294 inhabitants in the population schedule for the 1850 census. The *Alta* of March 1, 1853, as quoted in Bancroft, VI (p. 375), reported that some Mexicans, who had struck a vein of decomposed quartz near Curtisville frequently obtained 10 thousand dollars a day (!). Curtisville had a post office, 1853–1856. In 1856 the town could still support two butchers and one lawyer (Heckendorn, p. 89). The town has disappeared, but the creek is shown on the USGS Sonora 1939 quadrangle.

Cushenbury City [San Bernardino]. Six miles east of Holcomb Valley, along the road to the desert. The location is indicated on Crowell's map, 1903. The short-

lived "city" was laid out and named for John Cushenbury. It is mentioned in the Los Angeles *Star*, April 20, 1861, and also in the *Mining Press*, April 27, 1861, where it is stated that it probably petered out for lack of water. The site was doubtless near the present-day Permanente Cement Plant near Cushenbury Springs (La Fuze, I, pp. 59, 61, and note 28). The name is sometimes spelled Cushionberry.

Cut-eye Fosters: Bar, Camp [Sierra]. On the North Fork of Yuba River, below Goodyears Bar. Shown on Trask's 1853, Goddard's 1857, and Wescoatt's 1861 maps but not exactly in the same location. According to the County History, 1882 (p. 421), Foster was reputedly a professional horse thief, who employed a number of Indians to carry on his business. Downie describes him as philanthropic but dishonest. Newton Miller mined at the place from January, 1851, to July, 1852, and he gives a good description in his letters. In July, 1851, he built a wing dam with his partners, and the prospects were "too good to believe." The place is still shown on the USGS Strawberry Valley 1950 quadrangle and on the *Guidebook* map 9. The name Upper Fosters Bar may have been used to distinguish Cut-eye Fosters Bar from the well-known Fosters Bar. *See* Fosters Bar; Fosters Lower Bar.

Cut-Throat Bar [Sierra]. On the North Fork of Yuba River, west of Goodyears Bar. It was so named because a sick German miner had cut his own throat here (Co. Hist., 1882, p. 466). The place was later called Woodville Bar.

Cut-throat Gulch [Trinity]. About 1860, a Chinese prospector called "Blind Lee" was found here with his throat cut because it was thought that he had struck it rich (*California Place Names*).

Cuyamaca District [San Diego]. The Julian District is called Cuyamaca District in early reports of the Mining Bureau. In later reports it refers to the district south of the Julian-Banner District. *See* Stonewall Mine.

D**ads Gulch** [Yuba]. On the North Fork of Yuba River, north of Camptonville and Youngs Hill. The place is often mentioned by De Long, who spells the name Dadd. According to the County History, 1879 (p. 100), a Mr. Parsons, known as Dad, discovered gold here in 1851. The diggings were very rich and were still being worked in 1879. William Bull Meek mentions the place in his "Reminiscences" (p. 140).

Daggett [San Bernardino]. East of Barstow. It was not a gold town but a supply point on the Santa Fe main line for the many mines in the Calico Hills and surrounding area and the terminus for three short railroads built to haul the ore. In 1885 a 5-stamp custom mill for gold and silver was in operation (*Mining Bureau*, IX, p. 238), and later a second mill was built (Haenszel). The place was named for John Daggett, lieutenant governor of California, 1883–1887, who mapped the town and built the first house. *See* Waterman.

Dahlonegha [Kern]. The name was used for a mining district on the upper Kern River, according to Boyd (p. 43). It was probably named for a miner, or miners, who came from Dahlonegha, Lumpkin County, Georgia, where there was a gold rush in the 1830s.

Dale: District, town [San Bernardino, Riverside]. The district is in and near the northern and eastern part of Pinto Mountains. It includes Old Dale, about fifteen miles east of Twentynine Palms; New Dale, eight miles southeast of Old Dale; and numerous mines in the northern and eastern part of Pinto Mountains. Placer gold was first discovered in the early 1880s at Burt's (now Dale) Dry Lake. A well was dug and an arrastre built to mill the cemented gravel. The settlement which developed was called Virginia Dale, later

abbreviated to Dale, and in its heyday it reportedly had a population of 1,000. As placering gave out and quartz mines were discovered in the Pinto Mountains, the miners moved closer to them, and a new town called New Dale replaced Old Dale. By 1915 Old Dale had almost disappeared. The sites of both places are still shown on modern maps, including the current map of the Automobile Club of Southern California. Detailed accounts are given by Belden, June 23, 1957, and by R. D. Miller (pp. 13 ff.). The Virginia Dale, named after the town, was the first quartz mine located in the district, and it operated intermittently from about 1886 to the 1930s. The Supply Group was the most extensive, having produced about one million dollars by 1942. The Brooklyn Mine, on the border between the two counties, was discovered in 1893 and operated to 1930. These and other mines are listed and described in *Mining Bureau*, XXVII (pp. 289, 319) and XLIX (pp. 69 ff.).

Damascus [Placer]. On Humbug Creek, tributary to the North Fork of American River; about five miles southeast of Dutch Flat. Shown on Doolittle's map, 1868. According to the County History, 1882 (p. 377), it was founded in 1852 by Dr. D. W. Strong and was first called Strongs Diggings. Strongs Ravine marked the site of a claim for which notice was recorded on April 18, 1852 (Placer County Records, I, p. 86). When the post office was established November 15, 1856, it was named, like several other American places, after the ancient Arabic city. In 1855 a steam-driven mill with 10-stamps and two arrastres was built at the Damascus Mine (*State Register*, 1859). This mine, like the Mountain Gate and the Hidden Treasure, was a drift mine in the gravels of the Tertiary river channel. The Hidden Treasure was noted for its huge masses of quartz. (Gianella.) Browne in 1869 gives a detailed description of the Mountain Gate (pp. 99 f.) and another good description is given in 1882 in *Mining Bureau*, IV (part 2, pp. 183 f.). It was a cooperative, and during the twenty years it had been operating it yielded about 1.5 million dollars, forty percent of which was disbursed as dividends. Activities in the late 1880s are described in *Mining Bureau*, VIII (pp. 468 f.). The Damascus district, which includes the lode mines in the Pioneer-Humbug area in the north and the placer mines from Damascus to the Gas Hill area toward the south, is described in *Bulletin*,

193 (p. 43). The total production of the district was more than 12 million dollars for the drift mines and several millions more for the lode mines. The Pioneer is listed in *Bulletin*, 193 as the most productive lode mine, with a yield of one million dollars, and the Hidden Treasure the most productive placer mine with a production of 4 million dollars. Mining in the district continued intermittently until the 1930s with some prospecting in recent years. Damascus is shown on the USGS Colfax 1938 quadrangle.

Damnation Flat. An unidentified locality, listed in the Work Projects Administration project.

Dana Diggings [Placer]. The place is mentioned in a notice of a claim to the right to supply Dana Diggings with water conveyed through a flume from Dry Creek, recorded October 29, 1855 (Placer County Records, I, p. 313).

Dana Village [Mono]. In the Tioga District, on the mountain above the Sheepherder Tunnel. There was a small settlement here between 1879 and 1884. A fine stone cabin and ruins of other buildings still remain. It was named for its spectacular view of Mount Dana. (F. S. Wedertz.)

Danby [San Bernardino]. Near Highway 66. It was a trading center and post office (1898–1913) for the mines in the Old Woman Mountains to the south (*Register*, 1902).

Dan Cole [Sierra]. At the junction of Henness Pass Road and the road to Downieville. Shown on the County Map, 1874. There was a saw mill here which supplied lumber for the mines near the Mountain House area (R. Drury).

Darby Flat [Placer]. A notice of the sale of claims on Darby Flat in the Lone Star District, datelined Dry Creek, December 13, 1869, is listed in Placer County Records, V (p. 411).

Dardannelles Diggings [Placer]. On the Blue Lead, two miles east of Yankee Jims. Operations began in 1854, when the Crimean War made the name of the narrows between Europe and Asia Minor known everywhere. The four-mile long tunnels made the claim one of the best paying in the county. According to *Transactions*, 1858 (p. 298), twenty-four men took out 19 thousand dollars in one day, and a newspaper reported in January, 1856, that the yield of five and a half days washing was 334 ounces (Co. Hist., 1882, p. 221). In later years there was mainly hydraulic mining. The Dardanelles placer mine

yielded more than 2 million dollars (*Bull.*, 193, p. 50).

Dark Canyon [Butte]. In Concow township, north of Oroville. It was a transient, flourishing mining camp (Co. Hist., 1882, p. 253.)

Darlings Hill [Nevada]. Northeast of Red Dog; near Chalk Bluff Ridge. The extent of hydraulic mining is shown on Pettee and Bowman's map, 1879. The area is described by Pettee in Whitney, *Auriferous Gravels* (p. 170).

Darlings Ranch [El Dorado]. In the Hornblende Mountains north of Georgetown. Shown on Doolittle's map, 1868. In 1871 Raymond (IV, p. 105) reports rich gravel and lack of water. The Darling Mine, listed in the Mining Bureau reports until 1956, is in the Slate Mountains, northeast of Kelsey, and was active in the 1890s.

Darwin: town, District [Inyo]. Named for Dr. Darwin French, who led an expedition in search of the lost Gunsight Lode in 1860. The town served as the trading center and post office (established in 1875) for the silver, lead, and gold mines between the Coso and Argus ranges. The mines are listed and mapped in *Register*, 1902. The district produced large amounts of silver but only little gold.

Datons Bar [Placer]. *See* Dotans Bar.

Davis Ferry [Stanislaus]. On the Tuolumne River, between Empire City and Dickensons Ferry, on the way to the Southern Mines. Shown on Goddard's map, 1857.

Davis Flat [Tuolumne]. Near Confidence. The place is mentioned as "exceedingly rich" in *Mining Press*, June 6, 1862, and again in 1899 in *Mines and Minerals* (p. 358) as very rich.

Dawlytown [Butte]. On the Middle Fork of the Feather River, at the lower end of Bidwell Bar. Named for a Mr. Dawly, who had a store here in the summer of 1849. Delano and his party arrived October 10, 1850, and opened a store nearby (Delano, *Life*, p. 255, pp. 272 ff.).

Day Bar [Placer]. On the North Fork of American River, above Dead Mans Bar. The boundary of a claim here was recorded November 23, 1852, in Placer County Records, I (p. 157).

Daylors [Sacramento]. On the road to Jackson, at or near the crossing of Cosumnes River. Recorded on Judah's map, 1854, and on Goddard's, 1857. It was also known as Daylors Ranch. Dayler's Ferry is indicated on Trask's map, 1853. The place was on the Omuchumnes (Omochumnes) or Cosumnes rancho, granted in 1844 to Jared Sheldon, the partner of William Daylor, an English sailor who was a fellow worker employed by Sutter in 1840–1841 (Grimshaw, *Biographical Notes*) and who later became a brother-in-law of Sheldon. A post office established June 21, 1852 as Cosumne was moved to nearby Sloughhouse April 15, 1915.

Daytons Bar [Placer]. *See* Dotans Bar.

Dead Horse; Dead Mule Unidentified mining localities, listed in Hittell, *Resources*.

Dead Man's Bar [Placer]. On the North Fork of American River near Auburn. Shown on Trask's map, 1853, and Goddard's map, 1857. It was first called Neptunes Bar because it was worked mainly by sailors (Letts, p. 114). According to the Sacramento *Transcript*, April 26, 1850 (Bancroft Notes), Oregonians were working there when a party of Buckeye men also claimed the right to mine there, whereupon a fight ensued and the captain of the Oregonians was accidentally killed. Both parties then worked together peacefully and named the place Dead Man's Bar.

Dead Mans Bar [Tuolumne]. On the south side of Stanislaus River, just below Parrot's Ferry bridge. It is listed in the Giffen file. Shown on the USGS Columbia 1949 quadrangle as Deadman Bar.

Deadmans Cut [Nevada]. North of North San Juan. Three "Yankee Boys" from French Corral had cut twenty feet deep into a hill, when a cave-in killed them instantly (McKeeby, pp. 144 f; *Transactions*, 1858, p. 178). According to Vischer, it was the best known claim in the region.

Dead Mans Flat [Amador]. On Dead Man Creek, tributary to Dry Creek; northwest of Volcano. Ben Bowen lived here in September, 1854. The place was so named because three dead men were found here. The stream is shown on the County Map, 1866, and on the USGS Jackson 1938 quadrangle.

Deadmans Flat [Nevada]. An uncertain location, mentioned in the *Mining Press*, September 24, 1891 and February 13, 1892 (Foley).

Dead Mans Gulch [Plumas]. A tributary to the Middle Fork of Feather River. The place is listed in the Giffen file.

Dead Mans Gulch [Tuolumne]. West of Columbia, near Dead Mans Bar. The *Alta*, March 16, 1853, reprints an item stating that the miners made only average wages. The place is mentioned in the mining laws of Columbia District (Heckendorn, p. 9).

Shown on the USGS Columbia 1949 quadrangle as Deadman Gulch.

Dead Mans Hill [Calaveras]. Gold was discovered on or near Mountain Ranch before 1861, and the dirt paid up to twenty-five cents a bucket (*Mining Press*, February 22, 1861).

Dead Mans Hollow [El Dorado]. Near El Dorado. The place is mentioned by E. D. Perkins on Christmas day, 1849. It was named "for a couple of men having been murdered here for their gold past summer." The camp is mentioned again by Crockett in 1854. In 1857 there was a steam-driven mill with two stamps and two arrastres (*State Register*, 1859).

Dead Shot Flat. An unidentified camp, listed in Hittell, *Resources*.

Deadwood. A California slang word for "sure thing." Some of the mining localities might have been named in the literal sense.

Deadwood [Nevada]. On the Deadwood Ledge, two and a half miles from Nevada City. The place was located in 1856, and it is listed as a settlement in *Bean's Directory*, 1867.

Deadwood [Placer]. The Deadwood District included quartz, drift, and placer mines on Deadwood Ridge, Indian Creek, and the North Fork of the Middle Fork of the American River (*Mining Bureau*, XV, p. 317). Deadwood is shown on Goddard's map, 1857. Rich deposits were discovered in 1852, according to the *Directory* of Placer County, 1861 (Bancroft Notes). The County History, 1882 (p. 379), states that the place must have had between 500 and 600 inhabitants in its heyday, but by 1855 the glory had passed. In 1899 there was still a Herman mill with ten stamps in operation. The site of Deadwood is shown on the USGS Duncan Peak 1952 quadrangle.

Deadwood [Plumas]. About one and a half miles southeast of Spanish Peak. It is listed among placer mining localities in the vicinity that produced well in the early days of surface mining and were still yielding profitably in 1875 (Raymond, V, p. 115).

Deadwood [Sierra]. On the ridge between the North Fork of the North Fork of Yuba River and Canyon Creek. It is apparently the camp recorded on Trask's map, 1853. Shown on Crossman's map, 1867, and the County Map, 1874. M. Thomson (p. 15) mentions the place in 1856. Browne (p. 138) states that it was on the Blue Lead and was still flourishing in 1868, but the same authority (p. 141) reports that an investment of 115 thousand dollars yielded only 10 thousand dollars. The place is shown on the USGS Downieville 1907 quadrangle. A mine is listed in the Mining Bureau reports until 1941.

Deadwood [Siskiyou]. About ten miles north of Fort Jones. Shown on Goddard's map, 1857. Gold mining began in 1851, and in the spring of 1852 there were already more than 100 voters in the precinct. In 1854 McAdams (of McAdams Creek) discovered rich deposits just below the camp, and the place became second in importance to Yreka, according to the County History, 1881 (pp. 215 f.). Newspapers of the day reported "flattering prospects." Brewer (October 21, 1863) calls it "a busy little mining town." It is not certain whether it is the place that had a mine in operation in 1893 (*Mining Bureau*, XI, p. 446) and that was listed as a town in the *Register* of 1898 as "Old" Deadwood. The district was highly productive in placer gold and was later dredged (*Bull.*, 193, p. 135). W. M. Smith states that there are also several underground mines in the area.

Deadwood Creek [Yuba]. A tributary to the North Fork of the Yuba River, which has its source near Strawberry Valley. There was some gold mining in Rich, Kentucky, and Whiskey gulches along the creek in the early 1850s (Co. Hist. and County Map, 1879). Lecouvreur mentions Deadwood House, June, 1852, between Strawberry Valley and Grass Valley. Deadwood Mill is shown on the Creek southeast of Eagleville on Wescoatt's map, 1861. The Creek is shown on the USGS Bidwell Bar 1944 quadrangle.

Deadwood: Creek, District [Trinity]. The creek is a tributary to Trinity River, eight miles east of Weaverville. The deposits were discovered in 1851 but could not be exploited systematically because of Indian hostility, caused by the cruelty of the white man. (Cox, p. 25.) Later the district became a rich producer, and Deadwood was an important trading center. For a list of the mines and a map, see *Register*, 1898, and *Mining Bureau*, XXIX (p. 5–73). Brown Bear Mine, on Deadwood Creek, four miles northeast of Lewiston, was discovered in 1875 and was active intermittently until 1950 (*County Report*, IV, pp. 22 f.). The yield was reportedly between 7 and 10 million dollars.

Death Valley National Monument. Gold has been discovered, or said to have been discovered, at various times since 1849. The literature about the gold finds and lost mines is extensive but of very uneven value. L. Burr Belden's *Mines of Death Valley* and Harold O. Weight's *Lost Mines of Death Valley* are two of the interesting recent contributions. All important places where gold was found, or allegedly found, are treated separately in this book. *See* especially Breyfogle, Gunsight Lead, Goler Mine, Harrisburg.

Dedrick [Trinity]. On Canyon Creek, northwest of Weaverville. The place served as a trading center for the mines between the Trinity Alps and Trinity River. From 1891 to 1941 it had a post office. In 1898 there were three Huntington mills, one canon ball mill, and one arrastre in operation (*Register*, 1898). Mining in Dedrick District had developed in the 1880s and 1890s and activity continued until the 1930s, according to *Bulletin*, 193 (p. 135).

Deep Ravine [El Dorado]. The diggings were two miles from Kelsey. Drift mining yielded fair returns in 1851–52. According to William F. Reed's journal, the name was chosen at a meeting held October 14, 1851, by fifty claim holders.

Deer Creek [El Dorado, Sacramento]. In the western part of El Dorado County and the eastern part of Sacramento County. It parallels the Cosumnes River about a half mile to the north. The creek was first mined in the Gold Rush, and in the 1930s and early 1940s there was considerable dredging (*Bull.*, 193, p. 43).

Deer Creek [Nevada]. The important tributary to Yuba River was named in August, 1849, when a party had to abandon a freshly killed deer here (*California Place Names*). It became one of the best known minor streams of the gold region. The camps along the creek are often confused. James Marshall is said to have camped on the creek at the site of what later became Nevada City, while escorting a party of emigrants, and successfully panned for gold on several occasions (Lindgren, *Gold-Quartz Veins*, p. 17).

Deer Creek [Tehama]. A tributary to the Sacramento River. Bruff, in his journal entry of April 14, 1850 (II, p. 881), reports that he had found some gold here.

Deer Creek Crossing [Nevada]. This is a vanished camp about three miles from the junction of Deer Creek and Yuba River. Shown on Milleson and Adams' map, 1851. A. J. McCall, on November 24, 1849, gives a description of the camp and states that an enterprising individual had put up a shanty and opened a store there. De Long mentions the Anthony House, about four miles from the confluence, as shown on the USGS Smartsville 1943 quadrangle. It might have been the original camp and crossing. According to an item in the *Mining Press*, October 7, 1862, the claims (or most of them) were abandoned in 1856, but in 1862, the miners again averaged ten dollars profit a day.

Deer Creek Dry Diggings [Nevada]. *See* Nevada City.

Deer: Creek, Flat [Tuolumne]. West of Groveland. The Creek heads in the flat. The "Mountaineer," writing in 'the *San Joaquin Republican* of December 16, 1851, reports that lack of water prevented mining in Deer Flat, in which gold was in abundance. Carlo M. De Ferrari states that his grandfather and two brothers took out more than 10 thousand dollars in ground sluicing at Deer Flat. The *Annual Mining Review*, 1876 (p. 21), lists a 5-stamp steam-driven mill erected in 1865. The total gold production of Deer Creek, Big Oak Flat, and Groveland together is estimated at 25 million dollars (*Guidebook*, p. 47). Deer Creek and Deer Flat are shown on the USGS Sonora 1939 quadrangle.

Deer Park District [San Diego]. About six miles southeast of Cuyamaca Rancho State Park. It is listed in *Bulletin*, 193 (p. 171) as a district in which gold has been recovered in minor amounts from narrow quartz veins.

Deer Valley [El Dorado]. About ten miles northwest of Shingle Springs. It is a small lode gold mining district worked during the Gold Rush and prospected intermittently since then (*Bull.*, 193, p. 43).

Defender [Amador]. On the north side of Mokelumne River, near Contreras. The mine was one of the richest in the county, and it had a 10-stamp mill (*Register*, 1903). There was a post office from 1900 to 1915. The mine was still in operation in 1926 (*Mining Bureau*, XXIII, p. 164).

Deidesheimer [Placer]. Near Forest Hill, on the Blue Lead. By 1865 the diggings had yielded as much as 650 thousand dollars. Some of the boulders taken out contained 3,000 to 5,000 dollars worth of gold each (*Transactions*, 1860). The principal owner, Philip Deidesheimer, was a former student at the University of Heidelberg, Germany, and a well known mining engineer. He later went to Washoe, and his invention of "timbering" was used in the building of the Comstock mines (*CHSQ*, II, p. 206).

Delamar [Shasta]. The mining town was named in 1900 for J. H. Delamar, owner of the Bully Hill mines (*California Place Names*).

Delhi Mine [Nevada]. *See* North Columbia.

Delirium Tremens [Nevada]. *See* Alpha, Omega.

Delta [Shasta]. The place was so named because the level land at the top of the hill at the intersection of the Sacramento River with Dog Creek formed the shape of the Greek letter *delta*. No early mining records were found, but there were several stamp mills and arrastres along Dog Creek (*Register*, 1902), and the place had a post office between 1875 and 1880. Mines in the district are listed in the Mining Bureau reports until 1939.

Democrat Gulch [Trinity]. On Weaver Creek. Mentioned by Cox (p. 131) in 1858. A group of hydraulic mines were in operation in the 1930s (*Mining Bureau*, XXIX, p. 20). A correspondent to the *Trinity Journal*, February 10, 1860, gives a glowing account of mining at Galena Flat, Democrat Gulch.

Democrat Hill [Nevada]. Northwest of Dutch Flat. There was drifting in the 1870s and hydraulic mining where not prevented by overlying cemented lava (Raymond, VI, p. 117).

Dempster Gulch [Yuba]. Between the North and Middle forks of Yuba River. The place is mentioned in the County History, 1879 (p. 100).

Denny [Trinity]. *See* New River.

Dents Bar [Tuolumne]. Shown on Trask's map, 1853, on Stanislaus River and north of Montezuma. De Ferrari states that John Dent mined at Woods Diggings and Montezuma, and Dent's Tent is mentioned in at least one letter written from Woods Diggings in August, 1849, but the exact site of Dents Bar is undetermined. It is mentioned in the *Golden Era*, May, 1873.

Dents Ferry [Stanislaus]. The crossing over the Stanislaus River on the road from Stockton to the mines was a popular stopping place. William Perkins stayed here overnight, March 26, 1852 (p. 314). At that time it was called Dentville for John C. and Lewis Dent, who operated the ferry. *See* Knights Ferry.

Dents Ranch [Amador]. Four miles north of Volcano. Shown on the County Map, 1866. The place is often mentioned in Ben Bowen's diary, 1854–1859.

Dentville [Stanislaus]. *See* Dents Ferry, Knights Ferry.

Depot Camp [Plumas]. In the valley of the North Fork of Feather River. It was the base of Lassen's and other parties during the Gold Lake hunt. Bruff frequently mentions the place.

Depot Hill [Yuba]. Two miles north of Camptonville. Shown on Doolittle's map, 1868. De Long mentions the place, September 12, 1856. The Depot Hill hydraulic mine operated as early as 1855 and was worked every season when water was available, according to the owner in 1941. It was apparently the oldest operating hydraulic mine in the state at that time. The estimated production before 1927 was 1.25 million dollars or more. (*Mining Bureau*, XXXVIII, pp. 24 f.). The mine is still listed in 1952. *See* Jouberts Diggings.

Derbec Mine [Nevada]. *See* North Bloomfield.

Descanso [San Diego]. On Highway 80, south of Julian District. The name is the Spanish word for 'rest', 'repose', and apparently goes back to mission days. The post office was established in 1877. The gold mines of the district in 1900 are listed and mapped in the *Register*, 1902. Included are the Cascade, Free Coinage, and Independence.

Desert Lake [San Bernardino]. East of Ivanpah Dry Lake, near the Nevada state line. It is one of the few dry lakes of California which were successfully dredged, reportedly yielding twenty cents worth of gold per cubic yard. The Desert Gold Placers were reported idle in 1931 (*Mining Bureau*, XXVII, p. 293).

Devils Basin [Placer]. Northeast of Deadwood. In 1857 a steam-driven mill with two stamps and one arrastre was built (*State Register*, 1859). The consolidated claims of the diggings are listed in *Mining Bureau*, XV (p. 355). It is shown on Doolittle's map, 1868, along with Devils Throne and Hells Delight on the North Fork of the Middle Fork of American River. It is also shown, with nearby Devils Thumb, on the USGS Duncan Peak 1952 quadrangle.

Devils Elbow. An unidentified place, listed in the State Library Roster.

Devils Gate [Sierra]. Near Saint Louis. A lead seven to ten feet wide was struck in November, 1860 (*Mining Press*, December 7, 1860).

Devine Gulch [El Dorado]. Between Georgia Slide and Georgetown. According to Warren T. Russell (*Chispas*, pp. 213 ff.), the gulch was named for Caleb Devine, who discovered gold there in 1850. In 1892 a farmer found by accident a rich placer deposit in an abandoned miner's reservoir in the gulch and was reported to have taken out 10 thousand dollars in a short time.

Diamond Bar [Calaveras]. On the Mokelumne River, about seven miles west of Mokelumne Hill. It is shown on the Amador County Map, 1866.

Diamond Creek [Nevada]. A tributary to the South Fork of the Yuba River, east of Washington. Diamond Creek Diggings are shown on Doolittle's map, 1868. It is listed as a settlement by Bean, 1867 (p. 386). In the same year several companies were at work, with one claim yielding forty-four dollars per ton, according to a clipping from the Nevada *Transcript*, December 14, 1867 (Hayes Scrapbooks: Mining, IV, sec. 42). The consolidated mines at this place are listed in *Mining Bureau*, XIII (p. 241) and subsequent reports.

Diamond Mountain District [Lassen]. In the southern part of the county, about five miles south of Susanville. Placer mining began in the late 1850s and was followed by lode mining in the 1860s, which continued intermittently until the beginning of the twentieth century, with some activity again in the 1930s. The total production is estimated at a million dollars. (*Bull.*, 193, p. 43.)

Diamond Spring [El Dorado]. Three miles south of Placerville. The place is prominently shown on Trask's map, 1853, and all later maps. Some attribute the name to the finding of nice quartz crystals or "diamonds," which precipitated the rumor of the discovery of real diamonds; others attribute the name to the clear crystal springs at the site. Knapp (p. 512) reports a population of three to four thousand people in 1852. In 1853 the place had several stamp mills and a post office, and in June, 1854, it is mentioned as a jealous rival of Mud Springs (Welles, p. 284). Fire almost destroyed the town in August, 1856 (Bancroft, VI, p. 482). Diamond Springs and nearby Diamond Hill are mentioned by Crockett in 1858 or (?) 1859 (pp. 92 and 95). According to *Transactions*, 1860 (p. 60), the main industry was fruit raising at that time. However, the Larkin Mine, producing gold and copper, was in operation until the twentieth century. More details about the place may be found in *Resources* (p. 21) and in the County History, 1883 (pp. 215 ff.). Diamond Springs placer mines, partly hydraulic mined "many years ago," are still listed in the reports of the Mining Bureau until 1956. Diamond Spring (listed as Diamond Springs) is Historic Landmark 487. It is shown on the USGS Placerville 1931 quadrangle.

Diamondville [Butte]. Northeast of Chico, on Butte Creek. Shown on the County Map, 1862. According to an article in *Diggin's* (I:1, p. 14), a town was laid out in 1857 at newly discovered diggings at Rich Bar, which was first called Goatville, and later by vote was named Diamondville for James Diamond, a miner. There was a large Chinese settlement here at one time. *See* China Town and Rich Bar. Shown on the USGS Chico 1895 quadrangle.

Dickensons Ferry [Stanislaus]. On Tuolumne River, on the road to Mariposa, below present-day Roberts Bridge. It was established in the early 1850s by Gallant D. Dickenson, pioneer of 1846. Stephen Davis mentions it May 15, 1852. In 1862 John W. Roberts purchased the ferry, and it became known as Roberts Ferry.

Dickerhoff Mine [El Dorado]. *See* Cedar: Ravine, Springs.

Dicksburg Ravine [Yuba]. On Natchez Fork of Honcut Creek. Named for a man known as Dick, who settled here in 1850. An English firm built a quartz mill in 1851 but abandoned it after a year, with a loss of 40 thousand dollars. (Co. Hist., 1879, p. 90.) In the summer of 1852 Huntley (I, p. 193) speaks of Dicksburg as a town, and the Butte County History 1882 (p. 267) refers to it as having been "at one time lively and rich." Dicksburg Quartz Mill is shown on Wescoatt's map, 1861; on Doolittle's map, 1868, the name occurs as Vicksburgh.

Dickson Gulch [Butte]. Near Forbestown. It is mentioned as a rich gulch by Hutchings in his diary, November 1, 1855.

Diggers Bar [Nevada]. On the south side of the South Fork of Yuba River, one mile below Relief. It is shown on Trask's map, 1853.

Diggerville [Trinity]. This is another name for Minersville. It was so named because it was situated on Digger Creek. Hutchings lists Digger Creek as a town in 1855 but does not indicate the location.

Dillon: Creek, District [Siskiyou]. The creek is a tributary to the lower Klamath River. It was placer-mined during the Gold Rush, and the region around it was prospected in the 1930s. In 1951 the Siskon Mine was discovered, and it was worked between 1953 and 1960 with an estimated production of several million dollars. (*Bull.*, 193, p. 136.)

Diltz Mine [Mariposa]. *See* Sherlock Creek.

Dirty Bar. An unidentified place, mentioned by Guinn (p. 42).

Dirty Flat [El Dorado]. On the Blue Lead, northeast of Placerville. It was mentioned in 1875 by Raymond, VII (p. 96). Shown on the sketch map in Whitney, *Auriferous Gravels*, plate C.

Discovery Hill [Modoc]. Eight miles northwest of Fort Bidwell. The Bidwell Mines were discovered on the south slope of the hill after 1910. A description and a list of the claims may be found in *Mining Bureau*, XV (p. 245). The Fort Bidwell Consolidated Mines, on the north side of the hill, were reported idle in 1917.

Divide [Sierra]. Between the North and Middle forks of Yuba River, on the slope of Keystone Mountain. A 20-stamp, steam-driven mill was built in 1858 (*Annual Mining Review*, 1876, p. 22).

Diving Bell Bar [Amador]. On the Cosumnes River, north of Plymouth. It is shown on the County Map, 1866, below the forks, on the north side of the river.

Dixie Canyon [Plumas]. In Indian Valley district. In 1863 there was a water-driven, 6- (or 4-) stamp mill (*Annual Mining Review*, 1876, p. 22; Raymond, V, p. 96).

Dixon Creek [Plumas]. A branch of Nelson Creek. It is listed in the County History, 1882 (p. 288), as an important mining point.

Dixons Bar [Trinity]. On Trinity River, near Big Bar. It paid "extremely well" in the wet season, according to Cox (p. 83). In the summer of 1860, the diggings paid from five to eight dollars per day to the man (*Trinity Journal*, July 28, 1860).

Dixons Diggings [Nevada]. About eight miles above Little York. The *Alta*, March 18, 1854, reports that Dixon and company made twenty-five dollars per day to the hand.

Dobbins [Yuba]. On Dobbins Creek, southwest of Bullards Bar. Butler's map of 1851 shows it as Dobbins Ranch. It was settled in 1849 by William and Mark Dobbins (Co. Hist., 1879, p. 95). A post office was established in 1851. De Long mentioned the place on October 27, 1857. There was an 8-stamp mill in 1858 (*State Register*, 1859). The Bateman's mine with five stamps, which began work in July, 1867, yielded thirty dollars per ton (Browne, p. 155). The Dobbins or Indiana Ranch District is listed in 1919 in *Mining Bureau*, XV (p. 423). *See* Indiana Ranch.

Doble [San Bernardino]. Near the north shore of Baldwin Lake, at the east base of Gold Mountain in the San Bernardino Mountains. The town was established in 1900 and named for Budd Doble, son-in-law of E. J. ("Lucky") Baldwin, for many years owner of the Gold Mountain Mine (La Fuze, I, p. 132; II, p. 89). It was the trading center for a number of mines in the area (*Register*, 1902) and from 1900 to 1906 the post office. *See* Gold Mountain.

Dog Bar [Nevada]. On Bear River, southwest of Colfax. No mining records were found. In the 1930s it was mentioned as a place for a debris-storing dam site (*Mining Bureau*, XXXI, p. 351). There was also a Dog Bar Road.

Dog Creek [Shasta]. West of Delta. It is listed as a town by Hutchings in 1855. In December, 1860, an 18-ounce nugget was taken from a claim (*Mining Press*, December 14, 1860). The San Francisco *Courier* of July 28, 1865, reported that a miner picked up 6 thousand dollars worth of gold in 1865 (Bancroft Notes). The Dog Creek District is described in *Mining Bureau*, XIV (p. 775).

Dog Town [Amador]. North of Amador City. This was a gold mining camp also known as New Philadelphia. Both names were still used in 1893 in a report of the nearby Mayflower Mine (*Pamphlets*, III).

Dogtown [Butte]. On the West Branch of the North Fork of Feather River. Shown on the County Map, 1862. The original name of the camp was Mountain View. According to the account in the County History, 1882 (p. 252), the first cabin was built here in 1850 by a Mr. Bassett, whose wife raised dogs and sold them to the miners at a profit; hence the name Dogtown was given to the camp. In 1852 about 500 miners were at work there. In 1857 a post office was established and named Butte Mills, and in 1861 the name was changed to Magalia. The site of the old camp is now submerged by the Magalia Reservoir. The famous Dogtown nugget or Willard nugget was found about three miles east of Dogtown in the Willard hydraulic mine, of which Phineas Willard, Ira Wetherbee, and Wyatt M. Smith were the owners. According to the diary of Dr. A. K. Stearns, superintendent of the mine, the nugget was found April 15, 1859, and it weighed fifty-four pounds (fifty-two pounds after assaying). The value was 10,690 dollars. The site of the discovery is Historic Landmark 771. A "Gold Nugget Celebration," sponsored by the citizens of Magalia (for-

merly Dogtown) and the adjoining town of Paradise, is held annually at the two places. *See* Magalia.

Dogtown [Calaveras]. On San Domingo Creek, four miles north of Angels Camp. It was a mining camp in 1849, and was named because of a stray dog. Most of the claims were owned by German miners, who operated on a cooperative basis. A miner named Hammerschmidt, portrayed by Gerstaecker in "A Night in Mosquito Gulch," had a tunnel here which yielded well. A detailed account of the place is given by Demarest (pp. 20 f.) and by Raymond (IV, pp. 73 ff.). The site is recorded on the USGS Jackson 1938 quadrangle. *See* German Ridge.

Dogtown [El Dorado]. On the South Fork of Weber Creek, southeast of Placerville. Shown on Doolittle's map, 1868. It was a mining settlement that developed in a corral which had been used by Mormons (Co. Hist., 1883, p. 193).

Dogtown [Mariposa]. About four miles east and a little south of Coulterville, on Maxwell Creek. It is mentioned in *Bulletin*, 193 (p. 85) as part of the Kinsley district. On the USGS Coulterville 1949 quadrangle, extensive tailings are shown nearby. About four and a half miles to the southeast is Cat Town.

Dogtown [Mono]. On Dog Creek, near the junction of Clearwater and Virginia creeks; about halfway between Bridgeport and Mono Lake. The date of the discovery of placer gold here has not been definitely established. Leevining and his party were in the area as early as 1853, and they may have discovered gold here then, though no records exist. The discovery is gener-

Doble, San Bernardino Co.

ally attributed to Carl Norst, who settled here in 1857. Sometimes credit is errone- ously given to the Mormons, due to a mis- spelling of the name Moorman Meadows on some maps. The Meadows were not named for the Mormons but for Thomas J. Moorman, according to F. S. Wedertz. There was hydraulic mining in the region until fairly recently. *See* Monoville.

Dogtown [Tulare]. According to Nadeau (p. 238), Tailholt was originally called Dog- town. *See* Tailholt.

Don Juan [Trinity]. On Trinity River, near Cedar Flat. In 1858 the bar paid five to twenty-five dollars per hand in the rainy season (Cox, p. 83). A hydraulic Don Juan Point Mine was in operation in 1896 (*Mining Bureau*, XIII, p. 444). Don Juan Creek is recorded on the USGS Big Bar 1930 quadrangle.

Donkeyville [Nevada]. One mile above Nevada City. In the early 1850s some companies made ten to twenty-five and sometimes fifty dollars per day to the hand (Nevada *Journal*, reprinted in the *Alta*, June 4, 1854).

Donnells Flat [Stanislaus]. It was named for one of the partners of Donnell and Par- sons of Columbia, who built the first water system between Donnell Flat and Colum- bia in 1855. The name is preserved in Donnells Reservoir. (*California Place Names.*)

Donner [Placer]. Southeast of Soda Springs, near the road to Donner Pass. The *Register*, 1902, reports the presence of "sulphurets, quartz, free milling gold." "Sulphurets" or "sulfurets" refers to the sulfides in the ore, commonly pyrite, and possibly other sulfides (Gianella).

Don Pedros Bar [Tuolumne]. On the Tuolumne River, about six miles northeast of La Grange. Shown on Gibbes' map, 1852, and other early maps. The camp was named for Pierre ("Don Pedro") Sainse- vain, the well known pioneer of 1839, who was one of the first prospectors after the gold discovery. He mined successfully at Sutters Mill and Mormon Island after May, 1848. His presence in the Southern Mines is mentioned by Moerenhout, July 18, 1848. Later Sainsevain was a member of the California Constitutional Conven- tion. Among reports of rich yields is one in the Columbia *Gazette*, October 29, 1853, which tells of a company of ten men tak- ing out between 1,000 and 1,500 dollars per day. A good description of the camp is given by Carl Wheat in *James Carr* (note 21). The place is still mentioned as a city

by Mulford in 1863 (p. 242), and the post office existed until 1866. At the time of Lincoln's election, in 1860, 1,500 votes were cast here (Rensch-Hoover). When the reservoir was built by the San Fran- cisco Power and Light Company on the lower Tuolumne River, the site of the bar was inundated, but the name was pre- served. Don Pedro Bar and Dam are shown on the USGS Sonora 1939 quad- rangle.

Doodleburg [Nevada]. An unidentified set- tlement, mentioned in the Nevada *Journal*, June 17, 1859.

Doolittle Ranch [El Dorado]. Two miles northeast of Placerville, on the emigrant road to Carson Valley. Shown on 'Bowman's map, 1873. The *Alta*, November 25, 1855, reports that 700 dol- lars was obtained from a cartload of dirt (Bancroft Notes). The place is mentioned in the El Dorado County Records, November 11, 1857 (Mortgage Book C, pp. 201 f.).

Doolittle's Bridge [Nevada]. Doolittle's Suspension Bridge is shown on his map, 1868, on the South Fork of Yuba River, about four miles above Washington. The Bridge is mentioned in the County His- tory, 1880 (p. 132), along with another one built by Doolittle at Jefferson, below Washington. On Doolittle's map the name "Doolittle's and Ostrom's" designates an area extending northeastward from Rocky Bar toward Gods Country. The references are probably to A. J. Doolittle, maker and publisher of the 1868 map. *See* Bibliog- raphy.

Doolittles Diggings [Nevada]. About two and a half miles northeast of Nevada City. Shown on Doolittle's map, 1868, and probably for him. *See* Doolittles Point.

Doolittles Point [Nevada]. Just below Low- ell Hill. It was apparently named for A. J. Doolittle, one of the owners of a placer mine at nearby Liberty Hill and maker and publisher of the *Township and County Map of the Central Part of California*, 1868. Mr. Doolittle is mentioned in Raymond, VI (p. 117) and the place is shown on Doolittle's map.

Dorado [Plumas]. Prospering hydraulic min- ing in 1861 was reported in *Mining Press*, June 15, 1861 (p. 5).

Dorleska District [Trinity, Siskiyou]. In the Salmon Mountains, near the headwaters of Coffee Creek. The two most productive mines in the district, the Dorleska, discov- ered in 1897, and the Yellow Rose, have produced a total of about 300 thousand dollars. The Yellow Rose is on the opposite side of the ridge from the Dorleska, in the South Fork of Salmon River drainage. (*Bull.*, 193, p. 136.)

Doschs Store, Doschville [Amador]. Three miles northwest of Ione. It was not a gold mining camp but a stage stop on the road through Ione Valley to Sacramento in the 1850s (Cenotto). It is the site of the Dosch clay pit, described in *Bulletin*, 99 (p. 58), and of the ghost town Doschville, described by Andrews (pp. 68 f.). The name is sometimes spelled Dosh, as on the County Map, 1866.

Dos Palmas District [Riverside]. In the Orocopia Mountains, northeast of Salton Sea. There was some gold mining in the 1890s and some prospecting since that time. The mines are listed in *Bulletin*, 193 (p. 157).

Dotans Bar [Placer]. On the north side of the North Fork of American River, two miles above the mouth of the South Fork. Shown on Goddard's map, 1857. The name was variously spelled: Dotans, Dotens, Datons, Daytons. Stephen Wing mentions it in his journal, February 25, 1855, and Hittell includes it in his roster. The U.S. Bureau of the Census for 1850 gives the names of forty-two miners at "Dotons Bar" and another forty-two at "Dotons Bar and nearby Longs Bar." Hutchings describes it as a very busy little town in 1855, after it had obtained water from the North Fork Canal (Diary, April 26, 1855). The place is now under Folsom Lake.

Dotys: Flat, Ravine [Placer]. Near Ophir, west of Auburn and Sailors Ravine. Dotys Ravine is not shown on Doolittle's map, 1868. "Good diggings" were reported at the flat in the *Alta*, September 22, 1852. Stephen Wing mentions the places repeatedly in 1852, 1853, and 1855. On page 86 of volume I of his journal he records the laws of Dotys Flat District that were passed December 6, 1851. Doty Ravine and Doty Flat are shown on the USGS Auburn 1944 quadrangle.

Double Springs [Calaveras]. On a branch of Cosgrove Creek, at the fork of the old roads to Mokelumne Hill and San Andreas. Gold deposits were discovered on the land preempted by Charles L. Peck in 1848 or 1849. It was first called Two Springs. Jackson's map, 1850, shows the two springs. The phenomenal development made the place the county seat in 1850, and a post office was established July 10, 1851. Gibbes' map, 1851, and

Trask's, 1853, show it as a considerable town. In the spring of 1853, Murieta came to plunder the town, but the well-armed Doublespringers drove him off, and he went to Mariposa and death (Wiltsee, *CHSQ*, XI, p. 182). The decline of the town was as rapid as the rise. In 1860 the post office was discontinued, and today only a few structures remain. Part of the old court house built of lumber brought from China is still standing (G. Poore). *See* Valley Springs. Historic Landmark 264.

Douglas City [Trinity]. On Trinity River, south of Weaverville. It was at, or near Readings Bar, one of the places where Major P. B. Reading discovered gold in the summer of 1848. The town took its name when the post office was established December 23, 1859. John Carr (pp. 296 ff.) recalls the place as having been "quite pretentious" in 1859, and he gives an amusing account of the activities of the local newspaper. Brewer (pp. 326 ff.) gives a detailed account of the extensive hydraulic mining in 1862. Mining continued over a long period of time (*Mining Bureau*, XXIX, p. 61; XXXVII, p. 77). *See* Readings Bar [Trinity].

Douglass Flat [Calaveras]. Between Murphys and Vallecito, on the limestone belt. Shown on Trask's map, 1853, and Goddard's, 1857. The diggings were productive as early as 1849. The place is mentioned by Bachman, July 2 and 4, 1850. The *California Courier*, September 9, 1850, reported that two miners had taken out two pounds per day the previous week. In January, 1852, the first tunnel companies were organized to tap the riches of Table Mountain. In 1856 one company averaged thirty to fifty ounces a day. (Hittell Clippings, p. 76; Heckendorn, p. 97.) Later there was mainly hydraulic mining (*Guidebook*, p. 56). In 1867 Browne lists the active and idle claims, but the chief industry was then already fruit growing (*ibid.*, p. 520). The Flat is the scene of Gerstaecker's story "Der Ostindier." The place is recorded on the USGS Big Trees 1941 quadrangle. Historic Landmark 272. The name is also spelled Douglas Flat.

Douglasville [Tuolumne]. At the junction of Sawmill Flat Road with Sonora-Columbia Road, opposite Union Hill. It was a voting precinct. (Eastman.)

Downies Diggings [Plumas]. On Poorman Creek, a tributary to Nelson Creek. The place was mined by Downie and his party in the fall of 1850. It is repeatedly mentioned by Steele (pp. 162 ff.).

Downieville [Sierra]. At the junction of two branches of the North Fork of the Yuba River. It is one of the most important and most colorful towns of the northern mines. The gold deposits were discovered long before the Gold Lake hunt revealed the wealth between the Feather and the Yuba rivers, probably in 1848, certainly in 1849. The spot where the town later developed was known as Jim Crow Diggings, Washingtonville, Missouri Town, or simply The Forks. (Tucker, p. 99; Bancroft, VI, p. 490.) The name Marysville was also once proposed. In the winter of 1849–50 the town started on its phenomenal development. In the spring of 1850 it was named for Major William Downie with "general jollification" (Kane in *Miscellaneous Statements*). When David Demarest arrived there at the beginning of May, the town already had fifteen hotels and gambling houses, four bakeries, four butcher shops, and every piece of ground was claimed and occupied. In 1851 it reportedly had 5,000 inhabitants (Bancroft Scraps, V, p. 1806) and it polled 1,132 votes (Bancroft, VI, p. 490). When Sierra County was established in 1852, Downieville was named county seat. The town is recorded on all maps of the period; Gibbes', 1851, shows it as Downingville. Downie himself wrote a not entirely reliable chronicle, and many other writers tell the story of Downieville as well as stories about the place, including D. P. Barstow

(pp. 7 ff.)., Borthwick (p. 222 f.), Ainslee, Book IV. Mrs. Bates in Chapter XX tells the incredible story of a newly arrived woman who discovered gold when she swept the earthen floor of her kitchen and picked up 500 dollars worth the first day. The story of the Mexican woman who was hanged for having stabbed a man after the Fourth-of-July celebration, 1851, is one of the most often told tales of the Gold Rush. After the placers gave out and the diverting of the Yuba River failed, there was still considerable hydraulic and drift mining and some lode mining. But already in 1867 Browne (p. 148) records that the most important mills near the town were idle. The total output of gold is not definitely recorded, but in 1879 it was estimated at 15 million dollars (San Francisco *Call*, May 18, 1879, *in* Bancroft Scraps, V, p. 1806). The Oxford Mine and Mill, one mile north, operated with good results until the twentieth century. The Gold Bluff Mine, which was worked intermittently from 1851 to the 1950s, produced an estimated 1.5 million dollars (*Mining Bureau*, LII, p. 250). Descriptions of other mines in the area operating to World War II and later are given in the same report (pp. 237 ff.) and in *Bulletin*, 193 (p. 44).

Downings Ravine [El Dorado]. Five miles northeast of Coloma. John Steele (pp. 232 ff. and 280 ff.) mined here in the winters of 1851 and 1852.

Dragoon: Gulch, Flat [Tuolumne]. North of

Downieville, Sierra Co.

the junction of Sonora Creek with Woods Creek, sometimes spelled Dragon. The flat was apparently the camp occupied in the spring of 1849 by eighteen U. S. dragoons who had deserted from the army (*see* comment of De Ferrari in his edition of Stoddart, p. 66). According to Stoddart himself (p. 64), who dates the camp from 1848, the rich diggings were discovered when a drunken dragoon, on furlough from Grahams Dragoons, found a large lump of gold upon awakening from his sleep. William Perkins (pp. 225 f.) tells the story of the terrible murder of Captain George W. Snow here by Mexicans in 1851. This and several other misdeeds led to the formation of a vigilance committee. Hutchings lists Dragoon Gulch as a town in 1855. The *Mining Press*, March 23, 1861, reports that some Italians found a *chispa* worth one thousand dollars at this place. Shown on the USGS Sonora 1949 quadrangle.

Drakes Bar. An unidentified place, listed by Helper.

Drammonds Diggings [Placer]. On El Dorado Canyon, tributary to the North Fork of the Middle Fork of American River. Shown on Doolittle's map, 1868. This may be the same as Drummonds Point on El Dorado Canyon, mentioned by Lindgren (*Tertiary Gravels*, p. 156) as having been hydraulicked.

Draper Mine [Tuolumne]. See Soulsbyville.

Dredge [Sacramento]. See Natoma.

Dredgertown or Dredgerville [Yuba]. See Hammonton.

Dross Ravine [El Dorado]. Listed in Hittell's roster.

Drummonds Point [Placer]. See Drammonds Diggings.

Drummondsville [Amador]. Near Michigan Bar, off the main stage road through Arkansas Diggings. It is mentioned as a mining camp in the *Amador Ledger*, May 16, 1857.

Drunkards Bar [Placer]. On the Middle Fork of American River, above Spanish Bar. It is mentioned in the El Dorado County History, 1883 (p. 84), and is listed as a town by Hutchings in 1855.

Drunken Gulch [Mariposa]. On the easterly side of Mount Bullion, flowing into Sherlock Creek about one mile above the junction of Sherlock Creek and Merced River. Mining began here in 1854. It is listed in Bancroft, VI (p. 378).

Drunkers Bar [El Dorado]. On the Middle Fork of American River. It is mentioned in the El Dorado County Records, Record Book A (pp. 548 f.) in connection with Sailors Claim, June 9, 1852, and is probably the same as Drunkards Bar [Placer].

Dry Bar [Placer]. On the North Fork of American River. Notice of a claim was filed on October 10, 1852 (Placer County Records, I, p. 129).

Dry Bar [Tuolumne]. Probably near Jacksonville. Mulford, chapter XXXV, describes it from memory as "a lively camp in 1857," but it was only a ghost town when he saw it last.

Dry Bones Bar [Placer]. On the North Fork of American River, below Beals Bar. The County History of 1924 (p. 173) does not give a record of gold mining, but it tells a fantastic story about the origin of the name.

Dry Creek [Amador]. The stream joins Sutter Creek west of Ione. It is the best known of the many "Dry Creeks" and is the *Arroyo Seco* after which a Mexican land grant was named in 1840. The first prospectors were apparently Chilenos. The brothers Fowler mined here in October, 1849 (Journal of S. L. Fowler). According to an item in Bancroft Notes, the Chilenos were driven out in that year. The creek is often mentioned in Bowen's manuscript.

Dry Creek [El Dorado]. A tributary to Weber Creek, west of Placerville. Lyman and company mined here with fair success in July and August 1848 (Chester S. Lyman, pp. 188 ff.). The Pyramid Mine, four miles north of Shingle Springs was still operating in the 1930s, after a long period of idleness, and produced about one million dollars (*Mining Bureau*, LII, p. 423).

Dry Creek [Shasta]. South of Piety Hill. A detailed description is given in Raymond, VI (p. 143). One prospector took out 170 thousand dollars (!) in 1852 from the channel of the stream, in the vicinity of Piety Hill.

Dry Creek [Yuba]. There were three gold bearing Dry creeks in the county, one of which is apparently the Reeds Creek which appears on the USGS Smartsville 1943 quadrangle. It is a tributary to the Feather River, six miles above the mouth of Bear River, and is mentioned by Pringle Shaw (p. 123) as Dry Creek No. 2. It appears as Reeds Dry Creek on Wescoatt's map, 1861. Shaw implied Dry Creek No. 1 emptied into Bear River six miles northeast of the junction with the Feather River, and it is also shown on the above maps. Shaw also mentions Dry Creek No. 3, a stream forty miles long, which empties into the Yuba River at Ousleys Bar, and it also appears on both maps. In 1855 a 12-stamp steam-driven mill was erected at one of the Dry creeks (*State Register*, 1859), possibly at the last mentioned, on which Wescoatt indicates two quartz mills near the junction with the Yuba.

Dry Creekville [Amador]. *See* Drytown.

Dry Diggings. A number of places were so called because of the lack of water. The dirt had to be transported to a stream, or the water brought to the diggings. The best known early dry diggings were at the spot where Placerville developed. Of the many dry diggings mentioned in contemporary literature only those are listed here whose identity is established.

Dry Diggings [Calaveras]. On the Mokelumne River, between Mokelumne Hill and Campo Seco. Ryan (p. 59) and his party camped here in 1849.

Dry Diggings [El Dorado]. After Sutters Mill and Mormon Island, the diggings on Weber Creek were the next places where rich gold deposits were found. On Jackson's map, 1850, the entire length of Weber Creek is designated as Dry Diggings. Three of Sutter's men, William Daylor, Perry McCoon, and J. Sheldon must be credited with the discovery. Their camp in April and May, 1848, was on Weber Creek, two miles southwest of the site of Placerville. Haskins' statement (p. 134) that Oregonians discovered the dry diggings about March 1, 1848, is quite certainly incorrect. The Mason *Report* of August, 1848, containing the report of his visit in July of that year, states that Daylor and McCoon had cleared 17 thousand dollars in a short time, and that Sunol and Company nearby had contributed some specimens that Mason forwarded to the capitol at Washington. An excellent account of the early situation on and near Weber Creek is given by the French Consul Moerenhout, who visited the area between July 16 and 24, 1848 (Moerenhout, pp. 15 ff.). Sunols Washings on Weber Creek was probably the camp in which Moerenhout, on about July 17, 1848, came across José María Amador and a number of other prospectors, including the well-known pioneers "Don Pedro" Sansevain and Antonio Sunol, who with the help of twenty-five Indians had taken out 130 ounces of gold in one day's work. A letter of October 25, 1849, is datelined Dry Diggings City; this was probably the original name of Placerville (*CHSQ*, XXIV, p. 352). The Sacramento *Transcript*, May 15, 1851, reports that rich diggings had been found

in Dry Diggings on the ridge between Weberville and "Hangtown," where several hundred dollars worth of gold a day were found in some cases. For later developments, *see* Placerville. *See also* Dry Creek [El Dorado].

Dry Diggings [El Dorado]. Shown on Ord's map, 1848, east of Coloma, and on Derby's Sacramento map a little north of Coloma. It may be the same place mentioned by Wierzbicki in 1849 (p. 41). A letter published in the *Weekly Missouri Statesman*, January 4, 1850, may also refer to the same place. Doolittle's map, 1868, shows Dry Diggings about ten miles north of Coloma, on Canyon Creek, a tributary to the Middle Fork of American River.

Dry Diggings [Tuolumne]. *See* Columbia.

Dry Digginsville [Nevada]. On the Middle Fork of Yuba River. The diggings were worked mainly by Oregonians (San Franciso *Star*, December 2, 1848).

Dry Gulch [El Dorado]. On the North Fork of Cosumnes River. Extensive early mining is mentioned in the County History, 1883 (p. 89).

Drytown [Amador]. On Dry Creek, between Plymouth and Amador City. The camp is prominently shown on Trask's map, 1853. The first American miners were a company from New York who settled here in August, 1849. To be sure, according to a letter written to Henry L. Oak, an assistant to H. H. Bancroft, dated April 2, 1885, Seth Lee Beckwith built the first log house in November, 1848, at the place that was later known as Drytown, and he mined successfully until February, 1849. Bayard Taylor (chapter 25) describes the village as he found it in November, 1849, when there were between 200 and 300 miners established there for the winter. The digging was going on briskly, with an average good return, ranging from nothing to 114 dollars in two days. It was an election precinct in the November 13, 1849, state election (Berriman). In 1850 Albert Leonard had a trading post here. Stephen Fowler refers to the place as Dry Creekville in his journal of January, 1850. According to an entry of Doble, July 18, 1852, there were already 200 houses at the camp at that time. The same year the first stamp mill was built and a post office was established. In 1857 there were four mills with fifty-two stamps and three arrastres in and around the camp (*State Register*, 1859). The County History, 1881 (p. 87), records the burning of the Chileno section of the town in August, 1855, in the wake of the Lower Rancheria murders. In the same County History (pp. 229 ff.) a detailed account of the important mines and mills is given. The Fremont-Gover Mine, east of Drytown, operated intermittently to 1940 and produced more than 5 million dollars worth of gold (*Mining Bureau*, L, pp. 179 f.). Drytown is shown on the USGS Jackson 1938 quadrangle and is Historic Landmark 31.

Duartes Tableland [Los Angeles]. According to the Los Angeles *Star* of May 29 and June 5, 1852, surface gold was found on the land near the house of Andres Duarte. The washings yielded five to seven dollars per day to the man. (Hayes Scrapbooks: Mining (V, sec. 114 f.)

Duck Bar [Calaveras]. On the North Fork of Stanislaus River, six miles from Vallecito. The gold was found mainly in pot holes in limestone bedrock. It is mentioned in the Tuolumne County History, 1882 (p. 275), and the Duck Bar placer claims are listed until 1936 (*Mining Bureau*, XXXII, p. 338).

Dulzura District [San Diego]. About two miles southwest of Dulzura, near the Mexican border. Placer gold was discovered in 1877 by a Mexican boy, but nearby lode deposits were not worked until the 1890s. The Donahoe Mine, the chief mine, was worked on a small scale intermittently from about 1890 until 1915; the Johnston was operated in the 1890s without success; and the Doolittle mines were probably located in the 1930s. There was also some placer mining at the turn of the century, but without success. (*County Report*, III, pp. 122, 123 f., 151.)

Duncan Hill [Placer]. Two miles northwest of Auburn, in the Ophir district. Rich pocket mines of gold, silver, lead and copper were found in the region, according to *Mining Bureau*, XXIII (p. 247).

Duncan Peak District [Placer]. Twenty miles east of Forest Hill and six miles southeast of Last Chance. Mining began in the 1850s and has continued intermittently to the present time (*Bull.*, 193, p. 44). Duncan Peak was named for Thomas Duncan, an early miner.

Duncans Canyon [Placer]. The canyon is mentioned in a claim to water rights from Duncans Canon [!] through Millers Defeat to Cosmopolite Mining District. The notice was recorded July 18 [1854] in Placer County Records, I (p. 237). A description and map are given in *Mining Bureau*, XXI (pp. 275 f.).

Dunderberg [Mono]. *See* Castle Peak District.

Dungan Bar [Sierra]. It is listed by Coy (p. 67) as a place on the South Fork of Yuba River, above Downieville.

Dunning Claim [Calaveras]. East of San Andreas. The rich lead of the old river channel was discovered in early 1852 by Orson Murray of Murray Creek (San Francisco *Bulletin*, January 18, 1858).

Durgans Flat [Sierra]. On the North Fork of Yuba River, south of Downieville, and now a part of it. Recorded on Trask's map, 1853. The camp was called Washingtonville until James Durgan built a sawmill there in 1850. In 1851 there were 800 miners working here making good wages. (County History, 1882, pp. 456, 459.) According to an item in the San Francisco *Call*, May 18, 1879, the place yielded as much as 8 million dollars worth of gold (Bancroft Scraps, V, p. 1806).

Durham Ferry [San Joaquin]. *See* San Joaquin City.

Dusty Bar [Tuolumne]. Near Robinsons Ferry. The place is mentioned by Bachman, April 2, 1851.

Dustyville [El Dorado]. The Georgetown *News*, January 10, 1856, explains the name as follows. A company of miners did not wash their duds, but let them dry out and then beat them against rocks, causing a lot of dust.

Dutch, Dutchman. The term, an Anglicization of *deutsch*, 'German', was with few exceptions used for all miners from Germany, Switzerland, Austria, and the Netherlands.

Dutch-App Mine [Tuolumne]. On the Mother Lode, two miles southwest of Jamestown. The diggings there go back to the early 1850s. The present name stands for the consolidation of five rich mines, the Sweeney, Dutch, App, Heslep, and Hitchcock. The total production is not known, but 6.5 million dollars are attributed to the App-Heslep group and 2.5 to 3 million to the Dutch-Sweeney. (*U. S. Bulletin*, No. 424, pp. 36 ff.; *Mining Bureau*, XXIV, pp. 12 f.; *Bull.*, 193, p. 78). *See* App Mine, Heslep Mine.

Dutch Bar [Kern]. On the south side of Kern River, thirteen miles above San Emidio Creek. It is shown on Bancroft's map of 1868.

Dutch Bar [Placer]. On the north side of the Middle Fork of American River, above Yankee Bar, west of Spanish Dry Diggings. Shown on Doolittle's map, 1868, and on Bowman's, 1873. The Bar is mentioned in the notice of a claim dated August 6, 1855 (Placer County Records, I, p.

297). It is also mentioned in the Placer County History, 1882 (pp. 401 f.), and the El Dorado County History, 1883 (p. 84).

Dutch: Bar, Flat, Hill [El Dorado]. On the South Fork of American River, four miles west of Coloma. Recorded on Doolittle's map, 1868, on Bowman's map, 1873, and in the County History, 1883. It was probably this Dutch Bar that Ryan (p. 29) mentioned as a productive place in 1849. Stephen Wing bought a claim at Dutch Bar Flat, April 17, 1854; he mined at the bar and lived on Dutch Hill (Journal, I, p. 77).

Dutch Charleys Flat [Placer]. *See* Dutch Flat.

Dutch Creek [El Dorado]. A tributary to the South Fork of American River, near Coloma. Steele (pp. 280 f.) spent a terrible night here in November, 1852. The Dutch Creek vein is a continuation of the Mother Lode of Calaveras County (Raymond, VII, p. 91). Several mines are still indicated on the USGS Placerville 1931 quadrangle.

Dutch Creek [Mariposa]. A tributary to the North Fork of Merced River. It was named for "Dutch Frank" Laumeister, elected quartermaster of the Mariposa Batallion.

Dutch Diggings [Nevada]. Near Quaker Hill; between Osborn and Sapsucker ravines, tributaries to Greenhorn Creek. Shown on Pettee and Bowman's map, 1879. Pettee, of the Whitney Survey, found the gravel no more than fifty feet deep, with an extensive amount of the bedrock and a part of the rim to the channel uncovered (Whitney, *Auriferous Gravels*, p. 179).

Dutch Diggings [Plumas]. At the northern end of the La Porte gravel area. The place is mentioned by Lindgren (*Tertiary Gravels*, pp. 105, 107) in his discussioh of the ancient river channel in the area.

Dutch Flat [Butte]. On a branch of Honcut Creek, southwest of Forbestown. It is shown on the County Map of 1861.

Dutch Flat [Kern]. The place is mentioned in Boyd (p. 21). It is probably the same as the Dutch Flat which was originally in Tulare County, where rich quartz yielded thirty dollars per ton by the use of the arrastre (*Mining Press*, June 1, 1861).

Dutch Flat [Placer]. About two and a half miles northeast of Gold Run; near Interstate Highway 80. The rich Blue Lead in this region, near Bear River, was discovered in 1849. In 1851 Charles and Joseph Dornbach settled on the flat, and the place became known as Dutch Charlie's (or Charley's) Flat. This name was changed to Dutch Flat when the post office was established in 1856. By 1865 the population had reached more than 2,000. No records ot early mining were found, but when hydraulic mining was started in 1857, the town soon became one of the big mining centers of the county and remained so until the mines were closed by the antidebris injunctions of 1883. Good accounts of mining in the region may be found in Raymond (III, pp. 84 f.; IV, pp. 115 f.; VII, pp. 98 f.), and in Browne (pp. 105 ff.). James Teaff built the great tail sluice at a cost of 55 thousand dollars, and in 1868 he sank a shaft and reached the blue lead at a depth of 240 feet. In 1867 there were forty-five hydraulic claims within a radius of one and a half miles (San Francisco *Call*, April 9, 1867). A quartz boulder containing 5,760 dollars worth of fine gold was found in the Polar Star Mine in 1876 (Mining Bureau, *Report*, 1880–1882, part 1, p. 149), and in July, 1877, a Chinese company found a nugget worth 12 thousand dollars (Co. Hist., 1882, p. 229). The assay of gold at Dutch Flat showed as high as 970 degrees fineness (*Mining Bureau*, IV, p. 221). It was the first place at which the newly invented "giant powder" (dynamite) was extensively used in gold mining. The output of gold in the district before 1868 was about 3 million dollars (*Mining Bureau*, XXIII, p. 262), and according to *Bulletin*, 193 (p. 45), the total production is estimated at about 5 million dollars and possibly more. The town is Historic Landmark 397.

Dutch Gulch [Placer]. On the north branch of the Middle Fork of American River, near Michigan Bluff. Rich Diggings were found in 1850 (Hutchings' Diary, May 6, 1855). According to Whitney, *Auriferous Gravels* (p. 117), one man reportedly had taken out one thousand dollars from a single pan of dirt.

Dutch Hill [Plumas]. About eight miles east of Greenville, near the East Branch of the North Fork of Feather River. Shown on the Plumas County Map, 1886. It is an old placering district where the water for washing gold had to be raised by pumps until a 35-mile ditch was constructed in the late 1880s (Raymond, VI, p. 139; *Mining Bureau*, VIII, p. 482). The modern development is reported in Raymond, VII (pp. 158 f.) and in later reports of the Mining Bureau.

Dutchmans Gulch [Calaveras]. A tributary to Mokelumne River, northeast of Mokelumne Hill. Doble and partners mined here without much success in March, 1852.

Dutchmans Ranch [Sierra]. Near Scales Diggings, west of Downieville. Mentioned by De Long, July 7, 1857.

Dutchmans Ranch [Yuba]. *See* Notowa and Ramms Ranch.

Dutch Marys Ravine [Placer]. In the Forest Hill Divide. The *Mining Press*, Sept. 21, 1861, reports that mining was resumed by Chinese miners between this place and Shirt Tail Bend.

Dutch Mine [Tuolumne]. *See* App Mine and Dutch-App Mine.

Dutch Ranche [Mariposa]. West of Coulterville. The place is mentioned by Stephen Davis, May 16, 1852.

Dutch Ravine [Placer]. It joins Auburn Ravine one mile east of Virginia. Shown on Doolittle's map, 1868. "Good diggins" are reported in the *Alta*, September 22, 1852. The ravine is mentioned in Placer County Records on September 21, 1851 and November 24, 1855.

Dutch-Sweeney Mine [Tuolumne]. *See* Stent.

Dutchtown [El Dorado]. *See* Spanish Diggings.

Dutton Creek [Trinity]. Gold mining in 1872 was reported in an extract from the Weaverville *Journal* printed in the San Francisco *Bulletin*, February 23, 1872 (Hayes Scrapbooks: Mining, II, sec. 18). Mining was mainly at the confluence of Duttons Creek and Trinity River (H. E. Goodyear).

Duxbury Hill [Plumas]. Apparently near Nelson Point, on the Middle Fork of Feather River. It was a short-lived mining camp. Joseph Booth worked here without success in April and November, 1853.

E**agle Bird** [Nevada]. *See* Maybert.

Eagle Canyon [Yuba]. West of the North Fork of Yuba River, in Fosters Bar township. There were early, successful diggings, and they were still worked by Chinese in 1879 (Co. Hist., 1879, p. 95).

Eagle City [El Dorado]. On the Middle Fork of American River, near Georgetown. Abbott (pp. 120 f.) states that the camp had 500 voters in 1851. It may be the same as the Eagle Bar and City shown on the Map of the Volcanoville Quartz Mining District, on the north bank of the Middle Fork.

Eagle Creek [Shasta]. Near Ono. An old mining camp mentioned by Steger.

Eagle Gulch [Plumas]. About fifteen miles west of Sawpit Flat, on or near the Middle Fork of Feather River. In the 1860s six companies were engaged in drift mining (Browne, p. 167).

Eagle-Shawmut Mine [Tuolumne]. Between Chinese Camp and Jacksonville. In 1867 the Shawmut Mine (spelled Sharamut by Browne, p. 44) had a 10-stamp mill, which was idle at that time. According to *Mining Bureau*, XLV (p. 63), the mine, a consolidation of the Eagle and Shawmut claims, had a total recorded production of 7.38 million dollars at the time of its closure in 1947. Details of the modern development may be found in U. S. *Bulletin*, No. 424, (pp. 43 ff.); Mining Bureau (XXIV, pp. 14 ff. and XLV, p. 63); *Guidebook* (p. 48). The place is shown on *Guidebook* map 2.

Eagleville [Yuba]. Between the South Fork of Feather River and the North Fork of Yuba River, on the Butte County line. It was named after the Eagle Mine. Wescoatt's map, 1861, shows it as a considerable town. According to the County History, 1879 (p. 97), the town was first settled about 1851 and served as headquarters for the miners but disappeared when the deposits gave out. The Eagleville or North Star Mine, reported idle in 1916, was still listed in 1952 (*Mining Bureau*, XV, p. 452; XLVIII, p. 171). The name is recorded on the USGS Bidwell Bar 1944 quadrangle. *See* Strawberry Valley.

Early Mine [Mariposa]. *See* Sweetwater.

East Canyon [El Dorado]. Possibly a branch of Canyon Creek, near Georgetown. The U. S. Bureau of the Census in December, 1850, listed the names of forty-two inhabitants on East Canion in the vicinity of Oregon Canyon.

East Chinee [Tuolumne]. *See* Camp Salvado.

East Fork of Stuart Fork [Trinity]. This intermediate tributary of the Trinity River rises in the Salmon Mountains and empties into Stuart Fork about one and a half miles above the confluence with the Trinity. The important camps are listed in this dictionary under their specific names.

Eastman Diggings [Trinity]. On Eastman Gulch, a tributary to Trinity River, about five miles northeast of Lewiston. The deposits were discovered in 1851 by William Woodin, but the place was named for a Mr. Eastman, who later planted a large orchard there. According to Cox (p. 24), the diggings were rich and shallow. Both placer and lode gold mining were carried on until the twentieth century. The mines are listed and described in the *County Report*, IV (lode mines: pp. 72, 73, 77 and placer mines: pp. 81, 87, 94, 101). One of the principal placer mines, the Eastman or

Edwards Crossing, Nevada Co.

Jim Sing, was worked for many years before 1914 by Chinese. Water was brought through ditches three and five miles long to two hydraulic giants. In the early 1940s Martin and Setzer mined a part of the property by ground sluicing. (*County Report*, IV, p. 30; *Mining Bureau*, XIV, p. 905). Eastman Gulch is shown on the USGS Weaverville 1942 quadrangle.

Eastman Hill [Placer]. About 400 feet above Bear River, below the confluence with Dutch Flat Canyon and opposite Thompson Hill. Shown on Pettee and Bowman's map, 1879. When Pettee visited here in 1870, the gravel was almost entirely washed away, and only two or three men were still mining at the upper end of the hill (Whitney, *Auriferous Gravels*, p. 154).

Eastwood [San Diego]. North of Julian. In 1870 a town was laid out by Joseph Stancliff as a rival to Julian (Ellsberg, p. 18). *See* Julian. The name is preserved in Eastwood Creek and Hill, shown on the USGS Ysabel 1960 quadrangle.

Eclipse [Plumas]. South of Quincy. The place was the trading center and from 1897 to 1912 the post office for the quartz, drift, and hydraulic mines in the area (*Register*, 1900). According to *Mining Bureau*, XVI (Plumas, p. 42), Eclipse was an alternate name for Onion Valley in Saw Pit Flat Mining District.

Eddys Gulch [Siskiyou]. A tributary to the North Fork of Salmon River, south of Sawyers Bar. The *Annual Mining Review*, 1876, lists the following mills: Live Yankee, 8 stamps; Klamath, 12 stamps; Morning Star, 4 stamps. A quartz mill was hauled in by oxen in 1870 to the Ball Mine by Deacon Lee over the trail that is still known as the Deacon Trail, according to W. M. Smith. It is the opinion of Mr. Smith, who has long been familiar with the Salmon River mining scene, that this was the first quartz mill brought into the area. Besides the Ball Mine, which was one of the last to operate, were the Snowflake, the Fagundus, the Klim (later Joubert), and the Barry & Woodfield. According to *Bulletin*, 193 (p. 141), the estimated total production of the mines in Eddys Gulch was 4 million dollars.

Edwards Crossing [Nevada]. On the South Fork of Yuba River, on the road from Nevada City to North Bloomfield. There was a building at either end of the bridge, and placer mining was carried on at the river below (Foley). According to the County History, 1880 (p. 132), the bridge bore the name of its builder or owner successively. William E. Robinson built the first bridge in 1853; John Webber replaced it with a better structure in 1859; J. S. Wall replaced it in 1862 after a flood; J. M. Black bought it in 1865 and later sold it to William Edwards, whose name it still bears. Shown on the USGS Colfax 1938 quadrangle as Edwards Crossing.

Egg-Nog Settlement. An unidentified place, listed as a mining locality on an illustrated letter sheet published by Hutchings in 1855.

Elbow Bar [Yuba]. On the North Fork of Yuba River, near Missouri. Shown on Wescoatt's map, 1861. It was so named because of the shape of the bar. Gold was discovered in May, 1850, and apparently was worked out after one season, according to the County History, 1879 (p. 95). The name, however, still appears on Doolittle's map, 1868, and on the County Map, 1887.

El Dorado. At the time of the exploration of South America the Spanish term for 'gilded man', *el dorado*, was the designation given to a mythical Indian chief whose body was covered with gold dust. With the discovery of gold in California, it was simply used as a name for the gold region, and as such it spread throughout the world. Charles Preuss on his map of 1848 placed the name on the Plumas River and the South Fork of the American River.

El Dorado [Calaveras]. *See* Mountain Ranch.

El Dorado [El Dorado]. About four miles southwest of Placerville. Mud Springs was the name of the post office when it was established in 1851, but this name was changed to El Dorado on December 15, 1855. It appears as El Dorado on Goddard's map, 1857, and all later maps. The USGS Placerville 1931 quadrangle, however, still shows the name as Mud Springs. The principal mines in the area are listed by Browne in 1867 (p. 89). The *Register*, 1902, lists nine stamp mills in operation. The Pocahontas mine, three miles south of the town, was one of the oldest quartz mines in the state. It was first worked by Mexicans in 1852. Wells Fargo records show that between 800 thousand and 900 thousand dollars were shipped from the mine, according to the *Mountain Democrat*, Souvenir Edition, 1898. The most productive mines in the vicinity of El Dorado were the Church Mine and the Union Mine. The Church Mine yielded an estimated one million dollars, and the yield of the Union Mine was possibly as high as 5 millions (*Bull.*, 193, p. 45). *See* Uniontown I and Mud Springs. The town of El Dorado is Historic Landmark 486.

El Dorado [Yuba]. On the Feather River, below Marysville and Eliza. Shown on Gibbes' map, 1851. It was a speculative town founded to gain the miners' trade (Bancroft, VI, p. 487). Announcement of the sale of lots and description of location appeared in the Sacramento *Transcript*, April 8 and 30, 1850.

El Dorado: Bar, District [Placer]. On a north branch of the Middle Fork of American River. The code of laws for the district is recorded on July 13, 1852, in the Placer County Records, I (pp. 98 ff.). The Bar appears to be the same place as the camp near Michigan Bluff. *See* El Dorado; Creek, Camp, Canyon.

El Dorado: Bar, Flat [Calaveras]. Near Coyote Creek and Stanislaus River. The Independent Twelve Company established the camp at the Bar in the spring of 1849. It proved to be very rich. According to Harvey Wood (p. 24), the "Twelve" could clean out twenty-four to thirty-six ounces by ten o'clock, with the help of four to six bottles of brandy, and then quit for the rest of the day. Early in 1867 ten men took out 7 thousand dollars in four months at the Flat (Browne, p. 51).

El Dorado Canyon [El Dorado]. On a branch of Cosumnes River. It is mentioned by Lucius Fairchild, July 6, 1850, and is apparently the same as Big Canyon.

El Dorado: Creek, Camp, Canyon [Placer]. The stream is a tributary to the North Fork of the Middle Fork of American River, near Michigan Bluff. Recorded on Goddard's map, 1857. The canyon is mentioned in the Placer County Records, I (p. 215), when the El Dorado Water Company served notice of intention on February 4, 1854, to build a ditch near Michigan City, later Michigan Bluff. *See* El Dorado: Bar, District [Placer]; Ground Hog Glory. El Dorado Creek is shown on the USGS Colfax 1938 quadrangle.

El Dorado District [Kern]. Along Kelso Creek, on the eastern slope of the Piute Mountains. It is mentioned by Boyd (p. 43).

El Dorado Mine [Placer]. *See* Last Chance.

Eldoradoville [Los Angeles]. On the East Fork of San Gabriel River, where the stream bends north. From 1859 to 1862 it was the trading center for the mines on the East Fork, which had been worked intermittently since 1855. The place was washed away by flood the night of January 17–18, 1862. The Los Angeles *Star*, May 28, 1859, described it as a ramshackle town, consisting of three stores, a boarding house, livery stable, blacksmith shop, and butcher shop. It also had a half dozen saloons, with their gambling and dance halls "running wide open," according to the San Gabriel Canyon historian, Sedley Peck, and enjoyed the reputation of being "the Downieville of the South — a rough and tough miner's town." (J. W. Robinson, pp. 45 f.)

Eldridge Bar [Sacramento]. On the American River, between Sacramento and Negro Bar. It is mentioned in C. S. Wilson's *Report* to the stockholders of the Sacramento Valley Railroad, October 20, 1854. No mining record was found.

Elephant Bar [Plumas]. The bar is listed by Coy as having been on the Middle Fork of Feather River.

Eliza [Yuba]. On the Feather River, four miles below Marysville. In January, 1850, the Kennebec Company, of New Bedford, Massachusetts after having located Kennebec Bar on the Yuba in October, 1849, was looking for new business investments. It considered the waters at newly founded Marysville too low for navigation and arranged with Sutter to start a rival town a short distance above Hock Farm and opposite it. They named it for Sutter's daughter Anna Eliza. The speculative venture, along with several others, failed in its attempt to become the head of navigation and supply depot for the mines. (Ramey, *The Beginnings of Marysville*.)

Elizabeth Hill [Placer]. *See* Elizabethtown [Placer].

Elizabethtown [Placer]. A few miles northwest of present day Kings Beach. A short-lived settlement developed here in the early 1860s, when gold and silver were discovered north of Lake Tahoe in 1861 (*Bull.*, 193, pp. 124 f.). On August 17, 1863, Brewer stated that there were only two or three houses in the "town" that had been laid out.

Elizabethtown [Plumas]. About two miles northwest of Quincy. Gold was discovered in 1852, and soon afterwards the camp was named for Elizabeth Stark (later Mrs. W. A. Blakesley), daughter of Lewis Stark. It came to be known popularly as Betsyburg. There were rich diggings here, but they declined early (Co. Hist., 1882, pp. 276 f.). In the spring of 1861 a tempo-

rary revival was brought about by the discovery of a new ledge (*Mining Press*, March 23, 1861). In 1857 the place had a water-driven 3-stamp mill (*State Register*, 1859). In 1854 the town was a contender for the county seat, but lost out to Quincy. There was a short-lived post office from March 2 to December 17, 1855, when it was moved to its rival neighbor, Quincy. Historic Landmark 231.

Elizabethtown, Elizabeth Hill [Placer]. On the Iowa Hill Divide. The town is prominently recorded as Elizabeth on Trask's map, 1853, and it is mentioned in a miners' agreement of September 1, 1851, in the vicinity of Indian and Shirttail canyons (Placer County Records, I, p. 64). Elizabeth Hill is shown on Doolittle's map, 1868. According to the *Alta*, December 23, 1853, new rich diggings were discovered in 1853. The mines on the hill and their yields are listed in the County History, 1882 (p. 216). The place was apparently named for Elizabeth Hill, the owner of a large mine.

Elizaville [El Dorado]. The place is mentioned in the County History, 1883 (p. 191), as an early mining locality in Kelsey township.

Elizaville [Sierra]. *See* Forest City.

Elk Creek [Siskiyou]. A tributary to Klamath River. The diggings, which were struck in 1854 a short distance below Happy Creek, yielded from ten to fifteen dollars per day to the hand (Del Norte Co. Hist., 1881, p. 22.)

Ella Mine [Calaveras]. Seven miles northwest of Angels Camp. The operators of the mine experimented with roasting quartz for forty to seventy hours in superheated steam but gave up after having spent 25 thousand dollars (Browne, pp. 64 f.).

Ellises Ranch [Amador]. *See* Else: Creek, Ranch.

Elmer [Kern]. Northeast of Bakersfield. Also known as Granite. It is shown as Elmer on the map of the *Register*, 1904. The *Register* lists two quartz mines, one at Elmer and one at Granite, and a Huntington Mill at Elmer. There was a short-lived post office at Granite, December, 1875 to October, 1876, and one at Elmer, 1890–1914. The place was a stage stop and it was a principal sheep-shearing center; today it is known as Granite Station (R. C. Bailey).

Elmore Hill [Placer]. Northeast of Dutch Flat; above the confluence of Bear River and Little Bear River. Recorded as a settlement on Doolittle's map, 1868. The extent of hydraulic mining is indicated on Pettee and Bowman's map, 1879.

El Paso District [Kern]. North of Mojave. The mining activities are described in the *Mining Press*, July 6, 1863. The production continued until the middle of the twentieth century, but only a limited amount of gold was mined (*County Report*, I).

Else: Creek, Ranch [Amador]. A tributary to Sutter Creek, south of Volcano. The camp is mentioned as Ellises Ranch by Bowen, October 6, 1855. In 1855 and 1856 the name is spelled Else's Ranch in the assessor's books (Amador County clerk's office). It had a steam-driven stamp mill in 1861 (*Mining Press*, May 11, 1861).

Emigrant Canyon [Tulare]. Northeast of Walkers Pass. No records of mining were found, but the *Mining Press*, May 1, 1862, reports the discovery of a new mining region near the canyon with seventeen gold-bearing leads.

Emigrant Gap [Placer, Nevada]. Near the towns of Emigrant Gap and Blue Canyon, in the east central part of Placer and Nevada counties. It is both a lode and placer mining district. Mining began in the Gold Rush era and has continued intermittently. The Zeibright [Nevada] lode mine, which was worked on a large scale in the 1930s, yielded more than a million dollars. (*Bull.*, 193, pp. 45 f.)

Emigrant Ravine [El Dorado]. The ravine runs northeast of Placerville. It is shown on Bowman's map, 1873. "Fair wages" were made in 1849, according to Haskins (p. 135).

Emma Mine [Butte]. *See* Nimshew.

Emory Crossing [Yuba, Nevada]. Three miles northeast of North San Juan, on the Middle Fork of Yuba River. Shown on Wescoatt's map, 1861. It is listed in Brown and Dallison's *Directory*, 1856, and is mentioned as Emery Bridge by Borthwick (p. 196). De Long collected taxes from the miners here, March 23, 1855, and he "had a time with the Chinese." Emory Ford is shown on the USGS Smartsville 1943 quadrangle. A name that appears to be Emeri's R[anch] is shown on Trask's map, 1853, on the Upper Middle Fork of Yuba River, on the road from Oak Valley and Minnesota. It may not be the same location as Emory Crossing.

Empire Bar [Placer]. On the American River, one-half mile below Rattlesnake Bar. The bar is mentioned in connection with a claim recorded January 2, 1867, in Placer County Records, IV (pp. 236 f.).

Empire Bar [Yuba]. Shown on Trask's map, 1853, and Goddard's map, 1857, on the main Yuba River, below the confluence with Deer Creek.

Empire Canyon [El Dorado]. South of Georgetown. The U. S. Bureau of the Census lists the names of 84 inhabitants in the population schedule for the 1850 census. Stephen Wing prospected in Empire and Manhattan ravines in December, 1854, but could "get nothing more than the color" (Wing's Journal, II, p. 22). In 1874 there was hydraulic seam mining here (Raymond, VII, p. 83). Empire Creek and Manhattan Creek are shown on the USGS Placerville 1931 quadrangle.

Empire City [Sierra]. Seven miles southeast of Poker Flat. Empire House is shown on Goddard's map, 1857. In 1859 two companies built a 300-foot shaft to get air into their tunnel (*Mining Press*, October 27, 1860). The "city" did not develop, but the Empire Mine was in operation in the twentieth century. Recorded on the USGS Downieville 1907 quadrangle.

Empire City [Stanislaus]. On the south side of Tuolumne River, twenty miles from the mouth of the river and about one mile southwest of present-day Empire. Shown on Butler's map, 1851, and Goddard's, 1857. It is mentioned by Benjamin Deane on the way to the Southern Mines, May 21, 1850. From October, 1854 to December, 1855, it served as the county seat. By 1861 it had declined, but later a new town developed for the surrounding farming community (Stoddart, p. 107). Heckendorn (p. 103) mentions Empire Diggings but does not indicate the location.

Empire Creek [Siskiyou]. On the Klamath River, near Oak Bar. It is listed by Coy (p. 88).

Empire Flat [Nevada]. Near French Corral. It is mentioned in *Beans Directory*, 1867. Raymond, in 1870 (III, p. 39) describes the plans for building a tunnel 2,000 feet in length from the South Yuba side of the ridge, which would drain Empire and Kate Hayes flats and expose a bed of rich cement gravel forty feet deep. Both places are mentioned in 1879 in Whitney's *Auriferous Gravels* (p. 386).

Empire Flats [Placer]. Near Dotans Bar. The *Alta*, March 8, 1853, reprints an item from the *Placer Herald* that reports rich diggings but a lack of water.

Empire Hill [Nevada]. West of Little York. Shown on Pettee and Bowman's map, 1879, where the gravel of the southern part of the hill is shown as "more or less completely hydraulicked away." The area is described by Pettee in Whitney, *Auriferous Gravels* (pp. 154 f.).

Empire House [Yuba]. On the road from Marysville to Fosters Bar, about two miles east of Prairie Diggings. It is mentioned as a stage stop by William Bull Meek, stage driver (pp. 155 f.) and is shown on Doolittle's Map, 1868, below Peoria House.

Empire Mine [Nevada]. One mile southeast of Grass Valley. This is one of the oldest gold mines in California, having been in continuous operation from October, 1850, to the late 1950s (except during World War II). Detailed descriptions are given in *Mining Bureau* (XVI, Nevada, pp. 154 ff.; XXVI, pp. 105 ff.; XXXVII, pp. 392 ff.). In 1929 the Empire Star Mines Company took over and operated the Empire Mine, the North Star, and other mines, and at the time of the closure in 1957 the total production was 130 million dollars (*Mining Bureau*, XXXVII, p. 392; *Bull.*, 193, p. 54). Excellent pictures may be found in *Bulletin*, 193 and in Wagner's *Gold Mines of California*. Empire Mine is Historic Landmark 298. Shown on the USGS Smartsville 1943 quadrangle. *See* Ophir Hill.

Empire Ranch [Yuba]. Less than a mile south of Smartsville. Shown on Wescoatt's map, 1861, and Doolittle's, 1868. It was established as a hotel and trading post by Thomas Mooney in the early 1850s near an Indian rancheria, which continued to be maintained for several decades (Ramey). De Long refers to it in January, 1854, and the County History, 1879, mentions it (p. 83). Recorded on the USGS Smartsville 1943 quadrangle.

Empire Ravine [El Dorado]. Now in El Dorado city limits. It is mentioned in the County History, 1883 (p. 203).

Empire-Star Mine [Nevada]. *See* Empire Mine.

Engles Diggings [Shasta]. Near Roaring River. It was prospected in 1850 by Alonzo Engle and Alex Cunningham, according to Steger.

English Bar [Plumas]. On the Middle Fork of Feather River, between Nelson Point and Bells Bar. Shown on the USGS Downieville 1907 quadrangle.

English Bar [Yuba]. On the north side of the North Fork of Yuba River, two miles below Bullards Bar. Shown on Trask's map, 1853. Two Englishmen worked here with poor success in 1851, but the prospectors who occupied the camp later took out 90 thousand dollars the following summer (Co. Hist., 1879, p. 94). De Long collected miners' taxes here March 25, 1855.

English Mountain District [Nevada]. In the northeastern part of the county, near Bowman Lake. Mining began in the 1860s, and at the turn of the century gold and copper mines at English Mountain were worked (*Bull.*, 193, p. 46).

Enterprise [Butte]. On the South Fork of Feather River, five miles east of Bidwell Bar. It is shown as a sizeable camp on the County Map of 1861. Asa B. Smith datelined his letters from here between April, 1857 and November, 1859. Several stamp mills of the 1860s are listed in the *Annual Mining Review*, 1876 (pp. 21 f.). The place had a post office from 1878 to 1926, and the *Register*, 1903, indicates that it was the trading center for quartz mills in the vicinity at that time.

Enterprise [Nevada]. A small mining camp near Meadow Lake, consisting of a few houses and fifty to sixty inhabitants. It was named for the only mine of importance, discovered in 1865 and worked for several seasons. The shaft was down about ninety feet with several drifts. It was again worked on a small scale in 1880. (Co. Hist., 1880, p. 196.)

Erie Mine [Nevada]. *See* Graniteville.

Erskine Creek [Kern]. A tributary to Kern River, in the northeastern part of the county. The Glen Olive Mine in the region yielded a half million dollars (*Bull.*, 193, p. 46).

Escondido District [San Diego]. In the western part of the county, about twenty-five miles north of San Diego. Numerous claims and mines were worked during the 1890s and the early 1900s, but the production was small. The most important mines were the Escondido and the Oro Fino, about two miles southeast of the town. The Escondido was an old mine worked in the 1860s with an arrastre, and there are evidences that it was long before worked by Mexican miners. After 1897 it was called the Cleveland-Pacific Mine, and it operated until 1911. (*Mining Bureau*, XIII, p. 335; XIV, pp. 649 ff.; *County Report*, III, pp. 120 f.) *See* Rincon del Diablo Ranch.

Esmeralda [Calaveras]. On Indian Creek, about eight miles southeast of San Andreas. It was the trading post for the quartz and hydraulic mines in the area. The name of the post office, 1887–1943, was spelled Esmerelda. In 1899 the place had one stamp mill and two arrastres.

Esmeralda District [Mono]. North of Mono Lake and since 1864 in the state of

Nevada. *See* Hayes Scrapbooks: Mining, VI, for a collection of newspaper clippings on the district.

Esperanza [Calaveras]. On Esperanza Creek, a tributary to the North Fork of Calaveras River. The name is the Spanish word for 'hope'. Doble mentions it on May 9, 1852 as a camp of ten or twelve canvas houses and tents. It is recorded on Trask's map, 1853, and also on Goddard's map, 1857, where it appears as a sizeable place. The creek is shown on the USGS Big Trees 1941 and the Jackson 1938 quadrangles. The name is sometimes spelled Esperance.

Etna: Mills, Bar, Creek [Siskiyou]. On the west side of Scott Valley, at the foot of Etna Mountain (called Salmon Mountain locally). The place was settled in 1852 or 1853. In 1853 or 1854 the second grist mill in Scott Valley was built here. There were also two stores, two or three saloons, a blacksmith shop, and a saw mill. The settlement came to be known as Aetna Mills. It was the trading center for numerous quartz mines in the area until the flood of 1861–62, when it was absorbed by the neighboring camp Rough and Ready. (*Register*, 1898; Co. Hist., 1881, p. 214; W. M. Smith.) A post office had been established January 10, 1861, as Etna Mills (instead of Aetna Mills). In 1874 the state legislature changed the name of Rough and Ready to Etna, but the name of the post office remained Etna Mills until 1924, when it was abbreviated to Etna.

Euchre Bar [Placer]. On the North Fork of American River, just below the junction with the North Fork of the North Fork. Shown on Doolittle's map, 1868, and on the County Map, 1887. It is mentioned in the notice of a claim made November 16, 1851 (Placer County Records, I, p. 57). The place is also mentioned in the County History, 1882 (pp. 383 and 402). Shown on the USGS Colfax 1938 quadrangle.

Euchre Diggings [El Dorado]. Southwest of Placerville, near Shingle Springs. It was a camp of 1849. George F. Kent and associates named it "from the fact that more time was spent there during the winter in playing euchre than in digging gold." (*CHSQ*, XX, p. 39).

Eureka. The expression, 'eureka, I have found it', credited to the Greek geometrician Archimedes, was an extremely popular geographical name after the Constitutional Convention had the word inscribed on the great seal of California.

Eureka [Nevada]. South of the Middle Fork of Yuba River, and about seven miles northeast of Moores Flat. It is recorded on Goddard's map, 1857, and in other records as Eureka South to distinguish it from Eureka [North] in Sierra County. The camp was settled in 1850. Sometimes it had a winter population of 1,000 (Brown, *Directory*, 1856, p. 14). The rich placer deposits were exhausted about 1865. Quartz mining brought new prosperity, and in 1867 the total output of the township was estimated at 20 million dollars. The mines and mills are listed in *Bean's History and Directory* (pp. 402 ff.). The post office was established in 1867 and named Graniteville. The *Register* of 1900 still mentions the town as a trading center under the old name. *See* Graniteville.

Eureka Bar [El Dorado]. Below Horseshoe Bend, on the Middle Fork of American River. The place is shown on Doolittle's map, 1868; Bowman's map, 1873; and a map in *Mining Bureau*, IX (p. 275). A deed for a mining ditch is recorded in El Dorado County Records, Deed Book F (p. 78) for a mining ditch in Placer and El Dorado Counties from the lower end of Horseshoe Bar downstream and across the river to Eureka Bar, ending at Negro Bluff.

Eureka City [Sierra]. *See* Eureka North.

Eureka Flat [Sierra]. South of Gibsonville. Recorded on Trask's map, 1853. Eureka and Eureka Creek are shown on the USGS Downieville 1907 quadrangle.

Eureka Mills [Plumas]. *See* Eureka Peak.

Eureka Mine [Nevada]. Near the town of Grass Valley. The mine was located in 1851 but showed no remarkable development until 1863, after which it became highly productive. It was worked until the late 1870s and yielded more than 5.5 million dollars. Detailed description of Eureka Mine and others in the vicinity may be found in *Bean's Directory* (pp. 205 ff., 239 ff.); Browne (pp. 130 f.); Raymond (IV, pp. 124 f.); *Mining Bureau* (XVI, [Nevada], 166 f.); *Bulletin*, 193 (pp. 53 ff.). *See* Grass Valley.

Eureka Mines [Amador]. On Highway 49, south of the town of Sutter Creek. Before 1924 the Central Eureka and Old Eureka mines operated separately. Old Eureka, opened in 1852 with a 10-stamp mill, became part of the Hayward Mine, which by 1867 had fifty-six stamps and was the deepest mine in California (Browne, p. 75). It operated intermittently until its consolidation in 1924 with the Central Eureka. The latter had been active intermittently since 1855 and it reached a depth of 4,000 feet. After 1930 the production was shifted entirely to Old Eureka workings. It continued until 1942, when work was suspended until 1946. High cost of operation caused final closure in 1953. By the end of 1951 Central Eureka and Old Eureka together produced about 35 million dollars. (*Mining Bureau*, L, pp. 173 ff.; *Guidebook*, p. 64; *Bull.*, 193, p. 73.) The South Eureka Mine operated intermittently between 1891 and 1917; in the 1920s it was developed by the Central Eureka to a level of 4,100 feet, with no success. It was equipped with eighty stamps and reportedly produced 5.3 million dollars (*Mining Bureau*, L, pp. 192 f.).

Eureka North [Sierra]. On Eureka Creek, north of Goodyears Bar. Gold was discovered in 1850 and the diggings were rich. The place was first known as Eureka City. (Knights Scrapbooks, XIII, p. 73). Goddard's map, 1857, shows it as Eureka N. and the post office was called Eureka North, 1857–1861, to distinguish it from other Eurekas. On June 10, 1853, John Clark mentions a place called Ureka as a "small mining village" ten miles north of the Yuba. This is probably Eureka North. The place is also mentioned by M. Thomson in 1856 (p. 16), by Vischer in 1859 (pp. 238, 240), and in the *Mining Press*, July 2, 1862. In 1879 hydraulic mining and drifting still brought "princely revenues," according to the San Francisco *Call*, May 18, 1870 (Bancroft Scraps, V, p. 1806). The entire town was eventually washed away by hydraulicking and all that remains is a part of the old cemetery (R. Drury). In the 1930s there was intermittent mining on a small scale in the district (*Bull.*, 193, p. 45). Eureka, Eureka Creek, and several mines are shown on the USGS Downieville 1907 quadrangle.

Eureka: Peak, Mills [Plumas]. Between Nelson and Jamieson creeks, near Johnsville. Eureka is shown on Goddard's map, 1857. A rich ledge on the peak, elevation 7,490 feet, was discovered in 1850 by prospectors who were looking for Gold Lake. Work was begun in 1851 by the Eureka Company, the first company incorporated in California for the purpose of mining (Browne, p. 168), and in 1852 a 30-stamp water-driven mill was built (*Annual Mining Review*, 1876, p. 21). According to a clipping marked *Plumas County Argus*, October, 1858, in Hittell Clippings (verso of p. 103), two water-driven mills were running at that time, a mile-long railroad was

being built from the ledge to the mill, and enough quartz was being crushed to yield between 5 thousand and 18 thousand dollars per week. *Transactions*, 1858 (p. 201), reports that twenty-four tons were being crushed per day, with the average daily net profit more than 500 dollars. By 1870 the Eureka, Washington, and Rough and Ready ledges became the property of John Parrott, San Francisco financier, who sold his holdings in 1871 to the Sierra Buttes Company of London. With the purchase of the Mammoth ledge the firm became the owner of all the ledges on the mountain. (Raymond, VII, p. 94; Co. Hist., 1882.) By 1889 a 60-stamp mill was in operation with 229 men employed, and arrastres were used to work the tailings below (*Mining Bureau*, X, pp. 482 f.). Only thirty stamps were working about 1894, with 130 men employed (*Mining Bureau*, XII, p. 219). In 1905 the Sierra Buttes Company sold the Plumas-Eureka Mine to eastern capitalists, and it operated intermittently under various owners until 1943. Its production was more than 8 million dollars (*Bull.*, 193, p. 83). More details may be found in *Mining Bureau* (XVIII, pp. 604 f.; XXIV, p. 293; XXXIII, p. 112) and in the study W. Turrentine Jackson made for the Division of Beaches and Parks. Eureka Peak, Creek, and Lake are shown on the USGS Downieville 1907 quadrangle. Plumas-Eureka State Park includes Eureka Mine, Eureka Mills, and Jamieson City. These places are included with Johnstown (now Johnsville) in Historic Landmark 196.

Eureka South [Nevada]. *See* Eureka.

Eutaw Camp [Calaveras]. On the Stanislaus River, probably somewhere near Robinsons Ferry. The place was found mentioned only in Abrams' diary. He and his partners mined here successfully in September, 1849. In some instances Abrams calls the place Stanislaus Diggings.

Evans Bar [Butte]. On the north side of the Middle Fork of Feather River, above Kanaka Bar. Recorded on Trask's map, 1853, Goddard's map, 1857, and on modern maps.

Evans Bar [Trinity]. On the right bank of Trinity River, at the mouth of Evans Creek. The deposits were discovered in 1849 and yielded for many years. A Mr. Gross "of French birth" mined here in 1849 and built the first loghouse in the county. Cox (pp. 50 ff.) gives an extensive account of the camp. The claims were still yielding in 1861 (*Mining Press*, October 26,

1861), and in 1890 hydraulic mining was carried on. (*Mining Bureau*, X, p. 707.)

Evansville [Butte]. Five miles southwest of Forbestown. Shown on the County Map, 1861, and Doolittle's, 1868. It is probably the place near which a 26-ounce nugget was found in May, 1854 (*Alta*, May 30, 1854). In 1858 a mill with two arrastres was built (*State Register*, 1859). In a brief chronicle of the place the County History, 1882 (p. 267), states that it was named for the first settler in 1850. Browne (p. 162) indicates that there was still some mining about 1867.

Excelsior [Nevada]. According to *Bean's History* (p. 307 and *passim*) and the County History, 1880 (p. 72), Excelsior was the former name of the region around Meadow Lake and the name of the company under which Henry Hartley operated. *See* Meadow Lake. Excelsior was a favorite name for mines and claims. *See Consolidated Index*.

Excelsior [Sierra]. On Goodyears Creek, four miles northwest of Downieville, near Monte Cristo. The place was prospected before 1858 (Co. Hist., 1882, p. 489). It is on the Blue Lead, and mining was mainly by drifting. The decline started about 1860. (Browne, p. 138.)

Excelsior Hill [Nevada]. About two miles northeast of Remington Hill, southeast of Bald Eagle Diggings. Shown on Doolittle's map, 1868, as Excelsior. In the 1860s there was mainly drift mining, and where there was no underlying cement there was hydraulic mining. (Raymond, VI, p. 117). At one time one hundred ounces were washed in one week, according to the *Mining Press*, May 16, 1862.

Exchequer [Mariposa]. At the junction of Cotton Creek with Merced River. There were early placers of coarse gold here. The place is now under Lake McClure, but the nearby dam preserves the name.

Exchequer District [San Bernardino]. In the Vontrigger Hills, north of Goffs on the Santa Fe line. Shown on the County Map, 1892. It is listed in 1896 in *Mining Bureau*, XIII (p. 321), but the mines were not being worked because of lack of water.

Experimental Gulch [Tuolumne]. Tributary to the South Fork of Stanislaus River; heads about one and half miles northeast of Columbia. There were placer deposits here in the early 1850s. A small company took out fifteen hundred dollars the first part of March, 1853, according to the *Alta*, March 16, 1853. In 1854 an 8-stamp quartz mill was in operation (Columbia *Gazette*,

October 28, 1854). The place is mentioned in the "Mining Laws of Columbia District" (Heckendorn, p. 9) and in the *Mining Press*, November 2, 1861. The newspapers of the 1850s reported rich strikes. At Experimental Hill one claim prospected 150 to 200 dollars per pan according to the *Tuolumne Courier*, January 2, 1858. The Experimental Mine operated intermittently until the 1940s (*Mining Bureau*, XLV, p. 65). The total output together with Pine Log and Italian Bar was 3.5 million dollars in 1899 (*Mines and Minerals*, p. 358). Shown on the USGS Columbia 1949 quadrangle.

Extension Diggings [Placer]. At the head of El Dorado Canyon, tributary to the North Fork of the Middle Fork of American River. Shown on Doolittle's map, 1868.

F

Fagg Town [Trinity]. A part of Weaverville in the 1850s. It is mentioned by Cox (p. 131).

Fair Play [El Dorado]. Near Perry Creek, tributary to the Middle Fork of Cosumnes River. Shown on Doolittle's map, 1868. In 1853 the camp was mentioned as a prosperous little mining town with several stores and hotels (*Alta*, December 21, 1853). Later it became a trading center and post office for drift and hydraulic mines in the area. In the 1880s agriculture prevailed, but a 10-stamp mill was still in operation (*Resources of El Dorado County*, p. 21). The place is listed in the *Register* of 1902. Shown on the USGS Placerville 1931 quadrangle.

Fair Play [Sierra]. On Rock Creek, ten miles northwest of Downieville. Shown on the County Map, 1874. The mines were profitably operated, mainly by the hydraulic process (San Francisco *Call*, May 18, 1859). In later years they were a part of the Scales group (*Mining Bureau*, XXV, p. 188). *See* Scales.

Fales Hill [Plumas]. About four and a half miles north of Spanish Peak. Shown on the map in Raymond, VIII (p. 110) and described by J. A. Edman, who stated that the placer and hydraulic mines had long been profitably worked, but the gravels were nearly exhausted before 1875 (*ibid.*, pp. 118 f.).

Fales Station [Mono]. It was not a mining camp but a stage station on the Sonora-Mono wagon road, the route to Aurora and Bodie. It was established by Samuel

Fales, who developed the hot springs known as Fales Hot Springs in 1877.

Fallbrook [San Diego]. Small placer deposits in the region were worked mainly by Indians (*Mining Bureau*, XIV, p. 648).

Fall Creek [Nevada]. A tributary to the South Fork of Yuba River, east of Washington. A quartz ledge was discovered in 1861, but yielded only five and a half ounces of gold and silver to the ton (*Mining Press*, October 12, 1861). According to Foley, it was rich in gravel, however. It is mentioned as a settlement by Bean in 1867 (p. 385).

Fall River House [Plumas]. Eighteen miles from Forbestown, on Fall River, a tributary to the Middle Fork of Feather River. The place is shown as a settlement on the Butte County Map, 1862. Hutchings stayed here on his trip to the mines in 1855 (Diary, November 2, 1855).

Farley Gulch [Trinity]. On Digger Creek, near Minersville. It is mentioned in 1858 by Cox (p. 90).

Farmers Diggings [Sacramento]. On the south side of the American River, just below Sacramento Bar. Shown on Doolittle's map, 1868.

Farmers Hope [Mariposa]. *See* Whitlock.

Fashville [Calaveras]. This was a short-lived camp on the Calaveras River, named for the store keeper. Ayers mentions it in his reminiscences (p. 66). No other record was found.

Featherton [Yuba]. On the Feather River at the mouth of Honcut Creek, about fifteen miles above Marysville. It was founded by Covillaud of Marysville as a speculative venture to gain the miners' trade, but it had "no practical existence," according to Bancroft, VI (p. 487). In the *Placer Times*, May 3, 1850, Covillaud & Company announced a free boat ride from Marysville to the site as a means of selling lots. The name is shown on Bancroft's Map of the Northern Mines, 1849–50.

Feliciana Creek [Mariposa]. A tributary to Bear Creek. It heads near the Feliciana Mine and flows westerly into Bear Creek about one mile south of the junction of Bear Creek with Merced River. The diggings were opened in 1850 by Mexicans, who worked with arrastres. There was a 5-stamp mill here in 1866 and the mine was worked intermittently to the 1930s and early 1940s. A detailed description is given in *Mining Bureau*, LIII (p. 98). The creek marked Feliciana Creek on the USGS Yosemite 1938 quadrangle and on the Feliciana Mountain 1947 quadrangle is

Slate Gulch, which heads on the east side of Feliciana Mountain and flows northerly and into Merced River about two miles northeast of Briceburg.

Felix [Calaveras]. Near Salt Spring Valley Reservoir, between Milton and Copperopolis, about two miles from State Highway 15. It is listed as a quartz mining district in the Register, 1899. From 1896 to 1923 it had a post office. *See* Lost City.

Felters Ranch [Trinity]. On Oregon Gulch, east of Weaverville. Cox (p. 57) mentions some gold mining here in the 1850s.

Fenner [San Bernardino]. Near Highway 66, on the Santa Fe Railroad. The place was the trading center for the gold, silver, and copper mines of the district, and a post office was established there in 1892. The mines are listed but not mapped in the *Register* of 1902. Before the construction of the Goffs-Ivanpah branch railroad, Fenner was the shipping point via wagon road from mines in the Providence, New York, and Clark Mountains (Belden, August 12, 1956; San Bernardino City and County Directory, 1889; Haenszel).

Fergusons Bar [Butte]. On the North Fork of Feather River, above Shores Bar. Shown on the County Map, 1877. No mining records were found.

Fergusons Flat [San Bernardino]. In Holcomb Valley. In 1861 it was reported that some of the claims paid twenty-five to forty dollars a day (Bancroft Scraps, LI:1, p. 240). The name is sometimes spelled Furgusons.

Ferry Bar [Trinity]. On Trinity River, east of Douglas City. The camp was short-lived and was "unoccupied" as early as 1856 (Cox, p. 34).

Ferry Bar [Yuba]. On the North Fork of Yuba River, between Bullards and Fosters bars. It is shown on Trask's map, 1853. In 1849 a company of Chileans were brought to the camp and their success in mining led to a conflict with the men from Fosters Bar (Co. Hist., 1879, p. 99). The bar and the river bed were worked from 1849 to 1853 and proved to be very rich (*Marysville Directory*, 1853, p. xxv). James C. Flood, later one of the great promoters of San Francisco, started his career as a miner here, according to the County History (*ibid.*, p. 99).

Fiddlers Flat [Plumas]. On Nelson Creek. The County History, 1882 (p. 288), lists it among the important mining points along the creek.

Fiddlers Flat [Sierra]. Below Canyon Creek, near Portwine. Several companies paid fifteen to twenty dollars per day to the hand (*Mining Press*, May 16, 1862).

Fiddlers Gulch [Kern]. In the Rand District, southwest of Randsburg. Several mines were in operation until 1957 (*County Report*, I, 1962).

Fiddlers Gulch [Tuolumne]. Near Columbia. It is mentioned as a small gold camp, long since forgotten (Rensch, "Columbia, a Gold Camp," p. 4).

Fiddletown [Amador]. Northwest of Volcano. The place was settled in 1849, presumably by Missourians. It appears on Goddard's map, 1857, between Michigan Bar and Volcano. There was mainly placer mining and a little quartz mining. In 1865, however, a 10-stamp mill was built (*Annual Mining Review*, 1876, p. 23). A detailed account of the place is given in the County History, 1881 (pp. 222 f.). It was one of the many places where Joaquin Murieta is reputed to have been and where he was almost captured. The post office, established December 13, 1853, was called Fiddletown; in 1878 the name was changed to Oleta; and in 1932 the old name Fiddletown was restored. The origin of the name is uncertain. Some say it was named for the fiddle players among the Missourian miners; others give the credit to German fiddlers there. In his reminiscences Edwin A. Sherman (p. 167) tells the story of an old lady who claimed her family were the first settlers at the place, and that it was named Violin City because her husband, two sons, and one daughter played the violin. The town is Historic Landmark 35. The Fiddletown district is described in *Bulletin*, 193 (pp. 46 f.). In later years, the 1930s and early 1940s, there was some drift mining and dredging in the district, according to the report in this *Bulletin*.

Fielding [Shasta]. North of Redding. There was gold mining there at the turn of the century, and in 1902 the place had a Jones Rotary Mill (*Register*, 1902). A post office, established in 1897, continued until 1903.

Fienes Crossing [Nevada]. On Deer Creek, about one mile above the confluence with the main Yuba River. Shown on Hoffmann-Craven Great Gravel Map, 1873. It is mentioned in Nevada County History, 1880 (p. 133), as the site of the bridge built by Henry Fiene.

Filibuster Bar [Calaveras]. This was a place on the Mokelumne River which yielded 1,532 ounces of gold in one year, according to a clipping from the *Calaveras Chroni-*

cle (Hittell Clippings, p. 28) undated, but apparently in the year 1853.

Filibuster Bar [Trinity]. Between Readings Bar and Steiner Flat. It is mentioned by Cox (p. 43). Readings Bar, Filibuster Bar or Flat, and Cape Horn Bar were almost one continuous mining camp (H. E. Goodyear).

Fillmore Hill [Sierra]. In the southern part of the county. The *Sierra Democrat*, December 8, 1862, reports extensive mining, which paid eight to ten dollars per day to the hand.

Fine Gold: Creek, Gulch [Madera]. A tributary to the San Joaquin River, above Millerton Lake. The name is the Anglicized form of Oro Fino, a Sonorian camp (Derbec, p. 152). N. H. Stockton mined in the gulch in September and October, 1850, and made more than thirty dollars a day at times (Stockton's journal, October 12, 1850). On Gibbes' Map of the Southern Mines, 1852, the name appears as Fine Gold. The diggings are repeatedly mentioned in Eccelston's Mariposa War diary. Eccelston mined there after the campaign with little success. According to the *Alta*, July 10, 1852, there were few miners because of Indian attacks. In 1868 a 10-stamp steam-driven mill was built (*Annual Mining Review*, 1876, p. 22). The creek is shown on the USGS Millerton Lake 1945 quadrangle. Fine Gold district is described in *Bulletin*, 193 (p. 47). In recent years there has been some prospecting, mainly near Quartz Mountain.

Fine Gold Gulch [Tulare]. News of the discovery of new diggings, "the like of which had not been seen," reached Charles A. Kirkpatrick in February, 1851 (from his journal commenced in 1849).

Finleys [Yuba]. Wescoatt's map, 1861, records a settlement named Finleys on the south side of the North Fork of Yuba River, opposite Slate Range Bar.

Finleys Camp [Placer]. On Bear River. It was named for the captain of a party of immigrants. Mahlon Fairchild (pp. 18 f.) and his partner, van Wormer, mined here in the fall of 1849 with good success.

Fir Cap: Diggings, Ridge, Mountain [Sierra]. About four miles northwest of Downieville. About 1855 Downie (p. 136) observed a company driving a tunnel, called Alma, into Fir Cap Ridge, but he states that they gave up after having spent 14 thousand dollars. However, the San Francisco *Bulletin*, June 6, 1857, reports that the tunnel was finished in the summer of 1857, and rich pay dirt was found in addition to large petrified trees. The *Mountain Messenger*, in an issue of June, 1863, gives an account of a rich find at Fir Gap (!), where a pan of dirt prospected two ounces of coarse gold. A clipping from the *Occident*, June 21, 1867, contains a statement that a company at Fir Cap Diggings was building a tunnel into rich gravel deposits about 1,900 feet into the mountain (Hayes Scrapbooks: Mining, IV, secs. 26 and 37). The mountain is also known as Fir Top. *See* Fur Cap Diggings.

Fire Creek [Nevada]. Near Rough and Ready. Charles Nahl states in a letter dated, February 2, 1852, that he laid a claim here, but found no color.

Fir Top [Sierra]. *See* Fir Cap Diggings.

Fisher Bar [Placer]. On the north bank of the Middle Fork of American River, above Pleasant Bar. It is mentioned in Bancroft, VI (p. 354).

Fishers Bar [Sacramento]. On the American River, near Sacramento city. The camp is described by David Dustin who arrived there June 29, 1850 (his letter of August 14, 1850). He refers to the place as "Mississippi or Fishers Bar."

Fish Spring District [Inyo]. In the northwestern part of the county, about eight miles south of Big Pine. Fish Spring is mentioned in *Mining Bureau*, 1880–1882 (part 1, p. 177) and the district in *Bulletin*, 193 (p. 149). One of the mines, the New Era, was worked in the 1940s.

Fitchs Ferry [Trinity]. On Trinity River, about seven miles above Stewarts Fork. The crossing is mentioned by Coy (p. 80), and it is shown on his map (p. 77).

Five-Cent Gulch [Trinity]. On Weaver Creek, next to the diggings in Ten-Cent Gulch, at the east boundary of Weaverville townsite.

Five-Cent Hill [El Dorado]. On the Georgetown Divide, near Greenwood. Raymond, VII (p. 91) reports that there was gravel mining in 1874.

Five Mile Creek [Tuolumne]. A tributary to the South Fork of Stanislaus River, extending five miles from Summit Pass, north of Yankee Hill, to the site of a steam-driven sawmill built by the Tuolumne County Water Company in 1851–1852 for the purpose of providing lumber for wooden flumes (*Chispa*, VI, pp. 186 f.). Another source indicates the distance from Columbia as the source of the name. Recorded in 1853 on Wallace's map of the Water Company's canal. In 1864 a 5-stamp mill and in 1874 a 10-stamp mill were in operation (*Annual Mining Review*, 1876, pp. 22,

23). The Creek is shown on the USGS Big Trees 1941 quadrangle.

Flapjack Bar [Siskiyou]. On the south side of Salmon River, one mile above Sawyers Bar (Giffen file). There was a Slapjack Bar on the North Fork of Salmon River, above Sawyers Bar (Tickner).

Flat Creek [Shasta]. Ten miles northeast of Shasta, near Iron Mountain. In 1860 there was a camp here with about 100 miners, making five dollars a day to the hand (*Mining Press*, April 6, 1861). The Flat Creek District is described in *Mining Bureau*, X (p. 634).

Fleatown [El Dorado]. The place is mentioned as an early mining locality in Kelsey township (Co. Hist., 1883, p. 191).

Flea Valley [Butte]. Northeast of Magalia. It is not the Flea Valley shown on modern maps. According to the County History, 1882 (p. 253), it was once a flourishing mining camp.

Floras [El Dorado]. Two miles west of Volcanoville. Shown on a map (plate B) in Whitney, *Auriferous Gravels*. Hydraulic mining here is described in the same work (p. 96).

Florence City. An unidentified place, mentioned by Knapp (p. 517). It might have been in the state of Nevada.

Florida House [Sierra]. Above Old Mountain House, on the Sierra Turnpike Road to Downieville. It was a hostelry run by the Mrs. Romargi, a native of Florida, who was later the keeper of Nigger Tent, according to Meek (p. 124). Florida House was the last convenient camp for pack trains on the trail to Goodyears Bar, as well as a transfer point for stages going to Summit City via the old Henness Pass Road, according to Meek; however, Doolittle's map, 1868, shows Old Mountain House at this point, with Florida House just above it on the trail to Goodyears Bar.

Flyaway [Mariposa]. Seven miles southeast of Coulterville. It is recorded as Fly Away on Trask's map, 1853. The place is listed in Hittell's roster and in *Mining Bureau*, XIII (p. 218). There were eight claims with a 5-stamp mill, but production was only moderate. For other mines in the area, consult the map in *Mining Bureau*, LIII, and accompanying descriptions. Flyaway Gulch is shown on the USGS Sonora 1939 quadrangle.

Flying Dutchmans Camp [Sierra]. Near Downieville. No record of the place was found except Borthwick's charming account (pp. 237 ff.) of a group of American,

French, Italian, and Mexican miners who were lorded over by a German doctor, described as being in "a most dilapidated condition."

Folsom [Sacramento]. On the American River, twenty-one miles east of Sacramento. On an annotated copy of Judah's map, 1854, a townsite marked Granite City is inked in on the south side of the river adjoining and above Negro Bar. The handwriting is believed to be that of Theodore D. Judah, chief engineer of the Sacramento Railroad. *See* Negro Bar. The following year Judah laid out and named the town of Folsom at this site, the terminus of the first railroad in California. It was named for Captain Joseph L. Folsom, who had come to California as assistant quartermaster of Stevenson's Volunteers and had bought Rancho de los Americanos, part of the vast Leidesdorff estate, on which the station and town were built. (Judah's *Map of Folsom*, 1855.) Placer mining began as early as 1849. *See* Negro Bar. Many Chinese were engaged in sluicing and drift mining from the 1860s through the 1890s. The *Mining Press*, March 23, 1861, reported that many shafts had been sunk, and that the dirt paid fifty cents to the pan. The December 14, 1861 issue of the same journal stated that a tunnel yielded 400 dollars to each of two owners for many months. Drifting operations were generally on a small scale and limited to rich pay streaks of the Tertiary gravels. The mines between 1892 and 1896 are listed and described in *Mining Bureau* (XII, pp. 225 ff.; XIII, pp. 316 ff.). There was also some hydraulic mining in the area, but little lode mining (*Mining Bureau*, LI, pp. 142, 143). Dredging in Folsom District began in 1899. The district is described in *Bulletin*, 57 (pp. 178 ff.) and 193 (pp. 148 f.). The large dredging fields extended from Folsom southwest along the south side of American River, then to the town of Natoma to Nimbus, then to the east border of Mather Air Force Base. After operating for more than forty years they were closed down in 1962. The estimated output was more than 125 million dollars. *See* Natoma.

Fools Hill [Nevada]. On the Blue Lead, west of Dutch Flat (Bean, p. 369).

Forbes Diggings [Butte]. *See* Forbestown.

Forbestown [Butte]. East of Oroville, between the South Fork of Feather River and the North Fork of Yuba River. It is shown on Trask's map, 1853, and Goddard's, 1857, and is mentioned by Booth in 1852 and by Huntley in 1856. The place, sometimes called Forbes Diggings, was named for Ben F. Forbes, a native of Wisconsin who established a store there in 1850. It was called Forbestown in the *Statutes* of 1853, and the post office, established in 1854, also used this name. In its heyday, 1855, about 400 votes were cast. Hutchings reports that there were about 900 inhabitants in 1855 (Diary, November 1, 1855). He stated further that it was first settled in 1849 by a Mr. Toll and was known for some time as Tolls Old Diggings. *See* Tolls New Diggings [Yuba]. Tolls Dry Diggings, at which 400 to 500 miners were preparing to spend the winter of 1850–1851, are mentioned in the Sacramento *Transcript*, steamer ed., November 29, 1850 (Bancroft Notes: Butte County). This place may be the Tolls Old Diggings (later Forbestown) mentioned by Hutchings. Modern maps show Old Forbestown, now a ghost town, about a mile north of present Forbestown. Forbestown District is described in *Bulletin*, 193 (pp. 48 f.). There was both placer and quartz mining in the district. The Gold Bank Mine, a short distance northeast of Forbestown, operated on a large scale between 1888 and 1904 and produced 2 million dollars. Some mining continued in the district until the 1930s and there has been intermittent prospecting since then.

Fords Bar [Placer]. There were several places in Placer County named Fords Bar and several with Ford as the specific name. **Ford's Upper** [Bar] on the North Fork of American River is shown on Trask's map, 1853, above the confluence with the Middle Fork, below Iowa Hill. **Fords Bridge** is recorded on Doolittle's map, 1868, above Iowa Hill. **Fords Bar Bridge** is mentioned in the notice of a claim datelined Chioka Bar (on the North Fork), July 2, 1855, recorded in Placer County Records, I (p. 294). **Fords Lower Bar**, near Big Oak Bar, six miles above the mouth of the South Fork, is mentioned in the notice of a claim recorded January 24, 1852, in Placer County Records, I (recto of p. 69). This may be the Fords Bar mentioned in the County History, 1882 (p. 190), at which one claim yielded twenty ounces of gold on a Saturday in October, 1855. On the Middle Fork of American River above Spanish Bar there was a **Fords Bar**, mentioned by Wierzbicki in 1849 (p. 41). It is shown on Doolittle's map, 1868, at the junction with Otter Creek; Goddard's map shows it farther downstream, just above

Poverty Bar. Not specifically located is the place described in a somewhat doubtful item in Bancroft Notes, in which it is reported that John T. Little, later a storekeeper in Coloma, dug out sixty pounds of gold at Fords Bar in the spring and summer of 1849. A claim for a quartz lead which crossed Fords Ravine is datelined Fords Valley, September 1, 1851, in Placer County Records, I (p. 6). These places, likewise, are not located. *See* Fords Bar [Sacramento].

Fords Bar [Sacramento]. On the lower American River, below Farmers Diggings. Shown on Doolittle's map, 1868. No mining records were found.

Fordyce Valley [Nevada]. The place was a short-lived camp that developed in connection with the Meadow Lake gold rush in the 1860s. It is mentioned in *Bean's Directory*, 1867, and was apparently called Atlanta (Foley). The settlement is covered by Fordyce Dam.

Foremans [Calaveras]. Nine miles above Double Springs. In the early days David Foreman and Alexander Beritzhoff operated a hotel and a ferry at Fourth Crossing on San Antonio Creek, and the place was known as Foremans or Fourth Crossing. (*See* Fourth Crossing.) Foremans Upper and Lower Ranch is often mentioned by Bachman. The January 6, 1852 issue of the *Alta* has a story of a strange team composed of one man and two women. The man used pick and shovel and one of the women carried the dirt to a rocker that was operated by the other woman. The

correspondent expressed the wish that more women in California would rock the cradle instead of harassing their husbands with women's rights. (Bancroft Scraps, LI:1, p. 246.) The *Alta*, March 4, 1854, reprints an item from the Stockton *Journal* which reports that in February, 1854, placers were discovered in decomposed quartz and that a single pan of dirt yielded as much as two ounces of gold.

Forest [Sierra]. *See* Forest City.

Forest City [Sierra]. On a tributary to Oregon Creek, south of Downieville. The name is spelled Forrest City on Goddard's map, 1857, and the place is shown as an important crossroads. It is near or at the same place as Yumana on Oregon Creek mentioned by Trask, 1854 (doc. 9, pp. 62 f.). His map of 1853 shows a place labeled Indian V[illage] at the approximate site, south of Goodyears Bar. According to an article in the *Tuolumne Courier*, May 12, 1860, the first store was called Yomana Store, after the bluff above the town called Yomana by the Indians. The camp was settled in 1852, and according to the County History, 1882 (pp. 473 ff.), the original name was Brownsville, which was then changed to Elizaville and in 1854 to Forest City. The post office was established November 16, 1854, and the name was abbreviated to Forest in 1895. For the contradictory accounts of the name, *see California Place Names*. The *Alta*, March 16, 1854, reprints an item from the *Sierra Citizen*, according to which all companies in the district were doing well. Some miners earned 100 dollars per week to the hand, and some claims were sold for 1 thousand to 4 thousand dollars. In the same year, 1854, a lump of pure gold weighing forty-two ounces was found (*Alta*, July 7, 1854). For some years the camp prospered, but by the late 1860s the decline had begun. Browne (p. 140) states that in 1869 only one company was working, where formerly there had been twenty. The chief claim, the Live Yankee, was almost worked out at that time, but in 1872 and 1873 the Bald Mountain claim was discovered and developed with improved methods of drifting. The town soon regained its prosperity and by 1878 the population was reported at 800 (San Francisco *Call*, May 18, 1879). For a detailed account of the workings of the Bald Mountain claim, *see* Raymond, VII (pp. 151 ff.) and Whitney, *Auriferous Gravels* (pp. 436 f.) A description of the Forest or Alleghany District is given in *Bulletin*, 193

Forest City, Sierra Co.

(pp. 19 ff.), where it is stated that the Bald Mountain drift mine yielded 3.1 million dollars and the Live Yankee between three quarter and one million dollars.

Forest Hill [Placer]. On the Forest Hill Divide, between the North and Middle forks of American River. The town, situated on the Blue Lead gravels of the Tertiary Yuba River, became one of the most productive places of the gold region. The diggings were discovered before 1850, the year of a regular rush to Forest House on Forest Knoll. This was the designation of the hill as given on Trask's map, 1853. In 1853 the Dardanelles Company commenced work on a 20-mile long ditch, and by 1868 it had taken out more than 2 million dollars, first by drift then by hydraulic mining. The principal mines in the area and their profits are listed by Browne (pp. 93 ff.). In 1859 the mines shipped 100 thousand dollars worth of gold every month. A post office was established June 27, 1859. Soon afterwards the decline started, and in 1869 there were four mills with sixty stamps, all idle (Raymond, II, p. 41). Yet gold mining continued in a limited way until the middle of the twentieth century. Among the most productive placer mines in the Forest Hill district, with production figures given in *Bulletin*, 193 (p. 50) are the Mayflower, with over one million dollars; the Independent, New Jersey, and Jenny Lind together with more than 2.65 million, and the Paragon with the same amount; the Peckham Hill and Todd Valley together, with 5 million; the Georgia Hill, Yankee Jim, and Smiths Point together with 5 million; and the Dardanelles as mentioned above. Forest Hill is Historic Landmark 399.

Forest Home [Amador]. Eight miles north of Ione, near Willow Springs, on the road between Michigan Bar and Drytown. Shown on the County Map, 1866. The settlement, which developed around the tavern of the same name, is described in the *Amador Ledger*, May 9 and 16, 1857, as quite a little town with two stores, a billiard saloon, a barber shop, and an additional hotel. The previous year there were only ten miners, but after water was brought from the Cosumnes River and Michigan Bar Ditch, miners flocked in. The mines were worked out by 1868, according to Browne (p. 72), but a permit for hydraulic mining was issued around 1895 for a mine at Forest Home, probably at this location (*Mining Bureau*, XIII, p. 15). Later references are to copper mining in the area.

Forest Springs [Nevada]. On Wolf Creek, about three miles south of Grass Valley. Shown on Doolittle's map, 1868. The principal mine was the Norumbagua, which began operations in 1850 and for many years produced between forty and one hundred dollars per ton (Bean, pp. 216 ff., 230). It was worked at intervals until 1920, when it was closed; later it became part of the Banner Consolidated Mines (*Mining Bureau*, XVI, Nevada, p. 207; XVII, p. 436; XXVI, p. 102; XXXVII, p. 445). The total production of the Norumbagua Mine was more than one million dollars, according to *Bulletin*, 193 (p. 60). Forest Springs is shown on the USGS Smartsville 1943 quadrangle.

Forks of Butte [Butte]. At the junction of Big and West Butte creeks, west of Lovelock. The County Map of 1861 shows it as a sizeable settlement. Accounts of the operations of nearby drift mines (the Best, later the Royal Mine, and the John Dix Mine) may be found in *Mining Bureau* (XII, p. 85; XXVI, pp. 390, 405).

Forks of Salmon [Siskiyou]. The place was the trading center for numerous placer and hydraulic mines in the vicinity, and a post office was established in 1858. The *Register*, 1898, lists a stamp mill and arrastres. For a review of mining along the South Fork, *see* Jack Quinn's article *in Siskiyou Pioneer*, IV:1 (pp. 21 ff.).

Forks of the Cosumnes [Amador]. *See* Yeomet.

Forks of the Road [Calaveras]. This was the original name of Altaville.

Forks of Yuba [Sierra]. Rich diggings were reported in 1851 (Sacramento *Transcript*, February 14, 1851). *See* Downieville.

Forkville or Forksville [Sacramento, El Dorado]. On the North Fork of American River, at the junction with the South Fork. Butler's map, 1851, shows it about nine miles above the confluence, but Trask's map, 1853, and Goddard's, 1857, show it at the junction, above Beals Bar. The U. S. Bureau of the Census, 1850, lists the names of 378 miners at Beals Bar (Forksville), apparently the population of the two places.

Forlorn Hope Camp [Merced]. On the Merced River, east of modern Bagby. The place had a post office between 1854 and 1861, and in 1866 it was reestablished as Hopetown. Apparently between 1861 and 1866, the name was Hopeton. No mining records were found, but it was probably the name of a mine.

Forrest City [Sierra]. *See* Forest City.

Fort Ann [Amador]. On Dry Creek, three

miles north of Volcano. Shown on the County Map, 1866. Doble mentions it as Fort Ana, November 1, 1852. An account of the workings of the principal mine from 1895 to the early 1940s is given in *Mining Bureau*, L (p. 179). The origin of the name is not known. Andrews, in 1967, states that the outline of log barracks, headquarters, and stables were still traceable.

Fort Goff Bar [Siskiyou]. On the Klamath River, below Seiad. The place is mentioned in the County History, 1881 (p. 217). A hydraulic placer mine is listed in Mining Bureau *Reports* until 1935.

Fort Grizzley [El Dorado]. In Pi Pi Valley, near the South Fork of Cosumnes River. Doble (p. 209) mentions the place.

Fort Hill [El Dorado]. Northeast of Georgetown. It was probably so named for the shape of the hill. Reports on drift mining here may be found in Raymond (IV, p. 106; VII, p. 94).

Fort Jim [El Dorado]. A mining place of undetermined origin, east of Placerville. It is mentioned in the County History, 1883 (p. 193).

Fort John [Amador]. On Dry Creek, twelve miles northeast of Amador. Shown on the County Map, 1866. It was named for one John Stuart. P. Y. Cool, in a diary entry on April 15, 1851, states that he was named superintendent for the building of a Methodist Episcopal Church. This was probably the first church to be built in what is now Amador County (Berriman). The place had an excellent chronicler in Ben Bowen. In September, 1852, there were only five miners, two women, and five children, but in September, 1855, the voters numbered ten Democrats and thirty-five "Kin Saveys." The place declined soon afterwards. It is still listed, however, by the Mining Bureau in 1954.

Fort Jones [Siskiyou]. In Scott River Valley. The place was settled in 1851 and was first called Scottsville, then Wheelock. It was apparently not a mining town, but it became the trading center for a rich mining district. A post office was established December 29, 1854, under the name Ottitiewa, and in 1860 the name was changed to Fort Jones, after the military encampment which had been named in honor of Roger Jones, adjutant general of the U. S. Army.

Fosteria [Calaveras]. *See* Paloma.

Fosters Bar [Yuba]. On the North Fork of Yuba River; now covered by Bullards Bar Reservoir. It was one of the earliest and best known diggings on the Yuba and was named for William Foster, a survivor of the Donner party. In April, 1848, he formed a partnership in a cattle ranch south of the Yuba River with his brother-in-law, Michael C. Nye, who had been manager of Sutter's Hock Farm and major domo at Cordua's New Mecklenburg. Foster was one of the first miners on the lower Yuba in June, 1848, and a few months later he moved to the location later named for him. Buffum (pp. 35 ff.) states that Foster had a store there and a claim to a large part of the bar in November, 1848. According to Ramey, Foster managed the store when it was owned by Covillaud & Company, a partnership formed by Foster, Nye, and Covillaud in January, 1849. The last named was Charles Covillaud, who had been a partner of Theodor Cordua and later became one of the founders of Marysville. (*See* Ramey, *The Beginnings of Marysville*, pp. 10 ff.) Downie mentions Fosters Bar in the summer of 1849 (pp. 24 ff.). Borthwick (pp. 199 ff.) earned his living there as a portrait painter, and he gives an excellent description of the place. According to Frickstad, the post office was established March 5, 1852, but a post office is mentioned in a letter of Newton Miller as early as January 1, 1851. The place prospered for a decade, first by mining with coffer-dams and after 1854 by the hydraulic process. (Co. Hist., 1879, p. 93). In 1855 there were 300 inhabitants according to Hutchings (Diary, October 28, 1855). In 1866 the post office was transferred to Bullards Bar.

Fosters Lower Bar [Yuba]. Jackson's map and other early maps show the Bar further down-stream than the well-known Fosters Bar. Foster might have mined here before the name was given to the Bar north of the confluence of the North and the Middle forks of Yuba River. The name might also have been used to distinguish it from Cut-Eye Fosters Bar.

Four Hills [Sierra]. Near Plumas County line, fifteen miles from Downieville. Shown on the Plumas County Map, 1886. In 1861 a tunnel was built into the hills and a rich quartz vein discovered (*Mining Press*, April 6, June 1, 1861). The modern development is described in detail in *Mining Bureau* (XVI, Sierra, p. 87; XXV, pp. 164 f.). The total production of the Four Hills lode mine was 2 million dollars (*Bull.*, 193, p. 117).

Fourth Crossing [Calaveras]. On San Antonio Creek and Highway 49. The original Fourth Crossing was probably at the confluence of the creek with the South Fork of Calaveras River, and was the fourth time that the river had to be crossed from Stockton to the mines. The Fourth Crossing House is mentioned by Demarest. Jacob Bachman lived here after 1852 and was justice of peace for three terms. There was a 6-stamp water-driven mill here in 1871 (*Annual Mining Review*, 1876, p. 23), and in the *Register* of 1899 the place is still mentioned as a trading center with a post office (established 1855) for quartz and hydraulic mines in the area. The old bridge is still standing, and the historic Reddick Hotel is in use as a private home. The place is Historic Landmark 258. Shown on the USGS Jackson 1938 quadrangle. *See* Foremans.

Fowlers Diggings [Plumas]. South of Onion Valley Creek. It is mentioned in Stretch's "Report on the Onion Valley Ridge, 1881–1882."

Fox Creek [Siskiyou]. A tributary to the South Fork of Scott River. It was considered a rich creek, and mining was brisk. One claim yielded 15 hundred dollars in one day's work in 1862, according to the *Mining Press*, May 8, 1862.

Fox Gulch [Tuolumne]. Near Columbia, west of Experimental Gulch. It is mentioned in the Sacramento *Union*, May 22, 1855, where it is stated that two claims paid eighteen and twenty dollars to the hand and that one claim paid twenty-eight ounces in four days. Similar reports of rich yields are found in the newspapers of 1855. Reference to the place is made in the Heckendorn's "Mining Laws of Columbia District" (p. 9). The diggings were worked out in 1861, according to the *Mining Press*, November 23, 1861. Shown on the USGS Columbia 1949 quadrangle.

Francis [Trinity]. In the northwest corner of the county. It had a post office from 1881 to 1897. Placering in the vicinity was carried on until the end of the nineteenth century (*Register*, 1898).

Franklin Bar [Siskiyou]. On Scott River, between Hamburg and Scott Bar. Shown on Goddard's map, 1857. It is mentioned in the County History, 1881 (p. 217). Franklin Gulch appears on the USGS Seiad 1945 quadrangle.

Franklin City [Shasta]. *See* Whiskeytown.

Franklin Mine. *See* French Gulch [Shasta]; Placerville [El Dorado].

Frasers [Tuolumne]. Southeast of Columbia. It is shown on Trask's map, 1853, as the terminus of the road from Columbia.

Frazier Mountain District [Ventura]. In the

northeast corner of the county. There was early placer mining here, and in 1865 lode mining began and continued to about 1895, with minor prospecting since that time. The Frazier Mine yielded one million dollars. (*Bull.*, 193, p. 171.)

Fraziers Flat [Tuolumne]. On the Tuolumne River, south of Jacksonville. The deposits were discovered in 1859 and named for a "diabolical Scotchman" who mined here (Mulford, p. 103). The place is the scene of Mulford's story, "The Miner's Rainy Day." *See* Swetts Bar. It is not to be confused with Fraser Flat on the South Fork of Stanislaus River, west of present-day Pinecrest (De Ferrari).

Fredonia [Butte]. On the left bank of the Feather River, a few miles above Veazie City and below Oroville. A town was laid out in 1850, according to the County History, 1877 (p. 8). It was planned as a trading center for miners.

Freemans Crossing [Yuba, Nevada]. On the Middle Fork of Yuba River, northeast of North San Juan. Shown on Wescoatt's map, 1861, with the spelling Fremans Bridge. Gold was found here as early as 1850, and a ferry called Nyes Crossing was in operation at that time (Yuba Co. Hist., 1879, p. 100). (*See* Nyes Ferry.) In 1851 Thomas Hesse built a bridge, which was replaced in 1852, and the place was known as Hesse's Crossing (Brown's *Directory*, 1856). Thomas Freeman bought the bridge in 1854, and the name was changed to Freemans Crossing. The bridge was rebuilt in 1855 and was destroyed by high water in 1861. Freeman then moved from the site at the mouth of Oregon Creek and built a bridge farther downstream after two attempts. Shown on the USGS Smartsville 1943 quadrangle.

Freetown [Siskiyou]. Two miles above Humbug City. According to the County History, 1881 (p. 209), the place, which had two stores and several saloons, vanished in 1854, and the site was mined away.

Freezeout [Amador]. *See* Ione.

Freeze-Out [Butte]. On the west branch of Butte Creek. In the spring of 1861, Wells and Company completed a flume across the creek 100 feet high and 300 feet long. Their claim paid up to an ounce a day to the hand. (*Mining Press*, March 23, 1861.) Freeze-out was a typical miners expression found in other place names. Ione [Amador] was once so called.

Freiberg Tunnel [Inyo]. *See* Cerro Gordo.

Fremont [Yolo]. On the west bank of the

French Bar, Siskiyou Co.

Sacramento River, opposite Vernon. Shown on Trask's map, 1853. It was a trading center for miners on their way to the Feather River mines. It is mentioned by Peter Decker, August 31, 1849, and by Adolphus Windeler in February, 1850 (p. 53).

Frémont Estate [Mariposa]. John Charles Frémont, the best known of western explorers, played an important but controversial role in the Gold Rush, as well as in the early political history of California. In 1847 U.S. Consul Larkin bought the Alvarado land grant of 44,386 acres for Frémont. After Marshall's discovery, a great number of rich gold deposits were found on this grant. As a result, Frémont soon became the wealthiest man connected with the Gold Rush. After a bitter struggle with the squatters and miners, Frémont succeeded in having his grant confirmed by the courts in 1859. But within a few years he managed to ruin his rich holdings, and in May, 1867, they passed into the hands of a receiver. Among the numerous accounts, Browne (pp. 21 ff.) has given the best of the contemporary accounts, and Crampton's dissertation of 1941 gives a reliable modern account. The numerous gold towns, camps, and mines that developed on the vast estate are given under their specific names. *See* especially, Agua Fria, Bear Valley, Mount Bullion, Mount Ophir, Mariposa, Princeton. For a lively account of Frémont's family life in

Bear Valley from 1858 to 1861, *see* Jessie Benton Frémont, *Mother Lode Narratives*.

Fremont-Gover Mine [Amador]. *See* Drytown.

Fremont Peak [San Bernardino]. Eighteen miles southeast of Randsburg. The many claims on the west slope were gradually consolidated into the Fremont Peak Mine, which is reported in 1931 to have yielded twenty-five dollars per ton (*Mining Bureau*, XXVII, p. 295).

French. Probably the most common of the adjectives denoting nationality in the gold region toponymy. The French gold diggers were less numerous than the Germans, but the real French seldom associated with Americans, and their camps kept their national identity. The Canadians of French extraction were generally known as "French." Finally, some of the place names may have been family names.

French Bar [Amador]. On the Mokelumne River, about five miles southwest of Jackson, below Middle Bar. Shown on the County Map, 1866, and on Camp's map. It was also called Frenchmans Bar (Berriman, Cenotto). Goddard's map, 1857, shows a French Bar farther downstream, above Winters Bar, but across the river. Trask's map, 1853, shows a French Bar farther upstream, near the forks, opposite Rough and Ready Bar.

French Bar [Humboldt]. On the Klamath River, near Big Bar. A large hydraulic claim here discontinued operations in 1888 for lack of water (*Mining Bureau*, VIII, p. 219).

French Bar [Plumas]. *See* Carriboo.

French Bar [Siskiyou]. On Scott River, near the junction with Klamath River, below Scotts Bar. Shown on Goddard's map, 1857. A miners' agreement on water rights is dated February 18, 1854 (Siskiyou County Land Papers). Hutchings, who was here January 19, 1855, stated that it "bids fair to be a rival to Scotts Bar." It is also mentioned as a town by Metlar in 1856 (pp. 8, 10). According to the County History, 1881 (p. 217), the camp thrived in the 1850s but was then deserted and forgotten. A mine is still listed in 1914 for assessment only (*Mining Bureau*, XIV, p. 862).

French Bar [Stanislaus]. *See* La Grange.

French Bar [Tuolume]. On Tuolumne River. An unidentified camp listed in Giffen's file.

French Bar [Yuba]. On the North Fork of Yuba River, between Fosters and Slate Range bars. It is mentioned as a small bar in the *Marysville Directory*, 1858 (p. xxvii). A French Bar is shown on the USGS French Corral 1950 quadrangle on the main Yuba River, between Condemned Bar and the site of Rice Crossing. *See* Frenchmans Bar.

French Camp [Amador]. At the east base of Jackson Butte. Shown on Camp's map. Doble passed through what was apparently this place in the spring of 1852 (Diary, April 12, 1852), when it consisted of about fifty tents (Camp's note, p. 299). In 1857 there were about a dozen canvas houses and shanties occupied mainly by Frenchmen, according to an account in the Volcano *Weekly Ledger*, August 1, 1857. Another French Camp is shown on the County Map, 1866, about six miles northeast of Volcano, on the road marked Amador & Nevada Wagon Road, but no mining record was found.

French Camp [Amador]. About three miles northeast of Lancha Plana, just beyond Camp Union, on the road to Jackson. Shown on the County Map, 1866, and on Camp's map. The first miners were French, then Mexican and Chilean, and in 1854 a large band of Yaqui Indians mined here. An Italian reportedly traced the gravel range under the hills in 1856 and sometimes took out several thousand dollars a week. The camp had vanished in the 1870s. (Co. Hist., 1881, p. 202.) Andrews found two *hornos* (ovens) in the ruins, one

of which was still intact in 1967 (*Ghost Towns*, p. 34).

French Camp [Calaveras]. About one or two miles west of Murphys, on the French Gulch Road. The camp disappeared when the pay dirt gave out in the early 1850s, according to Demarest (p. 9).

French Camp [Mariposa]. Near the headwaters of Mariposa Creek; about four miles northwest of Mariposa. Shown on the Las Mariposas map, 1861. Bonnet Spring and mine suggest the reason for the name. Tailings piles still mark extensive placer diggings along the creek (Shirley Sargent.)

French Camp [Nevada]. Near Grass Valley. The *Alta*, March 4, 1854, reprints an item which reports that two Frenchmen took out 9 thousand dollars worth of gold in one month and that the profits for 1853 had been 29 thousand dollars, all apparently taken out by French miners.

French Camp [Stanislaus]. *See* La Grange.

French Camp [Trinity]. It is mentioned in Schoolcraft, III (p. 135) as a camp of French-Canadian miners on Pine Creek in 1851.

French Camp [Tuolumne]. North of the South Fork of Stanislaus River, northeast of Pine Log and about one and a half miles west of Italian Bar. It is mentioned by Dane (p. 3). The site is shown on the USGS Columbia 1948 quadrangle.

French: Canyon, Creek, Frenchtown [El Dorado]. Frenchtown, a camp of French Canadians established in 1850, was at the junction of Sawmill Creek and Forty Mile Creek, the point at which French Creek starts. Samuel F. Pond mentioned the canyon in his diary on August 23, 1850. In 1851 Pond and five men mined at the creek, making together between six and twenty dollars a day. The French Creek Mine to the south was revived about 1953 (*Mining Bureau*, LII, p. 414). It is indicated as Frenchtown Q. M. on Doolittle's map, 1868, about two miles southeast of Shingle Springs. Frenchtown and French Creek are shown on the USGS Placerville 1931 quadrangle.

French Corral [Nevada]. Near the South Fork of Yuba River, southwest of Birchville. According to Bean (p. 343), a Frenchman from Frenchmans Bar on the Yuba built an enclosure here in 1849. Milleson and Adams placed the name "Frenchmans Couill" on their map of 1851. This origin of the name has been generally accepted. It is shown on Goddard's map, 1857, as French Corral. Rich deposits were discovered in 1851 or 1852, and the town which developed became one of the important places between North San Juan and Grass Valley. McKeeby mined here with fair success in 1852, and he gives a good description. Other good contemporary accounts may be found in Brown's *Directory*, 1856; the *Alta*, March 20, 1857; N. C. Miller's letters; *Transactions*, 1858 (p. 175). Mrs. Bates gives a beautiful description of the place and of the road from Marysville (chapter XVIII). Rich hydraulic mining was carried on until the prohibition in 1884. In 1894 the U. S. Debris Commission granted limited hydraulic mining. A list of the mines in the district in 1871 is given in Raymond, IV (p. 117). The *Register* of 1900 mentions one stamp mill in operation. The town is shown on Doolittle's map, 1868, and on the USGS Smartsville 1943 quadrangle.

French Creek Bar [Butte]. On the Big Bend of the North Fork of Feather River, at the mouth of French Creek. The bar is recorded on the map of the County History, 1882 (p. 209).

Frenches Ravine [Sierra]. *See* French Ravine.

French Flat [Amador]. Between Amador and Sutter creeks, near Fiddletown. John Berry Hill mined here successfully in the early 1850s (Hill's *In the Gold Mines*, p. 27).

French Flat [Siskiyou]. Near Callahan's Ranch, two and a half miles up the South Fork of Scott River. A correspondent of the *Alta* in his report dated December 27, 1867, refers to this place as "a notable mining locality in its day," which was still active but in need of further capital to exploit its rich deposits (Hayes Scrapbooks: Mining, IV, sec. 52). It was considered a very rich flat and it was called French Flat because it was worked by a company of French miners (W. M. Smith).

French Flat [Tuolumne]. About one mile west of Rawhide Flat. It was sometimes known as French Gulch, but more commonly as French Flat (De Ferrari). French Flat is shown on the USGS Sonora 1897 quadrangle.

French Gulch [Calaveras]. Between Dogtown and Altaville; a branch of San Domingo Creek, tributary to the South Fork of Calaveras River. Mining was reported as prosperous in an article in the San Francisco *Bulletin*, January 27, 1857, cited in Bancroft Notes. The name is shown on the USGS Jackson 1938 quadrangle.

French Gulch [Trinity]. West of Weaverville. It is mentioned in Cox (p. 10). It may be

the same as French Town, part of Weaverville.

French Gulch [Tuolumne]. The western boundary of Gold Hill, near Columbia. It is mentioned by Jolly in his *Gold Spring Diary* (p. 92). According to the Columbia *Gazette*, February 12, 1853, it was paying well in many places. In the claim of George Camp and Company at the head of the Gulch four men were making about two ounces per day to the man, and others were doing equally well. There was another French Gulch in the old town of Sonora (De Ferrari). *See also* French Flat.

French Gulch: town; District [Shasta]. On Clear Creek, northwest of Whiskeytown. It was an important mining district, which had two water-driven quartz mills in 1851 (*State Register*, 1859) and a steam-driven 10-stamp mill in 1863 (*Annual Mining Review*, 1876, p. 22). On Goddard's map, 1857, French Creek, but no settlement is recorded. The post office was established February 18, 1856. In 1856 a lump of two pounds of gold was found here (*Alta*, August 5, 1856, in Bancroft Notes). Raymond, II (p. 85) reports that two mills with thirty-two stamps were operating in 1869, and the *Register* of 1902 lists nine stamp mills and two Huntington mills. The mines of French Gulch district operated until the middle of the twentieth century. *Bulletin*, 193 (p. 136 f.) lists the important ones, among which the most productive were the Brown Bear with a production of 15 million dollars, the Gladstone with 6.9 million, the Mad Mule with one million, the Milkmaid and Franklin together with 2.5 million, the Niagara with one million, and the Washington with 2.5 million. The Washington, discovered in 1851, was the first quartz mine worked in Shasta County. French Gulch is Historic Landmark 166. Shown on the USGS Weaverville 1942 quadrangle.

French Hill [Calaveras]. *See* Mokelumne Hill.

French Hill [Del Norte]. Between the Middle and South forks of Smith River, south of Gasquet. Mining began here in 1860 at one of the few old placer mines in the county. About five per cent of the value was platinum (*Mining Bureau*, XXIX, pp. 141 f.). According to the County History, 1881 (p. 136), mining had been suspended, but hydraulic mining is reported in the Mining Bureau reports until 1946 (XLVIII, p. 278).

Frenchmans Bar [Amador]. *See* French Bar.

Frenchmans Bar [Mariposa]. Probably on or

near Merced River. Allsop dates his last letter from this place, March, 1853.

Frenchmans Bar [Nevada]. On the South Fork of Yuba River, about three miles west of Washington. Shown on Doolittle's map, 1868.

Frenchmans Bar [Plumas]. Just above the junction of the East Branch with North Fork of Feather River. Shown on Trask's map, 1853. It is mentioned by Dame Shirley, October 29, 1851.

Frenchmans Bar [Yuba]. On the main Yuba River, between Condemned Bar and Rices Ford, west of French Corral. Shown on Wescoatt's map, 1861, and on Doolittle's, 1868. The place is mentioned by C. G. Whitcomb in a letter dated December 21, 1854. It is also mentioned by De Long on May 31, 1856, and it is listed in Brown's *Directory*, 1856 (p. 133). In the late 1870s only Chinese miners were working there, according to the County History, 1879 (p. 94). It is shown as French Bar on the USGS French Corral 1950 quadrangle.

Frenchmans Creek [Plumas]. A tributary to the Middle Fork of Feather River, north of Sierra Valley, in the southwestern part of the county. Claude François Seltier and his brother Simon, natives of France, came to Sierra Valley in 1858 and mined in the Frenchmans Creek area (Plumas County Historical Society, *Publication*, no. 13, pp. 8, 11 f.). Shown on the USGS Sierraville 1942 quadrangle.

Frenchmans Gulch [Tuolumne]. On Woods Creek, near Jamestown. It is mentioned by Heckendorn (p. 54). French Flat, northeast of Jamestown, is nearby.

Frenchmans Ranch [Yuba]. Near Forbestown. It is shown on Milleson and Adams' map, 1851. Lecouvreur (p. 230) refers to it in the summer of 1850 as "a cluster of five or six houses."

French Mine [Mariposa]. *See* Benton Mills.

French Ravine [El Dorado]. Now Clay Street in Placerville. The Ravine ran north to Clay Hill. (Schlappi-Ferguson.) Several deeds for property along the Ravine are recorded in El Dorado County Records (Deed Book C, p. 312, February 21, 1857; Book E, pp. 434 f., February 21, 1860).

French Ravine [Sierra]. The Mining Bureau *Report*, 1880–1882 (part 1, pp. 148 f.), records the find of a large nugget of 426 ounces valued at 8 thousand dollars in 1851, one of 532 ounces valued at 10 thousand dollars in 1855, and another of 93 ounces valued at 1,757 dollars in 1860. This may be the unidentified French Ravine which John Clark, a miner at Rab-

bit Creek in Plumas County, mentions in his account of January, 1856. He reports that a company at the camp washed out 345 ounces in one week. There is a Frenches Ravine southwest of Condemned Bar in Yuba County recorded on the USGS Smartsville 1943 quadrangle.

Frenchtown [Butte]. Near the West Branch of the North Fork of Feather River, in the vicinity of Yankee Hill. Shown on Trask's map, 1853, and on the County Map, 1862. It was once a flourishing mining camp, according to the County History, 1882 (p. 253), and it had a post office for a brief time in 1857–1858.

Frenchtown [El Dorado]. *See* French: Canyon, Creek.

Frenchtown [Siskiyou]. On Humbug Creek, two miles below the forks. The place was originally called Mowrys Flat, then Frenchtown because a number of Frenchmen had claims there about 1864. The change in name probably took place before 1853, for it was apparently this Frenchtown at which C. A. Holley mined and farmed at that time (Holley's letter, January 28, 1853).

French Town [Trinity]. The "town," mentioned by Cox (pp. 131 ff.), was a section of Weaverville in the 1850s.

Frenchtown [Yuba]. On Dry Creek, about nine miles west of North San Juan. Shown on Wescoatt's map, 1861. It was probably named by or for a Frenchman, Paul Vasseur, who settled here in 1854, owned 120 acres of land, and engaged in mining and winemaking. In spite of the decline in gold digging, he built a large arrastre in 1878. (Co. Hist., 1879, p. 89.) The place is recorded on the USGS Smartsville 1943 quadrangle.

Fresno Gulch [Madera]. Mining is reported after 1850. Many prospectors left because of the Indian troubles in connection with the Mariposa War (*Alta*, July 10, 1852).

Fresno River District [Madera]. The lower Fresno River was first placer-mined during the Gold Rush, when the Coarsegold and Grub Gulch districts to the northeast were being worked. Several small dredges were in operation in the late 1960s. (*Bull.*, 193, p. 50.)

Friant District [Fresno]. On the San Joaquin River, in the northeastern part of the county. The district is described in *Bulletin*, 193 (pp. 50 f.). During the construction of Friant Dam in 1940–1942, about 200 thousand dollars worth of gold was recovered in excavating the sand and gravel, and since 1946 as much as 25 thousand dollars worth of fine gold has been recovered annually from the sand and gravel plants there. (*See California Place Names.*)

Frogtown [Calaveras]. *See* Angels Camp.

Frogtown [Siskiyou]. A former name of Hawkinsville.

Frost Bar [Siskiyou]. On the Salmon River. It is listed as a mining camp of 1850–1851 in Bancroft, VI (p. 370).

Frytown [Placer]. In Auburn Ravine, two miles below Ophir. It was settled in 1849 and named for one of the owners of the general merchandise firm of Fry and Bruce (Co. Hist., 1882, p. 381). It is shown on Bancroft's map (Bancroft, VI, p. 368).

Fulda Flat [Placer]. A short distance below Texas Hill, about ten miles south and a little east of Emigrant Gap. Two men had a stamp mill here "at one time" and also a store and a saloon (*Placer Nuggets*, June, 1960).

Fur Cap Diggings [Sierra]. Northwest of Downieville, about three-fourths of a mile north of Monte Cristo. Shown on the County Map, 1874. It is probably the same as Fir Cap Diggings. *See* Fir Cap.

Furgusons Flat [San Bernardino]. *See* Fergusons Flat.

Gages Point [Sierra]. In Slate Creek Basin, northeast of La Porte. It is shown on the map in Raymond, V (preceding p. 89).

Galena Hill [Yuba]. In Horse Valley, about two miles north of Camptonville. Recorded on Wescoatt's map, 1861. According to the County History, 1879 (p. 100), a man from Galena, Illinois, mined here in 1852. The place is mentioned in a letter of November 3, 1853 (Whitcomb Family Papers) in connection with the surveying for the building of a ditch. De Long mentions it repeatedly after 1854. The diggings paid well after the Sierra Water Company provided water in 1858 (Hittell Clippings, p. 44). The *Mining Press*, May 11, 1861, reported well-paying hydraulic mining. A Galena Hill Mine is listed until 1896 (*Mining Bureau*, XIII, p. 15). Galena Hill is shown on the USGS Smartsville 1943 quadrangle. Galena House, mentioned by Lecouvreur in 1850 (p. 227) was apparently at a different location, on the Marysville-Fosters Bar Road, below Empire House and Peoria House (Rensch-Hoover).

Gales Ranch [Amador]. The location is not indicated. George L. Gale was justice of the peace in Volcano in 1855 (Berriman). In 1857 six stamps and two arrastres were in operation, according to the *State Register*, 1859.

Galice Creek [Del Norte]. On Smith River. Gold diggings of 1851 or 1852 are mentioned in the San Franciso *Bulletin*, March 29, 1859 (Bancroft Notes).

Galloway: Ranch, Hill [Sierra]. Near Downieville. Mentioned by Trask in 1854 (doc. 9, p. 62) and shown on his map, 1853. It was prospected in 1889 to bring back Downieville "to her old honored position," but the expected rich gravel ledge was never found (San Francisco *Call*, May 18, 1889).

Garden Bar District [Placer]. Northwest of Auburn, on Bear River. There was mainly copper mining, but some gold. The book of claims is contained in volume VI of Placer County Records, and the district is mentioned in the Placer County History, 1882 (p. 206), where the name is spelled Gardner.

Garden Gulch [Trinity]. A camp on Weaver Creek. Cox mentioned it in 1858 (p. 131). A dividend paying mine was in operation in 1914 and was listed until the 1940s (*Mining Bureau*, XIV, p. 905; XXXVII, pp. 78, 89). The gulch flows through Weaverville.

Garden Ranch Flat [Yuba]. In New York township, adjoining New York Ranch near Sharon Valley. The flat was settled in 1850 by Dr. Conduit and Mr. Hanley, who started mining there that year. In 1878 a flume was built from New York Flat and fourteen men worked day and night for Roberts and Kendall. (Yuba County History, 1879, p. 90.)

Garden Valley [El Dorado]. At the junction of Irish and Empire creeks, between Georgetown and Coloma. The camp had a post office as early as 1852, but the name is not recorded on Trask's or Goddard's maps. In 1857 a nugget worth 525 dollars was found here (*Mining Bureau*, II, part 1, p. 150). The Rosecrans Mine, which was worked previous to 1888, was reactivated between 1916 and 1918 and again in the 1930s. The Black Oak Mine produced about 1.25 million dollars by 1942 (*Mining Bureau*, XXXIV, p. 248; LII, pp. 409, 424). According to local tradition, the name arose because the people found it more profitable to raise vegetables than to dig for gold. *See* Johntown.

Garden Valley Ranch [Yuba]. On Willow Creek, a tributary to the North Fork of Yuba River. Garden Valley is shown on

Garden Ranch Flat, Yuba Co.

Wescoatt's map, 1861. According to a letter written by Clement Whitcomb, December 5, 1854, the entire Garden Valley was then being staked out for claims (Whitcomb family papers). The deposits were soon exhausted, and in 1879 only Chinese miners were left (Co. Hist., 1879, p. 99). There was extensive dredging in later years. The place is shown on the USGS Smartsville 1943 quadrangle.

Gardiners Point [Plumas]. On the county line, east of La Porte. Shown on Crossman's Map of Sierra County, 1867. Hydraulic and tunneling activities were reported in the *Mining Press*, April 27, 1861. The camp yielded about 500 thousand dollars by 1852 or thereabout. Soon afterward it was dormant for around ten years, when Colonel B. F. Baker purchased the property and consolidated it with adjoining mines. He not only put new life into the claim but found in it a small but flawless diamond. (Raymond, V, p. 83.)

Gardners Point [Sierra]. The camp mentioned by the *Mining Press*, June 21, 1862 is obviously the same as Gardiners Point on the Plumas-Sierra county line.

Garlock [Kern]. Northwest of Randsburg. It was named for Eugene Garlock, who built a stamp mill here in 1896. It had a post office from 1896 to 1904 and from 1923 to 1926, and according to the *Register*, 1904, two stamp mills. The mines are listed in the *County Report*, I, 1962. Originally the place was called Cow Wells, during the 1880s and early 1890s (R. C. Bailey).

Garota 1, Garota 2 [Tuolume]. *See* Garrote.

Garrote [Tuolumne]. Two placer camps northeast and east of Big Oak Flat were settled by Mexicans in 1850, or earlier. At the one that is now called Groveland a murderer was hanged in 1850, and the camp was called Garrote, the Mexican word for execution by strangulation. A similar incident occurred in the camp two miles to the southeast, and the two camps were accordingly called "The Garotes" (Heckendorn, p. 91). Buckbee gives a different account. On Trask's map, 1853, they are recorded as Garota 1 and Garota 2. The two names appeared on all later maps, often misspelled and confused. (*See* Savage Flat.) In June, 1850, there were nearly 2,000 Mexicans in the vicinity of Garrote 1, but an incident between Indians and white men caused the Mexicans to leave in fear, according to the "Mountaineer" in the *San Joaquin Republican*, December 16, 1851. The same year the U. S. Bureau of the Census lists 126 inhabitants for Gerote No. 1 and forty-two for Gerote No. 2 in the population schedule for the 1850 census. The post office was established November 29, 1851, at the northern camp under the name Garrotte. In 1875 the name was changed to Groveland. The southern camp retained the name Second Garrotte, and it still appears as such on the USGS Sonora 1939 quadrangle. Eccleston prospected here in September, 1850, and was disappointed, yet both places were lively around 1860. Second Garrote is Historic Landmark 460. The contention that Second Garrote is the locale of Bret Harte's "Tennessee's Pardner" is a figment of popular imagination. Nor has it been authenticated that Harte lived and wrote his stories in the cabin designated as such.

Garvey Bar [Siskiyou]. On Cottonwood Creek, about two miles below The Swallows (Giffen file).

Casburg [Siskiyou]. On the South Fork of Scott River; southwest of French Flat, near Camp Eden. It was a short-lived mining camp, mentioned in the *Siskiyou Pioneer*, IV:1 (p. 35).

Gas Canyon [Nevada]. A tributary to Greenhorn Creek, near Quaker Hill. Shown on Pettee and Bowman's map, 1879. Pettee describes the area and the extent of hydraulic mining by 1870 (Whitney, *Auriferous Gravels*, p. 181).

Gas Flat [Nevada]. *See* Gass Flat.

Gas Point [Shasta]. On the south side of Cottonwood Creek, about eight miles east of Horsetown. It yielded well for some time (*Mining Press*, December 7, 1860; March 16, 1861). The auriferous gravel is mentioned in *Mining Bureau*, XI, (p. 53). There was a post office here from 1875 to 1933, and between 1881 and 1890 the name of it was Pinckney, according to Frickstad. In 1859 the place was known as Janesville and it was "quite a flourishing village" (Sacramento *Union*, October 24, 1859). *See* Janesville.

Gass Flat [Nevada]. Near Rough and Ready. It was "quite a little settlement" in 1855, according to Hutchings, who spells the name Gas Flat in his diary of October 10. Bean, in 1867, likewise calls it a "settlement of importance" (p. 360).

Gaston, Gaston Ridge [Nevada]. In Washington township; the camp was six miles northeast of Washington, the Ridge extending to within four miles of Graniteville. The Ridge is shown on Doolittle's map, 1868. A ledge was located in 1856, and a primitive mill operated until 1863 (*Bean's Directory*). The renewal of gold mining in the 1880s is described in *Mining Bureau* (XVI, Nevada, pp. 170 f.). The consolidated mines are listed in the Mining Bureau report of 1941 (XXXVII, p. 451) and in *Bulletin*, 193 (p. 53), where the estimated production is given as 2 million dollars. Gaston Ridge and the site of the town Gaston are shown on the USGS Emigrant Gap 1955 quadrangle. *See* Graniteville.

Gate, or The Gate [Amador]. *See* Jackson Gate.

Gatesville [Yuba]. *See* Sucker Flat.

Gatons Tunnel [Nevada?]. According to an item in the *Alta*, April 14, 1854, it is the oldest tunnel in the so-called Blue Banks. It was started in 1851, and in the first week of April, 1854, almost 250 ounces of gold were taken out.

Gawleys Point [Tuolumne]. At or near Hawkins Bar. Mulford in his chapter "At the Gold Mines" tells the delightful story of Mr. Gawley, who buried his "pickle jars full of gold dust" here in 1849. Gardiner (p. 82) also mentions the place, calling it the Gauly claim, the richest spot on Hawkins Bar, which yielded thousands of dollars. The *Mining Press*, October 7, 1862, reports that rich gold and copper lodes were discovered in 1862.

Gazelle District [Siskiyou]. In the south-central part of the county. The main mine, the Dewey, was worked from the 1880s to about 1907 and produced about 900 thousand dollars (*Bull.*, 193, p. 137).

Geary Mine [Mariposa]. *See* Whitlock.

Genesee [Plumas]. On Indian Creek, tributary to the East Branch of the North Fork of Feather River, east of Taylorsville. The place was apparently named after the town in New York state. Between 1865 and 1868 the post office was called Geneseo. There was both drift and hydraulic mining, and according to the *Register*, 1900, two mills and one arrastre were in operation at that time.

Gentry Gulch [Mariposa]. A tributary to the North Fork of Merced River, eight miles east of Coulterville. In the early 1850s a lump of quartz found on top of the ground yielded 135 ounces of gold (Stephen Davis, April 3, 1853). The Hasloe Mine, later a consolidated mine that included the Gentry Gulch Mine, became a highly productive mine. (It is treated separately in this dictionary.) A mile west of the Hasloe was the Cherokee Mine, discovered in 1857 by a Cherokee Indian named Lovely Rogers; his mine was also known by his name. Some of the rich surface soil was worked in a hand mortar. The rock worked with arrastres yielded an average of 100 dollars per ton, according to Browne (p. 32). In 1859 when a steam-driven mill with eight stamps and two arrastres was built, the average yield was thirty-five dollars per ton; but it soon stopped, and the mill was sold at a sheriff's sale and was moved away in the early 1860s. In the 1880s and 1890s the mine was reactivated by the Shimer brothers (*Mining Bureau*, LIII, p. 122). On the North Fork of Merced River, at its confluence with Gentry Gulch, is the Bandarita Mine, discovered in 1856, first worked by arrastres, then by an 8-stamp water-driven mill, which produced as high as 100 dollars per ton, according to Browne (p. 33). The history of the mine to 1943 is continued in *Mining Bureau*, LIII (pp. 77 ff.). The total production exceeded 1.5 million dollars. Gentry Gulch and the Bandarita Mine are shown on the USGS Sonora 1939 quadrangle. *See* Hasloe Mine.

George Maker's [Nevada]. An unidentified place eight miles from Nevada City, listed in Brown's *Directory* (p. 133).

Georgetown [El Dorado]. The town was the center of the rich placer and seam diggings between the Hornblende and Slate mountains and the Middle and South forks of the American River. The first deposits were discovered by a young man named Hudson in the summer of 1849, according to a reliable contemporary source (Buffum, pp. 104 f.). He dug out 20 thousand dollars worth in six weeks. It is not known for which George the camp was named, George Phipps or George Ehrenhaft. *See California Place Names*. The camp is mentioned in the *Alta*, December 15, 1849, as Georgetown Dry Diggins with about "5,000 prosperous miners." Audubon (p. 239) mentions the place in 1850, and it appears on the maps of 1851 and in the name of the post office, October 7, 1851. Growlersburg was obviously only a nickname. Stephen Wing gives a description of the camp, October 20, 1854 (Journal, II, p. 16). The best early account is given by Lawson Patterson, who mined here from 1852 to 1862. The amount of gold mined in Georgetown Canyon by the spring of 1853 was 2 million dollars worth, as estimated by Haskins (p. 137). In 1867

eight mines were in operation and two were idle (Browne, p. 90). The Woodside Mine, described by Browne, yielded an average of thirty dollars per ton, using a concentrator invented by Mr. Woodside. The mine was discovered in 1860, but its existence was kept secret for a time. In 1866 a solid mass of gold was struck and more than 50 thousand dollars worth was produced in two days (Grass Valley *Union*, November 17 and 20, 1866). In 1876 there were forty stamps in operation at Georgetown (*Annual Mining Review*, 1876, p. 22) and in 1887 five mills with thirty-five stamps were operating (*Resources of El Dorado County*). The best later account of the district may be found in Raymond, VII (pp. 81 ff.). *See also* the County History, 1883 (pp. 187 f.). In 1902 there were still five stamp mills, one Huntington mill, and one arrastre listed in the *Register*, and some mining has continued until the present time with modern equipment. The Beebe Mine, a consolidation of Woodside-Eureka and other mines on the north side of Georgetown, is described in *Mining Bureau*, LII (pp. 406 f.). It produced 2 million dollars (*Bull.*, 193, p. 51). Edwin Markham taught school in Georgetown, and until recently the Talisman Press operated there. Historic Landmark 484.

George Town [Tuolumne]. North of Jamestown. Prominently shown on Trask's map, 1853. According to De Ferrari (p. 65), there was a short-lived attempt in late 1850 to form a new camp from the northern portion of Jamestown with the name Georgetown, but on May 25, 1851, the townspeople of the two camps held a meeting and voted to resume the name Jamestown. Both names appear, however, on Trask's map, 1853: George Tn on the north side of Woods Creek and James Tn to the south. The U. S. Bureau of the Census lists 462 inhabitants (in April, 1851) in the population schedule for Georgetown for the 1850 census and 791 inhabitants for Jamestown.

Georgia Bar [Merced]. On the north side of Dry Creek, two miles west of Merced River. Recorded on Trask's map, 1853.

Georgia Hill [Placer]. In Todds Valley, between the North and Middle forks of American River, south of Yankee Jims. Shown on Doolittle's map, 1868. The deposits were discovered accidentally by prospectors from Georgia in March, 1851, and they proved to be very rich (*Placer County Directory*, 1861, cited in Bancroft

Notes). Mining was later renewed on a large scale, and the total production by hydraulic mining (with Yankee Jims) prior to 1868 was 5 million dollars (*Mining Bureau*, XXIII, p. 262).

Georgia Slide [El Dorado]. On Canyon Creek, north of Georgetown. Rich seam deposits were worked here as early as 1850. In a letter datelined Oregon Canyon, January 19, 1851, Finley McDiarmid refers to Georgia Flatts, north of Georgetown. According to an informant in *Mining Bureau* (II, part 1, p. 150), a solid nugget of gold shaped like a goose egg, worth about one thousand dollars, was found at Georgia Slide in 1850. *See* Hudson Gulch. The *Annual Mining Review*, 1876 (p. 21), lists a 10-stamp water-driven mill, built in 1866. In 1887 it was still strictly a mining settlement with 100 inhabitants (*Resources of El Dorado County*, p. 91). Rich profits were made by a consolidated company until the enforcement of the law against hydraulic mining (*Mining Bureau*, LII, p. 436). The total production of the Georgia Slide mine is estimated at 6 million dollars (*Bull.*, 193, p. 51). Georgia Slide is usually considered the northern terminus of the Mother Lode. Recorded on the USGS Placerville 1931 quadrangle.

German. Despite the large number of German miners, the name is used for only a few camps and mines. Dutch was the general designation for people from Germany and central Europe.

German Bar [Nevada]. On the Middle Fork of Yuba River, on the road from Moores Flat to Alleghany, near the Sierra County line. Mining is said to have started in 1851. The bar is shown on Trask's map, 1853, and is mentioned in Trask's report of 1854 (document 9, p. 68). Hutchings lists it as German Diggings in 1855. A clipping from the Marysville *Express*, January 19, [1854?], records that three men of the German Bar Quartz Mining Company averaged 1 thousand to 3 thousand dollars a day, "unprecedented in the history of California" (Hittell Clippings, p. 23). Brown's *Directory* of 1856 lists it (p. 133). The bar was carried off by a flood in the winter of 1861–1862, but in the same year a rich lode was discovered, and it was said to have yielded as high as 100 thousand dollars a month (*Mining Press*, November 8, 1862). The German Bar Consolidated Mine is listed in 1940 in *Mining Bureau*, XXXVII (p. 451).

German Ridge [Calaveras]. On French Gulch and San Domingo Creek, north of

Angels Camp. It was so named because Germans operated a number of mines here with good success on a cooperative basis. Some mines were worked until the 1930s. A description is given in U. S. *Bulletin*, 413 (p. 133). *See* Dogtown.

Gerote No. 1; Gerote No. 2 [Tuolumne]. *See* Garrote.

Gibson Bar [Siskiyou]. On the Klamath River, near Gottville. No early mining records were found. The Gibson Bar Mine was reported idle in 1896, was reactivated in the 1920s (*Mining Bureau*, XXI, p. 43), and it is listed until 1935.

Gibsons Gulch [Tuolumne]. Between Martinez and Rattlesnake Gulch. It is mentioned as a placer camp in the Stockton *San Joaquin Republican*, May 16, 1854, and in the Columbia *Gazette*, May 20, 1854.

Gibsonville, Sierra Co.

Gibsonville [Sierra]. On Little Slate Creek near the Plumas County line. Shown on Trask's map, 1853. The camp was apparently named for a miner named Gibson, who was a partner of Captain Sears and who discovered new deposits on a ridge adjoining Sears Ridge (Hittell, *History*, III, pp. 96 f.) *See* Secret Ravine [Sierra]. According to a reprint from the Gibsonville *Trumpet* in the *Alta*, April 24, 1854, a rock of five tons was loosened, and from a small section of it eighty-four ounces of gold were realized after six days of labor with a small mortar. A post office was established June 18, 1855. John Clark in his journal, January 22, 1855, records that a miner in one day took out 18 hundred dollars worth of gold at the place called Gibson. Hutchings in his diary of November 8, 1855, gives a good description of the town, which had a population of about 700 at that time. The *Placer Press*, April 1,

1858, reports rich yieldings, and Vischer (p. 240) records mainly hydraulic mining in 1859. In the summer of 1862 many claims paid well, and a nugget of ninety-one ounces was picked up (*Mining Press*, July 16, 1862). According to Browne (p. 166), the deposits petered out in the late 1860s, but the County Map of 1874 shows the place as a sizeable town, and the San Francisco *Call*, May 18, 1879, reports that tunnel and hydraulic mining still paid. Some mines were still listed in 1942. The place is shown on modern maps.

Gilberts Ranch [Amador]. East of Fiddletown. Named for one of Ben Bowen's associates, who mined near by in 1854–55.

Gillespies [Trinity]. A camp of the 1850s on New River is mentioned by Cox (p. 106).

Gilson Mine [Tuolumne]. *See* Soulsbyville.

Gilta [Siskiyou]. In the extreme southwest corner of the county. It was the trading center and post office for the mines along Know-Nothing Creek. There was both placer and quartz mining in Gilta District. The *Register*, 1898, lists a 4-stamp mill. The Gilta Mine was worked mainly before 1900 and reportedly produced a million dollars (*Bull.*, 193, p. 137). *See also Mining Bureau*, XXXI (p. 283). Gilta is shown on the USGS Sawyers Bar 1945 quadrangle.

Git Up and Git. An unidentified place, listed in Hittell, *Resources*.

Gladstone Mine [Shasta]. *See* French Gulch and Jillsonville.

Gleason Mine [Placer]. *See* Iowa Hill.

Glen Aura [Nevada]. On the South Fork of Yuba River, probably under or near present Lake Spaulding. The name was given by A. J. McCall, who mined here with the New York Volunteers in 1849 (McCall, October 7, 1849).

Glencoe [Calaveras]. Ten miles northeast of Mokelumne Hill. Mexicans mined here in 1850. The post office for the place was named Musquito Gulch from 1873 to 1878, when it received the name of the historic town in Scotland. Both names were apparently used to designate the place. Raymond (VII, pp. 63 f.) mentions the Good Hope Mine, formerly worked by Mexicans with arrastres, which had an 18-stamp mill and was doing custom work in the Glencoe District in 1873. In 1899 the place was still the trading center and post office for quartz and drift mines (*Register*, 1899). Historic Landmark 280. *See* Mosquito Gulch.

Glines Canyon [Mono]. Above Green Lake. Charles Glines and others from Bridgeport, Connecticut, established a

mill and mining camp here in 1896. The chief claims were the Arnot and Par Value, the Par Value lending its name to a nearby lake. Ruins of the mill and the cabins and traces of the wagon road still remain. (F. S. Wedertz.)

Globe District [Tulare]. In the central part of the county. At the turn of the century there was some prospecting, particularly near Cow Mountain, north and west of the Tule River Indian Reservation (*Bull.*, 193, p. 52).

Goat Mountain [San Bernardino]. South of Barstow, in the Ord Mountains. Nine claims on the southwest slope were consolidated in the 1880s into the Gold Belt Mine, which operated until the 1930s (*Mining Bureau*, XXVII, p. 296; XXXVI, p. 235). It is still listed in 1953.

Goatville [Butte]. *See* Diamondville.

Godeys Gulch [Mariposa]. Shown on the Las Mariposas map, 1861, as a branch of Carson Creek, tributary to Agua Fria Creek, at Arkansas Flat. Alex Godey was probably the man who in 1849 found the first piece of gold-bearing quartz in this district (Crampton, p. 38). *See* Carsons.

Gods Country [Nevada]. North and east of Washington, between Canyon Creek and Little Canyon Creek, tributaries to the South Fork of Yuba River. Shown on Doolittle's map, 1868. According to Kinyon (pp. 133 ff.), it was once a well known area in the Gaston Ridge district, and a few shacks of a once prosperous camp were still standing in the summer of 1915. God's Country Ravine is given as the site of the Baltic lode mine, which had 20 stamps in operation at one time but was idle in 1918 (*Mining Bureau*, XII, p. 185; XVI, Nevada, p. 119). The Arctic Mine, at which a modern hydroelectric plant was installed in 1914, is described in *Mining Bureau* (XVI, Nevada, pp. 117 f.; XXXVII, pp. 384 f.), and other mines in the area are also described in these volumes. Gods Country has been almost completely denuded as the result of logging operations between 1945 and 1960 (Foley).

Goffs [San Bernardino]. About twenty-five miles northwest of Needles, on the main line of the Santa Fe. It was the southern terminus of the Nevada Southern (later California Eastern) Railroad, which served mines to the north as far as the Clark Mountain District and northeast as far as the Searchlight District in Nevada. Around 1920 and earlier, the community boasted a hotel, restaurant, store, and school, besides residences and railroad facilities. The post office was called Blake from 1896 to 1911. *See* Blake. (Belden, November 30, 1952; Haenszel.)

Gold Bank Mine [Butte]. *See* Forbestown.

Gold Bar [Nevada]. On the South Fork of Yuba River. Peter Decker mined here with good success in the summer of 1850 (Decker, July 26 and 29, 1850).

Gold Bar [Placer]. On the Middle Fork of American River, six miles east of Auburn. There was gold mining with intermittent success from the early 1850s. In 1875 a Gold Bar Mining Company with a capital of 10 million dollars was incorporated (*Pamphlets*, III, no. 9).

Gold Beach [Humboldt?]. The name, mentioned repeatedly in the *Alta* of June and July, 1850, refers apparently to the mining at Gold Bluffs and south of them. "Millions upon millions of dollars are lying on the beach."

Gold Bluff [Humboldt]. Near the town of Orick. According to the *Overland Monthly* (I, pp. 140 ff.), Hermann Ehrenberg and his party discovered the gold bluffs April 11, 1850, a few days before they discovered the mouth of Klamath River. Ehrenberg was a German-born veteran of the Texas War and later a famous Arizona pioneer. All newspapers reported the find, and the rush was exceeded only by the Gold Lake hunt. John Carr (pp. 89 ff.) gives a good account of the excitement. Gibbes' map, 1851, records the places as Gold Bluff and Beach. A chemist stated in the Sacramento *Transcript*, February 14 and 28, 1851 (Bancroft Notes) that one pound of the black sand yielded as much as seventy-five cents worth of gold, but that the sand was valueless unless an economic method of separation could be found. Details about mining the bluffs are given in Raymond, VI (pp. 144 ff.). The excitement helped to develop the Klamath-Trinity gold deposits. The washing of the sand for gold continued in a limited way for several decades, and the Gold Bluff Beach mines are listed in the reports of the Mining Bureau until 1888. The Gold Bluff Beach or Orick District is described in *Bulletin*, 193 (p. 180). According to this account, the estimated gold production by 1888 was more than one million dollars, and since that time there has been intermittent minor placer mining on the beaches in the region.

Gold Bluff [Sierra]. On the Middle Fork of the North Yuba River, north of Downieville. Shown on Trask's map, 1853. An 8-stamp mill, built in 1857, crushed about twenty tons of quartz daily and yielded an average of twenty dollars per ton (*Transactions*, 1858, pp. 193 f.). The mines operated almost continuously until 1902 and intermittently after 1914. The total production to 1954 is estimated at 1.5 million dollars (*Mining Bureau*, LII, p. 250). Nearby McKeebys Diggings were also called Gold Bluff.

Gold Bug Mine. *See* Canyon Creek [El Dorado]; Solomons Gulch [Mariposa].

Gold Camp [Kern]. On Tropico Hill, west of Rosamond. The *Desert Magazine*, June, 1963, published an illustrated article on this ghost mining camp.

Gold Canyon [Sierra]. At the foot of Table Rock, seven miles north of Downieville. It is shown as a settlement on the County Map of 1874. There was another Gold Canyon southeast of Alleghany, near the Nevada County line, where the Gold Cañon or Two Counties mine was discovered in the 1860s; it was still listed in 1942 (*Mining Bureau*, XVI [Sierra], pp. 89 f.; XXXVIII, p. 56. The production is estimated at between 750 thousand and one million dollars (*Bull.*, 193, p. 23).

Gold Cliff [Calaveras]. A productive mine in the town of Angels Camp. It was later operated by the Utica Company, which announced a total production of almost three million dollars. Shown on the *Guidebook* map 3.

Golden Center Mines [Nevada]. *See* Grass Valley.

Golden Chariot Group [San Diego]. In the Banner district. The quartz deposits were worked from 1871 to about 1876. There was intermittent mining until 1932, and since 1946 there has been limited exploratory work. The estimated production of 700 thousand dollars in gold ranks it second in the district. (*Mining Bureau*, XXX, pp. 350 f.; *County Report*, III, p. 124.) A detailed account is given by Ellsberg (pp. 45 ff.). *See* Banner City; Julian District.

Golden City [Trinity]. *See* Ridgeville.

Golden City [Tuolumne]. In the Tuolumne County *Great Register* of voters for 1872, Golden City is given as the residence of several miners, an assayer, a carpenter, a saloon keeper, and an engineer. No other record was found.

Golden Cross Mine [Imperial]. *See* Cargo Muchacho.

Golden Eagle Mine. *See* Hayden Hill [Lassen] and Indian Creek [Siskiyou].

Golden Gate: Creek, Mine [Amador]. The

Creek is a tributary to the North Fork of Sutter Creek. The County Map, 1866, indicates a mine and mill about three miles northeast of Volcano. It is listed in the *Register*, 1903. The Creek is shown on the USGS Jackson 1938 quadrangle.

Golden Gate Flume [Butte]. On Feather River, three miles above Oroville. The big flume was constructed in the 1880s to divert water from the river. A detailed description may be found in *Mining Bureau*, IX (pp. 271 f.). It was the same locale as the earlier Cape River Claim and the Union Cape Claim.

Golden Gate Hill [Calaveras]. Six miles northwest of San Andreas. It was also known as Golden Gate Butte. Recorded as Golden Gate on Trask's map, 1853. A branch of the rich old river channel of the county winds around it. A Golden Gate mine, one mile north of San Andreas, is listed in the Mining Bureau reports until 1936. Golden Gate Hill is shown on the USGS Jackson 1938 quadrangle.

Golden Gate: Mine, Tunnel [Plumas]. In a hill above Onion Valley, at the headwaters of Feather River. Gold was struck in 1856, and the vein gave out in 1865 (Quincy *Union*, December 16, 1865). The lead seemed to be a continuation of the great Blue Lead of Forest City, according to *Transactions*, 1858 (p. 202). A Golden Gate mine in the Sawpit District was relocated apparently in the early part of the twentieth century (*Mining Bureau*, XVI, Plumas, p. 91); it was still listed in 1937. Another Golden Gate mine was farther north at Round Valley, near Greenville. It is described by Browne (p. 169) as having had an 8-stamp water-driven mill in 1867, with an average yield of twenty-two dollars per ton.

Golden Point [Nevada]. Near Grass Valley. Rich yields were reported in the Grass Valley *Telegraph* in March, 1854 (Hittell Clippings, p. 26). *See* Gold Point.

Golden Queen Mines [Kern]. *See* Mojave Mining District.

Golden Rule Hill [Tuolumne]. South of Stent; between Stent and Sullivan Creek. It was on a slate vein containing gold. There was a 15-stamp water-driven mill here, and the average yield was about nine dollars per ton (Browne, pp. 42 f.). The Golden Rule Mine was productive until 1871, was later reopened, and was reported in operation in 1896 (*Mining Bureau*, XIII, p. 472). It is still being worked on a small scale (De Ferrari).

Golden Rule Mine [Placer]. Seven miles southwest of Auburn. It is shown on Doolittle's map, 1868, as Golden Rule Q. M. In 1867 a 20-stamp steam-driven mill was under construction. A detailed description is given by Browne (pp. 109 f.).

Golden Wedge. An unidentified place, listed in the Work Projects Administration project.

Gold Flat [El Dorado]. North of Diamond Springs. The miners of the Gold Flat district participated in a mass meeting at Diamond Springs, March 29, 1856 (Hayes Scrapbooks: Mining, I, sec. 34). The locality is also recorded in Crockett's account book, 1859.

Gold Flat [Nevada]. About one mile south of Nevada City. Shown on Doolittle's map, 1868. The diggings were discovered in 1850, and by 1851 a camp had developed with a population of around 300, about thirty cabins, two stores, six saloons, a butcher shop, four boarding houses, and a gambling house. Within a year the place was nearly deserted, was briefly revived in 1852 when claims were consolidated and sluicing operations were carried on, but by 1853 the town was gone. Gradually with the discovery and development of quartz mining, settlement was renewed, and in 1880 there were about sixty houses on the flat. (Co. Hist., 1880, pp. 86 f.) According to Bean (pp. 120 and 123), some mines yielded sixty to seventy dollars per ton, and for some time in 1862 one (Sneath and Clay) yielded as much as 180 dollars per ton. The Gold Flat-Potosi Mine, opened in 1851 with the Pittsburg, was a large producer operating as the Pittsburg Group and yielding an estimated 900 thousand dollars between 1862 and 1879 (*Mining Bureau*, XVI, Nevada, p. 234). Mines at Gold Flat are listed in the reports of the Mining Bureau until 1941.

Gold Gulch [Marin]. At Tomales Point. Gold was discovered in February, 1866, and according to the Petaluma *Journal*, February 15, 1866, the placers yielded sixteen dollars per day to the man. The County History, 1880 (p. 311), records extensive placering for two years, but the average daily yield was only two and a half dollars to the man.

Gold Gulch [Santa Cruz]. A creek and its tributary six miles from the mouth of San Lorenzo River. According to the *Pacific Sentinel*, Santa Cruz, June 14, 1856, some forty miners earned from three to ten dollars per day in the summer of 1855.

Gold Gulch Dry Diggings [Butte]. On the Middle Fork of Feather River, fifteen miles

northeast of Oroville. Recorded on Milleson and Adams' map, 1851.

Gold Hill [Amador]. Listed in Hittell's roster. The fineness of gold under the lava
bed was 968 degrees (Mining Bureau, IV,
p. 219). On the County Map, 1866, Gold
Hill is shown as a topographic feature just
west of Tunnel Hill, between Jackson and
Butte City.

Gold Hill [Calaveras]. There were several
hills so designated in the county. Poore
mentions a Gold Hill about a mile due
west of San Andreas, to which water was
brought from the Cave City area. This
may be the Gold Hill mentioned in an undated clipping, probably in the 1860s, in
Bancroft Scraps, LI:1 (p. 182), which reported the laying of a pipe from Cave City
to Gold Hill, where the reportedly rich
deposits had not been worked for lack of
water. Another Gold Hill, apparently also
called Tunnel Hill, was east of San Andreas on the divide between O'Neils and
San Antonio creeks, where rich deposits
were found at the end of the ancient river
bed from Table Mountain. The deposits,
under a cap of volcanic rock, were worked
for years with moderate success. (San
Francisco *Bulletin*, Jan. 18, 1858, in Bancroft
Notes.) Still another Gold Hill, mentioned
by Doble, is shown on Camp's map about
four miles northwest of San Andreas, at
approximately the location of Gold Hill
Mine recorded on the USGS Jackson 1902
quadrangle.

Gold Hill [El Dorado]. About five miles
northwest of Placerville, near Granite Hill.
Shown on Doolittle's map, 1868, and on
Bowman's, 1873. Stephen Wing mentions
Gold Hill two and a half miles from Coloma in his Journal (II, p. 77, April 15,
1854). In an item in the *Alta* of December
17, 1855, it is stated that the citizens
changed the name to Granite Hill to avoid
confusion with other places called Gold
Hill. *See* Granite Hill. Rensch-Hoover
states that the ruins of the town are still
visible, and the roofless wall of a sandstone building is still standing. A Gold
Hill Mine, northeastward, near Kelsey, is
mentioned in *Mining Bureau*, XVIII (p. 44).
Gold Hill Ditch is shown on Bowman's
map, 1873, northeast of Kelsey.

Gold Hill [Mariposa]. Near Mormon Bar.
Rich diggings were reported on the hill
after 1849; however, Allsop on November
27, 1852, indicates that there was no gold
worth working there at that time. The
Gold Hill listed in the table in Mining
Bureau, XXIV (p. 98) and in LIII (p. 264) is

shown on the Economic map of the USGS
Atlas, Sonora Folio, 1895, about one mile
northwest of Mount Bullion. It was a
former Las Mariposas Grant mine and
was active intermittently between 1910
and 1915.

Gold Hill [Nevada]. West of Washington,
near Jefferson Bar, on a tributary to the
South Fork of Yuba River. Shown on
Doolittle's map, 1868. The *Alta*, February
27, 1854, reports that one company of
three men took out 400 dollars one day
and 300 dollars another day. This is probably the Gold Hill to which Hittell refers in
Mining Bureau, IV (pp. 221, 224), where he
states that the yield with Rocky Bar was as
high as eighty dollars per ton, and the
gold fineness was up to 970°. The Nevada
Democrat, April 21, 1858, reported that one
company had taken out twenty-two
pounds of gold on one day at Gold Hill.

Gold Hill [Nevada]. In Grass Valley. It was
the richest and best known of the many
gold hills. Gold-bearing quartz was discovered in June, 1850. L. M. Schaeffer (pp.
120 f.) writes of the place as follows: "Direct opposite to my cabin was a hill seldom visited, except by an occasional
miner in search of firewood. By the merest
chance gold-bearing quartz was discovered upon its summit." According to
Vischer, the accidental discoverer was a
German prospector. Perhaps it was the
Dr. Wittenbach who erected the first experimental mill at the place (Bean, p. 187).
According to *Mines and Minerals* (p. 266),
the discovery was not made until October
of the same year. The first detailed description is given by Trask in 1854 (document 9, p. 84). The reports about the total
yield vary. Cronise (p. 580) states that it is
said to have reached as much as 5 million
dollars by 1865. Among the owners of
mines listed in *Annual Mining Review*, 1876
(p. 44), was George Hearst. Additional
descriptions may be found in *Guidebook* (p.
33); Bean (pp. 218 ff.); *Mining Press*, December 21, 1860. For the later developments *see* the bibliography in *Mining
Bureau* (XVI, Nevada, pp. 174, 211 ff. 218).

Gold Hill [Placer]. In Auburn Ravine, five
miles below Ophir. Shown on Trask's
map, 1853. This is obviously the Gold Hill
which John E. Banks reported as having
yielded richly in the winter 1851–52
(*Buckeye Rovers*, pp. 155 ff.). The deposits
were discovered in the spring of 1851 by a
party of miners from Georgia (*Directory* of
Placer County, 1861, cited in Bancroft
Notes). Hutchings stated that the diggings

were not remarkably rich, though as much as five dollars to the pan were found. At the time of the writing of his diary, April 29, 1855, the place was called Orr City. In 1868 a 4-stamp mill was in operation (*Annual Mining Review*, 1876, p. 21). The hill is still recorded on the USGS Auburn 1954 quadrangle. *See* Oro City; Mugginsville.

Gold Hill [Tuolumne]. At the northwest corner of Columbia. Shown on Wallace's map, 1853, just above the "Graveyard." Among the more than a score of claims between Gold Hill and French Gulch, its western boundary, listed in the Eastman file is the often mentioned Brainard (or Gregory and Company) claim, which yielded 17 hundred dollars in one week of June, 1854 (San Francisco *Evening News*, June 14, 1854), and in which a pound a day was not considered a great day's work (Columbia *Gazette*, June 3, 1854). The pay was ten to twenty dollars a day to the man (Columbia *Gazette*, May 27, 1854). Numerous large nuggets discovered at Gold Hill included one weighing 360 ounces, found imbedded in the ground and valued at about 65 hundred dollars (*Mining Bureau*, 1880–82, part 1, p. 148); another piece of 270 ounces in the Dalrymple claim, of which eight pounds was established as pure gold (San Francisco *Herald*, December 19, 1861); one weighing twenty-four ounces found in the Stearns claim the day after the owners had tried in vain to sell the claim for thirty dollars (Hittell Clippings, p. 31); another lump worth 300 dollars found in the tailings of an old claim (*Mining Press*, May 8, 1862). Similar reports are found in the San Jose *Pioneer*, February 16, 1878, and in *Mines and Minerals* (p. 357).

Gold: Hill, Canyon [Sierra]. Near Gibsonville. Rich yield was reported in 1858. A 48-ounce nugget of pure gold, worth 875 dollars was picked up in a tail race (Hittell Clippings, p. 28). Vischer in 1859 (p. 240) mentions that mainly tunnel work was carried on at the place.

Gold Lake. There are three Gold Lakes in Butte, Plumas, and Sierra counties. None of these lakes has anything to do with the famous Gold Lake hunt of 1849–50. Some gold was found in the Gold Lake northeast of Downieville, according to later reports. But the lake of the Stoddart stories and J. C. Tucker's tale, *To the Golden Goal*, is a phantom, and the hunt was started by a hoax. Its connection with the Gold Rush was that it led to the discovery and development of the rich deposits in the region of the Upper Feather River and that it brought about a noticeable shifting of the mining population in the Northern and even the Southern mines. The most detailed, but somewhat confusing, contemporary account is found in Bruff's *Gold Rush*. A very good contemporary account is given by Schaeffer ((pp. 81 ff.), who left Washington City on the South Fork of Yuba River with his party on June 7, 1850, in search of the lake but gave up in disgust after four days. Another contemporary, interesting but not very reliable account is that of Chris M. Waage, the ghost writer of Downie, *Hunting for Gold*. For a modern account *see* Jerry McKevitt's in *Journal of the West* (III, pp. 489–500) with an extensive bibliography. *See also California Place Names*. Hittell, *Mining*, (p. 25), reprints an item from the San Andreas *Independent* which tells the story of still another gold lake and the consequent excitement in the summer of 1861. It is probably only a warmed-up story of the previous hoax.

Gold Lake [Plumas]. On the boundary between Plumas and Butte counties, within the Granite Basin mining district. It is mentioned in *Mining Bureau* (XVI, Plumas, pp. 18 ff.). The lake is considered by some writers to be the phantom Gold Lake of 1850.

Gold Lake [Sierra]. Northeast of Downieville. In 1849 or 1850, a little gold was discovered in the sand of the lake, and exaggerated claims were made. Claims were taken up around the lake, with some success, but the metal in the sand of the lake was surface gold only. (San Francisco *Call*, May 18, 1879; Bancroft Scraps, V, pp. 1806 f.)

Gold Mountain [Amador]. Near Lower Rancheria, north of Sutters Creek. There is no record of early diggings, but in 1874 a 40-stamp mill was scheduled to be opened (Raymond, VI, p. 87). One mine, also known as Quartz Mountain Mine, was active in the 1880s and is still listed in the Mining Bureau reports until about 1954. (*Mining Bureau*, XI, p. 145; XII, p. 72; L, p. 246).

Gold Mountain [Nevada]. A camp near Grass Valley. A letter dated April 6, 1857, and several other letters by William Elder tell of rich quartz mining. The camp was apparently successful for some time. There were two crushing machines; and the people tried to establish a post office. It may be the same place mentioned in retrospect (1890) by Stewart Sheldon, at which gold was discovered on a "dare" in

1849 or 1850 (?), followed by a "rush" during which "hundreds of thousands of dollars a day" were taken out (Sheldon, p. 63).

Gold Mountain [San Bernardino]. Overlooking Lake Baldwin. The Gold Mountain (Doble) mine was operated from 1860 to 1900 by the well-known promoter, E. J. ("Lucky") Baldwin and by his successors into the 1940s (Nadeau, p. 252; *Mining Bureau*, XVII, p. 346; XLIX, p. 74). *See* Bairdstown; Doble.

Gold Point [Nevada]. Two miles east of Grass Valley. It was perhaps the same place as Golden Point, where rich deposits were reported in 1854. *See* Golden Point. *Mining Bureau* (XVI, Nevada, p. 176) records that a number of mines were consolidated in the Gold Point Group.

Gold Point [Sierra]. Six miles east of Downieville. In the early 1900s the Gray Eagle Mine up the ravine was being worked (Sinnott, *Sierra City*, p. 88).

Gold Reef District [San Bernardino]. In the Clipper Mountains, five miles northwest of Danby. Gold was discovered in 1915. The Clipper Mountain, Gold Reef, and Tom Reed mines were consolidated but were already idle in 1920. (*Mining Bureau*, XVII, p. 345; XXVII, p. 291; XLIX, table 38.)

Gold Run [Butte]. An unidentified place listed in the *State Register*, 1859, as having had a 16-stamp mill in 1852. A creek designated as Gold Run in the upper Sacramento Valley, northwest of Oroville, is shown on the USGS Oroville 1944 quadrangle.

Gold Run [Lassen]. The stream is a tributary to Susan Creek. Shown on the USGS Honey Lake 1899 quadrangle. No mining records were found, except the statement of Lindgren in 1911 (p. 115) that there was a little placer mining a few miles south of Susanville, the northernmost place in the Sierra Nevada at which gold mining was carried on.

Gold Run [Nevada]. The stream is mentioned on August 26, 1849: "on the banks of Deer Creek and Gold Run — as they have ever since been called — they struck some of the richest and most famous diggings ever known in California" (Wistar, I, p. 126). In April, 1850, claims sold from 5 thousand to 18 thousand dollars, according to Bancroft, VI (p. 358).

Gold Run [Placer]. About eight miles northeast of Colfax. The auriferous gravel in Gold Run Canyon was discovered in the spring of 1850 and proved to be so rich

that the price of some claims soon rose to as high as 18 thousand dollars (Sacramento *Transcript*, April 26, 1850, *in* Bancroft Notes). The place became known by the run through the camp. The post office was called Mountain Springs from 1854 to 1863. After the water supply was assured, first from Canyon Creek, then from Dutch Flat Ditch, and finally from South Yuba Ditch, the place developed into an important center of hydraulic mining. Detailed descriptions are given in Browne (p. 101 f.) and Raymond (VII, pp. 98 ff.). About 80 million cubic yards of gravel were mined hydraulically here (Lindgren, *Tertiary Gravels*, p. 145). This is about the quantity used to build Oroville Dam (Gianella). Between 1865 and 1878 more than 6 million dollars worth of gold were shipped from the Gold Run Express Office, according to *Bulletin*, 193 (p. 52). Moderate mining continued in the district until around 1915, with minor work in the twenties and thirties. Gold Run is Historic Landmark 405.

Gold Run, Placer Co.

Goldsboro [Shasta]. In the western part of the county, near the present settlement of Platina, in the vicinity of Bee Gum Creek. In 1900 a school district named Goldsboro was formed. (*Covered Wagon*, 1964, pp. 30 f.) No record of gold mining was found. Platina is in a platinum ore area (Steger).

Gold Spring [Tuolumne]. One mile northwest of Columbia. It was also called Gold

Springs. The camp was formerly a half mile west of the springs. Shown on Wallace's map, 1853, and Dart's, 1879. Gold was discovered and the place settled by Roderick S. Hatch in April, 1850 (Stoddart, p. 129). Jolly and partner located a claim here, built a ditch with another company to bring water from Gold Spring Gulch to Sandy Gulch, and prospered (Jolly's *Gold Spring Diary*, pp. 9 f.). In 1855 the camp had 500 inhabitants according to Heckendorn (p. 72). In 1854 a 9-ounce piece of pure gold was found (Hittell Clippings, p. 20), and about forty toms and several sluicing claims were in operation in the surrounding hills. In one claim an ounce of gold to the cart load was common, according to the Columbia *Gazette*, June 24, 1854. The Furnabaugh claim in the rear of Hatch's garden, east of Gold Spring, paid nine to fifteen dollars per day to the man (*San Joaquin Republican*, June 7, 1857); the Smith, Carver claim, repeatedly mentioned, yielded 266 ounces in one week with 106 ounces in a single afternoon (San Francisco *Bulletin*, January 8, 1863). Numerous similar reports are listed in the Eastman file. The Gold Springs District and Nigger Gulch District are reported to have produced 7.5 million dollars (*Mining Bureau*, XXIV, p. 42). The place is shown on the USGS Big Trees 1941 quadrangle.

Gold Springs [El Dorado]. On the creek tributary to Weber Creek, near Placerville. On Trask's map the settlement is shown west of Placerville and on Bowman's map, 1873, it is shown about four miles northwest of Placerville, and adjoining Gold Springs Flat is to the west. It is apparently the same as Cold Springs.

Goldstone [San Bernardino]. About thirty-five miles north of Barstow. The name designates a dry lake, a ghost town, and a mining district. The district is a twentieth century development. After 1912 there were three periods of gold mining activities. A detailed account is given by Belden, October 6, 1957. At first there was only dry washing in gulches where auriferous alluvium was deposited by erosion. In 1916 the Red Bridge Mine shipped ore assayed at 200 dollars per ton. (*Mining Bureau*, XV, pp. 804 ff.; XXVII, p. 310; XXX, p. 250; XLIX, table 23 following p. 259.) Shown on modern maps.

Goldtown [Kern]. In the Mojave Mining District. The township is shown on a map in *Mining Bureau*, (XIX, p. 156).

Goler: Gulch, Canyon, Placers [Kern]. Northwest of Randsburg. The discovery

of placer gold here in 1893 led to the development of the rich Randsburg-Johannesburg district. For many years the placers were well paying, mostly by dry washing; in the 1930s a washing and sluicing plant was built near the mouth of the canyon. In 1933 nuggets valued as high as 400 dollars each were found in test holes. (*Mining Bureau*, XXIX, p. 279; XXX, p. 245; XLV, p. 223; *County Report*, I, p. 154.) Although the place is miles away from Death Valley, the discoverers chose the name because they believed that they had come across the long-searched-for Goler mine or nuggets.

Goler Mine [Inyo]. It is one of the famous "lost mines" in Death Valley. Among the Argonauts who crossed Death Valley in 1849 were two Germans, Wolfgang Tauber and John Goller. Tauber claimed that he had found a rich gold deposit, and after his early death, Goller (or Goler, as his name was usually spelled) tried to locate the find, which then became known as Goler's mine or Goler's nuggets. The well-known carriage maker of Los Angeles may have been the same Goler, but Harris Newmark, who knew the pioneer well, does not mention the gold episode in his *Sixty Years in Southern California*. The Los Angeles *Star* in May, 1861, reported that a party was close to finding the lost mine but was driven back by hostile Indians (*Mining Press*, May 18, 1861, p. 8). A modern account is given by Weight (pp. 31 ff.).

Goler Wash [Inyo]. At the western boundary of Death Valley National Monument. This may have been the place where Wolfgang Tauber discovered gold early in 1850. Carl Mengel, once the partner of Shorty Harris and in 1912 owner of the Oro Fino Claim, found a small but rich pocket here (*Death Valley Guide*, p. 62). *See* Goler Mine.

Golls Diggins [Butte]. On the South Fork of Feather River. The place is mentioned by Hiram G. Ferris in a letter of December 29, 1850.

Gomorrah [Nevada]. South of the Middle Fork of Yuba River, west of Orleans. Shown on the map in Canfield's *Diary*. It is listed in the State Library Roster, and is mentioned in the Nevada County Historical Society *Bulletin*, April, 1949.

Good Hope Mine [Riverside]. *See* Pinecate.

Goodhues Camp [Sierra]. Breyfogle (p. 25) camped here March 2, 1850. The name is probably a misspelling of Goodyears.

Gibbes' map of 1851 shows it as Goodhues. *See* Goodyears Bar.

Goodyears: Bar, Creek [Sierra]. On the North Fork of Yuba River, southwest of Downieville. Miles and his brother Andrew Goodyear, the former a mountain man and founder of a fort in Utah before the advent of the Mormons, mined in the region of the North Fork of Yuba River and Goodyear Creek in the late summer of 1849. The post office was established October 7, 1851. In 1852 it was a contender for the county seat, but it lost out to Downieville. The newspapers reported rich yields (numerous items are in Bancroft Notes and Bancroft Scraps), and the name appears on the maps of 1851. The town began to decline around 1860, and in 1864 it burned down almost completely. But it continued as a post office and an election precinct. Mining was carried on with good success on the creek, according to the *Mining Press*, May 8, 1862, and it continued into the twentieth century. *See* Goodhues Camp.

Gopher City [Sierra]. Apparently in the Downieville region. It is mentioned in the Sacramento *Union*, December 19, 1854 (Bancroft Notes).

Gopher Flat [Amador]. Near Sutter Creek. An unidentified camp mentioned by John W. Winkley in "The Knave," September 22, 1963. The name apparently arose because of the tunneling from one hole to another close to the surface of the ground.

Gopher Hill [El Dorado]. On a ridge between two branches of Canyon Creek, about five miles northeast of Georgetown. Shown on Bowman's map, 1873. It was reported as favorably located for hydraulic mining and as having yielded well in the past, but in 1871 it was almost abandoned (Raymond, IV, p. 106).

Gopher Hill [El Dorado]. On Dutch Creek, east of Coloma. In 1874 there was mainly hydraulic mining, according to Raymond, VII (p. 95). The Gopher Hill Mine is recorded on the USGS Placerville 1931 quadrangle.

Gopher Hill [Nevada]. Near the South Fork of Yuba River, northeast of Nevada City. It is shown as a settlement on Raymond's map of the Great Gravel Deposit (VI, p. 108). The *Alta*, April 29, 1854, reports that some claims averaged only ten to twelve dollars because of the many boulders. It is apparently the same site as the Gopher Hill mentioned by Bean, by Browne (p. 122), and in the *Mining Press*, March 23, 1861.

Gopher Hill [Plumas]. Near Spanish Ranch. A large company mined here in the 1870s (*Annual Mining Review*, 1876, p. 49). A hydraulic Gopher Hill Mine is listed in 1894 in *Mining Bureau*, XII (p. 14).

Gopher Town [Placer]. Near Mountain Springs (later Gold Run). Notice of a claim for water rights on a section of the North Fork of American River near the junction with Blue Canyon is datelined Mountain Springs near Gopher Town, February 9, 1855 (Placer County Records, I, pp. 281 f.).

Gorda [Monterey]. In Los Burros District, near Jolon. Two small camps, Gorda and Los Burros, developed when a quartz vein was discovered in 1887. *See* Los Burros District. For the derivation of the name, *see California Place Names*.

Gordon Gulch [Tulare]. In the White River Mining district. According to a communication dated January 16, 1858, in an unidentified clipping in Hayes Scrapbooks: Mining, VII (sec. 23), the miners were making ten to sixteen dollars a day. Two companies had been working quietly since September, 1857, and when the news leaked out a "grand rush" ensued. The *Mining Press*, after mentioning varied results, reports June 9, 1862, the discovery of a rich quartz lead eight inches thick, of which one-fourth was gold.

Gosling Ravine [Placer]. On Canyon Creek, near Gold Run Ravine. The Gosling or Goosling Company started work in 1854 (Browne, p. 103). Mining did not prosper, however, until the big ditch from the South Fork of Yuba River brought water for hydraulicking in 1864.

Gospel: Flat, Gulch, Swamp [Calaveras?]. Unidentified places. All three are mentioned in the State Library Roster, and Gospel Gulch is also mentioned in Hittell, *Resources*, 1874 (p. 433). It might be the site of the Gospel Mine listed in Mining Bureau reports until 1935.

Gospel Swamp [Inyo]. At or near the town of Bishop Creek (later Bishop). The *Inyo Independent*, October 11, 1879, reports that plans were being made to build a Methodist Church at the cost of 3 thousand dollars on a piece of land on the corner of a ranch, apparently at the edge of Bishop, which was donated for the purpose. The town of Bishop already had the only church building in Mono and Inyo counties at that time, according to the newspaper account. No mining record was found for the place, but gold was mined nearby, particularly at the Cardinal or Wilshire-Bishop Mine, southwest of Bishop. *See* Bishop Creek District.

Gottville [Siskiyou]. Northwest of Yreka, on the Klamath River. It was a trading center and post office for the placers of this region on the Klamath River. A 5-stamp mill is listed in the *Register*, 1898. The place was named for William N. Gott, whose family owned one of the large mines here in the 1880s. Since 1934 the name of the post office has been Klamath River.

Gouge Eye [Nevada]. Near Greenhorn Creek, five miles northwest of Dutch Flat. The place was located about 1855 by a French company and was so named because a member of another company whose claim had been jumped lost one eye in the ensuing fight (*Nevada Directory*, 1895, p. 109). In 1892 the Gouge Eye Mine was profitably mined by Chinese (*Mining Bureau*, XI, p. 318). Respectable people called the place Hunts Hill. Browne, in 1867 (p. 122), lists both names as if they applied to separate places. *See* Hunts Hill.

Governor Mine [Los Angeles]. *See* Acton.

Grahams Ranch [Santa Cruz]. According to an undated clipping in Bancroft Scraps LI:1 (p. 175), a boulder of quartz was found in 1854 which yielded nearly 27 thousand dollars in gold. An extensive mining district developed, but the output of gold and silver was too small, and the diggings were soon abandoned. The report was not found confirmed elsewhere, but it might be the boulder found in a creek issuing from Ben Lomond Mountain. F. A. Hihn, who later founded Capitola, is said to have secured a large amount of gold from this boulder, according to *Mining Bureau*, XVII (p. 235). *See* Ben Lomond Mountain and Gold Gulch [Santa Cruz].

Grand Bar [Calaveras]. On the Stanislaus River. In 1857 one company netted 14 thousand dollars at the Bar (Hittell Clippings, p. 66½, from the Sonora *Herald*). According to his statements to Bancroft in 1877, Charles H. Chamberlain mined at Grand Bar in 1850, but he locates it on the Mokelumne River.

Granite [Kern]. *See* Elmer.

Granite Bar [Placer]. On the North Fork of American River, above Lacys Bar. It is mentioned in Bancroft Notes and in the County History, 1882 (p. 401). Rensch-Hoover locates it in El Dorado County.

Granite Basin [Plumas]. About six miles east of Buckeye. The place is mentioned in a letter by Asa B. Smith dated November 13, 1859. A correspondent of the Sacramento *Union* (Hayes Scrapbooks: Mining, IV, sec. 15) reports that the "rich hill diggings . . . through which ran a vein of solid gold" had a teeming and thrifty population a few years before but were deserted in 1864. However, the mines and the district are listed in the reports of the Mining Bureau until the middle of the twentieth century, and the basin is shown on the USGS Bidwell Bar 1944 quadrangle. The district is described in *Bulletin*, 193 (p. 52).

Granite City. *See* Folsom [Sacramento].

Granite Hill [El Dorado]. East of the town of Gold Hill. It is shown on early maps, but local residents recall that Granite Hill School was at Gold Hill (Schlappi-Ferguson). An item in the *Alta*, December 17, 1855, states that the citizens changed the name to Granite Hill in order to avoid confusion with other places called Gold Hill. Frickstad records that the post office at Cold (!) Springs was changed to Granite Hill in 1874. *See* Cold Springs and Gold Hill. Granite Hill is shown on the USGS Placerville 1931 quadrangle.

Granite Springs [Tulare]. In the Coso District. The *Mining Press*, June 9, 1862, reports that one company had to abandon a rich claim because of the approach of hostile Indians.

Granite Springs District [Mariposa; Tuolumne]. In the northwest corner of Mariposa County and the southwest corner of Tuolumne County, in the vicinity of Lake McClure and Don Pedro Reservoir, as outlined in *Bulletin*, 193 (p. 53). The mines were apparently last worked in the 1930s.

Granite Station [Kern]. *See* Elmer.

Graniteville [Nevada]. Two miles south of the Middle Fork of Yuba River. For early development *see* Eureka [Nevada]. The name Eureka was changed to Graniteville when the post office was established August 26, 1867. The place was a distribution point for reservoirs and ditches. In 1895 there were still thirty active mines in the region near Graniteville (*Nevada Directory*, 1895), and the *Register* of 1900 lists four stamp mills. According to *Bulletin*, 193 (p. 53), there was again activity in the Graniteville or Eureka district (which includes the Gaston mines) in the 1930s, and a few mines were worked briefly after World War II. Among the most productive mines were the Ancho-Erie, which yielded more than one million dollars; the Gaston, 2 million (?); and the Yuba, more than 2 million.

Grape Vine District [Calaveras]. Four miles

northwest of Columbia. Many mines and claims are listed in the 1850s. It is mentioned by Heckendorn (p. 104) as an area served by Valliceto [Vallecito] post office in 1856.

Grapevine District [Inyo]. In the northern part of Death Valley National Monument. At one time some gold was mined in Grapevine Canyon, at the north end of Grapevine Mountains, according to *Bulletin*, 193 (p. 149). No further details are given.

Grapevine District [San Bernardino]. North of Barstow. Shown on the County Map, 1892. There are several small lode-gold mines and dry placer deposits in the district, but apparently only one, the Olympus, has been worked. The famous Waterman Silver Mine is in the district. *See* Waterman.

Grapevine District [San Diego]. Grapevine Canyon is a tributary to San Felipe Creek, south of Banner. About 1903 the chief mine was the Dewey, which was equipped with a mill that was never used; in 1915 the principal claim was the Ready Relief (*Mining Bureau*, XIV, pp. 648 f.). The history of the Ready Relief Mine to 1903 is given in Ellsberg (pp. 42 f.).

Grass Flat [Sierra]. In Slate Creek Basin, three miles east of La Porte. Shown on Crossman's map, 1867. A detailed account of hydraulic mining in 1872 is given by Raymond (V, p. 83).

Grass Valley [Nevada]. On Highway 49, southwest of Nevada City. The nucleus of the town was the sawmill built in the fall of 1849. The place was known as Grass Valley from the beginning, although the post office name was Centreville from July 10, 1851 to August 20, 1852. According to Bancroft, VI (p. 357), D. Stump and two other Oregonians had discovered gold in 1848, and the placers in the Boston Ravine yielded 4 million dollars within six years. But the lucky strike which made Grass Valley famous came in 1850. In June, July, September, or October (the sources differ) a German carrying a bucket of water on Gold Hill stumbled over a piece of gold bearing quartz. When Heinrich Schliemann, the famous excavator of Troy, visited the place in May, 1851, there were already three mills in operation, and a fellow countryman told him that he cleared one thousand dollars in a week. The best contemporary accounts of the early days are by A. A. Sargent in Brown's *Directory*, 1856 (pp. 37–43), and by Eduard Vischer (pp. 244 f.). Edwin F. Morse, who

lived in Boston Ravine from 1852 to 1909, told his story in his old age. Hutchings states in his diary, October 4, 1855, that the population in 1855 was about 1,700, including many miners from Cornwall. The mills from 1851 to 1858 are listed in the *State Register*, 1859. In 1857 quartz mining apparently reached its peak, according to the reports in the newspapers. The principal mines and claims in the vicinity were on Gold, Ophir, New York, Osborne, Massachusetts, and Hueston hills. For more details, *see* the entries under these names. The annual production during the peak years was estimated at 5 million dollars, of which 4.2 million found their way to the mint (*Mining Press*, April 27, 1861). Professor B. Silliman esimates the total production between 1851 and 1866 to have been probably in excess of 23 million dollars (Browne, p. 111). The mines of Grass Valley were, with those of Dutch Flat, the first to introduce "giant powder" (dynamite), and in June, 1869, the miners went on strike against its introduction because the odor made people sick (*Alta*, June 7, 1869). A review of the conditions in the early 1870s is given in Raymond (II, p. 51; IV, p. 128; VI, pp. 117 f.; VII, p. 138). In 1875 there were still twenty-four mills in the township. The most convenient modern accounts of the area may be found in *Guidebook* (pp. 74 f.) and in *Bulletin*, 193 (pp. 13, 53 ff.). The Idaho-Maryland Corporation was a consolidation of mines, some of which went back to 1851. The total production of the group was 70 million dollars. The Empire-Star Company group, a consolidation of the North Star, Pennsylvania, Empire, and many small mines, is credited with having produced 130 million dollars, the highest among the lode mines of the state. The last of the Empire mines was closed in 1957, ending more than 100 years of mining in the region. The Golden Center Group, in the center of the town of Grass Valley, produced 2.5 million dollars. *See* separate entry for Eureka Mine. Total production of the lode mines in the district is estimated at 300 million dollars and the placer mines a few additional millions. For a description of the geologic structure, *see* Lindgren, *The Gold-Quartz Veins*. Excellent illustrations of the Grass Valley mines are given in *Bulletin*, 193 (pp. 53 ff.), in Wagner's *Gold Mines of California*, and in Morley's and Foley's *Grass Valley and Nevada City*. Alonzo Delano lived in Grass Valley from

Grass Valley, Nevada Co.

1850 until his death in 1878, and the town is the background for many of "Old Block's" delightful sketches and satires. The great entertainers, Lola Montez and Lotta Crabtree, are intimately connected with the town, and their homes are Historic Landmarks 292 and 293. John Rollins Ridge, poet and journalist, also lived here, and Josiah Royce, the famous American philosopher, was born here in 1855. Empire Mine is Historic Landmark 298.

Grass Valley [Plumas]. On the upper waters of the South Fork of Feather River. It is sometimes called Little Grass Valley. A camp developed probably in 1850 in connection with the Gold Lake hunt. Butler's map of 1851 and Milleson and Adams' map of the same year show it on the Middle Fork of Feather River, but both maps fail to record the "big" Grass Valley in Nevada County. Steele (p. 198) stopped here in an overcrowded hotel on February 23, 1851. Lecouvreur (pp. 235 ff.) tells a story about coming upon a deserted log house in June, 1852, where his company found, besides an immense number of empty bottles, a "two-gallon keg of old cognac of the very best quality." Goddard's map of 1857 shows the settlement on the south side of the river. The *Transactions*, 1858, (p. 202) states that the chief product was no longer gold but ice! Little Grass Valley and Grass Valley Hill, both geographical features, are shown on the USGS Downieville 1907 quadrangle. The Little Grass Valley Reservoir also keeps the name alive.

Grass Valley Creek [Trinity]. The stream joins the Trinity River about three miles from Lewiston. It is mentioned by Cox (pp. 29 f.). Good pay gravel was reported (Raymond, VI, p. 154).

Grass Valley House [Yuba]. North of the Middle Fork of Yuba River. It was an important way station on the trail from Nevada City to Fosters Bar. It is mentioned by Borthwick (p. 199).

Grass Valley Ranch [Amador]. On Grass Valley Creek, a tributary to Sutter Creek, eight miles east of the town of Sutters Creek. The first survey of Grass Valley Ranch was in September, 1851 (Berriman). It is shown as Grass Valley, a camp, on Trask's map, 1853. Doble describes it in April, 1852, as a ranch, store, and tavern on a beautiful flat. It is recorded again in Bowen's manuscript, September, 1854. In 1854 it was an election precinct (Co. Hist., 1881, p. 79), and in 1856 it had a 6-stamp mill.

Grass Valley Slide. A camp of uncertain location. The *Alta*, December 23, 1853, reprints an item with the sensational news that the Bosworth Company with three men washed out 922 dollars worth of gold in three days.

Gravel Hill [El Dorado]. Between Otter and Canyon creeks, north of Georgetown. In 1871 the deep gravel deposits were awaiting water, and by 1874 they were extensively worked by drifts and were yielding considerable gold (Raymond, IV, p. 105; VII, pp. 91, 95).

Gravel Hill [Sierra]. Near Gibsonville. Crossman's map, 1867, shows Gravel Diggings just below Gardners Point. In 1861 the miners at Gravel Hill made fourteen dollars a day to the hand (*Mining Press*, June 1, 1861).

Gravel Range District [Tuolumne]. About fifteen miles east of Groveland. Gold was mined in the late 1870s, mainly by the hydraulic process, at Dorseys and north of Smith Station, under the direction of Colonel Caleb Dorsey of Sonora (De Ferrari).

Graveyard Camp or Flat [Plumas]. Near Nelson Diggings, on the Middle Fork of Feather River. The place is listed in Bancroft, VI (p. 363) and in the County History, 1882 (p. 288).

Graveyard Canyon [Fresno]. Near Pine Ridge. Apparently the site of the Graveyard and Vulture Mine, listed in 1915 in *Mining Bureau*, XIV (p. 445).

Graveyard Hill [Shasta]. Near Horsetown. Rich pay dirt was discovered in the winter of 1864–65, and the whole hill was staked in claims, according to an extract from the *Shasta Courier*, in a clipping marked February, 1865 in Hayes Scrapbooks: Mining, IV (sec. 48, p. 99).

Graveyard Hill [Sierra]. In Slate Creek Basin, south of Chandlerville. Shown in Raymond, V, in his map of the Slate Creek Basin, Northern Part (opposite p. 88).

Graycrofts Diggings [Sierra]. On the Middle Fork of the North Yuba River; north of Downieville. Shown on the County Map of 1874. Coy lists the name as Graycrafts Diggings (p. 67).

Gray Eagle Bar [El Dorado]. On the Middle Fork of American River, below the confluence with Rubicon River and below Eureka Bar and Horseshoe Bar. It is prominently marked Grey Eagle on Trask's map, 1853. Huntley (p. 97) mentions Grey Eagle City as existing in the spring of 1852. Andrew S. Hallidie, the versatile Englishman, later of suspension bridge and San Francisco cable car fame, worked here in 1844–55, repairing the shooting irons of the miners (*CHSQ*, XIX, p. 145). The *Mining Press*, August 17, 1861, reported that two men took out 400 dollars in one day's washing. A drift mine, worked in the 1890s is still listed in 1950.

Grayson City [Stanislaus]. On the west bank of San Joaquin River, below the mouth of Tuolumne River; on the way to the Southern Mines. Shown on Butler's map, 1851. A. J. Grayson established a ferry here in 1850. The town was soon deserted, but the ferry continued to operate. In the late 1860s with the development of grain farming, a town was laid out and flourished until the middle 1880s (Stoddart, p. 107; Rensch-Hoover). The post office existed as Graysonville, then as Grayson, between 1870 and 1906, when it was moved to Westley.

Greaser Gulch [Madera]. Near Coarse Gold. Shown on Trask's map, 1853. Around 1900 it was the site of the Daisy Bell Mine (*Mining Bureau*, XIV, p. 541).

Greaser Gulch [Mariposa]. Between Toledo Gulch and Indian Gulch. Shown on Trask's map, 1853. It is mentioned by Eccleston, October 20, 1850. Shown on the USGS Indian Gulch 1920 quadrangle.

Greasers Camp. An unidentified place, listed in Hittell, *Resources*.

Greasertown [Calaveras]. On the Calaveras River, about five miles west of San Andreas. The San Andreas *Independent*, May 11, 1861, reports a serious fight between outnumbered white miners against Chinese. The marriage records of the 1860s indicate that there was a large Chinese population at that time. Camp's map shows the place about four miles southwest of San Andreas, with Petersburg as an alternate or former name, but Poore indicates that they were two separate places, now both under Hogan Reservoir. Petersburg was about one and a half miles west of Greasertown, which was a camp composed of Mexicans driven out of San Andreas by American miners.

Greaserville [Amador]. The place, somewhere near Jackson, is mentioned by Doble, May 19, 1852. Camp shows it tentatively west of Butte City. Berriman states that it was probably another name of Butte City, at least in early 1852, when it was used by the owners of Big Bar ferry.

Great Gravel Deposit [Nevada]. The name designates the very rich channel from Dutch Flat to Badger Hill and North Bloomfield. A map and description is given in Raymond, VI (pp. 108 f.).

Great Mogul District [Alpine]. On the East Fork of Carson River. The Virginia City *Union* (Bancroft Scraps LI:1, p. 215) had an optimistic article, according to which new deposits, probably mainly silver, were discovered in 1865. Although the Great Mogul Ledge is repeatedly mentioned, the district apparently never developed.

Greeley Hill District [Mariposa]. Seven miles northeast of Coulterville. The level table and timber land of Greeley Hill was named for Josiah Greeley, cousin of Horace Greeley (Sargent). The Red Cloud Mine, three and a half miles east of Greeley Hill, goes back to "early times," but was most active in the decade between 1885 and 1895. The total production is estimated at 1.5 million dollars. (*Mining Bureau*, LIII, p. 163.)

Green Emigrant [Placer]. On Quartz Prairie, three miles northwest of Auburn. Shown on Doolittle's map, 1868. The deposit was discovered in 1864. Numerous claims on Quartz and Bald hills of the Green Emigrant Quartz Lead were filed, December

24, 1864, in the Placer County Records, V (pp. 144 ff.) and later in the Lone Star District Book of Claims (also in Placer County Records). Newspapers of the following years reported enormous yields. Browne (p. 108) states that the owners refused definite information but that an estimated 100 thousand dollars was taken out in the first six months of 1867. The Green Emigrant Mine is listed in the Mining Bureau reports until 1936.

Green Flat Diggings [Tuolumne]. Eight miles from Sonora. According to the Sonora *Herald*, July 13, 1850, four Mexicans were almost lynched because they had been accused of having murdered two American miners. The exciting story is told by Heckendorn (pp. 40 f.). De Ferrari notes that another reference indicates, though not explicitly, that the place was near present-day Keystone.

Green Gulch [Mariposa]. Near Princeton. The discovery of rich gold-bearing quartz here is mentioned in the Report of the Nouveau Monde Gold Mining Company (postscript, dated October 28, 1854, p. 63). In the early 1860s a 40-stamp mill was built and was later moved to Mariposa (Browne, p. 29).

Greenhorn. The nickname for a new arrival was probably used more in the gold regions than elsewhere. Numerous stories were told about the old timers sending a "greenhorn" to prospect in the most unlikely places, and how in some cases the newcomer fooled them by striking it rich.

Greenhorn Bar [Placer]. On the North Fork of American River. A notice of a claim at Green Horn Bar was recorded May 23, 1852, in Placer County Records, I (p. 93). A Greenhorn Bar on the north bank of the Middle Fork of American River, above Pleasant Bar, is listed in Bancroft, VI (p. 354).

Greenhorn Bar [Yuba]. On the north side of Bear River, six miles east of Wheatland. Shown on the County Map of 1879.

Greenhorn Canyon [El Dorado]. Gold was discovered here in 1855, according to the Sacramento *Union*, February 10, 1855. A Greenhorn Canyon near Georgetown is mentioned in Book of Deeds F (p. 108) in the El Dorado County Records (Schlappi-Ferguson).

Greenhorn: Creek, Diggings, District [Siskiyou]. Southwest of Yreka. According to the County History, 1881 (p. 207), mining began in 1851 and a community developed along the stream. It was once a voting district although not a town, de-

pending largely on Yreka for supplies. The name arose because a greenhorn had been sent to an abandoned claim and struck it rich. The creek is mentioned in the sale of a mining claim dated November 30, 1854, recorded in the Siskiyou County Land Papers. Creek digging was still paying in 1862, according to the *Mining Press*, July 2, 1862. The district is listed in the reports of the Mining Bureau until 1914, and the Creek is shown on the USGS Yreka 1939 quadrangle. Since there was at least one more Greenhorn Creek in the county, some of the information given here may refer to another creek.

Greenhorn Diggings [Plumas]. *See* Argentine.

Greenhorn District [Nevada]. Along Greenhorn Creek, tributary to Bear River, in the region of Quaker Hill, Hunts Hill, Red Dog, and You Bet. The extent of hydraulic mining in the 1870s is shown on Pettee and Bowman's map, 1879. *Bean's History* (p. 229) refers to the quartz ledges located in 1861 south of Bannerville, separated from it by a cement and gravel hill. The camps in the district are listed separately in this dictionary.

Greenhorn: Gulch, Mountains, Caves [Kern]. The stream in the gulch rises in the Greenhorn Mountains and empties into Kern River. Gold is said to have been discovered in 1851 by a party (probably Godey's) sent out by Frémont. Rich placering was reported in the spring of 1855 (Boyd, pp. 2, 9). In 1858 two mills with six stamps and three arrastres were in operation, and in 1866 a steam-driven mill with twenty stamps (*State Register*, 1859; *Annual Mining Review*, 1876, p. 21). The Greenhorn Gulch mentioned in the *Mining Press* may be at the same location. An article reports that one mill turned out about eighty dollars per ton. Placer mining in the Greenhorn Caves, last known to be active in 1940, is described in *Mining Bureau*, XXIX (p. 307) and XLV (p. 223); and *County Report*, I (p. 155). Greenhorn district, four miles northwest of Miracle Hot Springs, is described in *Bulletin*, 193 (p. 60) and in *County Report*, I (p. 34). Mining in the region declined by 1890, and there has been only minor prospecting since that time. *See* Petersburg [Kern].

Greenhorn Hill [El Dorado]. In 1850 some miners jokingly sent a fellow to a place near Pilot Hill (between the Middle and South forks of American River) to dig in the shade of a tree. The Greenhorn took out a fortune in a few days and left the country. (Augustus Moore, "Experiences," pp. 5 f.).

Greenhorn Slide [Placer]. On the south side of the Middle Fork of American River. The head of Greenhorn [Slide?] is mentioned as the boundary of a claim recorded December 18, 1851, in Placer County Records, I (p. 52). The deposits were yielding "remarkably well," according to *Mining Press*, August 31, 1861. The total production was said to be one million dollars.

Green Lead: Creek, Mine [San Bernardino]. A small settlement on Greenlead Creek, two miles northwest of Holcomb Valley, developed around the quartz mine, which was operated from 1876 to the 1940s (Leadabrand, p. 87). The mine, also written Greenlead, was owned and operated by the Garvey family of Pomona (Belden, September 6, 1959). *See* Holcomb Valley.

Green Mountain [Plumas]. At Crescent Mills. Quartz mining started in the 1850s. A 60-stamp mill was listed in 1888 (*Mining Bureau*, VIII, p. 694). The Green Mountain Mine production between 1860 and 1890 was reportedly between one and two million dollars (*Mining Bureau*, XXIV, p. 289).

Green: Mountain, Canyon [Nevada]. Green Mountain is mentioned as a mining camp in Little York township (Bean's *Directory*, 1867). The Canyon is a tributary to Greenhorn Creek; between Hunts Hill and Quaker Hill. Shown on Pettee and Bowman's map, 1879. Pettee describes the gravels in the vicinity, where there had been drift mining (Whitney, *Auriferous Gravels*, pp. 180 f.).

Green Mountain Bar [Placer]. On the Middle Fork of American River, above the junction with the North Fork, between Hoosier and Main bars. Shown on Doolittle's map, 1868, and on Bowman's, 1873. A notice of a claim laid here, September 4, 1852, is recorded in the Placer County Records, I (p. 115). The bar is mentioned in the El Dorado County History, 1883 (p. 84).

Green Mountain District [Kern]. Between Piute post office on the west slope to the edge of Kelso Valley on the east side of Piute Mountains. There was mainly copper mining, but in 1863 the discovery of gold at the Green "Monster" caused quite an excitement. The assay was said to be 500 dollars to the ton of quartz, as the well-known mining engineer Henry Hanks reported (Bancroft Scraps, LI:1, p. 340). A number of mines, mainly idle, were still listed in 1949 (*Mining Bureau*, XLV, pp. 210 ff.).

Green Springs [El Dorado]. On Weber Creek, where trails to Coloma and to Mormon Island crossed. Shown on Derby's Sacramento map of 1849 and Jackson's map of 1850. Buffum, who was here on December 2, 1848 (p. 41), described the spring with its delicious water bubbling right on the road, surrounded by greenest verdure. It is mentioned again by Woods (p. 94) on December 25, 1849. No mining record was found. The place was probably only a way station. There was a store until 1868, a saloon, and a blacksmith shop, according to the County History, 1883 (p. 203).

Green Springs [Tuolumne]. Near the head of Green Springs Run, tributary to Stanislaus River. It is about seven miles from Hawkins Bar, at present-day Keystone. Gardiner and party passed through in the middle of December, 1849 (p. 109). Daniel B. Woods (p. 94) spent Christmas Eve, 1849, at Green Spring. Audubon made a sketch of the camp April 1, 1850 (reproduced in *CHSQ*, XXI, opposite p. 289, where it is located twelve miles west of Woods Diggings). No gold mining records were found, but the place is repeatedly mentioned by Stephen Davis, also by Heckendorn, and in the Sonora *Herald*, April 26, 1851. The camp had a post office from 1852 to 1869.

Green Valley [El Dorado]. Near a tributary to Weber Creek, northwest of Shingle Springs. Shown on Doolittle's map, 1868. It had two 5-stamp mills in 1887 (*Resources of El Dorado County*, p. 21). A post office was established February 4, 1854. Shown on the USGS Placerville 1931 quadrangle.

Green Valley [Placer]. On the North Fork of American River, near the junction with Blue Canyon, southeast of Dutch Flat. It is shown as a settlement on Doolittle's map, 1868. The valley was named in the fall of 1849 by Mahlon Fairchild's party (pp. 15 f.). When he and his companions arrived, they found a party of the Hudson's Bay Company who had built a wing dam. But Fairchild's party had no luck, although they were in the region of rich deposits. Hutchings lists Green Valley Bar as a town in 1855. Extensive mining was carried on in the 1870s by the Green [Valley] Blue Gravel Mining Company. The mine is listed by the Mining Bureau until 1936. (*Annual Mining Review*, 1876, p. 50; *Mining Bureau*, XXXII, p. 91.)

Greenville [Plumas]. On modern Highway 89, north of Crescent Mills. The camp developed around Mr. Green's hotel, which

Greenwood Valley, El Dorado Co.

was built in the 1850s. In the 1860s there were two mills, each with six or eight stamps (*Annual Mining Review*, 1876, p. 22; Browne, p. 170). A 5-stamp mill and one arrastre are still listed in the *Register* of 1900. A. R. Bidwell, in his historical sketch of Round Valley Reservoir (*in* Plumas County Historical Society *Publication*, no. 4, April, 1961), lists the quartz mills in the immediate vicinity. *See* Round Valley; Cherokee.

Greenville [Yuba]. On Rich Gulch, northwest of Bullards Bar. Shown on Wescoatt's map, 1861. The place was also called Oregon Hill. The deposits were discovered in 1851 and developed after a company of nine miners had built the Nine Horse Ditch (De Long, January 8, 1856; Co. Hist., 1879, p. 95). Shown on the USGS Smartsville 1943 quadrangle.

Greenwater [Inyo]. At the eastern boundary of Death Valley National Monument. Some gold and silver was mined here in the 1880s, but the place became well known when the copper deposits were developed by Arthur Kunz in 1906. Accounts may be found in various reports of the Mining Bureau.

Greenwood [Sierra]. In Slate Creek Basin, east of La Porte. Shown on the County Map of 1874. Tunnel mining was in operation from "earliest days" (clipping of an article in 1879 written by an editor of *Mountain Messenger* in Bancroft Scraps, V, p. 1805). The place is mentioned in the *Mining Press*, June 21, 1862, and by Raymond, V (p. 81). A placer mine is listed in the Mining Bureau report in 1942.

Greenwood: town, **Valley, Creek** [El Dorado]. Five miles southwest of Georgetown. Recorded on Trask's map,

1853, and on later maps. Bowman's map, 1873, shows it as a large place. Gold was discovered on Greenwood Creek in 1849. The name is generally connected with the old mountaineer and guide, Caleb Greenwood and, or his sons. According to John E. Banks of the Buckeye Rovers, who camped here March 24, 1850, the valley was named for a half-breed named Greenwood (probably Caleb's son John), who killed himself from too much hard liquor a short time earlier. Theodore T. Johnson in 1849 (pp. 171 ff.) also referred to the famous mountain man and emigrant guide who was living in the valley with his half-breed sons, one of whom was John. Frickstad records that the name of the post office established as Louisville on July 28, 1851 was changed to Greenwood, October 9, 1852. The County History, 1883 (p. 185), however, states that the town, originally called Long Valley, was named Lewisville in 1850 (also spelled Louisville), for the first-born child in the township, son of Lewis B. Meyers, storekeeper; but when the post office was established the name was changed to Greenwood because there was another Louisville in the county. In a letter datelined Greenwood Valley, November 10, 1850, Finley McDiarmid reports that the "village" at that time had between 1,000 and 1,500 inhabitants, and that he found the prospects for mining poor. Borthwick (p. 167) refers to the settlement Greenwood Valley, with a hotel, three stores, and a half dozen cabins in the summer of 1852. The *Annual Mining Review*, 1876 (p. 51), indicates extensive placer and hydraulic mining. In 1887 the 10-stamp

Revenge Mill was still in operation (*Resources*, p. 20), and three stamp mills and one arrastre are recorded in the *Register* of 1902. The Mining Bureau records a Greenwood quartz mine as late as 1938. There was other mining in the district in the 1930s (*Bull.*, 193, pp. 60 f.). The production of the Sliger Mine reached 2.85 million dollars and the Taylor Mine, one million. Since about 1955 skin divers have been mining in a small way on the Middle Fork of American River in the Greenwood District. The town Greenwood is Historic Landmark 521. (*See* Whistleburg.) The author of *Put's Golden Songster*, John A. Stone, known as Joe Bowers, lived in Greenwood and is buried there.

Greenwoods Camp [Nevada]. *See* Jefferson Bar.

Grey Eagle [Sierra]. Near Forest City and apparently the former Uncle Sam Claim. According to the *Mining Press*, May 16, 1862, the diggings yielded regularly 130 to 140 ounces per week.

Grey Eagle: Bar, City [El Dorado]. *See* Gray Eagle Bar.

Gridiron Bar. Unidentified place, listed in Hittell, *Resources*.

Grissell Bar [Nevada]. On the South Fork of Yuba River, opposite Rocky Bar, near Washington. It is mentioned in Bancroft, VI (p. 358), and according to the County History, 1880 (p. 205), it was worked by Chinese miners.

Grizzle Flat [El Dorado]. *See* Grizzly Flats.

Grizzly. The name of the most notable and most dreaded native animal of the California mountains is represented in numerous places and mines in our gold region. It was spelled in various ways, from Grizzler to Grisley.

Grizzly [Tuolumne]. Recorded on Goddard's map, 1857, near Big Oak Flat. It may refer to Grizzly Gulch, west of Big Oak Flat; the lower end of the Gulch ends at the town of Moccasin Creek (De Ferrari). A 20-stamp water-driven mill was erected in 1859 (*Annual Mining Review*, 1876).

Grizzly Bar [Placer]. On the North Fork of American River, one mile above the junction with the Middle Fork. Notice of intention to build a dam here was recorded October 14, 1851 (Placer County Records, I, p. 32).

Grizzly Bear House [Placer]. Between the North and the Middle forks of American River. Borthwick (pp. 175 ff.) gives a delightful account of the place in the summer of 1852. Hutchings includes it in his list of towns in 1855.

Grizzly: Canyon, Creek, Hill, Ridge [Nevada]. On Grizzly Creek, between North San Juan and North Bloomfield. It is on the gravel deposit of the county. According to an item in the *Alta*, April 29, 1854, the claims on the hill paid only eight to ten dollars a day. In 1855 the Middle Yuba Canal Company built a ditch from the canyon to supply North San Juan with water (Brown, *Directory*, p. 12). In 1861 a tunnel was bored into the ridge to reach the strata containing coarse gold (*Mining Press*, January 25, 1862). An extract from the Nevada *Transcript*, December 17, 1867, in Hayes Scrapbooks: Mining, IV (sec. 42), states that in 1867 several companies still made rich finds, and the rock from the ledge assayed about 18 hundred dollars per ton. The Ridge and some mines are listed in the Mining Bureau reports until the middle of the twentieth century. Grizzly Hill Road from North Columbia is a reminder of the old diggings. Grizzly Creek and Ridge are shown on the USGS Colfax 1938 quadrangle.

Grizzly: City, Gulch [Shasta]. Between Whiskeytown and Tower House. Grizzly Gulch was listed among the nine principal mining localities in the county in the state census of 1852. One issue of the Grizzly City *Gazette* was published, apparently about 1852, according to Steger.

Grizzly Flat [Placer]. Two miles southeast of Iowa Hill. Shown on Doolittle's map, 1868. Pay dirt is mentioned by Bowen, June 24, 1855. Mining claims are mentioned in an indenture, dated July 16, 1864 (Placer County Records, IV, p. 153).

Grizzly Flat [Plumas]. On Nelson Creek. It is listed in the County History, 1882 (p. 288), as one of the important mining points along the creek.

Grizzly Flats [El Dorado]. West of Grizzly Creek, a tributary to Steely Fork of the North Fork of Cosumnes River. The deposits were discovered and named in 1850 by three prospectors who killed a grizzly that pursued one of their jacks. D. B. Woods recorded in 1851 that ten members of the Grisly Company took out $20.37 per man a day (p. 174). In 1852 three water-driven stamp mills were in operation (Hittell clipping). John Doble was here April 15, 1852, and calls the camp Grizzly Flat, or Chickamasee. At that time it was a small, unpromising camp, but it already had bars, stores, boarding houses and a woman — "a rare thing in these mountains." Ezra Bourne mentions it as Grizzle Flat in the summer of 1852. The post office was established August 31, 1855 and named Grizzly Flats. The *Transactions*, 1860 (p. 82), gives a detailed description and mentions nine mills. In 1887 there were still three large stamp mills and one canon ball mill in operation (*Resources*, p. 83). A description of the mines in the district in the 1880s is given in *Mining Bureau*, VIII (pp. 177 ff.). The same source records in volume LII (p. 421) that the Mount Pleasant Mine produced more than one million dollars worth of gold between 1874 and 1914. The Blue Gouge or Berg Mine near Grizzly Flats was prospected extensively in 1896 by John W. Mackay and James C. Flood, the famed "Silver Kings" of the Comstock Lode. The work was stopped soon afterward, and later, about 1925, was resumed. In 1936 a small amount of activity was again carried on. (*Mining Bureau*, LII, p. 411.) The Grizzly Flats district is described in *Bulletin*, 193 (p. 61 f.). It is stated here that there was again some mining in the 1930s, and one mine on Hazel Creek, discovered in 1948, was worked for ten years and produced more than one million dollars. Grizzly Flat is shown on the USGS Placerville 1931 quadrangle.

Grizzly Fork [Trinity]. Joins the North Fork of Trinity River, eighteen miles above Trinity. Shallow placering began in the early 1850s. Forty to fifty miners averaged ten to twelve dollars a day. It was a short-lived camp with a store, butcher shop, and blacksmith shop. Cox (pp. 103 ff.) gives a gossipy account in 1858.

Grizzly Fort [Sierra]. On Fiddle Creek, tributary to the North Fork of Yuba River. Shown on the County Map of 1874. The camp is mentioned in 1856 in Brown's *Directory* (p. 133).

Grizzly Gulch [Yuba]. On Oregon Creek, between Camptonville and North San Juan. It is mentioned as a camp of 1853 in the County History, 1879 (p. 100).

Grizzly Hill [Amador]. On Sutter Creek, near Volcano. It was apparently a short-lived camp, mentioned in the newspapers in the early 1850s.

Grizzly Hill [Nevada]. Near the South Fork of Yuba River, on the Great Gravel Deposit, about two miles south of North Columbia. Shown on Doolittle's map, 1868, and mentioned by Raymond (VI, p. 108).

Grizzly Hill [Sierra]. About nine miles north of Downieville, near Poker Flat. Major

Downie mined here without success in 1852. Grizzly Creek is shown on the USGS Downieville 1907 quadrangle. Another Grizzly Hill, south of Brandy City, is shown on Doolittle's map, 1868.

Grizzly Mine [Tuolumne]. *See* Soulsbyville.

Groots Ferry [Siskiyou]. On the Klamath River. No mining reports could be discovered, but according to the *Mining Bureau* (II, pt. 1, p. 149), a nugget of 131 ounces, valued at 2,437 dollars, was found here.

Ground Hog Glory [Placer]. A vanished place in the Forest Hill Divide. Shown on Doolittle's map, 1868, and on the County Map, 1887, on the North Fork of the Middle Fork of American River, about two miles above the junction. Hutchings lists it as a town in 1855. It is mentioned in an undated clipping from the Nevada *Democrat* (1859 or 1860) among a number of settlements listed by T. Starr King, in Hayes Scrapbooks: Mining, I (sec. 64). According to an item in the Sacramento *Union*, December 23, 1852, an attempt was made to change the name to El Dorado Hill, but the old name prevailed. *See* El Dorado Creek [Placer].

Grouse Ridge [Nevada]. In Washington township, north of the South Fork of Yuba River, above Fordyce Lake. In 1867 a fine magnetic ore containing gold was discovered (Bancroft Scraps, LI:1, p. 142). Shown on the USGS Colfax 1938 quadrangle.

Groveland [Tuolumne]. For the early history *see* Garrote. This old, somewhat bloody place name was changed to Groveland in 1875 when the country became sensitive to obnoxious names. Some gold mining was continued after the name change. From 1888 to 1906 a British mining company was active, and the *Register* of 1903 records hydraulic mining. According to the *Guidebook* (p. 47), Groveland (and Garrote) were said to have produced with Big Oak Flat and Deer Creek 25 million dollars. Historic Landmark 446.

Growler Gulch [Del Norte]. Near Hurdy Gurdy Creek. According to the County History, 1881 (p. 135), a ditch from Hurdy Gurdy Creek was completed in 1880, and short-lived mining operations were carried on by the Big Flat Mining Company.

Growlersburg [El Dorado]. This is only a nickname for Georgetown. But according to the County History, 1883 (pp. 201 f.), there must have been a real Growlersburg at the site of Folsom Lake, named for an English sailor who was always growling.

Grub Flat [Plumas]. In Meadow Valley district. A large part of the lower gravel areas have been mined over, according to Lindgren (p. 99) in 1911.

Grub Gulch [Madera]. Seven miles north of Coarsegold. The camp was established probably about 1850. The Grub Gulch district is described in *Mining Burau*, XII (p. 157) and in *Bulletin*, 193 (p. 62). There was active mining from the 1880s through the early 1900s, but little since that time.

Grub Hill [Calaveras]. Near San Andreas. No early mining record was found, but the *Register* of 1899 lists a gold mine on the hill.

Grubstake Dry Placers [Kern]. On the slope of Black Mountain, northwest of Randsburg. Several dry washing machines were in operation in 1934 (*Mining Bureau*, XXX, p. 245).

Grubstake Hill [Kern]. About ten miles north of Cantil, near the head of Last Chance Canyon. In 1928 there was placer mining with water pumped from Last Chance Canyon (*Mining Bureau*, XXV, pp. 35 f.), and in 1934 several dry washing machines were in operation (XXX, 245). According to the *County Report*, I (p. 169), mining was mainly by short drifts into the gravel near the crest of the hill, with mined material probably sorted with dry screens, and the gold recovered by the wet method.

Guadaloupe River [Santa Cruz]. Gold placers were discovered in 1851 on a tributary of the stream and were worked with some success in 1853, but no settlement developed (extract from *Placer Times & Transcript*, June 27, 1853, in Bancroft Notes).

Guadalupe [Mariposa]. Seven miles south of Agua Fria. Recorded on Gibbes' Map of the Southern Mines, 1852, with the spelling Guadelupe. The name of the Virgin patron saint of Catholic Mexico was often used as a place name in California. The *San Joaquin Republican*, October 15, 1851, reports that at Camp Guadalupe, near Mariposa, quartz was worked with arrastres and was producing two to three ounces daily for the past three weeks and that plans were being made to lay out a town. Allsop (pp. 43 ff.) was at the place in February, 1852, and he gives an interesting account. In 1859 there was a 15-stamp steam-driven mill (*State Register*, 1859). An idle Guadalupe quartz mine is mentioned in 1920 in *Mining Bureau*, XVII (p. 117). The mountain and valley are recorded on the USGS Indian Gulch 1920 quadrangle. *See* Walloupa.

Guano Hill. An unidentified camp, listed in the State Library Roster.

Gullions Bar [Siskiyou]. On the west side of the Forks of Salmon River. Shown 'on Goddard's map, 1857. George Gibbs mined here without much success. He dated a letter from the bar on October 8, 1852.

Gulnacs Camp [Tuolumne]. Probably southwest of Tuttletown. Chester S. Lyman (p. 198) reached the place October 16, 1848, and a few days later examined the ravine from which a piece of pure gold, fifteen to twenty pounds, had been taken out. The place may have been named for William Gulnac, a pioneer of 1833, who was once the partner of Charles Weber at Stockton.

Gunsight Lode [Inyo]. This was one of the phantom gold (or silver) deposits allegedly discovered by some of the Jayhawkers of 1849–1850. For details *see* the two modern accounts of the mines in Death Valley: one by L. Burr Belden (pp. 15 ff.) and the other by Harold O. Weight (pp. 5 ff.) The *Inyo Independent*, April 10, 1875, reported the rediscovery of the Gunsight between Cerro Gordo and Panamint (Bancroft Notes). A story of the lode is told in *Mining Bureau*, III (pt. 2, p. 30). The Gunsite Mines in Inyo County, listed in the *Consolidated Index*, probably owed their name to the mysterious lode.

Gun Town [Nevada]. *See* Stockton Hill.

Guyamaca [San Diego]. A spelling variant of Cuyamaca. Cuyamaca District was a name used for Julian District in the early 1870s. *See* Julian District.

Gwin Mines [Calaveras]. Southwest of Mokelumne, at Lower Rich Gulch. The original mine was located in 1851, passed into the hands of U. S. Senator Wiliam M. Gwin about 1867, consolidated with two adjacent mines, and remained in control of the family until the end of 1882. From 1867 to 1871 forty stamps were constantly operating; by 1882 the mill was old and worn out. Total production by that time was more than two million dollars (*Mining Bureau*, VI (1885/86, pt. 2, pp. 31 ff.). The mine was reopened in 1894, and by 1903 one hundred stamps were operating. It was closed in 1908 (Logan, pp. 141 f.). The total production was about seven million dollars (*Bull.*, 193, p. 105). *See* Lower Rich Gulch (in the entry Rich Gulch). A resume of the history of the mine is given in *Las Calaveras*, January, 1968. There was a post office at the mine from 1870 to 1910. Gwin Mine, Paloma, and Lower Rich Gulch are

Historic Landmark 295. Other mines in the district are listed in the *Register*, 1899.

Hackberry Mountain District [San Bernardino].

About ten miles northwest of Goffs. There was mining here from the 1890s through the 1940s, with the most activity between 1904 and 1915 (*Bull.*, 193, p. 158).

Hackerman Bar [Trinity]. *See* Browns Bar.

Hacketville [Nevada]. Near Spenceville, near the Yuba County line. It was chiefly a copper mining settlement in Rough and Ready township (Co. Hist., 1880, p. 204).

Haightsville [Calaveras]. *See* Camanche.

Haines Flat [Del Norte]. Southeast of Gasquet at Gordon Creek, tributary to South Fork of Smith River. Hayne Flat is mentioned in Bancroft, VI (p. 370). It may be the same place as Haines Flat, where placering was carried on with modest success in 1877 (*Mining Bureau*, XXIX, p. 142). A Haynes Flat mine is listed in 1895 in *Mining Bureau* (XIII, p. 128) and again in 1952 (XLVIII, p. 303). Haines Flat is shown on the USGS Preston Peak 1944 quadrangle.

Haletown [Amador]. Between Clinton and Jackson. It is mentioned by Hutchings in his diary, July 12, 1855. No mining record was found. *See* Helltown [Amador].

Half-oz Gulch [Tuolumne]. Heckendorn (p. 89) locates it southeast of Sonora, but De Ferrari places it on Stanislaus River, below Robinsons Ferry.

Half Pound Gulch. An unidentified place, listed in the Works Project Administration project.

Halfway House [Tuolumne]. There were several Halfway houses in the County. Halfway House on Woods Creek, halfway betwen Sonora and Jamestown, was at the point now called Volpone Acres and formerly John Yorks. Barrys Halfway House, between Sonora and Columbia, near the intersection of Highway 49 and Parrots Ferry Road, was named for the proprietors H. and J. Barry. James Fosha and company took out a slug of gold here, which sold for one thousand dollars in May, 1858, according to an undated item from the Columbia *Courier* in Hittell Clippings. Near Barrys Halfway House was Campbells Halfway House. Another one was Per Johnsons Halfway House, a short distance above Sawmill road. (De Ferrari; Eastman.)

Halleck [San Bernardino]. *See* Oro Grande District.

Halloran Springs District [San Bernardino].

In the northeastern part of the county; about twelve miles northeast of Baker. To the north are the Turquoise Mountains, where the Indians formerly mined turquoise. Gold was first discovered about 1900 and was mined to 1914. In 1930 the discovery of gold at the Telegraph Mine led to a brief flurry of prospecting in the area, but the Telegraph Mine proved to be the only productive one. It was worked mainly between 1930 and 1938 and yielded an estimated 100 thousand dollars. (*Mining Bureau*, XXVII, pp. 320 ff.; XLIX, p. 82; *Bull.*, 193, p. 158.)

Halls Bar. An unidentified place in Helper's list (p. 151). Trask shows Halls Ferry on the Stanislaus River on his map, 1853. A Halls Mine on Cottonwood Creek in Shasta County is repeatedly listed in the reports of the Mining Bureau.

Halls Ranch [Sierra]. On the ridge below Eureka City, on the road to Brandy City. It was a combined ranch and stopping place (R. Drury).

Ham Bar [Sierra]. On the North Fork of Yuba River, above Goodyears Bar. River and bank diggings started in 1850–1851 (Sinnott, *Downieville*, p. 144). Three companies were still active in 1861 (*Mining Press*, July 20, 1861).

Hamburg Bar [Siskiyou]. On the Klamath River, near the junction with Scott River. Recorded on Goddard's map, 1857. It was founded and named by Sigmund Simon about 1850. *See* Simonville. His family owned the general store in Scotts Bar until 1906. There were "whole families all the way from Hamburg" at the German May festival here in 1859. (Buck, p. 117.) According to Brewer (p. 479), the placers were worked out in 1863, and the town was deserted except for a camp of Klamath Indians. However, it remained the trading center for numerous drift, placer, and hydraulic mines in the area (*Register*, 1898). A post office was established in 1878. Detailed description may be found in *Mining Bureau*, XXXVII (p. 125).

Hamburger Placers [San Bernardino]. Fifteen miles east of Atolia. Named for the owners, M. A. and D. A. Hamburger of Los Angeles. The place is mentioned in 1930 (*Mining Bureau*, XXVII, p. 300; XXX, p. 250). Shown on the USGS Fremont Peak 1954 quadrangle two and a half miles east of Fremont Peak.

Hamilton [Butte]. On the Feather River, below Oroville. Shown on Milleson and Adams' map, 1851. Bidwell picked up the first gold here in the spring of 1848, after his return from Sutters Mill. Windeler mentions the place December 23, 1850. The same year it was the first county seat and remained so until 1853. The town has disappeared, and it is sometimes confused with Hamilton City in Glenn County. Mansfield (p. 5) states that it was named for an early resident, a nephew of Alexander Hamilton. Another source states that it was reportedly named for William S. Hamilton, son of Alexander Hamilton, who mined on the Trinity River (Windeler, p. 214).

Hamilton Bar [Butte]. Above the Big Bend of the North Fork of Feather River. Shown on the County maps, 1862 and 1877. No mining record was found.

Hamilton Hill [Kern]. *See* Tropico Hill.

Hammonds Ravine [Placer]. Near Ophir. A claim for a quartz lead in the ravine, filed November 27, 1855 is recorded in the Placer County Records, I (p. 335).

Hammonton [Yuba]. About nine miles northeast of Marysville, on the main Yuba River. It was established in 1904–1905 as headquarters for dredging activities along the Yuba River and was first known as Dredgertown or Dredgerville. Before the post office was established in 1907 various names were suggested for the little gold dredging town: Hammon, Hammonville, Hammon City for the founder W. P. Hammon and Augustaville for his wife. However, the post office department chose Hammonton, to avoid confusion with Hamilton City [Butte] and Hammond [Tulare]. (Ramey.) Mansfield (p. 24) states that the founder is said to have gotten the idea of dredging when he had a well dug in his orchard in Oroville. According to *Bulletin*, 193 (p. 62), Hammon directed the first dredging in 1903, and in 1905 the Yuba Consolidated Gold Fields took over the operations, perfecting an unusually efficient method of mining placer gold. Their Yuba Dredge No. 20 was one of the largest in existence. Dredging continued until 1968, ending a period of almost seventy years, during which time more than a billion cubic yards of gravel were dredged.

Hampshire Mills [Yuba]. On Hampshire Creek, tributary to the North Fork of Yuba River. It was often mentioned by De Long. The name is derived from a sawmill, not a stamp mill. Hampshire Creek and Stores are recorded on Wescoatt's map of 1861. It was apparently only a trading center for the placers at Sucker Bar, Collins Riffle,

and Alabama Bar (County History, 1879, p. 97).

Hancock House [Sierra]. *See* Bassetts Station.

Hangmans Gulch [Tuolumne]. Near Sonora. It was so named because three men who had been hanged in 1857 were buried here, according to Buckbee (p. 404).

Hangtown [El Dorado]. The story still persists that Hangtown was the "original" name of Placerville. The first name of the camp was Dry Diggings, and Hangtown was its nickname. To be sure, this nickname was constantly used in contemporary literature by Borthwick, Carr, De Long, and others. But when the post office was established in 1850, it was named Placerville. Of the many contradictory stories about the name, McCall's story seems reliable. He reports as follows under date of October 17, 1849. A party of five men attacked and robbed a Mexican gambler at midnight, whereupon they were arrested and the next day tried and flogged. Three of them, who had previously been charged with robbery and attempted murder on the Stanislaus, were again tried by the crowd, declared guilty of robbery, and were hanged. The hanging of "Bloody Dick" on the same tree in July, 1850 was witnessed by Carr (pp. 64 f.). The tree was cut down a few days later. For another account of Hangtown by Buffum and for the history of the town, *see* Placerville.

Hangtown: Creek, Ravine [El Dorado]. The tributary to Weber Creek bears the nickname of the camp situated on its shores. The placers were very rich and for some time Leeper made fifty to a hundred dollars a day with a long tom. In 1850 most of the claims were deserted because of the Gold Lake hunt. (Leeper, p. 102; Carr, p. 69; Haskins, p. 78.) Hangtown Creek and Ravine are mentioned in 1857 by Crockett (pp. 80, 86).

Hanks Exchange [El Dorado]. Four miles southeast of Placerville. The place dates back to 1848 and was probably named for Captain Hanks (Chester Lyman, p. 187). Shown on the USGS Placerville 1931 quadrangle.

Hanselman Hill [Calaveras]. Between Albany Hill and Los Muertos. Named for Jacob Hanselman, one of the early prospectors. *See* Marble Springs.

Hansons Bar [Plumas]. An unidentified place on the Middle Fork of Feather River. It is listed in the Giffen file.

Hansonville [Yuba]. On South Honcut

Creek, about five miles southwest of Forbestown. Shown on Trask's map, 1853, and on Wescoatt's, 1861. It was originally in Butte County. James H. Hanson settled here in 1851 (Co. Hist., 1879, p. 91). In the same year the first stamp mill was built, and in 1852 there were seven stores, eight hotels, and 1,000 inhabitants. The post office was established in December, 1856. In 1859 the town had three mills with twenty-four stamps and five arrastres (State Register, 1859). The Butte County map of 1862 still shows the place as a sizeable town. Mining declined rapidly, however, and was replaced by agriculture (Browne, p. 148). A directory of 1884 lists only ten miners. In 1892 the post office was discontinued and the same year another post office named Rackerby was established. A Hansonville Mine, though idle in 1916 or before, is still listed in 1952 (Mining Bureau, XLVIII, p. 166). Hansonville is still shown on the USGS Smartsville 1943 quadrangle.

Happy Camp [Siskiyou]. Below the junction of Indian Creek with Klamath River; originally in Del Norte County. shown on Trask's map, 1853, and Goddard's, 1857. "Happy" was a favorite adjective used in names of camps and mines, and several stories have been told about the origin of the name in Siskiyou County. The camp was apparently first known as Murderers Bar. Reddick McKee, November 8, 1851, refers to "Mr. Roache's 'Happy Camp' at the place known as Murderer's bar, at the mouth of Indian Creek" (Indian Report, 1853, p. 178), but Gibbs (Schoolcraft, III, pp. 154 f.) calls the place Happy Camp and gives a description of it in October, 1851. According to the Del Norte County History, 1881 (p. 22), the camp had six or eight houses in 1854, and some sixty miners were making nine to fifteen dollars per day to the hand. The post office was established March 19, 1858, and the place became a trading center for numerous camps and mines. A recent account of the town is given in Siskiyou Pioneer, IV:1 (pp. 9 ff.). In 1861 the places below Happy Camp still paid well (Mining Press, October 12, 1861). Later hydraulic mining was carried on toward the south and southwest (Bull., 193, p. 139). The gold and copper mines of the district are listed in the 1914 report of the Mining Bureau. Happy Camp is shown on the USGS Seiad 1922 quadrangle.

Happy Valley [Calaveras]. One and a half miles east of Mokelumne Hill. It was described as a beautiful place with a brook "clear as mud" formed by six sluices (German Journal, June 18, 1855; Hittell Clippings, p. 62). The store of a Frenchman was standing until the middle of the twentieth century. According to Poore, the camp was established by French trappers of the Hudson's Bay Company.

Hardenberg: Mine, Mill, Ditch [Amador]. On the Mokelumne River, four miles south of Jackson. It was an old camp, no record of which was found. After 1890 the Hardenburg mine was reopened and a 20-stamp mill was built (Bull., No. 108, p. 84; Mining Bureau, XXIII, p. 166). A post office was established in 1893 with the name spelled Hardenburg.

Hardin Flat [Tuolumne]. On the Big Oak Flat road, west of Yosemite, at the head of Golden Rock Ditch. It is a small gold district in the East Gold Belt, described in Bulletin, 193 (p. 63). A number of small prospects are now worked intermittently, mostly by weekend prospectors. The settlement nearby was named for John Heardin, an Englishman commonly called "Little Johnny Heardin," who was in the area as early as 1854. He had a water-powered sawmill there to saw lumber for flumes to carry water to the mines; he also was one of the first locators of the water right on the South Fork of Tuolumne River that later resulted in the Golden Rock Ditch. The name was apparently misspelled when it was first placed on a map. It is variously spelled Hardin and Harden. Heardin was a very small man, who used to ride a very large horse, which he would lead to a stump or some other large object in order to mount. (De Ferrari.)

Hardisons Camp [Mariposa]. Near Mariposa. It was named for W. Hardison. Angus McIsaac, who mined on Mariposa Creek, mentions the camp in his journal of February 6, 1853, and later.

Hardscrabble [Amador]. See Ione.

Hardscrabble [Sierra]. On Rock Creek, five miles southeast of La Porte. Hardscrabble is a typical western American place name found repeatedly in the gold region. This camp was apparently established by miners from New Hampshire. J. A. Stuart mentioned the place, February 16, 1850, and mined with fair success in April, 1850 (pp. 102 ff.). According to the Mining Press, July 8, 1862, prospecting in the district started again in 1861, and tunnel and hydraulic mining was beginning to pay in 1862. Mines are listed in the reports of the Mining Bureau until 1942.

Hardscrabble [Tuolumne]. East of Columbia. It was a small camp, long since forgotten (Rensch, "Columbia, a Gold Camp," p. 4). Hardscrabble Gulch is east of the Sawmill Flat-Yankee Hill road. Dart's map, 1879, indicates Hardscrabble Quartz Mine at this location. Hardscrabble Gulch is shown on the USGS Columbia 1948 quadrangle.

Hardscrabble Gulch [Siskiyou]. On McAdams Creek, four miles north of Fort Jones. The mining camp was named in the 1850s by two former residents of Hardscrabble, Wisconsin (Luddy). According to the County History of 1881 (p. 216), it was a place on Hi You Gulch and was mined as early as 1854. A mine was worked successfully by Chinese after it had been given up as worked out in 1885 (*Mining Bureau*, XIII, p. 404).

Harlows Bar [Placer]. On the north side of the North Fork of American River, above the junction with the Middle Fork. Shown on Trask's map, 1853.

Harmony Ridge [Nevada]. The southwesterly extension of Washington Ridge, northeast of Nevada City. *See* Washington Ridge.

Harrisburg [Inyo]. In Death Valley National Monument, on the road through Emigrant Canyon. It was a short-lived camp, where "Shorty" Harris discovered gold deposits in 1905 or 1906, with his partner, Pete Aguerreberry. "Shorty" Harris was one of the most colorful and best-known "single-blanket jackass prospectors" of the Death Valley region. (*California Place Names*.) Shown on the USGS Ballarat 1908 quadrangle.

Harrison Gulch [Shasta]. A tributary to Cottonwood Creek. It was named for Judge W. Harrison, who settled here in 1852, according to *Bulletin*, 193 (p. 137). The Midas Mine, discovered in 1894, was worked on a large scale between 1896 and 1914, with a total production of about 4 million dollars.

Harrisons [Plumas]. Near Sly Creek, a branch of Lost Creek, tributary to the South Fork of Feather River, about six miles southwest of La Porte. It is shown as a settlement on Long and Montgomery's *Map of the Route of the South Feather Water Co's Main and Lateral Ditches*. It may be the same as Harrison Diggins, (mentioned in Plumas County Historical Society *Publication*, No. 13, p. 8) at which Claude F. Seltier, later of Frenchman Creek, had a store in 1856 for eighteen months, after which the camp disappeared.

Harrisons [Yuba]. On Honcut Creek. Mentioned by De Long, February 2, 1856. It was perhaps only a store.

Hart:town, District [San Bernardino]. At the south end of the Castle Mountains, five miles west of the Nevada state line. Gold was discovered in 1907, and for a few years the area flourished. Quite a town developed, which had eight saloons, a bookstore, a newspaper, and a post office, 1908–1915. It was apparently named for one of the discoverers, Jim Hart. For a while the town and the district were served by the Searchlight branch of the Santa Fe Railroad. The principal mines were the Oro Belle, the Valley View, and the Hart Consolidated. After 1920 mining was intermittent. The Valley View Mine was still operating in the early 1940s. (*Mining Bureau*, XXXIX, p. 464; XLIX, table following p. 257; Belden, September 30, 1956.)

Hartford Bar [Placer]. On the North Fork of American River, near Yankee Bar and Oregon Bar. It is mentioned in a claim recorded August 28, 1853, in Placer County Records, I (p. 186).

Hartley Butte [Nevada]. *See* Meadow Lake.

Hartman Bar [Plumas]. On the Middle Fork of Feather River, near Willow Creek; about five miles from the Butte County line. Rich deposits were discovered in 1850 in the wake of the Gold Lake hunt. The name is still recorded on the USGS Bidwell 1944 quadrangle.

Hartnells Ranch [El Dorado]. *See* Hartwells Ranch.

Harts Bar [Tuolumne]. Two miles below Jacksonville. Shown on Trask's map, 1853, and Goddard's, 1857. In 1851 Daniel B. Woods (pp. 142 ff.) gives a lucid account of the camp. The Harts Bar Draining and Mining Company worked with twenty-one men in the summer and fall of 1850. Peter Dean mentions the place in his "Statement," 1878 (p. 3).

Hartwells Ranch [El Dorado]. It is mentioned in the Mason *Report* as a contributor to gold specimens sent to Washington by Mason. This was doubtless a misprint, as it was probably the well-known pioneer, William E. Hartnell, who contributed the gold.

Harvard Mine [Tuolumne]. *See* Whiskey Hill.

Harveys [El Dorado]. It is mentioned by Crockett in 1854 (p. 42). No mining record was found.

Harveys Bar [Mariposa]. On Horseshoe Bend of Merced River. There was profitable mining for some years after 1849. Hiram Pierce passed the place in April, 1850 (Diary, p. 96), on his way to Savage's Camp on the Merced, about four miles distant. It is now inundated by Lake McClure.

Haskell Canyon [Los Angeles]. A branch of Bouquet Canyon. John C. Haskell mined here profitably, according to Arthur Perkins (p. 161), and his sons resumed digging during the 1929 depression.

Haskell Peak [Sierra]. About seven miles northeast of Sierra Buttes; near the Plumas County line. Shown on the County Map, 1874. There was a belief, or superstition, among early miners that the interior of the mountain was filled with gold. The proximity of one of the Gold Lakes may have had something to do with the legend. Pettee reports later, in 1879, that some believed that an ancient river channel could be traced from the Peak to Chips Hill east of Sierra City to Forest City. According to a letter received by Pettee in March, 1880, a prospecting tunnel had struck the channel and further work was intended (Whitney, *Auriferous Gravels*, p. 443). Further discussion of the location of the channel may be found in Lindgren, 1911 (pp. 112 f.).

Haskells [Amador]. An unidentified camp or ranch, recorded on Trask's map, 1853, northwest of Drytown.

Hasloe Mine [Mariposa]. Five and a half miles southeast of Greeley Hill and eight miles east of Coulterville, in Gentry Gulch. It was located in 1854 by John Funk and by 1868 reportedly had yielded 600 thousand dollars (Mariposa *Gazette*, 86th souvenir edition, p. 20). In the decade between 1880 and 1890 alone it reportedly produced more than 3 million dollars. Browne (p. 32) describes it when it was known as the Coward Mine. Its history to 1956 is continued in *Mining Bureau*, LIII (pp. 106 ff.). Shown on the USGS Buckhorn Peak 1949 quadrangle. *See* Gentry Gulch.

Hatchet Creek [Trinity]. Flows easterly into Trinity River about two miles above old Trinity Center. *See* Trinity Center. According to Cox (p. 18), placering yielded five to twenty dollars per hand in the early 1850s. In later years there was mainly hydraulic mining, which yielded a little more than thirty-three cents per cubic yard of gravel (*Mining Bureau*, X, pp. 698 f.).

Hatchs Garden [Tuolumne]. East of Gold Spring. According to the County History, 1882 (p. 104), a large number of holes were dug in 1852, and the output of gold was satisfactory in some cases. A few were paying well in 1853 (Columbia *Gazette*, June 22, 1853) *See* Gold Springs. There was another Hatchs Garden between the southern part of Knickerbocker Flat and Martinez (Eastman).

Hatchville [Amador]. West of Ione Valley. Recorded on Goddard's map, 1857. No mining record was found.

Havens [Sierra]. Opposite the ridge from Monte Cristo. It is mentioned by Monroe Thomson in 1856 (p. 15).

Havilah [Kern]. South of Kern River. The name of the biblical gold land was applied in 1864. The camp soon developed into a boom town. In 1866 it had about 3,000 inhabitants, a post office, and several stamp mills. (Boyd, p. 39; *Annual Mining Review*, 1876, pp. 22 f.) When Raymond (VII, p. 40) visited the place in 1873, he reported what he hoped was only a temporary relapse of prosperity. The *Register*, 1904, lists three mills and one arrastre still in operation. The mines around the town are listed in *County Report*, I, 1962. Historic Landmark 100.

Hawk Eye [Calaveras]. Four miles northwest of Angels Camp. Heckendorn (p. 99) lists only one miner in residence in 1856. Shown on the USGS Jackson 1938 quadrangle.

Hawkins Bar [Trinity]. On the lower Trinity River, between Salyer and Burnt Ranch. The deposits contained gold and platinum. In 1899 the place was still important enough to have a post office, which continued for several years, but the principal gold mine (hydraulic) became idle in 1909 (*Mining Bureau*, XIV, p. 907).

Hawkins Bar [Tuolumne]. On the north side of the Tuolumne River, below Jacksonville, near Red Mountain Bar. It was first settled in April, 1849, and named for "Old Hawkins," who kept a store here (*CHSQ*, XI, p. 170; Co. Hist., 1882, p. 52). The name appears on all maps after 1850, but on Trask's map, 1853, it is shown above Jacksonville on the south side of the river. It is probably mentioned in contemporary literature more often than any other place of its importance. In September of 1849 it already had a population of 1,000 men but no women (Schaeffer, pp. 35 f.). Gardiner, who arrived here with his party in September, 1849, was enthusiastic about the place, the landscape of which he found "fascinating and picturesque." Their rich claim was "jumped" and later was known as the Gauly claim (Gardiner, pp. 81 ff.). *See* Gawleys Point. Price was here October

22, 1849, and was impressed by the orderliness of the camp. Audubon came in March, 1850, and made two beautiful drawings of the place. In the same year the Hawkins Bar Company was at work with 108 members, but they averaged only a little more than four and a half dollars per day to the man (Daniel Woods, p. 173). James Carr (pp. 172 ff.) likewise reports only moderate success when he mined here in 1853–54. But in 1854 the town had a library which contained sets of the *Americana* and the works of Humboldt and Lyell. The decline did not start until 1858; in 1864 it was a ghost town, and in 1870 it was gone. The epilogue of this promising town was written by Prentice Mulford, who witnessed the decline and visited it twice in later years (*Prentice Mulford's Story*, pp. 90 ff.). The site is now under waters impounded by Don Pedro Reservoir.

Hawkinsville [Siskiyou]. On Yreka Creek, two miles north of Yreka. Recorded on Goddard's map, 1857. The place was named for an old settler (Co. Hist., 1881, p. 207). It had previously been called Frogtown. Hutchings, who was here February 20, 1855, states that the one-year-old town, also called Lower Town, was almost deserted. Four hydraulic claims below the settlement had considerable success (*Mining Press*, May 8, 1862). It was the trading center for surrounding placer mines (*Register*, 1898), with a post office established in 1888. Shown on the USGS Yreka 1939 quadrangle.

Hayden Hill [Lassen]. In the Modoc Plateau. One of the few places in the county where gold was discovered was on the hill named for J. W. Hayden, who located several claims in 1869 and later. Other names of the camp, situated on the stage line to Susanville, were Providence City and Mount Hope (Co. Hist., 1882, p. 399). Raymond (V, pp. 95 f.) describes the mines in 1873. He refers to the Haydon [!] Hill Company, which received 100 dollars a ton in gold and silver in 1872 from its mine on the north side of the mountain. The post office from 1871–1875 was called Hayden and between 1878 and 1919, Hayden Hill. The population in 1882 was 200, mainly miners. Between 1903 and 1910 mining was reactivated in the district, with large scale work at the Golden Eagle Mine, and in the 1930s there was again moderate activity, with intermittent prospecting since. The total production of the Golden Eagle Mine was more than a million dollars; the whole district produced about three million. (*Mining Bureau*, XXX, pp. 303 f.; XXXII, pp. 422 f.; *Bull.*, 193, p. 177.)

Haydensville [Mariposa]. *See* Bear Valley.

Hayfork [Trinity]. The stream is a tributary to the South Fork of Trinity River. Cox gives a detailed description (pp. 110 ff.). In 1858 there was only little gold mining. The town, on Highway 3, was the trading center, with a post office established in 1861, for a quartz and hydraulic mining district extending mainly along the creek, after which the town was named. *See Consolidated Index*.

Haynes Flat [Del Norte]. *See* Haines Flat.

Hayward Mine [Amador]. *See* Eureka Mines.

Hazel Creek [El Dorado]. Fifteen miles east of Placerville. Gold was discovered in 1948 in a logging road cut two miles southeast of Pacific House, and a successful mine was in operation in 1956. Sulfide concentrate may have assayed as high as 500 dollars per ton in gold and silver (*Mining Bureau*, LII, p. 416). The mine was operated until 1958 and produced an estimated one million dollars (*Bull.*, 193, pp. 61 f.).

Hazel Creek [Shasta]. A tributary to the Sacramento River, south of Dunsmuir. No early mining records were found, but *Mining Bureau*, XIV (p. 777) states that in early days placering was done "throughout its entire length." It is shown on modern maps.

Heath & Emory Ferry [Stanislaus]. On the Stanislaus River, about twenty-five miles from Stockton. Stephen Davis mentioned it May 15, 1852, and repeatedly later. The ferry was opened in 1849 by Nelson Taylor and was known as Taylors Ferry until it was acquired by Heath & Emory. Apparently there was no mining, but it was an important ferry on the way to the Mariposa mines.

Heckendorn [Tuolumne]. According to the *Mining Press*, February 3, 1863, John Heckendorn, the coauthor of the *Miners' Directory*, discovered here a quartz lead rich in gold and silver. The statement that a ton assayed at 879 dollars is probably a misprint or an exaggeration. John Heckendorn had the Shanghai Mine above Yankee Hill in June, 1857; the mine was supposedly rich, but Heckendorn did not work it for long (De Ferrari).

Hector Station [Mono]. At the base of the mountains northeast of Mono Lake. It was not a mining camp but a stage station, established in 1879–1880 by A. F. Hector on

Hedges, Imperial Co.

the road between Bodie and Lundy. The ruins remain today. (F. S. Wedertz.)

Hedges [Imperial]. In the Cargo Muchacho region, ten miles northwest of Yuma. In 1900 there was a large mill here with 140 stamps, according to the *Register* of San Diego County, 1902. When the post office was established in 1910, the name was changed to Tumco, coined from *The United Mines Company*. For a description of the Hedges District, *see Mining Bureau*, XIII (p. 339).

Helena [Trinity]. *See* North Fork.

Hell-out-for-noon City [Nevada]. A name mentioned in a clipping from *Golden Era* about 1856. The post office name was Alpha from 1855 to 1862.

Hells Delight [Placer]. It is listed in Hittell, *Resources*. Hutchings lists it as a town in 1855 on the Middle Fork Ridge of American River. Doolittle's map, 1868, shows it along with Devils Basin and Devils Throne on the North Fork of the Middle Fork of American River.

Hells Half Acre [Placer]. On the Forest Hill Divide. It is mentioned by Helper (p. 151) in 1855.

Hells Hollow [Mariposa]. A precipitous ravine descending 1,500 feet from Pine Tree Mine to Benton Mills. Shown as Hell's Hollow on the Las Mariposas Map, 1861. In 1859 Jessie Frémont wrote, "A fall into it is death," but excessive heat inspired its name (Sargent). Frémont engineered and financed a unique railway down the ravine to carry ore to his mills,

which began operating August 1, 1860. Ore-laden cars, controlled by brakes, descended by gravity, and empty cars were pulled back up by mules (*Alta*, August 7, 1860). Part of Highway 49 was built on the old roadbed. Shown as Hell Hollow on the USGS Sonora 1939 quadrangle.

Helltown [Amador]. An unidentified place, mentioned by J. H. Jackson (p. 370). It is possibly the Haletown between Clinton and Jackson mentioned by Hutchings in 1855. *See* Haletown.

Helltown [Butte]. On Butte Creek, northeast of Chico. Recorded on the County Map, 1862, and later maps, including the USGS Chico 1895 quadrangle. It is recorded as a mining camp in *Mining Bureau*, II (part 1, p. 188). The area along Butte Creek from about three miles southeast of Chico northeast to Centerville and Helltown was first placer mined in the Gold Rush, and was followed by hydraulic mining and some drift mining of the Tertiary gravels. At the beginning of the twentieth century it was worked with power shovels, then by dredging to the early 1920s, and later in the 1930s and 40s. (*Bull.*, 193, p. 32.)

Helvetia Hill [Nevada]. *See* North Star.

Hempstead [Mariposa]. On the road to Mariposa. Shown on Goddard's map, 1857.

Henley [Siskiyou]. *See* Cottonwood.

Henpeck Camp [Plumas]. On Nelson Creek, three fourths of a mile from Nelson Point. Hutchings refers to a Henpeck City in his Diary, November 13, 1855.

Hen Roost Camp. An unidentified place, listed in Hittell, *Resources*.

Henrys Diggings [El Dorado]. On a gulch near the Middle Fork of Cosumnes River, about three miles south of Grizzly Flat. Nathan Aldrich had a dry claim here during the summer in 1852–1853, according to letters written to his wife (Mrs. Henry J. Brown; Schlappi-Ferguson). The place is mentioned in the County History, 1883 (p. 195), as having good prospects. A drift mine, active in 1894, was worked again in 1949. Several other mines in the vicinity were also worked intermittently and are still listed in 1956. (*Mining Bureau*, LII.) Shown on the USGS Placerville 1931 quadrangle.

Hepsidam [Sierra]. On a channel of Slate Creek Basin. It was probably the name of an Indian village. Shown on the County Map, 1874. A tunnel, 4,500 feet deep, was built into a hill, and in 1877, more than a hundred men were working it (Co. Hist. 1882, p. 477).

Herbertville [Amador]. South of Amador City, on the main stage road to Drytown, via Upper Crossing. The camp was first described in 1854 by Trask (doc. 9, p. 86 f.). In 1852 there were twenty stamps and three arrastres in operation (*State Register*, 1859). According to the *Mining Press*, August 17, 1861, one of the deepest gold mine shafts was sunk in 1861. The principal mine, Talisman, had only moderate success, according to *Bulletin*, 108 (p. 91).

Hermitage [Butte]. North of Oroville. It was a flourishing but short-lived mining camp in Concow Township, according to the County History, 1882 (p. 253).

Hermitage Ranch [El Dorado]. Six miles south of El Dorado. In 1855 a 20-stamp steam-driven mill was erected here (*State Register*, 1857). In the 1890s the Hermitage Mine was part of the Sugar Loaf Quartz Mine (*Mining Bureau*, XIII, p. 158). This mine is listed in Mining Bureau reports until 1938.

Heslep Mine [Tuolumne]. On a vein of the Mother Lode, near Jamestown. The mine was in operation as early as 1850. The average output was eight dollars per ton. It had a 10-stamp mill in the 1860s (Browne, pp. 43 f.). In 1893 it was reopened by the App & Heslep Company with a 20-stamp water-driven mill, and again in 1923 with a 12-stamp mill. In 1912 it was consolidated with the Dutch and App mines. *See* App Mine; Dutch-App Mine.

Hesses Crossing [Yuba]. On the Middle Fork of Yuba River on the old road from North San Juan to Camptonville. Shown as Hess F[err]y on Trask's map, 1853. The name is usually spelled Hess Crossing. Thomas Hesse built a bridge at the site in 1851. Rich diggings were struck in 1853. Two young men took out as much as 500 dollars in one week (*Alta*, January 6, 1854). The place is often mentioned by De Long; on July 30, 1855, he collected for about eighty miner's licenses, mainly from Chinese. *See* Freemans Crossing.

Heuston Hill [Nevada]. *See* Hueston Hill and Houston Hill.

Hicks [Calaveras]. Four miles northwest of Copperopolis. The place is mentioned by Swan in the fall of 1848 and is recorded on Butler's map of 1851. A Hicks Rancho in the general region is mentioned in the *CHSQ*, XX (p. 100). A Hicks mine is listed in the reports of the Mining Bureau until 1936.

Hicorum [San Bernardino]. On the west side of the Providence Mountains. Gold was discovered here by a Chemehuevi Indian named Hi-corum, and the mining settlement and district became known by his name. He also discovered the gold deposits in the Bristol Mountains where the Orange Blossom Mine was developed. The mining settlement in the Providence Mountains was later known as Providence. (*California Place Names*; Belden, September 18, 1955.)

Hidden Treasure Mine [Placer]. Near Damascus. The deposits were discovered in 1875 by George Cameron, and the mine became the largest drift mine in the state. It was worked for thirty-two years and reportedly produced about 4 million dollars. (*Mining Bureau*, XXXII, pp. 65 f.) One of the numerous "lost mines" was the Hidden Treasure described in The Dutch Flat *Enquirer*, October 2, 1867, where it is reported that two Germans from Iowa Hill discovered "immense quantities" of gold near the headwaters of the North Fork of American River, but neither they nor several parties ever relocated the "Hidden Treasure" (Bancroft Notes). For references to other Hidden Treasure mines, *see* the *Consolidated Index*.

Higgins Point [El Dorado]. One quarter mile below Salmon Falls. "Very rich diggings" were discovered by the Mormons early in 1849. Shown on Bowman's map, 1873. The place was named for an Australian who opened the first store (Co. Hist., 1883, p. 202).

High Bank Diggings [Trinity]. On the Trinity River, above the junction with the

South Fork. The diggings are mentioned in 1858 by Cox (p. 83).

High Bar [Placer]. On the North Fork of American River, below Rattlesnake Bar. The place is mentioned in a notice of a claim of the High Bar Sluice Company, recorded December 4, 1851, and in later notices in the Placer County Records (I, pp. 50, 52, 192, 229). It is also known as Oakland Flat (Co. Hist., 1924, p. 176).

High Grade District [Modoc]. In the Warner Mountains, near the Oregon line. The discovery of gold deposits by a sheepherder 'in 1905 was followed by a rush in 1909–10. There has been minor activity since the 1930s (*Mining Bureau*, XV, p. 241; XXX, p. 304; *Bull.*, 193, pp. 149 f.).

High Rock Bar [Butte]. On the Feather River, above Oroville. Shown on the County Map of 1862. Asa B. Smith mentions the bar in a letter of October 8, 1860. The site is now under the Oroville Reservoir, but the High Rocks west of the vanished bar are still shown on detailed maps.

High State Bar [Mariposa]. On Maxwell Creek, near Coulterville. Church (p. 180) mined here in February, 1851, and made about nine dollars a day washing 100 buckets.

Highwaymans Bar. It is an uncertain name, mentioned by Helper (p. 151).

Hildreth [Madera]. The town, originally in Fresno County, was the trading center and from 1886 to 1896 the post office for the mining district described in *Mining Bureau*, VIII (pp. 202 ff.).

Hildreth Diggings [Tuolumne]. An early name for Columbia.

Hildreths Gardens [Tuolumne]. *See* Lorings Gardens.

Hillsburg [Nevada]. At Grass Valley. William Hill and E. P. Farnham built their metallurgical works here for the reduction of sulfurets by the chlorinizing process and within four years reduced 1,250 tons of sulfurets, mainly for the North Star and Rocky Bar mines. With a capacity of one ton a day, it ranked next to the Maltman works at Gold Flat, south of Nevada City, as the largest of its kind in the county. (*Bean's Directory*, p. 247.)

Hirshmanns Cut [Nevada]. *See* American Hill.

Hitchcock Mine [Tuolumne]. *See* Dutch-App Mine.

Hites Cove [Mariposa]. On the South Fork of Merced River, four and a half miles from El Portal. It was also designated as Hites Mine. Nearby Bunker Hill Mine was located in 1851 and was first called Squirrel Mine, because a squirrel had exposed gold quartz. It had one of the first quartz mills in the state, operated with wooden stamps (*Mining Bureau*, XIV, p. 578; XXXIV, p. 82; LIII, p. 246). The gold deposits at the Cove were not discovered until 1862, by John R. Hite. The work was first done by arrastres until a small stamp mill was built in 1866 (*Mining Bureau*, LIII, pp. 108 ff.). In 1874 there was a 20-stamp water-driven mill (*Annual Mining Review*, 1876, p. 22). The total production of the Hite Mine was estimated to have been about 3 million dollars (*U. S. Bull.*, 413, p. 145). The mine was reactivated in the early part of the twentieth century, and some prospecting has been done in the district in recent years (*Bull.*, 193, p. 64).

Hoaston Hill [Nevada]. *See* Houston Hill.

Hoboken [Trinity]. It was the principal mining and trading center of the New River diggings in 1858 (Cox, p. 106). There was a revival in the 1890s. The place had a post office for some time. The *Mining Bureau*, XIII (p. 449) records a hydraulic Hoboken and Grand Slide Mine in operation in 1896. The place is called Hoboken Bar or Grant's [!] Slide in *Bulletin.*, 92 (p. 92).

Hocumac Mine [San Bernardino]. *See* Mount Baldy district.

Hodson District [Calaveras]. The district extends ten miles, from the site of Hodson, near Copperopolis, to Salt Springs Valley. There was probably minor placer mining here in the Gold Rush era, according to *Bulletin*, 193 (p. 64). Around the turn of the century several mines were worked on a large scale. In 1903 a 120-stamp mill, one of the largest in California, was built at the Royal Mine, the total production of which was 5 million dollars. Another productive mine was the Mountain King, with an estimated production of one million dollars. In the 1930s and early 1940s there was again some gold mining. Recently there has been diamond drilling but very little gold mining.

Hog Canyon [Sierra]. Seven miles east of Downievile, in the Sierra Buttes. It was located on a rich quartz vein. The principal mine, owned by the Reis brothers, was evaluated at 300 thousand dollars in 1859 by Vischer (p. 243). In 1863 the place was an election precinct (Bancroft Scraps, V, p. 1780). In *Mining Press*, June 1, 1861, it was called Hoggs Cañon.

Hoggs Canyon [Sierra]. *See* Hog Canyon.

Hoggs Diggings [El Dorado]. Between the Middle and South forks of American

River, about three and a half miles southeast of Auburn. Shown on Doolittle's map, 1868, and Bowman's, 1873. The deposits were discovered probably in 1849 by John B. Hogg, an educated Tennesseean and a successful miner (Co. Hist., 1883, p. 182). In 1854 a piece of pure gold weighing sixty-seven ounces was picked up (Hittell Clippings, p. 21). The *Mining Press*, March 8, 1862, reports that two boys washed out a nugget of pure gold worth 400 dollars at Hog's Dry Diggings. In 1872, 18 hundred dollars worth of gold nuggets, one of which weighed ninety ounces, were washed out of the supposedly "worked out" diggings, according to an extract from the *Placer Herald*, March 2, 1872 (Hayes Scrapbooks: Mining, II, sec. 16).

Hog Hill [Calaveras]. Near Copperopolis. Prospecting for gold lead to rich copper deposits (*Mining Press*, July 6, 1861).

Hogs Back [Placer]. On the ridge between Bear River and North Fork of American River. It is mentioned in notice of a claim to water rights recorded February 15, 1855 in Placer County Records, I (pp. 281 f.).

Hogs Dry Diggings [El Dorado]. *See* Hoggs Diggings.

Hogtown [Amador]. An unidentified place, mentioned by Joseph Henry Jackson in *Anybody's Gold* (p. 189).

Holcomb Valley [San Bernardino]. North of Big Bear Lake. The discovery of gold in 1860 by William F. Holcomb led to a "rush" to the area. Hayes Scrapbooks: Mining, V (sec. 298–354) contain a collection of contemporary newspaper clippings pertaining to it. There was extensive placer and quartz mining for a number of years (Raymond, VI, pp. 62 f.; *Mining Bureau*, IX, p. 238; XXX, p. 250; La Fuze, I, pp. 54 ff., II, pp. 30 and *passim*). In the 1930s and early 1940s there was mining by power shovel (*Bull.*, 193, p. 171). An interesting account is given in *Desert Magazine*, February, 1962. During the Civil War the area was a center of renegade Confederate activity. Historic Landmark 619.

Holdens Garden [Tuolumne]. Now a part of Sonora Union High School campus, within Sonora city limits. Gold was discovered in Holden's vegetable garden in 1851. According to one source, it was found attached to the roots of an uprooted cabbage plant. Since Mr. Holden's fenced garden included much more land than a lawful claim, regular battles were fought until the property was divided into claims.

(James Woods, *Recollections* pp. 98 ff; Marryat, pp. 313 f.) In April, 1851 the Holden's garden chispa was discovered: a lump weighing more than twenty-eight pounds, twenty of which were estimated to be gold (quotation from Sonora *Herald* in Co. Hist., 1882, p. 63). This is doubtless the same as the mass of quartz and gold worth 30 thousand dollars discovered in 1850, mentioned in *Mining Bureau*, II, (part 1, p. 150).

Hole in the Wall [Yuba]. *See* Prairie Diggings.

Hollow Log [Sierra]. *See* Nigger Tent.

Holmes Camp [El Dorado]. On Weber Creek. Mr. Holmes, a mechanic from Connecticut, had his diggings here. Henry I. Simpson mined at the place with good success in August, 1848 (Simpson, pp. 13 ff.).

Holmes Camp [Shasta]. The camp was named for the Holmes who mined with Henry Simpson on Weber Creek. He mined again with Simpson, who claimed that he and his partner "dug upwards of 50 thousand dollars worth of gold" in ten days in September, 1848 (Simpson, pp. 16 f.).

Holts Canyon [San Bernardino]. On Lytle Creek near the summit of Cucamonga Mountain. Placer mines were discovered in the fall of 1869, according to an unidentified clipping dated September 18, 1869 in Hayes Scrapbooks, Mining, VII (Sec. Lytle Creek).

Holts Ravine [Butte]. An unidentified place, listed in Hittell's roster.

Homer District [Mono]. *See* Lundy.

Honcut: Creek, town, **City, District** [Yuba, Butte]. The name Honcut Creek in Yuba County appears in the *Statutes* of 1850 (p. 62) and on Gibbes', *A New Map of California* (Stockton: C. D. Gibbes, 1852). J. A. Stuart prospected along the Honcut in 1850 without success (pp. 99 ff.). In 1858 there was a water-driven mill with three arrastres at Honcut in Yuba County (*State Register*, 1859, p. 260). The town had a post office intermittently from 1856 to 1943 apparently at different sites in Yuba and Butte counties and under different names: Honcut [Yuba], Honcut [Butte], Bryden [Yuba], Moores Station [Butte], and finally Honcut [Butte]. For a discussion of the confused history, *see* Frickstad and *Diggin's*, XIV:4 (Winter 1970, pp. 10 f.). Doolittle's map, 1868, also shows Honcut post office and station on the California Northern Railroad. The town Honcut is shown on modern maps. There was another place called Honcut City in Butte County, southeast of Wyandotte and near the North Honcut. It is shown on the Butte County map, 1861; on Long and Montgomery's, 186?; and on Doolittle's, 1868. No post office is listed. The District is a gold dredging district in southwest Butte County, northeast of the town Honcut, along Honcut and Wilson Creeks. There was bucket line dredging from 1909 to about 1920 and some dragline dredging in the 1930s. (*Bull.*, 57, pp. 158 f. and 193, p. 65.) The name is derived from an Indian village. *See California Place Names.*

Hones Bar [Placer]. About ten miles above Auburn. Notice of a claim held by Chinese miners was recorded October 18, 1852 in Placer County Records, I (p. 127).

Honest Bar [Trinity]. The *Mining Press*, November 23, 1861, reports mining with good pay.

Honey Lake District [Lassen, Plumas]. South of Honey Lake. Among a few small lode mines is the Honey Lake or Badger Mine, which was discovered in 1900 and was worked during the 1920s and 1930s (*Bull.*; 193, p. 65).

Honolulu [Siskiyou]. On the Klamath River, near Gottville. It was a trading center and post office (1881–1885) for a group of placer and hydraulic mines. Listed in the *Register*, 1898.

Hoodoo Bar [Sierra]. On the North Fork of Yuba River, west of Goodyears Bar. It is said to have derived its name from the Indian pronunciation of "How-dye-do" (Co. Hist., 1882, p. 466). Hutchings spells the name Hudu in his diary, October 22, 1855.

Hoodville [Amador]. *See* Slabtown.

Hook and Ladder Mine [El Dorado]. *See* Smiths Flat.

Hoopa District [Humboldt]. In the Hoopa Indian Reservation. It is essentially a copper mining district, but some gold has been placer mined in the Trinity River and has also been produced as a byproduct in a copper mine which was active in 1965 (*Bull.*, 193, p. 138).

Hooperville [Siskiyou]. On Hooper Hill, on Indian Creek, tributary to Scott River, west of Fort Jones. Mining on the hill reportedly began as early as 1853, and the camp was named for Frank Hooper, an old prospector of Indian Valley (Co. Hist., 1881, pp. 212, 217). A mine on the hill, idle in 1916 for lack of water, is listed in *Mining Bureau*, XIV (p. 852). Some of the old buildings are still standing.

Hoosier Bar [El Dorado]. On the Middle Fork of American River, five miles above the junction. It is recorded on Doolittle's map, 1868, as Hosier Bar, and also on Bowman's map, 1873. It is mentioned in the County History, 1883 (pp. 84, 85).

Hoosier Hill [Siskiyou]. A half mile west of Hamburg Bar. The diggings were worked as early as 1856, but the production was apparently only small. Yet a Hoosier Hill Mine is listed in the reports of the Mining Bureau until 1935.

Hopetown [Merced]. *See* Forlorn Hope Camp.

Hope Valley District [Alpine]. About ten miles west of Markleeville. It is a small gold and tungsten mining district, first prospected in the early 1860s, with only intermittent minor prospecting since that time (*Bull.*, 193, p. 65).

Hopkinsville [Plumas]. Near the confluence of Hopkins and Poor Mans creeks. Shown on Milleson and Adams' map, 1851. Rich diggings were reported in 1850. McIlhany (p. 51) had a store here in 1852, and Lecouvreur (p. 241) mined here in June, 1852. Miners were still reported doing well in 1861 (*Mining Press*, September 28, 1861), and in the 1880s extensive hydraulic mining was carried on near the forks of Hopkins and Poormans creeks (Co. Hist., 1882, p. 321). The Creek is shown on the USGS Downieville 1907 quadrangle.

Hopland [Mendocino]. On Highway 101, twelve miles south of Ukiah. The only sizeable amount of gold mined in the county was at the platinum deposit near Hopland (*Mining Bureau*, XVII, p. 147).

Hornblende Mountains [El Dorado]. This was one of the richest placer and seam mining districts of the Georgetown Divide.

Hornbrook [Siskiyou]. On Highway 99. In the latter part of the nineteenth century the town was the trading center and from 1891 the post office for the mines along Cottonwood Creek (*Register*, 1898).

Hornitos [Mariposa]. Thirteen miles west of Mount Bullion. The place was settled in 1852 by Mexicans and was probably named after Los Hornitos in Mexico. For other theories about the naming, *see California Place Names.* A post office was established June 18, 1856, and in 1858 a quartz mill with two arrastres was operated by a 30 h.p. engine. It was alleged to have been superior to a stamp mill (Hittell Clippings, pp. 40 f.). In 1860 there was a steam-driven mill with 20 stamps (*Annual Mining Review*, 1876, p. 22). In 1861 some Mexicans found 500 dollars worth of quartz gold in two days (*Mining Press*, December 14, 1861). After 1900 three stamp mills were still in operation (*Register,* 1903). There is a story of a Murieta Tunnel here, where the legendary robber supposedly hid from a posse. The chocolate manufacturer, Domingo Ghirardelli, had a store here and the ruins are still standing. Historic Landmark 333. A description of the Hornitos District is given in *Bulletin,* 193 (p. 65 f.). One of the best mines was the Washington or Jenny Lind Mine. It was discovered in 1851 and was equipped with a 6-stamp mill as early as 1851, which reportedly produced for a time one thousand dollars worth of gold per day (!). The vertical depth of the Washington Mine was 1,600 feet and that of the Jenny Lind around 1,500 feet, and the workings connecting the two extended a distance of almost two miles. The estimated production to 1954 was 2.377 million dollars. (*Mining Bureau,* LIII, pp. 179 ff.) Some of the mines in the Quartzburg vein were numbered. The numbers one, five, eight, and nine operated until the twentieth century and are described in *Mining Bureau,* XXIV (pp. 104 f.), *Register,* 1903, and *Mining Bureau,* LIII (p. 144). The Prescott Vein, discovered in the early 1850s, is reported to have yielded 80 thousand dollars from surface diggings. Later it operated as the Badger Mine (*Mining Bureau,* LIII, p. 76). The Mount Gaines Mine is treated separately in this dictionary. The Ruth Pierce Mine, four miles east of Hornitos, produced about 600 thousand dollars (*Bull.,* 193, pp. 65 f.). For other mines in the district, consult the *Register,* 1903, *Mining Bureau,* LIII, and *Bulletin,* 193 (pp. 65 f.).

Hornswoggle Ravine [Yuba]. The strange name of a place situated somewhere between the North and Middle forks of Yuba River, is mentioned by De Long, November 27, 1855.

Horrs: Ranch, Ferry; Horrsville [Stanislaus]. On the Tuolumne River, a short distance above the junction with San Joaquin River. Shown on Trask's map, 1853. Horrs Ranch had a post office from 1851 to 1895, when the name was changed to Horr, and after a year it was moved to Waterford. Rensch-Hoover locates Horrsville near Roberts Ferry or Bridge, where Dr. B. D. Horr attempted to found a town in the 1860s.

Horse Bar [Yuba]. On the north bank of the main Yuba River just below the confluence of the South Yuba. Shown on Wescoatt's map, 1861, and on Doolittle's,

1868. It is mentioned in the County History, 1879 (p. 94), as a short-lived mining camp of 1851.

Horseshoe Bar [Placer, El Dorado]. In 1849 there were two Horseshoe bars on the American River, the lower one on the North Fork, below the junction of the North and Middle forks, and the upper one on the Middle Fork, between Stony Bar and Gray Eagle Bar. According to the Placer County History, 1882 (p. 401), the lower Horseshoe Bar, which was about seven miles above Beals Bar, was first worked by Mormons in 1848, and it became the trading center for neighboring bars. In 1852 it polled 300 votes. It is shown on Trask's map, 1853, and on Goddard's, 1857. The upper Horseshoe Bar, called Horseshoe (No. 2) in the County History, 1882 (p. 402), was on the Middle Fork at a point where the river makes a loop almost returning upon itself (*Mining Bureau,* VIII, p. 475; IX, p. 277). It is shown on Trask's map, 1853, on Doolittle's, 1868, and on the map in *Mining Bureau,* IX (p. 275). Andrew Smith Hallidie, later of San Francisco cable car fame, started his career at the upper bar in 1855 at the age of nineteen by building a suspension bridge and an aqueduct of a 220-foot span (*CHSQ,* XIX, p. 146). The *Mining Press,* August 31, 1861, reports that several companies had struck pay dirt, one of which after working their claims for six years, washed up forty ounces in one day and continued to have good success. According to the *Directory* of Placer County, 1861 (pp. 201 ff.), cited in Bancroft Notes, hundreds of miners rushed to the place when the first bedrock tunnel in the state was built there to drain the river. A town of tents and boards was set up, but early rains destroyed the dam and the camp was deserted. Letts (pp. 114 f.) states that neither bar "paid for the labor bestowed upon them."

Horseshoe Bend [Mariposa]. On the Merced River, about three miles southwest of Coulterville; now inundated by the waters of Lake McClure. Shown on Goddard's map, 1857. In 1850 there was a placer camp here with 400 inhabitants. By 1867 there were only a dozen small hydraulic claims, averaging four dollars a day to the man, according to Browne (p. 20). In the 1920s there was apparently some lode mining (*Mining Bureau,* XXIV, p. 90).

Horsetown [Shasta]. On Clear Creek, near Readings Bar. The original name was One Horse Town. Shown on Scholfield's

Horseshoe Bar, Placer Co.

map, 1851. There are numerous stories about the origin of the name. Gold was discovered here in March, 1848, by Major P. B. Reading. John S. Hittell mined here in 1849–1850. A post office was established October 12, 1852. The state census of 1852 lists it under the name One Horse Town and includes it among the nine principal mining localities of the county. Pringle Shaw in 1856 (p. 128) called it one of the important camps of the county. Hutchings in his diary, December 20, 1855, states that there were around 600 "Chinamen" in the vicinity of Horsetown. The production was only moderate until hydraulic mining was introduced in the fall of 1870 (Raymond, V, p. 90). It is mentioned as Horse Town as early as 1852 in a letter of S. G. George to John Bidwell, dated August 27, 1852 (Bidwell Papers, California State Library, California Section).

Horse Valley Diggings [Yuba]. One mile north of Camptonville. Horse Valley is shown on Wescoatt's map, 1861. Placer mines had been worked for fourteen years and were still yielding satisfactory returns in 1870, according to an item in the *Mining Press*, November 12, 1870.

Hosier Bar [El Dorado]. *See* Hoosier Bar.

Hot Springs [Mono]. The place is mentioned by Browne (p. 178) as the site of a 4-stamp water-driven mill, one of the three quartz mills in the county in 1867. The reference is probably to the Hot Springs that later became the town of Benton. *See* Benton.

Hottentot Bar [Plumas]. On the Middle Fork of Feather River, near Onion Valley. It is mentioned by Hutchings in his Diary, November 12, 1855.

Houghs Bar [Butte]. *See* Huffs Bar.

Houston Hill [Nevada]. South of Grass Valley. The *Alta* of June 10, 1854, reprints an item from the Grass Valley *Telegraph*, according to which a new lead yielded fifty to seventy-five dollars per ton of rock as it came out of a tunnel. The Sultana Mine on the hill is listed in the reports of the Mining Bureau until 1941. It is perhaps the same as Hueston Hill. Hoaston Hill, listed by Trask in 1856 (Senate doc. 14, p. 63) may also be the same place.

Howard Flat [Placer]. Unidentified place near Sears Diggings, mentioned in a clipping from the *Sierra Citizen* (Hittell Clippings, p. 72).

Howard Hill [Nevada]. Near Grass Valley. Several rich mines with mills are mentioned in the *Mining Press*, April 27, 1861. An extract from the Grass Valley *Union*, January 1, 1865, in Hayes Scrapbooks: Mining, IV (sec. 20) contains the statement that one company's claims averaged more than 100 dollars per ton at a cost of less than eight dollars per ton to obtain, crush, and amalgamate the bullion. Mines on the hill are listed in the 1942 report of the Mining Bureau.

Howard Ranch [Sierra]. *See* Bassetts Station.

Howards Ferry [Tuolumne]. On the Merced River, six miles above junction with the San Joaquin. Shown on Butler's map, 1851.

Howland Flat [Sierra]. In Gold Canyon, on the East Branch of Slate Creek, twelve miles north of Downieville. According to the County History, 1882 (p. 422), the camp was formed in 1850. The name is mentioned by John Clark in his manuscript, "The California Guide," August 19, 1853. In 1854 a shaft was sunk at the base of Table Mountain, where it struck a rich branch of the Blue Lead. The real prosperity of the town started when the great Yuba River Canal was completed (Vischer, p. 238), probably in 1856. The newspapers of the following years report rich production. According to the *Alta*, April 14, 1867, the population was still 1,200, and the total output to that time was 3.5 million dollars.

Hoyts Crossing [Nevada]. On the South Fork of Yuba River, one half mile below Edwards Crossing, on the road from Nevada City to Columbia Hill. About 1854 a bridge was built here by M. F. Hoyt (Co. Hist., 1880, p. 132).

Hoyts Diggings [Sierra]. On the Middle Fork of Yuba River. The camp is shown on Trask's map, 1853.

Hubbardville [Calaveras]. An unidentified place, listed in the Sacramento *Weekly Union*, February 2, 1852 (State Library) as a new mining settlement, with rich diggings in the vicinity.

Hubertville [Amador]. On the ridge between Amador and Sutter creeks. It is shown on an unidentified map of the mining region, about 1870. It is probably Herbertville (Berriman).

Hudson Gulch [El Dorado]. In Oregon Canyon, near Georgetown. The deposits were discovered in the summer of 1849 by the man whose name the place bears. The story of the rich discovery is told melodramatically, but probably correctly in the *Society of California Pioneers Quarterly*, I (pp. 18 ff.). Patterson (p. 73) states that it was on a "black lead" and that the nuggets were completely encrusted in black cement. By 1862 the estimated production was 1.5 million dollars. According to *Mining Bureau*, II (part 1, p. 150), the Gulch was apparently a part of Georgia Slide, where the one thousand dollar goose "egg" shaped nugget was found. *See* Georgia Slide.

Hueniche Bar [Del Norte]. *See* Craigs Creek.

Hueston Hill [Nevada]. South of Grass Valley. Named for the Hueston brothers who located the first mine in December, 1853. The Hueston Hill Company took out about half a million dollars from 1864 to 1867, averaging about forty-five dollars per ton (Bean, p. 225). *See* Houston Hill.

Huffs Bar [Butte]. East of Whiskey Bar, inside of the Big Bend of the North Fork of Feather River. Shown as Houghs Bar on the County Map of 1862; as Buffs Bar on the County Map of 1886; and as Huffs Bar on the map in the County History, 1882 (p. 209). There were bank diggings here, and the place is mentioned in the County History (p. 253) as a once flourishing mining camp.

Hughes Bar [Placer]. Near Ophir. Stephen Wing and companion mined here briefly in 1853, taking out as much as eighteen and a half dollars a day together (Wing's Journal, I, p. 42 and later).

Humboldt Flat [Sierra]. On the Middle Fork of the Yuba River, three miles below Minnesota. An item clipped from the *Mountain Echo* in Bancroft Scraps, LI:1 (p. 230) around 1865, reports the discovery of a lump of quartz which yielded 800 dollars worth of gold by pounding it in a common mortar.

Humbug. This was one of the favorite names during the Gold Rush. Some of the places so named turned out to be rich; others were named because discoverers of a new find thought the name would keep newcomers away.

Humbug [Nevada]. The old name of North Bloomfield. Bean (p. 395) tells the story of two Irishmen and one German who discovered gold in 1851 or 1852 on a tributary to the South Fork of Yuba River. One of the Irishmen was sent to Nevada City for provisions, and in his cups he told about the discovery. The next morning he was followed by about a hundred prospectors, who dubbed the stream Humbug Creek when they did not find the expected riches. However, after hydraulic mining developed, the town Humbug arose, and in 1855 it had a 24-stamp steam-driven mill (*State Register*, 1857). When the post office was established, June 1, 1857, the name was changed. *See* North Bloomfield.

Humbug [Plumas?] An unidentified place. Successful mining as well as grazing in May, 1858, is mentioned in an undated item in Hittell Clippings (p. 54). Humbug Valley in Plumas County is shown on the County Map, 1886, about ten miles east of Johnsville. Another Humbug Valley in Plumas County is shown on Keddie's map, 1892, near Longville, in the North Fork School District, in the northwestern part of the county.

Humbug: Bar, Canyon, Creek, Flat [Placer]. The creek is a tributary to the North Fork of American River, near Euchre Bar. It is recorded on Gibbes' map, 1851, and on Goddard's, 1857. According to the County History, 1882 (p. 383), the creek canyon was first called Mississippi Canyon, and the name was changed by prospectors when the amount of gold found was disappointing. Another account states that the canyon was first known as Tennessee Canyon (*Placer Nuggets*, February, 1971). Humbug Canyon is included in Hutchings' list of towns in 1855. Humbug Flat Ravine is mentioned in the Placer County Records, I (p. 238), July 24, 1854, and by Wing in 1852 and 1853 (Journal, I, p. 32). The mines are described in the County History, 1882 (p. 217). Humbug Creek and Bar are shown on the USGS Colfax 1938 quadrangle.

Humbug: Creek, Gulch, City, District [Siskiyou]. The creek is a tributary to Klamath River, northwest of Yreka. The deposits were discovered in 1850, but the placers were soon exhausted. Disappointed newcomers applied the name and left. More experienced miners went down to blue dirt and bedrock pitching and found rich deposits (Yreka *Union*, June 5, 1869, in Bancroft Notes). Some miners were making as high as fifty dollars per day to the man (*Alta*, February 18, 1852), and the profitable mining continued in a lesser degree, according to a reprint from the Yreka *Mountain Herald* in the *Alta* of March 29, 1854. Hutchings describes the extensive diggings at Humbug Gulch in his diary, January 30, 1855. In 1861 new findings, as reported in the *Mining Press*

(March 1, May 4, June 22, 1861), raised the hopes so high that even a post office was established — the only one in California with the name Humbug. It was probably at the place called Humbug City, mentioned in *Bulletin*, 193 (p. 38) "founded in 1851 and now almost disappeared." In 1872 there was a 15-stamp mill in operation (*Annual Mining Review*, 1876, p. 21). The district is described in *Bulletin*, 193 (p. 138), where it is stated that the total production of gold was about 15 million dollars, and that there has been dredging until the present day. Humbug Creek is recorded on the USGS Yreka 1939 quadrangle.

Humbug Ditch [Yuba]. Near Indian Valley. It is mentioned by De Long, September 29, 1856.

Humbug Flat [Nevada]. Near Grass Valley. The *Alta*, May 27, 1854, reports that the Old Ohio Company made ten to twelve dollars per day to the hand.

Humbug: Flat, Hill [Tuolumne]. Northwest of Jamestown, on the east side of Table Mountain. The diggings on the flat were started probably in 1850. Stephen Davis mentioned them April 14, 1852. The Columbia *Gazette*, February 12, 1853, reported that Humbug Hill was paying well. The *Alta*, June 24, 1854, reprints an item from the Columbia *Clipper* in which it was reported that a rich crevice was discovered in a vegetable garden, and agriculture "gave way to the pick and shovel." It may have been the same place that was named by the discoverers of a rich deposit mentioned in James Woods' *Recollections* (p. 98). Another account in the *Alta*, May 20, 1854, calls the place a gulch and states that some companies made fifty dollars per day to the man. The Humbug Gravel Mine is shown on Dart's map, 1879. The USGS Sonora 1939 quadrangle shows a Big Humbug Creek, north of Groveland, entering Tuolumne River above the mouth of Big Creek. There is also a Little Humbug Creek, tributary to Deer Creek, about three and a half miles northwest of Groveland (De Ferrari).

Humbug Gulch [Amador]. *See* Ballards Humbug.

Hungarian: Gulch, Hill [Plumas]. Twelve miles west of Saw Pit Flat. In 1867 three hydraulic and two drift claims paid about eight dollars per day to the man (Browne, p. 167). A Hungarian Hill placer mine is listed in the Mining Bureau reports until 1937.

Hungary Creek [Siskiyou]. It is mentioned

in Bancroft Scraps, LI:1 (p. 240) in a clipping of 1861. It is probably the same as Hungry Creek.

Hungry Creek [Siskiyou]. A tributary to Beaver Creek, which flows into the Klamath River west of Coles, near the Oregon border. There was mining probably as early as 1850. The *Mining Press*, May 1, 1862, reports that the tailings of previous mining were washed with good success. Hungry Creek Mining District is mentioned in 1892 in *Mining Bureau*, XI (p. 446), and mines in the district are listed until 1936.

Hungry Hill [Tuolumne]. *See* Six-Bit Gulch.

Hungry Hollow [Placer]. Near Auburn. It is mentioned by Coy (p. 39) and by Guinn (p. 42).

Huns Ranch [Nevada]. On the south side of the South Fork of Yuba River. Rich deposits, which yielded eighty dollars per pan, were discovered early in 1853, according to the *Alta*, March 6, 1853.

Hunter Canyon [Inyo]. In the Inyo Mountains, in Beveridge district. It is a remote area named for W. L. Hunter, who operated three arrastres there from the late 1870s to the early 1890s, but very little gold was produced (De Decker, pp. 49 f.). *See* Beveridge District.

Hunter Valley [Mariposa]. About five miles west of Bear Valley and extending northwest toward Lake McClure. It was named for William W. Hunter, well known engineer. In the 1850s there was extensive placer mining in the district. Browne (p. 31) mentions three lode mines in 1867, one of which was the Oakes and Reese Mine, at which a 12-stamp mill had been erected. The mine was discovered in 1863 and was active intermittently to 1938. It produced between 500 and 600 thousand dollars, mainly between 1863 and 1870 (*Mining Bureau*, XXIV, p. 106; LIII, pp. 145 ff.; *Bull.*, 193, p. 66).

Huntoon Station [Mono]. At the present site of the Savio Ranch in Huntoon Valley, north of Bridgeport. It was not a mining camp but a stage station established by A. Huntoon on the Sonora-Mono wagon road, which served the Bodie and Lundy travel (F. S. Wedertz).

Hunts Gulch [Amador]. Tributary to the Mokelumne River, southeast of Jackson. Shown on the County Map, 1866. Peters (pp. 13 f.) recounts from memory a history of the place. A miners' meeting to discuss miners' problems at Hunters Creek and Mokelumne River is reported in the *Alta*, July 7, 1849 (Berriman). The Gulch is listed

among remunerative mining localities in 1864 in an unidentified clipping dated July 2, 1864 in Hayes Scrapbooks: Mining, IV (sec. 20).

Hunts Hill [Nevada]. On Greenhorn Creek, tributary to Bear River; between Quaker Hill and Red Dog. Shown as a settlement on Doolittle's map, 1868, and the County Map, 1880. Borthwick stopped at Hunts Ranch when the place was still called Gouge Eye. *See* Gouge Eye. The gravel was first mined by drifting and was extremely rich in places (Whitney, *Auriferous Gravels*, p. 423). The bottom gravel was cemented and stamp mills were used to work it. Another account of the mining is given in *Mining Bureau*, XXIII (pp. 100, 101).

Huntsville [Calaveras]. Near the junction of Calaveras, San Joaquin, and Stanislaus counties. The town, named for a farmer in the valley in 1861, was supported by moderately paying surface mines and by agriculture, according to the San Andreas *Independent*, January 12 and 19, 1861. Descendants of Hunt are still in the cattle raising business here.

Hupps [Butte]. Between Big and Little Butte creeks, five miles north of Magalia. Rich gravel channels in the vicinity were worked from the 1860s to the 1920s (*Mining Bureau*, XI, p. 159; XXIV, p. 198; XXVI, p. 393). It was the site of John Hupp's sawmill from 1860 to about 1900 (*Diggin's*, X:3, p. 21). Shown on the USGS Chico 1944 quadrangle.

Hurdy Gurdy Creek [Del Norte]. A tributary to the South Fork of Smith River. There was considerable gold production prior to 1889. The gold was very coarse, and nuggets worth three to five dollars were said to have been common. Chinese worked here until 1906. (*Bull.*, 85, p. 61.) Shown on the USGS Preston Peak 1944 quadrangle.

Hurleton [Butte]. On Rocky Honcut Creek, east of Oroville. It was the trading center and post office for quartz mills in the vicinity (*Register*, 1903). In the 1860s it was a popular resort, first known as Boston Ranch, and later named for the owner of the ranch and hotel, Smith H. Hurles, according to the County History, 1882 (p. 267). The name was also spelled Hurlton.

Huse Bridge [Amador]. At the confluence of the North and Middle Forks of Cosumnes River; on the site of Yeomet. *See* Yeomet. Shown on the County Map, 1866. It was named for S. E. Huse, the proprietor of the bridge for a decade (El Dorado Co.

Hist., 1883, p. 199). Shown on the USGS Placerville 1931 quadrangle.

Hyampom [Trinity]. At the junction of Hayfork and South Fork of Trinity River. It was named for the remaining Indians who were here when the place was settled in 1855. It is described by Cox (pp. 127 f.). He spells the name Hyampum and records only sporadic gold mining in the vicinity. It was an early trading center for placer mines, and since 1890 it has had a post office. Shown on modern maps.

I**bex District** [San Bernardino]. Near the Ibex (now Ibis) railroad station in the Needles area. The main source of gold was the Ibex Mine. It was located in 1888, and in 1894 a mill was built (*Mining Bureau*, XI, p. 368; XIII, pp. 324 f.) This district is not to be confused with the Ibex district near Death Valley, which produced mainly lead, zinc, and silver.

Idaho-Maryland Group [Nevada]. *See* Grass Valley.

Idlewild [El Dorado]. *See* Taylors.

Ignis Fatuus Placer. An unidentified place, listed in Helper (p. 151).

Igo [Shasta]. On a fork of Clear Creek, southwest of Redding. For the derivation of the name, *see California Place Names*. Gold was mined as early as the 1850s. A post office was established July 14, 1873. Drift and hydraulic mines were very productive between the 1860s and 1880s, and many Chinese placer mined here at that time (*Bull.*, 193, p. 139). About 1900 one arrastre and one Justin mill were still in operation (*Register*, 1902). There was again activity in the Igo and Ono districts in the 1930s, when power shovels and dragline dredges were used (*Mining Bureau*, XXXV, pp. 140 f., 150 ff., and *Bull.*, 193, p. 38). *See* Ono.

Illinois Bar [Nevada]. On the north bank of the South Fork of Yuba River, on the road between North Columbia and Nevada City. It was the site of Coopers Bridge, built in 1856 by J. L. Cooper, and rebuilt in 1867 after having collapsed. Cooper and his partner, Joseph Kyle (or Kile) were robbed and murdered at the site in 1866. (Co. Hist., 1880, pp. 112 and 132). The bridge is also mentioned in the Nevada City *Democrat*, February 20, 1856, as part of a new wagon road to Eureka South, Moores Flat, Orleans Flat, and Minnesota.

Illinois Canyon [El Dorado]. The canyon heads in Georgetown and flows into Can-

yon Creek. According to Warren T. Russell, it was also known as South Canyon. Shown on Doolittle's map, 1868. Bowman's map, 1873, shows Illinois Ravine. In 1849 a one thousand dollar nugget was found in the canyon, and for some time it was known as Thousand Dollar Canyon (W. T. Russell, p. 98). The diggings were "seam diggings," and the ground was worked by hydraulic mining, but reportedly paid a little less than wages, according to the statement of W. A. Goodyear in 1871 (Whitney, *Auriferous Gravels*, p. 115).

Illinois Ravine [Nevada]. Near Nevada City. The Ravine heads near Newton (Newtown) and follows a northerly course to its junction with Rush Creek. There were rich shallow placers here at one time, according to Pettee (Whitney, *Auriferous Gravels*, p. 190).

Illinoistown [Placer]. On Interstate Highway 80, near Colfax. Shown on Trask's map, 1853, and Goddard's, 1857. It was settled as early as 1850 for the purpose of providing a supply depot for the mines, according to an item in Bancroft Notes taken from the Dutch Flat *Enquirer*, October 9, 1862. Gibbes records it as a town on his map of 1851, and Finley McDiarmid in a letter dated February 9, 1851, mentions that it had ten to twelve houses. Borthwick (p. 182) describes it as a "very romantic little place" with three shanties and one sawmill in the summer of 1852. The place was first known as Alder Grove and Upper Corral, according to Mahlon Fairchild (p. 17), who was here about the same time. A post office existed from 1853 to 1866, when it was transferred to Colfax. The Illinois Mining District is listed as late as 1915 in *Mining Bureau*, XV (p. 316). It is the same as the Colfax district (*Bull.*, 193, p. 38).

Independence [Plumas]. On or near the Middle Fork of Feather River, near Nelson Point. It was located in June, 1850, during the Gold Lake hunt. An interesting description and several letters dated in the fall of 1850 are in Alonzo Delano's *Life on the Plains and in the Diggings*, 1854 (pp. 344 f.; 347 f.). From 1871 to 1884 it was worked mainly by a British company. The County History, 1882 (p. 288), lists an Independence Bar as an important camp along Nelson Creek, tributary to the Middle Fork.

Independence [Sierra]. East of Downieville and north of Loganville, near the Columbo Mine. There was a settlement here from about 1858 to the middle of the 1870's (Sinnott, *Sierra City*, p. 89).

Independence Bar [Trinity]. Near the North Fork of Trinity River. The *Mining Press*, November 23, 1861, reports very good pay at gold mining here.

Independence Bar [Yuba]. On the main Yuba, six miles from Long Bar. It is mentioned by Lecouvreur in 1852 (pp. 222, 251).

Independence Hill [Nevada]. Near Red Dog. A company struck a rich lead here and worked with great success in the winter of 1860–61, with water from Chalk Bluff ditch (*Mining Press*, December 14, 1860). Pettee and Bowman's map, 1879, shows part of the area as "more or less completely hydraulicked away."

Independence Hill [Placer]. One mile above Iowa City, on the rich lead between the North and Middle forks of American River. Good deposits were discovered in 1854 (*Alta*, June 18, 1854). In 1855 Hutchings records having seen ditches with rushing water and on top of the hill a town of 200 inhabitants (Diary, May 4, 1855). The diggings are also mentioned in a notice of intention to construct a canal, filed December 24, 1855, in Placer County Records, I (p. 346). In 1860 there were 2,500 feet of tunnels with forty men working (*Transactions*, 1860, p. 85). It is possibly the same place as Independence Slope mentioned in the *Mining Press*, June 1, 1861, as "a truly gigantic mining operation."

Independence: town, **Creek, Flat** [Calaveras]. On Independence Creek, tributary to the South Fork of Mokelumne River; adjacent to Railroad Flat. Independence Flat is shown on Goddard's map, 1857. Bachman prospected here in July, 1852, without success. Doble mentions the place May 4, 1852.

Independent Mine [Placer]. *See* New Jersey.

Indiana Boys Camp [Nevada]. *See* Washington.

Indiana Creek [Yuba]. *See* Tolls New Diggings.

Indiana Hill [Placer]. Northwest of the confluence of Canyon Creek and the North Fork of American River; about one mile southeast of Gold Run, on the rich lead between Canyon Creek and Bear River. Shown on Doolittle's map, 1868. Browne (p. 104), in 1868, mentions three yielding claims and an 8-stamp mill with a hurdy-gurdy wheel. The Blue Gravel Mining Company still operated after 1936 (*Mining Bureau*, XXXII, p. 63).

Indiana Ranch [Yuba]. Between the North Fork of Yuba River and Dry Creek. Shown on Milleson and Adams' map just above Keystone Ranch. It was named by the Page brothers of Indiana, who discovered gold along the creek in 1851 (Co. Hist., 1879, p. 95). Lecouvreur (p. 228) calls it a Mexican ranch "which had not a very good reputation." The camp is mentioned repeatedly by De Long in 1855. In 1858 there was a 9-stamp steam-driven mill in operation (*State Register*, 1859). The population in 1858 was mostly French, Italian, and Portuguese, according to the *Marysville Directory*, 1858 (p. xxx). *See* Dobbins. After 1900 it was the most publicized mining district in the county, not through its gold production but through litigation. Eastern capitalists and promoters bought a number of early claims, and from 1908 to 1914 there was a series of court cases involving injunctions, damages, wages, slander, title, and embezzlement. Not enough gold was extracted to pay for the machinery needed to process the quartz (Ramey, from the Marysville *Appeal*, many issues between 1897 and 1914).

Indian Bar [Placer]. On the North Fork of American River. A notice of intention to flume the bed of the stream is recorded July 11, 1853, in Placer County Records, I (p. 171). It may be the same bar reported in the *Alta*, July 7, 1854, as earning two ounces a day to the man.

Indian Bar [Plumas]. On the East Branch of the North Fork of Feather River, near Rich Bar. Shown on Trask's map, 1853, as Indians Bar. Dame Shirley, who resided here from October, 1851 to November, 1852, describes the place as very rich, but when Windeler and his party were here on April 11, 1851, they struck bedrock five feet deep and made less than five and a half dollars.

Indian Bar [Siskiyou]. At the mouth of Indian Creek, tributary to the South Fork of Salmon River. The placer mines are mentioned in the *Siskiyou Pioneer*, II:10 (p. 7). The Mining Bureau lists the Indian Bar Mine as idle in 1914 (XIV, p. 859).

Indian Bar [Tuolumne]. On the Tuolumne River, five miles south of Jacksonville. Shown on Trask's map, 1853, but east of Jacksonville. It is mentioned as a bar of 1849 by Hawkins (p. 105). In 1854–55, when Gardiner had a store there, it was a small place and the population was mainly Chinese (pp. 229 ff.). Soon afterwards it was deserted. However, it is mentioned as a place of "considerable note" in 1856 by Heckendorn (p. 89). According to the *Mining Press*, August 10, 1861, the Sandborn claim yielded nearly 10 thousand dollars profit in one season. The place is shown on the USGS Sonora 1939 quadrangle. The site is now under Don Pedro Reservoir.

Indian Bar [Yuba]. Between the North and Middle forks of Yuba River. It is mentioned in the County History, 1879 (p. 100).

Indian Camp [Amador]. About two miles northeast of Jackson, near the headwaters of Squaw Gulch. Shown on the County Map, 1866. No mining record was found.

Indian: Camp, Creek [Trinity]. The creek is a tributary to the Trinity River, five miles south of Weaverville. An extract (probably February 21, 1872) from the Trinity *Journal* in Hayes Scrapbooks: Mining, II (sec. 21) contains a report of a rich find, prospecting two to four dollars worth of coarse gold per pan. According to Raymond, VI (p. 154), the gravel placers were mainly washed out in 1873, but hydraulic mining was carried on in the 1930s (*Mining Bureau*, XXIX, p. 63). The camp was about five miles upstream from the junction. The creek and a settlement are recorded on the USGS Weaverville 1942 quadrangle.

Indian Canyon [Placer]. Near Iowa Hill. It is "reputed to have been the richest cañon ever found in California" (Browne, p. 100). Henry S. Blom mentions it in his diary on August 30, 1851. The name is recorded in a miners' agreement dated September 1, 1851, and again in a document of March 30, 1869 (Placer County Records, I, p. 64; IV, pp. 377 ff.). Indian Canyon Mine is listed in the Mining Bureau report of 1936. Indian Creek is shown on the USGS Colfax 1938 quadrangle as a tributary to the North Fork of American River, flowing southeastward past Iowa Hill and Monona Flat.

Indian Creek [Calaveras]. On the limestone belt near Vallecito. Heckendorn mentions it (p. 104) as a camp in 1856. It was nearly exhausted in 1867 according to Browne (p. 58), but the *Annual Mining Review*, 1876 (p. 21), reported a 20-stamp mill in operation in 1871. Campo de los Muertos was once called Indian Creek.

Indian Creek [Siskiyou]. A tributary to Scott River, near Fort Jones. In 1855 there were 300 to 500 miners at work along the stream, and many claims paid from twenty to fifty dollars per day to the hand

(Sacramento *Union*, July 19, 1855). The claims above the mouth of French Gulch did not pay as well; still many miners made five to twelve dollars per day in the summer. Among the lode mines in the area the Golden Eagle, formerly the Indian Creek mine, idle since 1931, had an estimated total production of one million dollars. (*Mining Bureau*, XXXI, p. 319; XLIII, p. 437.) The Creek is shown on the USGS Yreka 1939 quadrangle. Another important gold bearing district was along Indian Creek which flows into the Klamath River from the northwest at Happy Camp. This Creek is shown on the USGS Seiad 1945 quadrangle.

Indian: Creek, Valley [Plumas]. Southeast of Lake Almanor. There were numerous well paying quartz mines in the valley, of which Crescent Mills Mine, Indian Valley Mine, and Taylors Mine were the most important. *See* Taylorsville. In the 1860s three steam-driven mills with eighty stamps were in operation. The mines had produced fifty dollars worth of gold per ton for years, but they were on the decline in 1872 (Raymond, V, pp. 64, 96). Two mines were still operating in the 1930s (*Mining Bureau*, XXX, p. 304). The Indian Valley Mine is estimated to have produced more than 1.8 million dollars (*Bull.*, 193, p. 42). The places are shown on the USGS Indian Valley 1940 quadrangle. *See* Crescent Mills.

Indian Diggins [El Dorado]. Between Indian and On It creeks, tributaries to the South Fork of the Cosumnes River. The diggings were started in 1849 or 1850. Doble prospected here in April, 1852, when the camp had fifty log cabins and two buildings housing hotels, stores, and gambling houses. A post office was established in 1853 with the name Indian Diggings, which was changed to Mendon in 1869 and to Indian Diggins in 1888 (to 1935). It is said that an early name given by the miners was Whorehouse Gulch. When ditches brought water from the Cosumnes River, the camp grew rapidly. In 1855 it had a population of 1,500, nine stores, five hotels, and many saloons (Browne, p. 85; Co. Hist., 1883, pp. 196 ff.). One of the early settlers was the grandfather of the historian Guy J. Giffen (San Francisco *Chronicle*, June 29, 1965, "Millie's Column"). Around 1900 the place was still a center of drift mines (*Register*, 1902), and several mines operated in the 1920s and 1930s (*Mining Bureau*, LII, pp. 433, 542, 552, 558, 567).

Indian District [Mono]. South of Mono Lake, west and south of Benton. There was mainly silver mining here, with some gold and copper. The district was organized in 1865 (Wasson's *Complete Guide*, p. 4), and in 1885 it was combined with the Clover Patch District. A description is given in *Mining Bureau*, VIII (pp. 378 f.). According to F. S. Wedertz, the district was named after the Indian Queen Mine, which was given its name because Indians had shown white people the location of the mine.

Indian Flat [Calaveras]. On the south side of Mokelumne River, opposite Lancha Plana, then called Sonora Bar. The diggings were located by A. Lascy and his partner in June, 1850.

Indian Flat [Nevada]. Near Rough and Ready. According to Bean (p. 360), it was a sizeable camp in 1850. It was probably the same place as Indian Springs. There is also an Indian Flat near Nevada City, where there was an Indian camp headed by Chief Oustamah, according to Foley.

Indian Gulch [Amador]. About five miles east of Jackson, on a tributary to the Mokelumne River. The gulch is described by Doble (pp. 60 f.) and is shown on Camp's map. The *Alta*, March 4, 1854, reprints an item from the Jackson *Sentinel* which reports that one company cleared 100 dollars daily here and in the neighboring Squaw Gulch. Bancroft, VI (p. 372) goes one better and reports that "many readily obtained $1,000 a day."(!)

Indian Gulch [Calaveras]. The creek joins the Stanislaus River below Robinsons Ferry. Harvey Wood (p. 21) mined at this place successfully in the fall of 1849. In February, 1854, an 8-pound lump of gold was dug up here (Hittell Clippings, p. 25). The steamer edition of the *Alta*, March 20, 1857 (Hittell Clippings, p. 30) reports that the Fritz company made twenty-five dollars per day to the hand at Indian Gulch in Calaveras County, but the exact location is not indicated; hence the reference may be to the Indian Gulch east of Mokelumne Hill.

Indian Gulch [Calaveras]. East of Mokelumne Hill, a short distance beyond Happy Valley. It was mentioned in a letter by William H. Moore, July 17, 1853. According to an item in the *German Journal*, June 18, 1855 (Hittell Clippings, p. 62), it was first worked by former members of the French *Garde Mobile*, who called their place Cagnade (!) Mobile. In 1855 it was occupied by Chinese miners, who said

they made "two bitty, one day, one man." — Indian Gulch was also the former name of West Point. *See* West Point.

Indian Gulch [Mariposa]. About four miles southeast of Hornitos. It was first mined by Mexicans and was called Santa Cruz (Crampton, p. 74). The elevation north of the Gulch is shown as Santa Cruz Mountain on the USGS Indian Gulch 1920 quadrangle. N. H. Stockton in his journal, November 9–19, 1850, states that he mined with no success, and that 200 miners were encamped there for the winter season. According to Angus McIsaac, March 5, 1853, it was a small mining district with two stores. Shown on the USGS Indian Gulch 1920 quadrangle. There is another Indian Gulch in the county, a tributary to the North Fork of Merced River, south of Gentry Gulch. It is the site of the Quail Mine, which began operations before 1873 and by 1954 had produced around 400 thousand dollars (*Mining Bureau*, LIII, pp. 75 f.). It is shown on the USGS Sonora 1939 quadrangle.

Indian Hill [El Dorado]. Between the South Fork of American River and Weber Creek, north of Placerville, on a spur of the county's Blue Lead. Shown on Bowman's map, 1873, and mentioned in the County History, 1883 (p. 88). These may be the same hill diggings which Haskins (p. 164) states were discovered in 1851. An Indian Hill Mine is still listed in 1938 (*Mining Bureau*, XXXIV, p. 263).

Indian: Hill, Creek [Sierra]. About five miles southwest of Goodyears Bar, south of the North Fork of Yuba River. Shown on Doolittle's map, 1868, and on the County Map, 1874. Downie (p. 133) mined here successfully in the winter of 1851–1852. On January 28, 1851, Steele (pp. 151 ff.) and his party camped here on a journey, of which he gives a remarkable account. The diggings paid well in spite of the inadequate water supply. Four men of one company washed out 100 dollars worth of coarse gold per day in thirty to fifty feet below the surface. An Indian Hill Mine is listed in the Mining Bureau reports until 1942. Indian Hill and Valley are shown on the USGS Downieville 1907 quadrangle.

Indian Springs [Butte]. North of Magalia, between Butte and Little Butte creeks. Rich gravel deposits were worked from 1860 until 1922 (*Mining Bureau*, XI, p. 159; XXIV, p. 198; XXVI, p. 394). A mine is still listed in 1949.

Indian Springs [Nevada]. Seven miles

southwest of Grass Valley. Shown on Doolittle's map, 1868, and the County Map, 1880. It was a short-lived placering camp, listed in Bean's *Directory*. It is probably the same as the Indian Flat and Indian Spring Flat mentioned in the *Alta*, December 23, 1853. A cluster of names, Indian Springs Hill, Indian Spring Creek, and a settlement, Indian Springs, is shown on the USGS Smartsville 1943 quadrangle.

Indian Valley [Sierra]. On the north side of the North Fork of Yuba River, about four and a half miles southwest of Goodyears Bar. Recorded on Gibbes' map, 1851. On Trask's map, 1853, and on the County Map, 1874, it is shown as an independent settlement across the river from Indian Hill. Morse (pp. 215 ff.) mined here in the fall of 1856. On the USGS Downieville 1907 quadrangle the canyon west of Humbug Creek is designated as Indian Valley, and the settlement Indian Hill nearby is also shown.

Indian Valley Mine [Plumas]. *See* Crescent Mills.

Industry Bar [Yuba]. On the main Yuba River, four miles above the confluence with Deer Creek. Shown on Milleson and Adams' map, 1851. In October, 1851, five men took out 5 thousand dollars in three days, according to the County History 1879 (p. 134). A formal duel with Colt revolvers was fought, November 1, 1851 (Brown, *Directory*, pp. 17 f.). With the development of hydraulic mining the bar was buried under gravel (*Alta*, November 7, 1867). According to *Mining Bureau*, XV (1915/16, p. 442), the river was still worked in the summers.

Ingrams Bar [Trinity]. On the Trinity River, east of Douglas City. It is mentioned by Cox (p. 34). In 1850 it was called Palmers Bar, according to *Trinity Journal*, December 19, 1891.

Inskips [Butte]. Near Butte Creek, not far from the Plumas County line. Shown on the County Map, 1862. Gold was discovered before 1857 reportedly by a "Dutchman" named Eenskip, and the camp was named for him. Successful mining was reported in May, 1858 (Hittell Clippings, p. 54), and in 1873 a 4-stamp mill was in operation (*Annual Mining Review*, 1876, p. 22). In 1859 there were five hotels (Bancroft, VI, p. 491), and the place had a post office from 1862 to 1915. Two mills with 10 stamps each are listed in the *Register*, 1902. An Inskip Mine is listed

in *Mining Bureau*, XV (p. 217). The old hotel is still standing.

Ione [Amador]. On Sutter Creek, about nine miles west of Jackson. The striving town was not one of the important "gold towns." Gold was washed in Ione Valley as early as 1848, and Ione City is mentioned in the *Alta*, March 3 and 23, 1852. In Book A of Calaveras County Deeds, (p. 272), it is mentioned as Ioneville. Bowen gives a pleasing picture under the date of January 23, 1855. In later years the production was mainly copper and coal. Among the former names attributed to the camp are Bedbug, Rickeyville, Freezeout, Hardscrabble, and Woosterville.

Ione [Nevada]. A settlement and a quartz mine are shown on Doolittle's map, 1868, to the southwest of Osborn Hill.

IOOF Bar [El Dorado]. On the Cosumnes River. Lucius Fairchild mined here in May and June, 1850, with moderate success. It was doubtless named by members of the Independent Order of Odd Fellows.

Iowa Bar [El Dorado]. Shown on Trask's map, 1853, on the upper South Fork of American River.

Iowa Cabins [Calaveras]. West of San Andreas; at the south end of Chili Gulch. Shown as Iowa Cabin on Camp's map. Ayers mentions it in the fall of 1849 (p. 44). A group of miners from Iowa built cabins here, and by the end of the year a hundred miners had settled in the camp, according to an article in *Las Calaveras*, October, 1957. According to Poore, the place is better known as North Branch.

Iowa: Diggings, Flat [Amador]. Three miles southeast of Jackson. The Sacramento *Union*, June 8, 1855, reported that two miners made 753 dollars in two days. The "new camp" of Iowa Flat, at the north base of Jackson Butte, is mentioned in the *Amador Ledger*, August 1, 1857, as having two hotels, the Butte Mountain House and the Iowa House (Berriman). In 1861 the place was an election precinct (Co. Hist., 1881, p. 97).

Iowa: Hill; City; Divide [Placer]. The camp was near the North Fork of American River, five miles east of Colfax. Shown on Trask's map, 1853, as Iova, and on Goddard's map, 1857, as Iowa Hill. But the post office, established June 16, 1854, was called Iowa City until 1901. It was one of the richest and most productive camps on the Blue Lead. Placering was probably done as early as 1849, but the rich diggings were not discovered until March, 1854. Soon about 1,000 men were working,

Iowa Hill, Placer Co.

and fifteen stores and eighteen hotels and restaurants were opened. The most exciting news since the discovery of gold was the report that the Jamieson claim yielded 200 ounces or more a day — temporarily at least. (Hittell Clippings, pp. 27, 32, 57, 58, 61.) The *Alta*, May 22, 1854, reprints an item from the *Empire Argus* which states that 22 hundred dollars had been washed out of a single pan of dirt (!), and the Sacramento *Union*, November 10, 1855, reports the find of a lump of fifty-eight ounces, valued at 1,177 dollars (Bancroft Notes). *Transactions*, 1860 (p. 86), gives a list of all the claims on Iowa Hill with statistics. Browne (p. 100) gives the production of the different claims in 1867 but adds the pessimistic note that the net gain is not much, and not one-third of the three dozen large tunnels paid expenses. In 1880 the gold production had fallen way behind the other hydraulic mining centers of Placer County: Michigan Bluff, Bath, Dutch Flat, Gold Run. In 1968 Iowa Hill was only a little hamlet, a post office, and Historic Landmark 401. Iowa Hill District is described in *Bulletin*, 193 (p. 67), where it is stated that drift mining continued through the early 1900s, and again in the thirties, with a few mines active in recent years. Among the mines listed, two produced more than one million dollars each, the Big Dipper and the Gleason.

Iowaville [El Dorado]. On Weber Creek, southeast of Placerville. Shown on Doolittle's map, 1868, and on Bowman's, 1873. It was a short-lived camp, mentioned in the County History, 1883 (p. 193).

Irish Creek [El Dorado]. A branch of Dutch Creek, tributary to the South Fork of American River, northeast of Coloma. Shown on Bowman's map, 1873. The U. S. Bureau of the Census lists the names of 252 inhabitants "On Irish Creek" in the population schedule for 1850. In 1855 a 20-stamp water-driven mill was erected, according to the *State Register*, 1859, yet Stephen Wing mined here with little success in September, 1855 (Journal II, pp. 33 ff.) — Some beautiful specimens of crystalline gold were found here (Hittell, *Mining*, p. 43). Shown on the USGS Placerville 1931 quadrangle.

Irish Hill [Amador]. Three miles northwest of Ione. It is shown as a settlement on the County Map, 1866. The place is reported as having been very rich in early days, was yielding satisfactorily in 1878, and was still being worked in 1881 with water coming from the Cosumnes River through the Plymouth ditch (*Pacific Coast Mining Review*, 1878, p. 75; Co. Hist., 1881, p. 192). Hydraulic mining completely obliterated the townsite (Andrews, pp. 71 ff.). The hill is shown on the USGS Sutter Creek 1944 quadrangle. Another Irish Hill is shown on the County Map, 1866, between Dry Creek and a branch of the Volcano Ditch, southwest of Fort John.

Irishmans Bar [Nevada]. On the South Fork of Yuba River. Peter Decker mined here in the summer of 1850 according to his diary of July 22, 1850.

Irishtown [Amador]. On the Middle Fork of Jackson Creek, near Pine Grove. It is mentioned by Ben Bowen, October 15, 1854. According to *California Historical Landmarks*, it was an "important stopping place for emigrants on their way to the southern mines." Historic Landmark 38. The marker is on the south side of Highway 88, but most of the remains of the town are on the north side, according to Andrews (pp. 69 ff.). Massive walls of adobe buildings were still standing until about thirty or forty years ago.

Iron Mountain [Calaveras]. Near West Point. Good deposits were apparently found in decomposed rock. It is listed in Bancroft, VI (p. 375).

Iron Mountain [Shasta]. Northwest of Keswick. This property was operated as a silver mine in the 1880s, as a copper mine (furnishing ore to Keswick Smelter) in the period 1896–1909, and as a gold mine, 1931–1941 (R. B. Eaton).

Irvine [Calaveras]. This was one of the Carson Hill claims, developed toward the end of the nineteenth century. It had three stamp mills and was the center of a number of quartz mines (*Register*, 1899). The post office was established in 1896.

Isabella [Kern]. On Highway 178, northeast of Bakersfield. It was the trading center for numerous mines on both sides of the road to Kernville (*Register*, 1904). A post office was established in 1896. According to R. C. Bailey, it was named by Steven Barton in 1893 in honor of Queen Isabella, patron of Christopher Columbus.

Island Bar [Butte]. There are records of two Island Bars on the Feather River. Trask's map, 1853, shows Island Bar on the Middle Fork, below Big Stony Bar. It was apparently near Island Bar Hill, which is shown on the USGS Bidwell Bar 1944 quadrangle, between the Middle and South forks, about six miles above the junction. The County Map, 1862, shows Island Bar as a sizeable camp on the Big Bend of the North Fork, and there is a picture of it in the 1880s in *Mining Bureau*, VI (part 2, p. 27). This Island Bar is also shown on the Bidwell Bar quadrangle. The Big Bend of the river forms almost an island.

Island Mountain [Trinity]. In the southwest corner of the county. It was so named in 1850 because it was almost encircled by streams. After 1915 the main production was copper and only a minimal amount of gold (*Mining Bureau*, LIII, p. 18).

Islips Ferry [Stanislaus]. On the Stanislaus River, west of Knights Ferry. Shown on Gibbes' map, 1851. It was also called Middle Ferry. No gold mining records were found. It was, however, an important crossing to and from the southern mines.

Audubon's party crossed here in January, 1850, and Christman (p. 150) in May, 1850.

Italian Bar [Amador]. On the Mokelumne River, four miles south of Jackson. Shown on the County Map, 1866.

Italian Bar [Placer]. On the South Fork of the North Fork of American River, about two miles above the confluence. Shown on Doolittle's map, 1868, and on the County Map, 1887. No mining records were found, but an Italian Mine is listed in 1936 in *Mining Bureau*, XXXII (p. 91).

Italian Bar [Tuolumne]. On the South Fork of Stanislaus River; about six miles northeast of Columbia. Italian Bar bridge is shown on Dart's map, 1879. The place is mentioned by Dane (p. 3) as having existed in 1850. Heckendorn mentions it in 1856. A 6-stamp steam-driven mill is listed in the *State Register*, 1859. According to the Columbia *Courier*, September 29, 1866, there was a 5-stamp mill at the Hazel Dell claim and the yield was twenty-five dollars per ton. The total production with nearby Pine Log and Experimental Gulch was 3.5 million dollars by 1899, according to *Mines and Minerals* (p. 358). Recorded on the USGS Big Trees 1941 quadrangle.

Italian Gulch [Trinity]. On Digger Creek, near Minersville. The diggings were "supposed to be rich" in 1858 (Cox, p. 90).

Ivanpah [San Bernardino]. The name was first applied to the now vanished mining camp at the foot of the Clark Mountains, near the Nevada state line. The development of the mines, mainly silver, with some gold, began in the early 1870s. However, the Montezuma Mine, which was located in 1872, showed evidence of having been worked long before, according to the San Bernardino *Guardian*, October 5, 1872. *See* Clark Mountains District. In 1901 the California Eastern Railroad built a branch into Ivanpah Valley to tap the mining business to the northwest, and it appropriated the name Ivanpah for the terminus. When the spur was discontinued in 1913, the name was transferred to the Leastalk station of the Union Pacific. (Myrick, II, pp. 844–848; Haenszel.)

Ivawatch Mountains [San Bernardino]. *See* Avawatz Mountains.

J**ackass.** Of the names of domesticated animals this was by far the most popular for camps and mines.

Jackass Flat [El Dorado]. At the head of a branch of Otter Creek, north of Georgetown. It was also known as Chris Ranch. Jackass Flat is listed in Raymond, IV (p. 105) and Jackass Hill in VII (p. 94). Jackass Flat is shown on Bowman's map, 1873.

Jackass Gulch [Amador]. Tributary to Clapboard Gulch, near Volcano. Doble (p. 102 and repeatedly) mined here with moderate success in 1852. Carlisle Abbott in his reminiscences (p. 93) mentions it as a mining locality of 1849.

Jackass Gulch [Nevada]. Probably on the Middle or South Fork of Yuba River. "The richest quartz in California, or perhaps in the world" was discovered here. This slight overstatement was published in the Nevada *Journal*, August 3, 1855, and similar statements appeared in other contemporary newspapers (Bancroft Notes). The deposits are said to have been discovered in July, 1855, by an old Kentucky negro. It may be the same place as Jackass Flat on the South Fork, listed in Bancroft, VI (p. 358).

Jackass Gulch [Trinity]. The original name of Canyon City. It was so named because a jackass fell over a precipice and "died from the shock" (Cox, p. 98). *See* Canyon: Creek, City.

Jackass Gulch [Tuolumne]. On the Stanislaus River, above Robinsons Ferry (Melones), on the road from the Northern to the Southern Mines. The gulch is recorded·on Trask's 1853 map, but not on Goddard's map, 1857. An often repeated story attributes the naming to the incident in which a runaway donkey led a miner to the rich deposit. Gerstaecker in "Die Entdeckung des Mosquitogulch" narrates the story that two jackasses were instrumental in leading miners to the place. Both accounts may be fictitious. Harvey Wood (p. 24) found rich profits in the fall of 1849. Stoddart (p. 62) tells of the enormous, probably somewhat exaggerated, finds at the place, and Heckendorn (p. 80) records rich diggings in 1848 and 1849. In 1851 a channel of the Carson Lead was struck. Jordan (pp. 183 ff.) records that he and another German mined here successfully in the summer of 1849, after the group of sailors who had been working with them left for richer diggings. In spite of the riches, the place was only short lived. In 1856, only twenty-two votes were cast at the election (Heckendorn, p. 80), and the place does not seem

to be recorded on any later maps. *See* Norwegian Gulch.

Jackass Hill [Tuolumne]. Northwest of Tuttletown. The stories told about the naming are probably all products of folk etymology. The Columbia *Gazette*, August 13, 1853, reported that the diggings had paid well in days gone by and were still being worked with considerable success. In 1859 there was a 5-stamp water-driven mill here (*Annual Mining Review*, 1876, p. 23). The deposits were worked until the 1920s (*Mining Bureau*, XXIV, p. 11; *Bull.*, 108, p. 159). Mark Twain lived nearby in a cabin which has been reconstructed and is Historic Landmark 138. The place is the background for his "Sage of Jackass Hill." Bret Harte's "Truthful James" has nothing to do with James W. Gillis, an old-timer near the Hill. The *Guidebook* (p. 54) and *California Historical Landmarks* (p. 33) have interesting stories, which could not be verified.

Jackassville [Sierra]. In Slug Canyon, southwest of Downieville. It is the popular name for the City of Six, said to be abbreviated from the Camp of Half a Dozen Jackasses. *See* City of Six Diggings.

Jack Fork [Riverside]. *See* Monson Canyon.

Jacksbury Diggings [Placer]. The first flat below Dotys in the Ophir region. The place is mentioned March 26, 1852, in Wing's Journal, I (p. 14). The "Rules and Regulations" of the Diggings, adopted October 13, 1850, are given in the same manuscript (p. 50).

Jackson: town, Creek [Amador]. The town, between Sutter Creek and Mokelumne River, became one of the important centers of the Mother Lode early in the Gold Rush. It was a favorite stopping place in 1848 because of the good spring, and the many bottles left there gave it the name Bottilleas when mining first started. Bayard Taylor (chapter 25) spent a night there at Cosgraves tent in the fall of 1849, when the community numbered about sixty people, who settled there for the winter, though the average amount of gold taken out was not more than half an ounce per day to the man. The following year the place had about 100 tents and houses (Co. Hist., 1881, pp. 167 ff.). The camp was named for Colonel Aldan Apollo Jackson, who mined there briefly in 1848 or early 1849 (Berriman) and for whom the town Jacksonville in Tuolumne County was also named. Butler's map, 1851, shows the name in big letters. The post office was established July 10, 1851; it was the county seat of Calaveras County, July, 1851 to May, 1852, and of Amador County from the date of its formation, May 11, 1854. Peters (pp. 15 ff.) recalls many details of the Jackson of 1851 and the following years. Doble (pp. 88 ff.) has a good description of the place in the summer of 1852. Borthwick (p. 287) states that the miners' population in the spring of 1853 was chiefly French, but when Ben Bowen visited the town, January 24, 1855, he reported that "the principal street is literally covered with Chinese stores." In 1859 the population was still 1,500, but agriculture had already crowded out mining (*Transactions*, 1859, p. 81). The oldest of the important mines was the Argonaut, which operated with short interruptions from 1850 to 1943 and produced more than 25 million dollars. An even larger producer was the Kennedy Mine, located at the "Gate" northeast of the town, in operation between 1856 and 1942, with an interruption between 1875 and 1885, and credited with a total production of about 34.2 million dollars. It is reported to be the deepest gold mine in the United States with a vertical depth of 5,912 feet. Among other large producers were the Oneida Mine, north of Jackson, which yielded 2.5 million dollars, and the Zeila, southeast of the town with a yield of more than 5 million dollars. The principal quartz mines of 1867 are listed in Browne (pp. 73 ff.). For later developments, *see Guidebook* (pp. 62 f.); *Mining Bureau*, L (pp. 182 ff.); *Bulletin*, 193 (pp. 69 ff.). Many reports of hanging, including some of Murieta's band, are found in early reports. Jackson was the birthplace of Anthony Caminetti, commissioner of immigration under President Wilson, and of Robert Aitken, noted astronomer. An excellent account of mining operations in the Jackson-Plymouth district, with many illustrations, is given in *Bulletin*, 193 (pp. 69 ff.).

Jackson Flat [Tuolumne]. Near Tuttletown, The *State Register*, 1859, lists it as having had a steam-driven 8-stamp mill in 1858.

Jackson Gate [Amador]. More than one mile north of the town of Jackson. Shown as "Gate" on Trask's map, 1853. "The Gate" was an election precinct in Calaveras County as early as 1850. The name is derived from a fissure in a reef of rock which crosses the creek here. It is shown as Jackson Gate on modern maps.

Jackson Gulch [Siskiyou]. Listed in the *Annual Mining Review*, 1876 (p. 21) as having a water-driven 8-stamp mill that was erected in 1870.

Jacksons Diggings [Plumas]. Near the Middle Fork of Feather River; southeast of Mohawk, near Wash. The gold-bearing gravel in shallow gulches of Wash and other creeks was first mined about 1868 and was still being washed in 1879 when visited by Pettee (Whitney, *Auriferous Gravels*, p. 479).

Jacksons Ferry [Tuolumne]. Over the Tuolumne River on the road from Empire City to Horseshoe Bend on the Merced River. Recorded on Trask's map, 1853. The ferry is mentioned by Benjamin H. Deane in his journal of May 22, 1850.

Jacksonville [Del Norte]. A gold camp in

Jackson, Amador Co.

1851 or 1852, mentioned in the *Alta*, March 29, 1854, as a rich and extensive district, which only lacked water.

Jacksonville [Tuolumne]. On the Tuolumne River, near the junction with Woods Creek. The place is shown on Gibbes' 1852 map and on other early maps. It was named for Colonel Aldan Apollo Moore Jackson, for whom the town Jackson in Amador County was also named. He is reported to have discovered gold here in 1849 (Coy, p. 56). Peter Dean (p. 2) mined here in the summer of 1849. According to the journal of William H. Townsend, July 8, 1849, there were at that time about forty people engaged in mining and store keeping here. The U. S. Bureau of the Census lists the names of 252 inhabitants in April, 1851. The post office was established October 7, 1851. The *Mining Bureau Report* of 1927 (XXIV, p. 42) reported that the gold output of the Jacksonville district (with Don Pedro and Stevens bars) had reached nine million dollars. Historic Landmark 419. According to *California Historical Landmarks* (p. 71), Julian Smart planted the first garden and orchard in the county at Jacksonville, and Colonel Jackson opened the first trading post in 1849.

Jacks Point [Sierra]. In the Slate Creek Basin, south of St. Louis. It is shown with placer mines on Raymond's map (vol. V, preceding p. 89).

James Bar [Amador, Calaveras]. On the lower Mokelumne River, northwest of Double Springs; below Middle Bar. It was recorded on the maps of Jackson, 1849, and Butler, 1851, as Lower Bar; and on Trask's map, 1853, and Goddard's, 1857, it appears as James Bar. Bayard Taylor describes Lower Bar of 1849 in chapters 8, 9, and 22 of *El Dorado*, and made a fine drawing of it. He tells the story of a miner who in disgust gave up a claim, apparently near Lower Bar, and a little German "jumped into his tracks" and cleared 800 dollars worth after one day of hard work. The bar was later named James Bar for Colonel George F. James, for whom Jamestown in Tuolumne County was likewise named. The deposits had been prospected in the fall of 1848, but were not worked successfully until the next year, when Mr. James began mining with a group of peons, who were driven off by white miners until a compromise was made. Bayard Taylor often mentions the Colonel, who once showed him a nugget of pure gold weighing sixty-two ounces. According to the recollections of Ayers (p. 78), Colonel James had taken up a bar below Middle Bar in the spring of 1850 and named it for himself. The site is inundated by Pardee Reservoir.

James Bar [Yuba]. On the north side of the main Yuba River, about five miles below the mouth of the South Fork. Shown on Trask's map, 1853.

James Point [Placer]. On the North Fork of American River, below Lacys Bar. It is mentioned in the County History, 1924 (p. 178), and in an article in *Placer Nuggets*, February, 1964 (p. 6).

Jamestown [Plumas]. *See* Poorman Creek.

Jamestown [Tuolumne]. The camp on Woods Creek, about four miles southwest

Jamestown, Tuolumne Co.

of Sonora, was one of the earliest important towns along the side of Table Mountain. It appears on all maps after Derby's of 1849. It was named for Colonel George F. James, a San Francisco lawyer, who served as alcalde and operated a store and hotel until his departure in May or June, 1849, following bankruptcy brought on by mining speculation (Stoddart, pp. 61, 65). Stoddart states that for a short time afterwards the camp was known as American Camp. However, late in 1850 it was apparently again called Jamestown (see George Town), and with the establishment of the post office on August 16, 1853, the old name was made official. Gunn mined here August 17, 1849, but found the diggings almost exhausted. Pringle Shaw (p. 117) found the town "retrogaded," in 1854. But with the development of the riches in Tunnel Mountain the place became important again. The New York Tunnel was probably the most profitable drift mine tunnel in the district. A three-pound lump, netting about one pound of pure gold, was found at Jamestown in June, 1854 (Hittell Clippings, p. 21). More details about the early heydays of the town can be found in Heckendorn (pp. 54 f.), Browne (p. 38), Sawtelle (pp. 11 f.), and in Stoddart's account. When Prentice Mulford taught school here in 1862, mining was still going strong. Three of his delightful stories deal with "Jimtown" (chapters eighteen to twenty). In 1881 the district was still the richest of the county. A Jamestown and Comet mine is listed as late as 1928. (Mining Bureau, II, part 1, pp. 184, 185; XXIV, p. 45.) Historic Landmark 431. The Jamestown district is described in Bulletin, 193 (p. 77 f.), where it is stated that there was considerable mining activity in the region again in the 1930s, with some prospecting in recent years. Among the mines listed the most productive were the App-Heslep with 6.5 million dollars (see App Mine), the Dutch Sweeney with 3 million (see Dutch-App Mine), the Harvard with 2 to 3 million, the Jumper with 5 million, the Rawhide with 6 million, and the Santa Ysabel with 1.5 million. The total production of the district is estimated at thirty million dollars.

Jamison City [Plumas]. North of Johnsville, on Jamison Creek, tributary to the Middle Fork of Feather River. Shown on Goddard's map, 1857. A 12-stamp mill operated as early as 1851 (Annual Mining Review, 1876), and in 1858 there were three mills with twenty-four stamps (State Register, 1859). The Jamison Mine operated until the 1930s, and its total production was more than 1.5 million dollars (Bull., 193, p. 83). Shown on the USGS Downieville 1907 quadrangle. Jamison City is part of the Plumas-Eureka State Park and is included in Historic Landmark 196. See Eureka [Plumas]. The name is also spelled Jamieson.

Janesville [Shasta]. On the North Fork of Cottonwood Creek. It is stated in the Mining Press, June 15, 1861, that hydraulic mining had started. The same newspaper reported on April 25, 1862, that some hill claims in the area yielded as high as thirty dollars a day to the hand. The name is sometimes spelled Jaynesville. According to the Sacramento Union October 24, 1859, the former name was Gas Point. See Gas Point.

Japses Bar [Placer]. On the Middle Fork of American River, below the junction with the Middle Fork of the Middle Fork. Shown on Doolittle's map, 1868, and on Bowman's, 1873.

Jawbone Canyon [Kern]. Sixteen miles north of Mojave. There was some gold mining in the hills as late as 1939. It is listed in California Place Names.

Jayhawk [El Dorado]. On a tributary to Weber Creek, ten miles west of Placerville. Shown on Doolittle's map, 1868. It was settled by Missourians and named for an early prospector, J. Hawk (Georgetown News, January 10, 1856; Co. Hist., 1883, p. 203). The post office name, 1860–1863, was spelled Jay Hawk, and it is so listed by Hutchings as a town in 1855.

Jefferson: Bar, City, Creek, Hill [Nevada]. The creek is a tributary to the South Fork of Yuba River, one mile below Washington. The bar was discovered in 1849 by a group of Oregonians known as Greenwood & Co., for whom it was first called Greenwoods Camp (Brown, Directory, pp. 9, 133). The camp with "one or two tents" is mentioned by Schaeffer (p. 93) on June 19, 1850, on his return from the Gold Lake hunt. Steele (pp. 143 f.) found the place entirely deserted in December, 1850. He and his companion took out more than 100 dollars worth in two days with a discarded rocker. The Alta, April 29, 1854, reprints an item from the Nevada Journal which reported that the average earnings on the hill were ten to twelve dollars a day to the hand, but one miner working alone took out forty-seven ounces in a week. Bean (p. 386) lists Jefferson Creek as a camp or settlement in 1867. The stream Jefferson Creek is shown on the USGS Colfax 1938 quadrangle.

Jeffersonville [Tuolumne]. About one mile southeast of Tuttletown. Shown on Dart's map, 1879. The *San Joaquin Republican*, August 9, 1856, reports that Stranahan took out a lump of gold four feet nine inches long and twelve inches in circumference from the New York Tunnel, and the gravel from which it was taken pays twenty-four ounces per day to the hand.

Jelly [Tehama]. On the Sacramento River, near the Shasta County line. It is one of the few places in Tehama County where gold mining was attempted. Chinese miners reportedly washed gold here by ground sluicing. In more recent years attempts were made to operate with dredges. The place was named for Andrew Jelly, who had a ferry here at one time (*Bull.*, 193, p. 138).

Jenkins Bar. An unidentified place. Guinn (p. 43) states that an ambitious tailor by the name of Jenkins stole a Digger Indian girl and was stabbed to death by her father.

Jenks Ranch [Calaveras]. East of San Andreas. According to the San Francisco *Bulletin*, January 18, 1858, there were several companies at work at that time (Bancroft Notes).

Jenny Bar [Calaveras]. On the lower Calaveras River. According to Coy (p. 46), the river cut through rich auriferous deposits at this place. It is probably the same as Jenny Lind.

Jenny Lind. When the great Barnum brought the "Swedish nightingale" to the United States in 1850 and the singer was received with great enthusiasm in the East, her name became a popular place name in the mining towns. The legend that she sang in California has persisted to the present day.

Jenny Lind [Calaveras]. On the Calaveras River, near Highway 8. The camp was the center of a mining district, and it had a post office as early as 1857. For various explanations of the naming, *see California Place Names*. Around 1900 it was still a center of hydraulic mining, although the *Register*, 1899, lists only one stamp mill. More recently there was dredging in the river (*Bull.*, 57, p. 14). Historic Landmark 266. Shown on the USGS Jackson 1938 quadrangle.

Jenny Lind Diggings [Nevada]. Near Lola Montez Diggings, in the vicinity of Grass Valley. The diggings, which had apparently been worked for some time, were deserted in 1870 (Whitney, *Auriferous Gravels*, p. 183).

Jenny Lind Flat [El Dorado]. Between the North and South forks of American River. It is now covered by Folsom Lake. There was gold mining here as early as 1852, according to the County History, 1883 (p. 202). The yield was reported to have been rich, "as high as $90 to the bucket," according to Hutchings in his diary, April 24, 1854. It is mentioned in the El Dorado County Records, May 11, 1876 (Mining Book A, p. 249), in connection with a claim near Massachusetts Flat. The name was misspelled Gene Lind Flat.

Jenny Lind: Flat, Tunnel [Placer]. Near Forest Hill, on the Blue Lead. It was "supposed to be richest pay to the hand ever realized in the state," 6 to 10 thousand dollars per day (but not to the hand). The total yield had reached a million dollars in the 1860s. It is mentioned in *Transactions*, 1858 (p. 189) and 1860 (p. 85). A Jenny Lind claim at or near the site was reported in 1936 as having been opened in 1915 and active intermittently since that time (*Mining Bureau*, XXXII, p. 59). *See* New Jersey.

Jenny Lind Mine [Mariposa]. *See* Hornitos.

Jerseydale [Mariposa]. Five miles south and high above Hites Cove. It had a post office from 1889 to 1930 and around 1900 three stamp mills (*Register*, 1903). The Jerseydale-Sweetwater District is listed in *Mining Bureau*, XVII (p. 97) and in *Bulletin*, 193 (p. 80). The streams in the region were mined in the Gold Rush era, and lode gold deposits were discovered not long afterwards. The greatest activity was from the 1870s to the early 1900s, with some mining activity again in the 1930s and since then occasional prospecting. *See* Feliciana Creek and Sweetwater.

Jersey Flat [Sierra]. One mile east of Downieville. Shown on the County Map, 1874. It was discovered in 1849 and first called Murraysville. In 1850 the Jersey Company acquired the place. It was repeatedly mentioned in the newspapers but was only of short duration. Downie (pp. 45 f.) camped here and tells the story of his party finding gold flakes in the water in which a salmon had been boiled. According to the San Francisco *Call*, May 18, 1879, the place "yielded at least 2 millions" (Bancroft Scraps, V, p. 1806).

Jersey Slide [Yuba]. Between the North and Middle forks of Yuba River. It is mentioned in the County History, 1879 (p. 100).

Jerusalem Bar [Trinity]. Near Jerusalem Creek, nine miles west of Ono. It is listed in *Mining Bureau*, XIII (p. 450).

Jesus Maria [Calaveras]. On the creek of the same name, a tributary to the North Fork of Calaveras River. It is mentioned in a letter of July 17, 1853, by W. H. Moore and is also mentioned as a mining place by Helper (p. 151). It was already a sizeable camp in 1852 and is shown on Trask's map, 1853, and other early maps. The name is derived from a Mexican who raised vegetables here for miners in the early 1850s. It had a large mixed population of Chinese, Mexicans, Chileans, French, and Italians. Historic Landmark 284. Shown on the USGS Jackson 1938 quadrangle.

Jillsonville [Shasta]. At the upper end of Clines Gulch, six miles northeast of French Gulch. Gold was discovered here between 1860 and 1870. Later the productive Gladstone Mine was developed at the site. In the summer of 1900 I. O. Gillson purchased the mine and modernized the mill, and within a decade 100 tons of ore were treated daily. In 1912 a "neat town" named Jillsonville was built. It was a company town and consisted of around twenty-three cottages. It has now all but disappeared. The total production of the Gladstone Mine has been variously estimated to have been between three and five million dollars. (Beatrice Nielson, *in Covered Wagon*, 1965, pp. 1 ff.)

Jim Crow Diggings [Sierra]. *See* Jim Crow Ravine and Downieville.

Jim Crow Ravine [Sierra]. Three miles east of Downieville. Shown on the County Map, 1874. Jim Crow, a Kanaka, mined here in 1849, and his name is repeatedly mentioned by Downie (pp. 35, 52, 90). The camp at the end of the Ravine was called Crow City. Downieville was at one time called Jim Crow Diggings. A Jim Crow Mine is listed in the Mining Bureau reports until 1942. Jim Crow Ravine is shown on the USGS Downieville 1907 quadrangle.

Jimmy Brown Bar [Nevada]. On the South Fork of Yuba River, above the mouth of Scotchman Creek, near Washington. It is listed in the Giffen file, in the Nevada County Records and in the County History, 1880 (p. 205).

Jims Diggings [El Dorado]. On Weber Creek, about five miles east of Weberville. Shown on Doolittle's map, 1868.

Jimtown [Tuolumne]. The popular name for Jamestown.

Joburg [Kern]. The nickname for Johannesburg.

Joe Lanes Bar [Siskiyou]. Near the Shasta River and Yreka Creek. Named in the fall or winter of 1851 for "General" Joe Lane who prospected here (Co. Hist., 1881). Joseph Lane was governor of the Oregon Territory.

Joes Gulch [Amador]. South of Jackson, north of Mokelumne River. It was apparently on a rich ledge and is mentioned by Raymond, VI (p. 86).

Joeville [Trinity]. Opposite Eastmans. The town was "improving slowly but surely," according to an item in Trinity *Journal*, March 14, 1868.

Joe Wallace Gulch [Calaveras]. A tributary to Alabama or Spring Gulch, near Watkins Bar. Doble (pp. 64 ff.) and companions mined here in March, 1852, with little success.

Johannesburg [Kern]. It was the best known town of the 1897 rush for Kern River gold. It was founded by Chauncey M. Depew and was named after the famous mining town in South Africa. The gold producing mines near Joburg, as it is popularly known, are listed and mapped in the *Register* of San Bernardino County, 1902, and in the *County Report*, 1962. There were three stamp mills in 1904 (*Register*, 1904). A description of the town may be found in *Bulletin*, 95 (p. 21).

John Bull Diggings [Calaveras]. On an ancient river bed near Golden Gate Hill and Campo Seco. The Bancroft Notes summarize an article on this river channel which appeared in the San Francisco *Bulletin*, January 18, 1858. John Bull Peak is shown on the USGS Jackson 1938 quadrangle.

Johnson Bar [Butte]. On the east side of Butte Creek, ten miles from Chico. It is listed in the Giffen file.

Johnson Flat [Mariposa]. Apparently near Hornitos, listed in Bancroft, VI (p. 378). One J. Johnson built a 2-stamp mill here in 1850. The reference is presumably to John F. "Quartz" Johnson, who discovered the Great Johnson Lode running from Horseshoe Bend on the Merced River south to Mount Ophir (*Sam Ward in the Gold Rush*, p. 37).

Johnsons Bar [El Dorado]. On the South Fork of American River, above Sailors (Russells) Bar (El Dorado County Records, Mining Location, I, pp. 21, 28). It may be the place where C. Johnson had a claim near Dutch Bar (*ibid.*, p. 66).

Johnsons Bar [Siskiyou]. On Scott River, near the junction with Klamath River south of Virginia Bar. Shown on Goddard's map, 1857. The *Alta*, March 21, 1852, reports the story of a miners' court that punished a thief with thirty-nine lashes and banishment (Bancroft Scraps, LI:1, p. 251).

Johnsons Canyon [El Dorado]. A tributary to the South Fork of American River, about five miles east of Placerville. Shown on Bowman's map, 1873. A. J. Graham mined here in 1855 and reported fair success in a letter of June 10, 1855 (*in* Asa H. Thompson letters). John C. Johnson, who opened the Johnson cutoff to the emigrant road in the fall of 1849 or spring of 1850, had a ranch in Johnsons South Canyon and a sawmill in Johnsons North Canyon (El Dorado County Records, Deeds Book B, p. 385; Leases Book A, p. 113). Johnsons Canyon is shown on the USGS Placerville 1931 quadrangle.

Johnsons Diggings [Nevada]. On the rich old river bed between French Corral and North San Juan. According to *Nevada County Historical Society Bulletin* April, 1953, it was named for David Johnson, who first mined here in 1851, and in 1853 the name was changed to Birchville. *See* Birchville.

Johnsons Humbug [Amador]. Near Volcano. Doble worked here with good success in 1853 (February 14, 1853).

Johnsonville [Mariposa]. *See* Bear Valley.

Johnston Bar [Placer]. On the North Fork of American River, near Negro Bar. A notice of a claim betwen the two bars is recorded September 18, 1854, in Placer County Records, I (p. 249).

Johnstown. *See* Johntown [El Dorado] and Johnsville [Plumas].

Johnsville [Plumas]. On Jamison Creek, tributary to the Middle Fork of Feather River, west of Mohawk Valley. In 1876 the Sierra Buttes Company, a London firm, owner of the Plumas-Eureka Mine, built a company town on Jamison Creek a half mile east of the mine and named it Johnstown, for the superintendent of the mine; later the name was changed to Johnsville. According to the *Register* of 1900, there were three stamp mills in operation at that time. An extensive bibliography and description of the district is given in *Mining Bureau*, XVI, Plumas County section (pp. 21 ff.). *See also* the description given by W. Turrentine Jackson in his study of the

Plumas-Eureka area made for the (California) State Division of Beaches and Parks and *Bulletin*, 193 (p. 82). There was intermittent mining in the district until about 1943. Apparently no record of the gold production exists; some estimates run as high as 20 million dollars. The town under the old name Johnstown, together with Jamison City, and Eureka Mine and Mills is Historic Landmark 196. *See* Eureka [Plumas]; Jamison City.

Johnsville [Sierra]. On the North Fork of Yuba River, southwest of Gold Lake. The *Register*, 1903, mentioned a 20-stamp mill driven by electricity. The St. John Ranch is shown on the USGS Downieville 1907 quadrangle.

Johntown [El Dorado]. North of Coloma, on Johntown Creek. Shown on Goddard's map, 1857. It was apparently discovered in 1848 by prospectors from Coloma, one of whose leaders was called John. D. P. Barstow stated in his manuscript that a sawmill was built in the spring of 1849. The *Alta*, May 22, 1854, reprints a report from the *Empire Argus* that rich hill diggings had been discovered between Johntown and Greenwood. Friends of Stephen Wing lived and mined in "Lower Johntown (Garden Valley)" in October, 1854, and Wing himself mined here with little success during the winter of 1854–55 (Journal, II, pp. 15 ff.). According to W. T. Russell, "Chispas," (pp. 58 ff.), the post office was in Garden Valley, .but the voting precinct was Johnstown. The Johnstown near American Flat along the Pilot and Rock Creek Canal mentioned in an unidentified Hittell Clipping (p. 73) dated April 26, 1856, is obviously a misspelling of Johntown. Johntown Creek is shown on the USGS Placerville 1931 quadrangle. *See* Garden Valley.

John Yorks [Tuolumne]. *See* Volpone.

Jolon Field [Monterey]. A part of the Los Burros Mining District.

Jones Bar [Placer]. On the North Fork of American River, above the confluence with Middle Fork. It is mentioned in the County History, 1882 (p. 402), and in a notice of intention to dam the river here datelined Jones Bar, December 14, 1852 in Placer County Records, I (p. 159).

Jones: Bar, Crossing [Nevada]. On the South Fork of Yuba River, about five miles northwest of Nevada City. Shown on Doolittle's map, 1868. It is listed in Bean's *Directory*, 1867, the County History, 1880 (p. 53), and in Hittell's roster. In an extract from the Grass Valley *Union*, November

26, 1867 (Hayes Scrapbooks: Mining, IV, sec. 16) reference is made to a recently made strike of a bed of cement "exceedingly rich in gold." Jones Bar is shown on the USGS Smartsville 1943 quadrangle.

Jones Camp [El Dorado]. Near Coloma. It was apparently a sizeable camp. Chester S. Lyman and a friend went there for religious services, July 2, 1848.

Jones Flat [Calaveras]. North of O'Neils Creek, four miles east of San Andreas. It is mentioned in the San Francisco *Bulletin*. January 18, 1858 (Bancroft Notes).

Jones Flat [Mariposa]. Five and a half miles northwest of Hornitos. The gravels were worked by hand methods in the "early days," and later by dragline dredges. (*Mining Bureau*, LIII, p. 32.) It is shown on the USGS Sonora 1939 quadrangle south of Exchequer Dam.

Jones: Hill, Canyon [El Dorado]. Jones Canyon is a tributary to the Middle Fork of American River, just above Canyon Creek; northwest of Georgetown. Shown on Bowman's map, 1873. It was named for its locator, James E. Jones, of Missouri (Co. Hist., 1883, p. 191). Trask in his Report (doc. 14, p. 71, published in 1855) mentions a placer mine at Jones Hill. Bowman's map, 1873, shows Jones Hill as a settlement, Jones Ravine, and Jones Hill Ditch. In 1875 there was gravel, seam, and hydraulic mining in the region, and the total output is estimated at from a half million to a million dollars (Raymond, IV, p. 106; VII, p. 95). Jones Hill hydraulic mine was active in 1892, again in 1907, and is still listed in *Mining Bureau*, LII (pp. 431, 553).

Jordan: Creek, Hill [Butte]. On the West Branch of the North Fork of Feather River, north of Cherokee. In 1865 there was a steam-driven 12-stamp mill here (*Annual Mining Review*, 1876, p. 23). Several promising quartz veins were opened on Jordan Hill in 1892 (*Mining Bureau*, XI, p. 157).

Jordan District [Mono]. About ten miles southwest of Bodie. The district was established in 1879, according to *Mining Bureau*, VIII (p. 363). The main activity was in the 1890s, when there was a town named Jordan (sometimes misspelled Jordon), with a large mill and a post office (F. S. Wedertz). The post office is listed as having been active 1891–1893 and 1896–1903.

Josephine [El Dorado]. North of Volcanoville. It served as a camp and post office (1895–1917) for the Josephine lode mine. The mine was active intermittently from the 1890s to 1935. A description is given in *Mining Bureau*, VIII, (pp. 165 f.) and LII (p. 511).

Jouberts Diggings [Sierra]. At the top of Depot Hill, five miles north of Camptonville, on the Sierra-Butte county line. Gold was discovered in 1852 by J. Joubert. The deposits were on blue gravel one hundred feet deep and three hundred feet wide and were hydraulicked for many years. Total production is not known, but it is estimated that at least one million dollars worth of gold was hydraulicked before 1927 (*Mining Bureau*, XII, 264, XVI, Sierra, 69, XXXVIII, 24). *See* Depot Hill.

Julian: District, town [San Diego]. About fifty miles northeast of the city of San Diego. Gold was first discovered on a creek near present-day Julian in the fall of 1869 by A. E. (Fred) Coleman, a negro, for whom the creek and a mining camp were named. *See* Coleman City. About February, 1870, Mike Julian and Drury Bailey, veterans of the Confederate Army, discovered quartz nearby, and soon numerous claims were located. In the George Washington claim, or mine, a lump of quartz weighing about ten pounds and yielding around 100 dollars was found, and according to the San Diego *Union*, March 10, 1870, a minor rush ensued. Fifty-four claims were reportedly recorded by the end of August (*Mining Bureau*, XXX, p. 350). A town was laid out and named Julian. On August 8, 1870, a post office was established. Soon several rival camps sprang up nearby — Branson City, Eastwood, Banner City. Among the early mines, besides the George Washington, were the Van Wert, Owens, Warlock, Eagle, and High Peak. Many others were developed in the region, including the Banner, Ready Relief, Golden Chariot, and Helvetia. The boom ended in 1876, and the mines in the district were dormant until the late 1880s, when the phenomenal success of the Stonewall Mine about three miles south of Julian District, brought about a revival in the Julian area. Several old mines were reopened, and in 1888 the Gold King and Gold Queen mines were discovered and mined until about 1900. There was again brief activity in the late 1920s and the 1930s. The total production of the Julian District (including the Banner District) is estimated at about 5 million dollars (*Bull.*, 193, p. 172). The town is Historic Landmark 412. Lists and descriptions of the mines are given in Raymond, V (pp. 23 ff.); *Mining Bureau*. XXX (pp. 348 ff.); *County Report*, III (pp.

Julian, San Diego Co.

116 ff., 136 ff.). A collection of contemporary newspaper clippings containing accounts of the Julian District, 1870–1872 is in Hayes Scrapbooks Mining (VIII, sec. San Diego). In these accounts the district is sometimes called Cuyamaca District. A detailed modern account is given in Ellsberg, *Mines of Julian. See* Banner City; Stonewall Mine.

Jumper-Golden Rule-New Era Group [Tuolumne]. At Stent, south of Jamestown. The group constitutes a consolidation of three rich old mines, which produced about five million dollars (U.S. *Bull.*, 424, pp. 41 ff; Logan, pp. 167 f.).

Jumper Mine [Tuolumne]. *See* Jamestown.

Junction Bar [Placer]. On the North Fork of American River, three miles from Auburn. A notice of intention by three Chinese to flume and mine here is recorded August 14, 1852 in Placer County Records, I (p. 103).

Junction Bar [Placer, El Dorado]. At the junction of the Middle Fork of American River with the North and South forks of the Middle Fork. Recorded on Trask's map (1853) as Jonction Bar, and as Junction Bar on Doolittle's map (1868) and Bowman's (1873). It is mentioned in the El Dorado County History, 1883 (p. 84), and in the Placer County History, 1882 (p. 402).

Junction Bar [Plumas]. At the junction of the East Branch and the North Fork of Feather River. Shown on Goddard's map, 1857. Dame Shirley, II (pp. 49 f.) gives a nice description and calls it "the most beautiful of all the Bars." It is also described in *Hutchings' Magazine*, II (p. 449, April, 1858).

Junction Bar [Siskiyou]. At the junction of Klamath and Scotts River. Shown on Goddard's map, 1857. It is mentioned in the County History, 1881 (p. 217). A mine operated by Chinese was still active in 1896 (*Mining Bureau*, XIII, p. 409).

Junction Bluff [Nevada]. *See* Sebastopol.

Junction City [Trinity]. On Highway 299, west of Weaverville, at the mouth of Canyon Creek. It became an important hydraulic mining center in the 1850s. The La Grange Mine, east of the town, is credited with having been the largest hydraulic mine in the world (*Mines and Minerals*, p. 376) in its period. *See* Weaverville. W. A. Knapp mentions the place in his recollections of 1851. It is the same as Milltown, which Cox (pp. 57 ff.) describes as "a town almost a city" in 1858. When the post office was transferred from Messerville, August 19, 1861, the new name was apparently chosen because of the town's situation at the juntion of roads to Canyon City, the lower Trinity, and Weaverville.

Junction House [El Dorado]. On the emigrant road, east of Placerville. Goddard's map, 1857, shows it at the crossing of the roads to Carson and Slippery Ford; Bowman's map, 1873, shows it at the cross roads from Georgetown and from Placerville to Virginia City.

Junction House [Yuba]. On the road from

Bullards Bar to Camptonville. Shown on the County Map, 1879, and on the USGS Smartsville 1943 quadrangle. Another name was Bogardus Rancho, named for E. Bogardus, the owner. Hutchings stopped here in October, 1855 (Diary, October 26).

Jupiter [Tuolumne]. *See* Philadelphia Diggings.

Kaiser Creek, Kaiser Creek Diggings [Fresno]. The Creek is a tributary to the San Joaquin River. Both Creek and Diggings were named for Fred Kaiser, who emigrated from Germany to San Francisco in 1851 and started to mine along the San Joaquin River in 1852 (C. F. Kaiser, grandson of Fred Kaiser). According to *Mining Bureau*, XIV (p. 446), there was placer mining along the creek on a small scale into the twentieth century. The stream is shown on the USGS Kaiser 1904 quadrangle.

Kanaka. The common designation for a native of the Hawaiian Islands was frequently used for place names in the gold rush because many of these people, including those that Sutter had imported, were in the mines in those days. In some places the name might have been applied in derision, or for Indians.

Kanaka Bar [Butte]. Above Bidwell Bar, on the east side of the Middle Fork of Feather River, near Island Bar Hill. Shown on Trask's map, 1853, and on Goddard's, 1857. It was apparently the same camp mentioned in the County History, 1882 (p. 253), as flourishing in the early days but extinct in 1882. Kanaka Bar is still listed in 1928 (*Mining Bureau*, XXIV, p. 199) when there was some prospecting.

Kanaka Bar [El Dorado]. On the South Fork of American River, between Coloma and Mormon Island. A rich lead was discovered, apparently in 1848, which yielded many thousands of dollars (Haskins, p. 137). It was so named "because it was occupied by several families of Sandwich Islanders and English sailors who had married Kanaka women" (Steele, p. 229). Kanacka (!) Valley is shown on Doolittle's map, 1868, along a tributary to the South Fork near Salmon Falls.

Kanaka Bar [El Dorado]. On the South Fork of American River, about eight miles above Coloma, above Chili Bar. It is mentioned in the El Dorado County Records in 1852 and 1853 (Mining I, p. 171; Mining Book A, pp. 21, 22).

Kanaka Bar [Trinity]. On the north side of Trinity River, at Douglas City, just below the mouth of Weaver Creek. There is no evidence that the place had anything to do with a relative of King Kamehameha of Hawaii. It may have been named for Indians in the service of Reading. In the 1850s it was developed by German settlers (Cox, p. 36). In 1862 a Chinese company is reported to have taken two hundred dollars a week, according to the *Mining Press*, May 8, 1862.

Kanaka Bar [Yuba]. On the North Fork of Yuba River; below Bullards, between English and Winslow bars. De Long collected taxes here, March 25, 1855. It is mentioned in the *Marysville Directory* of 1858 as entirely deserted at the time.

Kanaka; Bar, Creek [Shasta]. Tributary to Clear Creek. According to Steger (p. 41), gold was discovered at Kanaka Bar in the 1850s.

Kanaka: Bar, Creek [Tuolumne]. The Bar is at the junction of Kanaka Creek and Tuolumne River, between Jacksonville and Stevens Bar. Shown on Goddard's map, 1857. The stream is mentioned by Daniel B. Woods (p. 123) as Kanacca Creek. A Kanaka gravel mine, at another location, north of Groveland, on a gulch running into Tuolumne River, was idle in 1914 but is still listed in the Mining Bureau *Report* of 1928.

Kanaka Creek [Sierra]. Near Eureka Diggings (Eureka North). It is one of the three creeks or ravines in the county named for the Kanakas, according to R. Dury and to J. Sinnott (*Downieville*, p. 98). *See* Kanaka: Creek, Flat, City and Kanaka: Flat, Ravine.

Kanaka: Creek, Flat, City [Sierra]. The Creek is a tributary to the Middle Fork of Yuba River, below Forest City. It is shown on Goddard's map, 1857, Crossman's, 1867, Doolittle's, 1868, and the County Map, 1874. Doolittle's map also shows Kanaka Flat on the Creek below Chips Flat, and Kanaka City above Chips Flat. Browne, p. 147, f., gives a description of the quartz mines along the stream. A Kanaka Drift Mine, below Forest City, was in operation at the beginning of the twentieth century (*Mining Bureau*, XVI, Sierra, 44 f.), and placer mines were listed in 1942. *See* Canacer: Bar, Creek. *See also* Kanaka: Flat, Ravine.

Kanaka Diggings [El Dorado]. About two and a half miles southwest of Garden Valley, near the junction of Irish and Slate creeks. It was also known as Kanaka Town, but is shown as Kanaka Diggings on Derby's Sacramento map, 1849. According to Warren T. Russell (p. 133), it had a church and stores and a population of probably several hundred. In the 1880s three or four Kanakas were still living there and a few Chilenos.

Kanaka: Flat, Ravine [Sierra]. On the South Fork of the North Fork of Yuba River. Kanaka Flat was about six miles east of Downieville. It is shown on Crossman's map, 1867; Doolittle's, 1868; and the County Map, 1874. It was named for Downie's Hawaiians, two of whom were princes, according to an often repeated story. Downie was part owner of a store here in the fall of 1850, and he gives an account of a prospecting trip with four Kanakas in the fall of the same year (Downie, pp. 115 ff.). Crossman's map also shows a Kanaka Mine just north of Kanaka Flat. It was perhaps in Kanaka Ravine, where a 20-stamp water-driven mill was erected in 1865 (*Annual Mining Review*, 1876, p. 22). Browne (p. 148) stated that it was standing idle in 1868. In 1892 it was reported that the "Old Kanaka Mine," halfway between Downieville and Sierra City was reopened by two tunnels; the claim was still listed in 1918 (*Mining Bureau*, XI, p. 404; XVI, Sierra, p. 95). Kanaka Flat is now called Bee Ranch. *See* Kanaka: Creek, Flat, City.

Kanaka Hill [Siskiyou]. Four miles below Happy Cap. A hydraulic mine was operated here in the 1930s (*Mining Bureau*, XXXI, p. 290).

Kanaka Town [El Dorado]. *See* Kanaka Diggings.

Kane Flat [Sierra]. At the western end of Sierra City. It was also known as Buttes Flat. The place was the site of a large stamp mill of No. 9, Sierra Buttes Mine and of huge arrastres used for working the tailings of the mine in the 1880s and 1890s (Sinnott, *Downieville*, p. 202).

Kangaroo Bar. An unidentified place, listed in the Giffen file. A Kangaroo Mine in Mariposa County is listed in *Mining Bureau*, XXIV (p. 98).

Kansas Hill [Nevada]. It is mentioned as a mining camp in Hittell's roster.

Karneys Diggings [Amador]. *See* Whiskey Flat.

Kate Hayes Flat [Nevada]. Opposite the upper town of French Corral. It was an important mining ground on the gravel ridge which extends northeasterly to North San Juan. It is mentioned in *Bean's Directory*, 1867 (p. 335); by Raymond in 1870 (III, p. 39); and by Pettee in 1879

(Whitney, *Auriferous Gravels*, p. 386). Several mining localities were named for Kate (Catherine) Hayes, the Irish-born singer, who came to California in the early 1850s.

Kate Hayes Hill [Nevada]. Near Grass Valley. It is mentioned as a profitable placer mining locality in a predominantly quartz area, which turned out "fabulous amounts of free gold" (*Bean's Directory*, p. 189). A Kate Hayes Hill, or Oregon, quartz mine was reported idle in the Mining Bureau *Report* of 1894–1896, but was still listed in 1941 (*Mining Bureau*, XIII, p. 258; XXXVII, p. 455). Named for Kate (Catherine) Hayes, Irish-born soprano, who came to sing in Nevada City in 1852.

Katesville [Sacramento]. One and a half miles from Michigan Bar. Mining started here in 1852, but the place was deserted in 1862 (Co. Hist., 1880, p. 215). Hutchings mentions it in his diary, March 23, 1855.

Kavanaugh Ridge [Mono]. North of Dunderberg and above the East Fork of Green Creek. "Steve" Kavanaugh located claims on the ridge in 1898–1899 (Maule; Wedertz). Later he discovered the Chemung Mine in the Masonic District.

Kaweah River [Tulare]. One of the few places in the county where gold was found was on the Marble Fork of the River. Mining proved unsuccessful (*Bull.*, No. 92, p. 152).

Keane Wonder: Camp, Mine [Inyo]. On the west slope of the Funeral Range. The mine was discovered by Jack Keane and associates in 1903 (*California Place Names*). It reportedly produced one million dollars in gold and silver between 1908 and 1916. (*Mining Bureau*, XV, pp. 79, 81; XXII, p. 470; XXXIV, pp. 402 f.; *Desert Magazine*, May, 1942). Shown on the USGS Furnace Creek 1908 quadrangle.

Kearney [Yuba]. On Bear River, near Johnsons Crossing on Johnsons Rancho, a short distance above present-day Wheatland. The proprietors of Johnsons Rancho believed that Bear River could be made navigable for river boats and envisaged Kearney as one of the heads of navigation and a convenient depot for Yuba River diggings, but it never developed. It was an unsuccessful contender for the county seat in 1850. (Ramey.)

Kearsarge: City, District [Inyo]. On the eastern slope of the Sierra Nevada, about ten miles west of Independence. The district was organized September 19, 1864. It was named when the news was received that the Union warship *Kearsarge* had destroyed the raider *Alabama*, for whom the mines in the Alabama Hills had been named. According to the description given by W. A. Goodyear in *Mining Bureau*, VIII (p. 232 f.), some of the ore was very rich, both in gold and silver, one lot of ten tons having reportedly yielded 900 dollars per ton. There was a thriving camp for a brief period, and along the creek there were three quartz mills, one with ten stamps, one with five, and another with four. In 1888 when Goodyear visited the district, little was left of the mills, the town had disappeared entirely, and the mines in the district were abandoned except one, which was operated by a single man. The principal source of gold was from the Rex Montis Mine situated at an elevation of 12,000 feet. It operated from 1875 to 1883; a renewal was attempted in 1935, and in 1966 a project was underway to reach the vein at a lower level. Attempts to reopen other mines have met with no success. A detailed account of the district is given in De Decker (pp. 53 ff.).

Keeler [Inyo]. On Owens Lake bed. Named for Julius M. Keeler, mining superintendent. It was a trading center for the free milling gold mines east of Owens Lake. A post office was established in 1883.

Keelers: Flat, Ferry [Stanislaus]. Near Knights Ferry. The Ferry is recorded on Trask's map, 1853. According to the Sacramento *Transcript*, February 14, 1851, miners were making three or more ounces per day on the bar below the Ferry (Bancroft Notes). Heckendorn (p. 102) mentions the place in 1856.

Kehoe Canyon [Placer]. Below Little Horseshoe Bar, on the North Fork of American River. A suspended flume across the narrow gorge carried water for mining. It is mentioned in the Placer County History, 1924 (p. 173).

Keith District [Mono]. About eleven miles northwest of Mono Lake. The district was originally a part of the old Mono placer diggings, but in 1878 the miners discovered a quartz ledge and set aside this portion as a quartz mining district. The ore was treated in an arrastre, but the production was small. (*Mining Bureau*, VIII, p. 363.)

Kelloggs Diggings [Trinity]. On the Hayfork of Trinity River. There was placer mining as early as 1851, but the earnings were only five to seven dollars a day, according to Cox (p. 111).

Kelly Bar [Sierra]. An unidentified bar at the junction of Canyon Creek with the North Fork of Yuba River.

Kellys Bar [Placer]. On the North Fork of American River, near the junction with the Middle Fork, and above Calf Bar. Shown on Butler's and Gibbes' maps, 1851, and on most later maps. Notice of intention to drain the river through the Bar was recorded October 23, 1851, in Placer County Records, I (p. 37). Borthwick (p. 182) mentions the place in the early 1850s, and Weston (pp. 9 ff.) writes of an "awful slaughter of Indians" that took place here in May, 1853. — The name is sometimes spelled Kelleys.

Kellys Diggings [El Dorado]. About four miles east of Volcanoville, on a tributary to the South Fork of the Middle Fork of American River. Shown on Bowman's map, 1873. Raymond, in his *Report* for the year 1871 (IV, pp. 102 f.) describes the diggings as "discovered and superficially worked by a man named Kelly, a number of years ago." According to Kelly, it paid from fifteen to twenty dollars per day to the hand. Raymond states that several large hydraulics would be used upon the introduction of water.

Kelsey [El Dorado]. On Kelsey Canyon, tributary to the South Fork of American River. Shown on Trask's map, 1853, and on Goddard's, 1857. It was named for Benjamin Kelsey, a brother of Andrew of Kelseyville in Lake County. Rich diggings were reported as early as 1848. The place is mentioned as Kelseys Diggings by Wierzbicki in 1849 (p. 41). Barstow and Leeper (p. 103) mined here in the winter of 1849–50. The latter found "fair pickings" in the canyon because it was deserted on account of the Gold Lake hunt. James W. Marshall, the discoverer of gold at Sutters Mill, lived here later in life as a miner and blacksmith. His Blacksmith Shop is Historic Landmark 319. The Grey Eagle quartz mine, of which he was part owner, was just south of the town. *See* Theressa Gay (p. 343 f.). The Big Sandy Mine, also south of the town about three quarters of a mile, was located by Marshall. It had a 10-stamp mill and was active in the 1890s. In the 1930s the mine was worked for pocket gold and some fine specimens of crystallized gold were found. (*Mining Bureau*, LII, pp. 408 f.) In 1855 water reached the camp by a ditch from Pilot or Rock Creek (Hittell Clippings, p. 73). A post office was established March 3, 1856. In 1864 a 15-stamp water-driven mill was in operation, and in 1871 a

30-stamp steam-driven one. In the 1870s the Cincinnati and the Mansfield companies produced between one and two million dollars each. (*Annual Mining Review*, 1876, pp. 23, 41, 55.) At one time a young man picked up on the surface a nugget six inches long (Buffum, p. 107). The Kelsey or Lady Mine operated intermittently until 1941 (*Mining Bureau*, LII, p. 418). More information about the place may be found in the County History, 1883 (p. 191); Browne (p. 91); and *Resources* (p. 21). Kelsey is shown on most modern maps, on the road from Placerville to Georgetown.

Kelseys Bar [Placer]. On the North Fork of American River, next to Clinton Bar. It is mentioned in connection with a claim located November 23, 1883, and recorded in Placer County Records, I (p. 204). Buffum (p. 62) states that in 1848 two men at Kelseys Bar on the Middle Fork of American River washed out in two days fifty pounds of gold "amounting to nearly ten thousand dollars." There might have been some confusion about the location.

Kelseys Ravine [Nevada]. A small stream which flows through Nevada City from the northwest to the southeast. It was probably named for Edward Kelsey, prominent Nevada City financier and builder in the 1850s (Foley). It is also known as Oregon Ravine. The *Mining Press*, October 27, 1860, reports the discovery of a new rich quartz lead.

Kelso Canyon [Kern]. Thirty miles from Keyesville. Fair paying diggings were discovered in the spring of 1861 (*Mining Press*, August 24, 1861). Kelso Creek Placers, near Sageland, are listed as idle in 1933 in *Mining Bureau*, XXIX (p. 311); *County Report*, I (p. 163).

Kelso District [San Bernardino]. On the west slope of the Providence Range, east of the town of Kelso. Claims producing gold and silver include the Globe Mine at the head of Globe Canyon, the Equitibus Group, and the Frisco Group. Descriptions are given in *Mining Bureau*, XXVII (pp. 294 ff.).

Kemptons Crossing [Yuba]. *See* Robinsons Crossing.

Kennebec Bar [Placer]. On the north side of the Middle Fork of American River, four miles above the junction. Shown on Doolittle's map, 1868. The bar is mentioned in the *Placer Herald*, December 1, 1855 (Co. Hist., 1882, p. 190).

Kennebec Bar [Yuba]. On the main Yuba River, fifteen miles from Marysville. Recorded on Trask's map, 1853. It was founded in October, 1849, by the Kennebec Company of New Bedford, Massachusetts, who later founded the town of Eliza on the Feather River (Ramey). It is mentioned in a letter of C. W. Roach [?], dated November 15, 1850. According to the County History, 1879 (p. 84), gold was mined during the winter of 1849–1850, but the following spring the camp was abandoned. The *Marysville Directory*, 1858, however, reports that some good strikes had been made, but only a few miners were working at the bar in 1858.

Kennebec Hill [Nevada]. Southeast of North Columbia, on the Great Gravel Deposit. Shown on Doolittle's map, 1868, and mentioned by Raymond, VI (p. 108).

Kennebec Hill [Tuolumne]. *See* Columbia.

Kennedy Mine [Amador]. *See* Jackson.

Kennett [Shasta]. On the Sacramento River, north of Redding. This was the most important copper mining town in Shasta County and the site of Kennett Smelter, 1905–1919. The town was incorporated in 1911, with a population of 1,700. Both Kennett and Keswick smelters contributed to the gold industry by purchasing quartz for use as silica flux. (R. B. Eaton.)

Keno Bar [Nevada]. On the South Fork of Yuba River, just above Rocky Bar. It was developed in 1866 (Bean, p. 383), but the deposits were soon exhausted. It is listed in Bancroft, VI (p. 358) and is probably the same as Kino Bar.

Kenton Mine [Sierra]. *See* Alleghany.

Kentucky Bar [Placer]. On the North Fork of American River, near Willow Bar. The place is mentioned by Letts (p. 114). who states that in 1849, each of two partners washed 700 dollars each, "which was good wages." It is recorded July 10, 1851, and October 9, 1855, in the Placer County Records, I (pp. 8 and 309).

Kentucky Flat [Nevada]. On the road from Sacramento to Rough and Ready. It was settled by Kentuckians in 1850 and yielded remarkable profits (Brown, *Directory*, p. 13). It was probably the site of the Kentucky House mentioned by Schaeffer (p. 214). Kentucky Flat Creek is shown on the County Map, 1880. Hutchings gives the distance as seven miles from Nevada City (Diary, October 9, 1855). Kentucky Ravine is shown on the USGS Smartsville 1943 quadrangle.

Kentucky: Flat, Hill [El Dorado]. About six miles northeast of Georgetown, on a branch of Otter Creek, a tributary to the Middle Fork of American River. Shown on

Doolittle's map, 1868, and on Bowman's, 1873. It is on the Tertiary "white" channel running through El Dorado and southern Placer counties. There was extensive drift mining in 1874 (Raymond, VII, p. 93), and good drift and hydraulic mining was reported until about 1908 (*Mining Bureau*, XXXIV, p. 251; LII, pp. 431, 564). Shown on the USGS Placerville 1931 quadrangle.

Kentucky Gulch [Yuba]. *See* Deadwood Creek.

Kentucky Hill Diggings [Sierra]. Between Grizzly Creek, tributary to the North Fork of Yuba River near the Grizzly Hill south of Brandy City, and Oregon Creek, tributary to the Middle Yuba. Surface diggings were reported rich, and in 1855 "quite a town, composed of log cabins" had been built by the miners, according to the 1855 *Report* of the California State Surveyor General (p. 202).

Kentucky House [Calaveras]. Two miles south of San Andreas. During the Gold Rush it was an important trading center. It is shown on the *Guidebook* map (no. 4) and on the USGS Jackson 1938 quadrangle. Camp's map shows it with Third Crossing as an alternate name. *See* Third Crossing. A Kentucky House Mine, prospected in the 1890s, is listed in the reports of the Mining Bureau until 1936. It is the site of the Calaveras Cement Company Mill, a highly productive enterprise.

Kentucky Ranch [Yuba]. About two miles southwest of Dobbins Ranch, west of North San Juan, on the Marysville-Camptonville turnpike. Recorded on Doolittle's map, 1868. It is mentioned by De Long January 24 and February 10, 1856. Shown on the USGS Smartsville 1943 quadrangle.

Kenworthy [Riverside]. In Garner Valley, in the San Jacinto Mountains. The camp was established in 1897 and served the gold mines at nearby Hemet until the boom collapsed in 1899. It was named for Eugene Kenworthy, an Englishman who invested in the mines and lost everything when they failed. The place had a post office, hotel, store, stamp mill, sawmill and numerous cabins. The postmaster was Charles W. Lockwood, whose daughter Lela Noble, a resident of Hemet, lived in Kenworthy as a child. (John W. Robinson.)

Kern River Diggings. The name was given to the stream in 1845 in honor of Edward M. Kern, the topographer and artist of Frémont's third expedition. Placer gold may have been found here even before the discovery at Sutter's Mill. The discovery in larger quantities in 1854 led to the famous Kern River rush of 1855. A good account is given in H. G. Comfort's *Where Rolls The Kern*, 1934. The Sacramento *Union* of March 1, 1855, reports that the diggings paid between eight and fifty dollars per day to the man, and all other papers had similar reports. Other contemporary newspaper accounts may be found in Hayes Scrapbooks: Mining (V, sections 125 to 141). The placers extended about twelve miles, from Democrat Hot Springs to Hobo (now Miracle) Hot Springs (*Mining Bureau*, XXX, p. 245). Activities by dredging and pumping were reported in 1933, and in 1949 (*ibid.*, XLV, p. 219) dragline and other equipment was being installed. *See* Rio Bravo.

Kernville [Kern]. On Kern River, now inundated by Lake Isabella. Gold was reportedly discovered on the North Fork of Kern River in 1851 by a party sent out by the explorer Frémont. *See* Greenhorn Gulch. Placer mining in the area was soon to be replaced by quartz mining, when in the early 1860s Lovely Rogers accidentally discovered the Big Blue vein. By 1863 there was a camp called Quartzburg. *See* Quartzburg. Soon afterwards another camp named Williamsburg developed, about one mile down the river. The miners of Quartzburg referred to their neighboring camp as Whiskey Flat, but the residents themselves disliked this name and in 1864 decided to call their camp Kernville. For the story about the naming, *see* Boyd (p. 32) and *California Historical Landmarks* under the entry number 132. The mines north of Kernville (the former Williamsburg) are shown on the County Map, 1875. In 1875 seventy-five stamps were reported in operation in the Kernville area (*Annual Mining Review*, 1876, p. 23). Mining reached its peak in 1879, but the old town Kernville lived on for many years. In the early 1950s the Isabella Reservoir was built and the town disappeared under its waters. Its site is Historic Landmark 132. In 1951 a new town named Kernville was founded north of Lake Isabella. The Kernville Mine, southwest of the "new" Kernville, is included in the Big Blue Group, idle since 1943 (*County Report*, I, pp. 97 f.). *See* Cove District.

Keswick [Shasta]. Five miles northwest of Redding. Operations were begun at the turn of the century, with copper as the chief production, and little gold. It was named for Lord Keswick of London, president of the English-owned British Mountain Copper Company, Ltd. in 1896. It was the site of the Keswick Copper Smelter, 1896–1909. Around 1900 there were three stamp mills in the district (*Register, 1902*).

Keyesville [Kern]. Four miles west of Isabella. The camp was named for Richard Keyes, a pioneer of the Kern River mines even before the rush of the early 1850s. When the post office was established March 11, 1857, the name was misspelled Keysville, and this version is still often used for the ghost town. The place developed rapidly and was the center of the Keyes District for many years. In 1858 there were five water-driven mills with twenty-two stamps, the largest constructed in 1856 and owned by the company of Alexis von Schmidt, the noted engineer of Northern California (*State Register*, 1859; *Annual Mining Review*, 1876, p. 22). There was intermittent mining in the district to 1915 and some prospecting in the 1930s. Keyesville is Historic Landmark 98.

Keystone Mine [Amador]. One of the richest mines of the Mother Lode region. *See* Amador City; Spring Hill Mine.

Keystone Ranch [Yuba]. Southwest of Bullards Bar. It is shown on the County Map of 1879 and is mentioned by De Long, August 14, 1856, and repeatedly. In March, 1852, Henry Huntley (*California, its Gold*, V. 1, pp. 88 ff.) and an English company tried to build a stamp mill here without success. It is mentioned as a stage station between Oregon Hill (Greenville) and Old Fountain House (Meek, p. 151).

Keystone: Ravine, Mine, Mill [Sierra]. Between the North and Middle forks of Yuba River, southwest of Sierra City. The mine is shown on Crossman's map, 1867, and the Mill is shown as a settlement on the County Map, 1874. Major Downie of Downieville, was a member of the Keystone Tunnel Company about 1856. A terrible snowslide in March, 1868, killed five people and almost destroyed the mill (Bancroft Scraps). The fineness of the quartz gold was assayed at 933° (*Mining Bureau*, IV, p. 223). A Keystone Mine is listed in the Mining Bureau reports until 1942. Keystone Ravine and Mine are shown on the USGS Downieville 1907 quadrangle.

Keysville [Kern]. *See* Keyesville.

Killiams Bar [Placer]. On the North Fork of American River. A notice of the intention to flume the river about eight miles above Cold Spring to Killiams Bar is recorded June 15, 1853, in the Placer County Records, I (p. 169).

Killinger Hill [Shasta]. In the Pittsburg Mining District, near Copper City. An unidentified clipping datelined Shasta, April 20, 1864, in Hayes Scrapbooks: Mining, (IV, sec. 4), describes the deposits of copper, silver, and gold, and the tunneling activities on the hill.

Kimshew [Butte]. On Butte Creek, northeast of Stirling City. The name is derived from the Maidu Indian word for 'little water'. On the County Map of 1861 the name is applied for a township on both sides of Butte Creek. There was successful mining in May, 1858 (Hittell Clippings, p. 54). *See* Nimshew, Little Kimshew. For a description of Kimshew District, *see Bulletin*, 193 (p. 85). A number of gravel deposits of moderate size here have been mined by hydraulicking and drifting, and there are a few gold bearing quartz veins. Kimshew Table Mountain at the head of Little Kimshew Creek is described by Lindgren, *Tertiary Gravels* (pp. 95 ff.).

Kincades Flat [Tuolumne]. About three miles east of Jamestown, on the limestone belt. Shown on Dart's map, 1879, as Kincaid Flat. A detailed description is given by Browne (p. 38). Mining was continuous from 1850 to the 1870s. The richest pay was at water level, and in 1867 it was claimed that the Flat had yielded 2 million dollars. By 1899 the total production reached 3 million dollars (*Mines and Minerals*, p. 358). According to the reports of the Mining Bureau, production in later years was mainly crushed gravel. The place is famous as a locality where fossils of the mastodon and other animals were found in the auriferous gravels sixteen feet or more below the surface (Whitney, *Auriferous Gravels*, pp. 247, 257, 263).

Kinders Diggings [Nevada]. On Bear River; one and a half miles east of Lowell Hill. Shown on Hoffmann and Craven's Gravel Map, 1873. It is described by Pettee in Whitney, *Auriferous Gravels* (p. 175).

Kings: Diggings, Hill [Placer]. About six miles southwest of Iowa Hill; between Indian and Shirttail canyons, tributaries to the North Fork of American River. Shown as Kings Hill on Hoffmann and Craven's Gravel Map, 1873. On November 10, 1851, H. King and Company signed an agreement concerning the draining and fluming through Elizabethtown. The agreement is recorded under the name Kings Diggings in Placer County Records, I (p. 64). Kings

Hill is mentioned in a notice filed December 24, 1855, in Placer County Records, I (p. 346), and again in Raymond, VII (p. 108). Parks Hill was apparently an alternate name. According to Whitney, *Auriferous Gravels* (p. 112), the eastern rimrock of the hill reportedly "paid very richly, while the ground farther back in the hill did not pay expenses."

Kingsley [Mariposa]. *See* Kinsley.

King Solomon Mine [Mariposa]. *See* Bear Creek.

Kino Bar [Nevada]. Apparently near Washington City. In the spring of 1867 miners were engaged in sinking for an old bed of the Yuba River with good prospects, according to an extract from the Nevada *Transcript*, April 29, 1867 in Hayes Scrapbooks: Mining (IV, sec. 41). It is probably the same as Keno Bar.

Kinsley [Mariposa]. In the north central part of the county, about twelve miles east of Coulterville. Between 1896 and 1928 there was a post office with the name spelled Kingsley. The district is drained by Bull Creek and the North Fork of Merced River and is sometimes called Bull Creek District and Red Cloud District. Gentry Gulch is sometimes included, but in this dictionary Gentry Gulch is treated separately. The area was first placer mined. Lode mining was carried on from the 1860s to 1900, was reactivated in the 1930s, and in recent years there has been some prospecting. In 1947 the area along Bull Creek, north of the U. S. Forest Service Guard Station was dredged (*Mining Bureau*, LIII, p. 319). *See* Texas Hill, Marble Springs; Gentry Gulch (Hasloe and Bandarita); Greeley Hill (Red Cloud). For further information, consult *Mining Bureau* (XVII, pp. 95 f.; XVIII, pp. 365 f.; XXXI, p. 46); *Bulletin*, 193 (p. 85); and *Register*, 1903.

Kiotaville [Nevada]. *See* Coyoteville.

Kirkham Ranch [Sierra]. On the South Fork of the North Fork of Yuba River. Shallow placer mining here was followed by quartz mining. The place is mentioned by Sinnott, *Downieville* (p. 147).

Kitts [Yuba]. An unidentified place near New York House. It is mentioned by De Long, February 3, 1856.

Klamath [Siskiyou]. On the Klamath River, below Happy Camp. It was apparently a short-lived mining camp with a post office from 1866 to 1872, but it is listed as a "town" in the *Register*, 1898.

Klamath City [Del Norte]. At the mouth of Klamath River. It was founded and surveyed by Hermann Ehrenberg in April,

1850, after he and his party had discovered Gold Bluff and the mouth of the river. Twenty houses were erected, but the first fall storm threw a bar across the mouth of the river, rendering it useless as a harbor (*Overland Monthly*, I, pp. 140 ff.). The place served for some time as headquarters for gold seekers. The *Pacific News*, November 11, 1850, published a highly optimistic description of the town. Some claims were laid, but the output was meagre, and as early as the summer of 1851 George Gibbs (Schoolcraft, III, p. 149) reports that the miners had left.

Klamath River [Siskiyou]. *See* Gottville.

Klingermans Point [Yuba]. On the main Yuba River, between Condemned Bar (at the mouth of Dobbins Creek) and the junction with the South Fork of the Yuba. J. A. Stuart mined here successfully in January, 1851 (diary entries between December 28, 1850 and February 2, 1851). He locates the place two miles above the junction with the South Fork and six miles below Condemned Bar. The County Map, 1887, shows it as Clingmans Point. Wescoatt's map, 1861, however, leaves it unnamed, but places Clingmans Point farther up the river, between Condemned Bar and the junction of the North and Middle Forks, at present-day Rollins Point. The County History, 1879 (p. 94), likewise locates Clingmans Point here, describing it as a sharp bend in the river between Dobbins Creek and the Middle Yuba, where there had been "considerable mining."

Knapps Creek [Nevada]. A tributary to the South Fork of Yuba River, below North Bloomfield. It was the location of the Union Gravel Mining Company in the 1870s (Raymond, VI, p. 108). On modern maps the name appears as Spring Creek (Foley).

Knapps Ranch [Tuolumne]. On San Diego Hill, southeast of Columbia. It was on the Calaveras limestone vein. Because of the volcanic deroded material there were rich auriferous deposits near the surface (Browne, pp. 36 f.). The placers yielded richly for a short time around 1860. The Dutch Bill Claim paid at times one thousand dollars per month, and the Black Claim yielded five hundred ounces in March, 1861, after thirty days of washing. The surface ground of five acres yielded 200 thousand dollars by washing (Browne, p. 37; *Mining Press*, March 23, 1861). Here, as well as on nearby Gold Hill, large lumps and nuggets which yielded up to 8.5 thousand dollars worth of gold each were found (*Guidebook*, p. 54; *Mining Bureau*, II, part 1, p. 148; Knapp, p. 504). In the 1850s a 50-pound slab was also found at Knapps Ranch (*Bull.*, 193, p. 9).

Knapps Trinity Camp [Trinity]. Probably at or near the later Junction City. It is not a recorded name. Knapp (pp. 508 f.) and partners built a cabin and struck rich pay dirt in the fall of 1850. A few days later the Arkansas Dam broke and the Indians stole the equipment. They left in disgust, and it was reported that one hundred thousand dollars was later taken out of the same claim. It is probably the same place at which one company took out 4.2 thousand dollars in two months (*Mining Press*, December 21, 1861).

Knickerbocker Flat [Sierra]. Near Alleghany. A 2,000-foot tunnel was started in 1853 and began to pay richly in 1855 (*Transactions*, 1858, p. 189).

Knickerbocker Flat [Tuolumne]. South of Yankee Hill, on the canal of the Columbia and Stanislaus Water Company (Heckendorn, pp. 25, 74). According to an item in the Columbia *Gazette*, reprinted in the *Alta*, May 30, 1854, one company made six to twelve ounces a day. Similar reports of other companies are found in the *San Joaquin Republican* in the spring and summer of 1855 (Eastman File). The total production of Knickerbocker Flat and Yankee Hill by 1899 was estimated at 3.5 million dollars (*Mines and Minerals*, p. 358).

Knickerbocker Ranch [El Dorado]. Less than a mile north of Hoggs Diggings, southeast of Auburn. Knickerbocker Hotel is shown on Doolittle's map, 1868. According to the *Alta*, March 6, 1854, a lead was struck here from which the discoverers washed out fifty dollars in pieces of fifty cents to eight dollars worth from the first three loads of dirt.

Knights Creek [Tuolumne]. A tributary of Stanislaus River, north of the South Fork. One mine was said to have yielded fifty dollars per ton (*Mining Bureau*, IV, p. 224).

Knights Ferry [Stanislaus]. The crossing of the Stanislaus River was already a favorite stopping place on the road from Stockton to the mines in 1849 (Schaeffer, p. 44). William Knight of Indiana, an emigrant of 1841, started the ferry, apparently in 1848, and a town developed on the Stanislaus side of the river. When Knight died in 1849, John C. and Lewis Dent, brothers-in-law of General Grant, took over the business. According to Bancroft, VI (p. 514), the camp was called Dentville for a time. On Jackson's map, 1850, it is mistakenly spelled Nyes Ferry. It is recorded as Knights Ferry on Butler's map. The post office was established the same year. In 1856 Heckendorn lists some fifty American inhabitants, but the writer of a letter of April 10, 1856, to the Stockton *Republican* observed several companies of Chinese miners at work. In the winter of 1861–1862 rich gold deposits were discovered. This caused considerable excitement and resulted in the rebuilding of the town. (*Mining Press*, February 15, 1862.) For several years the place was the county seat. Historic Landmark 347. A description of Knights Ferry District is given in *Bulletin*, 193 (p. 85). It is stated here that there was dredging in the 1930s and early 1940s.

Knights Ferry, Stanislaus Co.

Knob [Shasta]. Near Highway 36, close to the Trinity line. It was a trading center and the post office (established 1896) for the surrounding quartz mines (*Register*, 1902). Knob Gulch placers are mentioned in 1914 in *Mining Bureau*, XIV (p. 776).

Know Nothing Creek [Butte]. The favorite nickname of the American Party in the 1850s was applied to a tributary to South Fork of Feather River. Shown on the County Map, 1862.

Know Nothing Creek [Siskiyou]. A tributary to the South Fork of Salmon River, where intensive mining, both placer and quartz, was carried on mainly before 1900. The Know Nothing Mine is listed in the Mining Bureau reports from 1887 to 1935. *See* Gilta.

Knoxville [Placer]. Near the mouth of Squaw Creek. It was one of several settlements that developed in the area when gold and silver were discovered in 1861 north of Lake Tahoe (*Bull.*, 193, pp. 124 f.). In August, 1863, there were about 600 miners in the district, and a town had been laid out (Brewer, p. 445).

Kohlbergs Humbug [Calaveras]. A gulch, tributary to the South Fork of Mokelumne River from the south, was named for a German prospector of the Eutaw, or Grunsky Company, who was for some time in charge of Rich Gulch. Doble mentions the camp June 21, 1852, but spells the name Colburg. *See* Alabama Gulch.

Kongsberg [Alpine]. On the Ebbets Pass Road, southwest of its junction with the Monitor Pass Road. The camp was founded around 1860 by Norwegian miners and was named after the mining town in Norway, and within a year the population was about 3,000 (*Bull.*, 193, p. 120). In 1863 a post office was established under the name Konigsberg; in 1865 the name was changed to Silver Mountain and in 1879 was discontinued. Despite the huge investment in the mines, mainly silver with some gold, activity soon declined, and by 1886 the place was abandoned. The total production in the Silver Mountain District is estimated at 200 thousand dollars (Maule, p. 27; *Bull.*, 193, p. 120).

Konigsberg [Alpine]. *See* Kongsberg.

Kramer Hills [San Bernardino]. South of Johannesburg and Randsburg, near the Kern County border. In April, 1926, the discovery of some high grade gold ores resulted in one of the twentieth century gold rushes, but only one mine produced profitably (*Mining Bureau*, XXVII, pp. 280 and 311 f.). The town of Kramer was an important supply center for the desert mines. It had a post office from 1896 to 1918, and it was the southern terminus of the Randsburg Railroad, a branch of the Santa Fe, which served the mines.

Kunkle [Butte]. On the West Branch of the North Fork of Feather River, north of Cherokee. It is shown on the County Map, 1862, as Kunkles. There was some mining until the end of the nineteenth century. Kunkle Reservoir is shown on the USGS Oroville 1944 quadrangle.

L**a Commodedad** [Tuolumne]. Five miles northeast of Pine Log Crossing. According to the Columbia *Gazette*, August 13, 1853, the camp consisted mainly of French and Spanish, with only a few Americans. It was reported that the discoverers had taken out as much as one hundred dollars to the pan, but wages were only average in 1853. (Eastman notes.)

Lacys Bar [Placer]. On the North Fork of American River, above Rattlesnake Bar. Shown on Jackson's map, 1850, Trask's, 1853, and later maps. It was also recorded as Laceys and Lacys Granite Bar. A pessimistic account is given in Letts (p. 114), but a newspaper account of October, 1856, in the County History, 1882 (p. 227), states that all claims were paying well. The U. S. Bureau of the Census of 1850 lists 252 inhabitants in the vicinity of Lacys Bar and nearby Manhattan Bar. Included are fifty-nine Kanakas and ninety-seven "Chinamen."

Ladies Canyon [El Dorado]. Tributary to the South Fork of American River, about two miles south of Kelsey. Shown on Doolittle's map, 1868. There is another Ladies Canyon, tributary to the Middle Fork of the American River, on the north side, just below Grey Eagle Bar; also shown on Doolittle's map. It is mentioned in the El Dorado County Records (Mortgage Book B, p. 194).

Ladies Canyon [Placer]. A tributary to the Middle Fork of American River, east of Forest Hill. Shown on Doolittle's map, 1868, and Bowman's, 1873. It is probably a euphonism for some unprintable name for "a place to which miners have given a number of aliases" (Patterson, p. 72). Hutchings saw a 37-ounce solid gold nugget taken from Ladies Kanyon when he was in nearby Michigan Bluff in 1855 (Diary, May 7, 1855). It is listed in Hittell's roster and is probably the same place which Crockett in 1859 (p. 94) calls Lady's Valley. A Ladies Canyon Mine is listed in the *Mining Bureau* report of 1936. Lady Canyon is shown on the USGS Colfax 1938 quadrangle.

Ladies Canyon [Sierra]. Tributary to the North Fork of Yuba River, between Downieville and Sierra Buttes. According to an extract from the Downieville *Messenger*, 1867, in Hayes Scrapbooks, Mining (IV, sec. 28), Ladies Canyon was regaining some of its old fame as a gold producing region. Shown on the USGS Downieville 1907 quadrangle.

Lady Emma Mine [El Dorado]. One mile east of Kelsey. The gold deposit was found by the divining rod of "Mr. Ai. Peck" and was prospected according to his predictions, with promise of further verification (*Annual Mining Review*, 1876, p. 53). The mine was active in the late 1890s and was again prospected in 1942 and 1947 (*Mining Bureau*, LII, pp. 512 f.).

Lafayette Hill [Nevada]. Two miles south of Grass Valley. A group of Frenchmen discovered gold here in 1851 and named the place for their countryman. In 1867 a mine and a mill were said to have had a monthly profit of 12 thousand dollars (Bean, pp. 212 f.). A Lafayette Mine on Osborne Hill is listed in the Mining Bureau reports until 1941.

La Grange [Stanislaus]. On the Tuolumne River, below Don Pedro Bar. A company of Frenchmen discovered rich placers here in 1849. The place was known as French Bar or Camp until the post office was established December 2, 1854. Shown on Goddard's map, 1857. The camp is described by Pringle Shaw (p. 120) in 1854, and by Heckendorn (pp. 93 ff.) in 1856. In 1859 the placers were exhausted and agriculture prevailed (*Transactions*, 1859, p. 90). After 1900 there was extensive gold dredging in the district, with an estimated production of 13 million dollars (*Bull.*, 193, p. 85). Historic Landmark 414.

La Grange Mine [Trinity]. *See* Weaverville.

Laguna Mountains District [San Diego]. *See* Pine Valley District.

Lake City [Nevada]. About two miles west of North Bloomfield. Shown on Doolittle's map, 1868. The town was laid out in 1858 (Bean, p. 396). It is on the rich gravel deposit where hydraulic mining yielded rich profits (Raymond, VI, p. 108; *Mining Bureau*, XVI, Nevada, p. 45). Shown on the USGS Colfax 1938 quadrangle.

Lake Mining District [Mono]. In the south-west corner of the county, about twenty-five miles south of Mono Lake. There are fifteen small lakes within ten miles of the center of the district, one of which is Mammoth Lake. The district is sometimes called Mammoth District. The principal mine was the Mammoth Mine, at which a 20-stamp mill was erected in 1878, with another twenty added the following year. Two mining camps, Mammoth City and Pine City, quickly developed, but the mill soon closed and the camps were quickly deserted. An account is given in *Mining Bureau*, VIII (pp. 373 ff.). *See* Mammoth City.

Lake Valley Diggings [Placer]. North of Lake Tahoe, near the Truckee River. According to an item in the *Placer Herald*, reprinted in the *Alta*, April 26, 1853, gold was discovered here in 1853 and miners made five to seven dollars a day to the man. The newspaper warned against a rush. No later reports were found.

Lancha Plana [Amador]. On the north side of Mokelumne River, now covered by Camanche Reservoir. Shown on the County Map, 1866. According to Bancroft, VI (p. 372), it was a Mexican camp in 1848, and according to Lascy in his reminiscences, it was first called Sonora Bar. Berriman indicates that it was the site of the miners' meeting mentioned by Kirkpatrick October 14, 1849. In 1850 the camp flourished, and Kaiser and Winter established a ferry made of a raft of casks lashed together. *See* Winters Bar. This created the new name Lancha Plana, 'flat boat'. Audubon mentions the flat boat ferry in his journal, April 24, 1850. In 1856 the place received an impetus from bluff mining, particularly on Chaparral Hill, and the population grew to 1,000 (Bancroft, VI, p. 372). A long but indefinite account of the early days is given in the County History, 1881 (p. 194). The diggings prospered until 1860: "No big strikes but average good pay" (*Mining Press*, January 18, 1861). The river was dredged from 1926 to 1932 (County Report, I, p. 201). It was one of the many places connected with the elusive Murieta, who is reported to have forced the ferryman and his party across the Stanislaus (!) River in January, 1853 (Ridge, p. 126 f.). Recorded on the USGS Jackson 1938 quadrangle. Historic Landmark 30.

Landecker Mine [El Dorado]. *See* Placerville.

Lander Bar [Yuba]. Above the junction of Yuba River and Dry Creek. Shown on Trask's map, 1853, and Wescoatt's, 1861.

According to the County History, 1879 (p. 84), it was situated at a point where the county line meets the mouth of Dry Creek and was the last of a chain of bars from Dry Creek to Long Bar. Placer mining was carried on as early as October, 1850 (Bean, p. 360). A Landers Bar placer mine, active in 1916/17, is mentioned in *Mining Bureau*, XV (p. 442) and was still listed in 1952.

Landrigans Garden [Tuolumne]. Near Sawmill Flat. The *Alta*, June 18, 1854, reported that the fine vegetable garden was gradually being dug up. The miners of one claim gained nine to twelve ounces, and a Chinese claim six to ten ounces a day. The name is sometimes spelled Lanigans.

La Panza [San Luis Obispo]. On Highway 178, at the foot of La Panza Range. The word is Spanish for 'paunch' and apparently originated long before the gold rush. Gold was mined in the creeks and gulches at various times, and in 1878 there was a veritable small-scale rush, which lead to the establishment of a post office. The washings were never very profitable (Co. Hist., 1883, pp. 248 ff.). Dredging for river gold was reported in 1922 (*Mining Bureau*, XVIII, p. 424). The La Panza District is described in *Bulletin*, 193 (p. 179). By 1888 the gold production was estimated at 100 thousand dollars, and mining continued through the early 1900s with some activity again in the 1930s and early 40s.

La Porte [Plumas]. In the southwest corner of the county; on Rabbit Creek, tributary to Slate Creek. The camp itself was first called Rabbit Creek, and as such it is recorded on Goddard's map, 1857. It was originally in Sierra County. The post office was established September 13, 1855, and named Rabbit Town. *See* Rabbit Creek. Unfortunately the colorful name was changed in 1857 to La Porte, after La Porte, Indiana, the hometown of Frank Everts, a local banker. Lotta Crabtree started her spectacular career here. The camp became an important mining center. It was on a channel of the Blue Lead which was not covered by lava and hence was excellent ground for hydraulic mining. Good accounts of mining here and in Plumas and Sierra counties in general are given in the *Mountain Messenger*, July 19, 1862, and the San Francisco *Bulletin*, July 30, 1862. Browne (pp. 164 ff.) states that fifty companies were operating profitably in 1857 with the annual yield of La Porte and vicinity estimated at 4 million dollars,

decreasing within the next ten years to two companies yielding one million dollars. According to *Transactions*, 1858 (pp. 199 f.), a 3,000-foot long tunnel was under construction to bring water from the South Fork of Feather River. The gold production in La Porte District by hydraulic mining was reportedly 60 million dollars or more in the period between 1855 and 1871 alone (Whitney, *Auriferous Gravels*, p. 449). There was also drift and lode mining in the district until World War I, and in the 1930s there was again some prospecting (*Bull.*, 193, p. 86).

Larkin Mine [El Dorado]. *See* Diamond Spring.

Last Chance. This was a term favored by prospectors for camps and mines. *See* California Place Names, and for the numerous mining locations *see* the Consolidated Index.

Last Chance [Butte]. A transient, flourishing camp in Concow Township, north of Oroville (Co. Hist., 1882, p. 253).

Last Chance [Kern]. The name was applied to the old consolidated claims on Tropico Hill in the Mojave District, four and a half miles northwest of Rosamond (*County Report*, I, p. 165).

Last Chance [Placer]. A mining district south of the main branch of the North Fork of the Middle Fork of American River; northeast of Michigan Bluff. Shown on the County Map, 1887. According to an often repeated story, the provisions of the prospectors were exhausted when one of them shot a deer with the last bullet; but according to the County Directory the shooting of a bird led to the discovery of gold. (Bancroft Notes.) The diggings were discov-

La Porte, Plumas Co.

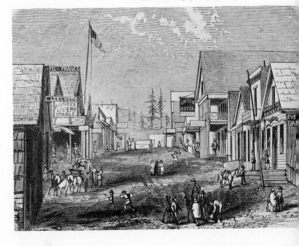

ered in 1850 and a permanent settlement developed in 1852. A post office was established, October 13, 1856. In 1871 local newspapers reported rich profits by hydraulic mining (Raymond, IV, p. 114). In 1927 the total production of the district was 2.5 million dollars, mainly from the El Dorado Mine (*Mining Bureau*, XXIII, p. 262), which continued to be worked intermittently until recent times. The camp at Last Chance was later called Caroline Diggings. *See* Caroline Diggings. The Last Chance Mine was run by the hydraulic method in a small way in the early 1970s (Gianella).

Last Chance: Camp, Creek [Plumas]. The stream is a tributary to the Middle Fork of Feather River, north of Onion Valley. This might be the place where a party of prospectors in search of the Gold Lake gave their guide a "last chance" to find the fictitious lake. No mining record was found. Creek and Camp are shown on the USGS Downieville 1907 quadrangle.

Last Chance Canyon [Kern]. In the Goler Placer District, northwest of Randsburg. It is mentioned in *Mining Bureau*, XXIX (p. 281).

Last Chance Hill [Mono]. Near Aurora. The Last Chance was one of the richest gold leads in the ridges surrounding Aurora (F. S. Wedertz).

Last Chance Mine [El Dorado]. On the north side of the South Fork of American River, opposite Coloma. According to the story, some prospectors were ready to give up when a Sacramento merchant staked them with provisions, and they developed a rich mine. There was a 10-stamp mill, and at one time five tons of dirt yielded 40 thousand dollars. It was owned by Danish prospectors, but the adjoining Danes Mine produced nothing (Browne, p. 91).

Latimers, Latimers Gulch [Calaveras]. The camp was near the Calaveras River, three miles northwest of San Andreas. It was named for David Latimer, who kept a store and boarding house here. Doble (pp. 33, 296) mined here briefly in February, 1852, when there were about fifty tents in the camp. The Benson Gravel Mine, which was worked in the 1890s, was reactivated as the Latimer Gulch Mine in the early 1930s (*Mining Bureau*, X, p. 152; XXXII, pp. 346, 360).

Latrobe [El Dorado]. On the old Sacramento-Placerville railroad. It is listed in Hittell's roster, but no other mining record was found.

Lattimore Bar [Butte]. Inside of the Big Bend of the North Fork of Feather River, northeast of Oroville. Shown on the County Map, 1862, and mentioned in the County History, 1882.

Laurence Hill [Nevada]. *See* Osborn Hill.

Lava Bed District [San Bernardino]. Thirty-five miles southeast of Barstow, in the Lava Bed Mountains. Shown on the County Map, 1892. There was mainly copper and silver production with only a few gold mining claims (*Mining Bureau*, XIII, p. 324). In the 1930s there was dry washing without much success in the Maumee Placers, on the south side of Argos Mountain (*Mining Bureau*, XXX, p. 250).

Lava Cap Mine [Nevada]. *See* Nevada City.

Lawler Bar [Trinity]. On Cañon Creek. Miners were reported to be making as much as twenty dollars per day to the man (*Trinity Journal*, February 18, 1860).

Lawnsdale Gulch [Tuolumne]. About one mile west of Columbia. The old Tuolumne Company Water Company sawmill was here. The *Alta*, June 14, 1854, reprints an item from the Columbia *Clipper* which reports that two men took out 218 dollars worth of gold in two days. Rich deposits had been found in 1853 (De Ferrari, in *Chispa*, V, p. 126). The Abel, Duchow claim was in the direction of the Lawnsdale mill, according to Eastman. In March, 1856, it yielded 800 to one thousand dollars per week from dirt thrown up the previous fall (*Alta*, March 21, 1856).

Lawrenceburg [El Dorado]. *See* Columbia Flat.

Lawson Flat [Nevada]. An unidentified place, listed in Hittell's roster.

Lazy Hollow. An unidentified place, listed in Hittell, *Resources*.

Leadfield [Inyo]. In Death Valley National Monument; at the head of Titus Canyon in the Funeral Range. The mining town was founded in 1926 by the "quack promoter, C. C. Julian," according to Nadeau (pp. 266, 267) in his book on ghost towns and camps in California.

Le Bars Ranch [Nevada]. Near Grass Valley. A gold mine that was located here in 1853 yielded forty-nine dollars per ton in 1867 (Bean, p. 228).

Ledge Bar [El Dorado]. On the South Fork of American River, near Coloma. It is mentioned in the County History, 1883 (p. 85).

Leek Spring [Amador]. At the Volcano cut-off from Carson Emigrant Road, which was completed June 28, 1852 (Berriman). Henry H. Bigler mentions Leek Spring in his diary, July 19, 1848. Doble prospected in the vicinity April 13, 1852. Shown on Goddard's map, 1857.

Lees Camp District [Death Valley National Monument]. In the Funeral Mountains, near the Nevada-California border. There are small mines and prospects in this area and in the adjoining Echo Canyon, but they have been idle for many years (*Bull.*, 193, p. 150). Lees Well is shown on the USGS Furnace Creek 1908 quadrangle.

Leevining: Canyon, Creek, town [Mono]. The town is near Mono Lake, on Highway 395, just above the junction with Tioga Pass road. The places were named for Leroy Vining, a native of Indiana. In the fall of 1852 soldiers of Lieutenant Tredwell Moore's detachment brought to Mariposa some specimens of quartz gold which they had picked up around Bloody Canyon (now in Yosemite Park). This inspired Vining to search for gold deposits east of the Sierra Nevada (Maule, pp. 5, 12). Some gold was apparently found, but no records exist.

Lehigh Bar [Placer]. On the Middle Fork of American River, next to Horseshoe Bar. According to Letts (p. 114) and to later reports, the bar was unproductive. The Lehigh Mine listed in the reports of the Mining Bureau until 1926 was in the Michigan Bluff District.

Lemmons [Calaveras]. On the Calaveras River, northwest of San Andreas. Shown on Jackson's, 1850, and Butler's 1851 maps. No mining record was found.

Les Fourcades [Calaveras]. The French name for Mokelumne Hill. See *CHSQ*, XXXV (p. 316 f.). It was named for the brothers Fourcade, French residents of Monterey, who mined at Mokelumne Hill in 1848 with great success (Moerenhout, p. 41).

Let-her-rip. This is probably a nickname for an unidentified place mentioned in a poem in the *Annual Mining Review*, 1876 (p. 18).

Letter Box [Plumas]. *See* Box.

Letts Bar [Placer]. Near Lacys Bar and Pilot Creek. It was apparently named for J. M. Letts, who mined here in the fall of 1849 (Letts, p. 113).

Lewis, Lewisville [Tuolumne]. The camp Lewis is shown on the road from Stockton to Mariposa on Gibbes' map of the Southern Mines, 1852. On Trask's map, 1853, Lewis Ferry is shown below the junction of Moccasin Creek with the Tuolumne River. De Ferrari, in "A Sketch of Early Tuolumne," *Chispa*, IV (p. 131), states that a camp, Lewisville, was established at the

head of Stevens Bar about 1850 by Daniel C. Lewis, who ferried passengers across the river on a log canoe. It is listed as Louisville in the U. S. Bureau of the Census population schedule for the 1850 census, with a population of eighty-four.

Lewiston [Trinity]. On Trinity River, below the junction with Deadwood Creek. It is shown as Liveston on Goddard's map, 1857. The place was named for B. F. Lewis, who settled here in 1854. Farming and some gold mining was reported as early as 1850 (Cox, pp. 26 ff.). Cox calls the place Louiston. A post office was established April 24, 1854. In 1860 claims yielded 1,400 dollars a week, according to the *Mining Press*, February 1, 1861, and on January 19, 1861, the Weaverville *Journal* reported the find of a 6-pound lump of gold. By 1873 mining was mostly replaced by agriculture, according to Raymond, VI (p. 154). Dredging operations, however, are listed in the reports of the Mining Bureau until 1941.

Lewisville. *See* Greenwood [El Dorado]; Lewis [Tuolumne].

Lexington House [Plumas]. On a tributary to Slate Creek, near the Butte and Yuba county lines. Shown on Eddy's, 1851, and Goddard's, 1857, maps. On Wescoatt's map, 1861, it is shown as Old Lexington House. Lecouvreur (p. 234) reached the place June 6, 1852, on the route to Grass Valley, and De Long mentioned it February 1, 1856. Lexington Hill is shown on the USGS Bidwell Bar 1944 quadrangle.

Liars Flat, Liases Flat [Yuba]. *See* Rices Crossing.

Liberty Cabbage Patch [Siskiyou]. *See* Sauerkraut Gulch.

Liberty District [Siskiyou]. In the southwestern part of the county, in the Salmon Mountains. The district is also known as Black Bear. There was placer mining in the 1850s and very productive lode mining between 1865 and about 1910, with some activity again in the 1930s and prospecting since that time (*Bull.*, 193, p. 139). *See* Black Bear.

Liberty Hill [Nevada]. About two miles south of Lowell Hill. Shown on Doolittle's map, 1868. The place is mentioned as a mining settlement in Little York Township in *Bean's Directory* of 1867. It is on the channel of the Blue Lead. Information about the mining is given in *Pacific Coast Mining Review*, 1878 (p. 248), and in Raymond, VI (p. 117). A Liberty Hill Mine is listed in the reports of the Mining Bureau until 1941. A seven-mile long telephone line was completed between Liberty Hill and Little York in January, 1878 (Foley).

Licking Forks [Calaveras]. On the Mokelumne River. A 6-stamp water-driven mill is mentioned in the *Register*, 1857.

Life Preserver [Placer]. North of Auburn. The *Placer Herald*, June 30, 1877 (Co. Hist., 1882, pp. 228 f.) tells the story of "Pike" Bell, a long-time resident of Bald Hill, who had been so unlucky that he was forced to pawn his wife's wedding ring. He kept on prospecting and in June, 1877, he hit a rich deposit, which he properly named Life Preserver. In three days he took out between 30 and 35 thousand dollars, and his place, later known as Nevada Hill, continued to produce, though not with the spectacular success of the first "strike."

Lightner Mine [Calaveras]. *See* Angels Camp.

Lights Canyon [Plumas]. In the north central part of the county. *Mining Bureau*, II (part 1, p. 188) records the production for the year 1879–80 at 5,999 dollars. A later report (*Mining Bureau*, XVI, Plumas, pp. 31 ff.) gives a description of the topography and geology of the district and states that prospecting began as early as 1850. Recently there has been some prospecting in the Lucky S lode mine (*Bull.*, 193, p. 86 f.).

Lime Kiln Gulch [Trinity]. On the Trinity River, opposite Point Bar. The *Mining Press*, December 28, 1861, reports new diggings "near the Forest House."

Limerick [Calaveras]. *See* Camanche.

Lincoln [Placer]. In the Garden Bar district, fifteen miles west of Auburn. There was mainly copper, but some gold mining. Notice of the sale of mining ground on the San Francisco ledge datelined Lincoln, May 9, 1863, is recorded in the Garden Bar book of claims in Placer County Records, VI (p. 38). A description of the Lincoln district is given in *Bulletin*, 193 (p. 87). It is stated here that considerable gold was obtained in the 1930s by dredging in lower Auburn Ravine and in Doty Ravine, and that it was at that time "probably the most profitable dragline dredge field in the state."

Lincoln Consolidated Mine [Amador]. In and near the town of Sutter Creek. Included are Lincoln, Wildman, and Mahoney mines, all of which were located about 1851 and operated separately and intermittently until consolidated in 1906, after which they worked at intervals until 1912. The combined production of

Wildman and Mahoney was about 5 million dollars and of Lincoln 2.2 million dollars. (*Bull.*, 108, p. 95; *Mining Bureau*, L, p. 186.)

Lincoln Hill [Plumas or Sierra]. On Canyon Creek, tributary to the North Fork of Yuba River. In 1861 good prospects with hydraulic mining were reported by the *Mining Press*, June 15, 1861. The *Annual Mining Review*, 1876 (p. 54), reports that a company with 10 million dollars capital started a development.

Linda [Yuba]. On the south bank of the main Yuba River, above Marysville. Shown on Gibbes' map, 1851, and Milleson and Adams', 1851. Bancroft, VI (p. 487) lists it among the ephemeral towns which were established as rivals to Marysville for miners' trade. It was the namesake of the pioneer steamer *Linda*, which was brought up the Feather River in the fall of 1849 by the Linda Company and was the first steamboat to enter the Yuba River, coming as far as John Rose's cattle ranch on the south side of the Yuba, near Roses Bar. The Company persuaded Rose to found the new town of Linda at the site they had demonstrated to be the head of navigation. After the county was organized in 1850 the large township south of the Yuba was named Linda. Today the name is applied to the large, sprawling unincorporated community containing farms, residences, stores, and industries. (Ramey, from Marysville *Appeal*, October 28, 1879; April 9, 1899.)

Linden [San Joaquin]. On Highway 8. Small scale mining was carried on here and along the Calaveras River mainly by Chinese (*Mining Bureau*, LI, p. 37).

Lindsays Bar [Butte]. In Concow Township, north of Oroville. According to the County History, 1882 (p. 253), it was a flourishing but only transient gold mining camp.

Linns Valley [Kern]. On Poso Creek, between Visalia and Walkers Pass. It was prospected by gold-seekers during the first Kern River rush. A post office was established in 1860 when the place was still in Tulare County. Named for William P. Lynn, an early prospector (Boyd, pp. 8, 21).

Lippards Bar [Nevada]. On the Yuba River, probably on the South Fork. Peter Decker mined here in April, 1850. The place was apparently named for a fellow miner, J. H. Lippard (Decker diary, April 12 and August 25, 1850).

Little Baltimore Ravine [Placer]. Near Baltimore Ravine, west of Auburn. According to the County History, 1882 (p. 227), two men dug out 1,200 dollars worth of nuggets, ranging from one to sixty dollars each in November or December, 1855.

Little Butte [Butte]. On Little Butte Creek. Two letters of October, 1853, by Seth and Asa Smith are datelined from here. Their washing paid only one and a half dollars a day. In 1930 a Little Butte Prospect is listed (*Mining Bureau*, XXVI, p. 396).

Little Deer Creek [Nevada]. Near Nevada City. Alex Barrington had a highly successful claim here in June and July, 1850 (*Miscellany*, p. 5). In 1854 three or four companies averaged between eight and fifteen dollars a day to the man (Hittell Clippings, p. 58). The *Mining Press*, June 9, 1862, reports that twenty hands here and at Gold Flat averaged sixty dollars a day each.

Little Grass Valley [Plumas]. The valley is along the South Fork of Feather River. A settlement, Grass Valley, on the south side of the river is shown on Goddard's map, 1857. *See* Grass Valley [Plumas]. In 1850, McIlhany (p. 49) speaks of American Grass Valley and a little later (p. 59) of Little Grass Valley. The diggings were probably discovered in the wake of the Gold Lake hunt. The valley is on the same channel as La Porte. The gold gravel was covered by a 300-foot lava bed, and there was only small scale drift mining. However, the place showed promise according to Browne (p. 166). Little Grass Valley and Little Grass Valley Hill are shown on the USGS Downieville 1907 quadrangle.

Little Grizzley [Sierra]. Seven miles north of Downieville. On the County Map of 1874 it appears larger than the camp called Grizzly several miles southwest. It is on the main Blue Lead. The mining was mainly drifting and was still going on in 1868 (Browne, p. 138). In 1869 a nugget of 107 ounces, valued at two thousand dollars, was discovered here (*Mining Bureau*, II, part 1, p. 149). A mine is listed in the Mining Bureau report of 1942.

Little Horseshoe Bar [Placer]. On the North Fork of American River, below Horseshoe Bar. It is recorded on July 10, 1852, in Placer County Records, I (p. 95).

Little Humbug Creek [Siskiyou]. A tributary to the Klamath River, named in analogy with the nearby rich Humbug district. According to *Mining Bureau*, XIV (p. 814), two million dollars worth of gold was extracted here by ground sluicing by 1914.

Shown on the USGS Yreka 1939 quadrangle.

Little Kimshew [Butte]. East of Inskip, on the Feather River. It was apparently a sizeable camp, shown on the County Map of 1861. According to the County History, 1882 (p. 252), this as well as Big Kimshew were once flourishing camps. Kimshew and Little Kimshew creeks are shown on modern maps.

Little Negro Hill [El Dorado]. *See* Negro Hill.

Little Oregon Bar [Placer]. On the North Fork of American River, probably near Oregon Bar. It is mentioned in Placer County Records, I (p. 42) in the notice of a claim filed November 15, 1851. In 1852 one company with forty men flumed 1,450 feet of the river and averaged a yield of 2,500 dollars per day, according to the County History, 1882 (pp. 225 f.).

Little Prairie [Trinity]. On the Trinity River, five miles below Big Bar. It was mentioned as a "promising settlement" by Cox (p. 81). Placer mining continued until the end of the century (*Mining Bureau*, XIII, p. 454).

Little Rattlesnake Bar [Placer]. On the North Fork of American River, about a mile southeast of Auburn. Shown on Doolittle's map, 1868. The bar is mentioned in the Placer County Records, I (p. 184), in connection with a claim recorded September 29, 1853. In 1855 the dirt paid about ten dollars to the wheelbarrow load (Co. Hist., 1882, p. 189).

Little Rich Bar [Sierra]. On the North Fork of Yuba River, west of Downieville. It was probably discovered in 1850 in the wake of the Gold Lake hunt, but according to County History, 1882 (p. 419), it was prospected in September, 1849, and named because it was near Rich Bar.

Little River Beach [Humboldt]. Ten miles north of Arcata. After the discovery of Gold Bluff, washing for gold in the fine sand was carried on for some time, and in the 1890s efforts were renewed. A report in *Mining Bureau*, XIII (p. 174) states that it was difficult to extract the fine gold and more profitable to get the coarser platinum.

Little Rock Creek [Butte]. It is listed in the County History, 1882 (p. 253), as a once flourishing mining camp.

Little York [Nevada]. Two miles southwest of Dutch Flat. Prominently marked on Trask's map, 1853. The ravine was first worked by forty-niners who came along the old Truckee road and found it convenient to camp here after the long trek. In the fall of 1850 the L. Karner party settled here. There was mainly dry digging. A pan yielded one dollar in 1852, according to the Nevada County Directory, 1895. When water was brought from Bear River a rapid development set in. The best early account is in Bean (pp. 367 ff.). In August, 1852, the town was organized and the miners from New York decided on the name over the southern opposition who wanted to call it St. Louis. The post office was established in 1855. When the placers gave out, quartz and hydraulic mining were taken up. In April 1867 there was still a sizeable population and two stamp mills were in operation (Bean, p. 372). The decline did not start until the prohibition of hydraulic mining in 1884. The post office was discontinued in 1886.

Live Oak [Sacramento]. On the Jackson Road, about a mile west of the Michigan Bar turnoff. Mining was started here before 1854, but it declined by 1861 (Co. Hist., 1880, p. 215). Hutchings, who was here March 22, 1855, refers to it as Live Oak City and describes it as one of the most picturesque villages in the mining district, which had grown within a year to a population of 400. In 1880 there was a small camp of Chinese miners nearby.

Live Oak Bar [Butte]. On the north side of the North Fork of Feather River, between Yankee Bar and Bardee Bar. Shown on the County Map, 1877.

Live Oak Bar [El Dorado]. Three miles upstream from Sutter's Mill. Shown on Doolittle's map, 1868. According to the not very reliable "Memoirs" of James Gregson (CHSQ, XIX, p. 134), he, James Marshall, and two companions prospected here and named the bar in February, 1848, and one day picked up a pint (!) of gold by hand. Besides Bigler's attempts west of Sutter's Fort, this would be the first bar discovered and named after the discovery at Sutter's Mill. — Two Live Oak quartz mines at different locations in the county are repeatedly recorded in the reports of the Mining Bureau.

Liveston [Trinity]. A misspelling of Lewiston, shown on Goddard's map, 1857. See Lewiston.

Live Yankee Claim [Sierra]. North of Forest City. According to Transactions, 1858 (p. 187), one company netted 116.4 thousand dollars from the summer of 1856 to the summer of 1858. The Mining Press, May 16, 1862, reported that almost 100 ounces, including a 60-ounce nugget, were mined in one day, and the Mining Bureau, II (part

1, p. 150) stated that between 1854 and 1862, twelve nuggets weighing thirty to 170 ounces each were discovered. In the main tunnel a big fossilized tree was found 900 feet below the surface. Raymond, VII (p. 152) states that the claim was exhausted in 1868. The total production of the Live Yankee was estimated to have been between three quarters and one million dollars (Bull., 193, p. 24).

Lizard Flat [Nevada]. Opposite Jefferson, at the mouth of Jefferson Creek, near Washington. A. J. Doolittle, took out "no less than 50 thousand dollars" here. It is listed in Bancroft, VI (p. 358).

Loafer: Flat, Gulch, Hill [Amador]. The Gulch is a tributary to the North Fork of Dry Creek, near Fiddletown. Shown on the County Map, 1866. On nearby Loafer Hill there was early hill mining (Co. Hist., 1881, p. 126).

Loafer Hill [Siskiyou]. Between Yreka and Hawkinsville. According to local tradition, the mining ground, rich in coarse gold, was left unclaimed for anyone "down and out" to make grubstake (Siskiyou Pioneer, II:4, p. 25).

Loafers Diggings [Butte]. According to a clipping from the Butte Record in 1854, some Frenchmen averaged here thirty dollars a day to the man (Hittell Clippings, p. 25).

Loafers Hollow [El Dorado]. Now in the corporate limits of El Dorado. There were two small mills in operation in 1857 (State Register, 1859).

Loafers Retreat. An unidentified place listed in Hittell's roster.

Lockwood Valley Placers [Ventura]. About eighteen miles west of Tejon Place. Apparently there were rich deposits, especially along Piru Creek, but only desultory mining in the 1930s (Mining Bureau, XXX, p. 251).

Logans Gulch [Trinity]. On the north side of Trinity River, a few miles below North Fork of Trinity River. There was a trading post here, and in 1850 one miner is reported to have made 250 dollars in one day with crude implements, according to Coy (p. 82).

Loganville [Sierra]. On the North Fork of Yuba River, two miles west of Sierra City. Shown on Doolittle's map, 1868, and on the County Map, 1874. It was probably settled as early as 1851. The chief mines were the Keystone, the Marguerite, and the Cleveland lode mines. There was also large scale hydraulic mining by the Dutch Company and the Romanos. (Sinnott, p.

124.) The old hotel is still used as a dwelling (R. Drury). The place is shown on the USGS Downieville 1907 quadrangle.

Log Cabin Ravine [El Dorado]. Now Bedford Avenue in Placerville. According to the reminiscences of Haskins (p. 134), the deposits were discovered by the Winslow brothers and yielded 250 thousand dollars. The ravine is mentioned by Lyman, who averaged one hundred dollars in eight days of washing (p. 193). Among the early miners were soldiers of Stevensons Regiment. A sailor was so lucky that he bought a barrel of liquor and let everybody help himself (Swan, pp. 13 ff.). Haskins (p. 70) tells a story of two slaves from Louisville, Kentucky, who worked hard and sent their master 2.3 thousand dollars in exchange for their freedom. In 1855 a large tunnel for quartz mining was built (Hittell Clippings, p. 53).

Logtown [El Dorado]. Two miles south of El Dorado (Mud Springs). Recorded on Trask's, 1853, and Goddard's, 1857, maps. The U. S. 1850 Census lists 420 inhabitants, mostly miners, at Logtown and vicinity. The place is mentioned by Finley McDiarmid in a letter datelined Oregon Canyon, January 19, 1851. The quartz mills operating for the district as early as 1856 are listed in the *State Register*, 1859, the *Annual Mining Review*, 1876 (p. 22), and in the County History, 1883 (pp. 93 f.). In a letter of George W. Browning, datelined Sacramento Valley, May 24, 1861, it is called a flourishing town in the midst of good diggings. The place is shown on the USGS Placerville 1931 quadrangle.

Logtown [Mariposa]. Near Mariposa, on the opposite side of Mariposa Creek from the Mariposa Public Cemetery. Shown on the Las Mariposas map, 1861. It was established in the spring of 1850 on higher ground than Mariposa when flood threatened to destroy the town (Crampton, p. 65).

Lola Montez: Hill, Diggings [Nevada]. Northwest of Grass Valley, near Slate Creek. Shown on Hoffmann and Craven's Great Gravel map, 1873. It is apparently the only place named for the popular actress and courtesan. According to an undated clipping from the Nevada *Democrat*, the Rock Tunnel Company, starting in July, 1853, worked for three years before it hit pay dirt here. The lead was two to three feet thick and prospected eight to ten dollars per day to the hand (Hittell Clippings, p. 72).

Lone Pine City [Inyo]. The town north of Owens Lake was the trading center and post office (established in 1870) for the silver, copper, and gold mines of the Cerro Gordo district and the Alabama Hills. *See* Raymond, V (1872, pp. 17 ff.).

Lone Star District [Placer]. Near Auburn. The popular name for mines was used for the district organized December 20, 1862 for mining copper, gold, and silver. The bylaws and claims are recorded in the Placer County Records, V.

Lone Star District [Tuolumne]. On Table Mountain. A number of large claims are listed in Heckendorn (p. 104).

Long Bar [El Dorado]. On the North Fork of American River, about three miles above the confluence with the South Fork, opposite Dotans Bar. Shown on Trask's map, 1853. It is mentioned in a letter by Henry V. D. Spiegel datelined Big Bar, June 7, 1850. According to the El Dorado County History, 1883 (p. 83), Long Bar and Dotans Bar both had 500 miners during the season. The place is now covered by Folsom Lake.

Long Bar [Nevada]. In Washington Mining District, just above the mouth of Scotchmans Creek, tributary to the South Fork of Yuba River. It is mentioned as a camp in 1849 in Nevada County Mining Records (Foley).

Long Bar [Placer]. On Bear River. It is mentioned as having been a very rich bar, a half mile long and 100 feet wide (*Placer Nuggets*, June, 1959, p. 3).

Long Bar [Placer]. On the Middle Fork of American River. Mentioned in Placer County Records, I (verso of p. 22) in the notice filed October 27, 1851, of intention to flume the river from the riffle low end of Dutch Bar to the middle of Long Bar.

Long Bar [Trinity]. On Trinity River, east of Weaverville. Mentioned repeatedly in the summer of 1850 by de Massey as a prosperous place with several stores. It may be the same Long Bar mentioned by Cox (p. 25).

Long Bar [Yuba]. On the main Yuba River, above the confluence with Dry Creek, near Parks Bar. In this vicinity the first gold on the Yuba River was discovered in June, 1848, by Jonas Spect of Pennsylvania (Bancroft, VI, p. 360). The place is recorded as Long Bar on Milleson and Adams' map, 1851, and on other early maps. Trask, 1853, records it as Long's Bar. According to the County History, 1879 (p. 86), it was the longest bar on the river. Peter Burnett, later governor of California, mined here in

November and December, 1848 (pp. 273 ff.), and he states that it was named for Dr. John P. Long and brother, Willis. At that time there were less than ninety people, one log cabin, and a number of tents and cloth shanties. In the spring of 1850 the population was 1,000, with six stores, eight hotels, and eight or ten saloons (Co. Hist., 1879, p. 86). Stephen Davis and brother had a store here in 1850–1851 (pp. 17–24). Lecouvreur mined here with fair success from February to June, 1852, and he gives an excellent description of the place (pp. 204 ff.). The post office was transferred from Dry Creek April 9, 1859. The diggings gave out in 1864 and the post office was discontinued the same year. In 1867 the bar was buried under the gravel from hydraulic mining upstream (Alta, November 7, 1867). Shown on the USGS Smartsville 1943 quadrangle.

Long Bar [Yuba]. On the North Fork of Yuba River, two miles above Fosters Bar. Shown on Wescoatt's map, 1861. Reference is made to it as a minor bar in Bancroft, VI (p. 360). De Long mentions it August 15, 1855, and later. In 1858 a large amount of ground was still unprospected and mining was declining because of lack of facilities to bring water, according to the Marysville Directory, 1858 (p. xxvii). The County History, 1879 (p. 94), states that fifteen Chinese miners were working there at that time.

Long Canyon [Mariposa]. Apparently on the Merced River, west of Horseshoe Bend. The only source found is the diary of Hiram Pierce, who mined here with some success in July and August, 1851.

Longfellow [Tuolumne]. On the Cerro Gordo, a mountain north of Big Oak Flat. The place was located in 1854. It had a 25-stamp mill and paid well until about 1914 (Mining Bureau, VIII, pp. 672 f.; XIV, p. 154).

Long Gulch [Siskiyou]. According to E. M. Anthony in his "Reminiscences of the Early Days in Siskiyou" (p. 13), mining operations started soon after gold was discovered in Shasta Butte City. The camp is mentioned in the Mining Press, May 8, 1862. One claim is said to have paid between 300 and one thousand dollars a week.

Long Gulch [Tuolumne]. About two miles south of Tuolumne. A lively town arose during the gold rush to Turnback Creek, but the miners stampeded to Sum-

mersville when the Eureka quartz lead was discovered in 1858 (Chispa, I, p. 1).

Long: Gulch, Canyon [Calaveras]. Near Angels Camp. It is mentioned as a small camp in Heckendorn (p. 99). A mine is listed in the Mining Bureau reports until 1936.

Long Hollow [Nevada]. Near Bear River. The Steamer edition of Alta, March 20, 1857, reported that four Chinese struck the main lead of Albion Diggings and took out 3 to 4 thousand dollars in a few days. It is listed in Hittell's roster.

Longs Bar [Butte]. On the Feather River, west of Bidwell Bar, near Oroville. Recorded on Milleson and Adams' map, 1851, and on Trask's, 1853. According to the recollections of Job F. Dye (Santa Cruz Sentinel, May 22, 1869), he was a member of a party of seven men who took out 70 thousand dollars worth of gold after forty-two days of work in the spring of 1848 at the rich diggings at Monterey Bar, later called Longs Bar. Bancroft, VI (p. 362) refers to it as Long Bar, mined in 1848, "turning out very rich, and counting at one time 4,000 diggers." It is mentioned by Webster in October, 1849, as a small town, and it is probably the same as Longs Bar mentioned by William Armstrong as existing in the fall of 1849, and by J. W. Booth, who was there in 1849 and later in 1852 (Booth's diary, pp. 32 f; 35 f.). Gerstaecker (p. 159) mentions the store at the place. J. A. Stuart reports that he and his company made ten cents each on their first day of mining, October 19, 1849. But Mansfield (p. 5) seems to remember after three-fourths of a century that the first pan of gold yielded 400 dollars. Ferguson (pp. 124 ff.) mined here in the summer of 1850 and helped build a wingdam, which was washed away after four weeks of labor. According to a clipping from the Alta, March 7, 1852, the camp prospered at that time and several hundred miners made good wages by washing in a rocker the ground which had been gone over twice before (Bancroft Scraps, LI:1, p. 250). In 1856 a 12-stamp mill was erected (State Register, 1859). In the County History, 1882 (p. 232), the bar is described as rich and for some time the most important camp of the region.

Long Tom District [Kern]. West of Poso Flat, about fifteen miles west of Kernville. The district was named after the principal mine. According to the Annual Mining Review, 1876 (p. 22), a 10-stamp steam-driven mill was in operation at the Long

Tom Mine as early as 1855. It was reported as quite active in the 1880s and again between 1925 and 1939 (*Bull.*, 193, p. 87).

Long Tom Ravine [Nevada]. Near Nevada City, in the vicinity of Cement Hill. Pettee mentions it in 1870 in his discussion of the ancient river channel in the area (Whitney, *Auriferous Gravels*, p. 184).

Long Valley [El Dorado]. *See* Greenwood.

Lookout [Inyo]. There was mainly silver and lead production and only traces of gold at this place (*Pacific Coast Mining Review*, 1878, p. 219).

Loraine [Kern]. *See* Paris.

Lorenz Bar [Placer, El Dorado]. Above Rattlesnake Bar, on both sides of the North Fork of American River. According to the Placer County History, 1924 (p. 177), it was a moderately rich bar in the early 1850s.

Lorings Gardens [Tuolumne]. Three-quarters of a mile west of Columbia, on the Matelot Gulch road. It was sometimes called Hildreths Gardens. Several claims between this place and Gold Springs were reported as doing well in 1853. One day in February one miner took out ten ounces, according to the Columbia *Gazette*, February 19, 1853.

Los Burros District [Monterey]. In the southern part of the Santa Lucia Range near Jolon. The district was organized in 1876 for quicksilver prospecting. In 1887 a quartz vein was discovered and a 3-stamp mill erected. *See* Gorda. By 1915 more than 150 thousand dollars worth of gold was produced. (*Mining Bureau*, VIII, p. 405; XXXI, p. 462.) This was a considerable amount for Monterey County. In 1953 and 1963 mining was again reported in the district, and in all 2,000 or more claims are believed to have been recorded (*Bull.*, 193, p. 179).

Los Coyotes [Tuolumne]. The camp is mentioned by William Perkins, January 25, 1852 (p. 300). It appears to be the same place as Coyote Diggings. There is a remote possibility that the reference may be to Coyote Creek in Calaveras County, where Perkins and his friend Ramon Navarro were mining about this time (De Ferrari).

Los Muertos [Calaveras]. Near Altaville. According to Ridge (p. 127), the trail of Murieta and his band was picked up here before the last stage of his career. The place, bearing the Spanish name meaning 'the dead', was apparently the same as the Mexican camp which was attacked and destroyed by Americans. *See* Campo de los Muertos.

Los Padres Mine [Los Angeles]. *See* Big Tujunga Canyon.

Lost. The adjective is found frequently in mining nomenclature. For a list of mines which were lost, or named for something that was lost, *see Consolidated Index.*

Lost Cabin Diggings [Siskiyou]. Of unknown location. In 1861 it was a new camp with 200 to 300 miners, who reportedly made ten to fifteen dollars a day to the man (Bancroft Scraps, LI:1, p. 240).

Lost Camp [Placer]. Northeast of Dutch Flat; one mile south of Blue Canon Railroad Station. Shown on Doolittle's map, 1868. It is mentioned in Placer County Records, I (p. 281), February 9, 1855, and in *Mining Press*, April 13, 1861. The workings of the Lost Camp hydraulic and drift mines are described in *Mining Bureau*, XIII (p. 282) and XV (p. 376 f.); and again in XXXII (p. 68), in which a report of a renewal of hydraulic mining in the 1930s is given.

Lost City [Calaveras]. Five or six miles north of Copperopolis, on the Von Offenheim ranch. In the 1850s there were apparently about twenty buildings, including dwelling houses, stores, and a nearby school, reportedly built by French miners, who left after gold mining failed. According to "The Knave," July 31, 1960, the location was near Felix, and former names were Stone City, Stone Creek Settlement. R. Coke Wood, however, locates the place on the Offenheim ranch, and states that the remains of about twenty stone houses may be found along a little creek and a stretch of terracing extending about a half mile. The best preserved building is called the "chalet," and an old French Basque lived there until recently. Old timers state that gold was panned and washed at the Stonehouse Mine.

Lost Hill [Nevada]. Within the limits of Nevada City, on the west side. The placer diggings were discovered in the spring of 1853 by Amos Laird, I. Williamson, I. N. Dawley, and others. They were first worked in a primitive way, with the sinking of small shafts and running of small drifts in different directions, and later were hydraulicked extensively (*Bean's Directory*, p. 129; *Mining Bureau*, XVI, Nevada, p. 38; Lindgren, *Gold-Quartz Veins*, p. 19). The name was given at the time the "lead" was lost (Foley).

Lost Infant Claim [El Dorado]. Near Placerville. Mentioned as a locality in Crockett's account book, 1859 (p. 94).

Lost Ravine [Nevada]. An unidentified place, listed in Hittell's roster.

Lotus [El Dorado]. On Highway 49, near Coloma. It was an old, rich but short-lived placer mining town. At one time the population was reportedly 2,000. The town was first called Marshall, then Uniontown in 1850, and when the post office was established January 6, 1881, the name was changed to Lotus. The *Register* of 1902 lists one stamp mill. The Stuckslager Mine, south of Lotus, was unusual because the gold found is associated with a rare mineral, roscoelite (*Guidebook*, p. 68). *See* Uniontown.

Loudens [Trinity]. *See* Lowden Ranch.

Louisa Mine. *See* Coulterville [Mariposa].

Louisiana Bar [El Dorado]. On the Middle Fork of American River, near the junction, as shown on Goddard's map, 1857. Trask, 1853, shows it on the South Fork. It is mentioned in the County History, 1883 (p. 83). A notice of the sale of claims below New York Bar is recorded October 11, 1851 in the Placer County Records, I (p. 9).

Louiston [Trinity]. *See* Lewiston.

Louisville [El Dorado]. On Dutch Creek, about four miles northeast of Coloma. Recorded on Gibbes' map, 1851. According to the *Guidebook* (p. 70), it was one of the great placer camps around 1850. In November, 1850, the U. S. Bureau of the Census listed the names of 420 inhabitants in Louisville and vicinity. The *Guidebook* states that the place was formerly called Spanish Flat; however, Doolittle's map, 1868, as well as the USGS Placerville 1939 quadrangle, show both Louisville and Spanish Flat about one mile apart. *See* Greenwood.

Louisville [Tuolumne]. *See* Lewisville.

Lousy Bar [El Dorado]. An unidentified name mentioned in Abbott's *Recollections* (p. 93).

Lousy: Level, Ravine, Bar [Nevada, Yuba]. On the main Yuba River. The camp is mentioned in Canfield's diary (p. 186) and is listed in Hittell, *Resources*, and in a Wells Fargo directory. *See* Rices Crossing.

Love Letter Camp. An unidentified place, listed in Hittell, *Resources*.

Lovelock [Butte]. North of Magalia and Hupps. The County Map of 1861 shows Lovelock's mill and store. Browne (p. 163) reports only one arrastre working in 1860, but the *Annual Mining Review*, 1876 (p. 23), lists a 4-stamp water-driven mill built in 1873. It is still shown on some modern maps, and is mentioned in *Bulletin*, 99 (p. 67).

Lovers Hollow. An unidentified place, listed as a mining locality on an illustrated letter sheet published by Hutchings in 1855.

Loves Bar [Tuolumne]. On Woods Creek, east of Montezuma. The place is mentioned by Heckendorn (p. 89).

Lowden Ranch [Trinity]. On Trinity River, southeast of Weaverville. It had a post office, 1874–1908, and placer mining was carried on until the end of the century (*Register*, 1898). Shown on the USGS Weaverville 1942 quadrangle. It is apparently the same place as Loudens, at the mouth of Grass Valley Creek, where William Spencer Louden built a bridge in 1855 (Cox, p. 29). The bridge pier and abutment are still in place (H. E. Goodyear).

Lowell Hill [Nevada]. About four miles northeast of Dutch Flat. Shown on Doolittle's map, 1868. In 1854 the miners made ten to twenty dollars a day to the hand (*Alta*, February 27, 1854). According to Raymond, VI (p. 117), one of the drift mines had the delightful name "Swamp Angel." In 1865 a 58-ounce nugget worth 1,100 dollars was found here (*Mining Bureau*, II, part 1, p. 149). When hydraulic mining was limited in 1884, there were still 400 men employed (*Nevada Directory*, 1895). The diggings were then worked mainly by Chinese. The Lowell District is listed in the Mining Bureau reports until 1918. The total gold production of the district is estimated at more than a million dollars (*Bull.*, 193, p. 87).

Lower Bar [Amador, Calaveras]. *See* James Bar.

Lower Calaveritas [Calaveras]. According to the *Annual Mining Review*, 1876 (p. 22), a 10-stamp water-driven mill was in operation at that time. *See* Calaveritas.

Lower Holcomb [San Bernardino]. At the junction of Poligue Canyon Road and the main road through Holcomb Valley. *See* Holcomb Valley. In later years the area became known as the Hitchcock Ranch. (Haenszel.)

Lower Indian Bar [Plumas]. On the north side of the North Fork of Feather River, two miles below Yellow Creek. Shown on the von Leicht-Craven map, 1874.

Lower Mines [Sacramento]. This was the original name used to designate the placers around Mormon Island. Recorded in July, 1848, on Ord's map and on the map in the Mason Report. It was used to distinguish them from the Upper Mines at Sutters Mill.

Lower Rancheria [Amador]. *See* Rancheria.

Lower Rich Gulch. *See* Rich Gulch [Calaveras].

Lower South Bar [El Dorado]. On the South Fork of American River, probably where Greenwood Creek joins the River. Theodore Johnson (pp. 176 ff.) and his partners mined here in the summer of 1849.

Lower Town. *See* Hawkinsville [Siskiyou]; Mosquito Valley [El Dorado].

Loyalton [Sierra]. *See* Smiths Neck.

Ludlow [San Bernardino]. On the Santa Fe main line, east of Barstow. It was not a mining town but an important supply point for the surrounding mines. It was also the terminus of the short line to Stedman and the southern terminus of the narrow-gauge Tonopah and Tidewater (Belden, February 7, 1854). The mines are listed but not mapped in the *Register*, 1902. From 1902 to 1926 the post office was called Stagg. *See* Stedman.

Lundy [Mono]. Six miles west of Highway 395, near the northern shore of Mono Lake. The town was the center for the rich gold and silver mining district. It had a post office from 1880 to 1914. The May Lundy, the chief mine, was discovered in 1877 and operated on a major scale until 1911, and on a limited scale in the 1930s, with minor prospecting since that time. The total production of gold was 3 million dollars, according to *Bulletin*, 193 (p. 64). De Decker (pp. 17 ff.) gives an account of Homer district, with a description of the town of Lundy and various mines in the area. The town and the lake on which it is situated was named for William O. Lundy, who had a timber patent here (*California Place Names*), and the mine was named for his daughter.

Lymans Diggings [El Dorado]. A few miles below Coloma. It was one of the first camps after the news of the discovery was spread. Chester Lyman (pp. 265 ff.) started mining with five partners, June 22, 1848, and washed eighty-six ounces in six days. When they heard of Charles M. Weber's success, they left for his camp.

Lynchburg [Butte]. One mile southeast of Oroville. Shown on Goddard's map, 1857, and on Doolittle's, 1868. The camp was named for George Lynch, the owner of the store. In 1854 it was a lively place, rivaling Ophir City (Oroville), according to the County History, 1882 (p. 238). The camp declined as early as 1854, but the name still appears on the von Leicht-Craven map, 1874.

Lynchburg [Placer]. On the Ralston Divide. It is listed by Hutchings in 1855. There

was hydraulic mining in the early 1870s, according to Warren T. Russell (p. 204). *See* Ralston Divide.

Lyonsdale [El Dorado]. A 20-stamp steam-driven mill was erected in 1864 (*Annual Mining Review*, 1876, p. 21). It is probably the Lyons Canon near Grizzly Flat mentioned by Crockett in 1856 (p. 40).

Lytle Creek Placers [San Bernardino]. About thirteen miles northwest of San Bernardino. The stream was named for Captain Andrew Lytle, who led a party of Mormons in 1851. Gold was discovered in the canyon in the early 1860s. A clipping from the Los Angeles *News*, marked May 23, 1864, in Hayes Scrapbooks: Mining, VII, contains a report that the mines along the creek were proving very rich. Other contemporary newspapers bring similar reports, some reporting earnings as high as forty dollars per day. The first large-scale hydraulic mining was carried on at Texas Point. *See* Texas Point. The flood of 1891 put a stop to most of the mining (Thrall, p. 242), but a claim was worked at the Hitching Ranch, 1920–1930, and during the depression individuals panned for gold earning as much as a dollar a day (Belden, April 11, 1954).

Lytles Bar [Siskiyou]. On the east side of Scott River, near the junction with Klamath River. Shown on Goddard's map, 1857. Hutchings was here January 19, 1855, on his travels to the mining country. The place is mentioned in the County History, 1881 (p. 217).

McAdams Creek [Siskiyou]. A branch of Moffett Creek, a tributary to Scott River, near Fort Jones. It was named for a Scot who discovered a rich vein here in 1854 (Co. Hist., 1881, p. 216). The *Mining Press*, July 6, 1861, reported that the Hardscrabble Company took out 30 ounces in one day. In 1880 the annual production of gold still amounted to almost 2,500 ounces (*Mining Bureau*, II, Part 1, p. 189), but the *Register* of 1898 lists only one Chinese claim. In later years there were dredging operations (*Bull.*, 85, p. 37). There was a McAdams post office, 1881–1882.

McBride Gulch [Siskiyou]. The gulch was prospected soon after the discovery of the rich digging near Shasta Butte City (E. M. Anthony, "Reminiscences," p. 13).

McCabes Creek [Butte]. A tributary to the South Fork of Feather River, five miles from Forbestown. Seth and Asa B. Smith mined here with variable success from 1855 to 1859 (Letters of Asa Smith).

McCall Gulch [Shasta]. On Dog Creek. According to an item in the *Shasta Courier*, January 11, 1868, several parties "made fortunes mining there," but the diggings were worked out after a time. (Hayes *Scrapbook*: Mining, IV, sec. 48.)

McCarty Flat [Sierra]. *See* O'Donnells Flat.

McClintock Ranch [El Dorado or Placer]. An unidentified place. The *Alta*, February 27, 1854, reprints an item, according to which one company averaged thirteen ounces a day.

McDonald Flat [Sierra]. *See* O'Donnells Flat.

McDowells Race [El Dorado]. *See* Pine Bar.

McDowellsville [El Dorado]. On the South Fork of American River, below Salmon Falls. According to the County History, 1883 (p. 203), McDowell Hill was a camp which once had four stores and one hundred inhabitants; but in 1883 it was a ghost town. It is mentioned as McDowellsville in *Resources of El Dorado County*, p. 138.

McGarveys [Tuolumne]. *See* McGarvis.

McGarvis [Tuolumne]. On the Stanislaus River, north of Jacksonville. The camp is recorded on Trask's map, 1853. The reference may be to McGarveys, southwest of Jamestown, at what is now known as Yosemite Junction, at the intersection of Highway 108 with 120, where McGarvey had a ranch (De Ferrari).

McGillivrays Bar [Trinity]. *See* Coopers Bar.

Maciys Bar [Mariposa]. An uncertain name of a bar on the Merced River, west of Coulterville, recorded on Trask's map, 1853.

McKeebys Diggings [Sierra]. Near Sebastapol. The diggings were developed by Lemuel McKeeby (pp. 45, 151) in 1852 and were worked successfully until 1863. He called the place Gold Bluff, but it was apparently not the same as the prosperous Gold Bluff near by.

McKenzie Bar [Merced]. On the Merced River. The *Alta*, January 4, 1854, reprints an item from the Stockton *Journal* which states that eight men of the McKenzie Company struck a lead which allegedly paid 100 dollars a day to the man.

McKenzies Gulch [Trinity]. A tributary to Weaver Creek, very near the northwest corner of Weaverville townsite. It is mentioned in 1858 by Cox (p. 131). A McKenzie and Timmerman Placer Mine, one and a half miles northwest of Weaverville is mentioned in 1941 in *Mining Bureau*, XXXVII (p. 87).

McKinneys Humbug [Calaveras]. On McKinneys Creek, nine miles east of San Andreas. It was also known as McKinneys Secret Diggings. The camp is mentioned by Bachman, November 1, 1851; by Heckendorn (p. 96); and also without "Humbug" repeatedly by Doble in the spring of 1852. The *Alta*, February 13, 1854, calls it one of the best camps of the county. It had more than 1,000 residents and should no longer have been called Humbug. In 1857 a 10-stamp water-driven mill was built (*State Register*, 1859). The Creek is shown on the USGS Jackson 1938 quadrangle.

Macksville [El Dorado]. On the Middle Fork of American River, apparently near El Dorado Canyon. The Sacramento *Transcript*, May 29, 1850, states that it was known by a dozen different names, and describes it as a prosperous town with many stores and gambling houses (Bancroft Notes).

McLaughlans Ravine [Placer]. A notice of a claim to water rights for mining was recorded September 27, 1853, in Placer County Records, I (p. 183).

McLeans: Bar, Ferry [Calaveras, Tuolumne]. Near the confluence of Coyote Creek and Stanislaus River, about one mile above Robinsons Ferry. Shown on Gibbes' map of 1851 and on later maps, sometimes spelled McLanes and McLains. The place is mentioned by diarists of 1849 and 1850: Harvey Wood (p. 21); Borthwick (p. 358); Bachman, February 4, 1850; in the Stockton *San Joaquin Republican*, June 11, 1853; and by Heckendorn in 1856. The ferry was established in the spring of 1849 by George McLean and was one of the first ferries, if not the first, on the upper Stanislaus River. It was also known as Upper Ferry. (De Ferrari, *in* Jolly's *Gold Spring Diary*, p. 60.)

Mad Canyon Diggings [Placer]. A tributary to the Middle Fork of American River, west of Michigan Bluff. Mad Canyon is shown on Bowman's map, 1873. It is mentioned in the Sacramento *Daily Transcript*, March 15, 1851; by Patterson, p. 72) and in Hittell's roster. Hutchings lists Mad Cañon as a town in 1855. Remarkable successes were reported in 1861 (*Mining Press*, August 31, 1861). The mines in the canyon are listed in Mining Bureau reports until 1936.

Madison Mine [Calaveras]. *See* Angels Camp.

Mad Mule Canyon [Shasta]. On Whiskey Creek, north of Whiskeytown. The California State Census of 1852 lists Mad

Mule Canon as one of the nine principal mining localities of the county. The place is mentioned by Helper (p. 151) and by Pringle Shaw (p. 128) as one of the important diggings of 1855. A beautiful nugget of crystalized gold, found in the Banghart Mine, was exhibited in the Paris Exposition of 1878 (*Mining Bureau*, II, part 1, p. 149). A consolidated mine operated until 1940, and is estimated to have produced more than a million dollars (*Mining Bureau*, XXIX, p. 35). Mad Mule Gulch is shown on the USGS Weaverville 1942 quadrangle.

Mad Ox Ravine [Shasta]. On Whiskey Creek, in the district of Mad Mule Canyon. The State Census of 1852 lists Mad Ox Cañon as one of the nine principal mining localities of the county. Mad Ox Ravine is mentioned by Helper in 1855, and by Shaw as an important Shasta County mining camp in 1856. According to items in Bancroft Notes (Shasta *Courier*, October, 1852, and San Francisco *Bulletin*, February 12, 1856) large nuggets up to forty-four ounces had been found here. The Mad Ox Mine was idle after 1911 (*Mining Bureau*, XIV, p. 791), but it is still listed in 1933 under Maddox Mining Company (*ibid.*, XXIX, p. 35). Mad Ox Gulch is shown on the USGS Weaverville 1942 quadrangle.

Magalia [Butte]. On the West Branch of the North Fork of Feather River, about five miles northeast of Paradise. The camp was formerly called Mountain View and Dogtown, and the post office was Butte Mills from 1857 to 1861. For the derivation of the name, see *California Place Names*. It was the center of extensive drift mining. Several large nuggets worth more than one thousand dollars each were discovered in the vicinity in the late 1850s and early 1860s, one of which, the Magalia or Dogtown nugget, netted more than 10 thousand dollars. (*Mining Bureau*, XV, pp. 198 ff.; II, part 1, p. 149.) See Dogtown. The Magalia or Perschbaker Mine, about three miles north of the town, was discovered in 1855 and is estimated to have produced more than a million dollars by the end of the century. It is described in *Mining Bureau*, XXVI, (pp. 398 ff.). In 1945 it was prospected and in 1947 was reported idle (*Mining Bureau*, XLV, pp. 428 f.). For other mines in the productive Magalia District, *see* the list and sketch map in *Bulletin*, 193 (p. 88) and the *Consolidated Index*. The district is reported to have yielded 40 million dollars, an exag-

gerated figure, according to William B. Clark, author of the *Bulletin* cited above.

Magnolia [El Dorado]. On the north side of the South Fork of American River, at the mouth of Greenwood Creek; three miles below Uniontown. Magnolia Ranch is shown on Doolittle's map, 1868. It is mentioned in the El Dorado County Records, Deed Book E. (p. 35 and p. 234), September 8, 1853. The camp is mentioned by Stephen Wing, March 2, 1855 (Journal, II, p. 28). A consolidated mine is listed in the *Register*, 1902. The place is shown on the USGS Placerville 1931 quadrangle.

Mahala Flat [Amador]. On the South Fork of Sutter Creek, southeast of Volcano. The place is shown on the County Map of 1866, and is mentioned in the County History, 1881 (p. 208). A hydraulic mine of 1856 paid wages until about 1868 (Browne, p. 73). The word Mahala is the Indian name for a dwarf ceanothus known as squaw's carpet (Hodge, p. 786), but the name is found repeatedly in old diaries with the meaning "squaw." There was a Mahala Mine in Calaveras County.

Mahoney Mine [Amador]. *See* Lincoln Consolidated Mine.

Main Bar [El Dorado]. *See* Maine Bar.

Maine Bar [El Dorado]. On the Middle Fork of American River, about five miles above the junction, between Green Mountain and Poverty bars. Shown on Doolittle's map, 1868, and on Bowman's map, 1873. According to an item in the San Francisco *Bulletin*, September 10, 1857, it had "the largest fluming operations going on within the state" (Bancroft Notes). The name is often spelled Main, as on Doolittle's map.

Maine Boys [Tuolumne]. In the Table Mountain district. It is mentioned by Heckendorn in 1856 (p. 104). According to Browne (p. 41), a tunnel built at the expense of 120 thousand dollars yielded only a little profit. But in 1871 Raymond, IV (p. 64) gives an optimistic account of the old Maine Boys ground. The Maine Boys claim in Columbia Gulch in the town of Columbia is reported to have paid eleven and a half pounds of gold in four days in October, 1853, equivalent to about 250 dollars to the man (Columbia *Gazette*, October 15, 1853).

Main Gulch [Tuolumne]. In the town of Columbia, and originally called Columbia Gulch. It extends from Saint Anne's Church to Jackson Street. The gulch was one of the richest "in the country." Several companies had sunk shafts to a depth of forty feet. One company averaged at least a half pound a day for a period of six weeks in March and April of 1853; another one was making around twenty dollars a day to the hand; others were not doing so well (Columbia *Gazette*, April 9, 1853). In 1854 one company took 23.5 ounces of dust in one day (Columbia *Gazette*, June 17, 1854). These are a few examples of local newspaper accounts of the day. The most important early claims in the gulch and nearby were perhaps the following: between the bridges — the Tiger claim, probably the best paying; the Columbia; the Luddy; the "Old Kennebec"; the Cascade (Windler Co.); "on the hill," the Smith; Portuguee Joe; the Cascade; the Tom Daly; the Bonnell; the Cannonade. Other early important claims in the gulch were the Maine Boys or "Old Hildreth," and the Pat Smith. The Cascade Claim reportedly took out sixty-three ounces as a result of one week's labor (Columbia *News*, August 26, 1858) and in May of 1860 took out $540.50 in one week (Columbia *Times*, June 7, 1860). The same company had been sued by the county in 1857 for having destroyed the road in its mining activities (*Weekly Columbian*, May 16, 1857). The Columbia claim, between the Cascade and the Tiger, cleaned up about 350 dollars in one week in June of 1862 (*Alta*, June 12, 1862). Information about these claims and numerous others may be found in the Eastman file.

Main Hill [Placer]. On the Iowa Hill Divide. The hill was apparently named after a drift mine called State of Maine Mine. The County History, 1882 (p. 216), lists the mines on the hill.

Maintop [Placer]. At the head of Volcano Canyon, northeast of Michigan Bluff. The camp is shown on Goddard's map, 1857.

Maith Creek [El Dorado]. It is mentioned as being near Diamond Springs by Crockett (p. 95) in 1858 or 1859. It may be the same as Matheneys Creek.

Malakoff District [Nevada]. West of North Bloomfield. The Malakoff Mine was one of the richest and best known mines, named after Malakoff Tower near Sebastopol during the Crimean War. The great tunnel was constructed along new lines in the 1850s by the hydraulic engineer, Hamilton Smith (J. W. Johnson, p. 201). Newton Miller, about 1865, was instrumental in making the first industrial use of the electric arc lamp here (Miller's letters). The *Nevada Directory*, 1895 (p. 115), gives the production of the Malakoff mine at 5 mil-

lion dollars, probably before the prohibition of hydraulic mining brought about by the Sawyer decision of 1884. Lindgren, however, gives the figure to 1900 at about 3.5 million dollars (*Professional Paper*, No. 73, p. 139). Pictures of the mine, which is more than 7,000 feet long, 3,000 feet wide, and as deep as 600 feet, are found in *Mining Bureau*, XXIII (p. 108) and *Bulletin*, 193 (p. 101).

Malay Camp [Yuba]. On the main Yuba River, north of Smartsville, opposite the mouth of Deer Creek. Shown on Wescoatt's map, 1861, and on the County Map, 1879. "A number of Malays" were working here in the early days (Co. Hist., 1879, p. 88).

Malcomb Bar [El Dorado]. On the upper Middle Fork of American River, below Gray Eagle Bar. Shown as Malcomb Cut on Doolittle's map, 1868, and as Malcomb Bar on Bowman's map, 1873.

Maloneys, Meloneys [Calaveras]. On the Stanislaus River, about two miles south of the town of Carson Hill. The place was found mentioned in two early newspapers. The *Alta*, June 16, 1851, reports a fight at Meloney's Diggings, in which several Americans and Mexicans were killed. The correspondent "Mountaineer" reports in the Stockton *San Juaquin Republican*, June 11, 1853, that Maloney's is only a site "excepting a few shanties inhabited by a few Mexicans." But he adds, "those hill-sides will pay to sluice, and I would not be at all surprised to see within a year a thrifty place spring up in this vicinity." Here we might have the origin of the famous diggings Melones. *See* Melones.

Maltmans [Nevada]. Between Nevada City and Gold Flat. Shown on Doolittle's map, 1868. It was the site of the Maltman Sulphuret Reduction Works, built in 1858 and operated by Oscar Maltman and G. F. Deetken. The first practical attempt to reduce auriferous sulfurets by the chlorinizing process was made here and by 1867 it was the largest of its kind in the county, the profits contributing greatly to the success of quartz mining in that area. *See* Hillsburg.

Malvina Mines [Mariposa]. *See* Coulterville.

Mameluke Hill [El Dorado]. In Oregon Canyon, on the Georgetown Divide. Shown on Doolittle's map, 1868. The hill diggings were discovered in 1851 by two miners, Klepstein and Keiser (Co. Hist., 1883, p. 191). They were apparently Germans, and this may account for the name. The corps of the Mamelukes was well known and feared in Germany during the Napoleonic wars. According to Patterson (pp. 41, 52), who prospected around Georgetown from 1850 to 1862, a quartz vein, only one foot wide but rich in gold, ran through the hill. The name is spelled Marmeluke Hill by De Long, March 2, 1854. On March 25, 1855 twelve pounds of pure gold were taken out of one claim, according to Hutchings (Diary, May 12, 1855). In 1874 there were still rich gravel diggings (Raymond, VII, pp. 91, 95). The Mameluke Mine is listed in Mining Bureau reports until the 1930s.

Mammoth [Plumas]. On Jamison Creek, a tributary to the Middle Fork of Feather River. A camp, or only a mine, is shown on Goddard's map, 1857.

Mammoth Bar [Mariposa]. Near Horseshoe Bend of Merced River. The bar is mentioned by Eccleston, October 20, 1850.

Mammoth Bar [Placer]. On the Middle Fork of American River, two and a half miles above the junction with the North Fork, below Kennebec Bar. A wire suspension bridge was built across the river to a point below Mammoth Bar, according to May Perry (*Placer Nuggets*, February 1, 1963. Doolittle's map, 1868, shows a wire sus-

Malakoff Diggings, Nevada Co.

pension at about this point. It was a rich bar, according to May Perry, and was worked successfully by Colonel W. S. Davis between 1879 and 1889, and by Howard Davis as late as 1900. The bar is also mentioned in the Placer County History, 1882 (p. 401). Shown on the USGS Auburn 1954 quadrangle.

Mammoth: City, District [Mono]. About fifty miles south of Bridgeport, near Mammoth Lake. Gold was discovered here in 1877, reportedly by miners who were looking for the so-called Lost Cement Mine. In 1878 the Mammoth Mining Company was formed to operate the Mammoth Mine, which took its name from the huge outcroppings. The district was called Lake District and sometimes Mammoth District. Headquarters were in the camp which quickly developed and was called Mammoth City. A post office was established in 1879, and the same year the population of Mammoth City and nearby Pine City was estimated at 1,500. A 20-stamp mill was erected in 1878 at neighboring Mill City and another twenty stamps were added the next year. Other mines were the Headlight, Monte Cristo, and Lisbon. By 1881 the Mammoth Mine had produced 200 thousand dollars, but expenses exceeded earnings, and the mine was closed. By 1888 only a half dozen prospectors were left. (*Mining Bureau*, VIII, pp. 373 ff.) There was again some mining in the district in the late 1890s and early 1900s, and later in the 1930s, according to *Bulletin*, 193 (p. 88). Between 1954 and 1958 the Beauregard Mine was in operation. The region is now a popular resort area.

Manhattan Bar [Placer]. Above Lacys Bar, near the confluence of the North and Middle forks of American River. Shown on Jackson's map, 1850. The Manhattan Company of New York built a canal and dam in 1849 as part of a well financed enterprise, which failed. The valuable quicksilver machines were soon abandoned for the common rocker, and the undertaking was given up in the fall (Letts, p. 113). Claims were later reported as all paying well, according to a newspaper account of October 6, 1856 (Co. Hist., 1882, p. 227). It was listed as a town by Hutchings in 1855. Manhattan Camp, on the North Fork, is mentioned in a letter of Jonas Winchester to this brother, dated October 24, 1849 (Winchester Papers, California State Library, California Section).

Manhattan: Canyon, Creek [El Dorado]. South of Georgetown. The *Alta*, March 6, 1853, reprints a report that miners earned five to eight dollars a day — a scant profit compared to other camps nearby. Stephen Wing and a partner laid a claim in a flat on the east side of the creek on November 25, 1855 (Journal, II, p. 19). *Mining Bureau*, II (part 1, p. 150) tells of the discovery of a nugget which coined 1,166 dollars in 1857, and W. T. Russell in his "Chispas" (p. 60) claims that one thousand dollars worth of gold was sluiced out of a boulder in the creek in 1885. According to Raymond, VII (p. 83), there was some hydraulic seam mining in the region in 1874. Manhattan Creek is shown on the USGS Placerville 1931 quadrangle.

Mankinsville [Shasta]. On Churn Creek, one and a half miles below Churntown. Hutchings found a boarding house and seven cabins, and poor diggings (Diary, December 27, 1855).

Mansanita [Calaveras]. Near Knights Ferry. The place is mentioned by Heckendorn (p. 104) in 1856. The name is probably a different spelling of manzanita the name of the common shrub, which was often used in the designation of mines and claims. But the Manzanita Mine in Calaveras County, often recorded in the reports of the Mining Bureau, was apparently not at this site.

Manvel [San Bernardino]. On the former railroad from Goffs to Ivanpah. It was a trading center and from 1893 to 1907 the post office for the gold and silver mines of the New York and the Ivanpah mountains. The mines are listed and mapped in the *Register*, 1902. The town was named for Allen Manvel, president of the Atlantic and Pacific Railroad, and was changed in 1907 to Barnwell by the Santa Fe Railroad (Haenszel).

Manzanita Bar [Siskiyou]. On the Klamath River, between Humbug Creek and Scott River. There are no early records, but *Mining Bureau*, XIV (p. 843), reports the Manzanita Bar Mine as the richest mine along this section of the river in 1913.

Manzanita Bar [Trinity]. On Trinity River, near Big Bar. Shown on Bancroft's Map of the Northern Mines. It was settled by five Oregonians in 1849. In 1854 a race six and a half miles long was built from Manzanita Creek, but apparently the diggings soon gave out. A full account, including the dramatic suicide of an Indian squaw, is given in Cox (pp. 76 ff.). Manzanita Creek is shown on the USGS Big Bar 1930 quadrangle. *See* Big Bar.

Manzanita Hill [Nevada]. In Bridgeport township, north of Sweetland, at the southern end of the body of gravel extending between Sweetland Creek and Kent Ravine near San Juan. Newton Miller made his home in this vicinity. In 1867 Sebastopol is mentioned in *Bean's Directory* as the residence of miners on Manzanita Hill and Junction Bluff. In 1868 Browne (p. 120) stated that McKeeley and Company claims, which yielded about 369 thousand dollars between 1855 and 1864, were worked out, but others were still active. In 1879 Pettee describes the gravel deposits and the extent of hydraulic mining (Whitney, *Auriferous Gravels*, pp. 385 ff.). A picture of the Manzanita Hydraulic Mine and description of the area is given in Lindgren, 1911 (pp. 20, 123). After the prohibition of hydraulic mining, the mine was given a permit for using the process by the United States Debris Commission in 1884 (*Mining Bureau*, XII, p. 14).

Manzanita Hill [Nevada]. On the ancient river channel which crosses the ridge east of the Sugar Loaf, about one mile north of Nevada City. The diggings were located in 1852 and proved highly profitable, according to *Bean's History* (p. 131). In 1856 one company blasted a tunnel and another built an elevator, unique at that time (Hittell Clippings, p. 67). By 1867 the estimated production of the claims, together with several to the north on the same channel, all within a distance of a little more than 3,000 feet, was more than 3 million dollars, according to Bean. The reports of the Mining Bureau (XI, p. 298; XVI, Nevada, p. 39) indicate that the production may have been 1.5 million by hydraulic mining and 3.5 million by drifting, and that work was carried on as late as 1894. Pettee, in 1870, describes in detail the operations of the Maltman claim, with sluices more than one mile long and a bedrock tunnel 2,400 feet long then under construction (Whitney, *Auriferous Gravels*, p. 189 f.).

Manzanita Hill [Nevada]. Between Steep Hollow Creek and Bear River; below Little York. The Hill is described by Pettee as the highest point on the ridge below Christmas Hill (Whitney, *Auriferous Gravels*, pp. 157 ff.). A large part of the gravel area is indicated on Pettee and Bowman's map, 1879, as "more or less completely hydraulicked away."

Marble Bar [El Dorado]. On the south side of the Middle Fork of American River, seven miles above the mouth. Recorded on Trask's map, 1853.

Marble Canyon [Inyo]. Near Big Pine. A nugget of nine ounces, the size of a lemon, was picked up as late as 1938 (*Desert Magazine*, October, 1938).

Marble Springs [Calaveras]. On Hanselman Hill, near Angels Camp. Shown on Goddard's map, 1857. The modern mines are recorded on *Guidebook* map 3. *See* Hanselman Hill.

Marble Springs [Mariposa]. On the North Fork of Merced River, east of Coulterville and south of Bower Cave. Shown on Trask's map, 1853, and on Goddard's, 1857. The deposits were discovered in 1851. They contained coarse gold in bluish quartz (Browne, p. 32). According to a letter dated May 3, 1856, in the *German Journal*, the discovery disproved the belief that no gold could be found near limestone rock. The gold contained twenty to thirty percent silver (Hittell Clippings, p. 53). It is said that the first mill of the state, with wooden stamps to be sure, was erected here, but the owner soon found the enterprise unprofitable. Mining was reactivated from time to time, and the place is listed and described until 1957 (*Mining Bureau*, XVII, p. 123; LIII, pp. 126 ff.). Hutchings listed it as a town in 1855. Shown on the USGS Buckhorn Peak 1949 quadrangle.

Marigold [Yuba]. South of the main Yuba River, about ten miles east of Marysville. It was a dredger town, which developed in the early 1900s at the site of the nineteenth century town of Martins. The name Marigold is supposed to be a contraction of the name of the *Marysville Gold* Mining Company. The company was later absorbed by the firm operating at nearby Hammonton to form the Yuba Consolidated Gold Fields. *See* Hammonton. (Ramey; Marysville *Appeal*, September 12 and December 19, 1905.)

Marion: Flat, Ravine [Plumas]. On the North Fork of Feather River, three miles below Big Meadows. The Flat is shown on the von Leicht-Craven map, 1874. Verne Richards refers to it as a "significant settlement" in a letter printed in *Plumas County Historical Society Publication*, No. 11, April, 1963.

Mariposa: Creek, City [Mariposa]. Near the southern terminus of Highway 49; also on Highway 140, about halfway between Merced and Yosemite Valley. James H. Carson (pp. 9 f.) claimed he discovered gold along Mariposa Creek early in the spring of 1849. This apparently gave rise to the assumption that Kit Carson had discovered gold here (*Guidebook*, p. 35; Coy, p. 57; *U. S. Bull.*, 424, p. 154; *Mining Bureau*, LIII, p. 128). Probably neither James nor Kit Carson had anything to do with the real discovery (*see* Carsons). The presence of gold in the region was doubtless known to Mexicans in 1848, and if we need a "discoverer," it was very likely Alex Godey in 1849 when he prospected the streams on Frémont's Mariposas grant. *See* Crampton (p. 38). There are numerous contemporary accounts of the digging on the Creek and in the camp: Christman (pp. 129–148) in April and May, 1850; Pancoast (pp. 287–293) in the spring of 1850; Eccleston (October 20, 1850); Rodney Odall (November 25, 1850). Eccleston mined here again with good success in the summer and fall of 1851, after his return from the Mariposa War, and he gives a detailed account including the daily profits. Other lengthy accounts are given by McIsaac, who mined here in 1852–53, and by Allsop, an observant Englishman, who mined in the district, 1851–1852. In October, 1849, a steam-driven quartz mill was in full operation (Eccleston) and perhaps the first in the state. Before Frémont started his operations, the squatters on his grant reportedly had taken out 200 thousand dollars worth of gold (Browne, p. 28). A post office was established on July 28, 1851, and on November 10 of the same year, the county seat was moved from Agua Fria. The camp is described in *Transactions*, 1859 (p. 92) as "strictly a mining town" with 500 inhabitants. Before Frémont sold the

Mariposa City, Mariposa Co.

town of Mariposa to J. F. "Quartz" Johnson in July, 1859, four streets were named Jessie, Charles, Bullion ("Old Bullion," the nickname of Frémont's father-in-law), and Jones, Frémont's brother-in-law (Pancoast). Bancroft, VI, gives many references which pertain to the rich yield around Mariposa in 1856. The Mariposa Mine of 1849, southeast of the town, was still in operation in 1955 and has alone produced almost 2.5 million dollars (*Mining Bureau*, LIII, p. 60). In recent times there has also been extensive placer mining with a drag line (*U. S. Bull.*, No. 424, p. 158).

Mariposa Grant [Mariposa]. The story and a detailed map of Frémont's Grant on Las Mariposas Rancho, a 44,500-acre "claim," appears in *Mining Bureau*, XXIV (pp. 97 ff.). *See also* Crampton. Situated on the grant were Mariposa, Bridgeport, Guadalupe, Arkansas Flat, Upper and Lower Agua Fria, Princeton, Mount Ophir, Bear Valley, Pine Tree and Josephine mines, Benton Mills, French Camp, Mormon Bar.

Mariposita [Mariposa]. On Mariposa Creek. Allsop was here January 28 and October 27, 1852. He calls it a rich "colony of Gauls and Mexicans." In the summer of the same year an attempt was made to drive out the French and Mexicans (*CHSQ*, XXXV, p. 318).

Marks Bar [Plumas, or Butte]. On the north side of the Middle Fork of Feather River, eleven miles above the junction with the South Fork. The bar is shown on Trask's map, 1853.

Marlette [Amador]. Near the North Fork of Mokelumne River. Marlette Mines, then still in Calaveras County, are mentioned by Ayers (p. 45) in 1849. They were rich, but had a high overhead layer. Browne (p. 74) mentions a 10-stamp mill as idle in 1866. An active Marlette Mine in 1886 is listed in *Mining Bureau*, VI (part 2, p. 22).

Marlows Camp [Tuolumne]. Between the North Fork of Tuolumne River and Turnback Creek. It is mentioned in the Bodie *Morning News*, November 6, 1879 as a camp of the late 1850s.

Marmeluke Hill [El Dorado]. *See* Mameluke Hill.

Marshall [El Dorado]. *See* Lotus and Union Town II.

Marshall Ravine [El Dorado]. About eight miles northeast of Georgetown, near Kentucky Flat. It is a short ravine that empties into Otter Creek. According to Warren T. Russell (p. 4), James Marshall, the discoverer of gold at Sutters Mill, built a cabin at the head of the ravine (later the site of the Tiedemann Mine, several miles south of Kentucky Flat) and mined there a short time, probably after he had sold his interest in the Marshall Ditch in 1868. He was still living there between 1872 and 1876. *See* Sardine Diggings. Theressa Gay (p. 309) indicates that Marshall had come to the Otter Creek mining area sometime during the year 1853. Marshalls Cañ. is shown on Doolittle's map, 1868.

Marshalls Bar [El Dorado]. Indistinctly marked on Butler's map, 1851, at the confluence of the North and Middle forks of American River.

Marsh Creek [Contra Costa]. A tributary to the San Joaquin River, which heads east and south of Mount Diablo. Named for John Marsh, the foremost pioneer since 1839 in the Mount Diablo district. The Antioch *Ledger* (June 17, 1871) and other papers reported the discovery of paying gold deposits along the Creek. The excitement was *very* short-lived.

Marsh Diggings [Yuba]. *See* Parks Bar.

Martell [Amador]. On Highway 49, north of Jackson. It was probably named for Louis Martell, a Canadian and before 1866 a resident of Jackson. Later it became a lumber town. Northeast of the town was the Oneida Mine, a rich lode mine with a 250-foot shaft, averaging forty dollars a ton in the 1860s. The total production was more than 2.5 million dollars. It was closed in 1913. (*Guidebook*, p. 64.) *See* Oneida Mine. South of the place was the even richer Argonaut Mine, listed separately.

Martinez [Tuolumne]. Southeast of Columbia, a short distance north of Shaws Flat. The name is also spelled Martinas. Stoddart (pp. 128, 144) states that the "Spanish" camp was named for a Mexican lady who brought in a large number of peons to work for her. According to *Mines and Minerals* (p. 357), a nugget worth 2,750 dollars was found in 1853. Thompson and Company paid between ten dollars and one ounce a day to the man (*San Joaquin Republican*, May 27, 1855) and Cervantes likewise paid good wages. In *Ghost Towns* it is stated that the great Murieta is said to have lived here for some time, hiding from his pursuers and poisoning wells as a pastime. The book even gives a picture of the site of his cabin. The place is shown on the USGS Columbia 1948 quadrangle.

Martinez Creek [El Dorado]. A tributary to the North Fork of Cosumnes River. It was an important center of quartz mines, including the rich Union and Church mines. *See* Uniontown I.

Martinez Hill [Mono]. One of the hills surrounding Aurora. The *Mining Press*, October 19, 1861, reports extensive lodes of gold and silver-bearing quartz "equal to any in the district." Other rich leads around Aurora were in the Middle and Last Chance hills.

Martin House [Yuba]. About two miles southwest of Oregon House, on the road from Fosters Bar to Marysville. Shown on Doolittle's map, 1868. It is mentioned by William B. Meek, stage driver (p. 155).

Martins [Yuba]. South of the main Yuba River, about ten miles east of Marysville. Shown on Wescoatt's map, 1861. It was established by miners along the river at nearby Swiss Bar and existed later as a stage stop on the road between Marysville and Smartsville (Ramey). *See* Marigold.

Martins Bar [Calaveras]. On the Mokelumne River, six miles southwest of Volcano. Shown on the Amador County Map, 1866.

Martins: Bar, Flat [Trinity]. On Trinity River, one mile above Taylor Flat. A mine is listed in 1896 in *Mining Bureau*, XIII (p. 455).

Martinsville [Nevada]. On the Middle Fork of Yuba River, where Rideout and Company were given a license to build a toll footbridge in August, 1850. It is probably the same as Martinville, mentioned in the Sacramento *Union*, September 4, 1851.

Marvin Ledge [Nevada]. Near Washington. It is mentioned as a settlement in *Bean's Directory*, 1867 (p. 386).

Mary Harrison Group [Mariposa]. *See* Coulterville.

Marysville [Sierra]. *See* Downieville.

Marysville [Trinity]. In the New River Mines district, three fourths of a mile from New River City. In the 1880s it was a rival town site with White Rock City, a half mile north, and with New River City. Shown on a map of New River Mines, by N. Wescoatt, printed in *Mining Press*, January 24, 1885 (p. 53). *See* New River. According to Florence E. Morris (*Trinity*, 1970), it was named in memory of the daughter of Mr. and Mrs. Peter Larcine, who operated a hotel there.

Marysville [Yuba]. The city was never a mining town, but it was the important metropolis of the Feather and Yuba river mines. The Sacramento *Transcript*, September 30, 1850 (steamer ed.) reports an unsuccessful attempt at dredging in the Yuba above Marysville. The Marysville

Herald in 1850–1851 tells of several projects including the *Phoenix*, which was a small boat rigged as a dredger and equipped with an amalgamator and given up as a failure after reaching Ousleys Bar in April, 1851. The entrepreneurs and capitalists of Marysville then turned their attention to quartz mining at Brownsville and other places in upper Yuba County. (Ramey.) John Rollins Ridge, author of the often reprinted yarn about Joaquin Murieta, worked as a county official in Marysville in 1853, when Captain Harry Love claimed the killing of the elusive Joaquin.

Marysville Buttes [Sutter]. *See* Sutters Buttes.

Masonic Bar [Siskiyou]. On Klamath River, two miles west of Seiad. It is mentioned in the County History, 1881 (p. 217). There was some mining in the "early days," and later mainly farming (*Mining Bureau*, XXI, p. 477). The mining was carried on largely by Chinese, according to *Siskiyou Pioneer*, II:10 (p. 30).

Masonic: District, town [Mono]. About twelve miles northeast of Bridgeport and about two miles from the Nevada state border. In 1862 a group of Masons from Aurora came to the region to prospect for gold, according to Maule (p. 27); hence, the name. There was, however, little mining until 1902, when the Pittsburg-Liberty Mine was located. It operated until 1910, producing around 700 thousand dollars, and in the 1920s it was apparently again reactivated. Among other mines in the district were the Serita, which produced about 500 thousand dollars and the Chemung, which was still operating in the 1940s. Descriptions of the mines are given in *Mining Bureau* (XV, p. 160, XVIII, pp. 415 f.) and *Bulletin*, 193 (p. 150). There was a post office at the town of Masonic between 1906 and 1927. Shown on the USGS Bridgeport 1958 quadrangle.

Massachusetts Bar [Placer]. On the North Fork of American River, shown on Trask's map, 1853, opposite Mineral Bar. A claim adjacent to the bar is recorded August 25, 1851, in the Placer County Records, I (p. 5).

Massachusetts Flat [El Dorado]. Between Condemned Bar and Negro Hill, near the confluence of the North and South forks of American River. Shown on Doolittle's map, 1868. According to the County History, 1883 (p. 202), it was opened in 1854 and paid well. Newton Miller in a letter dated May 28, 1854, states that many claims were paying "remarkably well"

there and that an English boy had taken out 800 dollars in two weeks. In 1855 it was a "thriving little town," and the population was mostly Portuguese and Negroes (Hutchings, Diary, April 24, 1855). Raymond, VII (pp. 91 and 96) refers to Massachusetts Flat and Negro Hill as the principal gravel mines of the Georgetown Divide, which had yielded richly in the past and were still yielding small amounts in 1874.

Massachusetts Hill [Nevada]. Southwest of Grass Valley. Situated on the same lode as Gold Hill. This lode is said to have produced five million dollars by 1865 (Cronise, p. 580). The first quartz was discovered at Massachusetts Hill early in January, 1850, and the same year two Germans built the first rude mill. (Bean, pp. 206 ff. and 228.) The deposits are mentioned by Schaeffer (p. 131). They were not as rich as those of Gold Hill. The *Mining Press*, May 8, 1862, reports that four men took out nearly 6 thousand dollars in six days from the Black Ledge on Massachusetts Hill. Several mines were still working with moderate success in 1867 and the Ben Franklin Mine on the south side of the hill yielded ninety dollars per ton in 1867 (Bean, p. 228). Raymond, VI (p. 118) lists the mines around the hill as idle in 1873. A renewal was attempted in 1896 (*Mining Bureau*, XIII, p. 251).

Matelot Gulch [Tuolumne]. Extends north from Columbia to Matelot Reservoir. The name also appears as Matloe, Matlock, and Matchlock. Since *matelot* is the French word for sailor, it may be assumed that French miners first mined here. Newspapers brought reports of rich diggings. One company struck a new lead and made 100 dollars in seven hours (San Francisco *Evening News*, June 14, 1854). Aiken and Company averaged six ounces per day and one Saturday took out twenty-three ounces (Sacramento *Union*, February 27, 1855); Stagman-Cunningham averaged ten to twenty dollars a day to the man (*San Joaquin Republican*, May 27, 1855); Porter paid seven dollars a day to the man (Sacramento *Union*, May 14, 1855). The place is mentioned in the letters of Charles W. Thompson in 1859 and reported as doing tolerably well. But in 1861 it was worked out because of the delay of the completion of the Columbia Gulch flume (*Mining Press*, November 23, 1861). Shown on the USGS Columbia 1948 quadrangle.

Matheneys; Creek, Diggings [El Dorado]. The diggings beside the creek are now within the city limits of El Dorado. They are mentioned as rich diggings by E. D. Perkins on December 25, 1849. They are also listed as a gold camp in the County History, 1883 (p. 203). The U. S. Bureau of the Census lists the names of 672 inhabitants on Mathinias (or Mathines) Creek in the population schedule for 1850. A Mathines Creek Mine is described in 1888 in *Mining Bureau*, VIII (p. 190), and it is still listed in 1916, though idle. The creek, a tributary to the North Fork of Cosumnes River, is shown on Doolittle's map, 1868, as Mathenas Creek. *See* Maith Creek.

Matheus [Nevada]. About three miles southeast of the junction of Deer Creek with Yuba River. Shown on Milleson and Adams' map, 1851.

Mathinas, Mathines, or Mathinias Creek [El Dorado]. *See* Matheneys Creek.

Matildaville [Nevada]. Near Blue Tent, on the road to Humbug. According to an article in the Nevada City *Transcript*, December 12, 1860 (quoted in Nevada County Historical Society *Bulletin*, June, 1952), it was a "brisk little mining village," named in honor of the first woman resident.

Matsells Creek [Mariposa]. *See* Maxwell Creek.

Maumee Placers [San Bernardino]. *See* Lava Bed District.

Maxwell Creek [Mariposa]. An intermittent stream which empties into Horseshoe Bend of Merced River. Shown on Trask's map, 1853, and Goddard's, 1857. The diggings were on both sides of Coulterville. The creek was named for George Maxwell (or Matsell), who mined here in 1849. Jim Savage mined here with his Indian relatives in 1849–1850 (Church, p. 184). Eccleston gives a good account of mining between the Tuolumne and Merced rivers in his diaries of October, 1850. In 1852 the average yield of placering was between fifteen and twenty dollars per day to the man (Browne, p. 20). A post office was established November 20, 1852; in 1872 the name was changed to Coulterville. For an account of lode mining here, *see* Coulterville.

Maybert [Nevada]. On the South Fork of Yuba River, five miles east of Washington. The *Nevada Directory*, 1895, lists the mines operating at that time, and the *Register* of 1900 lists a large stamp mill. The chief mine, the Eagle Bird (Diamond Creek Consolidated) operated intermittently from "early days" to 1934. There were several locations, extending from the South Fork of Yuba River to beyond the summit of the ridge in the direction of Bear Valley. A good description may be found in *Mining Bureau*, XII (p. 188) and XVI (Nevada, pp. 152 f.). Maybert and Eagle Bird are shown on the Economic Geology sheet of the USGS *Geologic Atlas*, no. 66 (Colfax Folio).

Mayflower Mine [Placer]. *See* Forest Hill.

May Lundy Mine [Mono]. *See* Lundy.

Mazourka Canyon [Inyo]. On the west slope of Inyo Mountains, northeast of Independence. There has been both lode and placer mining in the canyon and the area west of it (De Decker, p. 46). *See* Pops Gulch; Santa Rita Flat; Tibbetts District.

Mc alphabetized as Mac.

Meadow Flat [El Dorado]. The place is listed by Coy (p. 45) as being on the same tributary to an ancient river bed as Indian Diggings and Grizzly Flat.

Meadow Lake; Meadow Lake: City, Mining District [Nevada]. Practically at the summit of the Sierra crest, eight miles north of Cisco. It was the highest (7,100 feet) and one of the most interesting gold mining districts. Shown on Sierra County Map, 1874. The deposits were discovered in 1863 when gold mining in California was already on the downgrade. In 1858 the well-known Yuba Canal Company built a 300-yard stone wall across a little stream rising at 39° 25' latitude to supply water for the lower country. In June, 1863, Henry Hartley, an Englishman seeking health in the high mountains, noticed a number of ledges near the lake. He returned in August with two parties, discovered rich gold deposits, and formed the Excelsior Company. In 1865 the news reached the miners and a belated gold rush started. The newspapers of 1864 and 1865 are filled with contradictory reports. A post office was established, June 25, 1866, and the "city," first called Summit City (shown on Plumas County Map, 1886), had about 5,000 inhabitants, a bank, a stock exchange, a church, a brewery, two theaters, thirteen hotels, and the usual assortment of restaurants and hurdy gurdy houses. Good accounts of the palmy days are given by Wooster (pp. 149 ff.) in retrospect; Bean (pp. 305 ff.) in 1867, and in the *Overland Monthly*, November, 1874 (pp. 430 ff.). Browne (pp. 136 ff.) reported in 1868 that the sulfurets yielded by assay sixty to seventy dollars worth of gold per ton. Yet, the town never developed beyond the initial onslaught. The post office was discontinued September

20, 1869, and in 1872 the town was dead. The *Register* of 1900 still lists one stamp mill in operation. The best brief modern account is in *Mining Bureau*, XXXII (pp. 191 ff.), and a detailed and thorough account is given in the recently published monograph *Meadow Lake*, by Paul Fatout. Today all traces of the existence of the "city" are gone, except the usual debris. The site of the camp and Hartley Butte, honoring the discoverer are shown on the USGS Emigrant Gap 1955 quadrangle.

Meadow Valley [Plumas]. About seven miles west of Quincy and two miles south of Spanish Ranch. The settlement was a trading center and from 1855 the post office for numerous mines in the vicinity. In 1864 a correspondent of the Sacramento *Union* (Hayes Scrapbooks: Mining, IV, sec. 15) describes the place as being "once a notable distributing point to the rich placers which surrounded it, with a well-built town . . . now reduced to one store." The geology of the region is described in Raymond, V (pp. 119 ff.), *Bulletin*, 92 (p. 109), and in *Mining Bureau*, X (p. 485). The valley is shown on the USGS Bidwell Bar 1944 quadrangle. Spanish Ranch and Meadow Valley are Historic Landmark 481.

Meads Bar [Siskiyou]. On the Klamath River, below the mouth of Scott River. It is mentioned as an old bar in the County History, 1881 (p. 217).

Meeks Flat [Plumas]. On Nelson Creek. The County History, 1882 (p. 288), lists it as an important mining point along the creek.

Melbourne Hill [Nevada]. Less than a mile southwest of Remington Hill. Shown as a settlement on Doolittle's map, 1868. A small gravel deposit here is mentioned by Pettee in 1870 (Whitney, *Auriferous Gravels*, p. 175).

Mellens Camp [Los Angeles]. On the road to Tejon. According to the Los Angeles *Star*, March 28, 1862 (Hayes Scrapbooks: Mining, V, sec. 286), diggings were opened in the winter of 1862 but abandoned in the spring for lack of water. During the wet season "a great deal of gold" had been taken out.

Meloncitos [Calaveras]. The camp is situated at the foot of *Cerro de Melones*, the Mexican miners' name for Carson Hill, according to Vischer (p. 324).

Melones [Calaveras]. On the Stanislaus River, two miles north of Robinsons Ferry, and about two miles south of the town of Carson Hill. The name does not appear on early maps, but the *Alta*, June 16, 1851,

refers to Meloney's Diggings, and other newspapers refer to a Melones claim. Browne in 1867 (p. 59) states that after the discovery of the Morgan Mine at the summit of Carson Hill in 1850, the town of Melones on the south side of the hill became the largest mining camp in the state, with a population variously estimated from 3,000 to 4,000. Large scale mining was carried on at the Melones Mine between 1895 and 1918 (*Bull.*, 193, pp. 34 f.). It was then consolidated with the Morgan and Calaveras mines and was worked until 1926, and again between 1933 and 1942. The 100-stamp mill was in operation until it burned in 1942. *See* Morgan Ground; Carson Hill. In 1902 the name Melones was applied to the post office at Robinsons, formerly, Robinsons Ferry, on the Stanislaus River, two miles south of the site of the mining camp. In 1942 the post office was transferred to Angels Camp. The origin of the name Melones, which is still retained in the name Melones Reservoir, has not been determined. Edward Vischer in the summer of 1851 states that Carson Hill was called *el cerro de Melones* (hill of melons) and that there were several dry diggings called "Meloncitos" by Mexicans to differentiate them from the mountain (*CHSQ*, XI, p. 324). But Vischer does not explain the reason for the naming. Archie Stevenot, who was born at Carson Hill and later was the manager of the Melones Mine, claimed that his grandfather, Gabriel Stevenot, gave the name for the reason that the Mexican miners referred to the flakes of gold as *melones* because they looked like melon seeds (R. C. Woods). It has become a generally accepted theory that Mexicans found flakes of gold there in the shape of melon seeds. Gold flakes that resembled melon or cucumber seeds were actually found in various places in California (Browne, p. 51; Hittell, *Mining*, p. 46). This does not explain, however, why the Mexicans (or others) called a hill, or a camp Melones, which is the Spanish word for 'melons' not 'melon seeds'. It is quite possible that the place was named for a person (*California Place Names*). *See* Maloneys, Meloneys. There is a Melone family in Alamo and Saratoga, California, one of whose forbears came to the California mines in 1849, but there is no tangible evidence that he went to the Southern Mines, though there is a family tradition that he was connected with the camp Melones (Earl Melone and W. B. Melone). Another indication that the place may have been named for a person is the reference to a Melone family in Orange County, Virginia. In 1817 Susan Melone married John Robinson, and the two may have moved to California some time before or during the Gold Rush. In Calaveras County, about 1848, it is thought, John W. Robinson and Stephen Mead established Robinsons Ferry at the place also known as Melones. It is possible that John Robinson and Susan Melone Robinson have some connection with John W. Robinson of Robinsons Ferry, and also perhaps with a Mr. Melone who operated a saloon and trading post near the Ferry. Added to this, a claim was filed by the Melone's Consolidated Mining Company on August 8, 1879. These references do not prove that the camp Melones was named for a person, but they at least strengthen the case (De Ferrari, in *Chispa*, July–September, 1973, p. 435). *See* Maloneys, Meloneys; Robinsons Ferry.

Mendon [El Dorado]. This was the name of the post office for Brownsville from 1867 to 1888. Before and afterwards it was called Indian Diggings. The *Alta*, June 20, 1869, reports that one company had an eight-stamp mill and took out about fifty ounces per week. *See* Indian Diggins [El Dorado] and Brownsville [El Dorado].

Mendoza [Nevada]. In Meadow Lake District, near Enterprise. It is listed as a settlement in *Bean's Directory*, 1867. In 1866 it had a hotel, two restaurants, two stores, and a population of 500, but by 1880 not a house was standing (*Co. Hist.*, 1880, p. 196).

Menifee District [Riverside]. About eight miles south of Perris. It is a small district, which includes the Menifee, Lucky Boy, and Mammoth quartz mines. They were first worked in the early 1890s but were all reported idle by 1935. (*Mining Bureau*, XIII, p. 312; XXXI, p. 513 and *Bull.*, 193, p. 174.)

Menken Cut Bar [Eldorado]. Apparently on the Middle Fork of American River. It is mentioned in the County History, 1883 (p. 83).

Merced River Diggings [Mariposa]. Hiram Pierce mined here between April and September, 1850 with moderate success. In his excellent account of the area, he mentions Washington Flat, Harveys Bar, Horseshoe Bend, Maxwells Creek, Savages and Solomons Creek. Another good source of information about the river diggings is found in Robert Eccleston's diaries of the Mariposa Indian War. Several lists of newspaper references to the diggings in the region are given in Crampton's dissertation.

Merrimac [Plumas]. North of the Middle Fork of Feather River, on the Butte County line. Like several mines the place was named for the Confederate ironclad Merrimac of Civil War fame. It was a trading and milling center for the quartz mines of the district (*Register*, 1903), with a post office, 1883–1934.

Merrimac Hill [Nevada]. About two miles from Grass Valley. According to the Grass Valley *Directory* of 1865 (p. 76), one of the locators of the diggings in 1851 was George Hearst. The hill was worked only superficially until the Merrimac Mine was opened in 1864. The mine had a 10-stamp mill driven by a 30-h.p. motor (Bean, p. 202). Merrimack Q. M. is shown on Doolittle's map, 1868, about two miles northeast of Grass Valley. A mine on the hill is listed in the reports of the Mining Bureau until 1941.

Mesa Grande District [San Diego]. About eighteen miles east of Escondido. Gold was discovered in the late 1880s and mined to about 1896, and for a short time in the early 1930s. The chief mine was the Shenandoah, with a 10-stamp mill. The *Register*, 1902, also lists the Black Eagle Mine, with a 5-stamp mill. (*County Report*, III, p. 121.)

Mescal: District, town [San Bernardino]. In the Mescal and Ivanpah mountains; on the south side of U. S. Highway I 15. The mining town Mescal was two miles south of the highway, near Mescal Spring, and was sometimes called Nantan. There was a Nantan post office, 1887–1890. At Mescal Spring a 10-stamp mill was built in 1886. The Mollusk Mine, a half mile away, was operated from 1882 to 1888 and briefly in 1915. The Morning Star Mine, in the Ivanpah Mountains, was worked in the late 1920s and in the 1930s. (*Mining Bureau*, XLIX, p. 75 and table following p. 257; XXVII, p. 304.) For the origin of the name Mescal, *see California Place Names*.

Mesquite District [Calaveras]. The district is listed in 1882 in *Mining Bureau*, II (part 1, p. 176), as a very moderate producer of gold.

Mesquite Placers [Imperial]. On the southern spur of the Chocolate Mountains, north of the Southern Pacific line. Before 1900 water was brought in from Glamis to wash the gravels, and later in the 1930s there were unsuccessful attempts at dry placering in the washes (*Mining Bureau*,

XXII, pp. 258 f.; XXVIII, p. 245; *Bull.*, 193, p. 154). The mesquite is a desert tree of the acacia family. The name is of Aztec origin.

Messerville [Trinity]. Between Weaverville and Canyon Creek. It had a post office between April 2, 1860 and August 9, 1861, when it was transferred to Junction City. The place was formerly called Oregon Gulch, according to a correspondent of the *Trinity Journal*, January 21, 1860. There were 100 miners at work at that time making between six and twenty dollars per day. *See* Oregon Gulch.

Methodist Reserve Hill [Tuolumne]. Part of San Diego Hill; southeast of Columbia. Red Gulch and several other gulches have their source near the summit. Knapps' claim was on the summit. *See* Knapps Ranch. Other rich claims were Johnsons (Columbia *News*, August 28, 1858) and McCuloughs (Sacramento *Union*, February 20, 1856).

Mexican Flat [Tuolumne]. On the east side of Whiskey Hill, in the angle formed by Whiskey Hill and Table Mountain; west of Jamestown. The camp is mentioned by Heckendorn (pp. 103, 104). It is one of the few camps designated by the adjective "Mexican" instead of the commonly used "Spanish."

Mexican Mine [Mariposa]. *See* Benton Mills.

Michigan Bar [Sacramento]. On the Cosumnes River, about one mile north of the Michigan Bar turnoff from the Jackson Road. Shown on Goddard's map, 1857. D. A. Millington states in his journal of August 20, 1850, that he mined here briefly. The post office was established February 19, 1855, and continued until 1935. Extensive hydraulic mining was carried on for many years (*Mining Bureau*, LI, p. 143). At one time the camp counted more than 1,000 inhabitants; in 1880 only seventy white people and about 100 Chinese were left (Co. Hist., 1880, p. 214). In the 1930s and early 1940s the river was dredged and there was also some drift mining in the district (*Bull.*, 193, p. 90). Historic Landmark 468.

Michigan Bar [Siskiyou]. On the east side of Scott River, south of the junction. Recorded on Goddard's map, 1857. It is mentioned by Metlar in 1856 and in the County History, 1881 (p. 217).

Michigan: Bar, Flat [El Dorado]. On a tributary to the South Fork of American River, about two miles northwest of Coloma. The Flat is shown on Doolittle's map, 1868, and on Bowman's, 1873. This may be the site of the Michigan dam men-

tioned by Stephen Wing in his journal, October 12, 1854. Several sources claim that Leland Stanford had his store here (not at Michigan Bluff).

Michigan Bar, El Dorado Co.

Michigan: Bluff, City, District [Placer]. A half mile north of the Middle Fork of American River, seven miles from Forest Hill, between the headwaters of Skunk Canyon and Poor Mans Canyon. Prospectors from Michigan settled here in 1850. Shown prominently on Trask's map, 1853, as Michigen; on Blake's map, 1854, as Michigan City; and on Goddard's map, 1857, as Michigan Bluffs. The post office was established in 1854 as Michigan Bluff and continued until 1943. According to an item in the Doyle file, the diggings were first at a place called Michigan City, but the ground was so rich that the foundations of the buildings were nearly mined away and the town was moved a short distance away and was called Michigan Bluff. In 1857 fire destroyed the original town. Patterson (pp. 30, 31) mentioned the diggings in 1852, stating that one claim yielded 48 thousand dollars in five months, but that the only permanent building was a little log cabin. Hutchings reports that miners made eight to ten dollars per day in 1855 (Diary, May 7, 1855). Browne (p. 96) reports that the best years were between 1853 and 1858, when 100 thousand dollars were shipped per month, but by 1867 the amount was no more than 25 thousand dollars. The claims were first worked by drifting, later by hydraulic mining, and at one time it was one of the principal hydraulic camps in the state. The mines were on the Tertiary river channel. In 1866 the North American claim used nitroglycerin to break the hard cement. Included in the list of remarkable gold nugget discoveries recorded in *Min-*

ing Bureau, II (part 1, p. 149) is the 226-ounce nugget found near Michigan Bluffs in 1864. It was reportedly pure gold and sold for more than 4 thousand dollars. Accounts of the discovery vary. Leland Stanford earned the nucleus of his fortune here, not as a gold digger but as a purveyor of provisions in the early 1850s. Ed T. Planer dug up an interesting story about Stanford's first "store" in 1850 ("The Knave," November 6, 1941). Stanford was justice of the peace in 1855 (*CHSQ*, II, p. 203). The mines gave out about 1900, but *Mining Bureau*, XXIII (p. 90) still lists three mines in 1927. The total production (with Byrds Valley) by hydraulic mining as reported in 1927 was 5 million dollars. (*Mining Bureau*, XXIII, p. 262.) Among the placer mines listed in *Bulletin*, 193 (p. 91), the Big Gun or Michigan Bluff yielded more than a million dollars. *See Consolidated Index.* Historic Landmark 402.

Michigan Flat [Nevada]. An unidentified camp listed in Hittell's roster.

Midas Mine [Shasta]. *See* Harrison Gulch.

Middle Bar [Amador]. On Mokelumne River, near Mokelumne Hill. It is shown on Trask's map, 1853, and on Goddard's map, 1857. It was so named because it was situated between Upper and Lower bars. Bayard Taylor describes this and other camps of 1849 in chapters eight and nine of his *El Dorado*. Gerstaecker (I, pp. 272 ff.) gives an account of the place in the summer of 1850. D. A. Millington mined here in the fall of the same year (Journal, August 23 and September 1, 1850). Ayer recalls a lively gambling scene in the spring of 1850. The Stockton *Times*, March 3, 1850, carries advertisements of the Samuel Stenberger Store and the Gramm & Pages Ferry. A ferry license was issued June 15, 1850 to Martin & Peuch (Berriman). The first bridge over Mokelumne River was built here in 1851, was swept away by a flood in March, 1852; a new and higher bridge was completed in November, 1853, 459 feet in length and 32 feet above the water. Several mines are listed in the reports of the Mining Bureau until 1927. The name Middle Bar Bridge appears on the USGS Jackson 1938 quadrangle. The site, now at times inundated by Pardee Reservoir, is Historic Landmark 36.

Middle Bar [Plumas]. On the East Fork of the North Fork of Feather River, between Frenchmans Bar and Smith Bar. Shown on Trask's map, 1853.

Middle Bar [Tuolumne]. An unidentified place on Woods Creek, south of Sonora.

Middle Bar [Yuba]. At the mouth of Middle Fork of Yuba River. It is listed in the Giffen file.

Middle: Bar, Creek [Shasta]. The creek is a tributary to Sacramento River, three miles north of Redding. John Hittell stopped and mined here in September, 1849, after his arrival via the Lassen Cutoff. According to Petty (p. 42), fifty dollars a day for two men was considered a moderate yield in later years. In 1858 a water-driven 5-stamp mill was installed (*State Register*, 1859).

Middle Buttes [Kern]. Ten miles southwest of Mojave. Gold was discovered in the flat-topped hills at the end of the nineteenth century. A detailed description is found in *Mining Bureau*, XXXI (pp. 465 ff.). *See also County Report*, I, (p. 43).

Middle Ferry [Stanislaus]. *See* Islips Ferry.

Middle Hill [Mono]. Near Aurora. The *Mining Press*, October 19, 1861, reports that the hill has a number of valuable claims, rich in both gold and silver. There were also rich leads in nearby Last Chance and Martinez hills.

Middletown [Shasta]. Four miles from Shasta City. Hutchings describes it as "a bustling, busy little town with about 500 inhabitants" and during the rainy season nearly 1,400 (Diary, December 18, 1855). A post office was established June 18, 1856 and discontinued March 19, 1858. Steger states that the place was already deserted in the 1860s.

Middlewaters [Sierra]. Between Milton and Nebraska Diggings. It was a stage stop on the Henness Pass Road, recorded on Doolittle's map, 1868, as Mineral Waters Ranch, and as Middlewaters on the County Map, 1874.

Mile Gulch [Amador]. It is possibly the same site as Rattlesnake Flat. It was settled in 1849. In 1859 or 1860 a ditch from Rancheria Creek brought water to the place (Co. Hist., 1881, p. 231).

Mile Hill Ravine [Placer]. It was the site of a quartz mining company whose "partnership articles" were recorded March 15, 1862, in the Placer County Records, IV (p. 37).

Miles Ravine [Nevada]. An unidentified place listed in Hittell's roster.

Milkmaid Mine [Shasta]. *See* French Gulch.

Milk Punch Bar [Placer, El Dorado]. On the North Fork of American River, south of Auburn, above Whiskey Bar. It was on both sides of the river and is mentioned in the El Dorado County History, 1883 (p.

83), and in the Placer County History, 1882 (p. 401).

Milk Ranch [Yuba]. *See* Strouds.

Mill Bar [Sacramento ?]. An unidentified place, probably on the American River. It is listed in the Giffen file.

Mill City [Mono]. About a half mile below Mammoth City. A 40-stamp mill was built here in 1878 and 1879 by the Mammoth Mining Company. Some remains of the mill may still be seen today. (*Mining Bureau*, VIII, p. 375; Nadeau, pp. 215 f.) *See* Mammoth City.

Mill Creek [Fresno]. Tributary to the Kings River, in the eastern part of the county, near the town of Dunlap. It is a small district listed in *Bulletin*, 193 (p. 91), where it is stated that there was some placer mining in Mill Creek and other creeks in "early days," and small-scale lode mining from the 1880s to the end of the century.

Mill Creek [Yuba]. The creek is mentioned by Pringle Shaw (p. 122). In 1855 the region was an important district with fine gold and excellent lumber. In 1867 the claims of one company yielded five to eleven dollars per day to the hand, according to a clipping from the Quincy *National*, November 23, 1867, in Hayes Scrapbooks: Mining (IV, sec. 17).

Millers Bar [Butte]. On the Middle Fork of Feather River, two miles above the junction with the South Fork. Recorded on Trask's, 1853, map and on Goddard's, 1857. Ferguson (p. 132) mined here in the summer of 1850.

Millers Defeat [Placer]. On Deep Canyon, tributary to the North Fork of the Middle Fork of American River, about three miles south of Canada Hill. Shown on a sketch map in Whitney, *Auriferous Gravels* (p. 82). The camp is recorded in Hittell's roster and is mentioned on July 18 [1854] in a right-of-way claim for the construction of a ditch to the Cosmopolite mining district (Placer County Records, I, p. 237).

Millers Ranch [Butte]. On South Honcut Creek, south of Hansonville, on the Yuba County line. Shown on the von Leicht-Craven map, 1874. No mining record was found.

Millerton [Fresno]. *See* Rootville.

Millertown [Placer]. Near Ophir. According to the *Alta*, March 9, 1853, two men took seventy dollars worth of "beautiful fine gold" out of the north ravine. The camp is mentioned in connection with quartz leads April 4, 1853 and November 27, 1855 in Placer County Records, I (pp. 163 and 335). It is probably the same place as Mil-

lerton, shown on Goddard's map, 1857, north of Ophir.

Mill Town [Trinity]. On Trinity River, west of Weaverville. This is the original name of Junction City. Cox (pp. 57 ff.) gives a lengthy account of the place, calling it "a town, almost a city." *See* Junction City.

Milton [Calaveras]. On the Stanislaus County line, between Copperopolis and Stockton. The place was once the terminus of the old Copperopolis railroad. It was a trading center for the gold and copper mines in the area (*Register*, 1899). Extensive dredging was reported in the 1930s.

Milton [Sierra]. In the vicinity of Jackson Meadow, near the Sierra and Nevada county line. It was a stopping place on the Henness Pass Road. Shown on Doolittle's map, 1868, and the County Map, 1874, as Milton Ranch. Recorded as Milton on the USGS Downieville 1907 quadrangle.

Mine d'Or de Quartz Mountain [Madera]. *See* Quartz Mountain.

Mineral Bar [El Dorado]. On the South Fork of American River, below Coloma and Dutch Bar. It is mentioned in El Dorado County Records, Mining Locations, Book I (p. 83).

Mineral Bar [Placer]. On the south side of the North Fork of American River, above the junction with the Middle Fork, and above Barnes Bar. Shown on Trask's map, 1853, and on Goddard's, 1857. There was a well known bridge here on the road from Illinoistown to Iowa Hill (Hittell Clippings, p. 61). Notice of a claim near Mineral Bar was recorded September 15, 1851, in Placer County Records, I (p. 11). Hutchings lists the place as a town in 1855.

Mineral City [Amador]. Six miles west of Plymouth. Shown on the County Map, 1866. It is in a copper mining district, and no record of gold production was found.

Mineral: Hill, Park [Mono]. Near Mammoth Lake. From 1878 to 1880 mining of one of the richest deposits of the Mammoth Lake mines was carried on here.

Mineral King District [Tulare]. Near Sequoia National Park. The discovery of gold and silver in the area in 1873 brought about a short-lived rush (*Bull.*, 193, p. 91).

Mineral Point [Plumas]. A gold mining district, mentioned in the *Pacific Coast Mining Review*, 1878 (p. 249).

Mineral Slide [Butte]. On Little Butte Creek, east of Chico. A description of mining activities in the 1920s is given in *Mining Bureau*, XXIV (pp. 201 f.) and XXVI (pp. 400

Minnesota and Orleans Flat, Sierra Co.

f.). A number of mines are still listed in 1949. Shown on the USGS Chico 1944 quadrangle.

Mineral Waters [Sierra]. *See* Middlewaters.

Miners Ranch [Butte]. Near Bidwell Bar. Shown on the County Map, 1862. In January, 1854, beautiful specimens of gold were picked up off the surface after a heavy rain, according to an account in the *Butte Record* quoted in an unidentified Hittell clipping (p. 25).

Miners Ravine [Placer]. Near Auburn. A notice of intention to construct a ditch conveying the water of the ravine to Brules and Mississippi bars was recorded April 25, 1853, in Placer County Records, I (p. 165). The place is listed in Hittell's roster.

Minersville [Trinity]. On the East Fork of Stuart Fork of Trinity River, near the junction with Digger Creek. Numerous placer and quartz mines were worked as early as the 1850s. It was also called Diggerville or Diggersville. A talkative account is given in Cox (pp. 89 ff., 91 ff.). In later years there was mainly hydraulic mining. The post office existed intermittently from 1856 to 1954. According to an article in *Trinity*, 1962 (p. 9), it was successively at the Van Matre Ranch, Minersville, Unity Mine at Hayward Flat, and then back to Van Matre Ranch. The latter became known as Minersville, as distinguished from Old Minersville to the north. The mines are listed and described in *County Report*, IV.

Minerva [Placer]. On the North Fork of American River. It is mentioned in a letter written by Jonas Winchester to his wife, dated December 8, 1849 Winchester Papers, California State Library, California Section). No record of gold mining was found.

Minerva Bar [Plumas]. Listed in the County History, 1882 (p. 288), as one of the chief camps on the Middle Fork of Feather River. It is shown on modern maps below Rich Bar.

Ministers: Claim, Gulch [Amador]. On the south side of Amador Creek, at Amador City. In 1851 a Baptist preacher named Davidson and his associates discovered quartz gold here. This Ministers Claim became the nucleus of the large Original Amador Mine. (*Guidebook*, p. 65; Co. Hist., 1881, p. 145). *See* Amador City.

Minna Flat [Placer]. The camp is listed in Hittell's roster. It is probably the site of the Minna Ricca Mine (or Mina Rica), west of Auburn, listed in the Mining Bureau reports from 1882 until 1936, though it was long idle.

Minnesota [Sierra]. Between the Middle Fork of Yuba River and Kanaka Creek. Shown on Trask's map (1853), Goddard's (1857), Crossman's (1867) and the County Map (1874). The camp was apparently settled in 1851 by a man from Minnesota (Knights Scrapbooks, XIII, p. 81). The Blue Lead was discovered there in 1852. For some time there was excellent drift mining, and according to Browne (p. 139), 400 miners were at work in 1853, earning twelve to fifteen dollars a day. The geology is described by Trask (doc. 9, p. 64 f.)

in 1854. A steam-driven mill was built in 1855 (Hittell Clippings, p. 74). Vischer (p. 240) observed in 1859 that there was mainly tunnel work. The *Alta* and other papers of the 1850s reported rich yields. The Rapp Company at the Blue Tunnel reported one to four ounces a day to the man in 1854 and found a lump of 37 pounds of almost pure gold the same year (Hittell Clippings, pp. 21, 27, 29). Another big nugget of 266 ounces, valued at 5 thousand dollars is reported to have been found (*Mining Bureau*, II, part 1, p. 148). The decline started in the early 1860s, and in 1867 only four claims were still being worked (Browne, p. 139). The Minnesota Development Group is listed in the Mining Bureau reports until 1942.

Misery Flat [Amador]. East of Volcano. Andrews (p. 85 f.) mentions the camp, now vanished, which until recently had a layout for shoeing horses. Camp shows Misery Creek on his map.

Mississippi Bar [Sacramento]. On the north bank of the American River, about two and a half miles downstream from Folsom. The bar is shown on Trask's map, 1853, and on Goddard's, 1857. The place was named by Mississippians "in commemoration of the old folks at home," and when Edward Wilson was there in the spring of 1850, the "city" consisted of one wooden shanty and five tents (E. Wilson, p. 35). The 1850 United States Bureau of the Census lists 126 inhabitants at Mississippi Bar and an additional 252 apparently nearby. Barrington (*Miscellany*, p. 4) mined here ("Mississippi or Fishers Bar") with fair success in May, 1850. Newton Miller datelined letters from Mississippi Bar, January 26 and March, 1851. Notice of intention to build a ditch from Miner's Ravine to Mississippi Bar was recorded April 23, 1853 (Placer County Records, I, p. 165). This was apparently the ditch mentioned in the Sacramento County History, 1880 (p. 229), which brought water from the North Fork of American to Mississippi Township for mining the higher benches. Mining thereafter was brisk until 1870, but in 1880 only a few Portuguese and Chinese miners were left in the township. The first dredging operations on the American River began here in the spring of 1899 (*Bull.*, 57, pp. 178, 204). Mississippi Bar is shown on the USGS Folsom 1944 quadrangle. An alternate name was apparently Fishers Bar. *See* Fishers Bar.

Mississippi Bar [Yuba]. On the North Fork of Yuba River, eight miles below Big Can-

yon Creek. Shown on Trask's map, 1853. In the fall of 1852 about 150 Chinese inhabited the place. Borthwick (pp. 262 ff.) gives a classical description of the Chinese miners' mode of living and working. De Long collected taxes here March 19, 1855. It is mentioned as a small bar in the *Marysville Directory*, 1858 (p. xxvii).

Mississippi Canyon [Placer]. *See* Humbug Bar.

Mississippi Valley Mining District [Nevada]. Probably along the Kentucky Ravine. According to an excerpt from the Nevada *Democrat* in the *Alta*, May 21, 1854, valuable mines in the valley had been opened in 1853 or 1854. The name is mentioned in a bill of sale, July 14, 1860 (Newton Miller's letters).

Missouri Bar [Butte]. On the Middle Fork of Feather River, northeast of Bidwell Bar. Shown on Goddard's map, 1857. It is mentioned in the *Alta*, September 20, 1857.

Missouri Bar [El Dorado]. On the South Fork of American River, near Michigan Bar. It is mentioned in the County History, 1883 (p. 85).

Missouri Bar [Nevada]. On the South Fork of Yuba River, southeast of North Bloomfield. Shown on Doolittle's map, 1868. It is listed in Brown's *Directory*, 1856 (p. 133), and in Hittell's roster.

Missouri Bar [Placer]. On the North Fork of American River, below Negro Bar. Notice of a claim is recorded December 3, 1852, in Placer County Records, I (p. 145). Butler's map of 1851 shows a Missouri Bar near the source of the North Fork.

Missouri Bar [Plumas]. On the east branch of the North Fork of Feather River. Shown on Trask's map, 1853, a little below Rich Bar. It is often mentioned by Dame Shirley (p. 41 and *passim*).

Missouri Bar [Trinity]. On the Trinity River, opposite Steiners Ranch. It was a prosperous camp in the middle 1850s with water from Browns Creek (Cox, p. 47).

Missouri Bar [Tuolumne]. *See* Brazoria Bar.

Missouri Bar [Yuba]. There were apparently two Missouri bars in the county, somewhat confused in the records. Trask's map, 1853, shows a Missouri Bar on the main Yuba River, above Condemned Bar, between the North and South forks. This appears to be the Missouri Bar mentioned in the County History, 1879 (p. 94), at which "a company of white men and some Chinamen" were at work in that year. Wescoatt's map of 1861 and Doolittle's, 1868, show Missouri Bar on the

North Fork of Yuba River, north of Fosters Bar, between Sucker and Elbow bars. The County History, 1879 (pp. 95, 96), designates the bar at this place as Missouri Bar No. 2, stating further that it was located in March, 1850, by miners from Missouri, was once a large camp "with hotels, stores, and saloons," and was still worked in the summer season. Stephen Foster mined at Missouri Bar in 1852 (letter dated April 11, 1852) and De Long collected taxes here, March 18, 1855.

Missouri Canyon [El Dorado]. A tributary to Otter Creek, near Volcanoville. Shown on Doolittle's map, 1868, and Bowman's, 1873. Abbott, who was in the mines in 1850–1851, mined first at Missouri Canyon, according to his reminiscences (p. 87). The U. S. Bureau of the Census lists the names of 84 inhabitants in January, 1851, for the 1850 census. The canyon is mentioned April 8, 1856, by A. H. Saxton in a sales agreement. Mining in the area is described in 1872 and 1874 in Raymond (V, p. 52; VII, p. 93). Shown on the USGS Placerville 1931 quadrangle.

Missouri Canyon [Nevada]. A tributary to Greenhorn Creek, below Arkansas Canyon; near Red Dog. Shown on Pettee and Bowman's map, 1879, and mentioned by Pettee in Whitney, *Auriferous Gravels* (p. 164 and *passim*).

Missouri Flat [El Dorado]. Near Diamond Springs. An undated clipping in Hayes Scrapbook: Mining (I, sec. 34) reports the attendance of miners from Missouri Flat and neighboring districts at a mass meeting held at Diamond Springs, March 29, 1856.

Missouri Flat [Nevada]. One mile south of Grass Valley. The Lone Jack Mine, located in 1855, had yielded half a million dollars in gold by 1867 (Bean, p. 229).

Missouri Flat [Sierra]. About one mile west of Loganville. It is mentioned by Sinnott, *Downieville*, p. 201. No mining record was found.

Missouri Gulch [Mariposa]. Cuts through the town of Mariposa. Rich diggings developed in 1849. A quartz mine is still listed in 1894 (*Mining Bureau*, XII, p. 173).

Missouri Hill [Nevada]. Between Steep Hollow Creek and Bear River, east of Little York. Shown on Pettee and Bowman's map, 1879, on which a large part of the gravel is indicated as "more or less completely hydraulicked away." The area is described by Pettee in Whitney, *Auriferous Gravels* (pp. 154 ff.).

Missouri Tent [Yuba]. Between Strawberry Valley and Little Grass Valley, near the South Fork of Feather River. Shown on Milleson and Adams map, 1851. It is mentioned as Missouri House by Lecouvreur (p. 233) in a letter written in early July, 1852.

Missouri Town [Sierra]. *See* Downieville.

Moaning Cave [Calaveras]. The original name of the well-known landmark was Solomons Hole. Gold seekers believed that it had been worked for gold in Mexican or even Spanish times until Trask dispelled the tradition in 1851.

Mobile Bar [Amador]. On the north side of Mokelumne River, six miles west of Mokelumne Hill. Recorded on Trask's map, 1853. A Mobile Bar Mine in Calaveras County is listed in *Mining Bureau*, XXXII (p. 361).

Mobile Flat [Sierra]. On the North Fork of Yuba River, four miles east of Downieville. Shown on Doolittle's map, 1868, and on the County map, 1874. The settlement was later known as Newhouse Place and Shaughnessy Place (Sinnott, *Downieville*, p. 145).

Moccasin Creek [Tuolumne]. A tributary to Tuolumne River, southeast of Jacksonville. Spellings vary on early maps. The name appears as Mocosin on Gibbes', *A New Map of California*, Stockton, 1852; as Mocassin on Goddard's, 1857, map; but correctly on Trask's, 1853. Stories about the origin of the name vary. According to Pancoast (p. 297), the miners mistook the numerous water snakes for the mocassin snake of southern swamps; hence the name. When Gardiner mined here one week in the summer of 1852, he found the place deserted and "even the Chinamen passed it by" (p. 187). Hutchings, however, lists it as a town in 1855, and Heckendorn (p. 88) mentions it as a noted place in 1856. In 1859 there was a 12-stamp steam-driven mill (*State Register*, 1859). The post office was not established until 1923, when the Moccasin Power House was built. A Moccasin and Gold Key Mine, nine miles southeast of Jacksonville, is listed in the Mining Bureau reports until 1928. The creek is shown on the USGS Sonora 1939 quadrangle.

Mockingbird Mine [Mariposa]. *See* Colorado.

Modoc District [Inyo]. About ten miles east of Darwin, at the north end of the Argus Mountains. It is a lead-silver district, in which some gold has been recovered, but the mines have been idle for some time

(*Bull.*, 193, p. 150). There was a Modock post office between 1890 and 1903.

Mogul [Alpine]. Two miles from Monitor, in the vicinity of Markleeville. It was a mining camp of the 1860s and 1870s, and like its neighbor, Monitor, it produced some gold, along with silver and copper (Nadeau, p. 219). *See* Monitor.

Mohawk [Plumas]. In Mohawk Valley, on Highway 89. The place was named by descendants of German settlers from Mohawk Valley, New York. It was the trading center and from 1870 to 1926 the post office for neighboring quartz and copper mines. The region is described in *Mining Bureau*, XVI (Plumas, pp. 21 ff.).

Mojave Mining District [Kern]. In the southeastern part of the county, between the towns of Mojave and Willow Springs. It is also known as the Mojave-Rosamond district. The success of the Exposed Treasure Mine on Standard Hill, opened in 1894 by George Bowers, lead to the discovery of other mines in the district. The peak of production was between 1931 and 1942. During World War II, the mines were closed, but there has been some activity since then. The Standard Group yielded 3.5 million dollars; the Cactus Queen, discovered in 1934, yielded more than 5 million dollars; and the Golden Queen Group more than 10 million. The total production of gold and silver in the district is estimated at 23 million dollars. (*Bull.*, 193, p. 159.) Further details and lists of mines are given in *Mining Bureau*, XXIX (pp. 280, 283 f.) and XLV (pp. 218, 258); and in the *County Report*, I.

Mokelumne City [San Joaquin]. At the junction of the Cosumnes and Mokelumne rivers, less than a half mile east of Bensons Ferry. It is not the same as the town or camp shown on Butler's map, 1851, six miles northwest of the junction of the North and South forks of Mokelumne River in Calaveras County. The place was established in the early 1850s as a trading center and head of navigation for the mines. It prospered until 1862, when it was almost destroyed by the flood. The site of the vanished town is Historic Landmark 162.

Mokelumne: Diggings, Gulch [Calaveras]. In the vicinity of Mokelumne Hill. In June, 1849, Dr. Gillette came prospecting from nearby Upper Bar. He accidentally picked up a two-pound lump of gold during the noon hour. In two days he and his companion dug up fourteen pounds. When they started a day later from Upper Bar to the new diggings under the pretense of hunting, a number of miners suspected them and followed them. Soon the news spread and some of the men picked up several pounds a day at the start (Taylor, *El Dorado*, I, pp. 87 f.). Ryan (vol. 2, p. 59) refers to "Macalamo Dry Diggings" in a gulch at the foot of a hill. The *California Courier* reported September 9, 1850, that a party of "lucky hombres took out fifty pounds in eight days" from the rich gulch.

Mokelumne Hill [Calaveras]. The town on Highway 49 was one of the most important gold camps of the Southern Mines. It served as the county seat from 1852 to 1866. Recorded on Butler's map, 1851, and on all other early maps. The statement that the place was first called Big Bar is apparently erroneous. According to the San Andreas *Independent*, January 12, 1861, Mokelumne Hill was one mile distant from Big Bar. The first miners were Oregonians at Big Bar on the river in the fall of 1848, and the name Mokelumne Hill referred to the trading post on a hill above. As early as October, 1848, the French consul in San Francisco reported that four Frenchmen had returned with 138 (!) pounds of gold all picked up in a single gulch near Mokelumne Hill. (*CHSQ*, XIII, p. 271.) In another report, apparently somewhat exaggerated, it was stated that in the spring of 1851 three Frenchmen struck it rich on French Hill near the town and took out 180 thousand dollars worth of gold in a few days (Hittell Clippings, p. 62; Hittell, *History*, III, p. 114; Browne, p. 55). Since American prospectors claimed property rights, the discovery led to a bloodless "French War." December 15, 1851, the French in Les Fourcades, as they called the camp, numbered 6,000 to 8,000 [!] and had their own newspaper (*CHSQ*, XXXV, p. 316). However, Borthwick (pp. 286 ff.) claims that in the spring of 1853, the French numbered only one third of the population, and Vischer (p. 323), in 1859, states that the Anglo-Saxon and Teutonic elements had greatly increased. "Judge" Thompson (pp. 239 ff.) gives a detailed account of the vigilantes' committee of 1851–52. On May 26, 1854, the *Alta* reported the find of an extraordinary 80-ounce piece of pure gold in the shape of a pot hook (Bancroft Notes). When the original prosperity was gone, water made hydraulic mining possible. Murieta was, of course, in town, committed a few misdeeds, and presented himself in a hall of gamblers, a scene immortalized by Charles Nahl in a drawing, reproduced in the Grabhorn edition of Ridge's account (annotated by Francis P. Farquhar). For a description of Mokelumne Hill District, *see Bulletin*, 193 (pp. 91 f.). Both placer and lode mines are listed here, including the two lode mines near Mokelumne Hill: the Boston, two miles northeast which yielded 1 million dollars, and the Quaker City, four miles southwest of the town which yielded more than 1 million.

Monitor [Alpine]. On Monitor Creek, a tributary to East Carson River. It was a rich mining district with some gold. In the 1860s and 70s the camp had 2,000 inhabitants, and it had a post office from 1863 to 1888. Description and maps of the district may be found in *Mining Bureau*, XV (pp. 14 ff.) and XVII (pp. 399 ff.). The Monitor-Mogul District is described in *Bulletin*, 193 (p. 92). The decline in mining in this district in the 1880s was followed by renewed activity in the early 1900s and again in the 1930s; one mine, the Zaca, was worked in the 1960s. There is no record of the production of gold in the district, but the estimate ranges between 3 and 5 million dollars.

Mono Camp [Mariposa]. About three miles north of Mariposa and less than two miles southeast of Colorado. Recorded on the map in Crampton's dissertation. No mining record was found. Shown on the USGS Yosemite 1938 quadrangle.

Monona Flat [Placer]. On Indian Creek, two miles northeast of Iowa Hill. Doolittle's map, 1868, shows Mononatown at this location. Mining paid well in places here, according to Browne (p. 101). Specifications for the building of a 20-stamp mill are included in the indenture filed September 22, 1868, in Placer County Records, IV (pp. 344 ff.). The placers on the Tertiary gravels are described in *Bulletin*, 92 (p. 136). Shown on the USGS Colfax 1938 quadrangle.

Monoville [Mono]. About halfway between Bridgeport and Mono Lake, near Dogtown. Placer gold was discovered here in 1859, the year following the discovery of the diggings at Dogtown by Carl Norst. *See* Dogtown. The deposits proved rich and there was a "rush" to the place. Within a year the population was 900, according to the 1860 census figures, but when the gold and silver discoveries were made at Aurora, most of the miners left for the new location. Mining continued at Monoville in a small way, but by 1867 it

was at a standstill (Browne, p. 202). The most notable feature about Monoville, according to F. S. Wedertz, was the construction of ditches to supply water for placering. The *Mining Press*, June 29, 1869, reports that one company brought water a distance of thirteen miles, and Browne (p. 202) lists a 20-mile ditch from Virginia Creek, apparently to Monoville. Remains of ditches may still be traced along the hillside, and a reminder of hydraulic mining here is the Sinnamon Cut, a "1700 x 200-foot scar on the landscape" today (De Decker, p. 16). *See* Sinnamon Cut. Accounts of mining in the area are given in *Mining Bureau*, VIII (pp. 366 f.); De Decker (p. 15 f.); Nadeau (pp. 210 f.).

Monroeville [Glenn]. On Stony Creek; formerly in Colusa County. Lucius Fairchild gives details of placer mining here in letters written December 25, 1851 and February 4, 1852. William B. Ide mentions the place in a letter written to John Bidwell, September 10, 1852 (Bidwell Papers, California State Library, California Section). The place had a post office from 1853 to 1862. There is no evidence that gold was found to any extent in Glenn County.

Monson Canyon [Riverside]. In the Joshua Tree National Monument, north of Highway 60. The former name was Jack Fork. According to the *Desert Magazine*, October, 1940, there was an old deserted (gold or silver) mine here in 1939.

Monte Cristo [Mono]. About a half mile southeast of Star City, in the Patterson District. It was a small mining settlement of the 1880s. Other camps in the area were Belfort, Boulder Flat, all of which are indicated on the USGS Bridgeport 1911 quadrangle.

Monte Cristo [Sierra]. Three miles northwest of Downieville. Shown on Goddard's map, 1857. The name, taken from Alexander Dumas' popular novel, *The Count of Monte Cristo*, was repeatedly used in the mining region. Here the name was especially appropriate because the claims were situated on a steep cliff, accessible only on muleback. The diggings are on the main Blue Lead, and there was extensive drift mining as early as 1852. Deep tunnels with a maximum depth of 1,800 feet requiring two or three years to construct, struck pay dirt yielding about 18 thousand dollars a week, according to an item in the San Francisco *Bulletin*, July 3, 1857 (extracts in Bancroft Notes). John Clark states in his journal entry of October 17, 1855, that the pay was between ten and twenty dollars a day to the hand ("The California Guide"). Monroe Thomson mined here in the 1850s and wrote his interesting book, *The Golden Resources*, published 1856. Other early reports are by De Long (September 30, 1858), Vischer (p. 240) and in the *Transactions*, 1858 (pp. 194 f.). The *Mining Press*, March 16, 1861, reports that most claims still yielded thirty or more ounces per week; but the deposits gave out soon afterwards. Attempts at hydraulic mining failed because of the lack of water, and in 1868 the number of miners had dwindled to about a dozen (Browne, p. 140). A West Point-Monte Cristo Mine is listed in the reports of the Mining Bureau until 1942. The Monte Cristo Mine is recorded on the USGS Downieville 1951 quadrangle, and the settlement or camp Monte Cristo is shown on the 1907 quadrangle.

Monte Cristo Mine [Los Angeles]. *See* Big Tujunga Canyon.

Monte de Oro [Butte]. Four miles north of Oroville. There was a formation of auriferous quartz in Butte County known as the Monte de Oro formation. Shown on the USGS Chico 1895 and the Oroville 1944 quadrangles.

Monte Sana [Nevada]. On Deer Creek, two miles from Nevada City. The only record found is an item in the Nevada *Journal*, September 30, 1859, according to which a rich quartz district was discovered by a "good-for-nothing half-wit" (Bancroft Notes).

Monte Vista Quartz Mills [Butte]. A place shown prominently on the County Map of 1861. It was apparently at the foot of Yankee Hill.

Monterey Bar [Butte]. *See* Longs Bar.

Montezuma. The name of the Aztec chief when Cortes invaded Mexico was often used for mines, and in some cases it became a place name.

Montezuma [Tuolumne]. On the road from Chinese Camp to Sonora, south of Jamestown. The name is displayed prominently on Goddard's map, 1857. Trask records Montezuma Ferry as well as Montezuma on his map, 1853, but in different locations. Mining started in 1852 and the camp was quite a town by 1856 (Heckendorn, p. 80). Charles H. Chamberlain states that he mined there already in October, 1849 ("Statement of a Pioneer of 1849"). The post office was established at Oak Spring in 1851, but in 1854 the name was changed to Montezuma. An undated clipping from the Sonora *Union Democrat* reports the find of a six-pound nugget and a thirty-pound lump of gold, but does not reveal the source. In 1862 it must still have been a sizeable town, for it had a "doctor's shop" (Mulford, p. 165). In 1867 some placer mining was carried on (Browne, p. 38). Soon afterwards the diggings seem to have petered out. The post office was discontinued in 1887. The total production with Picayune Gulch in 1899 was one and a half million dollars (*Mines and Minerals*, p. 358). It is shown on the USGS Sonora 1939 quadrangle, but it is designated as a ghost town on the *Guidebook* map, No. 3. Historic Landmark, 122.

Montezuma-Apex Mine [El Dorado]. *See* Nashville.

Montezuma District [San Diego]. On the slope of San Ysidro Mountain; about six miles east of Warner Springs. The district was opened in 1896 and called Rice District, for the Rice Brothers of Warner Springs, who prospected here. In 1910 thirteen claims were relocated to form the Montezuma Mine, and the name of the district was changed to Montezuma. The important claims and mines are listed in *Mining Bureau*, XIV (p. 648) and *County Report*, III (pp. 122, 156). *See also Mining Bureau*, XIII (p. 344).

Montezuma Hill [Nevada]. About four miles northwest of Nevada City, near the South Fork of Yuba River. Shown on Doolittle's map, 1868. A ditch from Humbug Canyon brought water in 1853. It is listed in Brown's *Directory*, 1856 (pp. 12, 113), and is mentioned by De Long, June 1, 1856. According to the *Mining Press*, October 5, 1861, no other place in the county yielded as steady, rich returns for labor. Most of the work done here was drift mining, as conditions were unfavorable for hydraulic mining, according to Pettee, who visited the area in 1879. He found the drifts, which had been carried entirely through the hill, caved in and inaccessible; work had stopped in 1874 or 1875. (Whitney, *Auriferous Gravels*, p. 391.)

Montezuma River Claim [Siskiyou]. On the South Fork of Scott River. This was the largest placer gold producer of the Callahan Ranch. Gold was mined here as early as the 1850s. In later years it was in the hands of Chinese miners, and in 1893 the weekly cleanup still ran from 500 to 4,000 dollars (*Mining Bureau*, XI, p. 434). *See* Callahan.

Montgomery [Butte]. On the south side of the Middle Fork of Feather River, northeast of Bidwell Bar. Shown on Trask's, 1853, and Goddard's, 1857, maps.

Montgomery District [Mono]. On Montgomery Canyon, seven miles east of Benton. It was organized in 1863. There was far more silver than gold production (*Sierra Club Bulletin*, XIII, p. 42; *Mining Bureau*, VIII, p. 377.)

Monticello [Sierra]. An unidentified place, doubtless named for Jefferson's Virginia estate. It is situated on the main lode of the county near Sebastopol. It is mentioned by M. Thomson (p. 15) in 1856.

Monumental City [Sierra?]. The *Alta*, April 25, 1854, reprints a correspondence from the *Empire County* (!) *Argus* which reports rich diggings within six miles. The place is unidentified; it could be the same as the Monumental claim in Sierra County.

Monumental Claim [Sierra]. In the Sierra Buttes region. It was located in 1855 and was famous for "breasting" (side tunnelling) and for the large number of lumps of gold found there. A detailed description is found in *Transactions*, 1858 (p. 186). On August 18, 1860, a lump weighing 1,596 ounces troy was found in the mine. R. B. Woodward bought it for $21,636.52 and exhibited it in his famous gardens in San Francisco. After it was melted, it yielded only $17,654.94 (*Mining Bureau*, II, part 1, p. 148). An interesting but not authentic story of the find is given in Farish, *Gold Hunters* (pp. 39 f.).

Monumental District [Del Norte]. About forty-five miles northeast of Crescent City. It is a small lode-gold mining district, listed in *Bulletin*, 193 (p. 139). The Monumental Consolidated Mine, the chief producer in the district, has been worked intermittently since about 1900.

Mooney Flat [Nevada]. In Slacks Ravine, close to the Yuba County line. Shown on Wescoatt's map, 1861. It was named for Tom Mooney, who later owned the Empire Ranch, south of Smartsville. There was placer mining in the 1850s, and later hydraulic mining, which stopped with the prohibition in 1884, but drift mining continued. The place is listed in *Bean's Directory*, 1867. A drift mine is listed and described in *Mining Bureau*, XI (p. 316). Shown on the USGS Smartsville 1943 quadrangle.

Mooneys Flat [Trinity]. On Trinity River, north of Lewiston. It is mentioned by Cox (p. 27). There was mining on Mooneys Old Ranch apparently as early as the 1850s. In 1860 ten dollars per day to the man was not considered high when water

was available (Trinity *Journal*, April 21, 1860). Mooney Gulch is shown on the USGS Weaverville 1942 quadrangle.

Moonlight Flat [Plumas?]. An unidentified camp mentioned by Guinn (p. 42). A gold mining site at Moonlight Mountain [Plumas] is listed in *Mining Bureau*, II (part 1, p. 188).

Moonshine Creek [Yuba]. A tributary to the Middle Fork of Yuba River, near North San Juan. When the diggings were found in 1853, the discoverers failed to keep the secret, and "moonshiners" soon posted their claims (Co. Hist., 1879, p. 100). The diggings were soon worked out, but De Long collected taxes here, July 31, 1855. Shown on the USGS Smartsville 1943 quadrangle.

Moorehouse Bar [Tuolumne]. On Stanislaus River, above Parrots Ferry Bridge, north of Gold Springs. It was mentioned as rich in gold (*Mines and Minerals*, p. 358).

Moores Camp [Los Angeles]. According to the Los Angeles *Star*, March 28, 1862 (Hayes Scrapbooks: Mining, V, sec. 286) gold mining with ground sluices was steady during the rainy season.

Moores Flat [Nevada]. A short distance northeast of Woolseys Flat, southwest of Graniteville; above the great gravel deposit of the county. Shown on Doolittle's map, 1868. It was settled in 1851 or 1852 by H. M. Moore and family, who had driven cattle across the continent (Brown's *Directory*, 1856, p. 151). The rich gold deposits were mentioned in a letter from Marysville, November 16, 1853 (Hittell Clippings, p. 27) and in *Transactions*, 1858 (p. 183). In 1853 a ditch from Poormans Creek brought water. A post office was established in 1853 under the name Clinton, which was changed to Moores Flat in 1857. In the late 1860s the claims were bought by a few large companies that mined successfully for many years (Browne, p. 121). Lindgren (*Tertiary Gravels*, p. 141) states that the gravel was from 100 to 130 feet thick and that large boulders of quartz from two to six feet in diameter were found in the bedrock. An estimated 26 million cubic feet had been washed off, with perhaps 15 million remaining at the time Lindgren was writing, in 1911. The place is listed in *Mining Bureau*, XVI (Nevada, p. 45).

Moores Station [Butte]. *See* Honcut.

Mooretown [Butte]. Between the Middle and South forks of Feather River. Shown on the County Map, 1861. Asa B. Smith mentions the Mooretown Ditch in a letter to his brother, Seth, datelined McCabe Creek, January 1, 1859. Mooretown was the trading center and from 1888–1913 the post office for the surrounding quartz mines (*Register*, 1903). It was also a lumbering center.

Mooreville [Butte]. In the southeast corner of the county. Shown on the County Map, 1861. A large body of auriferous gravel was found, but hydraulic mining did not pay (Bancroft Scraps, 51:1, p. 5; Browne, p. 162). The name is preserved in Mooreville Ridge and in the name of the district. *See Bulletin*, 193 (p. 93).

Morgan: Ground, Slope [Calaveras]. On the north slope of Carson Hill. It was named for the president of the mining company which started in 1850 and did mainly tunnel work. Billy Mulligan and his gang drove the owners away and worked the rich deposits until legally ejected in 1853. (Browne, pp. 59 f.) Raymond, IV (p. 75) stated that the total production was reportedly 3 million dollars by 1871. The Reserve Mine, south of Morgan, opened in 1860, and produced, according to Hittell (*Mining Bureau*, IV, p. 223), 100 dollars worth of gold per ton of quartz. The tremendous tailing dumps still adorn the landscape. A 300 thousand dollar pocket of gold, five inches in diameter and four or five feet long, in the shape of a limb of a tree, reportedly "the largest single piece of quartz in the world [!] ever taken out of the ground," was from the Morgan Mine (*Mining Bureau*, XIV, p. 97). In 1918 the Morgan was consolidated with the Calaveras and Melones mines and was worked until 1926, and again from 1933 to 1942 (*Bull.*, 193, p. 35). *See* Carson Hill; Melones.

Morgans Bar [Tuolumne]. On Tuolumne

Mormon Bar, Placer and El Dorado Cos.

River, between Jacksonville and Don Pedros Bar. Shown on Trask's map, 1853, and Goddard's, 1857. It is probably the same bar as the one shown on Gibbes' map, 1851, in Mariposa County. Gardiner (p. 104) passed by in November or December, 1849. Mulford (p. 114) mentioned the place. In 1856 it was "of considerable note," according to Heckendorn (p. 89).

Morinose Gulch [Tuolumne]. *See* Mormon Gulch.

Mormon. The name is frequently used as a geographical name in the gold districts, because members of the Church of Latter Day Saints or Mormons played an important role in the early phases of the Gold Rush. Two organized units had arrived in California in 1846: the Mormon Batallion marching from Council Bluffs in Iowa to San Diego, and the shipload on the *Brooklyn* around Cape Horn. Many of them were employed by Sutter and some were present when gold was discovered, January 24, 1848.

Mormon Bar [Mariposa]. On Mariposa Creek, one mile southeast of Mariposa. Gold was discovered here in 1848 by Mormons, who left soon afterwards for Salt Lake City. For years Chinese worked over the area. Allsop was here at the end of January, 1852, and was greatly impressed by the richness. He was told at that time that the place had produced more than 2 million dollars worth of gold. Some miners working in gulches averaged as much as forty to fifty dollars a day, according to the *Alta*, March 1, 1852. It was reported (Hittell Clippings, p. 24) that a boy named Fritz found a lump of gold nearby weighing 193 pounds (!). Mining continued in the area until about 1870. In the 1930s there was again some mining with dragline dredges, and there has been minor prospecting since that time (*Bull.*, 193, p. 323). Mormon Bar is Historic Landmark 323.

Mormon Bar [Placer and El Dorado]. On the North Fork of American River, near Lacys Bar, on both sides of the river. Shown on Jackson's map, 1850. It was described by Letts in 1849 (pp. 71 ff., 82 ff.). The Sacramento *Union*, August 28, 1851, states that some 60 thousand dollars had been taken out two years before. Gardiner prospected there without success in September, 1851 (pp. 176 f.).

Mormon Diggings [Sacramento]. *See* Mormon Island.

Mormon Gulch [El Dorado]. On Mameluke Hill, near Georgetown. Patterson (p. 50)

Mormon Island, Sacramento Co.

worked here with good success from the fall of 1851 to the spring of 1853.

Mormon: Gulch, Creek, Diggings [Tuolumne]. The creek is a tributary to Stanislaus River, west of Sonora. It is shown on Jackson's map, 1850, and on most other contemporary maps. It is apparently the same as the place recorded as Morinose Gulch on Gibbes' map, 1851. Mormon Gulch was discovered by Mormons in 1848 and was the original name of the camp at the site of Tuttletown. *See* Tuttletown. It is mentioned by Gunn in September and October, 1849 and by Daniel B. Woods in December, 1849. The latter mined here with moderate success in the spring of 1850 and gives a good description. The rich diggings are often mentioned in Perkins' *Journal* in 1851; another account of October, 1851, is given by Marryat (pp. 306 ff.). Justesen (p. 52) mined here in 1851 and gives an exaggerated report: one greenhorn made 19 thousand dollars in one day at Mormon "Gulf," and Mormons carried away gold by the mule load. In 1852 the place was inhabited mainly by Chileans and Sonorians. The story that three Chileans were robbed and murdered in May, 1852, by a professional gambler, who was promptly hanged by a

vigilantes' committee, as told in *Two Eras in the Life of a Felon Grovenor I. Layton*, appears to be fiction. According to *Mines and Minerals* (p. 358), the total output of gold to 1899 was 2.25 million dollars. The "French Revolution" apparently had its beginnings here in June of 1850. *See* Stoddart (pp. 132 f.) and Gerstaecker's story, "The French Revolution."

Mormon Island [Sacramento]. On the South Fork of American River, three miles from the junction with the North Fork. It was not an island, but a sand bar separated by a ditch. *See* Natoma. It is now under Folsom Lake. The first regular gold camp after the discovery at Sutters Mill was established here. The first flakes were found March 2, 1848, by two Mormons returning from Coloma to Sutter's grist mill. When seven of Sutter's Mormons started their diggings here at the beginning of April, the place was known as Lower Mines or Mormon Diggings; this name is shown on Mason's map, 1848. For a full account *see* Bigler's diaries (pp. 103 ff. in *Bigler's Chronicle of the West*). The name is spelled Mormont on Derby's Map of General Riley's Route (1849), but correctly on his Sacramento Valley map and on Jarves' map of the same year. The rich initial findings at this place actually started the Gold Rush. Among the early visitors, besides Sam Brannan, was James Lick, who showed himself in May in a long overcoat and tall plug hat (*Pioneer Quarterly*, I, no. 2, p. 25). The first non-Mormon to prospect here was William S. Clark (of Clarks Point, San Francisco), who mined here from April to August, 1848. The first contemporary account besides Bigler's is by C. L. Lyman, who camped here June 17, 1848 (*CHSQ*, II, p. 186). The classical story of Mormon Island was written by J. M. Letts (pp. 71 ff.), who had a store at the place in 1849. The deposits were soon exhausted, and later accounts reported only moderate success. Historic Landmark 569.

Mormonitos [Tuolumne]. *See* Tuttletown.

Mormons Tavern [Sacramento]. Shown on Trask's map, 1853, just south of Mormon Island.

Morning Star Camp [Sierra]. Well-paying diggings are reported in the *Mining Press*, April 18, 1862.

Morning Star Hill [Placer]. Named after the principal mine. The mines are listed in the County History, 1882 (p. 216).

Morongo District [San Bernardino]. In the eastern San Bernardino Mountains, on the road from Baldwin Lake to Morongo Pass. Shown on the County Map, 1892. There were several small veins worked by Mexicans in the late 1880s. The Morongo King Group was worked from 1887 to 1895, when the 10-stamp mill was removed, and the main activity at the Rose Mine was between 1895 and 1903. *See* Rosemine. (*Mining Bureau*, VIII, p. 504; IX, pp. 226 f.; XII, p. 231; XIII, p. 325; XV, p. 800; XLIX, table following p. 259).

Morris: Bar, Ravine [Butte]. North of Oroville, in a "bend" of Table Mountain, above Thompson Flat. Shown on Trask's map, 1853. On Milleson and Adams' map, 1851, the name appears as Morrisons Ravine. It was probably named after Morris, Illinois, the home of the Armstrong brothers, butchers at nearby Longs Bar (Ferguson, pp. 125, 127). According to *Mines and Minerals* (p. 280), it was in May, 1848, the first camp on the Feather River after Bidwell's discovery. Ferguson (pp. 124 f.) mined here a short time in the summer of 1850. Seth Smith also mined at the bar and in the ravine in 1851 (letters of March 30 and June 30, 1851), and in 1853 and 1854 he mined with his brother Asa with varying success (letters of July–August, 1853 and December, 1853–June, 1854). In 1859 one

claim paid six to eight dollars per hand (May 1, 1859). John Swett, later state superintendent of schools, mined here from March to June, 1853, with little success. Browne, (p. 148) however, stated that the gulch was one of the richest in California. Hydraulic mining was unsuccessful but was followed by drifting, which continued until 1897, according to Lindgren (p. 89). In the Morris Ravine district drift and lode mining was renewed at the time of World War I, and again to some degree in the 1930s; in recent years the Morris Ravine has again been worked from time to time (*Bull.*, 193, p. 93; *Mining Bureau*, XLV, p. 429). Shown on the USGS Chico 1895 quadrangle.

Morrisons Flat [Sierra]. It is mentioned as a new and flourishing mining town, one mile from Craigs Flat (Sacramento *Daily Union*, July 1, 1856, *in* Hayes Scrapbooks: Mining, I, sec. 23).

Morrisons Ravine [Butte]. *See* Morris.

Morristown [Sierra]. On Canyon Creek, seven miles northwest of Downieville. Shown on Goddard's map, 1857. It was the headquarters for the mines on Craigs Flat (*Transactions*, 1858, p. 197). There was mainly hydraulic and drift mining, according to Vischer, 1859 (p. 240). In 1862 one company made 4 thousand dollars from a two weeks run (*Mining Press*, April 25, 1862). The degree of fineness of the gold was high, ranging from 942° to 965.5° for the year 1875–76, according to a report given to Pettee (Whitney, *Auriferous Gravels*, p. 458). The Morristown and Angora group of mines is listed in the Mining Bureau reports until 1942. Morristown is shown on the USGS Downieville 1907 quadrangle.

Morrowville [Shasta]. One and a half miles west of the present site of the town French Gulch. It was so known until 1854 (Steger).

Mosquito Creek [Butte]. East of Coutolenc. No early records were found, but a Mosquito Creek Mine is listed in 1896 in *Mining Bureau*, XIII (p. 89).

Mosquito Creek [Nevada]. An unidentified place listed in Hittell's roster.

Mosquito Creek [Plumas]. A tributary to the North Fork of Feather River. Rich diggings were reported in 1861 (*Mining Press*, April 20, 1861). A Mystery Gulch Mine at the creek is listed in 1937 in *Mining Bureau*, XXXIII (p. 114).

Mosquito Gulch [Calaveras]. On the South Fork of Mokelumne River, about eight miles northeast of Mokelumne Hill; on the

Mother Lode. In contemporary sources the name is usually spelled Musquito; likewise in the name of the post office, established June 2, 1858. "F.L.M." worked here in 1849–1851 and gave an interesting, anti-American account. Gerstaecker mined here in 1851, when it was almost exclusively occupied by Germans. He describes the place in his *Narrative* (pp. 234 ff.) and in his story "Eine Nacht in Mosquito Gulch" (I, p. 16). Doble mentioned the place June 21, 1852; it is shown on Camp's map. The *Calaveras Chronicle*, June 28, 1856, reports that forty arrastres were at work on a rich claim near Musquito Gulch, all owned by Mexican and Chilenos (clipping from Sacramento *Daily Union*, July 1, 1856, in Hayes Scrapbooks: Mining, I, sec. 23). According to another item in the *Calaveras Chronicle* about 1858, some Italians found a 20-pound block of quartz, which yielded five pounds of gold (Hittell Clippings, p. 29). A 10-stamp water-driven mill was built in 1864, an 18-stamp steam-driven mill in 1873 (*Annual Mining Review*, 1876, p. 21). Mining was typical "pocket mining." The deposits apparently petered out in 1878, when the post office was transferred to Glencoe.

Mosquito Gulch [Trinity]. A branch of Strope Creek. According to Cox (p. 91), it was the best settled and most improved of the tributaries to the east fork of Stuarts Fork.

Mosquito Valley [El Dorado]. Six miles northeast of Placerville, north of the South Fork of American River. Mosquito Road is recorded on Bowman's map, 1873. Rich placers were discovered in 1849. There were two camps, called Big House or Lower Town and Nelsonville. (Bowman's map shows Nelson Creek, but not Nelsonville.) In 1853 or 1854 a ditch from Slab Creek brought water. When the placers gave out, attempts at quartz mining were made, but the main activity was agriculture. (Co. Hist., 1883, p. 192.) The U. S. Bureau of the Census for 1850 lists the names of 126 inhabitants in Mosquito Canyon. A settlement, Mosquito, is shown on the USGS Placerville 1931 quadrangle.

Mound Springs [El Dorado]. Near Diamond Springs. An undated clipping in Hayes Scrapbooks: Mining (I, sec. 34) mentions the miners of Mound Springs as participants at a mass meeting held on March 29, 1856, at Diamond Springs. The camp is mentioned in 1859 by Crockett (p. 95).

Mound Springs [Tuolumne]. On Six Bit Gulch, about two miles west of Chinese Camp. Shown on Trask's map, 1853. Hutchings mentions it on July 20, 1855. Between the 1850s and 1860s it was a noted stage coach stop (De Ferrari).

Mountain Brow [Tuolumne]. In the Table Mountain district, on Highway 49, northwest of Shaws Flat. It was discovered in 1848 (Stoddart, p. 62). Heckendorn mentions the name in 1856 (p. 104).

Mountain Cottage [Yuba]. About two and a half miles southwest of Bullards Bar, on the ridge between Dobbins Ranch and Bullards Bar. Shown on Doolittle's map, 1868. It was mentioned as a stage stop by Meek and was later known as Summit House (p. 163 f.).

Mountaineer Lawsons Mining Camp [Sierra]. Apparently between the North and Middle forks of Feather River. It is mentioned by Steele, who reached this camp in Feburary, 1851, after a dangerous winter expedition (p. 185).

Mountaineer Mine [Nevada]. *See* Nevada City.

Mountain Gate Mine [Placer]. *See* Damascus.

Mountain House [Butte]. Between the Middle and North forks of Feather River, on Mountain House Creek. It was on the stage route between Oroville and Quincy, twenty-six miles northeast of Oroville. Shown on the County Map, 1862. A drift mine nearby was worked until the 1920s (*Mining Bureau*, XXIV, p. 202; XXVI, pp. 401 f.), and it is still listed in 1949. The Mountain Cottage, at which a lump of gold valued at 894 dollars was found (*Mining Press*, December 21, 1861), is shown on the same map just below Mountain House.

Mountain House [Plumas]. About three and a half miles north of Spanish Peak. It is mapped and listed by J. A. Edman (in Raymond, VIII, pp. 110 and 118), who states in 1875 that placer and hydraulic mines here had long been idle.

Mountain House [Shasta]. On Clear Creek, north of French Gulch at the end of the trail to the mining region. It is prominently shown on Goddard's map, 1857.

Mountain House [Sierra]. On Brush Creek, south of Goodyears Bar. Old Mountain House is shown on Crossman's map, 1867, and it is also recorded on the USGS Colfax 1938 quadrangle. It was a well known stage stop on the Sierra Turnpike. In the 1850s it was mentioned as an election precinct. A water-driven mill is listed in 1858 (*State Register*, 1859) and a steam-driven 10-stamp mill was built in 1868 (*Annual Mining Review*, 1876, p. 21). Near the camp a nugget worth 1,770 dollars was found (*Mining Bureau*, II, part 1, p. 149). The Brush Creek Ledge was considered the richest ledge in California, according to an item in an unidentified clipping of January, 1868, in Bancroft Scraps (LI: 2, pp. 624 f.). See Brush Creek. A Mountain House Mine is listed in the reports of the Mining Bureau until 1942.

Mountain King Mine. See Benton Mills [Mariposa]; Hodson [Calaveras].

Mountain Meadows District [Lassen]. In the southwestern part of the county, about fifteen miles northeast of Big Meadows. Placer gold was mined years ago. The deposits are in the Tertiary channel which extends to Taylorsville and Genessee districts. (*Bull.*, 193, p. 93.)

Mountain Ranch [Calaveras]. On El Dorado Creek, about ten miles southeast of Mokelumne Hill. The original name was El Dorado. It was a trading center for quartz and drift mines in the 1850s, with a post office established in 1858. Raymond (IV, p. 79) states that El Dorado was a decayed mining town in 1871, near which there were promising quartz ledges, with a 10-stamp mill on one claim (also listed in the *Annual Mining Review*, 1876, p. 23). In 1899 there were four stamp mills and one Tuster mill (*Mines and Minerals*, 1899). A placer mine is listed in the Mining Bureau report of 1936. Mountain Ranch is shown on the USGS Jackson 1938 quadrangle.

Mountain Springs [Placer]. About three miles southwest of Dutch Flat. A post office was established in 1854, and in 1863 the name was changed to Gold Run. See Gold Run. A claim for water rights was datelined Mountain Springs, near Gopher Town, February 9, 1855, in Placer County Records (I, p. 281). Doolittle's map, 1868, shows Mountain Springs Hotel less than a mile south of Gold Run.

Mountain View [Butte]. See Dogtown.

Mount Ararat [Butte]. An undetermined location, but apparently near Oroville. It is mentioned by Windeler (p. 105) as his "residence" while mining in the area in the winter of 1850–1851.

Mount Auburn [El Dorado]. Near Cedarville, between the Middle and South forks of Cosumnes River. It is listed in Hittell's roster.

Mount Auburn [Nevada]. About two miles northwest of Nevada City. The County Map, 1880, lists a quartz mine and indicates its location. The mine is described in

Mining Bureau, XVI (Nevada, p. 202), and it is listed until 1941.

Mount Baldy District [San Bernardino]. Mount San Antonio, the highest peak in the San Gabriel Mountains, is known locally as Mount Baldy, and the saddle on the Lytle Creek-San Antonio Canyon divide is called Baldy Notch. Gold was discovered on Baldy Notch and on upper San Antonio Creek in 1871 and mined intermittently to 1895. The major mine in the district was the Banks Mine, located in 1872 by James S. Banks and consolidated in 1894 with other placer mines in the area to form the Hocumac Mine (*Holcomb, Cushion, Mackay*). Large-scale hydraulic operations led to an injunction against the company for polluting the waters of San Antonio Creek, and by 1900 the mine was closed. On the southern slope of Mount Baldy a gold quartz vein was discovered in 1897, and there was a minor rush to the area, but by 1899 work was abandoned. A detailed account of the Mount Baldy District is given by J. W. Robinson (pp. 58 ff.).

Mount Buckingham [Mariposa]. About ten miles northeast of Mariposa. The first quartz mine was opened in 1850 by William Buckingham. An account of the mining activities in the first half of the twentieth century is given in *Mining Bureau*, XXIV (p. 102) and LIII (p. 133). Shown on the USGS Yosemite 1938 quadrangle.

Mount Bullion [Mariposa]. About five miles northwest of Mariposa, on Highway 49. It was on the Frémont grant. The camp was originally called Princeton. See Princeton. When the post office was established July 10, 1862, it was named after the mountain that had been given the nickname of Frémont's father-in-law, Senator Thomas Hart Benton. The history of the Princeton is summarized under the entry Princeton.

Mount Calvary [El Dorado]. Between Otter and Canyon creeks, north of Georgetown. The mines are listed in 1874 among the principal gravel mines of the Georgetown Divide (Raymond, VII, pp. 91, 95).

Mount Diablo [Contra Costa]. About twenty-five miles east of Oakland. The *Alta*, May 10, 1854, reported the finding of gold in the hills. It caused a brief excitement in Oakland, and companies were organized, but nothing developed.

Mount Echo District [Amador]. Bordering Dry Creek. In July, 1861, paying gold and silver mining was reported in *Mining Press*, July 20, 1861.

Mount Gaines [Mariposa]. Near Quartzburg, eight miles northwest of Mariposa. It was named for John Gaines, who came to the area from Texas in 1849 with his son John and cousin Edmond Gaines. The area was first placer mined in the 1850s and 1860s. In 1862 a 10-stamp steam-driven mill was built (*Annual Mining Review*, 1876, p. 22). The depth of the Mount Gaines mine shaft in 1911 was 1,322 feet, and thousands of feet of drifts were run. Between 1900 and 1911 the production was about one million dollars and by 1956 it reached 3.5 millions or more, ranking it among the five most productive mines in the county. A description is given in *Mining Bureau*, LIII (pp. 135 ff.). Shown on *Guidebook* Map 1.

Mount George [Nevada]. On Rush Creek, three miles from Nevada City. A quartz mill was established in 1852 (Trask, Senate Document 14, p. 63). According to the *Mining Press*, August 24, 1861, the mill was dismantled in 1861 and transferred to Washoe. A Mount George Mine is described in *Mining Bureau*, XII (pp. 193, 254), and it is listed until 1941.

Mount Gleason District [Los Angeles]. Eight miles south of Acton. Gold was discovered on the mountain in 1869 by George Gleason. There were many small mines on the slopes, which were active mainly in the 1890s, but only small amounts of gold were recovered. Mining continued intermittently in a small way until about 1930. (J. W. Robinson, p. 29; *Mining Bureau*, XII, p. 152; XV, pp. 476 f.; XXIII, p. 293; XXXIII, pp. 187 f.)

Mount Gregory [El Dorado]. West of the junction of Rubicon River and Long Canyon, on the road to Volcanoville. Shown on Goddard's map, 1857. A list of diggings and a description of the mining are given in Raymond (IV, p. 104; VII, p. 93). A placer mine is listed in Mining Bureau reports until 1937.

Mount Hope [Lassen]. *See* Hayden Hill.

Mount Hope [Yuba]. East of Forbestown, near the Butte County line. The place is shown as a sizeable camp on the Butte County Map, 1861. According to the County History, 1879 (p. 90), so-called winter diggings were worked from 1850 to 1856. In 1858 a quartz ledge was discovered, and a 5-stamp mill was built. A Mount Hope or Beehive Mine is listed in the reports of the Mining Bureau until 1952. Mount Hope House is shown on the USGS Bidwell Bar 1944 quadrangle.

Mount Ophir, Ophir [Mariposa]. Northwest of Mariposa. The white quartz-capped mountain is a prominent landmark along Highway 49. The first gold in the rich deposits was discovered apparently in 1848 by Mexicans, who were said to have taken out 217 thousand dollars in one week (!), according to Vischer (p. 243). The name was applied in 1851, and it is shown on Gibbes' map, 1852, and on other early maps. On February 20, 1852, the post office was established as Ophir, and on November 3, 1856, it was changed to Mount Ophir. According to tradition, the famous octagonal twenty and fifty dollar gold slugs were coined here from locally mined gold in a private mint built in 1850 by John L. Moffatt. A photograph of the ruins of the building purported to be the mint is reproduced in *Mining Bureau*, XIV (p. 591). The Merced Mining Company, of which Moffatt was one of the directors, commenced operations at Mount Ophir in April, 1851. A description of their installations is given in the report of the company in 1852. No mention of the mint is made in this report, nor in that of the Nouveau Monde Gold Mining Company, September 30, 1854. No other contemporary record of the existence of the mint was found, and Adams makes no mention of it. In 1858 there were twenty-four steam-driven stamps in operation (*Annual Mining Review*, 1876, p. 22). In 1859 the Mount Ophir Mine became a part of Frémont's grant and operations continued intermittently until 1914. The estimated production is between 250 thousand and 300 thousand dollars. (*Mining Bureau*, LIII, pp. 139 f.) Mount Ophir is shown on the *Guidebook* Map 1 as a ghost town.

Mount Oro [Nevada]. About three miles northeast of Quaker Hill. Shown on Doolittle's map, 1868. It is mentioned in Raymond, VI (p. 117) and in Whitney, *Auriferous Gravels* (p. 178).

Mount Pleasant [Sierra]. In the Slate Creek Basin, five miles south of La Porte. Shown on Crossman's map, 1867. The place was originally called Mount Pleasant Ranch. According to a letter of George Tufly to his brother, written from Mount Pleasant Ranch, April 10, 1855, the diggings were discovered there in the spring of that year. The *Mining Press*, May 25, 1861, reported that the mines were paying forty to fifty ounces a week. A detailed description of hydraulic mining in the region around 1872 is given in Raymond, V (p. 85). Pettee visited a hydraulic mine here in 1879 and stated in his report that there had been drift mining there in previous years, in the decade beginning about 1859

(Whitney, *Auriferous Gravels*, p. 450). Mount Pleasant is shown on the USGS Downieville 1907 quadrangle.

Mount Pleasant Mine [El Dorado]. *See* Grizzly Flats.

Mount Sinai District [Kern]. The district includes the mines on Kelso Creek, a tributary to the South Fork of Kern River. They were discovered and named by a party of prospectors in June, 1861. The rock was first worked by arrastres, and it is claimed that it yielded as high as 200 dollars per ton. (Havilah *Courier*, September 26, 1866, in Bancroft Notes.) *See* Claraville.

Mount Vernon Diggings [Sierra]. Two miles south of Downieville. Shown on Doolittle's map, 1868.

Mount Washington [Sierra]. It is mentioned as the site of a mine in Trask's *Report*, 1854 (doc. 9, p. 90).

Mount Zion [Nevada]. Between the Middle and South forks of Yuba River; about one and a half miles southeast of Snows Tent. Shown on Hoffmann and Craven's Gravel Map, 1873. Pettee in 1879 states that work had been carried on for more than twenty years and that a tunnel 1,400 feet in length reached bedrock. Drifting and hydraulic mining are also mentioned by Lindgren, 1911 (p. 141).

Mouth of Middle Yuba [Yuba]. This is the designation of a camp where many prospectors mined as late as 1879 (Co. Hist., 1879, p. 94).

Mowry's Flat [Siskiyou]. *See* Frenchtown.

Mud Canyon [Placer]. On the north bank of the middle Fork of American River, near Niggers Bluff and Missouri Canyon. Bancroft lists the place in his *History*, VI (p. 354) and states that the output was reportedly 3 million dollars.

Mud Flat [Nevada]. Near Nevada City. It is listed as a settlement in *Bean's Directory*, 1867.

Mud Hill [Butte]. Near Oroville. Named by Delano (*Correspondence*, p. 39) because he was "mud-bound" here for several weeks in the winter of 1849–1850. Delano does not give a mining record, but an interesting account is given at the end of chapter XVII of his *Life on the Plains*. The place is shown prominently on Trask's map, 1853.

Mud Springs [El Dorado]. About four miles southwest of Placerville. The name of the post office has been El Dorado since 1855, but the old name prevailed for many years and was even used by the Geological Survey on the Placerville quadrangle as late as 1931. It was applied in analogy to nearby Diamond Spring and was given because of the mud around the spring in which emigrants watered their cattle (Co. Hist., 1883, p. 203). The U. S. Bureau of the Census lists the names of 462 inhabitants at Mud Springs and vicinity in the population schedule for the 1850 census. The post office was established November 6, 1851. In 1854 the place reportedly had 2,500 inhabitants. In the same year a nugget of more than twenty-five ounces of nearly pure gold was picked up (*Alta*, September 7, 1854), probably the same nugget as the one weighing more than twenty-six ounces picked up by a Chinese miner and reported in the Sacramento *Union* (Hittell Clippings, p. 28). In 1858 there were three stamp mills and several arrastres in operation (*State Register*, 1859). *See* El Dorado.

Mugfuzzle Flat. An unidentified place mentioned in the (1856?) *Golden Era* (Guinn, p. 43).

Muggins. The name, repeatedly used for gold camps, is possibly derived from a personal name. Bret Harte and Mark Twain used it later, the former for "simpleton," the latter in reference to a card game. Marryat uses the expressions "fat Muggins" and "ignorant Foodle" on pages 288 f., but on page 367 he has a picture of the front of "Judge Muggins's Office" housed in a liquor store.

Muggins Bar [Plumas]. Below the junction of the East Branch with North Fork of Feather River. It was a mining camp of little importance in the fall of 1851 (Dame Shirley, p. 52). It may be the same as Mugginsville shown on Goddard's map, 1857, on the North Fork above the junction, and Muggingville mentioned in *Mining Press*, June 15, 1861.

Mugginsville [Calaveras?]. On the road from Stockton to Yosemite. Ralston stopped here with his bride in 1858 on his wedding trip (Haight, p. 3).

Mugginsville [Placer]. Hutchings lists it as a "town" in Placer County in 1855, but he does not locate it specifically. In the Sacramento *Union*, December 13, 1855, it is located a half mile below Gold Hill, about eight miles from Auburn. It came into existence about the same time as Gold Hill, in the early 1850s, but it appeared to be deserted in December, 1855. In the same item the name Oro is given as an alternate name. Curiously, Orr City is given as an alternate name of Gold Hill in 1855. See Gold Hill [Placer].

Mugginsville [Sierra]. Near Eureka North. It was in a hydraulic mining area. In 1862 one company averaged fifteen dollars a day to the hand, according to an item in the *Mining Press*, August 21, 1862. A Mugginsville placer mine is listed in the reports of the Mining Bureau until 1942.

Mugginsville [Siskiyou]. On Mill Creek, in Quartz Valley. The place is mentioned as a considerable camp in Bancroft, VI (p. 495). In 1858 it had a water-driven 6-stamp mill (*State Register*, 1859). The batteries and stamps of the old Morrison-Carlock 10-stamp mill are still standing (William Smith). In 1860 nearly 300 votes were cast at the camp (Co. Hist., 1881, p. 215). Shown on the USGS Yreka 1939 quadrangle.

Mugwump Mine [Sierra]. One quarter mile southwest of Forest. The mine, formerly known as Young America, is a combination lode and drift mine, with placer gold the major production. It was first worked in 1852 and intermittently from the 1890s to the late 1920s. In 1953 it was reactivated. The workings are described in the Mining Bureau *Report* of 1956 (p. 255). *See* Young American Flat. Mugwump is an Algonquian word for 'chief', but was used in American slang for persons convinced of their importance.

Mule Mountains [Shasta]. A district of quartz mines. The Black Bear Mine was still listed in 1939 (*Mining Bureau*, XXIX, p. 11; XXXV, p. 177). Shown on the USGS Weaverville 1942 quadrangle. *See* Muletown.

Mule Mountains District [Riverside]. About twenty miles southwest of Blythe, in the southeastern part of the county. There was some gold and copper mining here years ago, according to *Bulletin*, 193 (p. 161).

Mule Ravine [Nevada]. On the Blue Lead, west of Dutch Flat. It is mentioned in Bean (1867, p. 369).

Mule Springs [Nevada]. Above Little York. There was mining in the creek in the dry season only (*Alta*, December 20, 1853). A placer claim at Mule Springs Ranch in the Lowell District farther to the northeast was worked in the late 1930s and early 1940s (*Mining Bureau*, XXXVII, p. 434).

Muletown [Amador]. On Mule Creek, about one and a half miles north of Ione City. The name is shown on the County Map, 1866. The County History, 1881 (pp. 192 ff.), describes the place as a lively camp in the 1850s and gives a lengthy account, including the price of admission to a dance hall: single man, six dollars; with one lady, three dollars; with two ladies, free. According to the story, an Argentino often

washed out 100 dollars a day, and a Chinese miner once found a lump of gold weighing thirty-six ounces. The Quincy *Prospector*, March 3, 1855, and later issues, print the "Miners' Laws" for Muletown District. *See* Quincy [Amador].

Muletown [Shasta]. The original name, One Mule Town, was apparently given in analogy to nearby One Horse Town. In 1852 One Mule Town was listed in the state census as one of the nine principal mining localities of the county. Pringle Shaw, too, in 1856 calls it an important camp (p. 128). The Muletown District, which extends along Clear Creek, southwest of Redding, borders on the Igo and Ono districts. The first water-driven 6-stamp mill was erected in 1857 (*State Register*, 1859). The Muletown Consolidated Mines operated until 1938 (*Mining Bureau*, XXXV, pp. 149, 185).

Mumford Bar [Placer]. On the south side of the North Fork of American River, above Humbug Bar. The name is listed in the Giffen file, and it is shown on the USGS Colfax 1938 quadrangle and on the Duncan Peak 1952 quadrangle.

Mumfords Hill [Plumas]. About three miles southeast of Spanish Peak. Shown on the map in Raymond, VIII (p. 110). There was well-paying surface mining, and in 1875 hydraulic mining was still carried on profitably. The geology of the region is described by J. A. Edman in Raymond, VIII (pp. 109, 114, 115, 119).

Munckton [Mono]. *See* Castle Peak District.

Murchys Diggings [Nevada]. About a mile east of Nevada City. Shown on Doolittle's map, 1868. It was also known as Murchie Hill and Murchie Mine, located in 1861 by the Murchie brothers (*Bean's Directory*). The mine was later operated by the Empire Star Mines Company and was among two of the most important groups of gold quartz mines in the state (*Mining Bureau*, XVI, Nevada, pp. 202 f.; XXVI, pp. 118 f.; XXXVII, pp. 380, 458). It is shown on the USGS Colfax 1938 quadrangle.

Murderers Bar [El Dorado]. On the Middle Fork of American River, near its junction with the North Fork. Shown on Trask's map, 1853, and on most early maps. There are numerous accounts of the origin of the name, the most plausible probably the one told by Theodore Hittell in his *History*, III (pp. 76 f.). In the fall of 1848 five Oregonians were killed by Indians after the prospectors had killed three Indians who had tried to protect their women. Theressa Gay (in her biography of James W.

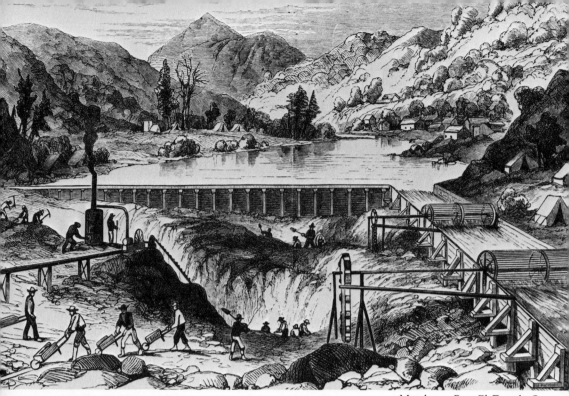

Murderers Bar, El Dorado Co.

Marshall, chapter 13) gives a detailed account, which she has based on contemporary reports. The diggings proved to be very rich. According to an item from the Sacramento *Transcript*, April 26, 1850 (Bancroft Notes), 100 to 150 men made two ounces per day to the man. Banks of the Buckeye Rovers (p. 135) tells the story of a miner who gave up a claim to an old man who made 9 thousand dollars from it. An item in the *Pacific News*, October 19, 1850, repeated in the *California Courier*, October 22, even claims that one company took out 132 ounces in one day and between 70 and 115 ounces daily in ten days. Marryat (pp. 235 ff.) shudders at the name but gives a pleasing account of the peaceful camp in July, 1851. The decline began in 1858, when only 200 miners, including Chinese, were left. (Sacramento *Union*, October, 1858, in Hittell Clippings, p. 67½.) A prospectus of 1875 claims the total production of the bar at 2.5 million dollars. The place is still shown on the USGS Auburn 1944 quadrangle.

Murderers Bar [Siskiyou]. Near the junction of Indian Creek with Klamath River. Gold mining started before 1851. The bar was so named because three miners were killed by Indians (George Gibbs, October 18, 1851, in Schoolcraft, III, pp. 155 f.). *See* Happy Camp.

Murderers Bar [Yuba]. On the main Yuba River, below present-day Englebright Dam. The name of the place is identified by two letters written by Alexander Rotchev, November 10, 1851 and February 23, 1852. They were published in *Archiv für Wissenschaftliche Kunde von Russland* and translated by Frederick C. Cordes in *CHSQ*, XXXIX (pp. 97 ff.). Rotchev, the last governor of Fort Ross, had sold the Russian colonies in California to Sutter for a song; now he had come back assuming that Sutter was wallowing in gold and could easily underwrite Rotchev's gold digging ideas. A. Erman, the editor of the German *Archiv*, had been in California in the 1830s and had called to the attention of Rotchev and the Russians the potential gold bearing soil of California.

Murderers Gulch [Amador]. North of Amador City. Placer mining was carried on as early as 1849. The place is mentioned in the County History, 1881 (p. 231), and in *Guidebook* (p. 65).

Murphys [Calaveras]. On Angels Creek and Highway 4. The town is one of the oldest and best known gold camps of the Southern Mines. It is shown on Trask's map, 1853, and all other early maps. The camp developed at the end of June, 1848, in connection with Charles M. Weber's Stockton Mining Company. It was named for John M. Murphy, one of the Murphys who had come from Canada with the Stevens-Murphy-Townsend party in 1844. It was the first immigrant party to bring wagons across the Sierra Nevada to Sutter's Fort. In 1857 the pioneer was already forgotten. When the Ralston-Frey wedding party passed the place, they were told "that it was named for a blundering Irishman" (Haight, p. 5). Chester Lyman camped with Murphy at Dry Creek on June 15, 1848 ("The Gold Rush", p. 185). A few weeks later (July 8) he found Murphy at a nearby site selling glass beads to the Indians in exchange for gold. This may have been the place known as Murphys Old Diggings. Some time later John and Daniel Murphy moved to the site on Angels Creek, and this camp became known as Murphys New Diggings, later shortened to Murphys, as in the name of the post office established November 6, 1851. Audubon made several nice drawings of the place. Gerstaecker describes the camp in a chapter entitled "Murphy's New Diggings" in his London, 1854 edition of his *Travels* (pp. 222 ff.). But he sometimes confuses the identity of the camps Stoutenburg and Murphys New Diggings. *See* Stoutenburg. The French miners dominated, with a mixture of Germans, Americans, and Mexicans. In 1851 the cooperative Union Water Company was organized to bring water from Stanislaus River, and the town enjoyed a phenomenal development (Hittell Clippings, p. 76). A suspension flume was constructed across the gorge, and in 1857 a drainage canal was built. Vischer (pp. 329 ff.) and *Transactions*, 1859 (p. 88) give a detailed description of the activities. Browne (pp. 57 f.) records that there were a dozen claims that were said to have averaged each one hundred thousand dollars or more. The Rhodes claim yielded thirty-seven pounds of gold one afternoon and sixty-three pounds the following morning. At least that is the report. The decline began in the middle 1860s. Although the placers were almost exhausted, there was still some hydraulic mining and also some lode mining. In 1867 there was one 3-stamp mill operating (Browne, p. 70) and in 1899 there were three mills. The district is described in *Mining Bureau*, XIII (p. 114). In recent years some of the mines have again been prospected (*Bull.*, 193, p. 96). Joaquin Murieta is, of course, connected with the town. According to an indestructible legend, the elusive character tried to make an honest living here, first as a miner, then as a monte dealer. The hanging of his half-brother turned him to banditry. (Ridge, pp. 11 f.) Murphys is the scene of several stories by Gerstaecker and two by

Dexter (no. 5 and 6). There is no evidence that Murphys was once called Wingdam — Bret Harte's "A Night in Wingdam" is fictitious. The Mitchler Hotel, established in the 1850s as the Sperry and Perry Hotel by J. L. Sperry (later of Sperry Flour fame) and John Perry, has operated continuously until the present day, and it preserves the old guest book with the names of well-known pioneers as well as national figures who were guests here in the past. Murphys is Historic Landmark 275 and Mitchlers Hotel is No. 267. *See* Vallecito.

Murphys Defeat [Tuolumne]. West of Columbia. The name is mentioned by Dane (p. 3) and was probably only a local nickname.

Murphys: Gulch, Ridge [Amador]. South of Jackson. Shown on the County Map, 1866. The Gulch is mentioned in Bancroft VI (p. 372) as having been one of the productive mining sites on the Mokelumne River.

Murrays Creek [Calaveras]. A tributary to the North Fork of Calaveras River, near Mountain Ranch. In 1857 two mills with sixteen stamps were in operation (*State Register*, 1859). The name appears on the USGS Jackson 1938 quadrangle, and the consolidated mines are listed in the Mining Bureau report of 1936.

Murraysville [Sierra]. *See* Jersey Flat.

Musquito. This was the spelling for Mosquito in several locations. For Musquito Gulch [Calaveras] *see* Mosquito Gulch and Glencoe.

Musser Diggings [Trinity]. Between East Weaver and Browns creeks. The diggings were paying well, according to the *Trinity Journal*, January 11, 1862.

Myers Diggings [Plumas]. Apparently the original name of Rich Bar (or a part of it) on the North Fork of Feather River. J. J. Myers was very likely one of the Germans who discovered the immensely rich deposits where Lassen had only found a trace of gold. Details are found in Bruff, August 18, 1850, and *passim*. *See* Rich Bar.

Myers Ravine [Nevada]. Near Nevada City. A settlement is listed under this name in *Bean's Directory*, 1867.

Myrtle Creek [Del Norte]. About ten miles above the mouth of Smith River. There was mainly coarse gold mining, and in 1854 the average yield was five to fifteen dollars a day to the hand. In June a miner made 400 dollars in two hours (Co. Hist., 1881, p. 21). A hydraulic mine was in operation until about 1900 but was reported as idle in 1925 (*Mining Bureau*, XI, p. 195; XXI, p. 293); it is still listed in 1952.

Mystery Gulch [Plumas]. *See* Mosquito Creek.

Nameless Point [El Dorado]. One of the Mount Gregory diggings, west of the junction of the Middle Fork of American River and Rubicon River.

Nantan [San Bernardino]. *See* Mescal.

Napa Bar [Siskiyou]. On a tributary to Klamath River, in the Cottonwood Mining District. According to *Mining Bureau*, VIII (p. 590), it was worked in 1888 by Chinese.

Nary Red [Placer]. A gravel hill between Dutch Flat and Alta. Shown on Pettee and Bowman's map, 1879, on which the extent of hydraulic mining is indicated. It is mentioned by Browne (p. 198) and by Lindgren (*Tertiary Gravels*, p. 145). The gravel was considered worthless; hence the name, derived from "never a red cent" referring to a copper cent.

Nashville [El Dorado]. On the North Fork of Cosumnes River, two miles north of the junction with the Middle Fork. The early name was Quartzville (El Dorado Co. Hist., 1883, p. 198) and this name appears on Trask's map, 1853. Amador County History, 1881 (p. 160), gives the name as Quartzburg. The present name was applied after Nashville, Tennessee, when the post office was established, March 5, 1852. The quartz vein was opened before 1851, and the camp was one of the first to introduce quartz crushing by arrastres and then by stamp mills. At one time 100 arrastres were observed with usually three Mexicans working each one (*Mountain Democrat*, souvenir edition, 1898). The first mill with 10 stamps was manufactured in Cincinnati and was brought around Cape Horn (*State Register*, 1857; *Guidebook*, pp. 33, 66). Some of the mines in the Nashville district produced profitably until the 1930s and 1940s, and there has been minor prospecting since (*Mining Bureau*, LII, pp. 411, 421; *Bull.*, 193, p. 96). The Montezuma-Apex Mine is credited with a production of one million dollars and the Nashville with 2 millions. Other productive mines mentioned in the reports of the Mining Bureau and elsewhere include the Buena Vista, the Central or Inez, the German, the Lone Star, and the Havilah (*Mining Bureau*, LII, pp. 421 ff.).

Natchez [Yuba]. On the Natchez Fork of Honcut Creek. Recorded on Trask's map, 1853 and on Goddard's, 1857. The camp began to develop in 1850, prospered for several years, and had a bad reputation for gambling and fighting (Co. Hist., 1879, p. 90). According to an undated item in the *Sierra Citizen*, one company took out three pounds in three days (Hittell clipping). In February, 1852, Huntley (p. 84) called the camp "almost deserted." But the ravines around the place paid well before they were exhausted.

National Bar [Yuba]. On the south side of the main Yuba River, fifteen miles above the confluence with Dry Creek. Shown on Trask's map, 1853.

Native American [Tuolumne]. Mentioned in 1856 by Heckendorn as a place in the Table Mountain District.

Native American Ravine [Nevada]. In the vicinity of Cement Hill near Nevada City. It is mentioned by Pettee in 1870 (p. 184) in his discussion of the ancient river channels in the area; and it is listed in Hittell's roster.

Natoma [Sacramento]. At or near Mormon Island. Recorded on Jackson's map, 1850, and Butler's, 1851. The name, also spelled Notoma, is Maidu Indian for 'east'. The place at Mormon Island was established in 1848 by Sam Brannan and was mentioned in 1849 by Wierzbicki as though it were the same place as Mormon Island. Notoma Valley Hotel is shown on Doolittle's map, 1868. The Natoma Ditch was a major source of mining around Folsom (*Mining Press*, October 26, 1861). The main canal was started in 1851, taking its water from the South Fork of American River at a point about two miles above Salmon Falls. (Natoma Dam in El Dorado County is shown on Doolittle's map, 1868.) The ditch reached Prairie City in 1853 and Folsom in 1854. The present-day town of Natoma, about one and a half miles southeast of Folsom, was called Dredge before 1909 (*Bull.*, 57, p. 201). It became the headquarters of the field offices and repair shops of the Natomas Company, a consolidation of three large dredging companies, and was the leading gold producer in California from 1946 to 1952 (*Mining Bureau*, LI, pp. 140 f.). *See* Folsom.

Natural Bar [Yuba]. Apparently on the main Yuba River near Englebright Reservoir. In 1867 it was buried under gravel (*Alta*, November 7, 1867).

Neals Bar [Nevada]. On the south side of Yuba River, eight and a half miles above Dry Creek. Recorded on Trask's map, 1853.

Neals Diggings [Butte]. On Butte Creek,

near Chinese Camp. The camp is shown on Trask's map, 1853, and was probably named for Sam Neal, the owner of the ranch on lower Butte Creek.

Neals Ranch [Mariposa]. In a gulch at the Chowchilla River. The *Mining Press*, April 25, 1862, reports that east of the ranch fifty dollars worth of gold were taken out by one person in three hours.

Nebraska: City, Flat [Sierra]. *See* Nebraska Diggings.

Nebraska Diggings [Sierra]. At the head of Jim Crow Ravine, southeast of Downieville. Shown on the County Map, 1874. It was also known as Nebraska City and Nebraska Flat (Sinnott, *Downieville*, p. 202). In 1853 a tunnel was built in solid rock, which did not pay. In 1858 a new, lower tunnel was started, which finally paid handsomely. (*Mining Press*, May 16, 1862.) It was a stopping place on the Henness Pass Road and was also called Cornish House. The name Cornish House is recorded on the USGS Downieville 1907 and 1951 quadrangles.

Nebraska Mine [Nevada]. *See* Washington Ridge.

Needles [San Bernardino]. On the Santa Fe Railroad, near the Arizona state line. The town, founded in 1883, was not a mining town but an important railroad and supply center for the large desert mining area surrounding it. Until after 1900 it was also the landing place for the Colorado River steamers, which hauled ore and heavy machinery for the mines (Delameter). A smelter was built in 1892 and enlarged in 1910, when more than twenty carloads of ore arrived there daily (*Needles Eye*, April 17, 1892; San Bernardino *Index*, May 20, 1910; Haenszel).

Needles Bar [Tuolumne]. Somewhere on the Tuolumne River. No mining record was found except Albert Leonard's report of unsuccessful prospecting in the spring of 1850.

Neenach [Los Angeles]. Small quantities of gold, about one hundred thousand dollars worth, were taken out in the Antelope Valley foothills between 1935 and 1938 (*Mining Bureau*, L, p. 494). The total production for the district is given at about two hundred thousand dollars in *Bulletin*, 193 (p. 175).

Negro. The term was frequently used in geographical names since the presence of one blackamoor was often sufficient to call the place for him. The nickname Nigger was still more often used, even in modern nomenclature. *See* Nigger.

Negro Bar [Placer]. On the North Fork of American River. A sluice claim from the upper end of Missouri Bar upstream 500 yards to Negro Bar was recorded December 3, 1852 in Placer County Records, I (p. 145).

Negro Bar [Sacramento]. On the American River, just downstream from Folsom. On Trask's map, 1853, and on Judah's, 1854, it is shown on the south side of the river; on Goddard's map, 1857, it appears on the north side. According to the County History, 1880 (p. 222), it was on the same side of the river as Folsom, where it began and ran nine-tenth of a mile downstream. The diggings were rich and in 1851 the camp had a population of 700. According to a manuscript note on an annotated copy of Judah's map, "upwards of two million dollars has been taken out at Negro Bar since 1849." In 1880 there was still some mining, mainly by Chinese. The U. S. Bureau of the Census in its population schedule for the 1850 census lists the names of 336 inhabitants at Negro Bar and "On the road." Hutchings found the place almost deserted but with a good hotel and "Chinamen everwhere" (Diary, April 23, 1855). The name Nigger Bar was apparently in use around 1909, when dredging was carried on between Dredge (Natoma) and Nigger Bar, as reported in *Bulletin*, 57 (pp. 180, 201). The USGS Folsom 1944 quadrangle shows Nigger Bar on the north side of the river, and it is now a part of a state park on the north bank (McGowan).

Negro Bar [Sierra]. Opposite Secret Canyon, east of Downieville. Downie's party mined here in October, 1849.

Negro Bar [Yuba]. On the main Yuba River, below the confluence with the South Fork. Shown on Milleson and Adams' map, 1851. The place was apparently named for a company of Negro prospectors. Breyfogle (p. 25) reports on February 24, 1850: "camped on Negro Bar with a company of negroes and was treated fairly." The *Alta* reported on November 7, 1867, that the bar was buried under gravel; but the County History, 1879 (p. 94), mentions a company of white men and some Chinese still at work in 1879.

Negro Bluff [El Dorado]. On the Middle Fork of American River, below Gray Eagle City. Shown on the Map of the Volcanoville Quartz Mining District. It is mentioned by A. H. Saxton in a sales agreement dated April 8, 1856.

Negro: Creek, Flat [Siskiyou]. Negro Creek

is a tributary to the South Fork of Salmon River. Negro Flat is at the mouth of the creek, about four miles above the Forks of Salmon. Shown on Goddard's map, 1857. The Flat is mentioned as one of the leading gold producers on the stream (Bancroft, VI, p. 370).

Negro Flat [El Dorado]. About five miles east of Placerville. Shown on Doolittle's map, 1868.

Negro Flat [Nevada]. Near Grass Valley. In 1854 the average pay was an ounce per day to the hand (*Alta*, April 8, 1854). Brown's *Directory*, 1856 (p. 133), mentions a Negro Flat fifteen and a half miles from Nevada City. The County Map, 1880, shows a Negro Creek, tributary to Deer Creek, about five miles west of Grass Valley.

Negro Gulch [Tuolumne]. Near Columbia. It is probably the same as Nigger Gulch near Nigger Hill, north of Columbia, in the vicinity of Gold Springs (De Ferrari). Eastman states that early deeds show these names as Negro Hill and Negro Gulch. The *Alta*, March 6, 1853, reports that there were diggings at Negro Gulch in 1850 and again in 1853, but the location is not indicated. There is a reference to a Negro Gulch near Columbia in the *Mining Press*, August 10, 1861, where it is stated that 106 ounces were taken out in one week by hydraulic operations, and that most of the claims took out large quantities of gold but did not report the profits.

Negro Hill [Calaveras]. East of Mokelumne Hill. According to the recollection of Charles Peters (p. 14), two negroes struck it rich in 1851. This caused such an excitement that a company decided to remove the top of the hill to find gold deposits. They succeeded, but the production was far less than expected and petered out in 1854 (*German Journal*, letter of June 18, 1855). In an item from the Mariposa *Chronicle* (Hittell Clippings, p. 26) the place is called Nigger Hill, and it is reported that Adams and Company exhibited (in 1854?) a unique amalgam of copper, silver, gold, and quartz found here.

Negro Hill [El Dorado]. On the South Fork of American River opposite Mormon Island, upstream eight miles from Salmon Falls. It is now under Folsom Lake. Shown on Judah's map of 1854 and on the Map of the American River and Natoma Water and Mining Company. It developed probably at the same time as Mormon Island in 1848. In 1853 the population was more than 1,000 according to Bancroft, VI (p.

352). The best description is in Newton Miller's letters, especially those of December 21, 1853, September 12 and December 26, 1854. Miller mined here successfully from 1853 to 1855, and his companies built a tunnel that paid rich dividends. He had a vegetable garden and a shower bath! There were originally two camps: Big and Little Negro Hill. In 1852 Dewitt, brother of Leland Stanford, opened a store here (Co. Hist., 1883, pp. 201 ff.). Hutchings gives the population at about 400 in 1855, "Whites, Negroes, and Portuguese" (Diary, April 24, 1855). In 1874 the riches were exhausted, but there was still some gold digging (Raymond, VII, p. 96). Historic Landmark 570. *See* Nigger Hill.

Negro Hill [El Dorado]. About three miles northeast of Placerville. Shown on a map in Whitney, *Auriferous Gravels* (p. 98). A. W. Goodyear in the same source (pp. 100 f.), in 1871, describes the gravels of two claims worked by the hydraulic process, one of which was said to be "very rich" in gold.

Negro Hill [Placer]. On the North Fork of American River, near Rattlesnake Bar. The place is mentioned in Hittell Clippings (p. 66½). The site of Rattlesnake Bar, now under Folsom Lake, is shown on the USGS Auburn 1954 quadrangle.

Negro Slide [Sierra]. On the south side of the North Fork of Yuba River, about two miles from Oak Valley, north of Camptonville. It is mentioned as a settlement by De Long, March 15, 1855. At one time the diggings paid eight to sixteen dollars to the hand (Sinnott, *Sierra City*, p. 165). The place was also known as Nigger Slide.

Negro Slide [Yuba]. On or near the North Fork of Yuba River; north of Camptonville. It is mentioned as a settlement by De Long, March 15, 1855.

Negro Tent [Sierra]. *See* Nigger Tent.

Nelighs Camp [El Dorado]. Near Placerville, just north of Webers Camp. Shown on the map accompanying Mason's Report, 1848, entitled "Positions of the Upper and Lower Gold Mines on the South Fork of the American River, California." Robert B. Neligh, an agent of Commodore Stockton, obtained 2 thousand dollars worth of gold here in three weeks. Mason visited the camp in July, 1848, and was given samples of gold. The camp is also mentioned by Lyman (p. 191).

Nelson: Creek, Diggings, Point [Plumas]. The Creek is a tributary to the Middle Fork of Feather River. Shown on Milleson and Adams' map, 1851, and most other early maps. The rich deposits were discovered in 1850 in the wake of the Gold Lake rush and were named for a "tall, sandy haired, thin faced, good natured hombre" (Delano, p. 19). The diggings proved to be one of the most profitable in the region. According to an item in the *Alta*, July 14, 1851, miners with a rocker made 500 dollars a day (Bancroft Notes). An undated clipping (Hittell, p. 26), as late as 1854, states that four men took out sixty-one

Nelson Point, Plumas Co.

ounces in one day. Other reports of the early years by Ferguson (p. 131), Lecouvreur (pp. 241 ff.), and Webster (pp. 156 ff.) were not as uniformly optimistic. An interesting description may be found in Delano's *Life on the Plains* (pp. 348 ff.). Until 1858 there was mainly ravine and river washing; the place could not be reached by teams (*Transactions*, 1858, pp. 205 f.). In 1862 several companies paid as high as twenty dollars a day to the hand (*Mining Press*, August 14, 1862). The riches were soon exhausted, but drift and placer mining is still recorded in the *Register* of 1900 and a mine in 1937 (*Mining Bureau*, XXXIII, p. 134). Nelson Creek and Point are shown on the USGS Downieville 1907 quadrangle. The post office was first established March 30, 1855, at Nelson Creek, then at Nelson Point.

Nelsons Bar [Butte]. On the east side of the West Branch of the North Feather River, about four miles above its mouth. Shown on Trask's map, 1853. It was reported extinct in 1880 (Co. Hist., 1882, p. 253). Shown on the USGS Oroville 1944 quadrangle.

Nelsonville [El Dorado]. *See* Mosquito Valley.

Neptune City [Placer]. North of Lake Tahoe. A settlement developed when gold and silver were discovered, but it was abandoned within a few years (*Bull.*, 193, pp. 124 f.). *See* Elizabethtown; Claraville; Knoxville.

Neptunes Bar [Placer]. *See* Dead Mans Bar.

Nesbits Bar [Placer]. In Auburn Ravine, near Gold Hill. The bar is mentioned in a mining lease recorded April 9, 1863 in Placer County Records, IV (pp. 87 ff.).

Nesbitts Flat [Butte]. An unidentified place. According to the *State Register*, 1859, a 12-stamp steam-driven mill was erected in 1857. It could refer to the John Nesbit ledge at Oregon City (Nopel).

Neutral Bar [Placer]. On the North Fork of American River, just below Euchre Bar. Notice of claim was recorded March 18, 1852, in Placer County Records, I (p. 82).

Nevada City [Nevada]. The rich auriferous deposits at Deer Creek were discovered in the fall of 1849 by a prospector named Hunt (Wistar, I, pp. 125 f.) and became known as Deer Creek Diggings or Deer Creek Dry Diggings. In September, 1849, the first log cabin was built, and in October Dr. A. B. Caldwell opened a store. The camp then became known as Caldwell's Upper Store. (Caldwell had previously built a store four miles down the creek at Beckville.) In March, 1850, at a public meeting, the inhabitants changed the name to Nevada (Brown and Dallison, pp. 18 ff.), and in December, 1850, when the post office was established, the name Nevada City was applied. The name Nevada City appears prominently on the 1851 maps of Butler and of Milleson and Adams. However, Gibbes' map, 1851, Trask's, 1853, and Goddard's, 1857, still show the name Nevada without the appellation "City." Gradually the name Nevada City prevailed to avoid confusion with the name of the county, established in 1851, and of Nevada Territory formed in 1861. The surface placers were rich and the camp grew quickly. Avery (in a letter published in *Bean's Directory*, pp. 74 ff.) recalls that in February, 1850, he found the ravines thick with miners, and American Hill covered with tents, brush houses, and a few log cabins. The great impetus came when the deep gravels of the ancient river bed were struck. According to various accounts, it happened when miners working in a ravine northeast of the camp found that the lead did not give out as usual but grew richer as they burrowed under the hill. The discovery caused great excitement and brought an influx of miners, who staked claims on the whole range of hills and sank shafts in an effort to trace the "lead." The yield was immense. A new camp sprang up and was named Coyoteville, after the method of mining likened to the burrowing of the coyote and called "coyoteing." (Brown and Dallison, pp. 17 f.; *Bean's Directory*, pp. 79 f.; Whitney, *Auriferous Gravels*, pp. 189 f.) *See* Coyoteville. The population of Nevada City as given in the schedule of the U. S. Census of 1850 was 1,067. By the fall of 1850 it had increased to about 6,000 in and about the town (Brown and Dallison, p. 22). A network of water ditches was begun in 1850, the first one in March from Mosquite Creek to Coyote Hill, another in May from Little Deer Creek to Phelps Hill. The Rock Creek Ditch, nine miles long, was completed in December, 1850. (Brown and Dallison, pp. 10 f.; Ferguson, p. 175). In 1851 the Deer Creek Water

Company was formed with William H. Folsom, later famous for building the Mormon Temple in Salt Lake City, as one of the organizers. Ground sluicing was introduced early in 1850 by William Elwell (Browne, pp. 118 f.) and came to be used extensively. The use of the water hose in sluicing operations was introduced near by by Anthony Chabot in 1852, and the following year the method of hydraulic mining was "invented" by Edward E. Matteson. *See* Buckeye Hill and American Hill. Quartz gold was found as early as 1850. The *Evening Picayune*, September 16, 1850, reported the finding of a lump weighing upwards of 400 pounds, for which the finders refused 25 thousand dollars. Other discoveries of quartz gold brought new excitement to the camp. The Merrifield, Providence, and Gold Tunnel veins were located in 1851. But difficulties were encountered in milling the quartz in early years. An undated clipping from the Nevada *Journal*, about 1854 (Hittell Clippings, p. 44) reports that earlier quartz-crushing undertakings along Deer Creek resulted in the loss of more than 125 thousand dollars. Vischer (p. 236) writes that an attempt by the Bunker Hill Company to separate gold by roasting quartz in a furnace ended in a complete failure.

Nevada City, Nevada Co.

The mills between 1851 and 1858 are listed in the *State Register*, 1859. There are two lengthy accounts of the early history of Nevada City and vicinity, one by A. A. Sargent in Brown and Dallison's *Directory*, 1856 (pp. 18–35), and one in *Bean's History*, 1867 (pp. 73–107). Contemporary accounts by individuals are numerous. Avery mined here while it was still called Deer Creek Diggings. Decker (pp. 233–257), Sawyer (pp. 118 ff.), and Steele (pp. 119 ff.) give interesting pictures of the situation in 1850. Other accounts are by Canfield who was here from May, 1850, to June, 1852, and by Borthwick (pp. 184 ff., 269 f.) who mined here in the spring and fall of 1852. For later developments, *see* *Bulletin*, 193 (pp. 97 ff.) where Nevada City district is described and the mines are listed and mapped. The district as outlined in this *Bulletin* includes the area from Indian Flat eastward through Nevada City, northeast to Willow Valley, and southeast through Canada Hill and Banner Hill toward the Lava Cap Mine. Drift mining continued to the end of the century. The lode mines did not become productive until the late 1860s; some operated into the 1890s. Large scale lode mining was resumed in the 1930s and continued until 1942. The most productive lode mine in the district was the Lava Cap, which yielded 12 million dollars between 1933 and 1942. Other productive lode mines were the Champion with a yield of 3 million dollars; the Mountaineer, 2 to 3 million; the Banner, the Canada Hill, the Pittsburgh, more than 1 million each; and the California Consolidated, 1 million. The author of *Bulletin*, 193, William B. Clark, estimates the total production of the district at more than 50 million dollars and possibly more than 70 million. For a description of the geologic structure of the region, *see* Lindgren, *Gold-Quartz Veins*.

Nevada Flat [El Dorado]. Between Otter and Canyon creeks, north of Georgetown. It is mentioned by Raymond in 1871 (IV, p. 105).

Nevada Hill [Placer]. *See* Life Preserver.

Newark [Placer]. On the north side of the North Fork of American River. Shown as Newark B., above Condemned Bar on Trask's map, 1853. A nugget of forty-four ounces, valued at 800 dollars, was found in the Swift Sure claims (*Mining Press*, October 26, 1861).

Newark [Sierra]. On Little Slate Creek, near the Plumas County line. The *Mountain Messenger*, July 19, 1862, mentioned the camp as "doing well" (Bancroft Notes), and it is mentioned as an election precinct in Township 8 (Bancroft Scraps, V, p. 1876). *Mining Press*, June 14 and 21, 1862, reports good yieldings. According to the County History, 1882 (p. 477), Newark was formerly known as Whiskey Diggings.

New Boston Company Bar [Calaveras]. On the south side of the South Fork of Mokelumne River, two miles above its mouth. Shown on Trask's map, 1853. Boston Company Bar is shown just above it. Both names appear without the designation Bar.

Newburg [Mono]. *See* Cameron.

Newcastle [Placer]. On Highway 40, three miles south of Ophir. Shown on Trask's map, 1853, and on Goddard's, 1857. Hutchings describes it as "a little gathering of old shanties called a town, with its poor eatables and flea-y bed, too short to stretch full length and too narrow to curl up on" (Diary, April 27, 1855). It was no real gold mining town, although the *Register* of 1902 reports some activity in quartz mining. In 1872 there was a 20-stamp mill here (*Annual Mining Review*, 1876, p. 23), apparently chiefly for custom work. The place is now a fruit shipping center with a population of around 800.

New Chicago [Amador]. North of Amador City. It was a mining camp of the 1850s; shown on the *Guidebook* map No. 5.

New Dale [San Bernardino]. *See* Dale.

New Diggings [Sacramento]. Between Folsom and Alder Creek. According to the County History, 1880 (p. 226), the old diggings here were worked in 1879 with better tools and good results.

New Diggings Ranche [Mariposa]. *See* New Years Diggins.

New Dry Diggings [Nevada]. Discovered early in 1854, half a mile from Round Tent on the Sacramento-Nevada road. The diggins yielded richly from the start (Hittell Clippings, p. 27). No later records were found.

New England Bar [Placer]. On the North Fork of American River. It is recorded in Placer County Records, I (p. 199) on October 15, 1853. The U. S. Bureau of the Census for 1850 lists New England Co. as a mining camp, apparently in the vicinity of Condemned Bar.

New England Mills [Placer]. On the North Fork of American River. According to the *State Register*, 1859, a mill with five stamps and three arrastres was erected in 1854, apparently only for custom work. The name is derived from a sawmill. The mines of the New England Mills or Weimar district are listed in *Mining Bureau*, XV (p. 319).

New Era [Butte]. On the Magalia Highway, south of Kunkle Reservoir. A New Era Mine is shown on the USGS Oroville 1944 quadrangle.

New Flats [Nevada]. Between the Middle and South forks of Yuba River. The camp is mentioned by Trask in his 1854 *Report* (doc. 9, p. 64).

New Forest City [Sierra]. Two miles from Forest City. The *Alta*, June 30, 1854 reprints an item from the Nevada *Democrat*, which states that new rich diggings were discovered in 1854.

New Gold Run [Nevada]. Between Grass Valley and Nevada City. A rich ravine was found in February, 1851, and within forty-eight hours the whole area was staked off. Miners were making sixteen to fifty dollars each, according to an item in the Sacramento *Transcript* (steamer ed.), February 28, 1851 (Bancroft Notes).

New Hartford Bar [Placer]. On the North Fork of American River. The name is recorded January 15, 1853, and September 11, 1853 in Placer County Records, I (pp. 148, 180).

Newhouse Place [Sierra]. *See* Mobile Flat.

New Jersey [Placer]. On the Blue Lead, near Forest Hill. By 1867 a claim had yielded 850 thousand dollars, according to Browne (p. 93). The combined production of the New Jersey, Independent, and Jenny Lind mines reached 2,653 million dollars (*Bull.*, 193, p. 50).

New London Bar [Placer]. On the North Fork of American River, opposite New Hartford Bar. The name is recorded in Placer County Records, I (p. 206).

New Mexican Camp [Mariposa]. In the western section of Bear Valley. Cristobal Ortega and a group of Mexicans discovered rich placers here in November, 1851. Although the camp was very short-lived (*Alta*, November 27, 1851), 250 thousand dollars' worth were said to have been taken out.

New Orleans [Nevada]. The name is mentioned repeatedly by Canfield and may refer to the camp Orleans Flat near the Middle Fork of Yuba River.

New Orleans Bar [Humboldt]. *See* Orleans Bar.

New Philadelphia [Amador]. North of Amador City. It was a camp of the 1850s, also known as Dog Town. It is shown on

the *Guidebook* map No. 5, and on Camp's map.

New Philadelphia [Butte]. It was apparently a miscarried attempt to give a new name to Thompsons Flat in 1854 ("The Knave," February 11, 1962). *See* Thompsons Flat.

New River; New River City [Trinity]. The stream is tributary to Trinity River, in the northwest part of the county. Cox (pp. 105 ff.) mentions a number of scattered camps along the stream and tells the story of a fight between two companies in 1851. They finally joined forces and developed the diggings. At first they were reported to be very rich, but in 1858 they yielded only four to eight dollars a day. The population of the camp at that time was about 129. A more optimistic report of the prospects in the district, particularly along Pony Creek, is given in *Mining Press*, December 21, 1861. In the 1880s new discoveries of both placer and lode mines were made. A description and map are given in the same journal, January 24, 1885, with three rival cities noted: New River City, Marysville, and White Rock. *See* Marysville [Trinity]. An alternate name for New River City was Denny, given by the miners for the owner of the store and chosen for the name of the post office in 1890. Both names persisted, however, and the *Register* of 1898 lists both Denny and New River City as trading centers for the mines in the region. The chief lode mine, the Mountain Boomer, had a 3-stamp mill in 1890 and by 1914 had produced 350 thousand dollars; it was reactivated in 1939 (*Mining Bureau*, XXXVII, p. 49). It is shown on the USGS Sawyers Bar 1945 quadrangle as Boomer Mine. The *County Report*, IV (pp. 62 ff.) lists the mines, mainly lode, in the region designated as Old Denny. The place now called Denny is at the site of Quimby (sometimes spelled Quinby), twenty miles downstream from Old Denny. According to Florence E. Morris (in *Trinity*, 1970), Old Denny was abandoned in 1920, and the store and post office were moved to the site of Quimby. The USGS Sawyers Bar 1945 quadrangle still shows Denny at the site of Old Denny; the Ironside Mountain 1951 quadrangle and all modern maps show it at the site of Quimby.

New Rocky Bar [Nevada]. On the west side of Wolf Creek, a mile and a half below Grass Valley. In 1918 it was a part of the immense property of the North Star Mine (*Mining Bureau*, XVI, Nevada, p. 211).

Newton [Nevada]. About five miles southwest of Nevada City. Shown as New Town on Trask's map, 1853, and as Newtown on Doolittle's map, 1868. According to Brown's *Directory* (p. 13), gold was discovered by a group of tars, and the place was accordingly first called Sailors Flat. Hutchings in his diary, October 9, 1855, mentions a "small, shaky, old-looking village called 'Newton'." Though the diggings were short lived, they were still mentioned in *Bean's Directory*, 1867. Later, in 1918, they were reported to have workable auriferous quartz veins (*Mining Bureau*, XVI, Nevada, p. 54). Shown on the USGS Smartsville 1943 quadrangle as Newtown.

Newtown [El Dorado]. On the south side of Weber Creek, seven miles southeast of Placerville and about a mile southwest of Dogtown. Shown on Doolittle's map, 1868. A post office was established June 17, 1854. Profitable mining was carried on as early as 1848. On their way from Sutters Fort and Mill, the Mormons built a corral here in July, 1848. In the winter of 1849–50, four men took out 64 thousand dollars in a small ravine (Haskins, p. 137). The town flourished after ditches brought water from Weber Creek in 1853. The Eureka Canal from the Cosumnes River was completed in 1856 (Hittell Clippings, p. 73). The *Register* of 1902 mentions drift and hydraulic mining.

Newtown [Nevada]. *See* Newton.

New Town [Placer]. Two miles from Virginiatown, on the north side of Dotys Ravine, on the road from Auburn to Marysville. Diggings discovered here in the winter of 1855 caused a town to grow up "double-quick," with three stores, three boarding houses, three butcher shops, and a half-dozen saloons (Sacramento *Union*, December 13, 1855).

Newtown [Shasta]. Near Churntown. Hutchings found the diggings the "worst dried up that I have yet seen" (Diary, December 27, 1855).

New Years Diggins [Mariposa]. On Browns Creek, seven miles north of Merced Falls. One of the early homesteaders here was Robert Prouty, who later became county sheriff (*Mariposa Gazette Centennial Edition*, 1954, p. 60). *Mining Bureau*, XXIV (p. 122) and LIII (p. 321) report hydraulic mining on Proutys Ranch along Browns Creek and its branches in 1927 and 1928. This may be the place mentioned by Stephen Davis as New Diggings Ranche, May 16, 1852.

New York Bar [Calaveras]. On the Stanis-laus River, near Grand Bar. According to an excerpt from the Sonora *Herald* in an undated clipping of 1858 (Hittell Clippings, p. 66½), the whole Bar was claimed by Dean & Sons, who employed fifty Chinese and were doing well. None of the modern New York mines in the county could be identified with this site.

New York Bar [Placer, El Dorado]. On the Middle Fork of American River, near the junction with the North Fork, between Louisiana Bar and Murderers Bar. Shown on Jackson's map, 1850, and other early maps. J. A. Stuart (p. 100) mined here in March, 1850 and stated that he never saw any gambling or a drunken man. In 1852 one company took out 550 dollars in one day with a tom, and another washed out 195 dollars from one pan of dirt (Placer Co. Hist., 1882, p. 225).

New York Bar [Trinity]. On Trinity River, eight miles below Taylor Flat. It is mentioned in 1858 by Cox (p. 82). A hydraulic New York Mine was still in operation in 1896 (*Mining Bureau*, XIII, p. 457).

New York Bar [Yuba]. On the North Fork of Yuba River, five miles north of Fosters Bar. Shown as N. Y. Bar on Wescoatt's map, 1861. The place is described by Borthwick (pp. 206 ff.) in the fall of 1852. He stated that the prospectors were all New Yorkers "brought up to professional and mercantile pursuits."

New York Bridge [Yuba]. The bridge crossed the North Fork of Yuba River just above the confluence with the Middle Fork. De Long collected taxes here September 19, 1855. No other mining records were found. Old New York Bridge is shown on Wescoatt's map, 1861, and on Doolittle's, 1868.

New York Cañon [Placer]. Near Wisconsin Hill. The sale of a mining claim in the canyon is recorded October 1, 1866 in Placer County Records, IV (pp. 229 ff.). Another New York Canyon, north of Canada Hill and Sailor Canyon, is mentioned in *Bulletin*, 193 (p. 34) and is shown on the USGS Colfax 1938 quadrangle.

New York: Creek, Ravine, Flat, Ranch [Yuba]. Near the Butte County line, between Brownsville and Forbestown. Hutchings mentions New York Ravine and Flat as rich (Diary, November 1, 1855). The situation of a large part of the flat on a marshy meadow with the gold deposits some twenty feet below the surface made the claims hard to work. In 1858 draining of the area was in progress (*Marysville Directory*, 1858). New York Ranch is men-

New York Flat, Yuba Co.

tioned in the County History, 1879 (p. 90), and is shown on Milleson and Adams' map, 1851, Wescoatt's, 1861, and the County Map, 1879. Mining had started in 1850; in 1857 the Nevada Company started work here and was still pursuing it in 1879. Browne (p. 162) described it as an important district in 1866 and well paying. New York Flat and Creek are shown on the USGS Smartsville 1943 quadrangle.

New York Flat [Sierra]. About one and a half miles east of Downieville. Shown on Doolittle's map, 1868. A small settlement developed here in the early 1850's (Sinnott, *Downieville*, p. 145). No mining records were found.

New York: Flat, Store [Amador]. New York Flat, now Gulch, is at the head of Ione Valley, below Drytown. It is mentioned by Doble on July 18, 1852. William W. White, who mined here in October and November, 1849, mentions New York Store, two miles below Drytown (*SCPQ*, IV, p. 210). New York Flat is shown on Camp's map.

New York Hill [El Dorado]. On the Georgetown divide, about two miles east of Georgia Slide. Shown on Bowman's map, 1873. Stephen Wing was here in 1855 and visited a tunnel that was reported as paying well (Journal, II, p. 26). In 1874 there were mainly gravel diggings here, according to Raymond, VII (p. 91).

New York Hill [Nevada]. On the west side of Wolf Creek, two miles south of Grass Valley. A rich vein once yielded 8 thousand dollars in half a day, and in about 1855, a lump of eleven pounds yielded 2 thousand dollars worth of gold (Hittell Clippings, p. 45). Various claims yielded a half million each before they were consolidated by the New York Hill Mining Company in 1864. In 1867 the sulfurets yielded between 100 and 200 dollars per ton (Bean, *History*, pp. 210 ff.). Later it became a part of the extensive area of the North Star Mines.

New York Hill [Placer]. On the North Fork of American River, four miles below Poverty Bar. The hill is mentioned in notice of a claim recorded August 28, 1854, in the Placer County Records, I (p. 245).

New York House [Yuba]. East of Brownsville. Shown on Wescoatt's map, 1861, and on the County Map, 1879. According to the County History, 1879 (p. 90), a hotel was built in 1850, and from 1860 on the place was mined and was called Union Flat. A Union Hotel is shown southwest of it on Wescoatt's map, 1861, and a Union Ranch is shown at this location on the County Map.

New York Mine [Los Angeles]. *See* Acton.

New York Mountains [San Bernardino]. In the northeast part of the county, northeast of Mid Hills and Providence Mountains. The County Map of 1892 shows a large New York Mining District on both slopes. The Darling Mine, four miles east of present-day Ivanpah, was a consolidation of twenty claims (*Mining Bureau*, XXVII, pp. 293, 317 ff.). *See* Manvel; Vanderbilt.

New York Point [Yuba]. Near New York Flat, east of Forbestown. The first claims were worked in 1853. A camp developed and had 600 inhabitants. It was only a mining town and soon disappeared (Co. Hist., 1879, p. 92).

New York Ranch [Amador]. Between Volcano and Jackson. It was a stage stop on the stage road, probably from 1850 on and later the site of a large hotel (Berriman).

New York Tent [Tuolumne]. Near the intersection of the Copperopolis Road and Highway 108, about a half mile west of Yosemite Junction. It is mentioned in the "Mining Laws of Montezuma District" (Heckendorn, p. 81).

Niagara Mine [Shasta]. *See* French Gulch.

Nicolaus Ferry [Sutter]. At the junction of the Feather River and Bear River. Shown on Jackson's map, 1850, and on Trask's, 1853. The name is also spelled Nicholaus, for Nicholaus Allgeier, a well known pioneer and one of Sutter's men, who operated a ferry at this point, an important crossing on the route from Sacramento to the mines on the lower Yuba River and Feather River. Allgeier also had a trading post at the place mentioned by Peter Decker, March 18, 1850, as a "town four weeks old." The U.S. 1850 Census lists 300 inhabitants, including fifty miners, at Nicolaus, Vernon, Oro City, Hock Farm, and vicinity.

Nigger. The nickname for negro was frequently used in mining days. The same places were often also called Negro.

Nigger Bar [Nevada]. On the north side of the North Fork of Yuba River, one mile below the mouth of the Middle Fork. Shown on Trask's map, 1853.

Nigger Bar [Placer]. On Bear River. It is mentioned in an article in *Placer Nuggets*, June, 1959 (p. 3).

Nigger Bar [Plumas]. On the Middle Fork of Feather River, listed in Bancroft, VI (p. 363).

Nigger Bar [Sacramento]. *See* Negro Bar.

Nigger Camp. An uncertain location, probably in Nevada County. It is mentioned in a poem in the *Annual Mining Review*, 1876 (p. 18).

Nigger Diggins [Sacramento]. Rich diggings were found one mile below Mormon Is-

land. According to the *Placer Times*, February 9, 1850, the yield was one or two ounces a day to the hand (Bancroft Notes).

Nigger Gulch [Calaveras]. A tributary to Mokelumne River, about five miles northeast of Mokelumne Hill. It is mentioned by Doble, February 27, 1852, and later; also repeatedly in the *Alta* of 1854. It is shown on Camp's map.

Nigger: Gulch, Hill [Tuolumne]. North of Columbia, near Gold Springs. The *Mining Press*, November 23, 1861, reported that the diggings in the gulch were nearly worked out. The completion of the Columbia Gulch flume apparently put new life into the place. According to the *Mining Bureau*, XXIV (p. 42), the production, together with nearby Gold Springs was 7.5 million dollars. *See* Negro Gulch; Gold Springs.

Niggerhead Bar [Placer]. On the north side of North Fork of American River, two miles below the mouth of the Middle Fork. Shown on Trask's map, 1853, as Nigerhead. It is recorded as the boundary of a claim, December 18, 1851, in Placer County Records, I (p. 53).

Nigger Hill [Calaveras]. *See* Negro Hill.

Nigger Hill [El Dorado]. The same as Negro Hill. Shown on Bowman's map, 1873, as Negro Hill. Patterson (pp. 36 ff.) calls it Nigger Hill. He found his first gold here in 1849 and claims that he was the first to introduce hill digging ("coyoteing"). Nigger Hill School is shown on the USGS Folsom 1944 quadrangle and Nigger Hill appears on the Auburn 1954 quadrangle. *See* Negro Hill [El Dorado] and Nigger Diggins [Sacramento].

Nigger Hill [El Dorado]. Near Placerville on a spur of the Blue Channel of the county, in the vicinity of Clay Hill and Indian Hill. It is mentioned in the County History, 1883 (p. 88).

Nigger Hill [Shasta]. On Watson Gulch. A promising claim was opened in 1861 (*Mining Press*, March 16, 1861). No gold mining records were found, but the Hill became known during World War II for its manganese deposits.

Nigger Hill [Siskiyou]. *See* Niggerville Creek.

Nigger Jacks Point [Tuolumne]. A well known lava point at the confluence of Green Springs Run and Stanislaus River, at O'Byrnes Ferry. It was named for a pioneer emancipated slave who lived near by. (De Ferrari.)

Nigger Ravine [Nevada]. The Ravine heads near the summit of Manzanita Hill and empties into Bear River near the junction with Steep Hollow Creek. Shown on Pettee and Bowman's map, 1879. The gravel formation of the area is described by Pettee in Whitney, *Auriferous Gravels* (pp. 157 f.).

Nigger Slide [Sierra]. *See* Negro Slide.

Nigger Tent [Sierra]. It was a way station on the Sierra Turnpike, about five miles below Goodyears Bar. The name was sometimes recorded as Negro Tent, as on Doolittle's map, 1868, and the County Map, 1874. Trask shows it as Niger Tent on his map, 1853, but refers to it as Negro Tent in his Report of 1854 (doc. 9, p. 62). Downie (p. 71) recalls that the place was known as Hollow Log in 1850, and this name appears on Milleson and Adams' map, 1851. Borthwick (p. 215) states that a negro had a way station at Nigger Tent in the fall of 1852, first in a tent, then in a cabin. According to an article in the Nevada County Historical Society publication of May, 1850, it was the site of a notorious hostelry established by "Italian gypsies" who came here in 1851 from Goodyears Bar. W. B. Meek, who was well acquainted with the area from the days of his youth, recalls in his "Reminiscences" (pp. 117 ff.) that the notorious hostelry was run by a Mrs. Romargi, a native of Florida, and that her husband had a mining claim two miles away, which rough characters and criminals are said to have used as a hideout. The site of Nigger Tent is shown on the USGS Pike 1951 quadrangle.

Niggers Bluff [Placer]. On the north bank of the Middle Fork of American River. It is listed in Bancroft, VI (p. 354).

Niggerville: Creek, Gulch; Nigger Hill [Siskiyou]. The Creek is a tributary to South Fork of Salmon River, opposite Knownothing Creek, in the rich mining district south of Forks of Salmon. There was mainly hydraulic mining. Niggerville Gulch and Nigger Hill are listed and mapped in the *Register*, 1898. A Nigger Hill placer mine is listed in the reports of the Mining Bureau until 1935. About a mile up Niggerville Creek a flume and a ditch were built to carry water around the mountain to the Nigger Hill Mine (W. M. Smith). The Creek is shown on the USGS Sawyers Bar 1945 quadrangle.

Nimshew [Butte]. On the Middle Fork of Butte Creek, northwest of Magalia. It is a Maidu Indian word and is said to mean 'big water'. In 1868 Browne (p. 160) mentions a mining tunnel under Table Moun-

tain. It was mainly a trading center and from 1880 a post office for the drift and quartz mines of the district (*Register*, 1903; *Mining Bureau*, XV, pp. 198 ff.). The Emma or Nimshew Drift Mine produced one million dollars or more by 1928 (*Mining Bureau*, XXIV, p. 196), and it is still listed in 1949. The location in Magalia district is indicated on the sketch map in *Bulletin*, 193 (p. 88). *See* Kimshew. The place is shown on the USGS Chico 1895 quadrangle.

Nixferschtay. An unidentified place. Guinn, who listed the name (p. 43), apparently took it from the *Golden Era* of about 1856. It is probably a nickname for a camp of German miners. The word is the phonetic spelling of the phrase 'nichts versteh', meaning 'I don't understand', the equivalent here of 'I don't speak English'.

No-eared Bar [Plumas]. An unidentified bar on the Middle Fork of Feather River, listed by Coy (p. 73). It is shown on modern maps on the south side of the river, below Minerva and Rich bars.

Nolton [Siskiyou]. At the junction of Thompson Creek with Klamath River, above Happy Camp. Toward the end of last century it was a trading center and post office for placer mines (*Register*, 1898). Recorded on the USGS Seiad 1945 quadrangle.

Norden Placer [Kern]. Two miles north of Randsburg. There was dry placer mining in the 1920s with poor success (*Bull.*, 95, pp. 145 ff.; *Mining Bureau*, XXV, p. 43).

Nordheimer Creek [Siskiyou]. Tributary to Salmon River, near the Humboldt County line. It was named for an early prospector, possibly the one who mined at Gold Bluffs in 1850. The Creek and ditch, which supplied water for Somes Bar, are mentioned in 1868 by Browne (p. 202). Later hydraulic mining was carried on (*Register*, 1898). A Nordheimer Placer is listed in the Mining Bureau reports until 1935. Shown on the USGS Sawyers Bar 1945 quadrangle. The mouth of the creek is about sixteen miles from the Humboldt County line, but the ridge around the head of the creek forms the line between Siskiyou and Humboldt counties.

North Bloomfield [Nevada]. There was an early mining camp here named Humbug, after Humbug Creek on which it was situated. In 1853 hydraulic mining came into use in the county and the town soon became an important mining center. When the post office was established, June 1, 1857, the name suggested was

Bloomfield, to which the post office department added the adjective to distinguish it from Bloomfield in Sonoma County. Between 1871 and 1881 the superintendent of the North Bloomfield Gravel Mining Company was Hamilton Smith, in 1875 the inventor of the hurdy-gurdy wheel and in 1886 the author of the standard book, *Hydraulics* (J. W. Johnson, pp. 200 ff.). After the prohibition of hydraulic mining in 1884 only a few mines continued operating cautiously (*Guidebook*, p. 77). Today it is a small community surrounded with huge heaps of mining debris. The yield for the famous Malakoff Mine near the town was about 3.5 million dollars, according to Lindgren (*Professional Paper*, 73, p. 139), and for the Derbec Mine between one and two million (*Bull.*, 193, p. 101). A detailed description and bibliography of the district is given in *Mining Bureau*, XVI (Nevada, pp. 45 ff.) and in *Bulletin*, 193 (p. 101). A map is given in Lindgren (*ibid.*, opposite p. 140). *See* Malakoff District.

North Branch [Calaveras]. A camp near the North Fork of Calaveras River, close to the junction with the South Fork. The place had a post office as early as 1852, but only meager mining records are available. A water-driven stamp mill is mentioned in the *Register* of 1899. A Hudson and North Branch quartz mine, listed in the Mining Bureau reports until 1936, was active in the 1870s, according to *County Report*, II (p. 158), and again in the 1890s, with prospecting in 1928 and 1929. The Pioneer Cemetery, Historic Landmark 271, is near the site of the old mining camp. The place is recorded on the USGS Jackson 1938 quadrangle. *See* Iowa Cabins; Second Crossing.

North Canyon [Plumas]. Between Greenville and Round Valley Reservoir, west of Indian Valley. It was so named because it lies north of the Reservoir. The history of the three successive dams built in the 1860s is given by John L. Peel and A. R. Bidwell in Plumas County Historical Society *Publication*, no. 4 (April, 1961). Bidwell also lists the quartz mills in the area, which continued operation into the 1870s. A 16-stamp water-driven mill is listed in 1872 (Raymond, V, p. 96). *See* Round Valley [Plumas]; Cherokee [Plumas].

North Columbia [Nevada]. Four miles west of North Bloomfield. It was so named to distinguish it from Columbia in Tuolumne County when the post office was established May 29, 1860. Hydraulic mining

was carried on in North Columbia district on a large scale from the middle 1850s to the early 1880s (*Bull.*, 193, pp. 101 f.). There was also lode mining in the area, with the Delhi Mine active between the 1860s and the 1890s, yielding around one million dollars. Chinese miners did small scale placering from about 1890 to the early 1900s. In the 1930s there was again some mining. The total production of the district is estimated at between 3 and 4 million dollars. *See* Columbia Hill.

North Fork [Mariposa]. At the confluence of North Fork with Merced River. According to the *State Register*, 1859, there was a 12-stamp steam-driven mill here in 1851, but the *Register* of 1903 lists no mill. Shown on the USGS Sonora 1939 quadrangle.

North Fork [Plumas]. On the south side of the North Fork of Feather River, south of Lake Almanor, at the site of present-day Seneca. The old mines on Dutch, Barker, Cummings, and Owl Hills were consolidated by the North Fork Mining Company in the 1870s. Mining activities are described in detail in Raymond, VII (pp. 158 ff.). The largest mine, the Glazier, was closed in 1941 and reopened in the late 1950s, according to the reminiscences of William J. McMillan in Plumas County Historical Society *Publication*, no. 25 (June, 1967, pp. 23 f.).

North Fork [Sierra]. Near Forest City, south of the North Fork of Yuba River. The *Alta*, March 2, 1854, reprints an item from the *Sierra Citizen* which reports that the price of individual claims is sometimes as high as 2.6 thousand dollars, and that the North Fork Tunnel yielded nearly 6 thousand dollars in one week. In the 1870s a high grade pocket worth 100 thousand dollars was found here (*Bull.*, 193, p. 11). The mile-long tunnel was worked until 1881 (Co. Hist., 1882, p. 479).

North Fork [Trinity]. At the junction of the forks of Trinity River, west of Weaverville. A confusing account of early mining is given by Cox (pp. 62 ff.); a better description is given in a letter by Franklin Buck (pp. 157 ff.) in 1856 and in the *Mining Press*, November 23, 1861. According to an article in the *Trinity Journal*, September 22, 1860, it was a thriving village destined to become "a second Weaverville" and until late years had been known as Bagdad. The *Register* of 1898 indicates that North Fork had two stamp mills and one Huntington Mill and was the milling center for the hydraulic mines in the area. It was also known as Helena, and a post office was established under this name in 1891. The present-day Helena post office, however, is about a mile and a half up the Trinity River from the old Helena post office or town of North Fork.

North Fork Dry Diggings [Placer]. *See* Auburn.

North Fork Mokelumne [Amador]. Two water-driven mills with sixteen stamps and four arrastres were erected here in 1857 (*State Register*, 1859).

North Fork of Coffee Creek [Trinity]. Coffee Creek is a tributary to Trinity River. The deposits on the North Fork were first worked by a company of Portuguese in 1856. The *Annals* (pp. 11 ff.) tell of a near tragedy which happened to a Mr. Rowland and family when they became lost in the snow on the way to their camp and remained without food and shelter for days, until finally rescued by hunters. — A hydraulic mine is still listed in 1896 (*Mining Bureau*, XIII, 458).

North Fork Tuolumne [Tuolumne]. Apparently it was only a milling center. In 1869 there were three water-driven mills with 40 stamps and one steam-driven mill with 5 stamps in operation (Raymond, II, p. 26).

North Hill [Calaveras]. North of Whiskey Hill. According to the San Andreas *Register*, July 21, 1866, rich placers were worked from here to Whiskey Hill and to Jenny Lind as early as 1849. The group of mines on North Hill, South Hill, Whiskey Hill, and other Hills in the area is listed in 1913/14 and is also mentioned in 1935 in *Mining Bureau* (XIV, p. 120; XXXII, p. 361).

North Ravine [Placer]. The creek was a tributary to the Middle Fork of American River, near Humbug Flat Ravine. The name is recorded in Placer County Records, I (p. 238).

North San Juan [Nevada]. Northwest of Nevada City, east of the junction of the North and Middle forks of Yuba River. Gold was not discovered here until January, 1853. One of the earliest claimants, Christian Kientz, a Mexican War veteran, saw in the hill above his claim a resemblance to the elevation at the entrance of Santa Cruz harbor, San Juan de Ulloa, and named it accordingly (Bean, *History*, pp. 335 ff.). In the spring of 1854 the Middle Yuba Canal brought water, and the camp enjoyed a fair prosperity (Vischer, p. 233). On May 21, 1857, a post office was established with the adjective "north" added to the name to distinguish it from San Juan in Monterey, later San

North San Juan, Nevada Co.

Benito County. It has been claimed that hydraulic mining really started here. In 1858 the poet Benjamin Parke Avery, after years of unsuccessful mining, bought the newspaper and published it as *Hydraulic Press*. A detailed description of the diggings is given in *Transactions*, 1858 (pp. 176 ff.) and 1860 (pp. 87 f.). A decade of great prosperity began August 5, 1859, when the completion of the 300-mile-long flume from the lakes around present Bowman Lake was celebrated. A description is found in the North San Juan *Hydraulic Press*, August 13, 1859. The Eureka Company cleaned up forty pounds of gold in a twelve-day run (*Mining Press*, February 22, 1861). The population of the town reached several thousands at times. It is one of the few gold towns that enjoyed a respectable library. The unpublished letters which Newton Miller wrote to his family present a veritable chronicle of the town between 1856 and 1864. The North San Juan Ridge along the ancient channel of the Yuba River was probably the richest hydraulic mining region in the state. For the later development, *see Mining Bureau*, XVI (Nevada, pp. 51 ff.).

North Star [Nevada]. On Lafayette Hill, two miles southwest of Grass Valley. The place was named after the North Star Mine, which operated as early as 1851. The North Star Mining Company was organized in 1861, and in 1866 it erected a 16-stamp mill with a 50-horsepower engine (Bean, p. 244). In the course of years the company "swallowed up" all the camps, claims, and mines west and southwest of Grass Valley. By 1913 it had produced more than 16 million dollars and by 1928 more than 33 million. (*Mining Bureau*, XVI, Nevada, pp. 211 ff.; XXVI, pp. 121 ff.) The Empire-Star Group, a consolidation of the North Star and Empire mines, operated in 1929 and with a short interruption during World War II until 1957. The total production was 130 million dollars. (*Bull.*, 193, p. 54.) An early name for this area was Helvetia Hill (Foley). *See* Empire Mine; Grass Valley.

Norton Diggings [Trinity]. At the junction of Strope Creek, the East Branch of Stuarts Fork. It was named for the Norton company, which built a water race with 250 sluice heads. According to Cox (pp. 90 f.), it was thought to be the richest camp in the county in 1858.

Norumbagua Mine [Nevada]. *See* Forest Springs.

Norwegian: Gulch, Mine [Tuolumne]. Be-

tween Tuttletown and Melones. Black Bart once robbed a stage carrying gold from the mine; this robbery led to his capture (*Guidebook*, p. 55). The Gulch is the same as Jackass Gulch. The Norwegian Mine, on the north slope of Jackass Hill, was worked in a small way as a pocket mine as early as 1851 and continued into the 1930s, or later, with a total production of about 200 thousand dollars (*Mining Bureau*, XIV, p. 157; *Bull.*, 108, p. 169; *Bull.*, 193, p. 126).

Norwegian: Tent, Gulch [Mariposa]. Near Mount Ophir, about five miles northwest of Mariposa. Shown on the Las Mariposas map, 1861. Allsop dated some of his interesting letters, April 28, 1852 and November 1, 1852 from Norwegian Flat. Shown on the USGS Bear Valley 1947 quadrangle.

Notoma [Sacramento]. *See* Natoma.

Notowa [Yuba]. The name is derived from a Yuba Indian rancheria on a flat that was later settled by John Ramm and named for him. There was apparently some gold mining, for De Long collected taxes here, February 10, 1852. *See* Ramms Ranch.

Nugget Bar [Siskiyou]. On the South Fork of Salmon River, eight miles above Forks of Salmon. No early mining records were found, but there was placer mining in the 1890s (*Mining Bureau*, XII, p. 289; XIII, p. 418). W. M. Smith states that the bar was worked by Chinese until about 1912 or 1913, and it was not worked to any extent until derricks were used to handle the large rocks.

Nugget Bar [Trinity]. Four miles north of Minersville. A hydraulic Nugget Bar Mine is listed in the Mining Bureau reports until 1940.

Nuggins Bar [Plumas]. An unidentified place listed in the Giffen file.

Number Nine [Mariposa]. *See* Hornitos.

Nutcake Camp. An unidentified place listed in the State Library Roster.

Nyes Ferry [Calaveras]. Across the Stanislaus River, on the road from Stockton to Jamestown. Recorded on Jackson's map, 1850. It is apparently a misspelling of Knights Ferry. *See* Knights Ferry.

Nyes: Ferry, Crossing [Yuba, Nevada]. On the Middle Fork of Yuba River, near Oregon Creek, shown on Trask's map, 1853. The ferry, established by Matthew Sparks in 1850, was an important crossing for the gold camps on the North Yuba until a bridge was built (Yuba Co. Hist., 1879, p. 100). *See* Freeman's Crossing.

Nyes Landing [Nevada]. *See* Bridgeport.

Nyman Consolidated Mines [Tuolumne]. *See* Quartz.

O**ahu** [Sierra]. About eight miles northwest of Downieville, on Craigs Flat. Hawaiians worked it first, and it was named after the island. There was tunneling, which paid six to eight dollars per day to the hand. (*Transactions*, 1858, p. 197.)

Oak Bar [Placer]. On the North Fork of American River. The bar is mentioned in the Placer County Records, I (verso of page 29) in connection with a notice of intention to dam and flume the river between Oak Bar and Fords, filed November 3, 1852.

Oak Bar [Siskiyou]. On Klamath River and Kohl Creek, above Hamburg. It was a trading center and from 1874 to 1928, a post office for numerous mines (*Register*, 1898). The bar was reported as a generous producer, but it was "nearly cleaned up" in 1888 (*Mining Bureau*, VIII, p. 592). Shown on the USGS Yreka 1939 quadrangle.

Oak Bottom [Shasta]. On Clear Creek. In 1861 two companies were engaged in fluming from Oak Bottom to Horsetown (*Mining Press*, August 3, 1861). The Oak Bottom Placer Syndicate was a large company that had mines in Shasta and Siskiyou counties.

Oak Flat [Sierra]. On Kanaka Creek, southwest of Chips Flat. Shown on Doolittle's map, 1868. It had an 8-stamp mill in 1868 (*Annual Mining Review*, 1876, p. 22).

Oak Flat [Tuolumne]. It is shown on Goddard's map, 1857, and is the same as Big Oak Flat.

Oak Grove House [Yuba]. On Dry Creek, twelve miles southwest of Fosters Bar. De Long stayed here at J. M. Abbott's house, October 19, 1855, and the next day subpoenaed him. Shown on the Smartsville USGS 1943 quadrangle.

Oakland [Mariposa]. A doubtful name, shown as a sizeable town east of Horseshoe Bend on Gibbes' map, 1851.

Oakland [Yuba]. On the Feather River, eleven miles north of Marysville. It was one of the speculative towns established in 1850 as a trading center for miners, but it soon disappeared. John Monet founded it on his ranch, which was between Featherton and Marysville. (Marysville *Herald*, September 20 and October 1, 1850; May 24, 1851.)

Oakland Flat [Placer]. On the North Fork of American River, below Rattlesnake Bar. It was also known as High Bar. *See* High Bar.

Oak Ranch [El Dorado]. Southwest of Grizzly Flat, near Placerville. The highly productive Crusen mine operated until 1883 (Co. Hist., 1883, p. 88). It was apparently the same as Oak Flat.

Oak Ranch [Sierra]. At the headwaters of Goodyears Creek. It was situated on what was called the lower reaches of the Poker Flat trail, at the junction of trails from Eureka North and Monte Cristo. It was important in early mining days because the owners raised vegetables and had an orchard. (R. Drury.)

Oak: Shade, Camp [Tuolumne]. The place is mentioned by Heckendorn (p. 103), but no mining records were found. It appears to have been about one quarter mile east of Yosemite Junction, on the south side of Highway 108 (De Ferrari).

Oak Spring [Tuolumne]. The place is mentioned in a letter written from Red Flat, January 12, 1853, by George W. Watson. It had a post office from 1851 to 1854, when it was transferred to Montezuma. *See* Montezuma.

Oak Tree Ranch [Yuba]. On Shady Creek, one mile south of North San Juan. It is mentioned by De Long, August 27, 1855, and is still shown on the USGS Smartsville 1943 quadrangle.

Oak Valley [Yuba]. Near Sierra County line, northwest of Camptonville. Shown on the Milleson and Adams' map, 1851. Borthwick (p. 214) mentions that there were three cabins and one hotel in the fall of 1852. De Long repeatedly refers to the place in his diaries in 1855. The diggings prospered after water became available (*Sierra Citizen* clipping in Hittell, p. 44). The population was mainly French, according to the "Reminiscences" of William Bull Meek (p. 137). Shown on the USGS Smartsville 1943 quadrangle.

O'Byrne Ferry [Calaveras]. *See* Byrnes Ferry.

Odin [Nevada]. *See* Washington Ridge.

O'Donnells Flat [Sierra]. Two miles east of Downieville, on Highway 49. Shown on Doolittle's map, 1868, and on the County Map, 1874. Downey camped here in October or December, 1849. In 1854 fifty-two votes were cast. The place was also known as McCarty Flat and McDonald Flat. (Sinnott, *Downieville*, pp. 144, 201.) It is mentioned in the County History, 1882 (p. 421).

Ogilby [Imperial]. A station on the Southern Pacific Railroad. From 1890 to 1942 it was

Ohio Flat, Yuba Co.

the post office for the American Girl and other profitable gold mines in the Cargo Muchacho Mountains (*Mining Bureau*, XXII, pp. 255 ff.; XXXVIII, pp. 113 f.).

Ohio Bar [Butte]. It was a flourishing transient mining camp north of Oroville, mentioned in County History, 1882 (p. 253).

Ohio Bar [Nevada]. On the Yuba River, one mile below the junction of the North and South forks of Yuba River. Shown on Trask's map, 1853, and on Goddard's, 1857. Peter Decker mentions it on March 30, 1850, and De Long on August 14, 1856. The bar is reported to have been rich and worked by Chinese until it was covered by water.

Ohio Diggings [Tuolumne]. Three miles north of Soulsbyville. It was a sizeable camp, mentioned by Heckendorn (p. 90). An Ohio Mine, apparently idle, is listed in the reports of the Mining Bureau until 1928.

Ohio Flat [El Dorado]. On the South Fork of American River. The flat is mentioned in the journal of Ezra Bourne of Union Flat in the summer of 1852.

Ohio Flat [Trinity]. On the south side of Trinity River near Poker and Point bars. In the spring of 1854 a large party of Ger-

mans found considerable coarse gold here (*Mining Press*, October 26, 1861).

Ohio Flat [Yuba]. About two miles and a half below Forbestown, adjoining Garden Ranch Flat, near New York Flat. Shown on Doolittle's map, 1868. Mining was reported as early as 1850. According to the *Marysville Directory*, 1858 (p. xxx), progress in digging a drainage ditch was slow because the land was mainly meadow and marsh land. In 1875 a 10-stamp mill was erected, and in 1879 a flume was completed from New York to Ohio Flat (Co. Hist., 1879, p. 90). The mine of the Ohio Flat Company is listed in *Mining Bureau*, XIII (p. 502).

Ohio Hill [Amador]. North of Jackson. Early rich placers are mentioned in the County History, 1881 (p. 181).

Ohio House [Siskiyou]. In Scott Valley, south of the Etna-Eastside Road. Shown on Goddard's map, 1857. It was a stage stop on the California-Oregon stage road as early as 1851.

Olancha [Inyo]. South of Owens Lake bed. The name is derived from a Shoshonean village. The place was a trading center and from 1870 served as a post office for the silver mines south of Owens Lake. There was only a minimal amount of gold production (*Register*, 1902).

Old Channel [Calaveras]. Listed in Hittell's roster.

Old Dad Mountain [San Bernardino]. On an unnamed mountain range about twelve miles southeast of Baker. A number of mines are mapped and described in *Mining Bureau*, XLIX (pp. 72 f., 76 f., 78 f.). The Brannigan Mine, on the west slope of the north extension, was located in 1905 and was active mainly between 1928 and 1935; the Oro Fino near by was first prospected in the 1890s but was not worked intensively until the period 1930–1945; and the Paymaster, north of the mountain, was opened in 1900 and worked into the 1950s. Old Dad Mountain is not to be confused with Old Dad Mountains, a range northeast of Bristol Mountains, where there was some mining about 1890, when several small ledges rich in gold were discovered (*Mining Bureau*, IX, p. 217).

Old Deadwood [Siskiyou]. At the confluence of Cherry and Deadwood creeks. Apparently it was near the later flourishing Deadwood Camp. It was listed as extinct in the 1850s (Co. Hist., 1881, pp. 212, 216), although the name still appears in the *Register*, 1898.

Old Denny [Trinity]. *See* New River.

Old Diggings [Shasta]. North of Redding, near Summit City. It is listed in the *State Register*, 1859, as having a steam-driven mill with two stamps in 1858. Old Diggings or Buckeye district is described in *Bulletin*, 193 (p. 140). It was a rich, productive district in the Gold Rush period and at first there was hydraulic mining; later there was lode mining, particularly between 1904 and 1909. The Reid Mine produced more than 2.5 million dollars. In the 1930s the region was again prospected. A map showing locations of the mines is given in *Mining Bureau*, XXIX (opposite p. 41). *See* Buckeye [Shasta].

Old Dry Diggings [El Dorado]. Both Placerville and the original Weber Camp were known by this name in 1848 and even later.

Old Eureka Mine [Amador]. *See* Eureka Mines.

Old Fountain House [Yuba]. About two miles north of Dobbins Ranch, on the road from Fosters Bar to Marysville. Shown on Doolittle's map, 1868. It is mentioned by William B. Meek, stage driver (p. 151).

Old Gulch [Calaveras]. Five miles southeast of San Andreas. It was also known as Washington Flat (San Francisco *Bulletin*, January 18, 1858, in Bancroft Notes). Heckndorn in 1856 lists only a butcher as an inhabitant. The San Francisco *Bulletin*, January 27, 1857, reports extensive diggings there, but no gold. An undated clipping (marked March, 1860) in Hayes Scrapbooks: Mining (I, sec. 63) reports a "good, paying hydraulic claim" in declining Old Gulch and lack of water at the rich diggings of nearby Washington Ranch, at which there are six paying claims. A settlement, Old Gulch, is shown on the USGS Jackson 1938 quadrangle, but today it is gone, except for one ruin at the edge of the quarry, where the Calaveras Cement Company has mined millions of tons of limestone (G. Poore).

Old Lexington House [Pluma]. *See* Lexington House.

Old Man Mountain [Nevada]. About three miles south and west of the site of Summit City (Meadow Lake). Frequent attempts have been made to exploit a series of fissure veins carrying a moderate amount of gold in the area between Old Man Mountain and Summit City, but generally without success (USGS *Geologic Atlas*, no. 66, Colfax Folio, p. 8). Shown on USGS Emigrant Gap 1955 quadrangle.

Old Mountain House. *See* Mountain House [Sierra].

Old Point Diggings [Nevada]. Near Grass Valley. It is mentioned as a favorable place in the *Alta*, April 8, 1854.

Old Rancheria [Amador]. *See* Rancheria.

Old Woman Mountains [San Bernardino]. Southeast of Danby. In the northwest part of the range, small ledges "very rich" in gold and silver were discovered about 1886, and a group of claims were worked around 1895. Between 1935 and 1939 the Blue Eagle Mine was active and between 1940 and 1942 the Long Shot Mine. (*Mining Bureau*, IX, p. 217; XIII, p. 325; XLIX, tables 26 and 46.)

Old Womans Gulch [Calaveras]. South of Mokelumne Hill. It is apparently a branch or a continuation of Chili Gulch. Rich pay dirt was discovered in 1860, when the Deep Blue Lead was struck (*Mining Press*, April 6 and June 15, 1861; U. S. *Bull.*, p. 63). The Gulch was named for an old Indian woman who mined here by herself, according to G. Poore.

Oleepa [Butte]. On the Feather River. Delano datelined two letters in May, 1850, from here (*Across the Plains*, pp. 127–128), but the place might only have been an Indian village.

Oles [Yuba]. Ten miles northeast of Marysville, on the old road to Downieville. It is an otherwise unidentified place recorded on the Milleson & Adams' map, 1851.

Oleta [Amador]. *See* Fiddletown.

Olney Creek [Shasta]. From the Muletown Mountains to the Sacramento River, south of Oregon Gulch and Redding. It was a rich mining stream, named for Nathan Olney of Oregon, who mined here with his Walla Walla Indians before the Gold Rush (Steger). The Illinois Insurance Company prospected here and on nearby Clear Creek in the fall and winter of 1849–1850, with headquarters at Camp Hill Springs and Campbell Springs (Weber-Biddle). Olney Creek is shown on the USGS Redding 1944 quadrangle.

Omega [Nevada]. Two miles southwest of the junction of Diamond Creek and the South Fork of Yuba River. It was settled in 1850 or 1851, and according to tradition, was first called Delirium Tremens. When the camp grew, the name became too obnoxious even to the unmellowed miners, and the last letter of the Greek alphabet was substituted. *See* Alpha. On April 29, 1854, the *Alta* reports that one company averaged half a pound of dust daily. The gold was up to 975° fineness (*Mining Bureau*, IV, p. 221). With the development of hydraulic mining the camp became an important center, and in 1857 a post office was established that lasted until 1891. By 1867 thirty gravel claims or mines had produced 1.5 million dollars, according to Bean (p. 378). The diggings were worked intermittently until 1949 and produced a total of 2.5 million dollars, according to a statement in Rensch-Hoover. The place is shown on the County Map, 1880, and on the USGS Colfax 1938 quadrangle. Historic Landmark 629.

Omit Bar [Butte]. On Butte Creek, just below Helltown. Shown on the County Map, 1877.

Omits Flat [Sierra]. East of Downieville, near Negro Bar, opposite Secret Canyon. The Flat is mentioned by Downie (p. 40).

Omo Ranch [El Dorado]. On Perry Creek, a tributary to the Middle Fork of Cosumnes River. No early mining records were found, but a post office was established in 1888 and the *Register*, 1902, lists four stamp mills. The Oak Mine was active in 1894; the Omo in 1896; and the Potosi to the east operated in 1908 (*Mining Bureau*, LII, pp. 521, 522, 526); the latter two mines

are listed in the Mining Bureau reports until 1938. The ranch is shown on the USGS Placerville 1931 quadrangle.

One Eye Canyon [El Dorado]. A tributary to Rock Creek, six miles north of Placerville. It was so named because one of the first prospectors had lost one eye (Co. Hist., 1883, p. 192). Shown on the USGS Placerville 1931 quadrangle.

One Horse Bar [Placer]. On the North Fork of American River, opposite the center of Green Valley. The name is recorded December 6 and 20, 1851, in the Placer County Records, I (p. 56).

One Horse Town [Shasta]. *See* Horsetown.

Oneida Mine and Mill [Amador]. Half way between Jackson and Sutter creeks; on the Mother Lode. According to Browne (p. 74 f.), the deposits were discovered in 1851 when a hunter chased a rabbit to some outcroppings of quartz containing gold. A steam-driven 60-stamp mill was erected as early as 1857 (*State Register*, 1859, p. 22). In 1867, sixty stamps were in operation and the net profit was twelve and a half dollars per ton (Browne, p. 75). The mines, which were worked until 1913, had reached a depth of 2,500 feet, and the total production was 2.5 million dollars (*Guidebook*, p. 64). The place, Martell, on the *Guidebook* map No. 5 marks the approximate site. *See* Martell.

O'Neils: Creek, Bar [Calaveras]. The creek is a branch of Calaveritas Creek, which is a tributary to the South Fork of Calaveras River. Ayers (p. 67) mentions it as being rich in 1850. It is shown on the USGS Jackson 1938 and the Big Tree 1941 quadrangles. The San Andreas *Independent*, March 9, 1861, reports that O'Neils Bar on Calaveritas Creek was one of the few places above Upper Calaveritas that was being worked at that time. The miners were mainly Germans.

One Mule Town [Shasta]. *See* Muletown.

Onion Valley [Plumas]. About ten miles from La Porte. Like many other places, the valley and the tributary to the Middle Fork of Feather River in the Sawpit Flat mining district were named for the profusion of wild onions. Gold was discovered here in 1850 in the wake of the Gold Lake hunt, and the name appears in 1851 on Butler's and Milleson & Adams' maps. There were about 400 miners in the Valley during the season of 1851, according to a conservative estimate given in the Quincy *Union*, December 2, 1865 (quoted by McKevitt, p. 499). Steele (pp. 189 ff.) stayed here three days in February, 1851, on his return from

Ophir, Placer Co.

the north, and he gives a dramatic and fascinating account of a large crowd of gold seekers marooned in the wilderness during a snowstorm. The elevation of Onion Valley is 6,300 feet (*Mining Bureau*, XVI, Plumas, p. 42). In 1851 the shrewd McIlhany built a large store. Charles C. Thomas also had a store the same year. He reports (Statement, p. 5) that there were twenty to thirty houses or more at that time, and that the place was the trading post for the surrounding mining camps. In June, 1852, Lecouvreur also calls the town "the central point for numerous surrounding camps" with ten or twelve stores and taverns (p. 240). August 18, 1855, Onion Valley became a post office. Contemporary reports in newspapers tell of astonishing finds. When the pay gravel gave out, the town declined as rapidly as it had grown. In 1870 the post office was discontinued; on the Sierra County Map, 1874, the town is shown as a small place. The gold deposits on Onion Valley Ridge are discussed in R. H. Stretch's "Report" (1881–1882). The district and mines are described in *Mining Bureau*, XVI (Plumas, pp. 42 ff.) and XXXIII (pp. 117, 134). The place is recorded on the USGS Downieville 1907 quadrangle and on most modern maps. *See* Eclipse.

Ono [Shasta]. Southwest of Redding, seven miles west of Igo. It was among several places in the West named after the biblical place. A post office was established in 1883. There was a Huntington Mill there in 1900 (*Register*, 1902), and limited quartz mining was carried on until around 1915 (*Mining Bureau*, XIV, p. 775). Drag-line dredges and power shovels were used in the 1930s in the Ono and Igo districts (*Bull.*, 193, p. 138). *See* Igo.

Ophir. The name of the biblical land of gold

was used frequently for claims and mines. Some of the names have been preserved until the present time.

Ophir [Butte]. The original name of modern Oroville. Gold was discovered in the fall of 1849. The name is prominently displayed on Butler's map, 1851. Windeler (pp. 98 and 111) mined here between September 22, 1850 and February 28, 1851. He stated that Ophir or Ophir City had about a dozen houses and the prospects were pretty good for the winter, but he had only fair success. Booth mined here profitably in May, 1852. When the post office was established, May 3, 1854, the name was changed because there was an Ophir post office in Mariposa County. For later development of the rich deposits, *see* Oroville.

Ophir [Mariposa]. *See* Mount Ophir.

Ophir, Ophirville [Placer]. On Auburn Ravine. Shown on Trask's map, 1853, and other early maps. The original name was Spanish Corral, but in October, 1850, Charles Giles of the Buckeye Rovers christened the place Ophir, believing that no other place by that name existed in California (*Buckeye Rovers*, p. 140). In 1850 there was only one log cabin, but in 1852 it was the "largest and most prosperous town in the county," if we believe the *Directory* of Placer County, 1861 (p. 20). Stephen Wing mentions the place frequently from 1852 to 1859. The post office was established as Ophirville, March 24, 1852. According to the County History, 1882 (p. 227), early in 1856 a Chinese found a nugget worth about 3.3 thousand dollars, and in September, 1859, the tailings of a quartz lode yielded 107 ounces of pure gold from thirty-three tons of refuse. Pringle Shaw (p. 121) states that the once-rich place had already started to decay in 1855 or 1856. There were three mills with thirty-six stamps and eight arrastres in 1856 (*State Register*, 1859), and even the *Register* of 1902 still lists four mills with forty-five stamps, at least in the district. There were mainly rich pocket mines with a considerable portion of silver. A description of the mines is given in 1874 in Raymond, VII (pp. 109 f.). The mines of the Ophir District are shown on the map of the *Mining Bureau*, XV (p. 319), and a detailed account is given in XXXII (pp. 28 ff.). The estimated gold production of Ophir District is more than 5 million dollars (*Bull.*, 193, p. 102). Ophir is now a ghost town, but it is still shown on modern maps. Historic Landmark 463.

Ophir Hill [Nevada]. One mile southeast of Grass Valley. The original Ophir Hill Mine, later owned and operated by the Empire Mining Company, opened in 1850, and in 1865 a 30-stamp mill was erected. The average yield was as high as forty-five dollars per ton, and the total production by 1864 was already one million dollars (Bean, pp. 223 ff.). *Mining Bureau*, XVI (Nevada, pp. 154 ff.) gives a history of the operation of Empire and other mines adjoining the Ophir Hill Mine. *See* Empire Mine.

Opopee: Creek, Bar [Butte]. The creek is a tributary to the North Fork of Feather River, on the Plumas County line, above Fergusons Bar. Shown on the County Map, 1877.

Orange Blossom Mine [San Bernardino]. *See* Bristol Mountains.

Ord District [San Bernardino]. The copper and gold mines in the Ord Mountains, twenty miles southwest of Barstow, were located in 1876; they are described in *Mining Bureau* (IX, p. 226; XV, pp. 808 f.; XXVII, p. 299; XXXVI, pp. 232 ff. and 257 ff.). Some work was again carried on in the 1930s (*Bull.*, 193, p. 161). *See* Goat Mountain.

Oregon. The name appeared in the mining regions more frequently than the name of any other state, not only because the Oregonians heard of the gold discovery a few months after the find at Sutters Mill, but because many immigrants preferred the route via Fort Hall and Oregon to the Humboldt River and the Sierra trek.

Oregon Bar [El Dorado]. On the North Fork of American River, below the junction with the Middle Fork, near Condemned Bar. The U. S. Bureau of the Census for 1850 lists forty-two inhabitants at Oregon Bar and nearby Rock Springs. The name Oregon Bar still appears on the USGS Auburn 1944 quadrangle, but farther upstream above Rattlesnake Bar. *See also* Oregon Bar [Placer].

Oregon Bar [Placer]. On the Middle Fork of American River, one and a half miles above Poverty Bar. Shown on Doolittle's map, 1868. The bar is mentioned as promising in the *Placer Herald*, November 3, 1855 (Co. Hist., 1882, p. 190). Recorded on the USGS Placerville 1931 quadrangle.

Oregon Bar [Placer]. On the North Fork of American River, above the confluence with the Middle Fork, near Barnes Bar and Mineral Bar. Judge Thompson (p. 238) and his company mined here in the fall of 1849. He describes the miners at this place as being "as fine a set of men as I have ever seen together." It is mentioned as one of the bars on the North Fork in an item in the Sacramento *Transcript* of June 29, 1850, cited in Bancroft Notes. The *California Courier*, July 15, 1850, reported that some claims yielded twenty dollars to the bucket. In the Placer County Records, I (p. 1) the Oregon Bar company is mentioned in connection with the Bay State Company, which was organized for the purpose of draining the North Fork of American River. The last three mentioned references do not indicate the location on the North Fork, and may therefore apply to the Oregon Bar in El Dorado County, below the junction with the Middle Fork of American River.

Oregon Bar [Siskiyou]. On the north bank of Klamath River, just above the mouth of Shasta River. An Oregon Bar Mine is listed in 1894 in *Mining Bureau*, XII (p. 289).

Oregon Bar [Yuba]. On the North Fork of Yuba River, northeast of Fosters Bar. Shown on Trask's map, 1853, and Wescoatt's, 1861. The *Picayune*, September 11, 1850, reports that the New York Damming Company in one morning took out 500 dollars' worth (Bancroft Notes). De Long collected taxes here December 10, 1855. In 1879 the place was deserted except for a few Chinese miners (Co. Hist., 1879, p. 94).

Oregon: Bar, Camp, Gulch [Amador]. On the Mokelumne River, one mile above Winters Bar. Shown on Trask's map, 1853. Alfred Green, who came to mine on the Mokelumne in the fall of 1848 tells (p. 12) of the arrival of a party of Oregonians, who had had some trouble with Indians before coming, and regarding them all as enemies, they started shooting them down without provocation. Lascy in his "Reminiscences" relates that the gulch was worked by Chilenos in 1849, and that Captain Winters mined at the bar the same year; and in 1850 he employed Mexicans in the building of a wingdam. The Bar proved to be rich and was worked for several seasons. The camp was an election precinct in 1849 (Berriman). The bridge of Palmer & Co., at Oregon Bar is mentioned in the *Calaveras Chronicle*, October 25, 1851. The site is now under the waters of Camanche Reservoir.

Oregon: City, Gulch [Butte]. Near the Middle Fork of Feather River, about seven miles above Oroville. Shown on the County Map, 1862. It was located on a rich quartz vein on which work began in 1851. In 1858 two large mills of eight and twelve stamps crushed ten and eighteen tons a day (*Transactions*, 1858, p. 217). According to the *State Register* of 1859, there were even four mills with thirty-two stamps and sixteen arrastres in operation. Browne (pp. 158, 163) lists the claims and mills in 1867. Shown on the USGS Oroville 1944 quadrangle.

Oregon Creek [Sierra]. A tributary to the Middle Fork of Yuba River, near Forest City. Shown on Goddard's map, 1857. Trask mentions it in 1854 (p. 62). A detailed description of the claims is given in *Transactions*, 1858 (pp. 187 f.). A high grade pocket worth about 200 thousand dollars was found at the Kate Hardy Mine in 1948. This mine has been worked intermittently to the present time and has produced 700 thousand dollars (*Bull.*, 193, pp. 11, 21, 23.)

Oregon Gulch [Shasta]. A tributary to Sacramento River, south of Redding. No early mining reports were found, but *Mining Bureau*, XIV (p. 776) states in 1914 that it had been "exceedingly rich" and prospected from its source to the valley.

Oregon Gulch [Trinity]. Between Weaverville and Canyon Creek. Gold was found in 1850 by two families from Oregon. John Carr (p. 110) prospected here in February, 1851, and he describes the place in *Pioneer Days in California* (pp. 262 ff.). It is apparently the same place of which Knapp makes exaggerated claims in his reminiscences (p. 505). According to Bancroft, VI (p. 371), three men made 300 dollars per day for some time. Later the place became known as Messerville. *See* Messerville.

Oregon Hill [El Dorado]. Apparently on the South Fork of American River, about six miles below Coloma. It is mentioned April 15, 1854, by Stephen Wing (Journal I, p. 77), who visited a friend who had a claim there, and again in a letter of October 2, 1856. An article in the *Mining Press*, datelined Placerville, March 8, 1870, refers to renewed activities in quartz mining on Oregon Hill (Hayes Scrapbooks: Mining, II, sec. 27).

Oregon Hill [Nevada]. North of Nevada City; just east of American Hill. The hill had been washed away completely when Pettee visited the area in 1870 and was reportedly the last to have carried any "fine quartz gold" (Whitney, *Auriferous Gravels*, p. 188).

Oregon Hill [Yuba]. On Oregon Creek, west of Fosters Bar. The place was worked successfully as early as 1851, and according to the *Marysville Directory* of 1858 (p. xxx), it was a lively town with hotels and shops on the thoroughfare from Marysville to the Northern Mines. It is often mentioned by De Long between 1854 and 1857. In 1857 a short-lived post office was established and named Greenville. Greenville is shown on the USGS Smartsville 1943 quadrangle.

Oregon House [Yuba]. On a tributary to Dry Creek; west of Dobbins Creek, tributary to the main Yuba River. Shown on Doolittle's map, 1868. There was a cabin in 1850, and the House was built in 1852 (Co. Hist., 1879, p. 88). The post office was established May 3, 1854. The place is often mentioned by De Long. Placering was carried on until the twentieth century (*Register*, 1905). Recorded on the USGS Smartsville 1943 quadrangle.

Oregon Ravine [Nevada]. *See* Kelseys Ravine.

Oregon: Ravine, Canyon [El Dorado]. North of Georgetown. The Canyon is shown on Bowman's map (1873) as a tributary to Canyon Creek. The Ravine had some of the richest seam deposits. It was discovered in 1848 or 1849 by three Oregonians, who left after having made excellent profits. According to Haskins (p. 136), there were already 200 miners in the locality in the fall of 1849. Cornelius, later U. S. senator from California, mined at Sailor Slide in Oregon Canyon with success. Charles Blake and companions mined at Oregon Cañon and took out fifty-nine dollars in six hours on Christmas Day, 1849 (*SCPQ*, VII, p. 25). One of Bancroft's informants, A. Barstow, claimed that there were 3,000 prospectors in March, 1849 (doubtless 1850). Another of Bancroft's informants, John T. Little, stated that four men brought to his store in Coloma 300 pounds of "ingots, coarse gold," which they had taken out of Oregon Canyon. They were weighed on his scales, and the estimated value of one lump was 2 thousand dollars. Another large nugget, which was sold for 1,250 dollars, is listed in *Mining Bureau*, II (part 1, p. 149). The total production of the seam deposits on Oregon Canyon and Canyon Creek was estimated at 3.5 million dollars in 1934 (*Mining Bureau*, LII, p. 436).

Orick District [Humboldt]. *See* Gold Bluff.

Oriental Mill [Nevada]. Near Nevada City. The steam-driven 8-stamp custom mill was erected in 1857. It is listed in *Bean's Directory* and in the *Annual Mining Review*, 1876 (p. 22). The Oriental Mine received permission for hydraulic mining in 1894.

Oriental Mine [Sierra]. Southwest of Alleghany. It is a lode mine, which produced 4.25 million dollars to 1956, figured at thirty-five dollars per ounce. More than 2 million dollars were produced before 1890. A description is given in *Mining Bureau*, LII (pp. 255 ff.). High grade pockets yielded 734 thousand dollars before 1890 and 100 thousand dollars in the 1930s (*Bull.*, 193, p. 11). The latter source (p. 24) gives the total production at 2.85 million dollars.

Oriflamme Canyon [San Diego]. In the Julian district, southeast of Banner. It was named after the Oriflamme quartz mine, which had a 10-stamp mill in 1886. It was located in the mid-1870s and was worked intermittently to about 1905. (*Mining Bureau*, VI, part 1, p. 89; *County Report*, III, p. 158). The mine was named after a boat that brought miners to San Diego County (O. F. Heckelman).

Original Amador Mine [Amador]. *See* Amador City; Spring Hill Mine.

Original Mine [Mariposa]. *See* Clearinghouse.

Orleans Bar [Humboldt]. On Klamath River, below the junction with Salmon River. Mining started in 1850. Although its name was originally New Orleans Bar, Gibbs called it Orleans Bar (Schoolcraft, p. 149) in the fall of 1851 and shows it on his manuscript map. This shorter form appears on Goddard's map and in the name of the post office established December 2, 1857. The place became a lively town after the Gold Bluff bubble burst in 1851. Carr mined here in January, 1851, unsuccessfully because of high water. The place became the trading center of mining along

the Salmon River. In 1860 the population counted 533 Chinese miners. Between 1870 and 1890 the mining and dredging was mainly carried on by a British syndicate. A detailed history of the place is found in *California Historical Society Quarterly*, XXXIX (pp. 53 ff.). A mine was in operation until 1913 (*Mining Bureau*, XXI, p. 310), and a hydraulic mine in the district was active in the 1930s (*Bull.*, 193, p. 140).

Orleans Flat [Nevada]. Near the Middle Fork of Yuba River, five miles northeast of North Bloomfield, in the lode and placer district of Moores Flat. Shown on Doolittle's map, 1868. Active placering began in 1851, and the town flourished (Bean, p. 402; *Transactions*, 1858, p. 183). In 1855 there were 600 persons here, many cabins and a number of stores (Hutchings' Diary, October 18, 1855). The diggings were shallow, however, and the decline began in 1857; and in 1867 only Mexican and Chinese worked the abandoned claims. According to Bancroft (VI, p. 486), the original name was Concord Bar. *See* Concord Bar.

Ormonde [Nevada]. Three miles from Washington. In 1895 it was only a site, but several mines were still active according to the *Nevada Directory*, 1895 (p. 127).

Oro [Sutter]. The Spanish word for 'gold' was naturally used for many camps and mines. The defunct town, also called Oro City, at the mouth of Bear River, was near present-day Nicolaus. It was founded as a trading post for the Northern Mines in 1850 and is shown prominently on Gibbes' map, 1851. The place soon disappeared, though it served briefly as the county seat (Bancroft, VI, p. 489). *See* Nicolaus Ferry.

Oro City [Placer]. In the Auburn Ravine. The camp was founded by a group of miners who had seceded from Gold Hill because of civic disagreements (*Directory of Placer County*, 1861). The place had a post office from 1853 to 1858. It is probably the same camp as Oro town, mentioned by Stephen Wing on April 5, 1853, as the "prettiest located place I have seen in this country." The miners in the vicinity were doing well, he reports, making as high as two ounces a day. *See* Gold Hill; Mugginsville.

Oro Fino [Madera]. *See* Fine Gold Creek.

Oro Fino [Siskiyou]. On Oro Fino Creek, a tributary to Scott River, west of Fort Jones. One company took out one thousand dollars in a week in 1862, according to *Mining Press*, April 1, 1862. The place was the trading center and post office (established 1861) for the numerous mines between Quartz and Chapparal hills. A water-driven 8-stamp mill was built in 1870 (*Annual Mining Review*, 1876, p. 22). Description of later development is given in *Mining Bureau*, XI (p. 437). The district is described in *Bulletin*, 193 (p. 140), where it is stated that in the 1930s and 1940s the mines were again active. There is still some quartz mining in the Oro Fino area, but the main activity now is farming (W. M. Smith).

Oro Fino Mine [El Dorado]. *See* Big Canyon, tributary to the Cosumnes River.

Oro Fino Placers [Butte]. West of modern De Sabla. Old placers paid especially well around 1890. Consolidated mines operated until the 1920s (*Mining Bureau*, XXIV, pp. 202 f.).

Oro Grande: District, town [San Bernardino]. Also called the Silver Mountain District. The town is on Highway 66, northwest of Victorville, near the center of the district. A trading post and a stamp mill were founded in 1878 and named Halleck for the chemist of the mill. A Halleck post office was established January 3, 1881. The quartz yielded twelve dollars per ton. Lack of water caused a decline after 1889 (*Mining Bureau*, IX, pp. 227, 237), but it remained the trading center and post office for the numerous gold and silver mines on both sides of the Mojave River. The individual mines are listed and mapped in the *Register* of 1902. The place gradually became known by the name of the nearby Oro Grande Mine, once the property of Edward L. Doheny, the oil tycoon (Santa Fe Coast Lines); the post office was renamed Oro Grande in 1925. In the 1930s there was mining activity again, and at present large amounts of cement are produced (*Bull.*, 193, p. 162).

Oro Grosso [Madera]. The Spanish name for 'coarse gold', probably at the site of modern Coarsegold on Highway 41. Derbec (pp. 140 ff.) datelines several letters in October of 1850, from Oro Grosso, and states that Mexicans named it thus because they found grains of gold worth several dollars each in the arroyo, later called Coarse Gold Creek. The camp was already nearly abandoned on October 23, 1850.

Oroleva [Butte]. Between the South Fork of the Feather and the North Fork of the Yuba rivers, in Strawberry Valley, five and a half miles east of Forbestown. It is shown as Orolewa, a sizeable place, on Trask's map, 1853, and on the County Map, 1862, and as Oroliva on Wescoatt's map, 1861. On the USGS Bidwell Bar 1944 quadrangle it appears as Oroleeve. Hutchings, who was there on his trip through the mines in 1855, found it a small deserted town, with one good hotel. It was started by a quartz mining company, and when the claims on the river failed, the town was abandoned. (Hutchings' Diary, November 5, 1855.) De Long mentioned the place on October 10, 1855, and again on January 3, 1857.

Oro Rico Mine [Mariposa]. *See* Peñon Blanco.

Oroville [Butte]. The camp on the Feather River was started as Ophir in 1849. *See* Ophir for early development. When the post office was established, May 3, 1854, the name had to be changed because there were two post offices in the state with similar names. When the Feather River Ditch was completed in the spring of 1856, the place became the center for the mining in the district (Hittell Clippings, p. 68). In 1856 the vote was 1,000 and the tributary population was 4,000 (Bancroft, VI, p. 490). It became the third county seat in 1856. The name is prominently shown on Goddard's map, 1857. It is reported that two miners working in the river above the town in 1857 took out 104 ounces of gold in one pan (Mansfield, p. 5). According to the same source (p. 24) a nurseryman hit upon the idea of dredging for gold when he built a well in his orchard. On Table Mountain, opposite Oroville, the famous Bracket Flume, which hung on brackets on the face of a cliff, was constructed when hydraulic mining was in its palmy days. In modern times dredging predominated. The *Register* of 1903 lists eleven dredging companies. In 1899 the total production within a radius of eight miles was estimated at 82 million dollars (*Mines and Minerals*, p. 280). For the extensive literature on the district, *see* Consolidated Index.

Orr City [Placer]. *See* Gold Hill; Oro City; Mugginsville — all in Placer County.

Ortega Mine [Mariposa]. *See* Princeton.

Osborn Hill [Nevada]. About two miles southeast of Grass Valley. Shown on Doolittle's map, 1868. In the 1860s there were about a dozen mines and at least one, the Wheal Betsy, yielded at times ninety dollars per ton (Bean, p. 226). According to the *Grass Valley Directory*, 1865, the name was applied to a ridge or mountain spur running north and south, parallel to Wolf Creek, about two miles east of

Grass Valley, and each knoll or hill on the ridge had a separate name — Prescott Hill, Laurence Hill, Redan Hill, Sebastopol Hill, Daisy Hill, Hueston Hill. Osborne Hill is shown on the USGS Smartsville 1943 quadrangle.

Osceola District [Nevada]. One mile south of Rough and Ready. There were at least six claims and mines in the state named for Osceola, the Indian leader in the Seminole War of 1835. In the fall of 1855 a group of prospectors discovered a ledge with a quartz pocket which yielded the incredible amount of 225 dollars of gold per ton. A company was formed and a 24-stamp mill was built at the Osceola mine. The output petered out like most of the quartz mines in this region. The mines of the district are listed in *Mining Bureau*, XVI (Nevada, p. 227). The consolidated Osceola Mine is listed until 1941.

Osdick [San Bernardino]. The group of mines in the Rand Mining district was named in 1905 for "Pete" Osdick, a pioneer miner. The name of the post office, established in 1922 as Osdick, was changed to Red Mountain in 1929, but the school district retained the old name. The group of silver and tungsten mines is listed under the name Osdick in the Mining Bureau reports until 1953.

Oskalousa Bar [Butte]. On the south side of the Middle Fork of Feather River, above the junction with the South Fork. Recorded on Trask's map, 1853. The place name Oscaloosa is found in several states. For the origin, *see American Place Names* by George R. Stewart.

Osoville [Nevada]. *See* Ossaville.

Ossaville [Nevada]. On Fordyce Creek, near Meadow Lake, on a site marked by huge boulders. John M. Wooster built a 10-stamp mill in the fall of 1865 in the wake of the Meadow Lake rush. Because of the composition of the quartz, the recovery of gold was difficult, and the settlement failed with the district. The editor of Wooster's "Reminiscences" calls the place Osoville from *oso*, 'bear' (*CHSQ*, XVIII, pp. 149 ff.), but the name is spelled Ossaville in *Bean's Directory*, 1867 (p. 313).

Ostro [El Dorado]. An unidentified place on the North Fork of the North Fork of Cosumnes River, shown on Butler's map, 1851.

Oswego Bar [Yuba]. An unidentified place listed in the Giffen file.

Ottawa Bar [Butte]. On the South Fork of Feather River, near Stringtown. Named after Ottawa, Illinois, from which the first

prospectors had come. It was founded by Delano and company in the spring of 1850. They built an expensive dam which had to be abandoned because of high water in the winter. In 1851 a company of Chinese took over the deserted claims and are said to have made fifty to one hundred dollars a day "for many days." Details are given in Delano, *Life* (pp. 279 f.).

Otter Bar [Calaveras]. On the Stanislaus River, near Vallecito. It is mentioned as a mining locality in *Chispa*, II (p. 34).

Otter Creek [El Dorado]. Tributary to the Middle Fork of American River, north of Bottle Hill. In the spring of 1851 the John Taylor Company discovered a vein on the Creek and built a 6-stamp mill near the trail from Georgetown to Volcano Bar, between the American River and Otter Creek. (*Alta*, April 25, 1852). Shown on the USGS Placerville 1931 quadrangle.

Ottitiewa [Siskiyou]. *See* Fort Jones.

Ousleys Bar [Yuba]. On the main Yuba River above Swiss Bar, about eight miles from Marysville. Shown on Milleson and Adams' map, 1851. Gibbes on his map of 1851 places it east of Auburn. In 1849 Dr. Ousley (or Owsley) of Missouri started to mine here and to practice medicine. According to Mrs. Thomas B. Porter, a descendant, the family name was spelled Owsley, and one of the Owsleys brought "a small army of Negroes to work the mines, which he did with profit" (James de T. Abajian). Breyfogle was at "Ousleys Bar" in February, 1850. Pringle Shaw writes interestingly about the place in 1855. At that time there were 750 inhabitants. In 1858 it was nearly deserted (*Marysville Directory*, 1858, p. xxviii), and by 1867 it was buried under gravel (San Francisco *Alta*, November 7, 1867).

Oustomah Hill [Nevada]. North of Nevada City; next to American Hill. The Neocene auriferous gravels in the region are described by Lindgren, *Auriferous Gravels* (p. 132). Mining began as early as 1853 according to Bean (pp. 153 f.), and during hydraulic mining a vein of quartz was discovered (*Mining Bureau*, XVI, Nevada, pp. 228 f.) After the property lay idle for many years, operations were resumed and continued until 1915, after which the 10-stamp mill was used for crushing chrome. The workings of the Oustomah lode mine are described in the report of the Mining Bureau cited above. The name is also spelled Oustamah.

Owens: Lake, River [Inyo]. According to the Los Angeles *Star*, July 3, 1858 (Hayes

Scrapbooks: Mining, VI, sec. 1), gold was discovered here in 1849 and the deposits were rediscovered in 1858. A party was organized to exploit the surface diggings on a stream that feeds the lake. The scrapbooks contain other clippings about mining at and near the lake. In the 1860s there was gold and silver mining in the valley and according to the *Annual Mining Review*, 1876 (p. 21), a water-driven 25-stamp mill had been built at a place on Owens River in 1870.

Owl Creek [Nevada]. A tributary to the South Fork of Yuba River, six miles west of Nevada City. A short tunnel was run into the lava near Key-Stone Sawmill, but the gravel did not prove to be rich. A few miles northeast of the sawmill, there were some surface diggings worked by Portuguese miners, but these also were reportedly not rich (Whitney, *Auriferous Gravels-*, p. 191).

Owl Creek [Placer]. A notice of a quartz vein claim is recorded December 16, 1851, in the Placer County Records, I (p. 37½). Doolittle's map, 1868, shows Owl Canŏn, tributary to the North Fork of American River, southwest of Yankee Jims.

Owlsburg, Owlburrow Flat [Calaveras]. At Murphys. The places are listed by Heckendorn and in Hittell's roster with different spellings. Browne (p. 58) calls the diggings rich. It was largely a placer mining area and extended north up the ridge to the Oro y Plata Mine, the richest mine in Murphys, which operated intermittently to 1900 (R. C. Wood). In 1860 a quartz mill with eight stamps and ten arrastres was erected. According to reports in the San Andreas *Independent*, it was "the most profitable quartz mill ever erected and worked in this county."

Oxbow Bar [El Dorado]. On the Rubicon River, near the junction with the Middle Fork of American River. Shown on Trask's map, 1853. It is mentioned in *California Historical Society Quarterly*, XII (p. 66).

P**acheco Pass** [Merced]. According to newspaper items quoted in Bancroft VI (p. 380), placers were discovered here in 1850 and yielded five to nine dollars a day for a brief time.

Pacific District [El Dorado]. In the east central part of the county, near Pacific House. Several hydraulic and drift mines were active in the 1850s and 1860s, and in the early 1920s some of the drift mines were worked again (*Bull.*, 193, p. 104).

Pacific Mine [El Dorado]. *See* Placerville.

Paint Pot Hill. An unidentified place listed in Hittell, *Resources*.

Palisade Mine [Napa]. *See* Silverado.

Palmers Bar [Trinity]. *See* Ingrams Bar.

Paloma [Calaveras]. Near Mokelumne Hill, at Lower Rich Gulch, tributary to Mokelumne River. It is mentioned in 1871 by Raymond, IV (p. 49). Paloma is the Spanish word for 'pigeon'. The Gwin Mine, which produced most of the gold for the district, was near the town of Paloma. *See* Gwin Mine. Shown on the USGS Sutter Creek 1944 quadrangle. According to Rensch-Hoover, Paloma is now called Fosteria. Paloma is Historic Landmark 295.

Palomas Canyon [Los Angeles]. The creek through the canyon is a tributary to Castaic Creek. *Mining Bureau*, XXIII (p. 291) and XXIX (p. 247) and elsewhere state that gold deposits in the area were mined by mission priests between 1834 and 1838. No evidence to prove this has been discovered. In 1888 *Mining Bureau*, VIII (p. 334), reports the finding of a piece of gold worth 1,900 dollars and in the next report, IX (p. 201), the Palamos Mining District with placering is mentioned.

Panamint [Inyo]. About eight miles northeast of Ballarat. The town developed in the 1870s and is said to have had a population of 2,500 at one time. It had a post office intermittently from 1874 to 1895. A 10-stamp steam-driven mill was listed in the *Annual Mining Review*, 1876 (p. 22). The mineral production was mainly silver, with only a little gold. With the lowering of the price of silver the place declined, and by the early 1930s silver mining was at a standstill, but there were still attempts to make gold mining profitable. (*Mining Bureau*, XXVIII, p. 358.) The town is shown on the USGS Ballarat 1908 quadrangle.

Panamint Range [Inyo]. William (or Charles) Alvord is credited with having discovered precious metal here, mainly silver, in 1860 while searching for the Gunsight Mine. Because of Indian troubles, prospecting was abandoned. The modern mines, Gold Bug, Gold Tooth or Schnellheist, Mountain Girl, Radcliff or Ratcliff, and others were not developed until after 1873. (Inyo *Independent*, June 12, 1873; *Mining Bureau*, XXVIII, pp. 364 ff.; XLVII, pp. 40 ff., with map.) *See* Pleasant Canyon.

Pancake Ravine. An unidentified place listed in Hittell, *Resources*.

Pancoast Diggings [Tuolumne]. Somewhere east of Knights Ferry. Charles E. Pancoast (pp. 293–296) worked here successfully with his partners in the summer of 1850. The place had a trading post but no real name.

Paradise [Placer]. Between the North and Middle forks of American River, about two miles northerly from Spanish Dry Diggings. Doolittle's map, 1868, shows it as Paradise Dry Diggings; Bowman's map, 1873, shows Paradise Diggings and Flat. In 1854 (?) a 27-ounce nugget was found here (Hittell Clippings, p. 26). A notice of a claim for water rights and for conveying the water in a ditch to Paradise Diggings, datelined Paradise, October 23, 1855, is recorded in Placer County Records, I (p. 311). Hutchings describes the place as "a dried-up village of shake houses and log cabins . . . , three-fifths German, one-fifth Chinese, and one-fifth made up of American Scotch, Irish, French and Chileno — all together" (Diary, May 10, 1855). According to the County History, 1882 (p. 227), in August, 1860, three men took out 3 thousand dollars in one week. Shown on the USGS Placerville 1931 quadrangle.

Paradise Flat [Siskiyou]. On the North Fork of Salmon River, near Sawyers Bar. Father Florian (Martin Francis Schweninger), native of Austria, served here as a Benedictine missionary in 1858. The church is about a half mile down the river from Sawyers Bar, and it is still standing today. (*CHSQ*, XL, p. 66; W. M. Smith.) The Paradise Flat Mine is listed in the Mining Bureau reports until 1935. The Paradise Group of mines, however, is in a different location, south of Happy Camp.

Paragon Mine [Placer]. *See* Forest Hill.

Paris [Kern]. On Indian Creek, north of Tehachapi. It is mentioned but not mapped in the *Register* of 1904. There was a post office here from 1903 to 1912 for the quartz mines in the region. The camp was established in 1902, and in 1912 the name was changed to Loraine (R. C. Bailey). The mines in the area are listed in *County Report*, I.

Paris [Nevada]. On the Relief Hill road, opposite the town of Washington. It is listed as a mining camp by Foley.

Paris Bar [Tuolumne]. On Tuolumne River, near Jamestown. It is mentioned in the *County History*, 1882 (p. 281) in a chronology dated March 1, 1863.

Park [El Dorado]. An abbreviation of Sly Park sometimes used in mining literature.

Parks Bar [Trinity]. On North Fork of Trinity River. An unidentified bar is mentioned in *Mining Bureau*, X (p. 706).

Parks Bar [Yuba]. The third camp from the point at which the Yuba River enters the valley. It is shown on Milleson & Adams' map of 1851, and all later maps. The diggings were discovered in May, 1848, and named Marsh Diggings for Dr. John Marsh, the pioneer of Contra Costa County and a member of the first company. In September, 1848, David Parks of Oregon opened a store in competition to Marsh's own store, and the place became known not for the pioneer but for the newcomer. According to the reminiscent account in the Sacramento *Weekly Review* (Bancroft Notes), Charles Covillaud, husband of Mary Murphy of Marysville, also had a store at Parks Bar in 1848, and employed a large number of Indians to mine for him. The early records are filled with astonishing reports of success. Parks left with 85 thousand dollars for New Orleans (Co. Hist., 1879, p. 88), and Marsh himself made about 40 thousand dollars, apparently in a short time (Lyman's biography, p. 279). The Sacramento *Transcript* reports on September 30, 1850, that five men took out 525 pounds of gold in a few days. Edwin F. Morse (pp. 218 ff.) mined here in the fall of 1850 and writes a very interesting account of his experiences. In May, 1851, Heinrich Schliemann, the famous excavator of ancient Troy, was here, referred to it as Parkis Bar, and wrote a description of the mining methods (p. 59). According to Hutchings' diary, September 25, 1855, Parks Bar had been one of the richest bars in California. The *Alta*, November 7, 1867, gives a list of the mines and their yield. Soon afterwards the old town was buried under the debris carried by the Yuba River from the hydraulic operations farther upstream.

Parks Hill [Placer]. In the Iowa Hill area. An agreement for fluming a canyon through Elizabethtown to Kings Diggings or Parks Hill was signed by C. Park and Company and others on November 10, 1850 (Placer County Records, I, p. 64.).

Parksville [Trinity]. Apparently at or near the headwaters of the East Fork of New River. Mining was mentioned in the *Trinity Journal*, October 20, 1860, and again April 27, 1861, with good results reported.

Parrotts Ferry [Tuolumne]. Across the Stanislaus River, on the road between

Parks Bar, Yuba Co.

Columbia and Vallecito. It was established in 1860 by Thomas H. Parrott, and operated until 1903, when the first bridge was built. Historic Landmark 438.

Partzwick [Mono]. Near Benton and the Blind Springs district. It was a settlement established in the late 1860s and named for Julius Partz (F. S. Wedertz).

Paso del Pino [Tuolumne]. North of Columbia, on the South Fork of Stanislaus River, near Experimental Gulch. It was mentioned as a mining locality of 1849 by Heckendorn (p. 6), by Stoddart (p. 116), and by Harris in his reminiscences, *The Gila Trail* (pp. 125 ff.). In February, 1850, Jewett found a tent village at Passo El-Pino or Pine Crossing, with nine companies working on ditches to turn the river (letter, February 1850). The same month William Perkins (p. 126) came upon Pine Crossing, described it as a bridge formed by two pine logs with an encampment of Americans of half a dozen tents. The place is shown on Gibbes' map, 1851, as Pine Crossing; on Wallace's map (1853) and Goddard's, 1857, as Pine Log. The *Picayune*, August 12, 1850 reports rich deposits at Pine Log Crossing, with lumps of one pound apparently no rarity. In a letter of Dr. John H. Wayman, datelined Shaws Flat, October 26, 1852, it is stated that some mines in the area of Paso La Pine

were being worked to good advantage. According to a report in the *Alta*, September 24, 1853, the place was then crowded with miners, many making ten to thirty dollars a day to the man. The Tuolumne County Land Papers register, on November 29, 1853, that a piece of land on the Paso del Pine River was claimed for mining purposes by a group of eight Frenchmen. Alexandre Dumas mentions Passo-del-Pin in his book *Un Gil Blas en Californie* (p. 143). According to an unidentified clipping of May, 1858, a Frenchman found a lump of more than fifty ounces at Pine Log, for which Sleeper & Co. paid 400 dollars. The place is mentioned as a city by Mulford (p. 202) about 1863. A Pine Log Mine is listed in the Mining Bureau reports until 1928. A detailed modern account is given by Jim Young in *Chispa*, VIII (pp. 281 ff.).

Patagonia Canyon [San Bernardino]. Near the Black Hill Range. In 1861 several tunnels yielded profitable gold, silver, and some platina. (*Mining Press*, August 17, 1861.)

Patens Bar [Tuolumne]. An unidentified place in the Giffen file.

Pat Goggins Diggings [Placer]. On the Ralston Ridge; in the southeastern part of the county, near Long Canyon. The diggings on the Tertiary gravels are mentioned by Lindgren, 1911 (p. 169). A place named Goggins is shown on the USGS Colfax 1938 quadrangle, and Goggin Mine is shown on the Duncan Peak 1952 quadrangle.

Patricks Bar [Placer]. On the North Fork of the American River, below Mormon Bar. The County History, 1924 (p. 178), reports that it was rich in early days, and that it was still being worked in the early 1920s.

Pats Bar [Amador]. *See* Puts Bar.

Pats Gulch [Sierra]. Two miles southeast of La Porte. Recorded on the County Map, 1874, and on the USGS Downieville 1907 quadrangle.

Patterson [Nevada]. Three miles east of North San Juan. It was the post office for Cherokee, established June 18, 1855. The name Cherokee could not be used because there was a post office by that name in Butte County. The place is mentioned in Newton Miller's letters of March 10 and July 16, 1856. Shown on the USGS Smartsville 1943 quadrangle as Paterson. *See* Cherokee [Nevada].

Patterson District [Mono]. It was a gold and silver producing district, named for James H. Patterson, discoverer of the deposits. The main period of mining activity was in the 1880s, and there was again some activity in the early 1900s and in the 1930s. The camps within the district were Belfort, Boulder Flat, Cameron, Clinton, Monte Cristo, and Star City. (F. S. Wedertz; *Bull.*, 193, p. 150.)

Patterson: Hill, Gulch [El Dorado]. In Oregon Canyon, one and a half miles northwest of Georgetown. The hill was first mined in November, 1849, by Lawson Patterson. He worked with varying success until May, 1861, when he struck a vein of decomposed quartz. His realistic account mentions the "black lead," where rounded nuggets up to 25 ounces each were found in black cemented lava (Patterson, pp. 38 ff.).

Pattersons Mill [El Dorado]. North of the junction of the North and South forks of Cosumnes River. Recorded on Goddard's map, 1857. It could have been only a saw mill, as no mining records were found. But again it might have been the site of the Patterson Mine near Indian Diggings, listed in the *Register*, 1902 (p. 10).

Pattison [Nevada]. One mile north of Washington, a half mile above the junction of Poorman Creek and the South Fork of Yuba River. It is listed as the site of the Red Point lode mine (Foley).

Paulinville [Yuba]. On the road from Marysville to Brownsville. It was settled in 1857 and later named by and for Pauline (or Paulin) Rauze. From 1866 to 1873 it had a post office. The County History, 1879 (p. 92), makes mention only of orchard and vineyard culture but no mining.

Paynes Bar [Tuolumne]. On the north side of Tuolumne River; south of Jacksonville. Shown on Trask's map, 1853. In 1850 the Payne Bar Company of twenty men worked here but averaged less than four dollars per day to the man (Daniel B. Woods, p. 174). In 1854 one company made one ounce to the pan (*Alta*, October 4, 1854).

Pearls Hill [Nevada]. Near Deer Creek; about one mile northwest of Anthony House. Pettee reports in 1879 that the tunnel at Pearls Hill had struck gravel but could be worked further only with increased water facilities (Whitney, *Auriferous Gravels*, pp. 195, 383 f.).

Peasoup Bar [Plumas]. On the East Branch of the North Fork of Feather River, opposite Indian Bar. It is mentioned by Rensch-Hoover and is listed by Giffen.

Peavine Flat [Sierra]. Near Chips Flat. A small camp of nine houses and one saloon, where several companies were mining in 1862 (*Mining Press*, April 18, 1862).

Peckham Hill [Placer]. About three miles southwest of Todds Valley. Shown on Doolittle's map, 1868. The Peckham Hill and Todds Valley Tertiary gravel mines together produced 5 million dollars worth of gold, according to *Bulletin*, 193 (p. 50).

Pecks Diggings [Nevada]. At the base of Cement Hill, near Nevada City; between Native American and Long Tom ravines. Pettee describes the gravel diggings in his discussion of the course of the ancient river channel in the region (Whitney, *Auriferous Gravels*, pp. 184 ff.).

Pecks Diggings [Tuolumne]. On Union Hill, southeast of Springfield. The story is told in the *San Joaquin Republican*, August 5, 1856, that Captain Peck came to Springfield in 1851, poor and out of luck, and was befriended by Murieta, who gave him a pan of gold from his claim on the hill, from which Peck washed twenty-five dollars. After Murieta was driven out, three men including Peck, realized 400 dollars per day for thirty-two days, one cartload having yielded 15 hundred dollars [!]. The claim lay idle for years, was worked again, and abandoned. Another story told in the *Tuolumne Independent*, February 1, 1879, tells of Peck's later location on Table

Mountain. After he sold the claims, allegedly misrepresenting the survey, five or six miners lost their lives by drowning in the rush of the water from Peck's old diggings, which had no drainage. Peck left the area, and the diggings were being reopened in 1879. The story of his dishonesty is repudiated in an issue of the newspaper the following week.

Pecks Ravine [Nevada]. An undetermined location, but probably near Grass Valley. Around 1851 a Captain Peck found a ledge in a place later known as Pecks Ravine, according to *Bean's History*, 1867 (p. 49), and built a quartz mill with several partners. When it failed and he lost his fortune, he committed suicide.

Pences [Butte]. The place is mentioned in Hittell Clippings (p. 54) as being successfully mined in May, 1858. It is apparently the same as the post office Pentz, near Oroville, which was named for Manoah Pence in 1864. It is shown as Pences, north of Oroville, on the County Map, 1861.

Pennsylvania Bar. Unidentified place listed in the Work Projects Administration project. More than ten mines or dredging companies named Pennsylvania are listed in the *Consolidated Index*.

Pennsylvania Gulch [Calaveras]. East of Murphys. A group of Pennsylvanians started mining here in December, 1849 (Heckendorn, p. 96). According to the *Register* of Calaveras County, 1899, it is the site of the Pennsylvania Coyote Creek Drift Mine. *See* Brownsville.

Penn Valley [Nevada]. Eight miles west of Grass Valley. Shown on Trask's map, 1853. There was mainly farming but some gold mining (Brown, *Directory*, 1856; Bean, 1867).

Penobscot [El Dorado]. On the Georgetown-Sacramento Road, about one mile west of Greenwood. There was a hotel and way station here as early as 1851 (Jerrett, p. 84).

Peñon Blanco [Mariposa]. Two miles northwest of Coulterville. The Spanish term for 'large white rock' was applied to the prominent landmark and apparently to Mexican diggings nearby. It is mentioned as Pino Blanco by Church (p. 184). In 1850 lumbermen from Maine built a handsome cabin but soon left it for Big Oak Flat. A Peñon Blanco House on the road from Stockton to Coulterville is mentioned by Stephen Davis, April 12, 1852. Water through the Golden Rock Ditch from Merced River apparently brought prosperity. In 1863 two miners washed

out 16 thousand dollars in two months of placering (Browne, p. 20). The Peñon Blanco or Oro Rico mine was within the limits of Frémont's grant, and according to the *Guidebook* (p. 35), it was one of "the longest claims on record." Its workings are described in Browne in 1867 (p. 35). It consisted of five patented claims and two unpatented in an area of more than 100 acres and operated with a 20-stamp mill. After 1912 there was little or no mining, but in 1934 there was some prospecting. (*Mining Bureau*, XIV, p. 593; XVII, p. 132; XXIV, p. 109; XXXI, p. 147, LIII, p. 147). The site of the mine is shown on the USGS Sonora 1939 quadrangle.

Penryn [Placer]. Between Loomis and Newcastle. There were several quartz mines nearby between 1860 and 1885. At one time a 10-stamp mill was in operation, but the workings petered out because the assay ran as low as four dollars per ton (*Mining Bureau*, XXIII, p. 250). The Alabama Mine in the Penryn district was still active in 1936 and produced a total of one million dollars (*Mining Bureau*, XXXII, p. 10; *Bull.*, 193, p. 105). The place was named by the owner of local granite quarries, after his home in Penrhyn, Wales.

Pentz [Butte]. *See* Pences.

Peoria Bar [Plumas]. On the Middle Fork of Feather River. It is mentioned in the County History, 1882 (p. 288), as one of the chief mining camps on the Middle Fork.

Peoria: Bar, Flat [Tuolumne]. On the Stanislaus River. The Bar is between Melones Dam and O'Byrnes Ferry, and the Flat is higher on the mountain, northeast of the Sierra Conservation Center, a state prison. Bancroft, VI (p. 375) quotes a reference, according to which some men took out of the Bar as much as five pounds of gold daily in 1850. In a clipping from the Sonora *Herald* of 1858 (Hittell Clippings, p. 66½) it is reported that the average wage in the river was eight dollars a day to the man. Heckendorn (p. 103) lists only one miner in residence. The Flat is listed as "rich" in *Mines and Minerals* (p. 358).

Peoria House [Yuba]. On the road from Fosters Bar to Marysville. Shown on Doolittle's map, 1868, northeast of Prairie Diggings. It is mentioned as a stage stop by Meek (p. 157), and the name has survived for a school district and a cemetery.

Pepper Box Flat [El Dorado]. Hutchings lists Pepper Box as a town in 1855, and Hittell includes Pepper Box Flat in his roster. In the El Dorado County Records (Mortgage

Book B, p. 697) mention is made of claims on Canyon Creek near Pepper Box Flat. There is a Canyon Creek in El Dorado County, tributary to the Middle Fork of American River.

Peppermint Gulch [Tuolumne]. At Peppermint Creek, a tributary to Woods Creek. Deposits were discovered in 1848 and were reported as "exceedingly rich" (Stoddart, p. 62). Shown on the USGS Sonora 1939 quadrangle.

Per Johnsons Halfway House [Tuolumne]. *See* Halfway House.

Perkins Bar [El Dorado]. On the South Fork of American River, eight miles from Placerville. Shown on Trask's map, 1853.

Perkins Coyote Diggings [Nevada]. On the East Fork of Greenhorn Creek, just north of Red Dog. According to the *Alta*, March 6, 1853, three men earned 2,100 dollars by sluicing, and an item in *Young America* (later Nevada City *Democrat*) reported that the previous season the claims yielded 18 to 20 thousand dollars to each partner in the Perkins Brothers' company within a span of four months. By 1854 the Perkins Brothers had sold out to Riggs & Company (L. L. White).

Perkins Ravine [Butte]. Near Forbestown. It is mentioned as a rich gulch by Hutchings in his diary, November 1, 1855.

Permit Mine [Mariposa]. *See* Whitlock.

Perrine Bar [Merced]. On the Merced River. The *Alta* of January 4, 1854, reprints an item from the Stockton *Journal* that reports that the Perrine company took out thirty to fifty dollars per day to the man.

Perris [Riverside]. *See* Pinecate.

Perrys Ranch [El Dorado]. Two miles from Indian Diggings. In the winter of 1853–1854 rich hill diggings were opened on the ranch. One company took out 450 dollars while cutting a tail race (*Alta*, April 17, 1854).

Perschbaker Mine [Butte]. *See* Magalia.

Persido Bar [Siskiyou]. An unidentified place on the Klamath River.

Perty Creek [Yuba]. A tributary to Dry Creek; eight miles southwest of Bullards Bar. Recorded on the County Map, 1879. Hydraulic mining was carried on in the 1870s.

Peru [El Dorado]. North of Kelsey, between Louisville and Spanish Flat. Shown on Doolittle's map, 1868. The U. S. Bureau of the Census lists the names of 168 inhabitants in the population schedule for Peru and vicinity for the 1850 census. Steele, who mined in nearby Downings Ravine, mentions the place (p. 296). Peru Bar

listed in the Work Projects Administration project is probably the same.

Pescadero Creek [Santa Clara]. Trask observed Mexicans placer mining in the summer of 1853 (Trask, 1854, p. 58).

Petersburg [Calaveras]. On the Calaveras River, about six and a half miles west of San Andreas. According to *Las Calaveras*, July, 1957, it was a mining camp started by Germans. Camp's map shows it as an alternate or former name for Greasertown, but Poore states that there were two separate camps about one and a half miles apart, and now both are under the waters of Hogan Reservoir.

Petersburg [Kern]. Between Kern River and Poso Creek, in the Greenhorn Mountains, near the Caves. Peter Gardett opened a store here during the first Kern River rush (Boyd, p. 10). Later it was sometimes known as Greenhorn. The quartz mills paid 80 to 135 dollars a ton (*Mining Press*, August 10, 1861). *See* Greenhorn: Gulch, Mountains, Caves [Kern].

Petersburg [Siskiyou]. On the South Fork of Salmon River, above the junction with the East Fork. It was a thriving camp in the 1860s and 1870s, with a Chinese settlement at one end of it (*Siskiyou Pioneer*, II:10, pp. 19 f.). A review of mining activities in the area into the twentieth century is given in the same publication (IV:1, pp. 21 ff.). There was a Petersburgh post office, 1869–1876.

Peters Flat [Sierra]. On the North Fork of the South Yuba River, east of Downieville. Recorded on Trask's map, 1853.

Petticoat Mine [Calaveras]. The richest mine in Railroad Flat. It is said to have yielded 100 dollars per one ton of quartz. According to Raymond (IV, p. 78), it was accidentally discovered by uncovering — not a skirt — but the outcrop in a placer claim, and was so named because the discoverers registered the claim in the names of their wives. The mine was reported idle in 1914 but is listed in the Mining Bureau until 1935.

Petticoat Slide [Sierra]. Near Poker Flat. According to the story, which might be true, one of a number of hurdy-gurdy girls who ventured into the camp, fell at the slippery entrance and slid into the camp, to the amusement of the miners. (Dressler, *Rabbit Creek*, p. 36; Downieville *Mountain Messenger*, March 29, 1930.) The name is mentioned in a poem in the *Annual Mining Review*, 1876 (p. 18). According to the *Sierra Democrat*, December 8, 1862, the Petticoat Company made eight to ten dollars per day to the hand. A Petticoat Claim is listed in *Mining Bureau*, XVI (Sierra, p. 112), but this is part of the Pilgrim Mine in the American Hill district, south of Downieville.

Phelps Hill [Nevada]. About two miles south of Washington. Shown on Doolittle's map, 1868. One of the earliest mining ditches was built from Deer Creek in May, 1850 (Brown, *Directory*, 1856, p. 10). Phelps Hill is listed as a settlement by Bean in 1867 (pp. 385 ff.). Tunnel and drift operations are described by Lindgren, 1911 (pp. 147 f.). According to the County History, 1880 (p. 206), seven acres yielded 600 thousand dollars in gold.

Phenix Mill [Plumas]. On the Middle Fork of Feather River, probably at or near the confluence with Onion Valley Creek. The mill was started in January, 1852. Booth and partners mined near here with good success early in 1852 (diary of February 29, 1852). Booth gives a good description of quartz mining along Feather River.

Phenix Quartz Mill [Sierra]. Northeast of Sierra City. Shown as a settlement on the County Map, 1874. It is doubtless the same site as Phoenix Mine shown on the USGS Downieville 1907 quadrangle and described in *Mining Bureau*, XVI (Sierra, p. 111).

Philadelphia Diggings [Tuolumne]. Between Eagle Creek and Knights Creek northeast of Columbia. Extensive hydraulic mining was carried on here in the late 1870s, when there was a ditch from the South Fork of Stanislaus River. The gravel mine and the ditch are shown on Dart's map, 1879. A post office was established in 1901 and named Jupiter (*Chispa*, II, p. 35).

Philadelphia House [Calaveras]. *See* Third Crossing.

Phillips [Madera]. On the Merced River, below Phillips Creek. Shown on Trask's map, 1853. It may have been a mining camp, although no mining records were found.

Phoenix Company Bar [Calaveras]. On the south side of Mokelumne River, ten miles above the mouth. Recorded in the Giffen file.

Picacho [Imperial]. Near the bend of the Colorado River, north of Yuma. It was named after the well known landmark Picacho Peak ('peak peak'). The superficial gold bearing gravel deposits in Picacho Basin were discovered about 1857 and were first mined mainly by Mexicans using the dry placering method on a small scale. Later, in the 1890s hydraulic mining was attempted without success. The Picacho Basin Quartz Mine, about five miles south of the village, was a consolidation of about thirty claims and operated from 1904 to 1910, with a reported production of about 2 million dollars (*Mining Bureau*, XII, p. 238; XIII, p. 343; XIV, pp. 729 ff.; XXII, pp. 260 ff.). In the 1930s there was a revival of placer and lode mining with little success (*Mining Bureau*, XXXVIII, pp. 112 ff.) and since then only minor prospecting (*Bull.*, 193, p. 162). The old mines are Historic Landmark 193.

Picaune Gulch [Calaveras]. Three miles from Mokelumne Hill. The place is mentioned in a letter of William Hanson datelined January 14, 1851, when he mined in nearby Rich Gulch. The name is a misspelling of Picayune.

Picayune Divide [Placer]. On the south side of Indian Creek, south of Iowa Hill. Picayune was at the time of the Gold Rush the smallest coin, and the name was used in the sense of paltry and insignificant. Although the Blue Lead runs through the hills, all attempts after 1856 to strike pay dirt by driving tunnels were failures. The Lebanon Claim struck gold bearing quartz in 1866 and built a 10-stamp mill, driven by a hurdy-gurdy wheel (Bancroft Scraps LI:1, p. 7).

Picayune Gulch [Tuolumne]. Between Jamestown and Chinese Camp. According to *Mines and Minerals* (p. 358), the place together with Montezuma had produced 1.5 million dollars by 1899. *See* Montezuma.

Picayune Point [Nevada]. An unidentified place listed in Hittell's roster.

Pickering Bar [Placer]. On the North Fork of American River, above the junction with the Middle Fork, below Euchre Bar. Hutchings describes the area on his trip through the mines in 1855 (Diary, May 4, 1855). The place is mentioned in the County History, 1882 (p. 402).

Pictos Bar [Butte]. On the west side of the North Fork of Feather River, two miles above Berry Creek. Shown on Trask's map, 1853.

Pierces Bar [Sierra]. Near St. Joe Bar, west of Goodyears Bar. Sinnott (*Sierra City*, p. 193) mentions it, stating that it is now called Convicts Bar, for the road crews that worked there between 1918 and 1920. No mining record was found.

Pierces Cabin [Nevada]. A settlement on the old Henness Pass Road, twenty miles from Bowman (Foley).

Pierson Hill [Tuolumne]. *See* Bensonville.

Piety Hill [Nevada]. Now a part of Nevada City. It is mentioned as a settlement by Bean, 1867.

Piety Hill [Shasta]. Southwest of Redding, about a mile east of Igo. According to Steger, the American residents gradually moved to Igo, and by 1880 only Chinese were left. Mining in nearby Clear Creek and Dry Creek in the 1850s and its revival in the early 1870s is described in Raymond (V, p. 99; VI, pp. 143 ff.). The Hardscrabble or Piety Hill Hydraulic Mine was a good producer until 1880 (*Mining Bureau*, XXII, p. 186). In the 1930s there was again activity with power shovels and dragline dredges in the district (*Bull.*, 193, p. 138).

Pike. The name was frequently used in gold camp geography and applied originally to gold diggers from Pike County, Missouri. Soon it was applied to people who were reluctant to tell where they came from. Still later it was applied to rough miners and new immigrants. Crosby (p. 20) gives a good account of the name.

Pike City [Sierra]. Between the Middle Fork of Yuba River and Oregon Creek. A letter of Daniel McLean to his brother A. G. is dated from this camp August 22, 1855. It is listed in Brown's *Directory*, 1856, and recorded on Doolittle's map, 1868. According to the *Register*, 1903, it was still a trading center and post office for a number of mines. A description of the Pike City mining district is given in *Mining Bureau*, XVI (Sierra, pp. 14 ff.). It is also described in *Bulletin*, 193 (p. 105), where it is stated that the Alaska Mine was worked on a large scale from 1863 to 1916; its production was more than one million dollars. The Pleasant View hydraulic mine was active between 1962 and 1963.

Pike County Bar [Trinity]. On the Trinity River, opposite Browns Creek. In characterizing the population of the camp Cox (p. 49) indicates that there was "not only a 'sprinkling', but that the predominant element must have been from Pike."

Pike Flat [Nevada]. In Grass Valley townsite. According to the Grass Valley *Telegraph*, October 6, 1853, the one and a half mile long flat, named in 1850 by the Pike Flat Company, yielded more than any other flat in the county. The *Alta* reports on December 23, 1853, that some claims yielded an average of 100 dollars a day, and on May 29, 1854, that one company took out 815 dollars on one Monday. This "beautiful spot" was soon destroyed by placer mining (*Mining Press*, July 6,

1861). It is still mentioned as a center of placering in 1867 by Bean (p. 189).

Pike Hill. An unidentified place listed in the State Library roster.

Pilgrims Camp [Siskiyou]. Near Mugginsville. According to a clipping from Yreka *Journal*, January 17, 1868, in Hayes Scrapbooks: Mining (IV, sec. 5), the diggings in the vicinity of Pilgrims Camp and Mugginsville are sufficient to give employment at "remunerative wages to a thousand miners."

Pilot Hill [El Dorado]. The camp Pilot Hill, halfway between the Middle and South forks of American River, northeast of the elevation, developed together with two other camps, Pittsville and Centreville. Pilot Hill is recorded on Gibbes' map, 1851, and on all other early maps. A post office was established April 18, 1854. According to the County History, 1883 (p. 181), the original name was Centreville; however, Bowman's map, 1873, shows both settlements. There was rich placer mining as early as 1849. In 1856 water for the camp was supplied by the Pilot and Rock Creek Canal (Hittell Clippings, p. 73). According to a report in Bancroft Notes, two miners found a boulder of quartz "literally gorged with gold." It was found in January, 1857, and a piece of it was sent to San Francisco, where it was assayed as containing 1,760 dollars worth of gold. It may have been the same boulder listed in *Mining Bureau*, II (part 1, p. 148), which was sold for 8 thousand dollars, but the date of the finding was given as 1867. According to the County History, 1883 (p. 90), the Pilot Hill Mine was better known as the Boulder Claim. The miners, meeting at Flume House on the Stockton Road July 3, 1858, adopted an interesting set of mining laws for the Pilot Hill district: "each company holding tunnel or shafting claims, in order to hold the same, shall be required to perform work to the amount·of twenty-five dollars each week for a period not to exceed twelve months" (Hittell Clippings, p. 39). Raymond in 1874 (VII, p. 95) mentions the seam diggings that had been worked to "a considerable extent" by "coyoteing" and arrastre milling. In the *Register* of 1902 Pilot Hill is still given as the center of a quartz mining district. The Zantgraf Mine, six miles southwest of Pilot Hill, on the east side of the American River, was first worked in 1888 with a 10-stamp mill, which was increased to twenty stamps during the 1890s. By 1901 the production reached about one

Pilot Peak and Onion Valley, Plumas Co.

million dollars. There was intermittent mining activity until 1941. (*Mining Bureau*, LII, p. 429). The stamp mill and the settlement were destroyed by fire in 1931 (Rensch-Hoover). In 1956 the land was the property of the U. S. government and was designated as a dam site. *See* Centerville.

Pilot Hill [Plumas]. Six miles northwest of Gibsonville. A quartz mine at the foot of the hill is still listed in 1895/96 (*Mining Bureau*, XIII, p. 303).

Pinacate [Riverside]. *See* Pinecate.

Pinchemtight [El Dorado]. The place is recorded as a settlement on Doolittle's map, 1868, and Bowman's, 1873, near Weber Creek. Pinchem Bar is mentioned in the El Dorado County Records (Mining Locations, I, p. 44) in connection with a claim filed December 2, 1850. It is said to be the same as Pinchem gut and probably the same as Pinch Gut Ravine mentioned in the *Alta*, March 29, 1854, from an item reprinted from Placerville *Mountain Democrat*, reporting that the miners made steady and remunerative wages. Hutchings, however, lists both Pinchumtight and Pinchgut as towns on "Weaver" Creek in 1855. The stories that a German

shoemaker and saloon keeper did the "tight pinching" of gold dust (Georgetown *News*, January 10, 1856; Co. Hist., 1883, p. 203) are clearly folk etymology. The place was a ghost town in 1883, but the Pinchem Ravine on Weber Creek is still a reminder.

Pinckney [Shasta]. *See* Gas Point.

Pine Bar [El Dorado]. Above the old Missouri Dam and the foot of McDowells Race, on the South Fork of American River. It is mentioned in the El Dorado County Records (Mining Locations, Book 1, p. 38). It may be near Missouri Bar on the South Fork near Michigan Bar.

Pinecate [Riverside]. At the site of modern Perris. The camp developed in the 1870s and had a post office from 1881 to 1887. It was spelled Pinacate, a more accurate spelling because it is the Mexican Aztec word *pinacatl*, 'black beetle'. It is listed in San Diego County as Pinecate in *Mining Bureau*, II (part 1, p. 181). Volume XV (pp. 529 ff.) of the *Report* gives a good description of the district and the mines which prospered between 1876 and 1882. The district is also described in *Bulletin*, 193 (p.

175), where it is called Pinacate. According to this account, the region between Perris and Elsinore had been placer mined in the 1850s. After the discovery of the Good Hope vein in 1874, there was activity until about 1903. The Good Hope Mine produced between one and two million dollars. In the 1930s there was again some mining in the district and some prospecting since that time.

Pine City [Mono]. On Mary Lake, above Mammoth City, at an elevation of 8,500 feet. It was a short-lived mining camp during the Mammoth Lake gold rush in the late 1870s. A picture of the camp is shown in *Mining Bureau*, XII (opposite p. 374). *See* Lake Mining District and Mammoth City.

Pine Crossing [Tuolumne]. *See* Paso del Pino.

Pine Grove [Amador]. Eight miles south of Sutter Creek. There were several important mines here dating back to the early 1850s. The settlement probably developed around "Pine Grove," the residence of Albert and Caroline Leonard, recorded as completed in 1855 (Berriman). A post office was established July 12, 1856. Mines and mills are shown on the County Map, 1866, and are fully described by Browne (pp. 78 f.). The Thoss Mine extracted 90 percent of the gold and silver from sulfurets by a special process. Besides gold and silver, tellurium was mined. Some mines were in operation until recent years (*Mining Bureau*, L, pp. 172, 177 f., 189, 192).

Pine Grove [Placer]. *See* Secret Ravine; Pino; Smithville; Stewarts Flat.

Pine Grove [Sierra]. In the Slate Creek Basin, at the Yuba County line. Shown on Trask's map, 1853, and on later maps. Lecouvreur was here in the summer of 1852, apparently before the gold deposits were discovered, and gives a poetic description of the place (pp. 231 f.). In September of the same year, John Clark calls it "a new place with 5 or 600 inhabitants" ("The California Guide"). According to Vischer (pp. 238, 240) and *Transactions*, 1858 (pp. 198 ff.), the mining was mainly tunnel work. The *Mining Press*, October 19, 1861, reports that 6 thousand dollars' worth was washed out from one tunnel in eight hours. A detailed account of the Comet, a cooperative mining undertaking, is given in Raymond, V (p. 81). In 1879 there was still some hydraulic mining, and the Hayes Mine is listed in Mining Bureau reports until 1942.

Pine Grove [Yuba]. Shown on Wescoatt's Map, 1861, as a camp or settlement on the old La Porte turnpike, south of Clipper Mill.

Pine Gulch [Tuolumne]. An unidentified place, in which a 23-pound nugget was found in 1854, according to *Mines and Minerals* (p. 357).

Pine Log [Calaveras]. In the Hodson area, three miles northwest of Copperopolis. Hittell's roster lists it in Amador County. According to *Mining Bureau*, XXXII (pp. 285 ff.) Pine Log was consolidated with other mines and called Royal Consolidated. The mine operated extensively between 1895 and 1905 and intermittently until 1936, when twenty of the 120 stamps were in operation. Pine Log no. 1 and 2 as well as Royal are listed in the *Register*, 1899. *Mining Bureau*, XXXII (p. 315) lists also Pine Log No. 3.

Pine Log; Pine Log Crossing [Tuolumne]. *See* Paso del Pino; Experimental Gulch.

Pine Tree [Kern]. Four miles south of Tehachapi. There was rich free gold mining until 1910 (*County Report* I, p. 178).

Pine Tree and Josephine Mine [Mariposa]. Two miles north of Bear Valley, on Highway 49. The deposits were discovered in 1849, probably soon after the discovery of lode-gold at the Mariposa Mine. The mines were originally separate, but they became part of the Frémont Las Mariposas Grant in 1859 and were worked jointly for many years. In spite of financial difficulties brought on by mismanagement the estimated yield exceeded 4 million dollars. The greatest production was between 1933 and 1944 under the management of the Pacific Mining Company. Operations ceased in the 1940s due to war-time conditions. Details are given in *Mining Bureau*, LIII (pp. 151 ff.). Shown on the *Guidebook* map 1.

Pine Valley District [San Diego]. On the west slope of Laguna Mountains, about nine miles east of Descanso. An alternate name is Laguna Mountains district. The principal mine is the Noble Mine, which was discovered in 1888, worked to 1914, and intermittently to the early 1940s. Numerous small claims were located mainly between 1910 and 1930 and worked on a small scale. In recent years there has also been some prospecting. (*Mining Bureau*, XIV, p. 6; *County Report*, III, pp. 121, 130; O. F. Heckelman.)

Pinery Diggings [Siskiyou]. Near Klamath River, south of Happy Camp. It was named after a nearby hill, on which manganese was later discovered. Gold was found in 1855, according to an item in the

Yreka *Union* June 5, 1869 (Bancroft Notes). There was also a Pinery Diggings in Quartz Valley on the old Quartz Valley-Kidder Creek Road (Tickner).

Piney Creek [Mariposa]. Tributary to Merced River, at the site of modern Lake McClure. There was placering after 1850, but it was soon exhausted. James D. Savage had one of his first trading posts at the mouth of the creek (Eccleston, *Mariposa*, p. 110).

Pino [Placer]. In the Secret Ravine. Shown on Doolittle's map, 1868. The name was apparently shortened from the commonplace name Pine Grove. It was an old gold mining camp which developed about 1850. According to John Winkley in the "Knave," August 12, 1945, it once had a population of 1,500 inhabitants. The post office was transferred from Smithville to Pino, December 6, 1869, and lasted until 1890.

Pino Blanco [Mariposa]. *See* Peñon Blanco.

Pioneer Claim [Sacramento]. About a half-mile below Mormon Island. An unsuccessful attempt to turn about forty rods of the American River from its channel was made in April, 1851, by John Steele and company. Steele (pp. 215 ff.) gives a fine description of this undertaking.

Pioneer Mine [Placer]. On the south side of American River Canyon, near Damascus. The mine operated from 1854 to 1862 and from 1880 to the 1920s; its production is estimated at nearly a million dollars. It had a 20-stamp mill and was one of the deepest gold mines in the county, with one vein opened to 1,440 feet below the apex. (*Mining Bureau*, VIII, p. 468; XXIII, p. 251; XXXII, pp. 31 ff.) There are or were at least twenty other Pioneer mines in the state.

Pi Pi [El Dorado]. Between the North and Middle forks of Cosumnes River, near Grizzly Flat and Indian Diggins. The name is apparently of Indian origin. Mines were opened in the 1850s and reactivated in the 1880s. Pi Pi Valley is mentioned by Alfred Doten, October 9, 1854 (Doble, p. 209), and the mining activities near Pi Pi are described in *Resources of El Dorado County* (pp. 88 f.).

Piru Creek [Ventura]. The only district in the county where a sizeable amount of gold was mined. It is in the northeastern part of the county. The deposits were apparently discovered in 1842 by Francisco Lopez after Andrés Castillero, later the discoverer of the New Almaden quicksilver mine, had called attention to

the existence of gold in the district. Theodore Hittell's account in his *History* (II, p. 312) is as vague and unreliable as numerous other accounts. The Piru Mining District is described in *Mining Bureau*, VIII (pp. 679, 680, 684). *See also Bulletin*, 193 (p. 176).

Pitchfork. An unidentified place, listed as a mining locality on a pictorial letter sheet published by Hutchings in 1855.

Pitiuna [Tulare?]. A Creek which emptied into the old Tulare Lake from the east. According to Bayard Taylor, I (p. 140), large quantities of gold were found there when he was in California in 1849.

Pittsburg Bar [Trinity]. On Trinity River, below Taylor Flat. It is mentioned in 1858 by Cox (p. 83). According to the *Shasta Herald*, a lucky hombre found a nugget of thirty-four and a half ounces (*Mining Press*, April 6, 1861). This place is not the modern Pittsburg Mine, which is on Canyon Creek.

Pittsburg Group [Nevada]. *See* Gold Flat *and* Nevada City.

Pittsburgh [Shasta]. On or near Pit River, north of Redding. Shown on Goddard's map, 1857. In the year 1880 the production of silver exceeded that of gold. It is listed in the Mining Bureau reports until 1924 as producing mainly copper.

Pittsburgh Bar [El Dorado]. Near the junction of the North and Middle forks of the Cosumnes River. The name is mentioned in the County History, 1883 (pp. 85 and 198), spelled with and without the final *h*.

Pittsburgh Bar [Yuba]. On the North Fork of Yuba River, north of Fosters Bar. Trask's map, 1853, and Wescoatt's, 1861, show it as Pittsburg Bar; Doolittle's map, 1868, shows it as Pittsburgh Bar. De Long collected taxes here in March and September, 1855. It is mentioned as Pittsburgh, a small bar, in *Marysville Directory*, 1858 (p. xxvii).

Pittsburg Hill [Yuba]. Between the North and Middle forks of Yuba River. Shown on the County Map, 1879. Gold was discovered by hunters in the spring of 1855 one mile east of the North Fork. Mining proved to be very rich and was still going on in 1879 (Co. Hist., 1879, p. 100), when there was drifting and tunneling, according to Pettee (Whitney, *Auriferous Gravels*, pp. 430 f.). In previous years there had been some attempts at hydraulic mining.

Pittsville [El Dorado]. *See* Pilot Hill.

Piute Mountains [Kern]. In the east-central part of the county, southeast of Bodfish. The mines and prospects in the crestal

Placerville, El Dorado Co.

part of Piute Mountains, around Clara-ville, are listed in the *County Report*, I (pp. 45 f.) and in *Bulletin*, 193 (p. 107). The periods of greatest activity in this area were from the 1860s to 1900 and from the 1930s to the early 1940s. The stage station of Piute, southwest of the Mountains, had a post office between 1875 and 1876 and again from 1894 to 1918. One stamp mill and one horse-drawn arrastre are recorded in the *Register*, 1904. For the name, *see California Place Names*. Shown on the USGS Mojave 1915 quadrangle.

Placer [Placer]. Apparently near Auburn. In the 1870s, the Green Mining Company did extensive tunnel mining (*Annual Mining Review*, 1876, p. 50).

Placerita: Creek, Canyon [Los Angeles]. The name of the tributary to Santa Clara River east of Newhall is a diminutive of placer, and is variously spelled. Gold was discovered in the region in 1842 by Francisco Lopez, six years before the discovery at Sutter's Mill, and was mined with moderate success until 1848 and intermittently until modern times. The actual site of the discovery is still a matter of conjecture, although it is indicated on the map of the National Geographic Society, 1954, and on other modern maps, and in 1956 the State of California established the Placeritas Historic Memorial Park. The date is fairly well established as March 9, 1842, by a petition dated April 4, 1842 (original in the National Archives; translation in *HSSCQ*, XXXI, p. 228). The most reliable accounts

are the articles by Joseph N. Bowman and Arthur B. Perkins published in *Historical Society of Southern California Quarterly* XXXI (pp. 224 ff.) and XL (pp. 149 ff.) and the survey "Pre-Marshall Gold in California" by Emil Bunje and James Kean. Not authenticated is the repeated claim in the publications of the Mining Bureau that the priests of the San Fernando and San Buenaventura missions had secretly been mining gold in the region since 1834. *See* Barric Mine; San Feliciana; San Fernando Placers.

Placerville [El Dorado]. After Sutter's Mill and Mormon Island, Placerville ranks as the third important location after the discovery of gold at Sutter's Mill. The washings at the camp of three of Sutter's men (Daylor, McCoon, and Sheldon) on Weber Creek were apparently older than those at the site of Placerville, about two miles to the northeast. *See* Dry Diggings [El Dorado]. According to the County History, 1883, an Indian in the employ of Sutter's men discovered the diggings on the north branch of Weber Creek (now Hangtown Creek), but the white men preferred their camp on Weber Creek and referred prospectors to the "new diggings," which curiously were called "Old Dry Diggings" until January, 1849. It is quite possible that Daylor's Camp became Old Dry Diggings after the deposits at Hangtown Creek and Cedar Ravine were discovered. Most sources of 1848 speak of

Placerville as Dry Diggings without the adjective "old." Buffum (p. 48) passed through Dry Diggings in the middle of December, 1848, and stated that about fifty log cabins had been erected. A letter to the St. Louis *Reveille* dated October 25, 1849, from Dry Diggins City (*CHSQ*, XXIV, p. 352) was reprinted in the St. Joseph *Adventure*. On January 22, 1849, two Frenchmen and one Chileno were hanged for stealing. Buffum (pp. 65 ff.) was an eyewitness to the scene, and his account of it is obviously more reliable than a dozen other stories that tried to explain why the Dry Diggings were burdened with the nickname Hangtown for a number of years. April 9, 1850, the post office was established and the name Placerville appears on a map for the first time in 1851 (Butler's map). According to the steamer edition of the Sacramento *Transcript*, February 1, 1851, the name was chosen because the streets of the town were almost impassable because of the numerous placering holes (Bancroft Notes). The early years of Placerville and its riches have been repeatedly described by contemporary writers: Buffum in 1848–49; Borthwick (pp. 112 ff.) in 1851–1852; and most detailed and most entertainingly (though only fairly reliable) by Haskins (chapters V to XII). J. M. Studebaker, the tycoon of the automobile industry, worked here in the early days as a blacksmith making wheelbarrows, which sold at ten dollars cash (Herbert L. Smith, I, p. 22). Philip D. Armour was a butcher in the town from 1852 to 1856; then he went to Chicago with a bag of gold dust worth 6 thousand dollars and started his packing firm. Abe and Rudolph Seligman, later the famous banking firm of London and New York, had a clothing store here. The mining activities in the Placerville district around 1870 are detailed in Browne (pp. 81 ff.) and in Raymond, VII (pp. 86 ff.). The record is continued to the 1930s in *Mining Bureau*, LII (pp. 422 f., 430 ff.) and in *Bulletin*, 193 (pp. 107 f.). Among the rich placer mines were the Coon Hollow, one mile south of Placerville, which was drifted (1852–1861), then hydraulicked (1861–1871) and produced 10 million dollars; the Spanish Hill (Little Spanish Hill in Placerville, Big Spanish Hill south of it), which produced 6 million dollars; Smith's Flat, east of Placerville, which produced more than 2 million; and White Rock, three miles northeast of Placerville, which was hydraulicked and produced 5 mil-

lion dollars. The total production of the placer mines alone is estimated at 25 million dollars or more. The principal gravel channels around Placerville are described and mapped in Lindgren, *Tertiary Gravels* (pp. 172 ff.). A Tertiary channel of the South Fork was developed by a 1,500-foot drift into the channel, and the gravel was sent through a 10-stamp mill and a 100-foot sluice at the Franklin Mine, two and a half miles east of Placerville. The Landecker Mine was another drift mine, one and a half miles southeast of Placerville. It was active in the early 1900s, in 1925, and in 1935 (*Mining Bureau*, LII, pp. 549, 555). Among the lode mines, the Pacific Quartz Mine in the southern part of the town of Placerville was operated by an English firm, the Placerville Gold Quartz Company, Ltd. The mine was active from 1852 to 1889 and again during 1914–1915, and its total was almost 1.5 million dollars. (*Mining Bureau*, LII, p. 422.)

Placerville Divide [El Dorado]. The rich region between the South Fork of American River and the North Fork of Cosumnes River is traversed by Weber Creek, which was named in honor of Charles M. Weber, the pioneer of the Divide. Raymond, VII (pp. 96 f.) gives a good description of the Divide, the Blue Lead, and the principal mines in 1874.

Plattsburg [Amador]. Near the Mokelumne River, opposite West Point. No mining record was found, but it was an election precinct in 1854, shortly before it was deserted. It was apparently named for a Colonel Platt, who tried his fortune at the Defender Mine, northwest of West Point. (Co. Hist., 1881, pp. 79, 216.)

Pleasant Bar [Placer]. Between Horseshoe Bar and Gray Eagle Bar on the Middle Fork of American River. Recorded on Trask's map, 1853. It is shown on Doolittle's map, 1868, above Horseshoe Bar. Little Pleasant Bar is also shown nearby. A Pleasant Bar Mine is listed in the reports of the Mining Bureau until 1936.

Pleasant Canyon [Inyo]. In the Panamint district, east of Ballarat. Shown on the County Map, 1884. The Gold Bug Mine was a consolidation of five unpatented claims and had a 5-stamp mill around 1895 (*Mining Bureau*, XXVIII, p. 368). It was relocated in 1940 as part of the Knob Group but was idle in 1951. The Radcliff or Ratcliff Mine, active between 1897 and 1915, and again between 1927 and 1942, with intermittent work since, was the richest mine in the area, having produced more than 1.3 million dollars (*Mining Bureau*, XLVII, pp. 45, 47 ff.; *Bull.*, 193, p. 146).

Pleasant Flat [El Dorado]. On the north side of the South Fork of American River, one mile above Coloma. Gold was discovered in the summer of 1852. Hydraulic mining was carried on until 1895. The flat is described by George Johnson in his "Notes".

Pleasant Flat [Nevada]. Three miles southwest of Nevada City, on the road to Grass Valley. Shown on Doolittle's map, 1868. It is mentioned in Nevada County Records (Pre-emptions, I) as a settlement in 1856.

Pleasant Hill [El Dorado]. Apparently near Mud Springs. The U. S. Bureau of the Census lists the names of 294 inhabitants, mainly miners, in its population schedule for 1850 at Pleasant Hill and vicinity.

Pleasant Springs [Calaveras]. On Alabama Gulch, below the junction of the North and Middle forks of Mokelumne River. Shown on Camp's map. It was an early mining center, where Charles Grunsky (later the well-known Stockton pioneer) opened a store and boarding house in 1849. Both establishments were taken over late in 1850 by his partner, D. L. Angiers. Doble and his company made their headquarters here from January to June, 1852, while mining in various gulches nearby (pp. 35 ff. and note, p. 297). There was a post office here between 1855 and 1857.

Pleasant Valley [El Dorado]. Between the Cosumnes River and Weber Creek, eight miles southeast of Placerville. Shown on Doolittle's map, 1868. The Mormons on their trek from Sutter's Fort to Salt Lake assembled here between June 17 and July 4, 1848. They named the spot and whiled away the time by washing gold, apparently with good success (Gudde, *Bigler's Chronicle*, p. 112). The rich drift gravel channel was discovered, or rediscovered, in the fall of 1893. It was actively prospected and an 8-stamp mill was erected (*Mining Bureau*, XII, p. 121). Shown on the USGS Placerville 1931 quadrangle.

Pleasant Valley [Mariposa]. On the Merced River, about six miles north of Exchequer, and now under water. It is mentioned by Benjamin H. Deane in his journal, July 1, 1850, while on his way from Horseshoe Bend on the Merced to Empire City on the Tuolumne River. From November 17, 1855 to September 16, 1856 it had a post office, and it was a voting and school precinct. Shown on the USGS Sonora 1939 quadrangle.

Pleasant Valley [Nevada]. Between Deer Creek and the South Fork of Yuba River, about four miles northwest of Rough and Ready. Shown on Doolittle's map, 1868. Mr. Rose of Rose's Corral had a trading post here, according to *Bean's Directory* (pp. 357 f.), probably in the summer or fall of 1849. Hutchings mentions the place on October 10, 1855.

Plughead Gulch. An unidentified place listed in the State Library roster.

Plugtown [Siskiyou]. *See* Riderville.

Plug Ugly Hill [Placer]. Between Dutch Flat Canyon and Squires Ravine, tributaries to Bear River. Recorded on Pettee and Bowman's map, 1879, where it is indicated that the gravel was "more or less completely washed away."

Plumas City [Yuba]. On the Feather River, above the confluence with Bear River. Shown on Milleson and Adams' map, 1851, and as Plumas on Gibbes' map, 1851, and Trask's, 1853. It was an ephemeral town, founded in 1850 by Sutter and Beach as a trading center for miners (Bancroft, VI, p. 487). There was a hotel and other buildings, and it was a favorite stop for excursion boats from Sacramento (*Placer Times*, March 30, 1850; Sacramento *Transcript*, April 1, 25 and June 22, 1850; Marysville *Herald*, May 27, 1851; Sacramento *Union*, November 3, 1851 and July 10, 1852). Sam Brannan and J. B. Starr were among the speculators.

Plumas-Eureka Mines [Plumas]. *See* Eureka [Plumas].

Plumbago Mine [Sierra]. *See* Chips Flat.

Plum Valley [Sierra]. Eight miles southwest of Alleghany, on the Henness Pass road. The hotel was built in 1854 by John Bope. Plum Valley post office, established in 1855 and discontinued in 1877, as well as Bope's Ranch and Hotel, are shown on Doolittle's map, 1868. Hutchings passed through on October 25, 1855. Plum Valley House is Historic Landmark 695.

Plunketts Ravine [El Dorado]. Listed in Hittell's roster.

Plymouth [Amador]. On Highway 49, north of Drytown. The place was a mining camp as early as 1852, and from the 1850s on, it was called Puckerville. It may have been called Pokerville or Poker Camp earlier (Berriman). Bancroft (VI, p. 372) states that it "absorbed the interests of the adjoining Pokerville Camp." When the post office was established September 18, 1871, the name was changed to Plymouth, after the nearby Hooper's Plymouth Mine. The various mines were consolidated in 1883.

The deepest shaft reached 4,450 feet, and the estimated total production of gold was 13.5 million dollars. Detailed descriptions are given in *Mining Bureau*, L (pp. 190 ff.); Logan (pp. 106, 111, 195); *Guidebook* (p. 65). *See* Puckerville. Historic Landmark 470, designates Plymouth Trading Post, established in 1857. Berriman, however, on the basis of a conversation with James B. Levaggi, states that the building was never called a trading post, except perhaps years later in the 1950s, by a person named Sam Turk. The proper designation would be Levaggi's Store, established in 1879, and also known as Empire Building.

Pocahontas Mine [El Dorado]. *See* El Dorado.

Poco Tempo Bar [Placer]. On the North Fork of American River, near Manhattan and Vigilance (Vigilant) bars. It was worked by Chilenos, according to the County History, 1924 (p. 178).

Point Bar [Trinity]. On the south side of Trinity River, south of Weaverville. The bar was worked with "good profit," according to Cox (p. 31), and in 1854 it had the reputation of being one of the best paying claims on the river. Mining was still going on in 1861 (*Mining Press*, September 28, October 26, 1861).

Point Lookout [Siskiyou]. In the vicinity of Happy Camp and Clear Creek. It is mentioned in the Del Norte County History, 1881 (p. 133), as an old mining locality worked with varying success.

Point of Timbers [San Bernardino]. *See* Cottonwood.

Poker Bar [Trinity]. On the north side of Trinity River, below the mouth of Grass Valley Creek; between Lewiston and Douglas City. Cox (p. 30) mentions it as Polka Bar. It had been worked with good profit since 1852 and was supplied with water from Grass Valley Creek by the German Ditch flumed across the river. A German company from Ohio Flat was reported as having found good paying ground at Poker Bar in 1856. It was still worked with modest success, six to eight dollars a day, in 1861 (*Mining Press*, September 28, October 26, 1861). In 1939 and 1940 a dragline dredge was in operation (*Bull.*, 36, p. 104; *Mining Bureau*, XXXVII, p. 85).

Poker Camp [Amador]. *See* Puckerville; Plymouth.

Poker Flat [Sierra]. In a narrow canyon of Canyon Creek, north of Downieville. Shown on Trask's map, 1853, and on later maps, sometimes spelled Pocker Flat. In the 1850s there was mainly horizontal tunneling, later drift and hydraulic mining. The town burned down several times. The Sacramento *Daily Union* of July 1, 1856, reports that only twelve families lived in the camp, but there were 400 miners within two miles (Hayes Scrapbooks: Mining, I, sec. 23). A good description is given by Henry Cohn who had a store here from 1857 to 1863. Brewer (p. 455) calls it a "miserable hole" in 1853. The San Francisco *Call*, May 18, 1879, includes it among the flourishing towns of the county (Bancroft Scraps, V, p. 1806). A Poker Flat placer mine is listed by the Mining Bureau in 1942. Poker Flat District is described in *Bulletin*, 193 (pp. 108 f.), and a bibliography of the district is given in *Mining Bureau*, XVI (Sierra, p. 17). The name Poker Flat is shown on the USGS Downieville 1907 quadrangle. Bret Harte's "The Outcasts of Poker Flat" has no connection with the camp except the name.

Pokerville [Amador]. *See* Plymouth; Puckerville.

Pole Cat Slide [El Dorado]. South of Kelsey, near Live Oak Bar. Shown on Doolittle's map, 1868. It is listed in the State Library roster.

Polka Bar [Trinity]. *See* Poker Bar.

Polk Springs District [Tehama]. In the eastern part of the county, about thirty miles southeast of Red Bluff. It is a small placer district, in which there has been hydraulic mining. A description is given in *Bulletin*, 193 (p. 111).

Pomfrets Hill [Calaveras]. Near Jenny Lind. It is mentioned as a mining locality in the San Andreas *Independent*, January 19, 1861.

Pontiac Hill [Nevada]. Near Nevada City, just west of Manzanita Diggings. In 1870, when Pettee visited the area, the hill was completely washed away (Whitney, *Auriferous Gravels*, p. 188).

Pony Bar [Trinity]. On Trinity River, about four miles east of Salyer. It is listed in the Mining Bureau *Report* of 1941 (XXXVII, p. 84) and in the *County Report*, IV (p. 106).

Pony Creek [Trinity]. The creek is a tributary to the East Fork of New River. On June 15, 1861, the *Mining Press* reported that the camp called Pony Creek was flourishing, with two stores, a hotel, and saloon; and the average gold yield was from five to twenty dollars a day to the man. The Hart claim, worked by four men, yielded an average of 400 dollars a week, according to the *Mining Press*, August 17, 1861. By 1923 the mines along the Creek were practically worked out; they had reportedly yielded about 3 million dollars (*Bull.*, 92, p. 93).

Pony Point [Trinity]. On Trinity River, one mile below Taylor Flat. A drift mine on the gravel bar is listed by the Mining Bureau in 1896 (*Mining Bureau*, XIII, Trinity, p. 459).

Poodle Town. An unidentified place listed in Hittell, *Resources*.

Poorman Creek [Nevada]. A tributary to South Fork of Yuba River, west of Washington. According to Steele (p. 163), it was named for a miner by that name; but on Butler's map, 1851, the same stream was apparently called Poor Creek, in contrast to another tributary, Rich Creek. Poorman Creek is listed in Brown's *Directory*, 1856 (p. 56). Steele (p. 150) and partners built a cabin here and mined profitably from December, 1850 to January, 1851. In spite of the name the early yield was estimated at one million dollars (Bancroft, VI, p. 357). *See* Poorman Creek [Plumas].

Poorman Creek [Plumas]. A tributary to Nelson Creek, east of Onion Valley. Shown as Poor Man's Creek on Milleson and Adams' map, 1851. It was also known as Poor Men's Creek. Noblet Herbert mentions the place December 27, 1850. The discovery of gold here was linked with the Gold Lake hunt in a statement by Thomas Spence, in which he claims that what Stoddart assumed to be a lake was really the overflow of the creek later known as Poor Man's Creek. *See* Gold Lake. Downie was at Poorman Creek in 1850 and once again before 1857 (pp. 123 ff., 136). A member of his party in October, 1850, tells of the rich diggings at what he termed the ironically named creek. McIlhany, too, (pp. 51, 55) stated that the rich deposits belied the name. He, himself, made good money there, not by mining, however, but by selling the carcass of a 450-pound grizzly bear to the prospectors at seventy-five cents a pound. The finding of a large specimen of gold was reported in the journal of John Clark, August 22, 1854. Extensive hydraulic mining on the creek was carried on in the 1880s by a company from Boston (Co. Hist., 1882, p, 321) and was renewed in 1907 (Plumas County Historical Society *Publication*, no. 15, pp. 18 f.). — The miners first called the place Jamestown, then Poorman's Creek North, to distinguish it from Poorman's creek on the South Fork of Yuba River. The latter had been named

for Richard Poorman, who claimed he had discovered gold at both places. (*Tuolumne Courier*, May 26, 1860.) *See* Poorman Creek [Nevada].

Poor Mans Bar [Siskiyou]. On Scott River, opposite Scott Bar. Recorded on Goddard's 1857 map. The Sacramento *Union*, June 15, 1855, reported that one thousand dollars was taken out in one day (Bancroft Notes).

Poor Mans Bar [Trinity]. On lower Canyon Creek. According to Cox (p. 97), the yield in 1855 was only five to eight dollars a day.

Poor Mans Gulch [Tuolumne]. *See* Six-Bit Gulch.

Poplar Bar [Plumas]. On the Middle Fork of Feather River. The County History, 1882 (p. 288), lists it as one of the chief bars on the Middle Fork.

Poppet Diggings. An unidentified place, listed as a mining locality on an illustrated letter sheet published by Hutchings in 1855.

Pop's Gulch [Inyo]. Near Santa Rita Flat, in the Mazourka Canyon area. In 1935 or 1936 a placer mining company from Los Angeles carried on a large-scale operation of hauling gravel by truck to a washing plant at Santa Rita Spring (De Decker, pp. 46 f.).

Porterfield [Amador]. Near Sutter Creek. In May of 1851 rich quartz deposits were found around the village of Porterfield, which consisted then of two or three cabins, and by the end of September there were 600 to 800 inhabitants according to an item in the *San Joaquin Republican*, October 8, 1851. A Mr. Porter found a 20-ounce piece of gold in his claim just 20 rods away from the store of W. I. Morgan at Volcano, but Morgan makes no mention of a village called Porterfield (Morgan diary, May 6, 1851).

Portuguese Bar [Placer]. Near the confluence of the North and Middle forks of American River, close to Calf Bar. Notice of a claim datelined Junction, August 3, 1853, is recorded in Placer County Records, I (p. 178).

Portuguese: Bar, Flat [Siskiyou]. Near the mouth of Portuguese Creek, a tributary to the Klamath River; about twelve miles west of Hamburg Bar. Hydraulic mining at the Flat in 1887 is described in *Mining Bureau*, VIII (pp. 595 f.). Intermittent mining at the Bar was reported to about 1925; in 1935 it was stated that machinery had been installed, but no work was being carried on at that time (*Mining Bureau*, XXI, p.

482; XXXI, p. 298). Portuguese Creek is shown on the USGS Seiad 1945 quadrangle.

Portuguese Flat [Shasta]. Near the upper Sacramento River, north of Dog Creek. An item in Hittell Clippings (p. 29) states that two prospectors took out 125 dollars in one day (in 1856?). According to Steger, the diggings had the reputation of being one of the roughest mining camps "in the North." Locally the name is pronounced pôr-tŭ-gˇe (*California Place Names*).

Portuguese Joes Bar [El Dorado]. Somewhere on the South Fork of American River. The story of the Portuguese sailor and his rich find is told by Haskins (pp. 130 ff., 137). No other records were found.

Port Wine [Sierra]. In the Slate Creek Basin; three miles southeast of La Porte. Recorded on Trask's map, 1853. The early surface placer mining petered out in 1851, but hydraulic mining instilled new life (Vischer, p. 240; *Mining Press*, May 25, 1861), and according to the *Alta*, February 24, 1854, between thirty and one hundred dollars' worth were the daily yield to the man. A newspaper clipping, dated July 9, 1863 (Bancroft Scraps, V, p. 1782) describes it as a religious and sober town, with a strong Welsh element. The claims that were still being worked in 1867 are listed by Browne (p. 166). Raymond, V (p. 84) lists the hydraulic companies and their profits in 1872. The various stories about the origin of the name are folk-etymological. Lecouvreur (p. 239) tells of finding a keg of cognac in a deserted place nearby, and a similar incident may have caused naming the place Port Wine. It is now a ghost town, but it had a post office between 1861 and 1865 and again between 1870 and 1918. It is still shown on the USGS Downieville 1907 quadrangle. A Port Wine Mine is listed in the Mining Bureau reports until 1942.

Poso: Creek, Flat [Kern]. An intermittent stream in the Greenhorn Mountains. Occasional mining along the creek has been reported since the 1860s. The important Poso Mine was not located until 1915 and was worked until 1938. In 1957 the equipment was still in fair condition. A description of it is found in *Mining Bureau*, XIX (p. 155) and *County Report*, I (pp. 119 ff.).

Possum Bar [Amador]. On the south side of Cosumnes River; south of Latrobe. Recorded on the County Map, 1866. It is mentioned in the *Amador Ledger*, June 13, 1857.

Potatoe Hill [Shasta]. South of Mount Shasta. Shown on Goddard's map, 1857. It is in a gold region but no mining records were found. Hutchings lists it as a town north of Shasta in 1855.

Potato Ravine [Placer]. Tributary to Canyon Creek, east of Gold Run. Browne (p. 104) mentions eight claims which tail into the ravine. A Potato Flatiron claim near Red Point is listed in the Mining Bureau reports until 1936.

Pot-Hole Bar [Tuolumne?]. Probably near Jacksonville. According to Mulford (chapter XXXV) the placers were exhausted in 1856. He saw it as a ghost town.

Pothole Placers [Imperial]. On the Colorado River, northeast of Yuma. The persistent story that gold was mined here in the eighteenth century is possible but not supported by convincing evidence. Harold O. Wright published an interesting account of "hidden gold" in the *Desert Magazine*, June, 1955. At the time of the Gold Rush placers were actually discovered here. According to the *Mining Bureau*, XXX (p. 245), there were at times between four and five hundred Mexican prospectors here, and the total production was reported at two million dollars. Dry washing on a small scale was still going on in 1934. Potholes district is described in *Bulletin*, 193 (p. 163).

Pot Luck City. An unidentified place, listed as a mining locality on an illustrated letter sheet published by Hutchings in 1855.

Potosi. The Spanish word for 'great wealth' was frequently used for claims and mines. The famous Potosi Mine in Bolivia was a silver producer as early as 1545. For the Potosi mines and claims in Amador, El Dorado, Mariposa, Nevada, Placer, and Shasta counties, *see* the *Consolidated Index*.

Potosi [Sierra]. In Gold Canyon, tributary to the East Branch of Slate Creek, near Howland Flat. Some of the claims justified the name (Raymond, V, p. 80). Shown on the USGS Downieville 1907 quadrangle.

Potosi Mine. *See* Coulterville [Mariposa]; Gold Flat [Nevada].

Potter Ridge District [Madera]. A moderate gold output is recorded in *Mining Bureau*, II (part 1, p. 177). It is now included in the Coarsegold District in the east-central part of the county (*Bull.*, 193, p. 38).

Potters Bar [Butte]. On the North Fork of Feather River, above the junction with the Middle Fork. Recorded on Trask's map, 1853. According to the Oroville *Mercury*, December 31, 1875, John Potter, a member of Bidwell's exploring party, mined here in 1848. It is mentioned by John Swett, March 19, 1853, and repeatedly. In 1855 one company took out 1,700 dollars in one day (Sacramento *Union*, April 29, 1855).

Poverty Bar [Calaveras]. On the south side of Mokelumne River, opposite and to the west of Lancha Plana. Shown on Goddard's map, 1857, and on the Amador County Map, 1866. A. Lascy in his "Reminiscences" mentions the bar as existing in May, 1850, with a single resident, a hunter who did not mine. According to Andrews (pp. 129 f.), the place was destroyed by the 1861–62 flood, when all bridges and ferries over the Mokelumne River disappeared. However, a post office is listed from 1854 to 1864. The site is inundated by Camanche Reservoir. The graves were removed to the old Pioneer Cemetery near San Andreas and the People's Cemetery in San Andreas (Rensch-Hoover).

Poverty Bar [El Dorado]. On the Middle Fork of American River, six miles above the junction. Recorded on Goddard's map, 1857, and on later maps. The bar is mentioned repeatedly in September, 1851, by Henry S. Blom, who stated that one day 1,900 dollars' worth was taken out from the claim of a company of six. According to an item in the Placer *Herald*, October 27, 1855, the Cromwell Company with forty hands took out as much as one hundred ounces on some days. About 1914 the place was the scene of one of the operations with a floating dredge (*Mining Bureau*, LII, p. 434). The Poverty Bar shown at the mouth of the American Canyon on the USGS Placerville 1931 quadrangle is obviously at the same location.

Poverty Bar [El Dorado]. On the South Fork of American River, below Indian Bar. A claim was located by Louis Speidel & Company, beginning at the foot of Indian Bar and running through Poverty Bar, December 16, 1850 (El Dorado County Records, Mining Location, I, p. 7). A mechanics lien was filed the same day (*ibid.*, Mechanics Liens Book, I, p. 7). The location on the river could not be determined.

Poverty Bar [Placer]. On the North Fork of American River. The bar is mentioned in a claim on the face of New York Hill, dated August 28, 1854, in Placer County Records, I, (p. 245). Hutchings includes it in his list of towns in 1855. It is also mentioned in the County History, 1924 (p. 179), and by May W. Perry in *Placer Nuggets*, February, 1964 (p. 6). The North

Fork Dam, built in 1880–1881, covered the place.

Poverty Bar [Plumas]. On the East Branch of the North Fork of Feather River, opposite Rich Bar. It is mentioned by Rensch-Hoover.

Poverty Bar [Tuolumne]. Near the confluence of Tuolumne River and Woods Creek. It is mentioned by Mulford (p. 116).

Poverty Bar [Yuba]. On the main Yuba River, below Ousley Bar, opposite Swiss Bar. Recorded on Trask's map, 1853. It is not the same Poverty Bar mentioned in the County History, 1879 (p. 94), as being in Foster Bar Township.

Poverty: Bar, Flat [Trinity]. On the Trinity River, in the Weaverville District. It was deserted in 1854 because of poor diggings; later it was reopened by Chinese who were said to have made good wages and "permanently settled" there from 1857 on (Cox, pp. 38 f.). A hydraulic mine at Poverty Flat, three and a half miles southeast of Weaverville, is described in 1913–1914 and is still listed in 1941 (*Mining Bureau*, XIV, p. 912; XXXVII, p. 85).

Poverty Flat [Mariposa]. It is apparently the same camp as Upper Agua Fria. The *Alta*, March 15, 1864, reprints an item that states that the Reynold's company of three men averaged seven to eight ounces per day for some time.

Poverty Flat [Plumas]. On the Middle Fork of Feather River. The County History, 1882 (p. 288), mentions it as one of the chief camps on the Middle Fork.

Poverty Gulch [Shasta]. Good pay dirt was struck in 1861, according to the Horsetown *Argus* (*Mining Press*, March 16, 1861).

Poverty Hill [Sierra]. Four miles south of La Porte. Recorded on the County Map, 1874. Vischer in 1859 (p. 240) reported mainly hydraulic mining. According to Raymond, V (p. 87), two million dollars' worth of gold had been taken out before the costly tunnels were built. Description of the district is given in *Mining Bureau*, XVI (Sierra, pp. 23 f.). Preparations for bucket line dredging at Poverty Hill are described in *Mining Bureau*, XXXVIII (pp. 35 f.). Shown on the USGS Downieville 1907 quadrangle.

Poverty Hill [Tuolumne]. Two and a half miles south of Jamestown. It was settled in 1850 by William Utter and was first called Utters Bar. In 1854 the camp was swept by fire, but apparently it was rebuilt by 1856, when it had five stores and thirty to forty dwellings. Heckendorn (p. 87) gives a description of it. When placer mining gave out in the 1860s, lode mining took its place. In July, 1869, there was a 15-stamp mill (Raymond, II, p. 26), and by 1899 the Hill, together with Chili Camp, had produced around 4 million dollars in gold (*Mines and Minerals*, p. 358). The post office was called Stent. *See* Stent. The Poverty Gulch mentioned in the Columbia *Gazette*, November 25, 1854, where Major Harmon and Company mined, may have been nearby.

Poverty Point [El Dorado]. On the east side of Big Canyon, two miles north of Placerville. Shown on Doolittle's map, 1868, and on Bowman's, 1873. Haskins (p. 135) speaks of rich ravines existing there. The Guilford Mine with a 15-stamp mill operated into the twentieth century and produced 200 thousand dollars between 1912 and 1917 (*Mining Bureau*, LII, p. 507).

Poverty Point [San Bernardino]. *See* Bear Valley.

Powelltown [Butte]. On the old Humboldt road, north of Magalia. It was settled in 1853 by R. P. Powell (Co. Hist., 1882, p. 259) and was the trading center; and from 1872–1906 it was the post office for the surrounding quartz mines (*Register*, 1903).

Powningville [El Dorado]. Shown as a settlement, near the South Fork of American River, about eight miles by road northwest of Coloma, on Bowman's map, 1873.

Prairie Buttes [Sutter]. *See* Sutters Buttes.

Prairie City [Sacramento]. On Alder Creek, two miles south of Folsom. Shown on Judah's map, 1854. Prairie Diggings was just north of Prairie City and Prairie House about two miles south on the Placerville road. The camp started in 1853. Within a year the population was more than 1,000, but by 1860 the decline had begun, according to the County History, 1880 (p. 225). Hutchings' estimate of the population was much lower. He stated that there were about 150 inhabitants in the spring of 1855, with probably 400 people getting their supplies there (diary, April 22, 1855). The place is mentioned in the *Mining Press*, May 4, 1861, as rich diggings that had attracted hundreds of prospectors. The name is preserved on the Prairie City road, which crosses Highway 50. Historic Landmark 464.

Prairie Diggings [Yuba]. North of the main Yuba River, about three miles northwest of Browns Valley. Wescoatt's map, 1861, shows it as a considerable settlement at the head of Prairie Creek, a tributary to Honcut Creek. It is also shown on Doolittle's map, 1868. The camp started in 1854 and enjoyed a few years of prosperity (Co. Hist., 1879, p. 87). The claims were abandoned in 1864 (Browne, p. 155). According to William B. Meek, a stage driver, it was considered a "hard camp" in bad repute and was also known as Hole in the Wall (p. 158).

Prattville [Plumas]. Shown on the map in the County History, 1882, below Big Meadows, the geographical feature. *See* Big Meadows. There was also a settlement called Big Meadows, which became known as Prattville when the post office was established in 1894 and named for Willard Pratt, first postmaster (Co. Hist., 1882, pp. 293 f.). After the failure of the Gold Lake hunt rich deposits were found in the region of Big Meadows. Modern maps show Prattville near the southwest shore of Lake Almanor, below the town of Almanor.

Prescott District [Mono]. On the summit of Mono Pass, on the old Mono Trail across the Sierra Nevada. Gold was first discovered in 1852 in Bloody Canyon by Lieutenant Tredwell Moore, U. S. Army, while pursuing Indians. It was rediscovered in 1879 and the Prescott Mining District was formed.

Prescott Hill [Nevada]. *See* Osborn Hill.

Priest [Tuolumne]. On Rattlesnake Creek, which heads in Big Oak Flat, one mile to the east. Before 1872 it was called Rattlesnake House and then usually Priest's Station, an early stage stop on the Big Oak Flat road. Later the road down Grizzly Gulch was called the Old Priest Grade. (De Ferrari.) One mile southwest of the place a number of mines operated before 1900. One pocket mine, the Bonanza, yielded two million dollars, according to *Mines and Minerals* (p. 354).

Princeton [Mariposa]. About five miles northwest of Mariposa; on Frémont's Las Mariposas Grant. The camp is mentioned in the *San Joaquin Republican*, August 21, 1854, and again September 4, where it is "dubbed" Princeton and described as a camp of about 200 Mexicans, who were working with arrastres. It was the site of the Princeton Mine, one of the richest gold mines in the state. It was opened in 1852 and from its beginnings produced seventy-five dollars per ton, according to Cronise (p. 577). When the 24-stamp steam-driven mill was built in 1860, it had become one of the richest mines in the state. From June to November of that year, 23,916 tons of quartz were crushed and yielded 527,633 dollars. The inclined depth of the shaft was 1,660 feet, the vertical depth about 1,350 feet. In 1867 the mine and mill became idle, but production continued intermittently into the twentieth century (*Mining Bureau*, XXIV, p. 111; *Guidebook*, p. 38.) The recorded production exceeds that of any mine in the county, and its size is exceeded only by the Pine Tree and Josephine Mine. The figure 4,397,743 dollars is authenticated, but estimates of production as high as 5 million dollars to the year 1929 have been given (*Mining Bureau*, LIII, pp. 156 ff.). Shown on the *Guidebook* map 1. The name of the camp or town Princeton was changed to Mount Bullion in 1862, when the post office was established. *See* Mount Bullion. The Ortega Mine to the south, on Highway 140, was discovered before 1856 by a member of the well known Spanish family and was worked successfully with arrastres until 1859, when it became part of Frémont's holdings. It was idle until 1934, after which it operated until World War II. In 1900 some of the ore from the old dumps was hauled to the custom mill at the Princeton Mine and yielded fourteen to twenty-seven dollars a ton (U. S. *Bull.*, 424, p. 131; *Mining Bureau*, LIII, pp. 148 f.)

Prior Ravine [Nevada]. Tributary to Greenhorn Creek; near the town Quaker Hill. Shown on Pettee and Bowman's map, 1879. Pettee describes the gravel formation at and near the site of Railroad Mine (Whitney, *Auriferous Gravels*, pp. 179 f.).

Prospect Flat [El Dorado]. East of Placerville. Shown on Bowman's map, 1873. There were rich diggings, with the Lyon claim alone having yielded 200 thousand dollars. A 10-stamp mill was in operation there (Co. Hist., 1883, p. 88).

Prospect Hill [Amador]. There was early hill mining, according to the County History, 1881 (p. 126).

Prospect Hill [Nevada]. Now a part of Nevada City. It is listed in *Bean's Directory*, 1867.

Prospect Hill [Placer]. Near Iowa Hill. The hill is mentioned in a notice of intention to construct a canal, datelined Iowa Hill, November 1, 1855, in the Placer County Records, I (p. 346). The Lebanon Company worked thirteen years and spent 100 thousand dollars on a tunnel before they struck the Blue Lead and pay dirt in 1866. These were Tertiary gravels. A 10-stamp

mill driven by a hurdy-gurdy wheel was erected (Bancroft Scraps, LI:1, p. 7).

Providence [San Bernardino]. *See* Hicorum.

Providence Camp [Tuolumne]. *See* Algerine Camp.

Providence City [Lassen]. Now Hayden Hill. The pious name was bestowed in 1870, when Reverend Harvey Haskins and party discovered gold here (Co. Hist., 1882, p. 399). *See* Hayden Hill.

Providence: Mountains, town [San Bernardino]. The mountain range runs northeast-southwest, in the eastern part of the county, about forty-five miles west of the Colorado River. The deposits, mainly silver, were discovered in the early 1880s, and some of the mines in the Providence or Trojan district operated until the late 1920s (*Mining Bureau*, IX, p. 223; X, p. 532; XXVI, pp. 281 ff.; XXVII, p. 354). The town of Providence on the east slope was mainly a company town for the rich Bonanza King silver mine, which was discovered in the 1870s, developed in the 1880s, and during one period of eighteen months reportedly produced almost one million dollars (Nadeau, pp. 252 f.). Belden gives an interesting account of the old ghost town (March 20, 1960). *See* Arrowhead District; Kelso District.

Prussian Hill [Calaveras]. Northeast of Esperanza Creek, tributary to the North Fork of Calaveras River; east of Mokelumne Hill. A rich vein was discovered about 1871, and well-paying quartz mines were in operation for several years (Raymond, IV, p. 79; VII, p. 63).

Puckerville [Amador]. On the ancient bed of Cosumnes River. It was a mining camp of the early 1850s and was called Pokerville and Poker Camp by Bancroft and other sources. It is recorded as Puckerville on the County Map, 1866. After 1870 it was called Plymouth. *See* Plymouth.

Puke Ravine. An unidentified place, listed in Hittell, *Resources*.

Pulga Bar [Butte]. On the North Fork of Feather River, near the Plumas County line. The name, meaning 'flea bar', may have been the original name of Big Bar (A. Drury, *California*, p. 505).

Puppytown. An unidentified place, listed in Hittell, *Resources*.

Purdon Crossing [Nevada]. On the South Fork of Yuba River, below Edwards Crossing, on the road from Nevada City to North San Juan. There was a ranch on the north side of the river and mining operations were carried on at the site of the crossing (Foley). Purdon Bridge is shown on the USGS Smartsville 1943 quadrangle.

Purdy [San Bernardino]. On the old California Eastern Railroad from Goffs to Ivanpah, near the Nevada state line. It is listed in *Register*, 1902, with the copper and gold mines south of New York Mountains. The station was named for Purdy Blake, daughter of Isaac Blake, who built the little Nevada Southern Railroad from Blake (Goffs) to this point to serve his mines in the New York Mountains (Belden, May 2, 1954).

Puritan Camp [El Dorado]. On the South Fork of American River, four miles below Coloma. Lucius Fairchild (pp. 72–88) spent the summer of 1850 there with a Wisconsin company which was building a dam and mining with apparently moderate success.

Push Coach Hill. An unidentified place, listed in Hittell, *Resources*.

Putah Creek District [Yolo]. On the southwestern part of the county. Early placer mining was carried on in a small way on lower Putah Creek. At one time there was a small mining camp on the site of present-day Winters, and in the 1930s there was minor placer mining here again. At one time also there was some sluicing on Cache Creek to the north, near the town of Capay. (*Bull.*, 193, p. 180.)

Puts Bar [Amador]. One and a half miles west of Lancha Plana. Shown on the County Map, 1866. It was discovered by a man named Putman, with only "wage claims," mined mainly by Chinese. It was an election precinct in 1861, when it produced not gold but melons and grapes. (Co. Hist., 1881, pp. 97, 198.) Coy's map shows it as Pats Bar.

Pyramid Mine [El Dorado]. *See* Dry Creek.

Quack Hill. An unidentified mining locality, listed in Hittell, *Resources*.

Quail Bar [Placer]. On the north side of the Middle Fork of American River, above Mammoth and Texas bars. It is mentioned in the Placer County History, 1882 (pp. 401 f.) and the El Dorado County History, 1883 (p. 84). Notice of a claim was recorded September 18, 1855 (Placer County Records, I, p. 302).

Quail Hill [Calaveras]. About six miles southwest of Copperopolis, near the Stanislaus County line. Both gold and copper were mined here. In 1867 there was a 20-stamp mill, and water was brought from Salt Spring Reservoir. A detailed description, including an account by Professor Silliman, is given by Browne (pp. 67 f.). Shown on the USGS Copperopolis 1939 quadrangle.

Quail Mine [Mariposa]. *See* Indian Gulch.

Quaker City Mine [Calaveras]. *See* Mokelumne Hill.

Quaker Hill [Nevada]. Five miles northwest of Dutch Flat, on the Great Gravel Deposit. Shown on Doolittle's map, 1868. In 1862 a company of five men took out over sixty ounces in ten days (*Mining Press*, May 8, 1862). In 1867 two 10-stamp mills with hurdy-gurdy wheels were in operation (*Bean's Directory*, p. 372). An account of later mining is given in *Mining Bureau*, XVI (Nevada, p. 65). Recorded on the USGS Colfax 1938 quadrangle.

Quartz [Tuolumne]. About two miles south of Jamestown; also known as Quartz Hill and Quartz Mountain. It was an important quartz mining and milling center as early as the 1850s. In 1854 it had four water-driven mills with thirty stamps and four arrastres (*State Register*, 1859). Details are given in Raymond (II, p. 26) and *Annual Mining Review*, 1876 (p. 22). In 1903 there was still a stamp mill (*Register*, 1903), and some mines were worked until modern times; the post office was not discontinued until 1924. *See* Stent for the production of the mines. Quartz Mountain is shown on the USGS Sonora 1939 quadrangle, and both Quartz Mountain and Stent appear on the *Guidebook* map, no. 3. The rich Nyman Consolidated Mines on Quartz Mountain yielded until 1926 (Logan, pp. 169 ff.).

Quartzburg [El Dorado]. *See* Nashville.

Quartzburg [Kern]. Near old Kernville. Gold was discovered by Lovely Rogers when he picked up a rock, was attracted by the weight, and found it full of gold (Chalfant, p. 26). He had accidentally discovered the Big Blue vein. For a summary of the activities which followed, *see* Cove District. The camp Quartzburg was first called Rogersville (Boyd, p. 32).

Quartzburg [Mariposa]. On Burns Creek, two miles northeast of Hornitos. Recorded on Butler's map (1851), Trask's (1853), and later maps. It is not certain whether it was the camp whose name was changed in 1851 from Burns (*Alta*, October 24, 1851), since it was not shown in exactly the same location. *See* Burns. In a letter of Andrew McFarlane datelined Quartz Vill (!)), October 12, 1851, he mentions working a quartz mill at the "celebrated burnses diggings." Sam Ward, a brother of Julia Ward Howe and a friend of Longfellow, was in the mining business at Quartzburg in 1851, and his interesting accounts of the camp and the region are reprinted in *Sam Ward in the Gold Rush* (pp. 27 ff.). Allsop (pp. 24 ff.) wrote about Quartzburgh in the winter of 1851–52. On June 25, 1851, a convention at Quartzburg established the "Mariposa Quartz Mining Law," which remained in force for many years, even in camps later detached from the county (Hittell Clippings, p. 40). The place is now only a memory and is sometimes confused with Quartzburg in Kern County. *See* Hornitos.

Quartzburg [Mariposa]. The place is shown on Butler's map, 1851, on Merced River about twelve miles northwest of Mariposa. It is probably the same as the important camp and was mistakenly placed in this location.

Quartz Canyon [El Dorado]. One mile from Volcanoville. It is listed in Hittell's roster, and a placer mine is described in *Mining Bureau*, XIII (p. 155).

Quartz Canyon [Yuba]. West of the North Fork of Yuba River, near Fosters Bar. In the 1870s the place was deserted (Co. Hist., 1879, p. 95).

Quartz Flat [Placer]. Apparently near Ophir. It is mentioned by Stephen Wing April 5, 1853, in connection with other localities in which the miners were doing well (Journal, I, p. 52).

Quartz Hill [El Dorado]. Shown on Bowman's map, 1873, one mile northwest of Placerville. It is now within the city limits, on the west side of Bedford Avenue, behind the Mother Lode Medical Center Hospital on Spring Street (Schlappi-Ferguson).

Quartz Hill [Shasta]. Three miles east of the Sacramento River, in the Churntown Mining District. It is mentioned in a clipping in Hayes Scrapbooks: Mining (IV, sec. 5) as an old gold mining town still holding its own in the spring of 1864. The hill is shown on the USGS Redding 1944 quadrangle.

Quartz Hill [Sierra]. Near Portwine. The *Mining Press*, June 21, 1862, reports that five companies and a newly opened hydraulic claim were at work and expecting good results.

Quartz Hill [Siskiyou]. On Scott River, opposite Scott Bar. Rich gold deposits were reportedly discovered in 1850 and were first placer mined. From the 1860s intermittently to World War II a mine was op-

erated both as a hydraulic and a lode mine, and in 1947 there was again some activity. A description is given in *Mining Bureau*, XLIII (p. 447) and *Siskiyou Pioneer* (II:10, pp. 27 f.).

Quartz Hills [Amador]. A collective name for the claims and mines on the rich ledge extending north from Mokelumne Hill. It is mentioned in the Bowen diary.

Quartz Mountain [Amador]. Two miles northeast of Amador City. It was probably an old mining site dating from the Gold Rush era. There was an extensive outcropping of quartz here, which made mining easy. In 1888 there were two mines, and one 10-stamp mill was in operation (*Mining Bureau*, VIII, p. 94).

Quartz Mountain [Madera]. Five miles south of Coarse Gold Gulch. It was originally owned by a French Company and was called Mine d'Or de Quartz Mountain. It had a 60-stamp mill in 1888, was vacated in 1906, and has been idle since that time (*Mining Bureau*, VIII, pp. 210 f.; XIV, p. 549). Shown on the USGS Mariposa 1938 quadrangle.

Quartz: Prairie, Hill [Placer]. The "prairie" is a high rolling ridge three and a half miles north of Auburn. The gold deposits discovered in 1864 were considered by old miners to be the richest in the state, according to the Auburn *Stars and Stripes*, December 28, 1864 (Hayes Scrapbooks: Mining, IV, sec. 19). In 1869 a 20-stamp mill was built, but the supposedly fabulous riches had given out and the mill was soon removed (Co. Hist., 1882, p. 228).

Quartz Ravine Bar [Placer]. On the North Fork of American River, above Rattlesnake and Kentucky bars. According to the County History, 1924 (p. 178), it was a very rich, deep bar, which was never fully worked out.

Quartz Township District [Plumas]. One of the two townships in which the Plumas section of Butte County was divided in 1851, which included the rich quartz ledge on Gold Mountain or Eureka Peak, discovered in the summer of 1851 in the wake of the Gold Lake Hunt and known later as Plumas Eureka Mine. The township included also City of Seventy-six, Jamison, Johnsville, and Mohawk Valley. (Co. Hist., 1882, pp. 241 ff.) The district is listed in *Mining Bureau*, II (part 1, p. 181) with a report of more than thirty thousand ounces of gold produced in the year ending May 31, 1880. The reports and bulletins of the Mining Bureau mention a number of mining places with the generic name Quartz. *See Consolidated Index.*

Quartz Valley [Siskiyou]. In the northwest corner of Scott Valley, separated from the main valley by a low ridge. There were rich extensive placer deposits. In the southern end of the valley they were worked by drifting and on the eastern side by sluicing and hydraulic operations. A detailed description is given in *Mining Bureau*, XI (pp. 434 ff.) and a summary in XIV (p. 822). There were also several quartz mines, but less productive. In 1859 two stamp mills are listed (*State Register*, 1859). William M. Smith doubts that there were stamp mills in this area before the late 1860s. Quartz Valley and Quartz Hill are shown on the USGS Yreka 1939 quadrangle.

Quartzville [El Dorado]. *See* Nashville.

Queen City [Nevada]. Southwest of Rough and Ready, near the Yuba County line. It is listed by Bean (pp. 355 f.), along with Spenceville, Hacketville, and Wilsonville as camps which arose during the copper "fever" of the winter of 1862–1863, none of which survived except Spenceville. Shown on the USGS Smartsville 1943 quadrangle.

Queen City [Sierra]. Near the Plumas County line, northeast of Port Wine. It is shown as a considerable settlement on the map (Southern Part) in Raymond V, on Crossman's map, 1867, and on the County Map, 1874. The large Golden Gate Tunnel is mentioned in *Mining Press*, April 13, 1861. The place is listed in 1919 in *Mining Bureau*, XVI (Sierra, pp. 19 f.). Shown on the USGS Downieville 1907 quadrangle.

Quicksilver Bar [Placer]. On Bear River. According to an article in *Placer Nuggets*, June, 1959 (p. 3), very fine gold deposits were found in 1851 but were not mined until later years.

Quimby [Trinity]. *See* New River.

Quincy [Amador]. Near Ione City. "Miners Laws of Quincy District" were published in the local weekly newspaper, *The Prospector*, September 22, 1855 (Bancroft Library). The town had a hotel and other buildings, including one to house *The Prospector*, published between May and November [?], 1855. The name of the town does not appear on the County Map, 1866.

Quincy [Plumas]. Shown on Goddard's 1857 map as Quinsy. Gold was apparently discovered on the American Ranch in the early 1850s. The town developed around H. J. Bradley's hotel and was named after Bradley's hometown in Illinois when it became the county seat in 1854. The post office was established in 1855. A detailed description of the Quincy District is found in *Mining Bureau*, XVI (Plumas, pp. 36 ff.). At the turn of the century two stamp mills and two arrastres were still in operation (*Register*, 1900). *See* American: Valley, Ranch.

Quincy Dam [El Dorado]. On the South Fork of American River, about four miles below Coloma. It is mentioned repeatedly by Lucius Fairchild, especially in a letter dated November 23, 1850.

Quinns Ranch [Nevada]. Near Graniteville (Eureka South). It is situated above the Magenta Flume and was the control center for the mining ditches in the area (Foley). The Magenta Flume (165 feet high) is indicated on Doolittle's map, 1868. The County History, 1880 (p. 172), describes the system of ditches and the storage reservoirs of the Eureka Lake and Yuba Canal Company. The largest of the storage reservoirs was the Eureka or French Lake, fourteen miles east of Eureka South. Another name of Quinns Ranch was Schands Ranch. It appears to be the name spelled Shands by Lindgren (*Tertiary Gravels*, p. 141).

Quito District [Kern]. The Spanish word for 'quits' was used for the diggings on the northeast side of Walkers Basin, south of Havilah (Boyd, p. 43).

Rabbit: Creek, Camp, Point [Plumas]. The stream is a tributary to Slate Creek. The camp owes its origin to the Slate Creek rush in the spring of 1852. It is shown on Goddard's map, 1857. John Clark mined here intermittently between 1852 and 1856 ("The California Guide," November 7, 1852 and later entries). In 1854 the place yielded twenty to thirty dollars per day to the hand (Hittell Clippings, p. 26). September 13, 1855 a post office called Rabbittown was established. In 1857 the colorful name was changed to La Porte, because the owner of the express company was born in La Porte, Indiana. In 1855 Lotta Crabtree started here on her spectacular career. According to the *Mountain Messenger*, July 19, 1862 (Bancroft Notes: Sierra County), the Dutch Company made 16 thousand dollars in one day cleaning up tailings in addition to a well-paid season. A. Dressler *in California's Pioneer Mountaineer of Rabbit Creek*, gives an entertaining and fairly dependable account. The creek is recorded on the Sierra County map of 1874. *See* La Porte.

Rabbittown [Plumas]. *See* La Porte; Rabbit Creek.

Racacous Creek [Plumas]. On the headwaters of Feather River. The name is probably a misspelling of Raccoon. Rich finds were made in October, 1850, by two miners who took out 800 dollars in one pan and averaged fifty dollars per day. (*Alta*, April 10, 1851).

Raccoon. A number of places were named after the once common *Procyon lotor*, but the name was almost invariably changed to the popular abbreviation. *See* Coon.

Rackerby [Yuba]. *See* Hansonville.

Radcliff (or Ratcliff) Mine [Inyo]. *See* Pleasant Canyon.

Rademacher District [Kern]. On the eastern border of the county, at the northeastern end of El Paso Mountains, about fifteen miles north of Randsburg. It was probably named for Alexander Rademacher, a resident of the region in 1879. Mining began in the 1890s, and the period of most activity was apparently before 1904 when many claims were worked by short adits and shafts. Later mining was intermittent, and in 1957 only one mine had a mill. The mines are mapped and described in *County Report* I (p. 47 and tables 133 ff.) with bibliographic references given.

Ragged Ass Bar [Trinity]. On lower Canyon Creek. It was named for the dilapidated miners who made only five to eight dollars a day (Cox, p. 97).

Ragged Breeches Bar [Calaveras, Tuolumne?]. On the Stanislaus River. It is listed as a town by Hutchings in 1855. It may refer to a Ragged Bar on the Stanislaus above Peoria Bar, mentioned, though not definitively, as having been on the north bank, in Calaveras County (De Ferrari).

Ragged Gulch [Trinity]. On Digger Creek, near Minersville. It once paid 100 dollars per day and in 1858 only three or four dollars (Cox, p. 90).

Ragged Tail Bar [Trinity]. On Canon Creek. According to *Trinity Journal*, February 18, 1860, miners were making seven to eight dollars per day.

Rag Gulch [Tulare]. In the White River Mining District. It was mentioned June, 1858, in the Mariposa *Democrat* (Hittell Clippings, p. 40). Rich placers were discovered in 1862, some of which yielded as high as fifty dollars to the pan (*Mining Press*, August 30, 1862).

Ragon Flat [Nevada]. Between Nevada City and Cement Hill. The geology of the area is described in Lindgren's *Tertiary Gravels* (pp. 125 ff.). The surface gravels are said to have paid well in early days, and a quartz lead was discovered in 1856 while working through the gravel in the old

Rabbit Creek, Plumas Co.

Empire Mine; in 1870 the Ragon incline
was sunk. Later workings of the mine are
described in *Mining Bureau*, XVI (Nevada,
pp. 238 f.); the early history is given in
volume XIII (pp. 260 f.).

Ragtown [El Dorado]. Somewhere southwest of Placerville. It is mentioned in the
County History, 1883 (p. 200).

Ragtown, Ragtown Hill [Calaveras]. About
four miles northeast of Camp Seco. Ragtown is shown on Goddard's map, 1857.
The Fourth of July Mine, on the hill, was
known for the extreme fineness of gold,
one mint having reported a fineness of
955° (U. S. *Bull.*, 413, p. 74).

Railroad: Diggings, Hill, Gulch [Yuba].
About three miles northeast of Camptonville. Recorded on Wescoatt's map, 1861.
McKeeby mined here in 1852 and gives a
good description of the place (p. 148). An
iron rail was built to convey the dirt to the
mines; hence, the name (Co. Hist., 1879,
p. 100). The Hill is mentioned repeatedly
by De Long in 1857. According to an undated clipping from the *Sierra Citizen* (Hittell Clippings, p. 44), claims at Railroad
Hill had paid as high as 1,100 dollars per
day. The place was on the route to be
supplied with water by the Sierra Mountain Water Company. There was still some
mining in the 1870s (Co. Hist., 1879, p.
100), but the town, which once had 100
inhabitants dwindled to eight or ten. William Bull Meek recalls in his "Reminiscences" (p. 136) that the population was
once 600.

Railroad Flat [Calaveras]. Ten miles east of
Mokelumne Hill. The place was settled in
1849 and later was so named because a
short track conveyed the lorries with ore
and waste to and from the diggings. No
early records were found and no recording on early maps, but the post office was
established in 1857. A stamp mill was built
in 1866, and by 1872 there were apparently five or six mills (Browne, p. 66; *Annual Mining Review*, 1876, pp. 21–23). At
the end of the century it was still the
center of quartz and drift mines, with two
stamp mills and one arrastre (*Register*,
1899). Historic Landmark 286. *See* Petticoat Mine.

Rainbow Mine [Sierra]. *See* Sixteen-to-One
Mine.

Ralston Divide [Placer]. In the southeast
part of the county, between Long Canyon
and the Middle Fork of American River.
The divide was named for William C.
Ralston, who had carried on hydraulic
mining at Ralstons, Lynchburg, and

Blacksmith Flat. Warren T. Russell tells
about these mining ventures in his "Chispas" (pp. 203 ff.). After Ralston's death in
1875, mining was resumed by several
companies. A Ralston Divide Gravel Mine
is listed in the Mining Bureau reports until
1936. All gravel mines on Ralston Divide
were in Tertiary river gravels.

Ramirez Mills [Yuba]. On the road from
Marysville to Camptonville, about three
miles above Dobbins Ranch. In the spring
of 1849, J. M. Ramirez brought a group of
Chilenos to Yuba County. The place is
mentioned by De Long, August 8, 1856.

Ramms Ranch [Yuba]. Northwest of
Camptonville. It is mentioned as a mining
settlement repeatedly by De Long in
1856–1857. Recorded on the County Map,
1879. It was also known as Dutchmans
Ranch and was famous for John Ramm's
grapes. John Ramm, who committed
suicide in 1886, was the father of Charles
A. Ramm who became a member of the
Catholic clergy of California, serving at
one time as secretary to Archbishop Rior-
dan at San Francisco (Ramey). Shown on
the USGS Smartsville 1943 quadrangle. *See*
Notowa.

Ramsey Bar [Butte]. On Little Kimshew
Creek, on the divide between the West
Branch and the North Fork of Feather
River; about five miles northeast of Stirling City. The creek was rich throughout
and was worked at Ramsey Bar in 1901,
according to Lindgren, 1911 (p. 95).

Ramseys Bar [Placer]. On the North Fork of
American River, below Rattlesnake Bar. It
is mentioned in the County History, 1924
(p. 176).

Ramshorn Bar [Sierra]. *See* St. Joe Bar.

Ramshorn Creek [Sierra]. Just west of
Goodyears Bar. There were apparently
rich diggings. Downie tried to mine here
but was driven out by the "St. Louis
Boys" (p. 134).

Rancheria [Amador]. About three miles
southwest of Drytown, on Rancheria
Creek. The camp took its name from the
Mexican-Spanish word for Indian village
and is variously spelled: Rancheree, Ranchoree, and Rancherie. Trask records it as
Rancheree on his map of 1853, northeast
of Amidor [Amador] City, and in his *Report*, 1854 (doc. 9, pp. 89 f.), he lists a mine
and a mill at Ranchoree. W. I. Morgan called it Rancheria in 1850 (pp. 47 and *passim*). A water-driven quartz mill was built
at Ranchorie as early as 1853, according to a
Hittell clipping (p. 74). A convention held
at Rancheria, June 7, 1851, established

quartz mining laws for miners at Dry, Rancheria, Amador, and Sutter creeks (Co. Hist., 1881, p. 146). In the 1850s Rancheria became known as Lower Rancheria (sometimes as Old Rancheria) to distinguish it from Upper Rancheria. (*see* below.) The camp at Lower Rancheria was predominantly Spanish speaking, until August 6, 1855, when a band of Mexicans murdered five men and one woman and cracked a safe. Three of the murderers were hanged, and a few weeks later two others were likewise executed. The story is told in Ben Bowen's diary under the dates August 7, 12, and September 14, 1855. The Mexicans, guilty or innocent, were driven from the region. The County History, 1881, tells a similar story and others, some doubtful (pp. 83 ff., 221). The Ranchoree or Rancheria Mine at this location, later known as Bunker Hill Mine, is described in *Bulletin*, 108 (p. 72) and *Mining Bureau*, L (p. 173). *See* Amador City. **Upper Rancheria** was situated about five miles northwest of Volcano, near a tributary to Rancheria Creek and at the end of a branch of Volcano Ditch. A short time before the murders were perpetrated at Lower Rancheria, three men had killed and robbed a man at Upper Rancheria and all escaped. (Bowen.) Rancheria Mine, five miles northwest of Volcano, apparently at the site of Upper Rancheria, is listed in 1913/14 in *Mining Bureau*, XIV (p. 45). Both Upper and Lower Rancheria are shown on the County Map, 1866.

Rancheria [Butte]. An unidentified site listed in Hittell's roster.

Rancheria: Creek, Gulch [Siskiyou]. A tributary to Klamath River, in the Henley-Hornbrook area. According to an extract dated Yreka *Union*, November 23, 1867, in Hayes Scrapbooks: Mining (IV, sec. 19), a company was engaged in running a tunnel through the bank of the creek in an attempt to reach the original bed of the stream, which had been rich in gold above that point. Placers on the gulch in the 1880s are mentioned in *Mining Bureau*, XII (p. 468).

Rancheria Gulch [Mono]. At Monoville. N. B. Hunnewill located a placer claim here around 1860 (F. S. Wedertz).

Ranch Gulch [Mariposa]. About six miles from Mariposa. McIsaac mentions March 25, 1853, that a Mr. Backman had rich claims here.

Ranchoree [Amador]. *See* Rancheria.

Rand District [Kern]. The rich gold fields around Randsburg and Johannesburg were named after the Rand Mountains in South Africa. The development of the district began after the discovery of placers in Goler Gulch and Canyon, northwest of Randsburg. The Yellow Aster Mine was located in 1895, and it became the heaviest producer in the district, with a total yield of 12 million dollars (*Mining Bureau*, XXIX, pp. 279 ff.). A 100-stamp mill was built in 1901, and others were soon to follow. The Butte Mine reportedly produced around 2 million dollars and several other mines produced a half million or more. Large scale mining continued in the district until 1918; in the 1930s and early 1940s there was again considerable activity, with intermittent work since then. The gold production is estimated at about 20 million dollars, the highest in Southern California. The Rand district was also known for its silver mines and for its production of tungsten. The mines are described and mapped in *Mining Bureau*, XLV (pp. 212 ff.); *Bulletin*, 193 (pp. 164 ff.); and *County Report*, I (pp. 47 ff.).

Randolph [Sierra]. Near Sierraville. Shown on the County Map, 1874. It was a stopping place on the road between Sierra City and Sierraville.

Randolph: Flat, Hill [Nevada]. The Flat is about one mile northeast of Rough and Ready. Randolph Flat Hotel is shown on Trask's map, 1853, and on Doolittle's, 1868. The camp was named after Randolph County, Missouri, and Kane mentions it among the places at which he mined in 1849–1850 (Miscellaneous Statements, 1878). The diggings were very successful in 1851 after water had been brought from Deer Creek to the Flat (*Brown and Dallison's Directory*, 1856, p. 11). One company at Randolph Hill made almost half a million dollars by ground sluicing in about two years (Bean, p. 357). According to a clipping from the Grass Valley *Telegraph*, the Randolph Company at Randolph Hill washed out 2,650 dollars in one day in August, 1853 (Hittell Clippings, p. 27). One nugget worth 1,018 dollars was found (*Alta*, February 22, 1853). On February 29, 1872, the Grass Valley *Republican* (quoted in the San Francisco *Monitor*, March 9, 1872) reported a rich vein at Randolph Flat, which yielded from two and a half dollars to three dollars a pan (Hayes Scrapbooks: Mining, II, sec. 14).

Randsburg [Kern]. Gold was discovered in 1895 and the camp was named the same year, after the famous Rand mines in South Africa. A listing of all the gold producing mines around the town, including references to previous reports of the Mining Bureau is given in *County Report*, I (p. 1962).

Ranshaws Bar [Placer or Nevada]. On the North Fork of American River. It is mentioned by Henry S. Blom, October 22, 1850 in his diary.

Rantedodler Bar [Sierra]. On the North Fork of Yuba River, a half-mile below Goodyears Bar. Downie (p. 131) mined here and built a cabin in the summer of 1851. The bar was considered to be without equal in 1854 (*Sierra Citizen*, August 12, 1854). The name is variously spelled: Rantedoddler, Ransedoddler, Rantedotler.

Rat Bar [El Dorado]. An unidentified place, listed in the Giffen file. It may refer to Rattlesnake Bar, west of Coloma.

Ratsburg [Los Angeles]. At the junction of Bouquet Canyon and San Francisquito Canyon roads. It is mentioned as a mining camp of the 1890s, where mining was carried on by drifting or tunneling (*HSSCQ*, XL, pp. 159, 161).

Rattlesnake Bar [El Dorado]. On the south side of the South Fork of American River, west of Coloma. Shown on Trask's map, 1853. It is mentioned in the Sacramento *Union* July 17, 1855.

Rattlesnake Bar [Nevada]. On the south side of the Middle Fork of Yuba River, two miles below Kanaka Creek. Shown on Trask's map, 1853.

Rattlesnake Bar [Placer]. On the North Fork of American River, below the junction with the Middle Fork; above Whiskey Bar. Shown on Doolittle's map, 1868. Mining on the bar was exhausted in 1850–51 because the claims were so situated that they could not be worked by natural water. In 1853, however, the flat bench above the bar was prospected with success and a town was built, taking its name from the Bar. Water was brought by the Bear River Ditch Company in July, 1853. (Co. Hist., 1882, p. 401.) A Mr. Qua started sluicing operations and made 30 thousand dollars, according to an undated account in the Sacramento *Union*, (Hittell Clippings, p. 66½). In 1854 the three men of the Rattlesnake Company made 6 thousand dollars in six weeks with one sluice (Hittell Clippings, p. 20). The production began to decline about 1855 (Pringle Shaw, p. 121), but according to the *Placer Herald*, October 27, 1855, the dirt still paid ten dollars to the wheelbarrow load. Mining activities in the Rattlesnake Bar district in the 1880s and 1890s and later in the 1930s are described in *Bulletin*, 193 (p. 112). The site of

Randsburg, Kern Co.

the Bar, now under Folsom Lake, is shown on the USGS Auburn 1954 quadrangle.

Rattlesnake Bar [Sierra]. Shown on Milleson and Adams' map, 1851, on the Middle Fork of Yuba River, about eight miles from the confluence with the North Fork.

Rattlesnake: Bar, Camp, Diggings [Sierra]. On Rattlesnake Creek, a tributary to the North Fork of the North Fork of Yuba River. Shown on Crossman's map, 1867, and on the County Map, 1874. This is probably the camp where Hodges mined 1848–1850. The camp was so named because Hodges had drawn the form of a rattlesnake on the sides of his tent with charcoal (p. 55). Rattlesnake Peak and Creek shown on the USGS Downieville 1907 quadrangle are reminiscent of the diggings. A Rattlesnake placer mine is listed in the Mining Bureau reports until 1941.

Rattlesnake Creek [Siskiyou]. A tributary to Scott River, west of Fort Jones. The stream is listed in *Mining Bureau*, II (part 1, p. 189). A moderate production of a little more than 300 ounces was shown in 1880.

Rattlesnake Creek [Tuolumne]. A camp on a tributary to Moccasin Creek. The main branch of the creek has its source above Big Oak Flat, flows through the middle of the town, and is joined by another branch called Slate Gulch about a half mile west of the town. It is probably the same as the camp recorded on Goddard's map, 1857. In his reminiscences, *The Gila Trail* (pp. 123 ff.), Benjamin Harris refers to the winter camp of about 1,500 miners at the "New Diggins" and the threat of an Indian attack in November or December of 1849. In May and June, 1850, a company worked here but made only a little more than eleven dollars per day to the man (Daniel B. Woods, pp. 136 ff.). But according to the "Mountaineer" in the *San Joaquin Republican*, December 16, 1851, all the claims along the three or more mile-long creek were extremely rich, one of which yielded an average of fifty dollars per day to the hand for several weeks early in the spring of 1850. Apparently it was lack of water that caused its later decline (Hittell Clippings, p. 73, from the Stockton *Argus*). It is shown on the USGS Sonora 1939 quadrangle.

Rattlesnake Diggings [Nevada]. Four miles south of Grass Valley. According to an item in the Grass Valley *Telegraph* (Hittell Clippings, p. 26), the gold was found mainly in large nuggets weighing between two and ten ounces. In March, 1854, a lump of forty-four ounces was found.

Rattlesnake Flat [Tuolumne]. Probably on Rattlesnake Creek, near Big Oak Flat, but shown on Gibbes' map, 1852, south of the South Fork of Tuolumne River.

Rattlesnake Gulch [Amador]. Near Drytown. It was one of the richest diggings in the region, mainly placering (Co. Hist., 1881, p. 231). It is mentioned in the *Guidebook* (p. 65).

Rattlesnake Gulch [Trinity]. The creek joins the North Fork of Trinity River twelve miles above Trinity. Good prospects were reported in 1854. In 1858 the camp had a store, butcher and blacksmith shops, and the sixty-odd miners made ten dollars a working day (Cox, p. 103).

Rattlesnake House [Tuolumne]. *See* Priest.

Rat Trap Slide. An unidentified place, listed in Hittell, *Resources*.

Ravenna [Los Angeles]. *See* Soledad Canyon.

Rawhide Ranch [Tuolumne]. Two miles northwest of Jamestown; the site of the once famous Rawhide Mine in Table Mountain district. The deepest shaft was 1,845 feet. It produced about six million dollars. There were two periods of prosperity: from the 1850s to 1867 and from 1891 to 1905. (*Guidebook*, pp. 54 ff.) In 1858 there was a 10-stamp water-driven mill (*State Register*, 1859); in 1860 twenty stamps and a forty horsepower engine were operating (Browne, p. 44; *Annual Mining Review*, 1876, p. 23). A detailed description of the modern development is given in U. S. *Bulletin*, 424 (p. 21). It is now a ghost town and is indicated on the USGS Sonora 1939 quadrangle.

Readings Bar [Shasta]. On Clear Creek, about four miles east of Igo. This place was near Pierson Reading's land grant, and he discovered gold here in the spring of 1848 before he found the deposits on Trinity River. *See* Clear Creek. Historic Landmark 32. *See also* Readings: Bar, Creek [Trinity].

Readings: Bar, Creek [Trinity]. On the Trinity River, at or near Douglas City. This is probably the second bar where Pierson B. Reading discovered gold in July, 1848, after his return from Sutter's Mill. *See* Douglas City [Trinity] and Readings Bar [Shasta]. The U. S. Geological Survey and the California State Mining Bureau, disregarding the name of the great pioneer, spell the name of the locality Redding, after the town in Shasta County. Reading started working here in July, 1848, with about sixty-five Indians, but gave up after six weeks because prospectors from Oregon objected to Indian labor. He is credited with having taken out 80 thousand dollars worth of gold, using only pan and rocker. (Cox, chapters 1 and 5; Weaverville *Journal*, April 20, 1874; Bancroft Notes). Leeper (pp. 116 f.) settled here in the spring of 1851. The pay dirt had to be carried to be washed in cradles and rockers; the average pay was ten to twenty dollars per day to the hand. The camp was abandoned in 1854. *See* the lengthy account in Cox (pp. 37 f.). The mines in the district are listed in the Mining Bureau reports until 1941, and the creek is recorded on the USGS Weaverville 1942 quadrangle. In both cases the spelling is Redding.

Readings Springs [Shasta]. *See* Shasta.

Rebel Hill [Sacramento]. Three miles south of Folsom. After the prohibition of hydraulic mining in 1884 drift mines operated here until the introduction of dredges in the late 1890s (*Mining Bureau*, LI, p. 142).

Rebel Ridge [Yuba]. Below Camptonville, near Wisconsin House. It is mentioned by Wheat in "Notes to the Journal of Charles E. De Long for 1854" (*CHSQ*, VIII, no. 3, p. 209). Meek relates (pp. 159 f.) that Southern sympathizers during the Civil War held their meetings at the Wisconsin House, which was considered an unsafe place by residents of nearby Camptonville.

Rectors Bar [Placer]. Above Horseshoe Bar No. 2, on the Middle Fork of American River, near the confluence of its North and Middle branches. It is mentioned by Wierzbicki (p. 41) in 1849 and was named for an Oregonian who mined here in 1848 (El Dorado Co. Hist., 1883, p. 182).

Redan Hill [Nevada]. *See* Osborn Hill.

Red Bank Mine [Mariposa]. *See* Benton Mills.

Red Bar [El Dorado]. On the South Fork of American River, west of Coloma. It is mentioned in the County History, 1883 (p. 85).

Red Bar [Trinity]. On Trinity River, below Douglas City. Gold mining started as early as 1850. In 1851 a Dutchman, working a rocker, and his wife digging and packing the dirt, netted several thousand dollars. After 1856 it was a flourishing camp, according to the detailed account by Cox (pp. 40 ff.).

Red Bird [Placer]. Although listed as a mining camp, it probably refers to the Red Bird mines near Weimar. The Red Bird Consolidated Mines are listed until 1935.

Red Cap Bar [Humboldt]. On the Klamath River, above the confluence with Trinity River. Shown on Goddard's map, 1857. It was named for an Indian subchief whose sole dress was ordinarily a greasy looking red woolen cap (Schoolcraft, III, pp. 148 ff.). Carr (p. 104) was here in January, 1851, but prospecting was poor. On Red Cap Creek, tributary to the Klamath River, there was limited gold and copper mining in the twentieth century (*Mining Bureau*, XIV, pp. 395, 400; XXXVII, p. 508; XXXIX, p. 79).

Red Cloud Mine [Mariposa]. *See* Greeley Hill.

Red Diamond [Nevada]. About three miles northeast of Quaker Hill. Shown on Doolittle's map, 1868. It is mentioned as an old camp in Raymond VI (p. 117).

Redding [Shasta]. The city, founded in 1872 by the Central Pacific Railroad, was the trading and shipping center for numerous gold, silver, and copper mines between the Sacramento River and the Trinity County line. For the municipally owned Blue Gravel Mine, *see* Blue Gravel Mine. Mining in the Redding area from the time of the Gold Rush to recent years is described in *Bulletin*, 193 (pp. 140 f.). An account of the naming is given in *California Place Names*.

Redding: Bar, Creek [Trinity]. *See* Readings Bar, Creek.

Red Dog [Nevada]. Four miles northwest of Dutch Flat, on the road from You Bet. Shown on Goddard's map, 1857, and Doolittle's, 1868. Three men, Henry Stehr and Joseph Clew of Arkansas and Charlie Wilson of Illinois, discovered gold in 1850 in a ravine, tributary to Greenhorn Creek, and they called the ravine Arkansas Ravine. They also found gold on the adjoining hill, which they named Red Dog Hill, after a hill in Illinois, where Wilson had mined in the lead-zinc mines. (Lyle L. White.) When the rush began in 1850–1851, two camps, Red Dog and Chalk Bluffs, were established, but the Chalk Bluffers soon recognized the superiority of the Red Dog townsite and moved over in a body. In 1852 or 1853 the residents changed the name by popular vote to Brooklyn, but when the post office was established in 1855, the name was rejected in favor of Red Dog because there already was a post office named Brooklyn in Alameda County (now a part of the City of Oakland). This version of the founding is essentially the same as given in *Bean's Directory* (pp. 370 f.). Brown's *Directory*, 1856, lists the place as Red Dog or Brooklyn. The map of Goddard, 1857, however, shows Brooklin as a separate location just south of Red Dog, and Doolittle's map, 1868, shows three different settlements: Red Dog; Brooklyn P. O., about one-quarter mile to the south; and Chalk Bluff, two miles east of Red Dog. An item in the *Alta*, December 16, 1853, reports that claims at Brooklyn were paying between ten and twenty dollars a day to the man, and in the same item Red Dog is also mentioned, apparently as a separate "village," at which there were already six or eight stores and four or five hotels. Another early description of the camp is given in the San Franciso *Bulletin*, July 13, 1857. The first water ditch to the Red Dog mines and townsite was Henry Stehr's, which brought water sometime in 1853 from the East Fork of Greenhorn Creek (Foley). Other ditches were the Perkins' ditch from Missouri Canyon to Independence Hill, and the Churchman ditch from Steep Hollow to the entire lower ridge (*Bean's Directory*, p. 371). When the surface placers gave out, hydraulic mining continued the prosperity. In November, 1860, four Germans cleaned up more than 5 thousand dollars in five days (*Mining Press*, December 7, 1860). The hydraulic washing uncovered silicified trees, which had been subjected to the violent current of the ancient river, along which the famous Blue Lead runs (Bancroft Scraps, LI:1, p. 11). In 1869 the rich diggings had begun to decline, and most of the miners moved to You Bet. Shown on the USGS Colfax 1938 quadrangle.

Red Flat [Trinity]. Four miles south of Dedrick. It is described by Cox (p. 97) in 1858. The earnings were fifteen to eighteen dollars a day. A Red Flat Mine was in operation until recent times (*Mining Bureau*, XIV, p. 912; XXXVII, p. 86).

Red Flat [Tuolumne]. About two miles southeast of Chinese Camp, on Highway 120. A letter of George W. Watson is datelined Red Flat, January 12, 1853, with Oak Springs Post Office, Southern Mines, as the mailing address. No other mention of the camp was found. Today only some tailings remain and indications of buildings said to have been of Chinese origin (De Ferrari).

Red Flat Hill [Calaveras]. Near Mokelumne Hill. In a letter of July 17, 1853, William H. Moore states that a large reservoir was built on top of the hill.

Red Gulch [Amador]. Near Volcano. Bowen recorded on October 22, 1854, that he and one of his friends prospected here and got out of "two sacks of dirt — two bits."

Red Hill [Calaveras]. The location could not be determined, and the only source is an undated (about 1854) item from the *Calaveras Chronicle* (Hittell Clippings, p. 27). Four Chilenos were ejected from Red Hill for not paying the foreigners tax. The Americans who bought their claim for twenty-five dollars found that it yielded abundantly. A nugget of twenty-two ounces of pure gold was found. The reference may be to the Red Hill west and south of Vallecito, where there was early placer mining, according to R. C. Wood. The back road from Vallecito to Frogtown goes over Red Hill.

Red Hill [Trinity]. On Trinity River, one mile north of Deadwood Creek. There were rich diggings in the early 1850s (Cox, p. 25). The Chamberlain and Red Hill mines were still listed in 1941 (*Mining Bureau*, XXXVII, p. 76). The Red Hill Mine, below Junction City, was one of the old hydraulic mines on the terraces on the west bank of the Trinity River operated by the Goldfield Consolidated Mines Company between 1938 and 1950 (*County Report*, IV, p. 31).

Red Hill Bar [El Dorado]. On the Middle Fork of American River, five miles above Poverty Bar. Recorded on Trask's map, 1853.

Red Hill Diggings [El Dorado]. There were two mining localities on or near the South Fork of American River named Red Hill. One was near Big Canon, a tributary to the South Fork, north of Placerville. Haskins, in his reminiscences (p. 135), describes the rich quartz vein as one eighth of a mile long and in places only about three inches wide. In the 1850s the yield was more than a quarter of a million dollars. The other Red Hill was five miles below Coloma, near Uniontown. Pond mentions the diggings in his diary, June 17, 1851. Wing mined here in the fall of 1856 (journal, II, p. 98) and the following year he was there again (Journal, III, pp. 50 ff.).

Red Hills [Amador]. Between Jackson and Butte City. It was reported in the *Amador Ledger*, December 6, 1856, that a large amount of dirt was taken from the tunnels during dry weather and was ready for washing. It may be the same place as Red Hill listed in Hittell's roster.

Red Hills [Trinity]. Between Weaverville and Junction City. It was a thriving mining town in the 1850s (Cox, p. 60). In 1861 the hills still had "first-rate" claims (*Mining Press*, November 23, 1861).

Red Mountain Bar [Tuolumne]. On the Tuolumne River, just below Six-Bit Gulch, and above Swetts Bar. Recorded on Trask's map, 1853. Gardiner mentioned the place in October, 1849 (p. 99). Hutchings lists it as a town in 1855. Mulford lived "off and on" at the Bar and gives a delightful picture of its end in "The Red Mountain Bar," chapter XVII of his *Story*. Shown on the USGS Sonora 1939 quadrangle.

Red Mountain District [Mendocino]. On the watershed between Russian River and Clear Lake. It is one of the few places in the county where small quantities of gold were mined (*Mining Bureau*, XII, p. 177).

Red Point [Placer]. In Humbug Canyon, at the North Fork of American River. It is listed as a place near drift mines (*Register*, 1902). Cross sections of the channel are sketched in *Mining Bureau*, IX (p. 115, plates 5 and 6).

Red Ravine [El Dorado]. A mining locality near Diamond Springs; mentioned by Crockett (p. 94) in 1859.

Red Ravine [Nevada]. Near Walloupa and Bear River. Recorded prominently on Trask's map, 1853.

Red Rock Canyon [Kern]. In the northeastern part of the county, twenty-nine miles north of Mojave. The placer deposits are described in 1894 and 1896 in *Mining Bureau*, XII (pp. 456 f.) and XIII (p. 195). Dry washing, which paid wages, was used exclusively. The Beryl of Bishop lode claims, which reportedly contained some gold, were known since 1931, were idle in 1949, and later were partially developed for uranium (*Mining Bureau*, XLIV, p. 210; *County Report* I, p. 338).

Red Rover Mine [Los Angeles]. *See* Acton.

Red Slide [Plumas]. On Poormans Creek. So named because pieces of deep red rock gradually slid into a creek. According to the Quincy *Union*, December 9, 1865, the Red Slide Company dug a tunnel in 1854 in the belief that the gold in the creek came from the rock. A disaster put an end to the undertaking. (Bancroft Notes.) A mine is listed in the Mining Bureau reports until 1937, but it apparently had been idle for some time.

Red Star Mine [Sierra]. *See* Sixteen-to-One Mine.

Reds Tent [Stanislaus]. Near Knights Ferry. No mining record was found, but Schaeffer (p. 46) was there November 23, 1849, and he gives a favorable picture.

Red Stone [Placer]. Ten miles north of Dutch Flat. In 1867 an 18-stamp mill was in the course of construction (Browne, p. 110).

Reece Ravine Diggings [Sierra]. Three miles south of Poker Flat. It is listed from 1894 to 1942 in the reports of the *Mining Bureau* (XII, p. 270, XXXVIII, p. 62). There was considerable development work here and a steam-driven stamp mill, according to R. Drury, apparently in the 1950s or later.

Reeces Bar [Butte]. The bar is shown on Trask's map, 1853, as Reeves Bar on a branch of Butte Creek. In the spring of 1850 Ferguson (p. 115) mentions the bar and gives an interesting account.

Reeves Bar [Butte]. *See* Reeces Bar.

Refuge Canyon [Placer]. A tributary to Shirttail Canyon, near Wisconsin Hill. It is shown on the map in Whitney, *Auriferous Gravels* (plate B) and sluicing operations are described (p. 91).

Regans [Calaveras]. About fifteen miles west of the confluence of the North and Middle forks of Mokelumne River. Shown on Butler's map, 1851.

Reid Mine [Shasta]. *See* Old Diggings.

Reinhart Bar [Plumas]. An unidentified place on the Middle Fork of Feather River listed by Coy (p. 73). It is shown on modern maps near the Butte County line.

Reis: Mine, Mill [Sierra]. *See* Sierra Buttes.

Relief Hill [Nevada]. About three miles southeast of North Bloomfield; on the Great Gravel Deposit. Shown on Doolittle's map, 1868. The place was settled in 1853 and was for a number of years a lively mining camp. It is mentioned by Bean (p. 396). In 1871 hydraulicking at several mines paid sixteen to thirty dollars per day to the hand (Raymond, IV, p. 118). The mines are listed in the Mining Bureau reports until 1941. Shown as Relief on the USGS Colfax 1938 quadrangle.

Remington Hill [Nevada]. Six miles northnortheast of Dutch Flat. Shown on Doolittle's map, 1868, and the County Map, 1880. It was probably named for the owner of the Remington-Pond cement mill in nearby Little York. The camp is mentioned in the *Alta*, February 27, 1854, as prosperous with a steady earning of sixteen dollars per day to the hand. In 1855 a nugget of 186 troy ounces valued at 3,500 dollars, and in 1867 another of 128 ounces valued at 2,400 dollars were found (*Mining Bureau*, II, part 1, p. 149). Drift and hydraulic mining was carried on in the early 1870s; in the 1930s drift mining was renewed on a small scale, and some old quartz mines or prospects were reopened (*Mining Bureau*, XXXI, pp. 10 ff.).

Rensomville [Amador]. An unidentified place, listed in Hittell's roster.

Republican Canyon [El Dorado]. A tributary to the Middle Fork of American River, west of Volcanoville. It is mentioned in Whitney, *Auriferous Gravels* (p. 84) and is shown on the map, (plate B).

Rescue [El Dorado]. Thirteen miles east of Folsom. No mining record was found, but a stamp mill is listed in the *Register* of 1902.

Reservoir Hill [El Dorado]. North of Placerville. Shown on Bowman's map, 1873. It is mentioned by Haskins (p. 98) retrospectively to 1852 or later. Browne (p. 84) lists ten or more claims working and paying in 1867.

Resters Bar [Placer]. On the Middle Fork of American River, near Stony Bar. There were rich diggings in 1849 and 1850 (*Directory* of Placer County, 1861, pp. 201–203).

Revere Mill [Nevada]. The camp of unknown location had produced 20 thousand dollars or more in two years, according to an item from the Nevada *Democrat* reprinted in the *Alta* of March 10, 1854. On a flat near the mill three men had earned 567 dollars in one week.

Reward [Inyo]. In the Russ district, ten miles north of Lone Pine. The Reward vein was discovered in 1878 and was worked intermittently from 1880 to 1936, when it was leased and reportedly produced an average of eleven dollars per ton in gold and silver. It is described in *Mining Bureau*, XXII (p. 473) and XXXIV (pp. 386 f.). The place was a trading center and from 1900 to 1906 the post office for numerous gold, silver, and lead mines on the creeks and canyons that disappear into Saline Valley (*Register*, 1902). In 1948 a new vein with lead, silver, and gold was exploited and reportedly assayed between 100 and 150 dollars per ton. It was still being worked in 1950. (*Mining Bureau*, XLVII, pp. 48 f.) Shown on the USGS Mount Whitney 1907 quadrangle. *See* Russ District.

Reynolds Bar [Merced]. On the Merced River. The *Alta*, January 4, 1854, reprints an item from the Stockton *Journal* that states that a company of six had taken out about 100 dollars a day to the man.

Reynolds Bar [Yuba]. *See* Roses Bar.

Reynolds Ferry [Calaveras]. On the Stanislaus River, west of Jamestown. Shown on Goddard's map, 1857. One company took out 5 thousand dollars worth in one week in the vicinity (*Alta*, March 6, 1854.) Heckendorn (p. 102) lists only a dozen miners still in residence in 1856. According to a clipping from the Sonora *Herald*, 1858, several large river claims were worked by Chinese (Hittell Clippings, p. 66½).

Rhode Island Bar [Tuolumne]. On the Tuolumne River, near Jamestown. According to Buckbee in *The Saga* (pp. 455 f.), one company netted one thousand dollars a week per man in the fall of 1854. No other reference was found.

Rhode Island Hill [Tuolumne]. *See* Bensonville.

Rhode Island Ravine [Nevada]. Near Grass Valley. According to the *Grass Valley Directory*, 1865 (pp. 10 and 80), there were good diggings in 1849–1850, and in 1861 the Good Hope Company, a group of Germans, apparently discovered a promising lead. It yielded twenty-five to thirty-six dollars per ton, or according to the *Mining Press*, February 8, 1861, even seventy-five dollars. In 1866 the La Crosse Mine was located and the owners were incorporated with a capital stock of 140 thousand dollars (Bean, p. 230). The Good Hope Mine, listed in *Mining Bureau*, XXXVII (p. 452), is probably at the same site as above.

Rhodes Diggings [El Dorado]. Near Diamond Springs. Crockett (p. 95) mentions in 1859 that the price of gold dust was seventeen and a quarter dollars.

Rhodes Diggings [Sacramento]. Three miles southeast of Folsom, at the head of Alder Creek, near Prairie City. Shown on Trask's map, 1853, on the trail from Sacramento to Mormon Island. This may be Rhodes Old Diggings, where in 1854 a nugget of 106 ounces was found, according to an item from the *Miners Advocate* in Hittell Clippings (p. 20). The *State Register*, 1859, states that in 1856 a steam-driven quartz mill with five stamps and two arrastres was erected at Rhodes Diggings. A drift mine was in operation in 1916 (*Mining Bureau*, LI, p. 142).

Ricardo Placer Mines [Kern]. On Highway 6. In Iron Canyon, near the station, extensive dry placer mining was done and there was a regular bonanza in 1894–96 (*Mining Bureau*, XXX, p. 246). A renewal was attempted in the 1930s without success (*County Report*, I, p. 183).

Rice District [San Diego]. *See* Montezuma District.

Rices Bar [Placer]. *See* Rich Bar.

Rices Crossing [Yuba, Nevada]. On the

main Yuba River, just above the confluence with the South Fork. Wescoatt's map, 1861, shows Rices' Bridge. Bancroft, VI (p. 359) lists Rice's Bar. The camp which developed near Mr. Rice's ferry was first called Lousy Level, then Liars Flat and Liases Flat. In 1879 only two white and several Chinese miners were left (Co. Hist., 1879, p. 94). Shown as Rices Ford on the USGS Smartsville 1943 quadrangle.

Richardson Hill [Placer]. A part of the Iowa Hill district. The *Alta*, April 27, 1854, reprints an item that reports rich diggings on the hill. A company of three took out 12 hundred dollars in one week.

Rich Bar [Amador]. On the Cosumnes River, about seven miles below the forks. Shown on the County Map, 1866. In the summer of 1857 at least seventy Chinese were at work sluicing at the once-famous bar, according to an item in the *Amador Ledger*, June 13, 1857, but at that time the place was better known for its luxurious garden, orchard, and nursery.

Rich Bar [Butte]. *See* Diamondville.

Rich Bar [Placer]. On the North Fork of American River. A claim is recorded August 21, 1851, in Placer County Records, I (p. 5). *See* Beaver Bar. Bancroft, VI (p. 355) lists a Rich Bar along with Calf, Jones, Mineral, and Pickering bars, all of which were above the junction with the Middle Fork. It is apparently the Bar labelled Rices Bar on Doolittle's map, 1868.

Rich Bar I and II [Plumas]. Of the many Rich bars, flats, and gulches the two bars on the Feather River were the best known and the most productive ones. One, Rich Bar I, is on the East Branch of the North Fork of Feather River and is still shown on modern maps between Belden and Virgilia, just south of Highway 70. The other one was on the Middle Fork of the river, near its confluence with Onion Valley Creek. Both were discovered by groups of prospectors consisting mainly of German miners, during the Gold Lake hunt in July, 1850. By a strange coincidence a lake which is now called Gold Lake is almost on a straight geometric line drawn between the two sites. Milleson & Adams' map, 1851, shows the bar on the North Fork; Trask's, 1853 and Goddard's, 1857 maps have both Rich Bars. It is only natural that the two bars were and still are confused in literature. It is still uncertain whether one of the bars is the same as Myers Diggings and which bar was called Barra Rica by the Chilenos. *See* Myers

Diggings. For Rich Bar I we have two excellent contemporary accounts. Mrs. Clappe resided here in the fall of 1851 and datelined some of her charming "Dame Shirley Letters" Rich Bar. Bruff mentions Rich Bar and Myers Diggings repeatedly in his diaries of the summer of 1850, but his account, detailed and extremely interesting, is somewhat confusing in spite of the scrupulous editing of Georgia Read and Ruth Gaines. Among the first who started the rush, according to the diary of George H. Baker, August 11, 1850, two men, a Dutchman and a Yankee, took out 22 thousand dollars. J. A. Stuart (pp. 111 f.) mined here in the summer of 1850 and gives a fascinating account, but his story was not written until 1895. Bancroft (VI, p. 364) cites a report from the San Francisco *Picayune*, that two Germans took out thirty-five pounds of gold in one day (!), and the Sacramento *Transcript*, November 29, 1850, reports that an Englishman found a lump valued at 300 dollars. As late as September 7, 1861, the *Mining Press* reports that the miners on the east fork were doing well and one company took out 800 dollars in one day. The Rich Bar II on the Middle Fork was apparently discovered shortly before the richness of the bar on the North Fork was found. According to Mansfield (p. 10), three Germans came upon the deposits and took out 36 thousand dollars worth in four days. Booth (pp. 13 ff.) mined here with varying success from July, 1852, to April, 1853, and gives an interesting and detailed account. The placers seemed to have given out soon, at least no mining records were found, while the deposits at the North Fork were mined until the 1860s. Rich as both bars were, the vast literature about them must be taken with a grain of salt. Many of the newspaper items were doubtless exaggerated and it is often uncertain to which of the two bars the information refers.

Rich Bar [Sierra]. Between Downieville and Goodyears Bar. Shown on Gibbes' map, 1851. In 1854 miners earned uniformly six to ten dollars a day to the hand, according to a reprint from the Gibsonville *Trumpet* in the *Alta*, April 24, 1854. Bancroft, VI (p. 362) lists both Big Rich Bar and Little Rich Bar.

Rich Bar [Trinity]. On Trinity River, eight miles below the junction with North Fork. According to the *Annals* (p. 8), a Frenchman, Mr. Gross, found here "treasures of gold" in 1848.

Rich: Bar, Flat [El Dorado]. On a tributary to the Middle Fork of American River, west of Georgetown. Recorded on Trask's map, 1853. In 1854 a Mr. Mott brought 200 ounces of gold to the mint (*Alta*, April 25, 1854). The flat is mentioned by Crockett in 1859 (p. 94).

Rich Creek [Nevada]. The Creek in conjunction with Poor Creek from the north forms the South Fork of Yuba River. Shown on Butler's map, 1851.

Rich Dry Diggings [Placer]. *See* Auburn.

Rich Flat [Nevada]. On Squirrel Creek, west of Grass Valley. According to Bean (p. 360), it was a settlement of importance in 1850, crowded with miners. It may be the same Rich Flat mentioned in the *Alta*, December 23, 1853, as being unsuccessful until water was brought from Deer Creek.

Rich Flat [Placer]. At the head of Rich Gulch in "Old Auburn" and south of the Fair Grounds.

Rich Flat [Sierra]. On the South Fork of Yuba River, east of Downieville. Recorded on Trask's map, 1853.

Rich Gulch [Butte]. East of the West Branch of the North Fork of Feather River. Shown on Trask's map, 1853, and Goddard's, 1857. The first store was opened in 1851, according to the County History, 1882 (p. 253), but the camp declined as nearby Yankee Hill developed. *See* Yankee Hill. — Rich Gulch was the former name of Thompsons Flat, north of Oroville. *See* Thompsons Flat.

Rich Gulch [Calaveras]. On the Mokelumne River, below James Bar. Shown on Trask's map, 1853. Coy mentions a Rich Bar near Winters Bar (p. 42), but no other record was found.

Rich Gulch [Calaveras]. There were two gulches and camps of this name in the county, both near the Mokelumne River. They are designated here as Lower Rich Gulch and Upper Rich Gulch. It is not always clear to which Rich Gulch contemporary accounts refer. Lower Rich Gulch was known for its quartz mines and Upper Rich Gulch for its placers. **Lower Rich Gulch.** The gulch is west of Mokelumne Hill and empties into Mokelumne River at James Bar, near Middle Bar. It is shown on Trask's map, 1853. Doten stated that "this gulch has been one of the richest in California" (Diary, June 22, 1851, quoted by Camp in his edition of *Doble*, note 7, p. 297). The San Andreas *Independent*, January 12, 1861, reported that the rich mines were discovered in August, 1849, and it was not uncommon

to take out lumps of pure gold weighing from thirty to forty ounces. This report presumably refers to Lower Rich Gulch. The *State Register*, 1859, lists two mills with twenty-four stamps in operation in 1857. The same year a post office was established at the camp. Browne (p. 70) records that a 15-stamp mill built in 1865 was idle in 1867. Lower Rich Gulch is the site of the famous Gwin Mine, at which a 60-stamp steam and water-driven mill was erected in 1868 (*Annual Mining Review*, 1876, p. 22). An extract from the Mokelumne Hill *Chronicle* in Hayes Scrapbooks: Mining (II, sec. 1), marked November 10, 1871, reports the discovery of rich strata at Gwin Mine "unparalleled in the history of quartz mining in this state." *See* Gwin Mine. **Upper Rich Gulch.** Between Mokelumne River and the North Fork of Calaveras River, about five miles northeast of Mokelumne Hill. It is shown on Butler's map, 1851, between the North and South forks of Mokelumne River. Charles Grunsky, progenitor of the Stockton pioneer family, mined here briefly in the winter of 1849–50 and also had a store in the camp. F. L. M. worked at Rich Gulch intermittently from 1849 to 1851 and gives an interesting, rather anti-American account. Some of the personal names mentioned by F. L. M. are the same as those in Gerstaecker's narrative. Gerstaecker visited the place in the summer of 1850 and calls it one of the best placer gulches (I, p. 374). Doble describes his visit to Rich Gulch in his diary of February 15, 1852. Tents were strung along it, and it had been dug up fifty feet wide for three or more miles. He states further that several "fortunes" had been taken out of it. The gulch and the settlement Rich Gulch are shown on the USGS Jackson 1938 quadrangle.

Rich Gulch [Kern]. A place mentioned by Boyd (p. 21).

Rich Gulch [Shasta]. Fair success was reported in the *Mining Press*, June 29, 1861.

Rich Gulch [Yuba]. A tributary to the North Fork of Yuba River, at the now flooded Bullard Bar. Shown on the USGS Smartsville 1943 quadrangle.

Rich Gulch Diggings [Trinity]. On the East Fork of the North Fork of Trinity River. Cox (p. 102) mentioned the camp in 1858, and another Rich Gulch (p. 131) on Weaver Creek, north of Weaverville townsite. An unidentified extract from a journal, December 10, 1864, in Hayes Scrapbooks: Mining (IV, sec. 19) states that a tunnel had extended some sixty feet into a ledge on Rich Gulch, a tributary to the lower East Fork.

Richmond Hill [Plumas]. Ten miles southeast of Quincy. In 1858 there were eight tunnels and some of the miners made twenty dollars a day to the man (*Transactions*, 1858, p. 203). When hydraulic mining was permitted in 1896 attempts were made to revive the rich diggings (*Mining Bureau*, XIII, pp. 17, 296).

Richmond Hill [Sacramento]. North of Mormon Island. There was drift mining until 1880 (Co. Hist., 1880, p. 231).

Richmond Hill [Sierra]. In the Slate Creek district. According to the *Mining Press*, July 16, 1862, five claims were paying about one ounce a day to the hand.

Rich Port [Nevada]. A settlement in Meadow Lake township (Foley). No mining record was found.

Rich Ravine [Placer]. In "Old Town" (lower Auburn), along Brewery Street (Spring Street). An editor of the Sacramento *Daily Union* observed in the January 15, 1855 issue of the newspaper, that the first use of the long tom in the state was in November, 1849, in Auburn Ravine, and that the long tom was in common use in January, 1850, in the Auburn diggings.

Rich Valley [Plumas]. At the North Fork of Feather River, south of Spanish Peak. Shown on Goddard's map, 1857.

Rickeyville [Amador]. *See* Ione.

Riderville [Siskiyou]. On Little Humbug Creek, east of Walker. According to the County History, 1881 (pp. 209 f.), there was a store here in 1851, but the town did not develop until 1859. It was first called Plugtown for a doctor who wore a plug hat. Later it was named for W. G. Rider, who had a claim at Rider Gulch. In its heyday it had about sixty cabins and a town hall. It vanished in 1866. The Rider Mine, listed in *Mining Bureau*, XIII (p. 422), may have preserved the name.

Ridgeville [Trinity]. Between Mule Creek, tributary to Stuarts Fork, and Digger Creek, tributary to East Fork of Stuarts Fork; northwest of Old Minersville. Shown on Goddard's map, 1857. Ridgeville Cemetery is shown on the map in the *County Report*, IV. The Sacramento *Union*, April 19, 1855, reported 1,000 persons in the new diggings, with some miners making from fifty to one hundred dollars per day. Cox (p. 94) states that there was a population of 700 in 1856, which dwindled to 150 in 1858. The place was also known as Golden City. It was described as the central mining camp among those on Strope, Coffee, Musquito, and Digger creeks. The region was known for large nuggets; a lump worth as much as 2 thousand dollars was reported. Fred Deiner was the principal owner, but there were many smaller claims (Raymond, VI, pp. 152 f.; Hittell Clippings, p. 65). This once lively camp has completely disappeared, except for the cemetery.

Ridleys Ferry [Mariposa]. On the Merced River, just below Benton Mills. Shown on Gibbes' 1851 and Goddard's 1857 maps. Thomas E. Ridley operated a ferry here in the summer of 1850. It is mentioned by Stephen Davis, April 24 and 26, 1852. Benton Mills and Bagby were later located on opposite sides of the river. On a chaparral mountain on the road to Bear Valley a Frenchman had apparently discovered a rich deposit in decomposed quartz, the location of which was lost but rediscovered in 1862 (*Mining Press*, April 25, 1862). Adolph Schwartz did a sketch of the ferry and Benton Mills which was reproduced in *Mother Lode Narratives* by Jessie Frémont.

Riggs [San Bernardino]. On the south side of the Silurian Hills; about eighteen miles north of Baker. It was a small mining town in connection with the Riggs gold mine and others in the area. It was also a station on the Tonopah and Tidewater Railroad. (Water Supply Paper, no. 224, pp. 55 f.; no. 490 B, pp. 202, 204; no. 578, p. 595; and Belden, June 21, 1959.)

Rincon del Diablo Rancho [San Diego]. Southeast of Oceanside. The remnants of mining activities on the property years ago indicated that Mexicans had operated here long before the recorded discovery of gold in San Diego County. Later, in 1860, a mine on the ranch yielded up to fifty dollars per ton with the use of arrastres, according to an item in Bancroft Notes. This is apparently the Escondido Mine, which was described in early reports as having been mined by Americans with an arrastre (*Mining Bureau*, VIII, pp. 524 f. and XIV, pp. 650 f.). *See* Escondido District.

Rincon Ranch [Santa Cruz]. According to an unidentified item in Hittell's Clippings (p. 51), this was one of the few places, probably in the Ben Lomond area, where gold mining was attempted with moderate success. There was placer mining as early as 1855, and in 1857 a company tried quartz mining. It was reported that a ton yielded as much as fifty dollars. The owner of the ranch, Major S. Hensley, received a percentage of the profits.

Ringgold [El Dorado]. Southeast of Placerville; actually the eastern part of Weberville. Shown prominently on Trask's map, 1853, and on Goddard's, 1857. It was mentioned by many emigrants who came over Carson Pass, because it was the first settlement on the road to the mines. H. L. Smith (p. 17) describes it on September [17] 1850, as "a sunny village, containing about 600 inhabitants." The Ringgold Lode Mine is listed in *Mining Bureau*, XXXIV (p. 266). Ringold Creek, a tributary to Weber Creek, is shown on the USGS Placerville 1931 quadrangle.

Rio Bravo [Kern]. At the mouth of Kern River Canyon, northeast of Bakersfield. The gold mining district was established in 1866 (Boyd, p. 43). Rio Bravo is an early name for Kern River. *See California Place Names*.

Rio Rico Mines [Calaveras]. On the Mokelumne River. The only source is the dateline of several letters written by W. A. George in 1850, published in the *Missouri Republican* (*CHSQ*, XXIV, pp. 348 f.). Other letters, written the same day, the writer datelined Rio Saco Mines.

Rio Saco Mines [Calaveras]. *See* Rio Rico Mines.

Rioters Bar. An uncertain place, mentioned by Helper (p. 151).

Rio Vista [Amador]. Listed in Hittell's roster.

Rising Sun Mine [Placer]. *See* Colfax.

Riverside: Mill, District [Tuolumne]. On the Stanislaus River. A 20-stamp mill was erected in 1874, according to the *Annual Mining Review*, 1876 (p. 23). The district is listed in the Table of Production for 1880 in *Mining Bureau*, II (part 1, p. 184).

Roaches Camp [Tuolumne]. On Wards Ferry road, between Sonora and the Tuolumne River; near the top of the grade on the north side of Tuolumne River canyon. It is mentioned by Heckendorn as a camp, (p. 89) and as diggings (p. 104). It once had 3,000 [!] inhabitants according to an article in *Chispa*, I:1, but now it is a ghost town.

Roach Hill [Placer]. About a mile east of Iowa Hill, on the rich north-south lead between the North and Middle forks of American River. In the 1850s the Dutch Company averaged ninety ounces weekly after mining eighteen months (Hittell Clippings, p. 64). Hutchings passed through here in May, 1855, and stated that it was supposed to be richer than Iowa

Hill (Diary, May 4, 1855). It is mentioned in 1867 as having had good claims (Browne, p. 100). The mines and their yields are listed in the County History, 1882 (pp. 216, 221).

Roaring Camp. Although it sounds like a typical name for a gold camp, no such place could be discovered in the literature and on the early maps which were checked. Coy's map (1948) shows it near Carson Hill. It seems that the name entered the geography of the gold region through Bret Harte's fictitious title, "The Luck of Roaring Camp." The Work Projects Administration project lists the name, and *Ghost Towns* published a photo of the *probable* site of Roaring Camp. The Roaring Camp adjacent to the Cowell State Park in Santa Cruz County is not "a typical pioneer California town of the Gold Rush era," but a miniature Walt Disney development with a small railroad.

Roaring River [Shasta]. A tributary to Cottonwood Creek. It is mentioned as paying nine to ten dollars a day to the hand, in *Mining Press*, March 16 and May 25, 1861. In the twentieth century there was mainly dredging.

Robbers Roost [Butte]. On Big Butte Creek, north of Paradise. There was placering as early as the 1850s. The name is preserved in the Robbers Roost Mining Company, which later operated the Oro Fino Mine (*Mining Bureau*, XXIV, p. 202).

Robbins Creek [Yuba]. A steam-driven stamp mill was in operation in 1858 (*State Register*, 1859).

Roberts Ferry [Stanislaus]. *See* Dickensons Ferry.

Robertson Flat [Placer]. In the eastern part of the county, in the Canada Hill district. It is mentioned in *Bulletin*, 193 (p. 34) and is shown on the USGS Colfax 1938 quadrangle south of Canada Hill and Sailor Flat. The name appears as Roberts Flat, east of Canada Hill, on a sketch map (Plate B) in Whitney, *Auriferous Gravels*.

Robinsons Crossing [Nevada]. *See* Edwards Crossing.

Robinsons Crossing [Yuba and Sutter]. Over Bear River, about two miles southwest of Wheatland. A man by that name settled here in 1849. Later it was called Kempton Crossing. (De Long, March 7, 1856.) It is shown as Kemptons Crossing on Wescoatt's map, 1861. In the Convention of 1878–79 James H. Keyes, a delegate, gave his address as Kemptons Crossing in Sutter County (Ramey).

Robinsons Ferry [Calaveras]. At the Stanislaus River, near the site of Melones. It is shown on Goddard's map, 1857, where it is placed on the Tuolumne side of the river. It was named for John W. Robinson, the partner of the Robinson and Mead store, just below the ferry. According to the *Alta*, March 4, 1854, the miners in the vicinity realized ten to fifty dollars to the hand. From 1856 to 1895 Harvey Woods operated the ferry but did not change the name; the post office was named Robinsons Ferry in 1879. The ferry did a tremendous business after the discovery of the rich lodes on Carson Hill, and in 1857 it was the seat of the White's Canal Company (Hittell Clippings, p. 48). In 1899 it was still the center and post office for the quartz mines of the region with three stamp mills and one arrastre (*Register*, 1899). February 10, 1902, the name of the post office was changed from Robinsons to Melones. Robinsons Ferry is Historic Landmark 276.

Robinsons Hill [Butte]. Near Virginia Flat. It is mentioned in an item in the early 1850s. (Hittell Clippings, p. 53).

Rochester: town, **District** [San Bernardino]. *See* Stedman.

Rock Bar [Placer]. On the north side of the North Fork of the American River. Shown on Trask's map, 1853, below Oregon Bar. No mining record was found.

Rock Creek [Butte]. In Concow Township, north of Oroville. It had a post office, 1858–1871, and is shown on the County Map of 1862. According to the County History, 1882, there were two once flourishing camps, Big and Little Rock Creek. *Mining Bureau*, XIII (p. 92) gives a description of mining in 1896, but calls the stream River.

Rock Creek [Calaveras]. A correspondent from Brushville to the San Andreas *Register*, July 21, 1866, reported that the quartz hauled to the mill far exceeded expectations of the owners of the claim, Hathaway and Austin.

Rock Creek [Nevada]. A tributary to the South Fork of Yuba River, near Nevada City. Shown on the von Leicht-Craven map, 1874. Canfield (p. xiii) states that his "diarist" had his diggings here in 1850. Bean lists several residents at Rock Creek in his *Nevada Township Directory*, 1867. The *Mining Press*, April 25, 1861, reports a miner took out about 6 thousand dollars' worth in a short time.

Rock Creek [Placer]. Wing prospected here without success in January, 1853 (Journal, I, p. 44). Notice of claims on the creek in

the 1860s are recorded in April, 1865 in Placer County Records, V (pp. 177, 183).

Rock: Creek, Diggings [Sierra]. The Creek is a tributary of the North Fork of Yuba River; the Diggings are about one mile south of Goodyears Bar. Shown on Doolittle's map, 1868, and on the County Map, 1874. Another Rock Creek to the northwest, a tributary to Canyon Creek, is also shown on the County Map. Both are shown on the USGS Downieville 1907 quadrangle.

Rock House Bar [Siskiyou]. On Scott River, apparently near Scott Bar. It is listed in a letter of February 22, 1856, published in a pamphlet on the Scott and Klamath rivers written by George W. Metlar, *A Practical Miner*.

Rock Island Bar [Yuba]. On the North Fork of Yuba River, northwest of Fosters Bar. Shown on Wescoatt's map, 1861. The name was applied in 1850 by a company of miners from Rock Island, Illinois (Co. Hist., 1879, p. 94). Gold mining was short-lived, but the place is still shown on the County Map, 1879.

Rock River [Tuolumne]. Southeast of Knights Ferry. It is shown on Trask's map, 1853, as a camp.

Rock Spring [Placer]. West of the North Fork of American River, about one mile southwest of Condemned Bar, below Carrolton. Shown on Doolittle's map, 1868, and on Bowman's, 1873. No mining record was found. The U. S. Bureau of the Census, 1850, lists forty-two inhabitants at Oregon Bar and nearby Rock Springs.

Rocklin District [Placer]. Two miles east of Rocklin and two miles south of Loomis. A gravel channel of the Tertiary American River traverses the area. A description is given in *Bulletin*, 193 (p. 113). The Lee drift mine, one of the chief sources of gold in the area, was operating in the early twentieth century (Gianella) and has also been prospected in recent years.

Rocky Bar [Butte]. On the south side of the Middle Fork of Feather River, between Bidwell Bar and Union Bar. Shown on the County Map, 1862.

Rocky Bar [El Dorado]. Two Rocky bars on the South Fork of American River are mentioned in the El Dorado County Records; one in 1851 about two miles above Coloma (Mining Locations, Book I, p. 99); another above Salmon Falls (Mining Book I, p. 182). (Schlappi-Ferguson.)

Rocky Bar [El Dorado]. On the Middle Fork of the Cosumnes River, near Coles. It was last worked in 1925 (*Mining Bureau*, XXII, p. 440).

Rocky Bar [El Dorado]. Half a mile east of Greenwood. *Mining Bureau*, XII (p. 122) records the old works in disrepair, but a mine is listed until 1956.

Rocky Bar [Nevada]. At the mouth of Scotchman Creek, tributary to the South Fork of Yuba River; one half mile above Washington. Shown on Doolittle's map, 1868. It was also called Boulder Bar. Prospecting started in 1852 and continued with moderate success until 1867. A description is given in Bean (pp. 379 ff.).

Rocky Bar [Nevada]. On Wolf Creek, south of Grass Valley and at the base of Massachusetts Hill. The Rocky Bar Mining Company built a 16-stamp mill here in 1856 (Grass Valley *Directory*, 1865, pp. 81 f.; *Bean's Directory*, 1867, p. 203). This was apparently the ill-fated Rocky Bar Mining Company that failed in its promotional scheme at the Rocky Bar on the Middle Fork of American River, below the junction with the Rubicon. *See CHSQ*, XII (pp. 65 ff.).

Rocky Bar [Placer]. On the Middle Fork of American River, below the junction with the Rubicon River, near Oxbow Bar. The Rocky Bar Mining Company was organized in July, 1849, for the purpose of quartz mining, but it turned out to be a promotional scheme, and the so-called "Labor Association" was short-lived. *See* Carl Wheat's story in *CHSQ*. XII (pp. 65 ff.)

Rocky Bar [Placer]. On the North Fork of American River, three miles east of Colfax. The *Alta*, February 27, 1854, reports that a company of five made as much as 700 dollars profit in one day. *Mining Bureau*, XV (p. 383) states that the miners had to wear diving suits to recover gold from the deep pools of the river. A Rocky Bar Mine is listed until 1936.

Rocky Bar [Plumas]. On the west side of the Middle Fork of Feather River; south of Quincy. Recorded on Trask's map, 1853, and on Goddard's, 1857.

Rocky Bar [Sacramento]. On the south side of American River, opposite Big Gulch (Ashland). Shown on Trask's map, 1853.

Rocky Bar [Siskiyou]. On Scott River. Listed in the Giffen file. It may be the same as Rocky Gulch, where in 1862 as high as seventy-five dollars to the pan was obtained (*Mining Press*, May 8, 1862).

Rocky Bar [Trinity]. Near the North Fork of Trinity River. The *Mining Press*, November 23, 1861, reports mining with good pay.

Rocky Point Slide [Placer]. On the lower

Middle Fork of American River, between Buckners Bar and Mammoth Bar. It is mentioned in *Placer County History*, 1882 (pp. 401 f.) and in El Dorado County History, 1883 (p. 84).

Rodgers Bar [Tuolumne]. Southeast of Don Pedro Bar. Recorded on Trask's map, 1853. It was a rich bar in 1850 and was still mentioned by Heckendorn (p. 89) as a "place of considerable note" in 1856. Rodgers Creek, which empties into Don Pedros Reservoir, is shown on the USGS Sonora 1939 quadrangle.

Rogersville [Kern]. *See* Quartzburg [Kern].

Roger Williams Ravine [Nevada]. Now within the town of Nevada City. Miners' cabins and camps began appearing here in 1850 (Foley).

Rollands Point [Yuba]. West of the North Fork of Yuba River; in Fosters Bar Township. In 1879 it was still worked by Chinese (Co. Hist., 1879, p. 95).

Rollin [Siskiyou]. South of Sawyers Bar, three miles up Eddys Gulch. It is listed in the *Register*, 1898, and was a trading center and post office for the quartz mines in Eddys Gulch. According to an article in *Siskiyou Pioneer*, IV:1 (p. 20), the place was named for Rollin Fergundes, discoverer of a rich pocket of gold. Shown on the USGS Sawyers Bar 1945 quadrangle.

Roma Mine [Mariposa]. *See* Bear Creek.

Root Hog. An unidentified place, listed in a poem in the *Annual Mining Review*, 1876 (p. 18).

Rootville [Fresno]. On the San Joaquin River, about one mile below Fort Miller. In 1850 Derbec (October 27) found the placers along the river among the poorest, with the best pay no more than four dollars a day, and the quicksilver machines abandoned everywhere. However, in later years rich placer mining was reported in the vicinity of Rootville. In 1861 a man employing Chinese labor took out as much as 400 dollars daily (*Mining Press*, October 26, 1861). In 1853 or 1854 the name Rootville had been changed to Millerton, after Fort Miller; it appeared as Millertown in the *Statutes* of 1854 (p. 222), but as Millerton on the maps. From 1856 to 1874 it was the county seat of Fresno County. The reservoir, formed by Friant Dam, has now obliterated the historic town, but it preserves the name. (*California Place Names.*)

Rosamond [Kern]. On Highway 23, south of Mojave. It was not a mining town but a trading center for the mines between Rosamond and Willow Springs, with a post office established in 1885. It is listed in the *Register*, 1904.

Rose Bar [Sierra]. On the South Fork of the North Fork of Yuba River, east of Downieville. Shown on Trask's map, 1853.

Rosecrans Quartz Lode [El Dorado]. One and a half miles northwest of Garden Valley. Shown on Bowman's map, 1873. The Rosecranz mine operated intermittently until 1939 (*Mining Bureau*, LII, pp. 423 f.).

Rose Hill [Nevada]. Near Grass Valley. An unidentified clipping in Hayes Scrapbook: Mining (I, sec. 43) reports that the crushing of quartz from Rose Hill yielded twenty-three dollars per ton in 1856. A Rose Hill Mine is listed in the Mining Bureau reports until 1941.

Rosemine, or Rose Mine [San Bernardino]. About six miles east of Baldwin, on a pioneer road to Yucca Valley. The name is presumably derived from the distinctive rose color of the iron-oxide ore. The mine was probably first worked in the 1860s, though it is said to have been mined by Mexicans many years earlier. The main activity was between 1895 and 1903, and the total production of gold and silver, with some copper, is estimated to have been between 450 thousand and 600 thousand dollars. The "town" at the mine was the trade center for the whole Morongo mining district. In 1899 it had a school, and in 1899–1900 a post office, with the name spelled Rosemine. (*Mining Bureau*, XLIX, pp. 79 f.; La Fuze, II, p. 71; Haenszel.)

Roses Bar [Yuba]. On the south bank of the main Yuba River, east of Timbuctoo Bend. It is recorded on all contemporary maps.

Roses Bar, Yuba Co.

Derby's Sacramento Valley map, 1849, and Jackson's map, 1850, record it as Rose and Reynolds Bar. At the spot where the bar developed, Jonas Spect discovered gold on June 2, 1848. After Cordua Bar it was apparently the first of the many washings and diggings along the lower Yuba River (Co. Hist., 1879, p. 83). John Rose, a Scottish pioneer of 1840 and part owner of the Nye and Sicard Rancho, opened a trading post here and the place became known by his name. It was probably here where two well-known San Francisco pioneers, Jacob Leese and Jasper O'Farrell, with their company mined first and were said to have taken out 75 thousand dollars in three months (McChristian). An interesting account is given by Edwin Sherman (pp. 349 f.) who mined here in the summer of 1849. In September, 1849, a dam was built across the river but it was washed away after several weeks (J. C. Merriam, p. 1). In 1850, 2,000 miners were working, and the camp had three stores, three boarding houses, and two saloons. Borthwick (pp. 254 ff.) tells a touching story of a boy, down and out, who was befriended by a cook. Theodore Hittell repeats the story in his *History*, III (p. 183), and that boy identified himself half a century later as Edwin F. Morse (Morse, pp. 217 f.). Descriptions of the beginnings of the camp are given in *Marysville Directory*, 1858, in the County History, 1879, and in Raymond, VII (pp. 144 ff.). By 1867 the bar was at least partly under gravel (*Alta*, November, 1867). The site is shown on the USGS Smartsville 1951 quadrangle.

Roses Corral [Nevada]. On Deer Creek, southwest of Nevada City. Apparently Mr. Rose's corral and adobe were here before he moved to Roses Bar. Brown's *Directory* 1856 (p. 9), mentions it as the earliest traceable settlement in the county (in the summer of 1848), at which Mr. Rose traded with the Indians; but it disappeared when no mines were found in the vicinity.

Rose Springs [Placer]. Near the junction of the North and South forks of American River. According to May W. Perry, in *Placer Nuggets*, February, 1964 (pp. 7 f.), water was taken from the North Fork Ditch and "plenty of coarse gold" was taken out.

Ross River [Siskiyou]. *See* Scott Bar.

Rotgut. An unidentified place, listed as a mining locality on an illustrated letter sheet published by Hutchings in 1855.

Rough and Ready, Nevada Co.

Rothrock Camp [Plumas]. On Nelson Creek in 1851. It is mentioned as a failure by Lecouvreur (pp. 241 f.).

Rough and Ready. The nickname of General (later President) Zachary Taylor was extremely popular after the Mexican War, and several camps and mines bore the name.

Rough and Ready [Nevada]. About seven miles southwest of Nevada City. The settlement was started in the fall of 1849 by the Rough and Ready Mining Company, formed in Shellsburg, Wisconsin, and headed by Captain A. A. Townsend, who had served under Taylor in the Mexican War. It is shown on Milleson & Adams' map, 1851. The diggings on the twelve-mile-long alluvial ledge from Buena Vista Ranch to Rough and Ready proved to be extremely rich. Townsend and his brothers took out 40 thousand dollars before the water failed in the spring of 1850 (Bean, p. 359). One thousand votes were cast in the election of 1850, and the people could indulge in the Don Quixotic idea of establishing an independent republic of Rough and Ready. A mile-long ditch from Deer Creek brought water to the diggings, according to Vischer (p. 237) in August, 1850, but probably later. The post office was established July 25, 1851. A few years of prosperity followed until the placers were exhausted. In 1855 a stamp mill was built, but only a little quartz was mined (Hittell Clippings, p. 74). In 1857 hydraulic mining was tried, but the supply of water was insufficient. Yet, in spite of the rapid decline, one of the claims sold three-fifths of its interest for 30 thousand dollars cash (*Transactions*, 1860, p. 85), and as late as February, 1861, a nugget of forty-five and a half ounces was exhibited in Delano's Bank. Bean lists 300 residents at Rough and Ready in 1867 (*Bean's History*, 1867). His account of the early history of the town (pp. 353 ff.) is the most detailed, though not entirely accurate. An account of later mining in the area is given in *Mining Bureau*, XVI (pp. 54 ff.). A brief resumé of the mining in Rough and Ready district from the Gold Rush era to the present day is found in *Bulletin*, 193, (p. 113). — In 1851 Charles and Arthur Nahl, the well-known artists, mined here, but they soon discovered that in the days before commercial photography, portrait painting was more lucrative than digging for gold. Another artist, William H. Folsom, later the builder of the Mormon Temple in Salt Lake City, mined here in the spring of 1850. Bret Harte's "The Millionaire of Rough and Ready" has nothing to do with the place except the name. The town is Historic Landmark 294.

Rough and Ready [Placer]. One mile east of

Forest Hill. No early mining records were found. The channel was probably exhausted in the early twentieth century, but a mine is listed in the reports of the Mining Bureau until 1936.

Rough and Ready [Sierra]. Shown as a camp or a mine on Jamison Creek, tributary to the Middle Fork of Feather River, on Goddard's map, 1857.

Rough and Ready [Siskiyou]. *See* Etna: Mills, Bar, Creek.

Rough and Ready [Tuolumne]. On Rough and Ready Creek, a branch of Tuolumne River, above Jacksonville. It is mentioned by Heckendorn in 1856 (p. 104) and recorded on Goddard's map, 1857. It is mentioned as "rich" in *Mines and Minerals* (p. 358) and by Browne (p. 41), who stated that not less than 200 thousand dollars were taken out by 1867. The creek is mentioned by Dexter in "The Major's Plum Puding." It is shown on the USGS Sonora 1939 quadrangle.

Rough and Ready Bar [Amador]. A camp on the north side of Mokelumne River, east of Mokelumne Hill, is shown on Trask's map, 1853.

Round Bar [Siskiyou]. On the east side of Klamath River, two miles east of Oak Bar. Listed in Giffen's file.

Round Tent Diggings [Nevada or Yuba]. On a branch of Dry Creek, near the county line. Shown on Trask's map (1853), Wescoatt's (1861), and the Yuba County Map (1879). In 1851 there was considerable surface mining, and the tent was built for a hotel by a man named Baker (Yuba Co. Hist., 1879, p. 79). Successful mining was reported in February, 1854 (Hittell Clippings, p. 25). The place is also mentioned in *Bean's History* (p. 353).

Round Valley [Mendocino]. In the northern part of the county. The meager gold output of the county was given a boost when the Marysville *Daily Appeal*, April 12, 1863, reported that "exceedingly rich" gold deposits had been discovered in the mountains east of Round Valley. Like other "lost mines," this one could not be found again (Bancroft Notes).

Round Valley [Plumas]. In the North Canyon, two miles from Greenville. An item in the *Mining Press*, December 14, 1861, tells of rich ledges which brought considerable activity in 1861. The *Annual Mining Review*, 1876 (p. 23), reports that there was a steam-driven mill there in 1862. By 1863 the camp was deserted, but after the completion of a third dam the following year, quartz mining was resumed and con-

tinued into the 1870s (J. J. Peel and A. R. Bidwell in Plumas County Historical Society *Publication*, no. 4, pp. 2, 4 ff.).

Rowdy Bar [Trinity]. On Trinity River, between Taylor Flat and Cedar Flat. The bar is mentioned by Cox (p. 83) in 1858.

Royal Mine [Calaveras]. *See* Hodson District.

Rubicon River District [Placer]. The South Fork of the Middle Fork of American River became known as Rubicon River. It is listed as a placer mining area in *Mining Bureau*, XXX (p. 243). Rubicon mines are still mentioned in 1955 in volume LII (p. 431). Rubicon River is shown on the USGS Placerville 1931 quadrangle.

Ruby Mine [Sierra]. Two and a half miles from Forest City, on the ridge above Goodyears Bar, in Alleghany District. It is a drift mine, located in 1865. There are three different channels, one of which is a lava boulder channel, where the lava capping is 800 feet over four feet of gravel (*Mining Bureau*, XI, p. 406). The mine is known for the 123 nuggets found here, each valued at more than one thousand dollars. The largest weighed more than fifty-two ounces and was worth 1,758 dollars. It is one of the three largest producers in the district, having yielded more than one million dollars (*Bull.*, 193, pp. 23, 24). Shown on the USGS Downieville 1951 quadrangle.

Ruch Creek [Trinity]. A tributary to the Hayfork of Trinity River. The stream with gold diggings was named after Ruch's ranch in 1852. The ranch was later sold to John Carr (Cox, p. 110).

Rum Blossom: Camp, Plain [Tuolumne]. The camp is listed in the Work Projects Administration project, and Rum Blossom Plain is listed as a town by Hutchings in 1855.

Rum Hollow [Mariposa]. Four and a half miles from Hornitos. It is mentioned by Hutchings in his diary, July 20, 1855.

Rush Creek [Butte]. *See* Brush Creek.

Rush Creek [Nevada]. A tributary to the South Fork of Yuba River, west of Nevada City. It is mentioned in the steamer edition of the *Alta*, March 6, 1853. In the spring of 1853 the miners averaged fifteen dollars a day to the hand. It is listed as a settlement in *Bean's Directory*, 1867. According to Bancroft, VI (p. 357), it was credited with a yield of three million dollars. Rush Creek is sometimes confused with Brush Creek, another tributary to the South Fork of the Yuba, northwest of Nevada City. Both creeks are shown on the USGS Smartsville 1943 quadrangle. *See* Brush Creek [Nevada].

Rush Creek [Trinity]. A tributary to Trinity River, east of Weaverville. Cox (pp. 27 ff.) gives a good account of the 1850s. According to Raymond, VI (p. 153), the creek was soon clogged up with tailings. About 1900 the gravels of the creek six miles northwest of Lewiston were worked by sluicing and later were hydraulicked. There was still activity in 1932 (*Mining Bureau*, XXIX, pp. 69 ff.).

Russ Diggings [Placer or El Dorado]. Somewhere on the Middle Fork of American River. In the fall of 1848, Adolph Gustav Russ and his father, Emanuel, both well-known San Francisco pioneers, mined here and took out four pounds of gold in a few hours, according to the Russ manuscript (p. 5).

Russ District [Inyo]. North of Owens Lake. In April, 1860, Colonel H. P. Russ of San Francisco organized the district when it was in Tulare County. The *Mining Press* July 6, 1861, reports rich silver but only sporadic gold production, and a map in the December 21st issue shows the region as a silver mining district. However, the statistics in *Mining Bureau*, II (part 1, p. 177) for 1879–80, show that the value of gold production surpassed that of silver. The largest source of gold was the Reward or Brown Monster group. *See* Reward.

Russell: Hill, Gulch, Diggings [Amador]. Russell Gulch is a tributary to South Dry Creek. Shown on the County Map, 1866. Bowen prospected on Russels (!) Hill and found the diggings profitable (Diary, November 11, 1854, December 11, 1855). Russells Diggings was an election precinct (Co. Hist., 1881, p. 79).

Russells Bar [El Dorado]. *See* Sailors Bar, below Johnsons Bar.

Russian Bar [Placer]. On the North Fork of American River. The bar is mentioned as the boundary to a claim recorded January 8, 1855, in Placer County Records, I (p. 275).

Russian Hill [San Francisco]. In the city of San Francisco. Mining claims were once staked off on Russian Hill after a Mr. McMurty found gold while digging his cellar, November 2, 1860 (*CHSQ*, XXXVIII, p. 339).

Russian River District [Sonoma]. Near the Fitch Ranch, in the vicinity of present day Healdsburg. The *Alta*, April 2, 6, 7, 1854, and other newspapers reported that gold was washed along the River, apparently mainly on Arroyo Seco on the eastern side

of the River and Sulphur Creek on the northern side, and paid three to five dollars per day to the hand. One particularly optimistic report in an unidentified newspaper (Hittell Clippings, p. 57) tells of the excitement caused for some time in the town of Petaluma, where merchants were busy outfitting the wagons of hundreds who were leaving the area to make the journey to the river to seek their fortune.

Russianville [Siskiyou]. At the junction of the Little North Fork with the North Fork of Salmon River, four miles downstream from Sawyers Bar. A colony of Russians mined here in the 1850s near a covered bridge, according to Kramer Adams in his *Covered Bridges of the West* (pp. 132, 139). Russianville school is shown on the USGS Sawyers Bar 1945 quadrangle.

Russville [Sacramento]. *See* Ashland.

Ruth Pierce Mine [Mariposa]. *See* Hornitos.

Sacets Gulch [Sierra]. In the Slate Creek Basin, east of La Porte. It is shown on the County Map, 1874, and is mentioned as Sackets Gulch in 1872 in Raymond, V (p. 81).

Sacramento. The chief city of the Gold Rush had a number of gold discoveries within the city limits. However, they were only hidden and forgotten deposits. The first excitement was in August, 1853, when the newspapers after August 10 spread the news, some believing that auriferous native gold had actually been discovered. According to the *State Tribune* in 1855, 700 dollars worth of gold was taken out in one day when the high water in the river had caused a cave-in. It was obviously a cache; a pair of trousers and a huge bowie knife were found at the same place (Hittell Clippings, p. 62). On August 8, 1860, another excitement was caused, when boys swimming in the river at the foot of M Street discovered several large gold nuggets (*CHSQ*, XXXVIII, pp. 337 f.).

Sacramento Bar [Sacramento]. On a branch of the American River Ditch, inside the bend of the American River, opposite Buffalo Creek. The bar is mentioned in the County History, 1880 (p. 229).

Sacramento District [San Bernardino]. In the Sacramento Mountains, about twelve miles west of Needles. Shown on the County Map, 1892.

Sageland [Kern]. In Kelso Canyon region, southeast of Lake Isabella. The place had a 10-stamp steam-driven mill, built in 1869 and another in 1872 (*Annual Mining Review*, 1876, pp. 21, 23).

Sailor. Sea-faring men, mostly deserters from ships in the San Francisco harbor, formed a sizeable portion of the early miners and left their traces in numerous names.

Sailor Bar [Plumas]. On the Middle Fork of Feather River, south of Quincy. Recorded on Trask's 1853 map, and as Sailors Bar on Goddard's 1857 map.

Sailor Bar [Sacramento]. On the American River, about one and a half miles below Mississippi Bar. Shown on Doolittle's map, 1868. It is frequently mentioned in old newspaper clippings. Around 1900 there was considerable dredging. Shown on the USGS Folsom 1944 quadrangle.

Sailor Bar [Yuba]. On the North Fork of Yuba River, between Elbow and Willow bars. Shown on Doolittle's map, 1868.

Sailor Boy Diggings [Sierra]. Near Brandy City. No early reports could be discovered, but there is a detailed description of hydraulic mining at the end of the twentieth century in *Mining Bureau*, XII (p. 273), and a mine is listed until 1942.

Sailor Boys Ravine [El Dorado]. One and a half miles from Placerville, on the trail to the American River. According to Haskins (pp. 162 f.), four Jack Tars, deserters from San Francisco, dug a hole on a hill down to bedrock and found "color," to the astonishment of the old timers. They made 20 thousand dollars in three months and departed.

Sailor Canyon [Placer]. East and north of Canada Hill. The canyon enters the North Fork of American River just west of Snow Mountain and opposite Granite Creek. There was gold-bearing gravel in the Sterret claim and farther down the canyon, below Oak Flat. Goodrich mentions the Sterret claim in 1871, stating that the gold found there was coarse in the bed rock but fine in the gravel above (Whitney, *Auriferous Gravels*, p. 114). The Sailor Canyon Drift Mine was reported active in the late 1880s and in the 1890s. In 1889–1890 a long bedrock tunnel was being driven to tap the channel, and by 1894–1896 it reached the gravel (*Mining Bureau*, X, p. 426; XIII, p. 285; XV, p. 372). There was also lode mining in the canyon. The Trinidad Mine, which had a 10-stamp mill, is described in *Mining Bureau*, XV (p. 343) and XXXII (p. 27). Sailor Canyon is shown on the USGS Granite Chief 1953 quadrangle. — The canyon is a noted fossil locality in which

early Jurassic and late Triassic marine fossils were found (Gianella).

Sailor Claim [Sierra]. Near Downieville. The *Alta* of September 9, 1852, reprints an item from the Downieville *Echo* which claims that eight men took out 615.5 ounces of gold in four days of labor.

Sailor Creek [El Dorado]. Shown on Bowman's map, 1873, as a tributary to Irish Creek.

Sailor Flat [El Dorado]. South of Johntown, above Irish Creek. Shown on Bowman's map, 1873. Stephen Wing prospected here without success in August, 1855 (Journal, II, p. 50).

Sailor Flat [Nevada]. Mentioned in *Bean's Directory* as a mining camp in Little York Township. It is shown on Doolittle's map, 1868, about a mile northeast of Quaker Hill, on the Great Gravel Deposit. The County Map, 1880, lists a placer mine at a location to the northwest, near Blue Tent. Pettee, in 1879, locates this mine east of Blue Tent, near the forks of Sailor Flat and Last Chance ravines, and describes the character of gravel and the extent of hydraulic mining at that time (Whitney, *Auriferous Gravels*, pp. 412 ff.).

Sailor Flat [Nevada]. Eight and a half miles above Nevada City. There was a deep channel, the bottom of which was never reached, according to *Bean's Directory*, 1867 (p. 132). It was believed to be a continuation of Scotch Flat channel.

Sailor Gulch [Calaveras]. Near the Middle Fork of Mokelumne River. It is mentioned in the *Alta*, March 13, 1854, in connection with building the Bunker Hill Canal from Mokelumne River.

Sailors Bar [El Dorado]. On the South Fork of American River, about four miles above Mormon Island. It is mentioned in the El Dorado County Records, Mining Locations, Book I (p. 46).

Sailors Bar [El Dorado]. Also called Russells Bar. On the South Fork of American River, below Johnsons Bar. It is mentioned in the El Dorado County Records, Mining Locations, Book I (p. 28). Johnsons Bar may have been near Dutch Bar at the point where C. Johnson and Company had a claim (*ibid.*, p. 66).

Sailors Bar [El Dorado]. On the South Fork of American River, about eight miles above Coloma. It is mentioned in the El Dorado County Records, Mining Locations, Book I (p. 172).

Sailors Bar [Placer]. On the north side of the Middle Fork of American River, opposite New York Bar. The bar is mentioned by

St. Louis, Sierra Co.

Coy (p. 37). It is apparently at or near Sailors Canyon on the Middle Fork.

Sailors Canyon [Placer]. On the Middle Fork of American River, near the junction with the North Fork. In 1850 the miners of this camp joined with those of Murderers Bar across the river and built a large flume. According to the El Dorado County History, 1883 (p. 83), it was swept away in September after the last nail had been driven.

Sailors Claim [El Dorado]. On the Middle Fork of American River, near Drunkers (Drunkards?) Bar. It is mentioned in the El Dorado County Records, June 9, 1852, Record Book A (pp. 548 f.).

Sailors Flat [Nevada]. *See* Newtown.

Sailors Ravine [Placer]. Northwest of Ophir. Shown on Doolittle's map, 1868. Stephen Wing prospected here without success, according to an entry in his journal, January 24, 1853.

Sailors Ravine [Sierra]. Tributary to the Middle Fork of North Fork of Yuba River. Shown on the County Map, 1874, and on the USGS Downieville 1907 quadrangle.

Sailors Slide [El Dorado]. *See* Oregon: Ravine, Canyon.

Saint Clairs Flat [Butte]. An otherwise unidentified flat opposite Oroville, mentioned in the *Mining Press*, February 1, 1862.

Saint Helena [Napa]. In the Napa Valley, between Yountville and Calistoga. About 1870, quartz veins were discovered on the mountain. The average assay was twenty-five dollars gold and twelve dollars silver per ton (Raymond, VI, p. 65). Some mining was done but it seems to have petered out soon.

St. Joe Bar [Sierra]. On Ramshorn Creek, about two miles west of Goodyears Bar. Shown on Trask's map, 1853. It is mentioned by Downie (p. 133) and in the County History, 1882 (p. 466). The diggings were reported as well paying in 1850. Later the place was known as Ramshorn Bar. (Sinnott, *Sierra City*, pp. 153, 157).

Saint Lawrenceville [El Dorado]. Near Greenwood. Shown on Bowman's map, 1873. Seam mining began in the 1850s. The rich deposits proved to be very easy to work because of the softness of the soil. The principal work was on the vein intersecting the Nagler or French Claim vein (Raymond, VII, pp. 77, 84 ff.). A Saint Lawrence Mine, one and a half miles southeast of Garden Valley, is listed by the Mining Bureau until 1956. It was active between 1867 and 1878, reaching a production figure of 465 thousand dollars. (*Mining Bureau*, LII, p. 530.) According to the 1898 *Souvenir Mountain Democrat* (p. 22), it had produced 2 million dollars when 500 feet was reached, and then the ledge disappeared.

St. Louis [Nevada]. East of Nevada City. The mill is mentioned in *Bean's Directory*, 1867 (p. 385), and a consolidated mine is listed by the Mining Bureau until 1941.

St. Louis [Sierra]. On a tributary to Slate Creek; on the road between La Porte and

Howland Flat. Shown on Trask's map, 1853, and on Goddard's, 1857. It was a rich mining town which started in the early 1850s. According to San Francisco *Whig and Commercial Advertiser*, June 11, 1853, St. Louis diggings were rich, with fifty houses in the camp and 100 or more on the flat (extract in Bancroft Notes). The post office was established in 1855. Henry Cohn had a store here, 1855–1863, and gives a good account in his *Jugenderinnerungen*. In 1859 Hendel and Company blasted a 6,000-foot tunnel into the hillside and hydraulic mining prevailed (Vischer, p. 241). The Committee of the Agricultural Society was so impressed by finding a two story building so high in the mountains that they proposed a silver medal for the express company of Everts, Wilson & Co. (*Transactions*, 1858, p. 199). In 1868 there were ten or twelve hydraulic companies at work (Browne, p. 138). The region is described in *Mining Bureau*, XVI (Sierra, pp. 19 ff.).

Salada [Tuolumne]. Near Chinese Camp. The place is mentioned in newspaper clippings, but no mining record was found. It is probably a misspelling of Salvado in Camp Salvado.

Salambo Flat [Tuolumne]. In the southwest part of the county, near the Mariposa County line. It is listed in the Work Projects Administration project, and it supposedly was once a settlement of 400 people. The Salambo Mine is listed in *Mining Bureau*, XXIV (p. 7).

Saleratus Ranch [Nevada]. On Rock Creek, north of Nevada City. It is mentioned by Canfield (p. 81) in his account of the early 1850s, and is shown on his map. Saleratus is potassium bicarbonate used by the miners as baking soda.

Salmon Falls [El Dorado]. On the South Fork of American River, a few miles from the junction with Middle Fork; now partly under Folsom Lake. Shown on Gibbes' map, 1851, and most other early maps. It was one of the earliest successful gold camps, probably discovered by Mormons from Sutter's grist mill before July, 1848. Daniel B. Woods, an educated Philadelphian, started mining here July 4, 1849. He was induced by the success of the two Jordan brothers, who had made 3 thousand dollars within a few weeks. Woods made only 390 dollars in three months, but he witnessed two Irishmen take out 422 dollars of fine scale gold in a vein of hard clay. He gives a good account of the summer of 1849 (pp. 49 ff.). A part

of the Connecticut Company mined here, apparently without success, in the fall of the same year (Lyman, September 30, 1849). Rich diggings were found around New Year, 1851. The steamer edition of the Sacramento *Transcript*, February 1, 1851, and other newspapers gave glowing accounts of the event. The population jumped to 3,000, and a post office was established October 7, 1851. In 1853 a canal was built from the Falls, providing water for many of the diggings which are now covered by Folsom Lake. Additional information is given in the County History, 1883 (pp. 202 f.). Historic Landmark 571.

Salmon Mountain [Siskiyou]. At the boundary of Siskiyou and Humboldt counties. There was both placer and underground mining here, and there were also a few small pockets (W. M. Smith). A company of eight or ten were reported to have dug for gold on the summit with satisfactory results (undated clipping from the *Shasta Courier*, 1855, in Hittell Clippings, p. 62). Shown on the USGS Sawyers Bar 1945 quadrangle. Etna Mountain, between Etna and the Salmon River country, is erroneously called Salmon Mountain locally.

Salmon River Diggings [Siskiyou]. The numerous diggings along the stream are shown on Butler's map, 1851. The Sacramento *Transcript* (steamer ed., pp. 5 and 8) reports, February 28, 1851, that new diggings were discovered at the head of Salmon River and east of it. The average earnings were twenty-four dollars a day to the man, and four prospectors got 1,840 dollars in one day. The event caused a minor rush (Bancroft Notes). In *Bulletin*, 193 (p. 134), it is stated that between 3,000 and 5,000 men had reportedly worked the Salmon River by means of flumes and wingdams, but the date is not indicated. Probably the richest part of the river was between Sawyers Bar and Forks of Salmon, a distance of seventeen miles, which had an estimated gold production of 25 million dollars. A general resumé of mining activities along the river is given in *Bulletin*, 193, and a detailed description of mining in 1892 is found in *Mining Bureau*, XI (pp. 432 ff.). *See also* the accounts in *Siskiyou Pioneer*, II:10.

Salomons Hill [Sierra]. In the Slate Creek Basin. It is in the placer district south of Chandlerville, and is shown on Raymond's map of Slate Creek Basin, Northern Part, in volume V (opposite p. 88).

Salt Pork Ridge [Shasta]. Three miles north of Shasta. Hutchings lists it as a town in 1855. It is mentioned by T. Starr King in an undated clipping (1860?) from the Nevada *Democrat*, in Hayes Scrapbooks: Mining (I, sec. 65).

Salt Springs [San Bernardino]. On Salt Creek, near the Amargosa River, thirty miles north of Baker. It was an important stop on the Santa Fe-Salt Lake Trail and the site of one of the earliest gold discoveries in California. L. Burr Belden wrote several detailed and informative articles in the San Bernardino *Sun-Telegram*, December 7, 1958, June 12, 1960, and January 5, 1964. He quotes an article by Von Blon in *Desert Magazine*, according to which horsemen of a Santa Fe trade caravan en route to Los Angeles panned gold here between 1826 and 1830. Whatever the truth may be, gold was seen here on December 1, 1849 by a Mr. Rowan and other members of a party led by Jefferson Hunt (Addison Pratt "Diary," p. 96; James S. Brown "Account," p. 124). David W. Cheesman reported that his party passed here, and at the Mojave River they met William T. B. Sanford hauling a mill to the Salt Springs mines in December, 1850 (Cheesman, pp. 296, 301). It is probably the place where in 1850 Frank Soulé, later editor of the *Alta* and a state senator, found the gold deposits, took samples, and organized a company in San Francisco that failed to develop (Miscellaneous Statements, pp. 42 f.). Raymond, III (pp. 14 f.) refers to the district as the Amargosa district, and the mines are shown as Amargosa Mines on H. H. Bancroft's Map of the Colorado Mines, 1863. Raymond states that gold was found in the general area in 1856, but the owners were forced to abandon the property to the Indians. In 1863 it was relocated and worked with success for more than a year. One surface pocket yielded 11 thousand dollars, and the average ore yield was estimated at eighteen to twenty dollars per ton. Raymond found the mines deserted in 1870. About 1865 it was reported in the Los Angeles *News* (Bancroft Scraps, LI:1, p. 212) that there was rich mining at Salt Springs, and a shipment of ore to Los Angeles was expected to yield 600 to one thousand dollars (per ton?). Though gold was plentiful, a succession of commercial mining ventures failed because of the remote location and the repeated attacks by the Piute Indians in the 1850s and 1860s. Operations have continued intermittently on a relatively small scale to the present times (Haenszel).

Salt Spring Valley [Calaveras]. Between Bear Mountains on the east and Gopher Ridge on the west, in the southwest part of the county, in the Hodson area. A gold belt extends from the vicinity of Copperopolis through Salt Spring Valley in a northwesterly direction to the region near Valley Springs. The geology of the area is described in *Mining Bureau*, XIII (pp. 118 f.). Shown on the USGS Jackson 1938 quadrangle.

Salvada [Tuolumne]. *See* Camp Salvado.

Salyer [Trinity]. On the Trinity River, about one and a half miles from the confluence of the South Fork of the Trinity. There was active mining in the area as early as the 1850s. When a post office was established in 1918, it was given the name of a prominent mining man, Charles Marshall Salyer (*California Place Names*).

Samaroo [Placer]. *See* Tamaroo Bar.

Sam Flat [Plumas]. An unidentified place near La Porte, listed by Coy (p. 74).

Sampsons Flat [Fresno]. In the foothills of the Sierra Nevada. There was placer mining in the early days. The claims are mentioned in *Mining Bureau*, XIV (pp. 441, 443). From the 1880s to about 1915 there was lode mining in the district (*Bull.*, 193, pp. 113 f.).

San Andreas, Calaveras Co.

San Andreas [Calaveras]. On the ancient channel of Mokelumne River. Shown on Butler's map, 1851, and most other contemporary maps. It was settled and named by Spanish Californians in 1848

(*Guidebook*, p. 61) and was an important gold mining center with an interesting history. In April, 1851, the French miners at Les Fourcades (Mokelumne Hill), after a fight with Irish miners there, retreated to San Andreas, where they defiantly raised the tricolor, which fluttered until the French consul came from San Francisco and restored order and they returned to their claims in Mokelumne Hill (Nasatir, in *CHSQ*, XXXV, pp. 317 ff.). Lucius Fairchild in a letter of December 24, 1850, had already complained bitterly about the many military organized French in the town. Murders and deprecations, which were numerous in the early 1850s, were credited to Murieta (Ridge, p. 110); indeed, according to Joseph Henry Jackson in *Anybody's Gold* (p. 354), the legendary Joaquin started his career here. Good descriptions of the rich camp are given by Borthwick (pp. 313 ff.) in the spring of 1853 and by Pringle Shaw in 1855. November 14, 1854, the post office was transferred from Third Crossing, and in 1855 it was the seat of the Pope's Ditch and the Union canal companies (Hittell Clippings, p. 48). In 1859 there were 1,000 inhabitants and two newspapers (*Transactions*, 1859, p. 84 — spelled Andres here). As late as 1867, the claims on the San Andreas Channel paid richly; The Plug Ugly Company made 11 hundred dollars in one day, and Marshall and Showalter took out nine pounds in one forenoon (Browne, pp. 53 ff.). The production came mainly from placer mining, but in 1873 there was a 10-stamp water-driven quartz mill (*Annual Mining Review*, 1876, p. 23). Mining activity in the San Andreas District is briefly reviewed in *Bulletin*, 193 (p. 114), tracing its development from the 1850s to the 1930s. Hydraulic and drift mining predominated from the 1850s through the 1880s, and some drifting has continued to recent years. Lode mining began in the 1870s, continued to the turn of the century, and was revived again in the 1930s.

San Antonio [Calaveras]. Ten miles east of Fourth Crossing; on San Antonio Creek, a tributary to the South Fork of Calaveras River. Recorded on Gibbes' map, 1851, as S. Antonia; on Trask's map, 1853, as Antoine. It was also known as San Antone, and the local name today is San Antone Camp. It was probably a Mexican camp dating from 1848 or 1849. In 1857 it was the seat of the San Antonio Ridge Canal Company (Hittell Clippings, p. 48). In 1853 and again a year or two later Hersey

Dexter mined in a camp near by; in chapters II, III, IV, and VIII of his book he tells from memory some delightful stories. The deposits were nearly exhausted in 1867 (Browne, p. 58). The San Antonio (or Lindsay) Mine, listed in the Mining Bureau reports until 1935, is farther south, between Altaville and Angels Camp.

San Antonio [Monterey]. Placer gold was discovered near the Mission in 1850, and in 1854 some Mexicans washed here with bateas (Trask, 1854, p. 58). According to an unidentified clipping in Hittell Clippings (p. 61), the Mexican miners here made three to five dollars a day. They said little about the diggings, but S. Regensburger, the storekeeper, informed the editor (of the *Alta California*?) that the Mexicans paid with gold in his store. The editor warned against excitement, advising that some experienced American miners examine the place. He told his readers that he had heard in 1850 that the Indians had found gold when the foundation for the mission was excavated in the previous century (1771), but that the padres had made them keep it a secret, threatening malediction. Small quantities of gold were mined in later years in the Santa Lucia Mountains, near the mission (Co. Hist., 1881, p. 95).

San Antonio Canyon [San Bernardino]. In the San Gabriel Mountains, north of Upland. Gold was discovered in a gulch near the head of the canyon in 1866 by a man named Banks. Soon afterward around 400 miners were mining farther down the canyon, below the Hogsback, according to the reminiscence of a pioneer. For thirty years miners worked the stream and its tributaries on the east side, but mud fouled the water supply for Ontario, and practically all mining activity was stopped, when the San Antonio Water Company served an injunction. *See* Mount Baldy District. In 1899 a quartz mill was hauled with extreme difficulty to the Gold Ridge Mine via Lytle Creek, but its use proved unprofitable. Glyde Maynard has given an account of mining in the region in *Pomona Valley Historian*, I (pp. 36 ff.).

San Bruno [Calaveras]. Near San Andreas. The Mosquito Mine in the vicinity was started by Mexicans about 1855; the mill first used mule-driven arrastres; later fifteen stamps were in operation. In the 1870s the nearby Bismarck Mine produced 100 to 125 dollars per ton (Raymond, VII, pp. 63 f.).

San Carlos [Inyo]. *See* Bend City.

Sand Flat [Yuba]. On the main Yuba River, south of Ousleys Bar. Shown on Wescoatt's map, 1861, and on the County Map of 1879. Hutchings states in his Diary, September 26, 1855, that miners were doing moderately well at Ousley Bar and Sand Hill Diggings below it, and that the population of the two places was about 300, mainly German, Spanish, and French. According to the County History, 1879 (p. 76), the diggings were said to have been rich, and still a little mining was done in 1879.

Sand Flats [Shasta]. Five miles east of the Sacramento River, near Buckeye. The old gold diggings were still holding their own in the spring of 1864, according to an unidentified clipping in Hayes Scrapbooks: Mining (IV, sec. 5).

Sand Hat [Yuba]. *See* Timbuctoo.

Sand Hill Bar [Yuba]. Near Timbuctoo. It is mentioned in the *Mining Press*, June 9, 1862. According to the County History, 1879 (p. 84), there were rich surface diggings in 1850, and later there was rich hydraulic mining.

San Diego, Santa Iago, Santa Ioga [Tuolumne]. San Diego is shown on Wallace's map, 1853, as a settlement less than a mile southeast of Columbia. It is the same place as Santa Ioga. Stoddart (pp. 115 f.) mistakenly locates it one mile northeast of the site of Columbia. He states that in the fall of 1849, before the Americans discovered gold at Columbia, some Mexicans were prospecting what was called the Main Gulch of that town, and finding a good prospect, they decided to camp in that locality. Stephen Davis mentions the camp on May 2, 1852. The best pay dirt was always four to six feet beneath the surface although some was taken at a depth of ninety feet (San Francisco *Evening News*, December 14, 1853). The newspapers of the day were filled with reports of rich finds. One company took out a lump weighing four and a half pounds, valued at 950 dollars (*Alta*, May 18, 1854). Green and Savage at the mouth of Santiago Gulch averaged about sixteen dollars a day to the man (Columbia *Gazette*, June 24, 1854). Riley and Mapes took out two and a quarter pounds one day (*San Joaquin Republican*, May 22, 1855). Kane's claim averaged ten dollars per day for most of the season (Columbia *Courier*, April 27, 1867). On February 16, 1878, the San Jose *Pioneer* reported that a gambler picked up a lump of gold worth 10 thousand dollars in an abandoned claim of 1854. San Diego Reservoir is situated on the campus of Columbia Junior College, southeast of Columbia. Santiago Hill, called Bell Hill since about 1918, northwest of the Reservoir is shown on the USGS Columbia 1948 quadrangle. It is the site of a marble quarry. Stoddart mentions another Santiago, called Flat of Santa Ioga, near Jamestown, from which Mexican miners moved to Sonora after some difficulty with the Americans. De Ferrari locates this place above Peppermint Creek, on the north side of Woods Creek at Jamestown.

San Domingo [Calaveras]. On San Domingo Creek, a tributary to the South Fork of Calaveras River. It is listed as a small camp in 1856 by Heckendorn (p. 99). From 1863 to 1867 four men took out of the limestone 100 thousand dollars (Browne, p. 58). Browne makes the incredible statement (p. 70) that a ton of limestone yielded 15 hundred dollars of gold, but the deposits were soon exhausted. A San Domingo Mine, three miles northeast of Altaville, which was hydraulicked "in the old days," was reactivated in the 1930s (*Mining Bureau*, XXXII, p. 350). The Creek is shown on the USGS Big Trees 1941 and Jackson 1938 quadrangles.

Sandusky Hill [El Dorado]. Near Coloma. The place is mentioned February 14, 1858, by Stephen Wing in his Journal, III (p. 99). He examined a claim for sale "but did not like the appearance of things."

Sandy Bar [Calaveras]. On the Mokelumne River, three miles above Big Bar. Shown on the Amador County map, 1866. Browne (p. 51) states that seven Frenchmen took out 107 pounds of gold in two days (!).

Sandy Bar [El Dorado]. On the Middle Fork of American River; north of Georgetown, above Volcano Bar. Recorded on Trask's map, 1853, and on Goddard's, 1857. It is mentioned in the *Alta*, April 25, 1852 (Bancroft Scraps, LI:1, p. 252). Carlisle Abbott (pp. 101 ff.) tells from memory an interesting story about the place. The Sandy Bar, between Grey Eagle and Volcano Bar, mentioned in the County History, 1883, is probably the same site. Bret Harte used this name (or that of another Sandy Bar) for his story "The Iliad of Sandy Bar."

Sandy Bar [Trinity]. On Trinity River, six miles below Taylor Flat, mentioned in 1858 by Cox (p. 82). A hydraulic mine was in operation in 1896 (*Mining Bureau*, XIII, p. 461).

Sandy Gulch [Calaveras]. A camp near the Mokelumne River, about three miles south, or southwest, of West Point. It is shown on Camp's map on a tributary to the Middle Fork of Mokelumne River, midway between the South and Middle forks. According to *Historical Landmarks*, it was a trading center in 1849 for mining camps in the area. Ben Bowen mentions the place on August 27, 1855. A canal was built in 1854 to bring water from the Mokelumne River to the rich deposits of the gulch and its tributaries, according to the *Alta*, March 13, 1854. In 1860 there was a water-driven 10-stamp mill in operation (*Annual Mining Review*, 1876, p. 22). Historic Landmark 253.

San Feliciano Canyon [Los Angeles]. A branch of Piru Creek, tributary to Santa Clara River, about twelve miles northwest of Newhall. It is shown on a sketch map in *Mining Bureau*, IX (p. 201) as S. Feliciana. The name is sometimes spelled Felicia. The date of discovery of gold here has not been definitely established, but it was probably soon after Francisco Lopez made his discovery in what became known as Placerita Canyon in 1842. J. N. Bowman in his reliable account indicates that San Feliciano or Santa Feliciana Canyon apparently became the "great center of activity" following the discovery at Placerita Canyon (*HSSCQ*, XXXI, p. 229), but he does not indicate the exact date. Arthur B. Perkins gives an account, basing it on various sources, some of which are doubtful (*HSSCQ*, XL, pp. 154 f.). Placering was renewed after the discovery at Sutters Mill. One Francisco Garcia took out 65 thousand dollars worth of gold in one season in the year 1854, according to *Mining Bureau*, VIII (p. 534). *See* San Fernando Placers; Placerita Creek.

San Felipe Canyon [San Diego]. Three miles from the center of the Julian Banner District. The Ready Relief Group and the Golden Chariot were the two most productive mines in the district. Both were located in 1870 and operated profitably until about 1875, but later attempts brought only small returns. Detailed descriptions are given in *County Report*, III (pp. 124 ff. and 132 ff.). Accounts are also found in Ellsberg, *Mines of Julian*.

San Fernando Placers [Los Angeles]. North of San Fernando Mission, in the foothills of the San Gabriel Mountains. The first authenticated discovery of gold in what is now the State of California was made in the creeks and canyons of this region. The placers have been designated as the San Fernando Placers and are treated in this book under their respective localities. The first discovery was made in 1842 — six years before Marshall's discovery at Sutters Mill. None of the numerous reports about earlier exploitation of gold deposits by the mission priests could be verified. Unfortunately, even one of the most reliable writers, Rossiter Raymond, fell for one of the spurious, or at least unverified stories. In his seventh *Report*, 1875 (p. 40), he tells it in these words: "The discovery of gold was made in Los Angeles County, near the mission of San Fernando, as early as 1812, and in 1828 gold was shipped from the port of San Diego." This statement has, regrettably, been repeated in one form or another in numerous publications. The mint in Philadelphia has actually an entry of January 30, 1838 that 820 ounces of gold from California was being deposited there (Guy J. Giffen, *California Gold*). This was either gold from Baja California, or from elsewhere. (Gold was brought into California for trading purposes; James Lick brought gold from South America to San Francisco in 1848.) Franciscan priests, or government officials, certainly would not have shipped Mexican gold to a United States mint directly, or through an American broker. The first real, tangible evidence of gold mining here is the shipment of twenty ounces of gold to Philadelphia made by Abel Stearns on November 22, 1842. After the discovery at Sutter's Mill mining in the San Fernando Placers was naturally resumed for a number of years, mainly by Mexican miners. Hayes Scrapbooks: Mining (V) have numerous clippings from the Los Angeles *Star* and other newspapers which report moderate production. A collection of pre-Marshall, or pre-Coloma items on gold production is in Bancroft Notes, also in Emil Bunje and James Kean, "Pre-Marshall Gold in California." *See* Placerita Creek; San Francisquito; and San Feliciano Canyon.

Sanfords Ranch [Nevada]. On the Middle Fork of Yuba River. Rich diggings, apparently a branch of the Coyote Lead, were found near by early in 1853 (*Alta*, March 6, 1853).

San Francisco Beach [San Franciso]. An account of gold washing on the beaches is given in *Bulletin*, 193 (p. 180). It was carried on by means of small washing plants, mainly south of Fleischacker Zoo. The gold was usually more plentiful after heavy rains. The estimated yield between 1939 and 1941 was about 13 thousand dollars.

San Francisquito Canyon [Los Angeles]. This is one of the San Fernando Placers, where gold was mined possibly as early as 1842. Arthur B. Perkins (p. 155) gives a short description and apparently considers it different from the other placer mines, but in most other accounts it is seemingly confused with San Feliciano. The annual publications of the Mining Bureau (XI, p. 248, and later) repeat the unproven story that the padres mined here from 1834 to 1839. Hayes Scrapbooks: Mining (V) have a number of clippings showing that there was very moderate placering in the 1860s. The real tangible evidence of gold deposits is in *Mining Bureau*, XXX (pp. 247 f.), where it is reported that during the late depression in the 1930s some gold was found in the debris on the eroded banks after the failure of Saint Francis Dam.

San Gabriel: Canyon, River [Los Angeles]. According to unverified accounts in the annual reports of the Mining Bureau (XV, p. 475; XXIII, p. 291; XXX, p. 247; and various others), the priests of the San Gabriel Mission had Indians wash gold in the canyon, presumably from 1834 until the discovery at Sutter's Mill became known. The gold deposits were not discovered until 1852 (Los Angeles *Star*, May 29, 1852, *in* Hayes Scrapbooks: Mining, V, sec. 114) and were worked with variable success until modern times. In the winter of 1858–1859 the canyon was mined for a distance of forty miles, according to the report of a correspondent to the Los Angeles *Star*, May 28, 1859, and miners were taking out between two and ten dollars per day to the man. In the summer of 1859 about 300 diggings along the river were worked, according to the *Southern Vineyard*, July 22, 1859 (Hayes Scrapbooks: Mining, V, sec. 246). The Roberts and Williams Stage Line scheduled tri-weekly trips from Los Angeles to the mouth of the canyon (J. W. Robinson, p. 45). A disastrous flood in January, 1862, brought an end to the boom and destroyed the mining town of Eldoradoville. *See* Eldoradoville. An unidentified clipping marked February 10, 1864, in Hayes Scrapbooks: Mining (V, sec. 258), reports that some miners were taking out ten to fifty dollars per day to the man in abandoned claims. The Los Angeles *Star*, February 19, 1870, reports that about one hundred were again work-

ing with good prospects after no mining had been done for several years. According to the Los Angeles *Evening Express*, May 29, 1872 (summarized in the Los Angeles folder of Bancroft Notes), placering was abandoned in 1868. Hydraulic mining started in 1871 with a race between Henry C. Roberts and William Ferguson to develop flumes, and it ended in 1874 because domestic water supplies in San Gabriel Valley were being polluted (J. W. Robinson, pp. 49 ff.; HSSCQ, XXXV, pp. 120 ff.; *Mining Bureau*, L, pp. 495 f.). *See* Crab Hollow.

San Geronimo [Marin]. About eight miles west and south of San Rafael. A drift gold mine was opened in October, 1878, one half mile from the station. It is said that the yield was as high as ninety dollars per ton (Co. Hist., 1880, p. 288). It petered out, like all gold mining activities in the county.

San Jacinto [Calaveras]. Near Murphys. It is mentioned as a small camp in Heckendorn, 1856 (p. 97).

San Joaquin City [San Joaquin]. On the west side of San Joaquin River, near the mouth of Stanislaus River. Shown on Butler's map, 1851. It was established in 1849 as a trading center on the route to the Southern Mines, but by 1861 it was, according to Stoddart (p. 107), a "mere ranch." Later it apparently was revived as a terminal for river boats and contributed to the development of grain farming and cattle raising (*California Historical Landmarks*). In 1880 it still had a hotel, warehouse, saloons, stores, and homes, but today only a plaque recalls the location near the old Durham Ferry (Rensch-Hoover). Historic Landmark 777.

San Juan: Hill, Ridge [Nevada]. The hill near the town of North San Juan was named in 1853 by a prospector, a veteran of the Mexican War, after San Juan de Ulloa in Mexico. It is on the Blue Lead and the auriferous gravel was only slightly covered. The claims of the Eureka Company, which built a tunnel between 1855 and 1860, yielded more than half a million dollars (Browne, p. 120). The ridge was the chief field of activity of Newton C. Miller, who built the Middle Yuba Canal and was instrumental in building the first long distance telephone circuit, sixty miles long, within three years after Bell's invention became known. Modern placering on the ridge is described in *Bulletin*, 92 (pp. 118 ff.).

San Pascal [Calaveras]. Shown on Trask's

map of 1853 on the road between Double Springs and McKinneys. It was apparently a mining camp of short duration.

San Pedros [Tuolumne]. A. Riley in a letter datelined San Pedros-Tuolamie, March 15, 1851, reports that two thirds of the miners had left the place for the Northern Mines, presumably to join the Gold Lake hunt. The reference may be to Don Pedro or Don Pedros. (De Ferrari).

Santa Anita Placers [Los Angeles]. Gold was discovered in Big Santa Anita Canyon, about eighteen miles from Los Angeles, and the placers were worked with modest success for several years. In July, 1858, hydraulic works were installed with great fanfare by the Santa Anita Mining Company and were operated until about 1861, when miners left for the more profitable mines on the San Gabriel River. (J. W. Robinson, pp. 41 f.)

Santa Ariba Farm [Los Angeles]. Reports of rich diggings in ravines and arroyos of the farm were received by the Los Angeles *Star*, June 5, 1852, and despite the heat, prospectors were at work and washed as much as four dollars from two barrels of dirt (Hayes Scrapbooks: Mining, V, sec. 115).

Santa Catalina Island [Los Angeles]. According to J. M. Guinn, George Yount of the Wolfskill party, 1831, discovered outcroppings of gold deposits on the island but neglected to explore further. After 1848 several attempts were made to find the lost "Yount Lode." In 1863 gold and silver were actually found and the San Pedro mining district and many claims were established. After two years the rush petered out. A description by J. M. Guinn, "The Lost Mines of Santa Catalina," is reprinted from *Overland Monthly in HSSC*, IX (pp. 43 ff.). According to Harris Newmark (pp. 318 f.), the boom did not peter out, but came to an end when the federal government suspected that the gold mining activities were a cloak for an attempt of the Confederates to establish a base for privateering.

Santa Clara River [Los Angeles, Ventura]. According to the Los Angeles *Star*, August 10, (?) 1854 (Hayes Scrapbooks: Mining, VII, sec. 17), a Mexican discovered gold on the tributary of the river in Ventura County. He and a companion took out 500 dollars worth in seven days, and the average amount made was twelve dollars a day, according to a "reliable source" (!). For the Santa Clara Canyon in the upper reaches of the river in Los Angeles County, *see* San Feliciano and San Fernando.

Santa Cruz Mountain [Mariposa]. *See* Indian Gulch.

Santa Feliciana [Los Angeles]. Obviously the same as San Feliciano. It is mentioned in *Mining Bureau*, XXIII (p. 291) and elsewhere with the unproven claim that priests from San Fernando and San Buena Ventura had had placers worked from 1834 to 1838.

Santa Iago [Tuolumne]. *See* San Diego [Tuolumne].

Santa Maria Gulch [Amador]. North of Mokelumne River, an eastern tributary to Grapevine Gulch (now partially inundated by Pardee Reservoir). Andrews describes the site of the remote camp, accessible only by pack trains and saddle horses, at which the only remains are fifteen or twenty chimneys, outlines of several quadrangles indicating structures, possibly adobes, and the outline of a street (*Ghost Towns*, pp. 95 f.). The gulch is shown on the USGS Sutter Creek 1944 quadrangle.

Santa Rita Flat [Inyo]. Near Mazourka Canyon. It was named after an early mine, according to De Decker (p. 46), where it is stated that the place had been worked intermittently until recent times. After a cloud burst in July, 1894, gold nuggets in various sizes ranging in value from ten cents to ten dollars were found nearby.

Santa Ynez [Santa Barbara]. It is one of the places near which small quantities of gold were found (Co. Hist., 1883, p. 99). An unidentified clipping marked October 27, 1855, in Hayes Scrapbooks: Mining (VII, sec. 17), contains an extract from the Santa Barbara *Gazette* reporting that the miners at Santa Ynez were making six to eight dollars per day.

Santa Ysabel Mine [Tuolumne]. *See* Jamestown.

Santiago [Tuolumne]. *See* San Diego [Tuolumne].

Sarahsville [Placer]. One and a half miles northeast of Forest Hill. Gold was discovered in 1850 at this place, first called Volcano. The next year the name was changed in honor of the first lady settler in the camp. The erection of the first steam-driven quartz mill is mentioned in Trask (doc. 9, p. 64), and the place is recorded on his map, 1853. Hutchings describes it as a quiet and industrious town in 1855 (Diary, May 7, 1855). The camp is mentioned in the *State Register*, 1859 (p. 259). When the post office was established

April 19, 1858, it was called Bath because there was a post office Sarahville in Amador County. Doolittle's map, 1868, shows Bath with Sarahsville as a former or alternate name.

Sarahville [Amador]. *See* Clinton.

Saratoga [El Dorado]. *See* Yeomet.

Sardine Bar [Placer]. On the Middle Fork of American River, above American Bar, near the junction with Rubicon River. It is mentioned in the Placer County History, 1882 (pp. 401 f.) and in the El Dorado County History, 1883 (p. 84).

Sardine Bar [Trinity]. Near Douglas City. The bar was abandoned in 1852, but worked again in 1855, paying eight to ten dollars a day to the man (Cox, p. 40).

Sardine Diggings [El Dorado]. Just west of Kentucky Flat, on the north side of the second Otter Creek. James W. Marshall mined here and later at Michigan Flat, apparently in 1853. He helped in the building of a ditch about a mile long to bring water from the second Otter Creek to Sardine Flat, and the ditch became known as Marshall Ditch. (Theressa Gay, pp. 309 f.) *See* Marshall Ravine.

Sardine Ravine [Nevada]. A branch of Wilcox Ravine, tributary to Steep Hollow Creek; east of You Bet. Shown on Pettee and Bowman's map, 1879. Pettee describes the area and extent of hydraulic mining by 1870 (Whitney, *Auriferous Gravels*, p. 168).

Satans Pride. An unidentified place, mentioned as a mining camp in a poem in the *Annual Mining Review*, 1876 (p. 18).

Sattley [Sierra]. *See* Churchs Corners.

Sauerkraut Gulch [Siskiyou]. Northwest of Forks of Salmon. Hydraulic mining was apparently carried on by a Chinese Company until the end of the nineteenth century (*Register*, 1898). Sauerkraut placers are listed by the Mining Bureau until 1935. Shown on the USGS Sawyers Bar 1945 quadrangle. During World War I the name of the gulch was changed from Sauerkraut to Liberty Cabbage Gulch, but in later years the old name was restored.

Savage: Flat, Diggings [Tuolumne]. The Flat is at the head of Big Creek, southeast of Second Garrote; near the Mariposa County line. Shown on Goddard's map, 1857. James D. Savage, an immigrant of 1846 and in 1851 in charge of the Mariposa Battallion, apparently grazed his horses here. It is a large meadow, green most of the year, and now a part of the Warren Burch Ranch (De Ferrari). Savages Diggings was a term applied to both Big Oak Flat and Garrote 1, although Savage is usually associated only with the former, according to De Ferrari. The sites of various localities in Mariposa, Tuolumne, and Merced counties, where Savage traded and had his Indians dig for gold are mentioned in the literature, creating some confusion. On the modern map by Crampton, a Savage Trading Post is shown at the junction of the two forks of Merced River, and Savage Tent at the junction of Merced River and Piney Creek. Historic Landmark 527 is placed at El Portal. Savage Monument stands above Fresno River, sixteen miles east of Madera (Rensch-Hoover). Savage camps or posts are also found on Mariposa Creek south of Agua Fria and on Horseshoe Bend of Merced River. The Savage Diggings near Rattlesnake Creek, ten miles from Jacksonville, and those mentioned in the *Mining Press*, November 16, 1861, might have been named for Charles Savage, one of Sutter's men and later a resident of Jacksonville.

Saw Hill [Sierra]. In the mining district of Slate Creek, west of Potosi. It is shown on Raymond's map in Raymond, V. It may be a misspelling of Saw Mill and having nothing to do with a mining camp.

Saw Mill Bar [Yuba]. On the main Yuba River, opposite Parks Bar. The diggings were started in the summer of 1849, and a sawmill which gave the name was built the same year. In September, 1850, the Canal company is said to have taken out almost 16 thousand dollars in five days (Co. Hist., 1879, p. 84).

Sawmill Flat [Shasta]. It is mentioned in Mining Bureau, II (part 1, p. 188) as a district with very moderate gold production. The location is not indicated.

Sawmill Flat [Tuolumne]. Three miles southeast of Columbia, where two saw mills had been built to provide timbers for the mines. Shown on Wallace's map, 1853. The camp was reported as flourishing in 1854, with new buildings, stores, and cabins in every direction (San Francisco *Herald*, June 19, 1854), and wages were from three to five ounces per day (Columbia *Gazette*, June 24, 1854). Many well paying claims are listed in Barbara Eastman's notes, and rich finds are reported in the newspapers of the day. In 1854 a nugget of twenty-five ounces was found, and probably soon afterwards a company struck a vein on Bald Mountain and took out a lump of nine pounds, which yielded five pounds of pure gold (Hittell Clippings, pp. 27, 31, 32). Among other reports, the Balaklava claim took out eight ounces per day for two continuous weeks (*San Joaquin Republican*, April 27, 1855). In 1867 Browne (p. 38) stated that two claims were still working and "the diggings here will last for a long time." According to *Mines and Minerals*, the total production to 1899 was 2.5 million dollars. Heckendorn (p. 75) tells the story that Murieta had his headquarters here in 1852. He poisoned the spring and intended to attack the Ira McCrea stores, but a small army saved the situation, and Mac had to stand the drinks and the pies consumed in his bakery. It is the site of "The Battle of Sawmill Flat." Sawmill Flat is Historic Landmark 424.

Saw Pit Flat [Plumas]. At Pilot Peak, in the southern part of the county. There were several well-paying claims, but washing was possible only from April to June because of the lack of water, according to an item in Bancroft Scraps, LI:1 (p. 169). The *Mining Press*, December 29, 1866, reports that all miners were working underground, and that the claims were prospecting very well. Both placer and lode mines in the Saw Pit District are listed in *Bulletin*, 193 (p. 114). In recent years skin divers have been prospecting the Middle Fork of Feather River.

Sawpit Gulch [Tuolumne]. Between Kennebec Hill and San Diego Hill, southeast of Columbia. Shown on Dart's map, 1871. It is mentioned in the "Mining Laws of Shaws Flat" (Heckendorn, p. 61). One company averaged ten to twenty dollars a day to the hand (*Alta*, June 24, 1853). John Clark reports in his "The California Guide" November 23, 1853, that a nugget of twenty-three ounces was found in Sawpit Gulch, but he does not give the location.

Sawyers Bar [Mendocino]. An unidentified place on Eel River, east of Fort Bragg. It is listed in Giffen's file.

Sawyers Bar [Siskiyou]. On the North Fork of Salmon River, on Trooks Flat. The bar was named in the 1850s for Dan Sawyer, who mined in the vicinity. New placers were struck in 1857 and the average yield with rockers was two to five ounces a day. A post office was established in 1858. At one time the camp had seven saloons, three hotels, and three stores. In later years a fire almost wiped out the town, and now there is a ranger station there, a small store, a saloon, and a gasoline station. (W. M. Smith.) Until the 1930s a number of mines and mills with modern equipment were operating in the vicinity (*Mining Bureau*, XXX, pp. 306 f.).

Saxton Creek [Mariposa]. A tributary to Merced River, about one and a quarter miles west of Briceburg. It is shown as Sextons Creek on Goddard's map, 1857, and on modern maps it appears as Saxon Creek. According to the reminiscences of David N. Hawley, he built a quartz mill in the fall of 1850 (other sources say in the summer of 1851), but like all other mills in the region at this time it failed, while miners earned eight or ten dollars a day by hand washing. (Hawley, p. 9.) Allsop mentioned the diggings as rich in December, 1851 and in January, 1852. On January 10, 1853, McIsaac's diary records the death of a Mexican by starvation. Among the mines is the Schroeder Group, the first deposits of which were discovered in July, 1877, by John Schroeder. Mining continued intermittently into the 1960s. (*Mining Bureau*, LIII, pp. 168 f.) The Rex, King Saxon, Queen Saxon, and Kid Saxon mines are still listed in the Mining Bureau report of 1957.

Scabby Hill [Yuba]. A steam-driven 4-stamp mill was in operation July 1, 1869 (Raymond II, p. 71). According to a report from the *Appeal*, January 26, 1872 (Hayes Scrapbooks: Mining, II, sec. 13), at that time about thirty miners made good wages in surface mining.

Scadden Flat [Nevada]. Near Grass Valley. The camp is mentioned in 1867 in *Bean's Directory*. A Scadden Flat Mine is listed in *Mining Bureau*, XXXVII (p. 463).

Scad Point [Plumas]. About one third of a mile north of Mumfords Hill; near Quincy. *Scad* is the miners' term for 'nugget'. J. A. Edman describes the geology of the region and states that there was still profitable hydraulic mining in 1875 (Raymond, VIII, p. 119).

Scales: Diggings, Ridge [Sierra]. Near Canyon Creek, about ten miles west of Downieville. Shown on Crossman's map, 1867. The camp is mentioned by John Clark in his guide October 24, 1856. It was perhaps named for Scales' saloon keeper (Bancroft Scraps, V, p. 1776), although Vischer (p. 243) states it was so named because the gold was found as scales in loose marl sand. There was mainly hydraulic mining, according to Vischer (p. 240) in 1859, and in Raymond, V (p. 85) in 1872. A post office was established in 1871. In 1903 the place was still a center of quartz and hydraulic mining (*Register*, 1903). Several mines were worked until

1925 (*Mining Bureau*, XXV, p. 188) and are listed until 1942. Shown on the USGS Downieville 1907 quadrangle.

Schands Ranch [Nevada]. *See* Quinns Ranch.

Schilling [Shasta]. *See* Whiskeytown.

Schirmer Ravine [Butte]. Seven miles north of Oroville. The diggings, under the old river bed below Table Mountain, never reached pay streak (Browne, p. 158). Shown on the USGS Oroville 1944 quadrangle.

Schleins Diggings [El Dorado]. On Tipton Hill, northeast of Georgetown. In 1874 the diggings were the most extensive workings of the whole section near the base of Tunnel Hill (Raymond, VII, p. 94).

Schroeder Group [Mariposa]. *See* Saxton Creek.

Sciad [Siskiyou]. *See* Seiad.

Scollans Camp [Calaveras]. On the South Fork of Calaveras River. It was named in the 1850s for John Scollan, alcalde of the Chili Gulch District. It is mentioned in the literature of the "Chilean War." *See* Chili Gulch.

Scorpion Gulch [Calaveras]. On the Stanislaus River, near Knights Ferry. The rich diggings were struck in May, 1850 (Harvey Wood, p. 26). It is mentioned by Heckendorn (p. 104) in 1856. The production was good, but the diggings had to be supplied with water.

Scotch, Scotchman, Scott. The large number of Scotts among the gold miners left its trace in California nomenclature. The names of some camps and districts were personal names.

Scotch Flat [Nevada]. Seven miles above Nevada City. There were fair returns from sluicing in the "early days," according to *Bean's Directory* (p. 132).

Scotch Flat [Plumas]. On Nelson Creek. The County History, 1882 (p. 288) lists it among the important mining points along the creek.

Scotchmans Creek [Nevada]. A stream between Alpha and Omega. It is mentioned as a camp by Bean (p. 385) in 1867.

Scotchmans Creek [Sierra]. It is mentioned by Downie (p. 136) and in Brown's *Directory*, 1856 (p. 133).

Scott Bar [Nevada]. On the south side of the North Fork of Yuba River, above the Middle Fork. Recorded on Trask's map, 1853.

Scott: Bar, Diggings, River, Valley [Siskiyou]. The river, a tributary to Klamath River, below Hamburg Bar, was called Beaver River by the trappers of the Hudsons Bay Fur Company. John E. Ross ("Narrative," p. 20) claims that he was responsible for the discovery of gold on the river in the summer of 1850, and that the stream was then named Ross River for him. He related that he gave the information about gold on the river to Joseph (!) Scott, who had rescued him from starvation, and under his "direction" Scott founded Scott Bar. The name of the river was then changed to Scott River. Ross is referring to John W. Scott, whose success started the Scott River rush and created an important cluster of names. A description is given by Gibbs in October, 1851 (Schoolcraft, III, pp. 159 f.). The diggings are first recorded on Butler's map, 1851. The gold was coarse and often came in lumps (Hittell Clippings, p. 87). Anton Roman mined here successfully 1850 to 1851 and invested his earnings, one hundred ounces of gold dust, in books, which started him on his career as bookdealer and publisher (Stewart, *Bret Harte*, p. 130). Another successful miner at the bar was Lucius Fairchild (*California Letters*, p. 155), later a general in the Civil War and governor of Wisconsin. In October, 1853 he and his partner bought a share in a claim for twenty-five dollars, which yielded them 2 thousand dollars each in a short time. The post office, established in 1856, was first called Scott River, then Scott Bar. The Yreka *Union* in 1856 reported that some quartz mills yielded as high as 200 dollars per ton, and the Yreka *Herald* in January, 1858, mentioned the find of a lump of 141 ounces almost en-

Scotts Bar, Siskiyou Co.

tirely pure gold (Hittell Clippings, pp. 23, 78). In November, 1860, four prospectors discovered a new quartz lead below Mill Creek, "the richest ever discovered in this county" (*Mining Press*, December 7, 1860, March 15, 1862). Sigmund Simon of Hamburg Bar had a store at the bar, which was in the hands of the family until mining declined at the beginning of the twentieth century. Several mills and arrastres are still listed in the *Register* of 1898. Scott Bar is still the trading center and post office for the surrounding mines, and gold dredging is still carried on in the River.

Scott Mountain [Siskiyou]. According to an undated item of 1855 from the Shasta *Courier*, gold was discovered high up on the mountain and a man could make an ounce a day with the use of a rocker (Hittell Clippings, p. 62; Cox, p. 10). The summit of the mountain marks the line between Siskiyou and Trinity counties. The first stage road into Scott Valley was over Scott Mountain, and there was mining on both sides. California State Highway 3 now crosses the mountain.

Scotts Bar [Plumas]. On the north side of the Middle Fork of Feather River, ten miles southwest of Quincy. It is listed in the Giffen file.

Scotts Bar [Siskiyou]. See Scott Bar.

Scotts Bar [Yuba]. On Scott Bar Creek, a tributary to the North Fork of Yuba River. The creek is shown on Wescoatt's map, 1861, above Indian Creek. According to the *Alta*, December 30, 1855, the yield was fifteen to eighteen dollars per day to the man in the year 1855, but it was of short duration. When De Long collected taxes here, October 16, 1855, the bar was mined mainly by Chinese.

Scottsburg [Amador]. On Dry Creek, near Ione City. The Quincy local newspaper, *The Prospector*, September 22, 1855, carries an advertisement for a general merchandise store for the miners in the issue of September 22, 1855.

Scotts Flat [Nevada]. On Deer Creek, east of Nevada City and about one and a half miles northwest of Quaker Hill. Shown on Doolittle's map, 1868. In 1854 the miners realized only six to ten dollars a day (*Alta*, June 4, 1854). Preparations for hydraulic mining are described in an extract from a clipping from the Nevada *Transcript*, January 21, 1865, in Hayes Scrapbooks: Mining (IV, sec. 18). The deep gravel mine is indicated on the County Map, 1880. By 1918 twelve million cubic yards of gravel had been removed from the vicinity

(*Mining Bureau*, XVI, Nevada, p. 63). According to *Bulletin*, 193 (p. 114) there was also drift mining in the district. In the 1930s there was some prospecting. Scotts Flat is shown on the USGS Colfax 1938 quadrangle.

Scotts Ravine [Nevada]. A tributary to Bear River; southeast of Little York. Shown on Pettee and Bowman's map, 1879. The extent of hydraulic mining in the area by 1870 is described by Pettee in Whitney, *Auriferous Gravels* (pp. 154, 159).

Scottsville [Amador]. Between Tunnel Hill and Jackson. In 1859 it was a small town, doing "a vast business" in hydraulic and tunnel mining (*Transactions*, 1859, p. 83). In January, 1861 a 20-stamp mill with a 30 horsepower engine was completed (*Mining Press*, January 4, 1861).

Scottsville [Sierra]. In Slate Creek Basin, south of St. Louis. It is shown on the map (Northern Part) in Raymond, V (opposite p. 88).

Scottsville [Siskiyou]. See Fort Jones.

Scott Town [Tuolumne]. Near Sonora. A party headed by Charles R. Scott started a rival camp below in 1848 or 1849, which apparently soon vanished (Stoddart, *in Tuolumne Courier*, February 23, 1861). De Ferrari, in his edition of Stoddart (p. 57), discounts Stoddart's identification of Scott as a Cherokee Indian and suggests that he is more likely to have been Charles G. Scott of Company B, Stevenson's Regiment.

Scottys Ranch [Sierra]. Near Minnesota. The diggings were worked by a company of Welch miners with fair success (*Sierra Democrat*, December 8, 1862).

Scraperville [Tuolumne]. On the east side of Table Mountain; about two miles west of Sonora. The Scraperville Gravel Mine is shown on Dart's map, 1879. The Columbia *Gazette*, August 13, 1853, refers to it as the "renowned village," which has no intention of drying up yet. Many were making only average wages; some lucky ones were doing very well. The Scraperville Tunneling Company tunnelled more than 900 feet and had not yet reached gravel dirt. Hutchings mentions it as a town in 1855, and Heckendorn mentions it as an important camp in 1856.

Sealeys Flat [Siskiyou]. It is mentioned by Trask in Document 9, 1854 (p. 90).

Searles [Kern]. On Highway 395; near the County line, now in the territory of the Naval Ordnance Test Station. It was named after the borax lake in San Bernardino County. The *Register* of 1904 records one stamp mill. The gold and silver mines in the southern Argus Range were served by the post office, which was active between 1898 and 1914.

Sears Dry Diggings [Sierra]. In the Slate Creek Basin, near Plumas County line. The deposits were discovered by a Captain Sears in 1850 in the wake of the Gold Lake hunt. It is not the same as St. Louis, although the diggings apparently became a part of it. Downie (p. 120) mentions the diggings in the fall of 1850, and John Clark refers to them September 3, 1852 and later. The story of the origin as given in Hittell's *History*, III (pp. 96 f.) is apparently fictitious. The *Alta*, in a December, 1853, issue reports that the mining is "very dull."

Sears Ridge [Sierra]. The divide between Slate and Canyon creeks was formerly known as Sears Ridge, named after Sears Diggings. Many gold camps sprung up along the bed of the glacial river — St. Louis, Portwine, Scales Diggings — especially after new deposits were discovered in February, 1854. Many sluices were built and the average earning was sixteen dollars a day to the hand (*Alta*, March 16, 1854, from the *Sierra Citizen*).

Sebastopol [Nevada]. One mile southwest of North San Juan. Shown on Doolittle's map, 1868. Like a number of other camps and mines it was named when the siege of the Russian fortress during the Crimean War in 1854 caused excitement in the world. McKeeby, who mined here and in the vicinity from 1852 to 1863, gives a good account of the early history (p. 151). Vischer (p. 233) mentions the place, and *Transactions*, 1858 (p. 176), reports that it "has for seven years paid hundreds of miners amply." It was populated by miners of Junction Bluff and Manzanita Hill (Bean, p. 342). Shown on the USGS Smartsville 1943 quadrangle.

Sebastopol [Sacramento]. About three miles along the old Ione Valley road (now Meiss road), which left Jackson road near Slough House. The camp was established in 1854, prospered until 1857, and was deserted in 1859, except for some Chinese (Co. Hist., 1880, p. 214).

Sebastopol [Sierra]. Near Canyon Creek, northwest of Downieville, on the main Blue Lead. Shown as Sevastopol on Crossman's map, 1867. It is also shown on the County Map, 1874. The camp is mentioned in 1856 by Thomson (p. 15). In 1867 Browne (p. 141) stated that there had been mining and prospecting since 1854, but

the "expenses had been double the receipts."

Sebastopol [Trinity]. On the east fork of Stewarts Fork above the junction. There was placering here before J. F. Chellis settled and named the place. An optimistic account is given by Cox (p. 82), but the mining was apparently short lived. According to an article in *Trinity*, 1962 (p. 9), the town once had a population of 600, but it disappeared by the turn of the century.

Sebastopol Hill [Nevada]. A knoll or hill on the Osborn Hill ridge, near Grass Valley (*Grass Valley Directory*, 1865). Hydraulic mining is mentioned in the *Mining Press*, February 1, 1861. The place had a custom mill with twelve revolving stamps until October, 1863, when it was moved to Boston Ravine (Bean, p. 203). This may have been the Ben McCauley mill, which crushed 12 thousand dollars' worth of gold from 190 tons, as reported in the *Mining Press*, August 31, 1861, and which was mentioned by Raymond in 1870 in connection with the highly successful Phoenix Mine on Sebastopol Hill (Raymond, III, pp. 44 f.) A Sebastopol Mine is listed in the Mining Bureau reports until 1941.

Second Crossing [Calaveras]. On the North Fork of Calaveras River, two miles northwest of San Andreas. It was the second crossing on Calaveras River between Stockton and Murphys. On Camp's map it is given as an alternate name for Iowa Cabins. According to Poore, it was also known as North Branch; Camp places it below North Branch (Old Site).

Second Garrote [Tuolumne]. *See* Garrote.

Second Ravine [Placer]. Near Auburn, next to the Spanish Ravine. Stephen Wing records on April 10, 1852, that he bought a claim here (Journal, I, p. 15).

Secret. The adjective "secret" was used frequently for names of mining places for various reasons. In Placer County there are three clusters of these names in different locations, the identities of which have been confused in the literature.

Secret Canyon [Sierra]. Southeast of Downieville. Shown on the County Map, 1874. In October, 1849, Downie's party found their first gold here. In the spring of 1850 Downie worked here again with good success, but his partner decamped with all the gold (Downie, p. 128). It was reported as paying well in the *Alta*, June 27, 1852, in an item taken from the Downieville *Echo*. Shown on the USGS Downieville 1907 quadrangle. A Secret Canyon Quartz

Mine is listed by the Mining Bureau until 1942.

Secret Diggings [Plumas]. Two miles south of La Porte. After 1856 there was mainly hydraulic mining (Vischer, p. 240). Shown on Crossman's map, 1867 and on the Sierra County Map, 1874. The best description is in *Transactions*, 1858 (pp. 200 f.). An extraordinary flume crossed the gorge at 2,000 feet above bottom to bring water. The net production at that time was about fifty dollars a day, apparently to the man. According to an item in *Mining Press*, June 22, 1861, a lucky strike of the Utah Company yielded for some time 200 dollars a day to the hand. In 1868, Browne (p. 166) reported that the Kingdom & Company had a 1,500-foot tunnel with fifty men at work, but the profits were only moderate.

Secret: Diggings, Canyon [Nevada]. Two miles from Nevada City, as listed in Brown's *Directory*, 1856 (p. 133). It is doubtless the Secret Canyon where Barrington (*Miscellany*, p. 5) prospected successfully in July, 1850.

Secreto or Secreta [Amador]. On a branch of Jackson Creek, near Clinton. It was apparently settled and named by miners from Chile. Doble, April 12, 1852, mentions that there were "mostly Chileans." It is mentioned again in the County History, 1881 (p. 167).

Secret Ravine [Placer]. The long ravine heads just south of Newcastle and runs southwesterly past Rocklin, draining finally into Dry Creek south of Roseville. Shown on Doolittle's map, 1868. There was extensive placer mining in the 1850s and 1860s in the vicinity of Newcastle, and also to the south around Stewarts Flat. Gardiner placer mined at Secret Ravine with fair success from October, 1850, to the summer of 1852. An unidentified clipping marked December 1, 1850 (in Hayes Scrapbooks: Mining, I, sec. 49) gives an optimistic account of the placer diggings, which extended for a distance of ten miles. Pine Grove, later Pino, was apparently the center of the ravine diggings at that time. The *State Register*, 1859, lists three mills, with a total of 22 steam-driven stamps and 8 arrastres, erected in 1858 at Secret Ravine, Placer County, indicating that there was also lode mining in the area — if in fact the reference is to this Secret Ravine. A post office named Secret Ravine was established in 1854, and for a few months in 1863 it was called Auburn Station. Hutchings lists Secret Ravine as a town in Placer County in 1855, but he does not locate it specifically. Secret Ravine is shown as a geographical feature on the USGS Auburn 1944 quadrangle.

Secret Ravine [Sierra]. Apparently near Onion Valley and Sears Ridge at a place where Captain Sears' partner, named Gibson, found gold in the early 1850s and kept its discovery secret from his partner. *See* Gibsonville.

Secret: Spring, Creek, Canyon, Hill [Placer]. The spring is shown on Goddard's map, 1857. The Creek issues from Canada Hill and empties into the North Fork of the Middle Fork of American River, northwest of Last Chance. Secret Canyon Ditch is shown on Doolittle's map, 1868; and Secret: Hill, Canyon, House, and Little Secret Canyon are shown on the Placer County Map, 1887. The Buckeye Rovers (pp. 120 f.) mention a Secret Canyon on May 5, 1850, while mining in El Dorado Canyon. They tell the story that several men had dug 10 thousand dollars' worth of gold, each within a few weeks, the previous fall. The *Annual Mining Review*, 1876, mentions a steam-driven 6-stamp mill at Secret Cañon, which had been built in 1864. The Whiskey Hill Mine near the head of the Canyon was not opened until 1882 (Co. Hist., 1882, p. 221). Secret Canyon, Secret House, and Little Secret Canyon are shown on the USGS Duncan Peak 1952 quadrangle.

Secret Town, Secret Ravine [Placer]. Secret Town is situated between three and four miles southwest of Dutch Flat and Gold Run. It is shown on Doolittle's map, 1868, as a station on the Central Pacific Railroad. The County Map, 1887, shows it at the same location, but the name is spelled in one word: Secretown. A notice of a claim in a ravine called Oregon Ravine "in Secret Town" is recorded on November 12, 1853, in Placer County Records, I (p. 198). The claim had previously been worked in 1849, according to the claimant. Recorded later in the same volume (pp. 281 f.) is the notice of intention to build a ditch to provide water for the camps Secret Town, along with Blue Canyon Hill, Dutch Flat, Hogs Back, Green, Lost Camp, Mountain Spring, Gopher Town, and Illinoistown. The water was to be taken from the North Fork of American River and Blue Canyon Creek. The settlement Secret Town is recorded on the USGS Chicago Park 1949 quadrangle, and southwest of it is shown the geographical feature Secret Ravine. The latter is not to be confused with the well known Secret Ravine southwest of Newcastle.

Segars Bar [Yuba]. A frequent misspelling of Sicards Bar.

Seiad: Creek, Valley town [Siskiyou]. On the Klamath River, at the junction with Seiad Creek. It was a center for drift and hydraulic mining (*Register*, 1898). The post office was established in 1858 and exists today. Seiad placer mines are listed in the Mining Bureau reports until the 1930s. The name was formerly spelled Sciad. It is an Indian name.

Selby: Flat, Hill [Nevada]. One mile north of Nevada City. Selby Flat is shown on Doolittle's map, 1868. Canfield (p. 4) gives a pleasant but somewhat doubtful and exaggerated account of the camp in May, 1850. The *Alta*, March 6, 1853, reports that sixty dollars per pan were taken out of one claim. In 1867 it was still a sizeable place (*Bean's Directory*).

Seneca [Plumas]. On the North Fork of Feather River, in Butt (or Butte) Valley, about three miles southwest of Greenville. The town was named after the township, which had been named in 1854 (*California Place Names*). It was an important center of mining during the Gold Rush era, according to *Bulletin*, 193 (p. 32). *See* North Fork [Plumas].

Seven by Nine Valley. Unidentified camp, listed in Hittell, *Resources*.

Seventy-Six [Pumas]. *See* City of 76.

Seven-up Ravine. An unidentified place, listed in Hittell, *Resources*.

Sextons Creek [Mariposa]. Recorded on Goddard's map, 1857. *See* Saxton Creek.

Shackleford Creek [Siskiyou]. In Quartz Valley. No early mining records were found, but according to the County History, 1881 (p. 215), John M. Shackleford built an 8-stamp quartz mill on the stream in 1852. There was some placer mining on Shackleford Creek, according to William M. Smith, but it is doubtful that there was a quartz mill there as early as 1852.

Shadow Creek [Siskiyou]. *See* Shadricks.

Shadow Mountain District [San Bernardino]. In the northeastern part of the county, about ten miles west of the Clark Mountains. Gold was discovered here in 1894, and mining continued for a few years (*Bull.*, 193, p. 167).

Shadricks [Siskiyou]. On a branch of the East Fork of Salmon River. It is a vanished mining camp, which developed in the 1880s (*Siskiyou Pioneer*, II:10, p. 21). The site is now a U. S. Forest Service campground and is called Shadow Creek.

Shady Creek [Nevada]. A tributary to the South Fork of Yuba River. In *Bean's Directory*, 1867, two mining settlements are listed, one in Bridgeport and the other in Bloomfield Township.

Shady Flat [Sierra]. Four miles east of Downieville and a half mile west of Mobile Flat, on Highway 49. It was an early day mining district, and later there was also lumbering (Sinnott, *Downieville*, p. 148).

Shady Run [Placer]. On the Southern Pacific Railroad, east of Dutch Flat and below Blue Bluffs. Shown on Doolittle's map, 1868. There was both hydraulic mining and drifting here; the drifting was carried on in 1896. The area is described by Lindgren, *Auriferous Gravels* (p. 146).

Shanghai Diggings [Nevada]. Near the Middle Fork of Yuba River; at the northwest extremity of Snow Point, above Orleans Flat. The gravel was being worked at the time Pettee visited the area in 1879 (Whitney, *Auriferous Gravels*, pp. 401, 402, 403). Shanghai Hill and City are listed but not identified in Hittell, *Resources*.

Sharamut Mine [Tuolumne]. *See* Eagle-Shawmut Mine.

Shasta [Shasta]. First called Reading Springs, then Shasta City. It was the metropolis of the far northern mines and is prominently shown on Goddard's map, 1857. It was the cross-roads and trading center of the placer mining area in the streams tributary to the Sacramento River in the central part of Shasta County. It was also at the head of the road and the beginning of the mule train to Trinity County, 1851–1857, and to Siskiyou County and Oregon, 1851–1860. A post office was established July 10, 1851, and the first public school in the county was established here in 1853. From 1851 to 1888 it was the

Shasta, Shasta Co.

county seat. Anton Roman had his bookstore here from 1853 to 1857, after he had mined with success on Scott River in Siskiyou County.

Shasta Butte City [Siskiyou]. *See* Yreka.

Shasta City [Shasta]. *See* Shasta.

Shasta Plain [Shasta]. There were rich diggings here in 1851, according to letters from Epaphroditus Wells to his wife.

Shaughnessy Place [Sierra]. *See* Mobile Flat.

Shawmut Mine [Tuolumne]. *See* Eagle-Shawmut Mine.

Shaws Flat [Tuolumne]. On the road from Sonora to Springfield. Shown on Gibbes' Map of the Southern Mines, 1852, and most later maps. The ghost town was once one of the most important gold camps on the limestone belt south of Columbia. The date of the discovery of gold here is uncertain. There had apparently been placering since 1848, and the place was first settled in 1850. A post office was established May 22, 1854. The repeatedly-told story that one Mandeville Shaw planted an orchard here in 1849 before the deposits were discovered could not be verified. The report that Senator J. W. Mandeville worked here during a recess of the legislature and averaged five dollars a day (Hittell Clippings, p. 28) might have something to do with the story. The place is mentioned by William Perkins repeatedly in 1851. A reliable account and an excellent picture is in Borthwick's book (pp. 342 f.). Pringle Shaw (p. 117) described the rich diggings as two miles long. According to Hittell, *Mining* (p. 48), a 26-ounce nugget was found in August and another on November 23, 1852. Many other rich yields are reported in contemporary newspapers, examples of which are taken from the Eastman file. In a day and a half one company took out more than 600 dollars, nearly 200 dollars of which was from one pan of dirt (Columbia *Gazette*, June 6, 1854). Burgess, Otis & Company took out 150 dollars to the hand in two and a half days (Sacramento *Union*, May 14, 1855). Pepper Grinder claim took out 92 ounces one week (same issue of the *Union*). On February 20, 1856, D. O. Mills, the banker, showed to the office of the Sacramento *Union* a bag of ten and a half pounds of gold dust that had been taken out of the Collins claim in three and a half days. The Portuguese Fluming Company took out 100 ounces of dust in one week (*Alta*, December 18, 1859). Two beautiful diamonds, pronounced "Simon pure" by Dr. Snell, geologist and chemist, were taken out of Helt and Pierce's claim (*Alta*, April 22, 1856). Such are the reports of contemporary newspapers! *Mines and Minerals* (p. 358) gives the total production of gold to 1899 as 6 million dollars. Additional information is given in Heckendorn (p. 60) and Browne (p. 35). *See* Caldwells Gardens. Historic Landmark 395. Shown on the USGS Big Trees 1941 quadrangle.

Sheepherder Lode [Mono]. In the Tioga district, on the summit of the Sierra Nevada, near the Tuolumne County line. In 1874 a sheepherder, W. Brusky, found the lode with claim notices of 1860 and a pick and shovel by the side of the location monument. In 1878 he returned, located a claim, and other prospectors followed him. The ore reportedly assayed on the average of twenty-five dollars per ton in gold and silver. (*Mining Bureau*, VIII, p. 675.) The discovery of the lode led to the development of the Great Sierra Mining Company, Bennettville and Dana Village.

Sheep Ranch [Calaveras]. North of Murphys. The deposits on the ranch, named after a sheep corral, were not discovered until 1866. The first stamp mill was built in 1872 (*Annual Mining Review*, 1876, p. 21), and a post office was established in 1877. The principal mine, of which George Hearst was one of the partners from 1874 to 1893, reportedly produced 4 million dollars worth of gold to the 1,300-foot level (*Mining Bureau*, XXI, pp. 158 ff.; XXXII, p. 288; *Bull.*, 18, pp. 104 f.). The mine was reopened in 1899 and worked intermittently to 1942, with minor activity since 1951 (*County Report*, II, pp. 69 ff.). The total production was 7 million dollars (*Bull.*, 193, p. 116). The Right Bower Mine in the district, which opened in the 1870s, was worked intermittently from the 1890s to the 1930s, was reactivated in 1954 (*County Report*, II, p. 67), and is again being reopened. The Old Pioneer Hotel at Sheep Ranch is still standing.

Sheldon [Sacramento]. The old Omochumnes Rancho of Jared Sheldon was along the north bank of the Cosumnes River, between Highway 50 and Jackson Road. *See* Daylors. It was important for mining history. Sheldon had built a dam for irrigation and the water flooded the diggings below. In July, 1851, the first serious fight took place in the struggle between farmers and miners, which was to last for more than a quarter of a century. (*Alta*, July 8, 1851; Bancroft Notes).

Shenanigan Flat [Sierra]. About a mile below Cherokee Bridge, on the north side of the North Fork of Yuba River. There was a settlement here on the pack trail from Downieville to Goodyears Bar, down past Brandy City and down Cherokee Creek (R. Drury).

Shenanigan Hill [Placer]. Opposite Spanish Diggings (Spanish Dry Diggings), on the Middle Fork of American River. The gold in the seam diggings here appeared irregularly in pockets, and miners were said to have made nothing or a fortune (Whitney, *Auriferous Gravels*, p. 115).

Shepley Ravine [Placer]. Notice of eight quartz claims laid by D. Shepley and associates February 2, 1853, are recorded in the Placer County Records, I (p. 161). It may be the site of the Shipley Mine and mill, listed in *Mining Bureau*, VIII (pp. 460, 694).

Sheridan [Placer]. No early records could be found. A post office was established in 1868, and the *Register* of 1902 records placer mining by dredging. It may be the same site as the village on the Southern Pacific Railroad.

Sherlock; Creek, Gulch, Diggings [Máriposa]. East of Bear Valley, on the south side of Merced River and well above it. Shown on Butler's map, 1851, and on later maps. Mining started early in 1849. One of the first outbreaks against Mexicans occurred here (*Alta*, October 25, 1849; *CHSQ*, XXXV, p. 38). The men who were driven out were apparently the Sonorians employed by the discoverers (T. T. Johnson, p. 230). The reliable Daniel Woods (pp. 84 f.) tells the following story of the discovery: The brothers Sherlock discovered the deposit accidentally and took out 30 thousand dollars from a "small square spot of ground." When they went to Monterey to deposit the gold, two sailors overheard them, took a furlough of seven weeks, followed the Sherlocks and returned to their ship with ninety pounds (!) of gold. Woods himself mined here in November, 1849, but was disappointed with the result. However, he met an old sailor who had kicked away a stone and found underneath it a nugget worth 500 dollars. A similar lucky find is reported in the Mariposa *Chronicle* of uncertain date: the John Marshall company found a nugget of almost eighty-six ounces with only little quartz; it had been thrown away because it was covered by a black mineral substance (Hittell Clippings, p. 26). In a letter of September, 1852, Allsop, who apparently had a claim here, speaks of successful operations in the creek with lit-

tle outlay. Several mines were active until recent years. The Diltz Mine, discovered in the 1860s, operated intermittently until about 1952 and is still listed in 1957. In the early 1930s several large masses of almost pure crystallized gold valued at 7 to 10.5 thousand dollars each at the old price were found. (*Mining Bureau*, XXXI, pp. 29 f.; LIII, pp. 91 ff.) The total production is estimated at between 750 thousand and one million dollars (*Bull.*, 193, p. 131). Sherlock Gulch with an intermittent stream is shown on the USGS Sonora 1939 quadrangle.

Shinbone Peak. An unidentified place, listed as a mining locality in Hittell, *Resources*.

Shingle Creek [El Dorado]. On the South Fork of American River, above Greenwood Creek. Early gold mining is mentioned by Coy (p. 29).

Shingle Springs [El Dorado]. About five miles southwest of Mud Springs. Gold was discovered here in 1848. In 1849 a shingle mill was put up here (Georgetown *News*, January 10, 1856; Kent, p. 39), and the camp took the name Shingle Springs. The first house was built in 1850 (Co. Hist., 1883, p. 200), and the post office was established in 1853. Lumps of gold worth 10 thousand dollars were taken out of the productive Gray Mine (Browne, p. 89). In 1887 there were still three mills with twenty, ten, and five stamps respectively (*Resources of El Dorado County*, p. 21). The Pyramid Mine, four miles north of Shingle Springs, was still operating in the 1930s after a long period of idleness. Its total production is estimated at about one million dollars (*Bull.*, 193, p. 117). The Big Canyon or Oro Fino Mine operated intermittently from the 1880s to 1940. *See* Big Canyon. The Crystal Mine, three miles from Shingle Springs on the road to Big Canyon, was one of the oldest locations in the county. Shingle Springs is Historic Landmark 456.

Shipleys Ravine [Placer]. Above Auburn. The place is mentioned by Stephen Wing on February 2, 1854 (Journal, II, p. 73). According to the County History, 1882 (pp. 195, 227), rich gold-bearing quartz was struck in 1855. An American and a "Dutchman" started digging at the head of the ravine and took out fifty-eight ounces in one day. Numerous claims, as well as the rules and regulations, are recorded in the Placer County Records of the same year (I, pp. 316 ff.). An 8-stamp steam-driven mill, built in 1857, and a 10-

stamp water-driven mill were in operation in 1876 (*Annual Mining Review*, 1876, p. 23). A mill is also listed in the Mining Bureau report of 1887/88.

Shirttail Canyon [El Dorado]. Near Oregon Bar. The Sacramento *Transcript*, steamer ed., June 29, 1850, refers to fairly profitable diggings in the canyon. According to the newspaper story, the name arose because a young miner was frightened one night by well imitated roars of a grizzly and fled in his "flannel" (Bancroft Notes).

Shirt Tail Canyon [Placer]. Neighboring Iowa Hill, in the Forest Hill Divide. Shown on the County Map, 1887. Knapp (p. 502) mined here in the spring of 1850; he made four to six ounces a day and maintained that "many made as high as one thousand dollars a day." The creek of the Canyon supplied water to Iowa Hill until July. The Buckeye Rovers mined here in August, 1850, and one of their members, Mr. Banks, narrates the story of a fight brought about by damming the stream. The place is mentioned as a town by Hutchings in 1855. In 1861 a company of Chinese miners resumed operations from Shirt Tail Bend to Dutch Marys Ravine (*Mining Press*, September 21, 1861). The mines of about 1880 are listed in the County History, 1882 (p. 217). One nearby mine still operated in 1888 (*Mining Bureau*, VIII, p. 466). The Canyon is shown on the USGS Colfax 1938 quadrangle.

Shirt-Tail Hill [Nevada]. The name is shown on Trask's map, 1853, southeast of Walloupa. According to *Miscellany* (p. 7), one Barrington had a good claim here in September, 1850, but no further record could be discovered.

Shively Diggings [Nevada]. Extended from Selby Hill, north of Nevada City, to Brush Creek. They were taken up in 1851 and were named for Henry Shively, one of the owners. The estimated yield to 1867 was one million dollars. The richest claims had long been worked out, but hydraulic mining and consolidation of claims were bringing regular profit (*Bean's Directory*, 1867, p. 129).

Shoemake [Tuolumne]. About two miles northeast of Chinese Camp, on Highway 120. Shown on Trask's map, 1853, north of Jacksonville, on the road to Campo Seco. It was both a ranch house and a road house, situated near the point now known as Chinese Station. It was also a stopping place on the Sierra Railroad for travelers to Big Oak Flat, Groveland, and other places "south of the river." (De Ferrari.)

Shores Bar [Butte]. North of Oroville, on the east side of the North Fork of Feather River, between Grizzly and Rock creeks. Shown on the von Leicht-Craven map, 1874, and on the County Map, 1877. It was a flourishing but transient mining camp, according to the County History, 1882 (p. 253).

Shorts Bar [Calaveras]. On Mokelumne River, northeast of Mokelumne Hill. Recorded on Trask's map, 1853.

Shortys Diggings [Sonoma]. On the Russian River. It was obviously a gold camp of a short duration, mentioned in the *Alta*, May 11, 1854.

Shumway Bar [Siskiyou]. On the North Fork of Salmon River, about one mile from the town of Forks of Salmon. It was named for Edward and Edwin Shumway, twin brothers, who mined here until they sold their property to a French company from San Francisco, about 1910 (William M. Smith).

Sicard: Bar, Flat [Yuba]. On a creek between Yuba River and Dry Creek; three miles northwest of Smartsville. It is recorded on most early maps. The bar was named for Pierre Sicard, a French sailor who had been in California since 1833, and was later one of Sutter's men, a part owner of Johnsons Ranch and of Cordua's lease and grant, and one of the founders of Marysville. He mined at the bar named for him in 1848 and opened a store in 1849. In contemporary literature the name was usually called Segar Bar. Emanuel Russ, the well known pioneer of San Francisco, and two of his sons mined here in the spring of 1849, but they gave up soon because they made only one ounce a day (A. G. Russ). McCall, September 23, 1849, apparently had no better luck. After the river (or the creek) was diverted, the bar enjoyed a short period of prosperity. The *Evening Picayune*, August 30, 1850, reports that a company from Ohio averaged between 600 and one thousand dollars a day. The *California Courier*, September 16, 1850, reports that fourteen pounds of gold were taken out in the forenoon. (Bancroft Notes.) Stephen Davis and his brothers were also here the same month. Another period of successful hydraulic operations was in the 1870s (Co. Hist., 1879, p. 88). A description of the Flat is given in Browne (p. 151). The gold is said to have had a high degree of fineness, some as high as 987°, according to Pettee (Whitney, *Auriferous Gravels*, p. 380). Sicard Flat is shown on the USGS Smartsville 1943 quadrangle. *See* Cigan Bar.

Sidewinder Mountain [San Bernardino]. Northeast of Victorville. The gold vein on the mountain was actively prospected in the 1880s, and the gold is reported to have assayed twenty-five to fifty dollars per ton (*Mining Bureau*, IX, p. 227). In 1953 the Mining Bureau reported that the mine, after which the mountain was named, was the largest gold operation in the Barstow-Victorville area. Sidewinder Mountain is shown on the USGS Apple Valley 1957 quadrangle.

Sidney Gulch [Trinity]. The creek is a tributary to Weaver Creek; near Weaverville. John Carr (p. 126) describes a lynching at the camp and the queer way in which its inhabitants took the law in their own hands in 1851. Carr's remark may indicate that it was a camp of Sidney ducks, as the gold diggers from the penal colonies in Australia were called. Sidney Hill Ditch, mentioned in 1896 (*Mining Bureau*, XIII, p. 561), is probably at the same site. Sidney Gulch is shown on the USGS Weaverville 1942 quadrangle.

Sidney Gulch [Tuolumne]. North of Sonora. It is mentioned in the "Mining Laws of Shaws Flat" (Heckendorn, p. 61).

Siebenthaler Lode [Amador]. *See* Volcano.

Sierra Buttes [Sierra]. The mountain north of Sierra City was one of the greatest producers of gold in the state. It was first called Yuba Buttes (Goddard's map, 1857). The mines on it were more than 8,000 feet high, and until modern times equipment and supplies had to be carried on mule back. The deposits were apparently discovered in the wake of the Gold Lake hunt in 1850. The large number of claims were gradually consolidated. Borthwick (pp. 246 f.) gives a fine description of the place. According to the *Annual Mining Review*, 1876 (p. 23), a 16-stamp water-driven mill was built in 1852. According to the reliable account in *Transactions*, 1858 (pp. 191 ff.), the ledge was opened in 1853 and a modest 3-stamp mill and two arrastres were put into operation. The heavy equipment, each stamp weighing 600 pounds, had to be dragged nine miles on sleds by men on snowshoes. The production was satisfactory in spite of the difficulties in transportation. The place took an enormous upswing when the Reis brothers, Ferdinand, Christian, and Gustav, bought the buttes, or most of them in 1857. The brothers, emigrants from Germany, had first mined in Mariposa and later had a supply store

in Downieville (Christian Reis, "Dictation"). Detailed descriptions of the rich mines are given in *State Register*, 1859, in *Alta*, July 26, 1867, and Browne (p. 147). In 1870 the Reis holdings were acquired by a London firm, which continued to develop the property. According to the San Francisco *Call*, May 18, 1879, three mills with ninety-six stamps and thirty-eight arrastres were in operation (Bancroft Scraps, V, p. 1,806). Between 1870 and 1904 or 1905 the production amounted to about 17 million dollars (*Mining Bureau*, XVI, Sierra, p. 121). This amount apparently did not include the mines outside of the Reis brothers property. Mining with modern equipment continued to recent times. About 1940 twenty tons of tailings at the Sierra Butte Mine yielded 146 ounces of gold and forty-six ounces of silver (*Mining Bureau*, XXXVIII, p. 44). It is shown as Buttes Mine on the USGS Downieville 1907 quadrangle.

Sierra City [Sierra]. On the South Fork of the North Yuba River, twelve miles above Downieville. The place developed as a trading center, and the post office, established in 1864, served the rich mines north of it. Downie (pp. 124 f.) claimed to have discovered gold here in the winter of 1850–51, but did not exploit it. Borthwick (pp. 242 ff.) described the place in 1852 before an avalanche destroyed it. It was rebuilt when the Reis brothers developed the famous Sierra Buttes mines. In 1857 the grand order of E Clampus Vitus was founded here. The city is shown on the County Map of 1874 and is described in the County History, 1882 (p. 470). In 1878 it had 400 inhabitants and the shipment of

Sierra City, Sierra Co.

gold by Wells Fargo was 288,380 dollars in that year (San Francisco *Call*, May 18, 1879; Bancroft Notes). A bibliography and detailed description of the region is found in *Mining Bureau* (XVI, Sierra, pp. 26 ff. *See also* volume XXXVIII, tables, pp. 50 f. and accompanying text). The activities in the district to the present time are described in *Bulletin*, 193 (p. 117), where it is stated that the estimated production is 30 million dollars or more. In 1860 a mass of gold weighing 1,596 ounces troy was found in the Monumental Mine, and in 1869 another mass 1,893 ounces in weight.

Sierra Rica Mine [Mariposa]. *See* Bear Creek.

Sierraville, Sierra Valley [Sierra, Plumas]. In the region between Yuba Pass and Beckwith Pass. There was some prospecting of gold and silver in early days, but later mainly farming and lumbering. The post office was established as Sierra Valley [Sierra] in 1862 but was changed to Sierraville in 1889. The Downieville *Mountain Messenger* announced a big festival of the *E. Clampus Vitus* in February, 1868 (Bancroft Scraps, V, p. 1,793), but this and other reports might be due to a confusion with Sierra City.

Sigl [Butte]. Apparently a bar, shown on Trask's map, 1853, on a branch of Butte Creek.

Signorita Bar [Tuolumne]. On the Tuolumne River, near Harts Bar. Daniel B. Woods (pp. 171 f.) gives the statement of the Signorita Bar Company, which operated at the bar between September 3 and October 25, 1850 with a total production of 9,700 dollars.

Silverado [Napa]. Five miles north of Calistoga. The vanished mining town, the chief product of which was silver, was named in analogy to El Dorado. The Silverado Mine was opened in 1872 and a 10-stamp mill was erected in 1874 (*Annual Mining Review*, 1876, p. 21; *Mining Bureau*, XIV, p. 270). The assay showed one dollar and ten cents' worth of gold and two dollars and sixty-five cents' worth of silver per ton. There was another more productive mine in the Silverado district, the Palisade Mine, which operated from 1876 to 1893, with a total production of 2 million dollars' worth of silver, some gold, copper, and lead (*Bull.*, 193, p. 178). The total production of gold in the district, sometimes known also as the Calistoga district, is estimated at 500 thousand dollars. The town of Silverado was made known through Robert Louis Stevenson, who lived at the deserted camp with his bride and wrote "The Silverado Squatters."

Silverado Canyon [Mono]. North of Ferris Canyon, near the Nevada state border. The Silverado Mine, on the eastern slope of Mount Patterson, produced mainly silver, with some gold. It is mentioned as having been active in 1888, and it was still operating in the 1930s when the mill was run by electric power (*Mining Bureau*, VIII, p. 362; XXXIV, p. 13).

Silver King District [Alpine]. About seventeen miles southeast of Markleeville. There are a few gold-bearing deposits, which were mined during the 1860s, but apparently there has been no activity since that time (*Bull.*, 193, p. 120).

Silver Lake [San Bernardino]. Eight miles north of Baker. It was not a mining town but a supply center for mines in a large surrounding area. It was on the main route from Daggett to Las Vegas, and at the crossroads of the route to Randsburg and the one from Ludlow to Shoshone and the south end of Death Valley. It was also an important station on the Tonopah and Tidewater Railroad. From 1907 to 1933 it had a post office. The town declined when it was bypassed by the Arrowhead Trail Highway (U.S. 91) in 1922. (Haenszel.)

Silver Mine Gulch [Tuolumne]. About five miles north of Columbia. A miner named Robinson and his partners were barely making grub, when in May, 1858, they found a lump of 265 ounces, which produced 112 ounces gold after crushing, according to an item from the Columbia *Courier* in Hittell's Clippings (p. 31).

Silver Mountain: town, **District** [Alpine]. *See* Kongsberg.

Silver Mountain District [San Bernardino]. *See* Oro Grande district.

Silver Queen District [Sonoma]. Five miles north of Cazadero. In the 1880s and early 1890s small amounts of gold were recovered from the Silver Queen Mine, and a little placer gold has also been mined in the area, according to *Bulletin*, 193 (p. 180).

Silver Valley [Alpine]. Formed by a tributary to the South Fork of Mokelumne River. It is shown as a camp on Trask's map, 1853, but it probably produced only silver.

Simonville [Siskiyou]. On Scott River, south of Scott Bar. It is mentioned as Simonsville in an undated clipping, about 1858. It was named for Sigmund Simon (*see* Hamburg

Bar), who was partner in a store here in 1854 (Co. Hist., 1881, p. 217).

Simpson Flat [Butte]. One and a half miles from Oroville. It was one of the oldest camps in the county, having been settled as early as 1849. Up to 1866 not a single "natural death" had occurred; all miners were doing well; there was plenty of water and good wages were paid (Sacramento *Union*, February 6, 1866).

Simpsons Bar [Tuolumne]. On the east side of Stanislaus River, six miles above Columbia. The bar is listed in the Giffen file.

Simpsonville [Mariposa]. *See* Bear: Valley.

Sinclairs Washings [Sacramento]. On the North Fork of American River, above the junction with the South Fork. John Sinclair was a well known Scottish pioneer, one of Sutter's men and later agent for Hiram Grimes, on whose Del Paso Rancho he lived. He was also alcade for Sacramento District from 1846 to 1849. In the early summer of 1848 he started mining here with fifty Indians, who mined fourteen pounds of clear gold for him in one week. The place is mentioned and mapped in the Mason *Report* in July, 1848.

Sinnamon Cut [Mono]. At the site of Monoville. A large hydraulic cut here was made by J. Sinnamon, who later, in the 1870s, engaged in ranching at Bridgeport. Nearby Sinnamon Meadows also bears his name. (F. S. Wedertz.) *See* Monoville.

Siskon Mine [Siskiyou]. *See* Dillon Creek.

Six-Bit Gulch [Tuolumne]. A camp on Six-Bit Gulch, a tributary to Tuolumne River, south of Chinese Camp. It was worked as early as 1849, and was still an inhabited camp when Mulford campaigned for the state legislature here in 1866 (Mulford, pp. 256 ff.). The nearby camps of Hungry Hill, Minnow Gulch, and Poor Mans Gulch, shown on the USGS Sonora 1948 quadrangle would indicate that the pickings were poor, unless these places were created by the whim of surveyors after 1897, when Six-Bit Gulch but not the other places were recorded.

Six-Mile Bar [Stanislaus or Tuolumne]. On the Stanislaus River, near Knights Ferry. Pringle Shaw (p. 116) calls it one of the principal bars on the river. Heckendorn mentioned it in 1856, and the Sonora *Herald* described it as very rich in 1858 (Hittell Clippings, p. 66). The bar is still listed as rich as late as 1898 in *Mines and Minerals* (p. 358).

Six-Mile Creek [Siskiyou]. A tributary to East Fork of Salmon River. The creek is old

placer mining ground, but no early reports were found. The Mining Bureau reports of the 1920s describe an active placer, which is still listed in 1935. The last placer mining in the region of the East Fork of Salmon River was carried on here (W. M. Smith).

Sixteen-to-One Mine [Sierra]. In Alleghany. The mine was located in 1896, and after it absorbed the holdings of the Tightner, Twenty-one, Rainbow, Red Star, and other lode mines (*see Bull.*, 193, p. 24), it became the largest producer in the district. It was active until late in 1965, after having operated for more than sixty years. Its total production was more than 25 million dollars. A description and bibliography is given in *Mining Bureau*, LII (pp. 262 ff.). *See* Alleghany.

Skeahan Bar [Siskiyou]. On Klamath River, above Swiss Bar. An unidentified place listed in Giffen's file.

Skidmore Flat. An unidentified place, listed in the Work Projects Administration project.

Skidoo [Inyo]. East of Emigrant Springs, in Death Valley National Monument. The name is derived from the popular slang expression, "twenty-three, skidoo." The gold deposits were discovered in 1906, reportedly by three tenderfoot prospectors, who sold their claims for 60 thousand dollars to Bob Montgomery of Rhyolite, Nevada (*Chuck-Walla*, February 15, 1907). A mill was built in 1907 and was operated by water brought through a pipeline from Telescope Peak, a distance of twenty-one miles, at a cost of more than 200 thousand dollars. By about 1915 the Skidoo Mine had produced more than 1.5 million dollars. (*Mining Bureau*, XV, pp. 83 f.) The town had a post office, 1907–1917, and reportedly had a population of 500. It had the reputation of being a "wild" place. Belden (pp. 44 f.) tells the story of a lynching, based on a contemporary account in the Skidoo *News*, dated April 5, 1908. The place is now a ghost town. The name is recorded on the USGS Ballarat 1908 and later quadrangles. Mines of the Skidoo District are listed in *Bulletin*, 193 (p. 151).

Skillman Flat [Nevada]. On Highway 20, above White Cloud. Listed as a mining camp by Foley.

Skinflint. An unidentified place, listed in Hittell, *Resources*.

Skull Flat [Calaveras]. Two miles northeast of West Point. The rock paid thirty to thirty-five dollars per ton. In 1867 the Skull Flat company owned claims on six or seven veins. (Browne, p. 66.) In 1873 there was a 10-stamp steam-driven mill (*Annual Mining Review*, 1876, p. 23).

Skunk Flat. An unidentified place, mentioned by Helper (p. 151).

Skunk Gulch [Placer]. A tributary to the North Fork of the Middle Fork of American River, south of Michigan Bluff. Shown on the sketch map of the auriferous gravel region visited by W. A. Goodyear of the Whitney Survey, May–December, 1871 (Whitney, *Auriferous Gravels*, Plate B). It is listed but not identified in Hittell, *Resources*.

Slab Ranch [Calaveras]. About one mile north and east of Angels Camp. It was a prosperous camp from 1850 to 1864, according to the recollections of Demarest's father (Demarest, pp. 9 ff.). However, Heckendorn in 1856 lists only two miners as inhabitants.

Slabtown [Amador]. Four miles east of Jackson. Recorded on the County map, 1866. Gold mining was developed in the early 1850s. The camp was first called Hoodville [or Hoodsville], according to George Harvey of Sacramento, whose great grandmother had a boarding house here. The *Amador Weekly Ledger*, August 1, 1857, bewailed the change of the name: "some sneaking scamp succeeded in fastening the title of 'Slabtown' to it, and you know a mean name sticks to it like a bur to a sheep's tail." The County History, 1881 (p. 181), states that the cabins in the early fifties were built of slabs from Huffaker's mill. The diggings were exhausted early, and the camp became a farming community.

Slap Jack Bar [Placer]. On the Middle Fork of American River. Henry W. Bigler and several other Mormons mined here in September and October, 1850. They were not very successful and rejoiced when they were called for duty in the Hawaiian Islands. (*Bigler's Chronicle*, p. 131.)

Slapjack Bar [Siskiyou]. On Scott River, south of Scott Bar. It is mentioned in the County History, 1881 (p. 217). There was also a Slapjack Bar and an Applesauce Bar on the North Fork of Salmon River, above Sawyers Bar, opposite Eddys Gulch (Tickner). *See* Flapjack Bar.

Slate Bar [Placer]. On the North Fork, American River. The Placer County Records, I (p. 274) record on January 2, 1855, a notice of a claim for the bed of the river at this place.

Slate Bar [Trinity]. On north side of Trinity River, west of Steiner Flat. It was discovered in 1850 by W. Jackman, who returned to Missouri and brought back a group of men who all "made their pile." An extensive account is given in Cox (pp. 47 ff.).

Slate: Bar, Hill [Sacramento]. On the west side of American River, between Folsom and the state prison. Shown on Judah's map of Folsom, 1854. It was a small camp engaged in crevice mining (Co. Hist., 1880, p. 229).

Slate Creek [El Dorado]. A tributary to Dutch Creek, about three miles northeast of Coloma. Shown on Bowman's map, 1873. The U. S. Bureau of the Census lists the names of 42 inhabitants "On Slate Creek" in the population schedule for the 1850 census.

Slate Creek Basin [Plumas, Sierra, Yuba]. The tributary to the North Fork of Yuba River with its basin was one of the important gold regions. Pringle Shaw (p. 121) describes the deposits as rich in coarse gold, deep layered and hard to extract. Downie (p. 134) tried to form a new mining district after 1853. The Slate Creek Ditch Company is mentioned by De Long, July 22, 1857. In the 1860s a three mile canal was built from the west branch of the creek to Gibsonville (Browne, p. 204). A detailed account and an excellent map of the Slate Creek Basin is found in Raymond, V (pp. 79 ff.).

Slate Creek Ledge [Nevada]. Above Willow Valley, near Nevada City. Listed in *Bean's Directory*, 1867.

Slate Gulch [Tuolumne]. Near Big Oak Flat, about one half mile west of which it joins Rattlesnake Creek. According to the "Mountaineer" in the *San Joaquin Republican*, December 16, 1851, the yield was an average of two ounces a day to the man in the spring of 1850.

Slate Mountain [El Dorado]. In 1887 there was a 10-stamp mill here (*Resources of El Dorado County*, p. 20). It may be the same Slate Mountain ten miles southeast of Georgetown mentioned in *Bulletin*, 193 (p. 120), at which there were a few lode mines.

Slate Range [San Bernardino]. East of Searles Lake, on the Kern county line. Shown on the County Map, 1892. The place had a post office between 1900 and 1911. Numerous gold and silver mines in the area are shown on the map of the *Register*, 1902.

Slate Range Bar [Yuba]. On Canyon Creek, above its confluence with Slate Creek. Shown on Gibbes' map, 1851, and on

Trask's and later maps. According to the County History, 1879 (p. 96), the bar was first worked by Mormons in 1849. Although the gold was found four feet under layers of slate, 60 thousand dollars worth were taken out in the summer of 1849, according to Buffum (p. 106). Borthwick (p. 214) passed the Slate Range House on the trail from Fosters Bar to Downieville in the fall of 1852 and gives a good account of the place. Many of the early writers mention the prosperity of the camp; it was "quite a lively town," as the Marysville *Directory* states in 1858. In the 1860s the place ceased to be the center of the numerous camps and mines in the vicinity, and there are no later mining records. The site of the camp differs on older maps. On the USGS Bidwell Bar 1944 quadrangle it is recorded on the North Fork of Yuba River, between Canyon and Deadwood creeks. A locality, Slate Range, is about two miles south of it.

Slaughters Bar [Sierra]. Opposite Goodyears Bar. It is mentioned in the County History, 1882 (p. 466).

Slayville Ranch [Sierra]. The name on Trask's map, 1853, is obviously another spelling of Sleighville.

Sleighville [Sierra]. Three miles northeast of Camptonville, between Oregon Creek and the North Fork of Yuba River; on the Sierra Turnpike. The hotel was built in 1849 by Peter Yore (Rensch), and the family operated the toll road to Downieville when it was opened in 1857 (R. Drury). It is mentioned by Downie (p. 71). Shown on Doolittle's map, 1868.

Sliger Mine [El Dorado]. *See* Spanish Diggings; Greenwood [El Dorado].

Slopeville [Sierra]. On the slope of Slate Creek, east of La Porte. Shown on Crossman's map, 1867. The map in Raymond, V (p. 88) shows numerous claims south of it. About 1865 the Monte Cristo Company took out gold "by the hundred ounces per week" at Slopeville, despite the insufficient amount of water (Bancroft Scraps, LI:1, p. 237).

Slug Canyon [Sierra]. One and a half miles south of Downieville. The Slug Canyon Company cleaned up 120 ounces of gold in a thirty day run of one arrastre (*Mining Press*, January 18, 1861). The place is listed by the Mining Bureau until 1941 (XXXVIII, p. 65).

Slug Gulch [El Dorado]. South of the Middle Fork of Cosumnes River. It is mentioned in the *Alta*, December 21, 1853. In 1867 Browne (p. 85) mentions it in connection

with Brownsville and Indian Diggings. The Slug Gulch hydraulic mine operated intermittently until 1930 (*Mining Bureau*, LII, p. 562). Recorded on the USGS Placerville 1931 quadrangle.

Sluice Fork. An unidentified name listed in Hittell, *Resources*.

Slumgullion [Calaveras]. The name is used as a place name by Bret Harte, who visited the region in December, 1855, and stayed a few days with Jim Gillis on nearby Jackass Hill. Neither Melones nor Carson Hill can be identified with it. Slumgullion, usually denoting a stew of meat and vegetables, is a miners' term for the muddy deposits in the sluices. Mulford (p. 247) mentions a slumgullion shovel. The 1936 edition of Delano's *Across the Plains* has a picture on page 149 showing the name.

Slumway Bar [Siskiyou]. *See* Shumway Bar.

Sly Park [El Dorado]. On Sly Park Creek, tributary to Camp Creek. Named July 5, 1848, for James Sly, one of the Mormons on their trek from Sutters Fort to Salt Lake (Bigler, p. 113). A fine description in the summer of 1854 is given by Welles (p. 287). *Resources of El Dorado County* (p. 21) lists a canon ball mill in 1887, and the *Register* of 1902 lists several quartz mines and two stamp mills. Recorded on the USGS Placerville 1931 quadrangle. The name is sometimes abbreviated to Park.

Smalta Bar [Plumas]. Doubtful name on the west branch of the North Fork of Feather River, recorded on Milleson and Adams' map, 1851.

Smartsville [Yuba]. South of the main Yuba River, near the Nevada County line; about one mile southeast of Timbuctoo. It was named for James Smart, who built the first house, a hotel, in 1856 (Co. Hist., 1879, p. 85). The place is mentioned by De Long, April 17, 1859. The camp did not develop until after the discovery of the Blue Gravel vein in 1854. A shaft was sunk, a tunnel built, and rich profits were reported. (*Alta*, March 13, 1867). In the 1870s when there was mainly hydraulic mining, profits increased. The deep mines around Smartsville are described and mapped in 1874 by Raymond (VII, pp. 142 f.). At that time the Blue Gravel Mine had become one of the most famous gravel mines in the state. By 1875 seven million dollars worth of gold had been taken out of the area and probably an additional 3 million before the days of deep mining. By 1879 it was reported at 13 million dollars (Whitney, *Auriferous Gravels*, p. 383). The total production is not known. For a later report of the area, *see Bulletin*, 92.

Smith Bar [Plumas]. On the East Fork of the North Fork of Feather River, below Rich, Indian, and Missouri bars. Shown on Milleson and Adams' map, 1851, and many later maps. This is apparently the famous bar named for a Mr. Messerschmidt or Messersmith, who played a conspicuous role in the Gold Lake hunt. Bruff (II, p. 810) identifies him as "Mr. Messer Smith from Pa-German extraction — We called him Smith." The name is frequently mentioned by Bruff and Dame Shirley. The latter states that "more gold has been taken from it [Smiths Bar] than from any other settlement on the river." This seems to be confirmed by newspaper articles that claim that the bar yielded one thousand dollars per hour (!) (Bancroft, VI, p. 364).

Smith Diggings [Sierra or Nevada]. In the spring of 1854, the *Alta* reprints items from local newspapers, according to which the miners averaged an ounce a day. One company took out 182 ounces in one week, and in the Dutch Tunnel a nugget of twenty-three ounces of solid gold was found in February according to the *Sierra Citizen* (reprinted in *Alta*, March 16, 1854).

Smith Flat [Trinity]. On the Trinity River, opposite Douglas City. According to the *Mining Press*, April 25, 1862, one company took out 800 dollars and another 500 dollars' worth of gold in two weeks of work.

Smith Flat District [Calaveras]. Includes a group of mining camps two miles west of Angels Camp (Demarest, p. 9). The principal mines of 1894 are listed in the *Mining Bureau*, XII (p. 97).

Smith's Flat Mine [El Dorado]. *See* Placerville.

Smith River [Del Norte]. Most of the gold produced in the county came from the small hydraulic placer mines along Smith River and its tributaries. The steamer edition of the Sacramento *Transcript*, January 14, 1851, reports that about 2,000 miners were at work with the average earning of twelve to fourteen dollars a day to the man. Smith River and its affluents are listed in the *Mining Bureau*, XIV (pp. 386 ff.). In later years there was extensive dredging.

Smiths Bar [Placer]. On west side of the North Fork of American River between Horseshoe Bar and Long Bar. Recorded on Jackson's map, 1850, and Goddard's, 1857. Gold was washed here in 1848 and the place was later named for the store-owner (McNeil, p. 49). Letts (p. 115) reports rich production in 1849, and Buffum, (p. 61) reports that five men dammed up the river in two weeks and then took out 15 thousand dollars in ten days. The U.S. Bureau of the Census lists the names of forty-two miners at Smiths Bar and another forty-two at nearby Long Bar in the population schedule for the 1850 census. The Bar is now covered by Folsom Lake.

Smiths Flat [El Dorado]. Three miles east of Placerville; on the Blue Channel of the county. Rich diggings were reported in 1849 (Haskins, p. 136). In March, 1854, a boulder of quartz with gold veins was found valued at 5 to 6 thousand dollars (Hittell Clippings, p. 23). In 1861 the Deep Channel Company introduced an improved cement crushing mill, the invention of a Mr. Woolsey, and the profits were increased considerably (*Mining Press*, April 13, 1861). A 10-stamp steam-driven mill was built in 1864 (*Annual Mining Review*, 1876, p. 22). The Toll House or Hook and Ladder Mine, a drift mine at Smiths Flat, was active before and during the 1890s and again from 1918 to 1932. It was on the Blue Lead and Gray Lead channels and was developed by 152-foot shaft and raises and several hundred feet of drifts (*Mining Bureau*, LII, p. 564). According to the *Mountain Democrat*, souvenir edition, 1898, the Hook and Ladder Mine had produced at least one million dollars by 1898. The total production of Smiths Flat placer mine was more than 2 million dollars (*Bull.*, 193, p. 108). Smiths Flat had a post office from 1876 to 1895. Recorded on the USGS Placerville 1931 quadrangle.

Smiths Flat [Sierra]. On the Blue Lead, between the Middle Fork of Yuba River and Oregon Creek, two miles from Forest Hill. The geology is described by Trask in 1854 (Doc. 9, pp. 65 f.). The flat is mentioned in the *Mining Press*, August 24, 1861. In 1864 a nugget of 140 ounces, worth 2,605 dollars was found, and again in 1866 a 146-ounce nugget worth 2,716 dollars (*Mining Bureau*, II, part 1, p. 149).

Smiths: Flat, Ferry [Mariposa]. Shown on Gibbes' map, 1851, on Merced River near the Horseshoe Bend. A license to operate the ferry was granted to J. L. Smith, May 21, 1851 (Mariposa County Records, Court of Sessions' Minutes, p. 34).

Smiths Neck [Sierra]. In the northeastern part of the county, near the Plumas County line. The settlement may have been so named because the Smith Mining Company was in operation there. In 1863 (or early 1864) the name was changed to Loyalton by the post office department at the suggestion of Rev. Adam G. Doom, the first postmaster, who considered the name expressive of the strong Union sentiment in the community (*California Place Names*). Later the place became a lumbering and ranching center. It is now the largest town in Sierra County.

Smiths Pocket [Stanislaus]. A fictitious name used by Bret Harte as the locale of his story "M'Liss". The location and characteristics of the town resemble those of La Grange in the middle fifties (Stewart, *Bret Harte*, pp. 44 f.).

Smiths Point [Placer]. Northwest of Forest Hill; between North and South Brushy canyons. Shown on Doolittle's map, 1868. It is repeatedly mentioned in Whitney, *Auriferous Gravels*, where it is stated (p. 118) that more than a million dollars is estimated to have been produced by drifting and hydraulic operations before 1879. The combined yield of Georgia Hill, Yankee Jims, and Smiths Point was about 5 million dollars (Lindgren, *Auriferous Gravels*, p. 150).

Smiths Ranche [El Dorado]. The place was visited in July, 1851, by Marryat (*Mountains and Molehills*, p. 245). It is the same location as Smiths Flat east of Placerville. In old deeds it is often called Smiths Rancho (Schlappi-Ferguson).

Smithville [Placer]. In Secret Ravine, about six miles southwest of Newcastle. Shown prominently as Smithville P. O. on Doolittle's map, 1868. It was about three-fourths of a mile southeast of Pino, the center of the Secret Ravine diggings in the 1850s and 1860s. The camp was named for the store keeper L. G. Smith (J. W. Winkley, "The Knave," August 12, 1945). From 1862 to 1869 it had a post office, which was transferred to Pino after its closure. *See* Secret Ravine; Pino; Stewarts Flat.

Snake Bar [Sierra]. On the North Fork of Yuba River, above Goodyears Bar. Recorded on Doolittle's map, 1868, and on the County Map, 1874. It was above the ancient bed of Yuba River and is obviously the same site as Snake F[lat] recorded on Trask's map, 1853. Sherman P. Sumner mined here in 1851 with good success (Letter of September 7, 1851). The *Alta*, March 16, 1854, reprints an item from the *Sierra Citizen*, according to which a company of five men averaged ten to fifteen ounces a day. It was an election precinct and still a busy camp in 1851 (*Mining Press*, July 20, 1861). The first white child born in Sierra County, Sierra Woodall, was born at Snake Bar (R. Drury).

Snake Gulch [Calaveras]. Listed in Hittell's roster.

Snake Ravine [Nevada]. West of Dutch Flat, on the Blue Lead (Bean, p. 369).

Sneath and Clay. *See* Gold Flat [Nevada].

Snelling [Merced]. On the Merced River, formerly in Mariposa County. Shown on Trask's 1853 and Goddard's 1857 maps. Gold mining apparently began as early as 1850. Before 1854 it was named Snellings Ranch for the owner of the hotel, Charles V. Snelling. It is mentioned in 1863 by Mulford, who lectured here. For some time it was the county seat. The placers were soon exhausted, but the place was the headquarters of the Snelling Gold Dredging Company (*Mining Bureau*, XXXI, p. 47). Dredging was carried on intermittently in the Snelling district between 1907 and 1952, and the total production of gold is estimated at 17 million dollars (*Bull.*, 193, pp. 120 f.).

Snow Canyon District [Inyo]. The district is listed in *Mining Bureau*, II (part 1, p. 177). The production of silver exceeded by far that of gold.

Snow Creek [Mariposa]. Several miles east of Mariposa. No mining record was found, but it had a 5-stamp mill in 1869 (*Annual Mining Review*, 1876, p. 21).

Snow: Point, Flat [Nevada]. South of the Middle Fork of Yuba River; about one and three quarter miles northeast of Moores Flat. Snow Point is shown on Doolittle's map, 1868. The valuable hill diggings date back to 1853. A miners' ditch was started in 1855, extending from the Yuba River to Snow Point and Orleans, Moores, and Woolsey flats. (Brown's *Directory*, 1856, pp. 12 f.) The place is mentioned in *Transactions*, 1858 (p. 183), and in Raymond, VI (p. 108). Pettee describes the geology of the gravel bank and some of the mining activity at the time of his visit in 1879 (Whitney, *Auriferous Gravels*, pp. 400, 401, 403).

Snows Diggings [Butte]. At the southern base of Kimshew Table Mountain. Hydraulic mining here is described by Lindgren (p. 96). Snows Mine is shown at this location on the USGS Bidwell Bar 1944 quadrangle.

Snow Tent [Nevada]. Two miles southeast of Moores Flat; south of the Middle Fork of Yuba River. Snow Tent Hotel is shown on Doolittle's map, 1868, on the gravel deposit which extends southwesterly to North Bloomfield. The place is mentioned in Brown's *Directory*, 1856 (p. 133), and in *Mining Bureau*, XVI (Nevada, p. 45). Snow Tent Spring is shown on the USGS Colfax 1938 quadrangle.

Snyders Bar [El Dorado]. On the South Fork of American River, three miles below Coloma. Steele (pp. 229 f.) mined here in the fall of 1851. It is mentioned by Stephen Wing as Snyder Bar in his journal of July 20, 1854. In the El Dorado County Records (Mining Locations, Book I, p. 110) reference is made to Snyders and Sutters Bar nearby.

Soap Weed [El Dorado]. An unidentified place. According to the *Annual Mining Review*, 1876 (p. 21), a quartz mill was in operation at that time.

Soda Creek [Siskiyou]. An unidentified place. According to the *Mining Press*, June 22, 1861, miners have "first rate prospects," It might be the same as Soda Springs in the northwest corner of Shasta County, recorded on Goddard's map, 1857. On modern maps Soda Creek is a tributary to the Sacramento River, crossing the border of the two counties near Castle Crag.

Soda: Creek, Bar [Plumas]. The Creek is a tributary to the East Fork of the North Fork of Feather River, about nine miles north of Quincy. Recorded on Trask's map, 1853. A Soda Bar and Eclipse placer mine is listed in 1893 in *Mining Bureau*, XIII (p. 306).

Soggsville [Nevada]. Near Nevada City. Named for Nelson Sogg, who built a stamp mill here in the 1850s (Bean, pp. 111, 117).

Sober & Parrish's Bridge [Amador, Calaveras]. *See* Big Bar.

Soldiers Bar [Trinity]. Three miles from Junction City. In 1861 several companies were at work with undetermined success (*Mining Press*, November 23, 1861).

Soldiers Gulch [Amador]. A tributary to Sutter Creek, near Volcano. Recorded on Trask's map, 1853. Gold is said to have been first mined here by soldiers from Stevenson's Regiment (Volcano *Ledger*, January, 1857). Doble describes the place, June 28, 1852, remarking that "the soldiers" first found gold here in 1848. The report that the bodies of two soldiers from the Regiment, who had died in their huts in the winter of 1848–49, were found the following spring by Mexican prospectors has not, however, been substantiated (Camp, *in* Doble, p. 301). Borthwick (p.

303) describes the Gulch as it was in the spring of 1853, reporting that the soil, held by stiff clay to the depth of forty feet, was equally rich in all strata. Bancroft's statement in VI (p. 372), that a pan of dirt could give several hundred dollars and that "many readily obtained one thousand dollars a day" is probably a slight exaggeration.

Soldiers Gulch [Tuolumne]. The gulch runs into Stanislaus River below Robinsons Ferry or Melones. Highway 49 runs partly down the gulch to the river crossing. According to Stoddart (p. 64), the diggings were discovered in 1848 by artillery soldiers, and large fortunes were made. One soldier accumulated 10 thousand dollars during his furlough, in spite of rude implements. Hutchings lists Soldiers Gulch as a town in 1855. An Atlas and Soldier Gulch Mine on Jackass Hill, north of Tuttletown, is listed until 1928 (*Mining Bureau*, XXIV, p. 22).

Soledad Canyon [Los Angeles]. Extends from Newhall through the mountains toward Mojave Desert; traversed by the Santa Clara River. In 1861 there was a copper mining boom, led by Manuela Ravenna of Los Angeles, who organized the Soledad Mining Company. The discovery of gold and silver added to the excitement and a town called Soledad soon developed. In 1868, when the post office was established, the name was changed to Ravenna to avoid confusion with Soledad in Montery County. It continued as a mining camp until 1877, when the miners moved to Acton and left Ravenna to become a ghost town. Arthur B. Perkins (*HSSCQ*, XL, pp. 162 ff.) and J. W. Robinson (pp. 20 ff.) give accounts of mining in the district. For a collection of contemporary newspaper clippings, *see* the section in Hayes Scrapbooks: Mining, VII. *See* Acton; Mount Gleason.

Solo District [San Bernardino]. North of the Mojave Sink. It is shown as a large district on the County Map, 1892. On Crowell's map, 1903, it includes Soda Mountains and the Old Dad Mountain range, at the north end of which gold was mined at the Oro Fino and other mines. Part of the district later became Halloran Spring District. *See* Old Dad Mountain; Halloran Spring District.

Solomons Gulch [Mariposa]. A tributary to the Merced River on the north side; east of Bagby. It is often mentioned as one of the auriferous gulches after 1850. According to Phillips' Coulterville *Chronicle* (ʄ 66),

Sonora, Tuolumne Co.

George Coulter had a store here in 1849 before he moved to Coulterville. Solomons is listed in Hittell's roster, apparently as a mine. The Black Bart Group and the White Porphyry Group, active mainly around the 1870s, and the Gold Bug in the 1880s and 1890s, are described in *Mining Bureau*, LIII (pp. 102, 181 f., 241). Solomons Gulch is shown on the USGS Sonora 1939 quadrangle.

Solomons Hole [Calaveras]. On Wadies Creek, six miles from Carson Hill. The miners used the name for Moaning Cave. It was a common belief that Mexicans had dug for gold here, until John D. Trask dispelled the tradition (*Alta*, December 7, 1851).

Solsbury, Solsby [Tuolumne]. *See* Soulsbyville.

Somerset [El Dorado]. On the old trail from Slys Park to Placerville. Named by the original settlers who came from Somerset, Ohio (Georgetown *News*, January 10, 1856). No mining record was found, but Somerset House is mentioned by John Winkley in "The Knave," March 16, 1961.

Somerville [Tuolumne]. *See* Summersville.

Somes Bar [Siskiyou]. Near the junction of the Klamath and Salmon rivers. There was placer mining on the bar probably as early as the 1850s. The post office (also spelled Somesbar, according to Frickstad) was established in 1875. The mines in the vicinity are listed and mapped in the *Register*, 1898.

Sonerita [Tuolumne]. *See* Sonorita.

Sonora [Tuolumne]. On the Mother Lode, southeast of Columbia. The camp is recorded on Derby's map, 1849 (misspelled Sororan Camp) and on all other early maps as Sonora or Sonorian. According to De Ferrari, *in* Stoddart (p. 86), the place was officially known as Stewart in 1850. In May, 1851, the U. S. Bureau of the Census designates it as Sonora. The camp was settled in 1848 by Mexicans from the state of Sonora, and for some time the population was almost exclusively Spanish-American, until the tax on noncitizen miners in 1851 made them leave. An account of the early troublesome years is given in Heckendorn (pp. 37–45). Among the numerous contemporary accounts are *Three Years in California* by Walter Colton, who visited the camp in 1848; the letters of Elizabeth Gunn, who lived here with her physician husband from 1851 to 1861; Marryat (pp. 258 ff.); Christman, editor of the Sonora *Herald* (pp. 169 f.); Pringle Shaw (p. 117); Daniel B. Woods (pp. 95, 141); Borthwick (pp. 329 ff.). The real chronicler of the early years was William Perkins, who lived in Sonora from 1849 to 1852, and wrote his account in retrospect. *See also* Gerstaecker, "The French Revolution" and Dumas, *Gil Blas*, chapter IX. The population was about 5,000 in 1849 and later. Contemporary newspapers reported astonishing finds. In one week the banks received 3,412 ounces of gold, according to the *Alta*, March 1, 1852 (Bancroft Scraps, LI:1, p. 249). One company took out 500 ounces in less than three months (Hittell Clippings, p. 24), and in August, 1855, three Frenchmen got three and a half pounds in less than three hours after opening their hole. Hittell, *Mining* (p. 48), states that more than twenty nuggets of between one and thirty pounds each were found from 1850 to 1858 in or near Sonora. *Mines and Minerals* (p. 357) even states that a thirty pound nugget was picked up on the street. Perkins notes in his *Journal* (pp. 118 and 213) that on two occasions nuggets weighing more than twenty pounds were dug up by three Mexicans, who in both cases invested the profits in drinking and gambling. Whatever the truth there may be in these reports, the richness of the diggings are confirmed by other sources. Browne (p. 38) states that Sonora in August, 1865, still shipped 102 thousand dollars' worth of gold to the mints. *Mines and Minerals* (p. 358) gives the total production at 11 million dollars. The placers were nearly exhausted in 1858, but quartz mining continued for years, first with arrastres, then with stamp mills (Browne, pp. 38, 48 ff.; *Mining Press*, May 11, 1861). Some mines of the district were in operation until the middle of the twentieth century. The most productive mines were the Bonanza Mine in the town of Sonora with a total production of 1.5 million dollars (*see* Bonanza Mine) and the Sugarman Mine, two miles north of Sonora, with a production of a million dollars (*Mining Bureau*, XLV, p. 72; *Bull.*, 193, p. 121). Sonora apparently had the first photographic atelier in the Gold Rush, opened in 1848 by W. H. Rulofson (*CHSQ*, XXXIV, p. 293). The omnipresent Murieta settled here in the fall of 1851, and soon a number of murders were committed (Ridge, p. 21). A vigilance committee was formed in the same year (Perkins, pp. 225 ff.). *See* Holdens Gardens.

Sonora Bar [Amador]. *See* Lancha Plana.

Sonorita [Tuolumne]. Near Arastraville. The camp is mentioned by William Perkins (p. 403) in a letter dated October 24, 1851. It had a water-driven 10-stamp mill (*Mining Bureau*, XIII, p. 491) and an idle quartz mill is listed until 1928. According to Stoddart, "Annals of Tuolumne County" (No. 1) in *Tuolumne Courier*, February 23, 1861, Sonerita, the misspelled diminutive, was used by the Mexicans for the upper part of the town of Sonora.

Sorefinger. An unidentified place. Goethe (p. 159) tells this story: Prospectors from Mississippi and Vermont discussed the name of their camp when "Shorty," a six-footer, caught a man raiding a sluice box and shot him in a finger, whereupon the miners gave him the nickname Sorefinger, and upon his sudden departure, named their camp likewise.

Soulsbyville [Tuolumne]. Eight miles east of Sonora. It was also known as Solsby, Solsbury, and Soulsbys Flat. A rich vein parallel to the Mother Lode was discovered in 1856 by the Platt Brothers while hunting for their cattle. In 1858 a large stamp mill was in operation and it is said that the quartz yielded up to 500 dollars per ton (Hittell Clippings, p. 39). Later Benjamin Soulsby and his sons took up a claim north of the Platt claim and struck it even richer, according to an undated clipping from the Mariposa *Gazette*. Browne (pp. 45 f.) gives a detailed description, including the unique system under which the miners worked. The place became known as the center of the temperance movement in the county. It is Historic Landmark 420. The Soulsby District, which includes the area around Soulsbyville, Tuolumne, and Buchanan, produced an estimated 20 million or more dollars worth of gold. The most productive mines were the Soulsby, which yielded 5.5 million dollars; the Black Oak, 3.5 million; the South United, 1.7 million; the Grizzly, 1.5 million; the Gilson, 1.25 million; and the Draper, 1 million (*Bull.*, 193, pp. 121 ff. with map).

South Bar [Plumas]. On North Fork of Feather River. Discovered in the wake of the Gold Lake hunt. According to the *Pacific News*, August 21, 1850, a streak was found which yielded 5 thousand dollars per day in lumps of a quarter pound to a half pound. Two men got fifty-six pounds in one day (Bancroft, VI, pp. 363 f.).

South Canyon [El Dorado]. *See* Illinois Canyon.

South Carolina Mine [Calaveras]. South of Carson Hill. From 1850 to 1853 it was leased to Mexicans who were said to have taken out 400 thousand dollars before the lease was cancelled. After five years of idling, a 10-stamp mill was erected and the rock yielded forty dollars per ton (Browne, p. 60). A mine at the site is listed in the Mining Bureau reports until 1936.

Southern Consolidated Mines [Mono]. *See* Bodie.

South Eureka Mine [Amador]. *See* Eureka Mines.

South Fork [Nevada]. On the South Fork of Poorman Creek, about three miles south of Graniteville. It was a rich camp, but the placers were soon exhausted. The place was also once a voting precinct. (Bean, 1867, p. 402.)

South Fork [Shasta]. In the 1870s there were two companies working (*Annual Mining Review*, 1876, p. 41), one with a 12 thousand dollar mill at Shasta.

South Fork [Yuba]. The place is mentioned in an item of the *San Joaquin Republican* May, 1854, as being on the canal of the Sierra Mountain Water Company.

South Fork Salmon [Siskiyou]. South of the Forks of Salmon. J. Carr states in his retrospective account, *Pioneer Days in California* (p. 105) that he mined here unsuccessfully in February, 1851. It is listed as a placer mining district in *Register*, 1898. A description is given in *Bulletin*, 92 (p. 97).

South Osborn Hill [Nevada]. South of Grass Valley. Bean (p. 227) lists a number of mines operating between 1858 and 1865.

South Point Dry Diggings [El Dorado]. About three miles northwest of Georgetown. Shown on Bowman's map, 1873.

South Spring Hill Mine [Amador]. *See* Spring Hill Mine.

South United Mine [Tuolumne]. *See* Soulsbyville.

Spangled Gold Gulch [Madera?]. The camp is mentioned in the *Alta*, July 10, 1852 as "almost deserted."

Spangler District [San Bernardino]. Northeast of Randsburg. The main production has been in the Spangler Mine, which has been worked intermittently since 1896, with an average yield of forty dollars per ton (*Mining Bureau*, XLIX, Table 58; *Bull.*, 193, p. 152).

Spanish. There were very few natives of Spain in the gold mines, but the adjective was commonly used for camps settled by Mexicans and other Spanish-speaking people.

Spanish Bar [Calaveras]. On the south side of Mokelumne River, opposite Whites Bar, about six miles southeast of Jackson. Recorded on the Amador County map, 1866. The rich diggings after 1849 were apparently short lived. However, a letter of October 30, 1855 states that miners were earning fifty to one hundred dollars per day to the man (Hittell Clippings, p. 63½).

Spanish Bar [El Dorado]. On the Middle Fork of American River, over the ridge from Spanish Dry Diggings, above Poverty Bar. Shown on Goddard's map, 1857. It is mentioned by Wierzbicki (p. 41) in 1849, and in the El Dorado County History, 1883 (p. 182). A letter dated October 7, 1849, written by Matthew Scott to his sister Caroline, is in the manuscript collection of the California State Library, California Section.

Spanish Bar [Tuolumne]. North of Sonora, on the Stanislaus River. It is mentioned by Buckbee (p. 292) as the scene of a murder of two gold miners in February, 1852. It may be the same bar mentioned in *Mining Press*, August 3, 1861, as paying well, but listed in Stanislaus County.

Spanish Camp [Tuolumne]. This may refer to Martinez, southeast of Columbia. This camp was a "Spanish" camp named for a Mexican lady who brought in a large number of peons to work for her, according to Stoddart (pp. 128, 144). *See* Martinez.

Spanish Canyon [El Dorado]. In the vicinity of Coloma. In November, 1850, the U. S. Bureau of the Census lists the names of 284 inhabitants in the population schedule for Spanish Canion.

Spanish Corral [Placer]. *See* Ophir, Ophirville.

Spanish Diggings [El Dorado]. The diggings five miles northwest of Georgetown, near the Middle Fork of American River are also known as Spanish Dry Diggings. They were discovered in 1848 by Andrés Pico, brother of the last Mexican governor of California, and are recorded on all early maps. They are first mentioned as Spanish Bar by Buffum (p. 52) in December, 1848. At first they were worked only by Sonorians, until Americans, Germans, and others followed. According to the County History, 1883 (p. 185), the first permanent camp was called Dutchtown and was later changed to Spanish Dry Diggings. The camps are described by Wierzbicki (p. 41), Tyson (p. 10), and as they were in the summer of 1852 by Borthwick (pp. 168 ff.). There are numerous reports of large nuggets discovered in the 1850s (Huntley, p. 96; Hittell Clippings, p. 20). A "cluster of beautiful dentric crystals of gold" of 101.4 ounces troy was found at the Grit claim in August, 1865 (*Mining Bureau*, II, part 1, p. 149). This is apparently the specimen given to the State Mining Bureau by the Fricot family and now on display in the Ferry Building in San Francisco, but the weight of the specimen is 201 ounces troy, according to *Bulletin*, 193 (p. 9). The Grit (Liddicoat, Spanish Dry Diggings) Mine was worked intermittently between 1852 and 1952 (*Mining Bureau*, LII, p. 415). The fineness of gold at the Sliger Mine was as high as 925°. This lode mine was active intermittently from 1864 to 1942, and in the decade between 1932 and 1942 more than 2.6 million dollars worth of gold was recovered (*Mining Bureau*, LII, pp. 425 ff.). Spanish Dry Diggings shown on the USGS Placerville 1931 quadrangle.

Spanish Flat [El Dorado]. Two miles north of Kelsey. Shown on Doolittle's map, 1868. Gold mining started probably as early as 1848. The first store was opened in 1849 (Co. Hist., 1883, pp. 191 f.). According to an item in the *Placer Herald*, a nugget worth 500 dollars was found in 1853 (Hittell Clippings, p. 21). A description of the camp in June, 1854, is given by Welles (pp. 280 f.). In 1855 water from the Pilot and Rock Creek Canal reached the place (item dated April 28, 1856, in Hittell Clippings, p. 73). The place had a post office from 1853 to 1872. The fineness of gold reached the high degree of 975 (*Mining Bureau*, IV, p. 220). Spanish Flat District includes the Alhambra Mine, which was active in the 1930s and 1940s and produced 1.25 million dollars. In 1939 one pocket yielding 550 thousand dollars was discovered in this mine. (*Bull.*, 193, pp. 11, 123 f.) *See* Louisville.

Spanish Flat [Plumas]. On Rabbit Creek, southeast of La Porte. Recorded on the Sierra County Map, 1874. John Clark ("The California Guide," January 3, 1853) mined here with success in the winter of 1853. Hayes Scrapbooks: Mining (I, sec. 50) marked December, 1860, gives a report from the *Mountain Messenger* describing the short-lived camp with its rich but not extensive diggings. The camp flourished between 1852 and 1857, but in 1860 only three families lived there.

Spanish: Flat, Gulch [Sierra]. In the Slate Creek Basin, southeast of La Porte. Shown on Crossman's map, 1867, and on Raymond's map in volume V. The *Alta*, December 30, 1853, reports the mining as "very dull," but according to the *Mountaineer* (Bancroft Scraps, LI:1, p. 237), it was a well-paying camp about 1865.

Spanish: Flat, Ravine [Placer]. One-half mile above Auburn. The Flat is shown on Trask's map, 1853. Notice of a claim dated October 20, 1851, is recorded January 10, 1852, in the Placer County Records, I,

(verso of p. 62). Stephen Wing worked his claim in the Ravine in the summer and fall of 1853, according to his journal (I). County History, 1882 (p. 228) records the finding of large nuggets, including one worth one thousand dollars, December 24, 1862.

Spanish Gulch [Amador]. Near Hunts Gulch. It is shown on the County Map, 1866, as a tributary to the Mokelumne River, just below Middle Bar. According to the County History, 1881 (p. 216), placering apparently started in 1850. In 1861 five arrastres were at work here (*Mining Press*, March 16, 1861). In 1967 Andrews, in his *Ghost Towns* (pp. 88 f.), reports finding a *tapia*, 'rammed earth house', still standing and most of the headstones in the cemetery undecipherable.

Spanish Hill [El Dorado]. There is a Little Spanish Hill in Placerville and a Big Spanish Hill south of it. Shown on Bowman's map, 1873. It is on the Deep Blue Channel. An interesting account is given in January, 1855, by Marks (pp. 53 f.). The production of gold reached the sum of 6 million dollars before 1911 (*Mining Bureau*, LII, p. 434).

Spanish: Ranch, Creek [Plumas]. Between the Middle and North forks of Feather River, seven miles west of Quincy. Recorded on Milleson and Adams' map, 1851, and Trask's, 1853. It was settled by Mexicans in 1850, apparently during the Gold Lake hunt. There were diggings on the creek above, and the owners of the ranch raised and sold pack animals to the miners. The place is mentioned repeatedly by Dame Shirley (p. 43, note). At the end of the century it was still the center for drift and hydraulic mining (*Register*, 1900). The Spanish Ranch post office was established in 1861 and was not discontinued until 1913. The mining district of 1917/18 is described in *Mining Bureau*, XVI (Plumas, pp. 46 ff.). Spanish Ranch and Creek are shown on the USGS Bidwell Bar 1944 quadrangle. Historic Landmark 481.

Spanish Ravine [El Dorado]. Near Placerville. Haskins (pp. 69 f.) tells an amusing story of a gentleman from Tennessee who brought three slaves to work for him in the winter of 1849–50. The claim was rich, but the negroes kept the gold, claiming that "Dey was now in a free country." Compare with Log Cabin Ravine.

Spanish Ridge [Nevada]. Three miles north of Washington. The deposits were not discovered until 1883. The low-grade quartz yielded at most one dollar and twenty-five cents worth of free gold per ton. At one time there were ten stamps and four Huntington mills in operation. The Spanish and other mines are listed and described in *Mining Bureau*, XVI (Nevada, p. 249). The Spanish mine is listed until 1941.

Spanishtown [Butte]. One mile northeast of Frenchtown, near Yankee Hill, east of the West Branch of the North Fork of Feather River. Shown on Goddard's map, 1857, and on the County Map, 1862. It was a temporary, flourishing camp, according to the County History, 1882 (p. 253). In a letter dated September 10, 1856 (reprinted in the County History, 1918, p. 71) it is stated that thirteen buildings had been erected within the past three weeks, and that a company of Chilenos had taken out three to five ounces per day to the hand; it is also stated that an old negro miner had taken out a little more than 700 dollars in three weeks work.

Speckled Diggings [Sierra]. About five miles northeast of Sierra City on a tributary to the South Fork of the North Fork of Yuba River. "New, rich and extensive diggings" were discovered in the summer of 1864 and were so-named because the cement boulders gave the appearance of being speckled or spattered (Sinnott, *Sierra City*, p. 11).

Spects Camp [Yuba]. On the main Yuba River, above Timbuctoo Ravine. It was a short-lived camp, where Jonas Spect discovered gold on June 2, 1848 (Co. Hist., 1879, p. 83).

Spenceville [Nevada]. On Dry Creek, close to the Yuba county line. It was an important station on the road from Sacramento to Grass Valley. In 1862 a well dug at Purtzman's ranch led to the discovery of the "Well Lede," which produced no gold but was for many years a rich producer of copper (Bean, p. 355; *Mining Bureau*, XVI, Nevada, p. 58; XXVI, p. 95). During World War II the place was used by Camp Beale as a simulated German village for war maneuvers. Shown on the USGS Smartsville 1943 quadrangle.

Split Rock Ferry [Mariposa]. On the Merced River, about four miles northwest of Bagby; about midway between Horseshoe Bend and Bagby. It is apparently the place mentioned by Stephen Davis, April 24 and 26, 1852. The site is shown on the USGS Coulterville 1949 quadrangle.

Spread Eagle Mine [Mariposa]. *See* Whitlock.

Spring Branch [Nevada]. On Little Deer Creek, now a part of Nevada City. The *Alta*, March 6, 1853, reports that fifty dollars per pan were washed out at this camp at that time.

Spring Creek [Nevada]. *See* Knapps Creek.

Spring Creek [Shasta]. A branch of the Sacramento River, near Keswick Dam. According to a clipping of April, 1864, in Hayes Scrapbooks: Mining, IV, sec. 5, a 20-stamp mill was constructed in the spring of 1864 near the mouth of the creek. In 1874 there was a 6-stamp steam-driven mill (*Annual Mining Review*, 1876, p. 22). In 1895 the mines were still making good showings (*Mining Bureau*, XI, p. 395). According to Steger the Creek was famous for its nuggets. One was discovered in 1870 and minted 33 hundred dollars; another one, a mixture of gold and quartz, was found near by in 1880 and was sold for 15 hundred dollars.

Springfield [Tuolumne]. Southwest of Columbia, on Mormon Creek; the two springs forming the headwaters. On Goddard's map, 1857, it is mistakenly recorded on Woods Creek. According to Eastman, the camp developed at a place called Tims Garden or Tims Springs. Heckendorn (pp. 65, 104) lists the principal claims and states that this was the only mining camp where a church was built before the first gambling house opened. In June, 1854, a three-pound lump of quartz was picked up containing one pound of pure gold (Hittell Clippings, p. 21). A good description of the camp is given by George Hobbs in a letter dated November 25, 1854 (*in* Letters of Asa H. Thompson). He states that it was considered the best camp in the vicinity. In the dry season the dirt was carted to the three large springs, which provided water for washing and gave the name to the place. According to Browne (p. 38), some cartloads were said to have yielded as much as one thousand dollars each, and the average earning in the early 1850s was ten to twenty dollars a day. In its heydays the place had 600 voters, in 1867 only one-tenth of that number. The post office, established in 1857, was discontinued in 1868. According to *Mines and Minerals* (p. 358), Springfield was one of the camps that contributed substantially to the 55 million dollar production of the Columbia district. A mine is listed until 1931, and the place is recorded on the USGS Big Trees 1941 quadrangle. It is Historic Landmark 432.

Springfield District [El Dorado]. North of the North Fork of Cosumnes River. It is sometimes also called El Dorado or Mud Springs District. The name Springfield is derived from the Springfield Mine, which became part of the Union Mine. It was a rich mining region and included the camps at El Dorado (Mud Springs), Aurum City, Uniontown, and Logtown. The Union (Springfield) Mine was considered the largest source of lode gold in the county, according to *Mining Bureau*, LII (pp. 426 f.). It was first worked in the early 1850s and operated at times with the nearby Church Mine and at times separately. The estimate of the total production varies between 2.7 million and 5 million dollars. It has been idle since 1940. The Church Mine, first worked in 1850, was closed in 1942; in 1953 a 20-stamp mill there was used as a custom chrome mill and later also to treat tungsten ore. (*Mining Bureau*, LII, p. 412). *See* Uniontown; El Dorado; Aurum City.

Spring Flat [El Dorado]. One-half mile north of Grizzly Flats. There was rich surface mining in 1853. The camp is mentioned by Crockett (p. 40) in 1856 and in County History, 1883 (p. 195).

Spring Garden, Spring Garden Ranch [Placer]. Southwest of Yankee Jims. The Ranch is recorded on Trask's map, 1853, and Doolittle's, 1868. The *Alta*, June 15, 1854, reprinted an item from the *Placer Democrat*, in which it was reported that placers at Spring Garden were discovered and paid two to eight dollars per pan. Wade H. Johnston mined here briefly in the fall of 1854 with fair success (Reminiscences). A Spring Garden Consolidated Placer Mine is listed in Mining Bureau reports until 1936. Spring Garden is shown on the USGS Colfax 1950 quadrangle and Spring Garden Ravine on the Georgetown 1949 quadrangle.

Spring Garden District [Plumas]. In the south-central part of the county. Years ago there was some hydraulic mining in the area around Spring Garden and Argentine Rock, according to *Bulletin*, 193 (p. 124), and in recent years there has been intermittent prospecting.

Spring Gulch [Butte]. The County History, 1882 (p. 253) lists Spring Gulch as a once-flourishing mining camp in Concow township.

Spring Gulch [Calaveras]. Six miles southeast of San Andreas, near Washington Ranch and Old Gulch. The San Francisco *Bulletin*, January 18, 1858, reports hydraulic mining with considerable success. An extract from the San Andreas *Independent* marked March, 1860, in Hayes Scrapbooks: Mining, I, sec. 64, calls it a new mining locality. Spring Gulch was apparently used as an alternate name for Alabama Gulch near Pleasant Springs. *See* Alabama Gulch.

Spring Gulch [Tuolumne]. About one and a half miles east of Columbia, on the Yankee Hill Road. Rich Diggings were reported in the 1850s. One claim prospected eight dol-

Springfield, Tuolumne Co.

lars to the pan (*Alta*, November 22, 1853), and another paid a half ounce per day to the man in 1855 (*San Joaquin Republican*, April 27, 1855). A French miner discovered a nugget of nearly pure gold, valued at more than 5 thousand dollars (*Mining Bureau*, II, part 1, p. 149). The Jellison claim had paid eight to ten dollars per day to the man for a long time (San Francisco *Evening Bulletin*, September 23, 1858), and Miller and Hawes' claim was paying handsomely in 1859 (*Tuolumne Courier*, November 12, 1859). Mulford (p. 255) campaigned here in 1866 as a candidate for the legislature.

Spring Hill Mine, Spring Mill [Amador]. Now in Amador City. Shown south of the creek on the County Map, 1866. According to the County History, 1881 (pp. 145, 153), gold was discovered in 1851 by a group of preachers and was named for the nearby springs and for an associate in the venture named Hill. In February, 1851, according to the story, quartz mining was attempted without success until later in the year, when a German who had mined in Peru introduced the arrastre. The company then took out seventy-five ounces a week, of which the German received one-third. A description of Spring Mill is given in *Transactions*, 1859 (p. 81). It was the oldest of five quartz mills near Amador City. According to *Guidebook* (p. 65), it was the nucleus of the Original Amador Mine. This mine operated intermittently between 1852 and 1937, with an estimated total production of 3.5 million dollars (*Mining Bureau*, L, pp. 188 ff.). South Spring Hill Mine was located in 1851, and by 1875 it had become highly productive (*Bull.*, 108, p. 91). In 1887 it had a 30-stamp mill and operated intermittently until 1920, when it was taken over by the Keystone Mining Company and was worked at intervals until 1942 (*Mining Bureau*, L, p. 193). Its production prior to 1902 was more than one million dollars. *See* Amador City.

Spring Town [Butte]. Shown prominently on Trask's map, 1853, but obviously only a misprint of String Town.

Springtown [Siskiyou]. On the South Fork of Salmon River, about three miles above the present-day town of Callahan. There were many Irish miners here (*Siskiyou Pioneer*, IV: 1, p. 35 and IV: 3, p. 77).

Spring Valley [Kern]. On Kern River. In 1858 it had a 4-stamp water-driven mill (*State Register*, 1859).

Spring Valley [Yuba]. Apparently on the Middle Fork of Yuba River, near the Sierra County line. It is described by Huntley (pp. 201 ff.) in May, 1852, and is mentioned by De Long, September 21, 1855.

Spring Valley Mine [Butte]. *See* Cherokee [Butte].

Spruce Flat [Trinity]. On South Fork of Trinity River. Moderate placer mining was reported in 1861 (*Mining Press*, September 21, 1861).

Squabbletown [Tuolumne]. On Woods Creek, less than one mile north of Browns Flat. It is now a ghost town, but the Squabbletown Mine is listed until 1928 (*Mining Bureau*, XXIV, p. 46). Shown on the USGS Columbia 1948 quadrangle.

Squaw Creek District [Shasta]. West of Kennett; the town is now under Shasta Lake. A number of rich diggings were reported in *Mining Press*, June 29, 1861. The Uncle Sam Mine is credited with a production of one million dollars before it closed down in the 1890s (*Mines and Minerals*, p. 375).

Squaw Gulch [Amador]. In the rich gravel bed east of Jackson. Shown on the County Map, 1866. The name is listed in Bancroft, VI (p. 372).

Squaw Hollow [Calaveras]. Near West Point and Bummerville, on a rich quartz lode. It is mentioned in the *Calaveras Chronicle*, May 1, 1878.

Squaw: Hollow, Creek [El Dorado]. The creek is a tributary to the North Fork of Cosumnes River. The diggings date from 1854; they are mentioned by Crockett in 1859 (p. 94). The Grand Victory Mine on Squaw Creek was in operation from 1857 to 1901, first with a 5-stamp mill, then one with 40 stamps. In the 1930s there was some prospecting (*Mining Bureau*, LII, p. 414). Squaw Hollow Creek is recorded on the USGS Placerville 1931 quadrangle. There is another Squaw Creek, which runs into the South Fork of American River, above Coloma.

Squires Canyon [Placer]. A branch of Bear River, south of Dutch Flat Canyon, in the Gold Run district. Shown on Pettee and Bowman's map, 1879. Browne (pp. 102 f.) lists seven claims in 1867, most of which were apparently opened after the South Yuba ditch brought water for hydraulic mining. The geology is described in Whitney, *Auriferous Gravels* (p. 153).

Squirrel Creek [Plumas]. According to a clipping from the *Plumas National*, February 29, 1872, in Hayes Scrapbooks: Mining II, sec. 20, a company made eighteen dollars a day to the hand on a flat near

Argentine, opposite the mouth of the creek.

Squirrel Creek Diggings [Nevada]. The creek is a tributary to Yuba River, near Grass Valley. In March, 1854, the average yield was reported to be sixteen dollars per day to the hand, (Hittell Clippings, pp. 26, 27) and according to the *Alta*, March 10, 1854, even twenty-five dollars. In 1867 several companies were working successfully (Bean, p. 357).

Squirrel Gulch [Siskiyou]. A tributary to Salmon River. According to the *Alta*, April 22, 1856, a lump of fifty ounces of pure gold was found here (Bancroft Notes).

Stag Flat [El Dorado]. On the Rock Creek Canal, east of Coloma. It is mentioned in the *Alta*, May 13, 1854. This may be Stagg Flat mentioned in the El Dorado County Records (Deed Book, D, p. 587).

Stagg [San Bernardino]. *See* Ludlow.

Standard Mines. *See* Bodie and Mojave Mining District.

Stanislaus Diggings [Calaveras]. There are several early references to diggings at or near the Stanislaus River, probably near Robinsons Ferry. On October 7, 1848, Francisco Coronel, a native of Mexico, who became mayor of Los Angeles in 1853, began working a claim near the Stanislaus river in a ravine in which Indians had discovered rich deposits. In three days he gathered about 134 ounces of gold with the help of two servants, and he worked with continued success for about a month. (Coronel, "Cosas de California," pp. 141 f.) Walter Colton visited a camp of Sonorians in the mountains near the Stanislaus, and in his journal of October 20, 1848, he mentions that a few weeks before a lump of nearly pure gold weighing twenty-three pounds, cubic in form, had been found. Abrams and his partners mined successfully in September, 1849, at a place he called Stanislaus Diggings. *See* Eutaw Camp. Ryan, who visited mining regions in California in the summer of 1849, describes mining on the lower Stanislaus in the first part of volume II of his *Personal Adventures in Upper and Lower California in 1848-9*. In 1868 Browne (p. 61) gives a detailed description of the Stanislaus quartz mine, just north of the river. The mine was remarkable in that much of the gold was in the form of a telluride. A description is also given in *Bulletin*, 108 (p. 133). It later became part of the Melones Consolidated Mines.

Stanislaus Mesa [Tuolumne]. *See* Table Mountain.

Stanshaw [Siskiyou]. *See* Stenshaw.

Star City [Mono]. About one and a half miles northwest of Cameron, in the Patterson District. It was a mining camp of the 1880s, along with Boulder Flat, Cameron, Monte Cristo.

Star City [Shasta]. On Star City Creek, a tributary to McCloud River. It was a prosperous mining district in the 1850s, probably named for John B. Star, who had a trading post there. Gold mining continued until the 1920s. Star City group is listed in the *Mining Bureau*, XVIII (p. 495).

Starr King Mine [Tuolumne]. Fifteen miles southeast of Sonora. Like the mountain in Yosemite National Park, it was named for Thomas Starr King, Unitarian clergyman and famous orator in the Civil War. In 1867 it had a 5-stamp mill, and the yield was as high as 150 dollars per ton (Browne, p. 46). It is listed, apparently as idle, in 1927 in *Mining Bureau*, XXIV (p. 20).

Startown [Placer]. Near the North Fork of the Middle Fork of American River; about a mile northeast of Last Chance. According to *Stars and Stripes*, June 15, 1871, it yielded richly by hydraulicking (Raymond, IV, p. 115). Shown on the USGS Colfax 1938 quadrangle.

Starvation Bar [Nevada]. On the South Fork of Yuba River, three miles above the mouth. It is listed in Giffen's file.

Starvation Flat [San Bernardino]. *See* Bear Valley.

Starvation Flat [Trinity]. A wide bar above a sharp bend of Trinity River, north of Lewiston and near Eastman Gulch. A Starvation Mine, discovered in 1932, was operating in 1941, using a nearby small quartz mill (*Mining Bureau*, XXXVII, pp. 59, 87). A dredger operated on the flat for years (H. E. Goodyear).

Steadman District [San Bernardino]. *See* Stedman district.

Steamboat Bar [Sierra]. On the North Fork of Yuba River, west of Downieville. Recorded on Trask's map, 1853. The Steamboat Company is said to have averaged 5 thousand dollars a day for some weeks in 1851 (Co. Hist., 1882, p. 457).

Stedman: town, District [San Bernardino]. About eight miles south of Ludlow. The greatest activity in the district was between 1904 and 1916, with some work again in the 1930s and 1940s and occasional prospecting since that time. The chief producer was the Bagdad-Chase Mine, which yielded more than 6 million dollars. Gold was discovered in 1899 by John Sutter, a Santa Fe Railroad man who was looking for water in the hills south of Ludlow. His claim, called the Bagdad Mine was later combined with nearby claims and operated by a group of capitalists as the Bagdad-Chase Mine. The officers of the corporation were Chauncey M. Depew, head of the New York Central Railroad as president; J. H. Stedman of Rochester, New York, as secretary; and Benjamin E. Chase also of Rochester, as treasurer. The principal town was called Stedman (sometimes spelled Steadman), and it was also known as Rochester, or Camp Rochester. The corporation built its own railroad from Stedman to a junction with the Santa Fe at Ludlow. As the town declined and disappeared, the tracks were removed in 1935. Stedman district was also known as Rochester District. (*Mining Bureau*, XLIX, pp. 71 f.; *Bull.*, 193, pp. 167 f.; Belden, November 23, 1952; Haenszel.) *See* Buckeye District.

Steelys Fork [El Dorado]. On the Cosumnes River, near Grizzly Flat. The camp was named for Victor J. W. Steely, who discovered gold here in the Mt. Pleasant mining district in March, 1852 (Co. Hist., 1883, p. 194). The place is mentioned as a settlement in 1856 by Crockett (p. 40), and the *State Register*, 1857, lists three mills in operation. The name is sometimes spelled Steeley.

Steep Gulch [Calaveras]. On the Mokelumne River. According to Gerstaecker (I, p. 377), rich diggings were discovered here by an Irishman who fell into the gulch while drunk.

Steep Hollow Diggings [Nevada]. North of Dutch Flat, on Steep Hollow Creek, tributary to Bear River. In September, 1849, the Buckeye Rovers did some not very successful prospecting here and on Bear River (pp. 90 ff.). The rich deposits were apparently discovered later: the *Alta* reports great excitement on April 16, 1852. In 1869 there were active diggings, according to an item in Bancroft Scraps (LI:3, p. 712). The Steep Hollow group of mines was idle around 1915, but it is still listed in the Mining Bureau reports as late as 1940. Steep Hollow Creek is recorded on the USGS Colfax 1938 quadrangle.

Steiners: Bar, Flat, Ranch [Trinity]. On Trinity River, southwest of Weaverville. The ranch was started by Benjamin Steiner in 1850 and developed into a rich placering district and an important trading center. It was also called Steinerville "by way of courtesy" (Cox, pp. 32, 42 ff.). Steiner Flat Mine is described as an "old producer"

(*Mining Bureau*, XIV, p. 914) and is listed until 1940. Steiner Flat is recorded on the USGS Weaverville 1942 quadrangle.

Stella [Shasta]. *See* Whiskeytown.

Stenshaw [Siskiyou]. On Klamath River, above Somes Bar. Placer mining was carried on until the end of the century (*Register*, 1898). Shown on USGS Sawyers Bar 1945 quadrangle. Stenshaw Placer is listed in Mining Bureau reports until 1935. The name is also spelled Stanshaw.

Stent [Tuolumne]. Two and a half miles south of Jamestown. It was formerly known as Poverty Hill (*Mining Bureau*, XIII, p. 479), on the summit of which it is situated. In the 1850s placer mining started at Stent and quartz mining at its twin camp Quartz, Quartzburg, or Quartz Mountain. Later both camps were centers of hardrock mining. The post office was first at Stent, then at Quartz, until it was discontinued in 1925. Among the most productive mines were the App-Heslep, which yielded 6.5 million dollars; the Jumper, 5 million; the Dutch Sweeney, 3 million; and the Santa Ysabel, 1.5 million (*Bull.*, 193, p. 78). *See* Poverty Hill; Quartz.

Stephens Bar [Tuolumne]. *See* Stevens Bar.

Sterling [Del Norte]. An unidentified gold camp of 1851, or 1852, mentioned in the San Francisco *Bulletin*, March 29, 1859 (Bancroft Notes).

Steubenville [Calaveras ?]. No mining records were found, but the "Steubenville" boys from Ohio were mentioned in the early gold days (Amador Co. Hist., 1881, p. 198). The name may be connected with Zane Steuben, who was in business with Crockett in 1854 (Crockett, pp. 1 ff.) at Smith Flat in Calaveras County.

Stevens [Trinity]. In the New River region. Placering was carried on until the end of the nineteenth century (*Register*, 1898). A Stevens Gulch Mine is listed in Mining Bureau reports until 1940.

Stevens Bar [Tuolumne]. On the Tuolumne River; near the confluence with Moccasin Creek, south of Jacksonville. According to Buckbee (p. 475), it was named in 1851 for its discoverer Simon Stevens. It is obviously the same place recorded as Stevensons Bar on Trask's map, 1853, and on Goddard's, 1857. It is spelled Stephens Bar by Daniel B. Woods, who states (p. 172) that the Stephen's Bar Damming & Mining Company, composed of thirty-eight men, took out 12 thousand dollars in the summer and fall of 1850. It is mentioned by Stephen Davis, April 21 and September 1, 1852. Apparently it was a sizeable place in 1856 (Heckendorn, p. 88). For some reason, *Mines and Minerals*, 1898 (p. 358) and *Mining Bureau*, 1927 (XXIV, p. 42) put it together with the rather distant places of Don Pedro's Bar and Jacksonville and give the total production of the three places at nine million dollars.

Stevens Hill [Placer]. In the Iowa Hill divide. No early mining reports were found, but six drift mines are still listed in the County History, 1882 (p. 216).

Stevensons Bar [Tuolumne]. *See* Stevens Bar.

Stewart [Tuolumne]. *See* Sonora.

Stewarts Flat [Placer]. In Secret Ravine, one mile east of Loomis. Shown on Doolittle's map, 1868. According to May W. Perry in *Placer Nuggets*, October, 1964 (p. 1), Stewarts Flat came into existence in the early 1850s, and at one time the population was around 1,500. A 5-stamp mill was established in 1864 (*Annual Mining Review*, 1876, p. 23). The yield was at first six dollars per ton, but it increased as the shaft was deepened. According to Browne (p. 110), the mine was worked from 1862 to 1864 and the average yield was fifteen dollars per ton, and if a report in County History, 1882 (p. 196), is correct, the Tom Seymour Mill, built 1862, turned out as much as sixty dollars per ton. It was apparently here that the Russ amalgamator was first used. According to Rensch-Hoover, the town of Stewarts Flat was abandoned in 1867 after the granite quarries were established at nearby Penryn, and today only the graveyard marks the site of the once populous town.

Stickness Gulch [Placer]. Below Michigan Bluff. Four tail sluices paid well from 1860 to 1863 (Browne, p. 96). The name is spelled Stickners in Whitney, *Auriferous Gravels* (p. 117).

Stillwagen [El Dorado]. Seven miles west of Fairplay. Listed in Hittell's roster. A Stillwagon lode mine operated intermittently between 1890 and 1914 and is listed by the Mining Bureau until 1956.

Stingtown [Plumas]. On the South Fork of Feather River, near the Sierra County line. Weston (pp. 17 ff.) gives a detailed account of the diggings in the summer of 1852. One of Weston's partners was severely stung by a scorpion; this might be the reason for naming the camp. There was a Stringtown farther down the river in Butte County.

Stockings Flat [Nevada]. Below Nevada City, near Randolph Flat. It is mentioned as a mining camp in Nevada City *Transcript*, May 21, 1875.

Stockton Creek [Mariposa]. A tributary to Mariposa Creek, about one mile south of Mariposa. It was originally called Ave Maria River, and it is so marked on Trask's map, 1853. There was a store and a corral at the junction of the two creeks before the influx of gold seekers, according to Crampton (p. 66). The Ave Maria Company worked here in 1852. *See* Ave Maria. Allsop speaks repeatedly of other operations on Stockton Creek. A water-driven quartz mill was listed in the *State Register*, 1857, and a Stockton Creek Mine, a half mile east and a little south of Mariposa, discovered in the 1850s, was worked intermittently to 1938 (*Mining Bureau*, XXIV, p. 188; LIII, p. 308; *Bull.*, 193, p. 89).

Stockton Hill [Calaveras]. On Chili Gulch; in Mokelumne Hill townsite. It was one of the richest mining areas in the state. According to the *Alta*, January 6, 1852, four men had washed out fifty ounces from the dirt of one (apparently real) coyote hole. Later an item in the *Calaveras Chronicle* reported that a nugget of fourteen ounces had been picked up (Hittell Clippings, p. 27). In 1854 a tunnel yielded seventy dollars in one hour (*Alta*, July 3, 1854). The San Francisco *Bulletin*, October 31, 1865, reported a rich find of opals. A Stockton Hill drift mine was active before 1900, and was reactivated in 1903–1904 and again in 1935–1936 (*Mining Bureau*, XXXII, pp. 352 f.; *County Report*, II, p. 207).

Stockton Hill [Nevada]. Two mining camps of this name are listed by Foley, one at North Bloomfield and one, also known as Gun Town, north of Weaver Lake, northeast of Graniteville.

Stone Cabin Gulch [Calaveras]. Two miles south of Campo Seco. In 1854 a nugget of ninety-three ounces, valued at 1,760 dollars, was found twenty feet below the surface (*Mining Bureau*, II, part 1, p. 149).

Stone: City, House, Creek, Settlement [Calaveras]. *See* Lost City.

Stone Creek [Amador]. Listed in Hittell's roster.

Stone Fort [Tuolumne]. Near Table Mountain; northwest of Jamestown. It was apparently a mining camp, but was found listed only in Nadeau's *Ghost Towns*. There was a so-called "stone fort" at New York Tent, at or near Yosemite Junction, but the so-called "loopholes" were, in the opinion of De Ferrari, actually placements for the ends of timber.

Stone House Bar [Butte]. In the Big Bend of

the North Fork of Feather River, opposite Stoney Creek. It was a flourishing but short-lived camp (Co. Hist., 1882, pp. 209, 253, and map).

Stoner Ravine [El Dorado]. It is mentioned by Crockett (p. 95) in 1858 as a locality near Diamond Springs.

Stonewall Mine [San Diego]. Seven miles south of Julian, southeast of Lake Cuyamaca. The mine was located about 1870 and was named for the famous Confederate leader in the Civil War, Stonewall Jackson. The original name was Stonewall Jackson Mine and was later abbreviated to Stonewall Mine. It was the most productive mine in the county, having yielded an estimated 2 million dollars. The period of highest production was after 1886 when Robert W. Waterman was governor of California, 1887–1891. Between 1889 and 1891 alone the yield was almost 1 million dollars. By 1893 most of the accessible ore was mined. In 1898 a cyanide reduction plant was installed and 35,000 tons were processed. Later attempts to reopen the mine were unsuccessful. In 1933 it was purchased by the State of California and it is now a part of the Cuyamaca Rancho State Park. A detailed description is given in *County Report*, III (pp. 133 f.). An account is also given in Ellsberg, *Mines of Julian*.

Stoney Bar [Yuba]. On the North Fork of Yuba River, near Fosters Bar. Shown on Trask's map, 1853. Clement G. Whitcomb refers to it in a letter dated September 10, 1854, as the "liveliest spot on the [Yuba] river this year" (Whitcomb Family Papers). De Long collected the miners tax here, September 26, 1855. According to the County History, 1879 (p. 94), about 500 men mined here in the early days; in 1879 only four French prospectors were left.

Stony Bar [Amador]. On the north side of Mokelumne River, southwest of Jackson. According to A. Lascy's reminiscences, the miners in 1849 had done well. Goddard's map, 1857, records a Stony Bar on the Mokelumne, east of Jackson.

Stony Bar [Butte]. On the Middle Fork of Feather River, between Kanaka Bar and Big Stony Bar. Goddard's map shows both Stony and Big Stony bars, but Trask's map, 1853, shows only Big Stony Bar.

Stony Bar [Butte]. On the north side of the North Fork of Yuba River, seven miles above the junction with Middle Fork. Shown on Trask's map, 1853.

Stony Bar [El Dorado]. At the junction of Otter Creek and the Middle Fork of American River. Shown on Goddard's map, 1857.

Stony Bar [El Dorado]. On the South Fork of American River, about five miles upstream from Coloma, above Live Oak Bar. It is recorded on Trask's map, 1853, and on Doolittle's, 1868, and is mentioned in the County History, 1883 (p. 85). A claim below the mouth of Kelsey Canyon is recorded in the El Dorado County Records (Mining Book A, p. 5) August 21, 1852.

Stony Bar [Nevada]. On north side of Rush Creek, one mile above its east branch. Shown on Trask's map, 1853. Stephen Jackson mined here in the fall of 1852 and describes it in a letter datelined Stoney Bar, November 20th.

Stony Bar [Placer]. On the North Fork of the Middle Fork of American River. Recorded on Gibbes' map, 1851. The Sacramento *Transcript*, August 30, 1850 (p. 2), reports that a company of nine men took out one thousand dollars in one day, and a pan of dirt yielded ten ounces of "clean gold" (Bancroft Notes). It is mentioned as a rich bar in the *Directory of Placer County*, 1861 (pp. 201 ff.). In the summer of 1850 the camp consisted of cloth tents and brush shanties. The Bradford Company built the first house (Augustus Moore, "Pioneer Experiences").

Stony Gulch [Tuolumne]. Near Columbia. According to an item in the Columbia *Courier*, a rich find was reported made in 1858 (Hittell Clippings, p. 31). Among the many Stony gulches in the county was one adjoining Sawpit Gulch, near Shaws Flat (De Ferrari).

Stony Point Bar [Butte]. On the south side of the South Fork of Feather River, eight miles above the mouth of the Middle Fork. Recorded on Trask's map, 1853. No mining record was found.

Stop Jack Bar [Amador or El Dorado]. An unidentified place on Cosumnes River. It is listed in the Giffen file.

Stoutenburg [Calaveras]. On Coyote Creek, near Murphys. In August, 1859, the election returns for Murphys Diggings were from Stoutenberg (R. C. Wood). The camp was named for a German whom Gerstaecker called Staudenburg (*Travels* London, 1854, p. 239), probably William E. Stoutenburgh, or Stoutenberg, a member of the West Coast Mining Company (New York *Herald*, June 27, 1849), who discovered gold in Vallecito probably in the spring of 1849 (San Andreas *Independent*, May 1, 1858; CHSQ, XXII, p. 82). Gerstaecker, who visited the place in the summer of 1850, describes it as a town of about fifty tents, nearly as many "bars," two or three block houses, a house built of planks, three American and four French dining rooms, two doctors' or drug shops, about twenty gambling tables, and a private post office. The first store was opened by Stoutenburg (or Staudenburg). There was also a duly elected alcalde, sheriff, and constable. (*Travels*, London, 1854, p. 239; *Narrative*, New York, 1855, p. 227.) The majority of the miners were French at that time, and the French Revolution, immortalized by Gerstaecker, really started here. Gerstaecker at times speaks of Stoutenburg as though it were the same place as Murphys New Diggings or Rich Diggings. (*Narrative*, London, 1853, Vol. 1, pp. 324 f.) *See* Murphys and Vallecito.

Stowgy Bar [Yuba]. Apparently on the North Fork of Yuba River, near Texas Bar. It is mentioned in the Marysville *Directory*, 1858 (p. xxvii), as nearly deserted at that time, although a large amount of gold had been taken from it in the past.

Straders: Bar, Ferry [Trinity]. The place on Trinity River, east of Douglas City, is mentioned by Cox (p. 34).

Strafford [Placer]. On the North Fork of American River, above Kellys Bar. It was so named because many of the miners had arrived on the bark Strafford. Recorded on Butler's map, 1851, and as Stratfords on Trask's map, 1853.

Stranahans [Nevada]. Apparently about three miles northwest of Quaker Hill. It is mentioned in Raymond, VI (p. 117), as one of several old camps in this area.

Strawberry Flat [Placer]. Three miles from Iowa Hill, at the terminus of a rich lead from Independence. Notice of intention to construct a canal, filed December 24, 1855, and an indenture regarding the sale of mining ground, dated March 30, 1869, are recorded in the Placer County Records (I, p. 346; IV, pp. 377 f.). Four drift mines are listed in the County History, 1882 (p. 216).

Strawberry Valley [Yuba]. On State Highway 20, near the Butte County line. Shown on Milleson and Adams' map, 1851, and on most later maps. According to Booth, June 6, 1852, it was actually named for the wealth of wild strawberries. Mining was profitable as early as 1850. In 1852 there were already five or six solid houses (Lecouvreur, p. 233). In 1855 a post office was established at Strawberry Valley, but De Long, January 21 and 26, 1856, calls it Straw Berry Valley. *See*

California Place Names. The Strawberry Valley District included Eagleville, Clipper Mills, and mines north of the North Fork of Yuba River. None was active in 1915/16 (*Mining Bureau*, XV, p. 423).

String Canyon [El Dorado]. A tributary to the North Fork of Cosumnes River, between Mount Pleasant and Grizzly Flat. Fifteen stamps and two arrastres were erected in 1852 (*State Register*, 1859), and rich quartz mining followed (Co. Hist., 1883, p. 194). It is mentioned by Crockett (p. 40) in 1856.

Stringer District [Kern]. Two miles south of Randsburg. The mines are listed in the *County Report*, I.

Stringtown [Butte]. On the South Fork of Feather River, near the junction with Middle Fork. It is recorded on Butler's and Milleson and Adams' maps of 1851, and is mentioned in Delano's *Life* (p. 276), and in several of his letters of 1850. There was mining as early as 1849 or 1850, but the place did not flourish until the river was flumed in 1852 (Co. Hist., 1882, p. 260). This book also tells (p. 210) the story of a hitherto unlucky miner who dug up a nugget in the "shape of a beef's heart," worth 15 hundred dollars. The camp had a post office from 1854 to 1858. Shown on the USGS Bidwell Bar 1944 quadrangle.

Strongs Diggings [Placer]. *See* Damascus.

Strope Creek [Trinity]. *See* Stroup Creek.

Stroubery Valley [Yuba]. The name is recorded on Trask's map, 1853, as a camp; but it is probably only a misspelling of Strawberry.

Strouds [Yuba]. Bob Stroud kept a hotel somewhere between Camptonville and Fosters Bar. The place is repeatedly mentioned by De Long in 1854–55 and was also known as Milk Ranch.

Stroup Creek [Trinity]. The creek above Minersville is mentioned by Cox (p. 90). It is the same as Strope Creek.

Strychnine City [Sierra]. *See* Brandy City.

Stuarts: Hill, Flat [Calaveras]. On the Calaveras River. According to an item in the *Calaveras Chronicle*, reprinted in the *Alta*, June 5, 1854, the hill was then profitably worked by a large number of miners. In the flats large amounts of gold had been taken out, and two miners returned to the Atlantic states with 16 thousand dollars each, earned after eight months of work.

Stuckslager Mine. *See* Lotus [El Dorado].

Stud Horse Bar [Placer]. On the North Fork of American River. The bar is mentioned in a notice of a claim laid August 7, 1852, and registered in the Placer County Records, I (p. 111).

Stud Horse Flat [Mariposa]. Three miles northwest of Bagby. The group of claims is described in 1920 in *Mining Bureau*, XVII (p. 139).

Sturdevants Ranch [Trinity]. The ranch between Junction City and Weaverville was a mining camp as early as 1849 or 1850. It was later named for a Mr. Sturdevant who built a sawmill and developed a farm in 1856. Miners netted eight to ten dollars a day, according to Cox (pp. 55 f.). The Sturdivant hydraulic mine, which later became a part of the La Grange operation, is described in 1912–14 (*Mining Bureau*, XIV, p. 914); and in 1950 the Oregon Gulch Dredging Company operated a dredge to mine the tailings accumulated near the mouth of Oregon Gulch from the workings of the La Grange Mine, but the recovery was poor and the dredge was soon shut down (*County Report*, IV, pp. 32, 35 f.).

Succertown [Amador]. *See* Suckertown.

Succor Flat [Placer]. About one and a half miles east of Iowa Hill. It was called Sucker Flat until the U. S. Board on Geographic Names in its sixth *Report* changed the name to Succor Flat. The place is shown on the County Map, 1887. It was a short-lived flourishing camp in the 1850s and 1860s, according to Rensch-Hoover (in the entry Iowa Hill). Raymond, VII (p. 108) mentions it in 1874 along with Grizzly Flat, Prospect Hill, and Wisconsin Hill, all in the vicinity of Iowa Hill and with a good potential for hydraulic mining. Succor Flat, apparently only a geographic feature is shown on the USGS Colfax 1938 quadrangle.

Sucker. The word is frequently found in the names of camps and mines. It could often not be ascertained whether it was for the carplike fish, or for a native of Illinois, the "Sucker state," or whether a camp was inhabited by "suckers."

Sucker Bar [Butte]. Probably on Sucker Run, tributary to the South Fork of Feather River, north of Forbestown. Booth mined here without much success from May to October, 1853. Sucker Run is recorded on the County Map, 1862, and on the USGS Bidwell Bar 1944 quadrangle.

Sucker Bar [Yuba]. On the North Fork of Yuba River, north of Fosters Bar, opposite Willow Bar. Shown on Trask's map, 1853. De Long collected miners' taxes here March 19 and September 23, 1855.

Sucker Creek [Del Norte]. The San Francisco

Bulletin, March 29, 1859, mentions gold diggings in 1851 or 1852 (Bancroft Notes).

Sucker Flat [Placer]. *See* Succor Flat.

Sucker Flat [Yuba]. Near the main Yuba River; one mile above Timbuctoo. Shown on Trask's map, 1853, and Wescoatt's 1861. It was first named Gatesville, for an early settler named Gates who came from Illinois, the "Sucker state." There was small scale placering as early as December, 1849. After water was brought from the Tri-Union and other ditches, mining improved steadily. (*Marysville Directory*, 1858, p. xxix; Co. Hist., 1879, p. 84). In *Transactions*, 1860 (p. 88), it is stated that the gold in one claim was termed "fine flour" and yielded as much as nineteen dollars per ounce. The Sucker Flat Channel extends from Timbuctoo to Smartsville. A description of the claims in this area is given in Browne (pp. 149 ff.). The claim owned by the Smartsville Blue Gravel Company was apparently the most productive, having yielded reportedly about one million dollars between 1864 and 1867. The estimated production of all the mines along the Channel is more than 2.5 million dollars, mostly before 1882. *See Mining Bureau*, XXXII (p. 79). Sucker Flat is shown on the USGS Smartsville 1943 quadrangle.

Sucker Riffle Bar [Butte]. On the Middle Fork of Feather River, near Kanaka Bar, close to the Plumas County line. Recorded on Trask's 1853 map, and on Goddard's 1857 map.

Sucker Run [Butte]. *See* Sucker Bar.

Suckertown [Amador]. Between Volcano and Fiddletown. Sucker Gulch is shown on the County Map, 1866. The miners were doing remarkably well in the winter of 1856 (*Amador Ledger*, March 8, 1856). Bowen mentions it as Succertown on April 10, 1855, in connection with the murder of two Chinese by Mexicans.

Sugar Loaf. Sugar was formerly delivered in a conoidal loaf to the grocer, who would break off pieces and sell it to customers by the pound. The familiar "sugar loaf" shape developed into a geographical generic term and was applied to a hill or mountain so shaped. The map of the United States became dotted with "sugar loafs," and California had its share of topographic features so named.

Sugar Loaf [El Dorado]. A mining district northwest of the confluence of the North and South forks of Cosumnes River. The hill which gave the name is shown about two miles northwest of Nashville on

Doolittle's map, 1868. It is mentioned by Crockett (p. 95) in 1859. The gold had a fineness of 968° (*Mining Bureau*, IV, p. 220). The famous Hermitage quartz mine near by, also shown on Doolittle's map, is described by Browne (p. 88). The hill is recorded as Sugar Loaf on the USGS Placerville 1931 quadrangle. Another Sugar Loaf is shown on the same quadrangle, about six miles west of Nashville. The Sugar Loaf Mine here is described in *Mining Bureau* LII (p. 426). It was a pocket ·mine worked in the early days of the Gold Rush by open cuts, and it was reactivated in the 1880s and worked to the 1950s. Still another Sugar Loaf, about a mile below Diamond Springs, is described in Whitney, *Auriferous Gravels* (p. 101). The Hill, after being drifted, was washed off, removing the whole top. The yield was reportedly about 3 million dollars.

Sugar Loaf [Nevada]. The name of the mountain just north of Nevada City, which yielded richly around 1855 (Hittell Clippings, p. 67).

Sugar Loaf [Nevada]. East of Red Dog; at the southern end of Chalk Bluff Ridge. Shown on Pettee and Bowman's map, 1879. Hydraulic mining here in 1870 is mentioned by Pettee in Whitney, *Auriferous Gravels* (p. 169).

Sugar Loaf Hill [Amador]. Between Clapboard and Indian gulches, near Volcano. There was considerable hydraulic mining here, exposing banks from seventy-five to eighty feet in height (Whitney, *Auriferous Gravels*, p. 102).

Sugar Loafs [Placer]. South of Iowa Hill, in the Blue Lead district. They are sometimes designated as No. 1 and No. 2 (Raymond, VII, p. 108). On the USGS Colfax 1938 quadrangle they are shown as Sugar Loafs.

Sugarman Mine [Tuolumne]. *See* Sonora.

Sugar Pine [Tuolumne]. On Sugar Pine Creek, about twelve miles east and north of Columbia. Shown on Dart's map, 1879. An extensive account of the diggings in 1862 is given in the *Mining Press*, June 9, 1862. In 1862 the famous Excelsior Mine was producing at the rate of 2 thousand dollars per day, according to the San Francisco *Bulletin*, August 21, 1862. By 1867 it had reportedly produced 300 thousand dollars, and its total production reached an estimated 500 thousand dollars (*Mining Bureau*, XIII, p. 478). The Invincible Mine was not true to its name and was discontinued after a good start; the Monitor Mine, which once claimed the sum of 300 dollars per ton, was likewise idle in 1867

(Browne, p. 47), but it was reactivated in 1893 (*Mining Bureau*, XII, p. 304). Dart's map of 1879 shows Sugar Pine G[ravel] Mine, Sugar Pine P[lacer] Mine, and Monitor, Excelsior and Mount Vernon Quartz mines. The settlement Sugar Pine is shown on the USGS Big Trees 1941 quadrangle.

Sulky Flat [Sacramento]. Near Folsom. Placer mining is mentioned in the *Pacific Coast Mining Review*, 1878 (p. 142), in the "once famous" mining district. In 1896 a mine one and a half miles southwest of Folsom was worked by Chinese (*Mining Bureau*, XIII, p. 318).

Sullivans: Creek, Diggings [Tuolumne]. A branch of Woods Creek; near Sonora. Recorded on Derby's map, 1849, and most other early maps. It was named for John Sullivan, a native of Ireland, who had come in 1844 with the Stevens Party, discovered the rich deposits in 1848, and opened a trading post (Buffum, p. 126; Perkins, p. 216). This part of the creek is south of Sonora, but Heckendorn (p. 104) mentions Sullivans: Creek, Dry Arroya, and Wet Arroya, three camps east of Sonora. The dry creek or arroyo heads in southern Sonora, while the wet creek is apparently the creek itself (De Ferrari). Our information refers to the lower part of the creek, which empties into Woods Creek, three miles south of Jamestown. Daniel B. Woods mentions the place repeatedly in 1849, and his narrative (pp. 94, 139) relates this incredible story: A Dutchman, following a vein under a rock, removed the rock with the help of some friends and in two hours took out forty pounds "of the precious ore" (!). A nugget of 408 ounces troy with an estimated value of 7,590 dollars was found in 1849. (*Mining Bureau*, II, part 1, p. 148.) In 1852 James Carr (p. 168) mentions the place as a heavy producer. Church, who was a partner, 1851–52, in the store at the confluence of Woods and Sullivan Creeks, gives an interesting account of the diggings (p. 184). In a letter of October 24, 1851 (pp. 402 f.), William Perkins made the exaggerated claim that the diggings on the creek had already yielded five and a half million dollars. He tells that the canyon diggings were then already reported exhausted (p. 215), but the rewashing with the use of long toms paid richly. In 1857 Street and Company built a dam and a reservoir, but soon after that the wealth appeared to be exhausted (Hittell Clippings, p. 50). *Mines and Minerals* (p. 358) gives the total production at 3 million dollars. A Sullivan Mine is still listed in 1927 *Mining Bureau*, XXIV (p. 46).

Sulphur Creek District [Colusa, Lake]. In the southwest corner of Colusa County and in adjacent Lake County. An account is given in *Bulletin*, 193 (p. 181). Gold was discovered in 1865, with the chief period of activity between 1880 and 1890. The total production is estimated at about 100 thousand dollars in gold. One of the mines, the Manzanita, was a mercury mine that also produced gold. There were also a few short-lived copper camps in western Colusa County (W. B. Clark).

Summersville [Tuolumne]. About two and a half miles southeast of Soulsbyville, in the Sierra Nevada East Gold Belt. In 1854 Franklin and Elizabeth Summers settled on Turnback Creek, tributary to the North Fork of Tuolumne River. In 1858 a quartz lode was discovered nearby, and the camp that developed was called Summersville, sometimes spelled Somerville. A post office was established here in 1888 and named Carters, for C. H. Carter, a local merchant. In 1908 the post office was discontinued and moved to the neighboring settlement Tuolumne. (*California Place Names*.) The mines in the area are mapped in *Bulletin*, 193 (p. 122). Summersville is Historic Landmark 407. Tuolumne is shown on the USGS Sonora 1939 quadrangle.

Summerville [Siskiyou]. On the South Fork of Salmon River, in the southwest corner of the county. The bar was completely mined off by the Salmon River Mining Company (W. M. Smith). The place is mentioned in the *Register*, 1898.

Summit City [Nevada]. *See* Meadow Lake.

Summit: City, Pass [Tuolumne]. About one mile from Columbia. Newspapers report rich yields in 1854 and later. The *Alta*, May 18 and 30, 1854, reports one company at the Pass making ten to twenty dollars per day to the hand and another washing out thirty ounces one day and fifty the next. The *San Joaquin Republican*, May 30, 1854, reports that more than four pounds were taken from one claim.

Summit Diggings [Kern, San Bernardino]. Northeast of Randsburg. In the early 1890s a placer was discovered on the summit of a spur of the El Paso Mountains where the highway to Searles Lake crossed, and considerable mining was carried on, mainly by dry washing. There was intermittent mining for short periods to the 1930s, mainly in San Bernardino County

(*Mining Bureau*, XII, p. 458; XXIX, p. 279; *County Report*, I, p. 189). The dry washing is illustrated in *Bulletin*, 92 (pp. 158, 159).

Summit House [Yuba]. *See* Mountain Cottage.

Sumneys Flat [Butte]. Near Stringtown. Asa B. Smith reports in a letter of January 30, 1859, that the claims on this flat were paying well in the winter.

Sunny Bar [Plumas]. It is mentioned as one of the chief camps on the Middle Fork of Feather River (Co. Hist., 1882, p. 288).

Sunny Hill [Shasta]. In the old prospecting ground, seven miles west of Ono. In 1892 *Mining Bureau*, XI (p. 396) reports that the ochre ore on the hill yielded allegedly 250 dollars of gold per ton. The Sunny Hill mines are listed by the Mining Bureau until 1939.

Sunols Washings [El Dorado]. Antonio Suñol of Sunol, Alameda County, had apparently mined with Sainsevain in May, 1848, at Coloma and Mormon Bar before he went to Weber Creek. His presence on Weber Creek the beginning of July is testified by Governor Mason and in Moerenhout's account (pp. 16, 23). He and his associates contributed samples of gold to the governor and the latter mentioned the diggings in his *Report* (30th Cong. 2nd sess. House Executive Doc. 1) as Sunolaco (map with *Report*) and Lunol & Co. (p. 58–64). *See* Dry Diggings.

Sunshine Valley [Mono]. In 1874 a 5-stamp gold mill was erected (*Annual Mining Review*, 1876, p. 21).

Supply Group [San Bernardino, Riverside]. *See* Dale District.

Surcease Mine [Butte]. *See* Yankee Hill [Butte].

Surf-Point Sal District [Santa Barbara]. The gold that has been washed from the beaches of Santa Barbara County may have contributed to the county's gold production, which in 1889 was recorded at 41 thousand dollars, according to *Bulletin*, 193 (p. 181).

Surprise Valley [Inyo]. In the Panamint District, west of the town of Panamint. Shown as Surprise Cañon on the County Map, 1884. There was mainly silver production, with some gold. Work began in 1873, and in 1894 there was still a 10-stamp mill, but the decline in the value of silver made mining unprofitable. In the 1930s there was some development and prospecting of the gold mines. (*Mining Bureau*, XII, p. 374; XXVIII, p. 358.)

Sutter Creek [Amador]. On Highway 49, between Amador City and Jackson. Shown

Sutter Creek Foundry, Amador Co.

as Sutter on Trask's map, 1853. The camp was named after the creek, on which Sutter had mined with Indians and Kanakas in 1848. The town developed in 1851 when quartz mining was introduced and continued as one of the principal gold mining centers. It was called Suttersville in the *Calaveras Chronicle*, October 25, 1851. When the post office was established in 1852, the name was Sutter Creek. A detailed history of the early days is found in the County History, 1881 (pp. 215 ff.). Knapp (pp. 513 ff.) gives an interesting description of 1852, including the appearance of the inevitable Joaquin Murieta. There were two quartz mills in 1851 (*Calaveras Chronicle*, October 25, 1851). In 1857 there were already six mills with 102 stamps; in 1881 seven mills with 134 stamps; and the *Register* of 1903 still lists six mills. The principal quartz mines of 1867 are listed by Browne (pp. 73 ff.). *See also* Logan (pp. 96 ff.). The first foundries in the gold region were at Sutter Creek and at Grass Valley [Nevada] (Berriman). The mines in and near Sutter Creek reached production figures as high as 36 million dollars. Sutter, for whom the place was named, did not participate in the wealth. *See* Eureka Mines and Lincoln Consolidated Mine. The town is Historic Landmark 322. For biographical notes on Sutter, *see* the Bibliography.

Sutters Bar [El Dorado]. *See* Snyders Bar.

Sutters Buttes [Sutter]. The dominant orographic feature of the Sacramento Valley was called Los Tres Picos in Sutter's grant and was known as the Bute, or Buttes, to the Hudson's Bay Company trappers in the early 1830s. On the maps of the 1830s and 1840s the name appears as Three Buttes, Sutters Buttes, *Los Picos de Sutter*, Prairie Buttes, or simply Butte Mountains. The Whitney Survey applied the name Marysville Buttes, and most maps used this name until the present name was made official in 1949 (U.S. Board on Geographic Names). (*California Place Names*). The three buttes have always been attractive to prospective miners, and mineral traces have been found, including gold and coal. However, the "pay dirt" was natural gas, which has been piped to neighboring communities (Ramey).

Sutters Mill [El Dorado]. Before the establishment of the Culloma (Coloma) post office November 8, 1849, the site of Marshall's discovery was generally known as Sutters Mill or simply The Mill.

Suttersville [Amador]. *See* Sutter Creek.

Swamp Angel Mine [Nevada]. *See* Lowell Hill.

Sweats Bar [Tuolumne]. *See* Swetts Bar.

Swedes Flat [Butte]. It is shown on Long and Montgomery's map, 186?, as a small town on an affluent of North Honcut Creek, about seven miles northeast of Honcut City. No mining record was found. Shown on the USGS Smartsville 1943 quadrangle.

Sweeney Mine [Tuolumne]. *See* Dutch-App Mine.

Sweetland [Nevada]. Two miles southwest

Sutters Mill, El Dorado Co.

of North San Juan. It is recorded on Trask's map, 1853, as Sweetlands. Brown, *Directory* (p. 14), refers to it as Sweetlands also, but *Bean's Directory*, uses the form Sweetland. It is one of the oldest settlements on the San Juan Ridge and was named for the three unmarried Sweetland brothers who started digging for gold here in 1850 (McKeeby, pp. 144 f.). In July, 1851, a ditch was built from Shady Creek, tributary to the South Fork of Yuba River (Brown, *Directory*, p. 12). According to a clipping from the Nevada *Democrat*, about 1857, the Monte Cristo Company built an extensive tunnel between Sweetland and Cherokee and struck it rich (Hittell Clippings, p. 88). A post office was established July 6, 1857. In 1858 the place is described as "mining village of a few hundred inhabitants, originally prospected by the man whose name it bears" (*Transactions*, 1858, p. 175). Recorded on the USGS Smartsville 1943 quadrangle.

Sweet Oil Diggings [Plumas]. About eight miles north of La Porte. The place is listed in Hittell's roster, and it is mentioned as the site of hydraulic mining "years ago" in *Bulletin*, 193 (p. 124).

Sweets Bar [Tuolumne]. *See* Swetts Bar.

Sweet Vengeance [Calaveras]. According to the *Annual Mining Review*, 1876 (p. 23), a 20-stamp steam-driven mill was built in 1865 at the cost of 55 thousand dollars.

Sweet Vengeance [Yuba]. One mile southeast of Prairie Diggings. It is mentioned as a stage stop on the road to Marysville. It was probably named for the nearby quartz

mine shown on Doolittle's map, 1868. Meek (p. 157) states that Portuguese truck farmers raised vegetables here.

Sweetwater [Mariposa]. At the head of Sweetwater Creek, a tributary to Merced River; northeast of Mariposa and about one mile west of Jerseydale. In 1853 there was a 12-stamp steam-driven mill (*Annual Mining Review*, 1876, p. 22). The Sweetwater Mine active intermittently until recent times (*Mining Bureau*, XXIV, p. 118; XXXI, p. 45; LIII, pp. 173 f.). The Early Mine was discovered and named by Thomas Early, county sheriff, 1855–1857, and it was worked intermittently from 1860 to the 1950s (Mariposa *Gazette*, September 2, 1862; *Mining Bureau*, LIII, pp. 164 f., 96 f.).

Swell Head Diggings. An unidentified place listed in Hittell, *Resources*.

Swetts Bar [Tuolumne]. On the Tuolumne River, above Don Pedro Bar, between Hawkins and Indian bars. It is shown on Trask's map, 1853, as Sweats Bar (but east of Jacksonville), and as Sweets Bar on Goddard's map, 1857. For some time the camp on the left bank was called Fraziers Flat. Mulford mined here in the late 1850s and tells the story in one of his delightful sketches, "Swetts Bar" (Chapter 12 in his *Story*). Gardiner visited here in 1851, and the following summer he mined here briefly without success, then engaged in truck gardening, and later located claims along the river and sold them to Chinese miners (p. 175). There is no evidence that the place was named for John Swett, who

later became California State Superintendent of Public Instruction (1863–1867).
Swett did make an attempt at mining in
Butte County, according to his sketchy
diary reprinted in *CHSQ*, XXIII, pp. 289 ff.

Swindle Hill [Placer]. The diggings near
Yankee Jims Gulch and Brushy Canyon
are mentioned in a sales agreement dated
June 9, 1862, and recorded in the Placer
County Records, IV (pp. 52 f.).

Swiss Bar [Calaveras]. On the south side of
Mokelumne River, four miles above Mid-
dle Bar. Shown on Trask's map, 1853. A
Swiss quartz mine, four miles east of Rail-
road Flat, idle in 1914, is still listed by the
Mining Bureau in 1935.

Swiss Bar [Siskiyou]. On the north side of
Klamath River, near Gottville. A mine is
listed as idle in 1896 in *Mining Bureau*, XIII
(p. 429).

Swiss Bar [Yuba]. On the main Yuba River;
nine miles above Marysville. It was the
first diggings above the mouth of the Yuba
River. Recorded on Trask's, 1853, and all
the later maps. Placer mining started in
1850 and paid well. In 1858 the bar was
nearly deserted (*Marysville Directory*, 1858,
p. xxiii) because of the debris from the
mines up the river. It soon disappeared,
although it was still shown on the County
Map, 1879.

Sycamore Flat District [Fresno]. East of
Fresno and north of Piedra. There was
superficial mining here at the time of the
Gold Rush and active lode mining from
the 1880s to about 1915, with minor prospecting since that time (*Bull.*, 193, p. 124).

Syndicate Mine [Mono]. *See* Bodie.

Syracuse Bar [Yuba]. On the main Yuba
River, three miles above Rose Bar. Recorded on Trask's map, 1853. Gravel from
the upper mines later buried the place
(*Alta*, November 7, 1867).

Table Mount [Siskiyou]. Gold mining
here is reported in the *Alta*, November 18,
1855 (Bancroft Notes).

Table Mountain [Butte]. Opposite Oroville
and extending eight miles northward to
Cherokee. The former name, Tancow,
probably of Indian origin, is shown on the
County Map, 1862. The Mountain, a
prominent landmark, is capped with a
thick basaltic cover, under which rich
gravel deposits were found and mined.
Water was brought in long aqueducts,
making the operation difficult and costly.

The mountain is described in Whitney,
Auriferous Gravels (pp. 207 f., 479 f.) and
Raymond, V (1872, p. 72 f.); it is described
and also mapped in Lindgren, 1911 (pp.
86 f.). The individual camps and topographical features are listed separately in
this dictionary.

Table Mountain [Sierra]. Near Poker Flat.
Shown on Crossman's map. The place is
mentioned as a mining camp in 1857 (Bancroft Scraps, V, p. 1,779).

Table Mountain [Tuolumne, Calaveras].
Along the Stanislaus River, from Columbia to Knights Ferry, about thirty miles
long. Stanislaus Mesa is another name
used for this striking feature in the landscape. It was covered with basalt, like the
Table Mountain in Butte County. A description is given in *Mining Bureau*, II (part
2, pp. 147 ff.). Tunnel mining started before 1850. Some of the mines assayed 950°
fineness (*Mining Bureau*, IV, p. 223), a
high degree for quartz gold. The Columbia and Sonora newspapers of the middle
1850s reported such rich yields that the
miners calculated their profits by the
pound (Hittell Clippings, pp. 28, 31). The
Transactions, 1859 (p. 90) reported that in
1853 a company struck a lead while digging a well in their garden and took out 75
thousand dollars worth of gold. In
November and December, 1855, the
newspapers were full of reports on "soap
mines" found at the foot of Table Mountain. Heckendorn lists the important
places in 1856 (p. 104); Browne (pp. 35, 38
ff.) lists the mines and claims on the
mountain in 1868. Browne adds (p. 35) the
pessimistic note: "This mountain has
yielded about 2 million dollars, but at a
cost of 3 million dollars." Much of the
waste of time, effort, and money was
caused by the individualistic system of
running tunnels into the mountain by
miners or companies of miners without
regard to the work and plans of other
miners and companies. Mulford (chapter
XXI, *Story*) tells in a humorous way of the
legal struggle between the Table Mountain Tunnel and the New York Tunnel
companies. The repeated assertion that
many of Bret Harte stories and poems are
based on camps at Table Mountain is
without foundation. The various camps at
the foot of the mountain are listed separately in this dictionary. Some mines are
listed in the reports of the Mining Bureau
until the 1960s. Another Table Mountain,
south of Soulsbyville, is mentioned in
several sources in the 1850s, but the Table

Mountain usually meant is the one described above (De Ferrari).

Table Mountain Humbug [Tuolumne]. According to *Mines and Minerals* (p. 358), the place had yielded half a million dollars by 1899. It may refer to the Humbug Mine on the east side of Table Mountain.

Table Rock [Sierra]. In the northwest corner of the county, near Howland Flat. Although the place is rarely mentioned in gold mining literature, it had a post office from 1857 to 1922, and its consolidated mines are listed in the Mining Bureau reports until 1941. Shown on the USGS Downieville 1907 quadrangle.

Table Rock [Tuolumne]. Apparently near Jacksonville. The *Mining Press*, May 11, 1861, has a report from the Jacksonville *Sentinel* that miners made average wages, and that a nugget worth thirty-five dollars was taken from one claim.

Tadpole Creek [Placer]. Near Iowa Hill. The *State Republican* in March, 1856, reports that a lump weighing nineteen pounds and containing about 14 hundred dollars worth of gold was found in old tailings, apparently thrown away in 1850 by a miner not sharp-eyed enough to see the gold in the quartz (Hittell Clippings, p. 22). It is mentioned as a settlement in 1874 by Raymond, VII (p. 108).

Taff Bar [Placer]. At the lower end of Canion (!). The camp is mentioned in the notice of a claim recorded October 12, 1852 in the Placer County Records, I (p. 125).

Tahoe District [Placer]. West and north of Lake Tahoe. In 1861 gold was discovered north of the lake and soon several short-lived settlements developed, including Elizabethtown and Neptune City near present-day Kings Beach, and Knoxville and Claraville near the mouth of Squaw Creek. The Tahoe Treasure Mine, west of Chambers Lodge, was located in 1932, and since that time it has been prospected intermittently. (*Bull.*, 193, pp. 124 f.)

Tailholt [Tulare]. It was the center of the mines along the White River (*Mining Press*, August 30, 1862) and was named White River when the post office was established in 1862. The camp was allegedly so called because a miner had nailed a cow's tail as a handle to the door of his cabin. An unidentified Tail-Holt Mill is mentioned in a poem in the *Pacific Mining Review*, 1878 (p. 163). *See* White River district; Dogtown [Tulare].

Tailors Bar [Plumas]. Recorded on Trask's map, 1853, on the south side of the North Fork of Feather River, below the junction with Rush Creek.

Talbots Hill [Calaveras]. East of Douglas Flat. It is shown as a large place on Trask's map, 1853, but no mining records were found.

Tamaroo Bar [Placer]. On the North Fork of American River, near Auburn. It is mentioned in notice of a claim recorded November 15, 1851, in the Placer County Records, I (p. 42½). In September, 1852, a company succeeded in washing out $92.82 worth of gold from one pan of dirt, according to Placer County History, 1882 (p. 225). In 1855 Greenwood's Company took out 15 hundred dollars worth of "beautiful gold" in one week (*Placer Herald*, October 27, 1855). In 1857 a dam was built here by the American River Ditch Company (Sacramento Co. Hist., 1880, p. 229). The name is misspelled Samaroo in Hutchings' list of towns in 1855.

Tancow [Butte]. This was the old name of Butte Table Mountain, apparently Indian. It is shown on the County map, 1862. *See* Table Mountain [Butte].

Tangle-Leg [Nevada or Placer]. Mentioned as a mining place in a poem in *Annual Mining Review*, 1876 (p. 18). There was a Tanglefoot Mine in Shasta County.

Tanyard [Amador]. Six miles west of Volcano. It was on the ridge stage road and was later called Tanyard Hill, according to Cenotto.

Taylor Flat [Trinity]. Between Burnt Ranch and Big Bar. It was probably here that an Algerian ex-colonel and his party had the first claims in July, 1850, and made 100 dollars a day to the man (de Massey, p. 101). French and Little French creeks, which join the Trinity here, are probably reminiscent of the lucky Frenchmen. An extensive account of the place before 1858 is given by Cox (pp. 81 f.). Hydraulic mining was carried on until modern times. A description of the mine ten miles below Big Bar is given in *Mining Bureau*, XIII (p. 463). Recorded on the USGS Big Bar 1930 quadrangle.

Taylor Gulch [Mono]. *See* Bodie.

Taylors [El Dorado]. Between Greenwood and Garden Valley. Recorded on Goddard's map, 1857. In the 1880s the average production was only twelve dollars per ton (*Mining Bureau*, II, part 1, p. 175). It was probably the site of the Taylor Mine, two miles northwest of Garden Valley, shown as Taylor Q[uartz] L[edge] on Doolittle's map, 1868. The Taylor Mine was also known as Idlewild. It had a 40-

stamp mill and produced an estimated one million dollars by 1934 (*Mining Bureau*, LII, p. 427).

Taylors Bar [Calaveras]. On the lower Calaveras River. Camp's map shows it about six miles southwest of San Andreas. Coy's map records it as Tailors Bar.

Taylors Ferry [Stanislaus]. Opened in 1849 by Nelson Taylor. *See* Heath and Emory Ferry.

Taylors Ravine [Placer]. In the vicinity of Crows Flat, in the southern part of the county. It is mentioned in connection with the sale of a water ditch, April 7, 1854, recorded in Placer County Records, I (p. 22).

Taylorsville [Plumas]. On a side road of Highway 83, east of Crescent Mills. Prospecting in the district began in 1850. Named for Jobe T. Taylor, who had a ranch and a grist mill here in 1856. According to the *Plumas National*, September 13, 1873, A. C. Light discovered a gold ledge in decomposed gneiss on the mountain south of the place and made good profits by washing alone with a hand mortar (Bancroft Notes). A post office was established in 1861, and it was still a center of the quartz mines at the end of the century (*Register*, 1900). A detailed account of the district in 1919 is given in *Mining Bureau*, XVI (Plumas, pp. 49 ff.). There has been intermittent prospecting in Taylorsville district in recent times (*Bull.*, 193, p. 125).

Tea: Bar, Creek [Siskiyou]. The Creek is a tributary to Klamath River, south of Cottage Grove. It is shown on the USGS Preston Peak 1944 quadrangle. The name of the old mining community at Tea Bar, also called Ti Bar, is derived from the Karok Indian village Ti'i. In 1896 a hydraulic Tea Bar Mine was operated by a Chinese cooperative (*Mining Bureau*, XIII, p. 429).

Tecumseh Mill [Nevada]. Two miles west of Omega. It is mentioned in *Bean's History* (p. 385). Tecumseh was a Pawnee chief who was killed in 1813. The name is also used for mines in Calaveras and Sierra counties.

Tehachapi Valley [Kern]. The exploitation of the gold deposits began in the early 1850s. An otherwise skeptical report, dated Los Angeles, June 6, 1855, in Hayes Scrapbooks: Mining (V, sec. 143), stated that the yield was as high as thirty dollars to the man. A clipping from the Los Angeles *Star*, August 24, 1861, reported that three men took out 45 hundred dollars worth in one season. Similar reports of moderate but steady success are in Hayes Scrapbooks. The *Mining Press*, April 18, 1862, likewise speaks of a well-paying district and a large amount of gold taken out in 1861–1862. In 1904 there were still two Huntington mills in operation (*Register*, 1904). The Pine Tree Mine near the town of Tehachapi was worked from 1876 to 1907 and reportedly produced a quarter million dollars worth of gold (*Bull.*, 193, p. 125). *See* Pine Tree [Kern].

Tehama Ravine [Nevada]. Near Graniteville. According to the *Alta*, February 22, 1853, a nugget worth 12 hundred dollars was found here in 1853.

Telegraph City [Calaveras]. About six miles southwest of Copperopolis, near the Stanislaus County line. According to the reminiscences of Robert B. Parks, descendant of the hotel owner, the town was established in the early 1860s, when several hundred miners prospected for copper in the vicinity. The name was reportedly given for the telegraph line between Stockton and Sonora. (*Las Calaveras*, January, 1961.) Shown on the USGS Copperopolis 1939 quadrangle.

Temescal Ranch [Los Angeles; Ventura]. The extensive gold deposits, fourteen miles northeast of Piru, were never thoroughly worked because of their low grade (*Mining Bureau*, XXVIII, p. 251), but plans were being made in the 1930s for large scale hydraulic operations.

Temperance Creek [Mariposa]. A tributary to Lake McClure, west of Bagby. A 4-stamp steam-driven mill was erected in 1860 (*Annual Mining Review*, 1876, p. 21). Shown on the USGS Sonora 1939 quadrangle.

Temperance Flat [Fresno]. On the south side of Millerton Lake. It is mentioned in *Mining Bureau*, XIV (p. 440), as an active mining camp in the early days. Placer mining in the region was followed by intermittent lode mining from 1853 to about 1915 and some prospecting in the 1930s (*Bull.*, 193, p. 125).

Temperance Flat [Placer]. Near Rock Creek. The camp is given as a mining district in a notice of a claim datelined Independence City, November 19, 1855, recorded in the Placer County Records, I (p. 329). According to a newspaper item of January 18, 1858, a mass of gold and quartz found here weighed ninety-five ounces and yielded one thousand and sixty dollars worth of gold (Co. Hist., 1882, p. 227).

Templar Ledge [Yuba]. West of North Fork of Yuba River in Foster Bar Township. In 1857 there was a 10-stamp quartz mill, which was removed to Oroville, and in 1864 another 10-stamp mill was built, which was given up after a loss of 40 thousand dollars; in 1879 a mill was again in operation (Co. Hist., 1879, p. 96). Several Templar mines are listed in *Mining Bureau*, XV (pp. 449, 456).

Ten-Cent Gulch [Trinity]. On Weaver Creek, in the center of Weaverville. Leeper built a solid log cabin nearby in the winter of 1850–1851 (p. 115). Carr and partners mined here in the spring of 1851 and made sixteen dollars a day with a rocker (p. 123). Five-Cent Gulch was next to it. A mine operated by Chinese was still in operation in 1914 (*Mining Bureau*, XIV, p. 914). One placer mine is listed until 1941.

Tennessee Bar [Siskiyou]. On Scott River. Some fine strikes were made in the winter 1853–1854, according to the *Yreka Mountain Herald* reprinted in the *Alta*, March 31, 1854.

Tennessee Canyon [Placer]. *See* Humbug Bar.

Tennessee Gulch [Tuolumne]. The Gulch runs from the base of Bale Mountain and enters Woods Creek at Browns Flat. It is mentioned in Heckendorn (p. 60). It was better known for its graphite deposits than for gold production. Shown on the USGS Columbia 1948 quadrangle.

Tennessee Hill [El Dorado]. Between the South Fork of American River and Weber Creek. The entire hill was rich with gold bearing gravel deposits (Co. Hist., 1883, p. 88).

Tennessee House [Yuba]. On the Marysville trail to Downieville. Recorded on Milleson and Adams' map, 1851, and described by Lecouvreur (pp. 227 f.). Tennessee Creek is shown on Wescoatt's map, 1861, as a tributary to the South Honcut.

Texana [Mariposa]. Near Pleasant Valley on the Merced River. It is mentioned by Benjamin H. Deane in his journal, July 21, 1850.

Texas Bar [Placer]. On the Middle Fork of American River, below Kennebec Bar, between Mammoth and Quail bars. It is mentioned in the Placer County History, 1882 (pp. 401 ff.) and in the El Dorado County History, 1883 (p. 84).

Texas Bar [Placer]. On the North Fork of American River, near Beals Bar, at the junction with the South Fork. Shown on Trask's map, 1853. It was paying well in 1856 according to an item in the *Placer Herald*, September 26, 1853 (Co. Hist., 1882, p. 190).

Texas Bar [Sierra]. About a quarter-mile below Goodyears Bar, opposite Hoodoo Bar. It is mentioned by Sinnott as having had good prospects (*Sierra City*, pp. 153, 164).

Texas Bar [Trinity]. On Trinity River, east of Douglas City. It is mentioned by Cox (p. 35). A productive mine, a half mile north of Douglas City, was in operation until 1914 (*Mining Bureau*, XIV, p. 914), and a Texas Bar Mine is listed as late as 1941.

Texas Bar [Tuolumne]. On Tuolumne River, about nine miles below Hawkins Bar. Gardiner visited a friend here in November or December, 1849 (pp. 104 ff.). Heckendorn (p. 89) mentioned it as a place of "considerable note."

Texas Bar [Yuba]. On the North Fork of Yuba River, near Fosters Bar. Shown on Trask's map, 1853. It is probably the same as Texas Ranche mentioned by Huntley in March, 1852, and by De Long, January 11, 1854.

Texas: Bar, Creek [El Dorado]. On the South Fork of American River, one half mile upstream from Chile Bar; about two miles north of Placerville. The Creek is shown near Kelsey Canyon on Bowman's map, 1873. Steele (pp. 270 ff.) mined at the Bar with his party from June to November, 1852, and he gives an excellent description of the camp. Notice of a claim at Texas Bar is recorded in the El Dorado County Records (Mining Location, Book A, p. 33, dated May 31, 1853).

Texas Canyon [Los Angeles]. Twelve miles northeast of Saugus. The placer mines were developed in the early 1900s. They produced quite fine gold but were worked only intermittently and with moderate success. (*Mining Bureau*, XXX, pp. 248 f.)

Texas Diggings [Placer]. Shown on the County Map, 1887, as a sizeable settlement on an affluent of the North Fork of the North Fork of American River, about seven miles northwest of Canada Hill. No mining record was found.

Texas Flat [Madera]. *See* Coarse Gold.

Texas Flat [Nevada]. Near Rough and Ready. It was a sizeable camp in 1850 (Bean, p. 360).

Texas Flat [Tuolumne]. Near Columbia, just below and south of Gold Springs. It is mentioned by Dane (p. 3). The *Alta*, March 16, 1853, reprints an item from the Columbia *Gazette*, which states that some miners left with five to ten thousand dollars profit.

Texas Gulch [Mariposa]. One mile southwest of Princeton. No mining records were found, but a quartz mine is listed in *Mining Bureau*, XIII (p. 223) and in the *Register*, 1903.

Texas Hill [El Dorado]. About two miles southeast of Placerville. It is situated on the Tertiary channel of the South Fork of American River. The *Alta*, November 15, 1852, reports the introduction of a new machine to wash gold. Between 1861 and 1871 hydraulic mining was carried on. In the report of the Mining Bureau, 1892–94, the Texas Hill drift mine is described. It was in the bend of the ancient river channel and was capped by 120 feet of andesite and was worked through a drift 1,500 feet long. The gravel was treated in a 10-stamp mill and a 100-foot sluice. About 10 million dollars worth of gold was produced in the area between Texas Hill and Coon Hollow. (*Mining Bureau*, XII, pp. 124 f.; LII, p. 563). The area is mapped in Lindgren, *Tertiary Gravels* (p. 173).

Texas Hill [Mariposa]. East of the North Fork of Merced River, two miles southwest of Kinsley. A mine was active intermittently from about 1865 to 1943, with little production (*Mining Bureau*, LIII, pp. 174 f.). Shown on the USGS Sonora 1939 quadrangle.

Texas Hill [Placer]. Nine or ten miles south and a little east of Emigrant Gap. It is primarily a logging settlement, but there was some mining in the district in the past. At one time there were 300 inhabitants. (*Placer Nuggets*, June, 1960.)

Texas Hill [Sacramento]. On the American River, below Negro Bar. A manuscript notation on Judah's map of 1854 shows it about two miles below Negro Bar on the east side of the river. Extensive gold mining was carried on here until 1855, according to the County History, 1880 (p. 225). The name still appears on Doolittle's map, 1868.

Texas Hill [Tuolumne]. An unidentified camp near Jamestown. A letter from one of the Smith brothers (p. 153) is dated from here January 2, 1856.

Texas House [Calaveras]. On the road from Stockton to Knights Ferry. Schaeffer (p. 47) mentions it in November, 1849.

Texas Point [San Bernardino]. In the Lytle Creek mining district. In 1867 the Hardpending Company of New York started the first large-scale hydraulic mining operation in the county, which proved to be successful. In 1868 or 1869 it was taken over by Louis Abadie and worked into the 1870s. Sometime before 1880 the operations were discontinued. An account

is given by Thrall in *Historical Society of Southern California Quarterly*, XXXII (p. 242) and by J. W. Robinson (p. 66). *See* Lytle Creek Placers.

Texas Springs [Shasta]. Near Horsetown. It is mentioned by Hutchings, December 20, 1855. Sandstone quarried here was used in nearby communities. Grace Grattan Masterson has written a reminiscent account of Horsetown and Texas Springs in the 1966 issue of the *Covered Wagon*.

Texas Tent [Yuba]. About fourteen miles northeast of Marysville, on the road to Downieville. Recorded on Milleson and Adams' map, 1851.

The Corners [Amador]. *See* Buena Vista.

The Forks [Sierra]. This was Downie's name for his camp in October, 1849; later it became Downieville. Here Forks refers to the junction of the North Fork of the North Fork with the North Fork of Yuba River. The former is now called Downie River.

The Gate [Amador]. *See* Jackson Gate.

The Hill [Nevada]. *See* Columbia Hill.

The Slide [Nevada]. In Grass Valley. A rich placer mine is mentioned in Bean (p. 189). The reference is to the "Grass Valley Slide," just inside of the Grass Valley north townsite line, near North Auburn and North Church streets (Foley).

Third Bar [Tuolumne]. On Tuolumne River. The Third Bar Company was organized July 25, 1850 with sixty Mexican laborers employed at five dollars each per day. In 4,260 working days there was no profit (Daniel B. Woods, p. 172).

Third Crossing [Calaveras]. Below San Andreas, on the South Fork of Calaveras River. The place was also known as Kentucky House and it was the trading center for miners in the area. It had a post office from 1852 to 1854. Shown on Camp's map.

Thomas Flat [Nevada]. It was a flourishing camp near Nevada City, listed in Hittell's roster. Hutchings mentions it in his diary, October 6, 1855.

Thompson Creek Bar [Siskiyou]. On Klamath River, between Seiad and Happy Camp. It is mentioned as an old bar in County History, 1881 (p. 217).

Thompson Hill [Placer]. Southwest of the town Dutch Flat. Recorded on Pettee and Bowman's map, 1879, where a large part of the gravel area is shown as "more or less completely hydraulicked away." A description is given by Pettee in Whitney, *Auriferous Gravels* (pp. 150, 154).

Thompsons Bar [Humboldt]. On Klamath

River between Weitchpec and Orleans, located in 1907. In 1914 hydraulic mining is listed in the *Mining Bureau*, XIV (p. 406).

Thompsons Dry Diggings [Siskiyou]. Gold was discovered here in March or April, 1851 by Abraham Thompson, a member of a prospecting party en route from Yreka Creek to Greenhorn Creek. The discovery led to the diggings which became the nucleus of Shasta Butte City, the forerunner of Yreka (Co. Hist., 1881, pp. 62, 196 ff.). *See* Yreka.

Thompsons Flat [Butte]. West of the Feather River, north of Oroville. It is shown as a sizeable town on the County Map, 1862. According to the County History, 1882 (p. 258), the first mining was along the river in 1848, and the place was called Rich Gulch. In 1852 George Thompson and others brought water in ditches, and two years later the camp on the hillside was moved to the flat and was named Thompsons Flat. By 1854 it was a thriving place with a population of "at least five hundred," three saloons, several stores, and a blacksmith shop. It had a post office from 1857 to 1870. In 1855 it was apparently also called New Philadelphia, as indicated in a letter of Asa B. Smith, datelined Thompsons Flat-New Philadelphia, January 21, 1855. The name is recorded on the USGS Chico 1895 quadrangle and the Oroville 1944 quadrangle.

Thoss Sulphuret Mill [Amador]. At Sutter and Grass Valley creeks, near Pine Grove. Shown on the County Map, 1866. Browne (pp. 79 f.) gives a detailed description of the mill owned by W. H. Thoss. Mr. Thoss employed a metallurgical process that he claimed yielded him as much as 600 dollars per ton of quartz or sulfurets.

Thousand Dollar Canyon [El Dorado]. Near Georgetown. According to *Mining Bureau*, II (part 1, p. 150), a nugget worth one thousand dollars was reported to have been found in 1849 or 1850 in this canyon, later called Illinois Canyon.

Three Buttes [Sutter]. *See* Sutters Buttes.

Three Pine Gulch [Tuolumne]. Midway between Columbia and Yankee Hill. Three Pine Mine is shown on Dart's map, 1879. The *Alta*, April 6, 1854, reports that an Italian who had hardly earned his board found a lump of pure gold weighing twenty-three pounds and eight ounces worth 48 hundred dollars. According to the *Mining Press*, November 23, 1861, the claims were worked out in 1861.

Ti Bar [Siskiyou]. *See* Tea Bar.

Tibbetts District [Inyo]. About ten miles northeast of Independence, in the Inyo Mountains. There was dry placer mining from 1894 to 1906 and some prospecting again in the 1930s (*Bull.*, 193, p. 152). *See* Mazourka Canyon.

Tichenors Gulch [Placer]. On the North Branch of the Middle Fork of American River. The mouth of the gulch, near Stony Bar, is mentioned in a claim recorded February 11, 1853 in the Placer County Records, I (p. 152). According to Hutchings, rich diggings were found in 1850 (*Diary*, May 6, 1855).

Tichners Secret [El Dorado]. The name for the diggings in El Dorado Canyon was probably given for the man whose discovery of gold at this place started a rush in the spring of 1850. The place is mentioned in the San Francisco *Bulletin*, March 1, 1859, in an item taken from the San Andreas *Independent* (Bancroft Notes).

Ticknor Basin [Kern]. On Kelso Creek, a tributary to Kern River. The diggings were opened in June, 1861, and were named for one of the prospectors (Havilah *Courier*, September 26, 1866).

Tiddletown [Amador]. The name appears to be a misprint for Fiddletown. Browne (p. 72) mentions that there were a few good hydraulic claims here in 1868.

Tiger Lilly [El Dorado]. Two miles southeast of Diamond Springs. The name is mentioned by Crockett (p. 94) in 1859. Recorded on the USGS Placerville 1931 quadrangle.

Tightner Mine [Sierra]. *See* Sixteen-to-One Mine.

Timbuctoo [Yuba]. Northwest of Smartsville. Shown on Wescoatt's map, 1861, and later maps. The placers near the main Yuba River were discovered in December, 1849. According to Farish (p. 73), the place was known as Sand Hat in 1854. For the name Timbuctoo, *see California Place Names*. It became a prosperous camp when hydraulic mining started in 1854, and the Tri-Union ditch brought water from Deer Creek (Co. Hist., 1879, pp. 84 f., 135 f.). A post office was established in 1858 and continued until 1883. Detailed accounts may be found in Browne (p. 149); *Alta*, November 7, 1867; Raymond, VII (p. 141); and Bayard Taylor, "Pictures of California Ten Years Later," (no. 15). Historic Landmark 320. Shown on the USGS Smartsville 1943 quadrangle.

Tims Spring [Tuolumne]. The original name of Springfield. It was also called Tims Gardens. The place was named for Timothy Eastman, who filed the first claim

May 15, 1850, and another September 2, 1850 (Barbara Eastman). *See* Springfield.

Tin-cup Diggings [Sierra]. On the North Fork of Yuba River, at or near Downieville. *Bulletin*, 193 (p. 44) locates it near Downieville and states that it was called Tin-cup Diggings because three men filled a tin cup with gold each day before quitting. R. Drury, however, states that the diggings were at the site of Downieville, at the junction of the North Fork of Yuba River and Downie River, and that they were so named because miners divided up the cleanup each day by measuring it out in a tin cup. Downie (p. 46) mined here in November, 1849, and made about one dollar to a pan.

Tinemaha [Inyo]. Between Bishop and Independence. It was the trading center and post office (1895–1910) for mines in the vicinity. The *Register*, 1902, lists eight mines that produced gold, with some silver and lead. The name was given for a legendary Piute chief and is preserved in a peak and a reservoir.

Tioga [Mono]. On the Old Tioga Road, near Yosemite Park boundary. A gold and silver mining district was established in 1878, when the famous Sheepherder mine was rediscovered. At one time there were 350 claims on the lode. The headquarters were at Bennettville (*Sierra Club Bulletin*, XIII, pp. 42 f.). *See* Sheepherder Lode; Bennettville. The Tioga Mining district is described in detail in *Mining Bureau*, VIII (p. 371). *See also* De Decker (pp. 21 f.). Despite the extensive plans for development of the district and the investments made, the total production of gold was small, probably not more than a few thousand dollars, according to *Bulletin*, 193 (p. 125).

Tippecanoe [Yuba]. *See* Tylers Diggings.

Tipton Hill [El Dorado]. Near the base of Tunnel Hill, seven miles northeast of Georgetown. There were only small ditches from Rock Creek, yet even without the aid of quicksilver, the washings yielded six dollars per day to the man. A description is given in Raymond (IV, p. 106; VII, p. 94). A placer mine, described as having been mined by drifting and hydraulicking "many years ago," is listed by the Mining Bureau until 1956.

Toadtown [Butte]. On Little Butte Creek, five miles north of Dogtown, now Magalia. In the early 1870s a 5-stamp mill was in operation and was reported as long idle in 1892 (*Mining Bureau*, XI, pp. 158 f.). In 1930 modern machinery struck high grade ore, and the same year the opening of a drift mine on the Nugget Channel at Toadtown is reported (*Mining Bureau*,

Timbuctoo, Yuba Co.

XXVI, pp. 372, 402). The location is indicated on a sketch map in *Bulletin*, 193 (p. 88). The town is also shown on modern maps.

Toby Moors Diggings [Amador]. *See* Alex Ranch.

Todds: Creek, Valley, Ravine [Placer]. Todds Creek is a tributary to the Middle Fork of American River, running northeastward from Oregon Bar. Shown on Gibbes' map, 1852. Todds Valley was named for Dr. F. Walton Todd, who was a cousin of Abraham Lincoln's wife (*CHSQ*, II, p. 204). Todd opened a store here in June, 1849. Knapp (p. 502) passed by in the spring of 1850, when Todd was building a cabin. Extensive diggings were found near the camp, and miners averaged one ounce a day (Sacramento *Transcript*, steamer ed., January 14, 1851). Claims at Todds Ravine were recorded September 6, 1851, in Placer County Records, I (p. 6). Miners were doing well in 1855 (Hutchings' Diary, May 9, 1855). A post office was established in 1856. Browne (pp. 93 f.) gives a pessimistic picture of activities here in 1867, stating that the Golden Calf Claim with an 1,800-foot tunnel had never paid, and that the 10-stamp mill of the Big Springs Claim was idle. According to an item in Bancroft Notes, the original diggings were covered by a landslide, but in the 1870s hydraulic mining was in full swing again. The total production of the Todd Valley Mine with Peckham Hill Mine was together 5 million dollars (*Bull.*, 193, p. 50). Todd Creek and

the settlement Todd Valley are shown on the USGS Placerville 1931 quadrangle.

Toledo Gulch [Mariposa]. A tributary to Burns Creek. The name may be confused with Tulitos. *See* Tulitos. Toledo Gulch is shown on the USGS Haystack 1919 quadrangle.

Tollgate Gulch [Kern]. North of Tehachapi Mountains, at lat. 35° 15', long. 118° 25'. There has been intermittent gold mining in recent times (*County Report*, I).

Tollhouse [Nevada]. Near Grass Valley. According to the *Mining Press*, April 18, 1862, a company struck a lead of blue gravel and mined with good success.

Tollhouse Mine [El Dorado]. *See* Smiths Flat.

Tolls: Dry Diggings, Old Diggings [Butte]. *See* Forbestown [Butte]; Tolls New Diggings [Yuba].

Tolls New Diggings [Yuba]. At or near Indiana Ranch, about six miles southwest of Fosters Bar. Milleson and Adams' map, 1851, shows Toll New Ranch, adjacent to Indiana Ranch. The diggings are mentioned by Lecouvreur (p. 228) in July, 1852, as a "pleasant little mining camp," and by De Long on October 25, 1855. According to the County History, 1879, gold was discovered along Indiana Creek in 1851, and the place was called Indiana Creek or Tolls New Diggings. *See* Indiana Ranch. Hutchings states in his diary, November 1, 1855, that Tolls Old Diggings was the name applied to Forbestown in 1849 and for some time later. The Sacramento *Transcript*, steamer ed.,

Todds Valley, Placer Co.

November 29, 1850, refers to rich deposits at Tolls Dry Diggings, at which 400 to 500 miners were preparing to winter in 1850–1851 (Bancroft Notes: Butte County); this was probably the Tolls Old Diggings to which Hutchings referred. See Forbestown [Butte].

Tolls Old Diggings [Butte]. See Forbestown.

Tolpekocking Flat [Sierra]. Near Chips Flat. It is mentioned in the *Mining Press*, June 22, 1861.

Tompkins House [Nevada]. In the Washington mining district. It was a stopover place for miners, operated by E. O. Tompkins (Foley).

Tooles Diggings [Yuba]. A camp near Fosters Bar, mentioned by Borthwick (p. 210) in the fall of 1852. It is probably the same as Tolls New Diggings.

Towerhouse, Towers [Shasta]. On Clear Creek, five miles northwest of Whiskeytown. Recorded on Goddard's map, 1857. The hotel called Towerhouse, a well known landmark, was built in 1852 by L. H. Tower (Steger). Hutchings called it "the best roadside house in California" (Diary, November 4, 1885). There was placer mining on the creek, but no quartz mining. It is mentioned in *Mining Bureau*, XI (p. 44). Tower House is shown on the USGS Weaverville 1942 quadrangle. According to an article in *Covered Wagon*, 1970 (p. 67), Towerhouse was first called "Free Bridge House" because of the toll free bridge built across Clear Creek by Mr. Tower. The "house" was destroyed by fire in 1919. The place is shown on the USGS Weaverville 1942 quadrangle.

Towle [Placer]. Near Dutch Flat. It is apparently a modern development of quartz mining. It had a post office, 1891–1935, and is listed with one nearby stamp mill in *Mines and Minerals* (p. 304) and in the *Register*, 1902. The Nevada County Map, 1880, indicates large holdings (largely lumber) of Towle Brothers extending into Nevada County northeast of Lowell Hill.

Town Creek [Shasta]. The *Mining Press*, June 29, 1861, reported that a company mined here with fair success.

Town Talk [Nevada]. Between Nevada City and Grass Valley. There was mainly drift mining on Town Talk Hill. The *Mining Press*, April 6, 1861, mentioned the "old Town Talk House." Glasscock, in *A Golden Highway* (p. 142), tells the story that the sign of the Town Talk saloon in Nevada City was carried down Deer Creek, and the miners posted it on the hill for the name of their camp.

Trabuco District [Orange]. In the Santa Ana Mountains, in the southeastern part of the county. Small amounts of placer gold have been mined here, mainly in Trabuco, Silverado, and Santiago canyons (*Bull.*, 193, p. 176).

Trasks Bar [Yuba]. On the North Fork of Yuba River, opposite Mississippi Bar. Recorded on Trask's map, 1853. It is also spelled Traskers Bar. Trask Bar is mentioned as a small bar in the *Marysville Directory*, 1858 (p. xxvii).

Treasure Mine [Amador]. See Amador City.

Tree Pine Gulch [Tuolumne]. The name is mentioned, after 1850, by Knapp (p. 504), who states that a Frenchman found a lump of gold "that weighed five thousand dollars." His good luck drove him insane and he died in an asylum in Stockton. Mr. Knapp obviously confuses the place with Three Pine Gulch.

Trinity Bar [Trinity]. On Trinity River, east of Douglas City. It was already exhausted in 1857 (Cox, p. 34).

Trinity Center [Trinity]. Near Swift Creek, a tributary to the Trinity River. It is recorded on Goddard's map, 1857, the terminal of the trail from Weaverville. The camp was settled by Moses Chadbourne in 1851, and miners made from ten to twenty dollars a day to the hand (Cox, pp. 18 f.). The post office was established in 1855, and the place became the trading center of the rich placer mines in the area. Farming gradually replaced gold mining, but in 1873 a number of companies were operating successfully, according to Raymond, VI (p. 152). In later years the river was dredged in this region. The Trinity (Clair Engle) Reservoir now covers (Old) Trinity Center. New Trinity Center was built about 1960 on Swift Creek, about two miles south of the old town.

Trinity River District [Trinity]. The name was given to the river in 1845 by Pierson B. Reading under the mistaken impression that it emptied into Trinidad Bay. The first reports of the rich washings and diggings on the stream were published in the *Alta*, August 2, 1849 (Bancroft Notes). A summary of the mining operations along the river and its tributaries is given in *Bulletin*, 193 (pp. 143 f.). Placer mining yielded an estimated 35 million dollars. Extensive dredging operations were carried on until recent years. Among the lode mines near the Trinity, the Bonanza King, about four miles east of Carrville, yielded 1.25 million dollars. The important camps along the

Trinity and its tributaries are listed separately in this dictionary.

Trojan District [San Bernardino]. Trojan district is on the east slope of Providence Mountains. Adjoining it on the south is the Arrowhead district. On the west slope of the mountains is Kelso District. *See* Providence Mountains.

Tropico: Hill, Mines [Kern]. Between Rosamond and Willow Springs. Gold was discovered on the hill in 1894, and successful mining was carried on until 1956. The hill was originally named for the discoverer, Ezra Hamilton. The present name arose in 1909 when the Tropico Mining and Milling Company was formed. Glen A. Settle, in his historical sketch of Tropico, estimates that the total production after sixty-two years of operation was between 6 and 8 million dollars. The *Mining Bureau*, XLV (pp. 234 f.) describes the modern crushing methods at the Tropico Mine and reports the total production by 1949 at about 3 million dollars.

Troy [Butte]. Apparently on or near the Feather River, the exact location of which has not been determined, according to the *County History*, 1877 (p. 9). It was one of the towns laid out by speculators to capture the miners' trade, probably below what is now Oroville.

Truetts Bar [Tuolumne]. Somewhere near Jacksonville. Mulford, in his *Story* (p. 182), refers to a miner living there in the fall of 1850.

Tryagain Tunnel [El Dorado]. Three miles southeast of Placerville. Shown on Doolittle's map, 1868. The unique name in the Blue Channel of the county is mentioned by Browne (p. 82). A Tryagain or Last Chance drift mine, on the Tertiary channel of the South Fork of American River, was worked about 1896 and is listed by the Mining Bureau until 1956.

Tulitos [Mariposa]. Between Hornitos and Indian Gulch. According to the centennial edition of the Mariposa *Gazette*, Tulitos was an early-day mining camp. An old mine, near the head of Toledo Gulch, is listed in 1957 (*Mining Bureau*, LIII, p. 312).

Tumco [Imperial]. *See* Hedges.

Tunnel Hill [Amador]. Between Jackson and Butte City. Shown on the County Map, 1866. As early as 1850 miners struck gravel on an ancient river bed. Drifting was difficult but paid between one and two ounces a cartload. The first tunnel was run in 1852; the second in 1854. Water was piped in and sluicing made mining more profitable. (Co. Hist., 1881, p. 179.)

In 1861 miners made five to ten dollars per day to the hand (*Mining Press*, January 4, 1862).

Tunnel Hill [Calaveras]. *See* Gold Hill.

Tunnel Hill [El Dorado]. Just below Coloma. An otherwise unidentified camp mentioned by Stephen Wing in his Journal (II, p. 84) as the scene of a robbery on February 23, 1856.

Tunnel Hill [El Dorado]. Eight miles east of Georgetown. The Pilot Creek Ditch from the junction of Rubicon River and Pilot Creek pierced a tunnel through the hill and on the west side came upon "rich beds of auriferous gravel" (Raymond, IV, pp. 101 f.). Recorded on the USGS Placerville 1931 quadrangle.

Tuolumne [Tuolumne]. *See* Summersville.

Tuolumne City [Stanislaus]. On the north bank of Tuolumne River, about three miles from the confluence with San Joaquin River. Shown on Butler's map, 1851. It was once a town on the route to the Southern Mines, but by 1861 there was only a tavern and a ferry (Stoddart, p. 107). Later it was revived as the center of a small farming community and during high water navigation was resumed (Rensch-Hoover). A post office existed between 1867 and 1872.

Tuolumne House [Tuolumne]. A roadhouse near Green Springs, at present-day Keystone. It is mentioned by Stephen Davis, December 24, 1852. At one time there was a Tuolumne House in Jacksonville and another in Sonora (De Ferrarri).

Turkey Hill [Placer]. Two miles east of Michigan Bluff. It was at or near the site of the famous Weske claim, which still brought thirty-eight dollars a day to the man during one five-day period in June, 1871 (Raymond, IV, pp. 114 f.). A consolidated mine is listed in the Mining Bureau reports until 1936.

Turnback Creek [Tuolumne]. A tributary to Tuolumne River, southeast of Sonora. According to Dexter (p. 134), a group of white and Cherokee miners pursuing thievish Indians had to turn back here after an undecided fight. It was the scene of a gold rush in 1856. In 1857 there were two water-driven mills and one horse-drawn with nineteen stamps and three arrastres (*State Register*, 1859). Shown on the USGS Sonora 1939 quadrangle.

Turners Bar [Trinity]. One mile west of the mouth of Readings Creek, on the south side of Trinity River. It prospered in the 1850s, according to Cox (p. 40). For years, beginning in 1855, it was mined by Peter

Paulsen and his company of Germans. He had a couple of ditches from Readings Creek and a 54-foot water wheel in the river. Paulsen was the great grandfather of Hal E. Goodyear of Weaverville. In 1862 the profits were still good, according to the *Mining Press*, April 25, 1862.

Turners Diggings [El Dorado?]. Mentioned by Crockett (p. 40) in 1856.

Turners Flat [Tuolumne]. On the south side of Table Mountain, west of the intersection of Highway 108 and Montezuma Road. Rich deposits were discovered in 1855 (Heckendorn, p. 81). The *San Joaquin Republican*, November 11, 1855, reported that Hoffmann & Company had sunk a shaft from which they washed one ounce per pan.

Turnersville [Calaveras]. Ten miles east of Double Springs. Recorded on Butler's map, 1851, prominently shown as Turnerville.

Turtle Mountains [San Bernardino]. In the southeastern part of the county, ten miles north of Rice, a station on the Parker branch of the Santa Fe. The Mountain King Group of mines is mentioned in *Mining Bureau* (XXVI, p. 245; XXVII, p. 305).

Tuttle Gulch, Tuttletown [Shasta]. An unidentified camp. Claims were paying remarkably well, as reported by Horsetown *Argus* (*Mining Press*, March 16, 1861).

Tuttletown [Tuolumne]. On Mormon Creek, between Angels Camp and Sonora. Gold was first mined by the Mormons in 1848 at the place that became known as Mormon Gulch or Mormonitos. When Anson A. H. Tuttle settled here, it was named for him. A letter written December 10, 1849 (quoted by De Ferrari *in* Stoddart, p. 65) mentions the fact that five men took out forty pounds of gold in five days. Eighty-four inhabitants are listed in the population schedule for the U.S. 1850 Census. Marryat (pp. 269 ff., 286 ff., 323 ff.) describes the place in September, 1851, and claims that the camp started to grow after his party had installed a new type of power-driven stamp mill. A post office was established in 1857. Harman & Company were grinding rock with arrastres, which were paying ninety dollars per ton (*San Joaquin Republican*, October 27, 1857). The first eighteen tons of quartz milled by the "Chaparel Mill" in 1858 [?] yielded 108 pounds of amalgam valued at 9 thousand dollars (Hittell Clippings, p. 43). In one day, reportedly, at least 15 thousand dollars worth of rock was taken out of a Table Mountain tunnel near Tuttletown in the

Cardinell claim (*San Joaquin Republican*, January 3, 1858). At the Bixel claim a boulder valued at 2 thousand dollars was taken out (*Alta*, July 21, 1858). The *State Register*, 1859, reports four mills with forty stamps in operation in 1858. In the same year Sleeper & Company exhibited a piece of quartz valued at 2 thousand dollars, one side of which was covered with gold (Hittell Clippings, p. 32). An old man discovered a pocket containing 10 thousand dollars worth of gold near the profitable Patterson mine, after having searched seven years for it (Browne, p. 44 f.). Pocket mining continued in the area until World War II, and some work has been done at two of the mines since that time (*Bull.*, 193, p. 126). The famous Arbona Mine is marked in *Guidebook* (map 3). Mark Twain spent five months in 1864–1865 on nearby Jackass Hill, but Bret Harte could not be identified with the place. Historic Landmark 124. *See* Mormon: Gulch, Creek, Diggings [Tuolumne].

Twelve Mile Bar [Plumas]. On the East Branch of the North Fork of Feather River. Recorded on Trask's map, 1853. It is mentioned in the summer of 1858 in William Taylor's *California Life* (p. 317). The *Mining Press*, October 7, 1862, reports new quartz lode discoveries.

Twentynine Palms; town, District [San Bernardino, Riverside]. The town is in the south central part of San Bernardino County, just north of the San Bernardino Base Line. Recorded on the County Map, 1892, and listed as a center of mines (*Register*, 1902). R. D. Miller lists the mines and describes the mining activities in the 1870s and 1880s in the vicinity of the oasis. Some of the ore worked with arrastres yielded 100 dollars per ton (pp. 9 ff.). He also describes later mining activities at Gold Park camp, situated eight miles south of the oasis, in the area extending into the little San Bernardino and Hexie mountains, and at the New Eldorado Mine at the northwest end of Pinto Basin (p. 48). Other accounts may be found in *Mining Bureau*, XV (p. 815) and in *Bulletin*, 193 (pp. 168 f.).

Twenty-one Mine [Sierra]. *See* Sixteen-to-one.

Twists Flat [Sierra]. Near Goodyears Bar. Mentioned by Downie (p. 71) as a "rich patch" opposite Negro Point. Shown on Trask's map, 1853, on the South Fork of the North Fork of Yuba.

Twists Ranch [Calaveras]. Near Angels

Camp. Heckendorn (p. 102) lists a dozen miners in residence in 1856.

Two-bit Gulch. An unidentified place, listed in the Work Projects Administration project.

Two Cents Ranch. An unidentified place listed by Guinn (p. 42).

Two Counties Mine [Sierra]. *See* Gold Canyon.

Two Cut Ranch. An unidentified place, listed as a mining camp in the State Library roster.

Two Mile Bar [Calaveras]. On the Stanislaus River, near Knights Ferry. Mentioned by Prentice Shaw, about 1854, as one of the principal bars on the river. According to an item in the Sonora *Herald* in 1858, the miners washing in the river were mainly Chinese (Hittell Clippings, p. 66½). It is reported as paying well in 1861 in the *Mining Press*, August 3, 1861.

Two Springs [Calaveras]. *See* Double Springs.

Tylers Diggings [Yuba]. A few miles above Camptonville; near Oregon Creek. The gravel deposits here and at nearby Tippecanoe were of little importance, according to Pettee (p. 431) and appeared to be deserted at the time of his visit in 1879.

Tyro Mine [Mariposa]. *See* Coulterville.

Tysons Hospital [Placer]. Near Emigrant Gap. This is not an actual place name. Dr. James L. Tyson established a tent hospital here in July, 1849, which was frequented by miners from Bear River and the North Fork of American River. This unique effort is excellently described by Tyson (pp. 69 ff.).

Ubehebe District [Inyo]. In the central part of the county. It is a copper-lead-silver district, in which some gold has been produced, mainly at the Lost Burro Mine. The mine was worked between 1906 and 1917, and again between 1934 and 1942, yielding about 100 thousand dollars. (*Bull.*, 193, p. 152.)

Ukiah [Mendocino]. On Highway 101, between Hopland and Willits. The discovery of gold four miles from Ukiah in December, 1860, caused a run, which soon petered out (*Mining Press*, December 7, 1860).

Uncle Sam Claim [Sierra]. On the old road from Alleghany to Nevada City in the Forest City region. It was reported as "a large operation" and having one of the finest tunnels (*Transactions*, 1858, pp. 186 f.). *See* Grey Eagle. The Uncle Sam Mine started work in 1850 and was operated intermittently until the 1940s. Listed in *Mining Bureau*, XVI (Sierra, pp. 60 f.) and XXXVIII (p. 66).

Uncle Sam Mine [Shasta]. *See* Backbone Creek; Squaw Creek District.

Uncle Toms [Placer]. Near the Rubicon River, some twenty miles east of Georgetown. It was situated on, or near a Tertiary channel, but little production is reported. It is mentioned and shown on the map in *Mining Bureau*, LII (p. 431).

Union. This was an extremely popular name for bars and camps in pre-Civil War days. There is still a large number of mines called Union, but only a few could be identified with old diggings.

Union Bar [Amador]. On the Mokelumne River, near Lancha Plana, Puts Bar, and Poverty Bar. According to an account in Andrews, *The Ghost Towns of Amador* (pp. 101 f.), the place was probably obliterated in the flood that swept away Poverty Bar and Puts Bar early in the 1860s. The Sacramento *Bee* (no date) reported that consignments of Springfield rifles and other military equipment had been made to the Union Guards of Union Bar. During the construction of Pardee Dam in recent years, a whole "grid" of stub masonry walls two to three feet thick were uncovered on the north bank of the river, presumably at the site of Union Bar. No other accounts to substantiate these reports were found.

Union Bar [Butte]. On the south side of the Middle Fork of Feather River, two or three miles above Bidwell Bar. Shown on Trask's 1853 and Goddard's 1857 maps. J. W. Booth, May 16, 1852, had a claim here. Shown on the Plumas National Forest map.

Union Bar [Calaveras]. On the Mokelumne River, near Clays Bar. Gold was found in pieces resembling melon seeds in size and shape (Bancroft Scraps, LI:1, p. 56). *See* Melones.

Union Bar [Placer]. On the North Fork of American River, near Lacys Bar. Sixty men, including sons of some of Philadelphia's first families, spent the summer of 1849 in hard labor. Many were in debt when the rainy season started. (Letts, pp. 113 f.) Notice of a claim on the bed of the river with intention to dam and flume it commencing at Union Bar, datelined Lacy's Bar, September 12, 1852, is recorded in Placer County Records, I (p. 117).

Union Bar [Yuba]. On the north side of the

main Yuba River, a few miles above the confluence with Deer Creek. Recorded on Milleson and Adams' map, 1851, and Wescoatt's, 1861. It was a small camp and the deposits were soon exhausted (Co. Hist., 1879, p. 88).

Union: Bar, Gulch, Hill [Trinity]. On Trinity River, east of Douglas City. The bar is mentioned by Cox (p. 34) in 1858. There was rich hydraulic mining until the twentieth century (Mining Bureau, XIV, p. 915). Union Gulch and Hill mines are listed in 1941. Union Hill Mill is recorded on the USGS Weaverville 1942 quadrangle.

Union Cape Claim [Butte]. On the Feather River, two miles above Oroville. A unique flume operation is fully described in Transactions, 1858 (p. 218). The claim yielded richly when the water was low. In October, 1860, a hundred men took out 900 to 12 hundred dollars a day (Mining Press, November 10, 1860). See Cape River Claim; Golden Gate Flume.

Union City [El Dorado]. West of Coloma. It is mentioned in the Sacramento Transcript, January 14, 1851, as rich diggings, paying twelve to twenty-four dollars per day to the hand. This is probably the later Uniontown, now Lotus.

Union Creek [Plumas]. A tributary to Nelson Creek. The County History, 1882 (p. 288) lists it as an important mining point.

Union Flat [Amador]. About one mile north of Volcano. Shown on the County Map, 1866. The Mining Press, August 31, 1861, reports that water from Volcano Ditch was replacing the high flumes. A hydraulic Union Flat Mine is listed by the Mining Bureau in 1927.

Union Flat [El Dorado]. On the South Fork of American River. It was named for the several members of the "Star Mining Company" who came from Union County, Indiana, when the organization was formed in the summer of 1852 to work the leads of gold on the Flat (Journal of Ezra Bourne).

Union Flat [Shasta]. On the north side of Cottonwood Creek. One claim paid regularly eight to fifteen dollars a day to the hand (Mining Press, March 16, 1861).

Union Flat [Sierra]. On the North Fork of Yuba River, five miles east of Downieville. Recorded on Crossman's map, 1867, and on the County Map, 1874. No mining records were found. It is the site of a U.S. Forest Service campground today.

Union Flat [Yuba]. West of Brownsville. The diggings around New York House, shown on the County Map, 1879, were called Union Flat around 1860 (Co. Hist., 1879, p. 90).

Union Gulch [Marin]. On Highway 1, northeast of Woodville. The copper company working here in 1863 produced some silver and gold (Mining Bureau, LI, p. 267). It was one of the few places in the county where gold was found.

Union Hill [Nevada]. Two miles east of Grass Valley. Gold mining is recorded as early as January 30, 1851. A number of mines yielded eighty dollars per ton at times. Sulfurets were said to yield as high as 420 dollars per ton. First arrastres were in use, then a number of stamp mills. (Bean, pp. 220 ff.)

Union Hill [Sierra]. On a tributary to Rock Creek, twelve miles west of Downieville. Shown as a settlement on the County Map, 1874.

Union Hill [Tuolumne]. East of Springfield and west of the Columbia-Sonora road. Eastman lists six claims in the years 1855 and 1856. Byrd, Dow & Company took out a quartz rock weighing several pounds, said to contain two pounds of gold (San Joaquin Republican, June 24, 1855). Holbrook & Quett Brothers struck a rich lode, which paid four to fifteen dollars to the pan. It was near the once famous Peck Diggings and believed to be a continuation of it (San Joaquin Republican, August 5, 1855). Shown on the USGS Columbia 1948 quadrangle.

Union Mills [Nevada]. Near Meadow Lake. There was a settlement here in which there were mills for processing gold in the area (Foley).

Uniontown [El Dorado]. There were two mining locations in the county named Uniontown, or Union Town, one near the North Fork of Cosumnes River, the other on the South Fork of American River. **Uniontown I.** On Martinez Creek, tributary to the North Fork of Cosumnes River, about two miles southeast of El Dorado (Mud Springs). Shown on Trask's map, 1853, but not on Goddard's, 1857. The name is derived from the Union Mine, which with the Church Mine was on the rich Union lode. The mines were worked from the early 1850s, when there was a town of two to three thousand miners — Mexicans and "whites" according to Mines and Minerals (p. 311). See Springfield District. **Uniontown II.** On the South Fork of the American River, one and a half miles below Coloma. It is recorded on Goddard's map, 1857, but not on Trask's, 1853. First it was called Marshall, presumably for James Marshall, discoverer of gold at Sutter's Mill; later the name was changed to Union Town. At one time the place had ten or twelve boarding houses and several stores, and at least a thousand miners were working there (Co. Hist., 1883, p. 180). Steele mentions the place (p. 326), when he was there in the summer of 1853. Stephen Wing refers to Union or Union Town in April and May of 1856 and datelines part of his journal of 1858 Union Town. The name was changed to Lotus when the post office was established January 6, 1881. *See* Lotus.

Union Town [San Bernardino]. In eastern Holcomb Valley, north of Arrastre Flat, at Union Flat. The general sentiment in the valley during the Civil War was Confederate, but some groups upheld the Union. Miners around Union Town and Clapboard Town were taking out from five dollars per day to as much as fifty ounces of gold per week. (Drake, pp. 16 f.; La Fuze, I, p. 61).

Union Valley [Placer]. Half way on the road from Nevada City to Sacramento. Steele was here March 25, 1851. No mining records were found.

Union Valley [Plumas]. A place mentioned by Browne (p. 167) as being north of Little Grass Valley and not very successful because of the lack of water.

Unionville [Nevada]. Three miles above Nevada City, on Little Deer Creek. It was established in 1863, and it is mentioned by Bean in 1867.

Unionville [Tuolumne]. Also called Uniontown. Above the North Fork of Tuolumne River, southwest of Long Barn. In 1862 the output was ten to twenty dollars per day to the hand (*Mining Press*, June 9, 1862).

United Mines [Tuolumne]. On the North Fork of Tuolumne River. A consolidation of nine patented claims was in operation until 1914. The total production is not known, but it was around 2 million dollars (*Mining Bureau*, XXIV, pp. 20 f.).

Upper Agua Fria [Mariposa]. *See* Agua Fria; Poverty Flat.

Upper Arkansas Bar [Placer]. On the North Fork of American River, opposite the center of Green Valley. It is mentioned in the notice of a claim recorded December 20, 1851, in the Placer County Records, I (p. 56).

Upper: Bar, Ferry [Amador, Calaveras]. *See* Big Bar.

Upper Calaveritas [Calaveras]. *See* Calaveritas.

Upper Corral [Placer]. *See* Alder Grove; Illinoistown.

Upper Crossing [Amador]. *See* Amador Crossing.

Upper Diggings [Sierra?]. Apparently a

Uniontown, El Dorado Co.

camp on the Feather River. It is mentioned in the *California Star*, December 2, 1848. Delano (*Correspondence*, p. 22) dates a letter from the place October 12, 1849.

Upper Ferry [Calaveras, Tuolumne]. *See* McLeans: Bar, Ferry.

Upper Fosters Bar [Sierra]. *See* Cut-Eye Fosters Bar.

Upper Holcomb [San Bernardino]. *See* Belleville.

Upper Mines [El Dorado]. The placers around Sutters Mill are thus recorded on Mason's map of the gold fields, July 20, 1848. Upper Mine Mill is indicated on Ord's map, July 25, 1848.

Upper Rancheria [Amador]. *See* Rancheria.

Upper Rich Gulch [Calaveras]. *See* Rich Gulch.

Upper Swedes Bar [Trinity]. Between Taylor Flat and Swede Creek. It is mentioned in 1858 by Cox (p. 83). A drift mine was still in operation in 1896 (*Mining Bureau*, XIII, p. 465).

Ural [Nevada]. One and a half miles southwest of Nevada City. It was obviously named after the Russian Mountain chain, where gold was mined long before Marshall's discovery. It was located in 1851, and a mill was built in 1852. The name Ural mine was later changed to Cornish Mine. It was worked with moderate success as late as 1867 (Bean, p. 111). It is still listed as a part of the Champion group by the Mining Bureau until 1941.

Ureka [Sierra]. *See* Eureka North.

Urisko [Nevada]. A camp between Columbia Hill and the Middle Fork of Yuba River, mentioned in the *Mining Press*, January 25, 1862.

Utica Mine [Calaveras]. *See* Angels Camp.

Utters Bar [Tuolumne]. *See* Poverty Hill.

V

Vail Ranch [Nevada]. Near Grass Valley. The place was located on one of the Phoenix ledges and turned out "some splendid rock" (Raymond, III, p. 44).

Valentine Hill [Calaveras]. North of Bummerville. There was early mining on the hill named for a prospector, Valentine Granados, according to an article in *Las Calaveras*, July, 1957.

Vallardville [Del Norte]. Rich diggings in 1856 were reported in the *Alta*, June 24, 1856. According to the County History, 1881 (p. 45), the town was laid out in 1856 and was named for a prominent citizen, A. Vallard. A company from San Francisco operated here with hydraulic power.

Vallecito [Calaveras]. On Coyote Creek and Highway 4. It is recorded on Trask's map, 1853, as Biacete, and on Goddard's map, 1857, as Vallesietta. The name, a diminutive form of Spanish *valle*, was found on maps and in literature with a great variety of spellings. A post office was established on August 17, 1854, under the name Vallicita. The various spellings of the name were finally replaced by the present one, Vallecito, when it was made official by the post office department, October 1, 1940. Gold was discovered in the area by Daniel and John Murphy. *See* Murphys. At first mainly "coyoteing" was carried on, but when rains flooded the shafts the miners turned to placering. In the early 1850s many large nuggets were found here, or in nearby places. *See* Coyote Gulch. The *Alta* of April 5, 1852, reported that a party of eight men had unearthed a lump of twenty-six pounds, of which twenty-five were gold (Bancroft Scraps, LI:1, p. 251). The same newspaper reported the following day that a piece of solid gold weighing 305 ounces had been deposited with the Adams Express Company at Sonora. It was found on March 24, 1852, in a hole fifty-four feet deep at Bayecito. A twenty-seven pound nugget was found apparently at this place, Biaceta, too, according to a letter written by James Carr (p. 166) on April 3, 1852. A single pocket of gold in the Isabel Mine, a half mile west of the town, yielded 50 thousand dollars (Browne, p. 71). Whatever may be the truth in the reports of these sensational findings, the camp flourished, and in 1854 it had a school, a church, a division of the Sons of Temperance, and a post office, which still exists. In the most flourishing period, between 1852 and 1855, 60 thousand dollars worth of gold was shipped monthly, and even in 1867 the monthly shipment was still 20 thousand dollars according to Browne (p. 58). In 1874 Raymond points out (VII, p. 63) that Vallecito no longer enjoyed the prosperity of former years, but hydraulic mining was still carried on extensively in the vicinity. In 1880 the town was still the largest producer in the county, except Mokelumne Hill (*Mining Bureau*, II, part 1, p. 188). In the 1930s there was drift mining in the District (*Bull.*, 193, p. 126). The source of the riches was the ancient river channel, on which the town is situated. For a description of the channel, *see* Lindgren (p. 202). For an excellent though partly fictitious account of the region, *see* the California section of Gerstaecker's *Narrative*. *See* Stoutenburg in this dictionary.

Valley Springs [Calaveras]. At the junction of State Highways 12 and 26. A gold bearing vein had been discovered a mile and a half to the west, but the place, Valley Springs, developed mainly as a center for quartz and drift mines in the area, with a post office established in 1872. It was the successor to the famous but short-lived town of Double Springs, which was a few miles to the northeast. *See* Double Springs. Historic Landmark 251. Shown on the USGS Jackson 1938 quadrangle.

Valley View [Placer]. Six miles northeast of Lincoln. Shown on Doolittle's map, 1868. Early gold, silver, and copper production is reported. The settlement had developed in connection with the Banker Mine. *See* Whiskey: Diggings, Hill. The place is listed and mapped in the *Register*, 1902. A Valley View Mine is listed by the Mining Bureau until 1943.

Vamco Bar [Yuba]. On the North Fork of Yuba River, near Deadwood Creek. Recorded on Wescoatt's map, 1861.

Vances Bar [Trinity]. On the north bank of Trinity River, opposite Cox Bar. It was settled in 1850, according to Cox (p. 78 f.). In an item in the *Trinity Journal*, April 11, 1891, it is stated that it was later called Cox's Bar. *See* Cox Bar.

Vance: Wing-Dam, Bar [Yuba]. A wing-dam was constructed on the North Fork of Yuba River in 1850 by a man named Vance, and profitable returns were reported in 1852 (Co. Hist., 1879, p. 94). Presumably the Bar was at the same place.

Vanderbilt [San Bernardino]. On the northwest side of the New York Mountains, about three miles from present-day Ivanpah. The place was the center of a number of mines in the mountain range (*Register*, 1902), and it had a post office from 1893 to 1900, when it was moved to Manvel. *See* New York Mountains. The Vanderbilt District is described in *Mining Bureau*, XII, 235, and in *Bull.*, 193, p. 169. Gold was discovered in the District in 1861, and the most productive period of mining was between 1892 and 1898, and again between 1931 and 1941, mainly at the Vanderbilt and Gold Bronze mines.

Van Dusen Canyon [San Bernardino]. South and east of Holcomb Valley. It was named for Jed Van Dusen, for whose young daughter Belleville was named. *See* Belleville. Van Dusen discovered and worked a rich mine in the canyon and was murdered by his partner. The mine became a

"lost" mine, was later found, and was lost again. (Leadabrand, pp. 85 ff.)

Van Matre Ranch [Trinity]. *See* Minersville.

Veazie City [Butte]. On the Feather River, near the junction with Honcut Creek, a few miles from the southern boundary of the county. It was laid out in 1850 (Co. Hist., 1877, p. 8), and was a popular stopping place on the road from Marysville to the Feather River mines. It is shown as Veza City or Charleys Ranch on Milleson and Adams' map, 1851; as Veazie on Trask's map, 1853; and as Charleys Ranch on Goddard's map, 1857. Windeler (p. 148, and *passim*) mentions it as Charleys Ranch.

Vermont Bar [Calaveras]. On the Stanislaus River, one and a half miles above New York Bar. Several well-paying claims, some worked by Chinese on shares, are mentioned in an issue of the Sonora *Herald* in 1858 (Hittell Clippings, p. 66). The site of Vermont Bar is shown above Melones Dam on the USGS Copperopolis 1942 quadrangle.

Vermont: Bar, Flat [Placer]. On the Middle Fork of American River, near the junction with the North Fork, opposite Murderers Bar. Shown on Coy's map. In 1850 the miners joined with those of Murderers Bar in building an enormous flume across the river, which was swept away the same year (El Dorado Co. Hist., 1883, pp. 83 f.). Notice of sale of water rights in a ravine, datelined Vermont Flat, February 9, 1854, probably refers to the same place [Placer County Records, I, p. 230).

Vernon [Mono]. At the eastern base of Copper Mountain, in the Jordan District. A mining camp developed around a placer mining claim located in 1881 by C. H. Howard. Later when Copper Mountain was developed, it became a copper town. (F. S. Wedertz.)

Vernon [Sutter]. On the east bank of the Sacramento River opposite the junction with the Feather River. Shown on Gibbes' map, 1851, and Trask's, 1853. It was laid out in the spring of 1849 as a trading center for the Feather and Yuba River mines by Elisha Crosby and associates. It flourished until the fall and was then superseded by Marysville (Crosby, *Memoirs*, p. 29).

Veza City [Butte]. *See* Veazie City.

Vicksburg [Yuba]. *See* Dicksburg Ravine.

Victor [San Bernardino]. Five miles southeast of Oro Grande, at the Upper Narrows of the Mojave River; on the main line of the Santa Fe Railroad. It was named for J.

N. Victor, construction superintendent of the California Southern Railroad, 1881–1888. A post office was established in 1886, and in 1903 the name was changed to Victorville. By 1889 it had become the milling and supply center not only for the mines to the northeast, such as the Sidewinder, but also for mines throughout the San Bernardino mountain area as far east as the Morongo District (San Bernardino City and County Directory, 1889; Belden, June 30, July 7, 1963). The mines are listed and mapped in the *Register*, 1902.

Vigilance Bar [Placer]. On the North Fork of American River, near Manhattan Bar. All through the summer of 1849 the miners slaved in the construction of a dam and a canal, but "they did not get enough pay for the provisions consumed during the construction." (John Letts, p. 114.) It is mentioned in the County History, 1924 (p. 178), as Vigilant Bar, last mined in 1860.

Vine Spring Garden [Tuolumne]. One and a half miles northwest of Columbia. It is on Marble Quarry road, which intersects Parrots Ferry road at the lower end of Gold Springs. There was plenty of water and some placer mining, but in 1852 the area was already devoted mainly to vegetable raising (James Carr, pp. 164 ff.). However, a Vine Spring Mine near the site, idle in 1914, is still listed by the Mining Bureau in 1928.

Violin City [Amador]. *See* Fiddletown.

Virgin: City, Creek [Trinity]. Favorable reports of gold mining were given in the *Mining Press*, August 17, 1861. The location is not indicated.

Virgin Flat [Nevada]. On the South Fork of Yuba River, in Washington township. It is listed in Hittell's roster and in Bancroft, VI (p. 358). The yield was small, estimated at around 40 thousand dollars, according to the County History, 1880 (p. 205).

Virginia [Placer]. *See* Virginiatown.

Virginia Bar [Siskiyou]. On Scott River, near the junction with the Klamath River. Recorded on Goddard's map, 1857. It is mentioned as a small mining camp in the County History, 1881 (p. 218), but is listed as a fairly productive bar in 1916 (*Mining Bureau*, XIV, p. 843).

Virginia Dale [San Bernardino]. *See* Dale.

Virginia Flat [Butte]. On the North Fork of Feather River, where it "debouches from the mountains." It is situated on a gold bearing vein three to six feet thick, twenty feet below the surface. In 1856 there were more than fifty claims here, and six companies were engaged in making a tunnel (Hittell Clippings, p. 53).

Virginia Mine [Mariposa]. *See* Coulterville.

Virginiatown [Placer]. Four miles east of Lincoln. Shown as Virginia on Doolittle's map, 1868. According to *California Historical Landmarks*, it was founded in June, 1851, and a freight railroad, California's first railroad, was built through here in 1852 to Auburn Ravine, one mile away. The place had a post office named Virginia from 1858 to 1860. Again, according to *California Historical Landmarks*, "over 2,000 miners worked rich *deposits*." (!) The County *Directory*, 1861, reported that lack of water retarded development of the place until a ditch was built from Bear River (Bancroft Notes). It was at Virginiatown that Philip Armour had his butcher shop, which is said to have been the nucleus of the great Armour meat packing business in Chicago. Historic Landmark 400.

Virner [El Dorado]. Between Georgetown and Kentucky Flat, near Gray Eagle Hill. The drift mines are listed in the *Register*, 1902. The place had a post office from 1897 to 1913. This is probably the place mentioned by Theressa Gay (p. 310) as Camp Virner, formerly Works Ranch, near which James Marshall, the discoverer of gold at Sutters Mill, built a cabin. *See* Marshall Ravine. Gray Eagle Hill is not the site of the Gray Eagle Mine, of which Marshall was part owner. *See* Kelsey.

Volcano [Amador]. Fifteen miles northeast of Jackson, on both sides and at the fork of Sutter Creek. Recorded on Trask's map, 1853. It is one of the important still-existing gold towns, situated on the rich limestone belt. John Doble, in his journal, June 26, 1852, states that the name was derived from the "supposed volcanic appearance that exists in and about it" and from the "cellular porous . . . burnt-looking rocks and the rough hills around." Professor Camp points out that Doble's observations are substantiated by contemporary newspaper reports, such as the Volcano *Ledger*, November 3, 1855, which suggests the evidence of volcanic action in the "granite rock," and the San Francisco *Bulletin*, October 7, 1857, which states that "the miners called the light, grey, yellow and reddish colored stone above the limestone, lava." This same kind of rock, a welded tuff formed by the fusion of volcanic ash and pumice during an eruption, and, as the miners knew, disintegrated by weathering, is now quarried for building stone and "picture rock." The notion that the town was situated on a crater apparently arose in the late 1850s and led to the nickname Crater City. Bayard Taylor's earlier indication that the blackened cave entrances at Doble's "pile of rocks" could be the exits of volcanic fires was mere speculation, and the early miners' interpretation that there had been a volcano in the vicinity was correct. (Camp in Doble, pp. 300 f.) The first prospectors may have been discharged soldiers from Stevenson's Regiment. Bayard Taylor testifies to the richness of the mines (chapter 23 of his *El Dorado*). In 1849 one miner took out 8 thousand dollars worth of gold in a few days, and another, a Mexican, got twenty-eight pounds of gold from a single pocket. In 1849 Volcano was an election precinct, and in 1851 the post office was established. W. I. Morgan had a store there from January, 1851 to January, 1853. Borthwick (pp. 303 ff.) describes the place in the spring of 1853. The real chronicler of the prospering town was

Doble, who lived here from 1852 to 1862. In April, 1852, there were already 300 houses built of clapboard and pine, and on May 8, 1853, Doble states that the place had eleven stores, six hotels, three bakeries, and three bars. In the election of 1855 the town cast 1,050 votes (Ben Bowen, September 6, 1855). Hydraulic operations were started in 1855. A new and better quality of quartz was later brought to the surface from the Siebenthaler lode, and the George L. Gale lode near the town produced 100 dollars per ton, according to items in the *Mining Press*, April 20 and May 11, 1861. In 1858 two mills with eight stamps and six arrastres were erected (*State Register*, 1859). Browne (pp. 73 f., 80) gives a good account in 1867. Most of the mines were already idle then. A description of the district may be found in *Bulletin*, 193 (p. 126) and *Bulletin*, 92 (p. 146). There was limited dredging in the region in the 1930s, and some prospecting has been done since then. Volcano is Historic Landmark 29. It has the honor of having

Volcano, Amador Co.

had the first private observatory in the state, built by George Madeira. On June 30, 1861, he discovered the brilliant comet "1861 II," only a few hours after its discovery in Europe. Its site is Historic Landmark 715.

Volcano [Placer]. *See* Sarahsville; Bath.

Volcano Bar [El Dorado]. On the south side of the upper Middle Fork of American River, opposite the mouth of Volcano Creek. Recorded on Jackson's map, 1850. Edward Wilson (p. 40) states that while he was there in the spring of 1850, a Mexican took out twenty-nine pounds in three days, and another lucky miner took out 8 thousand dollars in a week. Finley McDiarmid mentions the place in a letter datelined Oregon Canyon, January 19, 1851. The miners were reported to be doing remarkably well, according to the *Mining Press*, August 31, 1861. In 1854 a formal duel was fought here because of political differences (Co. Hist., 1883, p. 184).

Volcano Canyon [Placer]. Two miles north of Michigan Bluff. The *Alta*, March 29, 1854, reprints this sensational news: On a Monday in March a Mr. Bell found a nugget of pure gold weighing forty-one ounces, another weighing twenty-two and a half ounces, and in addition took out 425 dollars worth of fine gold!

Volcano Flat [Amador]. The place near Volcano is mentioned by Albert Leonard, who had an inn there in the 1850s. He stated that the diggings had failed. His statement made for H. H. Bancroft in 1888 is a retrospective account of his experiences in the mining regions. Browne (p. 73) reports in 1867 that four claims were still active, although they were nearing exhaustion.

Volcano Slide [El Dorado]. Near Georgetown, probably in the vicinity of Volcanoville. The *Alta*, March 6, 1853, reprints a highly optimistic report: The gold is "thickly distributed through a hard, black cement;" the earnings never fall short of fifty dollars per day to the hand, and some days the yield is as high as one thousand dollars (!).

Volcanoville [El Dorado]. In the Hornblende Mountains, six miles northeast of Georgetown. Recorded on Goddard's map, 1857. The name arose because a nearby mountain seemed to be an extinct volcano, and the miners had to work through lava cement. In April, 1852, a company working with a long tom discovered rich deposits (*Alta*, April 5, 1852). In

1855 a 12-stamp steam-driven mill was erected (*State Register*, 1859). In 1856 newspapers reported the finding of a 42.8-ounce nugget valued at 750 dollars (*Alta* and San Franciso *Bulletin*, March 24, 1856). In 1860 there were many Italian companies here (*Transactions*, 1860, p. 58). The Josephine Mine with a 20-stamp mill was still in operation in 1887 (*Resources*, p. 20). The district is described in *Mining Bureau*, XI (p. 206), and a mine is listed until 1938. *See* Volcano Slide.

Volpone [Tuolumne]. One mile north of Jamestown. The story of two Frenchmen who struck it rich here and buried their treasure of gold is told in *Ghost Towns*. When one of them came back after fifteen years, the Volpone (or Volponi) brothers, natives of Italy, were in possession of the land and were raising vegetables. Midway between Jamestown and Sonora, on Woods Creek, there was formerly a Halfway House at the point now called Volpone Acres and earlier as John Yorks (De Ferrari). *See* Barrys Halfway House.

Volunteer Camp [Nevada]. Between the South Fork of Yuba River and Bear River, probably near Omega. Knowing that old soldiers and drunken sailors were considered lucky and easily followed by other prospectors, a group of Stevenson's Volunteers established a well-hidden camp to prospect promising claims. A. J. McCall gives a delightful picture of finding his fellow countrymen in the fall of 1849 (entries September 24 to 28, 1849).

Wades Flat [Calaveras]. Near Vallecito. It is mentioned in 1856 by Heckendorn (p. 104) and is probably the same place as the one mentioned in Hittell's roster as Waites Flat and by Trask as Wadies Creek.

Wahoo [Sierra]. Near Canyon Creek, east of La Porte. Shown on the County Map, 1874. It is mentioned as Washoe in 1857 (Bancroft Scraps, V, p. 1,779). *Wahoo* is an Indian word for cork elm, Indian arrowwood, and other useful trees or shrubs. Wahoo mines are listed in the Mining Bureau reports until 1942.

Wakell Flat [Humboldt]. At the confluence of Wakell Creek with Klamath River, east of Gold Bluff. It is shown on Goddard's map, 1857, but no mining record was found.

Waldauer Claim [Placer]. Between Ophir and Dotys Flat. Mr. Waldauer struck a rich pocket 'on July 4, 1867, which yielded 18 thousand dollars in three days (Marysville *Weekly Appeal*, July 20, 1867).

Waldo [Yuba]. *See* Cabbage Patch.

Walker: Bar, Creek [Siskiyou]. On the south side of Klamath River, about seven miles below Hamburg Bar. In 1894 a placer mine owned by Chinese is listed in *Mining Bureau*, XII (p. 293). According to the County History, 1881 (p. 195), two Chinese companies worked the bar and another one across the river. Walker Creek and Gulch are shown on the USGS Seiad 1922 quadrangle. Another Walker Bar, on the north side of Klamath River, about fourteen miles below Happy Camp, was also owned by Chinese (*Mining Bureau*, XIV, p. 293).

Walker River Diggings [Mono]. They are mentioned in Hittell Clippings (p. 67) and are apparently the same as the diggings at Dogtown. Dogtown was on Virginia Creek, a tributary to East Walker River. The accounts about the discovery vary. *See* Dogtown.

Walkers Basin [Kern]. Near Havilah. There was a 20-stamp mill in 1866 (*Annual Mining Review*, 1876, p. 22) at the Joe Walker mine, seven miles northeast of Havilah, in the northern part of the Basin. The mine was active between 1865 and 1874, and for short periods intermittently to 1951 (*County Report*, I, p. 112).

Walkers Plains [Butte]. Between the North and Middle forks of Feather River, on the Plumas County boundary. The plains are mentioned in 1864 as a plateau of peculiar rock formation, which had been tunneled for gold and to which a ditch was being constructed (unidentified clipping in Hayes Scrapbooks: Mining, IV, sec. 15). The plateau is mentioned in *Bulletin*, 92 (p. 104) and is shown on the USGS Bidwell Bar 1944 quadrangle.

Wallace [Calaveras]. On the San Joaquin County line, south of Camanche. It was a center for quartz and drift mining (*Register*, 1899). A post office was established in 1883. It replaced Catts (or Cat) Camp, when the San Joaquin and Sierra Railroad was built and the town renamed for the surveyor. *See* Cat Camp.

Wallis Ravine [Sierra]. On Little Slate Creek, near the county line. In the 1860s the Go-Ahead Company sunk a 351-foot shaft with a steam engine to bedrock, with interesting results, but not enough gold was found to engage in commercial exploitation (Raymond, V, p. 86).

Walloomsac Bar [Placer]. An unidentified

bar on the North Fork of American River, listed in the Giffen file.

Walloupa [Nevada]. On the old road from Nevada City to Dutch Flat, near You Bet. Recorded on Trask's map, 1853, and Goddard's 1857. Gold was discovered in the summer of 1852 (Brown's *Directory*, 1856, p. 16) and the camp, which usurped the site of an Indian village, was named for an old Indian of Wemeh's (Weimar's) tribe. The name *Walloupe* was an early California corruption of Guadelupe. According to *Bean's Directory*, 1867, it was the first surveyed townsite in the county, surveyed in 1852 by Charles Marsh and others of Nevada City. After a ditch was built to bring water from Steep Hollow, the camp developed rapidly. Several tunnels produced good pay dirt (Hittell Clippings, p. 88). Hutchings lists the place as a town in 1855. The decline started in 1860 and most of the miners moved to You Bet (*Nevada Directory*, 1895).

Walls Bridge [Nevada]. *See* Edwards Crossing.

Walls Diggings [Sacramento]. Near Mormon Island. Walter Wall was a pioneer miner of Mormon Island (Co. Hist., 1880, p. 230). There was a Wall Town on Carson Creek, about four miles south of White Rock (McGowan).

Walsh Ravine [Nevada]. On Little Deer Creek, Nevada City. It is listed in Nevada County Pre-emptions, I, p. 404 (Foley).

Wambos Bar [Yuba]. On the North Fork of Yuba River, near Deadwood Creek. It appears on Trask's map, 1853, as Wambaugh and with different spellings in mining literature. The bar was apparently named for M. N. Wambaugh, who came to California in 1846 and was "wagon master" of an immigrant train in 1848. His name is often mentioned in Camp's edition of *James Clyman*. The bar is mentioned by Downie (p. 24). Borthwick (pp. 267 f.) gives an interesting account of his stay in 1852, and De Long collected taxes here, March 19, 1855. According to the *Marysville Directory*, 1858, the bar gave fortunes to some miners and was still worked in a limited way in 1858. John E. Ross (p. 18) claims to have discovered these and other diggings in 1849. The bar is shown on map 9 of the *Guidebook*.

Wards Diggings [Calaveras]. North of Vallecito. The Tertiary gravels of the ancient river channel reportedly yielded high values in coarse gold, and about a half mile to the east, a shaft was reportedly sunk to a

depth of 146 feet without reaching bedrock (Lindgren, *Tertiary Gravels*, p. 202).

Wards Ferry [Tuolumne]. On the Tuolumne
River, above its confluence with Deer
Creek. It is listed in Heckendorn (p. 104).

Warren Hill [Sierra]. In the Slate Creek Basin, northeast of La Porte. The camp is
mentioned by John Clark in "The California Guide," April 23, 1856. An undated
clipping in Hayes Scrapbooks: Mining (I,
sec. 50) states that the camp had its heyday between 1853 and 1857, that the
gravel banks disappeared as hydraulic
mining progressed in the direction of La
Porte, and that the camp was deserted by
1860. Yet, it is still recorded in 1873 on a
map in Raymond's *Report*, V.

Wash [Plumas]. On the Middle Fork of
Feather River, in Mohawk Valley. It
served as trading center and post office
(from 1875 to 1904) for the quartz mines of
the district (*Register*, 1900). In 1905 the
name, which had been given for a pioneer,
was changed to Clio. *See California Place
Names*. The old name, Wash, is still shown
on the USGS Downieville 1907 quadrangle.

Washington [Nevada]. On the south bank of
the South Fork of Yuba River, about five
miles east of North Bloomfield. Shown on
Goddard's map, 1857, and Doolittle's,
1868. The camp was known as Indiana
Boys Camp in the fall of 1849; by 1850 it
had a large population and was called
Washington (Brown, *Directory*, 1856, p. 9
f.). The name sometimes appeared as
Washington City. According to the
County History, 1880 (p. 91), probably
about 3,000 men were working at and near
Washington in 1850–1851. Steele, however, (p. 149) found the hotel, stores, and
a large number of cabins deserted in December, 1850. This was obviously the result of the Gold Lake excitement, and later
the place apparently recovered. Between
1852 and 1854 the post office was named
Washington South Yuba; in 1862 it was
reestablished as Washington. By 1867 the
population had declined to 350, including
"Mongolians," according to Bean's *History*
(p. 377). The place is shown on the USGS
Colfax 1938 quadrangle. Washington mining district is described in *Mining Bureau*,
VIII (pp. 435 ff.) and XVI (Nevada, pp. 59
ff.). For a brief summary of mining activities in the district from 1850 to recent
years, *see Bulletin*, 193 (p. 128).

Washington District [Kern]. At the mouth of
Kern River Canyon; established in 1866
(Boyd, p. 43).

Washington Flat [Mariposa]. On the north

side of Merced River, above Bagby, near
Bond Flat. Shown on the Las Mariposas
Map, 1861. There was placering after 1850,
but the camp was short lived. Washington
Flats, near Horseshoe Bend, is mentioned
by Benjamin H. Deane in his journal July
14, 1850. Hiram Pierce (p. 94) camped
there in April, 1850. There were five or six
tents there at that time. In 1859 Frémont
built his dam at Ridleys Ferry, which
backed up the water and flooded out the
miners (Mariposa *Gazette*, June 24, 1859).

Washington: Flat, Ranch [Calaveras]. *See*
Old Gulch.

Washington Hill [Plumas]. Near Sawpit
Flat. According to the Quincy *Union*, December 9, 1865, it was a striving camp in
1855. However, repeated tunneling to
reach the vein proved fruitless, and according to the *Mining Press*, November 30,
1861, the future was still uncertain.

Washington Mine. *See* French Gulch [Shas-
ta]; Hornitos [Mariposa].

Washington Ridge [Nevada]. A long, narrow ridge extending from Nevada City to
the northeast about twenty miles into the
Washington district. Among the drift
gravel mines on the ancient river channel
were the Manzanita (Manzanita Hill), the
Odin (formerly Nebraska and Live Oak),
the Harmony, the Young America, and
others. Detailed descriptions may be
found in *Mining Bureau* (XI, pp. 296 ff.;
XII, pp. 196 f.; XVI, Nevada, pp. 91 ff.);
Lindgren, 1911 (pp. 127 ff.).

Washingtonville [Sierra]. *See* Durgans Flat
and Downieville.

Washingtonville [Tuolumne]. *See* Camp
Washington.

Washoe [Sierra]. *See* Wahoo.

Wasson [Mono]. Near Lundy. It is mentioned as a small mining camp by De Decker (p. 18).

Waterman [San Bernardino]. At present-day
Barstow. It was named for Robert W.
Waterman, later governor of California. It
was first a camp or company town for the
Waterman Mill, which processed ore from
the Waterman Silver Mine in the hills
north of the Mojave River. *See* Grapevine
District. Waterman post office was estab-
lished in 1881, and the following year the
Southern Pacific built a station here on the
Mojave–Needles line. When the Santa
Fe built a railroad over Cajon Pass to join
the line at Waterman Junction in 1885, the
name was changed in 1886 to Barstow, for
William Barstow Strong, president of the
Santa Fe Railroad. The town continued as

a supply center for the mines. (Belden, September 15, 1963; Haenszel.)

Watkins Bar [Amador]. On the Mokelumne River, about six miles east of Jackson. Recorded on Goddard's map, 1857. No mining record was found.

Watson Bar [Trinity]. On Trinity River, below Taylor Flat. A hydraulic mine is listed in the Mining Bureau reports from 1896 to 1941.

Wauponsa Creek [Plumas]. About 1865 the *Plumas Standard* reported the discovery of rich gold deposits on the stream with an Indian name. It caused the then existing town of Plumas City to be temporarily "almost wholly deserted" (Bancroft Scraps LI:1, p. 237).

Waynes Bar [Calaveras, Tuolumne]. On the Stanislaus River, nine miles north of Columbia. Listed in the Giffen file.

Wayne Tunnel [Sierra]. Apparently near Downieville. The *Alta*, February 2, 1854, reprints an item from the *Mountain Echo* which states that the claims averaged an earning of 3 thousand dollars weekly.

Weaver Creek, Weaverville [El Dorado]. A frequent misspelling for Weber Creek and Weberville.

Weavers Diggings [Trinity]. About thirty-five miles northeast of Weaverville. Recorded on Butler's map, 1851.

Weaverton [El Dorado]. It is mentioned by E. D. Perkins, February 28, 1849. It is the same place as Weberville.

Weaverville [El Dorado]. *See* Weaver Creek.

Weaverville, Weaver Creek [Trinity]. The town and the creek are shown on most early maps after 1851. The rich finds on the creek, a tributary to Trinity River, were reported apparently for the first time in the Sacramento *Transcript*, April 26, 1850 (Bancroft Notes). The diggings soon surpassed in quantity all the other deposits in the county. The camp was established in 1850, if not earlier, and named for George Weaver, a prospector who built the first cabin. But the sources differ as to the identity of Mr. Weaver. According to the manuscript of John Martin, the youngest son of Alexander Hamilton opened the first store in December, 1850. Martin and other miners called the creek Weaver Creek, but he does not say who Mr. Weaver was. Carr (pp. 111 ff.) arrived in February, 1851, and found only one round tent and four log cabins. He lived in the town until 1866 and was the real chronicler of the important place. In March of 1851 he reports the lynching and scalping of three white men who had sto-

len the mules of a pack train (pp. 119 ff.). He also records the battle between the Chinese rival companies of the "Hong Kongs and Cantons" in 1854 (pp. 267 ff.). Knapp (pp. 506 ff.) gives another account of the early days but is apt to exaggerate. He mined here in the fall of 1851 without luck and gave his claim to a Mr. Is. Comstock, who took out 60 thousand dollars in two months. He gives a good account of the terrible slaughter of Indians accused of having killed a white man. Another good description is given in the letters of Franklin Buck who lived in the town from 1852 to 1866. According to him, the Chinese population in 1854 was about 1,000 and the place had four stores, four gambling saloons, and a restaurant. The *Union Democrat* in 1854 tells the story of a Mr. Sites and a company of five who dug a shaft in 1851 more than 700 feet deep and five feet in diameter all by hand — apparently the deepest "coyote" hole ever made. They found gold in every stratum. (Hittell Clippings, p. 25.) Brewer (pp. 329 ff.) gives a graphic account of life in the town in 1862, when there were twenty-eight saloons, and "liquor holes, and gambling, and fighting were favorite pastimes." Raymond, VI (pp. 148 ff.) gives a good description of mining on Weaver Creek and other tributaries to Trinity River. According to him, around 1870 Weaverville shipped about 1.5 million dollars worth of gold annually, and he reports that some estimates of the total production have been as high as 70 million dollars. Some of the mines near Weverville operated until recent times, and a number of dragline dredges also operated

Weaverville, Trinity Co.

Weberville, El Dorado Co.

in the district (*Bull.*, 193, pp. 145 f.). The La Grange Mine, four miles west of Weaverville, which was one of the largest hydraulic mines in the state, is described in *Mining Bureau*, XXII (pp. 39 ff.) and XXXVII (pp. 43 f.). Work began in 1851, and from 1862 to 1918 large scale hydraulic mining was carried on. Between 1932 and 1942 the State Highway Department excavated the mine by means of hydraulicking during the construction of the highway between Weaverville and Junction City and recovered some gold in the operation. The total production of the mine has been at least 8 million dollars, in the opinion of William B. Clark, author of *Bulletin*, 193 (pp. 145 f.). The mine is Historic Landmark 778.

Webbers Bridge [Nevada]. *See* Edwards Crossing.

Weber: Creek, Camp; Weberville [El Dorado]. Charles M. Weber was the pioneer of gold mining between the South Fork of American River and Cosumnes River. He moved into the district at the beginning of June, 1848, and employed Indians to dig and wash gold. He and his first partner, William Daylor (or Dalor) made 50 thousand dollars together in a short time (Buffum, p. 73). He moved his camp several times and finally settled at the confluence of Weber and Hangtown creeks. Here (or at a former camp) Governor Mason and his party visited him in July, 1848 and gave a glowing account of

the immense yield on the creek and the gulches obtained with the help of a large number of Indians. Weber contributed to the first gold to be sent to Washington. The creek is shown on Mason's sketch and on all the maps after 1850. The Royce family arrived at Weberville in October, 1849, and stayed two months. Mrs. Royce (*A Frontier Lady*, pp. 82 ff.) gives a charming account. The real chronicler was E. G. Buffum (pp. 65 ff.) who arrived December 3, 1848, and found a dozen rough log cabins. He mined very successfully, making 190 dollars one day. Other early accounts by Lyman (pp. 187 ff.); Borthwick (pp. 139 ff.); W. W. Call in September, 1849; Edmundson, October 6, 1850; Daniel B. Woods (pp. 60 ff.). The spelling changes continually between Weber, Webber, and Weaver. The U. S. Bureau of the Census uses the name Weaverville in its population schedule for the 1850 census, in which it lists the names of 906 inhabitants in the camp and vicinity. A picture of the now vanished Weberville was published in *California Historical Society Quarterly* VI (p. 238). *See* Old Dry Diggings.

Weber Divide [El Dorado]. Between the South Fork of American River and Weber Creek. Situated on the Gray Channel of very hard cemented gravel. The claims in 1867 are described in Browne (pp. 83 f.). Some were drift claims in summer and hydraulic in winter.

Weeds Point [Yuba]. Three miles northwest of Camptonville. It was named by a miner of that name, who abandoned the claim in 1853. In 1865 a company was formed and found the diggings very profitable (Co. Hist., 1879, p. 100). The County Map of 1879 shows the place as a sizeable town. The Weeds Point Mine was apparently in operation in 1915/16 (*Mining Bureau*, XV, p. 441). Shown on the USGS Smartsville 1943 quadrangle.

Weimar [Placer]. The place on Highway 40, named for an old Indian chief, Weimah, was not a gold camp, but it was the post office and center for a number of quartz mines (*Register*, 1902). The quartz mines of the Weimar district are listed in *Mining Bureau*, XV (p. 319).

Weimar Hill [Nevada]. Near Grass Valley. The North Star quartz vein on the hill is described in Professor Silliman's report quoted by Browne (p. 115).

Weitchpec Bar [Humboldt]. At the junction of Klamath River and Trinity River. Shown on Goddard's map, 1857, as Weitspeck. It was named after an Indian village. Hydraulic mining is mentioned in 1888, in *Mining Bureau*, VIII (p. 218), where the name is spelled Witzpeck. Some platinum along with gold was mined from the 1890s to the 1940s (*Mining Bureau*, XII, p. 135; XIV, p. 407; XXXVII, p. 515).

Weske Claim [Placer]. On the ridge between El Dorado and Volcano canyons. Named for Adolph Weske. *See* Turkey Hill.

Westall Diggings [Sierra]. East of Sierra City, about one mile north of Bassetts Station. The diggings were named for Alford Westall and sons, who worked them in the 1880s and 1890s (Sinnott, *Sierra City*, p. 132).

Westmorland [Tuolumne]. In the Table Mountain district. It is mentioned as a mining camp by Heckendorn (p. 104).

West Point [Calaveras]. Between the North and Middle forks of Mokelumne River, about five miles above the confluence. It was called Indian Gulch before 1854. The diggings prospered, and in 1856 a post office was established. The area became one of the richest pocket mine districts of the state. A high grade pocket valued at more than 300 thousand dollars was found at the Keltz Mine, four miles northwest of West Point (*Bull.*, 193, p. 11). In 1857 West Point was the seat of two canal companies, and in 1858 two mills were in operation (*State Register*, 1859). Browne (pp. 65 f.) refers to the several

hundred pocket mines in the area in the 1860s and lists the mines and mills of 1867, some of which were already idle then. Raymond, VII (p. 63) claims that quartz mining was still strong in 1874, and the *Register* of 1899 still lists five stamp mills and one arrastre. The productive Hageman Mine at West Point Powerhouse on the other side of the river was in operation until the 1950s (*Mining Bureau*, L, pp. 181, 187). The place is Historic Landmark 268. According to *California Historical Landmarks*, it was named by Kit Carson (apparently in 1846), and Bret Harte lived here for a period. For a map and resumé of mining activities in West Point district from the 1850s to the present day, *see Bulletin*, 193 (p. 129) and the table in *County Report*, II.

West Ravine [Sierra or Nevada]. According to the *Mining Press*, August 21 and 30, 1862, two companies took from their claims more than 800 dollars worth in one week.

Westville [Placer]. South of Emigrant Gap. No early mining records were found. Around 1900 it was the center and post office for quartz and drift mines and had two stamp mills (*Register*, 1902). Shown on the USGS Colfax 1938 quadrangle.

West Walker District [Mono]. In the northern part of the county, a few miles southwest of Coleville. It is listed as a small mining district, in which several quartz mines were active in the 1890s and early 1900s (*Bull.*, 193, p. 180).

West Weaver Creek [Trinity]. A rich deposit of gold in decomposed quartz was discovered in April, 1862, in a gulch which empties into the creek. Some nuggets worth up to ninety dollars were found, and a minor rush followed. (*Mining Press*, May 1 and 8, 1862.) *See* Weaver Creek.

Wet Gulch [Calaveras]. Near Whiskey Slide. On June 25, 1870, a group of Italian miners washed out a rusted tin box containing 1,572 dollars worth of gold coins, coined by Moffatt & Co., San Francisco. According to several newspaper accounts in Bancroft Notes, the coins had belonged to a Frenchman named "Cherry," who had kept a store here and was murdered in 1852. There were several Wet Gulch mines in the county. *See Consolidated Index* and *County Report*, II.

Wetherbys Ranch [San Diego]. Apparently in the gold mining district around Julian. According to the *Mining Press*, March 1, 1861, and April 18, 1862, the Los Angeles

Star had optimistic reports of the gold finds here, and the diggings paid well.

Wet Hill [Nevada]. Now a part of Nevada City. The camp is mentioned in the *Alta*, March 6, 1853. The steamer edition of the same newspaper of March 20, 1857, reports that in the preceding week a single pan of dirt had yielded 100 dollars worth of pure gold. The hill is listed in Bancroft, VI (p. 358) and is mentioned in *Mining Bureau*, XVI (Nevada, p. 38).

Wet Ravine [Sierra]. Near Alleghany. It is mentioned in the *Mining Press*, August 24, 1861, as famous for its rich lead. In 1860 it had an 8-stamp water-driven mill (*Annual Mining Review*, 1876, p. 23). Hutchings lists Wet Hill as a town in 1855.

Whale Boat Ferry [Amador, Calaveras]. On the Mokelumne River, between Big Bar and Lower Bar, near Frenchmans Bar (Cenotto; Calaveras County Deeds). *California Historical Landmarks* locates it at Big Bar and states that it was established in 1849 and maintained until the first bridge was built, about 1852.

Whales Bar [Calaveras]. On the Mokelumne River, east of Jackson. Recorded on Goddard's map, 1857.

Wheatland District [Yuba, Placer, Nevada]. On the lower Bear River, near Wheatland and Camp Far West. It is described in *Bulletin*, 193 (p. 130). During the Gold Rush the streams were placer mined; and in the 1930s gold was recovered from a copper mine by cyanidation and by dragline dredging in some of the ravines. The area described is in western Placer and southern Yuba counties; Ramey includes the area around Spenceville and Hacketville in southwestern Nevada County and gives Bear River district as an alternate name.

Wheeler Diggings [Amador]. On the North Branch of Sutter Creek, northeast of Volcano. It is mentioned in the County History, 1881 (p. 216), along with Ashland and Grizzly Hill.

Wheelock [Siskiyou]. *See* Fort Jones.

Wheelocks Ravine [El Dorado]. Located near Diamond Springs. It is mentioned in 1859 by Crockett (p. 95).

Whetstone Bar [Trinity]. On Trinity River, opposite Red Bar. There was well-paying placering as early as 1850. Water from Dutton Creek was brought across the river by a flume. A description is given in Cox (p. 42).

Whimtown [Tuolumne]. Near Shaws Flat, on the east side of Table Mountain. The name is derived from the many whims, devices for raising ore or water, from the mine shafts. The place is described in December, 1856, as a settlement of twelve or more houses around a flat near Caldwells Gardens and its rich claims (clippings from the *Democratic State Journal, in* Hayes Scrapbooks: Mining, I, sec. 28). Browne (p. 39) mentions it but does not report the gold production. A detailed description of the method of mining with whims is given in San Francisco *Evening Bulletin*, November 26, 1856.

Whipple Mountains District [San Bernardino]. In the southeast corner of the county. Gold was probably first mined here many years ago, according to *Bulletin*, 193 (p. 169), but the main period of activity was in the 1930s and 1940s. Copper and manganese mines, however, outnumbered the gold mines. *See* the map in *Mining Bureau*, XXXIX (plate 7). Among the gold mines described in *Mining Bureau*, XLIX (table following p. 257) are the Vidal, at the southwest base of Savahai Peak; the Roulette, north of Whipple Mountains; the Ethel Leona (gold and copper) on the south slope of the mountains; and the Islander (gold and copper) on the north slope, near Lake Havasu.

Whiskeyana Flat [Nevada]. On the South Fork of Yuba River. The *Alta*, June 27, 1852, reprints an item from the Downieville *Echo*, according to which the New York Company of twelve men averaged 296 dollars per day to the man (!). The flood of the river had made possible the large profits.

Whiskey Bar [Butte]. There were bank diggings on the north side of the Big Bend of the North Fork of Feather River. Recorded on the County Map, 1877, and on the map in the County History, 1882 (p. 209).

Whiskey Bar [El Dorado]. In the Horseshoe Bend of the North Fork of American River, near Rattlesnake Bar. Recorded on Doolittle's map, 1868, and on Bowman's 1873. Gardiner mined here in the summer of 1851 (pp. 162, 180). A wire rope bridge was built across the river at this point in 1854 (Co. Hist., 1883, p. 83). Hutchings mentions the bridge, April 26, 1855, and lists Whiskey Bar as a town in the same year. The site is now covered by Folsom Lake.

Whiskey Bar [Nevada]. Northwest of Nevada City. It is listed in the Giffen file.

Whiskey Creek Diggings [Shasta]. *See* Whiskeytown.

Whiskey Diggings [Sierra]. On Little Slate

Creek, near the Plumas County line. Shown as Whiskey on Trask's map, 1853. The camp is mentioned by John Clark in "The California Guide," September 3, 1852. The *Alta*, February 24, 1854, reprints an item from the Gibsonville *Trumpet* which reports that a greenhorn picked up a nugget of twenty-seven ounces on his first day of mining. There was prosperous tunnel work in progress when Vischer (p. 240) visited the place in 1859. One of the diggings averaged 700 dollars weekly in the winter of 1861 and in 1862 (*Mining Press*, March 16, 1861; July 16, 1862). The camp was also known as Whiskey and Newark (Bancroft Scraps, V, p. 1782). The place is still mentioned as a part of the Gibsonville district in 1918 (*Mining Bureau*, XVI, Sierra, p. 11).

Whiskey: Diggings, Hill [Placer]. On the Bald Hill Range, six miles northeast of Lincoln. Whiskey Diggings Ledge is mentioned in the notice of a claim of June 16, 1863 in the Placer County Records, VI (p. 36). In 1866 the location of the famous Banker Mine caused considerable notoriety due to Asbury Harpending, best known in connection with the Great Diamond Hoax. The complete story from various sources is told in the County History, 1882 (pp. 231 f.). Doolittle's map, 1868, shows Whiskey Diggings as a former (or alternate) name of Valley View and indicates the location of the Harpending and G. D. Roberts' Quartz Mine just north of it.

Whiskey Flat [Amador]. Near the Mokelumne River, southeast of Volcano. It was also known as Karneys Diggings. The County History of 1881 (p. 216) apparently by mistake calls the place Whiskey Slide, which is eight miles south in Calaveras County, and tells the following story. In 1855 Andy Karney mined here with a partner. One of them fell into a hole while slightly intoxicated and discovered a pocket of rich pay dirt.

Whiskey Flat [Butte]. On Butte Creek, near Magalia. Shown on the County Map, 1862, as a sizeable camp.

Whiskey Flat [Kern]. *See* Kernville.

Whiskey Flat [Mariposa]. About two miles north of Whitlock, near Sherlock Gulch. The Mariposa *Chronicle*, April 7, 1854, carried an advertisement of the store of Clement S. Simpson and George Ireton: WHISKY FLAT, Sherlock's Creek, Sign of the GROUND HOG. The place is mentioned in *Bulletin*, 193 (p. 131) as part of the Whitlock District, an area that was

placer mined soon after the beginning of the Gold Rush. Soon afterwards lode mining began. Shown on the USGS Sonora 1939 quadrangle.

Whiskey Flat [Nevada]. On the South Fork of the Yuba River, below Washington. It is listed in Bancroft, VI (p. 358).

Whiskey Flat [Placer]. About two miles northwest of Michigan Bluffs. Whiskey Flat Bridge is shown on Doolittle's map, 1868, across a branch of the Middle Fork of American River. No mining record was found.

Whiskey Gulch [Yuba]. *See* Deadwood Creek.

Whiskey; Gulch, Flat, Hill [Calaveras]. Southeast of Fourth Crossing. Bachman had a "fluming" at the gulch from December, 1856 to March, 1857, and at the flat from March, 1857 to November, 1858. A Whiskey Hill Mine, at a different location, near Jenny Lind, is listed in the *Register*, 1899.

Whiskey Hill [Tuolumne]. One mile southwest of Jamestown. Mining started in 1849. There was a 10- or 12-stamp water-driven mill here in 1857 (*State Register*, 1859). In 1869 one of the big mines, the Trio Mine, did not finish its tunnel because the yield was less than five dollars per ton (Browne, p. 44). According to Raymond, II (p. 26), there were four mills with twenty-nine stamps on the hill in 1869. The newspapers of the time give glowing accounts. Descriptions of the hill are found in U. S. *Bulletin*, 424 (p. 30); in *Mining Bureau*, XXIV (p. 40); and in *Bulletin*, 108 (pp. 165 f.). The Harvard Mine on the southeast slope, operating from 1850 to 1916, produced more than 2 million dollars. It is recorded on *Guidebook* map 3.

Whiskey Ravine [Placer]. A tributary to Canyon Creek, north of Gold Run Ravine. Recorded on Pettee and Bowman's map, 1879, where the gravel in nearby areas is shown as "more or less completely hydraulicked away."

Whiskey Slide [Calaveras]. On a tributary to the North Fork of Calaveras River, eight miles northeast of San Andreas. The camp is mentioned in the *Alta*, June 8, 1854. At that time the miners regularly washed two dollars to the pan. In 1857 it was the seat of the Whiskey Slide Canal Company (Hittell Clippings, pp. 22, 48). In 1871 a 10-stamp mill was erected after ten years of intermittent mining (Raymond, IV, p. 83). Shown on the USGS Jackson 1938 quadrangle.

Whiskeytown [Shasta]. About ten miles

northwest of Redding, on Whiskey Creek. Recorded on Goddard's map, 1857, as Whiskey. The place was settled in 1849 and was first called Franklin City. By 1852 it had become known as Whiskey Creek and was listed in the state census among the nine principal mining localities of the county. In 1856 a Whiskey Creek post office was established. In 1864 it was discontinued, but the name used locally was apparently Whiskeytown. In 1881 the post office was reestablished and bore successively the more respectable names Blair, Stella, and Schilling, until 1952 when the name was changed by popular demand to Whiskeytown. (*California Place Names*.) According to *Mining Bureau*, XIV (p. 775), the district around Stella produced more gold than any in the county, except French Gulch. In the twentieth century production was small, mainly from pocket mining (*Mining Bureau*, XXII, pp. 168 f.). Whiskeytown Dam and Reservoir were completed in 1963. The town is Historic Landmark 131.

Whistleburg [El Dorado]. Mentioned by Henry S. Blom in his diary April 6, 1851. It may have been a nickname for Greenwood.

White Cloud [Nevada]. Two miles southwest of Washington. Shown on Doolittle's map, 1868. The name was derived from the white cloud of dust stirred up by the approach of teams as they neared the area (Foley). The place is listed in Brown's *Directory*, 1856 (p. 133). No mining record was found. It is now a U. S. Forest Service Camp.

White Maple Spring [Yuba]. Southwest of Bullards Bar. It is mentioned by De Long, January 23, 1856, and is perhaps the site shown as Maple Grove Ranch on the USGS Smartsville 1943 quadrangle.

White Mountains [Mono]. In the southwestern part of the county. The streams in the region were mined in the 1860s and 70s and soon afterwards lode deposits were discovered (*Bull.*, 193, p. 152).

White Oak Flat [El Dorado]. In White Oak township, south of Salmon Falls township. Originally it was called Cart Wheel Valley. An interesting letter is datelined from White Oak Flats to Georgetown *News*, December 25, 1855 (Greenwood).

White Oak Flat District [Amador]. About ten miles northeast of Volcano. There was some placer mining years ago, according to *Bulletin*, 193 (p. 130), and recently the Marklee quartz mine has been prospected.

White Oak Springs. *See* Bovyers [Nevada].

White Porphyry Mine [Mariposa]. *See* Solomon Gulch.

White River District [Tulare]. In the southern part of the county. This was the only really productive gold region of the county. The *Alta*, July 22, 1851, reports rumors of rich diggings on Rio Blanco or White River. The news led to a rush that soon petered out (Bancroft Notes, from *Alta California*, July 22, 1851). However, in 1853 deposits were actually found and worked with moderate and intermittent success until 1930 (*Mining Bureau*, LIV, pp. 339 f.). The quartz vein encased in sandstone varied in thickness and yielded between 40 and 300 dollars per ton (Hittell Clippings, p. 40, from Mariposa *Democrat*). The trading center of the mines was Tailholt, a name changed to White River when the post office was established in 1862. *See* Tailholt. A chispa of thirteen ounces from White River was exhibited in Visalia in January, 1861 (*Mining Press*, February 1, 1861). There were several stamp mills in 1866 and 1867, and in 1873 the well-equipped Eclipse and Lee mill with fifteen stamps was in operation (*Annual Mining Review*, 1876, pp. 21 f., 45). The development of the district at the beginning of the twentieth century is described in *Mining Bureau*, XVIII (pp. 524 f.). Since 1906 there has been little activity. The estimated total production to 1914 was 750 thousand dollars (*Bull.*, 193, p. 131).

White Rock [Sacramento]. On the Sacramento-Placerville Wagon Road and on the railroad between Folsom and Placerville, about five miles south of Folsom (McGowan). Shown on Trask's map, 1853. It is mentioned in the president's report to the stockholders of the Sacramento Valley Railroad, 1854 (Wilson's report, p. 7).

White Rock Bar [Butte]. Northeast of Oroville, below Morris Bar. Recorded on Trask's map, 1853. According to a clipping from the Oroville *North Californian*, several claims worked here with good profits, 1852–1855 (Hittell Clippings, p. 68).

White Rock: Canyon, Hill [El Dorado]. About three miles northeast of Placerville. Recorded on Goddard's map, 1857. Haskins (p. 137) worked here successfully in the winter of 1849–50. The canyon is mentioned by McKeeby in the summer of 1850. Knapp (p. 517) states that Senator Stanford kept a store in the vicinity, and "his goods combined might almost have been put in a pack." According to Browne (p. 82), the place was on the Blue Channel of the county. The gold had a high degree of fineness: 965° (*Mining Bureau*, IV, p. 220). According to *Mining Bureau*, LII (p. 566), the White Rock diggings at White Rock Canyon yielded 5 million dollars by hydraulic operations "many years ago." Shown on the USGS Placerville 1931 quadrangle.

White Rock City [Trinity]. *See* Marysville and New River City.

Whites Bar [Amador]. On the north side of Mokelumne River, two and a half miles east of Mokelumne Hill. Recorded on Trask's map, 1853, Goddard's, 1857, and the County Map, 1866. The bar is mentioned by Doble, June 26, 1852. *See* Whit's Bar.

Whites Bar [Trinity]. On Trinity River, below Big Bar. It is mentioned as well paying by Cox (p. 81). A drift mine was in operation in 1896 (*Mining Bureau*, XIII, p. 466).

Whiteside Seam Diggings [El Dorado]. One and a half miles northeast of Johntown. Shown on Bowman's map, 1873.

Whiting Hill [Siskiyou]. On Scott River, near Simonsville. Named for Peter Whiting, who still lived there in 1881 in a cabin on the hill (Co. Hist., 1881, p. 217). In the 1850s a lump of 103 ounces of pure gold, estimated at one thousand eight hundred dollars was found (Hittell Clippings, p. 31). It is listed in a letter to George W. Metlar dated February 22, 1856, published in his pamphlet on Scott and Klamath River mines.

Whitlock [Mariposa]. About three and a half miles northwest of Mariposa. Around 1850 there was extensive placer mining in Whitlock Gulch and lode mining followed soon afterwards. In 1858 three mills with twenty-six stamps were in operation (*State Register*, 1859). The *Annual Mining Review*, 1876 (p. 21) mentions a 12-stamp mill having been built in 1863. The *Register*, 1903, lists three stamp mills in operation. Among the most productive mines was the Whitlock Group, which produced an estimated 500 thousand dollars by 1942, and the Spread Eagle Group, which produced 425 thousand dollars by 1939 (*Mining Bureau*, LIII, pp. 183 ff., 170 ff.). Other mines, including the Farmers Hope, the Nutmeg, the Permit, and the Geary are listed and described in *Mining Bureau* (XVII, p. 96; LIII, pp. 232 f.) and *U. S. Bulletin*, 434 (pp. 135 ff.). The post office was established March 15, 1899 and discontinued October 31, 1910.

Whitney Group [Plumas]. Near Crescent Mills, above Indian Valley. "In early days" rich surface pockets were found. The mines were reported idle in 1918 (*Mining Bureau*, XVI, Plumas, p. 171).

Whit's Bar [Calaveras]. On the Mokelumne River, probably near Mokelumne Hill. "Judge" Thompson (p. 246) mined here in 1853. It is doubtless the same as Whites Bar.

Whooping Boys Hollow [Tuolumne]. Probably a fictitious name used in a letter of December 23, 1852, by a man in the "dry diggings" near Columbia (*Miscellany*, p. 37).

Whorehouse Gulch [El Dorado]. *See* Indian Diggings.

Widow Harmans Ravine [Placer]. The location is not known, but it may have been the Widows Ravine near Gold Hill mentioned by Wing on January 25, 1853. Notice of a claim of December 2, 1854 is recorded in the Placer County Records, I (p. 270).

Wightman Camp [Nevada]. *See* Baltimore City.

Wilcox Ravine [Nevada]. A tributary to Steep Hollow Creek; near You Bet. Shown on Pettee and Bowman's map, 1879. Pettee describes the area in Whitney, *Auriferous Gravels* (pp. 164 ff.). Hittell lists the Ravine in his roster.

Wild Cat Bar [El Dorado]. On the south side of the Middle Fork of American River, five miles above the junction, between Kennebec and Hoosier bars. Shown on Doolittle's map, 1868, and Bowman's, 1873. The *Mining Press*, August 31, 1861, reports good yields in the mines.

Wild Emigrant [Nevada]. On Wolf Creek, ten miles south of Grass Valley. It was situated on a rich ledge, but there was only little surface mining because of the lack of water. (Raymond, III, 1870, p. 44).

Wild Goose Flat [El Dorado]. On the North Fork of American River, opposite Rattlesnake Bar. Doolittle's map, 1868, shows it below Rattlesnake Bar. It became a lively gold camp after the Pilot and Rock Creek Canal brought water in 1854 (Hittell Clippings, pp. 61½, 73). In 1874 the riches were gone, but it was still worked on a limited scale (Raymond, VII, p. 96). In 1887 it was a ghost town.

Wild Irish Bar [Plumas]. On the Middle Fork of Feather River, near the Butte County line. It was probably named in analogy to nearby Wild Yankee. Recorded on Trask's 1853 and Goddard's 1857 maps.

Wildman Mine [Amador]. *See* Lincoln Consolidated Mine.

Wild Rose Canyon [Inyo]. In Death Valley National Monument, in the Panamint Mountains. In the 1930s and 1940s there was some lode gold mining at the Burro, New Discovery, and Gem mines, and apparently there has also been some placer mining in the area (*Bull.*, 193, p. 152).

Wildwood [Trinity]. On Hayfork River and Highway 36. It served as a center for a quartz mining district and had a post office between 1888 and 1893. Later it was known mainly for manganese deposits.

Wild Yankee [Butte]. North of Berry Creek, on the trail to Rich Bar. Wild Yankee Ranch is recorded on Milleson and Adams' map, 1851. The camp is mentioned by Dame Shirley (I, p. 16; II, p. 135). In 1850 the Wild Yankee Company of fifteen members took out 4 thousand dollars in 450 days (Daniel B. Woods, p. 174). In 1915/16 there was apparently still active tunnel mining (*Mining Bureau*, XV, p. 223). Wild Yankee Hill is shown on the USGS Bidwell Bar 1944 quadrangle.

Willard Claim [Butte]. *See* Dogtown and Magalia.

Williams Bar [Yuba]. An unidentified place above Parks Bar, on the main Yuba River. A settlement farther north named Williams is shown on Wescoatt's map, 1861, less than a half mile north of New York Ranch on the road to Forbestown in Butte County.

Williamsburg [Kern]. *See* Kernville.

Williams Diggings [Trinity]. On the East Fork of Trinity River. It is mentioned by Cox (p. 102) in 1858.

Willow Bar [Amador]. On the north side of Mokelumne River, fifteen miles above Oregon Bar. Recorded on Trask's map, 1853.

Willow Bar [Calaveras]. On the Stanislaus River, two miles above Two Mile Bar. A company took out "10,662 dollars between August 2 and October 2 [1858?] as per mint receipts." (excerpted from Sonora *Herald*, undated, in Hittell Clippings, p. 66½).

Willow Bar [El Dorado]. On the lower Middle Fork of American River, between Wildcat Bar and Hoosier Bar. It is mentioned in the El Dorado County History, 1883 (p. 84) and in the Placer County History, 1882 (pp. 401 f.). Another Willow Bar, on the upper Middle Fork of American River, near the junction of the North and Middle forks of the Middle Fork, and above Boston Bar, is mentioned in El Dorado County Records (Mechanics Lien Book, III, p. 102), August 8, 1860. This

Willow Bar is shown on the map of the Volcanoville Quartz Mining District.

Willow Bar [Nevada]. On the Yuba River, west of French Corral. Shown on Trask's map, 1853.

Willow Bar [Placer]. On the Middle Fork of American River, between Upper Horseshoe Bar and Junction Bar. It is shown on the north side of the river on Trask's map, 1853. It may be the same as the Willow Bar mentioned in a claim recorded August 15, 1851, in Placer County Records, I (p. 3).

Willow Bar [Placer]. On the North Fork of American River, between Rattlesnake Bar and Lacys Bar. It is mentioned in the County History, 1924 (p. 178), and in *Placer Nuggets*, June, 1964. Willow Bar, above Rattlesnake Bar, is mentioned in Placer County Records, I (p. 278) in a claim for 150 yards of the river for "fluming" purposes, recorded January 29, 1855.

Willow Bar [Tuolumne]. An unidentified bar on Tuolumne River, about four miles south of Jacksonville. It might be the camp mentioned in the *Mining Press*, August 3, 1861, and again in *Mines and Minerals* (p. 358).

Willow Creek [Plumas]. On the Middle Fork of Feather River. It is mentioned in the County History, 1882 (p. 288) as one of the chief camps on the Middle Fork.

Willow: Creek, Bar [Yuba]. The Creek empties into the North Fork of Yuba River between Fosters Bar and New York Bar. The Bar is shown on Trask's map, 1853, and on Wescoatt's, 1861. Gold was struck here in 1852. It was worked until 1870, then abandoned to Chinese miners (Co. Hist., 1879, p. 97). It was repeatedly mentioned by De Long in 1855.

Willow District [Inyo]. East of Death Valley, in the Black Mountains; about fifteen miles west of Shoshone. The chief mines were the Confidence and the Ashford, the latter having produced about 135 thousand dollars (*Bull.*, 193, p. 152).

Willow Springs [Amador]. Five miles northwest of Amador. It is mentioned by Stephen L. Fowler in his journal October 26, 1849. Willow Springs: town, Flat, and Creek, are shown on the County Map, 1866. The place was important for its copper mines; the gold had been worked out by 1867 (Browne, p. 72). It was well known for its fine hotel on the road to Fiddletown.

Willow Springs [Calaveras]. On Willow Creek, a tributary to the South Fork of Calaveras River; one mile east of San Andreas. Lucius Fairchild mined here from

November, 1850, to about April, 1851, and he gives an interesting description. March 18, 1851 was his luckiest day, when he and his partners took 2 thousand dollars worth of gold "out of the hole." The creek is shown on the USGS Jackson 1938 quadrangle.

Willow Springs [Inyo]. In the Coso mining district. In 1861 or 1862 a stamp mill was erected, which crushed the output of three leads. A test showed 60 percent gold and 40 percent silver (*Mining Press*, September 11, 1862). The Springs are shown on the 1917 geological map of the county issued by the state Mining Bureau.

Willow: Springs, Diggings [Sacramento]. On the road from Sacramento to Placerville, about one mile southeast of Folsom, between Willow and Alder creeks. Shown on Jackson's map, 1850, and Judah's, 1854. According to the County History, 1880 (p. 225), mining started along Willow Creek and when the deposits were exhausted continued to the ridge, with water supplied by the Natoma Ditch of 1853. In its heyday there were twelve companies working here, and from the 2,000 or so acres it is estimated that "millions" were taken out, the eastern end of Willow Springs Hill having been very rich. A placer mining camp at Willow Springs is mentioned in *Pacific Coast Mining Review*, 1878 (p. 142) and in 1896 in *Mining Bureau*, XIII (p. 318).

Willow Valley [Nevada]. Near Nevada City. It is listed as a camp in *Bean's Directory*. Mining started in the early 1850s. In May, 1865, a new ledge was discovered, which failed to pay expenses after rich initial yield (*Bean's Directory*, p. 124). In 1882 the assay value was again forty dollars per ton (*Mining Bureau*, II, part 1, p. 180). The district is described in *Mining Bureau*, VIII (pp. 451 f.).

Wilshire-Bishop Creek Mine [Inyo]. *See* Bishop.

Wilson Creek [Calaveras]. Near San Andreas. In 1867 only one quartz mine with two arrastres was in operation.

Wilson Gulch [Yuba]. Between the North and Middle Forks of Yuba River. It is mentioned in the County History, 1879 (p. 100).

Wilsonville [Nevada]. In Rough and Ready Mining District. It is mentioned in Nevada County Mining Records (Foley) and is listed along with Spenceville, Hacketville, and Queen City, towns that arose during the copper "fever" of the winter of 1863–1864. None of them survived except Spenceville, which is shown on the USGS Smartsville 1943 quadrangle about ten miles southwest of Rough and Ready, near the Yuba county line.

Windsor [Sierra]. The camp is mentioned by Pringle Shaw (p. 124) as a "bustling little town" about 1856.

Windyville [Sierra]. North of Brandy City. Shown as Windaville on Wescoatt's map, 1861, and as Windyville on Doolittle's, 1868. The gravel deposit and the workings of the Arnott Mine are described by Pettee in 1879 (Whitney, *Auriferous Gravels*, pp. 461 f.). Water was brought in a ditch from Canyon Creek, and the washing season was limited to five months of the year. The gold was fine and scaly, with an occasional coarse nugget.

Wingate: Bar, Hill [Siskiyou]. On the Klamath River, below Happy Camp. Diggings were worked as early as 1851. George Gibbs passed here, October 16, 1851, and found a trading house and a party of miners (Schoolcraft, III, p. 154). The *Alta*, February 18, 1852, reported that the average daily earnings were twelve dollars to the man (Bancroft Scraps, LI:1, p. 249). Wingate Creek, a tributary to Klamath River, is shown on the USGS Seiad 1945 quadrangle. The Wingate Hill placer is listed in the Mining Bureau reports until 1935.

Wingdam. The term for a pier built into the river was quite common among miners. Ferguson (pp. 117 f.) describes a wingdam in detail. A Wing-Dam claim on the North Fork of American River is mentioned in *Placer Herald*, September 22, 1856. Bret Harte's name in "A Night in Wingdam" is just as fictitious as the story. *See* Murphys.

Winslow [Yuba]. On the west bank of the North Fork of Yuba River, below English Bar and Kanaka Bar, near the confluence of the Middle Fork. Shown on Butler's map, 1851, and on Trask's map, 1853. De Long collected taxes here, March 26, 1855. According to the *Marysville Directory*, 1858, (pp. xxiv f.), the place was named for Captain Winslow, who was among the first to import Chinese laborers to work in the mines. In 1879 the Winslow camp was still worked by Chinese, according to the County History, 1879 (p. 94).

Winslow Creek [El Dorado]. According to Haskins (p. 134), the Winslow brothers discovered gold in Log Cabin Ravine in 1848.

Winters [Yolo]. *See* Putah Creek District.

Winters Bar [Calaveras]. On Mokelumne

River, a short distance east of Lancha Plana. Recorded on Trask's map, 1853, as Winter Bar and on Goddard's map, 1857, as Winters Bar. According to A. Lascy's "Reminiscences" (pp. 4 f.), the bar was located in 1849 by Captain Winters, a store owner. Apparently he was a partner of the *lancha plana*. Charles Kirkpatrick (Journal, pp. 40 f.) mined and practiced medicine in the winter of 1849–50 but left in March because the river mining paid no more than ten dollars a day. According to a letter dated October 30, 1855, in Hittell's Clippings (p. 66). Henry Butler, a negro, netted the sum of 20 thousand dollars with his partners. One company took out forty-two ounces of gold from six wheelbarrows of dirt, according to the San Francisco *Bulletin*, December 24, 1855 (Bancroft Notes). *See* Lancha Plana.

Winters District [Modoc]. In the southwestern part of the county. The district was first prospected in 1890; in 1904 the Lost Cabin Mine was discovered and mining continued for a few years; in the 1930s there was again some prospecting (*Bull.*, 193, p. 177).

Winterton [Calaveras]. This is an old name of Altaville.

Wisconsin Bar [Amador]. On the Cosumnes River, about four miles south of Latrobe, near Rich Bar. Mentioned in El Dorado County History, 1883 (p. 85). Wisconsin Bar Bridge is shown on the County Map, 1866, and Doolittle's, 1868.

Wisconsin Bar [El Dorado]. On the North Fork of Cosumnes River, above Bucks Bar. Shown on Doolittle's map, 1868.

Wisconsin Flat [Nevada]. On Wolf Creek, south of Grass Valley. The famous Wisconsin ledge was located in 1854. A mine was working with variable success in 1867 (Bean, p. 211). The Wisconsin Mine is listed in 1941 and is described in detail in *Mining Bureau*, X (pp. 375 f.).

Wisconsin: Hill, Flat [Placer]. On the Blue Lead, between the North and Middle forks of American River, south of Iowa Hill, on a Tertiary river channel. Recorded on Goddard's map, 1857. The diggings developed in the early 1850s in the wake of the Iowa Hill boom. The newspapers reported rich yields. The Sacramento *Union*, July 30, 1855, reported that one claim netted 600 dollars in one day for three men. Another newspaper of August 2, 1855, cited in the County History, 1882 (p. 227), even reports the yield of 2 thousand dollars in one day, including a lump worth 139 dollars from the Bennet claim.

The population in 1855 was estimated at 1,500 (Bancroft Notes). The *Directory* of Placer County, 1861 (p. 45), states that the output began to dwindle in 1856. The 20-stamp Oriental Cement Mill, built in 1866, did not pay because the cemented gravel yielded only eighty cents per ton (Browne, p. 100). The drift and hydraulic mines are listed in the County History, 1882 (p. 216). The mines after 1900 are listed in *Bulletin*, 92 (p. 135).

Wisconsin House [Yuba]. About four miles southwest of Camptonville, on the road to Bullards Bar. Shown on Doolittle's map, 1868. It is mentioned repeatedly by De Long after 1854. It was situated on Rebel Ridge and was operated by a southern sympathizer, according to Meek's "Reminiscences" (pp. 159 f.) and was considered a rough and dangerous place, especially by residents of Camptonville, a Union town. *See* Rebel Ridge.

Wolf Creek [Nevada]. A tributary to Bear River. Shown on Goddard's map, 1857. In 1854 the claims of one company yielded an average of thirty-six to sixty-five ounces per week, according to a report of the Grass Valley *Telegraph* in the *Alta*, August 1, 1854. The place Wolf Creek is listed in Brown's *Directory*, 1856, twenty-six miles distant from Nevada City. The Creek is shown on Goddard's map, 1857. A post office was established at Wolf in 1888, and the place is listed in the *Register*, 1900. Wolf Creek appears on the USGS Smartsville 1943 quadrangle.

Wolf Creek [Sierra]. A tributary to the Middle Fork of Yuba River. Shown on Goddard's map, 1857. An 8-stamp water-driven mill was built in 1868 (*Annual Mining Review*, 1876, p. 22).

Wolf Gulch [Tuolumne]. The gulch runs into the Stanislaus River west of Gold Springs. The *Mining Press*, November 23, 1861, reports that the miners were waiting for the completion of the Columbia Gulch flume to resume activities.

Wolfs Bar [Butte]. Shown on Trask's map, 1853, on the south side of a branch of Butte Creek.

Wolfskill Ranch [San Diego]. Thirty-five miles northwest of San Diego. Gold bearing quartz was mined on a small scale, 1860–64 (Raymond, VII, p. 44). Apparently the first gold mining in the county was carried on here, before the development of the Julian district in 1870.

Wolverine [Placer]. About two miles northeast of Iowa Hill, near Monona Flat. It is listed as one of the important mining towns in the area between the North Fork of American River and its branch called Shirttail Canyon, which was visited by W. A. Goodyear of the Whitney Survey in 1871 (Whitney, *Auriferous Gravels*, p. 82). Shown on Hoffmann and Craven's Gravel Map, 1873.

Wolverine Bar [El Dorado]. On the South Fork of American River. Miners were making ten to twelve dollars a day to the man, with prospects for better wages in the future (Sacramento *Union*, August 27, 1856). The name was probably given to this and other places by miners from Michigan, the "wolverine" state.

Woodhouse [Calaveras]. About fifteen miles northeast of Mokelumne Hill, between the North and Middle Forks of Mokelumne River. The camp is mentioned in 1850 in Bayard Taylor's chapter on the "Journey to the Volcano" (in *El Dorado*), as under the command of a Virginian named Woodhouse. Doble describes the diggings on June 23, 1852. There were at that time two mills with ten stamps each, run by overshot wheels. It was perhaps the same site recorded as Wood Hill Co. on Trask's map, 1853. The Woodhouse Mine struck pay dirt 200–300 feet under the surface and paid well. The Holmes Mine, south of the place, opened in 1866 with a 10-stamp mill. Its sulfurets contained between 300 and 13 hundred dollars worth of gold per ton. A detailed description is given by Browne (pp. 66 f.). A Woodhouse mine operated intermittently until the 1930s (*Mining Bureau*, XXXII, p. 294).

Woodleaf [Yuba]. *See* Woodville.

Woodpecker: Ravine, Diggings [Nevada]. The ravine is on the south side of Pike Flat, now within the town of Grass Valley. The *Alta*, February 25 and March 18, 1854, reports good production: one company of nine men took out 15 thousand dollars worth of gold in one week, and the average earning was thirty dollars per day to the man, with seventy dollars a high yield. Placers were still yielding in 1867 (Bean, p. 189). A Woodpecker Ravine is shown near Birchville on the Hoffmann and Craven Great Gravel Map appended to Whitney, *Auriferous Gravels*. It is shown here as a tributary to the Middle Fork of Yuba River, which crosses the gravel channel running between French Corral and North San Juan. A Woodpecker Ravine on Deer Creek near Nevada City is mentioned in the Book of Deeds, Nevada County Records.

Woodpeck Hill [Nevada]. Apparently near Grass Valley. According to a *Directory* of Grass Valley of 1865 (Bancroft Notes), there were good diggings here in 1849–50. Morse (p. 224) mined here in the winter of 1850–51.

Woods Bar [Siskiyou]. On Klamath River, near Happy Camp. Work started in the summer of 1851 (*Alta*, February 18, 1852). An idle drift mine is listed in 1896 in *Mining Bureau*, XIII (p. 432), apparently at the same site.

Woods Bridge [Yuba]. North of Camptonville; shown on the County Map, 1879. It is mentioned as a settlement by De Long, March 15, 1855 and as Woods Ranch, August 19, 1855.

Woods: Creek, Crossing, Diggings [Tuolumne]. The tributary to Tuolumne River was one of the important gold streams of the district. The first deposits were discovered in 1848, probably by a prospector named Wood who may have come from Oregon and was killed early by Indians (Bancroft *Register*). He is identified by De Ferrari as Benjamin Wood (Stoddart, *Annals*, p. 56). The general assumption that Reverend James Woods discovered the gold is one of the traditional errors. The name is first recorded on Derby's map, 1849. Price (October 21, 1849) gives a gloomy picture of the place, except for the abundance of wine and champagne. The place is again mentioned on December 30th by Reverend Daniel B. Woods and March 27, 1850 by Audubon. Here the latter met a sick brother of Phineas T. Barnum, anxiously awaiting succor from his great brother. The creek is probably the one described October 19 and 20, 1848, by Lyman on his trading trip from San Jose. The place had a post office 1851–1853. In 1858 there were two mills with sixteen stamps on the creek and a water-driven 4-stamp mill at the crossing (*State Register*, 1859). A report in *Mining Bureau*, II (part 1, p. 150) states that a quartz lump of 150 pounds, of which seventy-five pounds was gold, was found in 1848 by William Gulnac, the partner of Charles M. Weber.

Woods Dry Diggings [Placer]. The dry diggings west of and around Auburn were first called North Fork Dry Diggings, later, Woods Dry Diggings (Co. Hist., 1882, p. 190).

Woodside Mine [El Dorado]. *See* Georgetown.

Woods Ravine [Nevada]. A tributary to Deer Creek, about two miles west of Nevada City. Woods Creek Ravine is shown on

Doolittle's map, 1868. Ferguson (pp. 140 ff.) described the camp as it was in 1850. Two quartz mines at or near the Ravine are listed in *Bean's Directory* (p. 126). Woods Crossing, listed as a settlement in 1867 by Bean (p. 364) was in Rough and Ready township.

Woodville [Yuba]. East of Forbestown, on the Butte county line. On Long and Montgomery's map it is shown as a small settlement on the South Feather Water Company's Ditch. It is also recorded on Wescoatt's map, 1861, and Doolittle's, 1868. The Plumas County Map, 1886, shows Woodville House. There was little mining, and according to the County History, 1879 (p. 92), there was mainly stock raising after 1850. It was a hotel-stage-stop on the Marysville-La Porte Road, southwest of Strawberry Valley. Later the name was changed to Woodleaf, probably when the post office was established in 1898. The *Register*, 1905, lists an 8-stamp mill. It is still shown as Woodville on the USGS Bidwell Bar 1944 quadrangle.

Woodville Bar [Sierra]. On the North Fork of Yuba River, west of Goodyears Bar. It was earlier called Cut-Throat Bar, according to the County History, 1882 (p. 466).

Woodworths Bar [Placer]. On the Middle Fork of American River; near Horseshoe Bar. In 1849 Letts (p. 114) saw three men working on an invention by Mr. Woodworth of New York. It looked like a large coffee mill, and Letts believed that the contraption would be suitable for gold mining. But the bar was apparently a failure.

Woody [Kern]. On Highway 142. It was not a gold town but a trading center for the quartz mines south of the place (*Register*, 1904) with a post office established in 1889. The place was named for Dr. Sparrell Walter Woody, pioneer rancher of the area (R. C. Bailey).

Woolseys Flat [Nevada]. Near the Middle Fork of Yuba River, four miles north of North Bloomfield. Shown on Doolittle's map, 1868. The flat is on the Great Gravel Deposit of the county. It was named for one of the first prospectors in 1851. A ditch from Yuba River brought water in 1855. One company cleaned up 6 thousand dollars in one week (Hittell's Clippings, p. 32). It is mentioned in *Transactions*, 1858 (p. 183), as on the road from North San Juan to Forest City. In 1867 there was still placering and the place was listed as a settlement (*Bean's Directory*). Browne (p. 121) says that the place had some of the deepest diggings in the county. It "gave up the ghost in 1874," according to the Nevada *Directory*, 1895, but Woolseys Cabin is still marked on the USGS Colfax 1938 quadrangle.

Woosterville [Amador]. *See* Ione.

Wyandotte [Butte]. Five miles southeast of Oroville. Recorded on Milleson and Adams' map, 1851, and later maps. The name is also spelled Wyandot. The Wyandott Mining Company was organized in 1849 by William Walker, a Wyandot Indian from Kansas, who was later provisional governor of Nebraska (Bruff, p. 608). A post office was established in 1859. The County Map, 1862, and Doolittle's map, 1868, show it as a sizeable town. Hutchings in 1855 had called it "a dried up town" (Diary, October 31, 1855). In 1867 gold was mined in several ravines and there were half a dozen hydraulic claims (Browne, p. 161). For modern gold dredging, *see Mining Bureau*, XXXII (p. 374).

Wyandotte Bar [Plumas]. Below the junction of the East Branch with North Fork of Feather River. It is mentioned by Dame Shirley (p. 42). J. A. Stuart (pp. 117 f.) mined here in November and December, 1850. The place is mentioned in a letter of John Robinson dated November 4, 1854 (California State Library, California Section).

Wyreka [Siskiyou]. *See* Yreka.

Y ankee. Next to Dutch, Yankee was the most common nickname used for camps and mines in California. All Americans who came from east of the Mississippi and north of the Ohio were called Yanks or Yankees (Haskins, p. 79).

Yankee Bar [Butte]. On the east side of the North Fork of Feather River, north of the Big Bend. Shown on the County Map, 1877.

Yankee Bar [Placer]. On the Middle Fork of American River, between Poverty Bar and Dutch Bar. Shown on Doolittle's map, 1868, on Bowman's map, 1873 (as Yankey Bar), and on the County Map, 1887. It is mentioned by Henry S. Blom in his diary, February 28, 1852, and in the Placer *Herald*, December 1, 1855 (Co. Hist., 1882, p. 190).

Yankee Bar [Placer]. On the North Fork of the American River. The bar is mentioned in a claim of December 25, 1851, recorded in Placer County Records, I (p. 67).

Yankee Bar [Yuba]. On the North Fork of Yuba River, above Willow and New York bars. Gold was mined here in 1852, but the deposits were soon exhausted (Co. Hist., 1879, p. 97).

Yankee Doodle. An unidentified camp, listed in Hittell, *Resources*.

Yankee Flat [Butte]. Near the Yuba County line. It is shown on Long and Montgomery's map, about five miles southeast of Enterprise, between South Honcut Creek and the South Fork of Feather River, on a lateral ditch of the South Feather Water Company. Rich diggings paid up to 100 dollars a day, according to the *Mining Press*, June 14, 1862.

Yankee Flat [El Dorado]. It is mentioned as an early mining locality in Kelsey township in the County History, 1883 (p. 191).

Yankee Hill [Amador]. East of Plymouth. Gold was mined with little success in 1850 (Co. Hist., 1881, p. 232). The camp is mentioned by Doble, January 25, 1853.

Yankee Hill [Butte]. East of the West Branch of the North Fork of Feather River, north of Cherokee. Gold was discovered in the area in 1850 by Chileans and Mexicans, and the first camps were known as Spanishtown and Rich Gulch, both of which are shown on Goddard's map, 1857. Nearby Yankee Hill was first a supply depot for the Frenchtown Canal and Mining Company, and by 1856 it developed into "a village," which at one time had three hotels and a population of 300, according to the County History, 1882 (pp. 253 ff.). In 1857 there were two steam-driven mills with twenty-five stamps in operation (*State Register*, 1859). On October 19, 1858 the post office was transferred from nearby Frenchtown. The County Map, 1862, shows the place as a considerable settlement. The Yankee Hill district, which includes the Concow and Big Bend areas, is described in *Bulletin*, 193 (p. 131). The Surcease lode mine in the Big Bend area operated on a major scale between 1933 and 1942, and its total production was more than one million dollars. Yankee Hill and Yankee Hill P. O. are shown on the USGS Oroville 1944 quadrangle and other modern maps.

Yankee Hill [Tuolumne]. One mile east of Columbia. Shown on Trask's map, 1853. Thomas Hill or Hills, a discharged drummer from Stevenson's regiment, and a party from Mokelumne Hill struck rich diggings here, May 17, 1849 (Stoddart, p. 89). In a letter of 1852, published by the San Joaquin Pioneer Society, 1953, Edmund Booth says: The discoverer's name was Hills, "and, being a Yankee, it sounded so much like the comic actor that the name fell on the place." Benjamin Harris in his reminiscences, *The Gila Trail* (p. 124), claims that he and his party named it in December, 1849, for Tony Hill, a member of the group. The mining population in 1856 was around 400, according to Bancroft, VI (p. 376). The early accounts report rich finds and nuggets. The J. R. Johnson company washed out 500 dollars worth in one day and found a nugget of fifty-five ounces. French miners found a nugget of 250 ounces, and a poor Italian who had been begging for the necessities of life found a lump of twenty-seven pounds one and a half feet under the surface. The Columbia *Gazette*, June 17, 1854, reports that one company took out nine and a half ounces in one day and in one pan washed out eighty-five dollars in fine dust. The average wage was twelve dollars per day to the man. (Hittell Clippings; Co. Hist., 1882, p. 108; Eastman file.) The Shanghai Mine working with arrastres yielded 100 dollars per ton in 1856 (Browne, p. 48). In 1858 there was a mill with four stamps and two arrastres (*State Register*, 1859); in 1862 a water-driven 10-stamp mill (*Annual Mining Review*, 1876 p. 23). Browne (p. 38) mentions rich hydraulic claims of the 1860s. The Columbia *Courier*, May 4, 1867, reports that there were fourteen working claims. In November of 1876 the Remington Gravel Claim cleaned up nearly 13 hundred dollars after a thirteen-day run (Sacramento *Union*, November 15, 1876). By 1899 the total production with adjacent Knickerbocker Flat was 3.5 million dollars (*Mines and Minerals*, p. 358). Shown on the USGS Big Trees 1941 quadrangle. A Yankee Hill Mine is still listed in the Mining Bureau report of 1927.

Yankee: Hill, Ravine [Sierra]. In the Slate Creek Basin, north of La Porte. Recorded on Raymond's map in volume V.

Yankee Jims [Placer]. On the road from Colfax to Forest Hill. Recorded on Trask's 1853 and Goddard's 1857 maps. According to the *Directory of Placer County*, 1861 (pp. 12 f. in Bancroft Notes), Yankee Jim was a Sydneyite named Robinson. He built a corral for stolen horses here and was hanged in 1852. John E. Ross, in his "Narrative" (1878), states that Yankee Jim was a member of Ross' party that discovered the diggings. Jim was a "very bad man" but very able and knew several languages perfectly. The place had a post office in 1852. Knapp (p. 512) calls it a lively town as early as 1852, and Steele (p. 310) tells a story of the camp fully as dramatic as Bret Harte's "Luck of Roaring Camp." The gravels mined are a part of the Tertiary river channel. For years the place was the center of the Forest Hill Divide and a pioneer place for hydraulic mining. According to a report, the method of using water under pressure for washing gravel was actually introduced here as early as the spring of 1852. It was a crude apparatus consisting of a rawhide hose, to which was attached a tin tube fashioned into a nozzle (*Mining Bureau*, II, part 2, p. 149). Credit for the invention of the hydraulic method, however, is generally given to Edward E. Matteson at American Hill in Nevada County. According to another account, in *Guidebook*, (p. 31), Colonel W. M. McClure visited Matteson at American Hill in 1853 and introduced Matteson's method at Yankee Jims that year. After the introduction of this type of mining, the newspapers were filled with reports of rich yields, many of which were exaggerated (*see* Placer County folder in Bancroft Notes). One item in the *Pacific*, September 24, 1855, predicted that the riches will not

be exhausted in thousands of years (Hittell Clippings, p. 63). The hydraulic mines at Yankee Jims and Georgia Hill had produced 5 million dollars prior to 1868 (*Mining Bureau*, XXIII, p. 262). Although tunnel and hydraulic mining had produced millions, the place was depopulated in 1875, according to Raymond, VII (p. 106). Today it is a ghost town, although the post office lasted until 1940. Historic Landmark 398. Shown on the USGS Colfax 1950 quadrangle.

Yankee Jims Dry Diggings [Placer]. In a gulch on the Middle Fork of American River. It is not the same camp as the one above, but it was perhaps named for the same person.

Yankee Slide [El Dorado]. On the Middle Fork of American River, above Volcano Bar. It is shown on Doolittle's map, 1868, and Bowman's, 1873, as Yankee Slide Bar. It is mentioned in the *Alta*, April 25, 1852 (Bancroft Scraps: LI:1, p. 252). According to the reminiscences of Carlisle Abbott (pp. 98 ff.), gold was discovered on the slide by five New Englanders. He tells several interesting stories about the place.

Yaqui Camp [Calaveras]. Southeast of San Andreas, on Willow Creek, tributary to the South Fork of Calaveras River. It is

Yankee Jims, Placer Co.

possible that the name was given to the camp because Yaqui Indians of New Mexico mined here. Ridge (p. 110) mentions the name, spelled Yackee, in connection with the ever-present Murieta; and the informant of Dumas' *Gil Blas* (p. 83) claims this as the locale of the "French Revolution." *See* Nasatir (*in* CHSQ, XXXV, p. 316); also Gerstaecker, "The French Revolution." Wade H. Johnston first mined here in the spring of 1854. In 1855 (?) the camp was the seat of the Bartlett-Bacon Canal Company (Hittell Clippings, p. 48). One company drifted dirt that paid ten dollars per day to the man in 1859, continuing similar success since 1855, according to a report in the San Andreas *Independent*, October 10, 1850 (quoted in *Las Calaveras*, July 1971). A Yaqui Camp mining claim still existed in 1936 (*Mining Bureau*, XXXII, pp. 258, 296).

Yates Beach [Del Norte]. One mile south of Crescent City. Small scale washing of the ocean sand was carried on in the early 1890s, and an attempt on a larger scale in 1913–1914 failed (*Mining Bureau*, XLVIII, p. 279).

Yatestown [Butte]. On the Feather River, opposite Fredonia. It was apparently named for James Yates, an English sailor who came from Mexico in 1842 and was one of Sutter's men. It is mentioned in November, 1849, in Delano's *Life* (pp. 275, 292) and again in his correspondence. It is also mentioned in the County History, 1877 (p. 9), and is listed in Bancroft, VI (p. 487), among the ephemeral towns which were established to gain the miners' trade.

Yellow Aster Mine [Kern]. Near Randsburg. The lode deposits were discovered shortly after the placer mines had opened in the Rand District in 1893. It operated from 1895 to 1918 and from 1921 to 1941, and probably yielded more than 12 million dollars (*Mining Bureau*, XLV, p. 237). For the extensive literature on its development, *see Bulletin*, 95 (pp. 121 ff.); *Desert Magazine*, November, 1964; and the *Consolidated Index*. According to R. C. Bailey, the name is derived from the title of a popular paperback novel of the period.

Yellow Jacket Gulch [Trinity]. On Weaver Creek. The camp is mentioned by Cox (p. 102) in 1858.

Yeomet [Amador]. At the junction of the forks of Cosumnes River, formerly in El Dorado County. According to *Hutchings' Magazine*, (II, p. 208), the name is derived from the waterfalls which are a half mile downstream called *yomet*, 'sounding rock', by the Indians. The place was also known as Forks of the Cosumnes and as Saratoga. The camp developed in 1849 or 1850 and prospered for a number of years (Knight's Scrapbooks, I, p. 91; El Dorado County History, 1883, p. 198). From 1854 to 1861 it had a post office with the name spelled Yornet. A number of mines and mills are shown in the vicinity on the Amador County Map of 1866. *See* Huse Bridge.

Yocumville [Siskiyou]. On the South Fork of Salmon River, opposite the mouth of Methodist Creek. It is mentioned as a vanished mining camp in the *Siskiyou Pioneer* (I:1, p. 4; II:6, p. 45). From 1869 to 1891 it had a post office.

Yokohl Valley [Tulare]. In the Blue Ridge country. The name is derived from a Yokuts tribe or village. An item from the Visalia *Delta*, August 22, 1872, in Hayes Scrapbooks: Mining, (V, sec. 5) reports rich gold bearing quartz leads in the vicinity, from which gold was panned. Ditches, traceable for two or three miles, gave evidence of ancient mining, but only little prospecting had been done recently. A Yokohl Copper Mine on Yokol Creek is listed in 1894, and the tungsten deposits of Yokohl Valley are listed in the Mining Bureau reports until recent years.

Yonpenhaff Gulch. An unidentified name, listed by Guinn (p. 43).

Yorktown [Tuolumne]. About a half mile from Povery Hill, near Jamestown. Shown on Trask's map, 1853. The camp may have been named for a Mr. York who, according to Lyman August 23, 1848, went south from Weber Creek. According to the somewhat unreliable reminiscences of Benjamin Harris, a Mexican miner found a 19-pound lump of gold mixed with quartz in the fall of 1849, and within a short time 7,000 people were reportedly on the spot [!] (*The Gila Trail*, p. 119). The camp is mentioned by Daniel B. Woods (p. 175), who recorded in 1849–50 that the York Bar company worked for many months without profit. Audubon, too, mentioned the camp, March 25, 1850, but the diggings seemed to have petered out soon afterwards. The U.S. Bureau of the Census lists 378 inhabitants in April, 1851, for the 1850 census.

Yorkville [Placer]. One and a half miles north of Yankee Jims. It was discovered in 1853, and for a number of years there was tunneling and hydraulicking. It is mentioned in the *Directory of Placer County*, 1861 (p. 54). The steamer edition of the

Alta, March 20, 1857, reported that the Washington Company made forty ounces in three days.

Yornet [Amador]. *See* Yeomet.

You Bet [Nevada]. Three miles west of Dutch Flat. Shown on Doolittle's map, 1868. The generally accepted, though not authenticated story of the origin of the name, is that 'you bet' was the favorite saying of the saloon keeper. Mining was carried on as early as 1849, but the camp did not develop until hydraulic mining was introduced. In 1867 it had a sizeable population, and a post office was established in 1868. The red gravel assayed up to 984° fineness. By 1871 most of the hydraulic claims had passed into the hands of British capital (Raymond, IV, p. 117). For twentieth century development of the district, *see Bulletin*, 92 (p. 133) and the *Consolidated Index*. The diggings of the district produced 3 million dollars worth of gold by 1918 (*Mining Bureau*, XVI, Nevada, p. 64). Although You Bet is a ghost town, it is still found on the USGS Colfax 1938 quadrangle and on many other modern maps. *See* Chalk Bluffs; Red Dog.

Young America Mine [Nevada]. *See* Washington Ridge.

Young America Mine [Sierra]. A lode mine about seven miles north of Sierra City, at an elevation of 7,200 feet. A description is given in *Mining Bureau*, X (pp. 643 ff.) and XXV (pp. 577 f.). It was located in 1883, and according to *Bulletin*, 193 (p. 117), it had a total production of 1.5 million dollars. Shown on the USGS Downieville 1907 quadrangle.

Yreka, Siskiyou Co.

Young American Flat [Sierra]. A quarter mile southwest of Forest. It was named after the chief mine in 1852. Listed in Hittell's roster. The mine was a combination drift and lode mine and operated intermittently until recent times. In the later years it was called Mugwump. (*Mining Bureau*, LII, p. 255.) *See* Mugwump.

Youngs Dry Diggings [El Dorado]. About three miles northeast of Greenwood. Shown on Bowman's map, 1873. Stephen Wing mentioned the camp on January 25, 1855 (Journal, II, p. 25). The diggings, described as shallow, surface excavations, are said to have paid well whenever water was available, according to W. A. Goodyear in Whitney, *Auriferous Gravels* (p. 115). The same source states that one little seam of quartz was struck here from which 25 to 30 thousand dollars were reportedly taken out within a short time.

Youngs Hill [Yuba]. On Beaver Creek; three miles north of Camptonville. Shown as a settlement on Wescoatt's map, 1861. It was named for William Young, the first claimant about 1851, or possibly for Nicodemus Young (note to De Long, February 17, 1857). McKeeby (p. 149) mentions it as a big camp in 1852. In 1855 De Long became part owner of a store. At that time the place had three hotels, three stores, four saloons, two dry goods stores, two butcher shops, two blacksmith shops, and a theater (!). (Co. Hist., 1879, p. 100.) Although it received water from the Sierra Mountain Water Company in 1858 (Hittell Clippings, p. 44), it does not seem to have survived long after that. It is still shown, however, on the County Map, 1879, and on the USGS Smartsville 1943 quadrangle.

Yount Lode [Los Angeles]. *See* Santa Catalina Island.

Yreka [Siskiyou]. The camp developed in May, 1851, after rich diggings were discovered in and around the site. It was first called Thompsons Dry Diggings, then Shasta Butte City. Gibbs, October 26, 1851, gives a good account of Shasté (!) Butte City (Schoolcraft, III, pp. 164 ff.). At that time it had already 1,000 inhabitants and 300 houses and huts. In a letter datelined Shasta Butte City, December 27, 1851, (printed in *CHSQ*, XXVI, p. 298), Hiram G. Ferris called it a town with thirty or more stores. On March 22, 1852 the name was changed to Wyreka and is so shown on Gibbes' 1852 and other maps for some time. *See California Place Names* for the development of the name. The post office was established August 19, 1853,

and the town remained the center of a
large district of hydraulic mining and
dredging. In 1898 it still had four mills
with about twenty-five stamps and two
arrastres (*Register*, 1898).

Yuba Buttes [Sierra]. *See* Sierra Buttes.

Yuba County House [Yuba]. On the road
from Fosters Bar to Marysville, northeast
of Prairie Diggings. Shown on Doolittle's
map, 1868. It is mentioned by Meek as a
stage stop "long since forgotten" (p. 157).

Yuba Mine [Nevada]. *See* Graniteville.

Yubaville [Nevada]. On the Middle Fork of
Yuba River, seven miles below Moores
Flat (*Mining Press*, June, 1867, p. 390).

Yubaville [Sierra]. About six and a half
miles southeast of Downieville, in a quartz
mining district north of the Middle Fork of
Yuba River. Shown on Doolittle's map,
1868.

Yumana [Sierra]. On Oregon Creek, near
Downieville. The camp is mentioned by

Trask in 1854, (Document 9, p. 62). *See*
Forest City [Sierra].

Zantgraf Mine [El Dorado]. *See* Pilot
Hill.

Zeibright Mine [Placer]. *See* Emigrant Gap.

Zeila Mine [Amador]. On Highway 49,
south of Jackson. The mine, opened in the
1860s, had a 1,700-foot shaft and one drift
was 3,000 feet long. It operated intermittently until 1914 and produced more than
5 million dollars. (*Guidebook*, p. 62.) The
name is sometimes spelled Zeile.

Zumwalt Flat [Sierra]. At the northeast end
of Downieville. Downie and his negros
worked here in November, 1849, and
washed out twelve ounces the first day.
The name was applied later, apparently
for Joseph Zumwalt who arrived in 1850.
It is shown on Trask's map, 1853, as Zu-
mont's F[lat].

Glossary & Bibliography

A COMBINED bibliography and glossary was considered more practical and useful to the reader than separate lists of books, manuscripts, maps, contributors, and technical expressions.

The bibliographical material in this section contains items that are repeatedly cited in the text. ("Text" refers to the place name entries.) Each source is listed in the Glossary and Bibliography with a key word (or some other convenient abbreviation), and this key word is used in the text as the reference. The page number is not given in references to books that have an alphabetical arrangement or a comprehensive index, or when the passage, as in diaries, can easily be identified by the date cited. For the maps, the key word is usually the name of the man who made the map and (or) was responsible for the names on it. Frequently, however, only the publisher of the map was known.

Many manuscripts, maps, and books exist in different versions or editions. An attempt has been made to indicate the version used in the text, but since the work on this dictionary extended over a number of years, there may be some discrepancies.

When the name of a person given in parentheses in the text indicates an informant, it does not mean that he is responsible for the wording of the entry, unless quotation marks are used.

Abajian. James de T. Abajian of San Francisco, librarian and historian, contributed information on mining localities for use in this dictionary.

Abbott. Carlisle S. Abbott, *Recollections of a California Pioneer* (New York: Neale, 1917). The author mined on the Middle Fork of American River, 1850–1851.

Abrams. William P. Abrams, "Diary" (1849–1851). 1 vol. MS in Bancroft Library.

A few entries in the diary are concerned with mining on the Stanislaus River in 1849.

Adams, Covered Bridges. Kramer Adams, *Covered Bridges of the West, A History and Illustrated Guide: Washington, Oregon, California* (Berkeley, Calif.: Howell-North, 1963).

Adams. Edgar H. Adams, *Private Gold Coinage of California, 1849–55; its History and its*

Issues (Brooklyn, New York: The Author, 1913).

Adit. An almost horizontal narrow passage leading from the surface into a mine.

The Agua Fria Gold Mining Company. *The Agua Fria Gold Mining Company, for the Working of the Agua Fria Mine, on the Agua Fria River, Mariposa County, California, U. S. A.* [London, 1851]. A prospectus.

Ainslie. Edward Maitland, *The Pilgrim and the Shrine*, by Herbert Ainslie [pseud.], (London, 1868). The account of a journey to Australia via the California gold mines is essentially a vehicle for the author's views on religion and morality. The California mining locale is Downieville and undefined places northerly in 1851.

Alexander. J. M. Alexander, "Letters to his Wife" (1851–1852). MS in Bancroft Library. 12 p. Several of the letters refer to mining in Tuolumne County.

Allsop. Thomas Allsop, *California and its Gold Mines* (London, 1853). An account of the Mariposa district in 1851–52 by an educated and observant Englishman, written in letters to a London periodical. He himself was interested in mining and was commissioned by English capitalists to report on the chances for mining in California.

Alluvial. Pertaining to material carried or laid down by running water.

Alta. *Alta California*, San Francisco. Jan. 4, 1849–June 2, 1891. Weekly, tri-weekly, daily newspaper. Follows *California Star* and *Californian*. For early history, *see* Kemble.

Amador. José M. Amador, "Memorias sobre la Historia de California." (1877). 229 p. MS in Bancroft Library. The author was a native of San Francisco, grantee of Rancho San Ramon, and later major-domo of Mission Jose. He went to the mines in 1848 and with several Indians established a mining camp near the present site of Amador City. In 1854 the county was named for him.

Amador County History. 1881: Jessie D. Mason, *History of Amador County, California* (Oakland: Thompson and West, 1881). Informative and more reliable than most county histories.

Amador County Map, 1866. J. M. Griffith, *Official Map of Amador County, California* (San Francisco: Britton & Rey, 1866).

Amador Quartz Mining District Map. (n.p.,n.d.). Copy in Bancroft Library.

Amalgamation. The process by which gold is extracted from pulverized ore with the aid of quicksilver.

American River and Natoma Water and Mining Company. [Map of the Company's Property] *ca.* 1859–1861. A copy of the map is in the California State Department of Parks and Recreation, Interpretative Services, Sacramento.

Amy's Marysville Directory. G. and O. *Amy's Marysville Directory* (San Francisco, 1856–1858). The 1858 edition contains a list of mining bars, placer and hill diggings.

Ancient Rivers. No longer existing streams of the Tertiary geologic age.

Andrews. John R. Andrews, *The Ghost Towns of Amador* (New York: Carlton Press, 1967). An informal account of ghost towns in Amador County.

Annals. *See* Cox.

Annual Mining Review. *Annual Mining Review and Stock Ledger*, San Francisco. Bancroft Library has only the 1876 issue. It contains a descriptive list of stamp mills and mining companies. There is also a long poem (pp. 18 f.) in which the names of many gold camps appear. It is essentially the same as the poem in the *Pacific Coast Annual Mining Review*, 1878.

Ansted. David Thomas Ansted, *The Goldseekers Manual* (New York: D. Appleton, 1849).

Anthony. E. M. Anthony, "Reminiscences of the Early Days of Siskiyou" (1869). 35 p. MS in Bancroft Library. A lecture delivered before the Siskiyou County Teachers Institute.

Armstrong. William Armstrong, "'49 Experiences" (1877). 14 p. MS in Bancroft Library. Dictation for H. H. Bancroft. The author was county recorder of Butte County. The account gives a description of his overland journey, Yuba City, and gold mining activities.

Arrastre. The term is derived from the Mexican *arrastrar*, 'to drag along the ground.' It is applied in California to the gold milling apparatus that was used to draw heavy weights over the ore in a circular pit by means of horse, mule, water, or man power. The arrastre was the simplest grinding apparatus used by the early miners. A good illustration may be found in *Hutchings' California Magazine*, October, 1857, p. 151.

Audubon. John Woodhouse Audubon, *Audubon's Western Journal* (Cleveland: A. H. Clark, 1906). The son of the famous ornithologist describes the arduous overland trip through northern Mexico and Texas to California, where he remained between September, 1849 to May, 1850. He was unsuccessful in mining, but he left delightful descriptions of his trips from Stockton to the Southern Mines and from Sutters Fort to Georgetown. Includes a set of beautiful drawings, republished by the Book Club of California in 1957.

Avery. Benjamin Parke Avery, *California Pictures in Prose and Verse* (New York, 1878). A delightful book but not actual source material.

Ayers. James J. Ayers, *Gold and Sunshine, Reminiscences of Early California* (Boston: R. G. Badger, 1922). Ayers was in the Calaveras mines, 1849–1850. Amost fifty years later he told his story in chapters IV–IX of his book.

Bachman. Jacob Henry Bachman, "The Diary of a 'Used-up' Miner," ed., Jeanne Van Nostrand. In *CHSQ*, XXII, pp. 67–83. Bachman, a descendant of a German Lutheran pioneer family of New York, was a relative of John Woodhouse Audubon and member of his California Company, who came overland to California in 1849. Outside of Audubon's account, Bachman's sketchy and intermittent diary is the only known extant one of the group. He mined with varying success in Calaveras County, mainly around Fourth Crossing.

Bailey. Richard C. Bailey, *Kern County Place Names* (Bakersfield: Kern County Historical Society, 1967). A list of place names with brief historical sketches. Mr. Bailey also contributed information directly for use in this dictionary.

Baird. *See* Illustrated Letter Sheets.

Baker. George H. Baker, *Map of the Mining Region of California* (Sacramento: Barber and Baker, 1855). Wheat, 273. Reissued in 1856 with little change. Wheat, 289. After having been in the diggings, George Baker published the newspaper *Granite Journal*, Folsom, and *Spirit of the Age*, Sacramento. He also became known for his maps and lithographs. The above mentioned map, published as a letter sheet, records many mining camps throughout the mining region of California. **Diary.** "Records of a California Residence," in *Society of California Pioneers Quarterly*, VIII, pp. 39 ff. The diary covers the period May 28, 1849 to August 11, 1850. It gives an interesting account of mining localities on the Feather River.

Ballenstedt. C. W. T. Ballenstedt, *Beschreibung meiner Reise nach den Goldminen Californiens* (Schöningen, 1851). A report

of a disillusioned gold seeker who mined along the Mokelumne River in the fall and winter of 1849–1850. The author does not refer to the camps by specific names.

Bancroft. When the name of the historian appears with a roman numeral, the reference is to *History of California*, by Hubert Howe Bancroft, 7 vols. [Vols. XVIII–XXIV of his *Works*], San Francisco, 1884–1890. Chapter 14 of vol. VI contains an extensive list of mining camps arranged in the somewhat confusing form of long footnotes in which many references are given, often adding to the confusion. Many of the statements used by Bancroft were made by participants in the gold rush, years later, however. **Bancroft's Register** refers to "Pioneer Register and Index," consisting of brief biographical entries, arranged alphabetically at the end of volumes II to V of his *History of California*. The pioneers are those who came to California before 1849. **Bancroft Notes** refers to "Bancroft's Reference Notes on Mines and Mining," consisting of three uncatalogued files in Bancroft Library. The first and most extensive file consists of notes, clippings, and references compiled by Bancroft's assistants. It is arranged in folders by counties. The second file of the "Reference Notes" consists of a list of references to mining items in selected California newspapers, 1850–1880. It is bound in spring back binders. The third file consists of notes and clippings pertaining to the discovery of gold in California before Marshall's discovery at Sutter's Mill. It is bound in a spring back binder. **Bancroft Scraps.** 105 vols. in 124. Scrapbooks of mounted newspaper clippings collected by Bancroft's assistants. Vols. I–V are arranged by California counties; vol. LI is devoted exclusively to California mining and is bound in 4 volumes cited as LI:1; LI:2; LI:3 and LI:4. "Bancroft Scraps" are not to be confused with "Bancroft Scrapbooks," now catalogued as "Knight's Scrapbooks." *See* "Knight's Scrapbooks." Both sets are in the Bancroft Library. **Bancroft's Map, 1868.** Hubert Howe Bancroft and Company, *Bancroft's Map of California and Nevada* (San Francisco: H. H. Bancroft, 1868). **Bancroft's Maps of the Mines, 1849–50.** In two parts: Northern Mines and Southern Mines, published in his *History of California*, VI, pp. 368 ff. **Bancroft's Map of the Colorado Mines.** (San Francisco: H. H. Bancroft, 1863).

Banks. John E. Banks. See **Buckeye Rovers.**

Bar. A ridge of sand or gravel across a

stream or a projection into the stream. In the California gold country the term was really used for any accumulation of sand, gravel, or rocks along running water or along a lake where gold was found.

Bari. Valeska Bari, *comp.*, *The Course of Empire; First Hand Accounts of California in the Days of the Gold Rush of '49* (New York: Coward-McCann, 1931). Includes "James Marshall, The Discoverer of Gold in California." Reprinted from Charles B. Gillespie in *Century*, February 1891.

Barnes. George A. Barnes, "Oregon and California in 1849" (1878). 30 p. MS in Bancroft Library. An interview by H. H. Bancroft. Barnes came to the California mines in 1849. Barnes Bar on the North Fork of American River was named for him.

Barstow. David P. Barstow, "Statement of Recollections of . . ., 1849–51, in California" (1878). 14 p. MS in Bancroft Library. A dictation recorded for H. H. Bancroft, in which he tells of his mining experiences at Sutters Mill, Coloma, and Downieville.

Batea. The Mexican term for a large wooden bowl in which gold-bearing earth or crushed ore was washed, as in a pan.

Bates. Mrs. D. B. Bates, *Incidents on Land and Water; or, Four Years on the Pacific Coast* (Boston, 1857). 3rd ed. Mrs. Bates and her husband kept a hotel in Marysville, 1851–1854. Next to Dame Shirley's *Letters*, hers is doubtless the best account of Gold Rush days written by a woman.

Bauer. John A. Bauer, "Statement of a Pioneer of 1849." (1877). 15 p. MS in Bancroft Library. Bauer was the first German druggist in California. He came here on a ship with Friedrich Gerstaecker and was a surveyor for Sutter.

Bayley. Thomas S. Bayley, "Recollections of California during the Gold Rush" (ca. 1900). 7 folders. MS in Bancroft Library. Contains the story of the sale of Sutters Fort (the big house) and Sutters Mill in 1849. It is a sketchy but very interesting account, though probably not entirely dependable, written by Bayley and his son fifty years later.

Bean. Edwin F. Bean, comp., *Bean's History and Directory of Nevada County* (Nevada [City], 1867). One of the best sources, especially for the later years, for gold mining localities in the county. The compiler is occasionally careless in giving directions, confusing east and west. Citations are to *Bean's History* or *Bean's Directory*.

Beauvais. A. B. Beauvais, Map of Columbia, 1871. *See* Dart.

Beckwith. Seth L. Beckwith, "Letter." San Francisco, April 2, 1885. 3 p. MS in Bancroft Library. Contains a brief autobiographical sketch with references to his mining at Drytown, Amador County and Angels, Calaveras County between October, 1848 and May, 1849.

Bedrock. The solid rock under soil, gravel, sand, or other surface formation.

Bekeart. Philip B. Bekeart, "James W. Marshall, Discoverer of Gold," in *Society of California Pioneers Quarterly*, I, pp. 7 ff. A good, though not entirely reliable, account of the discovery of gold, including previous reported, or real, discoveries.

Belden. L. Burr Belden, "History in the Making." Articles in the San Bernardino *Sun-Telegram*, 1950–65. When the name is given with the date, the latter refers to the date of the issue of the *Sun-Telegraph*. *Mines of Death Valley* (Glendale, Calif., 1966). This is one on the series on California mines published by La Siesta Press.

Bell. Horace Bell, *Reminiscences of a Ranger; or, Early Times in Southern California* (Santa Barbara: W. Hebberd, 1927).

Berriman. Clyde R. Berriman is a local historian of Amador County and an active member of the Conference of California Historical Societies.

Biddle. *See* Weber-Biddle.

Bidwell. John Bidwell, *Echoes of the Past* (Chico, Calif., 19—?). First edition, published shortly after his death. Republished by Lakeside Press, Chicago, 1928. John Bidwell (1819–1900), native of New York, came to California in 1841 and was Sutter's most faithful servant before the Gold Rush. In 1849 he acquired Arroyo Chico ranch and became the leader in the development of Butte County. In later years he was a congressman, general of the California militia, and in 1892 presidential candidate on the Prohibition ticket. In 1877 Bidwell wrote his reminiscences entitled, "California, 1841–48: An Emigrant's Recollections." MS in Bancroft Library. There is also a collection of Bidwell's correspondence and papers in the California State Library, California section.

Bigler. Henry W. Bigler, "Diary of a Mormon in California" (1872). 115 p. MS in Bancroft Library. Reminiscences and notes from his diary, 1846–48, sent to H. H. Bancroft. Important for his statements on the discovery of gold at Sutter's Mill. *See* Gudde, *Bigler's Chronicle of the West* for an account of the various versions of the journal in Bancroft Library; Huntington Library; Office of the Church

Historian of the Church of Latter Day Saints, Salt Lake City; Utah State Historical Society; and in private possession.

Billeb. William W. Billeb, *Mining Camp Days* (Berkeley, Calif.: Howell-North, 1968). The author, a resident of Bodie, California, 1908–1920, recounts from memory the story of Bodie and other mining camps in eastern California and Nevada. The book contains many interesting photographs of towns and camps.

Blake's Map, 1854. Charles T. Blake, Manuscript map of the region around Michigan City, Middle Fork of American River, included in a letter to his parents dated April 27, 1854. Wheat, 253. Photostat in Bancroft Library. Original in Anson Blake Collection in California Historical Society Library.

Bledsoe. *See* Del Norte County History.

Blom. *See* Bloom.

Bloom. Henry S. Bloom, "Tales of the Pioneers of the Kankakee," ed., Burton E. Burroughs (1931). 129 p. Typescript in Bancroft Library. The author describes his overland journey to California in 1850 and experiences in the northern mines, including Georgetown, Greenwood, Downieville.

Blue Lead. The auriferous gravel and cement in ancient river channels, which is often colored dark blue. There are several "Blue Leads" in different regions. The best known are probably those on the ancient river beds in Sierra, Nevada, and Placer counties.

Boggs. Mae Hélène Bacon Boggs, *My Playhouse was a Concord Coach . . .* (Oakland: The Author, 1942). An "anthology of newspaper clippings and documents" from 1839 to 1888; it contains excellent reproductions of a number of valuable maps and several lists of post offices of the 1850s.

Bonanza. The original Spanish term is now a common American term denoting a rich and profitable yield, not confined to gold mining.

Booth. Joseph W. Booth, "Diary" (1852–1853). 147 p. MS in Bancroft Library. The author was in the Northern Mines, particularly on the Middle Fork of Feather River. It is an excellent account.

Borthwick. J. D. Borthwick, *Three Years in California* (Edinburgh, 1857). Repeatedly reprinted under various titles. Borthwick was in the Northern and Southern Mines, 1851–1855, engaged in mining and sketching. He was an educated Englishman, observant and objective. He gives a good portrayal of the Americans, contrasting them with the foreign miners, especially the French. One of the best, if not the best book of the period. Excellent illustrations.

Bourne. Ezra Bourne, "Journal" (1850–1853). 52 p. MS in Bancroft Library. His diary covers mainly his overland journey followed by his mining experiences in the Placerville area.

Bowen. Ben Bowen, "Diary and Notebook" (1854–1859). 130 p. MS in Bancroft Library. The nineteen- or twenty-year-old Ben Bowen wrote a detailed, realistic, and objective chronicle of Fort John and central Amador County from September 1854 to February 1856. It is one of the best diaries.

Bowman. Amos Bowman, a member of the Geological Survey of California under the direciton of Josiah D. Whitney, explored the gravel region north of the North Fork of American River to the Middle Fork of Yuba River in the spring of 1870 and was joined in July by Professor W. H. Pettee, with whom he continued a study of the geology and the mapping of the topography during that year. Their surveys formed the basis of the map cited as **Pettee and Bowman's Map, 1879,** with corrections and revisions by Pettee. *See* Pettee. Their 1870 field work also contributed to the compilation of the map of the gravel area between the Middle Fork of American River and the Middle Yuba, cited as Hoffmann and Craven Map, 1873. *See* Hoffmann; Goodyear; Pettee. Both maps were published to accompany Whitney's *The Auriferous Gravels of the Sierra Nevada,* 1879–1880, in which detailed reports of the field work may be found. Another map cited as **Bowman's Map, 1873,** refers to his *Map of the Georgetown Divide, El Dorado County, Showing also Portions of the Placerville and Forest Hill Divide* (San Francisco: J. Jennings, 1873). *See* Whitney Survey.

Boyd. William H. Boyd, *Land of Havilah, 1854–1874* (Bakersfield: Kern County Historical Society, 1952). Contains a well-written account of the Kern River rush in the 1860s.

Bradley's Map. William W. Bradley, *Map Showing the Properties of the Grass Valley Mining District, Nevada County, California.* (Sacramento: Division of Mines, 1930). Accompanies C. A. Logan's report "Sacramento Division. Nevada County," *in* Division of Mines, *Report*, XXVI, pp. 90 ff.

Brannan. Samuel Brannan was in charge of Mormon colonization in California. In 1846 he brought a group of Mormons from

New York to settle in the state. After the discovery of gold at Sutters Mill, which he publicized far and wide, he became the most spectular financier and speculator in central California. Reva Scott has written about his experience in California in the book entitled *Samuel Brannan and the Golden Fleece* (New York: Macmillan, 1944).

Brewer. William H. Brewer, *Up and Down California in 1860–1864* (Berkeley: University of California Press, 1966). The book has appeared in three editions. It consists of letters written while the author traveled throughout California as an assistant to Josiah D. Whitney in the California State Geological Survey. *See* Whitney Survey.

Brewer Notes. Brewer's field notes, 1861–1864. Sixteen MS notebooks in Bancroft Library, as well as diaries and correspondence.

Breyfogle. Joshua D. Breyfogle, *Diary of J. D. Breyfogle, Sr., Covering his Experiences during his Overland Trip to California during the Gold Rush in 1849.* (n.p., n.d.). Contains a good account of mining on the Yuba River. The original MS of the diary is in Baker Library, Dartmouth College; a microfilm copy is in Bancroft Library.

Brierly. A. A. Brierly, former Inyo County Surveyor, is considered the dean of Inyo County historians. He furnished the author of this dictionary information about places where gold was found and mined in Inyo County.

Bristow. E. L. Bristow, "Rencounters with Indians, Highwaymen, and Outlaws" (1878). 16 p. MS in Bancroft Library. An interview made for H. H. Bancroft, which includes experiences in the Northern Mines in 1853.

Brockman. Christian F. Brockman, *A Guide to the Mother Lode Country* (Mariposa: Mariposa County Historical Society, 1948). A pamphlet giving brief descriptions of camps and towns.

Brown, *Directory. See* Brown and Dallison.

Brown. Mrs. Henry J. Brown is a descendant of Nathan Aldrich, who had a dry claim at Henrys Diggings in El Dorado County. This information was supplied by Jane Schlappi of Placerville.

Brown, History. *See* San Bernardino County History, 1922.

Brown. James S. Brown, "The Gold Discovery at Sutter's Mill" (1886). 5 p. MS in Bancroft Library. His account of the gold discovery, recorded for H. H. Bancroft. "James S. Brown's Account" refers to the journey of a group of Mormons from Salt Lake City to southern California in 1849 under the leadership of Jefferson Hunt.

Brown. John Brown, ed., *History of San Bernardino and Riverside Counties* (Madison, Wisc.: Western Historical Association, 1922). 3 vols.

Brown and Dallison. *Brown and Dallison's Nevada [City], Grass Valley, and Rough and Ready Directory, 1856, with an Historical Sketch of Nevada County by A. A. Sargent* (San Francisco, 1856). Contains the best, almost contemporary account of the three towns and the county, written by A. A. Sargent.

Browne. John Ross Browne, *Resources of the Pacific Slope* (New York: D. Appleton, 1869). J. Ross Browne was one of the most important publicists after 1848, and his *Resources* is an excellent source for the mining situation in 1867 and also for some previous history. The information was collected between May and July, 1867, and his report was submitted by the Treasury Department to the Speaker of the House in 1868 (and printed in 1869). The arrangement is sometimes misleading; the coverage is uneven for certain districts, and there is much repetition.

Browning. George W. Browning, "Letter to his Father." 4 p. MS in private possession; photostat in Bancroft Library. The letter is datelined Sacramento Valley, May 24, 1851, and includes a brief account of the diggings near Sutters Mill.

Bruff. Joseph Goldsborough Bruff, *Gold Rush; the Journals, Drawings, and Other Papers of J. Goldsborough Bruff*, ed., Georgia Willis Read and Ruth Gaines (New York: Columbia University Press, 1944). 2 vols. Another edition in one volume, 1949. Bruff was the captain of the Washington City and California Mining Association. His journal covers the period from April 2, 1849 to July 20, 1851, which includes the overland journey and experiences in the mines. Bruff and company arrived at Lassen's camp in August, 1850, and remained in the Feather River area until October, 1850. The rest of the journal is about his return east to the city of Washington. His journal is one of the best.

Buck. Franklin A. Buck, *A Yankee in the Gold Rush* (Boston: Houghton Mifflin, 1930). An excellent account of Weaverville between 1852 and 1866, written in the form of letters.

Buckbee. Mrs. Edna Bryan Buckbee, *Pioneer Days of Angels Camp* (Angels Camp: Calaveras Californian, 1932). *The Saga of Old Tuolumne* (New York: Press of the

Pioneers, 1935). Both books are written in the popular vein, with no references to sources of information given.

Buckeye Rovers. Howard L. Scamehorn, ed., *The Buckeye Rovers in the Gold Rush; an Edition of Two Diaries* (Athens, Ohio: University Press, 1963). The Buckeye Rovers were a party of Ohioans who broke up into smaller parties, most of whom mined successfully from 1849 to 1852 between the Middle and South forks of American River. It is an excellent account, in the form of the diaries of John E. Banks and J. Elza Armstrong.

Buffum. *Edward Gould Buffum, Six Months in the Gold Mines*, ed., John W. Caughey (Los Angeles: Ward Ritchie Press, 1959). Buffum was an officer of the New York Volunteers and had a chance to be in the Gold Rush from the beginning. He gives excellent accounts as a successful digger on the forks of American River. He was the chronicler of Weber Creek and was eye witness to the hangings that gave Dry Diggings (Placerville) the nickname Hangtown. The first edition was published in London, 1850. The 1959 edition is well edited by Professor Caughey.

Bulletin. (*Bull.*) California, Division of Mines, *Bulletin*, 1- (1880–).

Bulletin, (*Bull.*,) 193. California, Division of Mines, *Gold Districts of California*, by William B. Clark (Sacramento, 1970). An excellent guide to the gold districts of California, based on the author's research and on previous bulletins and reports of the California Dvision of Mines and Geology and its predecessor, the State Mining Bureau. The book gives the location, brief history, and description of the geology of each district.

Bullion. Uncoined precious metal, especially gold.

Bunje. Emil T. H. Bunje and James C. Kean, "Pre-Marshall Gold in California," Works Progress Administration Project. Typewritten. 2 vols. (Berkeley, 1938). An extensive survey of the literature on the subject.

Burnett. Peter H. Burnett, *Recollections and Opinions of an Old Pioneer* (New York: Appleton, 1880). Burnett, 1807–1895, was the first constitutional governor of California under American rule. He came to California in the fall of 1848 with the first party of gold seekers from Oregon and mined on the Yuba River between November 5 and December 19. Another edition was published in Oakland by Biobooks, in 1946.

Burns. Burns Ranche Gold Mining Company, *Quartz Mining* (New York, 1851).

An account of the company's activities in Mariposa County, with charter and related papers.

Butler's Map, 1851. B. F. Butler, *Map of the State of California. Compiled from the Most Recent Surveys and Explorations . . . Also a Complete Delineation of the Gold Region, Post Office Routes, etc.* (San Francisco: Butler, 1851). Wheat, 185. An important map, with only a few errors. A portion of the map from a little south of Monterey to the northern border of the state was published separately the same year as *Map of the Gold Region, California, 1851*. Wheat, 186.

Butte County Historical Society. *See* Diggin's.

Butte County History. 1877: *Butte County, California, Illustrations . . . with Historical Sketch of the County* (Oakland: Smith & Elliott, 1877). **1882:** Harry Laurenz Wells, *History of Butte County, California* (San Francisco, 1882). **1918:** George C. Mansfield, *History of Butte County* (Los Angeles: Historic Record Co., 1918).

Butte County Map. 1862: J. S. Hennings, *Map of Butte County, California* (San Francisco: W. B. Cooke, 1862). Approved in 1861 by the Board of Supervisors as the official map of the county, and sometimes cited as Butte County Map, 1861. **1877:** James McCann, *Official Map of the County of Butte, California* (San Francisco: Britton and Rey, 1877). **1886:** Another edition of McCann (San Francisco: Britton and Rey, 1886).

CHSQ. *California Historical Society Quarterly*, San Francisco, v. 1- (July 1922–   ).

Cain. Ella M. Cain, *The Story of Bodie*. With an Introduction by Donald L. Segerstrom (San Francisco: Fearon, 1956). The author, daughter-in-law of James S. Cain, is a lifetime resident of Bodie. Her father-in-law held an interest in the Standard Mine at Bodie and later he bought the Bodie Bank (1890). The book tells the story of the establishment of the town and gives many details about its colorful history.

Calaveras County Records. The early records in the office of the county recorder in San Andreas contain information on early mining localities. Information from them was supplied by L. Cenotto of the recorder's office.

California and its Gold. A privately printed pamphlet, by H. A., 1852, gives a brief history of the gold discoveries in California and Australia.

California Emigrant Letters. Compiled by Walker D. Wyman, in *CHSQ*, XXIV. A selection of letters, 1849–1850, published in Missouri newspapers. The letters concern the overland trip, mainly, but also include some from the mines.

California Folklore Quarterly. See *Western Folklore*.

California Gold Rush Letters (1849–18—). MS in Bancroft Library. A collection of various letters written by miners, mainly to relatives and friends "back home."

California Historical Landmarks. Sacramento: State of California, Division of Beaches and Parks, 1963. The landmarks are listed by number, with brief descriptions, and an index by county. The movement to preserve landmarks of historical importance or interest was inaugurated by the Native Sons of the Golden West. Since 1931 these landmarks have been registered and placed under the protection of the State of California Resources Agency.

California Historical Society Quarterly (*CHSQ*, San Francisco, v. 1- (July, 1922–).

California Illustrated. *California Illustrated Spirit of the Times*, San Francisco. 1855?-? Weekly newspaper. Numerous clippings are found in "Bancroft Scraps." The 1877 annual edition is also in Bancroft Library.

California Mother Lode Records. Daughters of the American Revolution, California. Peralta Chapter. California Mother Lode Records. (San Leandro, c. 1962–). 3 vols. in 2. Vol. 1–2: Marriage and death records from San Andreas, Calaveras. Vol. 3: Alpine County.

California Past and Present. *California: Its Past History; its Present Position; its Future Prospects . . . and a Minute and Authentic Account of the Discovery of the Gold Region* (London, 1850). The latter account is based chiefly on Vizetelly. See *Vizetelly*. The book has good pictures.

California Place Names. See *Gudde*.

California State Census, 1852. An abstract of the 1852 State Census, issued by the Secretary of State, appears in: California Legislature. Senate. Journal. 4th sess. (1853). Appendix. Doc. 14.

California State Surveyor General, *Report, 1855. In* California, Legislature, Assembly, sess. 1856, doc. 9. A number of mining camps are mentioned in the report.

Call. W. W. Call, "Recollections of Overland Journey to California, 1849" (n.d.). 15 p.

MS in Bancroft Library. Some notes on mining are included. Call arrived at Pleasant Valley in September, 1849; from there he went to Placerville by way of Weaverville, and then to Sacramento.

Camp. Charles L. Camp has edited John Doble's *Journal and Letters from the Mines, Mokelumne Hill, Jackson and Volcano, 1851– 1865* (Denver: Old West Publishing Company, 1862). His notes contain detailed information about mining camps in the region. **Camp's Map** refers to his "Map of the Central Mines," published in his edition of Doble's *Journal* mentioned above. The map indicates the localities mentioned by Doble and other places in the region extending from San Andreas in the south to the North Fork of the Cosumnes. Professor Camp also gave information about place names in Amador and Calaveras counties directly to the author of this dictionary.

Campo. The Spanish word for 'field' was used by Mexicans and Americans for a mining camp.

Canfield. Chauncey de Leon Canfield, *The Diary of a Forty-Niner* (New York: Morgan Shepherd, 1906). The diary is purported to have been written by a forty-niner named Alfred T. Jackson in the Grass Valley– Nevada City area. It is a romanticized story based on the recollections of a miner, Lewis Hanchett, and on the research of Canfield, the author. The book was republished in 1920 by Houghton Mifflin and in 1947 by J. L. Delkin, Stanford, California, with an introduction by Oscar Lewis.

Canyon. The now generally accepted spelling for the Spanish *cañon*, which in California has acquired the meaning of 'narrow valley', 'ravine', 'gulch'.

Carpenter. Gideon J. Carpenter, "Correspondence and Papers" (1853–1892). 43 pieces. MS in Bancroft Library. Some of the papers concern mining in El Dorado County.

Carr. James Carr, "The California Letters . . .," ed., Carl I. Wheat. In *CHSQ*, XI, pp. 157 ff. Carr came to California early in 1850 via Cape Horn. His letters to his family from Woods Creek and Hawkins Bar in the Southern Mines were written between February 1852 and April 1854.

Carr. John Carr, *Pioneer Days in California* (Eureka, Calif.: Times Publishing Co., 1891). An excellent retrospective account of a pioneer in Weaverville, 1850–1866, and a good account of Indians in Trinity and Humboldt counties. *A Vulcan among* *the Argonauts* (San Francisco: G. Fields, 1936) contains excerpts from the above memoirs.

Carson. James Carson, "Letter." Datelined Bucks Bar, August 15, 1856. *In* "California Gold Rush Letters." MS in Bancroft Library.

Carson Recollections. James H. Carson (d. 1853), *Early Recollections of the Mines, and a Description of the Great Tulare Valley* (Stockton: Published to accompany the steamer ed. of San Joaquin *Republican,* January 17–March 27, 1852). Repeatedly reprinted; contains nothing but generalities. It was probably written by a hack writer of the newspaper, but was highly praised by H. H. Bancroft, Theodore Hittell, and Robert E. Cowan. It is not to be considered as a historical source.

Castro Mining Claim. *In* Manuel de Jesús Castro, "Correspondence and Papers" (1830–1863). MS in Bancroft Library.

Caughey. John Walton Caughey, *Gold is the Cornerstone* (Berkeley: University of California Press, 1948). A comprehensive, scholarly account of the Gold Rush written for the general reader; with an extensive bibliography. *Rushing for Gold,* ed., Professor Caughey (Berkeley: University of California Press, 1949) is a series of papers on various aspects of the Gold Rush, published as a contribution to the centennial celebrations.

Cement. Heavily impacted gravel. A cement mill was a type of stamp mill designed to crush hardened material that could not be broken down by hydraulic operations.

Cenotto. Larry Cenotto of the Amador County Recorder's Office is a well-known historian of Amador County.

Central Mines. *See* Northern Mines.

Chalfant. Willie Arthur Chalfant, *Tales of the Pioneers* (Stanford, Calif.: Stanford University Press, 1942). Chalfant, for many years the editor and publisher of the *Inyo Register,* is considered the best authority on names and places in Inyo County and Death Valley.

Chamberlain. Charles H. Chamberlain, "Statement of a Pioneer of 1849" (1877). 4 p. MS in Bancroft Library. A dictation made for H. H. Bancroft concerning his experiences in gold mining and as a magistrate in Columbia.

Chamberlain, History. *See* Yuba County History.

Chamberlain. Newell D. Chamberlain, *The Call of Gold* (Mariposa, Calif.: Gazette Press, 1936). A resumé of the development of mining activities in Mariposa County. Includes extracts from contemporary newspapers, letters and writings of Mariposa County pioneers, according to the author. Parts appear to be fiction, however.

Chase. J. Smeaton Chase was an observant traveler, who related his experiences in three books published by Houghton Mifflin Company. One of these, *California Desert Trails,* 1919, makes reference to several gold camps.

Chavannes. H. de Chavannes de la Giraudière, *Les Petits Voyageurs en Californie* (Tours, 1853). The author tells the story of a French argonaut and his two young sons, who came to the gold mines along the American and Feather Rivers in 1849. It is not to be considered as a source but rather as an example of a beautifully produced book in the period of the gold rush, perhaps the finest.

Cheesman. David W. Cheesman, "By Ox Team from Salt Lake to Los Angeles, 1850; a Memoir," ed., Mary E. Fay. In *HSSCP,* XIV, pp. 271 ff.

Chile or Chilian Mill. An improved arrastre, used to grind quartz. Instead of "dragstones," two large stone wheels attached to an axle, rolled around on their edges, crushing the rock. The circular pit in which they revolved was smaller than that of an arrastre, and a mule was usually hitched to one end of the axle. Good illustrations may be found in *Hutchings' California Magazine,* October 1857, pp. 153, 154.

Chinard. *See* Trény.

Chispa. The Spanish term for 'nugget'.

Chispa. Sonora, California. V. 1 (July 1961–). Quarterly publication of the Tuolumne County Historical Society, formerly issued as *The Quarterly.*

Christman. Enos Christman, *One Man's Gold: The Letters and Journals of a Forty-Niner* (New York: Whittelsey, 1930). An interesting account of unsuccessful mining in Mariposa County and of conditions in Sonora in 1851–1852.

Chuckwalla. *Death Valley Chuck-walla.* Greenwater, January 1–June 1907.

Church. Andrew S. Church, "Memoirs." *In Society of California Pioneers Quarterly,* III, pp. 154 ff. A retrospective account of the Mariposa mines, written in 1901. Not entirely reliable.

Claim. The parcel of mining ground held by a miner or a company under local or government laws. The size of the average claim was originally about 600 by 1,500 feet but differed at different times and in different regions.

Clappe. *See* Dame Shirley.

Clark. Austin S. Clark, *Reminiscences of Travel, 1852–1865* (Middletown, Conn., 1897?). Includes a description of the author's experiences around Coloma.

Clark. Hiram C. Clark, "Reminiscences of Life and Adventures on the Pacific Coast, Twenty-Five Years Ago. By an Old Californian." 1 vol. Scrapbook in Bancroft Library. A series of articles printed in the Union City (Indiana) *Times* between December 3, 1874, and May 22, 1875. The author was a lawyer by profession who came to the California mines in the early 1850s and practised law in San Francisco. His "Reminiscences," as well as his "Statement of Historical Facts on California from 1851 to 1865," written for H. H. Bancroft in 1878, are not the usual account of personal experiences but rather a social commentary on events of the times.

Clark. John Clark, "The California Guide (1852–1856)." 206 p. MS in Coe Collection, Yale University Library. Microfilm in Bancroft Library. An excellent account of mining on the Feather and Yuba rivers.

Clark. William B. Clark, *Gold Districts of California. See Bull.*, 193.

Clark. William S. Clark, "Autobiographical Sketch." 31 p. Typescript in Bancroft; original in private possession. Clark came overland to San Francisco in 1846; built a wharf and warehouse at the foot of Broadway at the location later called Clarks Point; interrupted his business in the spring of 1848 to mine at Mormon Island, returning to San Francisco after an absence of eight months.

Clayton's Map, 1865? I. E. Clayton, *Map of Esmeralda and Mono* (San Francisco: Britton & Company, 1865?).

Clean-up. The operation of collecting the gold within a given time, or in a stamp mill, or in a hydraulic or placer mine.

Clyman. *James Clyman, Frontiersman. The Adventures of a Trapper and Covered Wagon Emigrant as Told in his Own Reminiscences and Diaries*, ed., Charles L. Camp, 2nd ed. (Portland, Ore.: Champoeg Press, 1960). Previously published by the California Historical Society, 1928. Clyman was a pre-Gold Rush emigrant to California, who settled in the Napa Valley. His observations on the extent and richness of the mining region are given in a letter dated December 25, 1848.

Cofferdam. A water-tight enclosure from which water was pumped to expose the bottom of a stream or river.

Cohn. Henry Cohn, *Jugenderinnerungen* (Stettin, 1914). Contains a good description of the region around St. Louis and Poker Flat. A part was translated from the German and published under the title "Saint Louis and Poker Flat in the Fifties and Sixties," in *CHSQ*, XIX, pp. 289 ff.

Color. Originally the tiny particles of gold that could not be weighed. Later it became a general miners' term for seeing gold. "At the depth of three feet we finally saw color."

Colton, Gardner Q. *See* Colton, Walter.

Colton. Walter Colton, *Three Years in California* (New York, 1850). Another edition: *The Land of Gold; or, Three Years in California* (New York, 1860). Colton came to California in 1846; was the first American alcalde at Monterey, 1846–48; edited and published with Robert Semple in Monterey the first California newspaper, *The Californian*, 1846–1847; visited the mines in October and November, 1848, meeting Governor Mason and Captain Sherman on their tour of observation of mining on the Stanislaus River. His brother, Gardner Quincy Colton, came to California in 1849 and makes mention of his brief stay in the mines in his *Boyhood and Manhood Recollections* (New York, 1897?).

Colusa County Map, 1855. De Jarnatt & Crane, *Official Map of Colusa County, California*, (San Francisco: Lith. Britton & Rey, 1885).

Comfort. Herbert G. Comfort, *Where Rolls the Kern; a History of Kern County, California* (Moorpack, Calif.: Enterprise Press, 1934).

Company. A vague term for an organization of miners for protection and cooperation. During the earliest gold mining years a company might have consisted of between two and one hundred miners. In later years the word designated usually a capitalistic enterprise.

Consolidated Index. California, Division of Mines, Bulletin no. 131 (San Francisco, 1945). *Consolidated Index of Publications of the Division of Mines and Predecessor, State Mining Bureau, 1880–1943, Inclusive.*

Cool Diary. P. Y. Cool, "Diary" (May 13, 1850 to July 3, 1852). MS in Bancroft Library and in Huntington Library. Records his experiences at the mines and in San Francisco.

Cordua. Theodor Cordua settled at the site of present-day Marysville in 1841 and called his farm Neu Mecklenburg, after his home province in Germany. *The Memoirs of Theodor Cordua*, reprinted from *CHSQ*, XII, no. 4, were edited by Erwin G. Gudde.

Coronel. Antonio F. Coronel, "Cosas de California." Dictation for Bancroft Library, 1877. MS in Bancroft Library. Pages 140 to 186 deal with Coronel's experiences in the mines. This section has been translated into English by Richard H. Morefield and is appended to his M.A. thesis (University of California, Berkeley), entitled "The Mexican Adaptation in American California: 1846–1875." It is also summarized in Bancroft's *History of California*, VI, pp. 78–81. Coronel, a native of Mexico, came to California in 1834, became mayor of Los Angeles in 1853; served as city councilman, 1864–1867, and as state treasurer, 1867–1871.

Country Rock. The rock traversed by or adjacent to an ore deposit.

County History. The annals of most counties in California have been recorded at some time in county histories, and some of them contain information about gold camps and towns. They are listed in this bibliography under the name of the county. The entry indicates the year, the publisher, and (when known) the editor of the publication.

County Map. Official maps of the county have been published by different county agencies. They are listed in this bibliography under the name of the county.

County Report. California, Division of Mines and Geology, *County Report* (San Francisco, 1962–65). I: *Kern County*; II: *Calaveras County*; III: *San Diego County*; IV: *Trinity County*. These are summaries and continuations of reports on mines and mining formerly issued in annual reports.

Cousin Jack. A nickname for a Cornishman.

Covered Wagon. The organ of the Shasta County Historical Society, published in Redding, September, 1941 to the present. The first issues were published elsewhere and were devoted to poetry and literary essays. In 1954 it absorbed the Society's *Yearbook*, and since that time it has been published annually.

Cox. Isaac Cox, *The Annals of Trinity County* (San Francisco, 1858). This may be considered the first county history; it covers one decade of the history of the region. The original, now rare edition was reissued by Harold C. Holmes in a John Henry Nash printing (Eugene, Oregon, 1940).

Coy. Owen C. Coy, *In the Diggings in Forty-nine* (Los Angeles: California State Historical Association, 1948). The author (1895–1952) was a professor of history at the University of Southern California and di-

rector of the California State Historical Association. *In the Diggings* is a survey (without citation of sources) of the mining camps, arranged and mapped by area. Unless otherwise indicated, citations are to *In the Diggings*. *Gold Days* (Los Angeles: L. A. Powell, 1930) is a popular account of the Gold Rush. *California County Boundaries* (Sacramento: California Historical Survey Commission, 1923) includes maps showing the changes in boundaries. A copy of his large map entitled "Map of a Portion of the Gold Mining Region of California" (San Francisco: California Historical Association, 1948), reproduced from manuscript, is in Bancroft Library.

"Coyoteing." The term is derived from the type of mining likened to the digging and burrowing of the coyote, the western American designation of the prairie wolf. This method of mining was apparently first used in 1850, when miners near Nevada City burrowed or drifted into and under hills in efforts to find "pay dirt" in the gravels along an ancient river channel. *See* Coyoteville in text.

Cradle or Rocker. A primitive portable device for washing gold-bearing earth, consisting of a short oblong box, fitted with a perforated hopper, a moveable slide or apron, and riffle bars. The apparatus was mounted on two rockers, similar to those on a baby's cradle; hence the name. The cradle or rocker was a one-man operation and was superseded by the "long tom." A good illustration is found in *Hutchings' California Magazine*, July 1857, p. 5.

Crampton. C. Gregory Crampton, "The Opening of the Mariposa Mining Region," Ph.D. diss. University of California, Berkeley, 1941. A thorough and detailed account with good maps and pictures.

Craven. *See* Hoffmann; Von Leicht-Craven Map, 1873.

Crites. Arthur S. Crites, *Pioneer Days in Kern County* (Los Angeles: Ward Ritchie Press, 1951).

Crockett. George H. W. Crockett, "Account and Memorandum Book" (1854–1862). 183 p. MS in Bancroft Library. Crockett's clientele was mainly in El Dorado County. He gives the names of people and the localities in which they lived. It is a useful source for place names in the area covered.

Cronise. Titus F. Cronise, *The Natural Wealth of California* (San Francisco: H. H. Bancroft, 1868). A comprehensive survey, including mining activities in individual counties and a resumé of various types of mining methods used.

Cropping-out. Parts of rock formation that appear above the ground, often leading to the discovery of gold.

Crosby. Elisha O. Crosby, *Memoirs of Elisha Oscar Crosby: Reminiscences of California and Guatemala from 1849 to 1864* (San Marino, Calif.: Huntington Library, 1945). Crosby, a member of the Constitutional Convention from the Sacramento district, had come to California in March, 1849. He practised law in the area and visited mines on the Yuba, Bear, and American rivers until his return to New York in 1860.

Crossman's Map, 1867. Crossman & Cochrane, *Map of the County of Sierra* (San Francisco: Britton & Rey, 1867).

Crowell's Map, 1903. Russell A. Crowell, *Miners Map of Death Valley and the Proposed Salt Lake Railroads* (Los Angeles, 1903). First published in 1902.

Crystalline Gold. Pieces of gold in the form of crystals, embedded in quartz; rarely found in placers.

Daingerfield. William P. Daingerfield, "Letters to his Family" (1850–1853). 27 p. MS in Bancroft Library. The letters are written mainly from Sacramento and from Shasta County.

Dame Shirley. Mrs. Louise Amelia Knapp Smith Clappe, *The Shirley Letters from the California Mines, 1851–52* (San Francisco, 1922). The letters of Mrs. Clappe to her sister "back home" depicting life in the diggings at Rich Bar on the East Branch of the North Fork of Feather River are remarkable for their chronicle of events as witnessed by a sensitive, observant woman. They are written in a charming, graceful style that has won them a unique place in Gold Rush literature. Originally published serially in San Francisco in 1854 and 1855 in *The Pioneer; or, California Monthly Magazine*, they were brought out in a small edition by Thomas C. Russell in 1922, in 1933 by the Grabhorn Press, and in 1949 in New York by Alfred A. Knopf, with an excellent introduction by Carl I. Wheat.

Damming a River. "I have been damming a river" was miners' jargon for having had bad luck.

Dane. G. Ezra Dane, *Ghost Town* (New York: Knopf, 1941). The stories about Columbia during the Gold Rush and later, as told to the author by "the oldest inhabitants," are a mixture of history, folklore, and fiction.

Dart. John Paul Dart, "A Mississippian in the Gold Fields" in *CHSQ*, XXXV, pp. 205 ff. A successful miner in Columbia and Sonora and for many years county surveyor of Tuolumne County. His diary, edited by Howard Mitcham, covers the period between November 10, 1849 and July 3, 1856. **Dart's Map of Columbia, 1871.** Tuolumne County, California. Surveyor's Office. The map is a detailed manuscript plat of the townsite, showing streets, lots, and names of lot owners. **Dart's Map of 1879.** *Map of the Principal Quartz and Gravel Mines in Tuolumne County, California* (San Francisco: A. L. Bancroft, 1879).

Davis. Harold P. Davis, *Gold Rush Days in Nevada City, with Historical Map* (Nevada City: Berliner & McGinnis, 1948). The late Mr. Davis was a well-known local historian.

Davis. Stephen Chapin Davis. *California Gold Rush Merchant* (San Marino: Huntington Library, 1956). The author was in California twice, in 1850–1851 and in 1852–1854. His journal includes the record of his experiences as a merchant in Long Bar on the Yuba River and in Coulterville in the Southern Mines. He gives many place names not found elsewhere and a good description of the road between Coulterville and Stockton.

Davis. William Heath Davis, *Sixty Years in California; a History of Events and Life in California . . .* (San Francisco: A. J. Leary, 1889). Published with additions as *Seventy-five years in California . . .* in San Francisco by John Howell in 1929 and 1967. Davis, prominent San Francisco merchant, who started his business career as a clerk in the Monterey store of his uncle, Nathan Spear, claims to have bought the first gold dust brought to San Francisco by the miners in June, 1848. He also claims to have handled some of the gold dust from the San Fernando Valley which Henry Mellus had obtained in 1840 from shopkeepers in Los Angeles.

Day. Sherman Day, 1806–1873, the son of Jeremiah Sherman, president of Yale College, was a noted civil and mining engineer. In 1855–1856 he located a wagon road across the Sierra Nevada. The same year he was a California state senator. From 1856 to 1864 he was superintendent of the quicksilver mine at New Almaden, Santa Clara County, California, and for a short time he was also superintendent of the Princeton Mine on the Las Mariposas Estate, Mariposa County. From September, 1868 to February, 1871 he served as surveyor general of the state of California. He was also a trustee of the College of California, which later became the University of California, Berkeley. A collection of letters written by Sherman Day to his father in the 1850s, mainly from New Almaden, is in the Bancroft Library. One of the letters is datelined Ion (Ione) Valley, July 19, 1856. Ione was an important mining camp in the 1850s in Amador County, and it was at this time, in 1856, that Day made his map of the vicinity, cited herein as **Sherman Day's Map of 1856.** The map is entitled: Map of Nine Sections of Land in Amador County; Surveyed by Sherman Day in July, August, and September, 1856 by Order of Andrés Pico and Ramon de Zaldo. A copy is on file in the Recorder's Office, Amador County.

Deadwood. California miner's slang for 'sure thing'.

Dean. Peter Dean, "Statement of Occurrences in California" (1878). 10 p. MS in Bancroft Library. The locale is Jacksonville and places on the Stanislaus River. Numerous mining localities are mentioned.

Deane. Benjamin H. Deane, "Journal" (1849–1851). 148 p. MS in Bancroft Library. An excellent account of the Southern Mines.

Death Valley Chuck-Walla. Greenwater, Calif. V. 1– v. 2, no. 1 (Jan. 1–June 1907).

Death Valley Guide. Works Project Administration Writers' Project, California, American Guide Series, *Death Valley, a Guide* (Boston, 1939). Contains a good map, but the gold finds are not properly treated.

Debris. The same as tailing.

Decker. Peter H. Decker, "Diaries" (1849–1871). MS in Society of California Pioneers Library, San Francisco. Vols. 2–7 (1850–1853) only pertain to mining in California. Decker mined on the South Fork of Yuba River and also had a store in Nevada City and at Parks Bar. His diaries are an excellent source for names of mining localities in these areas. Mrs. Helen S. Giffen has edited a part of the diaries under the title *The Diaries of Peter Decker, Overland to California in 1849 and Life in the Mines, 1850–1851* (Georgetown, Calif.: Talisman Press, 1966).

De Decker. Mary De Decker, *Mines of the Eastern Sierra* (Glendale, Calif.: La Siesta Press, 1966). A useful account, based on sound research.

De Ferrari. Carlo M. De Ferrari, Tuolumne County Recorder and County Historian, supplied much information on place names of the region. When the place name entry is followed by his name in parentheses, the information was given directly. De Ferrari has edited Stoddart's *Annals of Tuolumne County* (*see* Stoddart). References to his annotations to this book are so indicated; likewise reference to other writings of De Ferrari.

De Groot. Henry De Groot, *Glossary of Terms in Common Use among Miners in California.* *In* California Mining Bureau, *Report*, II (1882), pp. 280 ff. In the same *Report*, Part 2, pp. 133 ff.: *Hydraulic and Drift Mining. Recollections of California Mining Life* (San Francisco: Dewey, 1884). 16 p.

Delameter. John A. Delameter, "My Forty Years Pulling Freight" (as told to John Edwin Hogg). In *Touring Topics*, August, 1930.

Delano. *Alonzo Delano's California Correspondence*, ed., Irving McKee (Sacramento: Sacramento Book Club, 1952). The letters cover the period 1850–1851 around Bidwell Bar and Grass Valley. Considerable attention is given to Gold Lake. It is an interesting and important contribution. *Life on the Plains and Among the Diggings* (Auburn, New York, 1854). The book was repeatedly reprinted under various titles, including *Across the Plains and Among the Diggings* (New York: Wilson-Erickson, 1936). It is one of the best accounts, especially of the Yuba and Feather rivers and the Gold Lake country. Among his other books are *Pen Knife Sketches* (Sacramento, 1853), *The Miner's Progress* (Sacramento, 1853), *Old Block's Sketch Book* (Sacramento, 1856).

Del Norte County History, 1881. Anthony J. Bledsoe, *History of Del Norte County, California, with a Business Directory and Travelers' Guide* (Eureka: Wyman, 1881).

De Long. Charles E. De Long, "California's Bantam Cock" ed., Carl I. Wheat. In *CHSQ*, VIII–XI. De Long came to California as a youth in 1850, mined along the Yuba, collected the foreign miners' tax as deputy sheriff, 1855–1856, kept a store at Young's Hill, studied law and entered the bar in 1857, served in the state legislature, later entered politics in Nevada, and in 1869 was appointed U. S. minister to Japan. His diary, 1854–1863, carefully edited by Carl I. Wheat, is a faithful record of his activities and a valuable source for the history of mining along the Yuba in the 1850s.

Demarest. D. C. Demarest, *A Bit of Mother Lode History* (Oakland, 1951). Based on his own recollections and on the diaries of his father, David D. Demarest, the author gives the history of Angels Camp, Slabtown, and vicinity. His father's diary covering his journey to California in 1849 and his mining experiences in early 1850 is in the Bancroft Library, but the later diaries were apparently lost in the Berkeley 1923 fire.

De Massey. *See* Massey.

Derbec. Etienne Derbec, *A French Journalist in the California Gold Rush*, ed., A. P. Nasatir (Georgetown, Calif.: Talisman Press, 1964). Thirteen letters written between February 1850 and May 1851 provide an excellent source for the history of the Mariposa mines. A fine introduction and notes by Professor Nasatir enhance their value.

Derby's Maps. Lieutenant George H. Derby of the Topographical Engineers (known in literature as John Phoenix) was engaged in California exploration in 1849 and 1850. The two maps cited in this dictionary are described as follows. *Sketch of General Riley's Route through the Mining Districts, July and August, 1849* (New York: Ackermann's Lithogr., 1849). Wheat, 79. It is sometimes cited as J. Mc H. Hollingsworth. Published in U. S. 31st Cong., 1st sess., 1850, House Executive doc. no. 79. The second map is entitled *The Sacramento Valley from the American River to Butte Creek; Surveyed and Drawn by Order of Gen'l Riley . . . September and October, 1849*. Wheat, 149, marked Derby 1 (1850). Published in U.S. 31st Cong., 1st sess., 1850, Senate, Executive doc. no. 47, with his *Topographical Memoir*. The two maps described above are also reprinted in *CHSQ*, XI, no. 2, with Derby's *Reports* of the journeys on which they are based, and an introduction and biographical sketch by Francis P. Farquhar.

The Desert Magazine, Palm Desert, Calif. 1937– .

Dexter. A. Hersey Dexter, *Early Days in California* (Denver: Tribune-Republican Press, 1886). Delightful stories and poems. Based on recollections of experiences in the Southern Mines; hence to be used with care only.

Diggings. The term referred originally to the locations where placer mining was carried on, but it often simply meant places where gold was mined.

Diggin's. Oroville, California. V. 1 (Mar. 1957–). Quarterly publication of the Butte County Historical Society.

Dillon, Guillaume Patrice. *See* Nasatir.

Directory, Nevada County. *See* Bean.

Directory, Placerville. *See* Placerville Directory.

Dirt. The same as pay dirt.

District. *See* Mining District.

Doble. *John Doble's Journal and Letters from the Mines*, ed., Charles L. Camp (Denver: Old West Publishing Co., 1962). A detailed chronicle of Volcano and surrounding region, 1852–54, with excellent notes and maps by Professor Camp. Next to Bruff, it is probably the best of the published Gold Rush diaries.

Doolittle's Map, 1868. A. J. Doolittle, *Township and County Map of the Central Part of California* (San Francisco and Nevada City: A. J. Doolittle, 1868). A detailed and useful map, showing towns, post offices, roads, ranches, and proprietors.

Doten Diary. Alfred Doten, "Diary." The author spent some time in the California gold mines, and in the diary entries between September, 1854 and May, 1855, he mentions a number of mining localities in that region. Charles L. Camp makes a number of references to Doten's diary in his edition of *John Doble's Journal*, 1851–1865, which was published in 1962. A large part of Alfred Doten's experiences were in the state of Nevada, and the diary is now in the Manuscript Collection of the University of Nevada.

Downie. William Downie, *Hunting for Gold* (San Francisco: California Publishing Co., 1893). The reminiscences of "Major" Downie, a native of Scotland and founder of Downieville, were ghost written by Chris M. Waage and are quite accurate, though some of the quoted statements may be questioned. Downie mined at the forks of the Yuba in November, 1849.

Doyle File. Thomas B. Doyle ["California Place Names"]. 15 vols. MS in Bancroft Library. An extensive file of names of places in California, including mining camps and towns, collected for many years by the late Thomas B. Doyle of San Francisco.

Drake. Austin Drake, *Big Bear Valley, its History, Legends and Tales* (Big Bear Lake, California: Grizzly Little Press in the Pines, 1949).

Dredging. The method of mining, on a large scale, gold-bearing deposits of sand and gravel from present-day river channels and adjacent lands. Dredging in the Folsom district was carried on until 1962 and in the Hammonton district until 1968.

Dressler. Albert Dressler, *California's Pioneer Mountaineer of Rabbit Creek* (San Francisco, 1930). The sketches about Rabbit Creek, later LaPorte, in the 1850s and 1860s are based on reminiscences of pioneers, particularly John Thomas Mason, one-time bank messenger.

Drift, Drift Mining. A drift is a horizontal underground passage, following the vein. Drift mining is a method of mining deep deposits of auriferous gravel, or cement by means of sinking shafts and "driving a tunnel" or "drifting" until pay dirt is reached. *See* Tunnel Mining.

Drury. Aubrey Drury, "The Livermore Family" (1953). 95 p. MS in Bancroft Library. Contains letters of Horatio G. Livermore written from Big Bar on the Middle Fork of American River, where he mined and also operated a sawmill in 1851–1852. *California, An Intimate Guide* (New York: Harper, 1947), rev. ed. Contains a good chapter on the Mother Lode.

Drury. Ruth Drury, Curator of the Downieville Museum, furnished information about gold camps in Sierra County for this dictionary.

Dry Digging. In placer mining, the process of picking out small particles of gold with a knife after the "dirt" has been stripped off with a shovel. It is sometimes also applied to knife mining, in which gold in crevices in rocks along a stream is scraped out with a knife.

Dry Diggings. Placer mines where there is no natural water supply.

Dry Washing. Where water is insufficient for washing gold-bearing gravels, various schemes were devised to recover the gold. Among these is the "winnowing" method of repeatedly throwing a panful, or a blanketful of gravel into the air and catching it again. Other methods made use of Mexican hand bellows and of dry-washing machines employing small amounts of water and re-using it.

Duflot de Mofras. Eugène de Mofras, attaché of the French legation in Mexico, visited Oregon Territory and California in 1841–1842 and reported on the conditions of these territories to the French government in his *Explorations du Territoire de l'Oregon, des Californiens et de la Mer Vermeille, 1840, 1841, et 1842*. His *Carte de la Californie* (Paris, 1844) is part of his *Grande Carte*, based on his explorations.

Dumas. Alexandre Dumas, *A Gil Blas in California*, trans. by Marguerite Eyer Wilbur (Los Angeles: Primavera Press, 1933). Written by the French novelist and dramatist and published in Paris in 1852 as *Un Gil Blas en Californie*. Dumas claimed to have based the story of adventure on a contemporary journal, but it is more likely that it was based on the recollections of a Frenchman returned from California, as suggested by George R. Stewart (*CHSQ*, XIV, pp. 132 ff.). The gold digging scene was around Sonora, Pine Pass, and Murphys.

Dump. The quartz and gravel waste, especially from hydraulic mining and dredging, long ridges of which still adorn the landscape of the mining region.

Dustin. David (or Daniel?) Dustin, "Letters." 8 p. *In* "California Gold Rush Letters." MS in Bancroft Library. Two informative letters datelined Sacramento, August 14, 1850, and January 9, 1853.

East Belt. Designates the gold belt east of the Mother Lode, containing an extensive system of lode gold-bearing veins; described and mapped in *Bulletin*, 193, pp. 15, 17.

Eastman. Mrs. Barbara Eastman has spent many years compiling notes from documentary sources on the history of Columbia, Tuolumne County, and nearby towns and camps. Copies are deposited in the Bancroft Library. She has also written a series of articles on Columbia which were published in *Chispa*, the quarterly journal of the Tuolumne County Historical Society. *See* Columbia in text.

Eaton. Richard B. Eaton, Judge of the Superior Court, Shasta County, is an authority on the history of Shasta County and the author of articles on the history of the county. One of his articles is an account of Major P. B. Reading's discovery of gold at Readings Bar, Clear Creek, published in *Covered Wagon*, 1964.

Eccleston. Robert Eccleston, *The Mariposa War, 1850–1851*, ed., C. Gregory Crampton (Salt Lake City: University of Utah Press, 1957). Robert Eccleston was a member of the Frémont Association of New York, which came to California in 1849 to engage in cooperative mining. His diaries for 1850–1851 describe his experiences in the Mariposa mines, his participation in the Mariposa War, which occurred when miners intruded on Indian lands, and the discovery of Yosemite Valley by members of the Mariposa Battalion.

These diaries, carefully edited by Professor Crampton, are from the manuscript in the Bancroft Library. The first part, which covered the overland trip, was edited by Professor George P. Hammond for the Friends of the Bancroft Library in 1950, under the title *Overland to California on the Southwestern Trail, 1849*.

Idy's Map, 1851. *See* Milleson and Adams' Map. **Eddy's Map, 1853,** refers to the map compiled by State Surveyor General, W. M. Eddy, *Approved & Declared to be the Official Map of the State of California*, Passed March 25th, 1853 (New York: J. H. Colton, 1854). Wheat, 257. This much maligned map (*see* the criticism in *Report of the Surveyor General of California*, 1856, pp. 45, 236–237), is a good map, and certainly no worse than most other maps compiled before Goddard's.

Edmundson. William Edmundson, "Diary." Detached from *Annals of Iowa*, 3rd ser., VIII, No. 7 (Des Moines, 1908). In Bancroft Library. Covers mainly his overland journey and arrival at Weberville in El Dorado County.

Elder. William Elder, "Letters" (1850–1851). 11 letters. MS in Bancroft Library. The letters are datelined Centreville, Grass Valley, and Gold Mountain.

El Dorado County History, 1883: *Historical Souvenir of El Dorado County, California* (Oakland, 1883). comp., Paoli Sioli. One of the better county histories.

El Dorado County Records. The county records include Books of Deeds, Mining Localities, and other records dating back to the earliest days of mining in the county. They are under the jurisdiction of the County Recorder, Placerville.

Elephant. "To have seen the elephant" was an expression used by California miners to denote the experience of having sought one's fortunes in California's fabulous land of gold, ending usually in disillusionment and disappointment. "To see the elephant" generally denoted trying one's luck in the diggings.

Ellis' Map, 1850. Robert H. Ellis, *Map of the Gold Region of California* (New York: George F. Nesbit, Lith., 1850). Wheat, 154. Greatly resembles Jackson's map, 1850, with a few additional names.

Ellsberg. Helen Ellsberg, *Mines of Julian* (Glendale, California: La Siesta Press, 1972). One in the series on mines in southern California published by La Siesta Pess. It is a reliable, well-documented account.

Ely. Edward Ely, *The Wanderings of Edward Ely* (New York: Hastings, 1954). A fine retrospective account of a young Pennsylvania physician who visited in the mines around Placerville in the fall of 1851 en route to Bombay, India.

Evans. George W. B. Evans, *Mexican Gold Trail; the Journal of a Forty-Niner*, ed., Glenn S. Dumke (San Marino: Huntington Library, 1945). Contains a well-written account of the Mariposa diggings in 1849–1850 by a young attorney who mined in the area.

F.L.M. F. L. M., *Reise und Lebensbilder aus Neuholland, Neuseeland und Californien*, ed., W. Schulze (Magdeburg, 1853). Contains an account of mining in Mokelumne Hill, Rich Gulch, and Mosquito Gulch. It is strongly anti-American. Gerstaecker apparently used him and some of his companions as characters in his stories.

Fairchild. Lucius Fairchild, *California Letters* (Madison, Wisc.: Historical Society of Wisconsin, 1931). One of the finest contributions to Gold Rush literature, written by a young man from Wisconsin, who later became a general in the Civil War and several times governor of Wisconsin. The letters, written between 1851 and 1855, contain excellent descriptions of mining localities in a wide area extending from Calaveras County northward to Scott Valley near the Oregon border.

Fairchild. Mahlon D. Fairchild, "Reminiscences of a Forty-Niner," in *CHSQ*, XIII, pp. 4 ff. The author arrived in San Francisco in July 1849 and mined on Bear River, Deer Creek, and Yuba River in the early 1850s. His reminiscences were written at the age of seventy-seven and are to be used with care.

Farish. Thomas E. Farish, *The Gold Hunters* (Chicago: Donohue, 1904). A well-told account of the mining scene in California and personal recollections of mining in Butte and Plumas counties in the 1850s.

Farquhar. Francis P. Farquhar is the authority on place names of the High Sierra. His book entitled *Place Names of the High Sierra* was published by the Sierra Club in 1926. The author also edited three editions of Brewer's *Up and Down California, 1860–1864*. *See* Brewer and Whitney in this bibliography. Farquhar was a member of the committee which originally sponsored the publication of *California Place Names* in 1949. *See* Gudde.

Fatout. Paul Fatout, *Meadow Lake*

(Bloomington: Indiana University Press, 1969). A detailed, carefully documented account of the rush to Meadow Lake, 1865–1866, and its aftermath.

Fay. Albert H. Fay, *A Glossary of the Mining and Mineral Industry. In* U.S. Bureau of Mines, *Bull.*, 95. Washington, D.C., 1920.

Ferguson. Charles D. Ferguson, *The Experiences of a Forty-Niner during Thirty-four Years' Residence in California and Australia* (Cleveland, 1888). A highly interesting account, mainly of 1850, but edited much later. Ferguson mined first on the Feather River, then in Nevada City and vicinity. The book was partially reprinted by Biobooks in Oakland, 1948, under the title *California Gold Fields*.

Ferris. "Hiram Gano Ferris of Illinois and California" in *CHSQ*, XXVI, 289 ff. Joel E. Ferris has edited a group of letters of his father, written between 1850 and 1856. Ferris started mining near Coloma and moved northward toward the Oregon border. He was one of the organizers of Siskiyou County. A portfolio of his correspondence and papers in the Bancroft Library contains photostat copies of a number of his letters written from the mines, 1850–1855.

Ferry. Hypolite Ferry, *Déscription de la Nouvelle Californie* (Paris, 1850). An excellent comprehensive survey of the history, geography, and topography of California, its agriculture, mineral wealth, and its manners and customs. One chapter is on New Helvetia, one on the gold region, and another on the methods of mining.

Fish Journal. Isaac B. Fish, "Journal" (1854–1876). 3 vols. MS in the Charles Holbrook Library, Pacific School of Religion, Berkeley, California. The Reverend Fish was an itinerant Methodist Episcopal minister in the California mines from the early 1850s into the 1860s. Among the places mentioned in his journal, mainly in vol. 3, are Mokelumne Hill, Volcano, Jackson, Ione Valley, Sonora, Downieville, and Grass Valley.

Flour Gold. Fine particles of gold that can be recovered only by difficult processes.

Flume. A channel usually built of wood and often supported on a trestle to convey water for use in placer mining. "Fluming a river" denoted diverting the waters of the stream to lay bare the auriferous sand and gravel forming the bed. Good illustrations may be found in *Hutchings' Illustrated Magazine*, July 1857, pp. 10, 11 and September 1857, p. 105.

Foley. Doris Foley is a well-known local his-

torian of Nevada County, who furnished information about gold camps in the county directly to the author of this dictionary.

Folsom. William H. Folsom, "Dictation" (1886). MS in Bancroft Library. The author mined at Rough and Ready, Coyote Diggings, and Deer Creek in 1850. In the 1860s he built the Mormon Temple at Salt Lake City.

Fowler. Stephen L. Fowler, "Journal" (1849–1866). 2 vols. MS in Bancroft Library. Includes his mining experiences at Drytown and Downieville.

Freeman. Claire Freeman is a well-known historian of Placerville, one of the founders of the Heritage Association of El Dorado, and a contributor to the series of historical articles published in the Placerville *Mountain Democrat*.

Free Milling Gold. Gold that is free of combinations with other substances and does not require any treatment before being crushed in a stamp mill.

Frémont Estate. *See* Frémont, John Charles.

Frémont. Jessie Benton Frémont, *Mother Lode Narratives*, ed. and annotated by Shirley Sargent (Ashland, Oregon: L. Osborne, 1970). From unpublished letters and the book *Far West Sketches*, written by the wife of John Charles Frémont. It contains an account of family life on the Las Marpiposas Estate. (Reference to Frémont in text is to John Charles Frémont, unless otherwise specified.)

Frémont. John Charles Frémont, 1813–1890, was in California on two of his major expeditions, 1843–1844 and 1845–1846, and he is intimately connected with the acquisition of the province and the early history of the state. Details about these expeditions are found in his *Report of the Exploring Expedition to the Rocky Mountains . . . 1842, and to Oregon and North California . . . 1843–1844*, first printed as a Senate Document in 1845. Also his *Geographical Memoir upon Upper California . . .* 30th Congress, 1st sess (1848). Senate Misc. Doc. No. 148, and his *Memoirs of My Life . . .* (Chicago and New York, 1887), only one volume of which was published. Accompanying the above mentioned *Report* is a map usually credited to Frémont, but drawn by Charles Preuss, Frémont's cartographer on his first two expeditions. The map is entitled *Map of Oregon and Upper California*, but it includes a greater territory than indicated in the title. Of immediate interest to the history of gold camps in California is Frémont's acquisition of the rancho Las Mariposas, which had been granted to Juan B. Alvarado in 1844. Frémont acquired the 44,500-acre "claim" in 1847, and the subsequent discovery of gold on it led to the development of rich quartz mines. *See* the entry Mariposa Grant in the text of this dictionary. (Reference to Frémont in text is to John Charles Frémont unless otherwise stated.)

French. Dr. Darwin French led a party of fifteen into Death Valley in May of 1860, in search of the "lost" Gunsight Lode. They did not find the mine but left a number of place names.

Fresno County Map, 1874. George H. Goddard, *Map of Fresno County* (San Francisco: Britton, Rey, 1874).

Frickstad. *A Century of California Post Offices, 1848–1954*, compiled by Walter N. Frickstad (Oakland: Philatelic Research Society, 1955). A valuable contribution to the nomenclature of the state, giving the dates of establishment of all post offices; any change of name, or discontinuance.

Gannett. Henry Gannett, *The Origin of Certain Place Names in the United States*, 2nd ed., U.S. Geological Survey, Bulletin, no. 258 (Washington, 1905). The first edition appeared in 1902; in 1947 it was reprinted as *American Names: A Guide to the Origin of Place Names in the United States* (Washington: Public Affairs Press, 1947). The book contains many inaccuracies, together with some good information.

Gardiner. Howard C. Gardiner, *In Pursuit of the Golden Dream; Reminiscences of San Francisco and the Northern and Southern Mines, 1849–1857*, ed., Dale L. Morgan (Stoughton, Mass.: Western Hemisphere, 1970). During his stay in California, Gardiner mined first at Hawkins Bar and Sullivans Creek between August, 1849 and March, 1850; then in the Mariposa mines, April to July 1850; and from about May 1851, until his return home he mined at various places in the Northern and Southern mines. He has written a long, extremely interesting account of his experiences in retrospect. The book is carefully edited by Dale Morgan.

Gay. Theressa Gay; *James W. Marshall, the Discoverer of Gold. A Biography* (Georgetown, Calif.: Talisman Press, 1967). A detailed, carefully documented biography.

Geographic Board. *See* U.S. Board on Geographic Names.

Geological Survey. Unless otherwise indicated, all references are to the U.S. Geological Survey, established as an office under the Department of the Interior, March 3, 1879. *See* USGS Quadrangle.

Gerstaecker. Friedrich Gerstaecker, *Narrative of a Journey Round the World* (New York: Harper, 1853). This work of the popular German novelist was published in a number of English and American versions with different titles and minor text variations. The eleven chapters of the section entitled "California" give intimate pictures of the Gold Rush in 1849–1850. Unless otherwise stated the references are to 1853 Harper edition. Gerstaecker based his stories on personal experiences, first in the Northern Mines on Feather River in the fall of 1849 and the entire season of 1850 in the Southern Mines between the Mokelumne and Stanislaus rivers, *See* "Friedrich Gerstaecker: World Traveler and Author, 1816–1872" by Erwin G. Gudde, in *Journal of the West*, July, 1968.

Ghost Towns. *Ghost Towns and Relics of '49* (Stockton: Chamber of Commerce, n.d.). A brief illustrated guide to the Southern Mines.

Gianella. Vincent P. Gianella, geologist, mining engineer, and Professor *Emeritus* of the Mackay School of Mines (University of Nevada, Reno). Professor Gianella gave information on mining localities in Placer County to the author of this dictionary.

Gibbes' Maps. Charles D. Gibbes, *A New Map of the Gold Region in California* (New York: Sherman and Smith, 1851). Wheat, 192; and *Map of the Southern Mines* (San Francisco: Quirot & Co., Lith., 1852). Wheat, 218, published separately and in J. H. Carson's *Early Recollections of the Mines*. Another map of 1852, published in Stockton, California, is entitled *New Map of California*. . . . Gibbes' maps are historically important, though they are not always entirely accurate.

Gibbs. George Gibbs accompanied Colonel Redick McKee, U.S. Indian agent, on his expedition through northwestern California in the summer and fall of 1851. His journal of the expedition was published in Henry R. Schoolcraft, *Archives of Aboriginal Knowledge*, III, pp. 99 ff. *See* Schoolcraft. The journal, though not concerned with mining, is a valuable source for mining camps of the region. His manuscript map, showing the Trinity mines, is in the Indian Office, Washington, D.C. A copy is in the Bancroft Library (Wheat Collection), and a part of it was reproduced in Ernest de

Massey, *A Frenchman in the Gold Rush. See* Massey. His *Pacific Northwest Letters*, ed., Vernon Carstensen (Portland: Oregon Historical Society, 1954), include letters from the Forks of the Salmon, where he mined unsuccessfully in 1852.

Giffen. Guy J. Giffen, *California Gold* (n.p.n.d.). A brief resumé of the accounts of pre-Marshall gold discoveries in California. **Giffen File.** A card file of the gold mining bars in California, compiled by the late Mr. Giffen, is deposited in the Library of the Society of California Pioneers, San Francisco.

Giffen. Helen S. Giffen was a former librarian of the Society of California Pioneers, San Francisco. She is the author and editor of a number of books on California history, several of which deal with the Gold Rush. Among these is a compilation of *California Mining Newspapers, 1850–1880, a Bibliography* (Van Nuys, California: J. E. Reynolds, 1954) and an edition of *The Diaries of Peter Decker, Overland to California in 1849 and Life in the Mines, 1850–1851* (Georgetown, California: Talisman Press, 1966).

Gill. William Gill, *California Letters, Written in 1850 to his Wife Harriet Tarleton in Kentucky* (New York, 1922 ?). Includes the letters written from 1850–1851 while mining at Deer Creek, Trinidad, Weaverville, and Grass Valley.

Glasscock. Carl B. Glasscock, *A Golden Highway* (Indianapolis: Bobbs-Merrill, 1934). A popular account of the Gold Rush, based on personal interviews and sources listed by the author. *The Big Bonanza; the Story of the Comstock Lode* (Indianapolis: Bobbs-Merrill, 1931).

Goddard Maps. George H. Goddard, a native of England, emigrated to California in 1850 where he became a well known surveyor, civil engineer, and map maker. His famous 1857 map of California was published under the title *Britton and Rey's Map of the State of California* (San Francisco: Britton and Rey, 1857). Wheat, 302. It was the first map of the state based on actual surveys and the most accurate map published to that date. For the study of place names of the mining regions it is of greatest importance because of the detailed coverage. In 1969 a reproduction of the map was published as a keepsake of the Friends of the Bancroft Library, with a biographical sketch of the author written by Albert Shumate. *See also* Wheat, 302 for biographical information. Also cited in this dictionary is *Goddard's Map of a Survey of* the Mokelumne Hill Canal and a Reconnaissance of the Adjacent Country (San Francisco: Britton and Rey, 185?). Among other maps of sections of California made by him is a map of Fresno County, cited elsewhere. Goddard was associated with Whitney's Survey of the State of California, and in 1865 Mt. Goddard in the High Sierra was named in his honor by the Survey. Also an architect and artist by training, he designed the residential section South Park in San Francisco and made several sketches of San Francisco and a number of mining camps and towns, which were published as lithographs. Some of these were reproduced on illustrated letter sheets, popular among miners.

Goethe. Charles M. Goethe, *What's in a Name?* (Sacramento, 1949). Tales, historical and fictitious, about 111 California gold belt place names.

Gold Dust. Dust or gold dust used in the miners' jargon was not a fine powder or "dust" but was a general term for small particles of gold.

Golden Era. Published in San Francisco (Dec. 19, 1852–189-?). A weekly literary Sunday newspaper, which had a large circulation among the miners. Bancroft Library has a complete file for the years 1853–1867 and a broken file to March, 1893.

Gold Mines. *Gold Mines and Mining in California* (San Francisco: G. Spaulding, 1885). The book reviews the methods of mining and gives a list of the mining counties, with descriptions of their resources.

Gold Value. The value of gold in the early days was considered seventeen dollars, more or less, per ounce. An ounce a day per man was considered a good return. The official value was finally set at twenty-one dollars per ounce, which was raised in 1933 to thirty-five dollars per ounce.

Goodyear. Hal E. Goodyear, local historian of Trinity County and leader in the Conference of California Historical Societies. Mr. Goodyear furnished information on mining localities in Trinity County to the author of this dictionary.

Goodyear. W. A. Goodyear assisted Josiah D. Whitney in the exploration and survey of the gravel regions between the Mokelumne River and the North Fork of American River in the year 1871, and the results of his field work are published in Whitney's *The Auriferous Gravels of the Sierra Nevada*, 1879–1880. His route from

Georgetown northward to the North Fork of American River are shown on the sketch map opposite p. 82. His findings also contributed to the compilation of the *Map of the Tertiary Auriferous Gravel Deposits lying between the Middle Fork of the American and the Middle Yuba Rivers*, published in two parts to accompany *The Auriferous Gravels*. The same year, 1871, he covered the gravel regions, near the South Fork of American River, particularly around Placerville, and a sketch map of the distribution of the volcanic and gravel formations here appears opposite p. 98. The results of his exploration as far south as the Mokelumne are also described but not mapped. *See* Whitney Survey; Hoffmann; Pettee.

Grass Valley Directory. William S. Byrne, ed., *Directory of Grass Valley Township for 1865* (San Francisco, 1865).

Great Register. A list of the registered voters of a county. The older registers often give not only the name of the voter and his place of residence, but also his age, country, or state of nativity, date and place of naturalization, date of registration, and occupation.

Green. Alfred A. Green, "Life and Adventures of a 47er of California" (1878). A reminiscence dictated for H. H. Bancroft. MS in Bancroft Library. The author was in the mines on the Mokelumne River only briefly in the spring of 1850.

Greenwood. Robert Greenwood, publisher of Talisman Press, Georgetown, Calif., provided references and information from his newspaper files.

Gregson. James Gregson, "Statement" (1876). 11 p. MS in Bancroft Library. The author was working at Sutters Fort when Marshall brought the first gold from Sutters Mill. The Statement is also published in *CHSQ*, XIX, pp. 113–143, with Eliza M. Gregson's "Memoirs."

Grimshaw. William R. Grimshaw, *Narrative*, ed., J. R. K. Kantor (Sacramento: Sacramento Book Collectors Club, 1964). The manuscript of the account, written for H. H. Bancroft in 1872, covers the period of 1848–50 in the Sacramento area. Grimshaw was bookkeeper for Sam Brannan in Sacramento from the fall of 1848 to the fall of 1849, when he entered into partnership briefly with William Daylor on the Cosumnes. Bancroft considered his account one of the best of the period for the Sacramento area. Biographical notes on Jared Sheldon, William Daylor, and Perry McCoon are in the Manuscript Collection of Bancroft Library.

Ground Sluicing. Running or channeling water directly on the ground through a little ditch, into which cobblestones had been thrown as riffles to catch the gold. After the gravel or "dirt" was put through the ground sluice, it was generally "cleaned up" in a board sluice, or a long tom. *See also* Sluicing.

Grunsky. Clotilde Grunsky Taylor, " 'Dear Family', the Story of the Lives of Charles and Clotilde Grunsky, 1823–1891, as Revealed in Diaries and in Their Letters to Their Respective Families," trans., Carl Ewald Grunsky [their son] and Clotilde Grunsky Taylor [their granddaughter]. Reproduced from typescript (Berkeley, 1955). In Bancroft Library. Excerpts from early letters were translated by Charles E. Grunsky and published as Charles Grunsky, "Letters to his Wife," in *SCPQ*, X, pp. 9 ff. Grunsky, a native of Germany and well-known pioneer merchant of Stockton, came to California in 1849, mined briefly on the Mokelumne, had a store in Pleasant Springs, a freighting business to the mines, and later settled in Stockton.

Gudde. Erwin G. Gudde, *California Place Names, the Origin and Etymology of Current Geographical Names*, 3rd rev. ed. (Berkeley: University of California Press, 1969). The first edition appeared in 1949 as a contribution to the centennial celebrations of the state. The third revised edition includes a reference list to obsolete, alternate, and variant names mentioned in the text. References to *Bigler's Chronicle* refer to *Bigler's Chronicle of the West; the Conquest of California, Discovery of Gold, and Mormon Settlement as Reflected in Henry William Bigler's Diaries* (Berkeley: University of California Press, 1962). *See* Bigler. References to *Sutter's Own Story* refer to *Sutter's Own Story, the Life of General John Augustus Sutter and the History of New Helvetia in the Sacramento Valley* (New York: Putnam, 1936). *The Memoirs of Theodor Cordua*, ed., Erwin G. Gudde, were reprinted as a monograph from *CHSQ*, no. 4. *Exploring with Frémont: the Private Diaries of Charles Preuss, Cartographer for John C. Frémont on his First, Second, and Fourth Expeditions to the Far West*, trans. and ed. Erwin G. Gudde and Elisabeth K. Gudde, was published by the University of Oklahoma Press in 1958.

Guidebook. Olaf P. Jenkins, *Geologic Guidebook along Highway 49, Sierran Gold*

Belt; *The Mother Lode Country*, California, Division of Mines, *Bulletin*, no. 141 (San Francisco, 1948). Prepared for the centennial celebrations of the discovery of gold, this book with its many illustrations, geologic maps, and descriptions of mines, camps, and towns along the Mother Lode remains the standard guide to the region.

Guinn. James Miller Guinn, "Some California Place Names" in *HSSCP*, VII, part 1, pp. 39 ff. The author, an educator and historian, wrote a history of the state and several local histories.

Gulch. The American term, of uncertain origin, was used during the California gold mining period for any ravine, chasm, or canyon where gold was often discovered.

Gunn. Lewis C. Gunn and Elizabeth L. Gunn, *Records of a California Family: Journals and Letters* (San Diego, 1928). Anna Lee Marston has edited the journals of her father, 1849–1850, which covered the overland journey to California, several months of unsuccessful mining on Wood's Creek, and his practice as a physician in Jamestown and Sonora. His wife's letters continue the record of their sojourn in Sonora, 1851–61, where her husband later became part owner of the Sonora *Herald*.

HSSCP. *Historical Society of Southern California Annual Publication*, Los Angeles. V. 1–16 (1884–1934). **HSSCQ.** *Historical Society of Southern California Quarterly*. This is a continuation of the *Annual Publication* and is numbered v. 17–43 (1935–1961). The name was changed in 1962 to *Southern California Quarterly* and continues the numbering from v. 44 to date.

Haenszel. Arda Haenszel, a long-time resident and historian of San Bernardino County, has contributed extensively to the writing of both *California Place Names* and *California Gold Camps*. For many years she was active in the publication of *California Historical Landmarks*, issued by the California Department of Parks and Recreation.

Haight. Sarah (Haight) Tompkins, *The Ralston-Fry Wedding*, ed., Francis P. Farquhar (Berkeley: The Friends of the Bancroft Library, 1961). The diary of Miss Haight describes the wedding trip of William C. Ralston and Lizzie Fry to Yosemite Valley in May, 1858. The diarist was a member of the bridal party, all of whom had been invited to join the trip.

Hale. Edson D. Hale, *The County of San Ber-*

nardino (San Bernardino: The Board of Trade, 1888). A pamphlet outlining the resources of the city and county of San Bernardino.

Hale and Emory. C. P. Hale and Fred Emory, *Hale and Emory's Marysville City Directory* (Marysville, 1853). Includes a table of distances traversed by stage lines.

Haley. Charles S. Haley, *Gold Placers of California*, California State Mining Bureau, *Bulletin*, no. 92 (Sacramento, 1923). A good account of placer mining in the widest sense, with chapters on types of mining and explanation of mining terminology; locates principal lodes and districts. Contains good maps.

Hambly. David W. Hambly, "Autobiography" (ca. 1885). 120 p. MS in Bancroft Library. Recollections rewritten from diaries, including mining activities on the Feather River and other places in Plumas County in the early 1850s.

Hanna. Phil Townsend Hanna, *The Dictionary of California Land Names* (Los Angeles: Automobile Club of Southern California, 1946). Another edition, 1951. Contains current place names and some obsolete. No references to sources are given.

Hanson. William Hanson, "Letters" (1849–1852). 25 p. MS in Bancroft Library. The author mined near Mokelumne Hill.

Harris. Benjamin B. Harris, *The Gila Trail, the Texas Argonauts and the California Gold Rush*, ed., Richard H. Dillon (Norman: University of Oklahoma Press, 1960). A reminiscent account of the journey to California and experiences in the Southern Mines. The author is given to exaggeration in many instances.

Haskins. C. W. Haskins, *The Argonauts of California* (New York, 1890). A long reminiscent, yet important and apparently reliable account, especially in the first part of the book; in later chapters the author generalizes and tells many anecdotes. Chapters V–XII deal with early Placerville and vicinity. Names of many forty-niners are listed at the end of the book.

Hawley. David N. Hawley, "Hawley's Observations" (n.d.). MS in Bancroft Library. A dictation for H. H. Bancroft, including a brief account of quartz mining in Mariposa County.

Hayes Scrapbooks. References are to Benjamin I. Hayes, Scrapbooks: Mining. 13 vols. Part of a 130-volume set in the Bancroft Library. Benjamin I. Hayes, a prominent southern California attorney and member of the state legislature, came to California in 1850. His scrapbooks on mining are concerned chiefly with southern California. They consist for the most part of newspaper clippings between the 1850s and 1870s but contain also excerpts from official reports. The numbers of the sections are often difficult to find because of the way in which the volumes were bound. The Bancroft Library has a photocopy of Hayes, Emigrant Notes, in 5 volumes (San Diego, 1875). Only a small part relates to the mining scene in California.

Heckelman. O. F. Heckelman of Julian, California, furnished the author information on mining localities in San Diego County.

Heckendorn. J. Heckendorn and W. A. Wilson, *Miners and Business Men's Directory. For the Year Commencing January 1st, 1856. Embracing a General Directory of the Citizens of Tuolumne and Portions of Calaveras, Stanislaus and San Joaquin Counties. Together with the Mining Laws of Each District, a Description of the Different Camps, and Other Interesting Statistical Matter* (Columbia, Calif., 1856). Contains names of many places, with only few errors.

Helper. Hinton R. Helper, *The Land of Gold* (Baltimore, 1855). An informative, highly critical account, stressing the shady side of the mining scene. Contains nothing for gold geography except a list (p. 151) of fanciful names of bars and settlements, almost all of which are confirmed by other sources.

Herbert. "Noblet Herbert to Mrs. John Augustine Washington," ed., John A. Washington, in *CHSQ*, XXIX, pp. 297 ff. The letter, dated December 27, 1850, describes his experiences in the region around Onion Valley. Herbert's party was one of the first to mine there in the wake of the Gold Lake hunt.

Hill. James B. Hill, *In the Gold Mines in '50, '51, and '52.* El Dorado County Historical Society, Publication no. 3 (Coloma, 1966).

Hill. James H. Hill, *Historical Summary of Gold, Silver, Copper, Lead, and Zinc Produced in California, 1848–1926* (Washington: U. S. Bureau of Mines, Economic Paper, no. 3, 1929).

Hinkle. George Hinkle, *Sierra Nevada Lakes* (New York: Bobbs-Merrill, 1949). Useful with reference to a study of Gold Lake.

Historical Society of Southern California. *See HSSCP* and *HSSCQ*.

Historic Landmark. *See California Historical Landmarks*.

Hittell. John S. Hittell and his brother Theodore H. Hittell were important figures in California historiography. John Hittell came to California in 1849, spent the winter of 1849–1850 in the mines, served twenty-five years on the staff of *Alta California*, was a member of the state legislature and the author of numerous books. **Hittell Clippings** refers to Hittell's Scraps, vol. 3, "Mining Scraps." The set of scrapbooks is in Bancroft Library. **Hittell, Mining** refers to his *Mining in the Pacific States* (San Francisco: H. H. Bancroft, 1861), an important treatise, including explanations of mining terms. **Hittell, Resources** refers to his *Resources of California* (San Francisco: A. Roman, 1874), a popular book of the 1860s and 70s which appeared in seven editions, contains an excellent chapter on mining and one on topographical names, including a list of curious names of mining localities. References are to the 6th edition. **Hittell's List** or **Roster** refers to "Table Showing Fineness of California Gold," compiled from notes of John S. Hittell, *in* California, State Mining Bureau, 4th Annual *Report*, 1884, pp. 219 ff. Places are arranged by counties in two sections: Placer Mines and Quartz Mines. Theodore H. Hittell joined his brother John in California in 1855. A lawyer by profession, he was best known for his excellent history of California, which appeared in several editions. References are to his *History of California*, 4 vols. (San Francisco: N. J. Stone, 1897–1898) cited as **Hittell, History.**

Hodge. Frederick Webb Hodge, ed., *Handbook of American Indians* (Smithsonian Institution, Bureau of American Ethnology, *Bulletin* no. 30, Washington, D.C., 1907–1910). Citations are to the 2-volume edition, 1912. The monumental authority on Indians north of Mexico.

Hodges. Orlando J. Hodges, "Prospecting on the Pacific Coast" in *CHSQ*, XXXIII, pp. 49 ff. A short but interesting account of mining in the Northern Mines between 1848 and 1851.

Hoffmann. Charles F. Hoffmann, native of Frankfurt am Main, Germany, was chief topographer of the Geological Survey of California, 1860–1874, cited in the text as **Whitney Survey.** His **Topographical Map of Central California, 1873,** which includes also a part of Nevada, is a detailed and reliable map, but unfortunately was not entirely finished when the Survey was discontinued. The Southern Section only was published, in two parts, and the Northern Section, also in two parts, exists only as a sketch map, a copy of which is in

Bancroft Library. **Hoffmann-Craven Gravel Map, 1873.** *Map of the Tertiary Auriferous Gravel Deposits lying between the Middle Fork of the American and the Middle Yuba Rivers*, 1873, compiled by Hoffmann and his assistant A. Craven on the basis of the surveys of Amos Bowman, W. H. Pettee, and W. A. Goodyear, supplemented by surveys made by Hoffmann, particularly in the important gravel region between the South and Middle Yuba. This map, also called the **Great Gravel Map,** was published in two parts, to accompany Whitney's *The Auriferous Gravels of the Sierra Nevada*, 1879–1880. *See* Pettee; Goodyear. The official map of the Whitney Survey and for many years the best map of the State of California, entitled *Map of California and Nevada*, was drawn by F. von Leicht and A. Craven, revised by Hoffmann and Craven in 1874 and published by the University of California. *See* Whitney Survey.

Holley. C. A. Holley. "Letter" (1853). *In* "California Gold Rush Letters," Bancroft Library.

Holmes. Roberta E. Holmes, *The Southern Mines; Early Development of the Sonora Mining Region* (San Francisco: Grabhorn Press, 1930). An account of the development of the area, with a chapter on the author's visit to the diggings in 1925 and "statements" of pioneer residents of Columbia and Sonora.

Hoover. *See* Rensch.

Hoppe. J. Hoppe, *Californiens Gegenwart und Zukunft* (Berlin, 1849). Included in the author's treatise on California and its future is an article of Professor A. Erman, in which he refers to an entry in his diary written in San Francisco on December 8, 1829, expressing the opinion that gold might well be found in California.

Humboldt County Map, 1865. A. J. Doolittle, *Official Map of Humboldt County* (San Francisco: G. T. Brown, 1865).

Hunt. George Lundy Hunt, "Letters and Diary" (1867). 3 vols. MS in Bancroft Library. Vol. 1 contains typescript of a diary, January–November, 1867, written at Campo Seco, Calaveras County, describing life in the mines.

Huntley. Sir Henry V. Huntley, *California, its Gold and its Inhabitants*, (London, 1856), 2 vols. The account was also published as *Adventures in California*, 2 vols. Based on the author's journal of 1852 while representing an English mining company in the Northern Mines. It contains some good information, though the style of writing is somewhat confusing. Huntley had been in California in 1850 as chief superintendent of the Anglo-California Gold Mining Company and his report on the Mariposa district is printed in the Rocky-Bar Mining Company *Report*, 1851, pp. 11 ff.

Hurdy-Gurdy Wheel. A popular contraption in gold mining. The wheel was operated by the impact of water directly on the paddles. The miners' term hurdy-gurdy girls for a certain class of females was probably derived from it.

Hutchings. James Mason Hutchings. "Diaries" (May, 1848–October 1849 and 1855). 351 p. Photocopy of typed transcripts in Bancroft Library. Original diaries in the Library of Congress. After losing several years' earnings "in the diggings" through a bank failure, Hutchings embarked on a tour of the gold region selling stationery in the form of illustrated letter sheets to the miners. His diary of 1855 includes the distances between the camps he visited and also a list of California towns in 1855. Also included are copies of two letters written from "Hangtown," December 19, 1849, February 15, 1850, and one from Weaver Creek, April 4, 1851. After leaving the mines Hutchings published the popular *Hutchings' Illustrated California Magazine*, 1856–1861. A series of articles entitled "Mining for Gold in California," describing methods of mining and containing beautiful, clearcut illustrations, appears in the issues of July, September, and October, 1857. Reprinted in *Mining Bureau*, XLV, supplement. *See Miners' Own Book.* **Hutchings California Scenes.** A Hutchings' illustrated letter sheet with the subtitle "Methods of Mining" (Baird, p. 107), lists on the margin the names of 64 mining localities.

Hutchings California Magazine. *See* Hutchings.

Hydraulic Mining. A California gold mining term for breaking down banks of gold-bearing gravel by the application of strong streams of water with a hose or iron pipe. This type of mining (often spelled "hydraulick") was used from 1853, when a nozzle was first attached to a hose, until the 1880s, when it was prohibited by law in many sections of the gold region. *See* Sawyer Decision. *See also* American Hill, Buckeye Hill [Nevada]; Yankee Jims in text. A good early illustration of hydraulic mining and ground sluicing may be found in *Hutchings' California Magazine*, July 1857, and in the *Miners Own Book*.

Illustrated Letter Sheets. Stationery with illustrations, many of which are reproductions of drawings of California mining scenes made by well-known artists of the day. They were popular among miners who found it hard to write long letters to the "folks back home." J. M. Hutchings, later editor of *Hutchings Illustrated California Magazine*, traveled throughout the mining regions for a number of years selling his editions of letter sheets. A bibliography entitled *California's Pictorial Letter Sheets, 1849–1869*, compiled by Joseph A. Baird and published by David Magee (San Francisco, 1967), describes and locates copies of the letter sheets, all of which have become collectors' items. Baird's *Bibliograph* includes reproductions of selected sheets and indices of subjects and titles, artists, engravers, lithographers, publishers, etc.

Indian Report. 33rd Cong., spec. sess. (1853). Senate, Executive doc. no. 4. A lengthy report of the Secretary of the Interior, including correspondence from Indian agents and commissioners from California. **Indian Report** with the year added refers to the annual publications of the Commissioner of Indian Affairs.

Inyo County Map, 1884. J. B. Treadwell, *Map of the County of Inyo, State of California* (n.p.: 1884).

Jackson, Alfred T. *See* Canfield.

Jackson. Joseph Henry Jackson, *Anybodys Gold* (New York: Appleton-Century, 1941). Written for the general reader; based on sound research.

Jackson. Stephen Jackson, "Letters" (1849–1867). 15 letters. MS in Bancroft Library. Written mainly from Yuba and Nevada counties.

Jackson. W. Turrentine Jackson, *A History of Mining in the Plumas Eureka State Park Area, 1890–1943*. Professor Jackson's report prepared for the California Division of Beaches and Parks is available as *Publication*, no. 10 (November 1, 1962) of the Plumas County Historical Society.

Jackson's Map, 1850. William A. Jackson, *Map of the Mining District of California* (New York: Lambert & Lane, Lith., 1850), with a 12-page descriptive "appendix," dated Dec., 1849. Wheat, 161. In 1936 the Grabhorn Press, San Francisco, reproduced the map with the appendix for Thomas W. Norris. It records the impor-

tant mining camps and towns of 1849 and early 1850 and is important for any study of the mining region. *See* Ellis.

Janssens. Agustín Janssens, "Vida y Aventuras." MS in Bancroft Library. This account includes his two months unsuccessful mining experiences on the Stanislaus River. It was translated and edited by William H. Ellison and Francis Price under the title *Life and Adventures in California of Don Agustín* (San Marino, Calif.: Huntington Library, 1953).

Jarves Map, 1849. James J. Jarves, *A Correct Map of the Bay of San Francisco and the Gold Region* (Boston: James Munro, 1849). Wheat, 100. The "diggings" on the rivers from the Tuolumne to the Yuba and Feather rivers are indicated but generally not named on this early map.

Jayhawker Party. One of the parties of gold seekers who crossed Death Valley in 1849 and who are directly or indirectly responsible for a number of place names in the region. *See* John G. Ellenbecker, *The Jayhawkers of Death Valley* (1938); and Carl Wheat, in *HSSCQ*, pp. 102 ff.

Jerrett. Herman D. Jerrett, *Hills of Gold* (Sacramento, The Author, 1963). The book includes accounts of mining localities in El Dorado County.

Jewett. George E. Jewett, "Journal" (1849–1850). 30 p. Microfilm and typescript in Bancroft Library; original in private possession. The diary covers the overland journey in 1849 and experiences in the Southern Mines, particularly around Columbia and Sonora.

Jewett. William S. Jewett, "Some Letters of William S. Jewett, California Artist" in *CHSQ*, XXIII, pp. 149 ff. Jewett, a portrait painter, came to San Francisco in 1849. Among his paintings is a full length portrait of Sutter. A selection of his letters relating to his California experience is edited by Elliot Evans.

Johnson. George Johnson, "Notes, Reminiscences, etc." (1849–1942). 25 folders, 4 scrapbooks. MS in Bancroft Library. Contains an account of mining in El Dorado County, especially the Coloma area.

Johnson. Joe William Johnson, "Early Engineering Center in California" in *CHSQ*, XXIX, pp. 193 ff. An interesting article on water supply and the hydraulic process in mining days.

Johnson. Russ and Anne Johnson, *The Ghost Town of Bodie, a California State Park* (Bishop, California: Chalfant Press, 1967). The book contains excerpts from contemporary newspapers and many excellent pictures.

Johnson. Theodore T. Johnson. *Sights in the Gold Region, and Scenes by the Way* (New York, 1849). The author was in the mines in the vicinity of Coloma in the summer of 1849. His interesting account was the first authentic personal record of mining experiences to be published. The second edition (New York, 1850) with the same title, and the third, *California and Oregon; or, Sights in the Gold Region* (Philadelphia, 1851), repeat the contents of the first with some additions. Included is a map purported to be "From the actual survey by direction of Com. Jones, 1849" (!), which appears to be derived from Ord's map of 1848 (*see* Mason Report and Ord) with a number of localities that do not appear on Ord. The book was repeatedly issued until 1865. Citations are from the third, 1851, edition.

Johnston. Philip Johnston, *Lost and Living Cities of the California Gold Rush* (Los Angeles: Automobile Club of Southern California, 1948). A popular, interesting, and sound booklet on the Gold Rush. The author has written a number of articles for *Touring Topics*, including "Relics of the Gold Rush" (January 1932).

Johnston, Wade H. Effie E. Johnston, "Wade H. Johnston Talks to his Daughter." In *Las Calaveras*, April 1969. Reminiscences of Johnston's overland journey in 1854 and experiences in Placer and Calaveras counties.

Jolly. John Jolly, *Gold Spring Diary*, ed., Carlo M. De Ferrari (Sonora: Tuolumne County Historical Society, 1966). The diarist, who came to the Southern Mines directly from England in 1849, gives an account of his mining interests in the Gold Hill-Columbia area between April 12, 1854, and July 27, 1855. It is meticulously edited and annotated by De Ferrari, editor of Stoddart's *Annals of Tuolumne County*.

Jordan. Rudolph Jordan, "An Autobiography" in *Society of California Pioneers Quarterly*, IV, no. 4, pp. 174 ff. Written by a German who came to California when he heard about the discovery of gold while working in Cuba as a daguerrotypist. Unfortunately only one mining episode in California, at Jackass Gulch, is described.

Judah's Map, 1854. Theodore D. Judah, *Map of the Sacramento Valley Railroad from the City of Sacramento to the Crossing of American River at Negro Bar* (San Francisco: B. F. Butler's Lith., 1854). Judah was the chief engineer; later he located the Central Pacific across the Sierra Nevada. The map accompanies **Judah's Report, 1854,** published as Sacramento Valley Railroad, *Report of the Chief Engineer on the Preliminary Surveys and Future Business of the Sacramento Valley Railroad* (Sacramento, 1854). **Judah's Map of Folsom, 1855.** *Map of Folsom* (San Francisco: Lith., F. Kuhl, 1855).

Julihn. C. E. Julihn and F. W. Horton, *Mines of the Southern Mother Lode*. Part 1, Calaveras County; Part II, Tuolumne and Mariposa County (U.S. Bureau of Mines, *Bulletin*, 413 and 424). Washington, D.C., 1938 and 1940.

Jump. "Jumping a claim" was a California term for taking possession of a claim that was supposed or appeared to be abandoned.

Justesen. Peter Justesen, *Two Years' Adventures of a Dane in the California Gold Mines* (Gloucester, 1865). A good account of the mines around Sonora, 1850–51, written by a Danish seaman.

Kahn. Edgar M. Kahn, "Andrew Smith Hallidie," in *CHSQ*, XIX, pp. 144 ff. Hallidie mined in various localities in California between 1852 and 1857 and began the manufacture of wire rope at American Bar, near Gray Eagle Bar. This led to his construction of numerous suspension bridges and later the creation of San Francisco's cable railway system.

Keddie's Map. Arthur W. Keddie, *Map of Plumas County* (Quincy ?, 1892).

Keeler's Map, ca. 1884. J. M. Keeler, *Mining Map of Inyo County* (San Francisco, 1884?). Photostat in Bancroft Library.

Kemble. Edward C. Kemble, *A History of California Newspapers, 1846–1858*, ed., Helen Bretnor (Los Gatos: Talisman Press, 1962). Originally published in Sacramento *Union*, Dec. 25, 1858. The 1927 edition (New York: Plandome Press) was edited by Douglas C. McMurtrie. An invaluable reference work.

Kenny. William R. Kenny, "History of the Sonora Mining Region," Ph.D. diss., University of California, Berkeley, 1955.

Kent. George F. Kent, "Life in California in 1849," ed., John Walton Caughey, in *CHSQ*, XX, pp. 26 ff. Kent came to California in 1849 via Cape Horn. His impressions of San Francisco and Sacramento and his experiences in mining near Shingle Springs are given in his journal, the original MS of which is in Huntington Library.

Kern County History. *See* Comfort.

Kern County Map, 1875. *Official Map of Kern County* (San Francisco: Britton, Rey, 1875).

King, Clarence. *See* Whitney Survey.

King. Thomas Butler King, *Report on California*, in U.S., 31st Congress, 1st Sess., House, Executive Doc. 59. King's report of March 22, 1850, as special agent to California, was reprinted as *California, the Wonder of the Age* (New York, 1850) and later also in the appendix to Bayard Taylor's *El Dorado*. It includes a survey of the extent and future of California's gold mining with a proposal to tax miners and to exclude foreigners; also a recommendation to establish a mint in California. King was U.S. Collector of Customs in San Francisco.

Kinyon. Edmund Kinyon, *The Northern Mines; Factual Narratives of the Counties of Nevada, Placer, Sierra, Yuba, and Portions of Plumas and Butte* (Grass Valley, Nevada City: The Union Publishing Company, 1949). A gathering of feature stories written by Edmund Kinyon, well known local historian and journalist, long associated with the *Daily Union* of Grass Valley and Nevada City.

Kip. Leonard Kip, *California Sketches, with Recollections of the Gold Mines* (Albany, N.Y., 1850). The author, a younger brother of William Ingraham Kip, bishop of California, gives a dismal picture of the California mining scene, based on his brief experiences on the Mokelumne River.

Kirkpatrick. Charles A. Kirkpatrick, "Journal" (1849). MS in Bancroft Library. The journal covers the overland trip and is followed by an account of mining experiences in the Southern Mines, ending with his arrival at Fine Gold Gulch in Tulare County.

Knapp. W. Augustus Knapp, "An Old Californian's Pioneer Story" in *Overland Monthly* (ser. 2, X, 1887). Knapp was in various parts of the Mother Lode and in the Trinity mines. Almost forty years later he wrote a very interesting account, which to be sure, contains some mistakes and obvious exaggerations.

Knave. "The Knave" is a section devoted to local history published in the Sunday edition of the Oakland *Tribune*. For many years it was ably edited by the late Ad Schuster, whose work is continued by Leonard Verbarg. John Winkley, Henry Mauldin, and other local historians have made valuable contributions.

Knights Scrapbooks. Scrapbooks compiled primarily for the *Handbook Almanac for the Pacific States*, edited by W. H. Knight and published by H. H. Bancroft, 1862–1864. 40 vols. MS in Bancroft Library. These scrapbooks were formerly cited as Bancroft Scrapbooks but have been re-catalogued as Knights Scrapbooks.

Knoche. Johann E. Knoche, "Autobiography," in *SCPQ*, II, pp. 215 ff. Knoche and a party of four other Germans mined unsuccessfully in the Mariposa mines in the summer of 1850. He gives a brief, factual account.

Knopf. Adolph Knopf, *The Mother Lode System of California*, U.S. Geological Survey, Papers, no. 157 (1929).

La Fuze. Pauliena B. La Fuze, *Saga of the San Bernardinos* (Bloomington, Calif.: San Bernardino County Museum Association, 1971). 2 vols. A detailed well-documented history of the San Bernardino Mountains, based on contemporary newspapers, county records, and diaries and reminiscences of local pioneers.

Lang. *See* Tuolumne County History.

Lapham and Taylor's Map, 1856. California Register and Statistical Reporter, *Map of the State of California* (San Francisco: Lapham and Taylor, 1856).

Lardner. *See* Placer County History, 1924.

Larkin Papers. Thomas Oliver Larkin, *The Larkin Papers, Personal, Business, and Official Correspondence of Thomas Oliver Larkin, Merchant and United States Consul in California*, ed., George P. Hammond, 10 vols. and index (Berkeley: University of California, 1951–1964). The original papers are in the Bancroft Library. The printed volumes are arranged chronologically, with the Gold Rush years represented in volumes VII–IX. *See* Mason Report.

Las Calaveras, San Andreas. V. 1 (Oct. 1952)– . Quarterly publication of the Calaveras County Historical Society, originally issued as *Historical Bulletin*.

Lascy. A. Lascy, "Reminiscences" (n.d.). 50 p. MS in Bancroft Library. The author gives a very good retrospective account of gold mining in Calaveras County around 1850.

Las Mariposas Map, 1861. Sarony, Major, & Knapp, lithographers, in *Las Mariposas Estate, Mariposa County, California* (New York: Sarony, Major, & Knapp, 1861). Published with *The Mariposa Estate, its Past, Present and Future* (New York, 1868);

appeared previously in *The Mariposa Estate* (London, 1861).

Lassen County History, 1882: *Illustrated History of Plumas, Lassen and Sierra Counties* (San Francisco: Fariss & Smith, 1882).

Lead or Ledge. A miners' term used for lode or vein.

Leadabrand. Russ Leadabrand, *A Guidebook to the San Bernardino Mountains of California, including Lake Arrowhead and Big Bear* (Los Angeles: Ward, Ritchie Press, 1961).

Lecouvreur. Frank Lecouvreur, *From East Prussia to the Golden Gate*, trans., Julius C. Behnke (New York, 1906). Lecouvreur, an educated East Prussian, who settled in Southern California, mined on the Yuba River and Nelson Creek in 1852. He gives an excellent account in his journal and letters, edited for publication by his widow, Josephine Rosana Lecouvreur.

Leeper. David Rohrer Leeper, *The Argonauts of 'Forty-Nine'* (South Bend, Indiana, 1894). A delightful account of a "floating" miner, especially interesting for El Dorado and Trinity county mines. Published with many, somewhat primitive illustrations.

Leonard. Albert Leonard, "Statement to h. h. Bancroft" (1888). 9 p. MS in Bancroft Library. The author came to California in 1849 and recounts his unsuccessful experience in the mines, mainly in Amador County, and of life in Sacramento City.

Letts. John M. Letts, *California Illustrated; Including a Description of the Panama and Nicaragua Routes* (New York, 1852). Also published under the title *A Pictorial View of California* (New York, 1853). Letts mined between July and November, 1849, in the bars along American River and its tributaries, and he devotes twelve chapters to his experiences.

Level. The horizontal passage or drift into or in a mine.

Lindgren. Waldemar Lindgren, *The Tertiary Gravels of the Sierra Nevada of California* U.S. Geological Survey, Washington, D.C.: Professional Paper, no. 73, 1911.) *The Gold-Quartz Veins of Nevada City and Grass Valley Districts, California* (Washington, D.C.: Extract from U. S. Geological Survey, *Report*, XVII, Part 2, 1896.)

Little. John T. Little, "Statement of Events in the First Years of American Occupation of California" (1878). 16 p. MS in Bancroft Library. Recorded for H. H. Bancroft. Little came to California in 1849, went to the mines, and became a merchant in Coloma and also its postmaster.

Lode. As opposed to a placer deposit, it refers to quartz or other rock in place, which may contain gold. Early miners used the term lode, lead, and vein indiscriminately.

Logan. Clarence A. Logan, *Mother Lode Gold Belt of California*, California, Division of Mines, *Bulletin* 108 (Sacramento, 1934). The mines are listed and described by counties, accompanied by geological and claim maps.

Long and Montgomery's Map. Long and Montgomery, *Map of the Route of the South Feather Water Company's Main and Lateral Ditches* (n.p.: 186?). From Oroville and the junction of North and South Honcut creeks to La Porte, Butte County.

Long Tom. A trough twelve or more feet long, two feet wide at the upper end, and three feet at the lower. At least two men were required to work it. The tom replaced the shorter rocker or cradle as a gold washing device and was widely used until the sluice box and other inventions replaced it. A good illustration is found in *Hutchings' California Magazine*, July 1857, p. 6.

Loose. Warren Loose, *Bodie Bonanza, the True Story of a Flamboyant Past* (New York: Exposition Press, 1971). A detailed account based on contemporary newspaper stories.

Luddy. William Luddy, "Reminiscences of Hardscrabble," in *Scott Valley Advance* August 20, 1900.

Lund. Handel Lund, "Diary," March 18–July 1852. 22 p. Also transcripts of letters datelined Murphys, early in 1853. Microfilm in Bancroft Library.

Lyman. Albert Lyman, *Journal of a Voyage to California and Life in the Gold Diggings* (Hartford, Conn., 1852). A fine account of the Connecticut Mining and Trading Company that worked at Mormon Island and Salmon Falls.

Lyman. Chester S. Lyman, *Around the Horn to the Sandwich Islands and California, 1845–1850*, ed., Frederick J. Teggart (New Haven: Yale University Press, 1924). Extracts of the Journal, 1848–1849, were published as "The Gold Rush" in *CHSQ*, II, pp. 181 ff. Lyman interrupted his work as a surveyor in California with a two months' interval in the diggings around Weberville in July and August 1848 and a brief experience in the fall as trader of goods in the Southern Mines. He later became a professor at Yale University.

Lyman. George D. Lyman, *John Marsh, Pioneer; the Life-Story of a Trail Blazer on Six Frontiers* (New York: Scribners, 1931). John Marsh, noted California pioneer of 1836 and grantee of Los Meganos in Contra Costa County, mined on the Yuba River as early as May, 1848, where he located the diggings at the place later known as Parks Bar.

MacBoyle. Errol MacBoyle, *Mines and Mineral Resources of Nevada County* (San Francisco: California State Mining Bureau, 1918). Lists and describes the mines. Similar reports were issued for Plumas County and Sierra County.

McCall. A. J. McCall, *Pick and Pan: Trip to the Diggings in 1849* (Bath, N. Y., 1883). One of the finest accounts, modest and unpretentious; written by an educated New Yorker. The diggings described were on the upper Yuba in 1849.

McChristian. Pat McChristian, "Statement" (1875?). 11 p. MS in Bancroft Library. Mining experiences on the Yuba are described.

M'Collum. William M'Collum, *California as I Saw it; Pencillings by the Way of its Gold Diggers and Incidents of Land and Water*, ed., Dale L. Morgan (Los Gatos: Talisman Press, 1960). A contemporary account, originally published in 1850, of his experiences during his journey to California, January 28, 1849 to February 15, 1850, including his five-week stay in the Southern Mines and a brief later attempt at mining on the South Fork of American River.

McDiarmid. Finley McDiarmid. "Letters" 1850–1851. Portfolio. MS in Bancroft Library. The letters were written to his wife on the overland journey and from the gold fields, mainly of El Dorado County.

McFarlane. Andrew McFarlane, "Letters" (1851; 1855). MS in Bancroft Library *in* "California Gold Rush Letters." The letters were written from Mariposa County.

McGowan. Joseph A. McGowan, professor of history, California State University at Sacramento, and Norman Wilson, Interpretative Services, California State Department of Parks and Recreation, contributed information to the author on gold mining localities in Sacramento County.

McGrath. Hugh McGrath, "Correspondence" (1850–1873). 14 folders. MS in Bancroft Library. Contains letters from friends in various mining camps in California.

McIlhany. Edward W. McIlhany, *Recollections of a '49er* (Kansas City, 1908). The author was not a miner but a shrewd, successful trader, operating mainly between Grass Valley and northernmost mines. His

account is somewhat rambling and disjointed, but he gives good information on Onion Valley, Bidwell's Bar, and Little Grass Valley.

McIsaac. Angus McIsaac, "A Journal and Diary, Southern Mines" (1852–1853). Typescript. 35 p. From the papers of C. Grant Loomis in Bancroft Library; location of original MS not known. It is a well written journal written between December 5, 1852 and March 31, 1853, while mining on Mariposa Creek, near the town of Mariposa.

Mack. Effie Mona Mack, *Mark Twain in Nevada* (New York: Scribner's, 1947).

McKeeby. Lemuel C. McKeeby, "The Memoirs of Lemuel Clarke McKeeby" in *CHSQ*, III, pp. 45 ff.; 126 ff. A good account of a lawyer who was one of the few persistent and successful miners, from 1851 to 1867. He was in the region between the Middle and South forks of the Yuba River, at French Corral and Sebastopol.

McKevitt. Jerry McKevitt, "Gold Lake Myth Brought Civilization to Plumas County" in *Journal of the West*, III, pp. 489 ff. The story of the Gold Lake hunt is told here and the subsequent establishment of mining camps on the Middle Fork of Feather River and its tributaries, and on the North Fork of Feather River.

McKinstry. Byron N. McKinstry, "California Gold Rush Diary" (1850–1852). 193 p. Microfilm of MS in Bancroft Library. Contains a description of mining, experiences mainly in the vicinities of Placerville and Mokelumne Hill.

McLean. Daniel McLean, "Letters" (1855–1856). Portfolio. MS in Bancroft Library. The letters are written from Pike City, Sierra County.

McNeil. Samuel McNeil, *McNeil's Travels in 1849, to, through and from the Gold Regions in California* (Columbus, 1850). A plain account by a shoemaker from Lancaster, Pennsylvania, who returned home as soon as he had made a modest sum. His travels in the gold regions took him from the Stanislaus to the Trinity rivers.

Maitland. Edward Maitland. *See* Ainslie.

Mansfield. George C. Mansfield, *The Feather River in '49 and the Fifties* (Oroville, 1924). Interesting stories but little originality.

Marin County History, 1880. *History of Marin County, California* (San Francisco: Alley, Bowen, 1880).

Mariposa Reminiscences. An oral history interview conducted by Corinne Gilb. University of California, Berkeley. 1954.

MS in Bancroft Library. Recollections of "old-timers" of the early days of the Mariposa area, to be used with utmost care.

Marks. Bernhard Marks, "*A California Pioneer; the Letters of Bernhard Marks to Jacob Solis-Cohen* (1853–1857) (Baltimore, 1954). Reprinted from *Publication of the American Jewish Historical Society*, XLIV, no. 1. Concerns mainly Placerville and Cold Springs area.

Marriage Records. Daughters of the American Revolution, California, Peralta Chapter, California Mother Lode Records, 3 vols. in 2. (San Leandro, 1962–63). Vols. 1–2 include records of marriages, births, and deaths in San Andreas, Calaveras County.

Marryat. Frank S. Marryat, *Mountains and Molehills; or, Recollections of a Burnt Journal* (London, 1855). Marryat, an intelligent Englishman, visited the Northern Mines briefly in July, 1851, and in the fall he engaged in quartz mining in the vicinity of Tuttletown in Tuolumne County. His interesting and entertaining account was repeatedly reprinted. The London edition has beautiful illustrations by the author; eight are colored plates and eighteen are woodcuts.

Marsh. *See* Lyman, George D.

Marshall. George A. Marshall, "Mother Lode Memoir: Reminiscences." Ed., Richard Dillon. In *Journal of the West*, III, pp. 355 ff. Marshall was born in Hornitos, California, in 1881, and spent many years in San Francisco, mainly in the U.S. Customs Office, where he became the Collector of Customs in 1940. His forebears located the Whitlock Mine on Sherlock Creek, northeast of Mariposa, and they were among the first to engage in quartz mining in the state. They also mined at other places in Mariposa County — the Princeton Mine, the Washington Mine near Hornitos, Mount Gaines Mine, Red Cloud Mine above Coulterville, and finally they settled in Hornitos.

Marshall. "James Marshall's Own Account of the Discovery of Gold in California" *in* Valeska Bari's compilation *The Course of Empire; First Hand Accounts of California in the Days of the Gold Rush of '49* (New York: Coward-McCann, 1931.) For the biography of James Marshall, *see* Theressa Gay.

Marston. *See* Gunn.

Martin. John Martin, "Data regarding Trinity County" (1888). 5 p. Typescript in Bancroft Library. Included is information on the founding of Weaverville.

Marysville Directory. **1853:** *See* Hale and Emory. **1856–1858:** *See* Amy's *Marysville Directory.*

Mason Report. Published in U.S., 30th Congress, 2nd sess., House, Executive Document no. 1, to accompany President Polk's Message to Congress of December 5, 1848. It is the famous report of Colonel Richard B. Mason, military governor of California, to the War Department, dated August 17, 1848, reporting his visit to the mines in July (Congressional Serial Set no. 537). With his report are three topographical sketches or maps. One is entitled *Positions of the Upper and Lower Gold Mines on the South Fork of the American River, California, July 20th, 1848*. Wheat, 51. The numbers on this sketch correspond to the labels on the gold specimens which accompanied Mason's report. The other two sketches or maps are printed on a single page, entitled *Upper Mines and Lower Mines or Mormon Diggings*. Wheat, 52. Also published in this volume is an extract of Larkin's letter of June 1, 1848, announcing the discovery of gold, and E. O. C. Ord's *Topographical Sketch of the Gold and Quicksilver District of California, July 25th, 1848*.

Massey. Ernest de Massey, *A Frenchman in the Gold Rush*, trans., Marguerite Eyer Wilbur. Special Publication, no. 2 (San Francisco: California Historical Society, 1927). Also published in installments in *CHSQ*, V–VI: 1. Massey, a member of the French nobility, migrated to California in 1849 and returned to France in 1857. His letters to his family describe his experiences as merchant and book dealer in San Francisco and his unsuccessful venture at mining on the Trinity and Klamath rivers in the summer of 1850. His journal is an almost classical account, especially of Big Bar and vicinity.

Maule. William M. Maule, "A Contribution to the Geographic and Economic History of Carson, Walker and Mono Basins in Nevada and California." Mimeographed (San Francisco: California Region, U.S. Forest Service, 1938). An excellent study with good maps. Mr. Maule supplied some information directly.

May. Ernest R. May, "Benjamin Park Avery", in *CHSQ*, XXX, pp. 125 ff. Avery, who started as a miner in 1849, became editor and publisher of North San Juan's *Hydraulic Press* and the Marysville *Appeal*, an editor of the San Francisco *Bulletin*, and editor of the *Overland Monthly* succeeding Bret Harte. He also served as state printer and later was appointed minister to China.

May. Philip R. May, *On the Mother Lode* (Christchurch, New Zealand: University of Canterbury, 1971). The author traces the use of the widely used term, giving the various definitions and applications as found in California gold literature. *Origins of Hydraulic Mining in California* (Oakland, Calif.: Holmes Book Company, 1970). A well-documented discussion of the early development of this method of mining in California, stressing the contributions of Anthony Chabot and Edward E. Matteson.

Maynard. Glyde Maynard, "Development of of San Antonio Canyon." In *Pomona Valley Historian* I, pp. 33 ff., 73 ff., 125 ff.

Meek. William Bull Meek, "Reminiscences" (*ca.* 1915). Typescript in Bancroft Library. As the son of a merchant in Camptonville, the author became well acquainted with the mining region in Yuba and Sierra counties on his "delivery route" during his youth and later, 1878 to 1914, as a stage driver. His reminiscences were written at the age of sixty-two and contain much firsthand information about the stage routes, particularly between Marysville and Downieville.

Merced Mining Company, San Francisco. *Annual Report*, 1852. Report of the Committee of Investigation on the affairs of the Company at Mount Ophir.

Merriam. J. Chester Merriam, "Bars on the Yuba River" (Marysville: City Library, 1951), Mimeographed. Listed are bars, with locations and brief descriptions; some quartz mines are also listed.

Merriam File. C. Hart Merriam, "Correspondence and Papers" (1874–ca. 1938). 2 cartons. MS in Bancroft Library. Among the papers is an extensive California place name file, which includes mining localities. Merriam was a well-known biologist and ethnologist, and for many years he was chairman of the U.S. Board on Geographic Names.

Metlar. George W. Metlar, *Northern California. Scott & Klamath Rivers; Their Inhabitants and Characteristics . . . By a Practical Miner* (Yreka, 1856). Preceding the text of the pamphlet is a letter containing a list of mining camps in the region.

Mill. Unless otherwise stated, a mill in gold mining consisted of a number of pestles or stamps used in crushing rock to obtain the gold. The mill was driven by water or electric power. In the twentieth century the stamp mill was gradually replaced by more modern devices, but formerly ninety-five percent of the rock was crushed by square or rotary stamps.

Miller, Loye. The information was supplied by Loye Miler, professor of biology, emeritus, University of California, Los Angeles.

Miller. Newton C. Miller, "Letters to his Family" (1847–1892). 109 letters. MS in Bancroft Library. The letters from 1850 to the early 1860s are a valuable source of information for mining in the areas around Mississippi Bar, Negro Hill, Fosters Bar and on the San Juan Ridge.

Miller. Ronald D. Miller, *Mines of the High Desert* (Glendale, California: La Siesta Press, 1965).

Milleson & Adams' Map, 1851. M. Milleson and R. Adams. *A Complete Map of the Feather & Yuba Rivers, with Towns, Ranches, Diggings, Roads, Distances* (Marysville, Calif.: R. A. Eddy, 1851). Wheat, 189. The map was compiled by two engineers, Milleson & Adams, drawn by Milleson and published by R. A. Eddy, stationer and book dealer in Marysville. It was the first adequate map of the Northern Mines, many names appearing on it for the first time. It is often cited as Eddy's Map.

Millington. D. A. Millington, "Journal of a California Miner (1850–1851)." 71 exp. Microfilm in Bancroft Library. The author mined in the Placerville area.

Mine. Actually a subterranean place where gold is mined. In California the term was often used for any place where gold was obtained.

Miners' Advocate. A weekly newspaper published in Coloma, Sept. 1852–Sept. 1853 and continued in Diamond Springs, Oct. 1853–Dec. 1855. Bancroft Library has no file, but there are clippings in Bancroft Scraps.

Miners' Own Book. *The Miners' Own Book: California Mining, Illustrated and Described* (San Francisco: Hutchings and Rosenfeld, 1858). Precise descriptions of gold mining methods used in California, with clear cut illustrations, based on the series of articles entitled "Mining for Gold in California," which appeared in the July, September, and October, 1857 issues of *Hutchings' Illustrated California Magazine*. Reprinted in *The Magazine of History*, XLVII, no. 3, extra number, 187.

Mines and Minerals. California Miners' Association, *California Mines and Minerals* (San Francisco, 1899). Uneven in treatment of the counties, with excellent information on some and useless and sometimes misleading on others.

Mining Bureau. The reference is to California, Division of Mines, *Report of the State Mineralogist*, v. 1– (1880–1908/10, 1912/14–). Title varies. Excellent and indispensable for mines that operated until recent times. It is not entirely dependable on historical facts. Gordon B. Oakeshott, in the *Journal of the West*, X:1 (January, 1971), has outlined the history of the organization, growth, and function of the Division since its inception as the California State Mining Bureau in 1880, with Henry G. Hanks as first state mineralogist. The original emphasis was on studies and statistics of mineral resources, mining activities, and publication of annual reports. The year 1927 marked the beginning of its basic geologic function and the change of name to Division of Mines and Mining, Department of Natural Resources. In 1929 the name was shortened to Division of Mines, and Olaf P. Jenkins, eminent geologist, was appointed chief (and only) geologist under the state mineralogist, Walter W. Bradley. Jenkins was responsible for the 1938 state geologic map, and during his term of office, 1929–1958, the technical publications in geology and mineral resources became internationally known. In 1948 Gordon B. Oakeshott, well-known geologist, became his chief assistant, and in 1957 the project of publishing maps of the state on colored lithograph sheets was begun (and finished in 1970). In 1958, Oakeshott served an interim appointment as state mineralogist and chief of the Division of Mines. The following year, 1959, Ian Campbell, internationally known geologist and professor at California Institute of Technology, became the state mineralogist and chief of the Division, and during his term of office the staff of professional geologists was greatly enlarged, and its reputation in geology was enhanced. The name of the Division was changed in 1961 to Division of Mines and Geology, Department of Conservation, and Campbell became state geologist, making him the third state geologist and the last state mineralogist. At his retirement in 1961, Wesley G. Bruer, likewise a well known geologist, was appointed state geologist, and Gordon B. Oakeshott, deputy chief.

Mining Bureau Bulletin. *See Bulletin.*

Mining Bureau Map, 1891. California State Mining Bureau, *Preliminary Mineralogical and Geological Map of the State of California* (San Francisco: Britton & Rey, 1891).

Mining District. An uncertain term. Some districts were well organized and could almost be called administrative units. Most of them were so called for convenience and were named after a locality or outstanding geographical feature.

Mining Press. *Mining and Scientific Press*, San Francisco. (1860–Mar. 1922). V. 1–124. Title varies. The volumes for 1860 containing reports from the mining districts are very useful.

Mining Review. *See Annual Mining Review.*

Miscellaneous Statements. "Miscellaneous Statements on California History" (1878). 43 p. MS in Bancroft Library. Dictated for H. H. Bancroft. Reminiscent but containing some good information on mining activities in different areas.

Miscellany. Jane B. Grabhorn, ed., *A California Gold Rush Miscellany* (San Francisco: Grabhorn Press, 1934). Contains the short journal of Alexander Barrington, April–November 1850, and nine letters from various miners. The book has beautiful illustrations.

A Mississippian in the Gold Field. *See* Dart.

Mitchell. John D. Mitchell, *Lost Mines and Buried Treasures along the Old Frontier* (Palm Desert: Desert Magazine Press, 1953). The author tells the stories of the lost mines of the Old Southwest, based on historical fact and local tradition.

Moerenhout. Jacques Antoine Moerenhut. *The Inside Story of the Gold Rush*, trans. and ed., Abraham P. Nasatir (San Francisco: California Historical Society, 1935). Official letters of the French consul at Monterey to the French Ministry of Foreign Affairs, written between May 15, 1848 and October 28, 1849, in which he reports the discovery of gold in California and his visit in July, 1848, to the mining region from the Cosumnes to the Feather rivers. Historically important for the influence of the French on the rush to California.

Monterey County History. 1881: *History of Monterey County, California* (San Francisco: Elliott and Moore, 1881).

Moore. Augustus Moore, "Pioneer Experiences" (1878). 30 p. MS in Bancroft Library. Contains information about Stony Bar in Placer County. The author was the son-in-law of Alonzo Delano.

Moore. William H. Moore, "Letter" datelined Carson's Creek, Calaveras County, July 17, 1853. 3 p. MS in Bancroft Library. Gives an account of mining at Vallecito, Murphys, Mokelumne Hill, and vicinity.

Morgan. William Ives Morgan. "Gold Dust, the Log of a Forty-Niner, 1848, '50, '51,

'52, '54," ed., Florence Emlyn (Downs) Muzzy. MS in Bancroft Library. The diarist left Bristol, Connecticut, at the age of twenty-one for California. He worked mainly at Volcano and Rancheria, where he kept stores in 1851 and 1852.

Morley. Jim Morley and Doris Foley, *Grass Valley and Nevada City; Being a History and Guide to the Adventuresome Past of Two Picturesque Cities of the California Gold Country.* It is essentially a pictorial guide, depicting still-existing buildings and scenes in excellent photographs made by Jim Morley. The coauthor of the text, Doris Foley, is a well-known local historian.

Morley. S. Griswold Morley, *The Covered Bridges of California* (Berkeley: University of California Press, 1938). The book contains photographs of the bridges, with historical sketches. A number of the bridges are in the gold mining region.

Mormon Battalion. The organization of a battalion of Mormon volunteers to participate in the Mexican War was one phase of the westward movement of the Church of the Latter Day Saints. The Mormon Battalion, like Stevenson's New York Volunteer Regiment, is known in history chiefly because many of its members played an important role in the Gold Rush and in the early period of California. *See* Brannan.

Morse. Edwin F. Morse, "The Story of a Gold Miner" in *CHSQ*, VI (pp. 205 ff., 332 ff.). Morse dictated his reminiscences to his daughter. His account of mining in Grass Valley and vicinity rings true.

Mother Lode. A widely used, loosely defined term, sometimes applied to as wide an area as the entire gold country in the Sierra Nevada foothills. It was evolved from the early miners' concept of one main quartz vein, with other known veins believed to be offshoots thereof. The "Mother Lode" is currently defined by geologists as follows. "A 120-mile-long system of linked or en echelon gold-quartz and mineralized schist or greenstone that extends from the town of Mariposa, north and northwest to northern El Dorado County" (*Bull.*, 193, p. 15). Philip R. May, in his recently published monograph *On the Mother Lode*, traces the history of the concept of the "Great Vein" or "Great Quartz Vein of California," which led to the coinage of the term "Mother Lode" in the late 1860s and the widely divergent use of the term in literature since that time.

Mulford. Prentice Mulford, *Prentice Mulford's Story* (New York, 1889). Repeatedly reprinted. With Delano and Gerstaecker, Mulford is the best true story teller of the Gold Rush. He mined several years in Tuolumne County, taught school in Jamestown, lectured in the mines, campaigned unsuccessfully for a seat in the legislature, and wrote articles and essays for newspapers and magazines. A selection of his writings in the 1860s and 1870s is given in his *California Sketches* (San Francisco: Book Club of California, 1935), ed., Franklin Walker.

Myrick. David Myrick, *Railraods of Nevada and Eastern California* (Berkeley: Howell-North, 1962–63), 2 vols. Volume 1 deals with the northern roads and volume 2 with the southern roads.

N

adeau. Remi Nadeau, *Ghost Towns and Mining Camps of California* (Los Angeles: Ward Ritchie Press, 1965). The author gives descriptions, stories, and anecdotes of ghost towns and camps where gold, silver, and copper were mined. The book has many good illustrations.

Nahl. Charles C. Nahl, "Letters to his Family" (1846–1854). 1 portfolio. MS in Bancroft Library. Among the letters of the well known artist of the California scene is one written February 2, 1852, probably from Sacramento, in which he describes his brief mining experience at Rough and Ready, near Nevada City.

Nasatir. Professor Abraham P. Nasatir has published extensively on the contributions of the French in California. *See* his *French Activities in California: An Archival Calendar-Guide* (Stanford University Press, 1945). A number of his articles about Frenchmen during the Gold Rush have appeared in the *California Historical Society Quarterly*. Included is a biography of Guillaume Patrice Dillon, Irish born French consul in San Francisco, 1850–1856, (XXXV, pp. 309 ff.). *See also* Derbec and Moerenhut.

Nevada County Historical Society Bulletin, Nevada City. March, 1948–

Nevada County History. 1880: Laurenz Wells, *History of Nevada County, California* (Oakland: Thompson & West, 1880). **1924:** William B. Lardner, *History of Placer and Nevada Counties* (Los Angeles, Historic Record Co., 1924).

Nevada County Map, 1880. J. G. Hartwell, *Map of Nevada County* (San Francisco: Galloway, 1880).

Nevada County Records. Various records of

early mining in the county are kept in the recorder's office in Nevada City.

Nevada Directory, 1856: *See* Brown & Dallison. **1895:** John E. Poingdestre, *Nevada County Mining and Business Directory* (Oakland: Pacific Press, 1895?).

Newmark. Harris Newmark, *Sixty Years in Southern California* (New York: Knickerbocker Press, 1916; new ed., 1926). Indispensable for any study of the history of southern California.

Nopel. John H. Nopel of Oroville, educator and historian, contributed information on mining locations in Butte County for use in this dictionary.

Northern Mines. In the early days of the Gold Rush the term Northern Mines designated the mining regions tributary to the city of Sacramento and the term **Southern Mines** the region tributary to Stockton. When mining was extended beyond the head of the Sacramento River to the northwest part of the state, the term Northern Mines included that area. Bancroft's maps of the Northern Mines and the Southern Mines, 1849–1850 (*History*, VI) approximate this division. A later, more accurate division, created three sections: The Northwest Mines centered around Shasta City and along the Trinity, Klamath, and Scott Rivers and their tributaries; the Central Mines from Amador County northward including El Dorado, Placer, Nevada, Yuba, Sierra, Butte, and Plumas counties, as well as the trading areas in Sacramento County and in Sutter County around the junction of the Sacramento and Feather rivers; and the Southern Mines extending southward from Calaveras County to Tuolumne, Mariposa, and northern Stanislaus counties, the region along Fresno and Kern rivers, and the trading area at Stockton in San Joaquin County.

Nouveau Monde Gold Mining Company. *Proceedings of the General Meeting Held . . . in Paris, September 30, 1854* (with a Postscript, October 28, 1854). The Company operated mines in Mariposa County.

Nugget. A piece of gold usually weighing one ounce or more.

Odall. Rodney P. Odall, "Three Letters from a California Goldseeker to his Parents" (1850–1851). MS in Bancroft Library. Two of the letters are datelined from Mariposa and from Brown's Bar (Plumas County?).

Old Block. *See* Delano.

Ord's Map, 1848. Lieutenant E. O. C. Ord, *Topographical Sketch of the Gold and Quicksilver District of California, July 25th 1848*. Wheat, 54. Published in U.S., 30th Congress, 2nd Session, House, Executive Document no. 1, to accompany President Polk's Message to Congress of December (serial set no. 537). His map was "the first map to make any pretense at cartographical accuracy after the gold discoveries." *See* Mason Report.

Ore. Generally used for any natural mineral compound that contains gold (or other metals).

Osbun. Albert G. Osbun, *To California and the South Seas; the Diary of Albert G. Osbun, 1849–1851*, ed., John Haskell Kemble (San Marino: Huntington Library, 1966). Osbun, a physician, was in charge of a party who mined without much success in the summer and fall of 1849 on the Yuba River and the Upper Sacramento.

Overland Monthly. *Overland Monthly and Out West Magazine*, San Francisco. V. 1–15 (July 1868–Dec. 1875); ser. 2, v. 1–93:4 (1883–July, 1935).

Pacific Coast Mining Review, 1878. *Pacific Coast Annual Mining Review*, San Francisco, 1878. Contains reports of the principal gold and silver mines in California and Nevada; also a poem with many names of California gold localities (pp. 162–165), almost identical with the poem in *Annual Mining Review*.

Paden and Schlichtmann. Irene D. Paden and Margaret Schlichtmann, *The Big Oak Flat Road; an Account of Freighting from Stockton to Yosemite Valley* (San Francisco, Privately printed, 1955). The main part of the book is based on Mrs. Schlichtmann's personal interviews with old residents on the Big Oak Flat Road, supplemented by chapters on Stockton and Knights Ferry based on Mrs. Paden's research. The **Schlichtmann Collection** of pictures, correspondence and notes used in the writing of *The Big Oak Flat Road* is in the Bancroft Library.

Palmer. Theodore S. Palmer, *Place Names of the Death Valley Region in California and Nevada* (Washington: privately printed, 1948). A carefully documented list indicating location of places and origin of the names, compiled by Dr. T. S. Palmer, member of the biological expedition to

Death Valley in 1891, for whom Mount Palmer in Death Valley was later named.

Pamphlets. *Pamphlets on California Mines* (Binder's title), 4 vols. In the University of California, Berkeley, Main Library.

Pan. *See* Panning.

Pancoast. Charles E. Pancoast, *A Quaker Forty-Niner* (Philadelphia: University of Pennsylvania Press, 1930). A reminiscent account of the overland journey in 1849 and mining experiences in both Southern and Northern Mines. Like many retrospective accounts, it is not always accurate.

Panning for Gold. Washing earth, gravel, or sand in a pan by agitation with water, to separate the heavier gold particles. Mexican miners used the batea or wooden bowl for the purpose. The preferable pan used by early California miners was made of sheet iron, with a flat bottom about twelve inches in diameter and sides extending about six inches at an angle of forty-five degrees. The value of a placer was often determined by the amount of gold a pan yielded.

Parsons. George F. Parsons, *The Life and Adventures of James W. Marshall* (Sacramento, 1870). The author wrote a short biography of Marshall, apparently on the basis of statements of Marshall and a former mining partner, William Burke, for the purpose of gaining recognition and support for the discoverer of gold at Sutter's Mill. Another edition with introduction, notes, and an additional chapter by G. Ezra Dane was published in San Francisco in 1935 by G. Fields, printed by the Grabhorn Press. *See also* Theressa Gay.

Patterson. Lawson B. Patterson, *Twelve Years in the Mines* (Cambridge, 1862). A brief, realistic, and instructive account written by a resident and miner for twelve years in Georgetown and vicinity. It contains a description not found elsewhere of "black lead," one to twenty-five ounce slugs, always rounded, encrusted in black cemented lava. A complete weather table for every day of the year 1853 is given in the appendix.

Patton. Annaleone D. Patton, *California Mormons by Sail and Trail* (Salt Lake City: Deseret Book Company, 1961). A review of the contributions of the Mormons to early California history.

Paul. Rodman W. Paul, *California Gold* (Cambridge: Harvard University Press, 1947). A well-written, carefully documented survey, designated as "a brilliant study" by Wheat.

Pay Dirt. Soil that was worth digging for gold.

Pay Streak. A vein that was profitable to work.

Perkins. Arthur B. Perkins, "Mining Camps of the Soledad," in *HSSCQ*, XL, pp. 149 ff. A survey of the mining camps in the township of Soledad, the northwesterly boundary of Los Angeles County.

Perkins, E. D. Elisha D. Perkins, *Gold Rush Diary; Being the Journal of Elisha Douglass Perkins on the Overland Trail in the Spring and Summer of 1849*, ed., Thomas D. Clark (Lexington: University of Kentucky Press, 1967). The diary of the overland journey is continued through the fall and winter of 1849 to February 28, 1850, during which time Perkins recounts his discouraging mining experiences, mainly in El Dorado County, near the Cosumnes River. The record of his later activities until his death in 1852 is not recorded. Appended to Perkins' diary is a reprinting of a series of informative California Gold Rush letters that appeared in 1849–1850 in the Marietta (Ohio) *Intelligencer*. They were written by miners who had come from the vicinity of Perkins' home town.

Perkins. William Perkins, *Three Years in California: William Perkins' Journal of Life at Sonora, 1849–1852*, ed., Dale L. Morgan and James R. Scobie (Berkeley: University of California Press, 1964). The classical account of life in Sonora and Tuolumne County, 1849–1852, written about ten years after the author's departure and doubtless based on a diary and other personal memoranda. In the introduction to this edition the editors have given a comprehensive survey of the literature of the period on the Southern Mines.

Peters. Charles Peters, *The Autobiography of Charles Peters* (Sacramento: La Grave, 1915?). A brief review of his long life, including mining experiences in the vicinity of Jackson in the 1850s, followed by short accounts of incidents in various mining localities, taken from different sources.

Pettee. W. H. Pettee, a member of the Geological Survey of California under the direction of Josiah D. Whitney, participated in 1870 with Amos Bowman in the survey and mapping of the region north of the North Fork of American River to the Middle Fork of Yuba River, which with the surveys of W. A. Goodyear formed the basis of reports published in Whitney's *The Auriferous Gravels of The Sierra Nevada of California*, 1879–1880. **Pettee and Bowman's Map, 1879** was based on their 1870 field work, revised and corrected by Pettee in 1879, and published under the title *Map Showing the Extent of the Hydraulic Mining Operations near Gold Run, Dutch Flat, Little York, You Bet, Chalk Bluffs, Red Dog, Hunt's Hill, and Quaker Hill; on Bear River and Cañon, Steep Hollow and Greenhorn Creeks.* Pettee revisted part of the mining regions in 1879 and made a detailed study of portions of the gravel areas in Placer, Nevada, Yuba, Sierra, Plumas, and Butte counties; the report of which was published as an appendix to *The Auriferous Gravels.* Pettee and Bowman's surveys of 1870 also contributed to the compilation of the Great Gravel Map covering the regions between the Middle Fork of Yuba River and the Middle Fork of American River, cited herein as Hoffmann-Craven Gravel Map, 1873. Both maps were published to accompany Whitney's *The Auriferous Gravels. See* Hoffmann; Whitney Survey.

Petty. Claude R. Petty, "Gold Rush Intellectual: the California of John Schertzer Hittell" (1952). Ph.D. diss., University of California, Berkeley.

Pfeiffer. Ida Pfeiffer, *Meine Zweite Weltreise* (Wien, 1856). 4 vols. in 2. Repeatedly reprinted and translated into French and English. The author was in California in 1853–54 and visited briefly the diggings on the Yuba River.

Phillips. Catherine Coffin Phillips, *Coulterville Chronicle, the Annals of a Mother Lode Town* (San Francisco: Grabhorn Press, 1942). A wordy account in a beautifully produced book.

Phoenix, John. *See* Derby.

Picayune. A daily evening newspaper published in San Francisco with some interruptions between 1850 and 1854, including a French section. United with San Francisco News in 1854 to form *News and Picayune* (1854–1856). For details *see* Kemble.

Pictorial Letter Sheets. *See* Illustrated Letter Sheets.

Pierce. Hiram D. Pierce, "Diary of a Trip to California and Return to New York, March 6, 1849–Jan. 8, 1851." 113 p. MS in Bancroft Library. The author mined on the Merced River at the time of the Mariposa War. The account was published as *A Forty-Niner Speaks*, (Oakland, 1930). Unpublished letters of Hiram Pierce are in the California State Library, California Section.

Pioneer Quarterly. *See* SCPQ.

Pioneer Society. *See* SCPQ.

Pittman. Amos S. Pittman, "The California and Australia Gold Rushes," ed., Theressa Gay, in *CHSQ*, XXX, pp. 15 ff. The author mined without much success in the vicinity of Coloma in the winter of 1849–50; he left when he heard the news of the gold discovery in Australia.

Placer, Placer Mining. The term "placer" is applied to a mass of gravel, sand, or similar material derived from the crumbling and erosion of solid rock and containing particles of gold, or nuggets of gold. In "placer mining" the gold is obtained by washing with water. When water is applied by pressure to break down banks of gravel, the method is called "hydraulicking." Deep deposits that can not be extracted by surface mining are mined before being washed by the sinking of shafts and drifting until pay dirt is reached.

Placer County Directory, 1861. Often quoted in Bancroft Notes in Bancroft Library. *California Local History* lists: R. J. Steele and others, *Directory of the County of Placer for the Year 1861* (San Francisco, 1861).

Placer County History. 1882: Myron Angel, *History of Placer County* (Oakland: Thompson & West, 1882). One of the best early county histories, with several chapters on mining. **1924:** William B. Lardner, *History of Placer and Nevada Counties* (Los Angeles: Historic Record Co., 1924).

Placer County Map, 1887. Charles E. Uren, *Official Map of Placer County, California* (San Francisco: Britton & Rey, 1887).

Placer County Records. Placer County, California. "Records" (ca. 1850–1873). 6 vols. MS in Bancroft Library. Certified copies of the original documents. The collection contains records of mining claims, building liens, land surveys, leases, and agreements. Vol. 1 proved most useful for this dictionary.

Placer Nuggets. Auburn, California. v. 1, Feb. 1957– . Quarterly publication of the Placer County Historical Society.

Placerville Directory. *Directory of the City of Placerville and the Towns of Upper Placerville, El Dorado, Georgetown and Coloma* (Placerville, 1862).

Plumas County Historical Society, Publication, Quincy?. No. 1 (Nov. 1960–).

Plumas County History, 1882: *Illustrated History of Plumas, Lassen, and Sierra Counties* (San Francisco: Fariss & Smith, 1882).

Plumas County Map, 1886. Arthur W. Keddie, *Map of Plumas County and Portions of Lassen, Sierra, Nevada, Yuba, Butte, Tehama* *and Shasta Counties, California*, . . . (San Francisco: Britton & Rey, 1886).

Pond. Samuel F. Pond, "Diaries" (1850–1854). 5 vols. MS in Bancroft Library. The diaries record experiences in the mines, mainly in El Dorado County.

Poore. George Poore, curator of the Calaveras County Historical Museum, San Andreas, supplied information about mining camps in Calaveras County.

Pratt. Addison Pratt, "Diary," ed., LeRoy R. Hafen and Ann W. Hafen, in *Journals of Forty-Niners, Salt Lake to Los Angeles* (Glendale: A. H. Clark, 1954). Pratt was one of the first Mormon missionaries to the Samoan Islands. In May, 1848, he was in the gold diggings in California briefly with Sam Brannan. In September of the same year he started out on his second mission to the Pacific Islands. In 1852 the French drove the Mormons from the Islands and Pratt came back to California, where he spent the rest of his life.

Preuss Map, 1848. Charles Preuss, *Map of Oregon and Upper California, from the Surveys of John Charles Frémont and other Authorities* (Baltimore: E. Weber, 1848). The authorship is usually attributed to Frémont, but the map was actually drawn by Charles Preuss, his cartographer. For details of Preuss' account of his professional relationship to Frémont, *see* the edition of his private diaries written on the first, second, and fourth expeditions and published as *Exploring with Frémont* (translated and edited by Erwin G. Gudde and Elisabeth K. Gudde, and published by the University of Oklahoma Press, 1958).

Price. Lewis R. Price, "Mazatlan to the Estanislao, the Narrative of Lewis Richard Price's Journey to California in 1849," ed., W. Turrentine Jackson. In *CHSQ*, XXXIX, pp. 35 ff. Price, an Englishman, was sent by his firm in Mexico to survey mining conditions in California in the fall of 1849. In his account written the same year he describes his visit to Woods Creek on the Stanislaus and Hawkins Bar on the Tuolumne.

Professional Paper. United States Geological Survey, *Professional Paper*. The monographs in this series are listed under the names of the individual authors.

Prospecting. Searching for new deposits; also preliminary exploration to test the value of lodes or placers.

Put's Golden Songster. By John A. Stone (San Francisco, 1858). A collection of songs sung by the miners. There is also a list of "Mining Localities Peculiar to California," pp. 63 f.

Quadrangle. *See* USGS quadrangle.

Quartz, Quartz Mining. In California the term quartz was applied to any hard gold or silver ore, as distinguished from gravel or earth. Hence, quartz mining was distinguished from placer mining.

Quaternary. Applied to the later or more recent period of the Cenozoic era. The Quaternary deposits of gold are in and adjacent to present-day channels and were mined on a small scale during the Gold Rush, and later, on a large scale, by dredging.

Quicksilver. The metal mercury was commonly used in washing to hold the free gold.

Ralston-Fry. *See* **Haight.**

Ramey. Earl Ramey, *The Beginnings of Marysville* (San Francisco: California Historical Society, 1936). Mr. Ramey is an authority on the history of Marysville and Yuba County, and he contributed information for this dictionary and for *California Place Names*.

Raup. H. F. Raup, "Place Names of the California Gold Rush" in *Geographical Review*, XXXV, pp. 653 ff. Treats the names in Trinity, Amador, and Calaveras counties.

Raymond. Rossiter W. Raymond. U. S., Treasury Department, *Statistics of Mines and Mining in the States and Territories West of the Rocky Mountains; Being the [1st–8th] Annual Report of Rossiter W. Raymond, United States Commissioner of Mining Statistics* (Washington, 1869–1877). The first annual report is for 1868 (printed in 1869); hence, Raymond I–VIII refer to the year covered: I (1868), etc. The set continues the reports of J. Ross Browne and is continued by *Mineral Resources of the United States* published by the U.S. Geological Survey. **Raymond's Map.** The reference is to his map of the Slate Creek Basin, Sierra County, California, published in two parts in vol. V of his *Report*, 1872, following p. 88. **Raymond's Glossary.** *Glossary of Mining Terms. In* American Institute of Mining Engineers, *Transactions*, IX, pp. 99–192.

Read. Georgia Willis Read, *A Pioneer of 1850,*

George Willis Read, 1819–1880 (Boston: Little, Brown, 1927). The diary of a physician, who came overland to the gold region in 1850, arriving at Hangtown (Placerville) in August. The diary relates chiefly to the overland journey with a brief commentary on mining conditions upon his arrival.

Reed. William F. Reed, "Journal" (Feb. 8, 1849–April 3, 1853). 145 p. MS in Bancroft Library. Includes account of mining in the vicinity of Coloma and Kelsey.

Register. California, State Mining Bureau, *Register of Mines and Minerals* (Sacramento, 1897–1906). Lists, locates, and describes the mines of the period by county, one volume to a county, with maps. A valuable reference list; coverage for different counties, however, is uneven.

Reis. Christian Reis, "Statement," dictated for H. H. Bancroft. MS in Bancroft Library. The three brothers, Ferdinand, Christian, and Gustav, natives of Germany, first mined in Mariposa and later moved to Downieville, where they had a store. In 1857 they owned all or most of the Sierra Buttes.

Rémond, A. *See* Whitney Survey.

Rensch. Hero E. Rensch. "Columbia, a Gold Camp of Tuolumne," mimeographed (Berkeley, California: Department of Natural Resources, Division of Parks, 1936). **Rensch-Hoover.** *Historic Spots in California*. This important reference work comp. by Hero E. Rensch, Ethel G. Rensch, and Mildred Brook Hoover was originally published by Stanford University Press in three separate volumes: *The Southern Counties* (1932), *Valley and Sierra Counties* (1933), *Counties of the Coast Range* (1937). A revised edition in one volume, edited by Ruth Teiser, was published in 1948; and a third edition, revised and edited by William N. Abeloe, was published in 1966.

Resources of El Dorado County. El Dorado County, Board of Supervisors, *Resources of El Dorado County* (Placerville, 1887). Shows the change from mining to agriculture.

Rice. C. M. Rice, *Dictionary of Geologic Terms* (Ann Arbor: The Author, 1949).

Ridge. John Rollin Ridge, *The Life and Adventures of Joaquin Murieta, the Celebrated California Bandit. By Yellow Bird* (Norman: University of Oklahoma Press, 1955). This edition is a reprint of the only known copy of the original edition of 1854, with an introduction by Joseph Henry Jackson, reviewing the history of the legendary Murieta and its various adaptations. *See*

also the Grabhorn Press, 1935 edition, reprinted from the *California Police Gazette*, vol. I, nos. 34–43 (Sept. 3 to Nov. 5, 1859) under the title *The Life of Joaquin Murieta, The Brigand Chief of California*, ed. Francis P. Farquhar, with a bibliography of selected versions of the Murieta story.

Riffle. The grooves, cleats, or blocks placed in the sluice or the rocker to hold the quicksilver that catches the gold particles.

Riley. A. Riley, "Letter" datelined San Pedros—Tuolamie, March 15, 1851. MS in Bancroft Library.

Riley. Bennet Riley, "Report on his Tour to the Gold Regions, dated August 30, 1849", *in* U.S., 31st Congress, 1st sess., House Executive Document, no. 17, pp. 785–792. Riley, as governor of California, visited the mines from the Tuolumne River to the American River between July 5 and August 9, 1849, in order to observe personally the conditions in the mines, particularly the relations with foreign miners.

Ritchie. Robert W. Ritchie, *The Hell-Roarin' Forty-Niners* (New York: J. H. Sears, 1928).

Roach. C. W. Roach (?), "Letter." MS in Bancroft Library *in* "California Gold Rush Letters." The letter was datelined San Francisco, November 15, 1850.

Robinson. Fayette Robinson, *California and the Gold Region* (New York, 1849). A geographical and historical account, with a reprinting of Mason's *Report* and other related documents.

Robinson. John W. Robinson, *Mines of the San Gabriels* (Glendale, California: La Siesta Press, 1973). A history of the mining camps and the mines in the San Gabriel Mountains, including the San Fernando placers, where gold was reportedly found in 1842. The account is based on official reports, contemporary newspapers, and the author's travels in the region.

Rocker. *See* Cradle.

Roman. Anton Roman began selling books to the mining community in Shasta County in January, 1851, and later he extended his territory to Trinity and Siskiyou counties. In the fall of 1853 his purchases of books and stationery for the three counties amounted to 42 thousand dollars. (*Overland Monthly*, 2nd series, v. 32, July, 1898).

Ross. John E. Ross, "Narrative of an Indian Fighter" (1878). 26 p. MS in Bancroft Library. Written by one of H. H. Bancroft's assistants. It is a good story but probably not very dependable. The author was colonel in the state militia in the Modoc

War, brigadier general in command of Oregon state troops, and Oregon state senator. His statements about Murderers Bar and Scott River are of interest. He also mentions mining on the Feather, American, and Yuba rivers.

Rotchev. Alexander Rotchev, "Letters of A. Rotchev, Last Commandant at Fort Ross," tr. and ed., Frederick C. Cordes. In *CHSQ*, XXXIX, pp. 97 ff. Originally published in *Archiv für Wissenschaftliche Kunde von Russland*, vol. II, no. 4. Rotchev, who was commandant at Fort Ross for twelve years (1829–1841), came back to California in 1851 and mined at Murderers Bar on the Yuba River.

Royce. Sarah Royce, *A Frontier Lady; Recollections of the Gold Rush and Early California* (New Haven: Yale University Press, 1932). Mrs. Royce's charming account includes a description of Weberville, the Sacramento flood of January, 1850, Grass Valley, and San Francisco.

Run, Rush. The rushing of miners toward a new discovery of a gold deposit. Run may also refer to a gold-bearing stream, as in "Gold Run" in Placer County. Miners also designated as a run, the length of time a mining operation was carried on before the "clean-up."

Rushing for Gold. *See* Caughey.

Russ. Adolph G. Russ, "Life of Adolph Gustav Russ" (ca. 1890). 3 folders. MS in Bancroft Library. The biography was prepared for Bancroft's *Chronicles of the Builders of the Commonwealth*. Adolph and his father, Emanuel Russ, mined on the American River in 1848 and 1849. The father, a silversmith and jeweler, founded the family business in San Francisco and was prominent in the German community.

Russell. Warren T. Russell, "Chispas, by an Old Miner" (1947). 245 p. MS in Bancroft Library. The author, a native of Garden Valley, near Coloma, gives much information about mining in El Dorado and Placer counties.

Ryan. William R. Ryan, *Personal Adventures in Upper and Lower California in 1848-49*, 2 vols. (London, 1850). Ryan, a member of the New York Volunteers, was in the mines between the American and Stanislaus rivers in the summer of 1849. The account is highly personal in nature.

S

CHSP; SCHSQ. *See* HSSCP; HSSCQ.

SCPQ. *Society of California Pioneers Quarterly*, San Francisco. vols. 1–10 (March, 1924–

1933). Sometimes cited as *Pioneer Quarterly*.

Sacramento County History. 1880: George F. Wright, ed., *History of Sacramento County, California* (Oakland: Thompson & West, 1880). Facsimile reproduction in 1970 with introduction by Allan R. Ottley (Berkeley: Howell North). **1890:** Winfield J. Davis, *An Illustrated History of Sacramento County, California* (Chicago: Lewis Publishing Co., 1890).

Sacramento County Map, 1885. Fred A. Shepherd (San Francisco: Britton & Rey, 1885).

Sacramento Valley Railroad. *See* Judah's *Report*, 1854; C. S. Wilson's *Report*, 1854.

San Bernardino County Directory. *San Bernardino City and County Directory* (San Bernardino: Flagg and Wallsen, 1889).

San Bernardino County History. 1883: *History of San Bernardino County* (San Francisco: Wallace W. Elliott, 1883). **1904:** Luther A. Ingersoll, *Ingersoll's Century Annals of San Bernardino County, 1769 to 1904* (Los Angeles: 1904). **1922:** John Brown, ed., *History of San Bernardino and Riverside Counties*, 3 vols. (Madison, Wisconsin: Western Historical Association, 1922).

San Bernardino County Map. 1892. *Official Map of San Bernardino County, California* (n.p.: 1892).

San Luis Obispo County History. 1883: *History of San Luis Obispo County* (Oakland: Thompson and West, 1883).

Santa Barbara County History. 1883: *History of Santa Barbara County, California* (Oakland: Thompson & West, 1883). Also contains history of Ventura County.

Santa Fe Coast Lines. The reference is to the compilation of the Atchison, Topeka & Santa Fe Railway system entitled "History of the Santa Fe Coast Lines," a typewritten copy of which was placed at the author's disposal through the kindness of Lee Lyles and E. G. Ryder.

Sargent. *See* Brown and Dallison.

Sargent. Shirley Sargent, author of books and articles on the history of Yosemite Valley and Mariposa County, contributed directly to the author of this dictionary, information about the history of mining camps in Mariposa County. The book entitled *Mother Lode Narratives*, edited and annotated by Shirley Sargent, is based partially on unpublished letters of Jessie Benton Frémont and gives an intimate picture of the Frémont family on Las Mariposas Estate. *See* the entry Jessie Benton Frémont.

Sawtelle. C. M. Sawtelle, "Pioneer

Sketches." 1876. MS in Bancroft Library. 14 p. Dictated for H. H. Bancroft. Among the brief sketches is one about William C. Bennett, who struck it rich in Jamestown in 1849 and 1850; later he was engaged in trading and the lumber business in the area.

Sawyer Decision. In 1884 Judge Lorenzo Sawyer issued a decree prohibiting the dumping of debris from hydraulic mining into the Sacramento and San Joaquin rivers and their tributaries. The decision practically brought an end to hydraulic mining, except where debris storage dams were permitted to be built.

Sawyer. Lorenzo Sawyer, *Way Sketches; Containing Incidents of Travel across the Plains; with Letters Describing Life and Conditions in the Gold Region* (New York: E. Eberstadt, 1926). The letters are written from Nevada City and Sacramento between September and December, 1850. The author later became chief justice of the Supreme Court of California.

Saxton. A. H. Saxton, "Letters" (1857–1858). 10 letters. MS in Bancroft Library, *in* Gideon J. Carpenter Papers. Saxton mined in El Dorado County.

Scamehorn. *See* Buckeye Rovers.

Schaeffer. Luther Melanchton Schaeffer, *Sketches of Travel in South America, Mexico and California* (New York, 1860). Written on the basis of a diary and recollections. Schaeffer was at Hawkins Bar in the winter of 1849 and in the mines between Nevada City and Downieville in the summer of 1850. One of the chapters is devoted to the Gold Lake hunt.

Schist. Crystalline rock, having a slaty structure.

Schlappi-Ferguson. Jane Schlappi and Marilyn Ferguson are historians of El Dorado County, particularly Placerville and vicinity. They are members of the Heritage Association of El Dorado, under whose auspices their account of Placerville has been published.

Schlichtmann Collection. *See* Paden and Schlichtmann.

Schliemann. Heinrich Schliemann, *Schliemann's First Visit to America*, ed., Shirley H. Weber (Cambridge: Harvard University Press, 1942). Schliemann, the noted German archaeologist and excavator of Troy, had a banking house for the sale and exchange of gold dust in Sacramento in 1851. His account is interesting but contains little about the geography of the gold region.

Schmölder. B. Schmölder, *The Emigrant's Guide to California* (London, 1849?). Translated from parts of his *Neuer Praktischer Wegweiser für Auswanderer nach Nord Amerika* (1849). The author was a resident of California for twenty-four years before he wrote this guide for his German countrymen.

Scholfield's Map, 1851. Nathan Scholfield, *Map of Southern Oregon and Northern California* (San Francisco: Marvin and Hitchcock, 1851). Wheat, 206. It is one of the first maps that attempts to show the mining regions along the Trinity and Klamath rivers, but does not pretend to give the names of all the sites.

Schoolcraft. Henry R. Schoolcraft, *Archives of Aboriginal Knowledge* (Philadelphia, 1860). 6 vols. Vol. III of this work contains George Gibbs' "Journal . . ." *See* Gibbs.

Schulz. Paul E. Schulz, *Stories of Lassen's Place Names* (Mineral, California: Loomis Memorial Association, 1949). A reliable regional study done "in the field."

Schulze. *See* FLM.

Schwarz. J. L. Schwarz, *Briefe eines Deutschen aus Kalifornien* (Berlin, 1849). Among the letters is one datelined New Helvetia, September 29, 1848, reporting the discovery of gold and examples of rich earnings.

Scott. Reva Scott, *Samuel Brannan and the Golden Fleece* (New York: Macmillan, 1944). *See* Brannan in this bibliography.

Seam Diggings. Decomposed bed rock, filled with irregular seams of gold-bearing quartz.

Settle. Glen A. Settle, *History of Tropico Hill* (Rosamond, Calif., 1959). A brief history of mining in the Tropico Hill area in Antelope Valley, from the late 1870s to 1956, written by the assistant manager of the Burton Brothers, Inc. mining company.

Seyd. Ernest Seyd, *California and its Resources; a Work for the Merchant, the Capitalist and the Emigrant* (London, 1858). Contains a chapter on the conditions of gold mining at the time and the types and methods of mining. Beautifully illustrated.

Seymour. E. Sanford Seymour, *Emigrants Guide to the Gold Mines* (Chicago, 1849). Describes the land and sea routes to California and gives a brief general account of mining prospects but no specific information on localities.

Shaft. A pit sunk from the surface. A good early illustration of sinking a shaft may be found in *Hutchings' California Magazine*, July 1857, p. 8.

Shaw. Frederick Shaw, "Letter" (February 14, 1857). MS in Bancroft Library *in*

California Gold Rush Letters. Written from Brandy Flat, Nevada County.

Shaw. Pringle Shaw, *Ramblings in California* (Toronto, 1856?). A very interesting account of mining activities in California in the early 1850s, with references to the important camps and towns about 1855, followed by a number of anecdotes and sketches based on personal experiences and observations.

Shaw. William Shaw, *Golden Dreams and Waking Realities* (London, 1851). The author, a British sailor, mined in the vicinity of Angels Camp in 1849.

Sheldon. Jared Sheldon came to California probably in 1840; in 1844 he was grantee of the Omochumnes ranch on the Cosumnes River, where he was associated with William Daylor. Some of his papers are in the California Section of the State Library in Sacramento.

Sheldon. Stewart Sheldon, *Gleanings by the Way, from '36 to '89* (Topeka, 1890). Sheldon recalls briefly his experiences in the mines near Nevada City and on the Yuba River in 1849–50(?).

Sherman. Edwin A. Sherman, "Sherman was There," ed., Allen B. Sherman, in *CHSQ*, XXIII, no. 3–4; XXIV, no. 1–3. The recollections of Major Sherman contain some interesting material. He mined on the Yuba in the summer and fall of 1849 and again briefly on the Merced in the summer of 1850.

Sherman. William Tecumseh Sherman, *A Letter of Lieut. W. T. Sherman Reporting on Conditions in California in 1848* (Carmel, Calif.: T. W. Norris, 1947). Sherman, who was stationed in California at the time of the gold rush, gives his opinion of the effect of the event on the economy of California and on the army in California.

Sherwood. J. Ely Sherwood, *The Pocket Guide to California* (New York, 1849). Description of land and sea routes, the California gold region, including Mason's *Report*, and pertinent information for the gold seeker, with twenty-eight pages of advertisements for equipment and services. No specific information on localities is given.

Shinn. Charles H. Shinn, *Mining Camps; a Study in American Frontier Government* (New York: Scribner's, 1885). Reprinted with an introduction by Joseph Henry Jackson (New York: Knopf, 1948). A classic treatise, written fifty years after the Gold Rush, when the author was a student of history and government at Johns Hopkins University.

Shufelt. S. Shufelt, *A Letter from a Gold Miner, Placerville, California, October, 1850* (San Marino: Huntington Library, 1944). A realistic account of the rigors of mining in the winter of 1849–50.

Sierra Club Bulletin. San Francisco, v. 1– (1893/96–   ).

Sierra County Historical Society [Bulletin]. v. 1 (April 1969)–   Originally published as *Quarterly*.

Sierra County History, 1882: *Illusrated History of Plumas, Lassen and Sierra Counties* (San Francisco: Fariss and Smith, 1882).

Sierra County Map. 1867: *See* Crossman. 1874: Charles W. Hendel, *Topographical Map of Sierra County, California* (San Francisco: Britton & Rey, 1874).

Simpson. Henry I. Simpson, *Three Weeks in the Gold Mines; or, Adventures with the Gold Diggers of California in August, 1848* (New York, 1848). A typical early guide, probably one of the earliest published, for prospective gold diggers. It is preceded by what is purported to have been personal experiences by a member of the New York Volunteers. Dale Morgan (M'Collum, p. 11) points out that there was no Henry I. Simpson in the New York Volunteers and that the personal narrative as well as the guide were plagiarized.

Sinnott. James J. Sinnott, *History of Sierra County* (Volcano: California Traveler, 1972–). Two volumes have been published. Vol. 1: *Downieville, Gold Town on the Yuba* (1972). Vol. 2: *History of Sierra City; History of Goodyears Bar* (1973).

Siskiyou County History. 1881: Harry Laurenz Wells, *History of Siskiyou County, California* (Oakland: D. J. Stewart, 1881).

Siskiyou County Land Papers. (1854–1862). 3 folders. MS in Bancroft Library. One folder contains documents relating to mining, mainly mining claims.

Siskiyou Pioneer. *Siskiyou Pioneer in Folklore, Fact and Fiction, and Yearbook* (Yreka: Siskiyou County Historical Society). V. 1– (1947–   ).

Slickens. A term sometimes applied to the debris from hydraulic mining.

Sluice, Sluicing. Washing by running the auriferous soil through boxes or long troughs provided with devices to catch the gold. *See also* Ground sluicing. Good illustrations are found in *Hutchings' California Magazine*, July, 1857, p. 7.

Smith. Asa B. Smith. *See* Seth Smith.

Smith. Grant H. Smith, "Bodie, Last of the Old-Time Mining Camps," in *CHSQ*, pp. 64 ff.

Smith. Hamilton Smith, *Hydraulics* (New York: J. Wiley, 1886).

Smith. Herbert L. Smith, "Scrapbooks of notes and pictures." 5 vols. In Bancroft Library. A collection of notes and photographs relating to mining on the Placerville Road and on the gold and silver boom of 1877–1883 at Bodie. The final volume is a newspaper in typescript edited by H. L. Smith entitled "The Bodie Era, the Chronicles of the Last Old Time Mining Camp Excitement," vol. 1:1–8:2 (Nov. 1877–March 1883).

Smith. Seth Smith, "Letters of Seth and Asa B. Smith" (1850–1862). 158 letters. MS in Bancroft Library. Very good letters written from the California gold fields to their family in Baltimore.

Smith. William M. Smith has provided much interesting and reliable information about mining camps along the Salmon River. His grandfather was a miner in the region, having come there in the early 1850s. Smith himself was born at Forks of Salmon and is today a resident of Etna.

Smith Brothers. "Smith Family Correspondence" (1849–1870). 81 folders. MS in Bancroft Library. The letters of Pardon B. Smith and his brothers describe life in the mines, mainly at Campo Seco. The letters are transcribed in Lucile Aucutt's, "Life in California Mining Camps," MA thesis, University of California, Berkeley, 1931.

Society of California Pioneers. See SCPQ.

Soulé. Frank Soulé, "Statement" (1878). 4 p. MS in Bancroft Library. In his dictation made for H. H. Bancroft, Soulé makes mention of his mining experiences in 1849 and 1850 at Sullivans Creek, Murphys, and near Death Valley. He later was associated with the editorship of several San Francisco newspapers. From 1853 to 1858 he edited and published the *California Chronicle*, and he is the coauthor with John H. Gihon and James Nisbet of the *Annals of San Francisco*, published in 1855.

Southern Mines. See Northern Mines.

Spence. Thomas Spence, "Statement" (1878). 12 p. MS in Bancroft Library. Contains an account of the 1850 Gold Lake excitement, the Kern River rush, and other mining activities in California.

Spiegel. Henry V. D. Spiegel, "Letters to his Family" (1850–1852). 35 p MS in Bancroft Library. These are good letters written from the Northern Mines.

Stampede. A wholesale rush for a newly discovered deposit of gold.

Stamp Mill. See Mill.

State Library Roster. A list of names of early mining towns compiled by California State Library for George R. Stewart. In Bancroft Library.

State Register. *The State Register and Year Book Facts* (San Francisco, 1857, 1859). The first systematic attempt to publish a year book similar to the present Blue Book published by the state. Fairly complete lists of quartz mills are given; also mining ditches and canals.

Statutes. The Statutes of California published by the state since 1850 contain many reference to place names, including the official naming of places by act of the legislature.

Steamer Edition. A special edition of a newspaper for delivery by steamers to ports along their routes. Publication was irregular and content differed from the local edition of the same date.

Stearns Diary. The diary of Dr. A. K. Stearns, superintendent of the Willard Mine, Dogtown, Butte County, in the 1850s, recounts the finding of the famous Willard or Dogtown Nugget. It is a manuscript in private possession, a copy of which is in the library of Chico State University.

Steele. John Steele, *In Camp and Cabin*, ed., Milo Quaife, published with *Bidwell's Echoes of the Past* (Chicago: Lakeside Press, 1928). Reprinted from the 1901 edition published in Lodi, Wisconsin. A sequel to his *Across the Plains in 1850*, it is a fascinating account of mining in the Coloma district and on the Yuba and Feather rivers, 1850–53. It is one of the best of its kind. The book was written on the basis of the author's diary, fifty years after the events described.

Steger. Gertrude A. Steger, *Place Names of Shasta County* (Redding, 1945). One of the few satisfactory regional studies in California. The reference indicates that the information was taken from this edition or from the revised edition edited by Helen M. Jones (Glendale: La Siesta Press, 1966).

Stephens-Murphy-Townsend Party. In 1844 Elisha Stephens (sometimes spelled Stevens) led a party of about fifty persons to California via Fort Hall and Humboldt River. They were the first party to bring wagons across the Sierra Nevada to Sutters Fort.

Stevens-Murphy-Townsend Party. See Stephens-Murphy-Townsend Party.

Stevenson's Volunteers. The regiment of New York Volunteers under the command of Jonathan D. Stevenson came round the Cape Horn to California arriving in March and April, 1847. It was too late to participate in military operations, but many of its members took part in the Gold Rush.

Stewart. George R. Stewart is the author of *Names on the Land* (New York: Random House, 1945), *American Place Names* (New York: Oxford University Press, 1970) and other studies on place names. He was a member of the University of California committee which sponsored the original writing of *California Place Names* by Erwin G. Gudde. Stewart is also the author of *Bret Harte, Argonaut and Exile* (Boston: Houghton Mifflin, 1931), which was used in the writing of this dictionary.

Stockton. N. H. Stockton, "Journal" (1850). 171 p. MS in Bancroft Library. It is a diary recording the overland trip and arrival in the California gold diggings.

Stoddart. Thomas R. Stoddart, *Annals of Tuolumne County*, ed., Carlo M. De Ferrari (Sonora: Mother Lode Press, 1963). Originally published in *Tuolumne Courier*, Feb. 23–Sept. 28, 1861. The book is not entirely reliable, but most of the errors have been corrected by the editor in copious footnotes.

Stokes. William Lee Stokes, *Glossary of Selected Geologic Terms, with Special Reference to their Use in Engineering* (Denver: Colorado Scientific Society, 1955).

Stone. See *Put's Golden Songster*.

Storms. W. H. Storms, *The Mother Lode Region of California* (California, State Mining Bureau, *Bull.*, No. 18), Sacramento, 1900. Lists and describes the mines of the "Central Gold Belt" in El Dorado, Amador, Calaveras, Tuolumne counties.

Stowell. Levi Stowell, "Bound for the Land of Canaan, Ho!" in *CHSQ*, XXVII, 157 ff. Stowell's diary for April 4 to May 7, 1849 records his mining experiences at Angels Camp and Carson's Creek.

Stretch. Richard H. Stretch, "Report on the Onion Valley Ridge, Plumas County, California" (1881–1882). 15 p. MS in Bancroft Library.

Stripping. To remove the surface earth or rocks in placering and open-pit mining.

Stuart. Joseph A. Stuart, *My Roving Life*, 2 vols. (Auburn, Calif., 1895). Vol. I contains an excellent account of mining on the Yuba and Feather rivers as described in his diary entries between October 16, 1849, and September 29, 1851.

Sulfuret. In California gold mining, the undecomposed metallic ores, usually sulfides.

Sumner. Sherman P. Sumner, "Letters to his Brother" (1850–1851). 3 letters. MS in Bancroft Library. Relate to mining in Yuba County.

Sutter. John Augustus Sutter (1830–1880), native of Kandern, Germany, of Swiss origin, settled in the Sacramento Valley in 1839 at the site of what is now the city of Sacramento, and in 1841 began the construction of Sutters Fort, which became the terminus of the emigrant trail from Missouri. The discovery of gold on January 24, 1848, by James Marshall in the tailrace of Sutter's mill at Coloma precipitated the Gold Rush, which ultimately brought financial ruin to Sutter. For details of Sutter's important and colorful career, consult *Sutter's Own Story* by Erwin G. Gudde (New York, 1936) and *Sutter: the Man and his Empire*, the definitive biography by James P. Zollinger (New York and London, 1939).

Sutter County Map, 1873. J. C. Pennington, *Official Map of Sutter County* (n.p.: 1873).

Swan. John A. Swan, *A Trip to the Gold Mines of California in 1848*, ed., John A. Hussey (San Francisco: Book Club of California, 1960). A brief but interesting and reliable account of the "Dry Diggings" near Placerville and on Weber Creek in 1848, written in 1870 for H. H. Bancroft.

Swett. "John Swett's Diary, January 25 to November 16, 1853" in *CHSQ*, XXIII, pp. 289 ff. His sketchy diary contains an account of his attempts at mining in California in Butte County. In later years he became a school teacher in San Francisco, and from 1863–1867 California state superintendent of public schools.

Tailings. The debris left mainly from hydraulic operations and dredging.

Tailrace. In mining, the flume or channel to carry off the tailings or debris from a mining operation. But the tailrace at Sutters Mill, where Marshall picked up the nuggets in January, 1848, was simply a channel to relieve the surplus water from the sawmill.

Taylor. Bayard Taylor, *El Dorado; or, Adventures in the Path of Empire* (New York, 1850), 2 vols. The renowned traveler, poet, and literary critic visited the diggings between the Cosumnes and Mokelumne rivers in 1849, and he devotes several chapters to the account of his experiences there. A part of the book was first published in letters printed in the New York *Tribune*. The complete book was repeatedly reprinted. Ten years after his visit to California, he returned on a lecture tour, and these lectures were printed in the New York *Mercury* in 1859[?] under the title "Pictures of California Ten Years Later." A number of them were reprinted in the Sacramento *Union* between January 14 and May 15, 1860. Appended to his *El Dorado* is the *Report* of Thomas Butler King, March 22, 1850.

Taylor. Rinaldo Rinaldini Taylor, *Seeing the Elephant*, ed., John W. Caughey (Los Angeles: Ward Ritchie Press, 1951). A group of interesting letters include two from Mormon Island, written September 20 and October 22, 1849.

Taylor. William Taylor, *California Life Illustrated* (New York, 1858). The author, a Methodist missionary to California, arrived in San Francisco in the fall of 1849 and made preaching tours in the mines as late as 1855.

Tertiary. The earlier of two geologic periods in the Cenozoic era. The ancient rivers to which reference is made in gold mining literature were formed during this period, and the auriferous gravels in these channels are called Tertiary gravels.

Thomas. Charles C. Thomas, "Mining Reminiscences of 1849." Statement recorded for H. H. Bancroft, 1883. The author arrived in California in the fall of 1849, mined at Bidwell Bar and Rich Bar [!]; he also had a store in Onion Valley from 1850 to 1853 and branch stores at Gibsonville and Hopkinsville. Later he moved to Sierra County, where he remained until 1861, when he went to the Comstock mines.

Thompson. Asa H. Thompson, "Letters" (1853–1860). 122 p. MS in Bancroft Library. The letters, written by Asa, his brother Charles, and other members of the family are mainly about Columbia and vicinity.

Thompson. Charles W. Thompson. *See* Asa H. Thompson, Letters.

Thompson. " 'Judge' Robert Thompson" in *CHSQ*, XXX, pp. 237 ff. Based on personal papers and arranged for publication by his daughter, Augusta B. Warren. Thompson did a good business selling milk to the miners at Dry Creek and Mokelumne Hill in the early 1850s; later he became an attorney at law.

Thompson Family Letters. *See* Asa H. Thompson, "Letters."

Thomson. Monroe Thomson, *The Golden Resources of California* (New York, 1856). An excellent account of the Blue and Eureka

lodes in Sierra County; based party on Trask.

Thrall. Will H. Thrall, "Lytle Creek Canyon; From the Indian Days to 1900," in *HSSCQ*, XXXIII, pp. 237 ff.

Tickner. Bernita L. Tickner, whose forebears were miners in Siskiyou County, contributed information about mining camps in the county.

Tom. *See* Long Tom.

Townsend. William H. Townsend, "Experiences in California," June–August, 1849. 5 p. MS in Rhode Island Historical Society Library; transcript in Bancroft Library. Related to the Jacksonville area.

Transactions. California, State Fair and Exposition, *Report of the California State Agricultural Society* (Sacramento, 1858–60). The three volumes contain informative reports of the "Visiting Committee" sent out to examine resources of the state.

Trask. John B. Trask was a member of the Mexican boundary survey and became the first state geologist of California. Several of his reports and his map are cited in this dictionary. **Trask Report. Doc. 9,** refers to *Report on the Geology of the Coast Mountains, and Part of the Sierra Nevada* (California, Legislature, Assembly, 5th sess. 1854, doc. no. 9). **Trask Report, Doc. 14,** refers to *Report on the Geology of the Coast Mountains . . . also Portions of the Middle and Northern Mining Districts* (California, Legislature, Assembly, sess. 1855, doc. no. 14). **Trask Report, 1856,** refers to *Report on the Geology of Northern and Southern California* (California, Legislature, Senate, Session 1856, doc. no. 14). **Trask's Map, 1853.** In 1853 John B. Trask's map entitled *Topographical Map of the Mineral Districts of California* was published. Wheat, 247. It is a landmark in the cartography of the mining region, recording more place names than any map published to that date. It is unusual in that east is at the top of the map. The same year, his *Map of the State of California* (Wheat, 246) was published; however, this map is not as complete for the mining region as the map mentioned above. The references in this dictionary are to his *Topographical Map of the Mineral Districts,* unless otherwise specified. Both maps were published by Britton and Rey, San Francisco.

Trény. *La Californie Dévoilée,* 3d ed. (Paris, 1850). A translation by Désiré Fricot, entitled *California Unveiled,* was published with an essay on the French immigration to the gold rush, *When the French Came to California,* by Gilbert Chinard (San Francisco: California Historical Society, 1944). Trény's account of the mining situation in California was a promotional pamphlet of a company, "La Californienne," organized to bring gold seekers to California.

Trinity. 1955–   . Organ of the Trinity County Historical Society, published to the present day in Weaverville.

Trinity County History. *See* Cox, Isaac.

Tucker. Joseph C. Tucker, *To the Golden Goal and other Sketches* (San Francisco, 1895). The personal reminiscences and sketches written by a physician in Sacramento were prepared for publication by his widow. One of the sketches is an interesting story of the doctor's participation in the Gold Lake hunt in the spring of 1850.

Tufly. George Tufly, "Letter to his Brother," April 10, 1855. 3 p. Photostat in Bancroft Library. A letter written in German about mining at Mount Pleasant Ranch.

Tunnel Mining. Drifting or tunneling underground along gravel channels and bringing the pay dirt to the surface for sluicing. A good illustration may be found in *Hutchings' Illustrated Magazine*, July 1857, p. 9.

Tuolumne County Directory. *See* Heckendorn.

Tuolumne County Historical Society. *See* Chispa.

Tuolumne County History. **1861:** *See* Stoddart. **1882:** Herbert O. Lang, *A History of Tuolumne County, California* (San Francisco: B. F. Alley, 1882). **1892:** *A Memorial and Biographical History of the Counties of Merced, Stanislaus, Calaveras, Tuolumne and Mariposa* (Chicago: Lewis Publishing Company, 1892).

Tuolumne County Land Papers. Portfolio. MS in Bancroft Library. The documents include mining claims, 1850–1854.

Tuolumne County Map, 1879, John P. Dart, *Map of the Principal Quartz Mines in Tuolumne County, California* (San Francisco: A. L. Bancroft, 1879).

Two Eras. *Two Eras in the Life of the Felon Grovenor I. Layton* . . . (New Orleans, 1853). The story of a gambler who murdered three Chilians at Mormon Gulch in 1852 and was immediately hanged, as told here, appears to be fiction.

Tyson. James L. Tyson, *Diary of a Physician in California* (New York, 1850). Tyson came to California in 1849 for the purpose of practising medicine in the mines. He remained only briefly but wrote a very good account of his experiences in the Northern Mines.

Tyson. Philip T. Tyson, *Geology and Industrial Resources of California* (Baltimore, 1851). The first scientific report of the gold discoveries, first published in U.S., 31st Cong., 1st sess., 1850, Senate, Executive doc. no. 47, part 2. **Tyson's map, 1849,** entitled *Geological Reconnoissances in California*, accompanies the above mentioned book. The report and the map are based on personal investigations made in 1849. The map is cited in this dictionary as Tyson's map, 1849, but it may appear as 1850 or 1851.

U

.S. Board on Geographical Names. Established on December 23, 1891, for the purpose of making uniform the usage and spelling of geographical names. In 1906 its powers were extended to include the approval of new names submitted to the Board.

U. S. Bulletin. U. S., Department of the Interior, Bureau of Mines, *Bulletin*. *Bulletin* No. 95 has a complete glossary of mining terms; No. 424 has a thorough account of Tuolumne and Mariposa counties in 1940, with maps and lists of mines in operation. Other numbers are listed separately under name of author. Much of the information in the *Bulletin* is similar to the findings given in the *Report* of the California State Mining Bureau.

USGS Quadrangle. The reference is to the maps of the topographical quadrangles of California issued by the United States Geological Survey. The date given refers to the reprint date. A number of areas covered by these sheets are included in the folios of the Geologic Atlas of the United States, published by the United States Geological Survey.

V

ein. A gold-containing streak of ground, used indiscriminately by early miners for lode or ledge.

Veta Madre. The Spanish name for Mother Lode.

Vischer. Eduard Vischer, "A Trip to the Mining Regions in the Spring of 1859," tr., Ruth Frey Axe, in *CHSQ*, XI, pp. 224 ff., 321 ff. Eduard Vischer, born in Bavaria, Germany, was a merchant in San Francisco and is best known as an artist of California scenes. His excellent account of his visits to the Northern and Southern mines is illustrated with sketches showing the methods of mining.

Vizetelly. Henry Vizetelly, *Four Months among the Goldfinders in California, being the Diary of an Expedition from San Francisco to the Gold Districts, by J. Tyrwitt Brooks, M.D.* (New York: Appleton, 1849). It is a convincingly written book, which was exposed as early as 1853 as a hoax, but was long afterwards still recognized as an authentic account. *See* Douglas S. Watson, "Spurious Californiana," in *CHSQ*, XI, pp. 65 ff. and Erwin G. Gudde, "The Vizetelly Hoax," in *Pacific Historical Review*, XXVIII, pp. 233 ff.

Volcanoville Quartz Mining District. *Map of the Volcanoville Quartz Mining District* (n.p., n.d.).

Von Leicht-Craven Map. The reference is to the 1874 (2nd) edition of the official map of the State Geological Survey of California, entitled *Map of California and Nevada*. It was originally drawn by Ferdinand von Leicht and A. Craven in 1873, revised by Hoffmann and Craven and published by the University of California. For many years it was the best map of the state of California.

W **ages.** A common miners' term for the profits made in placering.

Wagner. Jack Russell Wagner, *Gold Mines of California* . . . (Berkeley: Howell North, 1970). An illustrated history of selected mines in California, with biographical information on their owners and operators. The book is written for the general reader, and it contains an excellent selection of pictures of mines and mining scenes.

Wallace's Map, 1853. John Wallace. "Map showing the installations of the Tuolumne County Water Company in the gold mining region of Tuolumne County: Sonora, Columbia, Shaws Flat, Springfield, Browns Flat, and surroundings," 1853. MS photostat in Bancroft Library. Original in the Museum at Columbia, California.

Walsh. Henry L. Walsh. *Hallowed Were the Gold Dust Trails; the Story of the Pioneer Priests of Northern California* (Santa Clara, Calif.: University of Santa Clara, 1946). A detailed account of Roman Catholic priests and their work in the gold mining regions.

Ward. *Sam Ward in the Gold Rush*, ed., Carvel Collins (Stanford, Calif.: Stanford University Press, 1949). Longfellow's friend wrote a rather loquacious account of his

experiences in the Southern Mines, 1851–52. It is valuable for its unique detailed account of Quartzburg in the Mariposa district.

Warren. *See* Thompson ("Judge Thompson").

Washer. Another term for rocker.

Wasson. Jos. Wasson, *Complete Guide to the Mono County Mines* (San Francisco, 1879). It is hardly a complete guide but contains good information on the Mono and Inyo counties' mines in their early days. In this book Wasson revises his statement about the discovery of gold at Bodie and the circumstances of the discovery as given in his *Bodie and Esmeralda*, published the previous year, 1878.

Water Supply Papers. U.S. Geological Survey, Water Supply Papers. The entries are given under the name of the author.

Watson. George W. Watson, "Letter," datelined Red Flat [Tuolumne] January 12, 1853. 4 p. MS in Bancroft Library.

Wayman. John H. Wayman. "Diary and Letters" (1852–1862). 2 vols. MS in Bancroft Library. Vol. I contains information on the Southern Mines; vol. II includes letters from Shaws Flat and Forest City.

Weber-Biddle. John B. Weber and B. R. Biddle, "Journal of the Illinois Mutual Insurance Company." *In* Springfield (Illinois) *Daily Journal*, Dec. 4, 1849–April 13, 1850. The journals are a record of the overland trip and the mining venture of a company that mined near the upper Sacramento River in Shasta County.

Webster. Kimball Webster, *The Gold Seekers of '49* (Manchester, N.H., 1917). A well-told, detailed, sometimes monotonous account, partly a diary, partly reminiscent, includes his experiences in the Northern Mines, 1849–1851.

Wedertz. Frank S. Wedertz, *Bodie, 1859–1900* (Bishop, Calif.: Chalfant Press, 1969). The book is based on contemporary reports and on the author's long acquaintance with the area. It is a reliable, factual account of the town and its vicinity. Mr. Wedertz also furnished much additional information on mining camps in Mono County for use in the compilation of this dictionary.

Weight. Harold O. Weight, *Lost Mines of Death Valley* (Twentynine Palms: Calico Press, 1953). Written for the general reader.

Welles. C. M. Welles, *Three Years Wanderings of a Connecticut Yankee in South America, Africa, Australia, and California* (New York, 1859). A pleasing account of a traveler who visited the Northern Mines in 1854 after he had seen the gold diggings in Australia.

Wells. Epaphroditus Wells, "Letters to his Wife" (1849–1850). 28 p. Typescript in Bancroft Library. The letters contain information on life in the Northern Mines.

Wescoatt's Map, 1861. N. Wescoatt, *Official Map of Yuba County* (San Francisco: Lith. Britton & Co., 1861).

West Belt. Designates the gold belt west of the Mother Lode, containing an extensive system of lode gold-bearing veins; described and mapped in *Bulletin*, 193, pp. 15, 17.

Western Folklore. (Berkeley: University of California Press, 1942–   ). Formerly *California Folklore Quarterly*.

Weston. Silas Weston, *Life in the Mountains; or, Four Months in the Mines of California* (Providence, 1854). A brief but very interesting account of mining experiences in 1853 (?), written by a teacher from Rhode Island.

Westways. (Los Angeles: Automobile Club of Southern California, 1909–   ).

Wheat. Carl I. Wheat, *Books of the California Gold Rush* (San Francisco: Colt Press, 1949), an annotated, selected bibliography. *The Maps of the California Gold Region, 1848–1857; a Biblio-cartography of an Important Decade* (San Francisco: Grabhorn Press, 1942). [When referred to in this dictionary the number following the name "Wheat" indicates the map number.] It is an invaluable tool for a study of the cartography of the period, with reproductions of maps not readily accessible. Additional maps and information may be found in vol. III to V of his monumental historical-cartographical work, *Mapping the Transmississippi West, 1540–1861,* 5 vols. in 6 (San Francisco: Institute of Historical Cartography, 1957–1963). Wheat also edited "The California Letters of James Carr" in the *CHSQ. See* Carr.

Whim. A machine for hoisting ore to the surface. *See also* Whimtown [Tuolumne].

Whitcomb Family Papers (1851–1877). Includes papers of C. G. Whitcomb. 1 box. MS in Bancroft Library. The papers include description of life in the mines of Yuba County.

White. Charles White, *Letter from California, March 18, 1848* (Los Angeles: Glen Dawson, 1955). The personal letter written to a friend in St. Joseph, Missouri, by the alcalde of San Jose describes the richness of California's gold mines.

White. Lyle L. White is a member of a research group engaged in the study of the history of Nevada County.

Whitney Survey. Josiah D. Whitney, eminent American geologist, was appointed California state geologist in 1860 and commissioned to direct a complete geological survey of the state and to furnish topographical maps and reports with descriptions of its rocks, fossils, minerals, and its botanical and zoological productions together with specimens thereof. Failure of the legislature to provide financial support cut short the field work in 1874 and curtailed publication of reports and maps. The report on the geology, which was published by the legislature in 1865, was limited to a progress report entitled *Geology*, vol. I, and only the appendix of vol. II was published, later, in 1882, by Whitney himself in collaboration with Harvard College Museum of Comparative Zoology. *Geology I* includes reports of the mining region along the western slope of the Sierra Nevada from Mariposa County to Plumas County, based largely on the field work of Whitney, C. F. Hoffmann, William Ashburner, Clarence King, W. H. Brewer, and A. Rémond. A table of quartz mills operating in 1861, compiled by Ashburner, appears in the appendix. The anticipated report on the auriferous gravels did not appear until 1879–1880, published under Whitney's auspices, again in collaboration with Harvard College Museum of Comparative Zoology (*Memoirs*, I:1), under the title *The Auriferous Gravels of the Sierra Nevada of California*. This detailed report concentrates largely on the distribution and description of the auriferous gravels of the west slope of the High Sierra and is based mainly on the field work carried on in 1870–1871 by W. A. Goodrich and by Amos Bowman and W. H. Pettee in areas assigned to them in the region between the Mokelumne River and the Middle Fork of the Yuba River. A supplement, which appears as an appendix, contains Pettee's report on a later visit, in 1879, to portions of Placer, Nevada, Yuba, Sierra, Plumas, and Butte counties; also Goodyear's review of his 1871 field notes, followed by a listing of altitudes of points in the gravel region. A number of small specialized maps and diagrams appear within the text. For the maps published on the basis of the Survey, *see* Bowman, Hoffmann, Pettee, von Leicht. A copy of the printer's proof of the *Geological Map of the State of California*, 1873, is in the Bancroft Library. For a biography of

Whitney, consult Edwin F. Brewer, *Life and Letters of Josiah D. Whitney* (Boston: Houghton Mifflin, 1909). *See also* W. H. Brewer in this Bibliography. Consult two recently published articles in *Journal of the West*: "The Whitney Survey: Its Conflict with the California Legislature," by Charlotte P. Holton, *in* VIII:2 (April, 1969) and "The California State Geological Surveys," by Gordon B. Oakeshott, *in* X:1 (January, 1971). Mr. Oakeshott, deputy chief of the California Division of Mines and Geology, Department of Conservation, precedes his outline of the history, growth and function of the Division (see *Mining Bureau* in this bibliography) with a resumé of the reports of geological studies of the state made by its forerunners: John C. Frémont, 1843–44; James D. Dana, 1849; Philip T. Tyson, 1850; Pacific Railroad Reports, 1853–54 (see *California Place Names*); John B. Trask, state geologist, 1851–56; Whitney Survey, 1860–74.

Wierzbicki. Felix P. Wierzbicki, *California as it is and as it may be; or, A Guide to the Gold Region* (San Francisco, 1849). Wierzbicki was a Polish exile who came to America in 1834, studied medicine, came to California in 1847 with Stevenson's Regiment and "saw the elephant" in 1848. On the basis of his experiences and observations as a miner and a physician, he wrote a factual guide to the gold mines. His book was the first book in English printed and published in California and appeared in September and again in December, 1849. In 1933 the Grabhorn Press published an edition with an introduction by George D. Lyman.

Wilson. Edward Wilson, *The Golden Land; a Narrative of Early Travels in California* (Boston, 1852). Cover title: *Travels in California*. A floating miner, at Mormon Island, Placerville, Coloma, etc., whose success as related by him seems to be too good.

Wilson. Norman Wilson, of the Interpretative Services of the California State Department of Parks and Recreation, collaborated with Joseph A. McGowan, professor of history at the California State University at Sacramento, in furnishing information on the history of gold camps in Sacramento County.

Wilson's Report, 1854. C. S [L?] Wilson, *Report of the President* (of the Sacramento Valley Railroad) *to the Stockholders* (Sacramento, 1854). The report includes a list of "destinations" for freight shipped to points between Sacramento and Negro Bar, or the vicinity thereof, via the Sacramento Valley Railroad in May 1854.

Wiltsee. Ernest A. Wiltsee, " 'Double Springs,' the First County Seat of Calaveras County" in *CHSQ*, XI, pp. 176 ff.

Winch. A man-powered hoisting contraption; also called windlass.

Winchester Papers. Family letters in the California State Library, California Section.

Windeler. Adolphus Windeler, *The California Gold Rush Diary of a German Sailor*, ed., W. Turrentine Jackson (Berkeley, Calif.: Howell-North, 1969). The author and his friend "Charley" (Carl F. Christendorff), both German sailors, arrived in San Francisco in December, 1849. They mined in the vicinity of Oroville in the winter of 1850–1851 and in the Rich Bar area on the East Branch of the North Fork of Feather River in 1851–1852. It is a carefully edited, interesting account.

Wing. Stephen Wing, "Gleanings in California," (January 12, 1852–September 2, 1860). 4 vols. MS in Bancroft Library. Contains his journal covering his trip to California via Panama, his mining experiences in Placer and El Dorado counties, and his return to Massachusetts. It is an excellent detailed, realistic account of life in the mines — one of the best.

Wing Dam. A dam built into a river to divert the water for real or expected easy picking on the bottom of the stream.

Winkley. See *Knave*.

Wistar. Isaac J. Wistar, *Autobiography . . . 1827–1905* (Philadelphia: Wistar Institute of Anatomy and Biology, 1914). 2 vols. In his autobiography the author recounts his experiences as a young man in California. He mined briefly in the Bear River region in the fall of 1849, later sold provisions to miners on the Salmon River, and finally studied and practised law in San Francisco until his return to Philadelphia in 1857, where he became a well known penologist.

Wood. Harvey Wood, *Personal Recollections*, ed., John B. Goodman, III (Pasadena, 1955). A keepsake publication of the Zamorano Club. Wood, a member of the Kit Carson Association of New York, was owner of Robinsons Ferry, 1856–1895.

Wood. R. Coke Wood, professor of history at the University of the Pacific, is the author of numerous books and articles of the history of Calaveras County, including the town of Murphys. He reviewed the entries on Calaveras County for this dictionary and offered additional information.

Wood. Raymund F. Wood, *California's Agua Fria; the Early History of* Mariposa County (Fresno: Academy Library Guild, 1954). An extensive account of the county and its first county seat.

Woods. Daniel B. Woods, *Sixteen Months at the Gold Diggings* (New York, 1851). The author, a clergyman and a keen observer, was in the mines, mainly in the Mariposa and Tuolumne areas, in 1849–50. His excellent day to day account is one of the finest books of the Gold Rush.

Woods. James Woods, *Recollections of Pioneer Work in California* (San Francisco, 1878). Rev. Woods, the author, was a Presbyterian minister in Stockton and vicinity in the 1850s. There are some references to mining localities.

Woodward. E. Morrison Woodward, "Diary" (1849–1850). 40 p. MS in Bancroft Library. The author mined in Calaveras and Tuolumne counties.

Wooster. Clarence M. Wooster, "Meadow Lake City and a Winter at Cisco in the Sixties" in *CHSQ*, XVIII, pp. 149 ff. A pleasing picture of the highest mining district.

Work Projects Administration Project. Refers to research materials used from U.S. Work Projects Administration, California, ca. 1935–1942 for *California Place Names*. 6 cartons. In Manuscript Division of Bancroft Library.

Wyllys. Rufus K. Wyllys, "The French in Sonora, 1850–1854." Ph.D. dissertation. University of California, Berkeley, 1964.

Wyman. *See* "California Emigrant Letters."

Wynn. Marcia R. Wynn, *Desert Bonanza* (Glendale: A. H. Clark, 1963).

Yale. Charles G. Yale, *List of Working Mines on the Pacific Coast* (San Francisco, 1882).

Yuba County Directory. *Yuba, Sutter, Colusa, Butte and Tehama Counties Directory, 1884–5* (Binder's title).

Yuba County History 1879: William Henry Chamberlain, *History of Yuba County . . .* (Oakland: Thompson and West, 1879). One of the best county histories, with a detailed atlas and lists of mining towns by townships.

Yuba County Map. 1861: *See* Wescoatt. **1879:** *In* William H. Chamberlain, *History of Yuba County, California* (Oakland: Thompson and West, 1879). **1887:** J. M. Doyle, *Official Map of Yuba County* (n.p.: 1887).

List of Places by Counties

Alpine County

Great Mogul District
Hope Valley District
Kongsberg
Konigsberg
Mogul
Monitor
Silver King District
Silver Mountain: town, District
Silver Valley

Amador County

Alex Ranch
Amador City
Amador Crossing
American Flat
American Hill
Aqueduct City
Argonaut Mine
Arkansas Diggings
Armstrongs Mill
Arroyo Seco
Ashland
Ballards Humbug
Bedbug
Big Bar
Blacks Gulch
Blood Gulch
Bloody Gulch
Boomville
Boonville
Boston Store
Bottileas
Bridgeport
Buena Vista
Bunker Hill Mine
Burns & Pope Ferry
Butte City
Camp Opera
Camp Union
Cape Cod Bar
Casco Mill

Central Eureka Mine
Central House
Chaparral Hill
China City
China: Gulch, Hill
Clapboard Gulch
Clinton
Columbia Bar
Contreras
Crater City
Dead Mans Flat
Defender
Dents Ranch
Diving Bell Bar
Dog Town
Doschs Store
Doshs Store
Douglasville
Drummondsville
Dry Creek
Dry Creekville
Drytown
Ellises Ranch
Else: Creek, Ranch
Eureka Mines
Fiddletown
Forest Home
Forks of the Cosumnes
Fort Ann
Fort John
Freezeout
Fremont-Gover
French Bar
French Camp
French Flat
Frenchmans Bar
Gales Ranch
Gate, or The Gate
Gilberts Ranch
Golden Gate: Creek, Mine
Gold Hill
Gold Mountain
Gopher Flat
Grass Valley Ranch

Greaserville
Grizzly Hill
Haletown
Hardenberg: Mine, Mill, Ditch
Hardscrabble
Haskells
Hatchville
Hayward Mine
Helltown
Herbertville
Hogtown
Hoodville
Hubertville
Humbug Gulch
Hunts Gulch
Huse Bridge
Indian Camp
Indian Gulch
Ione
Iowa: Diggings, Flat
Irish Hill
Irishtown
Italian Bar
Jackass Gulch
Jackson: town, Creek
Jackson Gate
James Bar
Joes Gulch
Johnsons Humbug
Karneys Diggings
Kennedy Mine
Keystone Mine
Lancha Plana
Leek Spring
Lincoln Consolidated Mine
Loafer: Flat, Gulch, Hill
Lower Bar
Lower Rancheria
Mahala Flat
Mahoney Mine
Marlette
Martell
Middle Bar
Mile Gulch
Mineral City
Ministers: Claim, Gulch
Misery Flat
Mobile Bar
Mount Echo District
Muletown
Murderers Gulch
Murphys: Gulch, Ridge
New Chicago
New Philadelphia
New York: Flat, Store
New York Ranch
North Fork Mokelumne
Ohio Hill
Old Eureka Mine
Old Rancheria

Oleta
Oneida Mine and Mill
Oregon: Bar, Camp, Gulch
Original Amador Mine
Pats Bar
Pine Grove
Plattsburg
Plymouth
Poker Camp
Pokerville
Porterfield
Possum Bar
Prospect Hill
Puckerville
Puts Bar
Quartz Hills
Quartz Mountain
Quincy
Rancheria
Ranchoree
Rattlesnake Gulch
Red Gulch
Red Hills
Rensomville
Rich Bar
Rickeyville
Rio Vista
Rough and Ready Bar
Russell: Hill, Gulch, Diggings
Santa Maria Gulch
Sarahville
Scottsburg
Scottsville
Secreto or Secreta
Siebenthaler Lode
Slabtown
Soher & Parrish's Bridge
Soldiers Gulch
Sonora Bar
South Eureka Mine
South Spring Hill Mine
Spanish Gulch
Spring Hill Mine, Spring Mill
Squaw Gulch
Stone Creek
Stony Bar
(?) Stop Jack Bar
Succertown
Suckertown
Sugar Loaf Hill
Sutter Creek
Suttersville
Tanyard
The Corners
The Gate
Thoss Sulfuret Mill
Tiddletown
Toby Moors Diggings
Treasure Mine
Tunnel Hill

Union Bar
Union Flat
Upper: Bar, Ferry
Upper Crossing
Upper Rancheria
Violin City
Volcano
Volcano Flat
Watkins Bar
Whale Boat Ferry
Wheeler Diggings
Whiskey Flat
White Oak Flat District
Whites Bar
Wildman Mine
Willow Bar
Willow Springs
Wisconsin Bar
Woosterville
Yankee Hill
Yeomet
Yornet
Zeila Mine

Butte County

Adams Bar; Adamsville
Adamstown
Ah-Moon Bar
American Bar
Antelope Spring
Bagdad
Balsam Hill
Bangor
Banner Ledge
Bardee Bar
Bartees Bar
Berdan
Bernard Flat
Berry Creek Bar
Bidwell Bar
Big Bar
Big Bend
Big Kimshew
Big Rock Creek
Big Stony Bar
(?) Bingham Bar
Blairtown
Bleakly Point
Bloomer: Bar, Hill
Boneyard
Boston Ranch
Browns Ravine
Brush Creek
Buchanan Hill
Buffs Bar
Bull Creek
Burwells Bar
Butte Creek District
Butte Mills

Campville
Cape River Claim
Carpenters Bar
Carpenters Flat
Carr Diggings
(?) Carrysville
Cascade Valley
Centerville
Chambers: Bar, Creek
Chaparral House
Charleys Ranch
Cherokee; Cherokee: Flat, Ravine
China Town
Chinese Camp
Chub Gulch
Clipper Mills
Columbia Flat
Columbiaville
Concow: Valley, Township
Crane Valley
Curley Flat
Dark Canyon
Dawlytown
Diamondville
Dickson Gulch
Dogtown
Dutch Flat
Emma Mine
Enterprise
Evans Bar
Evansville
Fergusons Bar
Flea Valley
Forbes Diggings
Forbestown
Forks of Butte
Fredonia
Freeze-Out
French Creek Bar
Frenchtown
Goatville
Gold Bank Mine
Golden Gate Flume
Gold Gulch Dry Diggings
Gold Lake
Gold Run
Golls Diggings
Hamilton
Hamilton Bar
Helltown
Hermitage
High Rock Bar
Holts Ravine
Honcut: Creek, City, town
Houghs Bar
Huffs Bar
Hupps
Hurleton
Indian Springs
Inskips

Island Bar
Johnson Bar
Jordan: Creek, Hill
Kanaka Bar
Kimshew
Know Nothing Creek
Kunkle
Last Chance
Lattimore Bar
Lindsays Bar
Little Butte
Little Kimshew
Little Rock Creek
Live Oak Bar
Loafers Diggings
Longs Bar
Lovelock
Lynchburg
McCabes Creek
Magalia
(?) Marks Bar
Millers Bar
Millers Ranch
Mineral Slide
Miners Ranch
Missouri Bar
Monte de Oro
Monte Vista Quartz Mills
Montgomery
Moores Station
Mooretown
Mooreville
Morris: Bar, Ravine
Morrisons Ravine
Mosquito Creek
Mountain House
Mountain View
Mount Ararat
Mud Hill
Neals Diggings
Nelsons Bar
Nesbitts Flat
New Era
New Philadelphia
Nimshew
Ohio Bar
Oleepa
Omit Bar
Ophir
Opopee: Creek, Bar
Oregon: City, Gulch
Oro Fino Placers
Oroleva
Oroville
Oskalousa Bar
Ottawa Bar
Pences
Pentz
Perkins Ravine

Perschbaker Mine
Pictos Bar
Potters Bar
Powelltown
Pulga Bar
Ramsey Bar
Rancheria
Reeces Bar
Reeves Bar
Rich Bar
Rich Gulch
Robbers Roost
Robinsons Hill
Rock Creek
Rocky Bar
Rush Creek
Saint Clairs Flat
Schirmer Ravine
Shores Bar
Sigl
Simpson Flat
Snows Diggings
Spanishtown
Spring Gulch
Spring Town
Spring Valley Mine
Stone House Bar
Stony Bar
Stony Point Bar
Stringtown
Sucker Bar
Sucker Riffle Bar
Sucker Run
Sumneys Flat
Surcease Mine
Swedes Flat
Table Mountain
Tancow
Thompsons Flat
Toadtown
Tolls: Dry Diggings, Old Diggings
Troy
Union Bar
Union Cape Claim
Veazie City
Veza City
Virginia Flat
Walkers Plains
Whiskey Bar
Whiskey Flat
White Rock Bar
Wild Yankee
Willard Claim
Wolfs Bar
Wyandotte
Yankee Bar
Yankee Flat
Yankee Hill
Yatestown

Calaveras County

Abbeys Ferry
Alabama: Gulch, Hill
Albany Flat
Altaville
Alto Mining District
Angelo
Angels: Camp, Creek
Angier House
Antoine
Average
Bakers Claim
Balaklava Hill
Bald Hill
Bayecito
Bear: Mountains, Creek
Biacete
Big Bar
Big Flat
Black Creek
Blue Mountain: City, District
Boston Companys Bar
Boston Mine
Bostwick Bar
Brownsville
Brushville
Buckeye: Flat, Hill, Gulch
Buena Vista Hill
Buntys Gulch
Burns & Pope Ferry
Busters Gulch
Butte Flat
Byrnes Ferry
Calaveritas: Creek, Hill
Camanche
Camp Catarrh
Camp Flores
Campo de los Muertos
Campo Seco
Camp Senorita
Camp Spirito
Capulope
Carson: Creek, Hill, Flat, town
Cat Camp
Catts Camp
Cave City
Cayote or Cayute
Central Hill; Central Hill Channel
Chaparral Hill
Chaparral Tunnel
Cherokee: House, Creek, Flat
Chichi
Chilean Gulch
Chili Camp
Chili Gulch
China Bar
Cisna Hill
Clays Bar
Colburg

Collierville District
Comanche
Copperopolis
Corons
Corral Flat
Coyote: Gulch, Creek
Dead Mans Hill
Diamond Bar
Dogtown
Double Springs
Douglass Flat
Dry Diggings
Duck Bar
Dunning Claim
Dutchmans Gulch
El Dorado
El Dorado: Bar, Flat
Ella Mine
Esmeralda
Esperanza
Eutaw Camp
Fashville
Felix
Filibuster Bar
Foremans
Forks of the Road
Fosteria
Fourth Crossing
French Camp
French Gulch
French Hill
Frogtown
German Ridge
Glencoe
Gold Cliff
Golden Gate Hill
Gold Hill
(?) Gospel: Flat, Gulch, Swamp
Grand Bar
Grape Vine District
Greasertown
Grub Hill
Gwin Mines
Haightsville
Hanselman Hill
Happy Valley
Hawk Eye
Hicks
Hodson District
Hog Hill
Hubbardville
Huntsville
Independence
Indian Creek
Indian Flat
Indian Gulch
Iowa Cabins
Iron Mountain
Irvine
James Bar

Jenks Ranch
Jenny Bar
Jenny Lind
Jesus Maria
Joe Wallace Gulch
John Bull Diggings
Jones Flat
Kentucky House
Kohlbergs Humbug
Latimers
Lemmons
Les Fourcades
Licking Forks
Lightner Mine
Limerick
Long: Gulch, Canyon
Los Muertos
Lost City
Lower Bar
Lower Calaveritas
Lower Rich Gulch
McKinneys Humbug
McLeans: Bar, Ferry
Madison Mine
Maloneys; Meloneys
Mansanita
Marble Springs
Martins Bar
Meloncitos
Melones
Mesquite District
Milton
Moaning Cave
Mokelumne: Diggings, Gulch
Mokelumne Hill
Morgan: Ground, Slope
Mosquito Gulch
Mountain King Mine
Mountain Ranch
(?) Mugginsville
Murphys
Murrays Creek
Musquito
Negro Hill
New Boston Company Bar
New York Bar
Nigger Gulch
Nigger Hill
North Branch
North Hill
Nyes Ferry
O'Byrne Ferry
Old Channel
Old Gulch
Old Womans Gulch
O'Neils: Creek, Bar
Otter Bar
Owlsburg, Owlburrow Flat
Paloma
Pennsylvania Gulch

Petersburg
Petticoat Mine
Phoenix Company Bar
Picaune Gulch
Pine Log
Pleasant Springs
Pomfrets Hill
Poverty Bar
Prussian Hill
Quail Hill
Quaker City Mine
(?) Ragged Breeches Bar
Ragtown; Ragtown Hill
Railroad Flat
Red Flat Hill
Red Hill
Regans
Reynolds Ferry
Rich Gulch
Rio Rico Mines
Rio Saco Mines
Robinsons Ferry
Rock Creek
Royal Mine
Sailor Gulch
Salt Spring Valley
San Andreas
San Antonio
San Bruno
San Domingo
Sandy Bar
Sandy Gulch
San Jacinto
San Pascal
Scollans Camp
Scorpion Gulch
Second Crossing
Sheep Ranch
Shorts Bar
Skull Flat
Slab Ranch
Slumgullion
Smith Flat District
Snake Gulch
Soher & Parrish's Bridge
Solomons Hole
South Carolina Mine
Spanish Bar
Spring Gulch
Squaw Hollow
Stanislaus Diggings
Steep Gulch
(?) Steubenville
Stockton Hill
Stone Cabin Gulch
Stone: City, House, Creek, Settlement
Stoutenburg
Stuarts: Hill, Flat
Sweet Vengeance
Swiss Bar

Talbots Hill
Taylors Bar
Telegraph City
Texas House
Third Crossing
Tunnel Hill
Turnersville
Twists Ranch
Two Mile Bar
Two Springs
Union Bar
Upper: Bar, Ferry
Upper Calaveritas
Upper Rich Gulch
Utica Mine
Valentine Hill
Vallecito
Valley Springs
Vermont Bar
Wades Flat
Wallace
Wards Diggings
Washington: Flat, Ranch
Waynes Bar
West Point
Wet Gulch
Whale Boat Ferry
Whales Bar
Whiskey: Gulch, Flat, Hill
Whiskey Slide
Whit's Bar
Willow Bar
Willow Springs
Wilson Creek
Winters Bar
Winterton
Woodhouse
Yaqui Camp

Colusa County

Sulphur Creek District

Contra Costa County

Marsh Creek
Mount Diablo

Del Norte County

Althouse; Althouse Creek
Big Flat
Black Gulch
Coon Flat
Craigs Creek
Crescent City
French Hill
Galice Creek
Growler Gulch
Haines Flat

Haynes Flat
Hueniche Bar
Hurdy Gurdy Creek
Jacksonville
Klamath City
Monumental District
Myrtle Creek
Smith River
Sterling
Sucker Creek
Vallardville
Yates Beach

El Dorado County

Alabama Bar
Alabama Flat
Alhambra Mine
Alpine Mine
American Flat
American House
Arum City
Auram City
Aurum City
Austin
Backs
Bacons Placer
Badger Hill
Bald Hill
Baltic Peak
Barley Flat
Bean Hill
Bean Poker Flat
Beaver Bar
Beebe Mine
Bells Diggings
Big Bar
Big Canyon
Big Crevice
Big House
Biglers Diggings
Big Negro Hill
Big Ravine (Big Canyon)
Big Sandy Mine
Black Oak Mine
Blind Mans Flat
Blue Gouge
Boston Bar
Bottle Hill Diggings
Boulder Hill
Bowlder Hill
Brewster
Brills Diggings
Brocklis Bar
Browns Bar
Brownsville
Buckeye Flat
Buckeye Hill
Bucks Bar
Budeville

Buffalo: Hill, Creek
Bull Diggings
California Bar
Camp: Creek, Springs
Canton
Canyon
Canyon Creek
Cart Wheel Valley
Cave Valley
Cedarbergs Quartz Lode
Cedar: Ravine, Springs
Cedarville
Cement Hill
Centerville
Centre Diggings
Centreville
Chambers Ravine
Chelalian Bar
Chickamasee
Chicken Flat
Child Bar
Chilean Bar
Chile Bar
Chili Bar
Chillean Bar
Chillian Bar
China Bar
Chris Ranch
Church Mine
Cincinnati
Clarkson
Clarksville
Clay Hill
Clipper: Canyon, Hill
Coffin Bar
Cold Springs
Coloma
Columbia Flat
Columbia Ranch
Condemned Bar
Cool
Cooleys Bar
Coon: Hollow, Hill
Cosumnes
Cox Station
Coyoteville
Cranes Gulch
Crusen Mine
Crystal Mine
Culloma, Cullumah
Darlings Ranch
Dead Mans Hollow
Deep Ravine
Deer Creek
Deer Valley
Devine Gulch
Diamond Spring
Dickerhoff Mine
Dirty Flat
Dogtown

Doolittle Ranch
Downings Ravine
Dross Ravine
Drunkers Bar
Dry Creek
Dry Diggings
Dry Gulch
Dustyville
Dutch: Bar, Flat, Hill
Dutch Creek
Dutchtown
Eagle City
East Canyon
El Dorado
El Dorado Canyon
Elizaville
Emigrant Ravine
Empire Canyon
Empire Ravine
Euchre Diggings
Eureka Bar
Fair Play
Five-Cent Hill
Fleatown
Floras
Forkville, or Forksville
Fort Grizzly
Fort Hill
Fort Jim
Franklin Mine
French: Canyon, Creek, Frenchtown
French Ravine
Frenchtown
Garden Valley
Georgetown
Georgia Slide
Gold Bug Mine
Gold Flat
Gold Hill
Gold Springs
Gopher Hill
Granite Hill
Gravel Hill
Gray Eagle Bar
Greenhorn Canyon
Greenhorn Hill
Green Springs
Green Valley
Greenwood: town, Valley, Creek
Grey Eagle: Bar, City
Grizzle Flat
Grizzly Flats
Growlersburg
Hangtown
Hangtown: Creek, Ravine
Hanks Exchange
Hartnells Ranch
Hartwells Ranch
Harveys
Hazel Creek Mine

Henrys Diggings
Hermitage Ranch
Higgins Point
Hoggs Diggings
Hogs Dry Diggings
Holmes Camp
Hook and Ladder Mine
Hoosier Bar
Hornblende Mountains
Horseshoe Bar
Hosier Bar
Hudson Gulch
Idlewild
Illinois Canyon
Indian Diggins
Indian Hill
IOOF Bar
Iowa Bar
Iowaville
Irish Creek
Jackass Flat
Jayhawk
Jenny Lind Flat
Jims Diggings
Johnsons Bar
Johnsons Canyon
Johnstown
Jones Camp
Jones: Hill, Canyon
Josephine
Junction Bar
Junction House
Kanaka Bar
Kanaka Diggings
Kanaka Town
Kellys Diggings
Kelsey
Kentucky: Flat, Hill
Knickerbocker Ranch
Ladies Canyon
Lady Emma Mine
Landecker Mine
Last Chance Mine
Latrobe
Lawrenceburg
Ledge Bar
Lewis
Little Negro Hill
Live Oak Bar
Loafers Hollow
Log Cabin Ravine
Logtown
Long Bar
Long Valley
Lorenz Bar
Lost Infant Claim
Lotus
Louisiana Bar
Louisville
Lousy Bar

Lower South Bar
Lower Town
Lymans Diggings
Lyonsdale
(?) McClintock Ranch
McDowells Race
McDowellsville
Macksville
Magnolia
Main Bar
Maine Bar
Maith Creek
Malcomb Bar
Mameluke Hill
Manhattan: Canyon, Creek
Marble Bar
Marmeluke Hill
Marshall
Marshall Ravine
Marshalls Bar
Martinez Creek
Massachusetts Flat
Matheneys: Creek, Diggings
Mathinas, Mathines or Mathinias Creek
Meadow Flat
Mendon
Menken Cut Bar
Michigan: Bar, Flat
Milk Punch Bar
Mineral Bar
Missouri Bar
Missouri Canyon
Missouri Flat
Montezuma-Apex Mine
Mormon Bar
Mormon Gulch
Mosquito Valley
Mound Springs
Mount Auburn
Mount Calvary
Mount Gregory
Mount Pleasant Mine
Mud Springs
Murderers Bar
Nameless Point
Nashville
Negro Bluff
Negro Flat
Negro Hill
Nelighs Camp
Nelsonville
Nevada Flat
Newtown
New York Bar
New York Hill
Nigger Hill
Oak Ranch
Ohio Flat
Old Dry Diggings
Omo Ranch

One Eye Canyon
Oregon Bar
Oregon Hill
Oregon: Ravine, Canyon
Oro Fino Mine
Ostro
Otter Creek
Oxbow Bar
Pacific District
Pacific Mine
Park
Patterson: Hill, Gulch
Pattersons Mill
Penobscot
Pepper Box Flat
Perkins Bar
Perrys Ranch
Peru
Pilot Hill
Pinchemtight
Pine Bar
Pi Pi
Pittsburgh Bar
Pittsville
Placerville
Placerville Divide
Pleasant Flat
Pleasant Hill
Pleasant Valley
Plunketts Ravine
Pocohontas Mine
Pole Cat Slide
Portuguese Joes Bar
Poverty Bar
Poverty Point
Powningville
Prospect Flat
Puritan Camp
Pyramid Mine
Quartzburg
Quartz Canyon
Quartz Hill
Quartzville
Quincy Dam
Ragtown
Rat Bar
Rattlesnake Bar
Red Bar
Red Hill Bar
Red Hill Diggings
Red Ravine
Republican Canyon
Rescue
Reservoir Hill
Rhodes Diggings
Rich: Bar, Flat
Ringgold
Rocky Bar
Rosecrans Quartz Lode
Russ Diggings

Russells Bar
Sailor Boys Ravine
Sailor Creek
Sailor Flat
Sailors Bar
Sailors Claim
Sailors Slide
Saint Lawrenceville
Salmon Falls
Sandusky Hill
Sandy Bar
Saratoga
Sardine Diggings
Schleins Diggings
Shingle Creek
Shingle Springs
Shirttail Canyon
Slate Creek
Slate Mountain
Sliger Mine
Slug Gulch
Sly Park
Smiths Flat
Smiths Ranche
Snyders Bar
Soap Weed
Somerset
South Canyon
South Point Dry Diggings
Spanish Bar
Spanish Canyon
Spanish Diggings
Spanish Flat
Spanish Hill
Spanish Ravine
Springfield District
Spring Flat
Squaw: Hollow, Creek
Stag Flat
Steelys Fork
Stillwagen
Stoner Ravine
Stony Bar
Stop Jack Bar
String Canyon
Stuckslager Mine
Sugar Loaf
Sunols Washings
Sutters Bar
Sutters Mill
Taylors
Tennessee Hill
Texas: Bar, Creek
Texas Hill
Thousand Dollar Canyon
Tichners Secret
Tiger Lily
Tipton Hill
Toll House Mine
Tryagain Tunnel

Tunnel Hill
(?) Turners Diggings
Union City
Union Flat
Uniontown, Uniontown II
Upper Mines
Virner
Volcano Bar
Volcano Slide
Volcanoville
Weaver Creek
Weaverton
Weaverville
Weber: Creek, Camp; Weberville
Weber Divide
Weberville
Wheelocks Ravine
Whiskey Bar
Whistleburg
White Oak Flat
(?) White Rock
White Rock: Canyon, Hill
Whiteside Seam Diggings
Whorehouse Gulch
Wild Cat Bar
Wild Goose Flat
Willow Bar
Winslow Creek
Wisconsin Bar
Wolverine Bar
Woodside Mine
Yankee Flat
Yankee Slide
Young Dry Diggings
Zantgraf Mine

Fresno County

Big Creek District
Big Dry Creek District
Cassadys Bar
Friant District
Graveyard Canyon
Kaiser Creek; Kaiser Creek Diggings
Mill Creek
Millerton
Rootville
Sampsons Flat
Sycamore Flat District
Temperance Flat

Glenn County

Monroeville

Humboldt County

Big Bar
Buena Vista District
French Bar

(?) Gold Beach
Gold Bluff
Hoopa District
Little River Beach
New Orleans Bar
Orick District
Orleans Bar
Red Cap Bar
Thompsons Bar
Wakell Flat
Weitchpec Bar

Imperial County

American Girl Mine
Cargo Muchacho: Mountains, Mining District
Chocolate Mountains
Golden Cross Mine
Hedges
Mesquite Placers
Ogilby
Picacho
Pothole Placers
Tumco

Inyo County

Alabama Hills
Argus Mountains
Ballarat
Bend City
Beveridge District
Big Pine
Bishop Creek District
Breyfogle Canyon
Cardinal Mine
Cerro Gordo
Chloride Cliff District
Chrysopolis
Coso District
Darwin: town, District
Death Valley National Monument
Fish Spring District
Goler Mine
Goler Wash
Grapevine District
Greenwater
Gunsight Lode
Harrisburg
Hunter Canyon
Keane Wonder: Camp, Mine
Kearsarge: City, District
Keeler
Leadfield
Lees Camp District
Lone Pine City
Lookout
Marble Canyon
Mazourka Canyon

Modoc District
Olancha
Owens: Lake, River
Panamint
Panamint Range
Pleasant Canyon
Pop's Gulch
Radcliff (or Ratcliff) Mine
Reward
Russ District
San Carlos
Santa Rita Flat
Skidoo
Snow Canyon District
Surprise Valley
Tibbetts District
Tinemaha
Ubehebe District
Wild Rose Canyon
Willow District
Willow Springs
Wilshire-Bishop Creek Mine

Kern County

Agua Caliente District
Amalie
Beartrap Flat
Big Blue Mine
Bodfish: Canyon, Creek, Camp
Butte Mine
Cactus Queen Mine
Caliente
Cantil
Claraville
Clear Creek Mining District
Cove District
Cow Wells
Dahlonegha
Dutch Bar
Dutch Flat
El Dorado District
Elmer
El Paso District
Erskine Creek
Fiddlers Gulch
Garlock
Gold Camp
Golden Queen Mines
Goldtown
Goler: Gulch, Canyon, Placers
Granite
Granite Station
Greenhorn: Gulch, Mountains, Caves
Green Mountain District
Grubstake Dry Placers
Grubstake Hill
Hamilton Hill
Havilah
Isabella

Jawbone Canyon
Joburg
Johannesburg
Kelso Canyon
Kern River Diggings
Kernville
Keyesville
Keysville
Last Chance
Last Chance Canyon
Linns Valley
Long Tom District
Loraine
Middle Buttes
Mojave Mining District
Mount Sinai District
Norden Placer
Paris
Petersburg
Pine Tree
Piute Mountains
Poso: Creek, Flat
Quartzburg
Quito District
Rademacher District
Rand District
Randsburg
Red Rock Canyon
Ricardo Placer Mines
Rich Gulch
Rio Bravo
Rogersville
Rosamond
Sageland
Searles
Spring Valley
Standard Mines
Stringer District
Summit Diggings
Tehachapi Valley
Ticknor Basin
Tollgate Gulch
Tropico: Hill, Mines
Walkers Basin
Washington District
Whiskey Flat
Williamsburg
Woody
Yellow Aster Mine

Lassen County

Diamond Mountain District
Golden Eagle Mine
Gold Run
Hayden Hill
Honey Lake District
Mountain Meadows District
Mount Hope
Providence City

Los Angeles County

Acton
Banks Mine
Barric Mine
Big Tujunga Canyon
Bouquet Canyon
Castaic Creek
Crab Hollow Diggings
Duartes Tableland
Eldoradoville
Governor Mine
Haskell Canyon
Los Padres Mine
Mellens Camp
Monte Cristo Mine
Moores Camp
Mount Gleason District
Neenach
New York Mine
Palomas Canyon
Placerita: Creek, Canyon
Ratsburg
Ravenna
Red Rover Mine
San Feliciano Canyon
San Fernando Placers
San Francisquito Canyon
San Gabriel: Canyon, River
Santa Anita Placers
Santa Ariba Farm
Santa Catalina Island
Santa Clara River
Santa Feliciana
Soledad Canyon
Temescal Ranch
Texas Canyon
Yount Lode

Madera County

Chowchilla District
Coarse Gold: Creek, Gulch
Fine Gold: Creek, Gulch
Fresno Gulch
Fresno River District
Greaser Gulch
Grub Gulch
Hildreth
Mine d'Or de Quartz Mountain
Oro Fino
Oro Grosso
Phillips
Potter Ridge District
Quartz Mountain
(?) Spangled Gold Gulch
Texas Flat

Marin County

Gold Gulch
San Geronimo
Union Gulch

Mariposa County

Adelaide and Anderson Mine
Agua Fria
Altons Bar
Arkansas Flat
Ave Maria
Badger Mine
Bagby
Baldwin
Bandarita Mine
Bandareta
Barrett City
Bear Creek
Bear Valley
Benton Mills
Biddles Camp
Black Bart Mine
Bondurant
Bondville
Bridgeport
Buckeye District
Buena Vista Mine
Buffalo Gulch
Bull Creek District
Bullion Knob
Bunker Hill Mine
Burns: Camp, Creek, Diggings, Ranch
Carson Creek
Carsons or Carson
Catheys Valley
Cat Town
Chamisal
Champion Mine
Cherokee Mine
Chuchilla Diggings
Clearinghouse
Colorado
Colorow
Corbet Creek
Cotton Creek; Cottonville
Coulterville
Cunningham Rancho
Diltz Mine
Dogtown
Drunken Gulch
Dutch Creek
Dutch Ranche
Early Mine
Exchequer
Farmers Hope
Feliciana Creek
Flyaway
Fremont Estate
French Camp
Frenchmans Bar
French Mine
Geary Mine
Gentry Gulch
Godeys Gulch

Gold Bug Mine
Gold Hill
Granite Springs District
Greaser Gulch
Greeley Hill District
Green Gulch
Guadalupe
Hardisons Camp
Harveys Bar
Hasloe Mine
Haydensville
Hells Hollow
Hempstead
High State Bar
Hites Cove
Hornitos
Horseshoe Bend
Hunter Valley
Indian Gulch
Jenny Lind Mine
Jerseydale
Johnson Flat
Johnsonville
Jones Flat
Kingsley
King Solomon Mine
Kinsley
Logtown
Long Canyon
Louisa Mine
Maciys Bar
Malvina Mines
Mammoth Bar
Marble Springs
Mariposa: Creek, City
Mariposa Grant
Mariposita
Mary Harrison Group
Matsells Creek
Maxwell Creek
Merced River Diggings
Mexican Mine
Missouri Gulch
Mockingbird Mine
Mono Camp
Mormon Bar
Mountain King Mine
Mount Buckingham
Mount Bullion
Mount Gaines
Mount Ophir
Neals Ranch
New Diggings Ranch
New Mexican Camp
New Years Diggins
North Fork
Norwegian: Tent, Gulch
Number Nine
Oakes and Reese Mine
Oakland

Ophir
Original Mine
Oro Rico Mine
Ortega Mine
Peñon Blanco
Permit Mine
Pine Tree and Josephine Mine
Piney Creek
Pino Blanco
Pleasant Valley
Potosi Mine
Poverty Flat
Princeton
Quail Mine
Quartzburg
Ranch Gulch
Red Bank Mine
Red Cloud Mine
Ridleys Ferry
Roma Mine
Rum Hollow
Ruth Pierce Mine
Santa Cruz Mountain
Saxton Creek
Schroeder Group
Sextons Creek
Sherlock: Creek, Gulch, Diggings
Sierra Rica Mine
Simpsonville
Smiths: Flat, Ferry
Snow Creek
Solomons Gulch
Split Rock Ferry
Spread Eagle Mine
Stockton Creek
Stud Horse Flat
Sweetwater
Temperance Creek
Texana
Texas Gulch
Texas Hill
Toledo Gulch
Tulitos
Tyro Mine
Upper Agua Fria
Virginia Mine
Washington Flat
Washington Mine
Whiskey Flat
White Porphyry Mine
Whitlock

Mendocino County

Big Valley
Hopland
Red Mountain District
Round Valley
Sawyers Bar
Ukiah

Merced County

Forlorn Hope Camp
Georgia Bar
Hopetown
McKenzie Bar
Pacheco Pass
Perrine Bar
Reynolds Bar
Snelling

Modoc County

Discovery Hill
High Grade District
Winters District

Mono County

Arrastre Creek
Aurora
Belfort
Bennettville
Benton
Biderman, Mount
Bloody Canyon
Bodie
Booker Flat
Boulder Flat
Callahans Station
Cameron
Castle Peak District
Clinton
Clover Patch District
Dana Village
Dogtown
Dunderberg
Esmeralda District
Fales Station
Glines Canyon
Hector Station
Homer District
Hot Springs
Huntoon Station
Indian District
Jordan District
Kavanaugh Ridge
Keith District
Lake Mining District
Last Chance Hill
Leevining: Canyon, Creek
Lundy
Mammoth: City, District
Martinez Hill
Masonic: District, town
May Lundy Mine
Middle Hill
Mill City
Mineral: Hill, Park
Monoville

Monte Cristo
Montgomery District
Munckton
Newburg
Partzwick
Patterson District
Pine City
Prescott District
Rancheria Gulch
Sheepherder Lode
Silverado Canyon
Sinnamon Cut
Star City
Sunshine Valley
Taylor Gulch
Tioga
Vernon
Walker River Diggings
Wasson
West Walker District
White Mountains

Monterey County

Carmel River
Gorda
Jolon Field
Los Burros District
San Antonio

Napa County

Calistoga District
Conn Valley
Palisade Mine
Saint Helena
Silverado

Nevada County

African Flat
Albany Hill
Albion: Diggings, Hills
Allison: Ranch, Diggings
Alpha
Alta Hill
American Bar
American Hill
Ancho-Erie Mine
Anthony House
Arctic Group
Aristocracy Hill
Arkansas Canyon
Atlanta
Badger Hill District
Balaklava
Bald Eagle Diggings
Baltic Mine
Baltimore City
Banner Mine

Bannerville
Beckmans Flat
Beckville
Berrington Hill
Birchville
Birdseye Creek
Blacks Bridge
Blue Tent
Borrjes Ranch
Boston Hill
Boston: Ravine, Flat
Boulder Bar
Bourbon Hill
Bovyers
Bowling Green
Bowmans Ranch
Brandy Flat
Brass Wire Bar
Bridgeport
Brookland
Brooklyn
Browns Hill
Brunswick
Brush Creek
Buckeye Hill
Buckeye: Hill, Ravine
Buena Vista
Bunker Hill
Bunkerville
Burks Bar
Burrington Hill
Butte Flat
Buzzards
Caldwells Upper Store
Caledonia Flat
California Consolidated Mine
Camden
Camp Beautiful
Canada Hill
Canal Bar
Cardinal Hill
Cariboo: Ravine, Diggings
Carlyle
Carson Flat
Cascade Diggings
(?) Cedar Grove
Celina Ridge
Cement Hill
Centreville; Centreville Ravine
Chalk: Mountain Range, Bluffs
Champion Mine
Chapparal Hill
Cherokee
Chicken Point
Chimney Hill
Christmas Hill
Church Hill
Cin Bar
Cincinnati Bar
Cincinnati Hill

Clinton
Colton Hill
Columbia Hill
Concord Bar
Cooley Hill
Coopers Bridge
Cornish Mine
Cotton Hill
Council Hill
Coyote Diggings
Coyote Hill
Coyoteville
Crumbecker Ravine
Culbertsons Station
Darlings Hill
Deadmans Cut
Deadmans Flat
Deadwood
Deer Creek
Deer Creek Crossing
Deer Creek Dry Diggings
Delhi Mine
Delirium Tremens
Democrat Hill
Derbec Mine
Diamond Creek
Diggers Bar
Dixons Diggings
Dog Bar
Donkeyville
Doodleburg
Doolittles Bridge
Doolittles Diggings
Doolittles Point
Dry Digginsville
Dutch Diggings
Eagle Bird
Edwards Crossing
Emigrant Gap
Emory Crossing
Empire Flat
Empire Hill
Empire Mine
Empire-Star Mine
English Mountain District
Enterprise
Erie Mine
Eureka
Eureka Mine
Eureka South
Excelsior
Excelsior Hill
Fall Creek
Fienes Crossing
Fire Creek
Fools Hill
Fordyce Valley
Forest Springs
Freemans Crossing
French Camp

French Corral
Frenchmans Bar
Gas Canyon
Gas Flat
Gass Flat
Gaston; Gaston Ridge
(?) Gatons Tunnel
George Maker's
German Bar
Glen Aura
Gods Country
Gold Bar
Golden Center Mines
Golden Point
Gold Flat
Gold Hill
Gold Mountain
Gold Point
Gold Run
Gomorrah
Gopher Hill
Gouge Eye
Graniteville
Grass Valley
Great Gravel Deposit
Greenhorn District
Green Mountain; Green Mountain Canyon
Greenwoods Camp
Grissell Bar
Grizzly: Canyon, Creek, Hill, Ridge
Grizzly Hill
Grouse Ridge
Gun Town
Hacketville
Harmony Ridge
Hartley Butte
Hell-out-for-noon City
Helvetia Hill
Heuston Hill
Hillsburg
Hirshmanns Cut
Hoaston Hill
Houston Hill
Howard Hill
Hoyts Crossing
Hueston Hill
Humbug
Humbug Flat
Huns Ranch
Hunts Hill
Idaho-Maryland Group
Illinois Bar
Illinois Ravine
Independence Hill
Indiana Boys Camp
Indian Flat
Indian Springs
Ione
Irishmans Bar
Jackass Gulch

Jefferson: Bar, City, Creek, Hill
Jenny Lind Diggings
Jimmy Brown Bar
Johnsons Diggings
Jones: Bar, Crossing
Junction Bluff
Kansas Hill
Kate Hayes Flat
Kate Hayes Hill
Kelseys Ravine
Kennebec Hill
Keno Bar
Kentucky Flat
Kinders Diggings
Kino Bar
Kiotaville
Knapps Creek
Lafayette Hill
Lake City
Laurence Hill
Lava Cap Mine
Lawson Flat
Le Bars Ranch
Liberty Hill
Lippards Bar
Little Deer Creek
Little York
Lizard Flat
Lola Montez: Hill, Diggings
Long Bar
Long Hollow
Long Tom Ravine
Lost Hill
Lost Ravine
Lousy: Level, Ravine, Bar
Lowell Hill
Malakoff District
Maltmans
Manzanita Hill
Martinsville
Marvin Ledge
Massachusetts Hill
Matheus
Matildaville
Maybert
Meadow Lake: City, Mining District
Melbourne Hill
Mendoza
Merrimac Hill
Michigan Flat
Miles Ravine
Mississippi Valley Mining District
Missouri Bar
Missouri Canyon
Missouri Flat
Missouri Hill
Monte Sana
Montezuma Hill
Mooney Flat
Moores Flat

Mosquito Creek
Mountaineer Mine
Mount Auburn
Mount George
Mount Oro
Mount Zion
Mud Flat
Mule Ravine
Mule Springs
Murchys Diggings
Myers Ravine
Native American Ravine
Neals Bar
Nebraska Mine
Negro Flat
Nevada City
New Dry Diggings
New Flats
New Gold Run
New Orleans
New Rocky Bar
Newton
New York Hill
Nigger Bar
Nigger Ravine
Norumbagua Mine
North Bloomfield
North Columbia
North San Juan
North Star
Nyes: Ferry, Crossing
Nyes Landing
Odin
Ohio Bar
Old Man Mountain
Old Point Diggings
Omega
Ophir Hill
Oregon Hill
Oregon Ravine
Oriental Mill
Orleans Flat
Ormonde
Osborn Hill
Osceola District
Osoville
Ossaville
Oustomah Hill
Owl Creek
Paris
Patterson
Pattison
Pearls Hill
Pecks Diggings
Pecks Ravine
Penn Valley
Perkins Coyote Diggings
Phelps Hill
Picayune Point
Pierces Cabin

Piety Hill
Pike Flat
Pittsburg Group
Pleasant Flat
Pleasant Valley
Pontiac Hill
Poorman Creek
Potosi Mine
Prescott Hill
Prior Ravine
Prospect Hill
Purdon Crossing
Quaker Hill
Queen City
Quinns Ranch
Ragon Flat
Randolph: Flat, Hill
Ranshaws Bar
Rattlesnake Bar
Rattlesnake Diggings
Redan Hill
Red Diamond
Red Dog
Red Ravine
Relief Hill
Remington Hill
Revere Mill
Rhode Island Ravine
Rich Creek
Rich Flat
Rich Port
Robinsons Crossing
Rock Creek
Rocky Bar
Roger Williams Ravine
Rose Hill
Roses Corral
Rough and Ready
(?) Round Tent Diggings
Rush Creek
Sailor Flat
Sailors Flat
St. Louis
Saleratus Ranch
Sanfords Ranch
San Juan: Hill, Ridge
Sardine Ravine
Scadden Flat
Schands Ranch
Scotch Flat
Scotchmans Creek
Scott Bar
Scotts Flat
Scotts Ravine
Sebastopol
Sebastopol Hill
Secret: Diggings, Canyon
Selby: Flat, Hill
Shady Creek
Shanghai Diggings

Shirt-Tail Hill
Shively Diggings
Skillman Flat
Slate Creek Ledge
(?) Smith Diggings
Snake Ravine
Snow: Point, Flat
Snow Tent
Soggsville
South Fork
South Osborn Hill
Spanish Ridge
Spenceville
Sneath and Clay
Spring Branch
Spring Creek
Squirrel Creek Diggings
Starvation Bar
Steep Hollow Diggings
Stockings Flat
Stockton Hill
Stony Bar
Stranahans
Sugar Loaf
Summit City
Swamp Angel Mine
Sweetland
(?) Tangle-Leg
Tecumseh Mill
Tehama Ravine
Texas Flat
The Hill
The Slide
Thomas Flat
Tollhouse
Tompkins House
Town Talk
Union Hill
Union Mills
Unionville
Ural
Urisko
Vail Ranch
Virgin Flat
Volunteer Camp
Walloupa
Walls Bridge
Walsh Ravine
Washington
Washington Ridge
Webbers Bridge
Weimar Hill
(?) West Ravine
Wet Hill
Wheatland District
Whiskeyana Flat
Whiskey Bar
Whiskey Flat
White Cloud
White Oak Springs

Wightman Camp
Wilcox Ravine
Wild Emigrant
Willow Bar
Willow Valley
Wilsonville
Wisconsin Flat
Wolf Creek
Woodpecker: Ravine, Diggings
Woodpeck Hill
Woods Ravine
Woolseys Flat
You Bet
Young America Mine
Yuba Mine
Yubaville

Orange County

Trabuco District

Placer County

Adams Diggings
African Bar
Alabama Mine
Alder Grove
Alta
American Bar
American Hollow
American Slide
Americaville
Antelope Ravine
Antoine or Antone Canyon
Applegate
Arkansas Bar
Askews Bar
Auburn: town, Ravine, District
Auburn Station
Ayres Diggings
Bachelor Hill
Badger Bar
Bakers Ranch
Bald Hill
Baltimore: Hill, Ravine
Bardwells Bar
Barnes Bar
Bath
Beals Bar
Bean Poker Flat
Beaver Bar
Benshy
Big Crevice
Big Dipper Mine
Big Gun Mine
Bigler Canal
Big Oak Bar
Big Spring
Bird: Flat, Gulch
Birds Valley

Blacksmith Flat
Blanchard Diggings
Blue Bluffs
Blue Canyon
Blue Gulch
Bogus Thunder Bar
Boston Flat
Bradshaws Bar
Browns Bar
Browns Cut
(?) Brules Bar
Brushy Canyon
Buckeye Bar
Buckeye Flat
Buckners Bar
Bunchs Bar
Butchers Ranch
Byrds Valley
Calf Bar
Canada Hill
Canyon Creek
Cape Horn Bar
Caroline Diggings
Carpenters Bar
Carrolton
Cedar Creek
Centreville
Chilean Bar
China Town
Chioko Bar
Cihota Bar
Claraville
Clinton Bar
Clydesdale Diggings
Cold Spring
Colfax
Condemned Bar
Coon Creek
Corcoran Diggings
Cosmopolite Mining District
Coyote Bar
Cranwells Bar
Crater Hill
Crees Flat
Croesus
Crows Flat
Damascus
Dana Diggings
Darby Flat
Dardanelles Diggings
Datons Bar
Day Bar
Daytons Bar
Dead Man's Bar
Deadwood
Deidesheimer
Devils Basin
Donner
Dotans Bar
Dotys: Flat, Ravine

Drammonds Diggings
Drummonds Point
Drunkards Bar
Dry Bar
Dry Bones Bar
Duncan Hill
Duncan Peak District
Duncans Canyon
Dutch Bar
Dutch Charleys Flat
Dutch Flat
Dutch Gulch
Dutch Marys Ravine
Dutch Ravine
Eastman Hill
El Dorado: Bar, District
El Dorado: Creek, Camp, Canyon
El Dorado Mine
Elizabeth Hill
Elizabethtown
Elmore Hill
Emigrant Gap
Empire Bar
Empire Flats
Euchre Bar
Extension Diggings
Finleys Camp
Fisher Bar
Fords Bar
Forest Hill
Frytown
Fulda Flat
Garden Bar District
Garden Ranch Flat
Georgia Hill
Gleason Mine
Gold Bar
Golden Rule Mine
Gold Hill
Gold Run
Gopher Town
Gosling Ravine
Granite Bar
Green Emigrant
Greenhorn Bar
Greenhorn Slide
Green Mountain Bar
Green Valley
Grizzly Bar
Grizzly Bear House
Grizzly Flat
Ground Hog Glory
Hammonds Ravine
Harlows Bar
Hartford Bar
Hells Delight
Hells Half Acre
Hidden Treasure Mine
High Bar
Hogs Back

Hones Bar
Horseshoe Bar
Howard Flat
Hughes Bar
Humbug: Bar, Canyon, Creek, Flat
Hungry Hollow
Illinoistown
Independence Hill
Independent Mine
Indiana Hill
Indian Bar
Indian Canyon
Iowa: Hill, City, Divide
Italian Bar
Jacksbury Diggings
James Point
Japses Bar
Jenny Lind: Flat, Tunnel
Johnston Bar
Jones Bar
Junction Bar
Kehoe Canyon
Kellys Bar
Kelseys Bar
Kennebec Bar
Kentucky Bar
Killiams Bar
Kings: Diggings, Hill
Knoxville
Lacys Bar
Ladies Canyon
Lake Valley Diggings
Last Chance
Lehigh Bar
Letts Bar
Life Preserver
Lincoln
Little Baltimore Ravine
Little Horseshoe Bar
Little Oregon Bar
Little Rattlesnake Bar
Lone Star District
Long Bar
Lorenz Bar
Lost Camp
Lynchburg
(?) McClintock Ranch
McLaughlans Ravine
Mad Canyon Diggings
Main Hill
Maintop
Mammoth Bar
Manhattan Bar
Massachusetts Bar
Mayflower Mine
Michigan: Bluff, City, District
Mile Hill Ravine
Milk Punch Bar
Millers Defeat
Millertown

Mineral Bar
Miners Ravine
Minerva
Minna Flat
Mississippi Canyon
Missouri Bar
Monona Flat
Mormon Bar
Morning Star Hill
Mountain Gate Mine
Mountain Springs
Mud Canyon
Mugginsville
Mumford Bar
Nary Red
Negro Bar
Negro Hill
Neptune City
Neptunes Bar
Nesbits Bar
Neutral Bar
Nevada Hill
Newark
Newcastle
New England Bar
New England Mills
New Hartford Bar
New Jersey
New London Bar
Newtown
New York Bar
New York Canon
New York Hill
Nigger Bar
Niggerhead Bar
Niggers Bluff
North Fork Dry Diggings
North Ravine
Oak Bar
Oakland Flat
One Horse Bar
Ophir; Ophirville
Oregon Bar
Oro City
Orr City
Owl Creek
Paradise
Paragon Mine
Parks Hill
Pat Goggins Diggings
Patricks Bar
Peckham Hill
Penryn
Picayune Divide
Pickering Bar
Pine Grove
Pino
Pioneer Mine
Placer
Pleasant Bar

Plug Ugly Hill
Poco Tempo Bar
Portuguese Bar
Potato Ravine
Poverty Bar
Prospect Hill
Quail Bar
Quartz Flat
Quartz: Prairie, Hill
Quartz Ravine Bar
Quicksilver Bar
Ralston Divide
Ramseys Bar
Rattlesnake Bar
Rectors Bar
Red Bird
Red Point
Red Stone
Refuge Canyon
Resters Bar
Rices Bar
Richardson Hill
Rich Bar
Rich Dry Diggings
Rich Flat
Rich Ravine
Rising Sun Mine
Roach Hill
Robertson Flat
Robinsons Crossing
Rock Bar
Rock Creek
Rocklin District
Rock Spring
Rocky Bar
Rocky Point Slide
Rose Springs
Rough and Ready
Rubicon River District
(?) Russ Diggings
Russian Bar
Sailor Canyon
Sailors Bar
Sailors Canyon
Sailors Ravine
Samaroo
Sarahsville
Sardine Bar
Second Ravine
Secret: Diggings, Ravine
Secret Ravine
Secret: Spring, Creek, Canyon, Hill
Secret Town
Shady Run
Shenanigan Hill
Shepley Ravine
Sheridan
Shipleys Ravine
Shirt Tail Canyon
Skunk Gulch

Slap Jack Bar
Slate Bar
Smiths Bar
Smiths Point
Smithville
Spanish Corral
Spanish: Flat, Ravine
Spring Garden; Spring Garden Ranch
Squires Canyon
Startown
Stevens Hill
Stewarts Flat
Stickness Gulch
Stony Bar
Strafford
Strawberry Flat
Strongs Diggings
Stud Horse Bar
Succor Flat
Sucker Flat
Sugar Loafs
Swindle Hill
Tadpole Creek
Taff Bar
Tahoe District
Tamaroo Bar
Taylors Ravine
Temperance Flat
Tennessee Canyon
Texas Bar
Texas Diggings
Texas Hill
Thompson Hill
Tichenors Gulch
Todds: Creek, Valley, Ravine
Towle
Turkey Hill
Tysons Hospital
Uncle Toms
Union Bar
Union Valley
Upper Arkansas Bar
Upper Corral
Valley View
Vermont: Bar, Flat
Vigilance Bar
Virginia
Virginiatown
Volcano
Volcano Canyon
Waldauer Claim
Walloomsac Bar
Weimar
Weske Claim
Westville
Wheatland District
Whiskey: Diggings, Hill
Whiskey Flat
Whiskey Ravine
Widow Harmans Ravine

Willow Bar
Wisconsin: Hill, Flat
Wolverine
Woods Dry Diggings
Woodworths Bar
Yankee Bar
Yankee Jims
Yankee Jims Dry Diggings
Yorkville
Zeibright Mine

Plumas County

American House
American Rancho
American: Valley, Ranch
Argentine
Badger Hill
Barnards Diggings
Barra Rica
Beckworth
Beldens Bar
Bells Bar
Bernard Diggings
Betsyburg
Big Meadows
(?) Bingham Bar
Black Hawk Diggings
Black Rock
Boones Bar
Bowens Bar
Box
Brays Bar
Browns Bar
Buck
Buckeye Bar
Buckeye Ranch Dry Diggings
Bucks Ranch
Burleys Bar
Burtons Gulch
Butte Bar
Butterfly: Creek, Valley, Diggings
Butte Valley
Butt Valley
Cap Orsburne's Ravine
Cariboo
Caribou
Cherokee
City of 76
Claremont Hill
Clio
Coyote Diggings
Crescent Mills
Cromberg
Crooked Bar
Dead Mans Gulch
Deadwood
Depot Camp
Dixie Canyon
Dixon Creek

Dorado
Downies Diggings
Dutch Diggings
Dutch Hill
Duxbury Hill
Eagle Gulch
Eclipse
Elephant Bar
Elizabethtown
English Bar
Eureka: Peak, Mills
Fales Hill
Fall River House
Fidlers Flat
Fowlers Diggings
French Bar
Frenchmans Bar
Frenchmans Creek
Gardiners Point
Genesee
Golden Gate: Mine, Tunnel
Gold Lake
Gopher Hill
Granite Basin
Grass Valley
Graveyard Camp *or* Flat
Greenhorn Diggings
Green Mountain
Greenville
Grizzly Flat
Grub Flat
Hansons Bar
Harrisons
Hartman Bar
Henpeck Camp
Honey Lake District
Hopkinsville
Hottentot Bar
(?) Humbug
Hungarian: Gulch, Hill
Independence
Indian Bar
Indian: Creek, Valley
Indian Valley Mine
Jackson Diggings
Jamestown
Jamison City
Johnsville
Junction Bar
La Porte
Last Chance: Camp, Creek
Letter Box
Lexington House
Lights Canyon
(?) Lincoln Hill
Little Grass Valley
Lower Indian Bar
Mammoth
Marion: Flat, Ravine
(?) Marks Bar

Meadow Valley
Meeks Flat
Merrimac
Middle Bar
Mineral Point
Minerva Bar
Missouri Bar
Mohawk
(?) Moonlight Flat
Mosquito Creek
Mountain House
Muggins Bar
Mumfords Hill
Myers Diggings
Mystery Gulch
Nelson: Creek, Diggings, Point
Nigger Bar
No-eared Bar
North Canyon
North Fork
Nuggins Bar
Old Lexington House
Onion Valley
Peasoup Bar
Peoria Bar
Phenix Mill
Pilot Hill
Plumas-Eureka Mines
Poorman Creek
Poplar Bar
Poverty Bar
Poverty Flat
Prattville
Quartz Township District
Quincy
Rabbit: Creek, Camp, Point
Rabbittown
Racacous Creek
Red Slide
Reinhart Bar
Rich Bar I and II
Richmond Hill
Rich Valley
Rocky Bar
Rothrock Camp
Round Valley
Sailor Bar
Sailors Bar
Sam Flat
Saw Pit Flat
Scad Point
Scotch Flat
Scotts Bar
Secret Diggings
Seneca
Seventy-Six
Sierraville; Sierra Valley
Slate Creek Basin
Smalta Bar
Smith Bar

Soda: Creek, Bar
South Bar
Spanish Flat
Spanish: Ranch, Creek
Spring Garden District
Squirrel Creek
Stingtown
Sunny Bar
Sweet Oil Diggings
Tailors Bar
Taylorsville
Twelve Mile Bar
Union Creek
Union Valley
Wash
Washington Hill
Wauponsa Creek
Whitney Group
Wild Irish Bar
Willow Creek
Wyandotte Bar

Riverside County

Arica District
Bendigo District
Chuckwalla District
Dos Palmas District
Good Hope Mine
Jack Fork
Kenworthy
Menifee District
Monson Canyon
Mule Mountains District
Perris
Pinacate
Pinecate
Twenty-nine Palms: town, District

Sacramento County

Alabama Bar
Alder: Creek, Springs
Ashland
Beams Bar
Big Bar
Big Gulch
Big Gun
Bowlesville
(?) Brules Bar
Buckeye Bar
Burying Ground Hill
Cooks Bar
Cosumne
Daylors
Deer Creek
Farmers Diggings
Fishers Bar
Folsom
Fords Bar

Forkville *or* Forksville
Granite City
Katesville
Live Oak
Lower Mines
Michigan Bar
(?) Mill Bar
Mississippi Bar
Mormon Diggings
Mormon Island
Mormons Tavern
Natoma
Negro Bar
New Diggings
Nigger Bar
Nigger Diggins
Notoma
Pioneer Claim
Prairie City
Rebel Hill
Rhodes Diggings
Richmond Hill
Rocky Bar
Russville
Sacramento
Sacramento Bar
Sailor Bar
Sebastopol
Sheldon
Sinclairs Washings
Slate: Bar, Hill
Sulky Flat
Texas Hill
Walls Diggings
(?) White Rock
Willow: Springs, Diggings

San Bernardino County

Alvord District
Amargosa District
Arlington District
Arrastre Flat
Arrastre Spring
Arrowhead District
Avawatz Mountains
Bagdad
Bagdad-Chase Mines
Bairdstown
Baldwin Lake District
Baldy Notch
Banks Mine
Barnwell
Barstow
Bear Valley
Belleville
Black Hawk: Canyon, District
Blake
Bonanza King Mine
Bristol Mountains

Buckeye District
Calico
Camp Cady
Camp Rochester
Castle Mountains District
Clapboard Town
Clark Mountains District
Columbia
Coolgardie Placer
Cottonwood
Crackerjack
Cushenbury City
Daggett
Dale: District, town
Danby
Desert Lake
Doble
Exchequer District
Fenner
Fergusons Flat
Fremont Peak
Furgusons Flat
Goat Mountain
Goffs
Gold Mountain
Gold Reef District
Goldstone
Grapevine District
Green Lead: Creek, Mine
Hackberry Mountain District
Halleck
Halloran Springs District
Hamburger Placers
Hart: town, District
Hicorum
Hocumac Mine
Holcomb Valley
Holts Canyon
Ibex District
Ivanpah
Ivawatch Mountains
Kelso District
Kramer Hills
Lava Bed District
Lower Holcomb
Ludlow
Lytle Creek Placers
Maumee Placers
Manvel
Mescal: District, town
Morongo District
Mount Baldy District
Nantan
Needles
New Dale
New York Mountains
Old Dad Mountain
Old Woman Mountains
Orange Blossom Mine
Ord District